difford's
Encyclopedia
of Cocktails

2600 recipes

difford's
Encyclopedia
of Cocktails

2600 recipes

Simon Difford
diffordsguide°

FIREFLY BOOKS

A Firefly Book

Published by Firefly Books Ltd. 2009

Publisher Cataloging-in-Publication Data (U.S.)
Difford, Simon.
    Diffords encyclopedia of cocktails : 2600 recipes / Simon Difford.
[496] p. : col. photos. ;   cm.
Includes index.
Summary: Recipes from the traditional to the new and inventive.
Each recipe has a color photograph of the drink in its assigned glass,
ingredient measures, directions, garnish, variations, and information on
the cocktail's origin.
ISBN-13: 978-1-55407-501-0
ISBN-10: 1-55407-501-7
1. Cocktails.   I. Title.
 641.874 dc22   TX951.D544 2009

Library and Archives Canada Cataloguing in Publication
Difford, Simon
    Diffords encyclopedia of cocktails : 2600 recipes / Simon Difford.
Includes index.
ISBN-13: 978-1-55407-501-0
ISBN-10: 1-55407-501-7
    1. Cocktails. I. Title.
TX951.D52 2009   641.8'74   C2009-902265-6

Published in the United States by
Firefly Books (U.S.) Inc.
P.O. Box 1338, Ellicott Station
Buffalo, New York 14205

Published in Canada by
Firefly Books Ltd.
66 Leek Crescent
Richmond Hill, Ontario L4B 1H1

Printed in China

INTRODUCTION

This tome is a comprehensive compilation of over 2,600 cocktails collected during the dozen years I have been visiting and writing about the world's best bars. It is the eighth edition of an ongoing project that I hope never to finish.

This book '#8' contains 400 more cocktails than '#7' and many of these 'NEW' drinks have been created in the period since our previous publication while others are rediscovered vintage recipes. In addition I have 'UPDATED' numerous other recipes, and I hope you'll agree, for the better.

I'd like to thank the many cocktail aficionados and professional bartenders who have shared their recipes and insights with me. In the course of testing, refining and standardizing recipes, I have 'tweaked' many drinks to what I consider the best balance. Some may have originally been created using brands other than the ones I recommend here. Others may have originally been made in different proportions.

I have also adapted a few recipes to make them simpler, avoid ingredients that are obscure or obsolete, or take advantage of new ingredients that improve the original while staying true to its essence. Throughout, I have endeavoured to credit drink inventors, while making it clear that my adaptation varies slightly from their original creation. I'd be the first to admit that some of the recipes are better than others (most definitely including my own), so I've graded cocktails on a scale of one to five and discreetly indicated this score by dots above each drink's name.

Anyone looking to treat themselves to their very own home cocktail cabinet should begin with the fourteen 'Key Ingredients' featured in the opening pages. These are the most frequently used cocktail ingredients and by combining them with such easy-to-find ingredients as fruits and juices you will be able to make literally hundreds of drinks. I have marked these key cocktails with our key symbol throughout this guide.

Cocktail recipes are a very personal thing, and I would love to hear what you think of the recipes in this book. Do you have a better version of a classic cocktail? Is one of your own creations worth inclusion? Drop me a line at simon@diffordsguide.com. I also write email newsletters with drinks, bar reviews and new cocktail recipes from all around the world. If you'd like to receive these, please email me direct, or sign up at our website 'diffordsguide.com'.

Cheers!
Simon Difford
simon@diffordsguide.com

BARTENDING BASICS

PLEASE READ THE FOLLOWING INSTRUCTIONS BEFORE ATTEMPTING TO FOLLOW THE RECIPES IN THIS GUIDE.

By definition any drink which is described as a cocktail contains more than one ingredient. So if you are going to make cocktails you have to know how to combine these various liquids. Firstly, as in cooking, there is a correct order in which to prepare things and with few exceptions, which runs as follows:

1. Select glass and chill or pre-heat (if required)
2. Prepare garnish (if required)
3. Pour ingredients
4. Add ice (if required - add last to minimise melt)
5. Combine ingredients (shake, stir etc.)
6. Add garnish (if required)
7. Consume or serve to guest

Essentially, there are four different ways to mix a cocktail: shake, stir, blend and build. (Building a drink means combining the ingredients in the glass in which the cocktail will be served.)

A fifth mixing method known as 'rolling' is not that frequently employed but offers the bartender a more gentle mixing method than shaking but more thorough than stirring.

A further construction method, 'layering', isn't strictly mixing. The idea here is to float each ingredient on its predecessor without the ingredients merging at all. At the heart of every cocktail lies at least one of these five methods. So understanding these terms is fundamental.

Shakers

When you see the phrase "shake with ice and strain" or similar in the method, you should place all the necessary ingredients with cubed ice in a cocktail shaker and shake briskly (in the same manner you might agitate the metal ball in a can of spray-paint) for around fifteen seconds. Then you should strain the liquid into the glass, leaving the ice behind in the shaker.

Shaking not only mixes a drink, it also chills, dilutes and aerates it. The dilution achieved by shaking is just as important to the resulting cocktail as using the right proportions of each ingredient. If you use too little ice it will quickly melt in the shaker, producing an over-diluted drink - so always fill your shaker at least two-thirds full with fresh ice. Losing your grip while shaking is likely to make a mess and could result in injury, so always hold the shaker firmly with two hands and never shake fizzy ingredients (unless in a minute proportion to rest of drink).

Although shakers come in many shapes and sizes there are two basic types.

Standard Shaker

A standard shaker consists of three parts and hence is sometimes referred to as a three-piece shaker. The three pieces are **1/** a flat-bottomed, conical base or 'can', **2/** a top with a built-in strainer and **3/** a cap.

I strongly recommend this style of shaker for amateurs due to its ease of use. Be sure to purchase a shaker with a capacity of at least one pint as this will allow the ice room to travel and so mix more effectively.

To use:

1/ Combine all ingredients in the base of the shaker
2/ Fill two-thirds full with ice.
3/ Place the top and cap firmly on the base.
4/ Pick up the closed shaker with one hand on the top and the other gripping the bottom and shake vigorously. The cap should always be on the top when shaking and should point away from guests.
5/ After shaking briskly for a count of around 15 seconds, lift off the cap, hold the shaker by its base with one finger securing the top and pour the drink through the built-in strainer.

Rolling

Sometimes also referred to as the 'Cuban Roll' after the origin of this method of mixing, 'rolling' offers more dilution and aeration than stirring but is more gentle than shaking. It is achieved by simply pouring the ingredients from one container to another.

To do this, assemble your ingredients in a mixing glass or base of your shaker. Add ice and strain into a second mixing glass increasing the distance between the two vessels as you pour. Then pour the partially mixed cocktail back into the first ice-filled container and strain into the second once again. Repeat this process several times and you will have 'rolled' your drink.

Dry Shake

It is common practice amongst some bartenders to first shake drinks containing cream and eggs without ice. Then to shake the drink a second time with ice added. This practice is known as 'dry shaking' and the theory is that first shaking without ice, and so at a higher temperature, better allows the drink to emulsify. If you are going to do this I recommend placing a spring from a strainer in the shaker during the first 'dry shake' as this acts as a whisk when the drink is shaken.

Boston Shaker

A Boston shaker comprises two flat-bottomed cones, one larger than the other. The large cone, or 'can', is made of stainless steel while the smaller cone can be either glass, stainless steel or even plastic.

Avoid Boston shakers that rely on a rubber ring to seal. I use Alessi Boston tins as I find these seal without a thump and open with the lightest tap. However good your Boston shaker, these devices demand an element of skill and practice is usually required for a new user to become proficient.

To use:

1/ Combine ingredients in the glass, or smaller of the two cans.

2/ Fill the large can with ice and briskly up-end over the smaller can (or glass), quickly enough to avoid spilling any ice. Lightly tap the top with the heel of your hand to create a seal between the two parts.

3/ Lift shaker with one hand on the top and the other gripping the base and shake vigorously. The smaller can (or glass) should always be on the top when shaking and should point away from guests.

4/ After shaking for around 15 seconds, hold the larger (base) can in one hand and break the seal between the two halves of the shaker by tapping the base can with the heel of your other hand at the point where it meets the upper can (or glass).

5/ Before pouring, place a strainer with a coiled rim (also known as a Hawthorne strainer) over the top of the can and strain the mixture into the glass, leaving the ice cubes behind.

Swizzle

To 'swizzle' a drink is simply to stir it using a particular tool and action. This style of drink mixing originated in the Caribbean and originally a twig with a few forked branches was used. Today 'swizzle sticks' are usually made of metal or plastic and have several blades or fingers attached to the base at right angles to the shaft.

To swizzle simply immerse the blades of your swizzle stick into the drink, hold the stick between the palms of both hands and rotate rapidly by sliding your hands back and forth against it. If you do not have a bona fide swizzle stick, try using a barspoon in the same manner.

Stir

If a cocktail recipe calls for you to 'stir with ice and strain' then you should stir in a mixing glass using a bar spoon with a long, spiralling stem. If a specially designed lipped mixing glass is not available, one half of a Boston shaker, or the base of a standard shaker, will suffice.

Combine the ingredients in the mixing glass, adding the ice last. Slide the back of the spoon down the inside of the mixing glass and stir the drink. You should stir a drink for at least 20 seconds, then strain into a glass using a strainer (or the top of a standard shaker if you are using a standard shaker base in place of a mixing glass).

Fine Strain

Most cocktails that are served 'straight up' without ice benefit from an additional finer strain, over and above the standard strain which keeps ice cubes out of the drink. This 'fine strain' removes small fragments of fruit and fine flecks of ice which can spoil the appearance of a drink and is particularly beneficial if the drink has been shaken rather than stirred (or rolled).

Fine straining is achieved by simply holding a fine sieve, like a tea strainer, between the shaker and the glass. Another popular term for this method is 'double strain'.

Blend

When a cocktail recipe calls for you to 'blend with ice', place all ingredients and ice into a blender and blend until a smooth, even consistency is achieved. Ideally you should use crushed ice, as this lessens wear on the blades. Place liquid ingredients in the blender first, adding the ice last, as always. If you have a variable speed blender, always start slowly and build up speed.

Layer

As the name would suggest, layered drinks include layers of different ingredients, often with contrasting colours. This effect is achieved by carefully pouring each ingredient into the glass so that it floats on its predecessor.

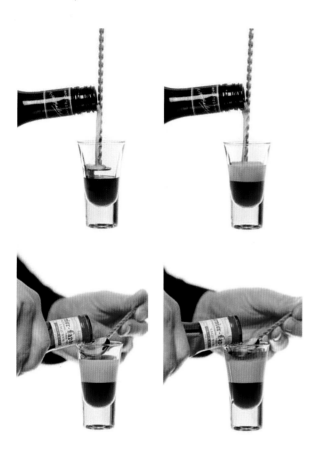

The success of this technique is dependent on the density (specific gravity) of the liquids used. As a rule of thumb, the less alcohol and the more sugar an ingredient contains, the heavier it is. The heaviest ingredients should be poured first and the lightest last. Syrups are non-alcoholic and contain a lot of sugar so are usually the heaviest ingredient. Liqueurs, which are high in sugar but lower in alcohol than spirits, are generally the next heaviest ingredient. The exception to this rule is cream and cream liqueurs, which can float.

One brand of a particular liqueur may be heavier or lighter than another. The relative temperatures of ingredients may also affect their ability to float or sink. Hence a degree of experimentation is inevitable when creating layered drinks.

Layering can be achieved in one of two ways. The first involves pouring down the spiral handle of a bar spoon, keeping the flat, disc-shaped end of the spoon over the surface of the drink. Alternatively you can hold the bowl end of a bar spoon (or a soup spoon) in contact with the side of the glass and over the surface of the drink and pour slowly over it.

The term 'float' refers to layering the final ingredient on top of a cocktail.

Muddle

Muddling means pummelling fruits, herbs and/or spices with a muddler (a blunt tool similar to a pestle) so as to crush them and release their flavour. (You could also use a rolling pin.) As when using a pestle and mortar, push down on the muddler with a twisting action.

Only attempt to muddle in the base of a shaker or a suitably sturdy glass. Never attempt to muddle hard, unripe fruits in a glass as the pressure required could break the glass. I've witnessed a bartender slash his hand open on a broken glass while muddling and can't over-emphasize how careful you should be.

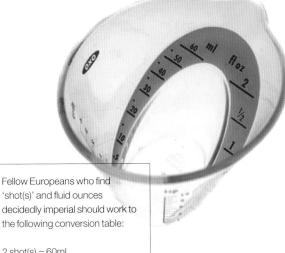

Measuring (Shots & Spoons)

Balancing each ingredient within a cocktail is key to making a great drink. Therefore the accuracy with which ingredients are measured is critical to the finished cocktail.

In this guide I've expressed the measures of each ingredient in 'shots'. Ideally a shot is 30ml or one US fluid ounce (29.6ml), measured in a standard jigger. (You can also use a clean medicine measure or even a small shot glass.) Whatever your chosen measure, it should have straight sides to enable you to accurately judge fractions of a shot. Look out for measures which are graduated in ounces and marked with quarter and half ounces.

The measure 'spoon' refers to a bar spoon, which is slightly larger than a standard teaspoon. Personally, I measure in ounces and count a slightly under-filled flat bar spoon as an 1/8 of an ounce.

Some bartenders attempt to measure shots by counting time and estimating the amount of liquid flowing through a bottle's spout. This is known as 'free-pouring' and in unskilled hands can be terribly inaccurate. I strongly recommend the use of a physical measure and a great deal of care.

Fellow Europeans who find 'shot(s)' and fluid ounces decidedly imperial should work to the following conversion table:

2 shot(s) = 60ml
1½ shot(s) 52.5ml
1 shot(s) = 30ml
¾ shot(s) = 22.5ml
½ shot(s) = 15ml
¼ shot(s) = 7.5ml
⅛ shot(s) = 4ml

Ice

A plentiful supply of fresh ice is essential to making good cocktails. When buying bagged ice avoid the hollow, tubular kind and the thin wafers. Instead look for large, solid cubes of ice. I recommend a Kold Draft (kold-draft.com) or Hoshizaki (hoshizaki.com) ice machines producing large (inch/25mm square) solid cubes.

When filling ice cube trays, use bottled or filtered water to avoid the taste of chlorine often apparent in municipal water supplies. Your ice should be dry, almost sticky to the touch. Avoid 'wet' ice that has started to thaw.

Whenever serving a drink over ice, always fill the glass with ice, rather than just adding a few cubes. This not only makes the drink much colder, but the ice lasts longer and so does not dilute into the drink. Never use ice in a cocktail shaker twice, even if it's to mix the same drink as before. You should always throw away ice after straining the drink and use fresh ice to fill the glass if so required. Not straining shaken ice and pouring it straight into the glass with the liquid will result in an overly diluted drink which will not be as cold as one where the drink is strained over fresh ice.

Unless otherwise stated, all references to ice in this guide mean cubed ice. If crushed ice is required for a particular recipe, the recipe will state 'crushed ice'. This is available commercially. Alternatively you can crush cubed ice in an ice-crusher or simply bash a bag or tea towel of cubed ice with a rolling pin.

If a glass is broken near your ice stocks, melt the ice with warm water, clean the container and re-stock with fresh ice. If this occurs in a busy bar and you are not immediately able to clean the ice chest, mark it as being contaminated with a liberal coating of red grenadine syrup and draw ice from another station.

Flame

The term ignite, flame or flambé means that the drink should be set alight. Please exercise extreme care when setting fire to drinks. Be particularly careful not to knock over a lit drink and never attempt to carry a drink which is still alight. Before drinking, cover the glass so as to suffocate the flame and be aware that the rim of the glass may be hot.

BARTENDER'S KIT

EVERYBODY LOVES A LITTLE RETAIL THERAPY SO HERE ARE SOME SUGGESTIONS AS TO WHAT COCKTAIL KIT TO INVEST IN.

1. Bar Bag

Professional photographer's equipment bags are perfect for storing and carry bar equipment. The one pictured by Tamrac (tamrac.com) is the one I use and features padded sections originally designed to house lenses but which are deep enough to accommodate shakers, mixing glasses and glassware. An abundance of front and side pockets, designed for holding films or other paraphernalia, snugly house bar spoons, measures, strainers and smaller bar tools.

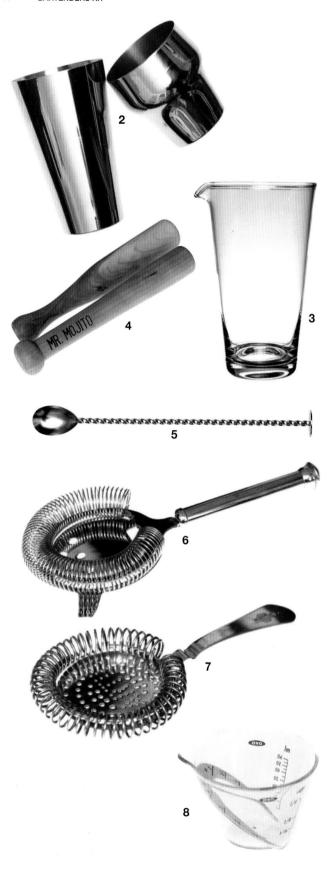

2. Shaker

There are numerous shapes and sizes of shaker and I own many examples. Personally I now favour a 'tin & tin' set given to me by those fab folk at Huitième Monde Bar Equipment in Paris but the tins are bashed from frequent use and their bottoms wrapped in insulating tape to add weight so less than photogenic.

When demonstrating cocktails I tend to use this Boston Shaker by Alessi (alessi.com) as the glass base allows onlookers to see the drink being assembled. The sides of an Alessi tin are firm yet flexible enough to make a tight seal against a Boston glass with the lightest of taps. Consequently, opening is effortless. The glasses which come with the tins are delicate so I've replaced mine with a cheaper and tougher alternative.

3. Mixing Glass

This (now discontinued) mixing glass comes from the good folk at Urban Bar. It's large enough to contain a great deal of ice, which means a colder, less diluted drink.

4. Muddlers

David Nepove's Mojitos are renowned in San Francisco and this is one of two shapes of muddler he has designed for his signature drink (mistermojito.com). I'm also very fond of Tony Abou-Ganim's 'Tag Bar' muddler (themodernmixologist.com) also pictured.

5. Barspoon by Bonzer

This very traditional barspoon is the most versatile of tools. The flat, disc shaped end can be used as a muddler (a risky business according to many barkeeps who have been stabbed by breaking spoons), for layering drinks and for stirring. Of course, the spoon end also comes in handy for measuring honey or lifting maraschino cherries out of jars. (mitchellcooper.com)

6. Sprung Strainer by Urban Bar

Hawthorn is to strainers what Hoover is to vacuum cleaners. Whoever makes them, sprung strainers with two or more prongs, designed to be used with Boston shakers, tend to be called Hawthorns. This one by Urban Bar (urbanbar.com) is well made with a tightly coiled spring.

7. Mixing Strainer

This is not a julep strainer. But I often call it one, because I use it as one would use a julep strainer – when pouring from a mixing glass. Rather than a bowl-shaped colander affair, this is sprung like a Hawthorn, but lacks the prongs. Thus it is held in the glass rather than on top. I bought it from a flea market.

8. Measure

This measure by Oxo, (oxo.com) may not look as slick as a stainless steel thimble measure but, with graduations from 1/4oz to 2oz (perfect for shots and fractions of a shot) and a milliliter scale on the side, it's a sight more practical. Not to mention being easier to read from above.

9. Fine Strainer

The challenge with fine strainers is to find one that is not so fine that liquid takes ages to flow through but that also has sufficient capacity to hold a decent volume. Fresh Strawberry Martinis tend to quickly clog most strainers.

10. Swivel Peeler

I like to cut generously sized long twists rather than the coin-sized circular variety and find a peeler such as this one by Oxo (oxo.com) infinitely better than a knife for cutting twists without too much pith.

11. Paring Knife

You'll need a sharp knife and cutting board, and when it comes to really sharp knives you have to look to Japan. Tanaka by Kin Knives (kinknives.com) have thirty two layers of alternating nickel and stainless steel surround a cutting core of powdered steel. Something that beautiful deserves real respect – sharpen with ceramic rather than steel.

12. Juicer

I have an industrial lever action citrus press on my bar but a simple glass juicer or hand press should suffice for domestic use.

13. Bar Blender

You'll need a blender for all those Frozen Daiquiris so choose one with a large capacity and a powerful motor. While you're at it you may as well have one that's also easy on the eye and my beautiful brushed chrome model by Kitchen Aid (kitchenaid.com) is certainly that.

14. Egg Separator

I'm a fan of using fresh egg whites in my cocktails and tend to use the shells to separate the white from the yolk where required. However, some may prefer this nifty tool from Oxo (oxo.com).

15. Citrus Zester & Canal Knife

I have a number of zesters and canal knives, none of which seem particularly sharp even when new. This one by Oxo combines both tools.

16. Waiter's Friend Cork Screw

I would love to claim that I use a Chateau Laguiole Master Sommelier (pronounced 'Shato Layol') but like so many others, I actually own, and have lost, numerous cheap Waiter's Friends which double as cork screw and bottle opener.

17. Ice Scoop

I use three ice scoops, one monster size plastic one for taking ice from the machine, a 12oz aluminum scoop for cubed ice and a 6oz aluminum scoop for crushed ice, the latter tending to channel crushed ice into the glass.

18. Nutmeg Grater

When selecting a nutmeg grater look for the type which also has a compartment for storing your nutmeg.

19. Powder Shaker

A shaker with a fine mesh of the type used in coffee shops to dust cappuccinos is perfect for applying chocolate and powdered cinnamon over cocktails.

1.   2.   3.   4.   5.   6.   7.

GLASSWARE

Cocktails are something of a luxury. You don't just ping a cap and pour. These drinks take time and skill to mix so deserve a decent glass.

Before you start, check your glassware is clean and free from chips and marks such as lipstick. Always handle glasses by the base or the stem to avoid leaving finger marks and never put your fingers inside a glass.

Ideally glassware should be chilled in a freezer prior to use. This is particularly important for martini and flute glasses, in which drinks are usually served without ice. It takes about half an hour to sufficiently chill a glass in the freezer.

If time is short, you can chill a glass by filling it with ice (ideally crushed, not cubed) and topping it up with water. Leave the glass to cool while you prepare the drink, then discard the ice and water once you are ready to pour. This method is quicker than chilling in the freezer but not nearly so effective.

To warm a glass ready for a hot cocktail, place a bar spoon in the glass and fill it with hot water. Then discard the water and pour in the drink. Only then should you remove the spoon, which is there to help disperse the shock of the heat.

There are thousands of differently shaped glasses, but if you own those mentioned here you have a glass to suit practically every drink and occasion. Failing that, a set of Collins, Martini and Old-fashioned or Rocks glasses, and possibly flutes if you fancy champagne cocktails, will allow you to serve the majority of drinks in this guide. Use a Martini in place of a Coupette and a Collins as a substitute for Hurricane and Sling glasses.

1. Martini

Those in the old guard of bartending insist on calling this a 'cocktail glass'. It may once have been, but to most of us today a V-shaped glass is a Martini glass. The recent resurgence in vintage cocktails has also led to a vogue for using a champagne saucer (AKA Coup) to serve straight-up drinks. Whatever your glassware preference, when choosing either a Martini or a Coup it should be no bigger than 7oz, as a true Martini warms up too much in the time it takes to drink such a large one. I'd suggest keeping your glasses in the refrigerator or even the freezer so they are chilled before use.

Capacity to brim: 7oz / 20cl

2. Sling

This elegant glass has recently become fashionable again – partly due to the popularity of long drinks such as the Russian Spring Punch.

Capacity to brim: 11oz / 32cl

3. Shot

Shot glasses come in all shapes and sizes. You'll need small ones if you're sensible and big ones if you're not!

Capacity to brim (pictured glass): 2oz / 6cl

4. Flute

Flutes are perfect for serving champagne cocktails as their tall, slim design helps maintain the wine's fizz. Chill before use.

Capacity to brim: 6oz / 17cl

5. Collins

In this guide I refer to a tall glass as a 'Collins'. A hi-ball is slightly squatter than a Collins but has the same capacity. A 12oz Collins glass will suffice for cocktails and is ideal for a standard 330ml bottle of beer. However, I favour 14oz glasses with the occasional 8oz for drinks such as Fizzes which are served tall but not very long.

Capacity to brim: 14oz / 40cl or 8oz / 24cl

6. Margarita

Named after the cocktail with the same name, this glass is still used predominately for the Mexican cocktail - the rim is crying out for salt.

Capacity to brim: 8oz / 24cl

7. Goblet

Not often used for cocktails, but worth having, if for no other reason than to enjoy your wine. An 11oz glass is big enough to be luxurious.

Capacity to brim: 11oz / 32cl

8. Boston

A tall, heavy conical glass with a thick rim, designed to be combined with a Boston tin to form a shaker. It can also be used as a mixing glass for stirred drinks.

Capacity to brim: 17oz / 48cl

9. Hurricane

Sometimes referred to as a 'poco grande' or 'Piña Colada' glass, this big-bowled glass is commonly used for frozen drinks. It screams out for a pineapple wedge, a cherry and possibly a paper parasol as well. Very Del Boy.

Capacity to brim: 15oz / 43cl

10. Old-fashioned

Another glass whose name refers to the best-known drink served in it. It is also great for enjoying spirits such as whiskey. Choose a luxuriously large glass with a thick, heavy base. Alternatively, the similarly shaped 'Rocks' glass has a thick rim and is usually made from toughened glass so better suited to drinks that require muddling in the glass.

Capacity to brim: 11oz / 32cl

11. Snifter

Sometimes referred to as a 'brandy balloon'. The bigger the bowl, the more luxurious the glass appears. Use to enjoy cocktails and deluxe aged spirits such as Cognac.

Capacity to brim: 12oz / 35cl

12. Toddy

Frequently referred to as a 'liqueur coffee glass', which is indeed its main use, this glass was popularised by the Irish Coffee. Toddy glasses have a handle on the side, allowing you to comfortably hold hot drinks.

Capacity to brim: 8.5oz / 25cl

13. Sour

This small glass is narrow at the stem and tapers out to a wider lip. As the name would suggest, it is used for serving Sours straight-up. I favour serving Sours over ice in an Old-fashioned but any of the recipes in this guide can be strained and served 'up' in this glass.

Capacity to brim: 4oz / 12cl

14. Rocks

Like an Old-fashioned with a thick rim, this is usually made from toughened glass - perfect for drinks that require muddling in the glass. A hardy glass, if there is such a thing.

Capacity to brim: 9oz / 27cl

GARNISHES

Garnishes are used to decorate cocktails and are often anchored to the rim of the glass. Strictly speaking, garnishes should be edible and can be anything from banana chunks, strawberries or redcurrants to coffee beans, confectionery, basil leaves and slices of fresh ginger. The correct garnish will often enhance the aroma and flavour as well as the look of a drink.

When deciding on what to garnish your cocktail with, use the ingredients within the drink as inspiration. For example if a drink is made using lime juice then a lime wedge is a safe option.

Fruit selected for high juice yields may not be ideal for garnishes. For example, larger limes juice well but smaller limes make more attractive garnishes. Whatever fruit you use - it should be unblemished and washed prior to use. Cut citrus fruits have a maximum shelf life of 24 hours when refrigerated.

Banana slice

Apple Slice

An apple slice garnish is quick, easy and looks great. Simply slice an apple finely using a mandolin and float the resulting disc on the surface of your drink. Alternatively cut a thicker slice and mount either the whole slice or a fraction of the slice on glass rim by means of diagonal cut in the slice. Apple slices are best cut to order as the cut fruit turns brown very quickly. You can prevent this oxidation by coating the cut sides with citrus juice.

Apple Wedge

Apple wedges can easily be secured to the rim of a glass - cut a wedge that is at maximum ¾ inch thick and slice diagonally to centre to allow placement on glass rim. Alternatively just drop the garnish into the drink - this is particularly effective in tall drinks. The fruit should be firm and fresh and not brown or bruised and the skin should be left on.

Apple Chevron

Using a quarter of an apple cut wafer thin slices down into the fruit but not all the way through – stop about a centimetre from the end of the apple wedge. Cut 5 or 6 slices into the fruit and then ease out these slices into a fan. Leave the skin of the apple on.

Apple Discs Caramelised

These are more time-consuming but worth the effort. Slice an apple finely using a mandolin. Then either coat the slices in sugar syrup or blanch them by dipping them into a simmering pan containing three parts granulated sugar and two parts water. Whichever option you choose, drain off the excess liquid and lay the slices on a baking tray lined with greaseproof paper. Place the tray in an oven set to 85°C (185°F) and bake for about three hours, until the discs are crisp and golden. You can store these in an air-tight container in the refrigerator for up to a fortnight.

Apricot Slice

Use either whole dried apricot or slice of dried apricot and slice into centre of fruit to allow placement on glass rim.

Banana Slice

Fruit should not be either green, bruised or overripe. Some like to remove the skin, others prefer to leave on for both appearance and ease of use. Slice into centre of fruit to allow placement on glass rim.

Berry Skewers

Berries such as blackberries, raspberries, strawberries and blueberries make an attractive and tasty garnish. Use fruit that is ripe but firm and not mushy. Berries can either be floated on the top of a drink or skewered (usually in threes) kebab-style on a cocktail stick and placed across the top of the glass.

Berry Skewers

Chocolate Dust

Grapes

Fruit stick   **Foam**

Celery Sticks

Celery sticks may be placed in drinks as stirring rods as is typical in a Bloody Mary. Choose firm sticks without bruises and cut to a length several inches longer than your glass so when placed inside it protrudes over the rim. Angled cuts tend to be more attractive than simply chopping at 90° to the stem. I like to leave a little of the leaf if possible.

Cherries

Fresh cherries make a tasty and attractive garnish and are less syrupy and sweet than maraschino cherries but with same visual effect. Use fruit that is ripe but firm and not mushy. It is common to cut a slit in cherries to allow them to be secured to the glass rim.

Chocolate Dust

The instruction 'dust with chocolate' refers to a fine coating of cocoa powder on the surface of a drink. The chocolate layer needs to remain very fine so as not to sink into drink. Use cocoa powder, rather than grated chocolate.

Chocolate Rim

Wipe a cut orange slice around the outside rim of glass to leave a line of juice with which to stick powder to glass (rather than lime juice when using salt). Also see 'salt rim' below.

Cinnamon Dust

The instruction dust with cinnamon refers to a fine coating of the spice on the surface of a drink. If using powdered cinnamon, use sparingly so layer does not become too thick and so sink into drink. Better to use a whole cinnamon stick and a fine grater to ensure that dusting is very light.

Cinnamon & Sugar Rim

Wipe a thin strip of sugar syrup around the outside rim of your glass and then roll this in a saucer containing a mixture of cinnamon powder and caster sugar. Also see 'salt rim' below.

Cinnamon Sticks

These are often placed whole in hot drinks and toddies. There are several lengths of dried cinnamon stick available so ensure that cinnamon is longer than the glass you are serving in.

Chilli

A small red eye chilli with a diagonal slice to allow it to sit firmly on the rim of the glass. Probably best not consumed, but each to their own. Also obviously take the usual precautions when handling chillies.

Coffee Beans

Simply float three coffee beans on the surface of the drink. Why three? The number signifies health, wealth and happiness and is said to bestow good luck on the drinker.

Cucumber Slice

Use fresh, moist, crisp cucumber as either a slice or stick. Slices can be cut thin enough to float on the surface of the drink, or, cut thicker, slit and secured to the glass rim.

Cucumber Stick

To make a stick cut length of cucumber to suit glass (should either sit an inch above the rim of the glass or fit exactly) then cut into 1/8 segment leaving skin on. These can be used as a stirrer much like a celery stick.

Flaming Zest Boat

Not only does this potentially dangerous garnish add to the theatrical style of Tiki drinks but my inner child finds floating fire boats irresistible.

Make your zest boat by chopping a lime or lemon lengthwise into four and scraping away the flesh from one wedge. Float your boat on top of the drink and carefully pour in its cargo of high-strength dark rum - for example Woods 100 or Pusser's Navy rum. Lastly, and very carefully please, ignite the rum.

This is almost certainly against nanny state rules and definitely constitutes a fire hazard. All the same, dear readers, I trust you to be responsible and careful. To prevent the predictable trail of carnage I will add:

1. Only use a fraction of a shot of rum or it will burn for ages.
2. Be aware that the flame may be blue and so almost invisible.
3. Don't move the glass, let alone drink from it, until the flame is out.
4. Don't blame me if your bar/home/life goes up in smoke.

Flamed Zest Twist

A flamed zest twist is a dramatic variation on the usual wide-cut zest twist and involves burning the aromatic oils emitted from citrus fruit zest as they are expressed over the surface of a drink. Lemons and limes are sometimes treated in this way but oranges are most popular and give the best results. Firm, thick-skinned navel oranges are best.

You will need to cut as wide a strip of zest as you can, wider than you would for a standard twist. Hold the cut zest, peel side down, between the thumb and forefinger about four inches above the drink and gently warm the skin of the twist with a match or lighter flame for approx 5 seconds. Then pinch the peel by its edges so that its oils squirt through the flame towards the surface of the drink - there should be a flash as the oils ignite. Finally, wipe the zest around the rim of the glass.

Whatever your twist, it should be cut from thoroughly cleaned citrus fruit without blemishes of spots on it skin. Ideally zests should be cut fresh for each drink but kept moist and refrigerated in a sealed box will have a shelf life of 1 day.

Flowers & Petals

Edible flowers and petals set afloat on the surface of a drink makes for an attractive garnish. Ensure the flowers used are edible and have not been sprayed. Suitable varieties include Dendrobium Orchids, Pansies, certain Rose varieties, Nasturtiums, Marigolds and Violets.

Foams

Foams can be made to float on the surface of any cocktail, the aroma and flavour of which usually contrasting with that of the drink beneath, so adding complexity. Foams are usually dispensed from a cream-whipping siphon. Gelatine or egg white is added to the flavoured mixture so when the siphon is charged with nitrous oxide, a foam is produced.

Popular base ingredients include cold tea and fruit juice but the foam can be made using pretty much any liquid provided that it is not oily. Both the ingredients and the charged siphon should be stored in a refrigerator as the colder the foam, the thicker it will be when discharged and the longer it will last on the top of the drink.

Nitrous oxide (N_2O), the key to these foams, is commonly known as laughing gas and is a colourless non-flammable gas with a pleasant, slightly sweet smell. Its nickname refers to the stimulating effects of inhaling it, which include spontaneous laughter, slight hallucinations and an analgesic effect. It is used in motor sport to boost power (nitrous oxide kit), and in surgery and dentistry as an analgesic. A 50/50 mixture of nitrous oxide and oxygen ('gas and air') is commonly used during childbirth. Nitrous oxide is a powerful greenhouse gas and you add to its global warming effect when opening a bag of potato chips as the gas is also used to displace staleness-inducing oxygen in snack food packaging.

WARNING - Inhaling nitrous oxide directly from a whipped cream charger or tank poses very serious health risks. These include potential lung collapse due to the high pressure and frostbite since the gas is very cold when released. I'm not suggesting you try this, but most recreational nitrous oxide users discharge the gas into a balloon before inhaling. Nitrous oxide can also cause mild nausea or dizziness and is unsafe to inhale while standing, as you are likely to fall over. I should also add that the possession of and recreational use of nitrous oxide is a criminal offence in much of the US and other areas of the world.

Fruit Stick

A fruit stick consists of one or more pineapple cubes and a maraschino cherry skewered kebab-style on a cocktail stick or specially designed plastic or wooden pick. Popularly used to garnish Tiki-style drinks the creation of the fruit stick is credited to Victor Jules Bergeron (A.K.A. Trader Vic) in the early 1930s.

Cut pineapple into quarters from top to bottom and remove woody core. Further cut into ½ inch or 1 centimetre cubes. Do not use overripe or mushy fruit. Cut pineapple will stay fresh for up to a day but it is of course preferable to cut to order.

Grapes

Grapes can be a simple and effective garnish. Either drop them into the drink or push three onto a cocktail stick and balance across the rim of the glass.

Kiwi slice

Lemon wedge

Grapefruit Zest Twist

Treat it as you would an oversized lemon and 'twist' a zest of the flavoursome oils over your drink.

Grated Chocolate

To sprinkle chocolate on the surface of a drink you can either shave chocolate using a vegetable peeler or dust with powder using a chocolate shaker with a fine mesh. Alternatively crumble a Cadbury's Flake bar in which case ensure fragments are small enough to prevent them sinking into drink.

Horse's Neck Peel

This classic garnish is usually used to garnish the drink of the same name and is basically a long ½ inch wide strip of peel cut in a continuous spiral and placed so as to overhang the rim of the glass. Lemon is most commonly used but a Horse's Neck can also be made from oranges and limes.

To achieve this hold a lemon lying horizontally in your hand with one end facing you. Use a canelle knife to cut into the far end of the fruit and pull towards you ¼ inch. Then turn the cut 90 degrees and start cutting around the lemon so that a ½ inch wide strip is left between the channels you cut. It is this wide strip left spiralling around the lemon that will form your Horse's Neck. Using a small knife carefully cut this strip from the lemon leaving as much of the white pith behind. This is placed in the glass spiralling up from the bottom to the top with the 'head' hooked over the rim of the glass. Place the ice inside the spiral before pouring your drink.

Kiwi Slice

Kiwi fruit slices prettily. Clean the fruit and slice using a slit in the side to secure to the rim of the glass.

Lemon Slice

Sometimes referred to as a 'lemon wheel' this is one of the truly classic garnishes. Wash fruit thoroughly and preferably use unwaxed lemons with uniform yellow skin (without green or brown discolouration). Cut 3/8 inch thick slices across the width of the fruit discarding both ends (poles). Slice to centre for placement on glass rim. Preferably cut as required or store cut fruit for a maximum of 6 hours.

Lemon Wedge

Wedges of lemons are often squeezed into drinks or fixed to the side of the glass as a garnish. A lemon wedge is an eighth segment of the fruit.

Wash fruit thoroughly and preferably use unwaxed lemons with uniform yellow skin (without green or brown discolouration). Cut the 'knobs' from either pole of the fruit, slice the fruit in half lengthwise, then cut each half into four equal wedges lengthwise. Cut a slit into the pointed flesh of each wedge to enable placement on glass rim. Preferably cut as required or store cut fruit for a maximum of 6 hours.

Marashino Cherries

Mint

Lime Slice

Sometimes referred to as a 'lime wheel'. Wash fruit thoroughly and preferably use unwaxed lemons with uniform green skin (without yellow or brown discolouration). Cut 3/8 inch thick slices across the width of the fruit discarding both ends (poles). Slice to centre for placement on glass rim. Preferably cut as required or store cut fruit for a maximum of 6 hours.

Lime Wedge

Fix lime wedge on side of glass or squeeze and drop into drink. A wedge is a sixth, or with large limes, an eighth segment of the fruit. The lime should have green skin without yellow or brown dis-colouration. Cut the 'knobs' from the top and bottom poles of the fruit, slice the fruit in half lengthwise, then cut each half into three (or for eighths, four) equal wedges lengthwise.

There are numerous ways to cut a slit into the fruit to fix onto glass but the most popular is by cutting into the pointed flesh at an angle. Lime wedges should be used within 6 hours of being cut and preferably cut as required.

Mangos

Fresh mangos are not generally used as a garnish. However, you can cut the flesh into cubes and skewer them on a cocktail stick or fix long thin wedge on the glass rim. Alternatively garnish mango cocktails with slices of dried mango on a stick.

Maraschino Cherries

Maraschino cherries were originally fresh cherries marinated in maraschino liqueur and such cherries are still made and available from Luxardo. However, nowadays the term typically refers to a preserved, sweetened cherries dyed bright red with food colouring and usually flavoured with almond.

Blue and yellow dyed maraschino cherries are also available and typically the green ones are peppermint-flavoured (green crème de menthe) while the blue ones are orange-flavoured (think blue curaçao). That said in the US it would appear they all have the same almond-maraschino flavour regardless of the colour.

Look for Opies stemmed maraschino cherries which, as the name would suggest, retain their stems to make a more attractive garnish (and for those with dexterous tongues to amaze their friends by tying said stems in a knot).

Maraschino cherries should be stored refrigerated and left in their own syrup/liqueur which should be saved as it is often used in recipes such as Sweet Manhattan. Drop cherry into drink.

Mint Leaf

A simple leaf or mint sprig atop a cocktail adds colour and a wonderful fresh fragrance. Boost the olfactory effect by smacking the mint between your hands before you drop onto the surface of the drink or drape over the rim.

Mint Sprig

When selecting a mint sprig for garnish, look for the tips of the sprig and use the top two inches or 50mm. There should be at least 6 leaves that push together and sit within drink.

Nutmeg Dust

The instruction 'dust with nutmeg' refers to a fine coating of the spice on the surface of a drink. It is preferable to grate fresh nutmeg as the powdered kind lacks flavour. Use a very fine grater and ensure that no one area becomes too heavily covered and so sinks into the drink.

Olives

The 'Oliver' from the 'Oliver Twist' duo classically graces a Dry Martini. It is essential to wash olives thoroughly to prevent oil from spoiling the appearance of a drink. Only remove sufficient olives required for a particular session from the jar.

Olives should be stored refrigerated and left in the oil or brine in which they were packaged. This brine may be used in a Dirty Martini.

Onions

Onions should be stored refrigerated and left in the oil or brine in which they were packaged and only removed from the jar when required. Small white cocktail onions are most notably used to garnish a Gibson Martini.

Orange Slice

Orange is a popular garnish. Slices (or wheels) are used whole in the drink or speared with cocktail sticks and cherries to make sails. It's also common to cut the slices in half.

Select (preferably unwaxed) fruit without brown discolouration and wash thoroughly. Cut 3/8 inch thick slices and store for a maximum of 6 hours or better, cut as required.

Orange Zest Twist

The fruit's bright skin adds flavoursome aromatic oils to a drink when used as a twist. If you are making twists, however, it is best to buy organically grown oranges, which are not sprayed with chemicals. See 'Twist' below.

Parasol (Umbrella)

A cocktail parasol is a miniature paper umbrella with cardboard ribs and a toothpick stem. It tends to be used to garnish rum based or 'Tikki' cocktails and is thought to have originally been introduced in the early 1930s by Don the Beachcomber at his Beachcomber restaurant in Hollywood, USA. Their purpose, amazingly, is not to shield delicate ice cubes from the rays of the sun but purely decorative.

Passion Fruit Boat

Despite its name, the fruit of love is remarkably ugly and garnishing can be a challenge. The two best garnishes utilising this fruit I know are 1), float half a fruit, cut side up, like a boat on the surface of your drink, or 2), if your cocktail uses crushed ice, cut a quarter of passion fruit and place it on the surface of the ice. Please discard the empty shells and don't even contemplate letting them anywhere near the rim of a glass.

Peach Slice/Wedge

Peaches should be firm not mushy and skin should remain on. Cut wedges at maximum ¾ inch thick as required and slice diagonally to centre to allow placement on glass rim.

Pear Slice/Wedge

Slices of pear can look great on the rim of a Martini glass. However, they oxidise very quickly, and should be rubbed with lemon juice.

Phsyalis

Leave fruit whole with leaves and stalk but wash before use. Carefully open the leaves and gently fold back against the stem and turn the stem and leaves in the opposite direction of the fruit half-a-turn. Then make a diagonal incision across the bottom of the fruit to facilitate placement on glass rim.

Pineapple Wedge

No Pina Colada or truly tropical cocktail is properly dressed without a wedge of pineapple, preferably with a maraschino cherry spiked into it. Cut the pineapple into ½ inch or 1cm thick rings and each ring into wedges as if cutting a cake and avoiding the woody core. A knife slit in the side of the wedge allows you to anchor it to the rim of a glass.

The skin adds to the appearance of this garnish so should remain on but golden is preferable to green. Do not use overripe or mushy fruit and either cut as required or store for maximum of 1 day.

Sail

A sail is a whole slice (or wheel) of citrus fruit, usually orange, served on a cocktail stick 'mast' and so known as a 'sail'. Usually the circular slice of fruit is folded around a maraschino cherry and the cocktail stick is skewered through both pieces of fruit.

Salt/Sugar Rim

Some recipes call for the rim of the glass to be coated with salt, sugar or other ingredients such as desiccated coconut or chocolate: you will need to moisten the rim first before the ingredient will hold. When using salt, wipe a cut wedge of lime around the outside edge of the rim, then roll the outside edge through a saucer of salt. (Use sea salt rather than iodised salt as the flavour is less biting.) For sweet ingredients like sugar and chocolate, either use an orange slice as you would a lime wedge or moisten a sponge or paper towel with a suitable liqueur and run it around the outside edge of the glass.

Whatever you are using to rim the glass should cling to the outside edge only. Remember, garnishes are not a cocktail ingredient but an optional extra to be consumed by choice. They should not contaminate your cocktail. If some of your garnish should become stuck to the inside edge of the glass, remove it using a fresh fruit wedge or a paper towel.

It is good practice to salt or sugar only two-thirds of the rim of a glass. This allows the drinker the option of avoiding the salt or sugar. If you rim glasses some hours prior to use, the lime juice or liqueur will dry, leaving a crust of salt or sugar crystals around the rim. The glasses can then be placed in a refrigerator to chill ready for use. If not kept ice cold, the juice and sugar can run down the glass.

A professional piece of equipment with the unfortunate title of a 'rimmer' has three sections, one with a sponge for water or lime juice, one containing sugar and another containing salt. Beware, as this encourages dipping the glass onto a moist sponge and then into the garnish, and so contaminating the inside of the glass.

Spicy Beans

Canadian readers will be well aware of these long, thin pickled beans. They are a popular alternative to celery in those parts as a garnish for 'Caesar' cocktails, a Canadian twist on the Bloody Mary. They originate with Blaze Denoon, who started picking beans in Vancouver in 1995. For more information see blazesbeans.com.

Star Anise

Star anise is the star-shaped pericarp of Illicium verum, a small native evergreen tree of southwest China. This dried spice is frequently floated on the surface of anise-flavoured drinks (so those who dislike this flavour should consider themselves warned).

Star Fruit

Star fruit can either be floated on the top of the drink and so a wafer thin slice should be cut to ensure the fruit does not sink. Otherwise a thicker slice can also be placed on the rim of the glass. Cut a slice of star fruit about ¼ inch or ½ cm thick and slice diagonally to centre to allow placement on glass rim.

Strawberry Fan

Cut wafer thin slices into strawberry and spear with a cocktail stick. Spread the slices apart to create a fan.

Zest Twist

This term refers to affecting the aroma and so perceived flavour of a drink by releasing the aromatic oils from a strip of citrus zest (lemon, lime, orange, grapefruit).

Using a knife or peeler, cut a ½ inch (12mm) wide length of zest from an unwaxed, cleaned fruit so as to leave just a little of the white pith. Hold it over the glass with the thumb and forefinger of each hand, coloured side down. Turn one end clockwise and the other anticlockwise so as to twist the peel and force some of its oils over the surface of the drink. Deposit any flavoursome oils left on the surface of the peel by wiping the coloured side around the rim of the glass. Some prefer to dispose of the spent twist but most drop the peel onto the surface of the drink as a garnish.

Citrus twists can also be thin, string like lengths of zest cut with a canelle knife and wrapped around a stirring rod to make a spring-like garnish, which is then slid off the stirrer and into the drink. Such thinly cut string-like twists can also be tied into a knot.

Physyalis

Salt/Sugar Rim

Sail

Orange Zest Twist

Olives

THE 14 KEY INGREDIENTS

| VODKA | GIN | RUM | TEQUILA | SCOTCH | COGNAC | BOURBON |

| TRIPLE SEC | ORANGE LIQUEUR | APRICOT LIQUEUR | BERRY LIQUEUR | DRY VERMOUTH | SWEET VERMOUTH | CHAMPAGNE |

WITH JUST THE 14 KEY INGREDIENTS ABOVE, A FEW MIXERS, SOME FRESH FRUIT, COPIOUS AMOUNTS OF ICE AND A HANDFUL OF KITCHEN BASICS YOU WILL BE ABLE TO MAKE MORE THAN 500 COCKTAILS IN THIS GUIDE.

LOOK FOR THE 🗝

FRIDGE & PANTRY ESSENTIALS

CRANBERRY JUICE	ORANGE JUICE	PRESSED APPLE JUICE	GRAPEFRUIT JUICE (PINK)	PINEAPPLE JUICE	TOMATO JUICE	COLA
SODA WATER	GINGER ALE & GINGER BEER	TONIC WATER	LEMONADE	LIME CORDIAL	ANGOSTURA BITTERS	MILK
FRESH LEMONS	FRESH LIMES	FRESH MINT	STRAWBERRIES	RASPBERRIES	MARASCHINO CHERRIES	EGGS
BLUEBERRIES	BANANAS	WHITE GRAPES	RED GRAPES	RUNNY HONEY	EARL GREY TEA	DOUBLE CREAM

SUGAR SYRUP

Many cocktails benefit from sweetening but granulated sugar does not dissolve easily in cold drinks. Hence pre-dissolved sugar syrup (also known as 'simple syrup') is used.

Make your own sugar syrup by gradually pouring and stirring two cups of granulated sugar into a saucepan containing one cup of hot water and simmer until the sugar is dissolved. Do not let the water even come close to boiling and only simmer for as long as it takes to dissolve the sugar. Allow syrup to cool and pour into an empty bottle. Ideally, you should finely strain your syrup into the bottle to remove any undissolved crystals which could otherwise encourage crystallisation. If kept in a refrigerator this mixture will last for a couple of months.

POMEGRANATE (GRENADINE) SYRUP

To make your own pomegranate syrup simply follow the instructions for sugar syrup above but use one cup of pomegranate juice (Pom Wonderful) in place of the water.

OUR RECIPES EXPLAINED

Bar
A dark bar indicates a new or updated drink, also stated next to the name. A light bar indicates a drink published in a previous edition.

Grade
Drinks are graded as follows:
1 circle = Disgusting,
5 circles = Outstanding

●●●●◑

Cocktail name

DAIQUIRI NO.2 UPDATED #8

Key
Indicates drinks which can be made using our 14 Key Ingredients (see page 26).

Glass
See pages 16-17 for glassware shapes and names.

Glass: Martini
Garnish: Lime wedge on rim
Method: SHAKE all ingredients with ice and fine strain into chilled glass.

2	shot(s)	**Bacardi Superior rum**
⅛	shot(s)	**Cointreau triple sec**
½	shot(s)	**Freshly squeezed orange juice**
½	shot(s)	**Freshly squeezed lime juice**
¼	shot(s)	**Sugar syrup** (2 sugar to 1 water)

Comment: A Daiquiri with subtle orange notes, but far from being a mere Orange Daiquiri.
Origin: Created circa 1915 by Constantino (Constante) Ribalaigua Vert at Floridita bar in Havana, Cuba.

Garnish
See pages 18-25 for full information on garnishes.

Ingredients
Recipes are laid out in the order we recommend adding to glass or shaker.

Method
See pages 6-13 for tips on how to shake, stir etc.

Origin
When, where and who created recipes.

Comment
Indication of taste or suitably flippant remark by Yours Truly.

Shot
Ideally a shot equals 30ml or 1oz but could be a shot glass or bottle cap.

A

A1 NEW #8

Glass: Martini
Garnish: Orange zest twist
Method: SHAKE all ingredients with ice and fine strain into chilled glass.

1¾	shot(s)	**Tanqueray London dry gin**
1	shot(s)	**Grand Marnier liqueur**
¼	shot(s)	**Freshly squeezed lemon juice**
⅛	shot(s)	**Pomegranate (grenadine) syrup**

Comment: Nothing subtle about this full-on orange, gin based short drink.
Origin: In W.J. Tarling's 1937 Café Royal Cocktail Book this cocktail is accompanied by the notation, "Invented by Albert". The recipe stated is "1 dash lemon juice, 1/3 Grand Marnier, 2/3 Dry Gin, Dash Grenadine."

A.B.C.

Glass: Shot
Method: Refrigerate ingredients then LAYER in chilled glass by carefully pouring in the following order.

½	shot(s)	**Luxardo Amaretto di Saschira**
½	shot(s)	**Baileys Irish cream liqueur**
½	shot(s)	**Courvoisier V.S.O.P. cognac**

Comment: A stripey shooter with almond, whiskey, cream and cognac.

'IN NEVADA… THE CHEAPEST AND EASIEST WAY TO BECOME AN INFLUENTIAL MAN… WAS TO STAND BEHIND A BAR, WEAR A DIAMOND CLUSTER-PIN, AND SELL WHISKEY.'
MARK TWAIN

A.B.C. COCKTAIL NEW #8

Glass: Martini (small)
Garnish: Lemon zest twist & cherry
Method: TEAR mint and place in shaker. Add other ingredients, SHAKE with ice and fine strain into chilled glass.

7	fresh	**Mint leaves**
1	shot(s)	**Courvoisier V.S.O.P. cognac**
1	shot(s)	**Warre's Otima tawny port**
¼	shot(s)	**Luxardo maraschino liqueur**
⅛	shot(s)	**Sugar syrup** (2 sugar to 1 water)
1	dash	**Angostura aromatic bitters**

Comment: Wonderfully delicate. Mint gives subtle freshness to the classic port and brandy combo.
Origin: Vintage cocktail of unknown origin.

ABACAXI RICAÇO

Glass: Pineapple shell (frozen)
Garnish: Cut a straw sized hole in the top of the pineapple and replace it as a lid.
Method: Cut the top off a small pineapple and carefully scoop out the flesh from the base to leave a shell with 12mm (½") thick walls. Place the shell in a freezer to chill. Remove the hard core from the pineapple flesh and discard; roughly chop the remaining flesh, add other ingredients and BLEND with one 12oz scoop of crushed ice. Pour into the pineapple shell and serve with straws. (The flesh of one pineapple blended with the following ingredients will fill at least two shells.)

1	fresh	**Pineapple**
3	shot(s)	**Bacardi Oro golden rum**
¾	shot(s)	**Freshly squeezed lime juice**
½	shot(s)	**Sugar syrup** (2 sugar to 1 water)

Origin: Adapted from David A. Embury's 1948 'Fine Art of Mixing Drinks'. Pronounced 'Ah-bah-Kah-shee Rich-kah-So', the Portuguese name of this Brazilian drink literally translates as 'Extra Delicious Pineapple'.
Comment: Looks and tastes great but a load of hassle to make.

ABBEY MARTINI

Glass: Martini
Garnish: Orange zest twist
Method: SHAKE all ingredients with ice and fine strain into chilled glass.

2	shot(s)	**Tanqueray London dry gin**
1	shot(s)	**Martini Rosso sweet vermouth**
1	shot(s)	**Freshly squeezed orange juice**
3	dashes	**Angostura aromatic bitters**

Origin: This 1930s classic cocktail is closely related to the better known Bronx.
Comment: A dry, orangey, herbal, gin laced concoction.

ABSINTHE COCKTAIL #1

Glass: Martini
Garnish: Mint leaf
Method: SHAKE all ingredients with ice and fine strain into chilled glass.

1	shot(s)	**La Fée Parisienne (68%) absinthe**
1	shot(s)	**Chilled mineral water**
¼	shot(s)	**Sugar syrup** (2 sugar to 1 water)

Variant: If grenadine (pomegranate syrup) is substituted for the sugar syrup this becomes a Tomate.
Origin: Dr. Ordinaire perfected his recipe for absinthe in 1792 and from day one it required the addition of water and sugar to make it palatable.
Comment: Absinthe tamed and served up.

ABSINTHE COCKTAIL #2

●●●●○○

Glass: Martini
Garnish: Lemon zest twist
Method: SHAKE all ingredients with ice and fine strain into chilled glass.

1	shot(s)	**La Fée Parisienne (68%) absinthe**
¼	shot(s)	**Almond (orgeat) syrup**
¼	shot(s)	**Marie Brizard anisette liqueur**
1	dash	**Angostura aromatic bitters**
¾	shot(s)	**Chilled mineral water** (reduce if wet ice)

Variant: Absinthe Frappé - served over crushed ice.
Origin: My adaptation of a classic recipe.
Comment: This aniseed flavoured mix tastes surprisingly tame but includes a shot of the notorious green fairy.

ABSINTHE DRIP COCKTAIL #1
(FRENCH METHOD)

●●●○○

Glass: Old-fashioned or absinthe glass
Method: POUR absinthe into glass. **PLACE** cube of sugar on a slotted absinthe spoon resting across the top of the glass. Using a bottle of chilled mineral water with a small hole in the cap, **DRIP** water over the sugar so it dissolves and drips into the glass. Traditionally the same amount of sugar is added as water but I find full strength absinthe requires more dilution. Add ice, stir and serve.

1½	shot(s)	**La Fée Parisienne (68%) absinthe**
1	large	**Sugar cube**
2	shot(s)	**Chilled mineral water**

Origin: This is the traditional method of serving absinthe. It was common until shortly before the First World War, when the drink was banned in most countries.
Comment: Patience is a virtue. Slow dripping of the water is essential to dissolve the entire sugar cube and give the drink enough sweetness to balance the absinthe.

ABSINTHE DRIP COCKTAIL #2
(CZECH METHOD)

●●●●○○

Glass: Old-fashioned or absinthe glass
Method: PLACE sugar cube on a slotted absinthe spoon resting across the top of the glass. **POUR** absinthe over the sugar cube into the glass. **LIGHT** the absinthe soaked cube and leave to burn and caramelise. Using a bottle of chilled mineral water with a small hole in the cap, **DRIP** water over what's left of the sugar so it dissolves and drips into the glass. Add ice, stir and serve.

1½	shot(s)	**La Fée Bohemian (70%) absinthe**
1	large	**Sugar cube**
2	shot(s)	**Chilled mineral water**

Origin: This supposedly bohemian method of serving absinthe came back in to being in 1998 with the UK launch of Hill's Absinth.
Comment: More about the theatrics involved in its making than the taste of the finished drink.

ABSINTHE DROP NEW #8

●●●○○

Glass: Old-fashioned
Garnish: None
Method: STIR all ingredients and strain into ice-filled glass.

1	shot(s)	**La Fée Parisienne (68%) absinthe**
¼	shot(s)	**Marie Brizard anisette liqueur**
2	shot(s)	**Chilled mineral water**

Comment: A fix for aniseed addicts.
Origin: Vintage cocktail of unknown origin.

ABSINTHE FRAPPÉ

●●●●○

Glass: Old-fashioned
Garnish: Mint sprig
Method: SHAKE all ingredients with ice and fine strain into glass filled with crushed ice. **CHURN** (stir) and serve with straws.

1½	shot(s)	**La Fée Parisienne (68%) absinthe**
½	shot(s)	**Marie Brizard anisette liqueur**
1½	shot(s)	**Chilled mineral water**
¼	shot(s)	**Sugar syrup** (2 sugar to 1 water)

Origin: Created in 1874 by Cayetano Ferrer at Aleix's Coffee House, New Orleans, which consequently became known as The Absinthe Room. Today the establishment is fittingly known as The Old Absinthe House.
Comment: Aniseed and the fire of absinthe are moderated by sugar and ice but still a dangerous combination.

ABSINTHE ITALIANO COCKTAIL

●●●○○

Glass: Martini
Garnish: Lemon zest twist
Method: SHAKE all ingredients with ice and fine strain into chilled glass.

1	shot(s)	**La Fée Parisienne (68%) absinthe**
½	shot(s)	**Marie Brizard anisette liqueur**
¼	shot(s)	**Luxardo maraschino liqueur**
1½	shot(s)	**Chilled mineral water** (reduce if wet ice)

Origin: A long lost classic.
Comment: Liqueurs sweeten and tame the absinthe burn in this milky green concoction.

ABSINTHE SOUR

●●●●○

Glass: Old-fashioned
Garnish: Lemon zest twist
Method: SHAKE all ingredients with ice and strain into ice-filled glass.

1	shot(s)	**La Fée Parisienne (68%) absinthe**
1	shot(s)	**Sugar syrup** (2 sugar to 1 water)
1	shot(s)	**Freshly squeezed lemon juice**
½	fresh	**Egg white**

Variant: Served 'up' in sour glass.
Comment: A touch of the sours for absinthe lovers.

A

ABSINTHE SPECIAL COCKTAIL

●●●●○○

Glass: Martini
Garnish: Lemon zest twist
Method: SHAKE all ingredients with ice and fine strain into chilled glass.

1	shot(s)	La Fée Parisienne (68%) absinthe
¼	shot(s)	Tanqueray London dry gin
¼	shot(s)	Marie Brizard anisette liqueur
1	dash	Angostura orange bitters
2	dashes	Angostura aromatic bitters
1½	shot(s)	Chilled mineral water (reduce if wet ice)

Origin: A long lost classic.
Comment: Tongue numbingly strong in flavour and alcohol.

ABSINTHE SUISESSE

●●●●○○

Glass: Old-fashioned
Garnish: Mint sprig
Method: SHAKE all ingredients with ice and strain into glass filled with crushed ice.

1½	shot(s)	La Fée Parisienne (68%) absinthe
½	shot(s)	Almond (orgeat) syrup
1	fresh	Egg white
½	shot(s)	Double (heavy) cream
½	shot(s)	Milk

Origin: New Orleans 1930s.
Variant: Also spelt 'Suissesse' and sometimes made with absinthe, vermouth, sugar, crème de menthe and egg white shaken and topped with sparkling water.
Comment: Absinthe smoothed with cream and sweet almond.

ABSINTHE WITHOUT LEAVE

●●●○○○

Glass: Shot
Method: Refrigerate ingredients then LAYER in chilled glass by carefully pouring in the following order.

¾	shot(s)	Pisang Ambon liqueur
¾	shot(s)	Baileys Irish cream liqueur
½	shot(s)	La Fée Parisienne (68%) absinthe

Origin: Discovered in 2003 at Hush, London, England.
Comment: This green and brown stripy shot is easy to layer but not so easy to drink.

ABSOLUTELY FABULOUS

●●●●○

Glass: Flute
Garnish: Strawberry on rim
Method: SHAKE first two ingredients with ice and strain into glass. TOP with champagne.

1	shot(s)	Ketel One vodka
2	shot(s)	Ocean Spray cranberry juice
Top up with		Perrier Jouet brut champagne

Origin: Created in 1999 at Monte's Club, London, England, and named after the Absolutely Fabulous television series where Patsy consumed copious quantities of Stoli and Bolly – darlings.
Comment: Easy to quaff – Patsy would love it.

ACAPULCO

●●●●●○

Glass: Collins
Garnish: Pineapple wedge on rim
Method: SHAKE all ingredients with ice and strain into ice-filled glass.

1	shot(s)	Don Julio reposado tequila
1	shot(s)	Bacardi Oro golden rum
1	shot(s)	Freshly squeezed grapefruit juice
2½	shot(s)	Pressed pineapple juice
½	shot(s)	Sugar syrup (2 sugar to 1 water)

Comment: An innocuous, fruity mixture laced with tequila and rum.

ACAPULCO DAIQUIRI

●●●●●○

Glass: Martini
Garnish: Lime wedge on rim
Method: SHAKE all ingredients with ice and fine strain into chilled glass.

1½	shot(s)	Bacardi Superior rum
½	shot(s)	Cointreau triple sec
¾	shot(s)	Freshly squeezed lemon juice
¾	shot(s)	Rose's lime cordial
½	fresh	Egg white

Comment: A smooth, yet citrus-rich Daiquiri.

ACE

●●●●○○

Glass: Martini
Garnish: Maraschino cherry on rim
Method: SHAKE all ingredients with ice and fine strain into chilled glass.

2	shot(s)	Tanqueray London dry gin
½	shot(s)	Pomegranate (grenadine) syrup
½	shot(s)	Double (heavy) cream
½	shot(s)	Milk
½	fresh	Egg white

Comment: Pleasant, creamy, sweetened gin. Add more pomegranate syrup to taste.

ACE OF CLUBS DAIQUIRI UPDATED #8

●●●●◑

Glass: Martini
Garnish: Dust with cocoa powder
Method: SHAKE all ingredients with ice and fine strain into chilled glass.

2	shot(s)	Bacardi Oro golden rum
½	shot(s)	White crème de cacao liqueur
½	shot(s)	Freshly squeezed lime juice
⅛	shot(s)	Sugar syrup (2 sugar to 1 water)

Comment: A Daiquiri with a hint of chocolate.
Origin: Created in the 1930s at a Bermudian nightclub of the same name.

B
C
D
E
F
G
H
I
J
K
L
M
N
O
P
Q
R
S
T
U
V
W
X
Y
Z

ACHILLES HEEL

Glass: Collins
Garnish: Apple slice
Method: SHAKE all ingredients with ice and strain into ice-filled glass.

2	shot(s)	**Zubrówka bison vodka**
¼	shot(s)	**Chambord black raspberry liqueur**
¼	shot(s)	**Peach Tree peach schnapps**
1	shot(s)	**Pressed apple juice**
½	shot(s)	**Freshly squeezed lemon juice**

Origin: Created in 2005 at Koba, Brighton, England.
Comment: If you like French Martinis you'll love this semi-sweet Tatanka with knobs on.

ADAM & EVE

Glass: Old-fashioned
Garnish: Lemon zest twist
Method: SHAKE all ingredients with ice and strain into ice-filled glass.

2	shot(s)	**Bulleit bourbon whiskey**
½	shot(s)	**Galliano L'Autentico liqueur**
¼	shot(s)	**Sugar syrup** (2 sugar to 1 water)
3	dashes	**Angostura aromatic bitters**

Comment: Lovers of the Sazerac will appreciate this herbal, bourbon-laced concoction.

ADAM & EVE #2 NEW #8

Glass: Martini
Garnish: Raspberries on stick & lemon zest twist
Method: SHAKE all ingredients with ice and fine strain into chilled glass.

1	shot(s)	**Tanqueray London dry gin**
1	shot(s)	**Courvoisier V.S.O.P. cognac**
1	shot(s)	**Crème de cassis liqueur**
⅛	shot(s)	**Freshly squeezed lemon juice**

Comment: Fruity but not too sweet.

ADDINGTON NEW #8

Glass: Martini
Garnish: Orange zest twist
Method: SHAKE first two ingredients with ice and fine strain into chilled glass. **TOP** with just the merest squirt of soda from chilled siphon.

2	shot(s)	**Martini Rosso sweet vermouth**
1	shot(s)	**Noilly Prat dry vermouth**
Top up with		**Soda** (from chilled siphon)

Comment: Substitute vermouths such as Antica Formula by Giuseppe B. Carpano dramatically alter the character of this cocktail.
Origin: Vintage cocktail of unknown origin.

ADDISON NEW #8

Glass: Martini
Garnish: Maraschino cherry
Method: STIR all ingredients with ice and fine strain into chilled glass.

1½	shot(s)	**Tanqueray London dry gin**
1½	shot(s)	**Martini Rosso sweet vermouth**

Comment: Basically a very wet, sweet Martini.

ADELAIDE SWIZZLE

Glass: Collins
Garnish: Lime slice
Method: POUR all ingredients into glass filled with crushed ice and **SWIZZLE.**

2	shot(s)	**Bacardi Superior rum**
½	shot(s)	**Freshly squeezed lime juice**
¾	shot(s)	**Velvet Falernum liqueur**
2	dashes	**Peychaud's aromatic bitters**

Origin: This is the signature cocktail at Café Adelaide's Swizzle Stick Bar, New Orleans, USA. There it is made with a liquid poured from a plain bottle marked 'top secret' but, having tried a drop, I think it is Falernum.
Comment: A slightly pink, dry, spicy long drink with rum and a hint of cloves and lime.

ADIOS

Glass: Shot
Method: Refrigerate ingredients then **LAYER** in chilled glass by carefully pouring in the following order.

¾	shot(s)	**Kahlúa coffee liqueur**
¾	shot(s)	**Don Julio reposado tequila**

Comment: Surprisingly tasty with a potent agave reminder of what you've just knocked back.

ADIOS AMIGOS COCKTAIL

Glass: Martini
Garnish: Lemon zest twist
Method: SHAKE all ingredients with ice and fine strain into chilled glass.

1	shot(s)	**Bacardi Supeior rum**
½	shot(s)	**Noilly Prat dry vermouth**
½	shot(s)	**Courvoisier V.S.O.P. cognac**
½	shot(s)	**Tanqueray London dry gin**
¼	shot(s)	**Freshly squeezed lime juice**
¼	shot(s)	**Sugar syrup** (2 sugar to 1 water)
½	shot(s)	**Chilled mineral water** (omit if wet ice)

Origin: Adapted from Victor Bergeron's 'Trader Vic's Bartender's Guide' (1972 revised edition).
Comment: To quote Vic, "You know that adios means good-bye. You drink two or three of these, and it's adios, believe me, it's adios."

A

ADIOS AMIGOS #2 NEW #8

●●●●○○

Glass: Martini
Garnish: Lemon zest twist
Method: SHAKE all ingredients with ice and fine strain into chilled glass.

1	shot(s)	**Tanqueray London dry gin**
½	shot(s)	**Courvoisier V.S.O.P. cognac**
½	shot(s)	**Bacardi Superior rum**
½	shot(s)	**Martini Rosso sweet vermouth**
½	shot(s)	**Freshly squeezed lemon juice**
⅛	shot(s)	**Sugar syrup** (2 sugar to 1 water)

Comment: I have added a dash of sugar to what was originally a bone dry recipe.

ADONIS

●●●●●○

Glass: Martini
Garnish: Orange zest twist
Method: STIR all ingredients with ice and strain into chilled glass.

2	shot(s)	**Tio Pepe fino sherry**
1	shot(s)	**Martini Rosso sweet vermouth**
2	dashes	**Angostura orange bitters**

Origin: Thought to have been created in 1886 to celebrate the success of a Broadway musical.
Comment: Surprisingly delicate, dry, aromatic oldie.

AFFINITY UPDATED #8

●●●●○

Glass: Martini
Garnish: Lemon zest twist
Method: STIR all ingredients with ice and fine strain into chilled glass.

1	shot(s)	**Johnnie Walker Scotch whisky**
1	shot(s)	**Martini Rosso sweet vermouth**
1	shot(s)	**Noilly Prat dry vermouth**
1	dash	**Angostura aromatic bitters**

AKA: Scotch Manhattan
Comment: Aperitif style cocktail which when shaken has an almost creamy, soft, mouth feel. Stir, as the recipe originally intended and the Scotch notes are more pronounced. I prefer mine shaken.
Origin: Fashionable in the 1920s.

AFTER EIGHT

●●●●○○

Glass: Shot
Method: SHAKE all ingredients with ice and fine strain into chilled glass.

½	shot(s)	**Ketel One vodka**
½	shot(s)	**White crème de cacao liqueur**
½	shot(s)	**Green crème de menthe liqueur**

Comment: Looks like mouthwash but tastes like liquid After Eight chocolates.

AFTER SIX SHOT

●●●○○

Glass: Shot
Method: Refrigerate ingredients then LAYER in chilled glass by carefully pouring in the following order.

½	shot(s)	**Kahlúa coffee liqueur**
½	shot(s)	**Giffard Menthe Pastille liqueur**
½	shot(s)	**Baileys Irish cream liqueur**

Comment: A layered, creamy, coffee and mint shot.

AFTERBURNER

●●●●○

Glass: Snifter
Method: POUR all ingredients into glass, swirl to mix, FLAMBÉ and then extinguish flame. Please take care and beware of hot glass rim.

1	shot(s)	**Giffard Menthe Pastille liqueur**
1	shot(s)	**Kahlúa coffee liqueur**
½	shot(s)	**Wray & Nephew overproof rum**

Comment: A surprisingly smooth and moreish peppermint-laced drink.

AGED HONEY DAIQUIRI

●●●●●

Glass: Martini
Garnish: Lime wedge on rim
Method: STIR honey with rum in base of shaker until honey dissolves. Add lime juice and water, SHAKE with ice and fine strain into chilled glass.

2	shot(s)	**Zacapa aged rum**
1½	spoons	**Runny honey**
½	shot(s)	**Freshly squeezed lime juice**
½	shot(s)	**Chilled mineral water** (omit if wet ice)

Comment: Sweet honey replaces sugar syrup in this natural Daiquiri. Try experimenting with different honeys. I favour orange blossom honey.

AGENT ORANGE

●●●●○

Glass: Old-fashioned
Garnish: Orange zest twist
Method: SHAKE all ingredients with ice and strain into ice-filled glass.

1	shot(s)	**Ketel One vodka**
½	shot(s)	**Grand Marnier liqueur**
½	shot(s)	**Cointreau triple sec**
2	shot(s)	**Freshly squeezed orange juice**

Comment: Fresh orange is good for you. This has all of the flavour but few of the health benefits.

AGGRAVATION

Glass: Old-fashioned
Garnish: Dust with freshly grated nutmeg
Method: SHAKE all ingredients with ice and strain into ice-filled glass.

2	shot(s)	**Johnnie Walker Scotch whisky**
¾	shot(s)	**Kahlúa coffee liqueur**
¾	shot(s)	**Double (heavy) cream**
¾	shot(s)	**Milk**
¼	shot(s)	**Sugar syrup** (2 sugar to 1 water)

Comment: If you like Scotch and enjoy creamy drinks, you'll love this.

AIR MAIL UPDATED #8

Glass: Collins
Garnish: Mint sprig
Method: SHAKE first 4 ingredients with ice and fine strain into ice-filled glass. **TOP** with champagne.

2	shot(s)	**Bacardi Oro golden rum**
¼	shot(s)	**Honey syrup** (4 honey to 1 water)
½	shot(s)	**Freshly squeezed lime juice**
½	shot(s)	**Freshly squeezed orange juice**
Top up with		**Perrier Jouet brut champagne**

Comment: This old classic is basically a Honeysuckle served long and topped with champagne. Rum, honey and a touch of citrus freshness make this one of the better champagne cocktails.
Origin: Adapted from a classic recipe, which first appears in the 1949 Esquire's Handbook for Hosts. This is a potent drink and the name could be a reference to airmail being the quickest way of getting a letter from A to B.

A.J. UPDATED #8

Glass: Martini
Garnish: Dust with cinnamon powder
Method: SHAKE all ingredients with ice and fine strain into chilled glass.

2	shot(s)	**Boulard Grand Solage calvados**
2	shot(s)	**Freshly squeezed grapefruit juice**
½	shot(s)	**Sugar syrup** (2 sugar to 1 water)

Comment: Amazingly simple and beautifully balanced. I hope you like apple brandy as much as I do.
Origin: The initials in the name stand for 'applejack', the American style of apple brandy this drink was originally based upon.

DRINKS ARE GRADED AS FOLLOWS:

● DISGUSTING   ●◐ PRETTY AWFUL   ●● BEST AVOIDED
●●◐ DISAPPOINTING   ●●● ACCEPTABLE   ●●●◐ GOOD
●●●● RECOMMENDED   ●●●●◐ HIGHLY RECOMMENDED
●●●●● OUTSTANDING / EXCEPTIONAL

AKU AKU

Glass: Large Martini (10oz)
Garnish: Pineapple wedge & cherry on rim
Method: BLEND all ingredients with 12oz scoop crushed ice. Serve with short straws.

1	shot(s)	**Bacardi Superior rum**
½	shot(s)	**Peach Tree peach schnapps**
1½	shot(s)	**Pressed pineapple juice**
½	shot(s)	**Sugar syrup** (2 sugar to 1 water)
¾	shot(s)	**Freshly squeezed lime juice**
10	fresh	**Mint leaves**

Origin: Adapted from Victor Bergeron's 'Trader Vic's Bartender's Guide' (1972 revised edition).
Comment: This Tiki classic looks a little like frozen stagnant pond water but tastes minty fresh and rather good.

ALABAMA SLAMMER #1

Glass: Martini
Garnish: Orange zest twist
Method: SHAKE all ingredients with ice and fine strain into chilled glass.

1½	shot(s)	**Ketel One vodka**
¾	shot(s)	**Southern Comfort liqueur**
1	shot(s)	**Freshly squeezed orange juice**
¼	shot(s)	**Pomegranate (grenadine) syrup**

Comment: None of the ingredients come from Alabama and the drink is served too long to slam. However, it's a good, rhythmic, rhyming name, if a little naff these days.

ALABAMA SLAMMER #2

Glass: Old-fashioned
Garnish: Peach wedge on rim
Method: SHAKE all ingredients with ice and strain into ice-filled glass.

1½	shot(s)	**Southern Comfort liqueur**
½	shot(s)	**Sloe gin liqueur**
½	shot(s)	**Luxardo Amaretto di Saschira**
2	shot(s)	**Freshly squeezed orange juice**
¾	shot(s)	**Freshly squeezed lemon juice**

Comment: Rich in flavour and quite sweet with a citrus bite. Surprisingly peachy!

ALABAZAM NEW #8

Glass: Collins
Garnish: Lemon slice
Method: SHAKE first 5 ingredients with ice and strain into ice-filled glass. **TOP** with soda.

2	shot(s)	**Courvoisier V.S.O.P. cognac**
1	shot(s)	**Grand Marnier liqueur**
1	shot(s)	**Freshly squeezed lemon juice**
½	shot(s)	**Sugar syrup** (2 sugar to 1 water)
1	dash	**Angostura orange bitters** (optional)
Top up with		**Soda water** (club soda)

Comment: Beware – this long fruity number packs a cognac charged punch.
Origin: Recipe adapted from William Schmidt's 1892 'The Flowing Bowl'.

A

THE ALAMAGOOZLUM COCKTAIL

Glass: Martini
Garnish: Pineapple wedge on rim
Method: SHAKE all ingredients with ice and fine strain into chilled glass.

1	shot(s)	**Bokma oude genever**
¾	shot(s)	**Yellow Chartreuse liqueur**
¾	shot(s)	**Wray & Nephew overproof rum**
¼	shot(s)	**Grand Marnier liqueur**
¾	shot(s)	**Sugar syrup** (2 sugar to 1 water)
1	shot(s)	**Chilled mineral water**
¼	shot(s)	**Angostura aromatic bitters**
¼	fresh	**Egg white**

Origin: Adapted from David A. Embury's 1948 'Fine Art of Mixing Drinks', where he writes, "This cocktail is supposed to have been a speciality of the elder Morgan of the House of Morgan, which goes to prove as a bartender he was an excellent banker."
Comment: Even Mr Embury would approve of this version. Overproof Jamaican rum and copious amounts of bitters make this drink.

ALAN'S APPLE BREEZE UPDATED #8

Glass: Collins
Garnish: Apple wedge on rim
Method: SHAKE all ingredients with ice and strain into ice-filled glass.

2	shot(s)	**Bacardi Superior rum**
½	shot(s)	**Bols apricot brandy liqueur**
1½	shot(s)	**Pressed apple juice**
1½	shot(s)	**Ocean Spray cranberry juice**
½	shot(s)	**Freshly squeezed lime juice**
¼	shot(s)	**Sugar syrup** (2 sugar to 1 water)

Comment: A sweet, tangy version of the Apple Breeze.
Origin: Created in 2002 by Alan Johnston at Metropolitan, Glasgow, Scotland.

ALASKA MARTINI

Glass: Martini
Garnish: Orange zest twist
Method: SHAKE all ingredients with ice and fine strain into chilled glass.

2½	shot(s)	**Tanqueray London dry gin**
¾	shot(s)	**Yellow Chartreuse liqueur**
1	shot(s)	**Tio Pepe fino sherry**
3	dashes	**Angostura orange bitters**

AKA: Nome
Origin: In his 1930 'The Savoy Cocktail Book', Harry Craddock writes, "So far as can be ascertained this delectable potion is NOT the staple diet of the Esquimaux. It was probably first thought of in South Carolina – hence its name." The addition of dry sherry is recommended in David Embury's 1948 'Fine Art of Mixing Drinks'.
Comment: If you like gin and Chartreuse, you'll love this strong and complex Martini.

ALASKA #2 NEW #8

Glass: Martini
Garnish: Maraschino cherry on stick
Method: SHAKE all ingredients with ice and fine strain into chilled glass.

2	shot(s)	**Tanqueray London dry gin**
1½	shot(s)	**Freshly squeezed lemon juice**
½	shot(s)	**Sugar syrup** (2 sugar to 1 water)
¼	shot(s)	**Crème de cassis liqueur**

Comment: The original recipe suggests adding the cassis separately after the drink is strained into the glass so it sinks. Looks great but the resulting drink is very sour until the cassis is stirred in.

ALASKAN MARTINI

Glass: Martini
Garnish: Lime zest twist discarded & mint leaf
Method: STIR all ingredients with ice and strain into chilled glass.

2½	shot(s)	**Tanqueray London dry gin**
¾	shot(s)	**Yellow Chartreuse liqueur**

Origin: Modern version of the Alaska.
Comment: Stir long and well – this needs dilution. The result will appeal to gin and Chartreuse fans.

ALBERTO MARTINI NEW #8

Glass: Martini/Coupette
Garnish: Orange zest twist
Method: STIR all ingredients with ice and strain into chilled glass.

1¼	shot(s)	**Tanqueray London dry gin**
1¼	shot(s)	**Noilly Prat dry vermouth**
1	shot(s)	**Tio Pepe fino sherry**
½	shot(s)	**Cointreau triple sec**

Comment: Dry, complex and aromatic. An equal parts gin and vermouth Martini with a good dose of fino sherry and a splash of triple sec.
Origin: In W.J. Tarling's 1937 Café Royal Cocktail Book the invention of this cocktail is credited to A.J. Smith.

ALESSANDRO

Glass: Martini
Garnish: Lemon zest twist
Method: SHAKE all ingredients with ice and fine strain into chilled glass.

1½	shot(s)	**Opal Nera black sambuca**
¾	shot(s)	**Tanqueray London dry gin**
¾	shot(s)	**Double (heavy) cream**
¾	shot(s)	**Milk**

Comment: Hints of aniseed, elderflower and gin emerge from this grey, creamy drink.

ALEXANDER UPDATED #8

●●●●○○

Glass: Martini
Garnish: Dust with freshly grated nutmeg
Method: SHAKE all ingredients with ice and fine strain into chilled glass.

2	shot(s)	**Tanqueray London dry gin**
1	shot(s)	**White crème de cacao liqueur**
1	shot(s)	**Double (heavy) cream**

AKA: Gin Alexander or Princess Mary
Comment: This gin based Alexander has sadly slipped from popularity, partly knocked by its successors, particularly the Brandy Alexander. Predictably, I've doubled the gin.
Origin: The original Alexander, equal parts gin, crème de cacao and cream, is thought to have originated in the twentieth century, certainly before 1917. It became a Prohibition favourite as the cream and nutmeg garnish helped disguise the rough taste of homemade 'bathtub' gin.

ALEXANDER THE GREAT

●●●●○○

Glass: Martini
Garnish: Dust with freshly grated nutmeg
Method: SHAKE all ingredients with ice and fine strain into chilled glass.

1½	shot(s)	**Ketel One vodka**
½	shot(s)	**Kahlúa coffee liqueur**
½	shot(s)	**White crème de cacao liqueur**
¾	shot(s)	**Double (heavy) cream**
¾	shot(s)	**Milk**

Comment: A tasty combination of coffee, chocolate and cream, laced with vodka.

'RUM, N. GENERICALLY, FIERY LIQUORS THAT PRODUCE MADNESS IN TOTAL ABSTAINERS.'
AMBROSE BIERCE

ALEXANDER'S BIG BROTHER

●●●●○○

Glass: Martini
Garnish: Physalis (cape gooseberry) on rim
Method: SHAKE all ingredients with ice and fine strain into chilled glass.

1½	shot(s)	**Tanqueray London dry gin**
¼	shot(s)	**Cointreau triple sec**
¾	shot(s)	**Bols blue curaçao liqueur**
¾	shot(s)	**Double (heavy) cream**
¾	shot(s)	**Milk**

Comment: Orangey in taste and creamy blue in colour - mildly better than pink for the macho out there.

ALEXANDER'S SISTER UPDATED #8

●●●○○○

Glass: Martini
Garnish: Dust with freshly grated nutmeg
Method: SHAKE all ingredients with ice and fine strain into chilled glass.

1½	shot(s)	**Tanqueray London dry gin**
¾	shot(s)	**Green crème de menthe liqueur**
¾	shot(s)	**Double (heavy) cream**
⅛	shot(s)	**Sugar syrup** (2 sugar to 1 water)

Comment: A green minty thing for dairy lovers.

ALEXANDRA

●●●●○○

Glass: Martini
Garnish: Dust with freshly grated nutmeg
Method: SHAKE all ingredients with ice and fine strain into chilled glass.

1½	shot(s)	**Pusser's Navy rum**
1	shot(s)	**Kahlúa coffee liqueur**
¾	shot(s)	**Double (heavy) cream**
¾	shot(s)	**Milk**

Comment: Surprisingly potent and spicy, despite the ladylike name.

ALFONSO

●●●●○○

Glass: Flute
Garnish: Twist of lemon
Method: Coat sugar cube with bitters and drop into glass. **POUR** Dubonnet and then champagne into chilled glass.

1	cube	**Sugar**
4	dashes	**Angostura aromatic bitters**
½	shot(s)	**Dubonnet Red** (French made)
Top up with		**Perrier Jouet brut champagne**

Origin: Named after the deposed Spanish king Alfonso XIII, who first tasted this drink while exiled in France.
Comment: Herbal variation on the classic Champagne Cocktail.

ALFONSO MARTINI

●●●●○

Glass: Martini
Garnish: Orange zest twist
Method: SHAKE all ingredients with ice and fine strain into chilled glass.

½	shot(s)	**Tanqueray London dry gin**
1	shot(s)	**Grand Marnier liqueur**
½	shot(s)	**Noilly Prat dry vermouth**
¼	shot(s)	**Martini Rosso sweet vermouth**
2	dashes	**Angostura aromatic bitters**
½	shot(s)	**Chilled mineral water** (omit if wet ice)

Origin: Adapted from Victor Bergeron's 'Trader Vic's Bartender's Guide' (1972 revised edition).
Comment: Dry yet slightly sweet with hints of orange, gin and warm spice.

A

ALGERIA

Glass: Martini
Garnish: Orange zest twist
Method: **SHAKE** all ingredients with ice and fine strain into chilled glass.

2	shot(s)	**Macchu pisco**
½	shot(s)	**Cointreau triple sec**
½	shot(s)	**Bols apricot brandy liqueur**
¾	shot(s)	**Chilled mineral water** (reduce if wet ice)

Origin: Modern adaptation of a classic.
Comment: Pisco, apricot and orange combine wonderfully in this medium dry, balanced cocktail with a tangy bite.

ALGONQUIN

Glass: Old-fashioned
Garnish: Cherry on stick
Method: **SHAKE** all ingredients with ice and strain into ice-filled glass.

2	shot(s)	**Rye whiskey (or bourbon)**
1¼	shot(s)	**Noilly Prat dry vermouth**
1¼	shot(s)	**Pressed pineapple juice**
2	dashes	**Peychaud's aromatic bitters**

Origin: One of several classic cocktails accredited to New York City's Algonquin Hotel in the 1930s. Its true origins are lost in time.
Comment: Pineapple juice adds fruit and froth, while Peychaud's bitters combine subtly with the whiskey in this dry, aromatic drink.

ALICE FROM DALLAS

Glass: Shot
Method: Refrigerate ingredients then **LAYER** in chilled glass by carefully pouring in the following order.

½	shot(s)	**Kahlúa coffee liqueur**
½	shot(s)	**Grand Marnier liqueur**
½	shot(s)	**Don Julio reposado tequila**

Comment: Coffee and orange spiked with tequila.

ALICE IN WONDERLAND

Glass: Shot
Garnish: Lime wedge
Method: Refrigerate ingredients then **LAYER** in chilled glass by carefully pouring in the following order.

| 1 | shot(s) | **Grand Marnier liqueur** |
| ½ | shot(s) | **Don Julio reposado tequila** |

Comment: Brings a whole new dimension to tequila and orange.

ALICE MINE NEW #8

Glass: Martini
Garnish: Orange zest twist
Method: **STIR** all ingredients with ice and strain into chilled glass.

1	shot(s)	**Grand Marnier liqueur**
½	shot(s)	**Tanqueray London dry gin**
½	shot(s)	**Noilly Prat dry vermouth**
¼	shot(s)	**Martini Rosso sweet vermouth**
1	dash	**Angostura aromatic bitters**

Comment: A medium-dry Martini with luscious orange notes.
Origin: Vintage cocktail of unknown origin.

ALIEN SECRETION

Glass: Collins
Garnish: Pineapple wedge & cherry
Method: **SHAKE** all ingredients with ice and strain into ice-filled glass.

2	shot(s)	**Ketel One vodka**
½	shot(s)	**Midori green melon liqueur**
½	shot(s)	**Malibu coconut rum liqueur**
3	shot(s)	**Pressed pineapple juice**

Origin: One of many 80s cocktails with a dodgy name.
Comment: Lime green and fruity but all too drinkable, with a distinct bite despite its mild sweetness.

ALL FALL DOWN

Glass: Shot
Method: Refrigerate ingredients then **LAYER** in chilled glass by carefully pouring in the following order.

½	shot(s)	**Kahlúa coffee liqueur**
½	shot(s)	**Don Julio reposado tequila**
½	shot(s)	**Pusser's Navy rum**

Comment: Too many of these and you will.

ALL WHITE FRAPPÉ

Glass: Old-fashioned
Garnish: Lemon zest
Method: **BLEND** ingredients with 6oz scoop of crushed ice. Pour into glass and serve with short straws.

1	shot(s)	**Luxardo Sambuca dei Cesari**
1	shot(s)	**White crème de cacao liqueur**
1	shot(s)	**Giffard Menthe Pastille liqueur**
1	shot(s)	**Freshly squeezed lemon juice**

Comment: Aniseed, chocolate, peppermint and lemon juice are an unlikely but tasty combination for summer afternoons.

ALLEGROTTINI

Glass: Martini
Garnish: Orange zest twist
Method: **SHAKE** all ingredients with ice and fine strain into chilled glass.

1½	shot(s)	**Ketel One Citroen vodka**
¾	shot(s)	**Cointreau triple sec**
¼	shot(s)	**Noilly Prat dry vermouth**
¾	shot(s)	**Freshly squeezed orange juice**
¼	shot(s)	**Freshly squeezed lime juice**

Origin: Discovered in 2005 at the Four Seasons Hotel, Prague, Czech Republic.
Comment: Strongly citrus but dry rather than bitter.

ALMOND MARTINI #1

Glass: Martini
Garnish: Sink 3 roasted almonds
Method: **SHAKE** all ingredients with ice and fine strain into chilled glass.

2	shot(s)	**Ketel One vodka**
½	shot(s)	**Freshly squeezed lemon juice**
½	shot(s)	**Almond (orgeat) syrup**
1	shot(s)	**Pressed apple juice**
2	dashes	**Fee Brothers peach bitters** (optional)

Origin: Created in 2004 by Matt Pomeroy at Baltic, London, England.
Comment: Almond inspired with hints of apple and lemon juice.

ALMOND MARTINI #2

Glass: Martini
Garnish: Sink 3 almonds
Method: **SHAKE** all ingredients with ice and fine strain into chilled glass.

2	shot(s)	**Almond flavoured vodka**
¾	shot(s)	**Luxardo Amaretto di Saschira**
¼	shot(s)	**Noilly Prat dry vermouth**
¾	shot(s)	**Chilled mineral water** (omit if wet ice)

Origin: Created in 2005 by Yours Truly (Simon Difford).
Comment: A delicate, almond flavoured Vodka Martini.

ALMOND OLD FASHIONED

Glass: Old-fashioned
Garnish: Orange zest twist
Method: **STIR** one shot of tequila with two ice cubes in a glass. Add amaretto, agave syrup, bitters and two more ice cubes. Stir some more then add another two ice cubes and the remaining tequila. Stir lots more so as to melt ice then add more ice. The melting and stirring in of ice cubes is essential to the dilution and taste of the drink.

2	shot(s)	**Don Julio reposado tequila**
¼	shot(s)	**Luxardo Amaretto di Saschira**
¼	shot(s)	**Agave syrup**
3	dashes	**Angostura orange bitters**

Origin: Created in 2005 by Mark Pratt at Maze, London, England.
Comment: One to please fans of both tequila and the Old Fashioned drinks genre.

AMALIA NEW #8

Glass: Coupette/Martini
Garnish: Pineapple foam
Method: **SHAKE** all ingredients with ice and fine strain into chilled glass.

2	shot(s)	**Bacardi Superior rum**
¾	shot(s)	**Freshly squeezed lemon juice**
¼	shot(s)	**Sugar syrup** (2 sugar to 1 water)
1	shot(s)	**Sauvignon Blanc wine**
⅛	shot(s)	**Gooseberry & mint cordial**

Origin: Created in 2008 by Sam Dean, Mobar, Nottingham, England.
Comment: Sip a gooseberry and mint influenced lemon Daiquiri though a foam topping.

AMANTE PICANTE NEW #8

Glass: Martini/Coupette
Garnish: Cucumber slice on the rim
Method: **MUDDLE** cucumber and coriander (cilantro). Add other ingredients, **SHAKE** with ice and fine strain into chilled glass.

2	slices	**Cucumber** (peeled & chopped)
2	sprigs	**Coriander** (cilantro)
1½	shot(s)	**Don Julio blanco tequila**
1	shot(s)	**Freshly squeezed lime juice**
½	shot(s)	**Agave syrup**
2	dashes	**Tabasco green sauce**

Origin: Created in 2008 by Francesco Lafranconi of Southern Wine & Spirits, USA.
Comment: So green and fresh that it must be good for you as well as tasting great.

AMARETTO SOUR

Glass: Old-fashioned
Garnish: Lemon slice & cherry on stick (sail)
Method: **SHAKE** all ingredients with ice and strain into ice-filled glass.

2	shot(s)	**Luxardo Amaretto di Saschira**
1¼	shot(s)	**Freshly squeezed lemon juice**
½	fresh	**Egg white**
2	dashes	**Angostura aromatic bitters**

Comment: Sweet 'n' sour – frothy with an almond buzz.

AMARITA NEW #8

Glass: Martini
Garnish: Long strings of lime zest twirled into glass
Method: **SHAKE** all ingredients with ice and fine strain into chilled glass.

1½	shot(s)	**Don Julio reposado tequila**
¾	shot(s)	**Aperol**
½	shot(s)	**Freshly squeezed lime juice**
3	shot(s)	**Fee Brothers grapefruit bitters** (optional)

Comment: Tequila predominates in this fairly bitter drink.
Origin: Created in 2007 by Neyah White, San Francisco, USA.

AMBER

Glass: Collins
Garnish: Apple wedge & nutmeg dust
Method: **MUDDLE** ginger in base of shaker. Add other ingredients, **SHAKE** with ice and strain into glass filled with crushed ice.

4	slices	**Fresh root ginger** (thumbnail sized)
1½	shot(s)	**Zubrówka bison vodka**
4	shot(s)	**Pressed apple juice**
½	shot(s)	**Sugar syrup** (2 sugar to 1 water)
½	shot(s)	**Berentzen apple schnapps**

Origin: Created in 2001 by Douglas Ankrah for Akbar at the Red Fort, Soho, London, England.
Comment: A fantastic combination of adult flavours in a long, thirst-quenching drink. Also great served up.

AMBER ROOM #1 NEW #8

Glass: Martini
Garnish: Lemon zest twist (discarded) and cherry
Method: **SHAKE** all ingredients with ice and fine strain into chilled glass.

1½	shot(s)	**Tanqueray London dry gin**
½	shot(s)	**Green Chartreuse liqueur**
½	shot(s)	**Martini Rosso sweet vermouth**
2	dashes	**Angostura orange bitters**
½	shot(s)	**Chilled mineral water** (omit if wet ice)

AKA: Golden Glow
Comment: Serious and packed with bold flavours. Fellow Chartreuse fans will approve.
Origin: This vintage cocktail originated from a layered or 'pousse-café' style drink called a Bijou. This original drink was so named after the French word meaning 'jewel' due to its trio of ingredients being coloured after the three most precious jewels: diamond (gin), ruby (sweet vermouth) and emerald (green chartreuse). Shaken rather than layered and the colours combine to make this aptly named amber coloured drink.

AMBER ROOM #2 NEW #8

Glass: Martini
Garnish: Lemon zest twist
Method: **STIR** all ingredients with ice and strain into chilled glass.

1½	shot(s)	**Tanqueray London dry gin**
1	shot(s)	**Noilly Prat dry vermouth**
¼	shot(s)	**St-Germain elderflower liqueur**
1	dash	**Angostura orange bitters**

Comment: A subtle, delicately floral Martini.
Origin: Adapted from a recipe created in 2007 by Stephan Berg, Munich, Germany.

AMBROSIA

Glass: Flute
Method: **SHAKE** first 4 ingredients with ice and strain into glass. **TOP** with champagne.

1	shot(s)	**Courvoisier V.S.O.P. cognac**
1	shot(s)	**Boulard Grand Solage calvados**
¼	shot(s)	**Freshly squeezed lemon juice**
¼	shot(s)	**Cointreau triple sec**
Top up with		**Perrier Jouet brut champagne**

Comment: Dry, fortified champers with a hint of apple.

AMBROSIA COCKTAIL

Glass: Martini
Garnish: Dust with freshly grated nutmeg
Method: **SHAKE** all ingredients with ice and fine strain into chilled glass.

¾	shot(s)	**Courvoisier V.S.O.P. cognac**
2	shot(s)	**Bols Advocaat liqueur**
1	shot(s)	**Cuarenta Y Tres (Licor 43) liqueur**
½	shot(s)	**Yellow Chartreuse liqueur**

Origin: I created this drink and named it after the Greek for 'elixir of life, the food of the gods'. In Britain Ambrosia is a brand of custard, so advocaat seemed appropriate, while, if there is a God, he/she/it surely drinks Chartreuse.
Comment: Easy-drinking but complex with a herbal edge.

AMERICAN BEAUTY #1

Glass: Large (10oz) Martini
Garnish: Float rose petal
Method: **SHAKE** first 6 ingredients with ice and fine strain into chilled glass. Use the back of a spoon to **FLOAT** red wine over drink.

2½	shot(s)	**Courvoisier V.S.O.P. cognac**
½	shot(s)	**Noilly Prat dry vermouth**
½	shot(s)	**Giffard Menthe Pastille liqueur**
½	shot(s)	**Freshly squeezed orange juice**
½	shot(s)	**Pomegranate (grenadine) syrup**
¾	shot(s)	**Chilled mineral water** (reduce if wet ice)
¼	shot(s)	**Shiraz red wine**

Origin: Adapted from David A. Embury's 1948 'Fine Art of Mixing Drinks'.
Variant: When served in a tall glass with crushed ice this is called an American Beauty Punch.
Comment: Both fresh and refreshing - a subtle hint of peppermint gives zing to this cognac cocktail.

HOW TO MAKE SUGAR SYRUP

To make your own sugar syrup, gradually pour **TWO cups of granulated sugar into a saucepan containing ONE cup of hot water.** Stir as you pour and carry on stirring and simmering until the sugar is dissolved. Do not let the water even come close to boiling and only simmer for as long as it takes to dissolve the sugar. Allow syrup to cool and pour into an empty bottle. Ideally, you should finely strain your syrup into the bottle to remove any undissolved crystals which could otherwise encourage crystallisation. If kept in a refrigerator this mixture will last for a couple of months.

AMERICAN BEAUTY #2

Glass: Martini
Garnish: Mint leaf
Method: SHAKE first 5 ingredients with ice and fine strain into chilled glass. Use the back of a soup spoon to **FLOAT** port over drink.

1	shot(s)	**Courvoisier V.S.O.P. cognac**
1	shot(s)	**Noilly Prat dry vermouth**
¼	shot(s)	**Giffard Menthe Pastille liqueur**
1	shot(s)	**Freshly squeezed orange juice**
½	shot(s)	**Pomegranate (grenadine) syrup**
½	shot(s)	**Warre's Otima tawny port**

Origin: Adapted from Victor Bergeron's 'Trader Vic's Bartender's Guide' (1972 revised edition).
Comment: Invigorating and peppermint fresh yet sophisticated and complex.

AMERICAN BREAKFAST NEW #8

Glass: Old-fashioned
Garnish: Grapefruit zest twist
Method: SHAKE all ingredients with ice and strain into ice-filled glass.

½	shot(s)	**Maple syrup**
2	shot(s)	**Bulleit bourbon whiskey**
1½	shot(s)	**Freshly squeezed grapefruit juice**

Comment: This citrus fresh Bourbon-laced drink would be great with your morning muesli.

AMERICAN PIE MARTINI

Glass: Martini
Garnish: Apple wedge on rim
Method: SHAKE all ingredients with ice and fine strain into chilled glass.

1½	shot(s)	**Bulleit bourbon whiskey**
½	shot(s)	**Berentzen apple schnapps**
½	shot(s)	**Crème de myrtille liqueur**
¾	shot(s)	**Ocean Spray cranberry juice**
½	shot(s)	**Pressed apple juice**
¼	shot(s)	**Freshly squeezed lime juice**

Origin: Adapted from a recipe discovered at Oxo Tower Restaurant & Bar, London, England.
Comment: This berry and apple pie has a tangy bite.

AMERICANA

Glass: Flute
Garnish: Peach slice
Method: Coat sugar cube with bitters and drop into glass. **POUR** bourbon and then champagne into chilled glass.

1	cube	**Sugar**
4	dashes	**Angostura aromatic bitters**
½	shot(s)	**Bulleit bourbon whiskey**
Top up with		**Brut champagne**

Comment: The Wild West take on the classic Champagne Cocktail.

AMERICANO

Glass: Collins
Garnish: Orange slice
Method: POUR Campari and vermouth into ice-filled glass and **TOP** with soda. Stir and serve with straws.

2	shot(s)	**Campari Bitter**
2	shot(s)	**Martini Rosso sweet vermouth**
Top up with		**Soda water** (club soda)

Origin: First served in the 1860s in Gaspare Campari's bar in Milan, this was originally known as the 'Milano-Torino' as Campari came from Milano (Milan) and Cinzano from Torino (Turin). It was not until Prohibition that the Italians noticed an influx of Americans who enjoyed the drink and so dubbed it Americano.
Comment: A bitter, fizzy, long refreshing drink, which you'll love if you like Campari.

> ## 'THE PROBLEM WITH THE WORLD IS THAT EVERYONE IS A FEW DRINKS BEHIND.'
> ## HUMPHREY BOGART

AMPERSAND NEW #8

Glass: Martini
Garnish: Orange zest twist
Method: STIR all ingredients with ice and strain into chilled glass.

1	shot(s)	**Old Tom gin**
1	shot(s)	**Courvoisier V.S.O.P. cognac**
1	shot(s)	**Martini Rosso sweet vermouth**
¼	shot(s)	**Grand Marnier liqueur**
1	dash	**Angostura orange bitters**

Comment: A brandy influenced wet, sweet Martini with a hint of orange.
Origin: First published in A. S. Crockett's 1935 'The Old Waldorf-Astoria Bar Book'. The name may be a reference to the '&' in Martini & Rossi, likely the brand of vermouth originally used.

AMSTERDAM COCKTAIL

Glass: Martini
Garnish: Orange zest twist
Method: SHAKE all ingredients with ice and fine strain into chilled glass.

2	shot(s)	**Bokma oude genever**
1	shot(s)	**Cointreau triple sec**
1	shot(s)	**Freshly squeezed orange juice**
3	dashes	**Angostura orange bitters**

Origin: Adapted from Victor Bergeron's 'Trader Vic's Bartender's Guide' (1972 revised edition).
Comment: Very orange, dry but wonderfully smooth.

A

THE ANCIENT DAIQUIRÍ NEW #8

●●●○○

Glass: Martini/Coupette
Garnish: None
Method: SHAKE all ingredients with ice and fine strain into chilled glass.

1	shot(s)	**Bacardi Superior rum**
½	shot(s)	**Drambuie liqueur**
½	shot(s)	**Green Chartreuse liqueur**
¾	shot(s)	**Freshly squeezed lime juice**
¼	shot(s)	**Vanilla sugar syrup**

Comment: Herbal liqueurs heavily influence this Daiquiri twist.
Origin: Created in 2008 by Lewis Jaffrey, Drambuie's Global Brand Ambassador and according to Lewis it is so named due to the ingredients having a combined age over 650 years.

AÑEJO HIGHBALL NEW #8

●●●●○

Glass: Collins
Garnish: Half orange slice & lime slice
Method: SHAKE first 4 ingredients with ice and strain into ice-filled glass.

2	shot(s)	**Zacapa aged rum**
1	shot(s)	**Orange curaçao liqueur**
1	shot(s)	**Freshly squeezed lime juice**
1	dash	**Angostura aromatic bitters**
Top up with		**Ginger beer**

Comment: Orange and rum with a hint of ginger spice. Long and thirst-quenching.
Origin: Created in the late 1990s by Dale DeGroff, New York City, USA.

AÑEJO MANHATTAN NEW #8

●●●●○

Glass: Martini
Garnish: Salami wrapped cherry on a pick
Method: STIR all ingredients with ice and strain into chilled glass.

2	shot(s)	**Don Julio añejo tequila**
½	shot(s)	**Martini Rosso sweet vermouth**
¼	shot(s)	**Cuarenta Y Tres (Licor 43) liqueur**
1	dash	**Angostura aromatic bitters**
1	dash	**Angostura orange bitters**

Comment: Tequila dominates this dry, serious Manhattan-like cocktail.
Origin: Created by Ryan Magarian, Seattle, USA.

ANGEL FACE

●●●●○

Glass: Martini
Garnish: Apple wedge on rim
Method: SHAKE all ingredients with ice and fine strain into chilled glass.

1	shot(s)	**Tanqueray London dry gin**
1	shot(s)	**Boulard Grand Solage calvados**
1	shot(s)	**Bols apricot brandy liqueur**

Origin: Adapted from Harry Craddock's 1930 'The Savoy Cocktail Book'.
Comment: Rich apricot and apple with a backbone of botanical gin. Balanced rather than dry or sweet.

ANGEL JUICE NEW #8

●●●●○

Glass: Martini/Coupette
Garnish: Apple fan
Method: SHAKE all ingredients with ice and fine strain into chilled glass.

1	shot(s)	**Pear flavoured vodka**
½	shot(s)	**St-Germain elderflower liqueur**
½	shot(s)	**Sauvignon Blanc wine**
½	shot(s)	**Pressed apple juice**
¼	shot(s)	**Sugar syrup** (2 sugar to 1 water)
½	shot(s)	**Freshly squeezed lime juice**
½	fresh	**Egg white**

Comment: Pear and elderflower lead this fruity drink.
Origin: Created in 2008 by Jay Decker at Paramount, London, England.

'IT'S BEEN SO LONG SINCE I'VE HAD CHAMPAGNE.' LAST WORDS OF ANTON CHEKHOV

ANGEL'S SHARE #1

●●●●●

Glass: Martini
Garnish: Orange zest twist
Method: STIR heaped spoon of orange marmalade with cognac in base of shaker until marmalade dissolves. Add other ingredients, SHAKE with ice and fine strain into chilled glass.

1	spoon	**Orange marmalade**
2	shot(s)	**Courvoisier V.S.O.P. cognac**
¼	shot(s)	**Cuarenta Y Tres (Licor 43) liqueur**
½	shot(s)	**Freshly squeezed lemon juice**
¼	shot(s)	**Sugar syrup** (2 sugar to 1 water)

Origin: Created in 2005 by Milo Rodriguez, London.
Comment: Tangy citrus fruit and cognac smoothed with a sweet hint of vanilla.

ANGEL'S SHARE #2

●●●●●

Glass: Snifter
Method: POUR the Chartreuse into glass and coat the inside of the glass with the liqueur by tilting and rotating it. DISCARD excess liqueur. Carefully set the liqueur on the interior of the glass alight and allow it to BURN for a few seconds. Extinguish flame by placing a saucer over the glass, add other ingredients and SWIRL to mix.
Beware of hot glass rim.

¼	shot(s)	**Green Chartreuse liqueur**
1½	shot(s)	**Courvoisier V.S.O.P. cognac**
¾	shot(s)	**Nocello walnut liqueur**
½	shot(s)	**Warre's Otima tawny port**

Origin: Adapted from a recipe created in 2005 by Jacques Bezuidenhout at Harry Denton's Starlight Room, San Francisco, USA.
Comment: A fabulous drink, especially when VEP Chartreuse, family reserve cognac and 20 year old tawny port are used as per the original Starlight Room recipe.

ANIS'TINI

Glass: Martini
Garnish: Star anise
Method: MUDDLE star anise in base of shaker. Add other ingredients, **SHAKE** with ice and fine strain into chilled glass.

2	dried	Star anise
1	shot(s)	Ketel One vodka
¾	shot(s)	Luxardo Sambuca dei Cesari
½	shot(s)	Pernod anis
1½	shot(s)	Chilled mineral water (reduce if wet ice)

Origin: Discovered in 2002 at Lot 61, New York City, USA.
Comment: Specks of star anise are evident in this aniseedy Martini.

ANITA'S ATTITUDE ADJUSTER

Glass: Sling
Garnish: Lemon slice & cherry on stick (sail)
Method: SHAKE first seven ingredients with ice and strain into ice-filled glass. **TOP** with champagne and gently stir.

½	shot(s)	Cointreau triple sec
½	shot(s)	Don Julio reposado tequila
½	shot(s)	Bacardi Superior rum
½	shot(s)	Tanqueray London dry gin
½	shot(s)	Ketel One vodka
½	shot(s)	Freshly squeezed lime juice
½	shot(s)	Sugar syrup (2 sugar to 1 water)
Top up with		Perrier Jouet brut champagne

Comment: Anita has a problem – she's indecisive when it comes to choosing base spirits.

ANTE

Glass: Martini
Garnish: Orange zest twist
Method: STIR all ingredients with ice and strain into chilled glass.

2	shot(s)	Boulard Grand Solage calvados
1	shot(s)	Dubonnet Red (French made)
½	shot(s)	Cointreau triple sec
2	dashes	Angostura aromatic bitters

Origin: Recipe adapted from one discovered in 2006 on drinkboy.com.
Comment: Medium dry, complex spiced apple with hints of orange.

APACHE

Glass: Shot
Method: Refrigerate ingredients then **LAYER** in chilled glass by carefully pouring in the following order.

¾	shot(s)	Kahlúa coffee liqueur
½	shot(s)	Midori green melon liqueur
½	shot(s)	Baileys Irish cream liqueur

AKA: Quick F.U.
Comment: A coffee, melon and whiskey cream layered shot.

APHRODISIAC

Glass: Collins
Garnish: Apple slice on rim
Method: MUDDLE ginger in base of shaker. Add other ingredients, **SHAKE** with ice and fine strain into ice-filled glass.

2	slices	Fresh root ginger (thumbnail sized)
2	shot(s)	Vanilla-infused Ketel One vodka
½	shot(s)	Green Chartreuse liqueur
2½	shot(s)	Pressed apple juice
1½	shot(s)	Sauvignon Blanc wine

Origin: Created in 2002 by Yannick Miseriaux at The Fifth Floor Bar, London, England.
Comment: As strong in flavour as it is high in alcohol.

APPLE & BLACKBERRY PIE

Glass: Martini
Garnish: Cinnamon dust & blackberry
Method: MUDDLE blackberries in base of shaker. Add vodka and apple juice, **SHAKE** with ice and fine strain into chilled glass. **FLOAT** cream on the surface of the drink by pouring over the back of a spoon and swirl to form a thin layer. You may need to add a touch of sugar syrup.

7	fresh	Blackberries
2	shot(s)	Ketel One vodka
1	shot(s)	Pressed apple juice
Float		Double (heavy) cream

Origin: Created in 2005 by Yours Truly (Simon Difford).
Comment: A dessert in a glass, but not too sweet.

APPLE & CRANBERRY PIE

Glass: Martini
Garnish: Dust with cinnamon powder
Method: SHAKE first 3 ingredients with ice and fine strain into chilled glass. **FLOAT** cream on surface of drink by pouring over the back of a spoon and swirl to form a thin layer.

1½	shot(s)	Ketel One vodka
¾	shot(s)	Berentzen apple schnapps
1	shot(s)	Ocean Spray cranberry juice
Float		Double (heavy) cream

Origin: Created in 2003 by Yours Truly (Simon Difford).
Comment: Sip apple and cranberry through a creamy cinnamon layer.

APPLE & CUSTARD COCKTAIL

Glass: Martini
Garnish: Apple wedge on rim
Method: SHAKE all ingredients with ice and fine strain into chilled glass.

2	shot(s)	Bols advocaat liqueur
1½	shot(s)	Boulard Grand Solage calvados
½	shot(s)	Berentzen apple schnapps
¼	shot(s)	Vanilla sugar syrup

Origin: I created this in 2002 after rediscovering advocaat on a trip to Amsterdam.
Comment: Smooth and creamy, this tastes like its name.

A

APPLE & ELDERFLOWER COLLINS

Glass: Collins
Garnish: Lemon slice
Method: SHAKE first 4 ingredients with ice and strain into ice-filled glass. **TOP** with soda, stir and serve with straws.

1½	shot(s)	**Tanqueray London dry gin**
1	shot(s)	**St-Germain elderflower liqueur**
1	shot(s)	**Berentzen apple schnapps**
1	shot(s)	**Freshly squeezed lime juice**
Top up with		**Soda water** (club soda)

Origin: Formula by Yours Truly (Simon Difford) in 2004.
Comment: A John Collins with lime in place of lemon and sweetened with apple and elderflower liqueurs.

APPLE & ELDERFLOWER MARTINI

Glass: Martini
Garnish: Float wafer thin apple slice
Method: SHAKE all ingredients with ice and fine strain into chilled glass.

1¾	shot(s)	**Ketel One vodka**
1	shot(s)	**St-Germain elderflower liqueur**
1¼	shot(s)	**Pressed apple juice**

Origin: Created in 2006 by Yours Truly (Simon Difford).
Comment: Light and easy - apple and elderflower laced with vodka.

APPLE & MELON MARTINI

Glass: Martini
Garnish: Apple wedge on rim
Method: SHAKE all ingredients with ice and fine strain into chilled glass.

2	shot(s)	**Ketel One vodka**
1	shot(s)	**Sour apple liqueur**
½	shot(s)	**Midori green melon liqueur**
½	shot(s)	**Freshly squeezed lime juice**

Comment: The ubiquitous Green Apple Martini with extra colour and flavour thanks to a dash of melon liqueur.

APPLE & SPICE

Glass: Shot
Garnish: Dust with cinnamon powder
Method: Refrigerate ingredients then **LAYER** in chilled glass by carefully pouring in the following order.

¾	shot(s)	**Boulard Grand Solage calvados**
¾	shot(s)	**Double (heavy) cream**

Comment: Creamy apple shot.

APPLE BLOSSOM NEW #8

Glass: Martini/Coupette
Garnish: Orange zest twist
Method: SHAKE all ingredients with ice and strain into chilled glass.

2	shot(s)	**Tanqueray London dry gin**
¼	shot(s)	**Boulard Grand Solage calvados**
1	shot(s)	**Freshly squeezed orange juice**
⅛	shot(s)	**Sugar syrup** (2 sugar to 1 water)
½	shot(s)	**Chilled mineral water** (omit if wet ice)

Comment: A Gin & Juice with a little extra interest courtesy of a dash of apple brandy. I've added the merest hint of sugar to lift Buckby's rather flat original recipe.
Origin: In W.J. Tarling's 1937 Café Royal Cocktail Book the invention of this cocktail is credited to one R.G. Buckby.

APPLE BLOSSOM COCKTAIL

Glass: Martini
Garnish: Apple wedge on rim
Method: SHAKE all ingredients with ice and fine strain into chilled glass.

2	shot(s)	**Boulard Grand Solage calvados**
2	shot(s)	**Martini Rosso sweet vermouth**

Origin: Adapted from Victor Bergeron's 'Trader Vic's Bartender's Guide' (1972 revised edition).
Comment: Stupidly simple to mix but complex to taste – spiced and concentrated apple juice.

APPLE BRANDY SOUR

Glass: Old-fashioned
Garnish: Lemon slice & cherry on stick (sail)
Method: SHAKE all ingredients with ice and strain into ice-filled glass.

2	shot(s)	**Boulard Grand Solage calvados**
1	shot(s)	**Freshly squeezed lemon juice**
¾	shot(s)	**Sugar syrup** (2 sugar to 1 water)
3	dashes	**Angostura aromatic bitters**
½	fresh	**Egg white**

Comment: Sour by name - balanced sweet and sour apple by nature.

APPLE BREEZE

Glass: Collins
Garnish: Apple wedge on rim
Method: SHAKE all ingredients with ice and strain into ice-filled glass.

2	shot(s)	**Zubrówka bison vodka**
2½	shot(s)	**Pressed apple juice**
1½	shot(s)	**Ocean Spray cranberry juice**

Variant: Substitute Ketel One vodka for Zubrówka bison vodka.
Comment: A lot more interesting than the better known Sea Breeze.

APPLE BUCK ●●●●○

Glass: Collins
Garnish: Apple wedge
Method: SHAKE first 4 ingredients with ice and strain into ice-filled glass. **TOP** with ginger ale.

1½	shot(s)	Boulard Grand Solage calvados
½	shot(s)	Sour apple liqueur
1	shot(s)	Pressed apple juice
½	shot(s)	Freshly squeezed lime juice
Top up with		Ginger ale

Origin: Adapted from a drink created in 2004 by Wayne Collins.
Comment: A refreshing long number with a taste reminiscent of cider.

APPLE CART ●●●●◐○

Glass: Martini
Garnish: Apple wedge on rim
Method: SHAKE all ingredients with ice and fine strain into chilled glass.

1½	shot(s)	Boulard Grand Solage calvados
1	shot(s)	Cointreau triple sec
1	shot(s)	Freshly squeezed lemon juice
½	shot(s)	Chilled mineral water (omit if wet ice)

AKA: Calvados Sidecar
Variant: Deauville
Origin: This classic cocktail is an adaptation of the even older Sidecar.
Comment: A serious combination of apple with orange and sweet with sour.

APPLE CRUMBLE MARTINI #1 ●●●●◐○

Glass: Martini
Garnish: Apple wedge on rim
Method: SHAKE all ingredients with ice and fine strain into chilled glass.

2	shot(s)	Johnnie Walker Scotch whisky
¼	shot(s)	Teichenné butterscotch schnapps
1	shot(s)	Pressed apple juice
½	shot(s)	Freshly squeezed lemon juice
¼	shot(s)	Sugar syrup (2 sugar to 1 water)

Comment: That's the way the apple crumbles - in this case enhancing the flavour of the Scotch.

APPLE CRUMBLE MARTINI #2 ●●●●○

Glass: Martini
Garnish: Dust with cinnamon powder
Method: SHAKE all ingredients with ice and fine strain into chilled glass.

2	shot(s)	Tuaca Italian liqueur
½	shot(s)	Freshly squeezed lemon juice
2	shot(s)	Pressed apple juice

Origin: Created in 2002 by Eion Richards at Bond's Bar, London, England.
Comment: Easy to make and equally easy to drink.

APPLE, CUCUMBER & ELDERFLOWER CUP NEW #8 ●●●●○

Glass: Martini/Coupette
Garnish: Float 3 cucumber slices
Method: MUDDLE cucumber in base of shaker. Add other ingredients, SHAKE with ice and fine strain into chilled glass.

2	inches	Cucumber (peeled & chopped)
2	shot(s)	Zubrówka bison vodka
½	shot(s)	St-Germain elderflower liqueur
½	shot(s)	Pressed apple juice

Comment: Apple and Zubrówka is a magic combination, as is and apple and elderflower. Here these flavoursome blends are enhanced and freshened by cucumber.
Origin: Discovered in 2007 at Public Restaurant, New York City, USA.

APPLE DAIQUIRI ●●●●○

Glass: Martini
Garnish: Apple wedge on rim
Method: SHAKE all ingredients with ice and fine strain into chilled glass.

2	shot(s)	Bacardi Superior rum
1½	shot(s)	Pressed apple juice
½	shot(s)	Freshly squeezed lime juice
¼	shot(s)	Sugar syrup (2 sugar to 1 water)

Origin: Formula by Yours Truly (Simon Difford) in 2004.
Comment: A classic Daiquiri with a very subtle hint of apple.

APPLE MAC ●●●●○

Glass: Martini
Garnish: Float apple slice
Method: SHAKE all ingredients with ice and strain into ice-filled glass.

2	shot(s)	Johnnie Walker Scotch whisky
1½	shot(s)	Pressed apple juice
½	shot(s)	Stone's original green ginger wine

Variant: Also suits being served over ice in an old-fashioned glass.
Origin: I created this twist on the classic Whisky Mac in 2004.
Comment: Scotch, ginger and apple are a threesome made in heaven.

DRINKS ARE GRADED AS FOLLOWS:

● DISGUSTING ●● PRETTY AWFUL ●● BEST AVOIDED
●●○ DISAPPOINTING ●●● ACCEPTABLE ●●●● GOOD
●●●● RECOMMENDED ●●●●● HIGHLY RECOMMENDED
●●●●● OUTSTANDING / EXCEPTIONAL

A

APPLE MANHATTAN #1

Glass: Martini
Garnish: Apple slice on rim
Method: SHAKE all ingredients with ice and fine strain into chilled glass.

2	shot(s)	**Bulleit bourbon whiskey**
1½	shot(s)	**Berentzen apple schnapps**
½	shot(s)	**Martini Rosso sweet vermouth**

Origin: My take on a drink created by David Marsden at First on First in New York City and latterly popularised by Dale DeGroff. Traditionalists may want to stir it.
Comment: Rusty gold in colour, this is a flavoursome number for bourbon lovers.

APPLE MANHATTAN #2

Glass: Martini
Garnish: Apple wedge on rim
Method: STIR all ingredients with ice and strain into chilled glass.

2	shot(s)	**Bulleit bourbon whiskey**
¾	shot(s)	**Berentzen apple schnapps**
¼	shot(s)	**Cointreau triple sec**
½	shot(s)	**Martini Rosso sweet vermouth**

Origin: Created in 2005 by Åsa Nevestveit and Robert Sörman at Grill, Stockholm, Sweden.
Comment: Exactly as billed – a Manhattan with a hint of apple.

APPLE MARTINI #1 (SIMPLE VERSION)

Glass: Martini
Garnish: Cherry in base of glass
Method: SHAKE all ingredients with ice and fine strain into chilled glass.

2½	shot(s)	**Ketel One vodka**
2	shot(s)	**Pressed apple juice**
¼	shot(s)	**Sugar syrup (2 sugar to 1 water)**

Variant: Sour Apple Martini, Caramelised Apple Martini
Origin: Formula by Yours Truly (Simon Difford) in 2004.
Comment: This is subtitled the simple version for good reason but, if freshly pressed juice is used, it's as good if not better than other Apple Martini recipes.

APPLE MARTINI #2

Glass: Martini
Garnish: Apple wedge on rim
Method: SHAKE all ingredients with ice and fine strain into chilled glass.

2	shot(s)	**Ketel One vodka**
¾	shot(s)	**Berentzen apple schnapps**
2	shot(s)	**Pressed apple juice**

Comment: There are as many different recipes for this drink as there are varieties of apple and brands of apple liqueur: this is one of the more popular.

APPLE MARTINI #3 (IBA SPEC) NEW #8

Glass: Martini
Garnish: Apple slice
Method: STIR all ingredients with ice and fine strain into chilled glass.

2	shot(s)	**Ketel One vodka**
¾	shot(s)	**Berentzen apple schnapps**
¾	shot(s)	**Cointreau triple sec**

Comment: Not really a Martini and not really much good.
Origin: This recipe is formulated according to International Bartender's Association 2008 proportions.

APPLE MOJITO

Glass: Collins
Garnish: Mint sprig
Method: Lightly **MUDDLE** (just to bruise) mint in base of glass. Add other ingredients, half fill glass with crushed ice and **CHURN** (stir) with bar spoon. Fill glass to brim with more crushed ice and churn some more. Serve with straws.

12	fresh	**Mint leaves**
2	shot(s)	**Bacardi Superior rum**
1	shot(s)	**Freshly squeezed lime juice**
1	shot(s)	**Berentzen apple schnapps**

Origin: Recipe by Yours Truly (Simon Difford) in 2005.
Comment: An enduring classic given a touch of apple. Those with a sweet tooth may want to add more apple liqueur or even a dash of sugar syrup.

THE APPLE ONE NEW #8

Glass: Collins
Garnish: Thinly sliced apple & mint leaf
Method: SHAKE all ingredients with ice and fine strain into ice-filled glass.

2	shot(s)	**Bulleit bourbon whiskey**
¾	shot(s)	**St-Germain elderflower liqueur**
¾	shot(s)	**Pressed apple juice**
½	shot(s)	**Freshly squeezed lime juice**

Comment: Whiskey, elderflower and apple with a refreshing burst of citrus.
Origin: Adapted from a recipe created in 2008 by Vincenzo Marianella at Doheny, Los Angeles, USA.

APPLE OF ONE'S EYE

Glass: Collins
Garnish: Apple wedge on rim
Method: SHAKE first 3 ingredients with ice and strain into ice-filled glass. **TOP** with ginger beer.

2	shot(s)	**Courvoisier V.S.O.P. cognac**
½	shot(s)	**Freshly squeezed lime juice**
1½	shot(s)	**Pressed apple juice**
Top up with		**Ginger beer**

Comment: This spicy concoction is long and refreshing.

APPLE PIE MARTINI

Glass: Martini
Garnish: Apple wedge on rim
Method: SHAKE all ingredients with ice and fine strain into chilled glass.

1½	shot(s)	Zubrówka bison vodka
½	shot(s)	Goldschläger cinnamon schnapps
2	shot(s)	Pressed apple juice
1	shot(s)	Ocean Spray cranberry juice

Origin: Created in 2000 by Alexia Pau Barrera at Sand Bar, Clapham, England.
Comment: There's a good hit of cinnamon in this apple pie.

APPLE PIE SHOT

Glass: Shot
Garnish: Dust with cinnamon powder
Method: SHAKE first 2 ingredients with ice and strain into chilled glass. **FLOAT** cream on drink by carefully pouring over the back of a spoon.

1	shot(s)	Berentzen apple schnapps
½	shot(s)	Frangelico hazelnut liqueur
¼	shot(s)	Double cream

Comment: Nuts, apple, cinnamon and cream – pudding, anyone?

APPLEISSIMO

Glass: Collins
Garnish: Apple slice on rim
Method: SHAKE first 3 ingredients with ice and strain into ice-filled glass. **TOP** with anis and serve with straws.

1½	shot(s)	Berentzen apple schnapps
2	shot(s)	Pressed apple juice
1½	shot(s)	Ocean Spray cranberry juice
1½	shot(s)	Pernod anis

Comment: Stir the anis in with straws before drinking. Anis is best added last as it reacts on contact with ice.

APPLE SPRITZ

Glass: Flute
Garnish: Peach or apple slice on rim
Method: POUR first 2 ingredients into glass and **TOP** with champagne.

¾	shot(s)	Berentzen apple schnapps
¼	shot(s)	Peach Tree peach schnapps
Top up with		Perrier Jouet brut champagne

Origin: Discovered in 2003 at Paramount Hotel, New York City, USA.
Comment: Sweet, fruity champagne – oh yeah, baby.

APPLE STRUDEL #1

Glass: Martini
Garnish: Dust with cinnamon powder
Method: SHAKE first 5 ingredients with ice and fine strain into chilled glass. Carefully **FLOAT** cream by pouring over the back of a spoon.

1	shot(s)	Berentzen apple schnapps
½	shot(s)	Goldschläger cinnamon schnapps
½	shot(s)	White crème de cacao liqueur
½	shot(s)	Brown crème de cacao liqueur
1	shot(s)	Pressed apple juice
¾	shot(s)	Double (heavy) cream

Variant: May also be served as a shot.
Origin: Created in 1999 by Alex Kammerling, London, England.
Comment: This sweet dessert cocktail tastes just like mum's home-made apple pie with cream.

APPLE STRUDEL #2

Glass: Martini
Garnish: Coat half rim with cinnamon and sugar
Method: SHAKE all ingredients with ice and fine strain into chilled glass.

1½	shot(s)	Vanilla-infused Ketel One vodka
½	shot(s)	Johnnie Walker Scotch whisky
½	shot(s)	Berentzen apple schnapps
½	shot(s)	Noilly Prat dry vermouth
1	shot(s)	Pressed apple juice

Origin: Recipe by Yours Truly (Simon Difford) in 2006.
Comment: Apple, vanilla and a hint of Scotch – reminiscent of the dessert but a good deal drier.

> **'WINE MAKETH MERRY: BUT MONEY ANSWERETH ALL THINGS.'**
> ECCLESIASTES 10:19

APPLE SUNRISE

Glass: Collins
Garnish: Apple slice
Method: SHAKE all ingredients with ice and strain into ice-filled glass.

2	shot(s)	Boulard Grand Solage calvados
½	shot(s)	Crème de cassis liqueur
3½	shot(s)	Freshly squeezed orange juice

Origin: Created in 1980 by Charles Schumann, Munich, Germany.
Comment: A pleasing blend of fruits with the apple punch of Calvados.

A

APPLE VIRGIN MOJITO (MOCKTAIL)
UPDATED #8

Glass: Collins
Garnish: Mint sprig
Method: **PLACE** mint, lemon, lime and sugar in glass. Half fill glass with crushed ice and **CHURN** (stir). Add more crushed ice to fill glass. Add apple juice, **TOP** with soda and **CHURN** some more. Serve with straws.

12	fresh	Mint leaves
½	shot(s)	Freshly squeezed lemon juice
½	shot(s)	Freshly squeezed lime juice
¾	shot(s)	Sugar syrup (2 sugar to 1 water)
3	shot(s)	Pressed apple juice
Top up with		Soda water (club soda)

Comment: A very refreshing driver's option.
Origin: Created in 2002 by Tony Conigliaro at Isola, London, England.

> 'WHY DOES MAN KILL? HE KILLS FOR FOOD. AND NOT ONLY FOR FOOD: FREQUENTLY THERE MUST BE A BEVERAGE.'
> WOODY ALLEN.

APPLESINTH

Glass: Old-fashioned
Garnish: Apple wedge on rim
Method: **SHAKE** all ingredients with ice and strain into glass filled with crushed ice.

1	shot(s)	La Fée Parisienne (68%) absinthe
1	shot(s)	Berentzen apple schnapps
2	shot(s)	Pressed apple juice
¾	shot(s)	Freshly squeezed lime juice
½	shot(s)	Passion fruit syrup

Origin: Created in 1999 by Alex Kammerling, London, England.
Comment: Hints of apple and liquorice combine to make a very moreish cocktail.

APPLES 'N' PEARS

Glass: Martini
Garnish: Apple or pear slice on rim
Method: **SHAKE** all ingredients with ice and fine strain into chilled glass.

1	shot(s)	Pear flavoured vodka
1	shot(s)	Boulard Grand Solage calvados
¾	shot(s)	Belle de Brillet pear liqueur
1½	shot(s)	Pressed apple juice

Origin: Created in 2005 by Yours Truly (Simon Difford).
Comment: 'Apples and pears' means stairs. Well worth climbing.

APPILY MARRIED

Glass: Martini
Garnish: Coat half rim with cinnamon and sugar
Method: **STIR** honey with vodka in base of shaker until honey dissolves. Add apple juice, **SHAKE** with ice and fine strain into chilled glass.

2	spoons	Runny honey
2½	shot(s)	Ketel One vodka
½	shot(s)	Pressed apple juice

Origin: Created in 2005 by Yours Truly (Simon Difford).
Comment: Apple and honey are indeed a marriage made in heaven, especially when laced with grainy vodka notes.

APRICOT COSMO

Glass: Martini
Garnish: Apricot slice
Method: **STIR** apricot preserve with vodka until preserve dissolves. Add other ingredients, **SHAKE** with ice and fine strain into chilled glass.

2	shot(s)	Ketel One vodka
1	spoon	Apricot preserve
1	shot(s)	Ocean Spray cranberry juice
¼	shot(s)	Passion fruit sugar syrup
½	shot(s)	Freshly squeezed lime juice
2	dashes	Angostura orange bitters

Origin: Created in 2004 at Aura Kitchen & Bar, London, England.
Comment: The apricot preserve adds a flavoursome tang to the contemporary classic.

APRICOT FIZZ

Glass: Collins (8oz max)
Garnish: Lemon wedge
Method: **SHAKE** first 3 ingredients with ice and strain into ice-filled glass. **TOP** with soda water.

2	shot(s)	Bols apricot brandy liqueur
1	shot(s)	Freshly squeezed orange juice
½	shot(s)	Freshly squeezed lime juice
Top up with		Soda water (from siphon)

Comment: This low-alcohol, refreshing cocktail is perfect for a summer afternoon.

APRICOT LADY SOUR

Glass: Old-fashioned
Garnish: Lemon slice & cherry on stick (sail)
Method: **SHAKE** all ingredients with ice and strain into ice-filled glass.

1½	shot(s)	Bacardi Superior rum
1	shot(s)	Bols apricot brandy liqueur
1	shot(s)	Freshly squeezed lemon juice
¼	shot(s)	Sugar syrup (2 sugar to 1 water)
½	fresh	Egg white

Comment: This seemingly soft and fluffy, apricot flavoured drink hides a most unladylike rum bite.

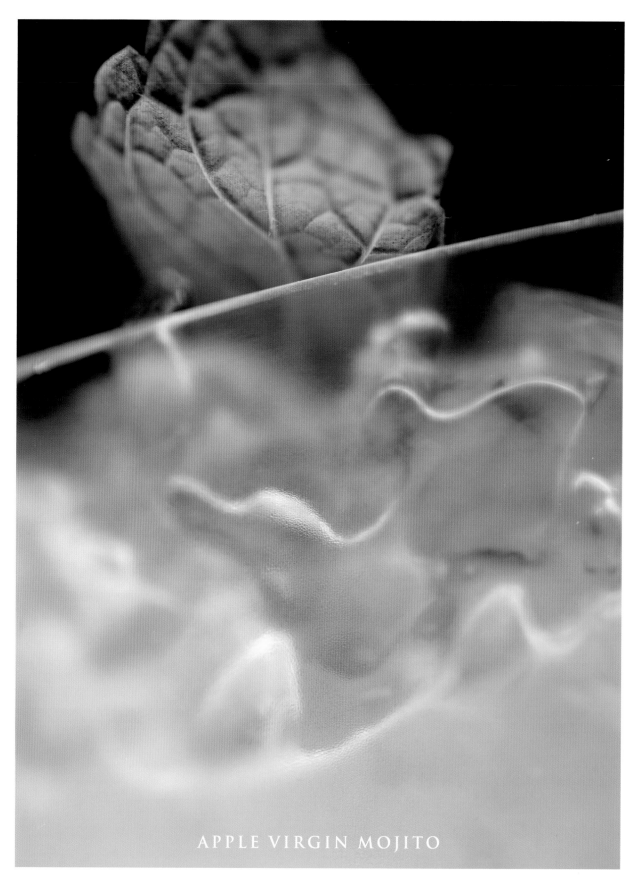

APPLE VIRGIN MOJITO

A

APRICOT MANGO MARTINI

Glass: Martini
Garnish: Mango slice
Method: MUDDLE mango in base of shaker. Add other ingredients, **SHAKE** with ice and fine strain into glass.

1	cupful	**Fresh diced mango**
2	shot(s)	**Tanqueray London dry gin**
½	shot(s)	**Bols apricot brandy liqueur**
¾	shot(s)	**Freshly squeezed lemon juice**
½	shot(s)	**Sugar syrup** (2 sugar to 1 water)

Variant: Use one-and-a-half shots of mango purée in place of fresh mango and halve amount of sugar syrup.
Comment: A simple, great tasting variation on the fresh fruit Martini.

APRICOT MARTINI

Glass: Martini
Garnish: Lemon zest twist
Method: SHAKE all ingredients with ice and fine strain into chilled glass.

1½	shot(s)	**Tanqueray London dry gin**
1	shot(s)	**Bols apricot brandy liqueur**
¼	shot(s)	**Freshly squeezed lemon juice**
⅛	shot(s)	**Pomegranate (grenadine) syrup**
3	dashes	**Angostura aromatic bitters**
¾	shot(s)	**Chilled mineral water** (omit if wet ice)

Comment: This scarlet cocktail combines gin, apricot and lemon juice.

APRICOT RICKEY NEW #8

Glass: Collins (small 8oz)
Garnish: Immerse length of lime peel in drink.
Method: SHAKE first 3 ingredients with ice and strain into ice-filled glass. **TOP** with soda.

1	shot(s)	**Tanqueray London dry gin**
1	shot(s)	**Bols apricot brandy liqueur**
½	shot(s)	**Freshly squeezed lime juice**
Top up with		**Soda water**

Comment: Light, fruity and refreshing, if a little on the sweet side.

APRIL SHOWER

Glass: Martini
Garnish: Orange zest twist
Method: SHAKE all ingredients with ice and fine strain into chilled glass.

2	shot(s)	**Courvoisier V.S.O.P. cognac**
½	shot(s)	**Bénédictine D.O.M. liqueur**
1½	shot(s)	**Freshly squeezed orange juice**

Comment: This mustard-coloured, medium dry, cognac-based drink harnesses the uniquely herbal edge of Bénédictine.

APRICOT SOUR

Glass: Old-fashioned
Garnish: Lemon zest twist
Method: STIR apricot jam (preserve) with bourbon until it dissolves. Add other ingredients, **SHAKE** with ice and fine strain into ice-filled glass.

2	spoons	**Apricot preserve**
1½	shot(s)	**Bulleit bourbon whiskey**
½	shot(s)	**Bols apricot brandy liqueur**
1	shot(s)	**Pressed apple juice**
½	shot(s)	**Freshly squeezed lemon juice**

Origin: Created in 2005 by Wayne Collins for Maxxium UK.
Comment: Short and fruity.

AQUARIUS

Glass: Old-fashioned
Garnish: Lemon slice & cherry on stick (sail)
Method: SHAKE all ingredients with ice and strain into ice-filled glass.

2	shot(s)	**Johnnie Walker Scotch whisky**
1	shot(s)	**Heering cherry brandy liqueur**
1½	shot(s)	**Ocean Spray cranberry juice**

Comment: A sweet cherry edge is balanced by the dryness of cranberry and Scotch.

ARBUZ NEW #8

Glass: Martini/Coupette
Garnish: Lemongrass through watermelon slice
Method: MUDDLE watermelon and lemon grass in base of shaker. Add other ingredients, **SHAKE** with ice and fine strain into chilled glass.

⅛	fresh	**Watermelon**
1	inch	**Lemon grass** (chopped)
1½	shot(s)	**Zubrówka bison vodka**
½	shot(s)	**Cointreau triple sec**
¼	shot(s)	**Pressed apple juice**

Comment: Summery watermelon with herbal grassy notes.
Origin: Created in 2008 by Andreas Cortes at Maze bar & Restaurant, London, England.

ARGENTINA COCKTAIL NEW #8

Glass: Martini
Garnish: Orange zest twist
Method: STIR all ingredients with ice and strain into chilled glass.

1	shot(s)	**Tanqueray London dry gin**
1	shot(s)	**Noilly Prat dry vermouth**
¼	shot(s)	**Cointreau triple sec**
¼	shot(s)	**Bénédictine D.O.M. liqueur**
1	dash	**Angostura orange bitters**
1	dash	**Angostura aromatic bitters**

Comment: A wet martini softened by liqueur and given a hint of citrus and spice.

APRICOT RICKEY

A

ARGHA NOAH NEW #8

●●●●○

Glass: Old-fashioned
Garnish: Orange zest twist
Method: STIR all ingredients with ice and strain into ice-filled glass.

2	shot(s)	**Zacapa aged rum**
1/8	shot(s)	**Honey syrup** (4 honey to 1 water)
1/4	shot(s)	**Drambuie liqueur**
1/8	shot(s)	**Matusalem Oloroso sherry**
1/2	shot(s)	**Ocean Spray cranberry juice**

Origin: Created in January 2009 by Yours Truly (Simon Difford) at the Cabinet Room, London, England.
Comment: Delicately spiced, honeyed and sherried aged rum.

THE ARGYLL

●●●○○

Glass: Martini
Garnish: Orange zest twist
Method: STIR all ingredients with ice and strain into chilled glass.

2	shot(s)	**Southern Comfort liqueur**
1	shot(s)	**Martini Rosso sweet vermouth**
1	dash	**Angostura orange bitters**

Comment: Southern Comfort lovers only need apply.

ARIZONA BREEZE

●●●●○

Glass: Collins
Garnish: Grapefruit wedge on rim
Method: SHAKE all ingredients with ice and strain into ice-filled glass.

2½	shot(s)	**Tanqueray London dry gin**
3	shot(s)	**Ocean Spray cranberry juice**
2	shot(s)	**Freshly squeezed grapefruit juice**

Comment: A tart variation on the Sea Breeze – as dry as Arizona.

ARMILLITA CHICO

●●●◐○

Glass: Martini (large 10oz)
Garnish: Lime wedge on rim
Method: BLEND all ingredients with 12oz scoop crushed ice.

2	shot(s)	**Don Julio reposado tequila**
1	shot(s)	**Freshly squeezed lime juice**
1/2	shot(s)	**Pomegranate (grenadine) syrup**
2	dashes	**Orange flower water**

Comment: Similar to a frozen Margarita but more subtle and dry.

ARMY & NAVY

●●●●○

Glass: Martini
Garnish: Lemon zest twist
Method: SHAKE all ingredients with ice and fine strain into chilled glass.

2	shot(s)	**Tanqueray London dry gin**
1/2	shot(s)	**Freshly squeezed lemon juice**
1/4	shot(s)	**Almond (orgeat) syrup**
1/2	shot(s)	**Chilled mineral water** (omit if wet ice)

Origin: This old classic was originally made to an 8:4:4 formula but I have borrowed this 8:2:1 formula from David A. Embury's 1948 'Fine Art of Mixing Drinks' (he describes the original formulation as "horrible"). The addition of water is a Difford touch.
Comment: Almond and lemon flavoured gin. Subtle, citrusy and dry.

ARMY MARTINI NEW #8

●●●●○

Glass: Martini
Garnish: Mint leaf
Method: SHAKE all ingredients with ice and fine strain into chilled glass.

2½	shot(s)	**Tanqueray London dry gin**
1/4	shot(s)	**Martini Rosso sweet vermouth**
1/4	shot(s)	**Pomegranate (grenadine) syrup**

Variant: Served 'dry' without the grenadine.
Comment: This rosé Martini is harder than it looks – perhaps that's where tha name comes from.

ARNAUD MARTINI

●●●●○

Glass: Martini
Garnish: Blackberry on rim
Method: STIR all ingredients with ice and strain into chilled glass.

1	shot(s)	**Tanqueray London dry gin**
1	shot(s)	**Noilly Prat dry vermouth**
1	shot(s)	**Creme de cassis liqueur**

Origin: A classic cocktail named after the pre-war stage actress Yvonne Arnaud.
Comment: An interesting balance of blackcurrant, vermouth and gin. Sweet palate and dry finish.

ARNOLD PALMER (MOCKTAIL)

●●●●○

Glass: Collins
Garnish: Lemon slice
Method: SHAKE all ingredients with ice and strain into ice-filled glass.

2	shot(s)	**Freshly squeezed lemon juice**
1	shot(s)	**Sugar syrup** (2 sugar to 1 water)
3	shot(s)	**Cold English breakfast tea**

Variants: Tom Arnold, John Daly
Origin: A popular drink throughout the United States. Named after and said to be a favourite of the legendary golfer.
Comment: Real lemon iced tea. Balanced and wonderfully refreshing.

ARTLANTIC

Glass: Collins
Garnish: Orange wedge
Method: SHAKE all ingredients with ice and strain into ice-filled glass.

1	shot(s)	**Sailor Jerry spiced rum**
½	shot(s)	**Luxardo Amaretto di Saschira**
½	shot(s)	**Bols blue curaçao liqueur**
½	shot(s)	**Freshly squeezed lime juice**
3	shot(s)	**Pressed apple juice**

Origin: Atlantic Bar & Grill, London, England.
Comment: This sea green cocktail tastes much better than it looks.

ASIAN GINGER MARTINI

Glass: Martini
Garnish: Ginger slice on rim
Method: MUDDLE ginger in base of shaker. Add other ingredients, SHAKE with ice and fine strain into chilled glass.

2	slices	**Fresh root ginger** (thumbnail sized)
1½	shot(s)	**Ketel One vodka**
2¼	shot(s)	**Sake**
¼	shot(s)	**Sugar syrup** (2 sugar to 1 water)

Origin: Adapted from a recipe created in 2004 by Chris Langan of Barnomadics.
Comment: Lightly spiced with ginger, distinctly oriental in character.

ASIAN MARY

Glass: Collins
Garnish: Lemongrass
Method: MUDDLE ginger in base of shaker and add vodka. Squeeze wasabi paste onto bar spoon and STIR with vodka and ginger until dissolved. Add other ingredients, SHAKE with ice and fine strain into ice-filled glass.

3	slices	**Fresh root ginger** (thumbnail sized)
3	peas	**Wasabi paste**
2	shot(s)	**Ketel One Citroen vodka**
1	spoon	**Soy sauce**
4	shot(s)	**Pressed tomato juice**
½	shot(s)	**Freshly squeezed lemon juice**

Comment: An aptly named Bloody Mary with plenty of Asian spice.

ASIAN PEAR MARTINI

Glass: Martini
Garnish: Pear slice on rim
Method: SHAKE all ingredients with ice and fine strain into chilled glass.

2	shot(s)	**Sake**
¼	shot(s)	**Belle de Brillet pear liqueur**
½	shot(s)	**Poire William eau de vie**
1½	shot(s)	**Freshly extracted pear juice**
¼	shot(s)	**Freshly squeezed lemon juice**

Origin: Created in 2002 by Yours Truly (Simon Difford).
Comment: Sake and pear juice with a kick.

ASSISTED SUICIDE

Glass: Shot
Method: SHAKE first 2 ingredients with ice and strain into chilled glass. TOP with Coca-Cola.

1	shot(s)	**Wray & Nephew overproof rum**
½	shot(s)	**Jägermeister liqueur**
Top up with		**Coca-Cola**

Comment: Not for the faint-hearted.

ASTOR NEW #8

Glass: Martini/Coupette
Garnish: Lemon zest twist
Method: SHAKE all ingredients with ice and fine strain into chilled glass.

1¼	shot(s)	**Tanqueray London dry gin**
1	shot(s)	**Swedish Punch**
¼	shot(s)	**Freshly squeezed lemon juice**
¼	shot(s)	**Freshly squeezed orange juice**

Variant: Waldorf Cocktail No.2
Comment: Citrus and the tang of Swedish punch add a distinctive flavour to gin in this tasty vintage cocktail.
Origin: Recipe adapted from Albert Stevens Crockett's 1931 'The Old Waldorf-Astoria Bar Book' where the drink accompanied by the following notation, "Perhaps [named] after William Waldorf, who built the original Waldorf. However, chances are, it was originated either at the old Astor House or the Astor Hotel, and took its name from its bar of nativity."

ASTORIA NEW #8

Glass: Martini/Coupette
Garnish: Lemon zest twist
Method: STIR all ingredients with ice and strain into chilled glass.

1	shot(s)	**Old Tom gin**
2	shot(s)	**Noilly Prat dry vermouth**
2	dashes	**Angostura orange bitters**

Comment: An Old Tom based super wet (two-thirds vermouth to one-third gin) Martini with a slug of orange bitters and served with a twist.
Origin: Recipe adapted from Albert Stevens Crockett's 1931 'The Old Waldorf-Astoria Bar Book' where the drink accompanied by the following notation, "After the big annex to the Old Waldorf, which at its opening, in 1897, became the main part of the establishment.
William Waldorf Astor built the original Waldorf Hotel, which opened in 1893, next door to his aunt's home, on the site of his father's mansion and today's Empire State Building. John Astor persuaded his aunt to move uptown and then built the Astor Hotel. The two hotels where connected and the combined Waldorf-Astoria became the largest hotel in the world at the time.

A

ASYLUM COCKTAIL

Glass: Old-fashioned
Method: POUR ingredients into glass without ice and **STIR**. Gently add ice and do NOT stir again. Consume once drink has turned cloudy.

1½	shot(s)	Tanqueray London dry gin
1½	shot(s)	Pernod anis
¼	shot(s)	Pomegranate (grenadine) syrup

Origin: Created by William Seabrook, famous for his account of eating human flesh, and first published in a 1935 book, 'So Red the Nose, or Breath in the Afternoon'.
Comment: Seabrook said of this drink, "look like rosy dawn, taste like the milk of Paradise, and make you plenty crazy." He must have been a Pernod lover!

ATHOLL BROSE

Glass: Martini
Garnish: Dust with freshly grated nutmeg
Method: Prepare oatmeal water by soaking 3 heaped tablespoons of oatmeal in half a mug of warm water. Stir and leave to stand for fifteen minutes. Then strain to extract the creamy liquid and discard what's left of the oatmeal.
To make the drink, **STIR** honey with Scotch until honey dissolves. Add other ingredients, **SHAKE** with ice and fine strain into chilled glass.

2	spoons	Runny heather honey
2	shot(s)	Johnnie Walker Scotch whisky
1½	shot(s)	Oatmeal water
¼	shot(s)	Drambuie liqueur
¼	shot(s)	Luxardo Amaretto di Saschira
½	shot(s)	Double (heavy) cream

Origin: My adaptation of a Scottish classic. Legend has it that Atholl Brose was created by the Earl of Atholl in 1475 when he was trying to capture Iain MacDonald, Lord of the Isles and leader of a rebellion against the king. Hearing rumours that MacDonald was drawing his drinking water from a small well, the Earl ordered it to be filled with honey, whisky and oatmeal. MacDonald lingered at the well enjoying the concoction and was captured.
Comment: Forget the porridge and kick start your day with an Atholl Brose.

ATLANTIC BREEZE

Glass: Collins
Garnish: Orange slice
Method: SHAKE all ingredients with ice and strain into ice-filled glass.

1½	shot(s)	Bacardi Superior rum
½	shot(s)	Bols apricot brandy liqueur
¼	shot(s)	Galliano L'Autentico liqueur
2½	shot(s)	Pressed pineapple juice
½	shot(s)	Freshly squeezed lemon juice

Comment: A fruity, tropical cocktail finished with herbal and citrus notes.

ATOMIC COCKTAIL

Glass: Martini
Garnish: Orange zest twist
Method: SHAKE first 3 ingredients with ice and fine strain into chilled glass. **TOP** with champagne.

1¼	shot(s)	Ketel One vodka
1¼	shot(s)	Courvoisier V.S.O.P. cognac
½	shot(s)	Amontillado dry sherry
Top up with		Perrier Jouet brut champagne

Origin: Created in the early 50s in Las Vegas. A-bomb tests were being conducted in Nevada at the time.
Comment: Golden and flavoursome – handle with care.

ATOMIC DOG

Glass: Collins
Garnish: Pineapple wedge and cherry
Method: SHAKE all ingredients with ice and strain into ice-filled glass.

1½	shot(s)	Bacardi Superior rum
¾	shot(s)	Midori green melon liqueur
¾	shot(s)	Malibu coconut rum liqueur
2½	shot(s)	Pressed pineapple juice
¾	shot(s)	Freshly squeezed lemon juice

Comment: A long, refreshing tropical drink with melon, coconut and pineapple juice.

ATTITUDE ADJUSTER 🔑

Glass: Hurricane
Garnish: Orange slice & cherry on stick (sail)
Method: SHAKE first 3 ingredients with ice and strain into ice-filled glass. **TOP** with Coca-Cola then **DRIZZLE** orange and coffee liqueurs.

2	shot(s)	Tanqueray London dry gin
1	shot(s)	Cointreau triple sec
¾	shot(s)	Freshly squeezed lime juice
Top up with		Coca-Cola
¼	shot(s)	Grand Marnier liqueur
¼	shot(s)	Kahlúa coffee liqueur

Comment: I've simplified and tried to improve this somewhat dodgy but popular cocktail – sorry, I failed!

THE ATTY COCKTAIL

Glass: Martini
Garnish: Lemon zest twist
Method: SHAKE all ingredients with ice and fine strain into chilled glass.

2¼	shot(s)	Tanqueray London dry gin
¾	shot(s)	Noilly Prat dry vermouth
¼	shot(s)	La Fée Parisienne (68%) absinthe
¼	shot(s)	Benoit Serres crème de violette

Origin: Adapted from Harry Craddock's 1930 'The Savoy Cocktail Book'.
Comment: Dry and aromatic with floral hints and aniseed notes.

AUNT AGATHA UPDATED #8

Glass: Old-fashioned
Garnish: Orange zest twist
Method: SHAKE first 3 ingredients with ice and strain into glass filled with crushed ice. **DASH** bitters over surface.

1½	shot(s)	**Pusser's Navy rum**
2	shot(s)	**Freshly squeezed orange juice**
1	shot(s)	**Pressed pineapple juice**
3	dashes	**Angostura aromatic bitters**

Comment: A most unusual looking, tropical tasting concoction.
Origin: Aunt Agatha was Bertie Wooster's terrifying aunt in P.G. Wodehouse's books.

AUTUMN LEAVES NEW #8

Glass: Old-fashioned
Garnish: Orange zest twist
Method: STIR all ingredients with ice and strain into ice-filled glass.

1	shot(s)	**Rye whiskey (or bourbon)**
1	shot(s)	**Boulard Grand Solage calvados**
1	shot(s)	**Martini Rosso sweet vermouth**
¼	shot(s)	**Strega liqueur**
2	dashes	**Angostura aromatic bitters**

Comment: Jeffrey's original recipe calls for Carpano Antica sweet vermouth in this whiskey, apple brandy, vermouth and herbal liqueur delightfully old-school combo. Serious drinkers need only apply.
Origin: Created in 2008 by Jeffrey Morgenthaler at Bel Ami Lounge, Oregon, USA.

> 'SO LONG AS ANY MAN DRINKS WHEN HE WANTS TO AND STOPS WHEN HE WANTS TO, HE ISN'T A DRUNKARD, NO MATTER HOW MUCH HE DRINKS OR HOW OFTEN HE FALLS UNDER THE TABLE.'
> WILLIAM BUEHLER SEABROOK

AUNT EMILY

Glass: Martini
Garnish: Apricot wedge on rim
Method: SHAKE all ingredients with ice and fine strain into chilled glass.

1½	shot(s)	**Tanqueray London dry gin**
1½	shot(s)	**Boulard Grand Solage calvados**
¾	shot(s)	**Bols apricot brandy liqueur**
¾	shot(s)	**Freshly squeezed orange juice**
⅛	shot(s)	**Pomegranate (grenadine) syrup**

Origin: A forgotten classic.
Comment: Aunt Emily is onto something as these ingredients combine to make a stylish fruity Martini.

AUTUMN MARTINI

Glass: Martini
Garnish: Orange zest twist
Method: Cut passion fruit in half and scoop out flesh into shaker. Add other ingredients, **SHAKE** with ice and fine strain into chilled glass.

1	fresh	**Passion fruit**
2	shot(s)	**Zubrówka bison vodka**
1	shot(s)	**Pressed apple juice**
½	shot(s)	**Passion fruit sugar syrup**
½	fresh	**Egg white**

Origin: Created in 2004 by Yours Truly (Simon Difford), inspired by Max Warner's excellent Autumn Punch.
Comment: An easy drinking, smooth, fruity cocktail with grassy hints courtesy of bison vodka.

AUNTIE'S HOT XMAS PUNCH

Glass: Toddy
Garnish: Cinnamon stick in glass
Method: POUR all ingredients into glass and stir. **MICROWAVE** for a minute (vary time depending on your microwave oven), stir again and serve.

¾	shot(s)	**Freshly squeezed lemon juice**
1½	shot(s)	**Noé Pedro Ximénez sherry**
2¼	shot(s)	**Courvoisier V.S.O.P. cognac**
3	shot(s)	**Pressed apple juice**
4	dashes	**Peychaud's aromatic bitters**

Origin: I created this drink to serve live on Christmas Eve 2002 during a broadcast on BBC radio. 'Auntie' is a nickname for the BBC and the drink uses the traditional punch proportions of 1 sour, 2 sweet, 3 strong and 4 weak.
Comment: A fruity seasonal warmer.

AUTUMN PUNCH

Glass: Sling
Garnish: Physalis (cape gooseberry) on rim
Method: Cut passion fruit in half and scoop out flesh into shaker. Add vodka, passion fruit sugar syrup, pear and lemon juice, **SHAKE** with ice and strain into ice-filled glass. **TOP** with champagne.

1	fresh	**Passion fruit**
2	shot(s)	**Zubrówka bison vodka**
¼	shot(s)	**Passion fruit sugar syrup**
1	shot(s)	**Freshly extracted pear juice**
½	shot(s)	**Freshly squeezed lemon juice**
Top up with		**Perrier Jouet brut champagne**

Origin: Created in 2001 by Max Warner at Baltic Bar, London, England.
Comment: Autumnal in colour with a wonderful meld of complementary flavours.

A

AVALANCHE

● ● ● ○ ○

Glass: Collins
Garnish: Banana slice on rim
Method: BLEND ingredients with 12oz scoop of crushed ice. Pour into glass and serve with straws.

2	shot(s)	Crème de banane liqueur
1	shot(s)	White crème de cacao liqueur
½	shot(s)	Luxardo Amaretto di Saschira
1	shot(s)	Double (heavy) cream
1	shot(s)	Milk
½	fresh	Peeled banana

Origin: Created in 1979 at Maudes Bar, New York City, USA.
Comment: Creamy, rich and smooth. Fluffy but lovely.

AVALANCHE SHOT

● ● ● ○ ○

Glass: Shot
Method: Refrigerate ingredients then **LAYER** in chilled glass by carefully pouring in the following order.

½	shot(s)	Kahlúa coffee liqueur
½	shot(s)	White crème de cacao liqueur
½	shot(s)	Southern Comfort liqueur

Comment: Rich, smooth and sticky – peculiarly, this has an almost nutty taste.

AVENUE UPDATED #8

● ● ● ● ○

Glass: Martini
Garnish: Orange zest twist
Method: Cut passion fruit in half and scoop flesh into shaker. Add other ingredients, **SHAKE** with ice and fine strain into chilled glass.

1	fresh	Passion fruit
1	shot(s)	Bulleit bourbon whiskey
1	shot(s)	Boulard Grand Solage calvados
¼	shot(s)	Pomegranate (grenadine) syrup
⅛	shot(s)	Orange flower water
1	dash	Angostura orange bitters
½	shot(s)	Chilled mineral water (omit if wet ice)

Comment: Passion fruit and orange flavours, laced with apple brandy and Bourbon. Fruity yet dry.
Origin: Adapted from the 1937 Café Royal Bar Book.

AVIATION NO.1 UPDATED #8

● ● ● ● ◐

Glass: Martini
Garnish: Lemon zest twist (& optional sugar rim)
Method: SHAKE all ingredients with ice and fine strain into chilled glass.

1¾	shot(s)	Tanqueray London dry gin
½	shot(s)	Luxardo maraschino liqueur
¼	shot(s)	Benoit Serres crème de violette
½	shot(s)	Freshly squeezed lemon juice
¼	shot(s)	Chilled mineral water (omit if wet ice)

Variant: Blue Moon
Comment: Benefits from a long shake. Citrus, floral gin with a slightly sour finish.
Origin: Recipe adapted from Hugo R. Esslinn's 1916 'Recipes for Mixed Drinks'.

AVIATION NO.2 UPDATED #8

● ● ● ● ◐

Glass: Martini
Garnish: Maraschino cherry (& optional sugar rim)
Method: SHAKE all ingredients with ice and fine strain into chilled glass.

1¾	shot(s)	Tanqueray London dry gin
¾	shot(s)	Luxardo maraschino liqueur
½	shot(s)	Freshly squeezed lemon juice
¼	shot(s)	Chilled mineral water (omit if wet ice)

Comment: This is a fantastic, tangy cocktail and dangerously easy to drink – too many of these and you really will be flying.
Origin: A well-established vintage cocktail. Formula by Yours Truly (Simon Difford).

AVIATOR #1 NEW #8

● ● ● ● ○

Glass: Martini
Garnish: Lemon zest twist
Method: SHAKE first 4 ingredients with ice and fine strain into chilled glass. **POUR** cassis into to centre of drink (it should sink).

2	shot(s)	Tanqueray London dry gin
½	shot(s)	Luxardo maraschino liqueur
½	shot(s)	Freshly squeezed lemon juice
½	fresh	Egg white
¼	shot(s)	Crème de cassis liqueur

Comment: An Aviation with egg white and a dash of cassis in the bottom but is actually better and more balanced when the cassis is shaken with the other ingredients.

AVIATOR #2 UPDATED #8

● ● ● ● ○ ○

Glass: Martini
Garnish: Lemon zest twist
Method: STIR all ingredients with ice and strain into chilled glass.

1	shot(s)	Tanqueray London dry gin
1	shot(s)	Noilly Prat dry vermouth
1	shot(s)	Martini Rosso sweet vermouth
1	shot(s)	Dubonnet Red (French made)

Comment: Bittersweet herbal notes of vermouth with a subtle hint of gin.
Origin: A classic cocktail of unknown origin.

DRINKS ARE GRADED AS FOLLOWS:

● DISGUSTING   ● ● PRETTY AWFUL   ● ● BEST AVOIDED
● ● ○ DISAPPOINTING   ● ● ● ACCEPTABLE   ● ● ● ● GOOD
● ● ● ● RECOMMENDED   ● ● ● ● ○ HIGHLY RECOMMENDED
● ● ● ● ● OUTSTANDING / EXCEPTIONAL

AWOL

Glass: Shot
Method: **LAYER** in chilled glass by carefully pouring ingredients in the following order. Then **FLAME** drink and allow to burn for no more than ten seconds before extinguishing flame and consuming. Take extreme care and beware of hot glass.

½	shot(s)	Midori green melon liqueur
½	shot(s)	Pressed pineapple juice
½	shot(s)	Ketel One vodka
½	shot(s)	Wray & Nephew overproof rum

Origin: Created in 1993 by Lane Zellman at Louis XVI Restaurant, St. Louis Hotel, New Orleans, USA.
Comment: A strong but surprisingly palatable shot.

AZTEC NEW #8

Glass: Martini/Coupette
Garnish: Flamed orange zest twist
Method: **STIR** all ingredients with ice and strain into chilled glass.

1¾	shot(s)	Bulleit bourbon whiskey
½	shot(s)	Benedictine D.O.M. liqueur
¼	shot(s)	White crème de cacao liqueur
1	drop	Tabasco pepper sauce

Comment: Whiskey with the merest touch of herbal and chocolate liqueurs spiced with a wisp of pepper.
Origin: Adapted from a recipe created in 2007 by Neyah White, Nopa, San Francisco, USA.

'IT'S NOT EVERY ONE THAT CAN SAY THAT HE HAS HAD CHOLERA THREE TIMES, AND CURED HIMSELF BY LIVING ON RED PEPPER AND BRANDY.'
SIR ARTHUR CONAN DOYLE

AZURE MARTINI

Glass: Martini
Garnish: Apple slice on rim
Method: **SHAKE** all ingredients with ice and fine strain into chilled glass.

2	shot(s)	Leblon cachaça
¼	shot(s)	Goldschläger cinnamon schnapps
1	shot(s)	Pressed apple juice
½	shot(s)	Freshly squeezed lime juice
¼	shot(s)	Sugar syrup (2 sugar to 1 water)

Origin: Created in 1998 by Ben Reed at the Met Bar, London, England, and originally made with muddled fresh apple.
Comment: A tangy cocktail – reminiscent of a cinnamon laced apple pie. Shame it's not blue.

B2C2

Glass: Martini
Garnish: Orange zest twist
Method: **SHAKE** first 3 ingredients with ice and strain into ice-filled glass. **TOP** with champagne.

1	shot(s)	Courvoisier V.S.O.P. cognac
1	shot(s)	Bénédictine D.O.M. liqueur
1	shot(s)	Cointreau triple sec
Top up with		Perrier Jouet brut champagne

Origin: Named after the four ingredients and created in France during World War II by American soldiers using ingredients liberated from retreating Germans.
Comment: Strong and sweet. This wartime drink can still be deadly if not handled with care.

B5200

Glass: Shot
Method: Refrigerate ingredients then **LAYER** in chilled glass by carefully pouring in the following order.

½	shot(s)	Kahlúa coffee liqueur
½	shot(s)	Baileys Irish cream liqueur
½	shot(s)	Wood's 100 rum

Origin: Discovered in 2003 at Circus Bar, London,.
Origin: Layering this drink is as easy as inflating a lifejacket – drink a few and you'll need one.

B-52 SHOT

Glass: Shot
Method: Refrigerate ingredients then **LAYER** in chilled glass by carefully pouring in the following order.

½	shot(s)	Kahlúa coffee liqueur
½	shot(s)	Baileys Irish cream liqueur
½	shot(s)	Grand Marnier liqueur

Origin: Named after B-52 bombers in Vietnam.
Comment: Probably the best-known and most popular shot.

B-53 SHOT

Glass: Shot
Method: Refrigerate ingredients then **LAYER** in chilled glass by carefully pouring in the following order.

½	shot(s)	Kahlúa coffee liqueur
½	shot(s)	Baileys Irish cream liqueur
½	shot(s)	Ketel One vodka

Comment: Why settle for a 52 when you can go one better?

B-54 SHOT

Glass: Shot
Method: Refrigerate ingredients then **LAYER** in chilled glass by carefully pouring in the following order.

½	shot(s)	**Luxardo Amaretto di Saschira**
½	shot(s)	**Kahlúa coffee liqueur**
½	shot(s)	**Baileys Irish cream liqueur**

Comment: Layered and sticky – but nice.

> ## 'MR EDITOR. I LEAVE WHEN THE PUB CLOSES.'
> ### WINSTON CHURCHILL

B-55 SHOT

Glass: Shot
Method: Refrigerate ingredients then **LAYER** in chilled glass by carefully pouring in the following order.

½	shot(s)	**Kahlúa coffee liqueur**
½	shot(s)	**Baileys Irish cream liqueur**
½	shot(s)	**La Fée Parisienne (68%) absinthe**

Comment: The latest and scariest of the B-something range of layered shots.

B-52 FROZEN

Glass: Old-fashioned
Garnish: Crumbled Cadbury's Flake bar
Method: **BLEND** ingredients with 6oz scoop of crushed ice. Pour into glass and serve with straws.

1	shot(s)	**Baileys Irish cream liqueur**
1	shot(s)	**Grand Marnier liqueur**
1	shot(s)	**Kahlúa coffee liqueur**

Comment: The classic shot blended with ice.

B & B

Glass: Old-fashioned
Garnish: Lemon zest twist
Method: **STIR** ingredients with ice and strain into ice-filled glass.

| 2 | shot(s) | **Bénédictine D.O.M. liqueur** |
| 2 | shot(s) | **Courvoisier V.S.O.P. cognac** |

Origin: Created in 1937 by a bartender at New York's famous 21 Club.
Comment: Honeyed and spiced cognac.

B & T NEW #8

Glass: Martini
Garnish: Lime zest twist
Method: **SHAKE** all ingredients with ice and fine strain into chilled glass.

| 2 | shot(s) | **Don Julio reposado tequila** |
| 1 | shot(s) | **Bénédictine D.O.M. liqueur** |

Comment: Delicately spiced and slightly sweetened tequila.
Origin: Adapted from a drink created in 2007 by Neyah White, San Francisco, USA. Originally this consisted of equal parts served unchilled in a brandy glass and using anejo tequila.

B. J. SHOT

Glass: Shot
Garnish: Thin layer of single cream
Method: Refrigerate ingredients then **LAYER** in chilled glass by carefully pouring in the following order.

| ½ | shot(s) | **Grand Marnier liqueur** |
| ½ | shot(s) | **Baileys Irish cream liqueur** |

Comment: You know what the letters stand for – hopefully tastes better.

BABO NATALE NEW #8

Glass: Martini
Garnish: Mint sprig
Method: **SHAKE** all ingredients with ice and fine strain into chilled glass.

5	fresh	**Mint leaves**
2	shot(s)	**Warre's Otima tawny port**
1	shot(s)	**Crème de framboise liqueur**

Comment: Richly flavoured and on the sweet side. One to chase a hearty dinner.

BABY BLUE MARTINI

Glass: Martini
Garnish: Orange zest twist
Method: **SHAKE** all ingredients with ice and fine strain into chilled glass.

2	shot(s)	**Tanqueray London dry gin**
¾	shot(s)	**Bols blue curaçao liqueur**
¾	shot(s)	**Freshly squeezed grapefruit juice**
¾	shot(s)	**Pressed pineapple juice**

Comment: Turquoise blue, easy drinking, fruity gin.

BABY GUINNESS

Glass: Shot
Method: Refrigerate ingredients then **LAYER** in chilled glass by carefully pouring in the following order.

1	shot(s)	**Kahlúa coffee liqueur**
½	shot(s)	**Baileys Irish cream liqueur**

Comment: Looks like a miniature pint of Guinness stout.

BABY WOO WOO

Glass: Shot
Garnish: Lime wedge
Method: SHAKE all ingredients with ice and fine strain into chilled glass.

½	shot(s)	**Ketel One vodka**
½	shot(s)	**Peach Tree peach schnapps**
½	shot(s)	**Ocean Spray cranberry juice**

Comment: Pink, sweet and all too easy to shoot.

BACARDI COCKTAIL UPDATED #8

Glass: Martini
Garnish: Maraschino cherry
Method: SHAKE all ingredients with ice and fine strain into chilled glass.

2	shot(s)	**Bacardi Superior rum**
½	shot(s)	**Freshly squeezed lime juice**
¼	shot(s)	**Pomegranate (grenadine) syrup**
½	shot(s)	**Chilled mineral water** (omit if wet ice)
⅛	shot(s)	**Sugar syrup** (2 sugar to 1 water)

Comment: This classic salmon-pinky drink perfectly combines and balances the subtle blue cheese notes I love in Bacardi with the rich sourness of lime juice and the sweetness of pomegranate syrup.
Origin: The Bacardi Cocktail originated in Cuba in 1917 and quickly grew in popularity with the growth of the cocktail culture in the USA after prohibition, so much so that it became known simply as 'the Bacardi'.

There are two schools of thought over the original ingredients - some believe it was originally simply a Daiquiri, containing rum, lime juice, and sugar but made using Bacardi rum and that the now ubiquitous grenadine version originated in New York sometime after Prohibition. However, others hold that the grenadine was there at conception – after all there is no doubt that the Daiquiri was originally made with Bacardi rum. However, the number of vintage cocktails books listing a Bacardi Cocktail without grenadine would seem to back up the inclusion of grenadine being a later addition.

Like the Daiquiri, The Bacardi Cocktail was sometimes served frozen and talking about this special iced version, Jack Doyle, former barman at Sloppy Joe's in Key West, then Bacardi Imports Inc. barman in New York, explained, 'The secret to the iced version was to shake the flaked iced until it looked like sherbet.' This technique became known as frappe.

As the Bacardi Cocktail rapidly grew in popularity a small number of establishments neglected to use Bacardi rum as the base ingredient, despite the brand being fundamental to the drinks name and taste. In 1936 this led the Bacardi Company to take the Barbizon-Plaza Hotel and the Wivel Restaurant in West Fifty-Fourth Street to court in New York City to ensure that when a customer asked for 'Bacardi' by name they were given Bacardi Rum, so protecting the company's trademark.

Bacardi's case at New York's Supreme Court involved the premise that theirs was a unique rum and Bacardi family members travelled from Cuba to New York to appear as witnesses. Even Enrique Schueg, the third President of the Bacardi Company, took to the witness stand. When asked by Justice Walsh, 'Well, how is this Bacardi Rum of yours made?' he replied, 'Oh! That is my secret.' Despite this secrecy, after deliberation, Justice John L. Walsh eventually affirmed that "Bacardi Rum is unique and uncopyable" and issued a ruling that a Bacardi Cocktail must legally be made with rum manufactured by the Compania Ron Bacardi.

BACARDI SPECIAL NEW #8

Glass: Martini
Garnish: Maraschino cherry
Method: SHAKE all ingredients with ice and fine strain into chilled glass.

1½	shot(s)	**Bacardi Superior rum**
¾	shot(s)	**Tanqueray London dry gin**
½	shot(s)	**Freshly squeezed lime juice**
¼	shot(s)	**Pomegranate (grenadine) syrup**
⅛	shot(s)	**Sugar syrup** (2 sugar to 1 water)
½	shot(s)	**Chilled mineral water** (omit if wet ice)

Comment: Hit the perfect proportions and you will strike a wondrous balance of flavoursome rum, gin botanicals, limey sourness and fruity sweetness.
Origin: Adapted from Harry Craddock's 1930 'The Savoy Cocktail Book' which also has the following notation to this vintage adaptation of the 'Bacardi Cocktail', "Made famous by Karl K. Kitchen, the well-known New York Newspaper Columnist."

BACCIO PUNCH NEW #8

Glass: Collins
Garnish: Slices of oranges & lemons
Method: SHAKE first 3 ingredients with ice and strain into ice-filled glass. **TOP** with champagne and soda water. Lightly stir and serve with straws.

1½	shot(s)	**Tanqueray London dry gin**
¾	shot(s)	**Marie Brizard anisette liqueur**
1½	shot(s)	**Freshly squeezed grapefruit juice**
1½	shot(s)	**Perrier Jouet brut champagne**
¾	shot(s)	**Soda water** (club soda)

Comment: A classic for aniseed lovers only.
Origin: The origin of this vintage cocktail is unknown but it in Italian its name means 'kiss'.

> ## 'NO WOMAN SHOULD MARRY A TEETOTALLER, OR A MAN WHO DOES NOT SMOKE.'
> ### ROBERT LOUIS STEVENSON

BAHAMA MAMA

Glass: Collins
Garnish: Pineapple wedge & cherry
Method: SHAKE all ingredients with ice and strain into ice-filled glass.

¾	shot(s)	**Pusser's Navy rum**
¾	shot(s)	**Zacapa aged rum**
1	shot(s)	**Malibu coconut rum liqueur**
1¾	shot(s)	**Freshly squeezed orange juice**
2½	shot(s)	**Pressed pineapple juice**
3	dashes	**Angostura aromatic bitters**

Comment: A tropical, fruity number laced with flavoursome rum.

BAHAMAS DAIQUIRI

●●●●●◐

Glass: Martini
Garnish: Pineapple wedge on rim
Method: SHAKE all ingredients with ice and fine strain into chilled glass.

1½	shot(s)	**Myers's dark Jamaican rum**
¾	shot(s)	**Malibu coconut rum liqueur**
¼	shot(s)	**Kahlúa coffee liqueur**
1½	shot(s)	**Freshly extracted pineapple juice**
½	shot(s)	**Freshly squeezed lime juice**

Origin: Adapted from the Bahamas Martini created in 2002 by Yannick Miseriaux at the Fifth Floor Bar, Harvey Nichols, London, England.
Comment: Totally tropical with a sweet tangy edge.

BAHIA

●●●●◐○

Glass: Collins
Garnish: Mint sprig, pineapple wedge & cherry
Method: BLEND all ingredients with 12oz scoop crushed ice and serve with straws.

2½	shot(s)	**Bacardi Superior rum**
3	shot(s)	**Pressed pineapple juice**
½	shot(s)	**Coco López cream of coconut**

Origin: Bahia is one of the 26 states of Brazil. It is also a pre-Prohibition drink containing dry vermouth, sherry, absinthe and bitters. This more recent Piña Colada style offering has more mass market appeal.
Comment: If you like Piña Coladas but are too embarrassed to order one then this drink is for you.

BAJAN DAIQUIRI

●●●●○

Glass: Martini
Garnish: Lime wedge
Method: SHAKE all ingredients with ice and fine strain into chilled glass.

2	shot(s)	**Bacardi Oro golden rum**
½	shot(s)	**Velvet Falernum liqueur**
¾	shot(s)	**Freshly squeezed lime juice**
½	shot(s)	**Chilled mineral water** (omit if wet ice)

Origin: Created in 2006 by Yours Truly (Simon Difford).
Comment: A full-flavoured Daiquiri with clove spice.

BAJAN MOJITO UPDATED #8

●●●●○

Glass: Collins
Garnish: Passion fruit slice or mint sprig
Method: Cut passion fruit in half and scoop flesh into glass. Add mint and gently **MUDDLE** (just to bruise mint). Add rum, lime juice and crushed ice. **CHURN** (stir) drink in glass to mix. **DRIZZLE** passion fruit liqueur and serve with straws.

1	fresh	**Passion fruit**
8	fresh	**Mint leaves**
2	shot(s)	**Bacardi Oro golden rum**
½	shot(s)	**Freshly squeezed lime juice**
½	shot(s)	**Sugar syrup** (2 sugar to 1 water)
¼	shot(s)	**Passoã passion fruit liqueur**

Comment: A laid-back fruity, slightly sweet Mojito.
Origin: Adapted from a recipe by Wayne Collins, London, England.

BAJAN PASSION

●●●●●○

Glass: Martini
Garnish: Float passion fruit slice
Method: Cut passion fruit in half and scoop flesh into shaker. Add other ingredients, **SHAKE** with ice and fine strain into chilled glass.

1	fresh	**Passion fruit**
1½	shot(s)	**Bacardi Oro golden rum**
½	shot(s)	**Bols apricot brandy liqueur**
1	shot(s)	**Freshly squeezed lime juice**
¼	shot(s)	**Sugar syrup** (2 sugar to 1 water)
¼	shot(s)	**Vanilla sugar syrup**

Origin: Created in 2004 by Wayne Collins for Maxxium UK.
Comment: A Daiquiri laced with fruit and spice.

BAJITO

●●●●◐

Glass: Collins
Garnish: Mint sprig
Method: Lightly **MUDDLE** mint and basil in glass just enough to bruise. Add rum, sugar and lime juice. Half fill glass with crushed ice and **CHURN** (stir) with bar spoon. Add more crushed ice and churn some more. Continue adding crushed ice and churning until glass is full.

6	fresh	**Basil leaves**
6	fresh	**Mint leaves**
2	shot(s)	**Bacardi Superior rum**
1	shot(s)	**Freshly squeezed lime juice**
¼	shot(s)	**Sugar syrup** (2 sugar to 1 water)

Origin: Discovered in 2004 at Excelsior Bar, Boston, USA.
Comment: Basically a Mojito with basil as well as mint.

BALABUSHKA NEW #8

●●●●◐○

Glass: Martini
Garnish: Apple slice on rim
Method: SHAKE all ingredients with ice and fine strain into chilled glass.

1½	shot(s)	**Ketel One vodka**
½	shot(s)	**Cointreau triple sec**
½	shot(s)	**Freshly squeezed lemon juice**
1	shot(s)	**Pressed apple juice**
⅛	shot(s)	**Almond (orgeat) syrup**

Comment: This vodka-based cocktail has flavours of apple, lemon, orange and almond.
Origin: Created in 2001 by Julien Escot at Langdon Hall Hotel, Cambridge, Ontario, Canada. Named in homage to George Balabushka, the legendary billiards cue maker.

BALALAIKA

Glass: Martini
Garnish: Orange zest twist
Method: SHAKE all ingredients with ice and fine strain into chilled glass.

1¼	shot(s)	**Ketel One Vodka**
1¼	shot(s)	**Cointreau triple sec**
1¼	shot(s)	**Freshly squeezed lemon juice**

Comment: Richly flavoured with orange and lemon.

BALD EAGLE SHOT

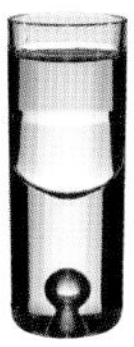

Glass: Shot
Method: Refrigerate ingredients then **LAYER** in chilled glass by carefully pouring in the following order.

½	shot(s)	**Giffard Menthe Pastille liqueur**
¾	shot(s)	**Don Julio reposado tequila**

Comment: Minty tequila – fresh breath tastic.

BALD EAGLE

Glass: Martini
Garnish: Salt rim
Method: SHAKE all ingredients with ice and fine strain into chilled glass.

2	shot(s)	**Don Julio reposado tequila**
¾	shot(s)	**Freshly squeezed grapefruit juice**
½	shot(s)	**Ocean Spray cranberry juice**
¼	shot(s)	**Freshly squeezed lime juice**
¼	shot(s)	**Freshly squeezed lemon juice**
¼	shot(s)	**Sugar syrup** (2 sugar to 1 water)

Origin: Created for me in 2001 by Salvatore Calabrese at The Lanesborough Library Bar, London, England.
Comment: If you like Tequila and you like your drinks on the sour side, this is for you.

BALI TRADER

Glass: Martini
Garnish: Banana chunk on rim
Method: SHAKE all ingredients with ice and fine strain into chilled glass.

2	shot(s)	**Ketel One vodka**
1	shot(s)	**Pisang Ambon liqueur**
1	shot(s)	**Pressed pineapple juice**

Comment: A tasty Caribbean combination of banana and pineapple.

BALLET RUSSE

Glass: Martini
Garnish: Lime wedge on rim
Method: SHAKE all ingredients with ice and fine strain into chilled glass.

2	shot(s)	**Ketel One vodka**
¾	shot(s)	**Crème de Cassis liqueur**
1	shot(s)	**Freshly squeezed lime juice**
¼	shot(s)	**Sugar syrup** (2 sugar to 1 water)

Comment: Intense sweet blackcurrant balanced by lime sourness.

BALM COCKTAIL NEW #8

Glass: Martini
Garnish: Olive
Method: SHAKE all ingredients with ice and fine strain into chilled glass.

3	shot(s)	**Manzanilla sherry**
½	shot(s)	**Cointreau triple sec**
⅛	shot(s)	**Pimento dram liqueur**
½	shot(s)	**Freshly squeezed orange juice**
1	dash	**Angostura orange bitters**

Comment: Medium dry sherry flavoured with orange and subtle spice.
Origin: Adapted from Harry Craddock's 1930 'The Savoy Cocktail Book'.

BALTIC SPRING PUNCH

Glass: Collins
Garnish: Mint sprig
Method: MUDDLE peach in base of shaker. Add next 3 ingredients, **SHAKE** with ice and fine strain into ice-filled glass and **TOP** with champagne.

1	ripe	**Peach** (skinned and diced)
1½	shot(s)	**Rose petal liqueur**
½	shot(s)	**Freshly squeezed lemon juice**
¼	shot(s)	**Sugar syrup** (2 sugar to 1 water)
Top up with		**Perrier Jouet brut champagne**

Variant: If using peach purée omit the sugar.
Origin: Created in 2002 at Baltic, London, England.
Comment: Just peachy, baby.

BALTIMORE EGG NOG UPDATED #8

Glass: Wine glass
Garnish: Dust with freshly ground nutmeg
Method: Vigorously **SHAKE** all ingredients with ice and fine strain into chilled glass.

1	shot(s)	**Courvoisier V.S.O.P. cognac**
1	shot(s)	**Goslings black seal rum**
½	shot(s)	**Madeira**
1	fresh	**Egg** (white & yolk)
½	shot(s)	**Sugar syrup** (2 sugar to 1 water)
½	shot(s)	**Double (heavy) cream**
½	shot(s)	**Milk**

Comment: A rich meal of a drink with a whole egg and cream – fortified with cognac, rum and madeira.
Origin: One of the most famous flip-style drinks.

BAMBOO #1 UPDATED #8

●●●●◐

Glass: Martini
Garnish: Orange zest twist
Method: STIR all ingredients with ice and strain into chilled glass.

2	shot(s)	Tio Pepe fino sherry
2	shot(s)	Noilly Prat dry vermouth
¼	shot(s)	Cointreau triple sec
3	dashes	Angostura orange bitters

Variants: Add 2 dashes of Angostura aromatic bitters in place of triple sec. Also see 'East Indian'.
Comment: For sophisticated palates only.
Origin: A classic and all but forgotten cocktail from the 1940s.

BAMBOO #2 NEW #8

●●●●○

Glass: Martini
Garnish: Accompanied with toasted almonds
Method: STIR all ingredients with ice and strain into ice-filled glass.

2	shot(s)	Tio Pepe fino sherry
1	shot(s)	Noilly Prat dry vermouth
1	shot(s)	Martini Rosso sweet vermouth

Comment: The combination of vermouth and fino makes for a fabulously complex cocktail.
Origin: Adapted from Harry Craddock's 1930 'The Savoy Cocktail Book'.

BANANA & ALMOND DAIQUIRÍ NEW #8

●●●◐○

Glass: Martini/Coupette
Garnish: Banana slice on rim
Method: BLEND all ingredients with crushed ice and serve in chilled glass.

1½	shot(s)	Bacardi Superior rum
1	shot(s)	Almond flavoured vodka
½	shot(s)	Freshly squeezed lemon juice
¼	shot(s)	Almond (orgeat) syrup
¼	fresh	Peeled banana

Comment: Just as it says on the tin – banana and almond flavoured Daiquiri.
Origin: Adapted from a drink created in 2008 by Apostol Bachev at Coq D'Argent, London, England.

BANANA BLISS

●●●●○○

Glass: Martini
Garnish: Banana chunk on rim
Method: STIR all ingredients with ice and strain into chilled glass.

2	shot(s)	Courvoisier V.S.O.P. cognac
1	shot(s)	Crème de banane liqueur
½	shot(s)	Chilled mineral water (omit if wet ice)
2	dashes	Angostura orange bitters

AKA: Golden Brown
Comment: Crème de bananes and cognac go shockingly well together.

BANANA BOOMER

●●●●○

Glass: Martini
Garnish: Banana chunk on rim
Method: SHAKE all ingredients with ice and strain into chilled glass.

1	shot(s)	Ketel One vodka
1	shot(s)	Crème de banane liqueur
½	shot(s)	Bols apricot brandy liqueur
½	shot(s)	Heering cherry brandy liqueur
¾	shot(s)	Freshly squeezed orange juice
¾	shot(s)	Pressed pineapple juice

Comment: Fortified bubble gum for the young at heart.

BANANA COLADA

●●●●○

Glass: Hurricane
Garnish: Banana chunk on rim
Method: BLEND ingredients with 12oz scoop of crushed ice. Pour into glass and serve with straws.

2	shot(s)	Bacardi Oro golden rum
½	shot(s)	Crème de banane liqueur
4	shot(s)	Pressed pineapple juice
1	fresh	Peeled banana
1	shot(s)	Coco López cream of coconut

Comment: Don't skimp, use a whole banana per drink for real flavour.

BANANA COW

●●●○○

Glass: Collins
Garnish: Banana chunk on rim
Method: BLEND all ingredients with 12oz scoop crushed ice and serve with straws.

1	shot(s)	Bacardi Superior rum
3	shot(s)	Fresh milk
1	dash	Vanilla extract
¼	shot(s)	Sugar syrup (2 sugar to 1 water)
1	fresh	Peeled banana
1	dash	Angostura aromatic bitters

Origin: Created by Victor J. Bergeron. This recipe is adapted from his 'Trader Vic's Bartender's Guide' (1972 revised edition).
Comment: The Trader writes of his drink, "The world's finest, greatest, oh-so good peachy hangover special. This'll do it when nothing else will." I think Vic is somewhat overselling this malty banana meal of a drink.

BANANA DAIQUIRI

Glass: Hurricane
Garnish: Banana chunk on rim
Method: **BLEND** all ingredients with 12oz scoop of crushed ice. Pour into glass and serve with straws.

2	shot(s)	**Bacardi Superior rum**
1	shot(s)	**Crème de banane liqueur**
½	shot(s)	**Freshly squeezed lime juice**
1	fresh	**Peeled banana**

Variant: Add a dash of maraschino liqueur.
Comment: A tangy banana disco drink that's not too sweet.

BANANAS & CREAM

Glass: Collins
Garnish: Banana chunk on rim
Method: **BLEND** ingredients with 12oz scoop of crushed ice. Pour into glass and serve with straws.

2	shot(s)	**Crème de banane liqueur**
1	shot(s)	**Luxardo Amaretto di Saschira**
1	shot(s)	**Baileys Irish cream liqueur**
1	shot(s)	**Double (heavy) cream**
2	shot(s)	**Milk**

Comment: Banana and cream frappé with hints of almond – one for a summer afternoon.

BANANA FLAMBÉ NEW #8

Glass: Old-fashioned
Garnish: Cinnamon Stick
Method: In a shallow dish flambé half a split banana with orange juice, sugar and cinnamon. **FLAMBÉ** until the banana softens completely and the orange juice reduces. Add cognac and flambé further. **MUDDLE** banana in the base of shaker, add other ingredients, **SHAKE** with ice and fine strain into chilled glass.

½	fresh	**Peeled banana**
1	shot(s)	**Freshly squeezed orange juice**
1	spoon	**Granulated sugar**
2	pinch	**Ground cinnamon**
½	shot(s)	**Courvoisier V.S.O.P. cognac**
1½	shot(s)	**Ketel One vodka**
½	shot(s)	**Leblon cachaça**
½	shot(s)	**Freshly squeezed lemon juice**
¼	shot(s)	**Sugar syrup** (2 sugar to 1 water)

Variant: Substitute the vodka for cachaça for a Banana Flambé Caipirinha.
Comment: As Tony says – "it's worth it".
Origin: Created in 2008 by Mauricio 'Tony' Harion from Mixing Bar Consulting, Belo Horizonte, Brazil.

BANDERA NEW #8

Glass: 3 x shot glasses
Method: **POUR** tequila and lime juice into separate shot (caballitos) glasses. To make Sangrita to fill third glass, **SHAKE** rest of ingredients with ice and fine strain into glass. Instruct drinker to sip from all 3 glasses alternatively.

2	shot(s)	**Don Julio reposado tequila**
2	shot(s)	**Freshly squeezed lime juice**
½	shot(s)	**Tomato juice**
½	shot(s)	**Pomegranate juice**
¼	shot(s)	**Freshly squeezed orange juice**
½	shot(s)	**Freshly squeezed lime juice**
⅛	shot(s)	**Pomegranate (grenadine) syrup**
2	drops	**Tabasco pepper sauce**
2	dashes	**Lea & Perrins Worcestershire sauce**
1	pinch	**Salt**
1	grind	**Black pepper**

Origin: A popular and classic way of serving tequila in Mexico. Sangrita means 'little blood' in Spanish and the drink is served with tequila in practicably every bar in Mexico.
Comment: In Mexico the quality of the homemade Sangrita can make or break a bar. The Sangrita in this trio is spicy and slightly sweet.

BANANA SMOOTHIE (MOCKTAIL)

Glass: Hurricane
Garnish: Banana chunk on rim
Method: **BLEND** ingredients with 12oz scoop of crushed ice. Pour into glass and serve immediately with straws.

3	shot(s)	**Pressed apple juice**
7	spoons	**Natural yoghurt**
3	spoons	**Runny honey**
1	fresh	**Peeled Banana**

Origin: Created in 2005 by Lisa Ball, London, England.
Comment: Serve with breakfast cereal and you'll be set up for the day. The high fresh banana content means this drink will quickly turn brown if left. This can be countered by adding fresh lemon juice and balancing with more honey but this detracts from the fresh banana flavour.

BANOFFEE MARTINI

Glass: Martini
Garnish: Dust with cocoa powder
Method: **MUDDLE** banana in base of shaker. Add other ingredients, **SHAKE** with ice and fine strain into chilled glass.

¼	fresh	**Peeled banana**
1½	shot(s)	**Vanilla flavoured vodka**
¾	shot(s)	**Teichenné butterscotch schnapps**
¾	shot(s)	**Crème de banane liqueur**
1	spoon	**Maple syrup**
½	shot(s)	**Double (heavy) cream**
½	shot(s)	**Milk**

Origin: Adapted from a recipe created in 2002 by Barry Wilson, Zinc Bar & Grill, Edinburgh, Scotland.
Comment: Thick and rich, one for after the cheese course.

BANSHEE

Glass: Shot
Method: SHAKE all ingredients with ice and fine strain into chilled glass.

½	shot(s)	**Crème de banane liqueur**
½	shot(s)	**White crème de cacao liqueur**
½	shot(s)	**Double (heavy) cream**

Comment: Creamy chocolate banana.

BARBARA

Glass: Martini
Garnish: Dust with freshly grated nutmeg
Method: SHAKE all ingredients with ice and fine strain into chilled glass.

1½	shot(s)	**Ketel One vodka**
¾	shot(s)	**White crème de cacao liqueur**
¾	shot(s)	**Double (heavy) cream**
¾	shot(s)	**Milk**

Comment: Quite neutral and subtle – the nutmeg garnish is as important to the flavour as cacao.

BARBARA WEST

Glass: Martini
Garnish: Lemon twist
Method: SHAKE all ingredients with ice and fine strain into chilled glass.

2	shot(s)	**Tanqueray London dry gin**
1	shot(s)	**Amontillado dry sherry**
½	shot(s)	**Freshly squeezed lemon juice**
¼	shot(s)	**Sugar syrup** (2 sugar to 1 water)
2	dashes	**Angostura aromatic bitters**

Origin: A classic from the 1930s.
Comment: Well balanced but for serious gin and sherry drinkers only.

BARBARY COAST HIGHBALL

Glass: Collins
Method: SHAKE all but soda with ice and strain into ice-filled glass. **TOP** with soda and stir.

1	shot(s)	**Bulleit bourbon whiskey**
1	shot(s)	**Tanqueray London dry gin**
1	shot(s)	**Brown crème de cacao liqueur**
½	shot(s)	**Double (heavy) cream**
½	shot(s)	**Milk**
Top up with		**Soda water** (club soda)

Variant: Omit soda and serve straight-up in a Martini glass.
Comment: Looks like a glass of frothy weak tea - bourbon and chocolate predominate.

BARBARY COAST UPDATED #8

Glass: Martini/Coupette
Garnish: Freshly grated nutmeg dust
Method: SHAKE all ingredients with ice and fine strain into chilled glass.

1	shot(s)	**Johnnie Walker Scotch whisky**
1	shot(s)	**Tanqueray London dry gin**
1	shot(s)	**White crème de cacao liqueur**
½	shot(s)	**Double (heavy) cream**
½	shot(s)	**Milk**

Comment: Cream and white chocolate liqueur smooth but don't smother gin and Scotch.
Origin: A Prohibition-era cocktail (1920-1933) of unknown origin.

ONE UNIT OF ALCOHOL CONTAINS MORE THAN 100 TRILLION BILLION (100,000,000,000,000,000,000,000) MOLECULES OF ALCOHOL.

BARNACLE BILL

Glass: Old-fashioned
Garnish: Mint sprig
Method: SHAKE all ingredients with ice and strain into glass filled with crushed ice.

½	shot(s)	**Yellow Chartreuse liqueur**
½	shot(s)	**Parfait Amour liqueur**
½	shot(s)	**Pernod anis**
½	shot(s)	**Chilled mineral water** (omit if wet ice)

Origin: Adapted from Victor Bergeron's 'Trader Vic's Bartender's Guide' (1972 revised edition).
Comment: This sweetie is great after a meal on a warm night.

BARNAMINT

Glass: Hurricane
Garnish: Oreo cookie
Method: BLEND ingredients with 12oz scoop of crushed ice. Pour into glass and serve with straws.

2	shot(s)	**Baileys Irish cream liqueur**
1½	shot(s)	**Green crème de menthe liqueur**
1	shot(s)	**Double (heavy) cream**
1	shot(s)	**Milk**
2	scoops	**Vanilla ice cream**
3	whole	**Oreo cookies**

Origin: This original TGI Friday's cocktail is named after the Barnum & Bailey Circus, which also inspired the red and white awnings outside Friday's restaurants.
Comment: If you're after a drinkable dessert, then this TGI classic may be the cocktail for you.

BARNEY BARNATO COCKTAIL

Glass: Martini
Garnish: Orange zest twist
Method: STIR all ingredients with ice and strain into chilled glass.

1½	shot(s)	**Dubonnet Red** (French made)
1½	shot(s)	**Courvoisier V.S.O.P. cognac**
¼	shot(s)	**Grand Marnier liqueur**
1	dash	**Angostura aromatic bitters**

Comment: Orange always works when mixed with cognac and here Dubonnet also tames and adds aromatic wine complexity.

Origin: This cocktail is named after Barney Barnato, who was born Barnett Issacs in 1852 in the Whitechapel slum of London and traded on his Jewish-Cockney wit and humour. With only a box of cigars to his name, in 1873 Barney fled poverty to join his brother in the South African diamond rush and changed his name. He formed the Barnato Diamond Mining Company and within ten years he had become a millionaire. He and his brother were eventually forced to sell out to Cecil John Rhodes for £5,338,650, then the single largest cheque that had been written. The fortune was little compensation for being beaten in the battle to control the Cape diamond mines - Rhodes went on to form the now mighty De Beers.

After a brief spell in South African politics Barnato died in 1897 when he was lost overboard near the island of Madeira, whilst on a passage home to England. It is still questioned as to whether he jumped, fell or was pushed. His body was recovered but the mysterious circumstances of his death were never resolved. He is buried at Willesden Jewish Cemetery, London.

His vast fortune was divided between his family, including his sister Sarah and her husband Abraham Rantzen, great-grandparents of TV presenter Esther Rantzen. Another beneficiary was his son, Woolf Barnato, who used part of this inheritance to become one of the so-called Bentley Boys racing drivers in the 1920s.

This recipe is adapted from Harry Craddock's 1930 'The Savoy Cocktail Book' which calls for a now defunct South African product called Caperitif. I have used Dubonnot Red in its place, but some consider white vermouth or aromatized wine a better substitute.

BARNUM (WAS RIGHT)

Glass: Martini
Garnish: Lemon zest twist
Method: SHAKE all ingredients with ice and fine strain into chilled glass.

2	shot(s)	**Tanqueray London dry gin**
1	shot(s)	**Bols apricot brandy liqueur**
½	shot(s)	**Freshly squeezed lemon juice**
2	dashes	**Angostura aromatic bitters**
½	shot(s)	**Chilled mineral water** (omit if wet ice)

Origin: 1930s classic resurrected by Ted Haigh in his 2004 book 'Vintage Spirits & Forgotten Cocktails'.
Comment: A classic cocktail flavour combination that still pleases.

BARRANQUILLA GREEN JADE

Glass: Martini
Garnish: Maraschino cherry & mint sprig
Method: SHAKE all ingredients with ice and fine strain into chilled glass.

2	shot(s)	**Tanqueray London dry gin**
1	shot(s)	**Green crème de menthe liqueur**
½	shot(s)	**Double (heavy) cream**
½	shot(s)	**Milk**
¼	fresh	**Egg white**

Comment: Lime green in colour, a tad minty and creamy smooth.

BARTENDER'S MARTINI

Glass: Martini
Garnish: Orange zest twist
Method: SHAKE all ingredients with ice and fine strain into chilled glass.

1	shot(s)	**Tanqueray London dry gin**
1	shot(s)	**Tio Pepe fino sherry**
1	shot(s)	**Dubonnet Red** (French made)
1	shot(s)	**Noilly Prat dry vermouth**
½	shot(s)	**Grand Marnier liqueur**

Comment: This classic cocktail resembles an aromatic Martini. Hints of sherry and orange are followed by a dry finish.

BARTENDER'S MUM NEW #8

Glass: Shot
Method: Carefully **LAYER** ingredients in the following order.

¾	shot(s)	**Teichenné butterscotch schnapps**
¾	shot(s)	**Baileys Irish cream liqueur**

Comment: Not sure mum would approve but as shots go...

BARTENDER'S ROOT BEER

Glass: Collins
Garnish: Lime wedge on rim
Method: POUR first 3 ingredients into ice-filled glass and **TOP** with Coca-Cola.

1	shot(s)	**Galliano L'Autentico liqueur**
1	shot(s)	**Kahlúa coffee liqueur**
¼	shot(s)	**Freshly squeezed lime juice**
Top up with		**Coca-Cola**

Comment: Not quite the root of all evil, but tasty all the same.

BARTON SPECIAL COCKTAIL NEW #8

Glass: Martini/Coupette
Garnish: Lemon zest twist
Method: STIR all ingredients with ice and fine strain into chilled glass.

1½	shot(s)	**Tanqueray London dry gin**
¾	shot(s)	**Boulard Grand Solage calvados**
¾	shot(s)	**Johnnie Walker Scotch whisky**

Comment: Dry and hardcore – gin, apple brandy and Scotch, tamed only by a little dilution and being chilled.
Origin: Thought to be named after the noted 'all American' Ad-man and political publicist, Bruce Fairchild Barton, who in 1919 co-founded the Barton, Durstine & Osborn advertising agency.

BASIL & HONEY DAIQUIRI

Glass: Martini
Garnish: Float basil leaf
Method: STIR honey and rum in base of shaker until honey dissolves. Add other ingredients, **SHAKE** with ice and fine strain into chilled glass.

2	spoons	Runny honey
2½	shot(s)	Bacardi Superior rum
3	fresh	Basil leaves
½	shot(s)	Freshly squeezed lime juice

Origin: Formula by Yours Truly (Simon Difford) in 2005.
Comment: Basil adds dry vegetable notes to this outstanding classic drink.

BASIL BEAUTY

Glass: Martini
Garnish: Pineapple wedge on rim
Method: Cut passion fruit in half and scoop flesh into shaker. Add other ingredients, **SHAKE** with ice and fine strain into chilled glass.

1	whole	Passion fruit
3	fresh	Basil leaves
2	shot(s)	Ketel One Citroen vodka
2	shot(s)	Pressed pineapple juice
¼	shot(s)	Freshly squeezed lime juice
½	shot(s)	Coconut syrup (or sugar syrup)

Origin: Created in 1999 by Wayne Collins, London, England.
Comment: Pineapple and passion fruit laced with citrus vodka and infused with hints of lime, basil and coconut.

BASIL GIMLET

Glass: Martini
Garnish: Lime wedge or cherry
Method: SHAKE all ingredients with ice and fine strain into chilled glass.

2½	shot(s)	Tanqueray London dry gin
¼	shot(s)	Freshly squeezed lime juice
1½	shot(s)	Rose's lime cordial
3	fresh	Basil leaves

Origin: Adapted from a drink discovered in 2006 at Stella, Boston, USA.
Comment: Tangy, citrus fresh and balanced.

BASIL BRAMBLE SLING

Glass: Sling
Garnish: Mint sprig
Method: MUDDLE basil in base of shaker. Add rest of ingredients, **SHAKE** with ice and strain into ice-filled glass. Serve with straws.

7	fresh	Basil leaves
2	shot(s)	Tanqueray London dry gin
1½	shot(s)	Freshly squeezed lemon juice
½	shot(s)	Sugar syrup (2 sugar to 1 water)
½	shot(s)	Crème de mûre liqueur

Origin: Created in 2003 by Alexandra Fiot at Lonsdale House, London, UK.
Comment: Wonderfully refreshing and balanced.

BASIL CRUSH NEW #8

Glass: Collins
Garnish: Basil leaf
Method: SHAKE all ingredients with ice and fine strain into ice-filled glass.

2	fresh	Basil leaves
1	shot(s)	Tanqueray London dry gin
¾	shot(s)	Cynar artichoke liqueur
1½	shot(s)	Pressed apple juice
1	shot(s)	Cold green tea
½	shot(s)	Fresh lime juice
¼	shot(s)	Honey syrup (4 honey to 1 water)

Comment: Green and herbal to the extent of almost being healthy. Bitter sweet and fruity.
Origin: This drink for Basil Brush fans is adapted from a recipe by Fabio Raffaelli, Restaurante Tristan, Mallorca.

BASIL GRANDE

Glass: Martini
Garnish: Strawberry and dust with black pepper.
Method: MUDDLE strawberries and basil in base of shaker. Add other ingredients, **SHAKE** with ice and fine strain into glass.

4	fresh	Strawberries (hulled)
5	fresh	Basil leaves
¾	shot(s)	Ketel One vodka
¾	shot(s)	Chambord black raspberry liqueur
¾	shot(s)	Grand Marnier liqueur
2	shot(s)	Ocean Spray cranberry juice

Origin: Created in 2001 by Jamie Wilkinson at Living Room, Manchester, England.
Comment: Fruity, with interest courtesy of the basil and grind of pepper.

BASIL MARY

Glass: Collins
Garnish: Basil leaf
Method: SHAKE all ingredients with ice and fine strain into ice-filled glass.

7	fresh	Basil leaves
2	shot(s)	Pepper-infused Ketel One vodka
4	shot(s)	Pressed tomato juice
½	shot(s)	Freshly squeezed lemon juice
8	drops	Tabasco pepper sauce
4	dashes	Lea & Perrins Worcestershire sauce
½	spoon	Horseradish sauce
½	shot(s)	Warre's Otima tawny port
2	pinch	Celery salt
2	grinds	Black pepper

Origin: Discovered in 2004 at Indigo Yard, Edinburgh, Scotland.
Comment: A Mary with a herbal twist.

DRINKS ARE GRADED AS FOLLOWS:

- DISGUSTING
- ○● PRETTY AWFUL
- ●● BEST AVOIDED
- ●●○ DISAPPOINTING
- ●●● ACCEPTABLE
- ●●●○ GOOD
- ●●●● RECOMMENDED
- ●●●●○ HIGHLY RECOMMENDED
- ●●●●● OUTSTANDING / EXCEPTIONAL

BASILIAN

Glass: Collins
Garnish: Lime slice & basil leaf
Method: MUDDLE cucumber and basil in base of shaker. Add next 4 ingredients, **SHAKE** with ice and fine strain into ice-filled glass. **TOP** with ginger ale.

1	inch	**Cucumber** (peeled & chopped)
5	fresh	**Basil leaves**
2	shot(s)	**Leblon cachaça**
¾	shot(s)	**Grand Marnier liqueur**
½	shot(s)	**Freshly squeezed lime juice**
¼	shot(s)	**Sugar syrup** (2 sugar to 1 water)
Top up with		**Ginger ale**

Origin: Created in 2005 by Duncan McRae at Dragonfly, Edinburgh, Scotland.
Comment: Vegetable notes with hints of orange and ginger. Healthy tasting!

BASILICO

Glass: Old-fashioned
Garnish: Basil leaf
Method: MUDDLE basil in base of shaker. Add other ingredients, **SHAKE** with ice and strain into glass filled with crushed ice.

7	fresh	**Basil leaves**
2	shot(s)	**Ketel One vodka**
½	shot(s)	**Luxardo limoncello liqueur**
½	shot(s)	**Freshly squeezed lemon juice**
½	shot(s)	**Sugar syrup** (2 sugar to 1 water)

Origin: Discovered in 2004 at Atlantic Bar & Grill, London, England.
Comment: A lemon Caipirovska with basil.

THE RICKEY WAS CREATED AT SHOEMAKER'S RESTAURANT, WASHINGTON, USA IN 1900, AND NAMED AFTER COLONEL JOE RICKEY WHO ORDERED IT.

BAT BITE NEW #8

Glass: Collins
Garnish: Lime wedge
Method: SHAKE all ingredients with ice and strain into ice-filled glass.

2	shot(s)	**Bacardi Superior rum**
1	shot(s)	**Crème de framboise liqueur**
2	shot(s)	**Ocean Spray cranberry juice**
½	shot(s)	**Freshly squeezed lime juice**

Comment: All too easy - light and fruity, lightly fortified with rum character.
Origin: Adapted from a cocktail promoted by Bacardi Superior.

BATANGA

Glass: Collins
Garnish: Salt rim
Method: POUR ingredients into ice-filled glass, stir and serve with straws.

2	shot(s)	**Don Julio reposado tequila**
½	shot(s)	**Freshly squeezed lime juice**
Top up with		**Coca-Cola**

Origin: The signature drink of the now legendary Don Javier Delgado Corona, the owner/bartender of La Capilla (The Chapel) in Tequila, Mexico. Still mixing, even in his eighties, Corona is noted for ritualistically stirring this drink with a huge knife.
Comment: Basically a Cuba Libre made with tequila in place of rum – an improvement.

'I COULD NEVER QUITE ACCUSTOM MYSELF TO ABSINTHE, BUT IT SUITS MY STYLE SO WELL.'
OSCAR WILDE

BATIDA DE ABACAXI NEW #8

Glass: Collins
Garnish: Pineapple wedge on rim
Method: SHAKE all ingredients with ice and strain into ice-filled glass.

2	shot(s)	**Leblon cachaça**
2½	shot(s)	**Pressed pineapple juice**
1	shot(s)	**Condensed milk**
½	shot(s)	**Sugar syrup** (2 sugar to 1 water)

Comment: This easy crowd pleaser is creamy, fruity and to taste – only vaguely alcoholic.
Origin: The Batida (meaning 'shake') is a traditional Brazilian drink and 'Abaci' means pineapple in Portuguese, the official language of Brazil.

Batida is a broad term for a drink usually containing fresh fruit, sugar and/or sweetened condensed milk (leite condensado). They are often blended with crushed ice or shaken and served over crushed ice.

BATIDA DE BANANA NEW #8

Glass: Collins
Garnish: Banana chunk on rim
Method: BLEND ingredients with 12oz scoop of crushed ice. Pour into glass and serve with straws.

2	shot(s)	**Leblon cachaça**
1	fresh	**Peeled banana**
1	shot(s)	**Condensed milk**

Comment: So thick that this is something of a liquid dessert – surprisingly yummy.
Origin: The Batida (meaning 'shake') is a traditional Brazilian drink.

A
B
C
D
E
F
G
H
I
J
K
L
M
N
O
P
Q
R
S
T
U
V
W
X
Y
Z

BATIDA DE CARNEVAL NEW #8

●●●●○○

Glass: Collins
Garnish: Mango slice
Method: BLEND all ingredients with 12oz scoop crushed ice and serve with straws.

2	shot(s)	**Leblon cachaça**
2	shot(s)	**Boiron mango purée**
1	shot(s)	**Freshly squeezed orange juice**
1	shot(s)	**Condensed milk**

Comment: So thick and fruity this easy, smoothie-style drink is something of a meal in itself – a three-course dessert that is.
Origin: The Batida (meaning 'shake') is a traditional Brazilian drink and 'Carneval' means mango in Portuguese, the official language of Brazil.

BATIDA DE COCO NEW #8

●●●○○

Glass: Collins
Garnish: Grate nutmeg over drink
Method: BLEND all ingredients with 12oz scoop crushed ice and serve with straws.

2	shot(s)	**Leblon cachaça**
2	shot(s)	**Coco López cream of coconut**
1	shot(s)	**Condensed milk**

Comment: As the name would suggest this is literally an alcoholic coconut-flavoured shake.
Origin: Literally meaning a shake of coconut, this is a traditional Brazilian drink.

BATIDA DE GOIBA NEW #8

●●●○○

Glass: Collins
Garnish: Mango slice
Method: SHAKE all ingredients with ice and strain into glass filled with crushed ice.

2	shot(s)	**Leblon cachaça**
2½	shot(s)	**Guava juice**
1	shot(s)	**Condensed milk**

Comment: An alcoholic guava-flavoured shake.
Origin: The Batida (meaning 'shake') is a traditional Brazilian drink and 'Goiba' means guava in Portuguese, the official language of Brazil.

BATIDA DE MILHO VERDE NEW #8

●●●●○○

Glass: Collins
Garnish: Cinnamon dust
Method: BLEND all ingredients with 12oz scoop crushed ice. Serve with straws.

2½	shot(s)	**Leblon cachaça**
70	grams	**Sweetcorn** (canned)
1½	shot(s)	**Sweetened condensed milk**

Comment: Quite possibly your first sweetcorn cocktail?
Origin: A classic Brazilian drink.

BATIDA DE MORANGO NEW #8

●●●○○

Glass: Collins
Garnish: Top with strawberries
Method: BLEND all ingredients with 12oz scoop crushed ice. Serve with straws.

2	shot(s)	**Leblon cachaça**
12	fresh	**Strawberries** (hulled)
1	shot(s)	**Crème de fraise liqueur**
½	shot(s)	**Condensed milk**

Comment: Strawberry milkshake laced with cachaça.
Origin: The Batida (meaning 'shake') is a traditional Brazilian drink and 'Morango' means strawberry in Portuguese, the official language of Brazil.

BATIDA ROSA NEW #8

●●●●○○

Glass: Large wine glass
Garnish: Pineapple wedge
Method: SHAKE first 3 ingredients with ice and strain into ice-filled glass. **TOP** with soda.

2	shot(s)	**Leblon cachaça**
1	shot(s)	**Freshly squeezed lemon juice**
1	shot(s)	**Pressed pineapple juice**
½	shot(s)	**Pomegranate (grenadine) syrup**
Top up with		**Soda water**

Comment: Cachaça pleasantly shines in this balanced fruity, Daiquiri style drink.
Origin: Adapted from a drink created in 2008 by Jeffrey Morgenthaler at Bel Ami Lounge, Oregon, USA.

BAY BREEZE

●●●●○○

Glass: Collins
Garnish: Pineapple wedge on rim
Method: SHAKE all ingredients with ice and strain into ice-filled glass.

2	shot(s)	**Ketel One vodka**
1½	shot(s)	**Ocean Spray cranberry juice**
2½	shot(s)	**Pressed pineapple juice**

Comment: Pink, fluffy, sweet and easy to drink.

BAZOOKA

●●●○○○

Glass: Shot
Method: SHAKE all ingredients with ice and fine strain into chilled glass.

¾	shot(s)	**Southern Comfort liqueur**
½	shot(s)	**Crème de banane liqueur**
⅛	shot(s)	**Pomegranate (grenadine) syrup**
¼	shot(s)	**Double (heavy) cream**

Comment: A sticky, pink shot.

BAZOOKA JOE

Glass: Shot
Method: Refrigerate ingredients then **LAYER** in chilled glass by carefully pouring in the following order.

½	shot(s)	Bols blue curaçao liqueur
½	shot(s)	Crème de banane liqueur
½	shot(s)	Baileys Irish cream liqueur

Comment: Banana and orange topped with whiskey cream.

BBC

Glass: Martini
Garnish: Dust with freshly grated nutmeg
Method: **SHAKE** all ingredients with ice and fine strain into chilled glass.

1¼	shot(s)	Courvoisier V.S.O.P. cognac
1	shot(s)	Bénédictine D.O.M. liqueur
¾	shot(s)	Double (heavy) cream
¾	shot(s)	Milk

Origin: Thought to have originated in the UK in the late 1970s and named, not after the British Broadcasting Company, but brandy, Bénédictine and cream.
Comment: Brandy and Bénédictine (a classic combo) smoothed with cream. Drier than you might expect.

BE-TON

Glass: Collins
Garnish: Squeezed lime wedge in glass
Method: **POUR** Becherovka into ice-filled glass, then **TOP** with tonic water and stir.

2	shot(s)	Becherovka liqueur
Top up with		Tonic water

Origin: Becherovka (or Carlsbad Becher as it's sometimes known) is the Czech national liqueur. Matured in oak, it contains cinnamon, cloves, nutmeg and other herbs.
Comment: This spicy drink is the Czech Republic's answer to the Gin 'n' Tonic.

BEACH BLONDE

Glass: Collins
Garnish: Banana slice on rim
Method: **BLEND** ingredients with 12oz scoop of crushed ice. Pour into glass and serve with straws.

½	fresh	Banana
1	shot(s)	Wray & Nephew overproof rum
3	shot(s)	Bols advocaat liqueur
3	shot(s)	Freshly squeezed orange juice

Origin: Created in 2002 by Alex Kammerling, London, England.
Comment: Fruity, creamy holiday drinking.

BEACH ICED TEA

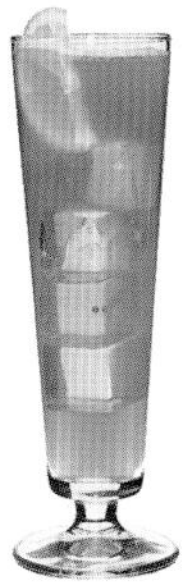

Glass: Sling
Garnish: Lemon slice
Method: **SHAKE** all ingredients with ice and strain into ice-filled glass.

½	shot(s)	Bacardi Superior rum
½	shot(s)	Tanqueray London dry gin
½	shot(s)	Ketel One vodka
½	shot(s)	Don Julio reposado tequila
½	shot(s)	Cointreau triple sec
1	shot(s)	Freshly squeezed lemon juice
½	shot(s)	Sugar syrup (2 sugar to 1 water)
3	shot(s)	Ocean Spray cranberry juice

Comment: A Long Island Iced Tea with cranberry juice instead of Coca-Cola.

BEACHCOMBER UPDATED #8

Glass: Martini
Garnish: Lime wedge on rim
Method: **SHAKE** all ingredients with ice and fine strain into chilled glass.

2	shot(s)	Bacardi Superior rum
½	shot(s)	Cointreau triple sec
¾	shot(s)	Freshly squeezed lime juice
¼	shot(s)	Luxardo maraschino liqueur
½	shot(s)	Chilled mineral water (omit if wet ice)

Comment: A Daiquiri with the addition of a dash of triple sec and maraschino.
Origin: Adapted from Patrick Gavin Duffy's 'The Official Mixer's Manual' (1956 James A. Beard edition).

> 'BACK IN MY RUMMY DAYS, I WOULD TREMBLE AND SHAKE FOR HOURS UPON ARISING. IT WAS THE ONLY EXERCISE I GOT.'
> W. C. FIELDS

BEACHCOMBER'S DAIQUIRI NEW #8

Glass: Martini/Coupette
Garnish: Lime slice
Method: **BLEND** all ingredients with one 6oz scoop crushed ice and serve with straws.

2	shot(s)	Bacardi Superior rum
1	shot(s)	Cointreau triple sec
¾	shot(s)	Freshly squeezed lime juice

Comment: Basically a frozen rum margarita.
Origin: Created by Ernest Raymond Beaumont-Gantt, A.K.A. Don The Beachcomber at his bar in Hollywood, California, USA.

BEACHCOMBER'S RUM BARREL NEW #8 ●●●●○○

Glass: Rum barrel mug or pint glass
Garnish: Pineapple wedge & cherry plus mint sprig
Method: BLEND all ingredients with 12oz scoop crushed ice and serve with straws.

2	shot(s)	**Bacardi Superior rum**
2	shot(s)	**Myers's dark Jamaican rum**
1	shot(s)	**Freshly squeezed orange juice**
1	shot(s)	**Pressed pineapple juice**
1	shot(s)	**Freshly squeezed grapefruit juice**
¾	shot(s)	**Freshly squeezed lime juice**
½	shot(s)	**Honey syrup** (4 honey to 1 water)
¼	shot(s)	**Pomegranate (grenadine) syrup**
¼	shot(s)	**World's End Pimento Dram liqueur**
¼	shot(s)	**Velvet Falernum liqueur**
⅛	shot(s)	**La Fée Parisienne (68%) absinthe**
1	dash	**Angostura aromatic bitters**

Comment: A foamy head hides a tasty (and be warned) rum laced, tangy fruity drink.
Origin: Created by Ernest Raymond Beaumont-Gantt, A.K.A. Don The Beachcomber at his bar in Hollywood, California, USA.

BEAM-ME-UP SCOTTY SHOT ●●●○○○

Glass: Shot
Method: Refrigerate ingredients then **LAYER** in chilled glass by carefully pouring in the following order.

½	shot(s)	**Kahlúa coffee liqueur**
½	shot(s)	**Crème de banane liqueur**
½	shot(s)	**Baileys Irish cream liqueur**

Comment: Coffee, banana and creamy whiskey. Very sweet but not too offensive and easy to layer.

BEARSKIN MARTINI NEW #8 ●●●●○

Glass: Martini
Garnish: Kalamata olives.
Method: STIR all ingredients with ice and strain into chilled glass.

2½	shot(s)	**Ketel One vodka**
⅛	shot(s)	**Kümmel liqueur**
⅛	shot(s)	**Noilly Prat dry vermouth**

Comment: A caraway influenced Martini.

THE BEAUTY BENEATH NEW #8 ●●●●○

Glass: Martini/Coupette
Garnish: Orange zest twist
Method: STIR all ingredients with ice and strain into a chilled glass.

1¾	shot(s)	**Zacapa aged rum**
½	shot(s)	**Martini Rosso sweet vermouth**
½	shot(s)	**Campari Bitter**
½	shot(s)	**Cointreau triple sec**
1	dash	**Angostura aromatic bitters**

Comment: Orange dominates this bitter-sweet Manhattan, come Daiquiri, come Negroni.
Origin: Created in 2008 by Jeffrey Morgenthaler at Bel Ami Lounge, Oregon, USA.

BEBBO ●●●●●◑

Glass: Martini
Garnish: Lemon zest twist
Method: STIR honey with gin in base of shaker until honey dissolves. Add other ingredients, **SHAKE** with ice and fine strain into chilled glass.

2	spoons	**Runny honey**
1½	shot(s)	**Tanqueray Londond dry gin**
1	shot(s)	**Freshly squeezed lemon juice**
½	shot(s)	**Freshly squeezed orange juice**
¼	shot(s)	**Chilled mineral water** (omit if wet ice)

Origin: A long lost relation of the Bee's Knees. This recipe is based on one from Ted Haigh's 2004 book 'Vintage Spirits & Forgotten Cocktails'.
Comment: Fresh, clean and citrusy with honeyed notes. Choose your honey wisely.

> **'A MAN WHO EXPOSES HIMSELF WHEN HE IS INTOXICATED, HAS NOT THE ART OF GETTING DRUNK.'**
> SAMUEL JOHNSON

BEE STING ●●●●○

Glass: Collins
Garnish: Apple slice
Method: STIR honey with whiskey in base of shaker until honey dissolves. Add tequila and apple juice, **SHAKE** with ice and strain into ice-filled glass. **TOP** with a splash of ginger ale.

1	spoon	**Runny honey**
1	shot(s)	**Rye whiskey (or bourbon)**
1	shot(s)	**Don Julio reposado tequila**
2	shot(s)	**Pressed apple juice**
Top up with		**Ginger ale**

Origin: Discovered in 2005 at The Royal Exchange Grand Café & Bar, London, England.
Comment: A delicately spiced, long, refreshing drink.

BEE'S KNEES #1 ●●●●○

Glass: Martini
Garnish: Orange zest twist
Method: STIR honey with rum until honey dissolves. Add other ingredients, **SHAKE** with ice and fine strain into chilled glass.

1¼	shot(s)	**Bacardi Superior rum**
1¼	shot(s)	**Pusser's Navy rum**
2	spoons	**Runny honey**
1	shot(s)	**Freshly squeezed orange juice**
½	shot(s)	**Double (heavy) cream**
½	shot(s)	**Milk**

Comment: Smooth and orangey to start, with a rum and honey finish.

BEE'S KNEES #2

Glass: Martini
Garnish: Orange zest twist
Method: In base of shaker **STIR** honey with gin until honey dissolves. Add lemon and orange juice, **SHAKE** with ice and fine strain into chilled glass.

2	shot(s)	**Tanqueray London dry gin**
3	spoons	**Runny honey**
1	shot(s)	**Freshly squeezed lemon juice**
1	shot(s)	**Freshly squeezed orange juice**

Variant: Made with light rum in place of gin this drink becomes a Honeysuckle Martini.
Origin: Adapted from David A. Embury's 1948 'The Fine Art of Mixing Drinks'.
Comment: This concoction really is the bee's knees.

BEE'S KNEES #3

Glass: Martini
Garnish: Lemon zest twist
Method: In base of shaker **STIR** honey with gin until honey dissolves. Add lemon juice, **SHAKE** with ice and fine strain into chilled glass.

2	shot(s)	**Tanqueray London dry gin**
3	spoons	**Runny honey**
¾	shot(s)	**Freshly squeezed lemon juice**

Comment: The combination of honey and lemon suggests flu relief but don't wait for an ailment before trying this soothing concoction.

BEETLE JEUSE

Glass: Collins
Garnish: Mint sprig
Method: Lightly **MUDDLE** mint in base of shaker just enough to bruise. Add other ingredients, **SHAKE** with ice and strain into ice-filled glass.

7	fresh	**Mint leaves**
1	shot(s)	**Green Chartreuse liqueur**
1	shot(s)	**Zubrówka bison vodka**
3½	shot(s)	**Pressed apple juice**
¼	shot(s)	**Passion fruit syrup**

Origin: Created in 2003 by Milo Rodriguez at Raoul's Bar, Oxford, and named after Beetlejuice, the Tim Burton black comedy about a young couple whose premature death leads them to a series of bizarre afterlife exploits.
Comment: Long and refreshing with a flavour reminiscent of caramelised apple.

DRINKS ARE GRADED AS FOLLOWS:

● DISGUSTING ●● PRETTY AWFUL ●● BEST AVOIDED
●●● DISAPPOINTING ●●● ACCEPTABLE ●●●● GOOD
●●●● RECOMMENDED ●●●●● HIGHLY RECOMMENDED
●●●●● OUTSTANDING / EXCEPTIONAL

'LET US DRINK FOR THE REPLENISHMENT OF OUR STRENGTH, NOT FOR OUR SORROW.'
CICERO

BEHEMOTH

Glass: Martini
Garnish: Lemon zest twist
Method: **SHAKE** all ingredients with ice and fine strain into chilled glass.

1½	shot(s)	**Bulleit bourbon whiskey**
1	shot(s)	**Martini Rosso sweet vermouth**
¾	shot(s)	**White crème de cacao liqueur**
¾	shot(s)	**Freshly squeezed lemon juice**
½	shot(s)	**Sugar syrup** (2 sugar to 1 water)
½	fresh	**Egg white** (optional)
2	dashes	**Peychaud's aromatic bitters** (optional)

Origin: This monstrous beast was created in 2004 by Yours Truly (Simon Difford).
Comment: Tangy, citrus bourbon with a hint of chocolate.

BEJA FLOR

Glass: Martini
Garnish: Banana chunk on rim
Method: **SHAKE** all ingredients with ice and fine strain into chilled glass.

2	shot(s)	**Leblon cachaça**
1	shot(s)	**Cointreau triple sec**
1	shot(s)	**Crème de banane liqueur**
½	shot(s)	**Freshly squeezed lemon juice**

Comment: Sharp and quite dry but with a sweet banana twang.

BELLA DONNA DAIQUIRI

Glass: Martini
Garnish: Wipe rim with lemon & dust with cinnamon powder
Method: **SHAKE** all ingredients with ice and fine strain into chilled glass.

1½	shot(s)	**Gosling's Black Seal rum**
1½	shot(s)	**Luxardo Amaretto di Saschira**
½	shot(s)	**Freshly squeezed lemon juice**
¼	shot(s)	**Sugar syrup** (2 sugar to 1 water)
½	shot(s)	**Chilled mineral water** (omit if wet ice)

Origin: Adapted from a drink discovered in 2003 at Bellagio, Las Vegas, USA.
Comment: This was the hit cocktail for diffords-guide staff at the Bellagio, Las Vegas, after working at the Nightclub & Bar Beverage Convention. Try one and see why.

BELLINI (DIFFORD'S FORMULA) UPDATED #8

●●●●◖

Glass: Flute
Garnish: Peach slice on rim
Method: SHAKE first 3 ingredients with ice and fine strain into chilled glass. Add prosecco and gently stir.

2	shot(s)	Boiron white peach purée
½	shot(s)	Crème pêche de vigne liqueur
¼	shot(s)	Freshly squeezed lemon juice
Top up with		Prosecco sparkling wine

Comment: It's hard not to like this blend of peaches and sparkling wine.
Origin: It has long been traditional in Italy to marinade fresh peaches in wine and the Bellini draws on this tradition, combining prosecco wine with puréed white peaches.
Giuseppe Cipriani created this drink at Harry's Bar, Venice, in 1945, fourteen years after he opened his tiny place on the edge of the Grand Canal, not far from St. Mark's Square. Cipriani named his cocktail after the 15th-century Venetian painter Giovanni Bellini due to the drink's pink hue and the painter's penchant for using rich pinks on his canvases.
Like many other legendary bars around the world, Harry's owes some of its notoriety to being patronised by probably the world's greatest drinker, Ernest Hemingway. It was also the haunt of Sinclair Lewis, Orson Welles, F. Scott Fitzgerald and Dorothy Parker, and continues to attract celebrities to this day. But you don't have to be a celebrity to go to Harry's Bar. Cocktail aficionados from around the world make pilgrimages to the birthplace of the Bellini to sample the original recipe.
White peaches are in season in Italy from May to September, so in Venice those bars that insist on only using fresh peaches rather than frozen puree sell the drink between May and October.

DURING THE REIGN OF WILLIAM III, PUNCH WAS SERVED FROM THE GARDEN FOUNTAIN. THE BARTENDER ROWED AROUND IN A SMALL BOAT, REFILLING GLASSES.

BELLINI-TINI

●●●●◐○

Glass: Martini
Garnish: Peach wedge
Method: SHAKE all ingredients with ice and fine strain into chilled glass.

2	shot(s)	Ketel One vodka
½	shot(s)	Peach Tree peach schnapps
2	shot(s)	Boiron white peach purée
3	dashes	Fee Brothers peach bitters (optional)

Comment: Peachy, peachy, peachy! Based on the Bellini, funnily enough.

BELLISSIMO

●●●○○

Glass: Old-fashioned
Garnish: Orange slice
Method: SHAKE all ingredients with ice and fine strain into ice-filled glass.

1	shot(s)	Frangelico hazelnut liqueur
1	shot(s)	Campari Bitter
1	shot(s)	Luxardo limoncello liqueur
½	shot(s)	Freshly squeezed lemon juice

Origin: Adapted from a drink created in 2003 by Ben Davidson at Posh Lounge, Sydney, Australia.
Comment: An unusual meld of flavours, but Campari lovers should give this a try.

BENSONHURST

●●●●◖

Glass: Martini
Garnish: Maraschino cherry
Method: STIR all ingredients with ice and strain into chilled glass.

2	shot(s)	Bulleit bourbon whiskey
1	shot(s)	Noilly Prat dry vermouth
½	shot(s)	Luxardo maraschino liqueur
¼	shot(s)	Cynar artichoke liqueur

Origin: Adapted from a drink created in 2006 by Chad Solomon and named after a neighbourhood close to his home in Brooklyn, New York City, USA
Comment: A refined and balanced Manhattan-style drink.

BENTLEY

●●●●◐○

Glass: Old-fashioned
Garnish: Orange zest twist
Method: STIR all ingredients with ice and strain into glass (no ice).

1½	shot(s)	Boulard Grand Solage calvados
1½	shot(s)	Dubonnet Red (French made)
2	dashes	Peychaud's aromatic bitters (optional)

Variant: Originally served straight-up.
Origin: Adapted from Harry Craddock's 1930 'The Savoy Cocktail Book'.
Comment: Dry, spiced wine impregnated with apple – pretty damn good.

BERMONDSEY BREEZE NEW #8

●●●◐○

Glass: Collins
Garnish: 3 slices of cucumber
Method: MUDDLE cucumber in base of shaker. Add other ingredients, SHAKE with ice and fine strain into glass filled with crushed ice.

1	inch	Cucumber (peeled & chopped)
12	fresh	Mint leaves
2	shot(s)	St-Germain elderflower liqueur
2	shot(s)	Sauvignon Blanc wine
1	shot(s)	Freshly squeezed lime juice
¼	shot(s)	Sugar syrup (2 sugar to 1 water)

Comment: Light and summery.
Origin: Created in 2008 by Scott Wallace at Village East, London, England.

BELLINI

BERMUDA COCKTAIL

Glass: Martini
Garnish: Orange zest twist
Method: SHAKE all ingredients with ice and fine strain into chilled glass.

2	shot(s)	Tanqueray London dry gin
½	shot(s)	Peach Tree peach schnapps
½	shot(s)	Freshly squeezed orange juice
¼	shot(s)	Pomegranate (grenadine) syrup

Origin: Adapted from Victor Bergeron's 'Trader Vic's Bartender's Guide' (1972 revised edition).
Comment: Gin with a sweetening touch of peach, orange and pomegranate.

ARTIFICIAL CARBONATION WAS FIRST ACHIEVED IN 1767.

BERMUDA ROSE COCKTAIL

Glass: Martini
Garnish: Apricot slice (dried or fresh) on rim
Method: SHAKE all ingredients with ice and fine strain into chilled glass.

2	shot(s)	Tanqueray London dry gin
½	shot(s)	Bols apricot brandy liqueur
¼	shot(s)	Pomegranate (grenadine) syrup
½	shot(s)	Chilled mineral water (omit if wet ice)

Origin: Adapted from Victor Bergeron's 'Trader Vic's Bartender's Guide' (1972 revised edition).
Comment: Delicate, floral and aromatic. A hint of sweetness but not so as to offend.

BERMUDA RUM SWIZZLE UPDATED #8

Glass: Collins
Garnish: Pineapple wedge & cherry
Method: SWIZZLE, or better and easier: SHAKE all ingredients with ice and strain into glass filled with crushed ice.

1	shot(s)	Bacardi Oro golden rum
1	shot(s)	Gosling's Black Seal rum
¾	shot(s)	Velvet Falernum liqueur
1	shot(s)	Pressed pineapple juice
1	shot(s)	Freshly squeezed orange juice
½	shot(s)	Freshly squeezed grapefruit juice
½	shot(s)	Freshly squeezed lime juice
¼	shot(s)	Freshly squeezed lemon juice
2	dashes	Angostura aromatic bitters

Comment: Your five-a-day fruits in a glass, laced with pungent rums and clove infused Falernum.
Origin: This recipe is adapted from one by Del Pedro, originally from Bermuda but now resident in New York City. It came my way (in 1997) courtesy of the LeNell Smothers, and apparently it originally heralds from the Swizzle Inn in Bermuda where their rather appropriate slogan is "Swizzle Inn, Swagger Out".

BERRY CAIPIRINHA

Glass: Old-fashioned
Method: MUDDLE lime and berries in base of glass. Add other ingredients and fill glass with crushed ice. CHURN drink with bar spoon and serve with short straws.

¾	fresh	Lime cut into wedges
3	fresh	Raspberries
3	fresh	Blackberries
2	shot(s)	Leblon cachaça
¾	shot(s)	Sugar syrup (2 sugar to 1 water)

Variant: Black 'N' Blue Caipirovska
Comment: A fruity version of the popular Brazilian drink.

BERRY NICE

Glass: Collins
Garnish: Blackberries
Method: MUDDLE blackberries in base of shaker. Add next 3 ingredients, SHAKE with ice and strain into ice-filled glass. TOP with ginger beer and serve with straws.

9	fresh	Blackberries
2	shot(s)	Ketel One vodka
¼	shot(s)	Chambord black raspberry liqueur
½	shot(s)	Freshly squeezed lemon juice
Top up with		Ginger beer

Origin: Adapted from a drink created in 2001 in the UK's The Living Room chain of bars.
Comment: Rich blackberry flavour with a ginger finish.

BERRY SMASH (MOCKTAIL) NEW #8

Glass: Old-fashioned
Garnish: Berries
Method: SHAKE all ingredients with ice and strain into glass filled with crushed ice.

7	fresh	Raspberries
3	fresh	Blackberries
2	shot(s)	Ocean Spray cranberry juice
1	shot(s)	Pressed apple juice
½	shot(s)	Freshly squeezed lemon juice
¼	spoon	Honey syrup (4 honey to 1 water)

Comment: Red berries with a splash of apple juice and honey served over crushed ice.

BESSIE & JESSIE

Glass: Collins
Garnish: Orange slice
Method: SHAKE all ingredients with ice and strain into ice-filled glass.

2	shot(s)	Johnnie Walker Scotch whisky
2	shot(s)	Bols advocaat liqueur
3½	shot(s)	Milk

Comment: Malty, creamy and eggy, but tasty.

BETWEEN DECKS

Glass: Collins
Garnish: Pineapple wedge, mint & cherry
Method: SHAKE all ingredients with ice and strain into ice-filled glass.

2½	shot(s)	Tanqueray London dry gin
1	shot(s)	Freshly squeezed orange juice
1	shot(s)	Ocean Spray cranberry juice
½	shot(s)	Freshly squeezed lime juice
¼	shot(s)	Sugar syrup (2 sugar to 1 water)
½	shot(s)	Chilled mineral water (omit if wet ice)

Origin: Adapted from Victor Bergeron's 'Trader Vic's Bartender's Guide' (1972 revised edition).
Comment: I've upped the ante on this drink with more gin and less fruit than the original - so beware.

BETWEEN THE SHEETS #1
(DIFFORD'S FORMULA) UPDATED #8

Glass: Martini
Garnish: Lemon zest twist
Method: SHAKE all ingredients with ice and fine strain into chilled glass.

¾	shot(s)	Bacardi Superior rum
¾	shot(s)	Courvoisier V.S.O.P. cognac
¾	shot(s)	Cointreau triple sec
¼	shot(s)	Freshly squeezed lemon juice
⅛	shot(s)	Sugar syrup (2 sugar to 1 water)
½	shot(s)	Chilled mineral water (omit if wet ice)

Comment: Classic proportions to this drink are most often quoted as being: 1 rum, 1 cognac, 1 triple sec and ¼ lemon juice but three shots of 40% alcohol and a splash of lemon juice make for a tart drink which should not be undertaken lightly. The formula above maintains the essential flavour and ingredients of the classic recipe but is a little more approachable.
Origin: Created in the early 1930s (during Prohibition) by Harry MacElhone of Harry's New York Bar in Paris, and derived from the Sidecar.

BETWEEN THE SHEETS #2
(WONDRICH'S FORMULA) NEW #8

Glass: Martini
Garnish: Garnish with flamed orange peel
Method: SHAKE all ingredients with ice and fine strain into chilled glass.

1	shot(s)	Courvoisier V.S.O.P. cognac
½	shot(s)	Bénédictine D.O.M. liqueur
½	shot(s)	Cointreau triple sec
¼	shot(s)	Freshly squeezed lemon juice
½	shot(s)	Chilled mineral water (omit if chilled)

Comment: Bénédictine takes the place of rum in this variation on a classic.
Origin: Formula adapted from recipe by David Wondrich. I've cut the lemon by a third, and when using fresh ice added a splash of water.

BEVERLY HILLS HOTEL MARTINI NEW #8

Glass: Martini
Garnish: Rosemary sprig
Method: SHAKE all ingredients with ice and fine strain into chilled glass.

2	shot(s)	Tanqueray London dry gin
1	shot(s)	St-Germain elderflower liqueur
1	shot(s)	Freshly squeezed grapefruit juice

Comment: Dry, but not oppressively so. Zingy grapefruit with gin complexity and delicate floral notes.
Origin: Adapted from a drink created in 2007 by Philip Spee at The Beverly Hills Hotel, California, USA.

BEVERLY HILLS ICED TEA

Glass: Sling
Garnish: Lime zest spiral
Method: SHAKE first 5 ingredients with ice and strain into ice-filled glass. TOP with champagne and gently stir.

¾	shot(s)	Tanqueray London dry gin
¾	shot(s)	Ketel One vodka
1	shot(s)	Cointreau triple sec
½	shot(s)	Freshly squeezed lime juice
½	shot(s)	Sugar syrup (2 sugar to 1 water)
Top up with		Perrier Jouet brut champagne

Comment: Very strong and refreshing.

BIARRITZ

Glass: Old-fashioned
Garnish: Orange & cherry on stick (sail)
Method: SHAKE all ingredients with ice and strain into ice-filled glass.

2	shot(s)	Courvoisier V.S.O.P. cognac
1	shot(s)	Grand Marnier liqueur
¾	shot(s)	Freshly squeezed lemon juice
½	fresh	Egg white
3	dashes	Angostura aromatic bitters

Comment: Basically a brandy sour with a little something extra from the orange liqueur.

BICARDAR NEW #8

Glass: Martini/Coupette
Garnish: Lemon zest twist
Method: STIR all ingredients with ice and strain into chilled glass.

2	shot(s)	Bacardi Superior rum
¼	shot(s)	Bols apricot brandy liqueur
¼	shot(s)	Luxardo marashino liqueur
⅛	shot(s)	Freshly squeezed lemon juice
1	dash	Angostura orange bitters
¼	shot(s)	Chilled mineral water (omit if wet ice)

Comment: Subtle and delicate with hints of apricot, cherry, lemon and orange.
Origin: Created in 2008 by Kashi Forootani at Seattle Hotel, Brighton, England.

BIG APPLE MARTINI

Glass: Martini
Garnish: Apple wedge on rim
Method: SHAKE all ingredients with ice and fine strain into chilled glass.

2½	shot(s)	**Ketel One vodka**
1	shot(s)	**Sour apple liqueur**
1	shot(s)	**Berentzen apple schnapps**

AKA: Apple Martini, Sour Apple Martini
Comment: There's no apple juice in this Martini, but it has an appealing light minty green hue.

THE BIG EASY

Glass: Collins
Garnish: Half orange slice
Method: SHAKE first 3 ingredients with ice and strain into ice-filled glass. **TOP** with ginger ale.

1¾	shot(s)	**Southern Comfort liqueur**
¾	shot(s)	**Cointreau triple sec**
2	shot(s)	**Freshly squeezed orange juice**
Top up with		**Ginger ale**

Comment: Fruity and refreshing with a hint of spice.

BIG JUICY (MOCKTAIL) NEW #8

Glass: Collins
Garnish: Lime wedge
Method: SHAKE first 5 ingredients with ice and strain into ice-filled glass. **TOP** with soda, stir and serve with straws.

2½	shot(s)	**Ocean Spray cranberry juice**
1½	shot(s)	**Pressed pineapple juice**
1	shot(s)	**Freshly squeezed lime juice**
¼	shot(s)	**Sugar syrup** (2 sugar to 1 water)
¼	shot(s)	**Pomegranate (grenadine) syrup**
Top up with		**Soda water** (club soda)

Comment: Everything about this drink is juicy, even its creator. A tasty way to top up your vitamin C levels.
Origin: Created in 2006 by Jose 'Juice' Miranda at Wd-50, New York City, USA.

BIGGLES AVIATION NEW #8

Glass: Martini
Garnish: Lime & ginger slice
Method: SHAKE all ingredients with ice and strain into ice-filled glass.

2	shot(s)	**Tanqueray London dry gin**
½	shot(s)	**Domaine de Canton ginger liqueur**
½	shot(s)	**Freshly squeezed lemon juice**
¼	shot(s)	**Sugar syrup** (2 sugar to 1 water)
¼	shot(s)	**Chilled mineral water** (omit if wet ice)

Origin: Created in 2008 by Simon Difford at the Cabinet Room, London, England. Named after the adventures of 'Biggles in Borneo' in which wartime flying heroes Ginger, Algy and Biggles battle the Japanese in the jungle.
Comment: A ginger influenced Aviation named after fictional flying heroes. The ginger used in Canton's liqueur is also sourced from Borneo. How neat.

BIGGLES SIDECAR NEW #8

Glass: Martini
Garnish: Lemon & ginger slice
Method: SHAKE all ingredients with ice and fine strain into chilled glass.

2	shot(s)	**Courvoisier V.S.O.P. cognac**
½	shot(s)	**Domaine de Canton ginger liqueur**
½	shot(s)	**Freshly squeezed lemon juice**
¼	shot(s)	**Sugar syrup** (2 sugar to 1 water)
1	dash	**Peychard aromatic bitters**
½	shot(s)	**Chilled mineral water** (omit if wet ice)

Comment: I set out to make an Aviation - but ginger cries out for cognac so I also ended up with this Sidecar twist.
Origin: Created in 2008 by Simon Difford, The Cabinet Room, London, England.
As a kid I was a Biggles reader and fan and I was working on a theme (see Biggles Aviation).

BIJOU UPDATED #8

Glass: Shot
Method: Carefully **LAYER** ingredients in the following order.

½	shot(s)	**Martini Rosso sweet vermouth**
½	shot(s)	**Green Chartreuse liqueur**
½	shot(s)	**Tanqueray London dry gin**

Comment: A shot loaded with bold flavours - fellow Chartreuse fans will approve.
Origin: This vintage layered, or 'pousse-café' style, drink is named after the French for 'jewel', apparently a reference to its trio of ingredients having the colours of the three most precious jewels: diamond (gin), ruby (sweet vermouth) and emerald (green chartreuse).
If all the ingredients, and so the colours, are shaken together the result is a rather better, aptly named drink called the Amber Dream. I wouldn't ponce about making this layered drink. Grab a shaker and enjoy an Amber Dream instead.

BIKINI MARTINI

Glass: Martini
Garnish: Orange zest twist
Method: SHAKE all ingredients with ice and fine strain into chilled glass.

2	shot(s)	**Tanqueray London dry gin**
¾	shot(s)	**Bols blue curaçao liqueur**
¼	shot(s)	**Peach Tree peach schnapps**
¼	shot(s)	**Freshly squeezed lemon juice**
½	shot(s)	**Chilled mineral water** (omit if wet ice)

Origin: Adapted from a cocktail created in 1999 by Dick Bradsell for an Agent Provocateur swimwear launch. The bikini swimsuit was named after Bikini Atoll, where A-bombs were tested after World War II, on the basis that such a revealing garment would cause as much shock as a thermonuclear device.
Comment: A vivid blue combination of lemon, orange and peach laced with gin.

BINGO

Glass: Collins
Garnish: Lemon slice
Method: **SHAKE** first 4 ingredients with ice and strain into ice filled glass. **TOP** with soda water.

1	shot(s)	**Ketel One vodka**
1	shot(s)	**Grand Marnier liqueur**
1	shot(s)	**Bols apricot brandy liqueur**
½	shot(s)	**Freshly squeezed lemon juice**
Top up with		**Soda water** (club soda)

Comment: Refreshing, fruity long drink.

BIRD OF PARADISE

Glass: Martini
Garnish: Dust with freshly grated nutmeg
Method: **SHAKE** all ingredients with ice and fine strain into chilled glass.

1¼	shot(s)	**Don Julio reposado tequila**
¾	shot(s)	**White crème de cacao liqueur**
½	shot(s)	**Luxardo Amaretto di Saschira**
1	shot(s)	**Double (heavy) cream**
¾	shot(s)	**Milk**

Comment: If you like tequila and creamy drinks, the two don't mix much better than this.

BISHOP

Glass: Toddy
Garnish: Dust with freshly grated nutmeg
Method: **MUDDLE** cloves in the base of shaker. Add boiling water and **STIR** in honey and other ingredients. Fine strain into glass and **MICROWAVE** for twenty seconds to boost temperature. **STIR**, garnish and serve.

7	dried	**Cloves**
3	shot(s)	**Boiling water**
2	spoons	**Runny honey**
2½	shot(s)	**Warre's Otima tawny port**
1	shot(s)	**Freshly squeezed orange juice**

Origin: My quick 'n' easy take on this variation of the 18th century Negus - reputedly a favourite of the writer Dr. Johnson. The traditional recipe begins with studding an orange with cloves and roasting it in the oven.
Comment: A flavoursome and warming variation on mulled wine.

BISON SOUR NEW #8

Glass: Old fashioned
Garnish: Lemon zest twist
Method: **SHAKE** all ingredients with ice and strain into ice-filled glass.

2	shot(s)	**Zubrówka bison grass vodka**
1	shot(s)	**Freshly squeezed lemon juice**
½	shot(s)	**Sugar syrup** (2 sugar to 1 water)
1	pinch	**Ground cinnamon**
½	fresh	**Egg white**

Comment: A flavour enhanced vodka sour.

THE BISTRO SIDECAR

Glass: Martini
Garnish: Lemon zest twist
Method: **SHAKE** all ingredients with ice and fine strain into chilled glass.

1½	shot(s)	**Courvoisier V.S.O.P. cognac**
½	shot(s)	**Tuaca Italian liqueur**
½	shot(s)	**Frangelico hazelnut liqueur**
¼	shot(s)	**Freshly squeezed lemon juice**
¼	shot(s)	**Freshly squeezed orange juice**

Origin: Adapted from a recipe by chef Kathy Casey of Kathy Casey Food Studios, Seattle, USA. Kathy's original recipe called for a sugar rim and tangerine juice.
Comment: Although significantly twisted from the classic, this is still recognisably a Sidecar in style.

BIT-O-HONEY

Glass: Shot
Method: Refrigerate ingredients then **LAYER** in chilled glass by carefully pouring in the following order.

| ¾ | shot(s) | **Teichenné butterscotch schnapps** |
| ¾ | shot(s) | **Baileys Irish cream liqueur** |

Variant: Layered with butterscotch, then honey liqueur and an Irish cream float.
Comment: A sweet but pleasant tasting shot.

BITCHES BREW NEW #8

Glass: Sour or Martini/Coupette
Garnish: Grate nutmeg over drink
Method: **DRY SHAKE** all ingredients without ice. Add ice, **SHAKE** again and fine strain into chilled glass.

1	shot(s)	**Martinique agricole rum**
1	shot(s)	**Zacapa aged rum**
1	shot(s)	**Freshly squeezed lime juice**
½	shot(s)	**Pimento Dram liqueur**
½	shot(s)	**Demerara sugar syrup**
1	fresh	**Egg** (white & yolk)

Comment: This flavoursome flip-style drink come served with a hint of Caribbean spice.
Origin: Created in 2008 by Daniel Eun at PDT, New York City, USA.

BITTER ELDER

Glass: Collins
Garnish: Lemon wedge
Method: **SHAKE** all ingredients with ice and strain into ice-filled glass.

2	shot(s)	**Tanqueray London dry gin**
1	shot(s)	**St-Germain elderflower liqueur**
2	shot(s)	**Pressed apple juice**
¾	shot(s)	**Freshly squeezed lemon juice**
3	dashes	**Angostura aromatic bitters**

Origin: Adapted from a short drink created in 2005 by Tonin Kacaj at Maze, London, England.
Comment: The eponymous elderflower is well balanced to make a dry refreshing long drink.

BITTER GRAPEFRUIT NEW #8

● ● ● ● ◑ ○ ○

Glass: Martini
Garnish: Grapefruit zest
Method: SHAKE all ingredients with ice and fine strain into chilled glass.

1½	shot(s)	**Ketel One vodka**
½	shot(s)	**Aperol**
1	shot(s)	**Martini Rosso sweet vermouth**
½	shot(s)	**Freshly squeezed grapefruit juice**

Comment: Grapefruit influenced and Negroni in style.
Origin: Discovered in 2007 at Public Restaurant, New York City, USA.

BITTER LADY NEW #8

● ● ● ● ○

Glass: Martini
Garnish: Grapefruit zest twist
Method: SHAKE all ingredients with ice and fine strain into chilled glass.

1½	shot(s)	**Tanqueray London dry gin**
1	spoons	**Runny honey**
¼	shot(s)	**Campari Bitter**
½	shot(s)	**Freshly squeezed lemon juice**
½	fresh	**Egg white**

Comment: I have dramatically cut the Campari and lemon in Mickael's original recipe to make a much lighter drink.
Origin: Adapted from a drink created by Mickael Perron from Bar Now On.

BITTER SWEET SYMPHONY

● ● ● ◑ ○ ○

Glass: Martini
Garnish: Apricot slice
Method: SHAKE all ingredients with ice and fine strain into chilled glass.

½	shot(s)	**Ketel One vodka**
1	shot(s)	**Cointreau triple sec**
1	shot(s)	**Bols apricot brandy liqueur**
½	shot(s)	**Freshly squeezed lime juice**
1½	shot(s)	**Freshly squeezed grapefruit juice**

Origin: Adapted from a drink created in 2003 by Wayne Collins for Maxxium UK.
Comment: This roller coaster ride of bitter and sweet mainly features apricot and grapefruit.

BITTEREST PILL

● ● ● ◑ ○ ○

Glass: Shot
Method: Refrigerate ingredients then LAYER in chilled glass by carefully pouring in the following order.

½	shot(s)	**Passion fruit sugar syrup**
½	shot(s)	**Campari Bitter**
½	shot(s)	**Ketel One vodka**

Origin: Created by Alex Kammerling, London, England
Comment: The bitterness of Campari, toned down by passion fruit sugar syrup.

BLACK & TAN

● ● ● ○ ○

Glass: Boston
Method: POUR lager into chilled glass then FLOAT Guinness on top.

½	pint	**Lager**
½	pint	**Guinness**

Comment: Lager downstairs, Guinness upstairs.

BLACK & VELVET

● ● ● ● ◑ ○

Glass: Boston
Method: POUR cider into chilled glass then FLOAT Guinness on top.

½	pint	**Cider**
½	pint	**Guinness**

Comment: Cider downstairs, Guinness upstairs.

BLACK & WHITE DAIQUIRI

● ● ● ● ◑

Glass: Martini
Garnish: Blackberry in drink
Method: MUDDLE berries in base of shaker. Add other ingredients, SHAKE with ice and fine strain into chilled glass.

12	fresh	**Blackberries**
2	shot(s)	**Malibu coconut rum liqueur**
1	shot(s)	**Bacardi Superior rum**
¾	shot(s)	**Crème de mûre liqueur**
½	shot(s)	**Freshly squeezed lime juice**
½	shot(s)	**Chilled mineral water** (omit if wet ice)

Origin: I named this drink after the black berries and the white Malibu bottle.
Comment: Blackberries and coconut add depth to the classic Daiquiri.

'ABSINTHE MAKES THE TART GROW FONDER.'
ERNEST DOWSON

BLACK BEARD

● ● ● ◑ ○

Glass: Boston
Method: POUR ingredients into glass and serve.

2	shot(s)	**Sailor Jerry spiced rum**
½	pint	**Guinness**
Top up with		**Coca-Cola**

Origin: Thought to have originated in Stirling, Scotland, during the late 1990s.
Comment: Something of a student drink, this tastes better than it sounds.

BLACK BISON MARTINI

Glass: Martini
Garnish: Apple wedge
Method: SHAKE all ingredients with ice and fine strain into chilled glass.

2	shot(s)	**Tanqueray London dry gin**
½	shot(s)	**Berentzen apple schnapps**
1½	shot(s)	**Pressed apple juice**
¼	shot(s)	**Noilly Prat dry vermouth**

Origin: Adapted from a drink discovered in 2001 at Oxo Tower Bar, London, England.
Comment: A fragrant cocktail with a dry finish. As the name suggests, also works well with Zubrówka bison vodka in place of gin.

BLACK FEATHER

Glass: Martini
Garnish: Lemon zest twist
Method: STIR all ingredients with ice and strain into chilled glass.

2	shot(s)	**Courvoisier V.S.O.P. cognac**
1	shot(s)	**Noilly prat dry vermouth**
½	shot(s)	**Cointreau triple sec**
1	dash	**Angostura aromatic bitters**

Origin: Adapted from a drink created in 2000 by Robert Hess and published on drinkboy.com.
Comment: Rounded cognac notes with a hint of orange. For dry, adult palates.

BLACK CHERRY MARTINI

Glass: Martini
Garnish: Fresh or maraschino cherry
Method: SHAKE all ingredients with ice and fine strain into chilled glass.

2½	shot(s)	**Ketel One vodka**
1	shot(s)	**Chambord black raspberry liqueur**

Comment: Subtle berry fruit tames vodka's sting.

BLACK FOREST GATEAU MARTINI

Glass: Martini
Garnish: Dust with cocoa powder
Method: SHAKE first 4 ingredients with ice and strain into chilled glass. **FLOAT** cream on drink.

2	shot(s)	**Ketel One vodka**
¾	shot(s)	**Chambord black raspberry liqueur**
¾	shot(s)	**Crème de fraise de bois liqueur**
¼	shot(s)	**Crème de cassis liqueur**
1	shot(s)	**Double (heavy) cream**

Origin: Created in 2002 at Hush, London, England.
Comment: Dessert by name and dessert by nature. Wonderfully moreish, naughty but very nice.

BLACK DREAM

Glass: Shot
Method: Refrigerate ingredients then **LAYER** in chilled glass by carefully pouring in the following order.

½	shot(s)	**Opal Nera black sambuca**
½	shot(s)	**Baileys Irish cream liqueur**

Comment: Slippery Nipple with black sambuca.

BLACK IRISH

Glass: Hurricane
Garnish: Dust with cocoa powder
Method: BLEND ingredients with 12oz scoop of crushed ice. Pour into glass and serve with straws.

1	shot(s)	**Ketel One vodka**
1	shot(s)	**Baileys Irish cream liqueur**
1	shot(s)	**Kahlúa coffee liqueur**
2	scoops	**Vanilla ice cream**

AKA: Frozen Black Irish
Comment: Like a very sweet, alcoholic, frozen caffè latte.

BLACK EYE NEW #8

Glass: Old-fashioned
Garnish: Berries & mint sprig
Method: MUDDLE first 3 ingredients in base of shaker. Add other ingredients, **SHAKE** with ice and strain into ice-filled glass.

2	fresh	**Blackberries**
5	fresh	**Raspberries**
5	fresh	**Mint leaves**
2	shot(s)	**Jameson Irish whiskey**
¾	shot(s)	**Drambuie liqueur**
¼	shot(s)	**Crème de cassis liqueur**

Comment: A fruity Rusty Nail variation.
Origin: Created in 2008 by Simon Lamont at Jardine, Cape Town, South Africa.

BLACK JACK SHOT

Glass: Shot
Method: Refrigerate ingredients then **LAYER** in chilled glass by carefully pouring in the following order.

¾	shot(s)	**Opal Nera black sambuca**
¾	shot(s)	**Jack Daniel's Tennessee whiskey**

Comment: Whiskey sweetened with sambuca.

BLACK JACK COCKTAIL

Glass: Martini
Garnish: Lemon peel twist
Method: **STIR** all ingredients with ice and strain into chilled glass.

1½	shot(s)	**Tanqueray London dry gin**
½	shot(s)	**Kirschwasser eau de vie**
½	shot(s)	**Crème de cassis liqueur**
¾	shot(s)	**Chilled mineral water** (reduce if wet ice)

Origin: The name Black Jack traditionally refers to a water bottle made from air dried leather. When the leather was dried it tended to turn black.
Comment: More burgundy than black but dark fruits of the forest dominate this medium dry cocktail.

BLACK JAPAN

Glass: Collins
Method: **POUR** melon liqueur into chilled glass then **FLOAT** Guinness on top.

1½	shot(s)	**Midori green melon liqueur**
Float & Top		**Guinness**

Origin: Black Japan is the name of a protective lacquer applied to metal.
Comment: This student-style drink will appeal to those with youthful exuberance and a sweet tooth.

BLACK MAGIC

Glass: Flute
Garnish: Black grape on rim
Method: **MUDDLE** grapes in base of shaker. Add liqueur, **SHAKE** with ice and fine strain into chilled glass. **TOP** with champagne.

12	fresh	**Seedless red grapes**
½	shot(s)	**Grand Marnier liqueur**
Top up with		**Perrier Jouet brut champagne**

Comment: More peachy in colour than black but balanced and tasty. Not sweet.

BLACK MARTINI

Glass: Martini
Garnish: Float grated white chocolate
Method: **SHAKE** all ingredients with ice and fine strain into chilled glass.

1½	shot(s)	**Bacardi Superior rum**
1½	shot(s)	**Brown crème de cacao liqueur**
1½	shot(s)	**Espresso coffee**

Origin: Created in 2004 by Yours Truly (Simon Difford).
Comment: This flavoursome mix of coffee and chocolate is further enhanced if vanilla-infused rum is used.

BLACK MUSSEL

Glass: Flute
Garnish: Orange zest twist (discarded)
Method: **POUR** first 2 ingredients into glass and **TOP** with champagne.

½	shot(s)	**Bols blue curaçao liqueur**
¼	shot(s)	**Crème de cassis liqueur**
Top up with		**Perrier Jouet brut champagne**

Comment: Blue curaçao adds a hint of orange to a Kir Royale.

BLACK 'N' BLUE CAIPIROVSKA

Glass: Old-fashioned
Method: **MUDDLE** berries in base of glass. Add other ingredients. Fill glass with crushed ice, **CHURN** (stir) with bar spoon and serve with straws.

6	fresh	**Blackberries**
10	fresh	**Blueberries**
2	shot(s)	**Ketel One vodka**
½	shot(s)	**Freshly squeezed lime juice**
¾	shot(s)	**Sugar syrup** (2 sugar to 1 water)

Comment: A great fruity twist on the regular Caipirovska.

BLACK NUTS

Glass: Shot
Method: **LAYER** in chilled glass by carefully pouring ingredients in the following order.

¾	shot(s)	**Opal Nera black sambuca**
¾	shot(s)	**Frangelico hazelnut liqueur**

Comment: It's something of a challenge to get the Hazelnut liqueur to float on the black sambuca. If you store the Opal Nera in a freezer and the hazelnut liqueur at room temperature, this helps.

BLACK ROSE NEW #8

Glass: Old-fashioned
Garnish: Lemon zest twist
Method: **STIR** all ingredients with ice and strain into (empty – no ice) chilled glass.

1	shot(s)	**Bulleit bourbon whiskey**
1	shot(s)	**Courvoisier V.S.O.P. cognac**
¼	shot(s)	**Pomegranate (grenadine) syrup**
3	dashes	**Peychaud's bitters**
1	dash	**Angostura aromatic bitters**

Comment: Sazerac-like but easier for the uninitiated.

DRINKS ARE GRADED AS FOLLOWS:

- DISGUSTING
- PRETTY AWFUL
- BEST AVOIDED
- DISAPPOINTING
- ACCEPTABLE
- GOOD
- RECOMMENDED
- HIGHLY RECOMMENDED
- OUTSTANDING / EXCEPTIONAL

BLACK RUSSIAN UPDATED #8

Glass: Old-fashioned
Garnish: Lemon slice & cherry on stick (sail)
Method: STIR all ingredients with ice and strain into ice-filled glass.

| 2 | shot(s) | **Ketel One vodka** |
| ¾ | shot(s) | **Kahlúa coffee liqueur** |

Variants: 1/ Served straight-up in a Martini glass. 2/ Topped with Coca-Cola and served over ice in a Collins glass. 3/ Made into a White Russian.
Comment: Most popularly served with cola. With or without, this drink is not that interesting.

BLACK STRAP NEW #8

Glass: Martini
Garnish: Orange zest twist
Method: STIR all ingredients with ice and strain into chilled glass.

2	shot(s)	**Gosling's Black Seal rum**
½	shot(s)	**Bénédictine D.O.M. liqueur**
½	shot(s)	**Brown crème de cacao liqueur**
2	drops	**Tabasco pepper sauce**

Comment: This drink benefits from the dilution, which comes with a lengthy stir.
Origin: Adapted from a recipe created in 2007 by Neyah White, San Francisco, USA.

BLACK VELVET UPDATED #8

Glass: Flute
Garnish: Shamrock or mint leaf
Method: Slowly POUR ingredients into chilled glass and gently stir.

| 3½ | shot(s) | **Guinness** |
| | Top up with | **Perrier Jouet brut champagne** |

AKA: Bismark
Variant: If porter is used instead of stout, this drink becomes simply a Velvet. If beer is used, it is known as the Halstead Street Velvet.
Comment: Full-flavoured stout and delicate champagne are an unlikely combination but this classic has stood the test of time. Some may wish to add a barspoon of sugar syrup.

Origin: Thought to have originated in 1861 at Brook's Club, London although some credit some credit the Shelbourne Hotel, Dublin, Ireland. What is certain is that this drink was created at the time when Britain was morning the death of HRH Prince Albert, husband of Queen Victoria.
The Black Velvet is often served to commemorate Saint Patrick's Day but is more fittingly served on 14 December as this is the day Prince Albert died of typhoid fever in 1861. Devastated, the Queen wore black for the rest of her life so this drink's shrouding of champagne is most appropriate.
In his 1948 'Fine Art of Mixing Drinks', David A. Embury writes of this drink, "I was first introduced to Black Velvet at the home of a very dear friend of mine in Montreal and I received one of the greatest of all the drinking surprises of my whole life. The combination of champagne and stout sounds terrifying - something like molasses and horseradish. Actually, its excellent. The champagne cuts the heavy, syrupy consistency of the stout, and the stout takes the sharp, tart edge off the champagne. Each is the perfect complement of the other. Be sure, however, that you use (a) a good bottle of stout, (b) an extra-dry champagne - preferably a brut or nature."

BLACK WIDOW

Glass: Martini
Garnish: Liquorice
Method: SHAKE all ingredients with ice and fine strain into chilled glass.

1	shot(s)	**Opal Nera black sambuca**
1	shot(s)	**Crème de fraise de bois liqueur**
1	shot(s)	**Malibu coconut rum liqueur**
½	shot(s)	**Double (heavy) cream**
½	shot(s)	**Milk**

Comment: This sticky, fruity, liquorice cocktail tastes a little like an Allsort sweet.

BLACKTHORN COCKTAIL

Glass: Martini
Garnish: Lemon zest twist
Method: STIR all ingredients with ice and strain into chilled glass.

1½	shot(s)	**Tanqueray London dry gin**
¾	shot(s)	**Dubonnet Red** (French made)
¾	shot(s)	**Kirschwasser eau de vie**

Comment: This drink benefits from a long, chilling and diluting stir. The result is Martini-style, fruity but dry.

BLACKTHORN ENGLISH UPDATED #8

Glass: Martini/Coupette
Garnish: Orange zest twist
Method: SHAKE all ingredients with ice and fine strain into chilled glass.

1½	shot(s)	**Sloe gin liqueur**
1	shot(s)	**Tanqueray London dry gin**
¾	shot(s)	**Martini Rosso sweet vermouth**
3	dashes	**Angostura orange bitters**
½	shot(s)	**Chilled mineral water** (omit if wet ice)

Comment: A fruit influenced yet dry and classic Martini.
Origin: A vintage classic whose origins are unknown.

BLACKTHORN IRISH

Glass: Martini
Garnish: Flamed lemon zest twist
Method: SHAKE all ingredients with ice and fine strain into chilled glass.

1½	shot(s)	**Jameson Irish whiskey**
1	shot(s)	**Noilly Prat dry vermouth**
¼	shot(s)	**Pernod anis**
4	dashes	**Angostura aromatic bitters**
½	shot(s)	**Chilled mineral water** (omit if wet ice)

Origin: A classic cocktail whose origins are unknown.
Comment: A dry and aromatic Martini with hints of anis. Some may prefer to add a dash of sugar syrup.

BLADE RUNNER

Glass: Collins
Garnish: Pineapple wedge & cherry
Method: SHAKE all ingredients with ice and strain into ice-filled glass.

2	shot(s)	**Bacardi Superior rum**
½	shot(s)	**Myers's dark Jamaican rum**
2½	shot(s)	**Pressed pineapple juice**
¼	shot(s)	**Sugar syrup** (2 sugar to 1 water)
2	dashes	**Angostura aromatic bitters**
½	shot(s)	**Freshly squeezed lime juice**

Origin: Discovered in 2005 at Zoulou Bar, Berlin, Germany.
Comment: Tangy and fruity but not too sweet.

BLIMEY

Glass: Old-fashioned
Garnish: Lime wedge & blackberries
Method: MUDDLE blackberries in base of shaker. Add other ingredients, SHAKE with ice and fine strain into glass filled with crushed ice. Serve with straws.

7	fresh	**Blackberries**
2	shot(s)	**Ketel One vodka**
¾	shot(s)	**Crème de cassis liqueur**
1	shot(s)	**Freshly squeezed lime juice**
⅛	shot(s)	**Sugar syrup** (2 sugar to 1 water)

Origin: Created in 2002 by Yours Truly (Simon Difford).
Comment: This blackberry and lime blend is both fruity and aptly named.

BLING! BLING! UPDATED #8

Glass: Shot
Method: MUDDLE raspberries in base of shaker. Add vodka, lime and sugar, SHAKE with ice and fine strain into glass. TOP with champagne.

7	fresh	**Raspberries**
½	shot(s)	**Ketel One vodka**
½	shot(s)	**Freshly squeezed lime juice**
¼	shot(s)	**Sugar syrup** (2 sugar to 1 water)
Top up with		**Perrier Jouet brut champagne**

Comment: An ostentatious little number.
Origin: Created in 2001 by Phillip Jeffrey at the GE Club, London, England.

BLINKER

Glass: Martini
Garnish: Lemon twist
Method: SHAKE all ingredients with ice and fine strain into chilled glass.

2	shot(s)	**Bulleit bourbon whiskey**
1	shot(s)	**Freshly squeezed grapefruit juice**
¼	shot(s)	**Pomegranate (grenadine) syrup**

Origin: A 1930s classic revisited.
Comment: Back in the 1930s David Embury wrote of this drink, "One of a few cocktails using grapefruit juice. Not particularly good but not too bad." How times have changed!

BLOOD & SAND #1 (CLASSIC FORMULA) UPDATED #8

Glass: Martini
Garnish: Orange zest twist
Method: SHAKE all ingredients with ice and fine strain into chilled glass.

¾	shot(s)	**Johnnie Walker Scotch whisky**
¾	shot(s)	**Heering cherry brandy liqueur**
¾	shot(s)	**Martini Rosso sweet vermouth**
¾	shot(s)	**Freshly squeezed orange juice**

Comment: One of the best classic Scotch cocktails but a little sweet.
Origin: Created for the premiere of the 1922 Rudolph Valentino movie, Blood and Sand. This equal parts formula comes from the 1930 edition of 'The Savoy Cocktail Book'.

> ## 'EVERYBODY HAS TO BELIEVE IN SOMETHING... I BELIEVE I'LL HAVE ANOTHER DRINK.'
> ### W.C. FIELDS

BLOOD & SAND #2 (DIFFORD'S FORMULA) NEW #8

Glass: Martini
Garnish: Orange zest twist
Method: SHAKE all ingredients with ice and fine strain into chilled glass.

1½	shot(s)	**Johnnie Walker Scotch whisky**
¾	shot(s)	**Heering cherry brandy liqueur**
¾	shot(s)	**Martini Rosso sweet vermouth**
¾	shot(s)	**Freshly squeezed orange juice**

Comment: A dry, more spirited Blood & Sand for those who like Scotch.
Origin: Formula by Yours Truly (Simon Difford) in 2006.

BLOODHOUND #1 NEW #8

Glass: Martini
Garnish: Raspberries on stick
Method: MUDDLE strawberries in base of shaker. Add other ingredients, SHAKE with ice and fine strain into chilled glass.

6	fresh	**Raspberries**
2	shot(s)	**Tanqueray London dry gin**
¾	shot(s)	**Noilly Prat dry vermouth**
¾	shot(s)	**Martini Rosso sweet vermouth**
¼	shot(s)	**Luxardo maraschino liqueur**

Variation: Made with raspberries in place of strawberries.
Comment: Looks like fruity disco drink fodder but is actually surprising dry and strong.
Origin: Unknown but in his 1922 'Mixing Cocktails', Harry McElhone credits the Duke of Manchester with this drinks creation. However, in his 1907 'World Drinks', William Boothby lists a Bloodhound, as does Tom Bullock in his 1917 'The Ideal Bartender'.

BLOODHOUND #2 UPDATED #8

Glass: Collins
Garnish: Lime wedge
Method: SHAKE all ingredients with ice and strain into ice-filled glass.

2	shot(s)	Campari Bitter
1	shot(s)	Ketel One vodka
3	shot(s)	Freshly squeezed grapefruit juice

Comment: A dry, tart, refreshing long drink.

BLOOD ORANGE NEW #8

Glass: Martini/Coupette
Garnish: Orange zest twist
Method: SHAKE all ingredients with ice and fine strain into chilled glass.

2	shot(s)	Tanqueray London dry gin
½	shot(s)	Campari Bitter
½	shot(s)	Noilly Prat dry vermouth
1	shot(s)	Freshly squeezed orange juice

Comment: Bone-dry but with full-on tangy fresh orange.
Origin: Created in 2008 by Jeffrey Morgenthaler at Bel Ami Lounge, Oregon, USA.

BLOOD SAGE NEW #8

Glass: Martini
Garnish: Sage leaf
Method: MUDDLE orange and sage in base of shaker. Add other ingredients, **SHAKE** with ice and fine strain into chilled glass.

½	shot(s)	Squeezed blood orange juice
2	fresh	Sage leaves
2	shot(s)	Tanqueray London dry gin
¾	shot(s)	Freshly squeezed lime juice
½	shot(s)	Sugar syrup (2 sugar to 1 water)
½	fresh	Egg white

Comment: Sage combines wonderfully with gin and orange in this beautifully balanced drink.
Origin: Adapted from a drink created by Ryan Magarian, Seattle, USA.

BLOODY BRONX NEW #8

Glass: Martini
Garnish: Maraschino cherry
Method: SHAKE all ingredients with ice and fine strain into chilled glass.

2	shot(s)	Tanqueray London dry gin
¼	shot(s)	Noilly Prat dry vermouth
¼	shot(s)	Martini Rosso sweet vermouth
1	shot(s)	Squeezed Blood orange juice

Comment: A Bronx made 'bloody' by the use of blood oranges.
Origin: A vintage cocktail adapted from the classic Bronx Cocktail, created in 1906 by Johnny Solon, a bartender at New York's Waldorf-Astoria Hotel, and named after the newly opened Bronx Zoo.

BLOODY CAESAR

Glass: Collins
Garnish: Pickled bean
Method: SHAKE all ingredients with ice and strain into ice-filled glass.

2	shot(s)	Ketel One vodka
4	shot(s)	Mott's Clamato juice
½	shot(s)	Freshly squeezed lime juice
7	drops	Tabasco pepper sauce
3	dashes	Lea & Perrins Worcestershire sauce
2	pinches	Celery salt
2	grinds	Black pepper

Origin: Created by Walter Chell in 1969 to celebrate the opening of Marco's Italian restaurant at the Calgary Inn, Canada. Walter was inspired by the flavours of Spaghetti Vongole (spaghetti with clams) and named the drink after the Roman emperor.
Comment: A peculiarly Canadian fishy twist on the classic Bloody Mary.

BLOODY JOSEPH

Glass: Collins
Garnish: Stick of celery
Method: SHAKE all ingredients with ice and strain into ice-filled glass.

2	shot(s)	Johnnie Walker Scotch whisky
4	shot(s)	Pressed tomato juice
½	shot(s)	Freshly squeezed lemon juice
8	drops	Tabasco pepper sauce
4	dashes	Lea & Perrins Worcestershire sauce
½	spoon	Horseradish sauce
½	shot(s)	Warre's Otima tawny port
2	pinches	Celery salt
2	grinds	Black pepper

Comment: A Bloody Mary with whisky.

BLOODY MARIA

Glass: Collins
Garnish: Salt & pepper rim plus celery stick
Method: SHAKE all ingredients with ice and strain into ice-filled glass.

2	shot(s)	Don Julio reposado tequila
4	shot(s)	Pressed tomato juice
½	shot(s)	Freshly squeezed lemon juice
8	drops	Tabasco pepper sauce
4	dashes	Lea & Perrins Worcestershire sauce
½	spoon	Horseradish sauce
½	shot(s)	Warre's Otima tawny port
2	pinches	Celery salt
2	grinds	Black pepper

Comment: Tequila adds a very interesting kick to the classic Bloody Mary.

DRINKS ARE GRADED AS FOLLOWS:

- DISGUSTING
- PRETTY AWFUL
- BEST AVOIDED
- DISAPPOINTING
- ACCEPTABLE
- GOOD
- RECOMMENDED
- HIGHLY RECOMMENDED
- OUTSTANDING / EXCEPTIONAL

BLOODY MARU

Glass: Collins
Garnish: Lemongrass stick
Method: SHAKE all ingredients with ice and strain into ice-filled glass.

3	shot(s)	**Sake**
3	shot(s)	**Pressed tomato juice**
½	shot(s)	**Freshly squeezed lemon juice**
8	drops	**Tabasco pepper sauce**
4	dashes	**Lea & Perrins Worcestershire sauce**
2	pinches	**Celery salt**
2	grinds	**Black pepper**

Origin: A Bloody Mary based on sake.

> 'THE SWAY OF ALCOHOL OVER
> MANKIND IS UNQUESTIONABLY
> DUE TO ITS POWER TO
> STIMULATE THE MYSTICAL
> FACULTIES OF HUMAN NATURE,
> USUALLY CRUSHED TO EARTH
> BY THE COLD FACTS AND
> DRY CRITICISMS OF THE
> SOBER HOUR.'
> WILLIAM JAMES

BLOODY MARY #1 (1930S RECIPE)

Glass: Old-fashioned
Garnish: Salt & pepper rim
Method: SHAKE all ingredients with ice and strain into empty glass.

2	shot(s)	**100-proof (50% A.B.V.) vodka**
2	shot(s)	**Thick pressed tomato juice**
¼	shot(s)	**Freshly squeezed lemon juice**
5	dashes	**Lea & Perrins Worcestershire sauce**
4	pinches	**Salt**
2	grinds	**Black pepper**
2	pinches	**Cayenne pepper**

Variant: Red Snapper
Origin: A 1933 version of the classic created in 1920 by Fernand Petiot at Harry's New York Bar, Paris, France.
Comment: Fiery stuff. The modern version is more user friendly.

BLOODY MARY #2 (MODERN RECIPE)

UPDATED #8

Glass: Collins
Garnish: Salt & pepper rim plus celery stick
Method: SHAKE all ingredients with ice and strain into ice-filled glass.

2	shot(s)	**Ketel One vodka**
4	shot(s)	**Pressed tomato juice**
½	shot(s)	**Freshly squeezed lemon juice**
7	drops	**Tabasco pepper sauce**
4	dashes	**Lea & Perrins Worcestershire sauce**
2	pinches	**Celery salt**
2	grinds	**Black pepper**

Comment: The classic brunch cocktail.
Origin: The creation of The Bloody Mary is a matter of some dispute, but is generally credited to Fernand Petiot. Whether this was in 1920 (or 1921), when Petiot was a young bartender at Harry's New York Bar in Paris, or in America, during the 1940s, after the comedian George Jessel had first popularised the unspiced combination of vodka and tomato juice, is not clear.

If you believe that Petiot first created it around 1920, then you will believe that the name is borrowed not from the English Queen Mary I, whose persecution of Protestants gave her that name, or for the silent movie actress Mary Pickford, but from one of Petiot's customers, apparently the entertainer Roy Barton. He had worked at a nightclub (or knew a bar) called the Bucket of Blood in Chicago, where there was a waitress known as 'Bloody Mary', and he said the drink reminded him of her. If you believe Petiot invented it in New York, where he worked at the St. Regis Hotel certainly from the end of Prohibition, then he may have had assistance in its creation from Serge Obolansky, the manager of the hotel, who asked him to spice up his 50-50 blend of vodka and tomato juice. According to this version, he attempted to rename the drink Red Snapper, after Vincent Astor, who owned the hotel, found the name too crude for his clientele. (now days a Red Snapper is a Bloody Mary made with gin).

The celery stick garnish apparently dates back to 1960 when a bartender at the Ambassador Hotel in Chicago noticed a lady stirring her drink with a celery stick. Whatever the precise story behind this fantastic drink, Bloody Mary recipes are as personal as Martinis. Purists will only use Tabasco, Worcestershire sauce, salt and lemon to spice up tomato and vodka but everything from oysters to V8 can be added. Variations include:

Asian Mary (with wasabi, ginger & soy sauce)
Bloody Bull (with beef consommé)
Bloody Caesar (with clam juice)
Bloody Joseph (with Scotch whisky)
Bloody Maria (with tequila)
Bloody Maru (with sake)
Bloody Shame (without alcohol)
Bullshot (with beef bouillon)
Cubanita (with rum)
Red Snapper (with gin)

BLOODY MARY #3 (DIFFORD'S RECIPE) NEW #8

Glass: Collins
Garnish: Salt & pepper rim plus celery stick
Method: MUDDLE pepper in base of shaker. Add other ingredients, SHAKE with ice and fine strain into ice-filled glass.

2	rings	**Yellow bell pepper (chopped)**
2	shot(s)	**Ketel One vodka**
3	shot(s)	**Pressed tomato juice**
½	shot(s)	**Freshly squeezed lemon juice**
¾	shot(s)	**Harvey's Bristol Cream sherry**
8	drops	**Tabasco pepper sauce**
4	dashes	**Lea & Perrins Worcestershire sauce**
2	pinches	**Celery salt**
2	grinds	**Black pepper**

Comment: My take on the Bloody Mary benefits from extra pepper spice and is sweetened and flavoured with sweet sherry.
Origin: Created in 2007 by Yours Truly (Simon Difford).

BLOODY MARY

BLOODY SHAME (MOCKTAIL)

Glass: Collins
Garnish: Celery stick
Method: SHAKE all ingredients with ice and strain into ice-filled glass.

5	shot(s)	**Pressed tomato juice**
½	shot(s)	**Freshly squeezed lemon juice**
8	drops	**Tabasco pepper sauce**
4	dashes	**Lea & Perrins Worcestershire sauce**
½	spoon	**Horseradish sauce**
2	pinches	**Celery salt**
2	grinds	**Black pepper**

AKA: Virgin Mary
Comment: Somehow missing something.

BLOOMSBURY MARTINI

Glass: Martini
Garnish: Lemon zest twist
Method: STIR all ingredients with ice and strain into chilled glass.

2	shot(s)	**Tanqueray London dry gin**
½	shot(s)	**Cuarenta Y Tres (Licor 43) liqueur**
½	shot(s)	**Noilly Prat dry vermouth**
2	dashes	**Peychaud's aromatic bitters**

Origin: Adapted from a drink created in 2003 by Robert Hess and published on drinkboy.com.
Comment: This pinky/rusty drink benefits from a good long stir but the result is an aromatic, medium dry, spicy vanilla Martini.

BLOW JOB

Glass: Shot
Method: SHAKE all ingredients with ice and fine strain into chilled glass.

½	shot(s)	**Grand Marnier liqueur**
½	shot(s)	**Crème de banane liqueur**
½	shot(s)	**Kahlúa coffee liqueur**

Comment: A juvenile but pleasant tasting sweet shot.

BLUE ANGEL

Glass: Martini
Garnish: Orange zest twist
Method: SHAKE all ingredients with ice and fine strain into chilled glass.

¾	shot(s)	**Bols blue curaçao liqueur**
¾	shot(s)	**Parfait Amour liqueur**
¾	shot(s)	**Courvoisier V.S.O.P. cognac**
¾	shot(s)	**Freshly squeezed lemon juice**
¾	shot(s)	**Double (heavy) cream**

Comment: This baby blue cocktail is sweet, creamy and floral.

BLUE BIRD

Glass: Martini
Garnish: Orange zest twist
Method: SHAKE all ingredients with ice and fine strain into chilled glass.

2	shot(s)	**Tanqueray London dry gin**
1	shot(s)	**Bols blue curaçao liqueur**
¾	shot(s)	**Freshly squeezed lemon juice**
¼	shot(s)	**Almond (orgeat) syrup**

Origin: Thought to have been created in the late 1950s in Montmartre, Paris, France.
Comment: A blue rinsed, orange washed, gin based 'tini' that benefits from being sweetened with almond rather than plain syrup.

BLUE BLAZER UPDATED #8

Glass: Toddy
Garnish: Lemon zest twist
Method: WARNING - do not attempt to make this drink. If you really must, then please practice with water first to perfect your method, stand on a non-flammable floor, have suitable fire fighting equipment and preferably a medical professional nearby. You will need two large silver-plated mugs with handles. Preheat the mugs with boiling water and warm the whisky. **POUR** the whisky into one mug and fresh boiling water into the other. Ignite the whiskey using a long match and while still blazing pour the whisky into the other mug. Then mix ingredients by pouring them from one mug to the other. The foolhardy increase the distance between the mugs as they pour, thus creating a spectacular long blue flame between the two mugs. Extinguish flame by covering mug, pour into glass and sweeten to taste by stirring in powered sugar.

2	shot(s)	**Cask strength Scotch whisky**
2	shot(s)	**Boiling water**
1	spoon	**Powdered sugar**

Comment: This is a showy way to make a simple hot whisky punch.
Origin: Created by 'Professor' Jerry Thomas, author of the first bartending book and travelling showman bartender. The Professor is said to have created this drink in the early 1860s while bartending at the Occidental Hotel in San Francisco.

BLUE CHAMPAGNE

Glass: Flute
Method: SHAKE first 4 ingredients with ice and strain into glass. **TOP** with champagne.

¾	shot(s)	**Ketel One vodka**
⅛	shot(s)	**Cointreau triple sec**
¼	shot(s)	**Bols blue curaçao liqueur**
¼	shot(s)	**Freshly squeezed lemon juice**
Top up with		**Perrier Jouet brut champagne**

Variant: With gin in place of vodka.
Comment: Fortified, citrussy champagne.

BLUE COSMO

Glass: Martini
Garnish: Orange zest twist
Method: **SHAKE** all ingredients with ice and fine strain into chilled glass.

2	shot(s)	**Ketel One Citroen vodka**
¾	shot(s)	**Bols blue curaçao liqueur**
1½	shot(s)	**Ocean Spray white cranberry**
¼	shot(s)	**Freshly squeezed lime juice**

Variant: Purple Cosmo
Comment: This blue rinsed drink may have novelty value but it is not as good as a traditional Cosmo.

BLUE EYED MARTINI NEW #8

Glass: Martini/Coupette
Garnish: Lemon zest twist
Method: **STIR** all ingredients with ice and strain into chilled glass.

1½	shot(s)	**Ketel One vodka**
½	shot(s)	**Tanqueray London dry gin**
⅛	shot(s)	**Bols blue curaçao liqueur**
¼	shot(s)	**Noilly Prat dry vermouth**

Comment: Matches your eyes – well at least it did when I served it to Michelle.

BLUE FIN

Glass: Martini
Garnish: Gummy fish
Method: **SHAKE** all ingredients with ice and fine strain into chilled glass.

2	shot(s)	**Ketel One Citroen vodka**
1	shot(s)	**Hpnotiq liqueur**
1½	shot(s)	**Ocean Spray white cranberry**

Origin: Created in 2003 at The Blue Fin, W Hotel, Times Square, New York, USA.
Comment: Citrussy, reminiscent of a blue Cosmo.

BLUE HAWAII NEW #8

Glass: Collins
Garnish: Pineapple wedge, cherry & paper parasol
Method: **POUR** blue curaçao into ice-filled glass. **SHAKE** the sugar syrup, pineapple and lime juice with ice and strain into ice filled glass so it forms a **LAYER** (carefully pour so floats on previous layer) over blue curaçao. Lastly **FLOAT** rum on top of drink.

½	shot(s)	**Bols blue curaçao liqueur**
3	shot(s)	**Pressed pineapple juice**
1	shot(s)	**Freshly squeezed lime juice**
½	shot(s)	**Sugar syrup** (2 sugar to 1 water)
1½	shot(s)	**Bacardi Superior rum**

Comment: Aloha!
Origin: Created in 1957 by Harry Yee at Henry Kaiser's Hawaiian Village Hotel (latterly the Hilton) in Waikiki, Oahu, Hawaii. The drink is named after the hit song from the 1937 Bing Crosby film, Waikiki Wedding, and not after what is generously described as a "musical-comedy" Elvis Presley 1961 film of the same name.

BLUE HAWAIIAN

Glass: Hurricane
Garnish: Pineapple wedge & cherry on rim
Method: **BLEND** ingredients with 12oz scoop of crushed ice. Pour into glass and serve with straws.

2	shot(s)	**Bacardi Superior rum**
1	shot(s)	**Bols blue curaçao liqueur**
1½	shot(s)	**Coco López cream of coconut**
3	shot(s)	**Pressed pineapple juice**
¼	shot(s)	**Freshly squeezed lemon juice**

Origin: Probably created by Don the Beachcomber in Los Angeles, USA.
Comment: A blue rinsed Piña Colada.

BLUE HEAVEN

Glass: Collins
Garnish: Pineapple wedge & cherry sail
Method: **SHAKE** all ingredients with ice and strain into ice-filled glass.

2	shot(s)	**Bacardi Superior rum**
1	shot(s)	**Bols blue curaçao liqueur**
½	shot(s)	**Luxardo Amaretto di Saschira**
½	shot(s)	**Rose's lime cordial**
4	shot(s)	**Pressed pineapple juice**

Comment: Actually more aqua than blue, this sweet concoction includes orange, almond, lime cordial and pineapple.

BLUE KAMIKAZE

Glass: Shot
Method: **SHAKE** all ingredients with ice and fine strain into chilled glass.

½	shot(s)	**Ketel One vodka**
½	shot(s)	**Bols blue curaçao liqueur**
½	shot(s)	**Freshly squeezed lime juice**

Comment: Tangy orange - but it's blue.

BLUE LADY

Glass: Martini
Garnish: Orange zest twist
Method: **SHAKE** all ingredients with ice and fine strain into chilled glass.

1	shot(s)	**Tanqueray London dry gin**
2	shot(s)	**Bols blue curaçao liqueur**
1	shot(s)	**Freshly squeezed lemon juice**
½	fresh	**Egg white**

Comment: Quite sweet with an orange, citrus finish.

BLUE LAGOON

●●●○○

Glass: Collins
Garnish: Orange slice
Method: BLEND ingredients with 18oz scoop of crushed ice. Pour into glass and serve with straws.

1	shot(s)	**Tanqueray London dry gin**
1	shot(s)	**Ketel One vodka**
1	shot(s)	**Bols blue curaçao liqueur**
1	shot(s)	**Freshly squeezed lime juice**
1	shot(s)	**Sugar syrup** (2 sugar to 1 water)

Variant: Vodka, blue curaçao and lemonade on the rocks.
Origin: Created in 1972 by Andy MacElhone (son of Harry) at Harry's New York Bar, Paris, France.
Comment: Better than the film – not hard!

'A MAN YOU DON'T LIKE WHO DRINKS AS MUCH AS YOU DO.' DYLAN THOMAS DEFINES AN ALCOHOLIC

BLUE MARGARITA

●●●●○○

Glass: Coupette
Garnish: Lime slice on rim
Method: BLEND all ingredients with one 6oz scoop crushed ice. Serve with straws.

2	shot(s)	**Don Julio reposado tequila**
1	shot(s)	**Bols blue curaçao liqueur**
1	shot(s)	**Freshly squeezed lime juice**
½	shot(s)	**Sugar syrup** (2 sugar to 1 water)

Comment: As the name suggests, a Margarita, only blue. This 'Disco Drink' looks scary but tastes pretty good.

BLUE MONDAY UPDATED #8

●●●●○○

Glass: Old-fashioned
Garnish: Orange zest twist
Method: SHAKE all ingredients with ice and fine strain into chilled glass.

1½	shot(s)	**Ketel One Citroen vodka**
¾	shot(s)	**Bols blue curaçao liqueur**
½	shot(s)	**Cointreau triple sec**
½	shot(s)	**Noilly Prat dry vermouth**
2	dashes	**Angostura orange bitters**

AKA: Caucasian
Comment: Disco blue but medium dry with a bittersweet orange taste.
Origin: My 2003 adaptation of Patrick Gavin Duffy's classic. The original consisted of ¾ vodka, ¼ triple sec, 1 dash blue food colouring.

BLUE MOON

●●●●○

Glass: Martini
Garnish: Orange zest twist
Method: SHAKE all ingredients with ice and fine strain into chilled glass.

2	shot(s)	**Tanqueray London dry gin**
¾	shot(s)	**Benoit Serres crème de violette**
½	shot(s)	**Freshly squeezed lemon juice**
½	fresh	**Egg white**

AKA: Blue Devil
Variant: Aviation
Origin: Adapted from David A. Embury's 1948 'The Fine Art of Mixing Drinks'. This long lost drink was originally made with the now extinct Crème Yvette liqueur. 'Blue Moon' is an astronomical term for the second of two full moons to occur in the same calendar month.
Comment: More dirty grey than blue but a must for Aviation lovers, whatever the colour.

BLUE MOUNTAIN COCKTAIL NEW #8

●●●●○

Glass: Martini/Coupette
Garnish: Orange zest twist (discarded) & 3 coffee beans
Method: SHAKE all ingredients with ice and fine strain into chilled glass.

1½	shot(s)	**Zacapa aged rum**
½	shot(s)	**Ketel One vodka**
½	shot(s)	**Kahlúa coffee liqueur**
1½	shot(s)	**Freshly squeezed orange juice**

Comment: A balanced wake-up call where the blue mountain means coffee and freshly squeezed orange juice.

BLUE PASSION

●●●●○

Glass: Old-fashioned
Garnish: Orange zest twist
Method: SHAKE all ingredients with ice and strain into glass filled with crushed ice.

1	shot(s)	**Bacardi Superior rum**
1	shot(s)	**Bols blue curaçao liqueur**
1¾	shot(s)	**Freshly squeezed lime juice**
1	shot(s)	**Sugar syrup** (2 sugar to 1 water)

Comment: This sweet and sour tangy drink is surprisingly good.

BLUE RIBAND

●●●○○

Glass: Martini
Garnish: Cherry dropped into glass
Method: STIR all ingredients with ice and strain into chilled glass.

2	shot(s)	**Tanqueray London dry gin**
1	shot(s)	**Cointreau triple sec**
1	shot(s)	**Bols blue curaçao liqueur**

Origin: The 'Blue Riband' was awarded to the liner that made the fastest Atlantic crossing. This cocktail is thought to have been created on one of these ships.
Comment: A sweetened, blue, orange & gin Martini.

BLUE SKY NEW #8

●●●○○

Glass: Martini
Garnish: Orange zest twist
Method: SHAKE all ingredients with ice and fine strain into chilled glass.

¾	shot(s)	**Tanqueray London dry gin**
¾	shot(s)	**Freshly squeezed lime juice**
¾	shot(s)	**Bols blue curaçao liqueur**
¼	shot(s)	**Luxardo maraschino liqueur**

Comment: Tis indeed blue. Orange and lime predominate.

BLUE STAR

●●●○○

Glass: Martini
Garnish: Orange zest twist
Method: SHAKE all ingredients with ice and fine strain into chilled glass.

1½	shot(s)	**Tanqueray London dry gin**
¾	shot(s)	**Noilly Prat dry vermouth**
¾	shot(s)	**Freshly squeezed orange juice**
¾	shot(s)	**Bols blue curaçao liqueur**

Comment: Gin, orange and a kick.

BLUE VELVET MARGARITA

●●●●○

Glass: Coupette
Garnish: Lime wedge on rim
Method: SHAKE all ingredients with ice and fine strain into chilled glass.

2	shot(s)	**Don Julio reposado tequila**
½	shot(s)	**Cointreau triple sec**
½	shot(s)	**Bols blue curaçao liqueur**
1	shot(s)	**Freshly squeezed lime juice**

Origin: Discovered in 2005 at Velvet Margarita Cantina, Los Angeles, USA.
Comment: May look lurid but is a surprisingly tasty Margarita.

BLUE WAVE

●●●○○

Glass: Hurricane
Garnish: Pineapple wedge on rim
Method: SHAKE ingredients with ice and strain into ice-filled glass.

1	shot(s)	**Tanqueray London dry gin**
1	shot(s)	**Bacardi Superior rum**
½	shot(s)	**Bols blue curaçao liqueur**
3	shot(s)	**Pressed pineapple juice**
1¾	shot(s)	**Freshly squeezed lime juice**
¾	shot(s)	**Sugar syrup** (2 sugar to 1 water)

Comment: A fruity holiday drink.

BLUEBERRY DAIQUIRI

●●●●○○

Glass: Martini
Garnish: Blueberries on stick
Method: MUDDLE blueberries in base of shaker. Add other ingredients, **SHAKE** with ice and fine strain into chilled glass.

20	fresh	**Blueberries**
2	shot(s)	**Bacardi Superior rum**
½	shot(s)	**Crème de myrtille liqueur**
½	shot(s)	**Freshly squeezed lime juice**

Origin: Created in 2002 by Yours Truly (Simon Difford).
Comment: Blueberry juice and liqueur lengthens and sweetens an otherwise classic Daiquiri.

BLUEBERRY MARTINI #1

●●●●○○

Glass: Martini
Garnish: Lemon zest twist (discarded) & blueberries on stick
Method: MUDDLE blueberries in base of shaker. Add other ingredients, **SHAKE** with ice and fine strain into chilled glass.

20	fresh	**Blueberries**
2	shot(s)	**Ketel One vodka**
¼	shot(s)	**Crème de myrtille liqueur**
⅛	shot(s)	**Sugar syrup** (2 sugar to 1 water)

Comment: Rich blueberry fruit fortified with grainy vodka. Not too sweet.

BLUEBERRY MARTINI #2

●●●●○

Glass: Martini
Garnish: Blueberries on stick.
Method: MUDDLE blueberries in base of shaker. Add other ingredients, **SHAKE** with ice and fine strain into chilled glass.

30	fresh	**Blueberries**
2	shot(s)	**Ketel One vodka**
¼	shot(s)	**Sugar syrup** (2 sugar to 1 water)
¾	shot(s)	**Sauvignon Blanc wine**

Comment: Rich blueberry fruit fortified with vodka – much more interesting with the additional splash of wine.

BLUEBERRY TEA

●●●●○

Glass: Toddy
Garnish: Lemon slice & cinnamon stick
Method: POUR first 2 ingredients into glass, **TOP** with tea and stir.

¾	shot(s)	**Luxardo Amaretto di Saschira**
¾	shot(s)	**Grand Marnier liqueur**
Top up with		**Hot black breakfast tea**

Comment: This does indeed taste just as described on the tin.

BLUEGRASS NEW #8

● ● ● ● ○

Glass: Martini
Garnish: Cucumber peel spiral
Method: MUDDLE cucumber in base of shaker
Add other ingredients, **SHAKE** with ice and fine
strain into chilled glass.

2	inches	**Cucumber** (peeled & chopped)
1½	shot(s)	**Bulleit bourbon whiskey**
¾	shot(s)	**Aperol**
⅛	shot(s)	**Sugar syrup** (2 sugar to 1 water)
1	dash	**Angostura aromatic bitters**
1	dash	**Angostura orange bitters**

Comment: Cucumber and Bourbon with a hint of
bitter sweet orange.
Origin: Created in 2008 by Hayden Lambert at
Merchant Hotel, Belfast, Northern Ireland and
named after the bluegrass that grows in Bourbon
County where some of the best horses in the world
are bred.

> THE BELLINI WAS FIRST
> CREATED IN 1945 BY GIUSEPPE
> CIPRIANI AT HARRY'S BAR,
> VENICE, ITALY.

BLUSH MARTINI

● ● ● ● ○

Glass: Martini
Garnish: Dust with cinnamon powder
Method: SHAKE all ingredients with ice and fine
strain into chilled glass.

1	shot(s)	**Ketel One vodka**
¾	shot(s)	**Vanilla schnapps liqueur**
½	shot(s)	**Luxardo Amaretto di Saschira**
¾	shot(s)	**Milk**
¾	shot(s)	**Double (heavy) cream**
¼	shot(s)	**Ocean Spray cranberry juice**

Origin: Created by Colin William Crowden, Mashed
Bar, Leicester, England.
Comment: Drier than it looks, but still one to follow
the dessert trolley.

BLUSHIN' RUSSIAN

● ● ● ● ○

Glass: Martini
Garnish: Float 3 coffee beans
Method: SHAKE all ingredients with ice and fine
strain into chilled glass.

1	shot(s)	**Ketel One vodka**
1	shot(s)	**Kahlúa coffee liqueur**
½	shot(s)	**Luxardo Amaretto di Saschira**
¾	shot(s)	**Double (heavy) cream**
¾	shot(s)	**Milk**

Comment: White Russian with a hint of almond.

BOBBY BURNS #1 UPDATED #8

● ● ● ● ○

Glass: Martini
Garnish: Accompanied by shortbread
Method: STIR all ingredients with ice and strain
into chilled glass.

2	shot(s)	**Johnnie Walker Scotch whisky**
1	shot(s)	**Martini Rosso sweet vermouth**
½	shot(s)	**Bénédictine D.O.M. liqueur**

Comment: Rich and slightly sweet, laced with
spice liqueur and a good dram.
Origin: Named after and commemorating Robert
Burns (1759–1796): poet, balladeer and Scotland's
favourite son. On the 25th January Scots honour the
great man's presumed birthday on what has
become known as Burn's Night with poem readings,
the ritualistic serving of haggis and a dram or two.

BOBBY BURNS #2 NEW #8

● ● ● ◐ ○

Glass: Martini
Garnish: Maraschino cherry in drink
Method: STIR all ingredients with ice and strain
into chilled glass.

2	shot(s)	**Johnnie Walker Scotch whisky**
1	shot(s)	**Martini Rosso sweet vermouth**
⅛	shot(s)	**La Fée Parisienne (68%) absinthe**
1	dash	**Angostura orange bitters**

AKA: Robert Burns
Comment: Scotch and vermouth with added
interest courtesy of absinthe and orange bitters.
Origin: Recipe adapted from Albert Stevens
Crockett's 1931 'The Old Waldorf-Astoria Bar
Book' where the drink is listed as 'Robert Burns'
accompanied by the following notation, "It may
have been named after the celebrated Scotsman.
Chances are, however, that it was christened in
honour of a cigar salesman, who "bought" in the
Old Bar [at the Waldorf-Astoria]."

BOBBY DE NIRO NEW #8

● ● ● ◐ ○

Glass: Martini
Garnish: Dried apricot on rim
Method: STIR jam with gin until jam is dissolved.
Add other ingredients, **SHAKE** with ice and fine
strain into chilled glass.

1	spoon	**Apricot preserve**
2	shot(s)	**Tanqueray London dry gin**
¼	shot(s)	**Bols apricot brandy liqueur**
½	shot(s)	**Freshly squeezed lemon juice**
1	dash	**Angostura orange bitters**

Comment: An apricot flavoured twist on the classic
Casino cocktail.
Origin: Adapted from a drink discovered in 2008 at
Westbourne House, London, England.

BOHEMIAN ICED TEA

Glass: Old-fashioned
Garnish: Lemon zest twist
Method: STIR all ingredients with ice and strain into ice-filled glass.

1½	shot(s)	**Becherovka liqueur**
½	shot(s)	**Ketel One Citroen vodka**
½	shot(s)	**Krupnik honey liqueur**
½	shot(s)	**Peach Tree peach schnapps**
2½	shot(s)	**Chilled earl grey tea**

Origin: Created by Alex Kammerling at Detroit, London, England. Originally stirred in a tea pot and served in tea cups.
Comment: A fruity and refreshing drink with surprising flavours.

BOHEMIAN MULE NEW #8

Glass: Collins
Garnish: Lime wedge
Method: POUR all ingredients into ice-filled glass and lightly stir.

1	shot	**La Fée Parisienne (68%) absinthe**
½	shot(s)	**Freshly squeezed lime juice**
Top up with		**Ginger beer**

Comment: Ginger beer and the length of this drink tame the absinthe within but its presence is most evident.
Origin: Created in 1990s by Giovanni Burdi, London, England.

BOILERMAKER

Glass: Boston & shot
Method: POUR whiskey to brim of shot glass and then manoeuvre shot glass so it is held tight up against the inside base of an upturned Boston glass. Then quickly flip the Boston glass over so that the bourbon is trapped in the now upside-down shot glass. Now pour beer into Boston glass over the whiskey filled shot glass.

1	shot(s)	**Bulleit bourbon whiskey**
1	pint	**Beer** (well chilled)

Origin: Unknown but in his book The Joy of Mixology Gary Regan credits steelworkers in western Pennsylvania.
Comment: When you get to the end of the beer the shot glass lifts and the whiskey is released as a chaser.

BOLERO

Glass: Martini
Garnish: Float apple slice
Method: STIR all ingredients with ice and strain into chilled glass.

1½	shot(s)	**Bacardi Superior rum**
¾	shot(s)	**Boulard Grand Solage calvados**
¼	shot(s)	**Martini Rosso sweet vermouth**

Origin: A classic of unknown origins.
Comment: A dry, challenging drink for modern palates. Be sure to stir well as dilution is key.

BOLERO SOUR

Glass: Old-fashioned
Garnish: Orange & lime zest twists (discarded)
Method: SHAKE all ingredients with ice and strain into ice-filled glass.

1	shot(s)	**Zacapa aged rum**
1	shot(s)	**Courvoisier V.S.O.P. cognac**
½	shot(s)	**Freshly squeezed orange juice**
1	shot(s)	**Freshly squeezed lime juice**
½	shot(s)	**Sugar syrup** (2 sugar to 1 water)
½	fresh	**Egg white**

Origin: Adapted from David A. Embury's 1948 'The Fine Art of Mixing Drinks'.
Comment: A beautifully balanced, flavoursome medley of sweet and sour.

BOLSHOI PUNCH

Glass: Old-fashioned
Method: SHAKE all ingredients with ice and strain into glass filled with crushed ice.

1½	shot(s)	**Wray & Nephew overproof rum**
1	shot(s)	**Crème de cassis liqueur**
¾	shot(s)	**Freshly squeezed lime juice**
½	shot(s)	**Sugar syrup** (2 sugar to 1 water)

Comment: Innocuous-seeming pink classic – richly flavoured and easy to drink.

BOMBAY NO. 2

Glass: Martini
Garnish: Orange zest twist
Method: SHAKE all ingredients with ice and fine strain into chilled glass.

1½	shot(s)	**Courvoisier V.S.O.P. cognac**
¾	shot(s)	**Noilly Prat dry vermouth**
¾	shot(s)	**Martini Rosso sweet vermouth**
¼	shot(s)	**Cointreau triple sec**
⅛	shot(s)	**La Fée Parisienne (68%) absinthe**

Origin: My 2006 adaptation of a recipe from Harry Craddock's 1930 'The Savoy Cocktail Book'.
Comment: A smooth, complex, Sazerac-style Martini.

BOMBER

Glass: Collins
Garnish: Lime wedge
Method: SHAKE first 3 ingredients with ice and strain into ice-filled glass. **TOP** with ginger beer, stir and serve with straws.

1	shot(s)	**Bacardi Superior rum**
1	shot(s)	**Sailor Jerry spiced rum**
1	shot(s)	**Freshly squeezed lime juice**
Top up with		**Ginger beer**

Origin: Created in 1998 by the B. Bar crew at The Reading Festival, England.
Comment: Cross between a Moscow Mule and a Cuba Libre.

BON BON

Glass: Martini
Garnish: Lemon zest twist (or a Bon Bon)
Method: SHAKE all ingredients with ice and fine strain into chilled glass.

1	shot(s)	**Vanilla-infused Ketel One vodka**
½	shot(s)	**Teichenné butterscotch schnapps**
¾	shot(s)	**Luxardo limoncello liqueur**
¾	shot(s)	**Freshly squeezed lemon juice**
¼	shot(s)	**Sugar syrup** (2 sugar to 1 water)
½	shot(s)	**Chilled mineral water** (omit if wet ice)

Origin: Adapted from a drink discovered in 2001 at Lab Bar, London, England.
Comment: Relive your youth and the taste of those big round sweets in this bitter-sweet, lemony cocktail.

BONNIE PRINCE CHARLES

Glass: Martini
Garnish: Lime wedge on rim
Method: SHAKE all ingredients with ice and fine strain into chilled glass.

2¼	shot(s)	**Courvoisier V.S.O.P. cognac**
¾	shot(s)	**Drambuie liqueur**
¾	shot(s)	**Freshly squeezed lime juice**

Origin: Recipe to proportions found in Victor Bergeron's 'Trader Vic's Bartender's Guide' (1972 revised edition).
Comment: Honeyed, spiced cognac with a touch of citrus. But is it fit for a Prince?

BONSONI NEW #8

Glass: Martini
Garnish: Orange zest twist
Method: STIR all ingredients with ice and strain into chilled glass.

2	shot(s)	**Martini Rosso sweet vermouth**
½	shot(s)	**Fernet Branca**
¾	shot(s)	**Chilled mineral water** (omit if wet ice)

Comment: Vermouth tames Fernet but will still only appeal to those with suitably old-school palates.
Origin: Vintage cocktail of unknown origin.

BOOMERANG

Glass: Martini
Garnish: Maraschino cherry
Method: SHAKE all ingredients with ice and fine strain into chilled glass.

1½	shot(s)	**Bulleit bourbon whiskey**
¾	shot(s)	**Noilly Prat dry vermouth**
¾	shot (s)	**Martini Rosso sweet vermouth**
¼	shot(s)	**Luxardo maraschino liqueur**
½	shot(s)	**Freshly squeezed lemon juice**
½	shot(s)	**Sugar syrup** (2 sugar to 1 water)
2	dashes	**Angostura aromatic bitters**

Comment: A very Sweet Manhattan with lemon juice.

BORA BORA BREW (MOCKTAIL)

Glass: Collins
Garnish: Pineapple wedge
Method: SHAKE first 2 ingredients with ice and strain into ice-filled glass.

3	shot(s)	**Pressed pineapple juice**
⅛	shot(s)	**Pomegranate (grenadine) syrup**
Top up with		**Ginger ale**

Comment: Fruity and frothy ginger beer.

BORDERLINE

Glass: Martini
Garnish: Orange twist
Method: SHAKE all ingredients with ice and fine strain into chilled glass.

2	shot(s)	**Bulleit bourbon whiskey**
½	shot(s)	**Maple syrup**
½	shot(s)	**Freshly squeezed lemon juice**
¾	shot(s)	**Punt E Mes**

Origin: Created in 2004 by James Mellor at Mint Leaf, London, England.
Comment: Bourbon sweetened with maple syrup, soured by lemon and made more complex by vermouth.

BOSOM CARESSER

Glass: Martini
Garnish: Orange peel twist (discarded)
Method: SHAKE all ingredients with ice and fine strain into chilled glass.

2	shot(s)	**Courvoisier V.S.O.P. cognac**
½	shot(s)	**Grand Marnier liqueur**
½	shot(s)	**Malmsey Madeira**
¼	shot(s)	**Pomegranate (grenadine) syrup**
1	fresh	**Egg yolk**

Comment: No bosoms to hand? Then caress your throat with this tasty drink.

BOSSA NOVA #1

Glass: Collins
Garnish: Lime slice
Method: SHAKE all ingredients with ice and strain into ice-filled glass.

2	shot(s)	**Bacardi Oro golden rum**
¾	shot(s)	**Galliano L'Autentico liqueur**
¾	shot(s)	**Bols apricot brandy liqueur**
2	shot(s)	**Pressed apple juice**
¾	shot(s)	**Freshly squeezed lime juice**

Origin: Named after the Brazilian dance which in turn comes from the Portuguese 'bossa', meaning 'tendency', and 'nova', meaning 'new'.
Comment: Apple with the added zing of rum, Galliano, apricot and lime juice.

BOSSA NOVA #2

Glass: Collins
Garnish: Pineapple wedge
Method: **SHAKE** all ingredients with ice and strain into ice-filled glass.

2	shot(s)	**Bacardi Oro golden rum**
½	shot(s)	**Galliano L'Autentico liqueur**
½	shot(s)	**Bols apricot brandy liqueur**
2	shot(s)	**Pressed pineapple juice**
½	shot(s)	**Freshly squeezed lemon juice**

Comment: Long and frothy with fruity rum and subtle anis notes. Not too sweet.

BOSTON

Glass: Martini
Garnish: Apricot slice on rim
Method: **SHAKE** all ingredients with ice and fine strain into chilled glass.

1¾	shot(s)	**Tanqueray London dry gin**
1	shot(s)	**Bols apricot brandy liqueur**
1	shot(s)	**Freshly squeezed lemon juice**
¼	shot(s)	**Sugar syrup** (2 sugar to 1 water)
⅛	shot(s)	**Pomegranate (grenadine) syrup**

Comment: Gin laced tangy fruit.

BOSTON FLIP

Glass: Wine goblet
Garnish: Dust with freshly grated nutmeg
Method: **SHAKE** all ingredients with ice and fine strain into chilled glass.

2	shot(s)	**Bulleit bourbon whiskey**
2	shot(s)	**Blandy's Alvada Madeira**
1	fresh	**Egg** (white & yolk)
¼	shot(s)	**Sugar syrup** (2 sugar to 1 water)

Comment: A good dusting of freshly grated nutmeg makes this old school drink.

BOSTON TEA PARTY

Glass: Collins
Garnish: Orange slice
Method: **SHAKE** first ten ingredients with ice and strain into ice-filled glass. **TOP** with Coca-Cola and serve with straws.

½	shot(s)	**Ketel One vodka**
½	shot(s)	**Johnnie Walker Scotch whisky**
½	shot(s)	**Noilly Prat dry vermouth**
½	shot(s)	**Cointreau triple sec**
½	shot(s)	**Pusser's Navy rum**
½	shot(s)	**Tanqueray London dry gin**
½	shot(s)	**Don Julio reposado tequila**
½	shot(s)	**Freshly squeezed orange juice**
1	shot(s)	**Freshly squeezed lime juice**
½	shot(s)	**Sugar syrup** (2 sugar to 1 water)
Top up with		**Coca-Cola**

Origin: Named after the revolt by early US settlers against the imposition of tax by the British Crown, which became the War of Independence.
Comment: Just about every spirit from the speedrail plus a splash of orange, lime and coke.

BOULEVARD

Glass: Martini
Garnish: Twist of orange (discarded) & maraschino cherries
Method: **STIR** all ingredients with ice and strain into chilled glass.

2½	shot(s)	**Bulleit bourbon whiskey**
1	shot(s)	**Noilly Prat dry vermouth**
½	shot(s)	**Grand Marnier liqueur**
2	dashes	**Angostura orange bitters**

Origin: A classic of unknown origins.
Comment: A Manhattan-style cocktail which takes no prisoners.

BOUQUET NEW #8

Glass: Martini
Garnish: Lemon zest twist
Method: **SHAKE** all ingredients with ice and fine strain into chilled glass.

1	spoon	**Runny honey**
2	shot(s)	**Tanqueray London dry gin**
½	shot(s)	**Freshly squeezed lemon juice**
¼	shot(s)	**Rose syrup**
½	shot(s)	**Chilled mineral water**

Comment: Rose delicately flavours gin with a sweet and sour balance provided by honey and lemon.
Origin: Adapted from a drink created in 2005 by Alex Pacumbo at Cocoon, London, England.

BOURBON BLUSH

Glass: Martini
Garnish: Strawberry on rim
Method: **MUDDLE** strawberries in base of shaker. Add other ingredients, **SHAKE** with ice and fine strain into chilled glass.

3	fresh	**Strawberries** (hulled)
2	shot(s)	**Bulleit bourbon whiskey**
¾	shot(s)	**Crème de framboise liqueur**
¼	shot(s)	**Maple syrup**

Origin: Created in 2003 by Simon King at MJU @ Millennium Hotel, London, England.
Comment: Strawberry and maple syrup combine brilliantly with bourbon in this drink.

BOURBON COOKIE

Glass: Old-fashioned
Garnish: Dust with cinnamon powder
Method: **SHAKE** all ingredients with ice and strain into ice-filled glass.

2	shot(s)	**Bulleit bourbon whiskey**
½	shot(s)	**Double (heavy) cream**
½	shot(s)	**Milk**
½	shot(s)	**Boiron mango or passion fruit syrup**
½	shot(s)	**Teichenné butterscotch schnapps**

Origin: Created in 2002 by Andres Masso, London, England.
Comment: Looks tame but packs a flavoursome punch.

BOURBON CRUSTA

Glass: Small wine goblet or flute
Garnish: See 'Crusta' for instructions
Method: SHAKE all ingredients with ice and fine strain into pre-prepared glass.

2	shot(s)	**Bulleit bourbon whiskey**
¼	shot(s)	**Cointreau triple sec**
⅛	shot(s)	**Luxardo maraschino liqueur**
½	shot(s)	**Freshly squeezed lemon juice**
¼	shot(s)	**Sugar syrup** (2 sugar to 1 water)
2	dashes	**Angostura orange bitters**
½	shot(s)	**Chilled mineral water** (omit if wet ice)

Variant: Brandy Crusta
Comment: Beautifully balanced bourbon and fresh lemon.

BOURBON MILK PUNCH

Glass: Martini
Garnish: Dust with freshly grated nutmeg
Method: SHAKE all ingredients with ice and fine strain into chilled glass.

1½	shot(s)	**Bulleit bourbon whiskey**
½	shot(s)	**Galliano L'Autentico liqueur**
1	shot(s)	**Double (heavy) cream**
1	shot(s)	**Milk**
¼	shot(s)	**Sugar syrup** (2 sugar to 1 water)

Comment: The character of bourbon shines through in this creamy number.

BOURBON RENEWAL NEW #8

Glass: Old-fashioned
Garnish: Seasonal berries
Method: SHAKE all ingredients with ice and strain into ice-filled glass.

2	shot(s)	**Bulleit Bourbon whiskey**
1	shot(s)	**Freshly squeezed lemon juice**
½	shot(s)	**Crème de cassis liqueur**
¼	shot(s)	**Sugar syrup** (2 sugar to 1 water)
1	dashes	**Angostura aromatic bitters**

Comment: Fruit supplements rather than dominates Bourbon in this easy long drink.
Origin: Created in 2008 by Jeffrey Morgenthaler at Bel Ami Lounge, Oregon, USA.

BOURBON SMASH

Glass: Collins
Garnish: Lime slice
Method: MUDDLE raspberries in base of shaker. Add other ingredients, **SHAKE** with ice and fine strain into ice-filled glass.

12	fresh	**Raspberries**
4	fresh	**Mint leaves**
2½	shot(s)	**Bulleit bourbon whiskey**
3	shot(s)	**Ocean Spray cranberry juice**
1	shot(s)	**Freshly squeezed lime juice**
½	shot(s)	**Sugar syrup** (2 sugar to 1 water)
2	dashes	**Angostura aromatic bitters**

Comment: This refreshing long drink has a sharp edge that adds to its appeal.

BOURBONELLA

Glass: Martini
Garnish: Stemmed cherry on rim
Method: STIR all ingredients with ice and fine strain into chilled glass.

1¾	shot(s)	**Bulleit bourbon whiskey**
¾	shot(s)	**Noilly Prat dry vermouth**
¾	shot(s)	**Cointreau triple sec**
¼	shot(s)	**Pomegranate (grenadine) syrup**
3	dashes	**Peychaud's aromatic bitters**

Comment: If you like bourbon, you'll love this fruity Manhattan.

BOXCAR NEW #8

Glass: Martini
Garnish: Sugar rim
Method: SHAKE all ingredients with ice and fine strain into chilled glass.

2	shot(s)	**Tanqueray London dry gin**
½	shot(s)	**Cointreau triple sec**
¾	shot(s)	**Freshly squeezed lime juice**
⅛	shot(s)	**Pomegranate (grenadine) syrup**
½	fresh	**Egg white**

Comment: A White Lady in a sugar-rimmed glass with the addition of a dash of grenadine and substituting lemon juice for lime.

BRADFORD

Glass: Martini
Garnish: Olive on stick or lemon zest twist
Method: SHAKE all ingredients with ice and fine strain into chilled glass.

2½	shot(s)	**Tanqueray London dry gin**
½	shot(s)	**Noilly Prat dry vermouth**
3	dashes	**Angostura orange bitters** (optional)

Origin: A Bradford is a Martini which is shaken rather than stirred. Like the Martini itself, the origin of the Bradford is lost in time.
Comment: More approachable than a stirred, traditional Dry Martini and downright soft compared to a Naked Martini.

BRAINSTORM

Glass: Martini
Garnish: Orange zest twist
Method: STIR all ingredients with ice and strain into chilled glass.

1½	shot(s)	**Bulleit bourbon whiskey**
1	shot(s)	**Noilly Prat dry vermouth**
¾	shot(s)	**Bénédictine D.O.M. liqueur**
½	shot(s)	**Chilled mineral water** (omit if wet ice)

Origin: Another long lost classic.
Comment: Spiced and slightly sweetened bourbon.

BRAKE TAG

Glass: Old-fashioned
Garnish: Orange zest twist
Method: SHAKE all ingredients with ice and strain into ice-filled glass.

1½	shot(s)	**Southern Comfort liqueur**
½	shot(s)	**Luxardo Amaretto di Saschira**
1	shot(s)	**Freshly squeezed orange juice**
1	shot(s)	**Ocean Spray cranberry juice**
3	dashes	**Peychaud's aromatic bitters**

Origin: Discovered in 2005 at Café Adelaide's Swizzle Stick Bar, New Orleans, USA.

BRAMBLE UPDATED #8

Glass: Old-fashioned
Garnish: Blackberries & lemon slice
Method: SHAKE first 3 ingredients with ice and strain into glass filled with crushed ice. **DRIZZLE** liqueur over drink to create a 'bleeding' effect in the glass. Serve with short straws.

2	shot(s)	**Tanqueray London dry gin**
1	shot(s)	**Freshly squeezed lemon juice**
½	shot(s)	**Sugar syrup** (2 sugar to 1 water)
½	shot(s)	**Crème de mûre liqueur**

Comment: One of the most enduring and endearing drinks to come out of the 1980s.
Origin: Created in the mid-80s by Dick Bradsell at Fred's Club, Soho, London, England.

BRAMBLETTE

Glass: Martini
Garnish: Orange zest twist
Method: SHAKE all ingredients with ice and fine strain into chilled glass.

2	shot(s)	**Tanqueray London dry gin**
1	shot(s)	**Benoit Serres crème de violette**
¾	shot(s)	**Freshly squeezed lemon juice**
¼	shot(s)	**Sugar syrup** (2 sugar to 1 water)

Comment: A martini style drink with a floral, gin laced palate.

BRANDY ALEXANDER

Glass: Martini
Garnish: Dust with freshly grated nutmeg
Method: SHAKE all ingredients with ice and fine strain into chilled glass.

2	shot(s)	**Courvoisier V.S.O.P. cognac**
½	shot(s)	**Brown crème de cacao liqueur**
½	shot(s)	**White crème de cacao liqueur**
½	shot(s)	**Double (heavy) cream**
½	shot(s)	**Milk**

AKA: The Panama
Origin: Created prior to 1930, this classic blend of brandy and chocolate smoothed with cream is based on the original Alexander which calls for gin as its base.
Comment: This after dinner classic is rich, creamy and spicy.

BRANDY BLAZER

Glass: Snifter & old-fashioned
Garnish: Lemon & orange zest twists
Method: POUR cognac into a warmed glass and rest the bowl of the glass on an old-fashioned glass so it lies on its side supported by the rim. **FLAME** the cognac and carefully move the glass back to an upright position sitting normally on your work surface. **POUR** in hot water (this will extinguish any remaining flame) and sugar. Stir, garnish and serve.

2	shot(s)	**Courvoisier V.S.O.P. cognac**
2	shot(s)	**Hot water**
¼	shot(s)	**Sugar syrup** (2 sugar to 1 water)

Origin: A variation on 'Professor' Jerry Thomas' Blue Blazer which involved theatrically pouring ignited brandy between two mugs. Please don't try this at home, kids.
Comment: One way to warm your winter nights.

THE USSR'S MIG-25 FIGHTER-BOMBER CARRIED HALF A TON OF ALCOHOL FOR BRAKE FLUID. IT WAS NICKNAMED THE 'FLYING RESTAURANT' BY ITS SOVIET CREWS.

BRANDY BUCK

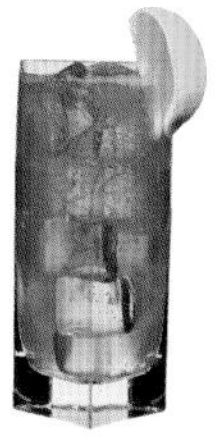

Glass: Collins
Garnish: Lemon wedge
Method: SHAKE first 3 ingredients with ice and strain into ice-filled glass. **TOP** with ginger ale and serve with straws.

2½	shot(s)	**Courvoisier V.S.O.P. cognac**
¼	shot(s)	**Grand Marnier liqueur**
¼	shot(s)	**Freshly squeezed lemon juice**
Top up with		**Ginger ale**

Comment: Lemon juice adds balance to the sweet ginger ale. Cognac provides the backbone.

BRANDY COCKTAIL NEW #8

Glass: Martini
Garnish: Lemon zest twist
Method: SHAKE all ingredients with ice and fine strain into chilled glass.

5	fresh	**Mint leaves**
2	shot(s)	**Courvoisier V.S.O.P. cognac**
¼	shot(s)	**Grand Marnier liqueur**
¼	shot(s)	**Sugar syrup** (2 sugar to 1 water)
1	dash	**Angostura aromatic bitters**

Origin: Vintage cocktail of unknown origin.
Comment: Subtle mint and citrus lightly flavour the cognac.

BRANDY CRUSTA

Glass: Small wine goblet or flute
Garnish: See 'Crusta' for instructions
Method: SHAKE all ingredients with ice and fine strain into pre-prepared glass.

2	shot(s)	**Courvoisier V.S.O.P. cognac**
¼	shot(s)	**Cointreau triple sec**
⅛	shot(s)	**Luxardo maraschino liqueur**
½	shot(s)	**Freshly squeezed lemon juice**
¼	shot(s)	**Sugar syrup** (2 sugar to 1 water)
2	dashes	**Angostura aromatic bitters**
¾	shot(s)	**Chilled mineral water** (reduce if wet ice)

Variant: Bourbon Crusta
Origin: Created in the 1840s-50s by Joseph Santina at Jewel of the South, Gravier Street, New Orleans, USA. The name refers to the crust of sugar around the rim. This recipe is adapted from David A. Embury's 1948 'The Fine Art of Mixing Drinks'.
Comment: This old classic zings with fresh lemon and is beautifully balanced by the cognac base.

> COUNT CAMILLO NEGRONI ASKED FOR AN AMERICANO WITH MORE KICK AT THE CASONI BAR, FLORENCE IN THE 1920s. THE RESULTING DRINK KEPT HIS NAME.

BRANDY DAISY NEW #8

Glass: Martini
Garnish: Mint sprig and cherry
Method: STIR all ingredients with ice and fine strain into chilled glass.

1½	shot(s)	**Courvoisier V.S.O.P. cognac**
½	shot(s)	**Yellow Chartreuse liqueur**
½	shot(s)	**Freshly squeezed lemon juice**
1	dash	**Angostura aromatic bitters**
½	shot(s)	**Chilled mineral water** (omit if wet ice)

Comment: Dry, and to be honest, a tad flat. A vintage cocktail for vintage palates.
Origin: Vintage cocktail of unknown origin.

BRANDY FIX

Glass: Old-fashioned
Garnish: Lemon zest twist
Method: SHAKE all ingredients with ice and strain into ice-filled glass.

2	shot(s)	**Courvoisier V.S.O.P. cognac**
½	shot(s)	**Pressed pineapple juice**
½	shot(s)	**Freshly squeezed lemon juice**
¼	shot(s)	**Sugar syrup** (2 sugar to 1 water)
⅛	shot(s)	**Yellow Chartreuse liqueur**

Comment: This wonderful classic is on the tart side of well balanced.

BRANDY FIZZ

Glass: Collins (8oz max)
Garnish: Lemon slice
Method: SHAKE first 3 ingredients with ice and fine strain into chilled glass (without ice). **TOP** with soda.

2	shot(s)	**Courvoisier V.S.O.P. cognac**
½	shot(s)	**Freshly squeezed lemon juice**
¼	shot(s)	**Sugar syrup** (2 sugar to 1 water)
Top up with		**Soda water** (from siphon)

Comment: A refreshing and tasty dry drink: cognac and lemon balanced with a little sugar and lengthened with soda.

BRANDY FLIP

Glass: Wine goblet or Martini
Garnish: Dust with freshly ground nutmeg
Method: SHAKE all ingredients with ice and fine strain into chilled glass.

1½	shot(s)	**Courvoisier V.S.O.P. cognac**
¼	shot(s)	**Sugar syrup** (2 sugar to 1 water)
¼	shot(s)	**Double (heavy) cream**
1	fresh	**Egg** (white & yolk)

Origin: A forgotten classic.
Comment: A serious alternative to advocaat for those without raw egg inhibitions.

BRANDY MILK PUNCH

Glass: Collins
Garnish: Dust with freshly grated nutmeg
Method: SHAKE all ingredients with ice and strain into glass filled with crushed ice.

2	shot(s)	**Courvoisier V.S.O.P. cognac**
3	shot(s)	**Milk**
1	shot(s)	**Double (heavy) cream**
¼	shot(s)	**Sugar syrup** (2 sugar to 1 water)
⅛	shot(s)	**Vanilla extract**

Origin: A New Orleans variant of the drink that enjoyed nationwide popularity during Prohibition.
Comment: This traditional New Orleans hangover cure beats your bog-standard vanilla milkshake.

BRANDY SMASH

Glass: Old-fashioned
Garnish: Mint sprig
Method: Lightly **MUDDLE** mint in base of shaker just enough to bruise. Add other ingredients, **SHAKE** with ice and fine strain into ice-filled glass.

7	fresh	**Mint leaves**
2	shot(s)	**Courvoisier V.S.O.P. cognac**
¼	shot(s)	**Sugar syrup** (2 sugar to 1 water)

Origin: A classic from the 1850s.
Comment: Sweetened cognac flavoured with mint. Simple but beautiful.

BRANDY CRUSTA

BRANDY SOUR

A
B
C
D
E
F
G
H
I
J
K
L
M
N
O
P
Q
R
S
T
U
V
W
X
Y
Z

BRANDY SOUR

Glass: Old-fashioned
Garnish: Lemon slice & cherry on stick (sail)
Method: SHAKE all ingredients with ice and strain into ice-filled glass.

2	shot(s)	**Courvoisier V.S.O.P. cognac**
1	shot(s)	**Freshly squeezed lemon juice**
½	shot(s)	**Sugar syrup** (2 sugar to 1 water)
½	fresh	**Egg white**
3	dashes	**Angostura aromatic bitters**

Comment: After the Whiskey Sour, this is the most requested sour. Try it and you'll see why – but don't omit the egg white.

BRASS MONKEY

Glass: Collins
Garnish: Lemon slice
Method: SHAKE all ingredients with ice and strain into ice-filled glass.

1	shot(s)	**Bacardi Superior rum**
1	shot(s)	**Ketel One Citroen vodka**
2½	shot(s)	**Freshly squeezed lemon juice**
1	shot(s)	**Sugar syrup** (2 sugar to 1 water)

Comment: Tangy, alcoholic, almost sherbety lemonade. Packed with Vitamin C.

BRASS RAIL

Glass: Martini
Garnish: Cape gooseberry
Method: SHAKE all ingredients with ice and fine strain into chilled glass.

1½	shot(s)	**Zacapa aged rum**
½	shot(s)	**Bénédictine D.O.M. liqueur**
½	shot(s)	**Freshly squeezed lemon juice**
½	shot(s)	**Sugar syrup** (2 sugar to 1 water)
½	fresh	**Egg white**
2	dashes	**Angostura orange bitters**
½	shot(s)	**Chilled mineral water** (omit if wet ice)

Origin: Adapted from a recipe by Tony Abou Ganim. He was apparently inspired by his cousin Helen's penchant for a nightcap after a special occasion; her favourite was Bénédictine.
Comment: Rather like a Daiquiri, yet subtly sweetened and spiced.

BRAZEN MARTINI

Glass: Martini
Garnish: Frozen blueberries & orange zest twist
Method: STIR all ingredients with ice and strain into chilled glass.

2½	shot(s)	**Zubrówka bison vodka**
¼	shot(s)	**Parfait Amour liqueur**

Comment: Not for the faint hearted – a great combination of strawy bison vodka with violet Parfait Amour.

BRAZILIAN BERRY

Glass: Old-fashioned
Garnish: Mint sprig
Method: MUDDLE fruit in base of shaker. Add other ingredients, SHAKE with ice and fine strain into glass filled with crushed ice. Serve with straws.

4	fresh	**Blackcurrants**
3	fresh	**Raspberries**
1½	shot(s)	**Sauvignon Blanc wine**
1	shot(s)	**Leblon cachaça**
1	shot(s)	**Crème de cassis liqueur**

Origin: Created in 2002 by Dan Spink at Browns, St Martin's Lane, London, England.
Comment: This drink combines wine, cachaça and rich berry fruits.

BRAZILIAN COFFEE

Glass: Toddy
Garnish: Float 3 coffee beans
Method: BLEND ingredients with 6oz scoop of crushed ice. Pour into glass and serve with straws.

1	shot(s)	**Leblon cachaça**
1	shot(s)	**Double (heavy) cream**
¾	shot(s)	**Sugar syrup** (2 sugar to 1 water)
2	shot(s)	**Espresso coffee**

Comment: Strong coffee and plenty of sugar are essential in this Brazilian number.

BRAZILIAN COSMOPOLITAN

Glass: Martini
Garnish: Orange zest twist
Method: SHAKE all ingredients with ice and fine strain into chilled glass.

1	shot(s)	**Leblon cachaça**
1	shot(s)	**Cointreau triple sec**
1½	shot(s)	**Ocean Spray cranberry juice**
½	shot(s)	**Freshly squeezed lime juice**

Comment: The distinctive character of cachaça bursts through the fruit in this twist on the contemporary classic.

BRAZILIAN MONK

Glass: Hurricane
Garnish: Cadbury's Flake in drink
Method: BLEND ingredients with two 12oz scoops of crushed ice. Pour into glass and serve with straws.

1	shot(s)	**Frangelico hazelnut liqueur**
1	shot(s)	**Kahlúa coffee liqueur**
1	shot(s)	**Brown crème de cacao liqueur**
3	scoops	**Häagen Dazs vanilla ice cream**

Comment: Nutty and rich dessert in a glass.

BREAKFAST AT TERRELL'S

Glass: Flute
Garnish: Kumquat half
Method: SHAKE first 4 ingredients with ice and strain into chilled glass. **TOP** with champagne.

¾	shot(s)	**Mandarine Napoléon liqueur**
¾	shot(s)	**Freshly squeezed orange juice**
¾	shot(s)	**Double (heavy) cream**
⅛	shot(s)	**Sugar syrup** (2 sugar to 1 water)
Top up with		**Perrier Jouet brut champagne**

Origin: Created by Jamie Terrell for Philip Holzberg at Vinexpo, Bordeaux, France, 1999.
Comment: This creamy orange champagne cocktail is almost as smooth as a Sgroppino.

BREAKFAST CLUB NEW #8

Glass: Martini
Garnish: Lemon zest twist
Method: STIR honey and marmalade with rum until dissolved. Add tea, **SHAKE** with ice and fine strain into chilled glass.

1	spoon	**Orange marmalade**
1	spoon	**Runny honey**
2	shot(s)	**Bacardi Superior rum**
1	shot(s)	**Cold lapsang souchong tea**

Comment: Slightly smoky with incredible depth of flavour. A perfectly balanced delight.
Origin: Recipe discovered in 2008 courtesy of DrinkBoy.com.

BREAKFAST MARTINI UPDATED #8

Glass: Martini
Garnish: Orange zest twist, slice of toast on rim
Method: STIR marmalade with gin in base of shaker until it dissolves. Add other ingredients, **SHAKE** with ice and fine strain into chilled glass.

1	spoon	**Orange marmalade**
2	shot(s)	**Tanqueray London dry gin**
½	shot(s)	**Cointreau triple sec**
½	shot(s)	**Freshly squeezed lemon juice**

Comment: The success or failure of this tangy drink is partly reliant on the quality of marmalade used.
Origin: Created in the late 1990s by Salvatore Calabrese at the Library Bar, London, England. It is very similar to the 'Marmalade Cocktail' created in the 1920s by Harry Craddock and published in his 1930 'The Savoy Cocktail Book' or you could describe this as being White Lady with marmalade in it.

Salvatore came up with the idea for this drink after his wife insisted he have breakfast one morning and served up toast and marmalade. He took the jar to work with him and this contemporary classic was the result. This drink was the inspiration for the many variations on the preserve (jam/marmalade) theme that have followed in the decade since Salvatore stopped for 'proper' breakfast rather than just his usual swift espresso.

BRIGHTON PUNCH

Glass: Collins
Garnish: Pineapple wedge & cherry
Method: SHAKE all ingredients with ice and strain into ice-filled glass.

1½	shot(s)	**Courvoisier V.S.O.P. cognac**
1½	shot(s)	**Bulleit bourbon whiskey**
1½	shot(s)	**Bénédictine D.O.M. liqueur**
2½	shot(s)	**Pressed pineapple juice**
2	shot(s)	**Freshly squeezed lemon juice**

Variant: With orange juice in place of pineapple juice.
Origin: Popular in the bars of Berlin, Germany.
Comment: Don't bother trying the version with orange juice but do try halving the quantities and serving up. Served long or short this is beautifully balanced.

THE BROADMOOR

Glass: Martini
Garnish: Flamed orange zest twist
Method: SHAKE all ingredients with ice and fine strain into chilled glass.

2	shot(s)	**Johnnie Walker Scotch whisky**
½	shot(s)	**Green Chartreuse liqueur**
½	shot(s)	**Sugar syrup** (2 sugar to 1 water)
4	dashes	**Angostura orange bitters**

Origin: Created in 2001 by Swedish bartender Andreas Norén at The Player, London, and popularised at Milk & Honey, London, England. Named after the infamous British mental institution.
Comment: Beautifully simple and seriously complex.

> 'OH NO, DARLING, YOU DIDN'T LISTEN. JULIAN SAID SHE'D GIVEN UP GIN - FOR BRANDY. SHE SAYS SHE CAN DRINK MORE BRANDY.'
> JOHN PAXTON

BROKEN SPUR NEW #8

Glass: Martini
Garnish: Freshly grated nutmeg dust
Method: SHAKE all ingredients with ice and fine strain into chilled glass.

3	shot(s)	**Taylor's Chip dry white port**
¼	shot(s)	**Tanqueray London dry gin**
¼	shot(s)	**Martini Rosso sweet vermouth**
⅛	shot(s)	**Marie Brizard anisette liqueur**
1	fresh	**Egg yolk**

Comment: Smooth rather than creamy and only lightly alcoholic. Perhaps one after a boozy dinner?
Origin: Vintage cocktail of unknown origin.

●●●●○

BRONX NO.1 #1 (ORIGINAL) UPDATED #8

Glass: Martini
Garnish: Maraschino cherry
Method: SHAKE all ingredients with ice and fine strain into chilled glass.

1½	shot(s)	**Tanqueray London dry gin**
¾	shot(s)	**Noilly Prat dry vermouth**
¾	shot(s)	**Martini Rosso sweet vermouth**
1	shot(s)	**Freshly squeezed orange juice**

Variants: 1/ Bloody Bronx – made with the juice of a blood orange. 2/ Golden Bronx – with the addition of an egg yolk. 3/ Silver Bronx - with the addition of egg white. 4/ Income Tax Cocktail – with two dashes Angostura bitters. Also see the Abbey Martini and Satan's Whiskers.
Comment: A serious, dry, complex cocktail – less bitter than many of its era, but still quite challenging to modern palates.
Origin: Created in 1906 by Johnny Solon, a bartender at New York's Waldorf-Astoria Hotel (the Empire State Building occupies the site today), and named after the newly opened Bronx Zoo. Reputedly the first cocktail to use fruit juice. The original recipe called for 2 shots gin, ¼ shot dry vermouth, ¼ shot sweet vermouth and 1 shot orange juice.

●●●●○

BRONZE ADONIS NEW #8

Glass: Martini
Garnish: Lemon spiral
Method: STIR all ingredients with ice and strain into a chilled glass.

1½	shot(s)	**Tio Pepe fino sherry**
1½	shot(s)	**Noilly Ambre vermouth**
½	shot(s)	**Manzanilla sherry**
2	dashes	**Angostura orange bitters**

Comment: A simple yet fabulous twist on the Adonis.
Origin: Created in 2008 by Julian de Feral at Bureau, London, England.

●●●●○

BROOKLYN #1

Glass: Martini
Garnish: Maraschino cherry
Method: STIR all ingredients with ice and strain into chilled glass.

2½	shot(s)	**Bulleit bourbon whiskey**
½	shot(s)	**Noilly Prat dry vermouth**
½	shot(s)	**Martini Rosso sweet vermouth**
¼	shot(s)	**Luxardo maraschino liqueur**
3	dashes	**Angostura aromatic bitters**

Origin: Though to have originated at the St George Hotel, Brooklyn, New York City, USA.
Comment: A Perfect Manhattan with maraschino liqueur.

●●●●○

BROOKLYN #2

Glass: Martini
Garnish: Maraschino cherry
Method: STIR all ingredients with ice and strain into chilled glass.

2	shot(s)	**Bulleit bourbon whiskey**
¾	shot(s)	**Noilly Prat dry vermouth**
½	shot(s)	**Luxardo Amaretto di Saschira**

Comment: A simple, very approachable Manhattan.

●●●●○

BRUBAKER OLD-FASHIONED

Glass: Old-fashioned
Garnish: Two lemon zest twists
Method: STIR malt extract in glass with Scotch until malt extract dissolves. Add ice and one shot of Scotch and stir. Add remaining Scotch, sugar and Angostura and stir some more. Add more ice and keep stirring so that ice dilutes the drink.

2	spoons	**Malt Extract**
2	shot(s)	**Johnnie Walker Scotch whisky**
¼	shot(s)	**Sugar syrup** (2 sugar to 1 water)
3	dashes	**Angostura aromatic bitters**

Origin: Created in 2003 by Shelim Islam at the GE Club, London, England. Shelim named this drink after a horse in the sports section of a paper (also a film made in the seventies starring Robert Redford).
Comment: If you like Scotch you should try this extra malty dram. After all that stirring you'll deserve one.

●●●●◐

BRUNSWICK NEW #8

Glass: Old-fashioned
Garnish: Orange slice & cherry on stick (sail)
Method: SHAKE first 3 ingredients with ice and fine strain into ice-filled glass. FLOAT claret on drink.

2	shot(s)	**Rye whiskey (or bourbon)**
¾	shot(s)	**Freshly squeezed lemon juice**
½	shot(s)	**Sugar syrup** (2 sugar to 1 water)
¾	shot(s)	**Claret red wine**

Comment: Has the good looks and also the flavour profile to back them up.
Origin: Recipe adapted from the 1935 'The Old Waldorf-Astoria Bar Book' in which Albert S. Crocket writes of this drink, "Invented at the Old Hotel Brunswick, once a resort for Fashion, and situated on the north side of Madison Square."

●●●○○

BUBBLEGUM SHOT

Glass: Shot
Method: SHAKE all ingredients with ice and fine strain into chilled glass.

½	shot(s)	**Midori green melon liqueur**
½	shot(s)	**Luxardo Amaretto di Saschira**
¼	shot(s)	**Double (heavy) cream**

Comment: As the name suggests, this tastes a little like bubble gum.

THE BUCK

Glass: Collins
Garnish: Lemon wedge
Method: POUR first 2 ingredients into ice-filled glass and **TOP** with ginger ale. Stir and serve with straws.

2½	shot(s)	**Tanqueray London dry gin**
½	shot(s)	**Freshly squeezed lemon juice**
Top up with		**Ginger ale**

Variant: The recipe above is for a Gin Buck, but this drink can also be based on brandy, calvados, rum, whiskey, vodka etc.
Comment: The Buck can be improved by adding a dash of liqueur appropriate to the spirit base. E.g. add a dash of Grand Marnier to a Brandy Buck.

BUCK'S FIZZ

Glass: Flute
Method: POUR ingredients into chilled glass and gently stir.

2	shot(s)	**Freshly squeezed orange juice**
Top up with		**Perrier Jouet brut champagne**

AKA: Mimosa
Origin: Created in 1921 by Mr McGarry, first bartender at the Buck's Club, London.
Comment: Not really a cocktail and not that challenging, but great for brunch.

BUENA VIDA

Glass: Old-fashioned
Garnish: Pineapple wedge on rim
Method: SHAKE all ingredients with ice and strain into glass filled with crushed ice.

2	shot(s)	**Don Julio reposado tequila**
1¾	shot(s)	**Freshly squeezed grapefruit juice**
¾	shot(s)	**Pressed pineapple juice**
½	shot(s)	**Vanilla sugar syrup**
3	dashes	**Angostura aromatic bitters**

Comment: The fruits combine brilliantly with the tequila and spice comes courtesy of Angostura.

BULLDOG

Glass: Collins
Method: SHAKE first 4 ingredients with ice and strain into ice-filled glass. **TOP** with Coca-Cola, stir and serve with straws.

1	shot(s)	**Bacardi Superior rum**
1	shot(s)	**Kahlúa coffee liqueur**
1½	shot(s)	**Double (heavy) cream**
1½	shot(s)	**Milk**
Top up with		**Coca-Cola**

Comment: Surprisingly nice – Coca-Cola cuts through the cream.

BULLFROG #1

Glass: Old-fashioned
Garnish: Maraschino cherry
Method: SHAKE all ingredients with ice and strain into glass filled with crushed ice.

1½	shot(s)	**Ketel One vodka**
¾	shot(s)	**Giffard Menthe Pastille liqueur**
1	shot(s)	**Double (heavy) cream**
1	shot(s)	**Milk**

Comment: Mint ice cream.

BULLFROG #2 NEW #8

Glass: Collins
Garnish: Lime wedge
Method: POUR vodka and lime into ice-filled glass and **TOP** with lemonade.

2	shot(s)	**Ketel One vodka**
½	shot(s)	**Freshly squeezed lime juice**
Top up with		**Lemonade/Sprite/7-Up**

Comment: Long, dry and fresh.

BULL SHOT NEW #8

Glass: Collins
Garnish: Celery Salt
Method: SHAKE all ingredients with ice and strain into ice-filled glass.

2	shot(s)	**Ketel One vodka**
4	shot(s)	**Cold beef bouillon**
½	shot(s)	**Fresh lemon juice**
3	dashes	**Lea & Perrins Worcestershire sauce**
3	dashes	**Tabasco pepper sauce**
1	pinch	**Salt**
1	grind	**Black pepper**

Comment: Cow broth replaces tomato in this Mary for carnivorous drinkers.

BULL'S BLOOD

Glass: Martini
Garnish: Orange zest twist
Method: SHAKE all ingredients with ice and fine strain into chilled glass.

½	shot(s)	**Bacardi Superior rum**
1	shot(s)	**Courvoisier V.S.O.P. cognac**
1	shot(s)	**Grand Marnier liqueur**
1½	shot(s)	**Freshly squeezed orange juice**

Comment: This beautifully balanced fruity cocktail has a dry finish.

BULL'S MILK

Glass: Collins
Method: SHAKE all ingredients with ice and strain into ice-filled glass.

1	shot(s)	**Gosling's Black Seal rum**
1½	shot(s)	**Courvoisier V.S.O.P. cognac**
4	shot(s)	**Milk**
½	shot(s)	**Maple syrup**

Comment: Dark spirits tamed by thick maple syrup and milk.

BULLDOG HIGHBALL NEW #8

Glass: Collins
Garnish: Orange slice
Method: SHAKE first 2 ingredients with ice and strain into ice-filled glass. **TOP** with ginger ale and lightly stir. Serve with straws.

2	shot(s)	**Tanqueray London dry gin**
1½	shot(s)	**Freshly squeezed orange juice**
Top up with		**Ginger ale**

Comment: Light and easy drinking. Gin and orange lightly spiced with ginger.

BUMBLE BEE

Glass: Shot
Method: Refrigerate ingredients then **LAYER** in chilled glass by carefully pouring in the following order.

½	shot(s)	**Kahlúa coffee liqueur**
½	shot(s)	**Luxardo Sambuca dei Cesari**
½	shot(s)	**Baileys Irish cream liqueur**

Comment: A B-52 with a liquorice kick.

BUONA SERA SHOT

Glass: Shot
Method: SHAKE all ingredients with ice and fine strain into chilled glass.

½	shot(s)	**Kahlúa coffee liqueur**
½	shot(s)	**Luxardo Amaretto di Saschira**
½	shot(s)	**Vanilla-infused Bacardi rum**

Comment: As sweet shots go, this is one of my favourites.

BURNING BUSH SHOT

Glass: Shot
Method: POUR ingredients into chilled glass.

1	shot(s)	**Don Julio reposado tequila**
6	drops	**Tabasco pepper sauce**

AKA: Prairie Dog, Prairie Fire
Comment: Hold onto your bowels!

BURNT TOASTED ALMOND

Glass: Martini
Garnish: Dust with freshly grated nutmeg
Method: SHAKE all ingredients with ice and fine strain into chilled glass.

1	shot(s)	**Ketel One vodka**
½	shot(s)	**Baileys Irish cream liqueur**
½	shot(s)	**Kahlúa coffee liqueur**
1	shot(s)	**Luxardo Amaretto di Saschira**
1	shot(s)	**Double (heavy) cream**
1	shot(s)	**Milk**

Variant: Toasted Almond
Comment: There's more than just almond to this sweety.

BUTTERFLY COCKTAIL NEW #8

Glass: Martini
Garnish: Lemon zest twist
Method: MUDDLE grapes in base of shaker. Add other ingredients and fine strain into chilled glass.

8	fresh	**Seedless white grapes**
3	fresh	**Basil leaves**
3	fresh	**Mint leaves**
1½	shot(s)	**Ketel One Citroen vodka**
¼	shot(s)	**St-Germain elderflower liqueur**
¼	shot(s)	**Freshly squeezed lemon juice**

Comment: Light and refreshing but with citrus complexity.
Origin: Created by Alex Kammerling, London, England.

BUTTERFLY'S KISS

Glass: Martini
Garnish: Cinnamon stick
Method: STIR all ingredients with ice and strain into chilled glass.

2	shot(s)	**Vanilla-infused Ketel One vodka**
1	shot(s)	**Frangelico hazelnut liqueur**
½	shot(s)	**Goldschläger cinnamon schnapps**
½	shot(s)	**Sugar syrup** (2 sugar to 1 water)
½	shot(s)	**Chilled mineral water** (omit if wet ice)

Origin: Adapted from a drink I discovered in 2003 at Bar Marmont, Los Angeles, USA.
Comment: Golden coloured Martini style drink complete with the odd gold flake and a hazelnut cinnamon twang.

BUTTERSCOTCH DAIQUIRI

Glass: Martini
Garnish: Butterscotch sweet in drink
Method: SHAKE all ingredients with ice and fine strain into chilled glass.

2	shot(s)	**Bacardi Superior rum**
1	shot(s)	**Teichenné butterscotch schnapps**
½	shot(s)	**Freshly squeezed lime juice**
½	shot(s)	**Chilled mineral water** (omit if wet ice)

Comment: A candified Daiquiri.

A
B
C
D
E
F
G
H
I
J
K
L
M
N
O
P
Q
R
S
T
U
V
W
X
Y
Z

BUTTERSCOTCH DELIGHT

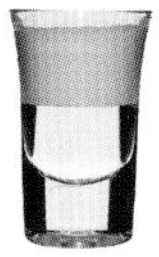

Glass: Shot
Method: Refrigerate ingredients then **LAYER** in chilled glass by carefully pouring in the following order.

| ¾ | shot(s) | Teichenné butterscotch schnapps |
| ¾ | shot(s) | Baileys Irish cream liqueur |

Origin: The origin of this drink is unknown but it is very popular in the bars in and around Seattle, USA.
Comment: Sweet connotations!

BUTTERSCOTCH MARTINI

Glass: Martini
Garnish: Butterscotch sweet
Method: **SHAKE** all ingredients with ice and fine strain into chilled glass.

2	shot(s)	Bacardi Oro golden rum
¾	shot(s)	Teichenné butterscotch schnapps
¾	shot(s)	White crème de cacao liqueur
⅛	shot(s)	Sugar syrup (2 sugar to 1 water)
½	shot(s)	Chilled mineral water (omit if wet ice)

Comment: Sweet and suckable.

BYCULLA NEW #8

Glass: Martini
Garnish: Slice ginger root on rim
Method: **SHAKE** all ingredients with ice and fine strain into chilled glass.

1	shot(s)	Tio Pepe fino sherry
1	shot(s)	Warre's Otima tawny port
½	shot(s)	Grand Marnier liqueur
½	shot(s)	Domaine de Canton ginger liqueur
½	shot(s)	Chilled mineral water (omit if wet ice)

Comment: Claret-come-mulled wine, but hold out for the warming ginger finish.
Origin: An adaptation of a vintage cocktail recipe of unknown origin. Believed to be named after a neighbourhood in South Mumbai, India.

BUZZARD'S BREATH

Glass: Hurricane
Garnish: Pineapple wedge on rim
Method: **BLEND** ingredients with 12oz scoop of crushed ice. Pour into glass and serve with straws.

2½	shot(s)	Leblon cachaça
1	shot(s)	Coco López cream of coconut
2	shot(s)	Pressed pineapple juice
¼	shot(s)	Double (heavy) cream

Comment: A Piña Colada made with cachaça.

BYZANTINE

Glass: Collins
Garnish: Basil leaf
Method: **MUDDLE** basil in base of shaker. Add other ingredients apart from tonic water, **SHAKE** with ice and strain into ice-filled glass. **TOP** with tonic water.

6	fresh	Basil leaves
1½	shot(s)	Tanqueray London dry gin
½	shot(s)	Passion fruit sugar syrup
2	shot(s)	Pressed pineapple juice
½	shot(s)	Lime & lemongrass cordial
Top up with		Tonic water

Origin: Created in 2001 by Douglas Ankrah for Akbar, Soho, London, England.
Comment: This fruity, herbal drink is even better made the way Douglas originally intended, with basil infused gin instead of muddled leaves.

THE C&C NEW #8

Glass: Shot
Garnish: None
Method: **LAYER** by carefully pouring ingredients in the following order.

| ¾ | shot(s) | Cointreau triple sec |
| ¾ | shot(s) | Courvoisier V.S.O.P. cognac |

Comment: The initial heat of brandy is chased and extinguished by sweet orange liqueur.

C C KAZI

Glass: Martini
Garnish: Lime wedge on rim
Method: **SHAKE** all ingredients with ice and fine strain into chilled glass.

1¾	shot(s)	Don Julio reposado tequila
1¾	shot(s)	Ocean Spray cranberry juice
½	shot(s)	Freshly squeezed lime juice
¼	shot(s)	Sugar syrup (2 sugar to 1 water)

Comment: A Rude Cosmo without the liqueur.

CABLE CAR

Glass: Martini
Garnish: Half cinnamon & sugar rim
Method: **SHAKE** all ingredients with ice and fine strain into chilled glass.

2	shot(s)	Sailor Jerry spiced rum
1	shot(s)	Cointreau triple sec
½	shot(s)	Freshly squeezed lemon juice
¼	shot(s)	Sugar syrup (2 sugar to 1 water)
½	fresh	Egg white

Origin: Created in 1996 by Cory Reistad at the Starlight Room, atop San Francisco's Sir Francis Drake Hotel. The Nob Hill cable cars pass by the bar, hence its catchphrase 'Between the stars and the cable cars'.
Comment: Vanilla and spice from the rum interact with the orange liqueur in this balanced, Daiquiri style drink.

CACHAÇA DAIQUIRI

Glass: Martini
Garnish: Lime wedge on rim
Method: **SHAKE** all ingredients with ice and fine strain into chilled glass.

2	shot(s)	**Leblon cachaça**
½	shot(s)	**Freshly squeezed lime juice**
¼	shot(s)	**Sugar syrup** (2 sugar to 1 water)
½	shot(s)	**Chilled mineral water** (omit if wet ice)

Comment: Might be in a Martini glass but it tastes like a Caipirinha.

CACTUS BANGER

Glass: Martini
Garnish: Lime wedge on rim
Method: **SHAKE** all ingredients with ice and fine strain into chilled glass.

1	shot(s)	**Don Julio reposado tequila**
1	shot(s)	**Grand Marnier liqueur**
2	shot(s)	**Freshly squeezed orange juice**
½	shot(s)	**Freshly squeezed lime juice**

Comment: A golden, sunny looking and sunny tasting drink.

CACTUS JACK

Glass: Martini
Garnish: Pineapple leaf
Method: **SHAKE** all ingredients with ice and fine strain into chilled glass.

1	shot(s)	**Don Julio reposado tequila**
¾	shot(s)	**Bols blue curaçao liqueur**
1¼	shot(s)	**Freshly squeezed orange juice**
1	shot(s)	**Pressed pineapple juice**
½	shot(s)	**Freshly squeezed lemon juice**

Comment: Vivid in colour, this orange led, tequila based drink has a balanced sweet and sourness.

CAFÉ GATES

Glass: Toddy
Garnish: Float 3 coffee beans
Method: Place bar spoon in glass, **POUR** first 3 ingredients and top up with coffee, then **FLOAT** cream by pouring over the back of a spoon.

¾	shot(s)	**Grand Marnier liqueur**
¾	shot(s)	**Kahlúa coffee liqueur**
¾	shot(s)	**Brown crème de cacao liqueur**
Top up with		**Hot filter coffee**
¾	shot(s)	**Double (heavy) cream**

Comment: Chocolate orange with coffee and cream.

CAIPI NEW #8

Glass: Old-fashioned
Garnish: None
Method: **MUDDLE** lime in base of shaker. Add rest of ingredients, **SHAKE** with 6oz scoop of crushed ice and pour without straining into glass.

¾	fresh	**Lime cut into wedges**
2	shot(s)	**Campari Bitter**
½	shot(s)	**Sugar syrup** (2 sugar to 1 water)

Comment: Bittersweet Campari and lime.

CAIPIGINGER

Glass: Old-fashioned
Garnish: Lime zest twist (discarded) & lime wedge
Method: **MUDDLE** ginger in base of shaker. Add other ingredients, **SHAKE** with ice and strain into glass filled with crushed ice. Serve with straws.

2	slices	**Fresh root ginger** (thumbnail sized)
2	shot(s)	**Leblon cachaça**
1	shot(s)	**Freshly squeezed lime juice**
¾	shot(s)	**Sugar syrup** (2 sugar to 1 water)

Comment: A ginger spiced take on the Caipirinha.

CAIPIRINHA #1 (BRAZILIAN SERVE) UPDATED #8

Glass: Old-fashioned
Method: **MUDDLE** lime in the base of a robust glass to release the juices and oils in its skin. Pour cachaça and sugar into glass, add ice and **STIR**. Serve with straws.

¾	fresh	**Lime cut into wedges**
2	shot(s)	**Leblon cachaça**
½	shot(s)	**Sugar syrup** (2 sugar to 1 water)

Comment: You are probably used to this drink being served with crushed ice but until you have tried it with cubed ice you have not really tried a Caipirinha.
Origin: Pronounced 'Kie-Pur-Reen-Yah', the name of this traditional Brazilian cocktail literally translates as 'little countryside drink'. It is made by muddling green lemons known as 'limon subtil', which are native to Brazil (limes are the best substitute when these are not available), and mixing with sugar and cachaça. Be sure to muddle in a sturdy, non-breakable glass.

In Britain and other 'new' cachaça markets it is common practice to serve this drink with crushed ice but in Brazil it is usually served with cubed ice. Capirinhas and variations on the theme are staples in cachaçerias, traditional Brazilian bars which specialise in cachaça.

DRINKS ARE GRADED AS FOLLOWS:

● DISGUSTING   ●● PRETTY AWFUL   ●● BEST AVOIDED
●●◐ DISAPPOINTING   ●●● ACCEPTABLE   ●●●◐ GOOD
●●●● RECOMMENDED   ●●●●● HIGHLY RECOMMENDED
●●●●● OUTSTANDING / EXCEPTIONAL

CAIPIRINHA #2 (CONTEMPORARY SERVE) NEW #8

Glass: Old-fashioned
Garnish: Serve with 2 short straws
Method: **MUDDLE** lime wedges in the base of shaker to release juice and oils in its skin. Add cachaça and sugar. **SHAKE** with 6oz scoop crushed ice and pour all without straining into glass.

¾	fresh	**Lime cut into wedges**
2	shot(s)	**Leblon cachaça**
½	shot(s)	**Sugar syrup** (2 sugar to 1 water)

Comment: There is much debate among bartenders as to whether granulated sugar or sugar syrup and if brown or white sugar should be used when making this drink. Those who favour granulated sugar argue that muddling with the abrasive crystals helps extract the oils from the lime's skin. Personally, I hate the crunch of sugar as inevitably not all the granulated sugar dissolves. Whether you should use brown or white sugar to make your syrup is another question. I prefer mine made the way it is in its native Brazil, with white sugar.
Origin: In its native Brazil it is usual to serve this drink with cubed ice but the drink travelled to the UK at a time when the use of crushed ice was fashionable and so in this and other 'new' cachaça markets use of crushed ice has become the norm.

CAIPIRISSIMA  UPDATED #8

Glass: Old-fashioned
Garnish: Serve with 2 short straws
Method: **MUDDLE** lime wedges in the base of shaker to release juice and oils in its skin. Add rum and sugar. **SHAKE** with 6oz scoop crushed ice and pour all without straining into glass.

¾	fresh	**Lime cut into wedges**
2	shot(s)	**Bacardi Superior rum**
½	shot(s)	**Sugar syrup** (2 sugar to 1 water)

Comment: A Daiquiri-like drink made in the style of a Caipirinha.

CAIPIROVSKA UPDATED #8

Glass: Old-fashioned
Garnish: Serve with 2 short straws
Method: **MUDDLE** lime wedges in the base of shaker to release juice and oils in its skin. Add vodka and sugar. **SHAKE** with 6oz scoop crushed ice and pour all without straining into glass.

¾	fresh	**Lime cut into wedges**
2	shot(s)	**Ketel One vodka**
½	shot(s)	**Sugar syrup** (2 sugar to 1 water)

Comment: Vodka replaces cachaça in this Caipirinha-style drink.

CAIPIRUVA UPDATED #8

Glass: Old-fashioned
Method: **MUDDLE** lime wedges and grapes in base of shaker to release juices. Add cachaça and sugar. **SHAKE** with 6oz scoop crushed ice and pour all without straining into glass.

½	fresh	**Lime cut into wedges**
4	fresh	**Seedless white grapes**
2	shot(s)	**Leblon cachaça**
½	shot(s)	**Brown sugar syrup** (2 sugar to 1 water)

Variant: Use pitted cherries instead of grapes.
Comment: A grape juice laced twist on the Caipirinha.
Origin: Created by Dale DeGroff, New York, USA.

CAJUN MARTINI

Glass: Martini
Garnish: Chilli pepper
Method: **STIR** vermouth with ice. Strain, discarding vermouth to leave only a coating on the ice. Pour pepper vodka into mixing glass, stir with coated ice and strain into chilled glass.

½	shot(s)	**Noilly Prat dry vermouth**
2½	shot(s)	**Pepper-infused Ketel One vodka**

Comment: A very hot vodka Martini. I dare you!

CALIFORNIAN MARTINI

Glass: Martini
Garnish: Orange zest twist
Method: **STIR** all ingredients with ice and strain into chilled glass.

2	shot(s)	**Ketel One vodka**
1	shot(s)	**Grand Marnier liqueur**
½	shot(s)	**Noilly Prat dry vermouth**
2	dashes	**Angostura orange bitters** (optional)

Comment: A medium dry, fragrant orange Martini.

CALIFORNIA ROOT BEER

Glass: Sling
Garnish: Lime wedge
Method: **SHAKE** first 3 ingredients with ice and strain into ice-filled glass. **TOP** with soda.

1	shot(s)	**Ketel One vodka**
½	shot(s)	**Kahlúa coffee liqueur**
¾	shot(s)	**Galliano L'Autentico liqueur**
Top up with		**Soda water** (club soda)

Variant: Bartender's Root Beer
Comment: Does indeed taste like root beer.

CALL ME OLD-FASHIONED

Glass: Old-fashioned
Garnish: Orange peel twist
Method: STIR sugar syrup and bitters with two ice cubes in a glass. Add one shot of cognac and two more ice cubes. Stir some more and add another two ice cubes and another shot of cognac. Stir lots more and add more ice.

2	shot(s)	**Courvoisier V.S.O.P. cognac**
¼	shot(s)	**Sugar syrup** (2 sugar to 1 water)
2	dashes	**Angostura aromatic bitters**

Origin: Created in 2001 by Yours Truly (Simon Difford).
Comment: An Old-Fashioned made with cognac instead of whiskey – works well.

CALVADOS COCKTAIL

Glass: Martini
Garnish: Orange zest twist
Method: SHAKE all ingredients with ice and fine strain into chilled glass.

1½	shot(s)	**Boulard Grand Solage calvados**
¾	shot(s)	**Cointreau triple sec**
1½	shot(s)	**Freshly squeezed orange juice**
2	dashes	**Angostura orange bitters**

Origin: Adapted from Harry Craddock's 1930 'The Savoy Cocktail Book'.
Comment: Tangy orange with an alcoholic apple bite.

CAMERON'S KICK

Glass: Martini
Garnish: Lemon zest twist
Method: SHAKE all ingredients with ice and fine strain into chilled glass.

1½	shot(s)	**Johnnie Walker Scotch whisky**
1½	shot(s)	**Jameson Irish whiskey**
¾	shot(s)	**Freshly squeezed lemon juice**
½	shot(s)	**Almond (orgeat) syrup**

Origin: Adapted from Harry Craddock's 1930 'The Savoy Cocktail Book'.
Comment: Peaty, honeyed whiskey with a cleansing hint of lemon rounded by almond.

CAMOMILE & BLACKFRUIT BREEZE

Glass: Collins
Garnish: Lemon slice
Method: SHAKE all ingredients with ice and strain into ice-filled glass.

2	shot(s)	**Ketel One Citroen vodka**
1	shot(s)	**Chambord black raspberry liqueur**
3	shot(s)	**Cold camomile tea**

Origin: Created in 2002 by Yours Truly (Simon Difford).
Comment: Adult, clean and subtle in flavour with a twang of fruit.

CAMPIRINHA NEW #8

Glass: Old-fashioned
Garnish: None
Method: MUDDLE lime and grapefruit in base of shaker to release juices. Add other ingredients, **SHAKE** with 6oz scoop crushed ice and pour all without straining into glass.

½	fresh	**Lime cut into wedges**
¼	fresh	**Ruby red grapefruit** (wedges)
2	shot(s)	**Campari Bitter**
½	shot(s)	**Sugar syrup** (2 sugar to 1 water)

Comment: This bright red fruit laden drink has the looks to appeal to all but its bitter-sweet flavour is specific to Campari convertees.
Origin: Adapted from a drink created in 2006 by Jamie Lawton at Orchid, Auckland, New Zealand.

CANADIAN APPLE (MOCKTAIL)

Glass: Collins
Garnish: Apple slice
Method: SHAKE all ingredients with ice and fine strain into ice-filled glass.

3½	shot(s)	**Pressed apple juice**
1½	shot(s)	**Freshly squeezed lemon juice**
¾	shot(s)	**Maple syrup**

Origin: Adapted from a drink discovered in 2005 at the Four Seasons Hotel, Prague, Czech Republic.
Comment: Refreshing and balanced with just the right amount of citrus acidity.

CANARIE

Glass: Collins (10oz/290ml max)
Method: POUR pastis and lemon syrup into glass. Serve iced water separately in a small jug (known in France as a 'broc') so the customer can dilute to their own taste (I recommend 5 shots). Lastly, add ice to fill glass.

1	shot(s)	**Ricard pastis**
½	shot(s)	**Lemon (citron) sugar syrup**
Top up with		**Chilled mineral water**

Origin: Very popular throughout France, this drink is fittingly named after the bird, which is typically bred for its bright yellow plumage.
Comment: The traditional French café drink with a twist of lemon sweetness.

CANARIES

Glass: Hurricane
Garnish: Pineapple wedge on rim
Method: SHAKE ingredients with ice and strain into ice-filled glass.

¾	shot(s)	**Bacardi Superior rum**
¾	shot(s)	**Cointreau triple sec**
¾	shot(s)	**Crème de banane liqueur**
¾	shot(s)	**Heering cherry brandy liqueur**
2	shot(s)	**Pressed pineapple juice**
2	shot(s)	**Freshly squeezed orange juice**

Comment: A long, fruity sweet drink that's only fit for consumption on a tropical beach.

CANARY FLIP

●●●●●◐

Glass: Martini
Garnish: Lemon zest twist
Method: SHAKE all ingredients with ice and fine strain into chilled glass.

2	shot(s)	**Bols advocaat liqueur**
2	shot(s)	**Sauvignon Blanc wine**
¾	shot(s)	**Freshly squeezed lemon juice**

Origin: Created in 2002 by Alex Kammerling, London, England.
Comment: A delightfully balanced drink.

CANCHANCHARA

●●●●◐○

Glass: Old-fashioned
Garnish: Lemon slice
Method: STIR honey with rum in the glass. Add lemon juice and ice. STIR and serve.

3	spoons	**Runny honey**
2	shot(s)	**Bacardi Superior rum**
1½	shot(s)	**Freshly squeezed lemon juice**

Origin: The Cuban forerunner of the Daiquiri, as drunk by Cuban revolutionaries fighting off the Spanish at the end of the nineteenth century. To be really authentic omit the ice. Origin and this recipe from Christine Sismondo's 2005 'Mondo Cocktail'.
Comment: Achieve the perfect balance between sweet honey and sour lemon and this is a great drink.

CANTEEN MARTINI

●●●●◐○

Glass: Martini
Garnish: Cherry in drink
Method: SHAKE all ingredients with ice and fine strain into chilled glass.

1½	shot(s)	**Bacardi Superior rum**
1½	shot(s)	**Southern Comfort liqueur**
½	shot(s)	**Luxardo Amaretto di Saschira**
½	shot(s)	**Freshly squeezed lime juice**

Origin: Originally created by Joey Guerra at Canteen, New York City, and adapted by author and columnist Gary Regan.
Comment: Tangy, sweet and sour – Southern Comfort drinkers will love this.

CAPE CODDER

●●●●◐○

Glass: Old-fashioned
Garnish: Lime wedge
Method: SHAKE all ingredients with ice and strain into ice-filled glass.

2	shot(s)	**Ketel One vodka**
3	shot(s)	**Ocean Spray cranberry juice**
¼	shot(s)	**Freshly squeezed lime juice**

Variant: Without lime juice this is a Cape Cod. Lengthened with soda becomes the Cape Cod Cooler.
Origin: Named after the resort on the Massachusetts coast. This fish shaped piece of land is where some of the first Europeans settled in the US. Here they found the cranberries which inspired this drink.
Comment: Dry and refreshing but not particularly interesting.

CAPITANO NEW #8

●●●○○

Glass: Martini/Coupette
Garnish: Orange zest twist
Method: SHAKE all ingredients with ice and fine strain into chilled glass.

1½	shot(s)	**Campari Bitter**
1½	shot(s)	**Carpano Antica Formula**
½	shot(s)	**Freshly squeezed lemon juice**
⅛	shot(s)	**Sugar syrup** (2 sugar to 1 water)

Comment: This bitter-sweet is one for Campari converts only.
Origin: Created in 2008 by Bernhard List.

CAPPERCAILLE

●●●●●○

Glass: Martini
Garnish: Pineapple wedge on rim
Method: STIR honey with whisky until honey dissolves. Add other ingredients, SHAKE with ice and fine strain into chilled glass.

2	spoons	**Runny honey**
2	shot(s)	**Johnnie Walker Scotch whisky**
½	shot(s)	**Cointreau triple sec**
½	shot(s)	**Bols apricot brandy liqueur**
1	shot(s)	**Pressed pineapple juice**
½	shot(s)	**Freshly squeezed lemon juice**

Origin: Created by Wayne Collins for Maxxium UK.
Comment: Wonderfully tangy, fruity Scotch.

CAPRICE

●●●●●○

Glass: Martini
Garnish: Orange zest twist
Method: STIR all ingredients with ice and strain into chilled glass.

1½	shot(s)	**Tanqueray London dry gin**
½	shot(s)	**Noilly Prat dry vermouth**
½	shot(s)	**Bénédictine D.O.M. liqueur**
1	dash	**Angostura orange bitters**

Comment: A long stir delivers the dilution necessary for this aromatic, spiced Wet Martini.

CAPTAIN COLLINS

●●●●◐○

Glass: Collins
Garnish: Orange slice & cherry on stick (sail)
Method: SHAKE first 3 ingredients with ice and strain into ice-filled glass. TOP with soda, stir and serve with straws.

2	shot(s)	**Canadian whiskey**
1	shot(s)	**Freshly squeezed lemon juice**
½	shot(s)	**Sugar syrup** (2 sugar to 1 water)
Top up with		**Soda water** (club soda)

Origin: Classic Collins variation.
Comment: Sweetened, soured and diluted whiskey.

CARAMEL MANHATTAN

Glass: Martini
Garnish: Lemon twist (discarded) & pineapple wedge on rim
Method: SHAKE all ingredients with ice and fine strain into chilled glass.

1½	shot(s)	**Bulleit bourbon whiskey**
¾	shot(s)	**Cartron Caramel liqueur**
½	shot(s)	**Martini Rosso sweet vermouth**
1	shot(s)	**Pressed pineapple juice**
2	dashes	**Peychaud's aromatic bitters**

Origin: Adapted from a drink created in 2002 by Nick Strangeway, London, England.
Comment: Flavours combine harmoniously with the character of the bourbon still evident.

CARAVAN

Glass: Collins
Garnish: Cherries
Method: POUR ingredients into ice-filled glass. Stir and serve with straws.

3	shot(s)	**Shiraz red wine**
½	shot(s)	**Grand Marnier liqueur**
Top up with		**Coca-Cola**

Origin: Popular in the French Alpine ski resorts.
Comment: A punch-like long drink.

CARDINAL PUNCH

Glass: Old-fashioned
Method: POUR cassis into ice-filled glass and **TOP** with wine. Stir and serve with straws.

1	shot(s)	**Crème de cassis liqueur**
Top up with		**Shiraz red wine**

Comment: A particularly fruity red.

CARDINALE

Glass: Old-fashioned
Garnish: Orange slice
Method: SHAKE all ingredients with ice and fine strain into chilled glass.

2	shot(s)	**Tanqueray London dry gin**
1½	shot(s)	**Campari Bitter**
1	shot(s)	**Noilly Prat dry vermouth**

Origin: A variation on the classic equal parts Negroni.
Comment: An extra dry Negroni for hardcore fans. I have to admit to being one.

CARIBBEAN BREEZE

Glass: Collins
Garnish: Pineapple wedge on rim
Method: SHAKE all ingredients with ice and strain into ice-filled glass.

1¼	shot(s)	**Pusser's Navy rum**
½	shot(s)	**Crème de banane liqueur**
2½	shot(s)	**Pressed pineapple juice**
2	shot(s)	**Ocean Spray cranberry juice**
½	shot(s)	**Rose's lime cordial**

Comment: A long drink with bags of tangy fruit flavours.

CARIBBEAN CRUISE

Glass: Collins
Garnish: Pineapple wedge on rim
Method: SHAKE all ingredients with ice and strain into ice-filled glass.

1½	shot(s)	**Bacardi Superior rum**
1½	shot(s)	**Malibu coconut rum liqueur**
4	shot(s)	**Pressed pineapple juice**
1	spoon	**Pomegranate (grenadine) syrup**

Comment: Long, frothy and fruity - one for the beach bar.

CARIBBEAN PIÑA COLADA

Glass: Hurricane
Garnish: Pineapple wedge & cherry
Method: BLEND ingredients with 12oz scoop of crushed ice. Pour into glass and serve with straws.

2	shot(s)	**Bacardi Supeior rum**
3	shot(s)	**Pressed pineapple juice**
½	shot(s)	**Coco López cream of coconut**
4	dashes	**Angostura aromatic bitters**
1	pinch	**Salt**

Comment: Angostura and salt make this a less sticky Colada.

CARIBBEAN PUNCH

Glass: Collins
Method: SHAKE all ingredients with ice and strain into glass filled with crushed ice.

2¼	shot(s)	**Wray & Nephew overproof rum**
½	shot(s)	**Luxardo Amaretto di Saschira**
½	shot(s)	**Malibu coconut rum liqueur**
¼	shot(s)	**Galliano L'Autentico liqueur**
¼	shot(s)	**Pomegranate (grenadine) syrup**
¾	shot(s)	**Freshly squeezed lemon juice**
3	shot(s)	**Pressed pineapple juice**

Comment: Red in colour and innocent looking, this flavoursome drink sure packs a punch.

CARIBE DAIQUIRI

Glass: Martini
Garnish: Lemon zest wedge
Method: SHAKE all ingredients with ice and fine strain into chilled glass.

2	shot(s)	**Bacardi Superior rum**
1	shot(s)	**Pressed pineapple juice**
½	shot(s)	**Freshly squeezed lemon juice**
¼	shot(s)	**Velvet Falernum liqueur**

Comment: A dry, fruity spicy Daiquiri.

CAROL CHANNING

Glass: Flute
Garnish: Raspberries
Method: SHAKE first 3 ingredients with ice and strain into chilled glass. **TOP** with champagne.

½	shot(s)	**Crème de framboise liqueur**
⅛	shot(s)	**Sugar syrup** (2 sugar to 1 water)
Top up with		**Perrier Jouet brut champagne**

Origin: Created by Dick Bradsell in 1984 with the milliner Stephen Jones. Named after the famously large mouthed American comedienne Carol Channing because of her appearance in the film 'Thoroughly Modern Milly', where, for some unknown reason, she spends much of the time running around shouting 'raspberries'.
Comment: Fortified raspberry and champagne.

CARROL COCKTAIL

Glass: Martini
Garnish: Pickled walnut or onion
Method: STIR all ingredients with ice and strain into chilled glass.

2	shot(s)	**Courvoisier V.S.O.P. cognac**
1	shot(s)	**Martini Rosso sweet vermouth**

Origin: Adapted from Victor Bergeron's 'Trader Vic's Bartender's Guide' (1972 revised edition).
Comment: Aromatic wine and cognac – dry yet easy.

CARROT CAKE

Glass: Martini
Garnish: Dust with cinnamon powder
Method: SHAKE all ingredients with ice and fine strain into chilled glass.

2	shot(s)	**Baileys Irish cream liqueur**
¾	shot(s)	**Goldschläger cinnamon schnapps**
1½	shot(s)	**Kahlúa coffee liqueur**

Comment: Tastes nothing like carrot cake - surely that's a good thing.

CARUSO MARTINI

Glass: Martini
Garnish: Mint leaf
Method: SHAKE all ingredients with ice and fine strain into chilled glass.

1	shot(s)	**Tanqueray London dry gin**
1	shot(s)	**Noilly Prat dry vermouth**
1	shot(s)	**Green crème de menthe liqueur**

Origin: The recipe is adapted from Harry Craddock's 1930 'The Savoy Cocktail Book'. The drink was created at The Savoy for the tenor Enrico Caruso in the early 20th century.
Comment: Emerald green with full-on mint. Good as a digestif after a tenor-sized meal.

CASABLANCA #1

Glass: Martini
Garnish: Orange zest twist
Method: SHAKE all ingredients with ice and fine strain into chilled glass.

2	shot(s)	**Bacardi Superior rum**
¾	shot(s)	**Cointreau triple sec**
¾	shot(s)	**Freshly squeezed lime juice**
½	shot(s)	**Luxardo maraschino liqueur**
½	fresh	**Egg white**

Origin: Named after Michael Curtiz's 1942 classic starring Bogie and Ingrid Bergman.
Comment: A rum based variation on the White Lady, with zingy citrus and sweet maraschino.

CASABLANCA #2

Glass: Martini
Garnish: Dust with freshly grated nutmeg
Method: SHAKE all ingredients with ice and fine strain into chilled glass.

1	shot(s)	**Ketel One vodka**
¼	shot(s)	**Galliano L'Autentico liqueur**
1	shot(s)	**Bols advocaat liqueur**
¼	shot(s)	**Freshly squeezed lemon juice**
1	shot(s)	**Freshly squeezed orange juice**
½	shot(s)	**Double (heavy) cream**

Comment: Creamy, fruity, alcoholic custard. Different!

CASANOVA

Glass: Martini
Garnish: Crumble Cadbury's Flake bar over drink
Method: SHAKE all ingredients with ice and fine strain into chilled glass.

1½	shot(s)	**Bulleit bourbon whiskey**
¾	shot(s)	**Blandy's Alvada madeira**
¾	shot(s)	**Kahlúa coffee liqueur**
¾	shot(s)	**Double (heavy) cream**
¾	shot(s)	**Milk**
⅛	shot(s)	**Sugar syrup** (2 sugar to 1 water)

Comment: Rich, medium-sweet and creamy with a mocha coffee finish.

CASCADE MARTINI

Glass: Martini
Garnish: Raspberries on stick
Method: SHAKE all ingredients with ice and fine strain into chilled glass.

8	fresh	**Raspberries**
2	shot(s)	**Ketel One vodka**
1	shot(s)	**Ocean Spray cranberry juice**
¾	shot(s)	**Freshly squeezed lemon juice**
¼	shot(s)	**Chambord black raspberry liqueur**
¼	shot(s)	**Vanilla sugar syrup**

Comment: Rich raspberry with hints of citrus and vanilla.

CASINO #1 UPDATED #8

Glass: Martini
Garnish: Maraschino cherry
Method: SHAKE all ingredients with ice and fine strain into chilled glass.

1½	shot(s)	**Tanqueray London dry gin**
¾	shot(s)	**Luxardo maraschino liqueur**
½	shot(s)	**Freshly squeezed lemon juice**
¼	shot(s)	**Chilled mineral water** (omit if wet ice)
1	dash	**Angostura orange bitters**

Variant: Bee's Knees, Blue Moon
Comment: Basically an Aviation dried and made more complex with a dash of orange bitters.
Origin: Recipe adapted from Harry Craddock's 1930 'The Savoy Cocktail Book'.

> ## 'GOT TIGHT LAST NIGHT ON ABSINTHE AND DID KNIFE TRICKS. GREAT SUCCESS SHOOTING THE KNIFE UNDERHAND INTO THE PIANO.'
> ### ERNEST HEMINGWAY

CASINO #2 NEW #8

Glass: Martini
Garnish: Maraschino cherry
Method: SHAKE all ingredients with ice and fine strain into chilled glass.

2	shot(s)	**Tanqueray London dry gin**
¾	shot(s)	**Luxardo maraschino liqueur**
½	shot(s)	**Freshly squeezed lemon juice**
½	shot(s)	**Freshly squeezed orange juice**
1	dash	**Angostura orange bitters**

Comment: Basically an Aviation but with a dash of orange juice and orange bitters.
Origin: Recipe adapted from David A. Embury's 1948 'Fine Art of Mixing Drinks'.

CASSE NOISETTE NEW #8

Glass: Martini
Garnish: Dust with grated nutmeg
Method: SHAKE first 3 ingredients with ice and strain into chilled glass. **FLOAT** thin layer of cream over drink.

1½	shot(s)	**Ketel One vodka**
¾	shot(s)	**Kahlúa coffee liquor**
¾	shot(s)	**Frangelico hazelnut liqueur**
¾	shot(s)	**Double (heavy) cream**

Comment: Sip hazelnut and coffee through a creamy topping. A dessert of a drink.
Origin: Adapted from a drink created in 2001 by Julien Escot at Hotel du Cap-Eden Roc in Cap d'Antibes (France). Casse Noisette won the overall contest at London's Drinks International Bartender's Challenge 2004.

CASSINI

Glass: Martini
Garnish: Blackberries on stick
Method: SHAKE all ingredients with ice and fine strain into chilled glass.

2	shot(s)	**Ketel One vodka**
1½	shot(s)	**Ocean Spray cranberry juice**
¼	shot(s)	**Crème de cassis liqueur**

Origin: Created in 1998 by Yours Truly (Simon Difford).
Comment: A simple but pleasant berry drink.

CASTRO

Glass: Martini
Garnish: Lime wedge on rim
Method: SHAKE all ingredients with ice and fine strain into chilled glass.

1½	shot(s)	**Zacapa aged rum**
¾	shot(s)	**Boulard Grand Solage calvados**
¼	shot(s)	**Freshly squeezed orange juice**
½	shot(s)	**Freshly squeezed lime juice**
¼	shot(s)	**Rose's lime cordial**
¼	shot(s)	**Sugar syrup** (2 sugar to 1 water)

Origin: Named after the Cuban.
Comment: Tangy and fruity.

CAUSEWAY

Glass: Collins
Method: SHAKE first 5 ingredients with ice and strain into ice-filled glass, **TOP** with ginger ale.

2	shot(s)	**Jameson Irish whiskey**
1	shot(s)	**Drambuie liqueur**
4	dashes	**Angostura aromatic bitters**
2	dashes	**Angostura orange bitters**
¼	shot(s)	**Freshly squeezed lemon juice**
Top up with		**Ginger ale**

Origin: Created by David Myers at Titanic, London, England.
Comment: Dry aromatic long whiskey drink.

CELERY MARTINI

Glass: Martini
Garnish: Salt rim & celery
Method: SHAKE all ingredients with ice and fine strain into chilled glass.

1¾	shot(s)	**Freshly extracted celery juice**
2	shot(s)	**Ketel One vodka**
¼	shot(s)	**Sugar syrup** (2 sugar to 1 water)

Origin: Created by Andreas Tsanos at Momos, London, England in 2001.
Comment: I only usually like celery when loaded with blue cheese - but I love this Martini.

CELTIC MARGARITA

Glass: Coupette
Garnish: Salt rim & lemon wedge
Method: SHAKE all ingredients with ice and fine strain into chilled glass.

2	shot(s)	**Johnnie Walker Scotch whisky**
1	shot(s)	**Cointreau triple sec**
1	shot(s)	**Freshly squeezed lemon juice**

Origin: Discovered in 2004 at Milk & Honey, London, England.
Comment: A Scotch Margarita – try it, it works.

CHAM 69 #1

Glass: Sling
Garnish: Berries
Method: SHAKE first 4 ingredients with ice and strain into ice-filled glass. TOP with lemonade, stir and serve with straws.

2	shot(s)	**Ketel One vodka**
¾	shot(s)	**Chambord black raspberry liqueur**
¾	shot(s)	**Luxardo Amaretto di Saschira**
¾	shot(s)	**Freshly squeezed lime juice**
Top up with		**Lemonade/Sprite/7-Up**

Origin: I created this drink back in 1998 and I've noticed it on cocktail menus across Europe. I was something of a beginner with a sweet tooth at the time but this new formulation is better balanced.
Comment: Medium sweet, long and fruity.

CHAM 69 #2

Glass: Sling
Garnish: Berries
Method: SHAKE first 4 ingredients with ice and strain into ice-filled glass. TOP with champagne, stir and serve with straws.

1	shot(s)	**Ketel One vodka**
½	shot(s)	**Chambord black raspberry liqueur**
½	shot(s)	**Luxardo Amaretto di Saschira**
¼	shot(s)	**Freshly squeezed lime juice**
Top up with		**Perrier Jouet brut champagne**

Origin: While re-examining my old creation in 2005 I decided champagne would be more appropriate considering the name.
Comment: Long, fruity and refreshing.

CHAM CHAM

Glass: Flute
Garnish: Berries
Method: POUR liqueur into chilled glass and TOP with champagne.

| ½ | shot(s) | **Chambord black raspberry liqueur** |
| Top up with | | **Perrier Jouet brut champagne** |

Comment: A pleasing blend of fruit and champagne to rival the Kir Royale.

CHAMPAGNE COCKTAIL UPDATED #8

Glass: Flute
Garnish: Orange zest twist (spray & discard)
Method: COAT sugar cube with bitters and drop into glass. POUR cognac over soaked cube, then TOP with champagne.

1	cube	**Brown sugar**
3	dashes	**Angostura aromatic bitters**
1	shot(s)	**Courvoisier V.S.O.P. cognac**
Top up with		**Perrier Jouet brut champagne**

Variant: Chicago, Prince of Wales
Comment: An over hyped classic cocktail that gets sweeter as you reach the dissolving cube at the bottom.
Origin: First recorded in Jerry Thomas's 1862 book 'How To Mix Drinks', or 'The Bon Vivant's Companion', where he almost certainly mistakenly specifies this as a shaken drink. That would be explosive. Another early reference to Champagne cocktails is in Mark Twain's 1869 novel, Innocents Abroad. It is thought the drink found popularity after a bartender named John Dougherty won an 1899 New York cocktail competition with a similar drink named Business Brace.

CHAMPAGNE CUP

Glass: Flute
Garnish: Maraschino cherry
Method: STIR first 3 ingredients with ice and strain into chilled glass. TOP with champagne and gently stir.

¾	shot(s)	**Courvoisier V.S.O.P. cognac**
½	shot(s)	**Grand Marnier liqueur**
¼	shot(s)	**Maraschino syrup** (from cherry jar)
Top up with		**Perrier Jouet brut champagne**

Comment: Sweet maraschino helps balance this dry drink.

CHAMPAGNE DAISY

Glass: Flute
Garnish: Pomegranate wedge
Method: SHAKE first 3 ingredients with ice and fine strain into chilled glass, TOP with champagne.

1	shot(s)	**Yellow Chartreuse liqueur**
⅛	shot(s)	**Pomegranate (grenadine) syrup**
1	shot(s)	**Freshly squeezed lemon juice**
Top up with		**Perrier Jouet brut champagne**

Comment: You'll need to like Chartreuse and citrus champagne to appreciate this drink.

CHAMPAGNE PICK-ME-UP NEW #8

Glass: Flute
Garnish: Orange zest twist (spray & discard)
Method: SHAKE first 3 ingredients with ice and fine strain into chilled glass. **TOP** with champagne.

1	shot(s)	Courvoisier V.S.O.P. cognac
1½	shot(s)	Freshly squeezed orange juice
¼	shot(s)	Pomegranate (grenadine) syrup
3	shot(s)	Perrier Jouet brut champagne

Comment: A subtle hint of biscuity champagne shines through this very quaffable drink.
Origin: There are many versions of this classic cocktail but I have taken this one from Dale DeGroff's 2008 'The Essential Cocktail' where Dale credits this recipe to the Ritz Bar Paris circa 1936.

CHAMPINO NEW #8

Glass: Flute
Garnish: Orange zest twist
Method: SHAKE first 2 ingredients with ice and fine strain into chilled glass. **TOP** with champagne.

1	shot(s)	Campari Bitter
1	shot(s)	Martini Rosso sweet vermouth
Top up with		Perrier Jouet brut champagne

AKA: Americano Royale
Comment: A champagne option for Negroni lovers.

CHAMPS-ELYSÉES

Glass: Martini
Garnish: Lemon zest twist
Method: SHAKE all ingredients with ice and fine strain into chilled glass.

1¾	shot(s)	Courvoisier V.S.O.P. cognac
¼	shot(s)	Green Chartreuse liqueur
½	shot(s)	Freshly squeezed lemon juice
½	shot(s)	Sugar syrup (2 sugar to 1 water)
3	dashes	Angostura aromatic bitters
¾	shot(s)	Chilled mineral water (omit if wet ice)
½	fresh	Egg white (optional)

Origin: Named after the touristy Parisian boulevard where (coincidentally) Rémy Cointreau have their offices.
Comment: A great after dinner drink for lovers of cognac and Chartreuse.

CHANCELLOR

Glass: Martini
Garnish: Orange zest twist
Method: SHAKE all ingredients with ice and fine strain into chilled glass.

2	shot(s)	Johnnie Walker Scotch whisky
1	shot(s)	Warre's Otima tawny port
½	shot(s)	Noilly Prat dry vermouth
¼	shot(s)	Sugar syrup (2 sugar to 1 water)
2	dashes	Angostura orange bitters

Origin: A classic of unknown origins.
Comment: Complex and sophisticated Scotch with fruity notes.

CHARENTE COLLINS

Glass: Collins
Garnish: Mint sprig & orange zest twist
Method: Lightly **MUDDLE** mint in base of shaker (just to bruise). Add other ingredients, **SHAKE** with ice and strain into glass filled with crushed ice. Serve with straws.

5	fresh	Mint leaves
2	shot(s)	Grand Marnier liqueur
1	shot(s)	Freshly squeezed lemon juice
1	shot(s)	St-Germain elderflower liqueur

Origin: Created in 2005 by Kieran Bailey, The Light Bar, London, England.
Comment: Refreshing orange and lemon with a hint of elderflower.

CHARLES DAIQUIRI

Glass: Martini
Garnish: Lime wedge on rim
Method: SHAKE all ingredients with ice and fine strain into chilled glass.

1	shot(s)	Bacardi Superior rum
1	shot(s)	Pusser's Navy rum
½	shot(s)	Cointreau triple sec
½	shot(s)	Freshly squeezed lime juice
⅛	shot(s)	Sugar syrup (2 sugar to 1 water)
½	shot(s)	Chilled mineral water (omit if wet ice)

Comment: Navy rum and triple sec add special interest to this Daiquiri.

CHARLIE CHAPLIN

Glass: Old-fashioned
Garnish: Lemon zest twist
Method: SHAKE all ingredients with ice and strain into ice-filled glass.

1½	shot(s)	Sloe gin liqueur
1½	shot(s)	Bols apricot brandy liqueur
1	shot(s)	Freshly squeezed lemon juice

Comment: This fruity number was originally served 'up' but is better over ice.

CHARTREUSE SWIZZLE NEW #8

Glass: Collins
Garnish: Pineapple wedge & cherry
Method: POUR ingredients into glass filled with crushed ice and **SWIZZLE** (or **SHAKE** all ingredients with ice and strain into glass filled with crushed ice).

1¼	shot(s)	Green Chartreuse liqueur
½	shot(s)	Velvet Falernum liqueur
1	shot(s)	Pressed pineapple juice
½	shot(s)	Freshly squeezed lime juice

Comment: A drink for people like me – Chartreuse lovers.
Origin: Created by Marco Dionysos at Tres Agaves, San Francisco, USA.

●●●●○

CHAS

Glass: Martini
Garnish: Orange zest twist
Method: SHAKE all ingredients with ice and fine strain into chilled glass.

1¾	shot(s)	Bulleit bourbon whiskey
½	shot(s)	Bénédictine D.O.M. liqueur
½	shot(s)	Luxardo Amaretto di Saschira
½	shot(s)	Cointreau triple sec
½	shot(s)	Grand Marnier liqueur

Origin: Created in 2003 by Murray Stenson at Zig Zag Café, Seattle, USA.
Comment: A wonderfully tangy cocktail with great bourbon personality and hints of almond and orange.

●●●●○

CHATHAM HOTEL SPECIAL

Glass: Martini
Garnish: Nutmeg dust
Method: SHAKE all ingredients with ice and fine strain into chilled glass.

2	shot(s)	Courvoisier V.S.O.P. cognac
¾	shot(s)	Warre's Otima tawny port
½	shot(s)	Brown crème de cacao liqeuer
¼	shot(s)	Double (heavy) cream
¼	shot(s)	Milk

Origin: This mid-1900s classic from New York's Chatham Hotel was resurrected by Ted Haigh in his 2004 book 'Vintage Spirits & Forgotten Cocktails'.
Comment: I've slightly changed the proportions and replaced the original lemon zest garnish with a little extra spice.

●●●●○

CHEEKY MONKEY UPDATED #8

Glass: Martini
Garnish: Orange zest twist
Method: SHAKE all ingredients with ice and fine strain into chilled glass.

1	shot(s)	Ketel One Citroen vodka
1	shot(s)	Yellow Chartreuse liqueur
1½	shot(s)	Freshly squeezed orange juice
1	dash	Angostura orange bitters

Comment: Firey yellow in colour, this drink features the distinctive flavour of Chartreuse with a citrus supporting cast.
Origin: Created in 2001 by Tony Conigliaro at Isola, Knightsbridge, London, England.

●●●●○

CHELSEA SIDECAR UPDATED #8

Glass: Martini
Garnish: Lemon zest twist
Method: SHAKE all ingredients with ice and fine strain into chilled glass.

1½	shot(s)	Tanqueray London dry gin
1	shot(s)	Cointreau triple sec
1	shot(s)	Freshly squeezed lemon juice
¼	shot(s)	Sugar syrup (2 sugar to 1 water)

Comment: Gin replaces cognac in this variation on the classic Sidecar.

●●●●○○

CHERRUTE UPDATED #8

Glass: Martini
Garnish: Grapefruit zest twist (discarded) & maraschino cherry
Method: SHAKE all ingredients with ice and fine strain into chilled glass.

2	shot(s)	Ketel One vodka
½	shot(s)	Heering cherry brandy liqueur
1½	shot(s)	Freshly squeezed grapefruit juice

Comment: Sweet cherry brandy balanced by the fruity acidity of grapefruit, laced with vodka.
Origin: Created in the early Noughties by Nicholas P J Snape at Mojo, Leeds, England.

●●●●○

CHERRY ALEXANDER

Glass: Martini
Garnish: Maraschino cherry
Method: SHAKE all ingredients with ice and fine strain into chilled glass.

1	shot(s)	Vanilla-infused Ketel One vodka
½	shot(s)	Heering cherry brandy liqueur
½	shot(s)	White crème de cacao liqueur
1	shot(s)	Double (heavy) cream
1	shot(s)	Milk

Origin: Created by Wayne Collins for Maxxium UK.
Comment: A fruity twist on the creamy classic.

●●●●○

CHERRY & HAZELNUT DAIQUIRI

Glass: Martini
Garnish: Cherry on rim
Method: SHAKE all ingredients with ice and fine strain into chilled glass.

2	shot(s)	Bacardi Superior rum
¾	shot(s)	Luxardo maraschino liqueur
1½	shot(s)	Frangelico hazelnut liqueur
½	shot(s)	Freshly squeezed lime juice
½	shot(s)	Chilled mineral water (omit if wet ice)

Origin: Adam Wyartt and I created this in 2003.
Comment: Nutty and surprisingly tangy.

CHERRY BLOSSOM

Glass: Martini
Garnish: Maraschino cherry in drink
Method: **SHAKE** all ingredients with ice and fine strain into chilled glass.

¾	shot(s)	**Heering cherry brandy liqueur**
¾	shot(s)	**Kirschwasser eau de vie**
½	shot(s)	**Cointreau triple sec**
1¼	shot(s)	**Freshly squeezed lemon juice**
¼	shot(s)	**Maraschino syrup** (from cherry jar)

Comment: Bundles of flavour – tangy and moreish.

CHERRY DAIQUIRI

Glass: Martini
Garnish: Cherry on rim
Method: **MUDDLE** cherries in base of shaker. Add other ingredients, **SHAKE** with ice and fine strain into chilled glass.

8	fresh	**Stoned cherries**
2	shot(s)	**Vanilla-infused Bacardi rum**
1	shot(s)	**Heering cherry brandy liqueur**
⅛	shot(s)	**Maraschino syrup** (from cherry jar)
½	shot(s)	**Freshly squeezed lime juice**
½	shot(s)	**Chilled mineral water** (omit if wet ice)

Origin: Created in 2003 by Yours Truly (Simon Difford).
Comment: Cherry sweetness paired with Daiquiri sharpness.

CHERRY MARINER NEW #8

Glass: Martini
Garnish: Morello or maraschino cherry
Method: **SHAKE** all ingredients with ice and fine strain into chilled glass.

2	shot(s)	**Tanqueray London dry gin**
1	shot(s)	**Heering cherry brandy liqueur**
¼	shot(s)	**Luxardo maraschino liqueur**
2	dashes	**Angostura orange bitters**

Comment: Rich cherry liqueurs fortified by gin and bittered with a hint of orange.
Origin: Adapted from a drink created by Mickael Perron from Bar Now On.

CHERRY MARTINI

Glass: Martini
Garnish: Lemon zest twist
Method: **SHAKE** all ingredients with ice and fine strain into chilled glass.

2	shot(s)	**Ketel One Citroen vodka**
¾	shot(s)	**Heering cherry brandy liqueur**
½	shot(s)	**Noilly Prat dry vermouth**
½	shot(s)	**Chilled mineral water** (omit if wet ice)

Origin: Created in 2005 by Yours Truly (Simon Difford).
Comment: A hint of cherry is balanced by citrus freshness, and dried and deepened by vermouth.

CHERRY MASH SOUR

Glass: Old-fashioned
Garnish: Lemon twist & cherry
Method: **SHAKE** all ingredients with ice and strain into ice-filled glass.

2	shot(s)	**Jack Daniel's Tennessee whiskey**
½	shot(s)	**Heering cherry brandy liqueur**
¾	shot(s)	**Freshly squeezed lemon juice**
½	shot(s)	**Sugar syrup** (2 sugar to 1 water)

Origin: Created by Dale DeGroff when Beverage Manager at the Rainbow Room Promenade Bar, New York City, USA.
Comment: The rich flavour of Tennessee whiskey soured with lemon and sweetened with cherry liqueur.

CHE'S REVOLUTION

Glass: Martini
Garnish: Pineapple wedge on rim
Method: **MUDDLE** mint with rum in base of shaker. Add other ingredients, **SHAKE** with ice and fine strain into chilled glass.

4	fresh	**Mint leaves**
2	shot(s)	**Bacardi Superior rum**
¼	shot(s)	**Maple syrup**
2	shot(s)	**Pressed pineapple juice**

Origin: Created in 2003 by Ben Reed for the launch party of MJU Bar @ Millennium Hotel, London, England.
Comment: Complex and smooth with hints of maple syrup and mint amongst the pineapple and rum.

CHICLET DAIQUIRI

Glass: Martini
Garnish: Banana slice on rim
Method: **BLEND** ingredients with a 12oz scoop of crushed ice and serve in large chilled glass.

2½	shot(s)	**Bacardi Superior rum**
½	shot(s)	**Crème de banane liqueur**
⅛	shot(s)	**Giffard Menthe Pastille liqueur**
½	shot(s)	**Freshly squeezed lime juice**
¼	shot(s)	**Sugar syrup** (2 sugar to 1 water)

Origin: Often found on Cuban bar menus, this was created at La Floridita, Havana.
Comment: A wonderfully refreshing drink on a summer's day with surprisingly subtle flavours.

CHIHUAHUA MAGARITA

Glass: Martini
Method: **SHAKE** all ingredients with ice and fine strain into chilled glass.

2	shot(s)	**Don Julio reposado tequila**
2	shot(s)	**Freshly squeezed grapefruit juice**
⅛	shot(s)	**Agave syrup**
3	dashes	**Angostura aromatic bitters**

Comment: Tequila and grapefruit juice pepped up with Angostura.

CHILL-OUT MARTINI

Glass: Martini
Garnish: Pineapple wedge on rim
Method: **SHAKE** all ingredients with ice and fine strain into chilled glass.

1	shot(s)	**Orange-infused Ketel One vodka**
1	shot(s)	**Malibu coconut rum liqueur**
1	shot(s)	**Baileys Irish cream liqueur**
1	shot(s)	**Freshly squeezed orange juice**

Comment: Smooth, creamy sweet orange and surprisingly strong.

CHIMAYO

Glass: Martini
Garnish: Float apple slice
Method: **SHAKE** all ingredients with ice and fine strain into chilled glass.

2	shot(s)	**Don Julio reposado tequila**
½	shot(s)	**Crème de cassis liqueur**
¾	shot(s)	**Pressed apple juice**
¼	shot(s)	**Freshly squeezed lemon juice**

Origin: Named after El Potrero de Chimayó in northern New Mexico, USA.
Comment: Apple juice and cassis take the sting off tequila.

CHIN CHIN UPDATED #8

Glass: Flute
Method: **STIR** honey with Scotch in base of shaker until honey dissolves. Add apple juice, **SHAKE** with ice and strain into chilled glass. **TOP** with champagne.

½	spoon	**Runny honey**
1	shot(s)	**Johnnie Walker Scotch whisky**
½	shot(s)	**Pressed apple juice**
Top up with		**Perrier Jouet brut champagne**

Comment: Golden honey in colour and also in flavour. An unusual and great tasting Champagne cocktail.
Origin: Created in 2002 by Tony Conigliaro at Isola, Knightsbridge, London, England.

CHINA BEACH

Glass: Martini
Garnish: Ginger slice on rim
Method: **SHAKE** all ingredients with ice and fine strain into chilled glass.

1	shot(s)	**Ketel One vodka**
1	shot(s)	**Domaine de Canton ginger liqueur**
2	shot(s)	**Ocean Spray cranberry juice**

Comment: Dry and lightly spiced.

CHINA BLUE

Glass: Collins
Garnish: Orange slice in drink
Method: **SHAKE** all ingredients with ice and strain into ice-filled glass.

1	shot(s)	**Bols blue curaçao liqueur**
1	shot(s)	**Soho lychee liqueur**
4	shot(s)	**Freshly squeezed grapefruit juice**

Origin: Emerged in Japan in the late 1990s and still popular along the Pacific Rim.
Comment: Looks sweet, but due to a generous splash of grapefruit is actually balanced and refreshing.

CHINA BLUE MARTINI

Glass: Martini
Garnish: Peeled lychee in drink
Method: **SHAKE** all ingredients with ice and fine strain into chilled glass.

1	shot(s)	**Bols blue curaçao liqueur**
1	shot(s)	**Soho lychee liqueur**
2	shot(s)	**Freshly squeezed grapefruit juice**
¼	shot(s)	**Freshly squeezed lemon juice**

Origin: An almost inevitable short adaptation of the original long drink above.
Comment: This simple cocktail with its turquoise colour tastes more adult and interesting than its colour might suggest.

CHINA MARTINI

Glass: Martini
Garnish: Orange zest twist & lychee in glass
Method: **STIR** all ingredients with ice and fine strain into chilled glass.

1½	shot(s)	**Tanqueray London dry gin**
½	shot(s)	**Soho lychee liqueur**
¼	shot(s)	**Cointreau triple sec**
½	shot(s)	**Noilly Prat dry vermouth**

Origin: Created in 2004 by Wayne Collins for Maxxium UK.
Comment: A complex, not too sweet lychee Martini.

CHINESE COSMOPOLITAN

Glass: Martini
Garnish: Flamed orange zest twist
Method: **SHAKE** all ingredients with ice and fine strain into chilled glass.

2	shot(s)	**Krupnik honey liqueur**
¾	shot(s)	**Soho lychee liqueur**
½	shot(s)	**Freshly squeezed lime juice**
1	shot(s)	**Ocean Spray cranberry juice**

Origin: Discovered in 2003 at Raoul's Bar, Oxford, England.
Comment: Oriental in name and style – perhaps a tad sweeter than your standard Cosmo.

CHINESE WHISPER MARTINI

●●●●○

Glass: Martini
Garnish: Lemon zest twist
Method: MUDDLE ginger in base of shaker. Add other ingredients, **SHAKE** with ice and fine strain into chilled glass.

2	slices	**Fresh root ginger** (thumbnail sized)
2	shot(s)	**Ketel One Citroen vodka**
1	shot(s)	**Soho lychee liqueur**
½	shot(s)	**Freshly squeezed lime juice**
¼	shot(s)	**Ginger syrup**

Origin: Adapted from a recipe discovered in 2003 at Oxo Tower Bar, London, England.
Comment: There's more than a whisper of ginger in this spicy Martini.

CHOC & NUT MARTINI

●●●○○

Glass: Martini
Garnish: Wipe rim with orange and dust with cocoa powder.
Method: SHAKE all ingredients with ice and fine strain into chilled glass.

2	shot(s)	**Ketel One vodka**
1	shot(s)	**Frangelico hazelnut liqueur**
1	shot(s)	**White crème de cacao liqueur**
¼	shot(s)	**Chilled mineral water** (omit if wet ice)

Comment: Surprise, surprise - it's sweet chocolate and hazelnut.

CHOCOLARITA

●●●●○

Glass: Coupette
Garnish: Chocolate rim
Method: SHAKE all ingredients with ice and fine strain into chilled glass.

2	shot(s)	**Don Julio reposado tequila**
¼	shot(s)	**Brown crème de cacao liqueur**
¼	shot(s)	**Kahlúa coffee liqueur**
1	shot(s)	**Freshly squeezed lime juice**
¼	shot(s)	**Sugar syrup** (2 sugar to 1 water)

Origin: Adapted from a recipe discovered in 2005 at Agave, Hong Kong, China.
Comment: As the name suggests – a Margarita with chocolate and coffee.

CHOCOLATE & CRANBERRY MARTINI

●●●●○

Glass: Martini
Garnish: Wipe rim with cacao liqueur & dust with cocoa powder
Method: SHAKE all ingredients with ice and fine strain into chilled, rimmed glass.

2	shot(s)	**Vanilla-infused Ketel One vodka**
½	shot(s)	**White crème de cacao liqueur**
½	shot(s)	**Noilly Prat dry vermouth**
1	shot(s)	**Ocean Spray cranberry juice**

Origin: Created in 2003 by Yours Truly (Simon Difford).
Comment: The chocolate rim sounds naff but makes this drink. Surprisingly dry.

CHOCOLATE BISCUIT

●●●○○

Glass: Martini
Garnish: Bourbon cream biscuit on rim
Method: SHAKE all ingredients with ice and fine strain into chilled glass.

2	shot(s)	**Courvoisier V.S.O.P. cognac**
1	shot(s)	**Kahlúa coffee liqueur**
1	shot(s)	**Brown crème de cacao liqueur**

Origin: Created in 1999 by Gillian Stanfield at The Atlantic Bar & Grill, London, England.
Comment: Sweet and rich, with coffee and chocolate – one to chase dessert.

CHOCOLATE MARTINI

●●●●○

Glass: Martini
Garnish: Wipe rim with cacao liqueur & dust with cocoa powder
Method: SHAKE all ingredients with ice and fine strain into chilled glass.

2	shot(s)	**Ketel One vodka**
1	shot(s)	**White crème de cacao liqueur**
1	shot(s)	**Noilly Prat dry vermouth**

Comment: Vodka and chocolate made more interesting with a hint of vermouth.

CHOCOLATE MINT MARTINI

●●●●○

Glass: Martini
Garnish: Wipe rim with cacao liqueur & dust with cocoa powder
Method: STIR all ingredients with ice and strain into chilled glass.

2	shot(s)	**Ketel One vodka**
½	shot(s)	**Giffard Menthe Pastille liqueur**
½	shot(s)	**White crème de cacao liqueur**
½	shot(s)	**Noilly Prat dry vermouth**

Comment: An after dinner sweety that tastes of chocolate mints.

CHOCOLATE PUFF

●●●●○

Glass: Old-fashioned
Garnish: Crumbled Cadbury's Flake bar
Method: SHAKE all ingredients with ice and fine strain into chilled glass.

1	shot(s)	**Bacardi Oro golden rum**
1	shot(s)	**Brown crème de cacao liqueur**
6	spoons	**Natural yoghurt**
2	zests	**Fresh orange**
¼	shot(s)	**Sugar syrup** (2 sugar to 1 water)

Origin: Created by Wayne Collins for Maxxium UK.
Comment: Smooth as you like. The orange is surprisingly evident.

CHOCOLATE SAZERAC

●●●●○

Glass: Old-fashioned
Garnish: Lemon twist (discarded) & apple wedge
Method: Fill glass with ice, **POUR** in absinthe, top up with water and leave the mixture to stand in the glass. Separately **SHAKE** bourbon, cacao, sugar and bitters with ice. Finally discard contents of glass (absinthe, water and ice) and strain contents of shaker into empty absinthe-coated glass.

½	shot(s)	La Fée Parisienne (68%) absinthe
2	shot(s)	Bulleit bourbon whiskey
½	shot(s)	White crème de cacao liqueur
¼	shot(s)	Sugar syrup (2 sugar to 1 water)
2	dashes	Peychaud's aromatic bitters

Origin: Created in 2005 by Tonin Kacaj at Maze, London, England.
Comment: This twist on the classic Sazerac pairs absinthe, bourbon and chocolate to great effect.

CHOCOLATE SIDECAR

●●●●○

Glass: Martini
Garnish: Wipe rim with cacao liqueur & dust with cocoa powder
Method: SHAKE all ingredients with ice and fine strain into chilled glass.

1	shot(s)	Courvoisier V.S.O.P. cognac
1	shot(s)	Brown crème de cacao liqueur
1	shot(s)	Taylor's Ruby port
1	shot(s)	Freshly squeezed lime juice
½	shot(s)	Sugar syrup (2 sugar to 1 water)

Origin: Created in 2005 by Wayne Collins for Maxxium UK.

IN 1867 LAUCHLIN ROSE PATENTED A PROCESS TO PRESERVE FRUIT JUICE WITHOUT ALCOHOL - ROSE'S LIME CORDIAL.

CHRYSANTHEMUM NEW #8

●●●●○

Glass: Martini/Coupette
Garnish: Orange zest twist
Method: STIR all ingredients with ice and strain into chilled glass.

2	shot(s)	Noilly Prat dry vermouth
1	shot(s)	Bénédictine D.O.M. liqueur
⅛	shot(s)	La Fée Parisienne (68%) absinthe

Comment: Herbal and aromatic, this benefits from the dilution that comes with a good long stir.
Origin: In his 1930 'The Savoy Cocktail Book', Harry Craddock writes of this drink: "Well-known and very popular in the American Bar of the S.S. Europa".

CHUBACABRAS DAIQUIRI NEW #8

●●●○○

Glass: Martini
Garnish: Maraschino cherry
Method: SHAKE all ingredients with ice and fine-strain into chilled glass.

2	shot(s)	Bacardi Superior rum
¾	shot(s)	Freshly squeezed lime juice
¼	shot(s)	Almond (orgeat) syrup
⅛	shot(s)	Luxardo maraschino liqueur
⅛	shot(s)	La Fée Parisienne (68%) absinthe
⅛	shot(s)	Orange blossom water

Comment: Absinthe, almond, maraschino and orange flower blossom water make for a highly flavoured daiquiri.
Origin: Created in 2008 by Marcis Dzelzainis, Quo Vadis, London, England. The name literally translates as 'goat sucker' and is the name given to a Latin American 'monster' that is said to kill goats and other small animals to then suck the blood out of them. The first reported incidences were in Puerto Rico during 1995 and more recently the band Super Furry Animals had a hit record with their ode to the chubacabra.

CHURCHILL MARTINI NEW #8

●●●○○

Glass: Martini
Garnish: Olive
Method: STIR gin with ice while glancing at an unopened bottle of dry vermouth. Strain into chilled glass.

2½	shot(s)	Tanqueray London dry gin

Comment: Gin served chilled and neat, other than with a little dilution courtesy of melting ice. A great man but not necessarily a great drink.
Origin: Legend has it that Sir Winston Churchill liked his Martinis served without the vermouth actually being added to the drink, just present in the same room. He is quoted as saying of the drink, "Glance at the vermouth bottle briefly while pouring the juniper distillate freely".

CICADA COCKTAIL

●●●●○

Glass: Martini
Garnish: Dust with freshly grated nutmeg
Method: SHAKE all ingredients with ice and fine strain into chilled glass.

2	shot(s)	Bulleit bourbon whiskey
1	shot(s)	Luxardo Amaretto di Saschira
½	shot(s)	Double (heavy) cream
¾	shot(s)	Sugar syrup (2 sugar to 1 water)

Origin: Those familiar with the Grasshopper cocktail (named for its green colour) will understand why this one is called the Cicada (they're a bit browner).
Comment: Smoothed whiskey with more than a hint of almond.

●●●●○

CIDER APPLE COOLER

Glass: Collins
Method: SHAKE all ingredients with ice and strain into ice-filled glass.

2	shot(s)	**Boulard Grand Solage calvados**
1	shot(s)	**Berentzen apple schnapps**
4½	shot(s)	**Pressed apple juice**

Comment: Not unlike the taste of strong dry cider.

●●●●○

CIDER APPLE MARTINI

Glass: Martini
Garnish: Apple wedge
Method: SHAKE all ingredients with ice and fine strain into chilled glass.

1½	shot(s)	**Boulard Grand Solage calvados**
¾	shot(s)	**Berentzen apple schnapps**
¾	shot(s)	**Freshly squeezed lemon juice**
1	shot(s)	**Pressed apple juice**
¼	shot(s)	**Sugar syrup** (2 sugar to 1 water)

Origin: Created in 1998 by Jamie Terrell at Lab, London, England.
Comment: As the name suggests, rich cider flavours with a sharp finish.

●●●●○

CIDER HOUSE RULES NEW #8

Glass: Old-fashioned
Garnish: Apple wedge
Method: SHAKE all ingredients with ice and fine strain into ice-filled glass.

2	shot(s)	**Don Julio reposado tequila**
1½	shot(s)	**Pressed apple juice**
½	shot(s)	**Freshly squeezed lemon juice**
¼	shot(s)	**Agave syrup**
½	spoon	**Ground cinnamon**

Comment: Margarita-style drink with tequila, lemon and apple juice.
Origin: Created by New York-based Brian Van Flandern, of Creative Cocktail Consultants Corp and named after the double Academy Award winning 1999 drama film and 1985 novel by John Irving of the same name.

●●●○○

CINDERELLA

Glass: Collins
Garnish: Lemon slice
Method: SHAKE first 5 ingredients with ice and strain into ice-filled glass. **TOP** with soda water.

2	shot(s)	**Freshly squeezed orange juice**
1½	shot(s)	**Pressed pineapple juice**
¾	shot(s)	**Freshly squeezed lemon juice**
⅛	shot(s)	**Pomegranate (grenadine) syrup**
3	dashes	**Angostura aromatic bitters**
Top up with		**Soda water** (club soda)

Comment: Long, fresh and fruity.

●●●●○○

CINNAMON DAIQUIRI

Glass: Martini
Garnish: Dust with cinnamon powder
Method: SHAKE all ingredients with ice and fine strain into chilled glass.

2	shot(s)	**Bacardi Superior rum**
½	shot(s)	**Goldschläger cinnamon schnapps**
½	shot(s)	**Freshly squeezed lime juice**

Origin: Created in 1999 by Porik at Che, London, England.
Comment: A subtle spicy cinnamon taste with tangy length.

●●●●○

CITRUS CAIPIROVSKA

Glass: Old-fashioned
Method: MUDDLE lemon in base of glass. Add other ingredients and fill glass with crushed ice. **CHURN** drink with bar spoon and serve with short straws.

¾	fresh	**Lemon cut into wedges**
2	shot(s)	**Ketel One Citroen vodka**
¾	shot(s)	**Sugar syrup** (2 sugar to 1 water)

Comment: Superbly refreshing balance of sweet and citrus sourness.

●●●●○

CITRUS MARTINI

Glass: Martini
Garnish: Orange zest twist
Method: SHAKE all ingredients with ice and fine strain into chilled glass.

1½	shot(s)	**Ketel One Citroen vodka**
1	shot(s)	**Freshly squeezed lemon juice**
¼	shot(s)	**Sugar syrup** (2 sugar to 1 water)
¼	shot(s)	**Cointreau triple sec**
3	dashes	**Angostura orange bitters**

AKA: Lemon Martini
Origin: Created by Dick Bradsell at Fred's, London, England, in the late 80s.
Comment: Orange undertones add citrus depth to the lemon explosion.

●●●●○

CITRUS RUM COOLER NEW #8

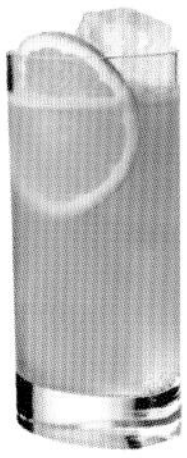

Glass: Collins
Garnish: Orange slice
Method: SHAKE first 3 ingredients with ice and strain into ice-filled glass. **TOP** with lemonade. Lightly stir and serve with straws.

1	shot(s)	**Bacardi Superior rum**
½	shot(s)	**Grand Marnier liqueur**
2	shot(s)	**Freshly squeezed orange juice**
Top up with		**Lemonade/Sprite/7-Up**

Comment: Light, fruit and refreshing.

CLARA ASTIÉ COCKTAIL NEW #8

Glass: Martini/Coupette
Garnish: Grapefruit zest twist (discarded) & dried apricot
Method: **STIR** jam with rum until jam dissolves. Add other ingredients, **SHAKE** with ice and fine strain into chilled glass.

2	shot(s)	Bacardi Superior rum
1	spoon	Apricot preserve
1	shot(s)	Noilly Prat dry vermouth
⅛	shot(s)	Luxardo maraschino liqueur
1	dash	Fee Brothers grapefruit bitters
½	shot(s)	Chilled water (omit if wet ice)

Comment: Tangy apricot with hints of maraschino dried by vermouth and fortified by light rum.
Origin: Adapted from a drink created in 2008 by Ian McLaren of Bacardi Brown-Forman Brands, UK. The name is in tribute to Doña Amalia's Godmother whose bequest revived the fortunes of Don Facundo Bacardi Massó allowing him to establish the rum brand we know today.

> 'THERE'S NOTHING WRONG WITH SOBRIETY IN MODERATION.'
> JOHN CIARDI

CLARET COBBLER

Glass: Goblet
Garnish: Mint sprig
Method: **SHAKE** all ingredients with ice and fine strain into glass filled with crushed ice. Serve with straws.

1½	shot(s)	Courvoisier V.S.O.P. cognac
1	shot(s)	Grand Marnier liqueur
2½	shot(s)	Shiraz red wine

Origin: My version of an old classic.
Comment: Fortified and slightly sweetened wine cooled and lengthened by ice.

CLAIRVOYANT NEW #8

Glass: Martini/Coupette
Garnish: Orange zest twist
Method: **STIR** all ingredients with ice and fine strain into chilled glass.

1½	shot(s)	Tio Pepe fino sherry
1½	shot(s)	Noilly Prat dry vermouth
¾	shot(s)	Frangelico hazelnut liqueur
1	dash	Angostura orange bitters

Comment: A hazelnut flavoured variation on the classic Coronation Cocktail.
Origin: Created in 2008 by Simon Difford in Jerez, Spain and named after Claire Hu, a fellow drinks hack on the same trip who was a fan of hazelnut liqueur.

CLARIDGE COCKTAIL UPDATED #8

Glass: Martini
Garnish: Lemon zest twist
Method: **SHAKE** all ingredients with ice and fine strain into chilled glass.

1½	shot(s)	Tanqueray London dry gin
1½	shot(s)	Noilly Prat dry vermouth
½	shot(s)	Cointreau triple sec
½	shot(s)	Bols apricot brandy liqueur

Comment: Gin for strength, vermouth for dryness and liqueur to sweeten – an interesting combination.
Origin: Adapted from Harry Craddock's 1930 'The Savoy Cocktail Book'.

CLASSIC COCKTAIL

Glass: Martini
Garnish: Lemon zest twist (optional sugar rim)
Method: **SHAKE** all ingredients with ice and fine strain into chilled glass.

2	shot(s)	Courvoisier V.S.O.P. cognac
½	shot(s)	Freshly squeezed lemon juice
½	shot(s)	Grand Marnier liqueur
½	shot(s)	Luxardo maraschino liqueur
½	shot(s)	Chilled mineral water (omit if wet ice)

Origin: Adapted from Harry Craddock's 1930 'The Savoy Cocktail Book'.
Comment: Reminiscent of a Sidecar with maraschino.

CLEMENTINE

Glass: Shot
Garnish: Sugar coated orange wedge
Method: Refrigerate ingredients then **LAYER** in chilled glass by carefully pouring in the following order. Instruct drinker to down in one and bite into the wedge.

| ½ | shot(s) | Luxardo limoncello liqueur |
| ½ | shot(s) | Mandarine Napoléon liqueur |

Comment: Short, sweet and very fruity.

CLIPPER COCKTAIL

Glass: Martini
Garnish: Lemon peel knot
Method: **SHAKE** all ingredients and fine strain into glass filled with crushed ice.

2	shot(s)	Bacardi Superior rum
2	shot(s)	Noilly Prat dry vermouth
½	shot(s)	Pomegranate (grenadine) syrup

Origin: Peggy Guggenheim's biography mentions that this cocktail was served during the 1940s on the Boeing flying boats known as Clippers.
Comment: Light, easy drinking and very refreshing.

CLOCKWORK ORANGE

Glass: Collins
Garnish: Orange slice in glass
Method: SHAKE all ingredients with ice and strain into ice-filled glass.

1½	shot(s)	**Courvoisier V.S.O.P. cognac**
1½	shot(s)	**Grand Marnier liqueur**
3	shot(s)	**Freshly squeezed orange juice**

Comment: Neither as memorable nor as controversial as the film but a pleasant orange drink all the same.

CLOVER LEAF COCKTAIL NO.1

UPDATED #8

Glass: Martini
Garnish: Float clover or mint leaf
Method: SHAKE all ingredients with ice and fine strain into chilled glass.

2	shot(s)	**Tanqueray London dry gin**
½	shot(s)	**Freshly squeezed lemon juice**
¼	shot(s)	**Pomegranate (grenadine) syrup**
½	fresh	**Egg white**

Variant: With raspberry syrup in place of pomegranate syrup.
AKA: Without the mint garnish this drink called a 'Clover Club'.
Comment: Smooth, aromatic, fruity and medium sweet.

CLOVER CLUB COCKTAIL NO.3 #1

(LOWE'S FORMULA) NEW #8

Glass: Martini
Garnish: None
Method: SHAKE all ingredients with ice and fine strain into chilled glass.

1	shot(s)	**Tanqueray London dry gin**
1	shot(s)	**Noilly Prat dry vermouth**
1	shot(s)	**Freshly squeezed lemon juice**
1	shot(s)	**Raspberry syrup** (1 juice to 1 sugar)
½	fresh	**Egg white**

AKA: With a mint leaf garnish this drink called a 'Clover Leaf'.
Comment: Balanced and complex with a fruity blast of raspberry – made interesting due to its inclusion of vermouth.
Origin: Recipe from 1909 Drinks - How to Mix and Serve, by Paul E. Lowe and courtesy of Dave Wondrich who says this is the earliest Clover Club recipe he has discovered. Lowe omits the lemon juice in his original recipe but this is thought to be a mistake. Albert Stevens Crockett credits the creation of this cocktail to the Bellevue-Stratford Hotel, Philadelphia in his 1931 'Old Waldorf Bar Days'.

CLOVER LEAF COCKTAIL NO.2

(MODERN FORMULA) UPDATED #8

Glass: Martini
Garnish: Float clover or mint leaf
Method: MUDDLE raspberries in base of shaker. Add other ingredients, SHAKE with ice and fine strain into chilled glass.

7	fresh	**Raspberries**
3	fresh	**Mint leaves**
2	shot(s)	**Tanqueray London dry gin**
¾	shot(s)	**Freshly squeezed lemon juice**
½	shot(s)	**Pomegranate (grenadine) syrup**
½	fresh	**Egg white**

AKA: With a mint leaf garnish this drink called a 'Clover Leaf'.
Comment: Carpet scaring red, this fruity adaptation perhaps has a wider appeal than the original Clover Leaf.

CLOVER CLUB COCKTAIL NO.3 #2

(DIFFORD'S FORMULA) NEW #8

Glass: Coupette/Martini
Garnish: Lemon zest twist (sprayed & discarded)
Method: SHAKE all ingredients with ice and fine strain into chilled glass.

1¾	shot(s)	**Tanqueray London dry gin**
¼	shot(s)	**Noilly Prat dry vermouth**
¼	shot(s)	**Martini Rosso sweet vermouth**
¼	shot(s)	**Freshly squeezed lime juice**
¼	shot(s)	**Pomegranate (grenadine) syrup**
½	fresh	**Egg white**

Comment: Creamy and easy – with notes of gin, citrus and spice.
Origin: Version of a vintage classic by Yours Truly (Simon Difford) at the Cabinet Room, London, England.

CLOYSTER NEW #8

Glass: Martini
Garnish: Grapefruit twist
Method: SHAKE all ingredients with ice and fine strain into chilled glass.

2	shot(s)	**Tanqueray London dry gin**
½	shot(s)	**Yellow Chartreuse liqueur**
½	shot(s)	**Freshly squeezed grapefruit juice**
¼	shot(s)	**Freshly squeezed lemon juice**
⅛	shot(s)	**Sugar syrup** (2 sugar to 1 water)
¼	shot(s)	**Chilled mineral water** (omit if wet ice)

Comment: There's a suitable subtle monastic influence to this complex, gin based, most learned of cocktails.
Origin: Adapted from a drink created in 2007 by John Deragon at PDT, New York City, USA.

CLUB COCKTAIL #1

Glass: Martini
Garnish: Orange zest twist
Method: **STIR** all ingredients with ice and strain into chilled glass.

1½	shot(s)	**Tio Pepe Fino sherry**
1½	shot(s)	**Warre's Otima tawny port**
1	dash	**Angostura orange bitters**

Origin: In his 1948 'The Fine Art of Mixing Drinks', David A. Embury writes, "Perhaps it would not be too much of an exaggeration to say there are as many Club Cocktails as there are clubs." This example is adapted from the same book.
Comment: Dry and incredibly aromatic. A perfect aperitif.

CLUB COCKTAIL #2

Glass: Martini
Garnish: Stuffed olive
Method: **SHAKE** all ingredients with ice and strain into chilled glass.

2	shot(s)	**Tanqueray London dry gin**
1	shot(s)	**Martini Rosso sweet vermouth**
⅛	shot(s)	**Yellow Chartreuse liqueur**

Origin: Adapted from Harry Craddock's 1930 'The Savoy Cocktail Book'.
Comment: A sweet Martini with a hint of Chartreuse.

CLUB COCKTAIL #3

Glass: Martini
Garnish: Maraschino cherry in drink
Method: **STIR** all ingredients with ice and fine strain into chilled glass.

2	shot(s)	**Bacardi Oro golden rum**
½	shot(s)	**Martini Rosso sweet vermouth**
½	shot(s)	**Noilly Prat dry vermouth**
½	shot(s)	**Maraschino syrup** (from cherry jar)
3	dashes	**Angostura aromatic bitters**
¾	shot(s)	**Chilled mineral water** (reduce if wet ice)

Origin: Adapted from a drink created in 2002 by Michael Butt at Milk & Honey, London, England.
Comment: An aromatic, spirited, classical cocktail.

CLUBLAND COCKTAIL *NEW #8*

Glass: Coupette/Martini
Garnish: Orange zest twist
Method: **STIR** all ingredients with ice and fine strain into chilled glass.

1½	shot(s)	**Ketel One vodka**
1½	shot(s)	**Taylor's Chip dry white port**
1	dash	**Angostura aromatic bitters**

Comment: Go easy on the bitters and this is a complex and rewarding Martini-style drink.
Origin: In W.J. Tarling's (Bill Tarling) 1937 Café Royal Cocktail Book Coronation edition the creation of this drink is credited to one A. Mackintosh. Originally made with a brand of port called Clubland, hence this drink's name.

COBBLED RASPBERRY MARTINI

Glass: Martini
Garnish: Mint leaf & raspberries on stick
Method: **MUDDLE** raspberries in base of shaker. Add other ingredients, **SHAKE** with ice and fine strain into chilled glass.

12	fresh	**Raspberries**
2	shot(s)	**Ketel One vodka**
1	shot(s)	**Shiraz red wine**
¼	shot(s)	**Sugar syrup** (2 sugar to 1 water)

Origin: Created by Yours Truly (Simon Difford) in 2004.
Comment: The addition of a splash of wine to a simple Raspberry Martini adds another level of complexity.

COBBLERS *UPDATED #8*

Glass: Goblet
Garnish: Mint sprig
Method: **SHAKE** all ingredients with ice and fine strain into glass filled with crushed ice. Serve with straws.

1½	shot(s)	**Courvoisier V.S.O.P. cognac**
1	shot(s)	**Grand Marnier liqueur**
2½	shot(s)	**Shiraz red wine**

Comment: Fortified and slightly sweetened wine cooled and lengthened by ice. This is my version of the classic recipe.

Origin: Cobblers emerged in the mid 1800s and circa 1880 the bartender Harry Johnson said of the Sherry Cobbler "This drink is without doubt the most popular beverage in this country, with ladies as well as with gentlemen. It is a very refreshing drink for old and young."

Cobblers are served with straws in a goblet filled with crushed ice and decorated with fruit and a sprig or two of mint. They are based on spirits and/or wine sweetened with sugar syrup or sweet liqueur. Classically Cobblers contain little or no citrus but modern variations often call for citrus and other fruits to be muddled. Personally I believe it's the lack of citrus that sets Cobblers apart. The best examples of these use the tannin and acidity in the wine to bitter and so balance.

Cobblers are also classically built in the glass. I prefer to shake mine to properly cool and mix them before straining over fresh crushed ice and stirring. I've taken to calling neo-Martinis which use wine in place of citrus 'Cobbled Martinis' (see Cobbled Raspberry Martini) although I understand that the name actually refers to the ice and not the fruit.

Interestingly, this drink is often cited for heralding in the paper straw which wasn't patented until 1888. Prior to that straws were just that, 'straw', usually rye, or even hollow pasta (macaroni or vermicelli).

EL COCO *NEW #8*

Glass: Martini/Coupette
Garnish: Lime zest twist
Method: **STIR** all ingredients with ice and fine strain into chilled glass.

2	shot(s)	**Bacardi Superior rum**
1	shot(s)	**Fresh coconut water**
¼	shot(s)	**Sugar syrup** (2 sugar to 1 water)
⅛	shot(s)	**Freshly squeezed lime juice**

Comment: Rum and coconut water with the merest hint of lime.
Origin: Created in 2008 by Richard Hunt at Mahiki, London, England and named after the coconut palm outside the original Bacardi distillery in Santiago de Cuba.

COCO CABANA

Glass: Martini
Garnish: Pineapple wedge on rim
Method: SHAKE all ingredients with ice and fine strain into chilled glass.

1½	shot(s)	**Malibu coconut rum liqueur**
½	shot(s)	**Midori green melon liqueur**
2	shot(s)	**Pressed pineapple juice**
¾	shot(s)	**Double (heavy) cream**
¾	shot(s)	**Milk**

Comment: A sweet, creamy tropical number for Barry Manilow fans.

COCO NAUT

Glass: Hurricane
Garnish: Pineapple wedge & cherry on rim
Method: BLEND ingredients with 12oz scoop of crushed ice. Pour into glass and serve with straws.

2	shot(s)	**Wray & Nephew overproof rum**
1½	shot(s)	**Coco López cream of coconut**
1	shot(s)	**Freshly squeezed lime juice**

Comment: This snow-white drink is hardly innocent with a double shot of overproof rum masked by the sweet coconut.

COCONUT DAIQUIRI

Glass: Martini
Garnish: Lime wedge
Method: SHAKE all ingredients with ice and fine strain into chilled glass.

2	shot(s)	**Bacardi Superior rum**
1	shot(s)	**Malibu coconut rum liqueur**
½	shot(s)	**Freshly squeezed lime juice**
½	shot(s)	**Coconut syrup**
¾	shot(s)	**Chilled mineral water** (omit if wet ice)

Variant: Blend with a 6oz scoop of crushed ice and a tad more coconut syrup.
Comment: That special Daiquiri flavour with a pleasing tropical touch.

COCONUT WATER

Glass: Martini
Method: STIR all ingredients with ice and fine strain into chilled glass.

2¼	shot(s)	**Malibu coconut rum liqueur**
1	shot(s)	**Ketel One vodka**
⅛	shot(s)	**Coconut syrup**
1¼	shot(s)	**Chilled mineral water** (reduce if wet ice)

Origin: Created in 2003 by Yours Truly (Simon Difford).
Comment: Have you ever drunk from a fresh coconut in the Caribbean? Well, this is the alcoholic equivalent.

COFFEE BATIDA

Glass: Old-fashioned
Garnish: Float 3 coffee beans
Method: BLEND all ingredients with crushed ice and serve with straws.

2	shot(s)	**Leblon cachaça**
1	shot(s)	**Espresso coffee**
1	shot(s)	**Kahlúa coffee liqueur**
½	shot(s)	**Sugar syrup** (2 sugar to 1 water)

Comment: Fortunately this caffeine and cachaça laced cocktail tastes a good deal better than it looks.

COFFEE COCKTAIL NEW #8

Glass: Small wine glass
Garnish: Dust with freshly ground nutmeg
Method: SHAKE all ingredients with ice and fine strain into chilled glass.

2	shot(s)	**Warre's Otima tawny port**
1	shot(s)	**Courvoisier V.S.O.P. cognac**
½	shot(s)	**Sugar syrup** (2 sugar to 1 water)
1	fresh	**Egg** (white & yolk)

Comment: As the anonymous writer of the 1887 edition comments, "The name of this drink is a misnomer, as coffee and bitters are not to be found among its ingredients, but it looks like coffee when it has been properly concocted."
Origin: Recipe adapted from Jerry Thomas's 1887 'The Bartender's Guide, or How to Mix All Kinds of Plain and Fancy Drinks'.

COFFEE & VANILLA DAIQUIRI

Glass: Martini
Garnish: Float 3 coffee beans
Method: SHAKE all ingredients with ice and fine strain into chilled glass.

2	shot(s)	**Vanilla-infused Bacardi rum**
1	shot(s)	**Kahlúa coffee liqueur**
½	shot(s)	**Freshly squeezed lime juice**
⅛	shot(s)	**Sugar syrup** (2 sugar to 1 water)
¾	shot(s)	**Chilled mineral water** (omit if wet ice)

Origin: Created in 2002 by Yours Truly (Simon Difford).
Comment: Coffee, vanilla, sweetness and sourness.

COLA DE MONO

Glass: Martini
Garnish: Dust with cinnamon powder
Method: MUDDLE cinnamon stick and pisco in base of shaker. Add other ingredients, **SHAKE** with ice and fine strain into a chilled glass.

1	inch	**Cinnamon stick**
2	shot(s)	**Macchu pisco**
1	shot(s)	**Espresso coffee**
1	shot(s)	**Kahlúa coffee liqueur**

Origin: I based this on a Chilean drink traditionally consumed at Christmas, the name of which translates as 'Tail of Monkey'. The original uses milk and sugar instead of coffee liqueur.
Comment: Coffee and cinnamon – a drink to be savoured.

COLD BLOODED NEW #8

Glass: Old-fashioned
Garnish: Rosemary sprig
Method: MUDDLE rosemary in base of shaker. Add other ingredients, **SHAKE** with ice and fine strain into ice-filled glass.

1	fresh	**Rosemary sprig**
1½	shot(s)	**Grand Marnier liqueur**
2	shot(s)	**Ocean Spray cranberry juice**
½	shot(s)	**Freshly squeezed lemon juice**
½	shot(s)	**Sugar syrup (2 sugar to 1 water)**

Comment: Red berry, orange and pine.
Origin: Adapted from a drink discovered in 2008 on Steve Olson's akawinegeek.com site.

COLD COMFORT

Glass: Old-fashioned
Method: SHAKE all ingredients with ice and strain into ice-filled glass.

2	shot(s)	**Wray & Nephew overproof rum**
6	spoons	**Runny honey**
1	shot(s)	**Freshly squeezed lime juice**

Origin: I discovered this while in Jamaica in 2001.
Comment: Take at the first sign of a cold, and then retreat under your bedcovers. Repeat dose regularly while symptoms persist. Warning – do not consume with other forms of medication.

THE COLD WINTER WARMER SOUR

Glass: Old-fashioned
Garnish: Orange slice & cherry on stick (sail)
Method: STIR honey with vodka in base of shaker until honey dissolves. Add other ingredients, **SHAKE** with ice and strain into ice-filled glass.

1	spoon	**Runny honey**
1	shot(s)	**Ketel One Citroen vodka**
½	shot(s)	**Bénédictine D.O.M. liqueur**
1	shot(s)	**Freshly squeezed lemon juice**
½	fresh	**Egg white**

Origin: Created in 2006 by Yours Truly (Simon Difford).
Comment: Flavours reminiscent of a hot toddy but served in a cold sour.

COLLAR & CUFF

Glass: Toddy
Garnish: Orange slice
Method: PLACE bar spoon in glass, add ingredients and **STIR**.

2	spoons	**Runny honey**
1	shot(s)	**Johnnie Walker Scotch whisky**
1	shot(s)	**Domaine de Canton ginger liqueur**
1	shot(s)	**Freshly squeezed lemon juice**
Top up with		**Boiling water**

Origin: Created in 2003 by Yours Truly (Simon Difford).
Comment: This blonde drink is warmed with ginger.

COLLECTION MARTINI

Glass: Martini
Garnish: Lime wedge
Method: SHAKE all ingredients with ice and fine strain into chilled glass.

¾	shot(s)	**Ketel One vodka**
¾	shot(s)	**Ketel One Citroen vodka**
¾	shot(s)	**Bénédictine D.O.M. liqueur**
¾	shot(s)	**Crème de mûre liqueur**
½	shot(s)	**Freshly squeezed lime juice**

Origin: Originally created by Matthew Randall whilst at The Collection, London, England.
Comment: Honey, spice and vodka enhanced by blackberries, with a very alcoholic edge.

COLLINS UPDATED #8

Glass: Collins
Garnish: Orange slice & cherry on stick (sail)
Method: SHAKE first 3 ingredients with ice and strain into ice-filled glass. **TOP** with soda, lightly stir and serve with straws.

2	shot(s)	**Bokma oude genever**
1	shot(s)	**Freshly squeezed lemon juice**
½	shot(s)	**Sugar syrup** (2 sugar to 1 water)
Top up with		**Soda water** (club soda)

Comment: Some say the John/Tom Collins was originally made with genever. So is this the original or an adaption on the Tom Collins. We will probably never know but whatever, it tastes great.
Origin: In England, this drink is traditionally credited to John Collins, a bartender who worked at Limmer's Hotel, Conduit Street, London. The 'coffee house' of this hotel, a true dive bar, was popular with sporting types during the 19th century, and famous, according to the 1860s memoirs of a Captain Gronow, for its gin-punch as early as 1814.

Others say that the Tom Collins originated in New York, and takes its name from the Great Tom Collins Hoax of 1874, a practical joke which involved telling a friend that a man named Tom Collins had been insulting them, and that he could be found in a bar some distance away, and took the city by storm. This is supported by the fact that the first known written occurrence of a Tom Collins cocktail recipe is found in the 1876 edition of Jerry Thomas' 'The Bartender's Guide'.

An alternative story attributes the drink to a Collins who started work at a New York tavern called the Whitehouse in 1873 and started pouring a thirst quencher made with gin. Another identifies a different Tom Collins, who worked as a bartender in New Jersey and New York area. There are apparently also versions of its creation in San Francisco and Australia, and it is not impossible that the drink evolved in two or more places independently.

There is also debate as to whether Old Tom gin, London Dry gin or Dutch genever was the original spirit base. Other spirits have since spawned an entire family of Collins' variants as follows:

Captain Collins (with Canadian whiskey)
Colonel Collins (with bourbon)
Jack Collins (with vodka)
Jock or Sandy Collins (with Scotch whisky)
Joe Collins (with vodka)
John Collins (with London dry gin)
Mike Collins (with Irish whiskey)
Pedro Collins (with light white rum)
Pepito Collins (with tequila)
Pierre Collins (with cognac or brandy)
Tom Collins (with old tom gin)
Vodka Collins (AKA Joe Collins)

COLONEL COLLINS

Glass: Collins
Garnish: Orange slice & cherry on stick (sail)
Method: SHAKE first 3 ingredients with ice and strain into ice-filled glass. **TOP** with soda, stir and serve with straws.

2	shot(s)	**Bulleit bourbon whiskey**
1	shot(s)	**Freshly squeezed lemon juice**
½	shot(s)	**Sugar syrup** (2 sugar to 1 water)
Top up with		**Soda water** (club soda)

Origin: Classic Collins variation.
Comment: Sweetened, soured and diluted bourbon.

COLONEL T

Glass: Sling
Garnish: Pineapple wedge
Method: SHAKE all ingredients with ice and strain into ice-filled glass.

2	shot(s)	**Bulleit bourbon whiskey**
1	shot(s)	**Bols apricot brandy liqueur**
2½	shot(s)	**Pressed pineapple juice**

Comment: Mellow and long with pineapple, apricot and bourbon.

COLONEL'S BIG OPU

Glass: Collins
Garnish: Orange slice & cherry on stick (sail)
Method: SHAKE first 3 ingredients with ice and strain into ice-filled glass. **TOP** with champagne and serve with straws.

1	shot(s)	**Tanqueray London dry gin**
1	shot(s)	**Cointreau triple sec**
½	shot(s)	**Freshly squeezed lime juice**
Top up with		**Perrier Jouet brut champagne**
1	dash	**Angostura orange bitters** (optional)

Origin: Adapted from a recipe created by Victor J. Bergeron and taken from his 'Trader Vic's Bartender's Guide' (1972 revised edition), where he writes "This is one of our old drinks. The colonel's big opu: the colonel's big belly."
Comment: A long, fruity yet dry drink charged with champagne.

COLONIAL ROT

Glass: Collins
Garnish: Mint sprig
Method: Lightly **MUDDLE** mint in base of shaker just enough to bruise. Add next 4 ingredients, **SHAKE** with ice and fine strain into ice-filled glass. **TOP** up with half soda and half lemonade.

7	fresh	**Mint leaves**
½	shot(s)	**La Fée Parisienne (68%) absinthe**
1	shot(s)	**Ketel One Citroen vodka**
½	shot(s)	**Sugar syrup** (2 sugar to 1 water)
½	shot(s)	**Freshly squeezed lime juice**
Top up with		**Half soda and half lemonade**

Comment: Long and green with more than a touch of the green fairy.

COLONY NEW #8

Glass: Martini
Garnish: Grapefruit zest twist
Method: SHAKE all ingredients with ice and fine strain into chilled glass.

1½	shot(s)	**Tanqueray London dry gin**
¾	shot(s)	**Freshly squeezed grapefruit juice**
¼	shot(s)	**Luxardo maraschino liqueur**

Comment: Grapefruit and maraschino balance each other in the gin based classic.
Origin: Created during the Prohibition period at New York's Colony speakeasy, possibly by bartender Marco Hattem. The Colony attracted an upmarket Clientele, including the Vanderbilts and Windsors. The liquor was kept in an elevator which would be sent to either that attic or the basement if federal agents raided.

COLORADO BULLDOG

Glass: Collins
Method: SHAKE first 4 ingredients with ice and strain into ice-filled glass. **TOP** with Coca-Cola.

1½	shot(s)	**Ketel One vodka**
1	shot(s)	**Kahlúa coffee liqueur**
1	shot(s)	**Double (heavy) cream**
1	shot(s)	**Milk**
Top up with		**Coca-Cola**

Variant: Colorado Mother (with tequila in place of vodka).
Comment: This dog's bite is hidden by cream.

COLUMBUS DAIQUIRI

Glass: Martini
Garnish: Lime wedge on rim
Method: SHAKE all ingredients with ice and fine strain into chilled glass.

1	shot(s)	**Bacardi Oro golden rum**
1	shot(s)	**Bols apricot brandy liqueur**
1	shot(s)	**Freshly squeezed lime juice**
½	shot(s)	**Chilled mineral water** (omit if wet ice)

Comment: A tangy, apricot flavoured Daiquiri.

THE COMET

Glass: Martini
Garnish: Lemon zest twist
Method: MUDDLE grapes in base of shaker. Add other ingredients, **SHAKE** with ice and fine strain into chilled glass.

7	fresh	**Seedless white grapes**
2	shot(s)	**Courvoisier V.S.O.P. cognac**
¾	shot(s)	**Grand Marnier liqueur**
1	dash	**Angostura aromatic bitters**

Origin: Created by Eddie Clark at the Albany Club, Albemarle Street, London, to celebrate the launch of the Comet jetliner in 1952.
Comment: Cognac with freshly extracted grape juice and a splash of orange liqueur.

COMMODORE #1

Glass: Martini
Garnish: Maraschino cherry
Method: SHAKE all ingredients with ice and fine strain into chilled glass.

2	shot(s)	Bacardi Oro golden rum
½	shot(s)	Freshly squeezed lemon juice
¼	shot(s)	Sugar syrup (2 sugar to 1 water)
⅛	shot(s)	Pomegranate (grenadine) syrup
½	fresh	Egg white

Origin: Adapted from David A. Embury's 1948 'The Fine Art of Mixing Drinks', where he writes, "Another version of the Commodore calls for whisky instead of rum, omits the egg white, and uses orange bitters in place of the grenadine. Obviously, the two Commodores command two different fleets."
Comment: A smooth, sweet Daiquiri with flavoursome rum.

> ## 'I'D RATHER HAVE A BOTTLE IN FRONT OF ME THAN A FRONTAL LOBOTOMY.'
> ### TOM WAITS

COMMODORE #2

Glass: Martini
Garnish: Maraschino cherry
Method: SHAKE all ingredients with ice and fine strain into chilled glass.

2	shot(s)	Bulleit bourbon whiskey
¾	shot(s)	White crème de cacao liqueur
½	shot(s)	Freshly squeezed lemon juice
¼	shot(s)	Pomegranate (grenadine) syrup
2	dashes	Angostura orange bitters (optional)

Comment: Fruity, tangy Bourbon - surprisingly dry.

CONCEALED WEAPON

Glass: Old-fashioned
Garnish: Lemon zest twist
Method: SHAKE all ingredients with ice and strain into ice-filled glass.

1	shot(s)	La Fée Parisienne (68%) absinthe
1	shot(s)	Chambord black raspberry liqueur
¾	shot(s)	Freshly squeezed lemon juice
½	shot(s)	Sugar syrup (2 sugar to 1 water)
1	dash	Peychaud's aromatic bitters
1	dash	Angostura aromatic bitters
½	fresh	Egg white

Origin: Created in 2000 by Danny Smith at Che, London, England.
Comment: Absinthe is the 'weapon' that's 'concealed' in this full-on short berry drink.

CONGO BLUE

Glass: Martini
Garnish: Lemon zest twist
Method: SHAKE all ingredients with ice and fine strain into chilled glass.

1¼	shot(s)	Zubrówka bison vodka
½	shot(s)	Midori green melon liqueur
1	shot(s)	Pressed apple juice
½	shot(s)	Crème de mûre liqueur
¼	shot(s)	Freshly squeezed lemon juice

Origin: Created in 1999 by Marc Dietrich at Atlantic Bar & Grill, London and apparently named after the beauty of the Congo sunset.
Comment: Flavoursome and sweet.

COOL MARTINI

Glass: Martini
Garnish: Apple slice chevron
Method: SHAKE all ingredients with ice and fine strain into chilled glass.

1½	shot(s)	Midori green melon liqueur
1	shot(s)	Don Julio reposado tequila
1½	shot(s)	Ocean Spray cranberry juice

Comment: Tastes nothing like the ingredients - which include melon, tequila and cranberry juice. Try it and see if you taste toffee.

COOL ORCHARD

Glass: Old-fashioned
Garnish: Pineapple wedge & cherry
Method: MUDDLE ginger in base of shaker. Add other ingredients, SHAKE with ice and fine strain into ice-filled glass.

2	slices	Fresh root ginger (thumbnail sized)
1½	shot(s)	Zacapa aged rum
½	shot(s)	Ginger sugar syrup
¼	shot(s)	Almond (orgeat) syrup
1	shot(s)	Pressed pineapple juice
½	shot(s)	Vanilla schnapps liqueur
¼	shot(s)	Freshly squeezed lime juice

Origin: Created in 2001 by Douglas Ankrah for Akbar, Soho, London, England.
Comment: An unusual line up of cocktail ingredients combine to make a great drink.

COOLMAN MARTINI

Glass: Martini
Garnish: Orange zest twist
Method: SHAKE all ingredients with ice and fine strain into chilled glass.

1¾	shot(s)	Zubrówka bison vodka
½	shot(s)	Cointreau triple sec
2	shot(s)	Pressed apple juice
¼	shot(s)	Freshly squeezed lemon juice

Origin: Created in 2001 by Jack Coleman at The Library Bar, Lanesborough Hotel, London, England.
Comment: Fragrant and complex. Integrated hints of apple and orange are laced with grassy vodka.

COOPERSTOWN MARTINI NEW #8

Glass: Coupette/Martini
Garnish: Orange zest twist (discarded) & mint sprig
Method: STIR all ingredients (including mint) with ice and fine strain into chilled glass.

8	fresh	**Mint leaves**
2½	shot(s)	**Tanqueray London dry gin**
¼	shot(s)	**Noilly Prat dry vermouth**
¼	shot(s)	**Martini Rosso sweet vermouth**

Comment: A minty Perfect Martini which is made more widely appreciated by the addition of half a barspoon of sugar syrup.

COPPER ILLUSION

Glass: Old-fashioned
Garnish: Orange zest twist
Method: STIR all ingredients with ice and strain into ice-filled glass.

1½	shot(s)	**Tanqueray London dry gin**
¾	shot(s)	**Campari Bitter**
¾	shot(s)	**Cointreau triple sec**

Variant: Negroni
Origin: Unknown but brought to my attention in 2005 courtesy of Angus Winchester and alconomics.com.
Comment: Basically a Negroni with liqueur replacing sweet vermouth. Like the Italian classic this is both bitter and sweet.

COQUETAIL AU VANILLA

Glass: Old-fashioned
Garnish: Maraschino cherry
Method: SHAKE all ingredients with ice and strain into glass filled with crushed ice. Serve with straws.

2	shot(s)	**Vanilla-infused Bacardi rum**
¼	shot(s)	**Velvet Falernum liqueur**

Origin: My adaptation of a classic.
Comment: This drink may look fluffy and sweet but it's dry and lightly spiced. Perfect for a sunny afternoon.

CORDLESS SCREWDRIVER

Glass: Shot
Garnish: Sugar coated half orange slice
Method: POUR vodka and champagne into chilled glass and serve. Instruct drinker to down in one and then bite into the orange wedge.

1	shot(s)	**Orange-infused Ketel One vodka**
Top up with		**Perrier Jouet brut champagne**

Comment: A slammer style drink for those looking for a fruity alternative to tequila.

CORNWALL NEGRONI NEW #8

Glass: Coupette/Martini
Garnish: Orange zest twist (flamed)
Method: STIR all ingredients with ice and strain into chilled glass.

2	shot(s)	**Tanqueray London dry gin**
½	shot(s)	**Campari Bitter**
½	shot(s)	**Punt e Mes**
½	shot(s)	**Martini Rosso sweet vermouth**
2	dashes	**Regan's Orange #6**

Comment: A bone-dry cocktail for very adult experienced palates. Cheers Gary.
Origin: Created in 2006 by Chad Solomon at Pegu Club, New York, USA as a tribute to Gary Regan who is originally from Cornwall.

CORONATION

Glass: Collins
Garnish: Maraschino cherry
Method: STIR first 5 ingredients with ice and strain into ice-filled glass. TOP with soda, stir and serve with straws.

1	shot(s)	**Tio Pepe fino sherry**
1	shot(s)	**Noilly Prat dry vermouth**
2	shot(s)	**Sauvignon Blanc wine**
¼	shot(s)	**Luxardo maraschino liqueur**
2	dashes	**Angostura aromatic bitters**
Top up with		**Soda water** (club soda)

Comment: Light and aromatic.

CORONATION COCKTAIL NO.1

Glass: Martini
Garnish: Orange zest twist
Method: STIR all ingredients with ice and strain into chilled glass.

1½	shot(s)	**Tio Pepe fino sherry**
1½	shot(s)	**Noilly Prat dry vermouth**
¼	shot(s)	**Luxardo maraschino liqueur**
2	dashes	**Angostura orange bitters**

Origin: Adapted from Harry Craddock's 1930 'The Savoy Cocktail Book'.
Comment: Medium dry and wonderfully aromatic.

CORPSE REVIVER NO.1 #1

Glass: Martini
Garnish: Orange zest twist
Method: STIR ingredients with ice and strain into chilled glass.

1½	shot(s)	**Courvoisier V.S.O.P. cognac**
¾	shot(s)	**Boulard Grand Solage calvados**
¾	shot(s)	**Martini Rosso sweet vermouth**
½	shot(s)	**Chilled mineral water** (omit if wet ice)

Origin: Created by Frank Meier, Ritz Bar, Paris, France. This recipe is adapted from Harry Craddock's 1930 'The Savoy Cocktail Book', where he writes, "To be taken before 11am, or whenever steam and energy are needed."
Comment: Dry and potent. A 'pick-me-up' hangover cure – or possibly put-you-right-back-down-again!

CORPSE REVIVER NO.1 #2

(GILBERG'S RECIPE) NEW #8

Glass: Martini
Garnish: Lemon zest twist
Method: STIR all ingredients with ice and strain into chilled glass.

2	shot(s)	**Boulard Grand Solage calvados**
¾	shot(s)	**Courvoisier V.S.O.P. cognac**
¾	shot(s)	**Martini Rosso sweet vermouth**

Comment: Strong enough to awaken the dead.
Origin: In his book 'The Joy of Mixology', Gary Regan recommends this version of the Corpse Reviver, which he writes was originally created in 2001 by Steve Gilberg, publisher of happyhours.com.

CORPSE REVIVER NO.2 #1

(SAVOY RECIPE) NEW #8

Glass: Martini
Garnish: Lemon zest twist
Method: SHAKE all ingredients with ice and fine strain into chilled glass.

¾	shot(s)	**Tanqueray London dry gin**
¾	shot(s)	**Cointreau triple sec**
¾	shot(s)	**Noilly Prat dry vermouth**
¾	shot(s)	**Freshly squeezed lemon juice**
⅛	shot(s)	**La Fée Parisienne (68%) absinthe**

Comment: Well balanced with zesty lemon and absinthe just shinning above other ingredients.
Origin: Adapted from 1930 Savoy Cocktail Book where Harry Craddock says of this drink, "Four of these taken in swift succession will unrevive the corpse again". Harry originally stipulated Kina Lillet as dry vermouth.

CORPSE REVIVER NO.2 #2 NEW #8

Glass: Martini
Garnish: Lemon zest twist
Method: STIR all ingredients with ice and strain into chilled glass.

¾	shot(s)	**Tanqueray London dry gin**
¾	shot(s)	**Yellow Chartreuse liqueur**
¾	shot(s)	**Noilly Prat dry vermouth**
¾	shot(s)	**Freshly squeezed lemon juice**
⅛	shot(s)	**La Fée Parisienne (68%) absinthe**

Comment: If a mouthwash tasted great and kicked you in the balls, then this would be it.
Origin: I noticed this version is popular with modern day bartenders, who, where possible follow Harry Craddock's original stipulation for Kina Lillet as dry vermouth.

DRINKS ARE GRADED AS FOLLOWS:

- DISGUSTING
- PRETTY AWFUL
- BEST AVOIDED
- DISAPPOINTING
- ACCEPTABLE
- GOOD
- RECOMMENDED
- HIGHLY RECOMMENDED
- OUTSTANDING / EXCEPTIONAL

CORPSE REVIVER #3

Glass: Martini
Garnish: Lemon zest twist
Method: SHAKE all ingredients with ice and fine strain into chilled glass.

¾	shot(s)	**Tanqueray London dry gin**
¾	shot(s)	**Swedish Punch**
¾	shot(s)	**Cointreau triple sec**
⅛	shot(s)	**La Fée Parisienne (68%) absinthe**
¾	shot(s)	**Freshly squeezed lemon juice**

Origin: Adapted from Victor Bergeron's 'Trader Vic's Bartender's Guide' (1972 revised edition).
Comment: Perhaps a tad sweet but the kill or cure alcohol is well masked. Steady!

> 'WHEN I PLAYED DRUNKS I HAD TO REMAIN SOBER BECAUSE I DIDN'T KNOW HOW TO PLAY THEM WHEN I WAS DRUNK.'
> RICHARD BURTON

COSMOGRONI NEW #8

Glass: Martini
Garnish: Orange zest twist
Method: SHAKE all ingredients with ice and fine strain into chilled glass.

½	shot(s)	**Tanqueray London dry gin**
1	shot(s)	**Campari Bitter**
¼	shot(s)	**Martini Rosso sweet vermouth**
1½	shot(s)	**Ocean Spray cranberry juice**

Comment: One for Campari lovers.
Origin: Recipe adapted from one discovered on DrinkBoy.com in February 2008. If this is your drink, please let me know.

COSMOPOLITAN #1

(DIFFORD'S FORMULA) UPDATED #8

Glass: Martini
Garnish: Flamed orange zest twist
Method: SHAKE all ingredients with ice and fine strain into chilled glass.

1	shot(s)	**Ketel One vodka**
1	shot(s)	**Cointreau triple sec**
1½	shot(s)	**Ocean Spray cranberry juice**
½	shot(s)	**Freshly squeezed lime juice**
1	dash	**Angostura orange bitters** (optional)

Comment: An authentic Cosmopolitan should be made with citrus vodka and this formula also works well if flavoured vodka is substituted. However, I prefer the simplicity of this recipe which when quality juice with at least 24% cranberry is used, the balance of vodka, citrus, berry fruit and sweetness is perfect.
Origin: The Cosmopolitan is one of those drinks that has had various incarnations through the ages – some of them, quite probably, independent of one another. And during the 1990s, the familiar blend of cranberry, citrus and vodka was one of the most popular cocktails in London and New York.

Most people agree a Cosmopolitan appeared on the West Coast of America at some point during the 1980s, and travelled from there to New York and beyond. Cheryl Cook has a claim to have invented the drink during the latter half of the 1980s while head bartender at The Strand on Washington Avenue, South Beach, Miami. She apparently based her drink on the newly available Absolut Citron vodka and added a splash of triple sec, a dash of Rose's lime and, in her own words, "just enough cranberry to make it oh so pretty in pink".

Her version is believed to have travelled by way of San Francisco to Manhattan where Toby Cecchini is credited with first using fresh lime juice in place of Rose's at his Passerby bar.

A likely early ancestor of the Cosmopolitan is the Harpoon, a drink promoted by Ocean Spray during the 1960s which consisted of vodka, cranberry juice and a squeeze of fresh lime. And a long-forgotten 1934 book of gin recipes, 'Pioneers of Mixing Gin at Elite Bars', contains a recipe for a Cosmopolitan that is very similar to today's drink, only with lemon in place of lime, gin in place of vodka, and raspberry in place of cranberry.

Whatever the origin, however, it was Sex And The City's Carrie Bradshaw who popularised the drink when she swapped Martinis for Cosmos. And New York's Dale DeGroff played a large part in refining today's popular recipe.

> **'I'M A CHRISTIAN, BUT THAT DOESN'T MEAN I'M A LONG-FACED SQUARE. I LIKE A LITTLE BOURBON.'**
> PRESIDENT CARTER'S MOTHER.

COSMOPOLITAN #2
(DEGROFF'S FORMULA) UPDATED #8

Glass: Martini
Garnish: Flamed orange zest twist
Method: SHAKE all ingredients with ice and fine strain into chilled glass.

1½	shot(s)	**Ketel One Citroen vodka**
½	shot(s)	**Cointreau triple sec**
1	shot(s)	**Ocean Spray cranberry juice**
¼	shot(s)	**Freshly squeezed lime juice**

Comment: This is the definitive Cosmo recipe from the man most associated with the drinks development and popularity.
Origin: Although it is generally agreed that the Cosmopolitan originated on America's West Coast sometime during the 1980s, this drink is most closely identified with New York City where bar legend, Dale DeGroff, and HBO's 'Sex and the City' perfected the drink and made it stylish.

This recipe is from Dale's 2002 'The Craft of the Cocktail' where he also explains that while he did not invent the Cosmopolitan, in his own words, "What I did do was popularize a definitive recipe that became widely accepted as the standard."

Dale put the drink on his menu at New York's Rainbow Room in 1996 and shortly after it was reported that Madonna had enjoyed one. As a result Dale received calls from all over the world asking for the recipe, which he had perfected by adding a dash of Cointreau and a flamed orange peel twist. New York Magazine credited Dale with the drinks invention, other publications followed this and he was asked to present it on several television stations.

When the HBO television series, 'Sex and the City', debuted in 1998, its creators decided the cosmopolitan would be the perfect accompaniment to Carrie Bradshaw's fashionista Manhattan lifestyle. Carrie, Miranda, Charlotte and sexpot Samantha where frequently shown sipping Cosmos and when the series hit the big screen in 2007, the film closed with the girls questioning why they had ever stopped drinking them.

COSMOPOLITAN #3 (1934 RECIPE)

Glass: Martini
Garnish: Orange zest twist
Method: SHAKE all ingredients with ice and fine strain into chilled glass.

2	shot(s)	**Tanqueray London dry gin**
½	shot(s)	**Cointreau triple sec**
¾	shot(s)	**Freshly squeezed lemon juice**
¼	shot(s)	**Raspberry syrup** (or pomegranate)

Origin: Recipe adapted from 1934 'Pioneers of Mixing Gin at Elite Bars'.
Comment: Reminiscent of a Sidecar and, dependent on your syrup, well balanced. Thanks to drinkboy.com forum for first bringing this drink to my attention.

COSMOPOLITAN DELIGHT

Glass: Martini
Garnish: Flamed orange zest twist
Method: SHAKE all ingredients with ice and fine strain into chilled glass.

1½	shot(s)	**Courvoisier V.S.O.P. cognac**
½	shot(s)	**Grand Marnier liqueur**
1¼	shot(s)	**Shiraz red wine**
¾	shot(s)	**Freshly squeezed lemon juice**
¼	shot(s)	**Almond (orgeat) syrup**
¼	shot(s)	**Sugar syrup** (2 sugar to 1 water)

Origin: Adapted from Dale DeGroff's book, 'The Craft of the Cocktail'. He credits the original recipe to a 1902 book by Charlie Paul.
Comment: No relation to the modern Cosmopolitan, this is a mellow, balanced blend of citrus, brandy and red wine.

COUNTRY BREEZE

Glass: Collins
Garnish: Berries
Method: SHAKE all ingredients with ice and strain into ice-filled glass.

2	shot(s)	**Tanqueray London dry gin**
½	shot(s)	**Crème de cassis liqueur**
3½	shot(s)	**Pressed apple juice**

Comment: Not too sweet. The gin character shines through the fruit.

COVADONGA

Glass: Martini
Garnish: Orange slice
Method: SHAKE all ingredients with ice and fine strain into chilled glass.

1½	shot(s)	**Campari Bitter**
1	shot(s)	**Martini Rosso sweet vermouth**
1	shot(s)	**Freshly squeezed orange juice**
½	shot(s)	**Pomegranate (grenadine) syrup**
5	dashes	**Angostura aromatic bitters**

Origin: Adapted from Victor Bergeron's 'Trader Vic's Bartender's Guide' (1972 revised edition).
Comment: Sweet, tart and fruity. My kinda girl!

COWBOY HOOF MARTINI UPDATED #8

Glass: Martini
Garnish: Orange zest twist
Method: SHAKE all ingredients (including mint) with ice and fine strain into chilled glass.

7	fresh	**Mint leaves**
3	shot(s)	**Tanqueray London dry gin**
½	shot(s)	**Sugar syrup** (2 sugar to 1 water)
3	dashes	**Angostura orange bitters** (optional)

Variant: Detroit Martini, The Cooperstown
Origin: Created in the early 90s by Dick Bradsell at Detroit, London, England.
Comment: Sweetened gin shaken with fresh mint.

COX'S DAIQUIRI

Glass: Martini
Garnish: Cox's apple slice (in memory of Jennings Cox)
Method: SHAKE all ingredients with ice and fine strain into chilled glass.

2½	shot(s)	**Vanilla-infused Bacardi rum**
½	shot(s)	**Freshly squeezed lime juice**
¼	shot(s)	**Vanilla sugar syrup**
1	shot(s)	**Freshly pressed pineapple juice**

Origin: One of two cocktails with which I won 'The Best Daiquiri in London Competition' in 2002. It is named after Jennings Cox, the American mining engineer credited with first creating the Daiquiri.
Comment: Vanilla and pineapple bring out the sweetness of the rum against a citrus background.

CRANAPPLE BREEZE

Glass: Collins
Garnish: Lime slice on rim
Method: SHAKE first 5 ingredients with ice and strain into ice-filled glass. TOP with ginger ale and stir.

1	shot(s)	**Ketel One Citroen vodka**
1	shot(s)	**Cointreau triple sec**
1	shot(s)	**Ocean Spray cranberry juice**
1	shot(s)	**Pressed apple juice**
½	shot(s)	**Freshly squeezed lime juice**
Top up with		**Ginger ale**

Origin: Created in 2002 by Wayne Collins.
Comment: A refreshing cooler for a hot day by the pool.

CRANBERRY COOLER

Glass: Collins
Garnish: Orange slice
Method: SHAKE all ingredients with ice and strain into ice-filled glass.

2	shot(s)	**Luxardo Amaretto di Saschira**
2	shot(s)	**Ocean Spray cranberry juice**
2	shot(s)	**Freshly squeezed orange juice**

Comment: Easy drinking for those with a sweet tooth.

CRANBERRY DELICIOUS (MOCKTAIL)

Glass: Collins
Garnish: Mint sprig
Method: MUDDLE mint in base of shaker. Add other ingredients, SHAKE with ice and strain into ice-filled glass.

12	fresh	**Mint leaves**
1	shot(s)	**Freshly squeezed lime juice**
½	shot(s)	**Sugar syrup** (2 sugar to 1 water)
4	shot(s)	**Ocean Spray cranberry juice**
3	dashes	**Angostura aromatic bitters**

Origin: Adapted from a drink created in 2006 by Damian Windsor at Bin 8945 Wine Bar & Bistro, West Hollywood, USA.
Comment: Cranberry juice given more interest with mint, lime and bitters. This drink contains trace amounts of alcohol but remains an effective driver's option.

CRANBERRY & MINT MARTINI

Glass: Martini
Garnish: Dried cranberries in base of glass & float mint leaf.
Method: Lightly MUDDLE mint in base of shaker, just enough to bruise. Add other ingredients, SHAKE with ice and fine strain into chilled glass.

9	fresh	**Mint leaves**
2	shot(s)	**Ketel One vodka**
1½	shot(s)	**Ocean Spray cranberry juice**
¼	shot(s)	**Pomegranate (grenadine) syrup**

Origin: Created in 2003 by Yours Truly (Simon Difford).
Comment: This little red number combines the dryness of cranberry, the sweetness of grenadine and the fragrance of mint.

CRANBERRY SAUCE

Glass: Martini
Garnish: Lime wedge
Method: SHAKE all ingredients with ice and fine strain into chilled glass.

2	shot(s)	**Ketel One vodka**
¾	shot(s)	**Lapponia cranberry liqueur**
2½	shot(s)	**Ocean Spray cranberry juice**
¼	shot(s)	**Freshly squeezed lime juice**

Origin: Created in 2003 by Yours Truly (Simon Difford).
Comment: Rich and fruity with that customary dry cranberry finish.

CRAPPLE (MOCKTAIL) NEW #8

Glass: Collins
Garnish: Lime wedge
Method: SHAKE all ingredients with ice and strain into ice-filled glass. Serve with straws.

2½	shot(s)	**Ocean Spray cranberry juice**
2	shot(s)	**Pressed apple juice**
1	shot(s)	**Freshly squeezed lime juice**
½	shot(s)	**Sugar syrup** (2 sugar to 1 water)

Comment: Cranberry, apple and lime. Simple but refreshing and decidedly fruity.

CREAMSICLE

Glass: Martini
Garnish: Orange zest twist
Method: SHAKE all ingredients with ice and fine strain into chilled glass.

1½	shot(s)	**Orange-infused Ketel One vodka**
1	shot(s)	**Grand Marnier liqueur**
½	shot(s)	**Double (heavy) cream**
½	shot(s)	**Milk**
⅛	shot(s)	**Sugar syrup** (2 sugar to 1 water)

Comment: A milky orange number with a surprisingly pleasant taste.

CREAM CAKE

Glass: Martini
Garnish: Crumbled Cadbury's Flake bar
Method: SHAKE all ingredients with ice and fine strain into chilled glass.

1¼	shot(s)	**Baileys Irish cream liqueur**
1¼	shot(s)	**Peach Tree peach schnapps**
1¼	shot(s)	**Luxardo Amaretto di Saschira**
1	shot(s)	**Double (heavy) cream**

Comment: Creamy pleasure for the sweet of tooth.

CREAMY BEE

Glass: Martini
Garnish: Cinnamon rim & raspberry
Method: SHAKE all ingredients with ice and fine strain into chilled glass.

1½	shot(s)	**Krupnik honey liqueur**
½	shot(s)	**Baileys Irish cream liqueur**
½	shot(s)	**Chambord black raspberry liqueur**
½	shot(s)	**Frangelico hazelnut liqueur**
¼	shot(s)	**Goldschläger cinnamon schnapps**

Origin: Created in 2002 at Hush, London, England and originally made with cinnamon syrup in place of Goldschläger.
Comment: Creamy cinnamon with hints of honey, nuts and berries.

CRÈME ANGLAISE MARTINI

Glass: Martini
Garnish: Dust with cocoa powder
Method: SHAKE all ingredients with ice and fine strain into chilled glass.

1	shot(s)	**Vanilla-infused Ketel One vodka**
2	shot(s)	**Bols advocaat liqueur**
1	shot(s)	**Milk**

Origin: Created in 2004 by Yours Truly (Simon Difford).
Comment: Very reminiscent of alcoholic crème anglaise.

CREAM SODA NEW #8

Glass: Collins
Garnish: Lemon slice
Method: SHAKE first 3 ingredients with ice and strain into ice-filled glass. **TOP** with lemonade and serve with straws.

1½	shot(s)	**Vanilla-infused Ketel One vodka**
1	shot(s)	**Bacardi Superior rum**
½	shot(s)	**Cuarenta Y Tres (Licor 43) liqueur**
	Top up with	**Lemonade/Sprite/7-Up**

Comment: An alcoholic cream soda created for Debbie Rizzo who expressed a desire for just such a thing.
Origin: Created in 2008 by Simon Difford at The Cabinet Room, London, England.

CRÈME BRÛLÉE MARTINI

Glass: Martini
Garnish: Dust with cinnamon powder
Method: SHAKE all ingredients with ice and fine strain into chilled glass.

2	shot(s)	**Vanilla-infused Ketel One vodka**
½	shot(s)	**Cartron caramel liqueur**
¾	shot(s)	**Cuarenta Y Tres (Licor 43) liqueur**
1	shot(s)	**Double (heavy) cream**
½	fresh	**Egg yolk**

Origin: Adapted from a drink created in 2002 by Yannick Miseriaux at the Fifth Floor Bar, London, England.
Comment: OK, so there's no crust, but this does contain egg yolk, caramel, vanilla, sugar and cream. Due to the cinnamon, it even has a brown top.

CREAMY CREAMSICLE

Glass: Martini
Method: SHAKE all ingredients with ice and fine strain into chilled glass.

½	shot(s)	**Orange-infused Ketel One vodka**
1¼	shot(s)	**Luxardo Ameretto di Saschira**
1	shot(s)	**Freshly squeezed orange juice**
¾	shot(s)	**Double (heavy) cream**
¾	shot(s)	**Milk**

Comment: Ultra smooth and creamy. Dessert, anyone?

CRÈME DE CAFÉ

Glass: Old-fashioned
Method: SHAKE ingredients with ice and strain into ice-filled glass.

1	shot(s)	**Kahlúa coffee liqueur**
¾	shot(s)	**Bacardi Oro golden rum**
¾	shot(s)	**Luxardo Sambuca dei Cesari**
1	shot(s)	**Double (heavy) cream**
1	shot(s)	**Milk**

Comment: Coffee predominates over the creaminess with hints of aniseed and rum.

CREOLE COSMO

Glass: Martini
Garnish: Lime zest twist
Method: SHAKE all ingredients with ice and fine strain into chilled glass.

1	shot(s)	**Martinique agricole rum**
1	shot(s)	**Clément Creole Shrubb liqueur**
1	shot(s)	**Ocean Spray cranberry juice**
½	shot(s)	**Freshly squeezed lime juice**

Comment: Dry, tangy and more sophisticated than your bog-standard Cosmo.

CRIMEA

Glass: Martini
Garnish: Float coriander leaf
Method: MUDDLE coriander in base of shaker. Add other ingredients, SHAKE with ice and fine strain into chilled glass.

5	fresh	**Coriander leaves**
2	shot(s)	**Tanqueray London dry gin**
1	shot(s)	**Pressed apple juice**
¼	shot(s)	**Freshly squeezed lemon juice**
⅛	shot(s)	**Sugar syrup** (2 sugar to 1 water)
½	shot(s)	**Chilled mineral water** (omit if wet ice)

Origin: Adapted from a drink discovered in 2006 at the Ballroom, London, England.
Comment: Fragrant, herbal gin with a hint of citrus.

CRIMSON BLUSH

Glass: Martini
Garnish: Berries
Method: SHAKE all ingredients with ice and fine strain into chilled glass.

2	shot(s)	**Ketel One Citroen vodka**
½	shot(s)	**Chambord black raspberry liqueur**
2	shot(s)	**Freshly squeezed grapefruit juice**
¼	shot(s)	**Sugar syrup** (2 sugar to 1 water)

Origin: Created in 2004 by Jonathan Lamm at The Admirable Crichton, London, England.
Comment: Well balanced, fruity sweet and sour.

CROSSBOW

Glass: Martini
Garnish: Orange zest twist
Method: SHAKE all ingredients with ice and fine strain into chilled glass.

2	shot(s)	**Tanqueray London dry gin**
½	shot(s)	**Cointreau triple sec**
¼	shot(s)	**White crème de cacao liqueur**
½	shot(s)	**Chilled mineral water** (omit if wet ice)

Origin: Adapted from a drink discovered in 2005 at Bar Opiume, Singapore.
Comment: Surprisingly dry orange and chocolate laced with gin.

CROUCHING TIGER

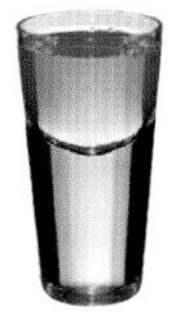

Glass: Shot
Method: SHAKE all ingredients with ice and fine strain into chilled glass.

¾	shot(s)	**Don Julio reposado tequila**
½	shot(s)	**Soho lychee liqueur**

Comment: Tequila and lychee combine harmoniously in this semi–sweet shot.

THE CROW COCKTAIL

Glass: Martini
Garnish: Lemon zest twist
Method: SHAKE all ingredients with ice and fine strain into chilled glass.

2	shot(s)	**Johnnie Walker Scotch whisky**
1	shot(s)	**Freshly squeezed lemon juice**
½	shot(s)	**Pomegranate (grenadine) syrup**

Origin: Adapted from Harry Craddock's 1930 'The Savoy Cocktail Book'.
Comment: If you use great syrup and have a penchant for Scotch then you could be pleasantly surprised by this drink.

CROWN STAG

Glass: Old-fashioned
Garnish: Lemon slice
Method: SHAKE ingredients with ice and strain into ice-filled glass.

1½	shot(s)	**Ketel One vodka**
1½	shot(s)	**Jägermeister liqueur**
1	shot(s)	**Chambord black raspberry liqueur**

Comment: A surprisingly workable combination.

CRUEL INTENTION

Glass: Martini
Garnish: Lime slice on rim
Method: SHAKE all ingredients with ice and fine strain into chilled glass.

2	shot(s)	**Bulleit bourbon whiskey**
¼	shot(s)	**Bols apricot brandy liqueur**
¼	shot(s)	**Luxardo Amaretto di Saschira**
1	shot(s)	**Pressed pineapple juice**
½	shot(s)	**Freshly squeezed lime juice**

Origin: Discovered in 2005 at The Mansion, Amsterdam, The Netherlands.
Comment: Bourbon with a hint of apricot, almond, pineapple and lime. Hardly cruel!

THE CROW COCKTAIL

CRUSHED STRAWBERRY FIZZ NEW #8

Glass: Collins (8oz max)
Garnish: Strawberry on rim
Method: MUDDLE strawberries in base of shaker. Add other ingredients apart from soda, **SHAKE** with ice and fine strain into chilled glass (without ice). **TOP** with soda.

3	fresh	**Strawberries** (hulled)
2	shot(s)	**Old Tom gin**
1	shot(s)	**Freshly squeezed lemon juice**
½	shot(s)	**Sugar syrup** (2 sugar to 1 water)
Top up with		**Soda water** (from siphon)

Origin: This Gin Fizz adaptation was created circa 1880 at the St. Nicholas Hotel, New York City.
Comment: Fruity and all too easy to drink. Don't hold back, the lack of ice in this tall drink requires you consume while still cold. But responsibly, of course.

CRUSTAS (GENERIC NAME) UPDATED #8

Glass: Small wine goblet or flute
Garnish: The trick is to find a lemon or a small orange. I favour lemon, which fits into a small wineglass tightly enough to act as a watertight extension to the glass. Cut off both ends of the fruit and carefully remove the pulp to leave a barrel-shaped shell of skin. Place in the top of the glass - wineglasses tend to curve in on themselves and this helps retain the fruit. Wet the edge of the glass and exposed fruit shell with sugar syrup and dip in caster sugar to frost the edge of both peel and glass. Leave for a couple of hours to form hard crust.
Method: SHAKE all ingredients with ice and fine strain into pre-prepared glass.

2	shot(s)	**Spirit** (whisk(e)y, gin, rum etc.)
½	shot(s)	**Freshly squeezed lemon juice**
¼	shot(s)	**Sugar syrup** (2 sugar to 1 water)
1	dash	**Angostura aromatic bitters**

Comment: Some cocktail historians, Ted Haigh included, consider the Crusta the forerunner of the Sidecar and in turn the Margarita. It's a very logical argument.
Origin: The invention of the Crusta is credited to a Joseph Santina at the Jewel of the South or a Joseph Santini at the City Exchange in New Orleans sometime during the 1840s or 1850s. It first appeared in print as 'The Brandy Crusta' in Jerry Thomas' 1862 bartender's guide.

Crustas always contain a spirit, lemon juice and sugar – sometimes in the form of a liqueur or liqueurs. They are so named due to their sugar rim, which should be applied hours before the drink is made so that it is dried hard, or indeed crusty, when the drink is served. Crustas are also distinguished by being garnished with a band of orange or lemon zest, and are drunk from the rim of the fruit, rather than the rim of the glass.

As David A. Embury writes in his 1948 'The Fine Art of Mixing Drinks', "The distinguishing feature of the Crusta is that the entire inside of the glass is lined with lemon or orange peel. The drink may be served in either a wineglass or an Old-Fashioned glass, although it is much harder to make the peel fit in the Old-Fashioned glass." Embury goes on to say, "While the 'Brandy Crusta' is the most common form of this drink, it is, after all, merely a Sour-type drink served in fancy style. Substitution of a different liquor as a base will give a Gin Crusta, a Rum Crusta, an Applejack Crusta, A Whisky Crusta, and so on."

CRUX

Glass: Martini
Garnish: Orange zest twist
Method: SHAKE all ingredients with ice and fine strain into chilled glass.

1	shot(s)	**Courvoisier V.S.O.P. cognac**
1	shot(s)	**Dubonnet Red** (French made)
1	shot(s)	**Cointreau triple sec**
1	shot(s)	**Freshly squeezed lemon juice**

Comment: The 'crux' of the matter is rarely as tasty as this fruity and none too sweet cognac.

CUBA LIBRE UPDATED #8

Glass: Collins
Garnish: Lime wedge
Method: SHAKE rum and lime juice with ice and fine strain into ice-filled glass. **TOP** with Cola-Cola and serve with straws.

2	shot(s)	**Bacardi Superior rum**
½	shot(s)	**Freshly squeezed lime juice**
Top up with		**Coca-Cola**

Variants: Cuba Pintada & Cuba Campechana
Comment: Basically a rum and coke with a squeeze of lime – but Cuba Libre has much more of a ring about it. And it is much more of a drink – the squeeze of lime adds layers of complexity and balances the sweetness of the cola.
Origin: The Cuba Libre was born out of Cuba's War of Independence with the Spanish, a war in which, like most Cubans, the Bacardi family were involved. In the late 1890s, Cuba's anti-colonial fighters were called the Mambí. Emilito Bacardi, eldest son of Emilio Bacardi, was one of them. He began his military service as aide de camp to Major General Antonio Maceo, Cuba's 'Bronze Titan', fighting the Spanish from Cuba's dense forests, or 'manigua'. During the war he was promoted to colonel, and became known as 'El Coronel'.

The war was scarcely over when, in late 1898 Warren Candler (brother of Asa Candler, then owner of Coca-Cola) sailed for Cuba, the first of twenty such trips. As a result of Warren's visits to Cuba, there in May 1899 the company hired a sales merchant to sell Coca-Cola syrup for use in soda fountains and appointed Jose Parejo, a Havana wine merchant as the Cuban distributor for Coca-Cola.

By 1900 Coca-Cola was both popular and widely available in Cuba so it is not surprising that American solders still garrisoned there started ordering Bacardi Cuban Rum and Coke with a squeeze of the ubiquitous lime. One solider in particular, Captain Russell of the US Signal Corp, is credited with starting this trend when one day in August 1900 he ordered the combination in a Havana bar. Naturally his drink sparked interest from the soldiers around him and before long the entire bar was drinking it. The Captain proposed a toast, 'Por Cuba libre!' in celebration of a 'free Cuba'. Fortunately for posterity, the event is supported by an affidavit from a witness, Fausto Rodriguez.

Rodriguez was a personal messenger to General Wood, appointed the military governor of Cuba after entering Santiago de Cuba on 17th July 1898, after Roosevelt's victory at the battle of San Juan Hill. After the Republic of Cuba was born on 20th May 1902, General Wood left Cuba and Fausto Rodriguez returned to Santiago de Cuba. Sixty-five years later, on 21st December 1964, Rodriguez told Emilito Bacardi the following story, affirmed under oath:

"During the period of military intervention, two Americans opened and operated a bar called The American Bar on Neptuno Street, between Consulado and Prado in Havana. It was patronized almost exclusively by American soldiers and by American civilians who worked in the various government offices in Havana.

"While I was employed at the office of the Signal Corps, I became quite friendly with an American whose last name was Russell (I do not remember his given name). He worked in the office of the Chief Signal Officer. Mr Russell frequently took me to The American Bar where we used to drink Bacardi Rum and Coca-Cola.

"One afternoon in August 1900, I went to The American Bar with Mr Russell, and he drank his usual Bacardi Rum and Coca-Cola. I just drank Coca-Cola, being only 14 years old. On that occasion, there was a group of American soldiers at the bar, and one of them asked Mr Russell what he was drinking. He told them it was Bacardi Rum and Coca-Cola and suggested they try it, which they did.

"The soldiers who drank the Bacardi Rum and Coca-Cola said they liked it, and wanted to know what the drink was called. When Mr Russell told them that the drink did not have a name, one of the soldiers said, "Let's give it a name". Another said, "How about calling it 'Cuba Libre'?" They all agreed and ordered another round of Bacardi Rum and Coca-Cola, calling it a Cuba Libre. To my best knowledge, this is the first time this phrase 'Cuba Libre' has been applied to a drink. Thus, the first Cuba Libre consisted of Bacardi Rum and Coca-Cola.

"During the American intervention, the words Cuba Libre – meaning Free Cuba – had a special political significance, and were used a great deal by the Cubans and Americans in Cuba. It seemed quite natural that the American soldiers selected and applied this popular slogan to this drink, which they considered indigenous to Cuba, consisting of Bacardi Rum and Coca-Cola. The name caught on quickly, and has remained popular to the present time." (sic)

The Cuba Libre peaked in popularity during the 1940s, partly aided by the Andrews Sisters who in 1945 had a hit with 'Rum and Coca-Cola', named after the drink's ingredients. During the war, all spirits production went over to industrial alcohol - in the absence of whiskey and gin, Americans turned to imported rum. The Cuba Libre is an enduring classic, still made with Bacardi rum and still enjoyed the world.

CUBA PINTADA

Glass: Collins
Garnish: Lime wedge
Method: POUR ingredients into ice-filled glass, gently stir and serve with straws.

2	shot(s)	**Bacardi Superior rum**
1	shot(s)	**Coca-Cola**
Top up with		**Soda water**

Variant: Cuba Campechana – rum with half soda and half cola; Cuba Libre – rum, cola and a dash of lime.
Origin: The name of this popular Cuban drink literally means 'stained Cuba' and there is just enough cola in this rum and soda to stain the drink brown.

CUBAN COCKTAIL NO.2 #1

Glass: Martini
Garnish: Lemon peel twist
Method: SHAKE all ingredients with ice and fine strain into chilled glass.

1½	shot(s)	**Bacardi Superior rum**
⅛	shot(s)	**Luxardo maraschino liqueur**
⅛	shot(s)	**Pomegranate (grenadine) syrup**
¼	shot(s)	**Freshly squeezed lemon juice**
1	dash	**Angostura orange bitters**
½	shot(s)	**Chilled mineral water** (omit if wet ice)

Origin: Adapted from Victor Bergeron's 'Trader Vic's Bartender's Guide' (1972 revised edition).
Comment: Perfumed yet not sweetened rum.

'IT HAD NEVER OCCURRED TO US THAT THE KREMLIN'S NEW ANTI-BOOZE CAMPAIGN WOULD APPLY TO JOURNALISTS. NOW, THAT'S A HUMAN-RIGHTS VIOLATION.'
P. J. O'ROURKE

CUBAN COCKTAIL N0.3 #2

Glass: Martini
Garnish: Lemon zest twist
Method: SHAKE all ingredients with ice and fine strain into chilled glass.

1½	shot(s)	**Bacardi Oro golden rum**
¼	shot(s)	**Courvoisier V.S.O.P. cognac**
½	shot(s)	**Bols apricot brandy liqueur**
½	shot(s)	**Freshly squeezed lime juice**
1	dash	**Angostura orange bitters**
½	shot(s)	**Chilled mineral water** (omit if wet ice)

Origin: Adapted from Victor Bergeron's 'Trader Vic's Bartender's Guide' (1972 revised edition).
Comment: Like much of the Caribbean, this drink has French influences. Thank goodness for Admiral Rodney.

'A REAL HANGOVER IS NOTHING TO TRY OUT FAMILY REMEDIES ON. THE ONLY CURE FOR A REAL HANGOVER IS DEATH.'
ROBERT BENCHLEY

CUBAN HEAL NEW #8

Glass: Martini/Coupette
Garnish: Lemon zest twist
Method: STIR all ingredients with ice and strain into chilled glass.

2½	shot(s)	**Bacardi Superior rum**
¼	shot(s)	**Cynar artichoke liqueur**
¼	shot(s)	**Luxardo limoncello liqueur**
¼	shot(s)	**Honey syrup** (4 honey to 1 water)
2	dashes	**Peychaud's aromatic bitters**

Comment: Honey-ed and initially sweet with herbal spirity rum notes adding depth.
Origin: Created in 2008 by Matthew Keegan at Blanch House, Brighton, England. The ingredients were chosen due to their historically being believed to be remedies.

CUBAN ISLAND

Glass: Martini
Garnish: Orange zest twist
Method: SHAKE all ingredients with ice and fine strain into chilled glass.

2	shot(s)	**Bacardi Superior rum**
½	shot(s)	**Noilly Prat dry vermouth**
½	shot(s)	**Freshly squeezed lemon juice**
¼	shot(s)	**Sugar syrup** (2 sugar to 1 water)

Origin: Adapted from a drink discovered in 2005 at DiVino's, Hong Kong, China.
Comment: The Daiquiri meets the Wet Martini. Interesting!

CUBAN MASTER

●●●○○

Glass: Collins
Garnish: Pineapple wedge
Method: SHAKE all ingredients with ice and strain into ice-filled glass.

1½	shot(s)	**Bacardi Superior rum**
1	shot(s)	**Courvoisier V.S.O.P. cognac**
1½	shot(s)	**Freshly squeezed orange juice**
1½	shot(s)	**Pressed pineapple juice**
½	shot(s)	**Freshly squeezed lemon juice**
¼	shot(s)	**Sugar syrup** (2 sugar to 1 water)

Origin: A classic cocktail I discovered in 1999 during a trip to Cuba.
Comment: Well balanced, wonderfully fruity.

CUBAN SPECIAL

●●●○○

Glass: Old-fashioned
Garnish: Orange zest twist
Method: SHAKE ingredients with ice and strain into ice-filled glass.

1½	shot(s)	**Bacardi Superior rum**
¾	shot(s)	**Cointreau triple sec**
2	shot(s)	**Pressed pineapple juice**
¼	shot(s)	**Freshly squeezed lime juice**

Comment: Not that special, but certainly OK.

CUBANITA UPDATED #8

●●●●○

Glass: Collins
Garnish: Lime wedge
Method: SHAKE all ingredients with ice and strain into ice-filled glass.

2	shot(s)	**Bacardi Superior rum**
3½	shot(s)	**Pressed tomato juice**
½	shot(s)	**Freshly squeezed lemon juice**
7	drops	**Tabasco pepper sauce**
4	dashes	**Lea & Perrins Worcestershire sauce**
½	spoon	**Horseradish sauce**
2	pinches	**Celery salt**
2	grinds	**Black pepper**

Comment: The Bloody Mary returns - this time with rum.

CUBATA NEW #8

●●●●○

Glass: Collins
Garnish: Lime wedge
Method: SHAKE gin and lime with ice and strain into ice-filled glass. TOP with Coca-Cola and serve with straws.

2	shot(s)	**Tanqueray London dry gin**
½	shot(s)	**Freshly squeezed lime juice**
Top up with		**Coca-Cola**

Comment: Hard to hate but the cola and lime dominate the subtle gin flavours.
Origin: The gin-based equivalent to the rum-based Cuba Libre. This drink is popular in Spain where gin is the dominant spirit.

CUCUMBER MARTINI

●●●●◐

Glass: Martini
Garnish: Strip of cucumber
Method: MUDDLE cucumber in base of shaker. Add other ingredients, SHAKE with ice and strain into glass.

2	inches	**Cucumber** (peeled & chopped)
1	shot(s)	**Zubrówka bison vodka**
1	shot(s)	**Ketel One vodka**
½	shot(s)	**Sugar syrup** (2 sugar to 1 water)

Origin: There are many different Cucumber Martini recipes; this is mine.
Comment: Cucumber has never tasted so good.

CUCUMBER & MINT MARTINI

●●●●◐

Glass: Martini
Garnish: Cucumber slice
Method: MUDDLE cucumber and mint in base of shaker. Add other ingredients, SHAKE with ice and fine strain into chilled glass.

2	inches	**Cucumber** (peeled & chopped)
7	fresh	**Mint leaves**
2	shot(s)	**Ketel One vodka**
1	shot(s)	**Pressed apple juice**
¼	shot(s)	**Sugar syrup** (2 sugar to 1 water)

Origin: Created in 2004 by David Ramos in the Netherlands.
Comment: A well balanced fortified salad in a glass – almost healthy.

CUCUMBER SAKE-TINI

●●●●○

Glass: Martini
Garnish: Float 3 cucumber slices
Method: MUDDLE cucumber in base of shaker. Add other ingredients, SHAKE with ice and fine strain into chilled glass.

1½	inch	**Cucumber** (peeled & chopped)
1½	shot(s)	**Ketel One vodka**
1½	shot(s)	**Sake**
¼	shot(s)	**Sugar syrup** (2 sugar to 1 water)

Origin: Created in 2004 by Lisa Ball, London, England.
Comment: Subtle and dry. Cucumber and sake are made for each other.

CUMBERSOME

●●●●○

Glass: Martini
Garnish: Physalis (cape gooseberry) on rim
Method: MUDDLE cucumber in base of shaker. Add other ingredients, SHAKE with ice and strain into a chilled Martini glass.

4	inch	**Cucumber** (peeled & chopped)
2	shot(s)	**Tanqueray London dry gin**
½	shot(s)	**Campari Bitter**
1	shot(s)	**Freshly squeezed orange juice**
½	shot(s)	**Sugar syrup** (2 sugar to 1 water)

Origin: Created in 2002 by Shelim Islam at the GE Club, London, England.
Comment: Interesting and fresh as you like with a pleasant bitterness.

'ALCOHOL IS LIKE LOVE.
THE FIRST KISS IS MAGIC,
THE SECOND IS INTIMATE,
THE THIRD IS ROUTINE. AFTER
THAT YOU TAKE THE GIRL'S
CLOTHES OFF.'
RAYMOND CHANDLER

CUNNINGHAM NEW #8

Glass: Martini
Garnish: Cherries & flamed blood orange twist
Method: SHAKE all ingredients with ice and fine strain into a chilled glass.

1½	shot(s)	**Johnnie Walker Scotch whisky**
½	shot(s)	**Freshly squeezed lemon juice**
½	shot(s)	**Squeezed blood orange juice**
¼	shot(s)	**Bénédictine D.O.M. liqueur**
¼	shot(s)	**Heering cherry brandy liqueur**

Comment: Tangy citrus fruit and Scotch with a herbal and cherry liqueur garnish makes for a damn tasty, fruity dram.
Origin: Created by Marco Dionysos at Tres Agaves, San Francisco, USA and in memory of Johnny Cunningham (1957 - 2003), one of the world's all-time great Scottish fiddlers.

CUPPA JOE

Glass: Martini
Garnish: Lemon zest twist
Method: SHAKE all ingredients with ice and fine strain into chilled glass.

1½	shot(s)	**Ketel One vodka**
1½	shot(s)	**Frangelico hazelnut liqueur**
1½	shot(s)	**Espresso coffee**

Origin: Created in 2003 at Cellar Bar, New York City, USA.
Comment: Nutty coffee fortified with vodka – well balanced.

CURDISH MARTINI

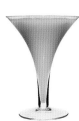

Glass: Martini
Garnish: Lemon zest twist
Method: STIR lemon curd with gin in base of shaker until curd dissolves. Add other ingredients, SHAKE with ice and fine strain into chilled glass.

2	spoons	**Lemon curd**
2	shot(s)	**Tanqueray London dry gin**
½	shot(s)	**Sour apple liqueur**
½	shot(s)	**Freshly squeezed lemon juice**

Origin: Created in 2001 by Tadgh Ryan at West Street, London, England.
Comment: Beautifully balanced with the tang of lemon curd.

THE CURRIER

Glass: Martini
Garnish: Float mint leaf
Method: SHAKE all ingredients with ice and fine strain into chilled glass.

1½	shot(s)	**Bulleit bourbon whiskey**
½	shot(s)	**Kümmel liqueur**
¼	shot(s)	**Freshly squeezed lime juice**
¼	shot(s)	**Rose's lime cordial**

Origin: Recipe submitted in July 2006 by Murray Stenson at ZigZag Café, Seattle, USA.
Comment: A wonderfully cleansing after dinner cocktail with bourbon and lime plus hints of caraway and fennel courtesy of the Kümmel.

CUSTARD TART

Glass: Shot
Garnish: Physalis (cape gooseberry) on rim
Method: MUDDLE physalis fruits in base of shaker can. Add other ingredients, SHAKE with ice and strain.

3	fresh	**Physalis fruits**
¾	shot(s)	**Bacardi Superior rum**
½	shot(s)	**Peach Tree peach schnapps**
¼	shot(s)	**Freshly squeezed lime juice**
½	shot(s)	**Bols advocaat liqueur**

Origin: Created by Alex Kammerling in 2001.
Comment: Custardy, strangely enough.

CVO FIREVAULT

Glass: Martini
Garnish: Orange zest twist
Method: SHAKE all ingredients with ice and fine strain into chilled glass.

1½	shot(s)	**Orange-infused Ketel One vodka**
¾	shot(s)	**Campari Bitter**
¾	shot(s)	**Freshly squeezed orange juice**
¾	shot(s)	**Pressed pineapple juice**

Origin: Discovered in 2005 at CVO Firevault, London, England.
Comment: Fruity yet slightly bitter. Orange predominates with strong bursts of Campari.

CYDER PRESS

Glass: Martini
Garnish: Float wafer thin apple slice
Method: SHAKE all ingredients with ice and fine strain into chilled glass.

2	shot(s)	**Boulard Grand Solage calvados**
½	shot(s)	**St-Germain elderflower liqueur**
1	shot(s)	**Dry cider**
¾	shot(s)	**Pressed apple juice**

Origin: Created in 2006 by Yours Truly (Simon Difford).
Comment: Fresh, fermented and distilled apple juice with a hint of elderflower.

DAIQUIRI AUTHENTICO NEW #8

Glass: Martini
Garnish: Lime wedge
Method: SHAKE all ingredients with ice and fine strain into chilled glass.

2	shot(s)	**Bacardi Superior rum**
¼	shot(s)	**Galliano L'Autentico liqueur**
½	shot(s)	**Freshly squeezed lime juice**
¼	shot(s)	**Sugar syrup** (2 sugar to 1 water)

Origin: A simplification of a drink created in 2008 by Erik Lorincz at Purple Bar, Sanderson Hotel, London, England.
Comment: A lightly peppermint spiced influenced daiquiri.

DAIQUIRI NO.1 NATURAL
(DIFFORD'S 10:3:2 FORMULA) UPDATED #8

Glass: Coupette
Garnish: Lime wedge on rim
Method: SHAKE all ingredients with ice and fine strain into chilled glass.

2½	shot(s)	**Bacardi Superior rum**
¾	shot(s)	**Freshly squeezed lime juice**
½	shot(s)	**Sugar syrup** (2 sugar to 1 water)
½	shot(s)	**Chilled water** (omit if wet ice)

Comment: Crisp, light and refreshing. Perfectly balanced complexity of flavours.
Origin: Pronounced 'Dye-Ker-Ree', this drink bears a close relationship to the Canchanchara, a 19th century Cuban blend of rum, lemon, honey and water, but the Daiquiris creation is credited Jennings Stockton Cox, an American engineer.

In 1898, after Roosevelt's victory at the Battle of San Juan Hill, the Americans began to exploit Cuba's iron-ore mines and Cox led one of the initial exploratory expeditions. Cox and his team worked in the Sierra Maestra Mountains on the south-eastern shore of Cuba where the small town of Daiquirí lies and is where that he created his classic drink.

The engineers received substantial salaries and generous tobacco rations, after all there had to be some inducements for these qualified engineers to leave secure positions in the USA and brave the threat of yellow fever in Cuba. Thankfully our hero also requested they each received a monthly ration of the local rum, Bacardi Carta Blanca, and noticing that the Cuban workers often mixed Bacardi with their evening coffee, he began to experiment himself.

Drinks legend has it that another engineer called Pagliuchi was viewing mines in the region and met with Cox. During their meeting they set about making a drink from the ingredients Cox had to hand: rum, limes and sugar. Cox's granddaughter recounts a slightly different tale; namely that Cox ran out of gin when entertaining American guests. Wary of serving them straight rum, he added lime and sugar. However Cox came to concoct the drink, the result was sublime.

On page 38 of his 1928 book, 'When it's Cocktail Time in Cuba', Basil Woon writes that this drink was popular with a group who used to meet in Santiago's Venus bar every morning at eight o'clock.

"The boys used to have three or four every morning. Most of them worked in the Daiquiri mines, the superintendent of which was a gentleman named Cox – Jennings Cox. One morning in the Venus Cox said: "Boys, we've been drinking this delicious little drink for some time, but we've never named it. Let's christen it now!" The boys milled around a bit and finally Cox said: "I'll tell you what, lads – we all work at Daiquiri and we all drank this drink first there. Let's call it a Daiquiri."

Basil Woon's account documents the origin and naming of the Daiquiri and unlike many other cocktails where there creation is lost in time, that of the Daiquiri is well substantiated, including the original recipe, recorded by Jennings Cox in his personal diary.

The Daiquiri seems to have travelled back to America with US Admiral Lucius Johnson, who fought in the Spanish-American war of 1898. He introduced the drink to the Army & Navy Club in Washington DC and a plaque in their Daiquiri Lounge records his place in cocktail history.

The Perfect Daiquiri Recipe
In his seminal 1948 'Fine Art of Mixing Drinks', David A. Embury writes, "The Daiquiri, like the Old-Fashioned, deserves an even greater popularity than it now enjoys. For example, it is in my opinion, a vastly superior cocktail to the Manhattan, yet most bars sell more Manhattans than Daiquiris. So far as I can ascertain there are two main reasons why more Daiquiris are not sold: the use of inferior rums and the use of improper proportions." To address those two points...

In his personal diary Jennings Cox records his original Daiquiri recipe (to serve six) as follows:

The juice of six lemons
Six teaspoons full of sugar
Six Bacardi cups ('carta blanca')
Two small cups of mineral water
Plenty of crushed ice

This original recipe and other such historical references specify 'Bacardi Carta Blanca' (now known as Bacardi Superior) as the rum used to make a Daiquiri. Thus to make a truly authentic Daiquirí you should use this rum as it is still made using the same strain of cultured yeast and recipe so maintains its original flavour profile. Bacardi Superior has a delicate blue cheese note, which adds a distinctive character to the finished drink.

Although Cox's recipe records the use of lemons it is most likely that he is actually referring to limes which are native to Cuba and that the confusion arises due to the common Cuban term for lime being 'limón'. Again to quote from Embury, "Actually lemons are almost unknown in Cuba, whereas lime trees grow in everyone's own yard."
Embury's own recipe calls for sugar syrup and this is something with which I whole-heartedly agree as granulated or caster sugar does not as readily dissolve in cold liquid. If you must insist in 'spooning' your sugar please use a mortar and pestle to first crush caster sugar to a fine powder, often termed 'bar sugar' or 'powdered sugar'.

Better still, make your own sugar syrup by pouring one mug of filtered water into a saucepan and over a very low heat, so as to not even come close to boiling, stir in two mugs of caster sugar. Allow to cool, bottle and store in a refrigerator where it will last for a couple of months.
Thus we have our ingredients: Bacardi Superior, freshly squeezed lime juice and 2-to-1 (double strength) sugar syrup. Now to the perfect proportions.

London's most famous bartender, Dick Bradsell, originally taught me Embury's 8:2:1 Daiquiri formula and I used to believe this was the best (I still do when making Daiquiris with aged rum). David Embury's 8:2:1 Daiquiri consists: 8 parts (2 shots) white label Cuban rum, 2 parts (½ shot) lime juice and 1 part (¼ shot) sugar syrup.

Some bartenders make Daiquiris according to the classic Margarita formula with twice as much lime. I have experimented with this but found that while tequila is robust enough to shine above the citrus flavour it tends to overpower the more delicate flavours of light rum. However, I do prefer a small increase in lime but also found a small increase in the rum beneficial. After all a mere two measures of rum would hardly satisfy great Daiquiri drinkers such as Hemingway. Thus I have now settled on the 10:3:2 formula above.

Embury's mixing instructions are, "Shake vigorously with plenty of finely crushed ice and strain into chilled cocktail glasses." This is to add dilution, a crucial aspect to perfecting the Daiquiri. As crushed ice is so variable in its wetness and so also the amount of dilution it adds to a drink, instead I prefer to shake with large cubes of double frozen ice taken from a freezer with the addition of 1/2 shot iced water. (I 'double freeze' cubed ice produced by ice machine). I shake with such vigour that there is indeed crushed ice left in the shaker when I strain the drink. This makes for an ice-cold Daiquiri with the controlled dilution essential to great straight-up Daiquiris.

What's in the Name
I first visited Cuba with Jamie Terrell back in the days when he was still working behind the stick at London's Atlantic Bar & Grill and not living a cachaça laced jet-set lifestyle in New York.

Fortunately Jamie spoke reasonable Spanish thanks to a sun-drenched season bartending on the Costa del Sol so as we toured Havana's bars in search of the perfect Daiquiri we were able to question the bartenders. Our first lesson was that asking for a mere 'Daiquiri' would result in being handed a blended Daiquiri. We quickly learnt that in Cuba you need to ask for a 'Natural Daiquiri' if you seek your Daiquiri shaken rather than blended.

Wherever you are in the world, when ordering a Daiquiri you need to convey to the bartender exactly what Daiquiri you desire. It is essential to be specific otherwise ordering just a 'Daiquiri' could result in your being asked, "What flavour would you like - strawberry, banana, mango or pineapple?" In such cases answering "just lime please" often leaves the questioner perplexed.

To further confuse the ordering of a Daiquiri, the great Ribalagua listed his Daiquiri adaptations as Daiquiri No.2, No.3, No.4 and No.5. Thus a simple 'original' or 'classic' Daiquiri should properly be termed 'Daiquiri No.1' and this can be served either 'Natural' (straight-up), 'On-The-Rocks' or 'Frozen'.

DAIQUIRI NO.1 NATURAL

● ● ● ● ●

DAIQUIRI NATURAL NO.1 #2
(EMBURY'S 8:2:1 FORMULA) UPDATED #8

Glass: Martini
Garnish: Lime wedge on rim
Method: SHAKE all ingredients with ice and fine strain into chilled glass.

2	shot(s)	**Zacapa aged rum**
½	shot(s)	**Freshly squeezed lime juice**
¼	shot(s)	**Sugar syrup** (2 sugar to 1 water)
½	shot(s)	**Chilled mineral water** (omit if wet ice)

Comment: Traditionally a Natural Daiquiri should always be based on light rum but if I should feel like breaking with tradition and using aged rum, I find Embury's 8:2:1 formula works particularly well.
Origin: According to David A. Embury's 1948 'Fine Art of Mixing Drinks' the classic proportions of a daiquiri are: 8 parts (2 shots) white label Cuban rum, 2 parts (1/2 shot) lime juice and 1 part (1/4 shot) sugar syrup. I have added the optional addition of water for increased dilution.

● ● ● ● ●

DAIQUIRI NO.1 FROZEN
(DIFFORD'S 16:6:6:1 FORMULA) UPDATED #8

Glass: Martini
Garnish: Maraschino cherry
Method: BLEND well all ingredients with 6oz scoop of crushed ice. **STRAIN** blended drink through a fine strainer to remove ice fragments.

2	shot(s)	**Bacardi Superior rum**
¾	shot(s)	**Freshly squeezed lime juice**
¾	shot(s)	**Sugar syrup** (2 sugar to 1 water)
⅛	shot(s)	**Luxardo maraschino liqueur**

Variant: Floridita Daiquiri or with fruit and/or fruit liqueurs.
Comment: Blend with too much ice and you will have a tasteless slushy drink that will give you brain-ache if you drink it too fast. However, made correctly and fine strained this is a superbly refreshing drink on a hot day.
Origin: Daiquiris were originally shaken and served 'straight-up' or 'on-the-rocks'. The frozen, blended version is said to have first been produced by Emilio Gonzalez at the Plaza Hotel in Cuba. However, it was made famous by Constantino (Constante) Ribalagua Vert who presided over the bar at Havana's La Florida (later renamed Floridita to distinguish it from the restaurant of the same name) for some forty years until his death in early December 1952.

In his 1948 'The Fine Art of Mixing Drinks', David A. Embury writes of Havana's Floridita, "This restaurant, at the corner of Obispo and Monserrate streets in Havana, became known as 'La Catedral del Daiquiri' – The Temple of the Daiquiri – and Ribalagua as the Cocktail King – 'El Rey de los Coteleros'. The title was, indeed, well deserved. His limes were gently squeezed with his fingers lest even a drop of the bitter oil from the peel get into the drink; the cocktails were mixed (but not overmixed) in a Waring Blender; the stinging cold drink was strained through a fine sieve into the glass so that not one tiny piece of the ice remained in it. No smallest detail was overlooked in achieving the flawless perfection of the drink."

Ernest Hemingway, the hard-drinking, Nobel prize-winning author, lived in Cuba for years, indulging his passions for fishing, shooting and boozing. In the 30s and the 40s he would often work his way through twelve of the Floridita's frozen Daiquiris - often doubles, renamed 'Papa Dobles' in his honour. The Hemingway Special Daiquiri, which includes grapefruit, was created for him. In his book 'Islands in the Stream', Hemingway's hero stares deep into his frozen Daiquiri, and Hemingway writes, "It reminded him of the sea. The frappéd part of the drink was like the wake of a ship and the clear part was the way the water looked when the bow cut it when you were in shallow water over marl bottom. That was almost the exact colour."

● ● ● ● ●

DAIQUIRI NO.1 ON-THE-ROCKS
(DIFFORD'S 10:3:2 FORMULA) NEW #8

Glass: Old-fashioned
Garnish: Lime slice & cherry on stick (sail)
Method: SHAKE all ingredients with ice and fine strain into ice-filled glass.

2½	shot(s)	**Bacardi Superior rum**
¾	shot(s)	**Freshly squeezed lime juice**
½	shot(s)	**Sugar syrup** (2 sugar to 1 water)

Comment: Light and refreshing. No one flavour predominates - sweet and sour are in harmony with the rum.
Origin: In my formative Daiquiri drinking years I followed the convention that a Daiquiri No.1 should be served 'straight-up'. However, I have now reverted to drinking my Daiquiris 'on-the-rocks' and interestingly Cox's original recipe (see Daiquiri No.1 Natural) suggests that this may also be the way he originally intended the drink to be served. In his diary Cox stipulates, "Put all ingredients in a cocktail shaker and shake well. Do not strain as the glass may be served with some ice." And as Albert S. Crockett notes of this drink in his 1935 'The Old Waldorf-Astoria Bar Book', "Personal preference dictates serving the cocktail with finely shaved ice in the glass."

Obviously serving a drink over ice will add dilution so rendering the additional dash of water to my 10:3:2 Daiquiri formula superfluous. Having tried 'up' and 'on-the-rocks' Daiquiris made to the same 'No.1' formula next to each other I have to admit that more nuances are found in the 'up' when compared to 'on-the-rocks'. However, I prefer holding and drinking from a big heavy old-fashioned glass rather than a V-shaped Martini or curvaceous Coupette. Thus I now vary my serve according to mood but with 1/2 shot of water added when served 'up' and omitted when served 'on-the-rocks'.

'I LIKE GIN. YOU CAN SEE THROUGH IT. BEER IS LIKE A FISH-POND... I CAN DRINK TWENTY GLASSES IN THE COURSE OF A DAY, EASY.' VICTORIAN TAILOR QUOTED BY HENRY MAYHEW

● ● ● ● ◑

DAIQUIRI NO.2

Glass: Martini
Garnish: Lime wedge on rim
Method: SHAKE all ingredients with ice and fine strain into chilled glass.

2	shot(s)	**Bacardi Superior rum**
⅛	shot(s)	**Cointreau triple sec**
½	shot(s)	**Freshly squeezed orange juice**
½	shot(s)	**Freshly squeezed lime juice**
¼	shot(s)	**Sugar syrup** (2 sugar to 1 water)

Comment: A Daiquiri with subtle orange notes, but far from being a mere Orange Daiquiri.
Origin: Created circa 1915 by Constantino (Constante) Ribalagua Vert at Floridita bar in Havana, Cuba.

DAIQUIRI NO.1 #2

A B C D E F G H I J K L M N O P Q R S T U V W X Y Z

DAIQUIRI NO.3 UPDATED #8

●●●●●

Glass: Old-fashioned
Garnish: Lime wedge on rim
Method: SHAKE all ingredients with ice and strain into glass filled with crushed ice. Serve with short straws.

2	shot(s)	**Bacardi Superior rum**
½	shot(s)	**Freshly squeezed lime juice**
½	shot(s)	**Sugar syrup** (2 sugar to 1 water)
¼	shot(s)	**Freshly squeezed grapefruit juice**
⅛	shot(s)	**Luxardo maraschino liqueur**

Comment: A Daiquiri No.1 with a tang of grapefruit and hint of maraschino. Essentially a Hemingway Special Daiquiri (Papa Doble Daiquiri) for folk without the great author's constitution or love of the sours.
Origin: Thought to have been created by Constantino (Constante) Ribalaigua Vert at the Floridita bar in Havana, Cuba, circa 1915. If this was invented as early as 1915, then this was the predecessor of the Hemingway Daiquiri, since Hemingway did not arrive in Cuba until 1928.

DAIQUIRI NO.4 (FLORIDA STYLE) NEW #8

●●●●○

Glass: Martini
Garnish: Lime wedge on rim
Method: SHAKE all ingredients with finely crushed ice and strain into chilled glass.

2	shot(s)	**Bacardi Oro golden rum**
½	shot(s)	**Freshly squeezed lime juice**
¼	shot(s)	**Sugar syrup** (2 sugar to 1 water)
¼	shot(s)	**Luxardo maraschino liqueur**
½	shot(s)	**Chilled water (reduce if wet ice)**

Origin: Created by Constantino (Constante) Ribalaigua Vert at the Floridita bar in Havana, Cuba. This recipe is adapted from a 1937 Bar Florida (later renamed Floridita) menu, also in Havana, Cuba.
Comment: Maraschino cherry liqueur flavours this finely balanced golden rum based Daiquiri.

DAIQUIRI NO.5 (PINK DAIQUIRI) UPDATED #8

●●●●◐

Glass: Martini
Garnish: Lime wedge on rim
Method: SHAKE all ingredients with ice and fine strain into chilled glass.

2	shot(s)	**Bacardi Superior rum**
⅛	shot(s)	**Luxardo maraschino liqueur**
¼	shot(s)	**Pomegranate (grenadine) syrup**
½	shot(s)	**Freshly squeezed lime juice**
¼	shot(s)	**Sugar Syrup** (2 sugar to 1 water)

AKA: Pink Daiquiri
Origin: Created by Constantino (Constante) Ribalaigua Vert at the Floridita bar in Havana, Cuba.
Comment: Classically tangy Daiquiri but sweetened with pomegranate syrup and a splash of maraschino.

DAIQUIRI ELIXIR

●●●●●

Glass: Martini
Garnish: Lime wedge on rim
Method: SHAKE all ingredients with ice and fine strain into chilled glass.

2	shot(s)	**Bacardi Superior rum**
½	shot(s)	**Freshly squeezed lime juice**
¼	shot(s)	**Martinique cane juice syrup**
⅛	shot(s)	**Green Chartreuse liqueur**
½	shot(s)	**Chilled mineral water** (omit if wet ice)

Origin: Another Daiquiri variation from Yours Truly (Simon Difford).
Comment: Freshly pressed sugar cane syrup and the French elixir Chartreuse add complexity to the classic Daiquiri.

> ## 'CLARET IS THE LIQUOR FOR BOYS; PORT FOR MEN; BUT HE WHO ASPIRES TO BE A HERO MUST DRINK BRANDY.'
> ## SAMUEL JOHNSON

DAIQUIRI DE LUXE

●●●●○

Glass: Martini
Garnish: Lime wedge on rim
Method: SHAKE all ingredients with ice and fine strain into chilled glass.

2	shot(s)	**Bacardi Superior rum**
¼	shot(s)	**Rose's lime cordial**
½	shot(s)	**Freshly squeezed lime juice**
¼	shot(s)	**Almond (orgeat) syrup**
¼	shot(s)	**Chilled mineral water** (omit if wet ice)

Comment: A classic Daiquiri but with lime cordial and almond syrup replacing sugar as the sweetener.

DAIQUIRI NOIR NEW #8

●●●●◐

Glass: Martini/Coupette
Garnish: Mint sprig
Method: Lightly MUDDLE mint in base of shaker. Add other ingredients, SHAKE with ice and fine strain into chilled glass.

7	fresh	**Mint leaves**
2	shot(s)	**Zacapa aged rum**
½	shot(s)	**Drambuie liqueur**
½	shot(s)	**Freshly squeezed lime juice**
¼	shot(s)	**Sugar syrup** (2 sugar to 1 water)

Comment: Drambuie adds herbal consistency to this minty fresh aged rum Daiquiri.
Origin: Discovered in 2008 at Hugos Bar Pizza, Sydney, Australia.

DAISY CUTTER MARTINI

Glass: Martini
Garnish: Float mint leaf
Method: Lightly **MUDDLE** mint in base of shaker (just to bruise). Add other ingredients, **SHAKE** with ice and fine strain into chilled glass.

3	fresh	**Mint leaves**
1½	shot(s)	**Ketel One vodka**
1	shot(s)	**St-Germain elderflower liqueur**
1	shot(s)	**Noilly Prat dry vermouth**
¼	shot(s)	**Yellow Chartreuse liqueur**

Origin: Created in 2006 by Yours Truly (Simon Difford). I named it not for the bomb but after the cricketing term for a ball bowled so incompetently that it skims along the ground.
Comment: Floral, minty and herbal with a dry finish.

DAISY DUKE

Glass: Old-fashioned
Garnish: Berries
Method: SHAKE all ingredients with ice and strain into glass filled with crushed ice. Serve with straws.

2	shot(s)	**Bulleit bourbon whiskey**
1	shot(s)	**Freshly squeezed lemon juice**
½	shot(s)	**Pomegranate (grenadine) syrup**

Origin: Created in 2002 by Jake Burger at Townhouse, Leeds, England.
Comment: This bright red drink tastes more adult than it looks.

DAMN-THE-WEATHER

Glass: Martini
Method: SHAKE all ingredients with ice and fine strain into chilled glass.

1	shot(s)	**Tanqueray London dry gin**
1	shot(s)	**Martini Rosso sweet vermouth**
½	shot(s)	**Cointreau triple sec**
1½	shot(s)	**Freshly squeezed orange juice**

Comment: Gin and herbal notes emerge in this predominantly orange drink.

DAMN IT JIMMY NEW #8

Glass: Martini
Garnish: Blue cheese stuffed olive
Method: STIR all ingredients with ice and fine strain into chilled glass.

1½	shot(s)	**Sake**
1½	shot(s)	**Bacardi Superior rum**
¼	shot(s)	**Tio Pepe Fino sherry**
¼	shot(s)	**Noilly Prat dry vermouth**
¼	shot(s)	**Sugar syrup** (2 sugar to 1 water)

Origin: Created in August 2008 by Simon Difford at The Cabinet Room, London, England.
Comment: Delicately flavoured and ever so slightly sweet.

DAMSON IN DISTRESS

Glass: Shot
Method: SHAKE all ingredients with ice and fine strain into chilled glass.

1½	shot(s)	**Damson gin liqueur**
½	shot(s)	**Luxardo Amaretto di Saschira**
¼	shot(s)	**Freshly squeezed lemon juice**

Origin: Discovered in 2003 at Hush, London, England.
Comment: Damson and amaretto sharpened by lemon juice.

DANDY COCKTAIL

Glass: Martini
Garnish: Lemon and orange zest twists
Method: SHAKE all ingredients with ice and fine strain into chilled glass.

1½	shot(s)	**Bulleit bourbon whiskey**
1½	shot(s)	**Dubonnet Red** (French made)
½	shot(s)	**Cointreau triple sec**
1	dash	**Angostura aromatic bitters**

Origin: Adapted from Harry Craddock's 1930 'The Savoy Cocktail Book'.
Comment: This complex Manhattan variant is a well balanced combo of spirit, liqueur and aromatic wine.

DARK DAIQUIRI

Glass: Martini
Garnish: Lime wedge
Method: SHAKE all ingredients with ice and fine strain into chilled glass.

1½	shot(s)	**Zacapa aged rum**
½	shot(s)	**Pusser's Navy rum**
½	shot(s)	**Freshly squeezed lime juice**
½	shot(s)	**Sugar syrup** (2 sugar to 1 water)
¾	shot(s)	**Chilled mineral water** (omit if wet ice)

Comment: The fine sweet and sour balance of a great Daiquiri with hints of molasses.

DARK & STORMY

Glass: Collins
Garnish: Lime wedge
Method: SHAKE first 3 ingredients with ice and strain into ice-filled glass. **TOP** with ginger beer, stir and serve with straws.

2	shot(s)	**Gosling's Black Seal rum**
1	shot(s)	**Freshly squeezed lime juice**
½	shot(s)	**Sugar syrup** (2 sugar to 1 water)
Top up with		**Ginger beer**

Origin: The national drink of Bermuda, where ginger beer and Gosling's rum are produced.
Comment: This deliciously spicy drink is part of the Mule family - but is distinctive due to the strong flavour of the rum.

DARLINGTON NEW #8

●●●○○

Glass: Martini
Garnish: Orange zest twist
Method: SHAKE all ingredients with ice and fine strain into chilled glass.

2	shot(s)	**Tanqueray London dry gin**
½	shot(s)	**Boulard Grand Solage calvados**
½	shot(s)	**Bols blue curaçao liqueur**
1	shot(s)	**Noilly Prat dry vermouth**
1	shot(s)	**Freshly squeezed lemon juice**
¼	shot(s)	**Sugar syrup** (2 sugar to 1 water)

Comment: Gin, orange and lemon made Martini-like by a drying splash of vermouth.
Origin: In W.J. Tarling's 1937 Café Royal Cocktail Book (Coronation Edition), the invention of this cocktail is credited to J.B. O'Brien.

D'ARTAGNAN

●●●●○

Glass: Martini
Garnish: Lemon zest twist
Method: SHAKE first 4 ingredients with ice and fine strain into chilled glass. **TOP** with champagne.

½	shot(s)	**Armagnac**
½	shot(s)	**Grand Marnier liqueur**
2	shot(s)	**Freshly squeezed orange juice**
¼	shot(s)	**Sugar syrup** (2 sugar to 1 water)
Top up with		**Perrier Jouet brut champagne**

Comment: Use genuine freshly pressed juice and you'll have a tasty Mimosa-style drink.

DC MARTINI

●●●●○

Glass: Martini
Method: STIR all ingredients with ice and strain into chilled glass.

2	shot(s)	**Vanilla-infused Bacardi rum**
¼	shot(s)	**Frangelico hazelnut liqueur**
¼	shot(s)	**Giffard white crème de cacao**
¼	shot(s)	**Sugar syrup** (2 sugar to 1 water)
½	shot(s)	**Chilled mineral water** (omit if wet ice)

Origin: Discovered in 2000 at Teatro, London, England.
Comment: Vanilla, chocolate and a hint of nut. Add more sugar to taste.

DE LA LOUISIANE #1

●●●●○

Glass: Martini
Garnish: Lemon zest twist
Method: STIR all ingredients with ice and strain into chilled glass.

2	shot(s)	**Bulleit bourbon whiskey**
¼	shot(s)	**Bénédictine D.O.M. liqueur**
1	dash	**Angostura aromatic bitters**
½	shot(s)	**Chilled mineral water** (omit if wet ice)

Origin: The signature cocktail of the Restaurant de la Louisiane in New Orleans which opened in 1881.
Comment: Whiskey with hints of honey and spice.

DE LA LOUISIANE #2

●●●●●

Glass: Martini
Garnish: Maraschino cherry
Method: STIR all ingredients with ice and strain into chilled glass.

1	shot(s)	**Bulleit bourbon whiskey**
1	shot(s)	**Bénédictine D.O.M. liqueur**
1	shot(s)	**Martini Rosso sweet vermouth**
⅛	shot(s)	**La Fée Parisienne (68%) absinthe**
3	dashes	**Peychaud's aromatic bitters**

Origin: Recipe adapted from Stanley Clisby Arthur's 1938 'Famous New Orleans Drinks and How to Mix 'Em'.
Comment: Full flavoured and complex, yet fairly sweet, with herbal notes and a touch of absinthe.

DE LA LOUISIANE #3

●●●●○

Glass: Martini
Garnish: Orange zest twist
Method: STIR all ingredients with ice and strain into chilled glass.

1½	shot(s)	**Bulleit bourbon whiskey**
1	shot(s)	**Dubonnet Red** (French made)
¼	shot(s)	**Cointreau triple sec**
2	dashes	**Peychaud's aromatic bitters**
½	shot(s)	**Chilled mineral water** (omit if wet ice)

Origin: Another variation on this New Orleans classic.
Comment: Beautifully balanced. This fruity whiskey drink manages to be both approachable and serious.

DEAD MAN'S MULE

●●●●○

Glass: Collins
Garnish: Lime wedge on rim
Method: SHAKE first 4 ingredients with ice and strain into ice-filled glass. **TOP** with ginger beer.

¾	shot(s)	**La Fée Parisienne (68%) absinthe**
¾	shot(s)	**Goldschläger cinnamon schnapps**
¾	shot(s)	**Almond (orgeat) syrup**
½	shot(s)	**Freshly squeezed lime juice**
Top up with		**Ginger beer**

Origin: Discovered in 2003 at the Met Bar, London, England.
Comment: Strong in every respect. Big, full-on flavours of aniseed, cinnamon and ginger.

DEAN'S GATE MARTINI

●●●●○

Glass: Martini
Garnish: Orange zest twist
Method: SHAKE all ingredients with ice and fine strain into chilled glass.

2	shot(s)	**Bacardi Superior rum**
1	shot(s)	**Drambuie liqueur**
1	shot(s)	**Rose's lime cordial**
¾	shot(s)	**Chilled mineral water** (omit if wet ice)

Comment: Rich and strong with a warm, honeyed citrus flavour.

DEATH BY CHOCOLATE

●●●●○

Glass: Hurricane
Garnish: Chocolate shavings (crumbled Cadbury's Flake bar)
Method: BLEND all ingredients with two 12oz scoops of crushed ice and serve with straws.

1	shot(s)	**Ketel One vodka**
1½	shot(s)	**Bailey's Irish cream liqueur**
1	shot(s)	**Brown crème de cacao liqueur**
3	scoops	**Chocolate ice cream**

Comment: Unsophisticated but delicious. Don't be cheap – use deluxe ice cream

DEATH IN THE AFTERNOON

●●●○○

Glass: Flute
Garnish: Float rose petal
Method: SHAKE first 3 ingredients with ice and fine strain into chilled glass. **TOP** with champagne.

¼	shot(s)	**La Fée Parisienne (68%) absinthe**
½	shot(s)	**Freshly squeezed lemon juice**
¼	shot(s)	**Sugar syrup** (2 sugar to 1 water)
Top up with		**Perrier Jouet brut champagne**

Origin: Created by Ernest Hemingway (not just named after his book), this recipe was the author's contribution to a 1935 cocktail book titled, 'So Red the Nose, or Breath in the Afternoon'.
Comment: Bravado (absinthe) dominates this drink, alongside hints of citrus and biscuity champagne.

DEATH IN THE GULF STREAM NEW #8

●●●●○

Glass: Collins
Garnish: Lime wedge
Method: SHAKE all ingredients with ice and strain into glass filled with crushed ice. **CHURN** (stir) and add more ice until glass is filled.

2	shot(s)	**Bokma oude genever**
1	shot(s)	**Freshly squeezed lime juice**
½	shot(s)	**Sugar syrup** (2 sugar to 1 water)
4	dashes	**Angostura aromatic bitters**
1	grated	**Lime zest**

Origin: According to 'Gentleman's Companion' this libation was a favourite of Ernest Hemingway. "... we got Hemingway's other picker-upper, and liked it. Take a tall thin water tumbler and fill it with finely cracked ice. Lace this broken debris with four good purple splashes of Angostura, add the juice and crushed peel of one green lime, and fill the glass almost full with Holland gin . . . No sugar, no fancying. It's strong, it's bitter - but so is English ale strong and bitter, in many cases. We don't add sugar to ale, and we don't need sugar in a Death In The Gulf Stream – or at least not more than one teaspoon. Its tartness and its bitterness are its chief charm. It is reviving and refreshing; cools the blood and inspires renewed interest in food, companions and life."
Comment: Remembering that Hemingway was a diabetic so has a very sour tooth, I believe this drink needs more than "one teaspoon" of sugar. Thus I have added half a shot of syrup to the original recipe. It also needs dilution, so be sure to shake well and churn in the glass.

DEAUVILLE #1

●●●●○

Glass: Martini
Garnish: Lemon zest twist
Method: SHAKE all ingredients with ice and fine strain into chilled glass.

1	shot(s)	**Boulard Grand Solage calvados**
1	shot(s)	**Courvoisier V.S.O.P. cognac**
¾	shot(s)	**Cointreau triple sec**
½	shot(s)	**Freshly squeezed lemon juice**
⅛	shot(s)	**Sugar syrup** (2 sugar to 1 water)
½	shot(s)	**Chilled mineral water** (omit if wet ice)

Variant: Apple Cart, Calvados Sidecar
Origin: A classic drink of unknown origin.
Comment: A well-balanced appley twist on the classic Sidecar.

DEAUVILLE #2

●●●●◐○

Glass: Martini
Garnish: Lemon zest twist
Method: SHAKE all ingredients with ice and fine strain into chilled glass.

1	shot(s)	**Boulard Grand Solage calvados**
1	shot(s)	**Courvoisier V.S.O.P. cognac**
1	shot(s)	**Cointreau triple sec**
1	shot(s)	**Freshly squeezed lemon juice**
¼	shot(s)	**Sugar syrup** (2 sugar to 1 water)

Origin: A classic drink of unknown origin.
Comment: The classic recipe omits the sugar syrup, which makes this drink too sour for my taste. Duly sweetened, it is very much in the Sidecar vein.

DEEP SOUTH

●●●○○

Glass: Old-fashioned
Garnish: Lime wedge
Method: MUDDLE ginger in base of shaker. Add other ingredients, **SHAKE** with ice and fine strain into glass filled with crushed ice.

2	slices	**Fresh root ginger** (thumbnail sized)
1½	shot(s)	**Clément Creole Shrubb liqueur**
1½	shot(s)	**Freshly squeezed orange juice**
¾	shot(s)	**Freshly squeezed lime juice**

Origin: Discovered in 1999 at AKA Bar, London, England.
Comment: Citrussy with delicate orange and ginger.

THE DELICIOUS SOUR UPDATED #8

●●●●◐

Glass: Old-fashioned
Garnish: Lemon slice & cherry on stick (sail)
Method: SHAKE all ingredients with ice and strain into ice-filled glass. **TOP** with soda.

2	shot(s)	**Boulard Grand Solage calvados**
1	shot(s)	**Crème pêche de vigne liqueur**
1	shot(s)	**Freshly squeezed lemon juice**
¼	shot(s)	**Sugar syrup** (2 sugar to 1 water)
½	fresh	**Egg white**
Top up with		**Soda water** (club soda)

Origin: Adapted from William Schmidt's 1892 book, 'The Flowing Bowl'.
Comment: Tis rather.

DELMARVA COCKTAIL NO.1

Glass: Martini
Garnish: Float mint sprig
Method: SHAKE all ingredients with ice and fine strain into chilled glass.

2	shot(s)	**Bulleit bourbon whiskey**
½	shot(s)	**Noilly Prat dry vermouth**
½	shot(s)	**Giffard Menthe Pastille liqueur**
½	shot(s)	**Freshly squeezed lemon juice**

Origin: Created by Ted 'Dr. Cocktail' Haigh, who hails from America's Delmarva Peninsula.
Comment: A minty fresh, dry, whiskey-based palate cleanser.

DELMARVA COCKTAIL NO.2

Glass: Martini
Garnish: Lemon zest twist
Method: SHAKE all ingredients with ice and fine strain into chilled glass.

2	shot(s)	**Bulleit bourbon whiskey**
½	shot(s)	**Noilly Prat dry vermouth**
½	shot(s)	**White crème de cacao liqueur**
½	shot(s)	**Freshly squeezed lemon juice**

Origin: Gary Regan adapted Ted Haigh's original Delmarva Cocktail and published this version in his 'Joy of Mixology'.
Comment: Whiskey's distinctive character shines through but is softened and flavoured by chocolate and a hint of citrus.

DELMONICO

Glass: Martini
Garnish: Orange zest twist
Method: STIR all ingredients with ice and strain into chilled glass.

1¼	shot(s)	**Courvoisier V.S.O.P. cognac**
1½	shot(s)	**Martini Rosso sweet vermouth**
1¼	shot(s)	**Noilly Prat dry vermouth**
3	dashes	**Angostura aromatic bitters**

Variant: If orange bitters are used in place of Angostura this becomes a Harvard.
Origin: A classic from the 1930s.
Comment: A Perfect Manhattan with cognac substituted for the whiskey.

DELMONICO SPECIAL

Glass: Martini
Garnish: Orange zest twist
Method: STIR all ingredients with ice and strain into chilled glass.

2¼	shot(s)	**Tanqueray London dry gin**
¼	shot(s)	**Courvoisier V.S.O.P. cognac**
¾	shot(s)	**Noilly Prat dry vermouth**
3	dashes	**Angostura aromatic bitters**

Origin: A classic from the 1930s.
Comment: A Wet Martini dried with a splash of cognac.

THE DEMOCRAT NEW #8

Glass: Collins
Garnish: Lemon slice
Method: SHAKE with ice and strain into glass filled with crushed ice.

2	shot(s)	**Bulleit bourbon whiskey**
½	shot(s)	**Crème pêche de vigne liqueur**
½	shot(s)	**Honey water** (4 honey to 1 water)
1½	shot(s)	**Freshly squeezed lemon juice**

Origin: Created in 2007 by Jon Santer at Bourbon & Branch, San Francisco, USA as "a kind of ode to the south – a democratic stronghold for so long."
Comment: The base spirit is inspired by Harry Truman, 33rd President, who only drank bourbon and is considered by many to be the last great Democrat.

DEMPSEY UPDATED #8

Glass: Martini
Garnish: Maraschino cherry
Method: SHAKE all ingredients with ice and fine strain into chilled glass.

1½	shot(s)	**Tanqueray London dry gin**
1½	shot(s)	**Boulard Grand Solage calvados**
⅛	shot(s)	**La Fée Parisienne (68%) absinthe**
½	shot(s)	**Pomegranate (grenadine) syrup**

Origin: A vintage cocktail of unknown origins.
Comment: Just on the right side of sweet but as hard as nails.

DEPTH BOMB

Glass: Old-fashioned
Garnish: Lime wedge
Method: SHAKE all ingredients with ice and strain into ice-filled glass.

1	shot(s)	**Boulard Grand Solage calvados**
1	shot(s)	**Courvoisier V.SO.P. cognac**
½	shot(s)	**Freshly squeezed lemon juice**
¼	shot(s)	**Pomegranate (grenadine) syrup**
⅛	shot(s)	**Sugar syrup** (2 sugar to 1 water)

Comment: Brandy and apple brandy benefit from a sour hint of lemon, balanced by grenadine.

DEPTH CHARGE

Glass: Boston & shot
Method: POUR lager into Boston glass. **POUR** vodka into shot glass. **DROP** shot glass into lager and consume.

1	glass	**Lager**
1½	shot(s)	**Ketel One vodka**

Variant: Boilermaker
Comment: One way to ruin good beer.

DERBY DAIQUIRI

Glass: Martini
Garnish: Orange zest twist
Method: SHAKE all ingredients with ice and fine strain into chilled glass.

2	shot(s)	**Bacardi Superior rum**
¾	shot(s)	**Freshly squeezed orange juice**
½	shot(s)	**Freshly squeezed lime juice**
¼	shot(s)	**Sugar syrup** (2 sugar to 1 water)

Comment: A fruity twist on the Classic Daiquiri.

DERBY FIZZ

Glass: Collins (8oz max)
Garnish: Lemon slice
Method: SHAKE first 6 ingredients with ice and strain into chilled glass. **TOP** with soda.

1¾	shot(s)	**Bulleit bourbon whiskey**
½	shot(s)	**Bacardi Superior rum**
¼	shot(s)	**Grand Marnier liqueur**
1	shot(s)	**Freshly squeezed lemon juice**
½	shot(s)	**Sugar syrup** (2 sugar to 1 water)
½	fresh	**Egg white** (optional)
Top up with		**Soda water** (from siphon)

Comment: An elongated sour with perfectly balanced strength, sweetness and sourness.

DESERT COOLER

Glass: Collins
Garnish: Orange slice
Method: SHAKE first 3 ingredients with ice and strain into ice-filled glass. **TOP** with ginger beer.

2	shot(s)	**Tanqueray London dry gin**
¾	shot(s)	**Heering cherry brandy liqueur**
1½	shot(s)	**Freshly squeezed orange juice**
Top up with		**Ginger beer**

Comment: Sandy in colour - as its name suggests - with a refreshing bite.

DETOX

Glass: Shot
Garnish: Lime wedge on drink
Method: Refrigerate ingredients then **LAYER** in chilled glass by carefully pouring in the following order.

½	shot(s)	**Peach Tree peach schnapps**
½	shot(s)	**Ocean Spray cranberry juice**
½	shot(s)	**Ketel One vodka**

Comment: Hardly a detox but tasty all the same.

DETROIT MARTINI UPDATED #8

Glass: Martini
Garnish: Float mint sprig
Method: SHAKE all ingredients (including mint) with ice and fine strain into chilled glass.

7	fresh	**Mint leaves**
3	shot(s)	**Ketel One vodka**
½	shot(s)	**Sugar syrup** (2 sugar to 1 water)
⅛	shot(s)	**Freshly squeezed lime juice**

Variant: Cowboy Hoof Martini
Origin: Created by Dick Bradsell in the mid 90s and based on his Cowboy Hoof Martini.
Comment: Vodka doused mint with the merest hint of lime. Clean and flavoursome.

DETROPOLITAN

Glass: Martini
Garnish: Flamed orange zest
Method: SHAKE all ingredients with ice and fine strain into chilled glass.

1	shot(s)	**Ketel One vodka**
½	shot(s)	**Cointreau triple sec**
¼	shot(s)	**Crème de cassis liqueur**
1½	shot(s)	**Ocean Spray cranberry juice**
½	shot(s)	**Freshly squeezed lime juice**

Origin: Created at Detroit, London, England.
Comment: Yet another twist on the Cosmopolitan.

DEVIL'S COCKTAIL

Glass: Martini
Garnish: Lemon zest twist
Method: SHAKE all ingredients with ice and fine strain into chilled glass.

2	shot(s)	**Warre's Otima tawny port**
1½	shot(s)	**Noilly Prat dry vermouth**
¼	shot(s)	**Freshly squeezed lemon juice**

Origin: Vintage cocktail of unknown origin.
Comment: Lemon predominates with the richness of port fighting to be heard.

DEVIL'S MANHATTAN

Glass: Martini
Garnish: Lemon zest twist
Method: STIR all ingredients with ice and strain into chilled glass.

2	shot(s)	**Bulleit bourbon whiskey**
1	shot(s)	**Southern Comfort liqueur**
½	shot(s)	**Martini Rosso sweet vermouth**
3	dashes	**Peychaud's aromatic bitters**

Comment: A Sweet Manhattan with a hint of the south.

DEVIL'S SHARE NEW #8

Glass: Old-fashioned
Garnish: Orange zest twist
Method: MUDDLE ginger in base of shaker. Add other ingredients, **SHAKE** with ice and fine strain into ice-filled glass.

2	slice(s)	**Fresh root ginger** (thumbnail sized)
2	shot(s)	**Bulleit bourbon whiskey**
¾	shot(s)	**Freshly squeezed orange juice**
1	shot(s)	**Freshly squeezed lemon juice**
½	shot(s)	**Sugar syrup** (2 sugar to 1 water)

Origin: Created in 2006 by Pete Kendall at Match Bar, London, England.
Comment: Ginger, bourbon and lemon makes for a spicy and tasty little devil.

DIABLE ROUGE

Glass: Martini
Garnish: Berries on stick
Method: SHAKE all ingredients with ice and fine strain into chilled glass.

2	shot(s)	**Ketel One vodka**
2	shot(s)	**Pressed pineapple juice**
¼	shot(s)	**Crème de cassis liqueur**

Comment: Not quite as rouge as the name would suggest. Hard to hate.

EL DIABLO

Glass: Collins
Garnish: Lime wedge
Method: SHAKE first 3 ingredients with ice and strain into ice-filled glass. **TOP** with ginger beer.

2	shot(s)	**Don Julio reposado tequila**
¾	shot(s)	**Crème de cassis liqueur**
1	shot(s)	**Freshly squeezed lime juice**
Top up with		**Ginger beer**

Origin: Thought to have originated in California during the 1940s. The name translates as 'The Devil'.
Comment: The tequila, red fruit and ginger aren't exactly subtle, but there's a time and place for everything.

DIAMOND DOG

Glass: Old-fashioned
Garnish: Orange slice
Method: SHAKE all ingredients with ice and strain into ice-filled glass.

1	shot(s)	**Campari Bitter**
1	shot(s)	**Noilly Prat dry vermouth**
1	shot(s)	**Rose's lime cordial**
1	shot(s)	**Freshly squeezed orange juice**

Origin: Discovered in 2005 at Four Seasons George V, Paris, France.
Comment: Bittersweet and refreshingly different.

DIAMOND FIZZ

Glass: Collins (8oz max)
Garnish: Lemon slice
Method: SHAKE first 3 ingredients with ice and strain into chilled glass. **TOP** with champagne.

2	shot(s)	**Tanqueray London dry gin**
1	shot(s)	**Freshly squeezed lemon juice**
½	shot(s)	**Sugar syrup** (2 sugar to 1 water)
Top up with		**Perrier Jouet brut champagne**

Origin: A long lost classic.
Comment: Why top a Fizz with soda when you can use champagne?

DIANA'S BITTER

Glass: Martini
Garnish: Split lime wedge
Method: SHAKE all ingredients with ice and fine strain into chilled glass.

2	shot(s)	**Tanqueray London dry gin**
1	shot(s)	**Campari Bitter**
1	shot(s)	**Freshly squeezed lime juice**
½	shot(s)	**Sugar syrup** (2 sugar to 1 water)

Comment: A drink for the Campari aficionado: bittersweet and strong.

DICKENS' MARTINI UPDATED #8

Glass: Martini
Garnish: No garnish
Method: STIR vermouth with ice and strain to discard excess, leaving the mixing glass and ice coated with vermouth. **POUR** gin over vermouth coated ice, **STIR** and strain into chilled glass.

| ¾ | shot(s) | **Noilly Prat dry vermouth** |
| 2½ | shot(s) | **Tanqueray London dry gin** |

Comment: A Dry Martini served without any garnish (i.e. no olive or twist). The name is a reference to Charles Dickens' novel Oliver Twist.

DIFFORD'S DAIQUIRI

Glass: Old-fashioned
Garnish: Lime zest twist
Method: SHAKE all ingredients with ice and strain into ice-filled glass.

2½	shot(s)	**Zacapa aged rum**
½	shot(s)	**Freshly squeezed lime juice**
1	shot(s)	**Difford's Daiquiri Water**

Origin: Created in 2005 by Yours Truly (Simon Difford) and served exclusively at the Cabinet Room Bar, London, England.
Comment: The better the rum, the better the Daiquiri. However, this recipe can even make a light white rum Daiquiri taste like it has been well aged.

DETROIT

DIFFORD'S OLD-FASHIONED

Glass: Old-fashioned
Garnish: Orange zest twist
Method: STIR all ingredients with ice and strain into ice-filled glass.

| 2½ | shot(s) | **Bulleit bourbon whiskey** |
| 1 | shot(s) | **Difford's Daiquiri Water** |

Origin: Created in 2005 by Yours Truly (Simon Difford) and served exclusively at The Cabinet Room, London, England.
Comment: Due to the use of Daiquiri Water, this tasty Old-Fashioned doesn't require the arduous stirring and dilution traditionally associated with the drink.

DIKI-DIKI

Glass: Martini
Garnish: Half sugar rim
Method: SHAKE all ingredients with ice and fine strain into chilled glass.

2	shot(s)	**Boulard Grand Solage calvados**
½	shot(s)	**Swedish Punch**
½	shot(s)	**Freshly squeezed grapefruit juice**

Origin: Adapted from Harry Craddock's 1930 'The Savoy Cocktail Book'.
Comment: Fruity yet tart. The sourness is a challenge initially but very rewarding.

DIMI-TINI NEW #8

Glass: Martini
Garnish: Grapefruit zest twist
Method: SHAKE all ingredients with ice and fine strain into chilled glass.

7	fresh	**Raspberries**
2	shot(s)	**Ketel One vodka**
¼	shot(s)	**Heering cherry brandy liqueur**
½	shot(s)	**Freshly squeezed lime juice**
⅛	shot(s)	**Sugar syrup** (2 sugar to 1 water)

Comment: Like Dimi – this drink's easy to like.
Origin: Adapted from a recipe by Dimitri Lezinska, the Grey Goose Ambassador, originally using Grey Goose vodka.

DINGO

Glass: Collins
Garnish: Orange slice
Method: SHAKE all ingredients with ice and strain into ice-filled glass.

1	shot(s)	**Bacardi Superior rum**
1	shot(s)	**Bulleit bourbon whiskey**
½	shot(s)	**Luxardo Amaretto di Saschira**
2	shot(s)	**Freshly squeezed orange juice**
1	shot(s)	**Freshly squeezed lemon juice**
¼	shot(s)	**Pomegranate (grenadine) syrup**
¼	shot(s)	**Sugar syrup** (2 sugar to 1 water)

Comment: Very fruity but with a rum and whiskey kick.

DINO SOUR

Glass: Old-fashioned
Garnish: Lemon slice & cherry on stick (sail)
Method: SHAKE all ingredients with ice and fine strain into chilled glass.

1	shot(s)	**Bacardi Superior rum**
1	shot(s)	**Gosling's Black Seal rum**
1	shot(s)	**Freshly squeezed lemon juice**
½	shot(s)	**Sugar syrup** (2 sugar to 1 water)
½	fresh	**Egg white**

Comment: Two diverse rums combine brilliantly in this classic sour.

DIPLOMAT

Glass: Old-fashioned
Garnish: Orange zest twist
Method: STIR all ingredients with ice and strain into ice-filled glass.

2	shot(s)	**Noilly Prat dry vermouth**
1	shot(s)	**Martini Rosso sweet vermouth**
⅛	shot(s)	**Luxardo maraschino liqueur**
2	dashes	**Angostura orange bitters**

Origin: Adapted from Harry Craddock's 1930 'The Savoy Cocktail Book'.
Comment: Wonderfully aromatic and dry. Too good to waste on diplomats.

DIRTY BANANA

Glass: Collins
Garnish: Banana slice on rim
Method: BLEND all ingredients with 12oz scoop crushed ice. Serve with straws.

1½	shot(s)	**Zacapa aged rum**
1	shot(s)	**Kahlúa coffee liqueur**
1	shot(s)	**Crème de banane liqueur**
1	fresh	**Peeled banana**
1	shot(s)	**Double (heavy) cream**
1	shot(s)	**Milk**

Origin: A popular cocktail in Jamaica.
Comment: Long, creamy and filling banana drink with a 'dirty' flavour and colour courtesy of coffee liqueur.

DIRTY-DRY-DIRTY MARTINI NEW #8

Glass: Martini/Coupette
Garnish: Three olives & lemon zest twist
Method: STIR all ingredients with ice and fine strain into chilled glass.

2	shot(s)	**Tanqueray London dry gin**
¼	shot(s)	**Noilly Prat dry vermouth**
⅛	shot(s)	**Freshly squeezed lime juice**
⅛	shot(s)	**Olive brine** (from olive jar)

Comment: However hard you think you are, this one is harder.

DIRTY MARTINI

Glass: Martini
Garnish: Olive on stick
Method: **STIR** all ingredients with ice and strain into a chilled glass.

2½	shot(s)	**Tanqueray London dry gin**
¼	shot(s)	**Olive brine** (from olive jar)
¼	shot(s)	**Noilly Prat dry vermouth**

AKA: F.D.R. Martini after the American president Franklin Delano Roosevelt.
Variant: Substitute vodka for gin.
Origin: Some attribute the creation of this drink to Roosevelt: the 32nd president was a keen home bartender, although his cocktails were reportedly 'horrendous', and there is no evidence that he used olive brine in his Martinis.
Comment: This drink varies from delicious to disgusting, depending on the liquid in your jar of olives. Oil will produce a revolting emulsion: make sure that your olives are packed in brine.

> **'I'VE BEEN DRUNK FOR ABOUT A WEEK NOW, AND I THOUGHT IT MIGHT SOBER ME UP TO SIT IN A LIBRARY.'**
> F. SCOTT FITZGERALD

DIRTY SANCHEZ

Glass: Collins
Garnish: Lime slice
Method: **SHAKE** first 4 ingredients with ice and strain into ice-filled glass. **TOP** with ginger beer.

2	shot(s)	**Don Julio reposado tequila**
¾	shot(s)	**Agavero tequila liqueur**
½	shot(s)	**Chambord black raspberry liqueur**
½	shot(s)	**Freshly squeezed lime juice**
Top up with		**Jamaican ginger beer**

Origin: Created in 2001 by Phillip Jeffrey and Ian Baldwin at the GE Club, London, England.
Comment: A wonderfully refreshing and complex long summer drink.

DIVINO'S

Glass: Martini
Garnish: Chocolate shavings
Method: **SHAKE** all ingredients with ice and fine strain into chilled glass.

½	shot(s)	**Ketel One vodka**
2½	shot(s)	**Barolo wine**
1	shot(s)	**Brown crème de cacao liqueur**

Origin: Discovered in 2005 at DiVino, Hong Kong.
Comment: The chocolate liqueur takes the acidity off the wine without masking its flavour.

DIXIE COSMOPOLITAN NEW #8

Glass: Martini/Coupette
Garnish: Flamed orange zest twist, cinnamon & sugar rim
Method: Break up section of cinnamon and drop into shaker. Add other ingredients, **SHAKE** with ice and fine strain into chilled glass.

2	inch	**Cinnamon stick**
1	shot(s)	**Southern Comfort liqueur**
1	shot(s)	**Cointreau triple sec**
¼	shot(s)	**Rose's lime cordial**
½	shot(s)	**Freshly squeezed lime juice**
1½	shot(s)	**Ocean Spray cranberry juice**

Comment: Slightly sweet and somewhat reminiscent of jellybean sweets.
Origin: Created circa 2005 by Matthew Dakers, a globetrotting professional bartender.

DIXIE DEW

Glass: Martini
Garnish: Orange zest twist
Method: **SHAKE** all ingredients with ice and fine strain into chilled glass.

2	shot(s)	**Bulleit bourbon whiskey**
½	shot(s)	**Giffard Menthe Pastille liqueur**
½	shot(s)	**Cointreau triple sec**
¾	shot(s)	**Chilled mineral water** (omit if wet ice)

Comment: A peppermint fresh, bourbon laced drink.

DNA #1

Glass: Martini
Garnish: Orange zest twist
Method: **SHAKE** all ingredients with ice and fine strain into chilled glass.

1½	shot(s)	**Tanqueray London dry gin**
¾	shot(s)	**Bols apricot brandy liqueur**
1	shot(s)	**Freshly squeezed lemon juice**
¼	shot(s)	**Sugar syrup** (2 sugar to 1 water)
2	dashes	**Angostura orange bitters** (optional)

Origin: Created by Emmanuel Audermatte at The Atlantic Bar & Grill, London, England, in 1999.
Comment: Slightly sharp and very fruity, but pleasantly so.

DNA #2

Glass: Martini
Garnish: Lemon zest twist
Method: **SHAKE** all ingredients with ice and fine strain into chilled glass.

1	shot(s)	**Tanqueray London dry gin**
1	shot(s)	**Damson gin liqueur**
¾	shot(s)	**Bols apricot brandy liqueur**
½	shot(s)	**Freshly squeezed lime juice**
2	dashes	**Angostura aromatic bitters**
½	shot(s)	**Chilled mineral water** (omit if wet ice)

Origin: Created in 2005 by Tonin Kacaj at Maze, London, England.
Comment: Tangy, fruity and gin laced.

DOCTOR #1

Glass: Martini
Garnish: Lime zest twist
Method: SHAKE all ingredients with ice and fine strain into chilled glass.

1½	shot(s)	**Zacapa aged rum**
1½	shot(s)	**Swedish Punch**
¾	shot(s)	**Freshly squeezed lime juice**

Origin: In David Embury's classic, 'The Fine Art of Mixing Drinks', my hero lists four wildly different drinks using Swedish Punch. Trader Vic's 'Bartender's Guide' lists two variations of a single drink, for which the above is my own recipe.
Comment: Retitled 'Swedish Daiquiri', this could be a hit.

DOCTOR #2 NEW #8

Glass: Martini
Garnish: Lime zest twist
Method: SHAKE all ingredients with ice and fine strain into chilled glass.

2	shot(s)	**Swedish Punch**
1	shot(s)	**Freshly squeezed lime juice**

Origin: Vintage cocktail of unknown origin.
Comment: Lime combines wells with the aromatics spices in Swedish Punch.

DOCTOR FUNK

Glass: Sling
Garnish: Lime wedge
Method: SHAKE first 6 ingredients with ice and strain into glass filled with crushed ice. TOP with soda and serve with straws.

2½	shot(s)	**Gosling's Black Seal rum**
¼	shot(s)	**Pernod anis**
½	shot(s)	**Freshly squeezed lemon juice**
¼	shot(s)	**Freshly squeezed lime juice**
¼	shot(s)	**Pomegranate (grenadine) syrup**
¼	shot(s)	**Sugar syrup** (2 sugar to 1 water)
Top up with		**Soda water** (club soda)

Origin: A Tiki drink adapted from one created circa 1937 by Don The Beachcomber.
Comment: Too many and you'll need your very own doctor.

> '[GRANT] STOOD BY ME WHEN I WAS CRAZY, AND I STOOD BY HIM WHEN HE WAS DRUNK; AND NOW WE STAND BY EACH OTHER ALWAYS.'
> GENERAL WILLIAM SHERMAN

DOHENY PISCO PUNCH NEW #8

Glass: Collins
Garnish: Mint sprig & very thin slice of pineapple
Method: Lightly MUDDLE (just to bruise) mint in base of shaker. Add next 5 ingredients, SHAKE with ice and strain into ice-filled glass. TOP with ginger beer.

12	fresh	**Mint leaves**
1½	shot(s)	**Pressed pineapple juice**
2	shot(s)	**Macchu pisco**
¾	shot(s)	**Freshly squeezed lemon juice**
¼	shot(s)	**Vanilla sugar syrup**
1	dash	**Angostura aromatic bitters**
Top up with		**Ginger beer**

Comment: Vincenzo's twist on the San Franciscan classic.
Origin: Adapted from a drink created in 2007 by Vincenzo Marianello at Doheny, Los Angeles, USA.

DOLCE-AMARO

Glass: Martini
Garnish: Orange zest twist
Method: STIR all ingredients with ice and strain into chilled glass.

1½	shot(s)	**Campari Bitter**
1½	shot(s)	**Noilly Prat dry vermouth**
¾	shot(s)	**Luxardo Amaretto di Saschira**

Comment: The very apt name translates as 'bittersweet'.

DOLCE HAVANA

Glass: Martini
Method: SHAKE all ingredients with ice and fine strain into chilled glass.

1¼	shot(s)	**Bacardi Superior rum**
½	shot(s)	**Campari Bitter**
½	shot(s)	**Cointreau triple sec**
1¼	shot(s)	**Freshly squeezed orange juice**
1¼	shot(s)	**Freshly squeezed lime juice**
⅛	shot(s)	**Sugar syrup** (2 sugar to 1 water)

Origin: Created by Fabrizio Musorella in 2000 at the Library Bar, Lanesborough Hotel, London, England.
Comment: A melange of Mediterranean fruit.

LA DOLCE VITA NEW #8

Glass: Martini
Garnish: Lemon zest twist
Method: MUDDLE grapes in base of shaker. Add vodka, honey and bitters, SHAKE with ice and fine strain into chilled glass. TOP with prosecco.

4	fresh	**Seedless white grapes**
1	shot(s)	**Ketel One vodka**
1	spoon	**Runny honey**
1	dash	**Angostura orange bitters**
Top up with		**Prosecco sparkling wine**

Origin: Created in 2002 by Tony Conigliaro at Isola, London, England.
Comment: Complex, yet easy to quaff with grape juice, vodka, honey and a touch of fizz.

DOLORES #1

Glass: Martini
Garnish: Lemon zest twist
Method: SHAKE all ingredients with ice and fine strain into chilled glass.

2	shot(s)	**Zacapa aged rum**
2	shot(s)	**Dubonnet Red** (French made)
1	shot(s)	**Tio Pepe fino sherry**

Origin: A classic. Some recipes include a splash of orange juice.
Comment: Aromatic and well balanced, provided you use French-made Dubonnet.

DOLORES #2

Glass: Martini
Garnish: Dust with grated nutmeg
Method: SHAKE all ingredients with ice and fine strain into chilled glass.

1½	shot(s)	**Courvoisier V.S.O.P. cognac**
¾	shot(s)	**Heering cherry brandy liqueur**
¾	shot(s)	**White crème de cacao liqueur**
1	fresh	**Egg white**

Comment: A chocolaty after dinner libation.

DON DAISY NEW #8

Glass: Martini/Coupette
Garnish: Lemon zest twist
Method: SHAKE all ingredients with ice and fine strain into chilled glass.

1½	shot(s)	**Bacardi Superior rum**
½	shot(s)	**Noilly Prat dry vermouth**
½	shot(s)	**St-Germain elderflower liqueur**
¼	shot(s)	**Freshly squeezed lemon juice**
¼	shot(s)	**Sugar syrup** (2 sugar to 1 water)
½	fresh	**Egg white**

Comment: This zesty, silky smooth and easy drink is laced with light rum.
Origin: Created in 2008 by James Tait, UK.

DONEGAL

Glass: Martini
Garnish: Orange zest twist
Method: SHAKE all ingredients with ice and fine strain into chilled glass.

1½	shot(s)	**Jameson Irish whiskey**
1¼	shot(s)	**Noilly Prat dry vermouth**
½	shot(s)	**Luxardo maraschino liqueur**
½	shot(s)	**Mandarine Napoléon liqueur**

Comment: Aromatised Irish whiskey with cherry and orange.

DON JUAN

Glass: Martini
Garnish: Orange zest twist
Method: SHAKE all ingredients with ice and fine strain into chilled glass.

1¾	shot(s)	**Courvoisier V.S.O.P. cognac**
1	shot(s)	**Cuarenta Y Tres (Licor 43) liqueur**
1	shot(s)	**Freshly squeezed orange juice**
½	shot(s)	**Double (heavy) cream**
½	shot(s)	**Milk**

Comment: A lightly creamy orange affair with vanilla spice.

> **'LET'S GET OUT OF THESE WET CLOTHES AND INTO A DRY MARTINI.'**
> HOLLYWOOD PRESS AGENT

DONNA'S CREAMY'TINI

Glass: Martini
Garnish: Cherry on rim
Method: SHAKE all ingredients with ice and fine strain into chilled glass.

1	shot(s)	**Luxardo Amaretto di Saschira**
1	shot(s)	**Heering cherry brandy liqueur**
1	shot(s)	**Brown crème de cacao liqueur**
1	shot(s)	**Double (heavy) cream**

Origin: Adapted from a drink created in 2002 by Yannick Miseriaux at the Fifth Floor Bar, London, England.
Comment: A fine example of an alcoholic liquid pudding.

DON'S DELIGHT NEW #8

Glass: Martini/Coupette
Garnish: Lime wedge
Method: SHAKE all ingredients with ice and fine strain into chilled glass.

2	shot(s)	**Don Julio añejo tequila**
½	shot(s)	**Bulleit bourbon whiskey**
⅛	shot(s)	**Luxardo amaretto liqueur**
1¼	shot(s)	**Freshly squeezed lime juice**
½	shot(s)	**Sugar syrup** (2 sugar to 1 water)
1	fresh	**Egg white**

Comment: When made with Don Julio 1942, as this drink originally was, this is another memorable trick by the affable Brian Van Flandern.
Origin: Created in 2008 by Brian Van Flandern (Don Julio Global Brand Ambassador) in New York City, USA.

DON'S PASSION NEW #8

Glass: Coupette/Martini
Garnish: Half a passion fruit
Method: Cut passion fruit in half and scoop out flesh and seeds into shaker. Add next 4 ingredients, **SHAKE** with ice and fine strain into chilled glass. Pour grenadine into centre of drink (should sink to bottom).

1	fresh	Passion fruit
2	shot(s)	Bacardi Superior rum
½	shot(s)	Galliano L'Autentico liqueur
1	shot(s)	Freshly squeezed lime juice
½	shot(s)	Freshly squeezed orange juice
¼	shot(s)	Grenadine (pomegranate) syrup

Comment: Passion fruit and Galliano influence this Bacardi Cocktail style drink.
Origin: Created in 2008 by Symeon White at Avon Gorge Hotel, Bristol, UK.

DORIAN GRAY

Glass: Martini
Garnish: Orange zest twist
Method: SHAKE all ingredients with ice and fine strain into chilled glass.

1½	shot(s)	Bacardi Superior rum
¾	shot(s)	Grand Marnier liqueur
1	shot(s)	Freshly squeezed orange juice
¾	shot(s)	Ocean Spray cranberry juice

Origin: Discovered in 1999 at One Aldwych, London, England. This cocktail takes its name from Oscar Wilde's novel, in which a socialite's wish to remain as young and charming as his own portrait is granted. Allured by his depraved friend Lord Henry Wotton, Dorian Gray assumes a life of perversion and sin. But every time he sins the painting ages, while Gray stays young and healthy.
Comment: Fruity and rum laced, not overly sweet.

'IF YOU DRINK, DON'T DIAL.'
PHONE OPERATOR, 1950s

DOROTHY PARKER

Glass: Martini
Garnish: Sugar rim
Method: SHAKE first 4 ingredients with ice and fine strain into chilled glass. **TOP** with champagne.

1½	shot(s)	Ketel One Citroen vodka
½	shot(s)	Cointreau triple sec
¼	shot(s)	Chambord black raspberry liqueur
½	shot(s)	Freshly squeezed lemon juice
Top up with		Perrier Jouet brut champagne

Origin: Discovered in 2007 at Town Hall, San Francisco, USA, and named for the wit and drinker.
Comment: Light, fruity and easy to drink.

DOUBLE GRAPE MARTINI

Glass: Martini
Garnish: Grapes on stick
Method: MUDDLE grapes in base of shaker. Add other ingredients, **SHAKE** with ice and fine strain into chilled glass.

12	fresh	Seedless white grapes
2	shot(s)	Ketel One vodka
¾	shot(s)	Sauvignon Blanc wine
½	shot(s)	Sugar syrup (2 sugar to 1 water)

Origin: Created by Yours Truly (Simon Difford) in 2004.
Comment: The wine adds complexity to a simple Grape Martini.

DOUBLE VISION

Glass: Martini
Garnish: Blackcurrants on stick
Method: SHAKE all ingredients with ice and fine strain into chilled glass.

1	shot(s)	Ketel One Citroen vodka
1	shot(s)	Raspberry flavoured vodka
1	shot(s)	Pressed apple juice
½	shot(s)	Freshly squeezed lime juice
¼	shot(s)	Sugar syrup (2 sugar to 1 water)
3	dashes	Angostura aromatic bitters

Comment: Citrus fresh with strong hints of apple and red berries.

DOUGHNUT MARTINI

Glass: Martini
Garnish: Segment of doughnut
Method: SHAKE all ingredients with ice and fine strain into chilled glass.

1½	shot(s)	Bacardi Superior rum
¾	shot(s)	Bulleit bourbon whiskey
½	shot(s)	Vanilla schnapps liqueur
½	shot(s)	Cuarenta Y Tres (Licor 43) liqueur
⅛	shot(s)	Teichenné butterscotch schnapps
¾	shot(s)	Chilled mineral water (omit if wet ice)

Origin: Created in 2003 by Yours Truly (Simon Difford).
Comment: My attempt at mimicking the taste of a Krispy Kreme Original Glazed doughnut without ending up with an overly sweet cocktail.

DOWA

Glass: Old-fashioned
Garnish: Lime wedge
Method: STIR honey and vodka in base of shaker until honey dissolves. Add lime juice, **SHAKE** with ice and strain into glass filled with crushed ice. Serve with straws.

4	spoons	Runny honey
2½	shot(s)	Ketel One vodka
¼	shot(s)	Freshly squeezed lime juice

Origin: This cocktail is particularly popular in upscale hotel bars in Kenya where it is enjoyed by the safari set. The name translates as 'medicine'.
Comment: Very similar to the Caipirovska in its use of vodka, lime and crushed ice: the honey makes the difference.

DOWNHILL RACER

Glass: Martini
Garnish: Pineapple wedge on rim
Method: **SHAKE** all ingredients with ice and fine strain into chilled glass.

1¾	shot(s)	**Zacapa aged rum**
¾	shot(s)	**Luxardo Amaretto di Saschira**
1¾	shot(s)	**Pressed pineapple juice**

Comment: Aged rum sweetened, softened and flavoured with pineapple and amaretto.

DR ZEUS

Glass: Old-fashioned
Method: **POUR** Fernet Branca into ice-filled glass, **TOP** with chilled mineral water and leave to stand. Separately **MUDDLE** raisins in base of shaker, add other ingredients and **SHAKE** with ice. Finally **DISCARD** contents of glass and strain contents of shaker into the Fernet Branca coated glass.

1	shot(s)	**Fernet Branca**
20	dried	**Raisins**
2	shot(s)	**Courvoisier V.S.O.P. cognac**
¼	shot(s)	**Sugar syrup** (2 sugar to 1 water)
⅛	shot(s)	**Kahlúa coffee liqueur**
1	dash	**Angostura orange bitters**

Origin: Created by Adam Ennis in 2001 at Isola, Knightsbridge, London, England.
Comment: Not that far removed from a Sazerac cocktail, this is innovative and great tasting.

DRAGON BLOSSOM

Glass: Martini
Garnish: Maraschino cherry
Method: **SHAKE** all ingredients with ice and fine strain into chilled glass.

1¾	shot(s)	**Rose petal vodka**
¼	shot(s)	**Soho lychee liqueur**
¼	shot(s)	**Maraschino syrup** (from cherry jar)
1¾	shot(s)	**Ocean Spray cranberry juice**

Comment: Light, aromatic, semi-sweet and distinctly oriental in style.

DRAMATIC MARTINI

Glass: Martini
Garnish: Grate nutmeg over drink
Method: **SHAKE** all ingredients with ice and fine strain into chilled glass.

1	shot(s)	**Tuaca Italian liqueur**
1	shot(s)	**Grand Marnier liqueur**
1	shot(s)	**Irish cream liqueur**
1	shot(s)	**Milk**

Comment: Creamy and sweet with orangey, herbal notes.

DREAM COCKTAIL

Glass: Martini
Garnish: Orange zest twist
Method: **SHAKE** all ingredients with ice and fine strain into chilled glass.

1½	shot(s)	**Courvoisier V.S.O.P. cognac**
¾	shot(s)	**Cointreau triple sec**
¼	shot(s)	**Marie Brizard anisette liqueur**
½	shot(s)	**Chilled mineral water** (omit if wet ice)

Comment: An after dinner drink with brandy, orange liqueur and a refreshing burst of aniseed.

DREAMSICLE

Glass: Martini
Method: **SHAKE** first 3 ingredients with ice and fine strain into chilled glass. **FLOAT** cream.

1½	shot(s)	**Kahlúa coffee liqueur**
¾	shot(s)	**Cointreau triple sec**
1	shot(s)	**Freshly squeezed orange juice**
¾	shot(s)	**Double (heavy) cream**

Comment: Sweet coffee and orange smoothed by a creamy top. A veritable dessert in a glass.

DREIKLANG (THREE OF A KIND) NEW #8

Glass: Old-fashioned
Garnish: Orange zest twist
Method: **STIR** sugar syrup with 2 ice cubes, add xoxolate mole and stir again. Add more ice plus tequila and **STIR** some more.

2	shot(s)	**Don Julio reposado tequila**
½	shot(s)	**Sugar syrup** (2 sugar to 1 water)
5	drops	**Xoxolate Mole** (bittermens.com)

Comment: Named after the German word for 'three of a kind' due to the trio of flavours encountered in this drink; orange, agave and chocolate.
Origin: Created in 2007 by Heiko Tagawa, Germany.

DROWNED OUT

Glass: Collins
Garnish: Lime wedge
Method: **POUR** ingredients into ice-filled glass, stir and serve with straws.

2	shot(s)	**Pernod anis**
1	shot(s)	**Freshly squeezed lime juice**
Top up with		**Ginger ale**

Comment: Ginger combines with aniseed rather than drowning it.

DRY DAIQUIRI NEW #8

● ● ● ● ◐ ○

Glass: Martini/coupette
Garnish: Lime wedge on rim
Method: SHAKE all ingredients with ice and fine strain into chilled glass.

2	shot(s)	**Zacapa aged rum**
½	shot(s)	**Freshly squeezed lime juice**
¼	shot(s)	**Sugar syrup** (2 sugar to 1 water)
⅛	shot(s)	**Campari Bitter**
⅛	shot(s)	**Passion fruit syrup**

Origin: Created in 2007 by Kevin Armstrong, Match Group, London.
Comment: Passion fruit syrup is powerful stuff and a little goes a long way in this drink.

DRY ICE MARTINI

● ● ● ● ● ◐

Glass: Martini
Garnish: Orange zest twist
Method: STIR all ingredients with ice and strain into chilled glass.

2	shot(s)	**Ketel One vodka**
½	shot(s)	**Noilly Prat dry vermouth**
¾	shot(s)	**Icewine**

Origin: Created by Yours Truly (Simon Difford) in 2004.
Comment: Despite the name, this is slightly honeyed rather than dry.

DRY MARTINI #1 (TRADITIONAL)

● ● ● ● ●

UPDATED #8

Glass: Martini
Garnish: The 'Oliver Twist' choice between an olive (stuffed or otherwise) or a lemon zest twist is traditional and these are the two most common garnishes for a Dry Martini. There are, however, a number of variants. A 'Dickens' is a Martini without a twist, a 'Gibson' is a Martini with two onions instead of an olive or a twist and a 'Franklin Martini' is named after Franklin Roosevelt and has two olives.
Method: STIR vermouth with ice and strain to discard excess, leaving the glass and ice coated with vermouth. POUR gin over vermouth coated ice, STIR and strain into a chilled glass.

¾	shot(s)	**Noilly Prat dry vermouth**
2½	shot(s)	**Tanqueray London dry gin**
1	dash	**Angostura orange bitters** (optional)

Origin: The Martini and its origins is a topic that can raise temperatures among drinks aficionados and, as so often, no one really knows.

Today the drink is a blend of dry gin or vodka with a hint of dry vermouth. Yet it seems to have evolved from the Manhattan via the Martinez, a rather sweet drink based on Dutch genever or Old Tom gin with the addition of sweet vermouth, curaçao and orange bitters. The Martini, like the Martinez, was initially sweet, not dry (hence the need to specify that its descendant was a 'Dry' Martini), and very heavy on the vermouth by modern standards.

Martinis were known in the late 1880s but the Dry Martini most likely appeared with the emergence of the London Dry gin style. In 1906 Louis Muckenstrum wrote about a dry Martini Cocktail which, like the Martinez, benefited from curaçao and bitters as well as vermouth. Yet, unlike earlier versions, both the gin and the vermouth were dry. According to Gary Regan, the marketers at Martini & Rosso vermouth were advertising a Dry Martini cocktail heavily at that time.

One myth attributes the creation of the Dry Martini to one Martini di Arma di Taggia,, head bartender at New York's Knickerbocker Hotel, in 1911, although this is clearly too late. It is also no longer believed that the name relates to Martini & Henry rifles, the first of which was launched in 1871.

The Dry Martini seems to have got drier and drier over the years. Curaçao rapidly left the drink, but orange bitters remained a usual ingredient until the 1940s (interestingly, these are now coming back into vogue in some bars).

There is some debate as to whether a Martini should be shaken or stirred. It should be stirred. If shaken, it becomes a 'Bradford'. Shaking the drink increases the dilution and introduces air bubbles into the drink, making it taste fresher and colder but making the drink appear cloudy due to the introduction of tiny air bubbles.

The following are some of the most popular variations on the classic Dry Martini:

Dickens' Martini – without a twist.
Dirty Martini – with the brine from an olive jar.
Franklin Martini – named after Franklin Roosevelt and served with two olives.
Gibson Martini – with two cocktail olives.
Vesper Martini – James Bond's Martini, made with gin and vodka.
Vodkatini – very dry, vodka based Martini.
Wet Martini – heavy on the vermouth.
Comment: The proportion of gin to vermouth is a matter of taste; some say 7 to 1, others that one drop is sufficient. I recommend you ask the drinker how they would like their Martini, in the same manner that you might ask how they have their steak. If the drinker orders a 'Sweet Martini', use sweet red vermouth rather than dry and use a cherry as garnish instead of an olive.

DRY MARTINI #2 (NAKED) UPDATED #8

● ● ● ● ○

Glass: Martini (frozen)
Garnish: Chilled olive on stick or lemon zest twist
Method: POUR water into glass, swirl around to coat and place in freezer for at least two hours, alongside gin, until the inside of the glass is covered in a thin layer of ice and the gin is frozen. POUR vermouth into icy glass and swirl to coat the ice with vermouth. POUR frozen gin into glass and serve immediately.

¼	shot(s)	**Chilled mineral water**
⅛	shot(s)	**Noilly Prat dry vermouth**
2½	shot(s)	**Tanqueray London dry gin** (frozen)

Variant: Use an atomiser to coat glass with vermouth. Based on vodka.
Origin: After the Second World War, vermouth proportions in the classic Dry Martini dropped rapidly, and this 'Naked' style of serve began to appear. Tradionally both vermouth and gin had been stirred with ice. In a Naked Martini the merest hint of vermouth is swirled around a well-chilled glass and then frozen gin is poured into the vermouth-coated glass.

The trick to a good Naked Martini is still achieving some dilution by the addition of a splash of water in the glass before freezing. This is a trick I learnt from Salvatore Calabrese, who originally tended bar at London's Duke's Hotel – famous for its Dry Martinis.
Comment: Dilution is achieved as the water you have frozen in the glass begins to melt. Both glass and gin must be freezing cold so that the temperature masks the strength of the alcohol. You have been warned!

DRY ORANGE MARTINI

● ● ● ● ● ◐

Glass: Martini
Garnish: Grapefruit twist
Method: STIR all ingredients with ice and strain into chilled glass.

2	shot(s)	**Tanqueray London dry gin**
¾	shot(s)	**Noilly Prat dry vermouth**
¼	shot(s)	**Cointreau triple sec**
2	dashes	**Angostura orange bitters**

Origin: Created in 2003 by Wayne Collins for Maxxium UK.
Comment: Bone dry, orangey, aptly named Martini.

DRY MARTINI #1

DUBLINER

Glass: Martini
Garnish: Maraschino cherry
Method: STIR all ingredients with ice and strain into chilled glass.

2	shot(s)	**Jameson Irish whiskey**
½	shot(s)	**Grand Marnier liqueur**
½	shot(s)	**Martini Rosso sweet vermouth**
1	dash	**Angostura orange bitters**

Origin: Adapted from a recipe by Gary Regan and discovered in 2007 at Death & Company, New York City, USA.
Comment: Irish whiskey shines through the spicy orange.

THE DUBONNET COCKTAIL #1 UPDATED #8

Glass: Old-fashioned
Garnish: Lemon zest twist
Method: STIR all ingredients with ice and strain into ice-filled glass.

2	shot(s)	**Tanqueray London dry gin**
2	shot(s)	**Dubonnet Red** (French made)
2	dashes	**Angostura aromatic bitters**

Origin: A classic that was popular in Britain during the 1920s.
Comment: Simple yet complex. Dry and aromatic.

THE DUBONNET COCKTAIL #2 NEW #8

Glass: Martini
Garnish: Lemon zest twist
Method: SHAKE all ingredients with ice and fine strain into chilled glass.

1½	shot(s)	**Tanqueray London dry gin**
1½	shot(s)	**Dubonnet Red** (French made)
¼	shot(s)	**Freshly squeezed lemon juice**

Origin: Vintage cocktail of unknown origin.
Comment: Gin and Dubonnet with a hint of citrus. Be sure your Dubonnet is the French stuff.

DULCHIN

Glass: Martini
Garnish: Orange zest twist
Method: SHAKE all ingredients with ice and fine strain into chilled glass.

2	shot(s)	**Macchu pisco**
½	shot(s)	**Grand Marnier liqueur**
½	shot(s)	**Bols apricot brandy liqueur**
¼	shot(s)	**Rose's lime cordial**
¼	shot(s)	**Pomegranate (grenadine) syrup**
¾	shot(s)	**Chilled mineral water** (omit if wet ice)

Comment: This dry, amber coloured, fruity cocktail carries a pisco punch.

DURANGO

Glass: Collins
Garnish: Orange slice
Method: SHAKE first 3 ingredients with ice and strain into ice filled glass. **TOP** with soda.

2	shot(s)	**Don Julio reposado tequila**
¾	shot(s)	**Luxardo Amaretto di Saschira**
1	shot(s)	**Freshly squeezed grapefruit juice**
Top up with		**Soda water** (club soda)

Comment: This sandy coloured drink makes tequila, amaretto and grapefruit juice into unlikely but harmonious bedfellows.

DUTCH BREAKFAST MARTINI

Glass: Martini
Garnish: Orange zest twist
Method: SHAKE all ingredients with ice and fine strain into chilled glass.

1½	shot(s)	**Tanqueray London dry gin**
1½	shot(s)	**Bols advocaat liqueur**
1	shot(s)	**Freshly squeezed lemon juice**
¼	shot(s)	**Sugar syrup** (2 sugar to 1 water)
⅛	shot(s)	**Galliano L'Autentico liqueur**

Origin: Created in 2002 by Alex Kammerling, London, England.
Comment: A tasty, aromatic, almost creamy alternative to a fry-up.

DUTCH COURAGE

Glass: Collins
Garnish: Lemon slice
Method: SHAKE all ingredients with ice and strain into ice-filled glass.

1	shot(s)	**Tanqueray London dry gin**
1	shot(s)	**Bols advocaat liqueur**
¾	shot(s)	**Freshly squeezed lemon juice**
3	shot(s)	**Pressed apple juice**

Origin: Created in 2002 by Alex Kammerling, London, England.
Comment: A refreshing alternative to a traditional English lemonade.

DUTCH MASTER NEW #8

Glass: Martini
Garnish: 2 grapes on stick
Method: STIR all ingredients with ice and strain into chilled glass.

2	shot(s)	**Ketel One vodka**
⅛	shot(s)	**Tio Pepe fino sherry**
⅛	shot(s)	**St-Germain elderflower liqueur**
1	shot(s)	**Tonic water**

Comment: It's a vodka and tonic but not like you know it.
Origin: Created in 2007 by Bruce Borthwick in Fife, Scotland.

DYEVITCHKA

Glass: Martini
Garnish: Orange zest twist
Method: SHAKE all ingredients with ice and fine strain into chilled glass.

1	shot(s)	**Ketel One vodka**
1	shot(s)	**Cointreau triple sec**
½	shot(s)	**Freshly squeezed lime juice**
¼	shot(s)	**Sugar syrup** (2 sugar to 1 water)
1½	shot(s)	**Pressed pineapple juice**

Comment: Pineapple replaces cranberry in this Cosmo-like cocktail.

EARL GREY FIZZ

Glass: Flute
Garnish: Lemon knot
Method: SHAKE first 3 ingredients with ice and strain into chilled glass. **TOP** with champagne.

1	shot(s)	**Zubrówka bison vodka**
½	shot(s)	**Strong cold earl grey tea**
¼	shot(s)	**Sugar syrup** (2 sugar to 1 water)
Top up with		**Perrier Jouet brut champagne**

Origin: Created in 2002 by Henry Besant at Lonsdale House, London, England.
Comment: Looks like a glass of champagne but has a well judged little extra something.

> ## 'A MAN SHOULDN'T FOOL WITH BOOZE UNTIL HE'S FIFTY; THEN HE'S A DAMN FOOL IF HE DOESN'T.'
> WILLIAM FAULKNER

EARL GREY MAR-TEA-NI

Glass: Martini
Garnish: Lemon zest twist
Method: SHAKE all ingredients with ice and fine strain into chilled glass.

2	shot(s)	**Tanqueray London dry gin**
1¼	shot(s)	**Strong cold earl grey tea**
¾	shot(s)	**Freshly squeezed lemon juice**
½	shot(s)	**Sugar syrup** (2 sugar to 1 water)
½	fresh	**Egg white**

Origin: Adapted from a drink created in 2000 by Audrey Saunders at Bemelmans Bar at The Carlyle, New York City.
Comment: A fantastic and very English drink created by a New Yorker. The botanicals of gin combine wonderfully with the flavours and tannins of the tea.

EAST INDIA #1 UPDATED #8

Glass: Martini
Garnish: Orange zest twist
Method: SHAKE all ingredients with ice and fine strain into chilled glass.

2½	shot(s)	**Courvoisier V.S.O.P. cognac**
⅛	shot(s)	**Grand Marnier liqueur**
⅛	shot(s)	**Luxardo maraschino liqueur**
¼	shot(s)	**Pomegranate (grenadine) syrup**
1	dash	**Angostura aromatic bitters**

Origin: An old classic. This recipe is adapted from one in Ted Haigh's book 'Vintage Spirits & Forgotten Cocktails'.
Comment: Wonderfully complex and rounded – a serious drink for serious drinkers.

EAST INDIA #2

Glass: Martini
Garnish: Orange zest twist & nutmeg dust
Method: SHAKE all ingredients with ice and fine strain into chilled glass.

1½	shot(s)	**Courvoisier V.S.O.P. cognac**
¾	shot(s)	**Grand Marnier liqueur**
1½	shot(s)	**Pressed pineapple juice**
2	dashes	**Angostura aromatic bitters**

Origin: A version of the East India classic, thought to originate with Frank Meier at the Ritz Bar, Paris.
Comment: A rich yet bitter short drink based on cognac.

EAST INDIA HOUSE

Glass: Martini
Garnish: Lemon zest twist
Method: SHAKE all ingredients with ice and fine strain into chilled glass.

2	shot(s)	**Courvoisier V.S.O.P. cognac**
½	shot(s)	**Zacapa aged rum**
½	shot(s)	**Cointreau triple sec**
½	shot(s)	**Pressed pineapple juice**
2	dashes	**Angostura orange bitters**

Origin: I've adapted this recipe from a classic cocktail which is thought to have been created in the 19th century by Harry Johnson: I've doubled the quantities of everything but cognac.
Comment: Dry and challenging – rewarding for some.

EAST INDIAN

Glass: Martini
Garnish: Olive on stick
Method: STIR all ingredients with ice and strain into chilled glass.

2	shot(s)	**Tio Pepe fino sherry**
2	shot(s)	**Noilly Prat dry vermouth**
¼	shot(s)	**Sugar syrup** (2 sugar to 1 water)
3	dashes	**Angostura orange bitters**

Variant: Bamboo
Comment: Dry and pretty flat (like much of India) but perfectly balanced with subtle hints of orange zest.

EAST MEETS WEST JULEP NEW #8

Glass: Old-fashioned
Garnish: Mint sprig, pomegranate seeds
Method: SHAKE all ingredients with ice and fine strain into glass filled with crushed ice.

¾	shot(s)	**POM Wonderful pomegranate juice**
7	fresh	**Mint leaves**
2	shot(s)	**Bulleit bourbon whiskey**
½	shot(s)	**Honey syrup** (4 honey to 1 water)
¼	shot(s)	**Pomegranate (grenadine) syrup**

Comment: Reminiscent of honeyed Mint Julep with pomegranate fruit.
Origin: Adapted from a drink created in 2008 by Nidal Ramini at Montgomery Place, London, England.

EAST VILLAGE ATHLETIC CLUB NEW #8

Glass: Martini/Coupette
Garnish: Lime wedge on rim
Method: SHAKE all ingredients with ice and fine strain into chilled glass.

¾	shot(s)	**Don Julio blanco tequila**
¾	shot(s)	**Yellow Chartreuse liqueur**
¾	shot(s)	**Grand Marnier liqueur**
¾	shot(s)	**Freshly squeezed lemon juice**

Origin: The Last Word, a vintage cocktail classic, was first documented in Ted Saucier's Bottoms Up in 1951 where its creation was attributed to the Detroit Athletic Club. In 2008 the folk at New York's PDT tinkered with the recipe to create this drink named after their own hood.
Comment: Essentially a Last Word with tequila instead of gin.

> ## 'HE WAS WHITE AND SHAKEN, LIKE A DRY MARTINI.'
> ### P. G. WODEHOUSE

EASTER MARTINI

Glass: Martini
Garnish: Grated chocolate (crumbled Cadbury's Flake bar)
Method: MUDDLE cardamom pods in base of shaker. Add other ingredients, **SHAKE** with ice and fine strain into chilled glass.

4	pods	**Green cardamom**
2	shot(s)	**Vanilla-infused Ketel One vodka**
1	shot(s)	**White crème de cacao liqueur**
¼	shot(s)	**Sugar syrup** (2 sugar to 1 water)
½	shot(s)	**Chilled mineral water** (omit if wet ice)
½	fresh	**Egg white**

Origin: Created in 2003 by Simon King at MJU Bar, Millennium Hotel, London, England.
Comment: A standard Chocolate Martini with extra interest thanks to the clever use of vanilla and cardamom. The egg white was my own addition. It seemed appropriate given the Easter in the title.

EASTERN MARTINI

Glass: Martini
Garnish: Japanese ume plum in drink
Method: SHAKE all ingredients with ice and fine strain into chilled glass.

2	shot(s)	**Ketel One vodka**
1½	shot(s)	**Choya Umeshu plum liqueur**
1	shot(s)	**Pressed apple juice**

Origin: Created in 2003 by Chris Langan, Barnomadics, Scotland.
Comment: Light, fragrant and fruity – distinctly oriental.

EASTERN PROMISE

Glass: Martini
Garnish: Lemon zest twist
Method: SHAKE all ingredients with ice and fine strain into chilled glass.

2	shot(s)	**Orange-infused Ketel One vodka**
¼	shot(s)	**Bols apricot brandy liqueur**
½	shot(s)	**Rose syrup**
½	shot(s)	**Freshly squeezed lemon juice**
½	shot(s)	**Chilled mineral water** (omit if wet ice)

Origin: Adapted from a drink discovered in 2004 at Oxo Tower Bar, London, England.
Comment: Citrus dominates this drink but the result is floral rather than tart.

EASTERN RASPBERRY SIDECAR NEW #8

Glass: Martini
Garnish: Half sugar rim/floating raspberry
Method: MUDDLE raspberries in base of shaker. Add other ingredients, **SHAKE** with ice and fine strain into chilled glass.

7	fresh	**Raspberries**
1	shot(s)	**Courvoisier V.S.O.P. cognac**
1	shot(s)	**Sake**
½	shot(s)	**Cointreau triple sec**
½	shot(s)	**Freshly squeezed lemon juice**
½	shot(s)	**Sugar syrup** (2 sugar to 1 water)

Origin: Created by Ryan Magarian, Seattle, USA.
Comment: Refreshing, fruity, easy drinking.

EASTERN SIN NEW #8

Glass: Martini
Garnish: Pineapple wedge on rim
Method: SHAKE all ingredients with ice and fine strain into chilled glass.

1½	shot(s)	**Johnnie Walker Scotch whisky**
1½	shot(s)	**Heering cherry brandy liqueur**
½	shot(s)	**Cointreau triple sec**
½	shot(s)	**Martini Rosso sweet vermouth**
½	shot(s)	**Pressed pineapple juice**

Origin: In W.J. Tarling's 1937 Café Royal Cocktail Book the invention of this cocktail is credited to J. Stoneham. I have cut the amount of cherry brandy by a third compared to the Café Royal formula.
Comment: Fruity and slightly sweet but toned by a hint of Scotch.

EASY TIGER

Glass: Martini
Garnish: Orange zest twist
Comment: MUDDLE ginger in base of shaker. Add honey and tequila, and **STIR** until honey is dissolved. Add other ingredients, **SHAKE** with ice and fine strain into chilled glass.

2	slices	**Fresh root ginger** (thumbnail sized)
2	spoons	**Runny honey**
2	shot(s)	**Don Julio reposado tequila**
1	shot(s)	**Freshly squeezed lime juice**
¾	shot(s)	**Chilled mineral water** (omit if wet ice)

Origin: Created in 1999 by Alex Kammerling.
Comment: Tangy and zesty with rich honey and ginger.

> **'AN INTELLIGENT MAN IS SOMETIMES FORCED TO BE DRUNK TO SPEND TIME WITH HIS FOOLS.'**
> FOR WHOM THE BELL TOLLS, ERNEST HEMINGWAY

ECLIPSE

Glass: Collins
Garnish: Mint leaf & raspberry
Method: MUDDLE raspberries in base of shaker. Add other ingredients, **SHAKE** with ice and strain into glass filled with crushed ice. Serve with straws.

12	fresh	**Raspberries**
2	shot(s)	**Bulleit bourbon whiskey**
1	shot(s)	**Chambord black raspberry liqueur**
½	shot(s)	**Freshly squeezed lime juice**
2	shot(s)	**Ocean Spray cranberry juice**

Origin: Signature cocktail at the chain of Eclipse Bars, London, England.
Comment: A fruity summer cooler which I challenge anyone not to like.

EGG CUSTARD MARTINI

Glass: Martini
Garnish: Dust with freshly ground nutmeg
Method: SHAKE all ingredients with ice and fine strain into chilled glass.

1½	shot(s)	**Ketel One vodka**
1	shot(s)	**Bols advocaat liqueur**
½	shot(s)	**Vanilla-infused Ketel One vodka**
½	shot(s)	**Bulleit bourbon whiskey**
¼	shot(s)	**Sugar syrup** (2 sugar to 1 water)

Origin: Created in 2002 by Alex Kammerling, London, England.
Comment: Just as custardy as the name would suggest but surprisingly potent.

EDEN

Glass: Collins
Garnish: Orange zest string
Method: SHAKE first 3 ingredients with ice and strain into ice-filled glass. **TOP** with tonic water.

2	shot(s)	**Orange-infused Ketel One vodka**
½	shot(s)	**St-Germain elderflower liqueur**
1½	shot(s)	**Pressed apple juice**
Top up with		**Tonic water**

Origin: Adapted from a drink created in 2003 by Sylvain Solignac at Circus, London, England.
Comment: Orange zest predominates in a long, refreshing drink that's perfect for warm days.

EGGNOG #1 (COLD)

Glass: Collins
Garnish: Dust with freshly grated nutmeg
Method: SHAKE all ingredients with ice and strain into ice-filled glass.

2½	shot(s)	**Courvoisier V.S.O.P. cognac**
½	shot(s)	**Sugar syrup** (2 sugar to 1 water)
½	shot(s)	**Double (heavy) cream**
1	fresh	**Egg**
2	shot(s)	**Milk**

Comment: Lightly flavoured alcoholic egg custard. Also try swapping dark rum for the cognac.

EDEN MARTINI

Glass: Martini
Garnish: Orange zest twist
Method: SHAKE all ingredients with ice and fine strain into chilled glass.

2½	shot(s)	**Tanqueray London dry gin**
½	shot(s)	**Parfait Amour liqueur**
¼	shot(s)	**Rose water**
¼	shot(s)	**Freshly squeezed lemon juice**
¼	shot(s)	**Chilled mineral water** (omit if wet ice)

Origin: Adapted from a recipe discovered in 2003 at Oxo Tower Bar, London, England.
Comment: Rich purple in colour with rose, vanilla, almond, citrus and gin.

EGGNOG #2 (HOT)

Glass: Toddy
Garnish: Dust with freshly grated nutmeg
Method: POUR ingredients into heatproof glass and **STIR** thoroughly. **HEAT** in microwave oven for a minute (adjust time as appropriate to your oven) and **STIR** again. Alternatively, mix and warm in pan over heat – do not boil.

2½	shot(s)	**Courvoisier V.S.O.P. cognac**
½	shot(s)	**Sugar syrup** (2 sugar to 1 water)
½	shot(s)	**Double (heavy) cream**
1	fresh	**Egg** (white & yolk)
2	shot(s)	**Milk**

Comment: A warming, spicy and filling meal in a glass.

THE 1862 NEW #8

●●●●○

Glass: Martini
Garnish: Orange zest twist (discarded) & maraschino cherry
Method: DRY SHAKE (without ice) all ingredients to emulsify. Add ice, **SHAKE** again and fine strain into a chilled glass.

2½	shot(s)	**Bacardi Superior rum**
¾	shot(s)	**Tio Pepe fino sherry**
¼	shot(s)	**Luxardo maraschino liqueur**
¼	shot(s)	**Freshly squeezed lemon juice**
¼	shot(s)	**Sugar syrup** (2 sugar to 1 water)
1	dash	**Angostura orange bitters**
½	fresh	**Egg white**

Origin: Adapted from a drink created in 2008 by Scott Ingram at MC Bar, Abode Hotel, Glasgow, Scotland. The name is a reference to the year when Facundo M. Bacardi established his first distillery.
Comment: Fantastically complex with notes of rum, maraschino, sherry and orange.

EIGHTEEN'97 NEW #8

●●●●◑

Garnish: Martini
Garnish: Orange zest twist (discarded), white grapes on stick
Method: MUDDLE kumquats in base of shaker. Add next 3 ingredients, shake and fine strain into a chilled glass. **FLOAT** wine.

5	fresh	**Kumquats** (chopped)
1½	shot(s)	**Francoli Moscato grappa**
1¼	shot(s)	**St-Germain elderflower liqueur**
¼	shot(s)	**Sugar syrup** (2 sugar to 1 water)
¼	shot(s)	**Merlot red wine**

Origin: Created in 2008 by Raffaello Dante at Salvatore's at FIFTY, London, England.
Comment: Looks great and, with the citrus freshness of kumquat combined with the oily character of grappa, it also tastes great.

'I DO NOT LIVE IN THE WORLD OF SOBRIETY.'
OLIVER REED

EL BURRO

●●●●○

Glass: Collins
Garnish: Lime slice
Method: SHAKE first 4 ingredients with ice and strain into ice-filled glass. **TOP** with ginger beer.

2	shot(s)	**Don Julio reposado tequila**
½	shot(s)	**Freshly squeezed lime juice**
¼	shot(s)	**Sugar syrup** (2 sugar to 1 water)
3	dashes	**Angostura aromatic bitters**
Top up with		**Ginger beer**

AKA: Mexican Mule
Origin: Created by Henry Besant and Andres Masso, London, England. The name of this Mexican version of the Moscow Mule translates from Spanish as 'The Donkey'.
Comment: Ginger spice and tequila soured with lime.

EL ESTRIBO UPDATED #8

●●●○○

Glass: Martini
Garnish: Berries on stick
Method: SHAKE all ingredients with ice and fine strain into chilled glass.

2	shot(s)	**Don Julio reposado tequila**
¼	shot(s)	**Crème de cassis or Chambord**
1	shot(s)	**Pressed pineapple juice**
½	shot(s)	**Double (heavy) cream**
½	shot	**Milk**

Comment: Pink and creamy but with a tequila kick.
Origin: The signature drink at El Estribo, Mexico City, which sadly closed in 2005. The drink and this once legendary tequila bar's name 'estribo' is used to say "one for the road" in Mexico... before you get into the stirrups and ride away.

EL PRESIDENTE NO.1 #1

●●●●◑

Glass: Martini
Garnish: Lime wedge on rim
Method: SHAKE all ingredients with ice and fine strain into chilled glass.

2	shot(s)	**Bacardi Superior rum**
¾	shot(s)	**Pressed pineapple juice**
½	shot(s)	**Freshly squeezed lime juice**
¼	shot(s)	**Pomegranate (grenadine) syrup**

Origin: Classic variation on the Daiquiri, of unknown origin.
Comment: Rum and pineapple combine wonderfully and the Daiquiri is the king of cocktails.

EL PRESIDENTE #2

●●●●◑

Glass: Martini
Garnish: Lime zest twist
Method: SHAKE all ingredients with ice and fine strain into chilled glass.

2	shot(s)	**Bacardi Superior rum**
1	shot(s)	**Noilly Prat dry vermouth**
1	dash	**Angostura aromatic bitters**

Comment: Bone dry. Rather like a rum based, old school Martini.

EL PRESIDENTE #3

●●●○○

Glass: Martini
Garnish: Orange zest twist
Method: SHAKE all ingredients with ice and fine strain into chilled glass.

2	shot(s)	**Bacardi Superior rum**
1	shot(s)	**Noilly Prat dry vermouth**
½	shot(s)	**Cointreau triple sec**
¼	shot(s)	**Pomegranate (grenadine) syrup**

Origin: Adapted from Victor Bergeron's 'Trader Vic's Bartender's Guide' (1972 revised edition). Vic writes of this drink, "This is the real recipe".
Comment: A sweeter version of #2 above.

EL PRESIDENTE #4

Glass: Martini
Garnish: Orange zest twist
Method: STIR all ingredients with ice and strain into chilled glass.

1½	shot(s)	**Bacardi Superior rum**
¾	shot(s)	**Noilly Prat dry vermouth**
½	shot(s)	**Cointreau triple sec**

Comment: Dry but not bone dry, with balanced fruit from the triple sec and vermouth.

EL TORADO

Glass: Martini
Garnish: Float thin apple slice
Method: SHAKE all ingredients with ice and fine strain into chilled glass.

2	shot(s)	**Don Julio reposado tequila**
½	shot(s)	**Noilly Prat dry vermouth**
1½	shot(s)	**Pressed apple juice**

Origin: Popular throughout Mexico.
Comment: Dry, sophisticated and fruity, with tequila body.

ELDER & WISER

Glass: Old-fashioned
Garnish: Lemon zest twist
Method: SHAKE all ingredients with ice and fine strain into ice-filled glass.

2	shot(s)	**Bulleit bourbon whiskey**
1	shot(s)	**St-Germain elderflower liqueur**
1	shot(s)	**Pressed apple juice**

Origin: Created in 2006 by Yours Truly (Simon Difford) and named for its original base, Wiser's Canadian whisky.
Comment: Apple and elderflower combine wonderfully with bourbon.

THE ELDER AVIATOR

Glass: Martini
Garnish: Lemon zest twist
Method: SHAKE all ingredients with ice and fine strain into chilled glass.

2	shot(s)	**Tanqueray London dry gin**
½	shot(s)	**St-Germain elderflower liqueur**
¼	shot(s)	**Luxardo maraschino liqueur**
½	shot(s)	**Freshly squeezed lemon juice**
½	shot(s)	**Chilled mineral water** (omit if wet ice)

Origin: Created in 2006 by Yours Truly (Simon Difford)
Comment: Fans of the classic Aviation may appreciate this floral twist.

ELDER FASHIONED

Glass: Old-fashioned
Garnish: Orange zest twist
Method: STIR one shot of bourbon with two ice cubes in a glass. **ADD** elderflower liqueur, orange bitters and two more ice cubes. **STIR** some more and add another two ice cubes and the rest of the bourbon. **STIR** lots more and add more ice.

2	shot(s)	**Bulleit bourbon whiskey**
¾	shot(s)	**St-Germain elderflower liqueur**
1	dash	**Angostura orange bitters**

Origin: Created in 2006 by Yours Truly (Simon Difford).
Comment: Whiskey and elderflower served in the Old-Fashioned style. The elderflower liqueur smoothes the bourbon.

ELDER SOUR

Glass: Old-fashioned
Garnish: Lemon slice & cherry on stick (sail)
Method: SHAKE all ingredients with ice and strain into ice-filled glass.

2	shot(s)	**St-Germain elderflower liqueur**
1	shot(s)	**Freshly squeezed lime juice**
½	fresh	**Egg white**
1	dash	**Angostura orange bitters** (optional)

Variation: Served 'up' in a sour glass.
Origin: Created in 2006 by Yours Truly (Simon Difford).
Comment: So smooth it's almost fluffy. A great after-dinner drink.

ELDERFLOWER COLLINS #1

Glass: Collins
Garnish: Lemon slice
Method: SHAKE first 4 ingredients with ice and strain into ice-filled glass. **TOP** with soda.

2	shot(s)	**Tanqueray London dry gin**
1½	shot(s)	**St-Germain elderflower liqueur**
1	shot(s)	**Freshly squeezed lemon juice**
⅛	shot(s)	**Sugar syrup** (2 sugar to 1 water)
Top up with		**Soda water** (club soda)

Comment: A hint of elderflower adds interest to the classic Collins cocktail – long, balanced and refreshing.

ELDERFLOWER COLLINS #2

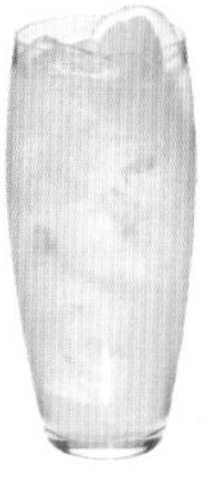

Glass: Collins
Garnish: Lemon slice
Method: SHAKE first 4 ingredients with ice and strain into ice-filled glass. **TOP** with soda.

2	shot(s)	**Ketel One Citroen vodka**
⅛	shot(s)	**Luxardo maraschino liqueur**
¼	shot(s)	**St-Germain elderflower liqueur**
¾	shot(s)	**Freshly squeezed lemon juice**
Top up with		**Soda water** (club soda)

Comment: Long and refreshing with a floral, cherry and citrus flavour.

ELDERFLOWER COSMO

Glass: Martini
Garnish: Lime zest twist
Method: SHAKE all ingredients with ice and fine strain into chilled glass.

1½	shot(s)	**Ketel One vodka**
1	shot(s)	**St-Germain elderflower liqueur**
½	shot(s)	**Pressed pineapple juice**
¼	shot(s)	**Freshly squeezed lime juice**

Origin: Created in 2006 by Yours Truly (Simon Difford).
Comment: Despite the absence of citrus vodka, orange liqueur and cranberry, this delicate blend is still Cosmopolitan in style.

ELDERFLOWER DAIQUIRI

Glass: Martini
Garnish: Lime wedge on rim
Method: SHAKE all ingredients with ice and fine strain into chilled glass.

2	shot(s)	**Bacardi Superior rum**
1	shot(s)	**St-Germain elderflower liqueur**
½	shot(s)	**Freshly squeezed lime juice**

Origin: Created in 2006 by Yours Truly (Simon Difford).
Comment: Elderflower liqueur adds floral interest to the classic Daiquiri.

ELDERFLOWER MANHATTAN

Glass: Martini
Garnish: Maraschino cherry
Method: SHAKE all ingredients with ice and fine strain into chilled glass.

2	shot(s)	**Bulleit bourbon whiskey**
1	shot(s)	**St-Germain elderflower liqueur**
½	shot(s)	**Noilly Prat dry vermouth**
2	dashes	**Angostura aromatic bitters**

Origin: Created in 2006 by Yours Truly (Simon Difford).
Comment: Elderflower replaces sweet vermouth in this 'perfect' and aromatic Manhattan.

ELDERFLOWER MARTINI #1

Glass: Martini
Garnish: Lime zest twist
Method: SHAKE all ingredients with ice and fine strain into chilled glass.

2	shot(s)	**Zubrówka bison vodka**
1	shot(s)	**St-Germain elderflower liqueur**
½	shot(s)	**Noilly Prat dry vermouth**

Comment: This veritable shrubbery is floral and grassy with dry borders.

ELDERFLOWER MARTINI #2

Glass: Martini
Garnish: Lemon zest twist
Method: SHAKE all ingredients with ice and fine strain into chilled glass.

1	shot(s)	**Ketel One vodka**
1	shot(s)	**Zubrówka bison vodka**
1	shot(s)	**St-Germain elderflower liqueur**
½	shot(s)	**Noilly Prat dry vermouth**

Comment: Dry but not bone dry with aromatic hints of grass and elderflower.

ELDERFLOWER MOJITO

Glass: Collins
Garnish: Mint sprig
Method: Lightly **MUDDLE** (just to bruise) mint in base of glass. Add other ingredients, half fill glass with crushed ice and **CHURN** (stir) with bar spoon. Fill glass to brim with more crushed ice and churn some more. Serve with straws.

12	fresh	**Mint leaves**
2	shot(s)	**Bacardi Superior rum**
1	shot(s)	**St-Germain elderflower liqueur**
1	shot(s)	**Freshly squeezed lime juice**

Comment: The enduring classic benefits from a touch of elderflower.

ELEGANTE MARGARITA

Glass: Coupette
Garnish: Lime wedge & salted rim (optional)
Method: SHAKE all ingredients with ice and fine strain into chilled glass.

1½	shot(s)	**Don Julio reposado tequila**
½	shot(s)	**Cointreau triple sec**
½	shot(s)	**Rose's lime cordial**
¾	shot(s)	**Freshly squeezed lime juice**
½	shot(s)	**Sugar syrup** (2 sugar to 1 water)

Origin: Created in 1999 by Robert Plotkin and Raymon Flores of BarMedia, USA.
Comment: One of the best Margarita recipes around. Richly endowed with flavour.

ELIXIR

Glass: Collins
Garnish: Mint sprig
Method: Lightly **MUDDLE** mint in base of shaker. Add next 3 ingredients, **SHAKE** with ice and strain into ice-filled glass. **TOP** with soda, stir and serve with straws.

7	fresh	**Mint leaves**
1½	shot(s)	**Green Chartreuse liqueur**
1	shot(s)	**Sugar syrup** (2 sugar to 1 water)
¾	shot(s)	**Freshly squeezed lime juice**
Top up with		**Soda water** (club soda)

Origin: Created in 2003 by Gian Franco Pola for Capannina in Cremona and Coconuts in Rimini, Italy.
Comment: A minty, herbal, refreshing summer drink.

ELIXIR 66 NEW #8

Glass: Martini
Garnish: Coriander leaf
Method: Lightly **MUDDLE** coriander in base of shaker. Add other ingredients, **SHAKE** with ice and fine strain into chilled glass.

1	sprig	**Fresh coriander**
1	shot(s)	**Green Chartreuse liqueur**
¼	shot(s)	**La Fée Parisienne (68%) absinthe**
⅛	shot(s)	**Berentzen apple schnapps**
½	shot(s)	**Freshly squeezed lime juice**
1	shot(s)	**Pressed apple juice**
¼	shot(s)	**Sugar syrup** (2 sugar to 1 water)
½	shot(s)	**Chilled mineral water** (omit if wet ice)

Comment: Bright green and intensely flavoured but considering it is flavoured with absinthe and chartreuse, it is surprisingly subtle.
Origin: Created in 2003 by Ben Davidson of Elixir Group, Australia.

> 'ABSTAINER: A WEAK PERSON WHO YIELDS TO THE TEMPTATION OF DENYING HIMSELF A PLEASURE.'
> AMBROSE BIERCE

ELIXIRITA NEW #8

Glass: Martini
Garnish: None
Method: **SHAKE** all ingredients with ice and fine strain into chilled glass.

2	shot(s)	**Don Julio blanco tequila**
1	shot(s)	**Fresh Squeezed lime juice**
½	shot(s)	**Agave syrup**
¼	shot(s)	**Courvoisier V.S.O.P. cognac**

Origin: Created in 2007 by H. Joseph Ehrmann, this is the signature Margarita at his bar 'Elixir' in San Francisco, USA. He dedicated it to the Boston College Eagles.
Comment: Basically a Tommy's Margarita with a splash of cognac served straight-up.

ELK MARTINI

Glass: Martini
Garnish: Lemon zest twist
Method: **STIR** all ingredients with ice and fine strain into chilled glass.

1	shot(s)	**Tanqueray London dry gin**
1	shot(s)	**La Vieille Prune plum brandy**
¼	shot(s)	**Noilly Prat dry vermouth**

Origin: Adapted from Harry Craddock's 1930 'The Savoy Cocktail Book'.
Comment: Craddock calls for this drink to be shaken, but in this instance stirring seems more in order.

ELLE FOR LEATHER

Glass: Collins
Garnish: Vanilla pod
Method: **SHAKE** first 4 ingredients with ice and strain into glass filled with crushed ice. **TOP** with champagne.

1½	shot(s)	**Johnnie Walker Scotch whisky**
1	shot(s)	**Vanilla schnapps liqueur**
¼	shot(s)	**Freshly squeezed lemon juice**
⅛	shot(s)	**Sugar syrup** (2 sugar to 1 water)
Top up with		**Perrier Jouet brut champagne**

Origin: Created in 2001 by Reece Clark at Hush Up, London, England.
Comment: A long, cool champagne cocktail pepped up with Scotch whisky and vanilla schnapps. Easy drinking - yet adult.

ELYSIAN

Glass: Martini
Garnish: Float apple slice
Method: **STIR** all ingredients with ice and strain into chilled glass.

2	shot(s)	**Boulard Grand Solage calvados**
½	shot(s)	**Martini Rosso sweet vermouth**
½	shot(s)	**Noilly Prat dry vermouth**
¼	shot(s)	**Maple syrup**
3	dashes	**Angostura aromatic bitters**
3	dashes	**Peychaud's aromatic bitters**

Origin: Created in 2004 by Mickael Perron at Millbank Lounge Bar, London, England.
Comment: Dry and aromatic, although not for all tastes.

EMBASSY COCKTAIL

Glass: Martini
Garnish: Orange zest twist
Method: **SHAKE** all ingredients with ice and fine strain into chilled glass.

1	shot(s)	**Courvoisier V.S.O.P. cognac**
1	shot(s)	**Bacardi Superior rum**
1	shot(s)	**Cointreau triple sec**
¾	shot(s)	**Freshly squeezed lime juice**
1	dash	**Angostura aromatic bitters**

Origin: Created in 1930 at the famous Embassy Club speakeasy in Hollywood, USA.
Comment: Bone dry – one for hardened palates.

EMBASSY ROYAL

Glass: Martini
Garnish: Orange zest twist
Method: **SHAKE** all ingredients with ice and fine strain into chilled glass.

1¾	shot(s)	**Bulleit bourbon whiskey**
1	shot(s)	**Drambuie liqueur**
1	shot(s)	**Martini Rosso sweet vermouth**
1	shot(s)	**Freshly squeezed orange juice**

Comment: An aromatic, herbal and altogether pleasant concoction.

EMERALD MARTINI

Glass: Martini
Garnish: Sprayed and discarded lemon & lime zest twists plus mint leaf
Method: STIR all ingredients with ice and strain into chilled glass.

2	shot(s)	Lime flavoured vodka
1	shot(s)	Green Chartreuse liqueur
1	shot(s)	Chilled mineral water

Origin: Discovered in 2005 at Bugsy's, Prague, Czech Republic.
Comment: A serious drink that's rammed with alcohol and flavour.

ENCHANTED

Glass: Collins
Garnish: Lychee or mint sprig
Method: MUDDLE grapes in base of shaker. Add next 3 ingredients, **SHAKE** with ice and fine strain into ice-filled glass. **TOP** with ginger ale.

7	fresh	Seedless white grapes
1½	shot(s)	Courvoisier V.S.O.P. cognac
½	shot(s)	Soho lychee liqueur
½	shot(s)	Freshly squeezed lime juice
Top up with		Ginger ale

Origin: Created by Wayne Collins, UK.
Comment: Light, fruity and easy drinking with lychee and ginger dominating.

EMPEROR'S MEMOIRS

Glass: Collins
Garnish: Orange & lemon zest twists
Method: SHAKE first 4 ingredients with ice and strain into ice-filled glass. **TOP** with ginger beer.

1	shot(s)	Tanqueray London dry gin
½	shot(s)	Punt E Mes
¼	shot(s)	Ginger cordial (non-alcoholic)
¼	shot(s)	Freshly squeezed lemon juice
Top up with		Ginger beer

Origin: Created in 2001 by Douglas Ankrah for Akbar, Soho, London, England.
Comment: Not particularly alcoholic, but strong in a gingery, spicy way.

ENGLISH BREAKFAST MARTINI

Glass: Martini
Garnish: Orange zest twist
Method: SHAKE all ingredients with ice and fine strain into chilled glass.

1	shot(s)	Tanqueray London dry gin
1	shot(s)	St-Germain elderflower liqueur
1	shot(s)	Cold English breakfast tea
½	shot(s)	Freshly squeezed lemon juice

Origin: Created in 2006 by Yours Truly (Simon Difford).
Comment: Light and fragrant, thanks to tea, elderflower and the botanicals in the gin.

EMPIRE COCKTAIL

Glass: Martini
Garnish: Apricot slice on rim
Method: SHAKE all ingredients with ice and fine strain into chilled glass.

1½	shot(s)	Tanqueray London dry gin
¾	shot(s)	Boulard Grand Solage calvados
¾	shot(s)	Bols apricot brandy liqueur

Origin: Adapted from Harry Craddock's 1930 'The Savoy Cocktail Book'.
Comment: Apricot dried by gin and apple brandy.

ENGLISH CHANNEL

Glass: Martini
Garnish: Lemon zest twist
Method: SHAKE all ingredients with ice and fine strain into chilled glass.

¾	shot(s)	Grand Marnier liqueur
¾	shot(s)	Bénédictine D.O.M. liqueur
2	shot(s)	Cold earl grey tea

Origin: Adapted from a drink discovered in 2005 at Bellini, Auckland, New Zealand.
Comment: The earl grey tannins balance the spice and orange in the liqueurs to make a harmonious aperitif.

ENCANTADO

Glass: Martini
Garnish: Mint sprig
Method: SHAKE all ingredients with ice and fine strain into chilled glass.

1½	shot(s)	Don Julio reposado tequila
½	shot(s)	Courvoisier V.S.O.P. cognac
½	shot(s)	Peach Tree peach schnapps
½	shot(s)	Chambord black raspberry liqueur
½	shot(s)	Freshly squeezed lime juice

Comment: Essentially a Margarita with a hint of peach and raspberry. Not too sweet.

ENGLISH GARDEN

Glass: Collins
Garnish: Three slices of cucumber
Method: SHAKE all ingredients with ice and strain into ice-filled glass.

2	shot(s)	Tanqueray London dry gin
2½	shot(s)	Pressed apple juice
1	shot(s)	St-Germain elderflower liqueur
½	shot(s)	Freshly squeezed lime juice

Comment: Quintessentially English in flavour – anyone for tennis?

ENGLISH MARTINI

Glass: Martini
Garnish: Rosemary
Method: Strip rosemary leaves from stem and **MUDDLE** in base of shaker. Add other ingredients, **SHAKE** with ice and fine strain into chilled glass.

1	fresh	**Rosemary sprig**
2½	shot(s)	**Tanqueray London dry gin**
1	shot(s)	**St-Germain elderflower liqueur**

Origin: Adapted from a drink created in 2003 at MJU, Millennium Hotel, London, England.
Comment: Rosemary and sweet elderflower combine wonderfully with the gin botanicals to make an interesting and approachable Martini.

ENGLISH ROSE

Glass: Martini
Garnish: Maraschino cherry
Method: STIR all ingredients with ice and strain into chilled glass.

1¾	shot(s)	**Tanqueray London dry gin**
¾	shot(s)	**Noilly Prat dry vermouth**
½	shot(s)	**Parfait Amour liqueur**
¼	shot(s)	**Freshly squeezed lemon juice**
⅛	shot(s)	**Pomegranate (grenadine) syrup**

Comment: A dry, complex, gin laced drink. Stir well.

ENVY

Glass: Martini
Garnish: Star fruit on rim
Method: SHAKE all ingredients with ice and fine strain into chilled glass.

½	shot(s)	**Ketel One vodka**
2	shot(s)	**Midori green melon liqueur**
1	shot(s)	**Peach Tree peach schnapps**
¾	shot(s)	**Frangelico hazelnut liqueur**
¼	shot(s)	**Freshly squeezed lime juice**

Comment: Green with … melon, oh, and a hint of hazelnut. A tad on the sweet side.

EPESTONE DAIQUIRI

Glass: Martini
Garnish: Lime wedge
Method: SHAKE all ingredients with ice and fine strain into chilled glass.

2	shot(s)	**Bacardi Superior rum**
½	shot(s)	**Crème de cassis liqueur**
½	shot(s)	**Freshly squeezed lime juice**
½	shot(s)	**Chilled mineral water** (omit if wet ice)

Comment: A pleasant, maroon coloured, blackcurrant flavoured Daiquiri.

EPIPHANY

Glass: Martini
Garnish: Berries on stick
Method: SHAKE all ingredients with ice and fine strain into chilled glass.

1¾	shot(s)	**Bulleit bourbon whiskey**
½	shot(s)	**Crème de mûre liqueur**
2	shot(s)	**Pressed apple juice**

Origin: Created in 2004 by Naomi Young at Match, London, England.
Comment: Not sure what a fruity bourbon drink has to do with the manifestation of Christ.

EPISCOPAL UPDATED #8

Glass: Old-fashioned
Method: STIR ingredients with ice and fine strain into ice-filled glass.

| 1½ | shot(s) | **Green Chartreuse liqueur** |
| ¾ | shot(s) | **Yellow Chartreuse liqueur** |

Origin: A well-established drink promoted by the marketeers at Chartreuse and named due to the combining of the clerical colours of yellow and green.
Comment: My favourite way to enjoy Chartreuse. Especially good when made with V.E.P. Chartreuse.

BESSIE BRADDOCK: 'WINSTON, YOU'RE DRUNK.' WINSTON CHURCHILL: 'BESSIE, YOU'RE UGLY. BUT TOMORROW I SHALL BE SOBER.'

ESCALATOR MARTINI

Glass: Martini
Garnish: Pear slice on rim
Method: SHAKE all ingredients with ice and fine strain into chilled glass.

1	shot(s)	**Poire William eau de vie**
½	shot(s)	**Zubrówka bison vodka**
2	shot(s)	**Pressed apple juice**
⅛	shot(s)	**Sugar syrup** (2 sugar to 1 water)

Origin: Created in 2002 by Kevin Connelly, England. It's called an escalator because the 'apples and pears', rhyming slang for 'stairs', are shaken.
Comment: This orchard-fresh concoction was originally made with Korte Palinka (Hungarian pear schnapps) - if using that or Poire William liqueur in place of Poire William eau de vie, little or no sugar is necessary.

ESPECIAL DAY

Glass: Martini
Garnish: Blackberry & discarded lemon zest twist
Method: MUDDLE blackberries in base of shaker. Add other ingredients, **SHAKE** with ice and fine strain into chilled glass.

3	fresh	**Blackberries**
2	shot(s)	**Bacardi Superior rum**
½	shot(s)	**Martini Rosso sweet vermouth**
¾	shot(s)	**Crème de mûre liqueur**
½	shot(s)	**Pressed pineapple juice**
3	dashes	**Peychaud's aromatic bitters**

Origin: Created in 2005 by Tonin Kacaj at Maze, London, England.
Comment: Beautifully balanced, aromatic, rum laced and fruity.

ESPECIE NEW #8

Glass: Martini/Coupette
Garnish: Lime zest twist
Method: SHAKE all ingredients with ice and fine strain into chilled glass.

2½	shot(s)	**Bacardi Superior rum**
1	shot(s)	**Velvet Falernum liqueur**
¾	shot(s)	**Chilled mineral water** (omit if wet ice)
2	dashes	**Angostura aromatic bitters**

Comment: Rum laced and rust coloured with hints of clove and jasmine. A touch syrupy.
Origin: Created in 2008 by Juraj Ivan at Coq D'Argent, London, England.

ESPRESSO DAIQUIRI

Glass: Martini
Garnish: Float 3 coffee beans
Method: SHAKE all ingredients with ice and fine strain into chilled glass.

2	shot(s)	**Bacardi Superior rum**
1¾	shot(s)	**Espresso coffee**
½	shot(s)	**Sugar syrup** (2 sugar to 1 water)

Variant: Espresso Martini
Comment: Rum based twist on the ubiquitous Espresso Martini.

ESPRESSO MARTINI

Glass: Martini
Garnish: Float 3 coffee beans
Method: SHAKE all ingredients with ice and fine strain into chilled glass.

2	shot(s)	**Ketel One vodka**
1¾	shot(s)	**Espresso coffee**
½	shot(s)	**Sugar syrup** (2 sugar to 1 water)

Variants: Espresso Daiquiri, Insomniac, Irish Coffee Martini, Jalisco Espresso, Jolt'ini.
Comment: Forget the vodka Red Bull, this is the connoisseur's way of combining caffeine and vodka.

ESQUIRE #1

Glass: Martini
Garnish: Orange zest twist
Method: SHAKE all ingredients with ice and fine strain into chilled glass.

2	shot(s)	**Bulleit bourbon whiskey**
¾	shot(s)	**Grand Marnier liqueur**
¾	shot(s)	**Freshly squeezed orange juice**
1	dash	**Angostura aromatic bitters**
½	shot(s)	**Chilled mineral water** (omit if wet ice)

Comment: Spicy bourbon laden with orange fruit.

ESQUIRE #2

Glass: Martini
Garnish: Blackberry
Method: STIR all ingredients with ice and strain into chilled glass.

1½	shot(s)	**Ketel One vodka**
¾	shot(s)	**Raspberry flavoured vodka**
¾	shot(s)	**Parfait Amour liqueur**

Origin: Created in the 1990s by Dick Bradsell for Esquire Magazine.
Comment: One for hardened Martini drinkers.

FREDERICK THE GREAT OF PRUSSIA TRIED TO BAN THE CONSUMPTION OF COFFEE. HE INSISTED THAT HIS PEOPLE DRANK ALCOHOL INSTEAD.

ESTES

Glass: Collins
Garnish: Raspberry & thin strips of lime zest
Method: MUDDLE raspberries in base of shaker. Add other ingredients, **SHAKE** with ice and fine strain into glass filled with crushed ice.

7	fresh	**Raspberries**
1¾	shot(s)	**Don Julio reposado tequila**
½	shot(s)	**Chambord black raspberry liqueur**
1¾	shot(s)	**Ocean Spray cranberry juice**
½	shot(s)	**Agave syrup**
¾	shot(s)	**Freshly squeezed lime juice**

Origin: Created in 2005 by Henry Besant and Andres Masso, London, England, and named in honour of Tomas Estes, the official Tequila Ambassador in Europe.
Comment: This rich, fruity long drink is a real crowd pleaser.

ESTILO VIEJO

Glass: Old-fashioned
Garnish: Lime zest twist
Method: **STIR** half of the tequila with two ice cubes in a glass. Add agave syrup and Angostura and two more ice cubes. Stir some more and add another two ice cubes and the rest of the tequila. Stir lots more and add more ice. The melting and stirring of the ice is essential to the dilution and taste of the drink.

2½	shot(s)	**Don Julio reposado tequila**
½	shot(s)	**Agave syrup**
3	dashes	**Angostura aromatic bitters**

Origin: The name of this drink literally translates from Spanish as 'Old Style'. It is basically a Tequila Old-fashioned.
Comment: Even better when made with añejo tequila.

E.T.

Glass: Shot
Method: Refrigerate ingredients and **LAYER** in chilled glass by carefully pouring in the following order.

½	shot(s)	**Midori green melon liqueur**
½	shot(s)	**Baileys Irish cream liqueur**
½	shot(s)	**Ketel One vodka**

Comment: Fortified creamy melon.

EUREKA COCKTAIL NEW #8

Glass: Martini
Garnish: Lemon zest twist
Method: **SHAKE** all ingredients with ice and fine strain into chilled glass.

1	shot(s)	**Boulard Grand Solage calvados**
¾	shot(s)	**Sloe gin liqueur**
½	shot(s)	**Heering cherry brandy liqueur**
½	shot(s)	**Freshly squeezed lemon juice**
½	shot(s)	**Chilled mineral water** (omit if wet ice)

Origin: Recipe adapted from a 1937 Bar Florida (later renamed Floridita) menu, Havana, Cuba.
Comment: A punchy, full-flavoured, veritable basket of fruit.

EVERY-BODY'S IRISH COCKTAIL

Glass: Martini
Garnish: Green cherry on stick
Method: **SHAKE** all ingredients with ice and fine strain into chilled glass.

2	shot(s)	**Jameson Irish whiskey**
½	shot(s)	**Green Chartreuse liqueur**
¼	shot(s)	**Green crème de menthe liqueur**

Origin: In his 1930 'The Savoy Cocktail Book', Harry Craddock writes of this drink, "Created to mark, and now in great demand on, St. Patrick's Day."
Comment: Like the Incredible Hulk, this drink packs a dangerous green punch.

EVITA

Glass: Martini
Garnish: Orange zest twist
Method: **SHAKE** all ingredients with ice and fine strain into chilled glass.

2	shot(s)	**Ketel One vodka**
½	shot(s)	**Midori green melon liqueur**
1	shot(s)	**Freshly squeezed orange juice**
½	shot(s)	**Freshly squeezed lime juice**

Comment: A tangy, lime green, medium-sweet combination of melon, orange and lime.

EXOTIC PASSION

Glass: Collins
Garnish: Pineapple wedge & strawberry
Method: **SHAKE** all ingredients with ice and strain into ice-filled glass.

1½	shot(s)	**Ketel One vodka**
¾	shot(s)	**Passoä passion fruit liqueur**
¾	shot(s)	**Crème de fraise de bois liqueur**
1½	shot(s)	**Pressed pineapple juice**
1½	shot(s)	**Freshly squeezed grapefruit juice**

Comment: Bittersweet and floral - one for the poolside.

EXTRADITION

Glass: Old-fashioned
Garnish: Strawberry on rim
Method: **MUDDLE** strawberries in base of shaker. Add other ingredients, **SHAKE** with ice and fine strain into ice-filled glass.

3	fresh	**Strawberries** (hulled)
2	shot(s)	**Macchu pisco**
2	shot(s)	**Pressed apple juice**
¾	shot(s)	**Passion fruit syrup**

Origin: Created in 2001 by Francis Timmons at Detroit, London, England.
Comment: A light, fruity drink for a summer afternoon.

F-16 SHOT

Glass: Shot
Garnish: Split stemmed cherry on rim
Method: Refrigerate ingredients then **LAYER** in chilled glass by carefully pouring in the following order.

½	shot(s)	**Kahlúa coffee liqueur**
½	shot(s)	**Baileys Irish cream liqueur**
½	shot(s)	**Bacardi Superior rum**

Origin: Named for the F-16 jet and closely related to the B-52.
Comment: May not break the sound barrier but at least it layers well.

F. WILLY SHOT

Glass: Shot
Method: SHAKE all ingredients with ice and fine strain into chilled glass.

½	shot(s)	**Ketel One vodka**
½	shot(s)	**Bacardi Superior rum**
½	shot(s)	**Luxardo Amaretto di Saschira**
½	shot(s)	**Cointreau triple sec**
¼	shot(s)	**Rose's lime cordial**

Comment: Not as bad as it looks or sounds.

FACUNDO'S FLARE NEW #8

Glass: Martini/Coupette
Garnish: None
Method: SHAKE all ingredients with ice and fine strain into chilled glass.

1½	shot(s)	**Bacardi Superior rum**
½	shot(s)	**Aperol**
1	shot(s)	**Freshly squeezed orange juice**
½	shot(s)	**Vanilla sugar syrup**
2	dashes	**Fee Brothers peach bitters**
½	fresh	**Egg white**

Comment: So smooth this drink is almost creamy. Vanilla dominates with fruity hints of rum.
Origin: Created by Bruce Hamilton at Tigerlily, Edinburgh, Scotland.

FAIR & WARMER COCKTAIL

Glass: Martini
Garnish: Orange zest twist
Method: SHAKE all ingredients with ice and fine strain into chilled glass.

2	shot(s)	**Bacardi Superior rum**
1	shot(s)	**Martini Rosso sweet vermouth**
½	shot(s)	**Cointreau triple sec**

Origin: Adapted from Harry Craddock's 1930 'The Savoy Cocktail Book'.
Comment: Sure to warm and fairly good.

FAIRBANKS COCKTAIL NO.1

Glass: Martini
Garnish: Maraschino cherry
Method: SHAKE all ingredients with ice and fine strain into chilled glass.

1	shot(s)	**Tanqueray London dry gin**
1	shot(s)	**Noilly Prat dry vermouth**
1	shot(s)	**Bols apricot brandy liqueur**
¼	shot(s)	**Freshly squeezed lemon juice**
¼	shot(s)	**Pomegranate (grenadine) syrup**
½	shot(s)	**Chilled mineral water** (omit if wet ice)

Origin: Adapted from Harry Craddock's 1930 'The Savoy Cocktail Book'.
Comment: Apricot liqueur dominates this cocktail but the dry vermouth and dilution save it from excessive sweetness.

FALCONI NEW #8

Glass: Martini/Coupette
Garnish: Orange zest twist
Method: STIR all ingredients with ice and strain into chilled glass.

2	shot(s)	**Rye whiskey (or bourbon)**
1	shot(s)	**Noilly Prat dry vermouth**
1	shot(s)	**Warre's Otima tawny port**
1	dash	**Angostura orange bitters**

Comment: Dry and subtly aromatic.

FALLEN ANGEL NEW #8

Glass: Martini
Garnish: Float mint leaf
Method: SHAKE all ingredients with ice and fine strain into chilled glass.

2	shot(s)	**Tanqueray London dry gin**
1	shot(s)	**Freshly squeezed lemon juice**
¼	shot(s)	**Green crème de menthe liqueur**
¼	shot(s)	**Sugar syrup** (2 sugar to 1 water)

Origin: Vintage cocktail of unknown origin.
Comment: Gin laced lime and fresh mint. A somewhat acquired taste.

FALLEN LEAVES

Glass: Martini
Garnish: Lemon peel zest
Method: STIR all ingredients with ice and strain into chilled glass.

1½	shot(s)	**Boulard Grand Solage calvados**
1½	shot(s)	**Martini Rosso sweet vermouth**
½	shot(s)	**Noilly Prat dry vermouth**
¼	shot(s)	**Courvoisier V.S.O.P. cognac**

Origin: Created in 1982 by Charles Schumann in Munich, Germany, and first published in his book 'American Bar'.
Comment: Suitably autumnal in colour. The vermouths and brandies are in harmony.

FANCY BRANDY

Glass: Martini
Garnish: Lemon peel zest
Method: SHAKE all ingredients with ice and fine strain into chilled glass.

2	shot(s)	**Courvoisier V.S.O.P. cognac**
¼	shot(s)	**Cointreau triple sec**
⅛	shot(s)	**Sugar syrup** (2 sugar to 1 water)
1	dash	**Angostura aromatic bitters**
½	shot(s)	**Chilled mineral water** (omit if wet ice)

Origin: Adapted from a recipe by Charles Schumann, Munich, Germany, and published in his 'American Bar'. Very similar to Jerry Thomas' Fancy Brandy Cocktail, published in his 1862 edition.
Comment: This appropriately named brandy based drink benefits from dilution, hence my addition of a splash of water.

FANCY DRINK

Glass: Sling
Garnish: Lemon slice & kumquat
Method: SHAKE first 3 ingredients with ice and strain into ice-filled glass. **TOP** with bitter lemon.

1	shot(s)	**Grand Marnier liqueur**
1	shot(s)	**Bacardi Superior rum**
2	shot(s)	**Freshly squeezed grapefruit juice**
Top up with		**Bitter lemon**

Comment: Tasty and tart! Refreshingly sour.

FANCY FREE

Glass: Martini
Garnish: Maraschino cherry
Method: SHAKE all ingredients with ice and fine strain into chilled glass.

2	shot(s)	**Bulleit bourbon whiskey**
½	shot(s)	**Luxardo maraschino liqueur**
2	dashes	**Angostura aromatic bitters**
2	dashes	**Angostura orange bitters**
½	shot(s)	**Chilled mineral water** (omit if wet ice)

Comment: Aromatised, tamed bourbon.

FANTASIA (MOCKTAIL)

Glass: Collins
Garnish: Lime wedge
Method: SHAKE first 4 ingredients with ice and strain into ice-filled glass. **TOP** with lemonade, stir and serve with straws.

¼	shot(s)	**Freshly squeezed lime juice**
¼	shot(s)	**Freshly squeezed lemon juice**
¼	shot(s)	**Sugar syrup** (2 sugar to 1 water)
5	dashes	**Angostura aromatic bitters**
Top up with		**Lemonade/Sprite/7-Up**

Origin: Discovered in 2004 at Claris Hotel, Barcelona, Spain.
Comment: A Spanish twist on the popular Australian LLB.

FAT SAILOR

Glass: Old-fashioned
Garnish: Lime wedge
Method: SHAKE all ingredients with ice and strain into glass filled with crushed ice.

1½	shot(s)	**Bacardi Oro golden rum**
¾	shot(s)	**Pusser's Navy rum**
¼	shot(s)	**Kahlúa coffee liqueur**
1	shot(s)	**Rose's lime cordial**
½	shot(s)	**Freshly squeezed lime juice**

Origin: Tiki style drink of unknown origin.
Comment: A tasty, suitably calorie laden, rum concoction.

FAT TIRE

Glass: Old-fashioned
Garnish: Orange zest twist
Method: SHAKE all ingredients with ice and fine strain into ice-filled glass.

1½	shot(s)	**Zacapa aged rum**
1	shot(s)	**Averna Amaro Siciliano**
½	shot(s)	**Freshly squeezed orange juice**
½	shot(s)	**Pressed pineapple juice**

Origin: Discovered in San Francisco in 2006, hence the American spelling of 'tyre'.
Comment: This flavourful, bittersweet aperitif won't be to everyone's taste.

FBI

Glass: Collins
Garnish: Crumbled Cadbury's Flake bar
Method: BLEND all ingredients with 18oz scoop of crushed ice and serve with straws.

2	shot(s)	**Ketel One vodka**
1	shot(s)	**Baileys Irish cream liqueur**
1	shot(s)	**Kahlúa coffee liqueur**
3	scoops	**Häagen Dazs vanilla ice cream**

Comment: Yummy alcoholic milkshake with coffee and whiskey cream.

FEATHER DUSTA CRUSTA

Glass: Martini
Garnish: Lemon zest twist & optional sugar rim
Method: SHAKE all ingredients with ice and fine strain into chilled glass.

1½	shot(s)	**Boulard Grand Solage calvados**
½	shot(s)	**Luxardo maraschino liqueur**
¾	shot(s)	**Freshly squeezed grapefruit juice**
½	shot(s)	**Freshly squeezed lemon juice**
¼	shot(s)	**Passion fruit syrup**
¼	shot(s)	**Pomegranate (grenadine) syrup**
2	dashes	**Peychaud's aromatic bitters**

Origin: Created in 2006 by Gregor de Gruyther at Ronnie Scott's, London, England. It is "quite a light Crusta", hence the name.
Comment: In Gregor's own words, "Based on the father of the Sidecar, the granddad of the Margarita, Laydeez an' Gennulmen! The Brandy Crusta."

LA FEUILLE MORTE

Glass: Collins (10oz/290ml max)
Method: POUR first 3 ingredients into glass. Serve iced water separately in a small jug (known in France as a 'broc') so the customer can dilute to their own taste. (I recommend five shots.) Lastly, add ice to fill glass.

1	shot(s)	**Ricard pastis**
½	shot(s)	**Pomegranate (grenadine) syrup**
½	shot(s)	**Mint (menthe) syrup**
Top up with		**Chilled mineral water**

Origin: Pronounced 'Fueel-Mort', the name literally means 'The dead leaf', a reference to its colour.
Comment: A traditional French way to serve pastis.

FIESTA

Glass: Martini
Garnish: Pomegranate seeds in drink
Method: SHAKE all ingredients with ice and fine strain into chilled glass.

1	shot(s)	**Bacardi Superior rum**
1	shot(s)	**Boulard Grand Solage calvados**
1	shot(s)	**Noilly Prat dry vermouth**
⅛	shot(s)	**Freshly squeezed lime juice**
⅛	shot(s)	**Pomegranate (grenadine) syrup**

Comment: With the right amount of quality pomegranate syrup, this is a great drink.

FIFTH AVENUE SHOT

Glass: Shot
Method: Refrigerate ingredients then **LAYER** in chilled glass by carefully pouring in the following order.

½	shot(s)	**Brown crème de cacao liqueur**
½	shot(s)	**Bols apricot brandy liqueur**
½	shot(s)	**Double (heavy) cream**

Comment: A sweet, apricot and chocolate creamy shot.

FIFTH DEGREE NEW #8

Glass: Martini/Coupette
Garnish: Lemon zest twist
Method: STIR Campari with ice (to coat ice and glass) and then strain to discard excess. Add other ingredients, **STIR** with coated ice and strain into chilled glass.

⅛	shot(s)	**Campari Bitter**
2	shot(s)	**Ketel One Vodka**
1	shot(s)	**Martini Rosso sweet vermouth**
¼	shot(s)	**Luxardo maraschino liqueur**

Origin: Created in 2008 and promoted by Diageo's Reserve Brands division. Apparently this drink was inspired by the classic Martinez.
Comment: Bitter sweet.

FIFTY-FIFTY MARTINI

Glass: Martini
Garnish: Olive on stick
Method: SHAKE all ingredients with ice and fine strain into chilled glass.

1½	shot(s)	**Tanqueray London dry gin**
1½	shot(s)	**Noilly Prat dry vermouth**

Origin: Adapted from Harry Craddock's 1930 'The Savoy Cocktail Book'.
Comment: A very 'wet' but wonderfully dry Martini which demands an olive, not a twist. Before you start – Craddock calls for it to be shaken.

57 T-BIRD SHOT

Glass: Shot
Method: SHAKE all ingredients with ice and fine strain into chilled glass.

½	shot(s)	**Ketel One vodka**
½	shot(s)	**Grand Marnier liqueur**
½	shot(s)	**Luxardo Amaretto di Saschira**

Variants: With California Plates add ½ shot orange juice; with Cape Cod Plates add ½ shot cranberry juice; with Florida Plates add ½ shot grapefruit juice; with Hawaiian Plates add ½ shot pineapple juice.
Comment: A '57 T-bird, or 1957 Ford Thunderbird to give it its full title, immortalised in the Beach Boys' song 'Fun Fun Fun', was the classic car for any 1950s teenager. Top down, radio up, girl next to you...

ACCORDING TO H.L. MENCKEN, 17,864,392,788 DIFFERENT COCKTAILS CAN BE MADE FROM THE INGREDIENTS 'ORDINARILY AVAILABLE IN A FIRST-RATE BAR'.

FIG SUPREME NEW #8

Glass: Old-fashioned
Garnish: Fig wedge on rim
Method: Scoop out the flesh of figs and **MUDDLE** in base of shaker. Add other ingredients, **SHAKE** with ice and fine strain into glass filled with crushed ice.

2	ripe	**Figs**
2	shot(s)	**Don Julio añejo tequila**
½	shot(s)	**Freshly squeezed lime juice**
¼	shot(s)	**Grand Marnier liqueur**
¼	shot(s)	**Pomegranate (grenadine) syrup**

Origin: Created by Salvatore Calabrese at Salvatore At Fifty, London, England.
Comment: Fig and pomegranate add an extra dimension to this Margarita-style cocktail.

FINAL WARD NEW #8

Glass: Martini
Garnish: None
Method: SHAKE all ingredients with ice and fine strain into chilled glass.

¾	shot(s)	**Rye whiskey (or bourbon)**
¾	shot(s)	**Green Chartreuse liqueur**
¾	shot(s)	**Luxardo maraschino liqueur**
¾	shot(s)	**Freshly squeezed lemon juice**

Origin: Adapted from a drink created in 2007 by Phil Ward at Death & Co., New York City, USA.
Comment: Mr Ward's variation on the classic vintage drink 'The Last Word'.

FIFTY FIFTY MARTINI

FINE & DANDY UPDATED #8

Glass: Martini
Garnish: Lemon zest twist
Method: SHAKE all ingredients with ice and fine strain into chilled glass.

1¾	shot(s)	**Tanqueray London dry gin**
¾	shot(s)	**Cointreau triple sec**
½	shot(s)	**Freshly squeezed lemon juice**
¼	shot(s)	**Sugar syrup** (2 sugar to 1 water)
½	shot(s)	**Chilled mineral water** (omit if wet ice)
1	dash	**Angostura aromatic bitters**

Comment: A gin based drink that's soured with lemon and sweetened with orange liqueur.

FINITALY

Glass: Martini
Garnish: Blueberries or raspberries.
Method: SHAKE all ingredients with ice and fine strain into chilled glass.

1½	shot(s)	**Cranberry flavoured vodka**
½	shot(s)	**Martini Rosso sweet vermouth**
½	shot(s)	**Chambord black raspberry liqueur**
¾	shot(s)	**Chilled mineral water** (omit if wet ice)

Origin: Created by Michael Mahe at Hush, London, England.
Comment: A simple, berry led Martini.

FINN ROUGE

Glass: Martini
Garnish: Lemon zest twist
Method: MUDDLE raspberries in base of shaker. Add other ingredients, **SHAKE** with ice and fine strain into chilled glass.

5	fresh	**Raspberries**
1¾	shot(s)	**Cranberry flavoured vodka**
½	shot(s)	**Crème de framboise liqueur**
¾	shot(s)	**Ocean Spray cranberry juice**
¼	shot(s)	**Freshly squeezed lemon juice**
⅛	shot(s)	**Sugar syrup** (2 sugar to 1 water)
1	grind	**Black pepper**

Origin: Adapted from a drink created in 2005 by Jamie Stephenson, Manchester, England.
Comment: A rather red, rasping, berry rich drink.

FINNBERRY MARTINI

Glass: Martini
Garnish: Cranberries
Method: SHAKE all ingredients with ice and fine strain into chilled glass.

2	shot(s)	**Cranberry flavoured vodka**
2	shot(s)	**Ocean Spray cranberry juice**
1	shot(s)	**Lapponia cloudberry liqueur**

Origin: I created this in 2002 after a trip to Finland with Finlandia vodka.
Comment: This rich berry Martini can be varied by using other berry liqueurs in the Lapponia range – try using two with a half shot of each.

FIREBALL

Glass: Shot
Method: SHAKE all ingredients with ice and fine strain into chilled glass.

1	shot(s)	**Goldschläger cinnamon schnapps**
3	drops	**Tabasco pepper sauce**

Comment: Down this in one and be prepared for a sweet cinnamon palate quickly followed by a hot, spicy finish.

FIREMAN'S SOUR NEW #8

Glass: Old-fashioned
Garnish: Orange slice & cherry on stick (sail)
Method: SHAKE all ingredients with ice and strain into ice-filled glass.

2	shot(s)	**Bacardi Superior rum**
1	shot(s)	**Freshly squeezed lime juice**
½	shot(s)	**Pomegranate (grenadine) syrup**
½	fresh	**Egg white**

Origin: Circa 1930s, USA.
Comment: Smooth and balanced with great rum character. Lime fresh and fruity sweet.

FIRST OF JULY

Glass: Martini
Garnish: Apple slice & blackberry on stick
Method: MUDDLE blackberries in base of shaker. Add other ingredients, **SHAKE** with ice and fine strain into chilled glass.

4	fresh	**Blackberries**
2	shot(s)	**Boulard Grand Solage calvados**
1	shot(s)	**Chambord black raspberry liqueur**
2	shot(s)	**Freshly squeezed grapefruit juice**

Origin: Created on 1st of July 2004 by David Guidi at Morton's, London, England.
Comment: Rich blackberry fruit with a hint of grapefruit acidity.

FISH HOUSE PUNCH #1 UPDATED #8

Glass: Collins
Garnish: Lemon slice
Method: SHAKE all ingredients with ice and strain into ice-filled glass.

1	shot(s)	**Courvoisier V.S.O.P cognac**
1	shot(s)	**Bacardi Oro golden rum**
¾	shot(s)	**Crème pêche de vigne liqueur**
¾	shot(s)	**Freshly squeezed lemon juice**
¼	shot(s)	**Sugar syrup** (2 sugar to 1 water)
2	shot(s)	**Chilled mineral water**

Comment: This fruit laced mix is neither too sweet, nor too strong. It is perfect.
Origin: Probably the most famous of all punch recipes, this originated in 1732 at a Philadelphia fishing and social club called the 'State in Schuylkill'. Many modern variations use soda water (club soda) in place of mineral water. The inclusion of peach liqueur is a modern substitute for the traditional peach brandy. However, it's believed the Schuylkill original omitted peach entirely.

FISH HOUSE PUNCH #2 UPDATED #8

Glass: Collins
Garnish: Lemon slice
Method: SHAKE all ingredients with ice and strain into ice-filled glass.

1	shot(s)	**Courvoisier V.S.O.P cognac**
1	shot(s)	**Bacardi Superior rum**
1	shot(s)	**Crème pêche de vigne liqueur**
1½	shot(s)	**Strong cold English breakfast tea**
1	shot(s)	**Freshly squeezed lemon juice**
¼	shot(s)	**Sugar syrup** (2 sugar to 1 water)

Origin: Formula by Yours Truly (Simon Difford).
Comment: Over the decades this recipe has constantly morphed. The inclusion of cold tea is the latest adaptation.

FITZGERALD NEW #8

Glass: Old-fashioned
Garnish: Lemon wedge
Method: SHAKE all ingredients with ice and strain into ice-filled glass.

2	shot(s)	**Tanqueray London dry gin**
½	shot(s)	**Sugar syrup** (2 sugar to 1 water)
1	shot(s)	**Freshly squeezed lemon juice**
2	dashes	**Angostura aromatic bitters**

Comment: A gin sour without the egg white
Origin: Adapted from a drink created in the early 1990s by Dale DeGroff at the Rainbow Room, New York City, USA.

> 'NOW FOR DRINKS, NOW FOR SOME DANCING WITH A GOOD BEAT.'
> HORACE

FIX (GENERIC NAME) NEW #8

Glass: Old-fashioned
Garnish: With fruit used in recipe
Method: SHAKE all ingredients with ice and strain into ice-filled glass.

2	shot(s)	**Spirit** (rum, gin, whisk(e)y etc.)
1	shot(s)	**Freshly squeezed lemon juice**
1	shot(s)	**Sweet fruit juice** (often pineapple)
½	shot(s)	**Sugar syrup** (2 sugar to 1 water)

Origin: A Fix is a classic style of drink that constitutes of a spirit, lemon juice, and some kind of sweet fruit served short.
Comment: Match the juice and spirit and this formula works every time.

FIZZ (GENERIC NAME) UPDATED #8

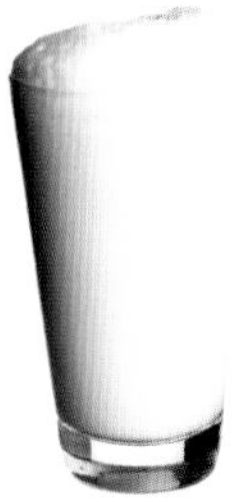

Glass: Collins (8oz max)
Garnish: Lemon slice
Method: SHAKE first 4 ingredients with ice and strain into chilled glass (no ice in glass). **TOP** with soda dispensed from a siphon.

2	shot(s)	**Spirit** (gin, whisk(e)y, vodka etc.)
1	shot(s)	**Freshly squeezed lemon/lime juice**
½	shot(s)	**Sugar syrup** (2 sugar to 1 water)
½	fresh	**Egg white** (optional)
Top up with		**Soda water** (from siphon)

Origin: Like the Collins, this mid-19th century classic is basically a sour lengthened with charged water and at first glance there is little difference between a Fizz and a Collins. However, there are several distinguishing features. A Collins should be served in at least a twelve ounce, and ideally a fourteen ounce tall glass, while that used for a Fizz should be no bigger than eight ounces. A Collins should be served in an ice-filled glass, while a Fizz should be served in a chilled glass without ice.

A Fizz should also be made using charged water from a siphon in preference to soda from bottles or cans. The burst of pressure from the siphon bulb generates tiny bubbles which give off carbonic acid, benefiting the flavour and the mouth-feel of the drink.

For the correct proportions I have turned to David A. Embury's seminal 'The Fine Art of Mixing Drinks'. He recommends "1 - or a little less – sweet (sugar, fruit syrup, or liqueur), 2 sour (lime or lemon juice), 3 - or a little more - strong (spirituous liquor), and 4 weak (charged water and ice). I interpret this as follows: 2 shots spirit (gin, whiskey, vodka, brandy), 1 shot lemon or lime juice, ½ shot sugar syrup, topped up with soda. I also like to add half a fresh egg white, which technically makes the drink a 'Silver Fizz'.
Comment: I recommend the Derby Fizz with its combination of liqueur and spirits over these more traditional versions.

FIZZ Á LA VIOLETTE NEW #8

Glass: Small Collins (8oz)
Method: 1/ Flash **BLEND** first 6 ingredients without ice (to emulsify mix). Then pour contents of blender into shaker and **SHAKE** with ice. Strain into chilled glass (no ice in glass) and **TOP** with soda from siphon. ALTERNATIVELY: 2/ Vigorously **DRY SHAKE** first 6 ingredients without ice until bored/tired. Add ice to shaker, **SHAKE** again and strain into chilled glass (no ice). **TOP** with soda water from siphon.

1½	shot(s)	**Old Tom gin**
¼	shot(s)	**Benoit Serres crème de violette**
1	shot(s)	**Freshly squeezed lemon juice**
½	shot(s)	**Sugar syrup** (2 sugar to 1 water)
1	shot(s)	**Double (heavy) cream**
1	fresh	**Egg white**
Top up with		**Soda water** (from siphon)

Note: The so called 'dry shake' allows the cream and egg white to emulsify thus giving this drink its legendary silky mouth feel without the over dilution which would result from a prolonged shake with ice.
Variation: Blend rather than shake.
Origin: An adaptation of the Ramos Fizz. In his 1939 'the gentleman's Companion', Charles H. Baker Jr. credits this dinks creation to Ahmed Soliman a manufacturer and seller of Perfume Essences in the Khan el Kalili Bazaar, Cairo.
Comment: A delicate floral drink that is so creamy smooth that it is almost fluffy.

FLAME OF LOVE MARTINI NEW #8

●●●●◐○

Glass: Martini/Coupette
Garnish: Flamed orange zest twist
Method: Pour sherry into chilled glass, swirl to coat inside and discard excess. Using a match or lighter, express and ignite the oils from the orange peel so the burn oil coats the inside of the sherry-coated glass. **SHAKE** the vodka with ice and fine strain into the coated glass.

¼	shot(s)	**Tio Pepe Fino sherry**
3	twists	**Orange peel**
2	shot(s)	**Ketel One vodka**

Comment: Bone dry but fresh and most definitely citrussy.
Origin: Created at Chasen's, a legendary Hollywood restaurant that opened in 1936 and was a haunt of movie stars and even royalty until its eventual demise in 1995. The memorabilia that decorated the restaurant was held in storage and in 1997 Maud and Dave Chasen's grandson opened another Chasen's on Beverly Hills' Cañon Drive which sadly failed due to a lack of patrons.

During the original Chasen's heyday its star-studded clientele enjoyed drinks created by its noted bartender Pepe Ruiz. Of these the Flame of Love is his most famous creation, partly due to its originally being made for Dean Martin. The legend of this drink is further embellished by Dean dragging his old pal Frank Sinatra to Chasen's to try the drink. The story goes that Frank was so impressed that he ordered one for everyone in the place.

> 'WHEN I SELL LIQUOR, IT'S BOOTLEGGING. WHEN MY CUSTOMERS SERVE IT ON LAKESHORE DRIVE, IT'S HOSPITALITY.'
> AL CAPONE

FLAMING DR PEPPER

●●○○○

Glass: Shot & Boston
Method: POUR beer into Boston glass. **LAYER** amaretto and rum in chilled shot glass by carefully pouring amaretto and then rum. **IGNITE** the rum and carefully lift shot glass then drop (bottom first) into Boston glass.

1	bottle	**Lager**
½	shot(s)	**Luxardo Amaretto di Saschira**
½	shot(s)	**151° overproof rum**

Origin: So named as the end result resembles the taste of the proprietary Dr Pepper soft drink. This drink inspired an episode of The Simpsons featuring a similar drink titled the 'Flaming Homer' and later the 'Flaming Moe' (after the programme's bartender).
Comment: Please consider the likelihood of burning yourself while attempting to lift the flaming shot into the beer.

FLAMING FERRARI

●●○○○

This flaming drink (to be downed in one) requires an assistant to help the drinker consume the concoction.

Step 1.
Glass: Martini
Method: LAYER ingredients by carefully pouring in the following order.

½	shot(s)	**Pomegranate (grenadine) syrup**
1	shot(s)	**Galliano L'Autentico liqueur**
1	shot(s)	**Opal Nera black sambuca**
1	shot(s)	**Green Chartreuse liqueur**

Step 2.
Glass: Two shot glasses.
Method: POUR each ingredient into its own shot glass.

1	shot(s)	**Grand Marnier liqueur**
1	shot(s)	**Pusser's Navy rum**

Step 3.
Method: IGNITE the contents of the Martini glass. Give two long straws to the drinker and instruct them to drink the contents of the Martini glass in one go. As they do so, slowly **POUR** the contents of the two shot glasses into the flaming Martini glass.

Variant: Flaming Lamborghini with coffee liqueur and blue curaçao in the shot glasses.
Comment: Not recommended if you want to remember the rest of the evening and please be careful – alcohol and fire is a risky combination.

FLAMING HENRY

●●●●◐○

Glass: Shot
Method: LAYER by carefully pouring ingredients in the order below. Finally **IGNITE** bourbon. Extinguish flame prior to drinking and beware of hot glass rim.

½	shot(s)	**Luxardo Amaretto di Saschira**
½	shot(s)	**Baileys Irish cream liqueur**
½	shot(s)	**Bulleit bourbon whiskey**

Origin: Created by Henry Smiff and friends in the South of France and popularised by one of their number, John Coe, the successful London drinks wholesaler.
Comment: Flaming good shot.

FLAMINGO #1

●●●●◐○

Glass: Martini
Garnish: Banana chunk on rim
Method: SHAKE all ingredients with ice and fine strain into chilled glass.

1	shot(s)	**Bulleit bourbon whiskey**
¾	shot(s)	**Crème de banane liqueur**
1½	shot(s)	**Freshly squeezed orange juice**
¾	shot(s)	**Freshly squeezed lemon juice**
½	fresh	**Egg white**

Comment: It's not pink but it has bourbon, banana, orange and lemon smoothed with egg white.

FLAMINGO #2

●●●○○

Glass: Martini
Garnish: Star fruit
Method: SHAKE all ingredients with ice and fine strain into chilled glass.

2	shot(s)	**Zacapa aged rum**
1½	shot(s)	**Pressed pineapple juice**
½	shot(s)	**Freshly squeezed lime juice**
⅛	shot(s)	**Pomegranate (grenadine) syrup**

Origin: Classic of unknown origins.
Comment: A tasty, pink drink with a frothy top.

'WHAT'S WRONG, A LITTLE PAVEMENT SICKNESS?' RUSSIAN SAYING

FLATLINER

●○○○○

Glass: Shot
Method: POUR sambuca into chilled glass. **LAYER** tequila by carefully pouring over sambuca. Lastly **DRIP** pepper sauce onto drink. This will sink through the tequila to form an orange line on top of the sambuca.

¾	shot(s)	**Luxardo Sambuca dei Cesari**
¾	shot(s)	**Don Julio reposado tequila**
8	drops	**Tabasco pepper sauce**

Comment: A serious combination of sweetness, strength and heat. Looks weird and tastes weirder.

FLIP (GENERIC NAME) UPDATED #8

●●●●◐

Glass: Sour or Martini
Garnish: Dust with freshly grated nutmeg
Method: SHAKE all ingredients with ice and fine strain into chilled glass.

2	shot(s)	**Spirit** (brandy, gin, whisk(e)y etc.)
1	shot(s)	**Sugar syrup** (2 sugar to 1 water)
1	fresh	**Egg** (white & yolk)
½	shot(s)	**Double (heavy) cream**

Variant: Served hot in a toddy glass - heat in a microwave oven or mix in a pan over heat.
Comment: I favour creamy, spicy, bourbon based Flips.
Origin: Flips basically consist of any fortified wine or liquor shaken with a whole egg and sweetened with sugar. They can also contain cream and are typically garnished with a dusting of nutmeg and served in a sour glass or small Martini glass. They can be served hot or cold.
The very first Flips, which emerged as early as the late 1600s, consisted of tankard of ale to which a mixture made from sugar, eggs and spices was added before being heated with a red-hot iron poker from the fire. Later they came to mean any fortified wine or liquor shaken with a whole egg and sweetened with sugar.

FLIP THAT'S GOOD NEW #8

●●●●◐

Glass: Sour (or Martini/Coupette)
Garnish: Grate nutmeg over drink
Method: SHAKE all ingredients with ice and strain into chilled glass.

2	shot(s)	**Zacapa aged rum**
½	shot(s)	**Sugar syrup** (2 sugar to 1 water)
½	shot(s)	**Double (heavy) cream**
1	fresh	**Egg yolk**

Comment: Basically an aged rum flip with the sugar level reduced and egg white omitted.
Origin: Created in December 2008 by Yours Truly (Simon Difford) at the Cabinet Room, London, England.

FLIP WILLIAMS NEW #8

●●●●○

Glass: Sour glass (or Martini/Coupette)
Garnish: Grate nutmeg over drink & swirl 3 drops of Angostura bitters
Method: SHAKE all ingredients with ice and fine strain into chilled glass.

1½	shot(s)	**Bulleit bourbon whiskey**
¾	shot(s)	**Poire William eau de vie**
¼	shot(s)	**Sugar syrup** (2 sugar to 1 water)
½	shot(s)	**Double (heavy) cream**
2	dashes	**Angostura aromatic bitters**
1	fresh	**Egg yolk**

Comment: Velvety smooth with hints of whiskey and pear.
Origin: Created in 2008 by Julian de Feral at Bureau, London, England.

THE FLIRT

●●●●○○

Glass: Martini
Garnish: Lipstick on rim
Method: SHAKE all ingredients with ice and fine strain into chilled glass.

2	shot(s)	**Don Julio reposado tequila**
¾	shot(s)	**Bols apricot brandy liqueur**
¾	shot(s)	**Freshly squeezed lime juice**
1	shot(s)	**Ocean Spray cranberry juice**

Origin: Created in 2002 by Dick Bradsell at Lonsdale House, London, England.
Comment: A fruity drink to upset glass washers throughout the land.

FLIRTINI #1

●●●●○

Glass: Martini
Garnish: Pineapple wedge on rim
Method: SHAKE all ingredients with ice and fine strain into chilled glass.

2	shot(s)	**Ketel One vodka**
1½	shot(s)	**Pressed pineapple juice**
¼	shot(s)	**Chambord black raspberry liqueur**

AKA: French Martini
Origin: Made famous on television's Sex And The City. Said to have been created in 2003 for Sarah Jessica Parker at Guastavinos, New York City, USA.
Comment: It's a French Martini! Hard not to like.

FLIRTINI #2 UPDATED #8

Glass: Martini
Garnish: Maraschino cherry
Method: SHAKE first 3 ingredients with ice and fine strain into chilled glass. **TOP** with champagne.

¾	shot(s)	**Ketel One vodka**
¾	shot(s)	**Cointreau triple sec**
2	shot(s)	**Pressed pineapple juice**
Top up with		**Perrier Jouet brut champagne**

Origin: Adapted from a recipe by the New York bartender Dale DeGroff.
Comment: A flirtatious little number that slips down easily.

THE FLO ZIEGFELD

Glass: Martini
Garnish: Pineapple wedge on rim
Method: SHAKE all ingredients with ice and fine strain into chilled glass.

2	shot(s)	**Tanqueray London dry gin**
1	shot(s)	**Pressed pineapple juice**
¼	shot(s)	**Sugar syrup** (2 sugar to 1 water)

Origin: Named after Florenz Ziegfeld, the Broadway impresario, whose widow recalled the recipe for the 1946 'Stork Club Bar Book'.
Comment: The original recipe omits sugar but was probably made with sweetened pineapple juice.

FLORAL MARTINI

Glass: Martini
Garnish: Edible flower petal
Method: STIR all ingredients with ice and fine strain into chilled glass.

2	shot(s)	**Tanqueray London dry gin**
½	shot(s)	**St-Germain elderflower liqueur**
¼	shot(s)	**Noilly Prat dry vermouth**
¼	shot(s)	**Rosewater**
½	shot(s)	**Chilled mineral water** (omit if wet ice)

Origin: Adapted from a drink created in 2003 at Zander Bar, London, England.
Comment: This aptly named gin Martini is soft but dry.

FLORIDA COCKTAIL (MOCKTAIL)

Glass: Collins
Garnish: Orange slice & cherry on stick (sail)
Method: SHAKE first 4 ingredients with ice and strain into ice-filled glass, **TOP** with soda.

1	shot(s)	**Freshly squeezed grapefruit juice**
2	shot(s)	**Freshly squeezed orange juice**
½	shot(s)	**Freshly squeezed lemon juice**
¼	shot(s)	**Sugar syrup** (2 sugar to 1 water)
Top up with		**Soda water** (club soda)

Comment: The Florida sun shines through this fruity, refreshing drink.

FLORIDA DAIQUIRI

Glass: Martini
Garnish: Maraschino cherry
Method: SHAKE all ingredients with ice and fine strain into chilled glass.

2	shot(s)	**Bacardi Superior rum**
½	shot(s)	**Freshly squeezed lime juice**
¼	shot(s)	**Sugar syrup** (2 sugar to 1 water)
½	shot(s)	**Freshly squeezed grapefruit juice**
⅛	shot(s)	**Maraschino syrup** (from cherry jar)
¾	shot(s)	**Chilled mineral water** (omit if wet ice)

Comment: The classic blend of rum, lime and sugar, but with a hint of freshly squeezed grapefruit juice and maraschino. A user-friendly version of a Hemingway Special.

FLORIDA SLING

Glass: Sling
Garnish: Redcurrants/berries
Method: SHAKE all ingredients with ice and strain into ice-filled glass.

2	shot(s)	**Tanqueray London dry gin**
¼	shot(s)	**Heering cherry brandy liqueur**
2	shot(s)	**Pressed pineapple juice**
¾	shot(s)	**Freshly squeezed lemon juice**
¼	shot(s)	**Pomegranate (grenadine) syrup**

Comment: A tall, pink, dumbed down Singapore Sling.

> ‘I SAW A WEREWOLF DRINKING A PINA COLADA AT TRADER VIC'S, AND HIS HAIR WAS PERFECT.’
> WARREN ZEVON

EL FLORIDITA DAIQUIRI NO.1

Glass: Martini
Garnish: Maraschino cherry
Method: BLEND all ingredients with 6oz scoop of crushed ice. Pour into glass and serve.

1½	shot(s)	**Bacardi Superior rum**
⅛	shot(s)	**Luxardo maraschino liqueur**
¼	shot(s)	**Freshly squeezed grapefruit juice**
½	shot(s)	**Freshly squeezed lime juice**
½	shot(s)	**Sugar syrup** (2 sugar to 1 water)

Variant: Hemingway Daiquiri
Origin: Emilio Gonzalez is said to have first adapted the Natural Daiquiri into a frozen version at the Plaza Hotel in Cuba. However, Constantino Ribalaigua Vert of Havana's Floridita bar made the frozen daiquiri famous with a recipe that included grapefruit.
Comment: Great on a hot day, but the coldness masks much of the flavour evident when this drink is served straight-up.

EL FLORIDITA DAIQUIRI NO.2

Glass: Martini
Garnish: Lime wedge on rim
Method: SHAKE all ingredients with ice and fine strain into chilled glass.

2	shot(s)	**Bacardi Superior rum**
½	shot(s)	**Martini Rosso sweet vermouth**
½	shot(s)	**Freshly squeezed lime juice**
¼	shot(s)	**White crème de cacao liqueur**
⅛	shot(s)	**Pomegranate (grenadine) syrup**

Variant: With fruit.
Comment: Like other Daiquiris, this complex version benefits from dilution so consider adding a dash of water.

FLORIDITA MARGARITA

Glass: Coupette
Garnish: Lime wedge & salted rim (optional)
Method: SHAKE all ingredients with ice and fine strain into chilled glass.

1½	shot(s)	**Don Julio reposado tequila**
½	shot(s)	**Cointreau triple sec**
½	shot(s)	**Ocean Spray cranberry juice**
¼	shot(s)	**Rose's lime cordial**
1½	shot(s)	**Freshly squeezed grapefruit juice**
¾	shot(s)	**Freshly squeezed lime juice**
½	shot(s)	**Sugar syrup** (2 sugar to 1 water)

Origin: Created in 1999 by Robert Plotkin and Raymon Flores of BarMedia, USA.
Comment: A blush coloured, Margarita-style drink with a well-matched amalgamation of flavours.

FLOWER POWER MARTINI

Glass: Martini
Garnish: Orange zest twist
Method: SHAKE all ingredients with ice and fine strain into chilled glass.

2	shot(s)	**Tanqueray London dry gin**
½	shot(s)	**St-Germain elderflower liqueur**
½	shot(s)	**Noilly Prat dry vermouth**
¼	shot(s)	**Benoit Serres crème de violette**

Origin: Created in 2007 by Yours Truly (Simon Difford).
Comment: A Dry Martini served super-wet with more flower power than Austin Powers.

FLUFFY DUCK UPDATED #8

Glass: Collins
Garnish: Orange slice
Method: SHAKE first 4 ingredients with ice and strain into ice-filled glass. **TOP** with soda.

1½	shot(s)	**Tanqueray London dry gin**
1½	shot(s)	**Bols advocaat liqueur**
1	shot(s)	**Cointreau triple sec**
1	shot(s)	**Freshly squeezed orange juice**
Top up with		**Soda water** (club soda)

Comment: Light, creamy and easy drinking. The gin's character prevents it from being too fluffy.

FLUTTER

Glass: Martini
Garnish: Orange zest twist
Method: SHAKE all ingredients with ice and fine strain into chilled glass.

2	shot(s)	**Don Julio reposado tequila**
1	shot(s)	**Kahlúa coffee liqueur**
1¼	shot(s)	**Pressed pineapple juice**

Origin: Created in 2003 by Tony Conigliaro at Lonsdale House, London, England.
Comment: The three ingredients combine brilliantly.

FLY LIKE A BUTTERFLY

Glass: Martini
Garnish: Orange zest twist
Method: SHAKE all ingredients with ice and fine strain into chilled glass.

1½	shot(s)	**Noilly Prat dry vermouth**
1½	shot(s)	**Martini Rosso sweet vermouth**
¾	shot(s)	**Dubonnet Red** (French made)
¾	shot(s)	**Freshly squeezed orange juice**

Origin: My take on a classic called a 'Lovely Butterfly'.
Comment: This light, aromatic, sweet and sour beauty has a grown-up, quinine-rich flavour but lacks the 'sting like a bee' finish.

FLYING DUTCHMAN MARTINI

Glass: Martini
Garnish: Orange zest twist
Method: STIR all ingredients with ice and strain into chilled glass.

2½	shot(s)	**Bokma oude genever**
¼	shot(s)	**Cointreau triple sec**
2	dashes	**Angostura orange bitters**
¾	shot(s)	**Chilled mineral water**

Comment: A Martini with more than a hint of orange.

FLYING GRASSHOPPER

Glass: Martini
Garnish: Chocolate powder rim & mint leaf
Method: SHAKE all ingredients with ice and fine strain into chilled glass.

1	shot(s)	**Ketel One vodka**
¾	shot(s)	**White crème de cacao liqueur**
½	shot(s)	**Giffard Menthe Pastille liqueur**
¾	shot(s)	**Double (heavy) cream**
¾	shot(s)	**Milk**

Comment: A Grasshopper with vodka – tastes like a choc mint ice cream.

FLYING SCOTSMAN UPDATED #8

●●●●○

Glass: Old-fashioned
Garnish: Orange zest twist
Method: STIR all ingredients with ice and strain into ice-filled glass.

2	shot(s)	**Johnnie Walker Scotch whisky**
2	shot(s)	**Martini Rosso sweet vermouth**
¼	shot(s)	**Sugar syrup** (2 sugar to 1 water)
3	dashes	**Angostura aromatic bitters**

Comment: Sweetened Scotch with plenty of spice: like a homemade whisky liqueur.

'THIS IS DISGRACEFUL… I AM AS DRUNK AS A LORD – BUT IT DOESN'T MATTER, BECAUSE I AM A LORD!'
BERTRAND RUSSELL

FLYING TIGRE COCTEL

●●●●○

Glass: Martini
Garnish: Orange zest twist
Method: SHAKE all ingredients with ice and fine strain into chilled glass.

1¾	shot(s)	**Bacardi Superior rum**
¾	shot(s)	**Tanqueray London dry gin**
¼	shot(s)	**Sugar syrup** (2 sugar to 1 water)
⅛	shot(s)	**Pomegranate (grenadine) syrup**
3	dashes	**Angostura aromatic bitters**
¾	shot(s)	**Chilled mineral water** (omit if wet ice)

Origin: Adapted from a recipe in the 1949 edition of Esquire's 'Handbook For Hosts'. The drink is credited to an unnamed Captain serving in the US Marines, Amphibious Group Seven, at Santiago de Cuba in 1942.
Comment: Light, aromatic and complex – one to sip.

FOG CUTTER #1

●●●●○

Glass: Collins or tiki mug
Garnish: Orange slice
Method: SHAKE first 6 ingredients with ice and strain into ice-filled glass. FLOAT sherry on top of drink and serve without straws.

1½	shot(s)	**Bacardi Superior rum**
¾	shot(s)	**Courvoisier V.S.O.P. cognac**
½	shot(s)	**Tanqueray London dry gin**
1½	shot(s)	**Freshly squeezed orange juice**
½	shot(s)	**Freshly squeezed lemon juice**
½	shot(s)	**Almond (orgeat) syrup**
½	shot(s)	**Amontillado dry sherry**

Origin: A version of what became a Tiki classic, sometimes credited to Trader Vic and/or Don the Beachcomber. In his 'Bartender's Guide' (1972 revised edition) Vic remarks, "Fog Cutter, hell. After two of these, you won't even see the stuff."
Comment: Don't be fooled by the innocuous colour. This long, fruity drink packs a serious kick.

FOG CUTTER #2

●●●●○

Glass: Old-fashioned
Garnish: Orange slice
Method: SHAKE first 5 ingredients with ice and strain into glass filled with crushed ice. DRIZZLE cherry brandy over drink and serve with straws.

1	shot(s)	**Bacardi Superior rum**
½	shot(s)	**Courvoisier V.S.O.P. cognac**
½	shot(s)	**Tanqueray London dry gin**
½	shot(s)	**Freshly squeezed lime juice**
¼	shot(s)	**Sugar syrup** (2 sugar to 1 water)
¼	shot(s)	**Heering cherry brandy liqueur**

Comment: A well balanced (neither too strong nor too sweet), short, fruity drink.

FOG HORN

●●●○○

Glass: Old-fashioned
Garnish: Lime wedge
Method: POUR ingredients into ice-filled glass and stir.

2	shot(s)	**Tanqueray London dry gin**
½	shot(s)	**Rose's lime cordial**
Top up with		**Ginger ale**

Comment: Different! Almost flowery in taste with the spice of ginger beer.

FONTAINEBLEAU SPECIAL

●●●○○

Glass: Martini
Garnish: Star anise
Method: SHAKE all ingredients with ice and fine strain into chilled glass.

1½	shot(s)	**Courvoisier V.S.O.P. cognac**
1½	shot(s)	**Marie Brizard anisette liqueur**
¾	shot(s)	**Noilly Prat dry vermouth**

Comment: Cognac, aniseed and vermouth combine in this pleasant after dinner drink which has a taste reminiscent of liquorice.

FORBIDDEN FRUITS

●●●●○

Glass: Collins
Garnish: Berries on stick
Method: MUDDLE berries in base of shaker. Add next 3 ingredients, SHAKE with ice and strain into glass filled with crushed ice. TOP with ginger beer.

4	fresh	**Blackberries**
4	fresh	**Blueberries**
4	fresh	**Strawberries** (hulled)
4	fresh	**Raspberries**
2	shot(s)	**Tanqueray London dry gin**
1	shot(s)	**Freshly squeezed lime juice**
½	shot(s)	**Sugar syrup** (2 sugar to 1 water)
Top up with		**Ginger beer**

Origin: Created in 2001 by Andres Masso at Lab Bar, London, England.
Comment: Long and fruity with something of a bite.

THE FORMOSA NEW #8

Glass: Martini
Garnish: Orange zest twist
Method: STIR all ingredients with ice and strain into chilled glass.

| 2 | shot(s) | **Sake** |
| 2 | shot(s) | **Taylor's Chip dry white port** |

Comment: Light and easy to drink. Wine-like.

FORT LAUDERDALE

Glass: Martini
Garnish: Orange zest twist
Method: SHAKE all ingredients with ice and fine strain into chilled glass.

1½	shot(s)	**Bacardi Superior rum**
½	shot(s)	**Martini Rosso sweet vermouth**
1	shot(s)	**Freshly squeezed orange juice**
¼	shot(s)	**Freshly squeezed lime juice**

Comment: Rum, vermouth, lime and orange form a challenging combination in this golden drink.

FOSBURY FLIP

Glass: Collins
Garnish: Apricot slice on rim
Method: SHAKE all ingredients with ice and strain into ice-filled glass.

2	shot(s)	**Zacapa aged rum**
1	shot(s)	**Frangelico hazelnut liqueur**
1	shot(s)	**Bols apricot brandy liqueur**
2 ½	shot(s)	**Freshly squeezed orange juice**
¾	shot(s)	**Freshly squeezed lime juice**
⅛	shot(s)	**Pomegranate (grenadine) syrup**
1	fresh	**Egg yolk**

Origin: Created in 2002 by Salvatore Calabrese at the Library Bar, Lanesborough Hotel, London, England, for Kirsten Fosbury. The Fosbury Flop is the style of high jump used by almost all successful high jumpers today and introduced by the American Dick Fosbury, who won the Gold Medal at the 1968 Olympic Games.
Comment: This richly flavoured, yellow, velvety drink is almost custardy in consistency.

FOUR LEAF CLOVER NEW #8

Glass: Martini
Garnish: Physalis fruit
Method: MUDDLE clove in base of shaker. Add other ingredients, **SHAKE** with ice and fine strain into chilled glass.

1	dried	**Clove**
2	shot(s)	**Bacardi Superior rum**
1	shot(s)	**Pressed apple juice**
¾	shot(s)	**Freshly squeezed lime juice**
½	shot(s)	**Honey syrup** (4 honey to 1 water)

Comment: Originally based on vodka but seemed a shame not to try it as a Daiquiri.
Origin: Created in 2008 by Denis Broci at Maze bar & Restaurant, London, England.

FOUR W DAIQUIRI

Glass: Martini
Garnish: Grapefruit wedge on rim
Method: SHAKE all ingredients with ice and fine strain into chilled glass.

2	shot(s)	**Bacardi Oro golden rum**
1½	shot(s)	**Freshly squeezed grapefruit juice**
¾	shot(s)	**Maple syrup**
2	dashes	**Angostura aromatic bitters**
½	shot(s)	**Chilled mineral water** (omit if wet ice)

Origin: My version of an old drink created by Herb Smith and popularised by his friend Oscar at the Waldorf, New York City. The drink was named in honour of the Duke of Windsor and his bride, formerly Wallis Warfield Simpson. The four 'W's stand for Wallis Warfield Windsor Wallop.
Comment: The oomph of rum, the sourness of grapefruit and the richness of maple syrup, all aromatised by bitters.

> **'I GAVE HER A DRINK. SHE WAS A GAL WHO'D TAKE A DRINK IF SHE HAD TO KNOCK ME DOWN TO GET THE BOTTLE.'**
> JOHN PAXTON

FOURTH OF JULY COCKTAIL

Glass: Martini
Garnish: Cinnamon dust
Method: POUR bourbon and Galliano into warm glass, **IGNITE** and sprinkle cinnamon while flaming. **SHAKE** last 3 ingredients with ice and strain into glass over extinguished bourbon and Galliano base.

---first layer---

1	shot(s)	**Bulleit bourbon whiskey**
1	shot(s)	**Galliano L'Autentico liqueur**
	dust	**Cinnamon over flame**

---second layer---

1	shot(s)	**Kahlúa coffee liqueur**
1	shot(s)	**Freshly squeezed orange juice**
1	shot(s)	**Double (heavy) cream**

Comment: More a stage show than a cocktail but rich and tasty all the same.

FOURTH OF JULY SHOT

Glass: Shot
Method: LAYER Refrigerate ingredients then **LAYER** in chilled glass by carefully pouring in the following order.

¼	shot(s)	**Pomegranate (grenadine) syrup**
½	shot(s)	**Bols blue curaçao liqueur**
½	shot(s)	**Ketel One vodka**

Comment: Looks cool… tastes less so!

FRANK SULLIVAN COCKTAIL

Glass: Martini
Garnish: Sugar rim & lemon zest twist
Method: SHAKE all ingredients with ice and fine strain into chilled glass.

1	shot(s)	**Courvoisier V.S.O.P. cognac**
1	shot(s)	**Cointreau triple sec**
1	shot(s)	**Noilly Prat dry vermouth**
1	shot(s)	**Freshly squeezed lemon juice**

Origin: Adapted from Harry Craddock's 1930 'The Savoy Cocktail Book'.
Comment: A Sidecar made dry with vermouth: it needs the sweet rim.

THE FRANKENJACK COCKTAIL

Glass: Martini
Garnish: Orange zest twist
Method: SHAKE all ingredients with ice and fine strain into chilled glass.

1½	shot(s)	**Tanqueray London dry gin**
1½	shot(s)	**Noilly Prat dry vermouth**
½	shot(s)	**Bols apricot brandy liqueur**
½	shot(s)	**Cointreau triple sec**

Origin: Adapted from Harry Craddock's 1930 'The Savoy Cocktail Book'.
Comment: Dry, sophisticated orange and apricot.

FRANKLIN MARTINI

Glass: Martini
Garnish: Two olives
Method: STIR vermouth with ice and strain to **DISCARD** excess, leaving the glass and ice coated with vermouth. **POUR** gin over vermouth coated ice, **STIR** and strain into chilled glass.

| ¾ | shot(s) | **Noilly Prat dry vermouth** |
| 2½ | shot(s) | **Tanqueray London dry gin** |

Comment: A Dry Martini garnished with two olives.

FREDDY FUDPUCKER

Glass: Collins
Garnish: Orange slice
Method: SHAKE all ingredients with ice and strain into ice-filled glass.

2	shot(s)	**Don Julio reposado tequila**
3½	shot(s)	**Freshly squeezed orange juice**
½	shot(s)	**Galliano L'Autentico liqueur**

Variant: Harvey Wallbanger
Comment: A Harvey Wallbanger made with tequila in place of vodka. It's usual to build this drink and 'float' Galliano over the top. However, as the Galliano sinks anyway it is better shaken.

FREE TOWN

Glass: Martini
Garnish: Maraschino cherry
Method: SHAKE all ingredients with ice and fine strain into chilled glass.

2	shot(s)	**Bacardi Superior rum**
1	shot(s)	**Warre's Otima tawny port**
½	shot(s)	**Sugar syrup** (2 sugar to 1 water)
2	dashes	**Peychaud's aromatic bitters**

Origin: Created in 2004 by Alexandra Fiot at Lonsdale, London, England.
Comment: Great for sipping after dinner.

FRENCH 75 UPDATED #8

Glass: Flute
Garnish: Lemon zest twist (knot)
Method: SHAKE first 3 ingredients with ice and strain into chilled glass. **TOP** with champagne.

1½	shot(s)	**Tanqueray London dry gin**
½	shot(s)	**Freshly squeezed lemon juice**
¼	shot(s)	**Sugar syrup** (2 sugar to 1 water)
Top up with		**Perrier Jouet brut champagne**

Comment: Fresh, sherbet, clean, sophisticated - very drinkable and hasn't dated.
Origin: Legend has it that the drink was created by Harry MacElhone at his Harry's American Bar, Paris, in 1925 and was named after the 75mm Howitzer field gun used by the French army during the First World War (1914 to 1918). However, like other drinks in the first (1919) edition of Harry's own book, 'The ABC of Mixing Drinks', he credits the drink to Macgarry of Buck's Club, London, England.

However, its creation is now commonly attributed to the USA during the Prohibition era (1920-1933). Although the Howitzer was mounted on American tanks my issues with the American origin theory are that the Great War was well over by the time Prohibition started and I question whether an American, now or then, would name a drink after a metric measurement. Being a Brit, I favour The French 75 being an English drink that gained in popularity in France during the Prohibition era and found its way to the US with returning officers.

FRENCH 76

Glass: Flute
Garnish: Maraschino cherry
Method: SHAKE first 3 ingredients with ice and strain into chilled glass. **TOP** with champagne.

1	shot(s)	**Ketel One vodka**
½	shot(s)	**Freshly squeezed lemon juice**
¼	shot(s)	**Sugar syrup** (2 sugar to 1 water)
Top up with		**Perrier Jouet but champagne**

Variant: Diamond Fizz
Comment: A Vodka Sour topped with champagne. Works well.

FRENCH 77

Glass: Flute
Garnish: Lemon zest twist
Method: POUR first 2 ingredients into chilled glass, and **TOP** with champagne.

1	shot(s)	St-Germain elderflower liqueur
¼	shot(s)	Freshly squeezed lemon juice
Top up with		Perrier Jouet brut champagne

Origin: I created this twist on the classic French 75 in 2006.
Comment: Elderflower liqueur adds flavour to champagne while a splash of lemon juice balances the sweetness.

FRENCH APPLE MARTINI

Glass: Martini
Garnish: Float wafer thin apple slice
Method: SHAKE all ingredients with ice and fine strain into chilled glass.

¾	shot(s)	Ketel One vodka
¾	shot(s)	Apple flavoured vodka
1	shot(s)	St-Germain elderflower liqueur
¼	shot(s)	Noilly Prat dry vermouth

Origin: Created in 2006 by Yours Truly (Simon Difford).
Comment: Dry, subtle apple with a delicate hint of elderflower.

FRENCH BISON-TINI

Glass: Martini
Garnish: Raspberries on stick
Method: SHAKE all ingredients with ice and fine strain into chilled glass.

2	shot(s)	Zubrówka bison vodka
2	shot(s)	Pressed pineapple juice
¼	shot(s)	Chambord black raspberry liqueur

Comment: A French Martini with the distinctive taste of Zubrówka.

FRENCH CONNECTION NEW #8

Glass: Old-fashioned
Garnish: Lemon zest twist
Method: STIR all ingredients with ice and strain into ice-filled glass.

| 2 | shot(s) | Courvoisier V.S.O.P. cognac |
| 1 | shot(s) | Luxardo Amaretto di Saschira |

Comment: The apricot and almond notes in amaretto combine perfectly with cognac in this simple drink.

FRENCH DAIQUIRI

Glass: Martini
Garnish: Lime wedge on rim
Method: SHAKE all ingredients with ice and fine strain into chilled glass.

2	shot(s)	Bacardi Superior rum
1	shot(s)	Chambord black raspberry liqueur
½	shot(s)	Freshly squeezed lime juice
¾	shot(s)	Chilled mineral water (omit if wet ice)

Comment: A classic Daiquiri with a hint of berry fruit.

FRENCH DAISY

Glass: Martini (champagne saucer)
Garnish: Lemon zest twist
Method: SHAKE first 4 ingredients with ice and fine strain into chilled glass. **TOP** with champagne.

1	shot(s)	Courvoisier V.S.O.P. cognac
½	shot(s)	Crème de cassis liqueur
½	shot(s)	St-Germain elderflower liqueur
1	shot(s)	Freshly squeezed lemon juice
Top up with		Perrier Jouet brut champagne

Origin: Adapted from a drink created by Wayne Collins, London, England.
Comment: Rich blackcurrant with hints of elderflower, citrus and champagne. Slightly sweet.

FRENCH KISS #1

Glass: Martini
Garnish: Star anise
Method: SHAKE first 3 ingredients with ice and fine strain into chilled glass. **POUR** grenadine into centre of drink. (It should sink.)

1	shot(s)	Ketel One vodka
¾	shot(s)	Pernod anis
2	shot(s)	Freshly squeezed orange juice
⅛	shot(s)	Pomegranate (grenadine) syrup

Comment: Looks like a Tequila Sunrise but tastes of anis and orange.

FRENCH KISS #2

Glass: Martini
Garnish: Raspberries on stick
Method: SHAKE all ingredients with ice and fine strain into chilled glass.

1½	shot(s)	Ketel One vodka
½	shot(s)	Chambord black raspberry liqueur
½	shot(s)	White crème de cacao liqueur
½	shot(s)	Milk
½	shot(s)	Double (heavy) cream

Comment: Smooth creamy chocolate and raspberry.

FRENCH LEAVE

Glass: Collins
Garnish: Orange slice
Method: SHAKE all ingredients with ice and strain into ice-filled glass.

1½	shot(s)	**Ketel One vodka**
½	shot(s)	**Pernod anis**
3½	shot(s)	**Freshly squeezed orange juice**

Comment: An easy drinking blend of vodka, anis and orange juice.

FRENCH MARTINI UPDATED #8

Glass: Martini
Garnish: Pineapple wedge on rim
Method: SHAKE all ingredients with ice and fine strain into chilled glass.

2	shot(s)	**Ketel One vodka**
1½	shot(s)	**Pressed pineapple juice**
½	shot(s)	**Chambord black raspberry liqueur**

AKA: Flirtini
Comment: Raspberry and pineapple laced with vodka. Easy drinking and very fruity.

FRENCH MOJITO

Glass: Collins
Garnish: Raspberry & mint sprig
Method: Lightly **MUDDLE** mint in base of glass (just to bruise). Add rum, liqueur and lime juice. Half fill glass with crushed ice and **CHURN** (stir) with bar spoon. Continue to add crushed ice and churn until drink is level with glass rim.

12	fresh	**Mint leaves**
2	shot(s)	**Bacardi Superior rum**
½	shot(s)	**Chambord black raspberry liqueur**
1	shot(s)	**Freshly squeezed lime juice**
¼	shot(s)	**Sugar syrup** (2 sugar to 1 water)

Comment: A classic Mojito with a hint of berry fruit.

FRENCH MONKEY

Glass: Old-fashioned
Garnish: Lemon zest twist
Method: SHAKE first 3 ingredients with ice and strain into ice-filled glass. **TOP** with just a splash of soda.

2	shot(s)	**Johnnie Walker Scotch whisky**
½	shot(s)	**St-Germain elderflower liqueur**
½	shot(s)	**Pressed apple juice**
1	shot(s)	**Soda water** (club soda)

Origin: Created in 2006 for my French friend, Xavier Padovani.
Comment: Apple, Scotch and elderflower, honeyed and floral.

FRENCH MULE

Glass: Collins
Garnish: Sprig of mint
Method: SHAKE first 4 ingredients with ice and strain into ice-filled glass. **TOP** with ginger beer, stir and serve with straws.

2	shot(s)	**Courvoisier V.S.O.P. cognac**
1	shot(s)	**Freshly squeezed lime juice**
1	shot(s)	**Sugar syrup** (2 sugar to 1 water)
3	dashes	**Angostura aromatic bitters**
Top up with		**Ginger beer**

Comment: This French answer to the vodka based Moscow Mule uses cognac to make a more flavoursome, long, refreshing drink.

FRENCH SHERBET

Glass: Martini
Garnish: Orange zest twist
Method: SHAKE all ingredients with ice and fine strain into chilled glass.

1	shot(s)	**Tanqueray London dry gin**
1	shot(s)	**Cointreau triple sec**
1	shot(s)	**Freshly squeezed orange juice**
1	shot(s)	**Freshly squeezed lime juice**

Comment: Not particularly French or sherbety – just a fresh orange wake-up call.

FRENCH SPRING PUNCH UPDATED #8

Glass: Sling
Garnish: Strawberry
Method: SHAKE first 4 ingredients with ice and strain into ice-filled glass. **TOP** with champagne and serve with straws.

1	shot(s)	**Courvoisier V.S.O.P. cognac**
½	shot(s)	**Crème de framboise liqueur**
½	shot(s)	**Freshly squeezed lemon juice**
¼	shot(s)	**Sugar syrup** (2 sugar to 1 water)
Top up with		**Perrier Jouet brut champagne**

Origin: Created by Dick Bradsell and Rodolphe Sorel at Match EC1, London, England, during the late 1990s.
Comment: Not as popular as the Russian Spring Punch but still a modern day London classic.

FRENCH TEAR #1

Glass: Martini
Garnish: Pineapple wedge on rim
Method: SHAKE all ingredients with ice and fine strain into chilled glass.

1¾	shot(s)	**Sailor Jerry spiced rum**
¾	shot(s)	**Grand Marnier liqueur**
2	shot(s)	**Pressed pineapple juice**

Origin: Discovered in 2000 at Quo Vadis, London, England.
Comment: Light, flavoursome, easy drinking. Altogether very gluggable.

FRENCH MULE

FRENCH WHISKY SOUR

Glass: Old-fashioned
Garnish: Lemon slice & cherry on stick (sail)
Method: SHAKE all ingredients with ice and strain into ice-filled glass.

2	shot(s)	**Johnnie Walker Scotch whisky**
½	shot(s)	**Ricard pastis**
1	shot(s)	**Freshly squeezed lemon juice**
½	shot(s)	**Sugar syrup** (2 sugar to 1 water)
½	fresh	**Egg white**
3	dashes	**Angostura aromatic bitters**

Comment: Pastis adds a pleasing hint of anise and liquorice to the classic Whisky Sour.
Origin: Created in 2006 by Simon Difford and inspired by Tony Conigliaro's Liquorice Whisky Sour.

FRESCA NOVA UPDATED #8

Glass: Flute
Garnish: Quarter orange slice
Method: SHAKE first 4 ingredients with ice and fine strain into chilled glass. Slowly **TOP** with champagne.

1½	shot(s)	**Grand Marnier liqueur**
¾	shot(s)	**Freshly squeezed orange juice**
¼	shot(s)	**Sugar syrup** (2 sugar to 1 water)
1	shot(s)	**Double (heavy) cream**
Top up with		**Perrier Jouet brut champagne**

Origin: Created by Jamie Terrell for Philip Holzberg at Vinexpo 1999.
Comment: Cream, orange and champagne work surprisingly well.

FRENCH ARTIST AND NOTABLE ALCOHOLIC HENRI DE TOULOUSE-LAUTREC CARRIED A VIAL OF ABSINTHE IN HIS WALKING STICK AT ALL TIMES.

FRISCO SOUR NEW #8

Glass: Old-fashioned
Garnish: Orange slice & cherry on stick (sail)
Method: SHAKE all ingredients and strain into ice-filled glass.

2	shot(s)	**Bulleit bourbon whiskey**
½	shot(s)	**Bénédictine D.O.M. liqueur**
½	shot(s)	**Freshly squeezed lemon juice**
¼	shot(s)	**Sugar syrup** (2 sugar to 1 water)
½	fresh	**Egg white**

Comment: A bourbon rich sour with monastic herbal notes.

FRESA BATIDA

Glass: Collins (8oz)
Garnish: Strawberry
Method: MUDDLE strawberries in base of shaker. Add other ingredients, **SHAKE** with ice and strain into glass filled with crushed ice.

7	fresh	**Strawberries** (hulled)
2½	shot(s)	**Leblon cachaça**
½	shot(s)	**Freshly squeezed lemon juice**
½	shot(s)	**Sugar syrup** (2 sugar to 1 water)

Origin: The Batida is a traditional Brazilian style of drink and 'Fresa' means strawberry in Portuguese, the official language of Brazil.
Comment: A long, very refreshing strawberry drink laced with cachaça.

FRIAR TUCK

Glass: Martini
Garnish: Dust with freshly ground nutmeg
Method: SHAKE all ingredients with ice and fine strain into chilled glass.

1	shot(s)	**Frangelico hazelnut liqueur**
1	shot(s)	**Brown crème de cacao liqueur**
1	shot(s)	**Double (heavy) cream**
1	shot(s)	**Milk**

Variant: With amaretto and ice cream.
Comment: Round, jolly and creamy with chocolate and hazelnut.

FRESCA

Glass: Martini
Garnish: Lemon zest twist
Method: SHAKE first 4 ingredients with ice and fine strain into chilled glass. **TOP** with lemonade.

1½	shot(s)	**Ketel One Citroen vodka**
½	shot(s)	**Chambord black raspberry liqueur**
1	shot(s)	**Freshly squeezed grapefruit juice**
½	shot(s)	**Freshly squeezed lemon juice**
Top up with		**Lemonade/Sprite/7-Up**

Comment: The sweet, fizzy topping is essential to lengthen and balance this drink.

FRIDA'S BROW

Glass: Martini
Garnish: Dust with cinnamon powder
Method: SHAKE all ingredients with ice and fine strain into chilled glass.

2	shot(s)	**Don Julio reposado tequila**
½	shot(s)	**White crème de cacao liqueur**
¼	shot(s)	**Pomegranate (grenadine) syrup**
½	shot(s)	**Double (heavy) cream**
½	shot(s)	**Milk**

Origin: Discovered in 2005 at Velvet Margarita Cantina, Los Angeles, USA.
Comment: Creamy, sweetened tequila with hints of chocolate.

FRENCH WHISKY SOUR

A
B
C
D
E
F
G
H
I
J
K
L
M
N
O
P
Q
R
S
T
U
V
W
X
Y
Z

FRISKY BISON

Glass: Martini
Garnish: Float apple slice
Method: Lightly **MUDDLE** mint in base of shaker (just to bruise). Add other ingredients, **SHAKE** with ice and fine strain into chilled glass.

7	fresh	**Mint leaves**
2	shot(s)	**Zubrówka bison vodka**
1	shot(s)	**Berentzen apple schnapps**
1	shot(s)	**Pressed apple juice**
½	shot(s)	**Freshly squeezed lime juice**
¼	shot(s)	**Sugar syrup** (2 sugar to 1 water)

Origin: Created by Tony Kerr in 1999 at Mash & Air in Manchester.
Comment: Sweet 'n' sour, fruity, minty and fresh.

FRISKY LEMONADE

Glass: Collins
Garnish: Lime wedge
Method: **POUR** ingredients into ice-filled glass and lightly stir.

2	shot(s)	**Lime flavoured vodka**
½	shot(s)	**Noilly Prat dry vermouth**
Top up with		**Lemonade/Sprite/7-Up**

Origin: Created by Aaron Rudd in 2002 at Home, London, England.
Comment: Reminiscent of alcoholic lemon barley water.

FROTH BLOWER COCKTAIL

Glass: Martini
Garnish: Lemon zest twist (spray & discard)
Method: **SHAKE** all ingredients well with ice and fine strain into chilled glass.

2	shot(s)	**Tanqueray London dry gin**
¼	shot(s)	**Pomegranate (grenadine) syrup**
1	fresh	**Egg white**

Origin: Adapted from Harry Craddock's 1930 'The Savoy Cocktail Book'.
Comment: Salmon-pink and very frothy but surprisingly complex and tasty.

FROUPE COCKTAIL

Glass: Martini
Garnish: Orange zest twist
Method: **STIR** all ingredients with ice and strain into chilled glass.

1½	shot(s)	**Courvoisier V.S.O.P. cognac**
1½	shot(s)	**Martini Rosso sweet vermouth**
¼	shot(s)	**Bénédictine D.O.M. liqueur**

Origin: Adapted from Harry Craddock's 1930 'The Savoy Cocktail Book'.
Comment: A bittersweet, herbal old-school drink that's in line for rediscovery.

FROZEN MARGARITA

Glass: Martini
Garnish: Maraschino cherry
Method: **BLEND** all ingredients with 6oz scoop of crushed ice. Serve heaped in the glass and with straws.

1½	shot(s)	**Don Julio reposado tequila**
¾	shot(s)	**Cointreau triple sec**
¾	shot(s)	**Freshly squeezed lime juice**
½	shot(s)	**Sugar syrup** (2 sugar to 1 water)

Variant: With fruit and/or fruit liqueurs.
Comment: Citrus freshness with the subtle agave of tequila served frozen.

FRU FRU

Glass: Flute
Garnish: Split strawberry
Method: **SHAKE** first 3 ingredients with ice and strain into glass. **TOP** with champagne.

¾	shot(s)	**Passoã passion fruit liqueur**
¾	shot(s)	**Crème de fraise de bois liqueur**
¾	shot(s)	**Freshly squeezed grapefruit juice**
Top up with		**Perrier Jouet brut champagne**

Comment: Dry, bitter grapefruit complimented by passion fruit and strawberry.

FRUIT & NUT CHOCOLATE MARTINI

Glass: Martini
Garnish: Crumbled Cadbury's Flake bar
Method: **SHAKE** all ingredients with ice and fine strain into chilled glass.

1	shot(s)	**Raspberry flavoured vodka**
½	shot(s)	**Frangelico hazelnut liqueur**
½	shot(s)	**White crème de cacao liqueur**
½	shot(s)	**Chambord black raspberry liqueur**
½	shot(s)	**Baileys Irish cream liqueur**
¾	shot(s)	**Double (heavy) cream**
¾	shot(s)	**Milk**

Comment: Naughty but nice – one for confectionery lovers.

FRUIT & NUT MARTINI

Glass: Martini
Garnish: Orange zest twist & almond flakes
Method: **SHAKE** all ingredients with ice and fine strain into chilled glass.

1	shot(s)	**Vanilla-infused Ketel One vodka**
1	shot(s)	**Frangelico hazelnut liqueur**
½	shot(s)	**Noé Pedro Ximénez sherry**
1	shot(s)	**Ocean Spray cranberry juice**
½	shot(s)	**Freshly squeezed orange juice**

Origin: Created by Yours Truly (Simon Difford) in 2004.
Comment: A rich Christmas pudding of a Martini.

FRUIT PASTEL

Glass: Martini
Garnish: Fruit Pastille sweets
Method: SHAKE all ingredients with ice and fine strain into chilled glass.

1½	shot(s)	**Ketel One Citroen vodka**
½	shot(s)	**Parfait Amour liqueur**
½	shot(s)	**Berentzen apple schnapps**
¼	shot(s)	**Freshly squeezed lime juice**

Comment: Tastes distinctly like a Fruit Pastille sweet.

FRUIT SALAD

Glass: Sling
Garnish: Fruit Salad chewy sweet or banana slice
Method: SHAKE all ingredients with ice and strain into ice-filled glass.

2	shot(s)	**Ketel One vodka**
½	shot(s)	**Crème de banane liqueur**
2½	shot(s)	**Freshly squeezed orange juice**
½	shot(s)	**Galliano L'Autentico liqueur**
¼	shot(s)	**Pomegranate (grenadine) syrup**

Comment: This variation on the Harvey Wallbanger tastes like Fruit Salad 'penny chew' sweets.

FRUIT SOUR UPDATED #8

Glass: Old-fashioned
Garnish: Lemon zest twist
Method: SHAKE all ingredients with ice and strain into ice-filled glass.

1	shot(s)	**Bulleit bourbon whiskey**
1	shot(s)	**Cointreau triple sec**
1	shot(s)	**Freshly squeezed lemon juice**
½	fresh	**Egg white**

Comment: An orange influenced, sweet and sour whiskey cocktail.

FRUITS OF THE FOREST

Glass: Martini
Garnish: Rasberries on stick
Method: SHAKE first 5 ingredients with ice and fine strain into chilled glass. **POUR** Chambord into the centre of the drink: it should sink to the bottom.

2	shot(s)	**Zubrówka bison vodka**
½	shot(s)	**St-Germain elderflower liqueur**
1	shot(s)	**Freshly squeezed orange juice**
½	shot(s)	**Freshly squeezed lime juice**
½	fresh	**Egg white**
¼	shot(s)	**Chambord black raspberry liqueur**

Origin: Adapted from a drink created in 2004 by Stuart Barnett at TGI Friday's, Reading, England.
Comment: Grassy, floral, citrus and smooth, but look out for the fruity bottom.

FRUIT TREE DAIQUIRI UPDATED #8

Glass: Martini
Garnish: Half grapefruit wedge & cherry
Method: SHAKE all ingredients with ice and fine strain into chilled glass.

2	shot(s)	**Bacardi Superior rum**
¾	shot(s)	**Bols apricot brandy liqueur**
¾	shot(s)	**Freshly squeezed grapefruit juice**
¾	shot(s)	**Freshly squeezed lime juice**
¼	shot(s)	**Maraschino syrup** (from cherry jar)
½	shot(s)	**Chilled mineral water** (omit if wet ice)

Comment: A restrained Papa Doble with apricot liqueur.

FUEGO MANZANA NO.2

Glass: Martini
Garnish: Small red chilli on rim
Method: MUDDLE chilli in base of shaker. Add other ingredients, **SHAKE** with ice and fine strain into chilled glass.

1	inch	**Fresh red chilli** (deseeded & chopped)
2	shot(s)	**Don Julio reposado tequila**
½	shot(s)	**Berentzen apple schnapps**
1	shot(s)	**Pressed apple juice**
½	shot(s)	**Freshly squeezed lime juice**
⅛	shot(s)	**Sugar syrup** (2 sugar to 1 water)

Origin: Created by Danny Smith at Che, London, England, initially using rum instead of tequila. 'Fuego Manzana' is Spanish for 'Fire Apple'.
Comment: A hint of chilli heat adds interest to an Apple Margarita, creating a full flavoured contemporary classic.

'WHEN YOU CAN'T WALK TO A GREAT PUB, THIS COUNTRY ISN'T WORTH LIVING IN ANY MORE.'
ANDREW JEFFORD, BBC RADIO 4, 7 JULY 2001

FULL CIRCLE

Glass: Collins
Garnish: Pineapple wedge on rim
Method: SHAKE all ingredients with ice and strain into ice-filled glass.

3	shot(s)	**POM Wonderful pomegranate juice**
2	shot(s)	**Tanqueray London dry gin**
¾	shot(s)	**Pressed pineapple juice**

Origin: Adapted from a drink discovered in 2004 at Mandarin Oriental, New York City, USA. The name is a reference to the bar's location - Columbus Circle, where the world's first one-way rotary system (roundabout) was implemented in 1904.
Comment: Fruity and easy drinking, yet with complexity from the gin.

●●●●○

FULL MONTE NEW #8

Glass: Sling
Garnish: Lemon slice
Method: SHAKE first 8 ingredients with ice and strain into ice-filled glass. **TOP** with champagne, lightly stir and serve with straws.

½	shot(s)	**Bacardi Superior rum**
½	shot(s)	**Tanqueray London dry gin**
½	shot(s)	**Ketel One vodka**
½	shot(s)	**Don Julio blanco tequila**
½	shot(s)	**Luxardo maraschino liqueur**
1	shot(s)	**Freshly squeezed lemon juice**
¼	shot(s)	**Sugar syrup** (2 sugar to 1 water)
2	dashes	**Angostura aromatic bitters**
Top up with		**Perrier Jouet brut champagne**

Variant: Beverly Hills Iced Tea
Comment: Champagne replaces cola and maraschino liqueur replaces triple sec in this sophisticated adaptation of a Long Island Iced Tea.
Origin: Created by Audrey Saunders at Pegu Club, New York City, USA.

●●●●○

FU MANCHU DAIQUIRI

Glass: Martini
Garnish: Pineapple wedge on rim
Method: SHAKE all ingredients with ice and fine strain into chilled glass.

2	shot(s)	**Bacardi Superior rum**
1	shot(s)	**Freshly squeezed lime juice**
½	shot(s)	**Sugar syrup** (2 sugar to 1 water)
¼	shot(s)	**Cointreau triple sec**
¼	shot(s)	**Giffard Menthe Pastille liqueur**
¾	shot(s)	**Chilled mineral water** (omit if wet ice)

Origin: Adapted from a recipe by David Embury.
Comment: A natural Daiquiri with a refreshing, clean, citrussy, minty edge.

●●●●○○

FUMIGATOR FLIP NEW #8

Glass: Sour glass (or Martini/Coupette)
Garnish: Nutmeg & cherry
Method: WASH chilled glass with whisky (swirl to coat inside and shake to discard excess). **SHAKE** other ingredients with ice and fine strain into whisky coated chilled glass.

¼	shot(s)	**Lagavulin 16yo malt whisky**
2	shot(s)	**Zacapa aged rum**
1	shot(s)	**Heering cherry brandy liqueur**
⅛	shot(s)	**Sugar syrup** (2 sugar to 1 water)
½	shot(s)	**Double (heavy) cream**
1	fresh	**Egg yolk**

Origin: Created in 2008 by Julian de Feral at Bureau, London, England.
Comment: Subtle notes, smoky malt with rum and cherry, smoothed by egg and cream.

●●●●○

FUNKY MONKEY

Glass: Goblet (or coconut shell)
Garnish: Toasted coconut strips
Method: BLEND all ingredients with 12oz scoop of crushed ice and serve with straws.

1	shot(s)	**Bacardi Oro golden rum**
¾	shot(s)	**Crème de banane liqueur**
¾	shot(s)	**White crème de cacao liqueur**
1	shot(s)	**Coco López cream of coconut**
1	shot(s)	**Double (heavy) cream**
1	shot(s)	**Milk**
1	small	**Peeled banana**

Origin: Created in 1998 by Tony Abou-Ganim, Las Vegas, USA.
Comment: Be sure to use a ripe or even over-ripe banana in this tropical style drink.

●●●○○

FUZZY NAVEL

Glass: Collins
Garnish: Lemon slice
Method: SHAKE all ingredients with ice and strain into ice-filled glass.

2	shot(s)	**Peach Tree peach schnapps**
4	shot(s)	**Freshly squeezed orange juice**

Variant: Hairy Navel with the addition of a shot of vodka.
Origin: A not very well regarded but extremely well-known cocktail whose origins are lost.
Comment: The hairy version is a slightly more interesting, drier, less fluffy concoction. So why have a fluffy navel when you can have a hairy one?

●●●●○

G & TEA

Glass: Collins
Garnish: Lemon slice
Method: SHAKE first 3 ingredients with ice and strain into ice-filled glass. **TOP** with tonic water.

1½	shot(s)	**Tanqueray London dry gin**
1	shot(s)	**St-Germain elderflower liqueur**
1	shot(s)	**Cold English breakfast tea**
Top up with		**Tonic water**

Origin: Created in 2006 by Yours Truly (Simon Difford).
Comment: Dry, floral, long and refreshing.

●●●●○○

GALVANISED NAIL

Glass: Old-fashioned
Garnish: Lemon zest twist
Method: STIR all ingredients with ice and strain into ice-filled glass.

2	shot(s)	**Johnnie Walker Scotch whisky**
½	shot(s)	**Drambuie liqueur**
¼	shot(s)	**St-Germain elderflower liqueur**
½	shot(s)	**Pressed apple juice**
½	shot(s)	**Freshly squeezed lemon juice**

Origin: Created in 2003 by Yours Truly (Simon Difford), taking inspiration from the Rusty Nail.
Comment: A blend of Scotch and honeyed spice with lemon freshness plus hints of apple and elderflower.

GANSEVOORT FIZZ

Glass: Collins
Garnish: Lemon slice
Method: **SHAKE** first 4 ingredients with ice and strain into ice-filled glass. **TOP** with soda.

2	shot(s)	**Zacapa aged rum**
1	shot(s)	**Drambuie liqueur**
1	shot(s)	**Freshly squeezed lemon juice**
2	dashes	**Peychaud's aromatic bitters**
Top up with		**Soda water** (club soda)

Origin: Created for 5 Ninth in Manhattan and originally published in David Wondrich's 2005 'Killer Cocktails'.
Comment: A potent, flavoursome herbal cooler based on aged rum.

GARIBALDI

Glass: Collins
Garnish: Orange slice
Method: **POUR** Campari into ice-filled glass. **TOP** with orange juice, stir and serve with straws.

2	shot(s)	**Campari Bitter**
Top up with		**Freshly squeezed orange juice**

Origin: Appears on cocktail lists throughout Italy. Named after the famous revolutionary general who helped liberate and reunify Italy.
Comment: Reminiscent of red grapefruit juice.

GATOR BITE

Glass: Coupette
Garnish: Salt rim
Method: **SHAKE** all ingredients with ice and fine strain into chilled glass.

1	shot(s)	**Green Chartreuse liqueur**
1½	shot(s)	**Cointreau triple sec**
1	shot(s)	**Freshly squeezed lime juice**
¾	shot(s)	**Sugar syrup** (2 sugar to 1 water)

Comment: Looks like a Margarita, but instead of tequila features the unique taste of Chartreuse. Yup, it bites.

GAUGUIN

Glass: Old-fashioned
Garnish: Maraschino cherry
Method: **BLEND** all ingredients with 6oz crushed ice and serve with straws.

2	shot(s)	**Bacardi Superior rum**
½	shot(s)	**Freshly squeezed lime juice**
½	shot(s)	**Freshly squeezed lemon juice**
½	shot(s)	**Passion fruit syrup**

Comment: The passion fruit shines through in this drink, which is very much a frozen Daiquiri in style.

GE BLONDE

Glass: Martini
Garnish: Apple wedge
Method: **SHAKE** all ingredients with ice and fine strain into chilled glass.

1¾	shot(s)	**Johnnie Walker Scotch whisky**
1¼	shot(s)	**Sauvignon Blanc wine**
1	shot(s)	**Pressed apple juice**
½	shot(s)	**Sugar syrup** (2 sugar to 1 water)
¼	shot(s)	**Freshly squeezed lemon juice**

Origin: A combined effort by the staff of London's GE Club in January 2002, this was named by Linda, a waitress at the club who happens to be blonde. She claimed the name was inspired by the cocktail's straw colour.
Comment: This delicate drink demands freshly pressed apple juice and a flavoursome Scotch with subtle peat.

GEISHA MAR-TEA-KNEE

Glass: Martini
Garnish: Open tea pearl
Method: **SHAKE** all ingredients with ice and fine strain into chilled glass.

1½	shot(s)	**Tanqueray London dry gin**
¾	shot(s)	**Zen green tea liqueur**
1	shot(s)	**Cold jasmine tea**

Origin: Created in the USA in 2006.
Comment: Surprisingly fresh and light, this starts slightly sweet but finishes with refreshing bitter tannins. Tea pearls - hand-rolled balls of tea leaves - make a wonderful garnish.

GENTLE BREEZE (MOCKTAIL)

Glass: Collins
Garnish: Lime wedge
Method: **POUR** ingredients into ice-filled glass, stir and serve with straws.

4	shot(s)	**Ocean Spray cranberry juice**
2	shot(s)	**Freshy squeezed grapefruit juice**

Comment: A Seabreeze without the hard stuff.

GEORGETOWN PUNCH

Glass: Collins
Garnish: Pineapple wedge
Method: **SHAKE** all ingredients with ice and fine strain into ice-filled glass.

1	shot(s)	**Bacardi Superior rum**
¾	shot(s)	**Gosling's Black Seal rum**
1½	shot(s)	**Malibu coconut rum liqueur**
1	shot(s)	**Ocean Spray cranberry juice**
1	shot(s)	**Pressed pineapple juice**
¾	shot(s)	**Freshly squeezed lime juice**

Origin: Adapted from a drink discovered in 2005 at Degrees, Washington DC, USA.
Comment: A Tiki-style, fruity rum punch.

GEORGIA JULEP

Glass: Metal mug or Collins glass
Garnish: Mint sprig and slice of lemon
Method: Lightly **MUDDLE** (only to bruise) mint in base of shaker. Add other ingredients, **SHAKE** with ice and strain into chilled glass half filled with crushed ice. **CHURN** (stir) the drink using a bar spoon. Top up the glass with more crushed ice and churn again. Continue adding crushed ice and churning until the drink meets the rim of the glass then serve with long straws.

12	fresh	**Mint leaves**
2½	shot(s)	**Bulleit bourbon whiskey**
1	shot(s)	**Peach Tree peach schnapps**
⅛	shot(s)	**Sugar syrup** (2 sugar to 1 water)
3	dashes	**Angostura aromatic bitters**

Origin: This classic was originally made with peach brandy in place of peach liqueur. It is also sometimes made with apricot brandy.
Comment: Bourbon, peach and mint are flavours that combine harmoniously.

> 'I HAVE MADE AN IMPORTANT DISCOVERY... THAT ALCOHOL, TAKEN IN SUFFICIENT QUANTITIES, PRODUCES ALL THE EFFECT OF INTOXICATION.'
> OSCAR WILDE

GIBSON UPDATED #8

Glass: Martini
Garnish: Two chilled cocktail onions on stick
Method: **STIR** vermouth with ice in a mixing glass. Strain and discard excess vermouth to leave only a coating on the ice. **POUR** gin into mixing glass containing coated ice and **STIR**. Finally strain into chilled glass.

½	shot(s)	**Noilly Prat dry vermouth**
2½	shot(s)	**Tanqueray London dry gin**

Origin: Today a Gibson is a Dry Martini served with two onions. Charles Dana Gibson produced hugely popular pen-and-ink drawings between the 1890s and 1930s. His illustrations of girls were as iconic as modern-day supermodels, and it is said this drink was named after the well-endowed Gibson Girls - hence the two onions.

However, a cocktail book published in 1917 includes a Martini-like drink named Gibson but without the onions, and a separate Onion cocktail which we might today call a Gibson. Gibson was a member of New York's The Players' club and a bartender there by the name of Charley Connolly is credited for at least adding the garnish, if not actually creating the drink.
Comment: A classic Dry Martini with cocktail onions in place of an olive or twist.

GIMLET #1 UPDATED #8

Glass: Martini
Garnish: Lime wedge or cherry
Method: **STIR** all ingredients with ice and strain into chilled glass.

2½	shot(s)	**Tanqueray London dry gin**
¾	shot(s)	**Rose's lime cordial**

Variant: Other spirits, particularly vodka, may be substituted for gin.
Origin: In 1747, James Lind, a Scottish surgeon, discovered that consumption of citrus fruits helped prevent scurvy, one of the most common illnesses on board ship. (We now understand that scurvy is caused by a Vitamin C deficiency and that it is the vitamins in citrus fruit which help ward off the condition.) In 1867, the Merchant Shipping Act made it mandatory for all British ships to carry rations of lime juice for the crew.

Lauchlin Rose, the owner of a shipyard in Leith, Scotland, had been working to solve the problem of how to keep citrus juice fresh for months on board ship. In 1867 he patented a process for preserving fruit juice without alcohol. To give his product wider appeal he sweetened the mixture, packaged it in an attractive bottle and named it 'Rose's Lime Cordial'.

Once the benefits of drinking lime juice became more broadly known, British sailors consumed so much of the stuff, often mixed with their daily ration of rum and water ('grog'), that they became affectionately known as 'Limeys'. Naval officers mixed Rose's lime cordial with gin to make Gimlets.

A 'gimlet' was originally the name of a small tool used to tap the barrels of spirits which were carried on British Navy ships: this could be the origin of the drink's name. Another story cites a naval doctor, Rear-Admiral Sir Thomas Desmond Gimlette (1857-1943), who is said to have mixed gin with lime 'to help the medicine go down'. Although this is a credible story it is not substantiated in his obituary in The Times, 6 October 1943.
Comment: A simple blend of gin and sweet lime.

GIMLET #2 (SCHUMANN'S RECIPE)

Glass: Martini
Garnish: Lime wedge or cherry
Method: **SHAKE** all ingredients with ice and fine strain into chilled glass.

2½	shot(s)	**Tanqueray London dry gin**
¼	shot(s)	**Freshly squeezed lime juice**
1¼	shot(s)	**Rose's lime cordial**

Origin: A shaken twist on an already established drink by the famous bartender and cocktail author Charles Schumann of Munich, Germany.
Comment: Generously laced with gin and wonderfully tart.

GIN & FRENCH NEW #8

Glass: Old-fashioned
Garnish: Lemon slice
Method: **STIR** all ingredients with ice and strain into ice-filled glass.

2	shot(s)	**Tanqueray London dry gin**
2	shot(s)	**Noilly Prat dry vermouth**

Origin: Traditionally Italian vermouth was sweet while French vermouth was dry. Hence this drink is simply gin and dry vermouth.
Comment: Bone dry but botanically rich.

GIMLET

GIN & IT UPDATED #8

●●●●○○

Glass: Old-fashioned
Garnish: Orange slice
Method: STIR all ingredients with ice and strain into ice-filled glass.

2	shot(s)	**Tanqueray London dry gin**
2	shot(s)	**Martini Rosso sweet vermouth**
1	dash	**Angostura aromatic bitters**

Origin: The name is short for 'Gin and Italian', a reference to the sweet vermouth, which was traditionally Italian while French vermouth was dry. In his 'Craft of the Cocktail', Dale DeGroff states that this drink was originally known as a 'Sweet Martini' and as such was a popular drink during the 1880s and 1890s at the Hoffman House and other New York bars. Later it became known as "Gin & Italian", until during Prohibition it was shortened to "Gin & It".
Comment: Simple but tasty combination of botanicals, wine and spirit.

'TIME IS NEVER WASTED WHEN YOU'RE WASTED ALL THE TIME.'
CATHERINE ZANDONELLA

GIN & JUICE NEW #8

●●●○○

Glass: Collins
Garnish: Orange slice
Method: SHAKE all ingredients with ice and strain into ice-filled glass.

2	shot(s)	**Tanqueray London dry gin**
2½	shot(s)	**Freshly squeezed orange juice**
1½	shot(s)	**Freshly squeezed grapefruit juice**

Origin: Possibly the inspiration behind the Top 10 single 'Gin and Juice' by rapper Snoop Doggy Dogg, from his debut album Doggystyle.
Comment: Gin and fruit juice. OK, but really nothing to sing about.

GIN & SIN UPDATED #8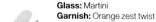

●●●●○

Glass: Martini
Garnish: Orange zest twist
Method: SHAKE all ingredients with ice and fine strain into chilled glass.

2	shot(s)	**Tanqueray London dry gin**
1	shot(s)	**Freshly squeezed orange juice**
½	shot(s)	**Freshly squeezed lemon juice**
¼	shot(s)	**Pomegranate (grenadine) syrup**
½	shot(s)	**Chilled mineral water** (omit if wet ice)

Comment: This is one of those drinks that benefits from a little dilution to prevent the citrus and gin becoming too aggressive.

GIN & TONIC

●●●●●○

Glass: Collins
Garnish: Run lime wedge around rim of glass. Squeeze and drop into drink.
Method: POUR ingredients into ice-filled glass, stir and serve without straws.

| 2 | shot(s) | **Tanqueray London dry gin** |
| Top up with | | **Tonic water** |

Origin: The precise origin of the G&T is lost in the mists of time. Gin (or at least a grain based juniper spirit) was drunk for medicinal reasons from the 1600s onwards. Quinine, the pungent bark extract which gives tonic its distinctive bitterness, had been used against malaria for even longer. The first known quinine-based tonics were marketed during the 1850s.

The popularity of tonic in the British colonies, especially India, is clear. Schweppes launched their first carbonated quinine tonic in 1870, branding it Indian Tonic Water. The ladies and gentlemen of the Raj also drank phenomenal quantities of gin. It is therefore accepted that gin and tonic emerged in India during the second half of the nineteenth century and was drunk partly to ward off malaria.
Comment: This might not be considered a cocktail by most, but it is actually classified as a Highball. Whatever, it's one of the simplest and best drinks ever devised, hence its lasting popularity.

GIN ATOMIC

●●●●○○

Glass: Collins
Garnish: Lemon zest twist
Method: Lightly **MUDDLE** (just to bruise) basil in base of shaker. Add other ingredients apart from tonic, **SHAKE** with ice and strain into ice-filled glass. **TOP** with tonic water and serve with straws.

3	fresh	**Basil leaves**
2	shot(s)	**Tanqueray London dry gin**
1	shot(s)	**St-Germain elderflower liqueur**
½	shot(s)	**Freshly squeezed lemon juice**
2	dashes	**Fee Brothers lemon bitters** (optional)
Top up with		**Tonic water**

Origin: Created in 2007 by Brendan Mainini at The Ambassador Bar, San Francisco, USA.
Comment: A nuclear gin and tonic – or at least, one that simply radiates flavour.

GIN BERRY

●●●●○○

Glass: Martini
Garnish: Lime zest twist
Method: SHAKE all ingredients with ice and fine strain into chilled glass.

1½	shot(s)	**Tanqueray London dry gin**
½	shot(s)	**Chambord black raspberry liqueur**
½	shot(s)	**Freshly squeezed lime juice**
1½	shot(s)	**Ocean Spray cranberry juice**

Origin: Adapted from a drink created in 2004 by Chris Lacey, UK.
Comment: Berry flavours combine harmoniously with gin – what an appropriate name.

GIN COCKTAIL

Glass: Martini
Garnish: Lemon peel twist
Method: STIR all ingredients with ice and strain into chilled glass.

2½	shot(s)	**Tanqueray London dry gin**
⅛	shot(s)	**Cointreau triple sec**
⅛	shot(s)	**Sugar syrup** (2 sugar to 1 water)
2	dashes	**Angostura aromatic bitters**

Origin: A classic that was already well-established when Jerry Thomas recorded his version of the recipe in 1862.
Comment: A pink gin made more approachable by a splash of triple sec and sugar syrup.

GIN DAISY

Glass: Goblet
Garnish: Maraschino cherry
Method: SHAKE all ingredients with ice and strain into glass filled with crushed ice. **CHURN** (stir) drink with ice and serve with straws.

2½	shot(s)	**Tanqueray London dry gin**
¼	shot(s)	**Yellow Chartreuse liqueur**
¼	shot(s)	**Pomegranate (grenadine) syrup**
¼	shot(s)	**Freshly squeezed lemon juice**

Origin: A classic Daisy variation.
Comment: If correctly made this serious, gin dominated cocktail should be blush, not pink.

GIN DAISY #2 (JERRY THOMAS STYLE) NEW #8

Glass: Martini
Garnish: Seasonal berries
Method: SHAKE all ingredients with ice and fine strain into chilled glass. **TOP** with a splash of soda from a siphon.

2	shot(s)	**Bokma oude genever**
½	shot(s)	**Grand Marnier liqueur**
¾	shot(s)	**Freshly squeezed lemon juice**
¼	shot(s)	**Sugar syrup** (2 sugar to 1 water)
1	splash	**Soda water** (from siphon)

Variation: Use almond (orgeat) syrup in place of sugar.
Origin: The origins of the Daisy are lost in time but the first written reference to it is in an 1866 novel called 'Gay Life in New York, or Fast Men and Grass Widows' by Henry Llewellyn Williams. This recipe is adapted from Jerry Thomas' 1876 'How to Mix Drinks'.
Comment: The rich style of genever combines wonderfully with orange liqueur in this balanced classic.

GIN DAISY #3 (MODERN LONG STYLE)

NEW #8

Glass: Collins
Garnish: Seasonal berries
Method: SHAKE first 3 ingredients with ice and strain into ice-filled glass. **TOP** with soda and serve with straws.

2	shot(s)	**Tanqueray London dry gin**
1	shot(s)	**Freshly squeezed lemon juice**
½	shot(s)	**Pomegranate (grenadine) syrup**
Top up with		**Soda water** (club soda)

Origin: Daisies can be served in a goblet filled with crushed ice, straight-up or as in this case in a Collins glass.
Comment: Fruit and botanicals served long and refreshing.

GIN FIX

Glass: Goblet
Garnish: Lemon slice
Method: SHAKE all ingredients with ice and strain into glass filled with crushed ice. **CHURN** (stir) drink with ice and serve with straws.

2	shot(s)	**Tanqueray London dry gin**
1	shot(s)	**Freshly squeezed lemon juice**
½	shot(s)	**Sugar syrup** (2 sugar to 1 water)

Origin: The Fix is an old classic that's very similar to the Daisy.
Comment: A Gin Sour served over crushed ice in a goblet.

GIN FIXED

Glass: Martini
Garnish: Lemon slice
Method: SHAKE all ingredients with ice and strain into glass filled with crushed ice. **CHURN** (stir) drink with ice and serve with straws.

2	shot(s)	**Tanqueray London dry gin**
¼	shot(s)	**Cointreau triple sec**
1	shot(s)	**Pressed pineapple juice**
½	shot(s)	**Freshly squeezed lemon juice**
¼	shot(s)	**Sugar syrup** (2 sugar to 1 water)

Comment: Sweet and sour with a spirity pineapple twang.

HOW TO MAKE SUGAR SYRUP

To make your own sugar syrup, gradually pour TWO cups of granulated sugar into a saucepan containing ONE cup of hot water. Stir as you pour and carry on stirring and simmering until the sugar is dissolved. Do not let the water even come close to boiling and only simmer for as long as it takes to dissolve the sugar. Allow syrup to cool and pour into an empty bottle. Ideally, you should finely strain your syrup into the bottle to remove any undissolved crystals which could otherwise encourage crystallisation. If kept in a refrigerator this mixture will last for a couple of months.

A
B
C
D
E
F
G
H
I
J
K
L
M
N
O
P
Q
R
S
T
U
V
W
X
Y
Z

ABSINTHE HAS NEVER BEEN BANNED IN THE UK.

GIN FIZZ UPDATED #8

●●●●○

Glass: Collins (8oz max)
Garnish: Half lemon slice & mint sprig
Method: **DRY SHAKE** first 3 ingredients with ice and strain into chilled glass (no ice in glass). **TOP** with soda.

2	shot(s)	**Old Tom gin**
1	shot(s)	**Freshly squeezed lemon juice**
½	shot(s)	**Sugar syrup** (2 sugar to 1 water)
Top up with		**Soda water** (from siphon)

Variants: With the addition of egg white this drink becomes a 'Silver Fizz'; with egg yolk it becomes a 'Golden Fizz'. A Royal Fizz includes one whole egg, a Diamond Fizz uses champagne instead of charged water, a Green Fizz has a dash of green crème de menthe and a Purple Fizz uses equal parts of sloe gin and grapefruit juice in place of gin and lemon juice.
Origin: A mid-19th century classic.
Comment: Everyone has heard of this clean, refreshing, long drink but few have actually tried it.

GIN GARDEN

●●●●○

Glass: Martini
Garnish: Float cucumber slice
Method: **MUDDLE** cucumber in base of shaker. Add other ingredients, **SHAKE** with ice and fine strain into chilled glass.

1	inch	**Cucumber** (chopped & peeled)
2	shot(s)	**Tanqueray London dry gin**
1	shot(s)	**St-Germain elderflower liqueur**
1	shot(s)	**Pressed apple juice**

Origin: Adapted from a drink that Daniel Warner at Zander and Tobias Blazquez Garcia at Steam collaborated on in London, England, in 2001.
Comment: A veritable English shrubbery with flowers, fruit and vegetables flourishing in harmony.

GIN GENIE

●●●●○

Glass: Collins
Garnish: Mint sprig
Method: Lightly **MUDDLE** mint in base of shaker (just to bruise). Add other ingredients, **SHAKE** with ice and strain into glass filled with crushed ice.

8	fresh	**Mint leaves**
1½	shot(s)	**Tanqueray London dry gin**
1	shot(s)	**Sloe gin liqueur**
1	shot(s)	**Freshly squeezed lemon juice**
½	shot(s)	**Sugar syrup** (2 sugar to 1 water)

Origin: Adapted from a drink created in 2002 by Wayne Collins, UK.
Comment: A fruit-led long drink for gin-loving Bowie fans.

GIN GIN NEW #8

●●●●○○

Glass: Old-fashioned
Garnish: Lemon zest twist
Method: **STIR** all ingredients with ice and strain into ice-filled glass.

2	shot(s)	**Tanqueray London dry gin**
1	shot(s)	**Stone's original green ginger wine**

Comment: Gin and ginger – as simple as that. Surprisingly good.

GIN GIN MULE

●●●●○

Glass: Collins
Garnish: Lime wedge
Method: **MUDDLE** ginger in base of shaker. Add next 4 ingredients, **SHAKE** with ice and fine strain into ice-filled glass. **TOP** with ginger beer.

2	slices	**Fresh root ginger** (thumbnail sized)
2	shot(s)	**Tanqueray London dry gin**
½	shot(s)	**Freshly squeezed lime juice**
¼	shot(s)	**Sugar syrup** (2 sugar to 1 water)
3	dashes	**Angostura aromatic bitters**
Top up with		**Ginger beer**

Origin: Adapted from a drink created in 2004 by Audrey Saunders, New York City, USA.
Comment: Fresh ginger and the herbal notes from gin make this much more than another take on the Moscow Mule.

GIN PUNCH #1 UPDATED #8

●●●●◐

Glass: Collins
Garnish: Lemon slice
Method: **SHAKE** all ingredients with ice and fine strain into chilled glass.

2	shot(s)	**Tanqueray London dry gin**
¾	shot(s)	**Freshly squeezed lemon juice**
¾	shot(s)	**Sugar syrup** (2 sugar to 1 water)
2	shot(s)	**Chilled mineral water**
1	dash	**Angostura aromatic bitters**

Origin: This is a version of the drink for which Limmer's Hotel in London was most famed: a Captain Gronow recalled it in his 1860s memoirs as one of the top, if filthy and seedy, sporting hangouts of 1814, thanks in part to its 'famous gin-punch'. A bartender named John Collins worked there later in the 19th century, and was famous enough to inspire a limerick, so many believe he created the Collins, which is similar to gin punch, although the drink is not named in the rhyme which goes as follows:

My name is John Collins,
 head waiter at Limmer's,
Corner of Conduit Street,
 Hanover Square,
My chief occupation is filling
 brimmers
For all the young gentlemen
 frequenters there.

Comment: Light and refreshing – akin to alcoholic real lemonade.

GIN PUNCH #2 NEW #8

Glass: Collins
Garnish: Seasonal berries
Method: SHAKE all ingredients with ice and strain into ice-filled glass. Serve with straws.

3	shot(s)	**Bokma oude genever**
½	shot(s)	**Freshly squeezed lemon juice**
¼	shot(s)	**Raspberry syrup** (1 juice to 1 water)
¼	shot(s)	**Sugar syrup** (2 sugar to 1 water)
¼	shot(s)	**Freshly squeezed orange juice**
⅛	shot(s)	**Pressed pineapple juice**
⅛	shot(s)	**Luxardo maraschino liqueur**
2	shot(s)	**Chilled mineral water**

Origin: Adapted from Hebert Asbury's 1928 reprint of Jerry Thomas' 1862 How to Mix Drink, or The Bon Vivant's Companion.
Comment: Easy on the palate yet incredibly complex. Linseed oil notes of genever shine through.

GIN SLING UPDATED #8

Glass: Sling (or Collins)
Garnish: Lemon slice
Method: SHAKE first 3 ingredients with ice and strain into ice-filled glass. **TOP** with soda and serve with straws.

2	shot(s)	**Tanqueray London dry gin**
½	shot(s)	**Freshly squeezed lemon juice**
¼	shot(s)	**Sugar syrup** (2 sugar to 1 water)
Top with		**Soda water** (club soda)

Origin: 'Sling' comes from the German word 'schlingen', meaning 'to swallow' and is a style of drink that was popular from the late 1700s.
Comment: Sugar balances the citrus juice, the spirit fortifies and the carbonate lengthens.

GIN SOUR UPDATED #8

Glass: Old-fashioned
Garnish: Lemon slice & cherry on stick (sail)
Method: SHAKE all ingredients with ice and strain into ice-filled glass.

2	shot(s)	**Tanqueray London dry gin**
1	shot(s)	**Freshly squeezed lemon juice**
½	shot(s)	**Sugar syrup** (2 sugar to 1 water)
½	fresh	**Egg white**
3	dashes	**Angostura aromatic bitters**

Comment: This 4:2:8 formula is a tad sourer than the classic sour proportions of 3:4:8: three quarter part of the sour ingredient (lemon juice), one part of the sweet ingredient (sugar syrup) and two parts of the strong ingredient (gin).

GINA UPDATED #8

Glass: Sling
Garnish: Berries on stick
Method: SHAKE first 3 ingredients with ice and strain into ice-filled glass. **TOP** with soda.

2	shot(s)	**Tanqueray London dry gin**
½	shot(s)	**Crème de cassis liqueur**
½	shot(s)	**Freshly squeezed lemon juice**
Top up with		**Soda water** (club soda)

AKA: Cassis Collins
Comment: The lemon and blackcurrant mask the character of the gin.

GINGER BEER DAIQUIRI (MOCKTAIL) NEW #8

Glass: Old-fashioned
Garnish: Lime wedge
Method: SHAKE all ingredients with ice and strain into ice-filled glass.

1	shot(s)	**Freshly squeezed lime juice**
½	shot(s)	**Sugar syrup** (2 sugar to 1 water)
2	shot(s)	**Ginger beer** (homemade)
2	dashes	**Angostura aromatic bitters***

*****Note:** Angostura aromatic bitters contain alcohol but in the finished drink the alcohol level is negligible.

Origin: Created in 2006 by Audrey Saunders, New York, USA.
Comment: Audrey, I love you but where's the rum?

GINGER & LEMONGRASS MARTINI

Glass: Martini
Garnish: Float thinly cut apple slice
Method: MUDDLE ginger and lemongrass in base of shaker. Add other ingredients and **STIR** until honey dissolves. **SHAKE** with ice and fine strain into chilled glass.

1	slice	**Fresh root ginger** (thumbnail sized)
½	stem	**Lemongrass** (chopped)
2	spoons	**Runny honey**
2	shot(s)	**Tanqueray London dry gin**
¼	shot(s)	**Noilly Prat dry vermouth**
¼	shot(s)	**Pressed apple juice**
¾	shot(s)	**Chilled mineral water** (omit if wet ice)

Origin: Created in 2005 by Yours Truly (Simon Difford).
Comment: Consider infusing the lemongrass in gin instead of muddling.

HOW TO MAKE SUGAR SYRUP

To make your own sugar syrup, gradually pour TWO cups of granulated sugar into a saucepan containing ONE cup of hot water. Stir as you pour and carry on stirring and simmering until the sugar is dissolved. Do not let the water even come close to boiling and only simmer for as long as it takes to dissolve the sugar. Allow syrup to cool and pour into an empty bottle. Ideally, you should finely strain your syrup into the bottle to remove any undissolved crystals which could otherwise encourage crystallisation. If kept in a refrigerator this mixture will last for a couple of months.

GIN-GER & TONIC

Glass: Collins
Garnish: Lime wedge
Method: MUDDLE ginger in base of shaker, add gin and sugar, **SHAKE** with ice and strain into ice-filled glass. **TOP** with tonic water.

2	slices	**Fresh root ginger** (thumbnail sized)
2	shot(s)	**Tanqueray London dry gin**
¼	shot(s)	**Sugar syrup** (2 sugar to 1 water)
Top up with		**Tonic water**

Comment: A dry, refreshing long drink for those that like their G&Ts gingered.

GINGER COSMO

Glass: Martini
Garnish: Slice of ginger on rim
Method: SHAKE all ingredients with ice and fine strain into chilled glass.

2	shot(s)	**Ketel One Citroen vodka**
¾	shot(s)	**Domaine de Canton ginger liqueur**
1¼	shot(s)	**Ocean Spray cranberry juice**
¼	shot(s)	**Freshly squeezed lime juice**
⅛	shot(s)	**Sugar syrup** (2 sugar to 1 water)

Origin: Emerged during 2002 in New York City.
Comment: Just what it says on the tin – your everyday Cosmo given extra vitality courtesy of a hint of ginger spice.

GINGER COSMOS

Glass: Collins
Garnish: Basil leaf
Method: MUDDLE ginger and basil in base of shaker. Add other ingredients, **SHAKE** with ice and fine strain into glass filled with crushed ice. Stir and serve with straws.

2	slices	**Fresh root ginger** (thumbnail sized)
5	fresh	**Basil leaves**
2	shot(s)	**Tanqueray London dry gin**
1½	shot(s)	**Pressed pineapple juice**
1½	shot(s)	**Pressed apple juice**
¼	shot(s)	**Freshly squeezed lime juice**
¼	shot(s)	**Sugar syrup** (2 sugar to 1 water)

Origin: Created in 2003 by Massimiliano Greco at Zander, London, England. 'Cosmos' is a reference to the botanical name for pineapple, Ananas comosus.
Comment: Warming ginger spice in a very cooling, fruity drink.

GINGER MARGARITA

Glass: Coupette
Garnish: Lime wedge on rim
Method: SHAKE all ingredients with ice and fine strain into chilled glass.

2	shot(s)	**Don Julio reposado tequila**
1	shot(s)	**Domaine de Canton ginger liqueur**
1	shot(s)	**Freshly squeezed lime juice**

Comment: A Margarita spiced with ginger.

GINGER MARTINI

Glass: Martini
Garnish: Brandy snap biscuit
Method: MUDDLE ginger in base of shaker. Add other ingredients, **SHAKE** with ice and fine strain into chilled glass.

2	slices	**Fresh root ginger** (thumbnail sized)
2	shot(s)	**Ketel One vodka**
¾	shot(s)	**Stone's original green ginger wine**
¾	shot(s)	**Pressed apple juice**
½	shot(s)	**Freshly squeezed lime juice**
¼	shot(s)	**Sugar syrup** (2 sugar to 1 water)

Origin: Discovered in 2003 at Hurricane Bar and Grill, Edinburgh, Scotland.
Comment: This Martini may be served chilled but its flavour is distinctly warming.

GINGER MOJITO

Glass: Collins
Garnish: Mint sprig
Method: MUDDLE ginger in base of shaker. Add mint and lightly **MUDDLE** (just to bruise). Add next 3 ingredients, **SHAKE** with ice and fine strain into glass filled with crushed ice. **TOP** with ginger ale.

3	slices	**Fresh root ginger** (thumbnail sized)
12	fresh	**Mint leaves**
2	shot(s)	**Bacardi Superior rum**
½	shot(s)	**Freshly squeezed lime juice**
½	shot(s)	**Sugar syrup** (2 sugar to 1 water)
Top up with		**Ginger ale**

Comment: A spiced variation on the classic Mojito.

GINGER NUT

Glass: Collins
Garnish: Lemon wedge
Method: POUR ingredients into ice-filled glass and stir.

1½	shot(s)	**Frangelico hazelnut liqueur**
1½	shot(s)	**Ketel One Citroen vodka**
Top up with		**Ginger beer**

Comment: A long, refreshing meld of strong flavours.

GINGER PUNCH

Glass: Collins
Garnish: Lime wedge
Method: MUDDLE ginger in base of shaker. Add honey and rum and **STIR** until honey is dissolved. Add lime juice and sugar, **SHAKE** with ice and fine strain into ice-filled glass. **TOP** with ginger ale.

2	slices	**Fresh root ginger** (thumbnail sized)
2	spoons	**Runny honey**
2½	shot(s)	**Bacardi Oro golden rum**
¾	shot(s)	**Freshly squeezed lime juice**
¼	shot(s)	**Sugar syrup** (2 sugar to 1 water)
Top up with		**Ginger ale**

Comment: A ginger spiced rum punch.

●●●●○

GINGER SNAP NEW #8

Glass: Collins
Garnish: Lemon zest twist
Method: SHAKE first 5 ingredients with ice and strain into an ice-filled glass. TOP with soda and serve with straws.

1½	shot(s)	**Tanqueray London dry gin**
½	shot(s)	**Domaine de Canton ginger liqueur**
½	shot(s)	**Cointreau triple sec**
½	shot(s)	**Freshly squeezed lemon juice**
1	dashes	**Angostura aromatic bitters**
Top up with		**Soda water** (club soda)

Comment: This balanced Gin Collins is sweetened by ginger and orange liqueurs.
Origin: Created in 2007 by Gary Regan, New York, USA.

●●●●○

GIN-GER TOM

Glass: Collins
Garnish: Lime squeeze & mint sprig
Method: MUDDLE ginger in base of shaker. Add other ingredients, SHAKE with ice and fine strain into ice-filled glass.

2	slices	**Fresh root ginger** (thumbnail sized)
2	shot(s)	**Tanqueray London dry gin**
1	shot(s)	**Freshly squeezed lime juice**
½	shot(s)	**Sugar syrup** (2 sugar to 1 water)
Top up with		**Soda water** (club soda)

Origin: Adapted from a drink created in 2003 by Jamie Terrell at Lab, London, England.
Comment: A Tom Collins with lime and ginger – very refreshing.

●●●●○

GINGERBREAD MARTINI

Glass: Martini
Garnish: Slice of root ginger
Method: SHAKE all ingredients with ice and fine strain into chilled glass.

1½	shot(s)	**Bulleit bourbon whiskey**
¾	shot(s)	**Teichenné butterscotch schnapps**
¾	shot(s)	**Stone's original green ginger wine**
2	shot(s)	**Pressed apple juice**

Origin: Created by Yours Truly (Simon Difford) in 2004.
Comment: Sticky, warming and spicy.

●●●●○

GINGERTINI

Glass: Martini
Garnish: Orange zest twist
Method: SHAKE all ingredients with ice and fine strain into chilled glass.

2	shot(s)	**Tanqueray London dry gin**
½	shot(s)	**Domaine de Canton ginger liqueur**
¼	shot(s)	**Noilly Prat dry vermouth**
¼	shot(s)	**Sugar syrup** (2 sugar to 1 water)
½	shot(s)	**Chilled mineral water** (omit if wet ice)

Origin: Created by Yours Truly (Simon Difford) in 2002.
Comment: A delicate Martini with a warming hint of ginger.

●●●●○

GIUSEPPE'S HABIT

Glass: Martini
Garnish: Star anise
Method: Spray the oils from 2 lemon zest twists into the cocktail shaker, wipe them around the rim of the glass and drop them into the shaker. Pour other ingredients into shaker. SHAKE with ice and fine strain into chilled glass.

2	twists	**Lemon zest**
1½	shot(s)	**Galliano L'Autentico liqueur**
¾	shot(s)	**Frangelico hazelnut liqueur**
¾	shot(s)	**Cointreau triple sec**
1¼	shot(s)	**Pressed apple juice**

Origin: Created in 2002 by Leon Stokes at Zinc Bar & Grill, Birmingham, England.
Comment: An intriguing drink that combines hazelnut, orange, apple, aniseed and peppermint.

●●●●○

GIVE ME A DIME

Glass: Martini
Garnish: Crumbled Cadbury's Flake bar
Method: SHAKE all ingredients with ice and fine strain into chilled glass.

1½	shot(s)	**White crème de cacao liqueur**
1½	shot(s)	**Teichenné butterscotch schnapps**
1½	shot(s)	**Double (heavy) cream**

Comment: Creamy, sweet and tasty.

●●●○○

GLAD EYE COCKTAIL

Glass: Martini
Garnish: Star anise
Method: SHAKE all ingredients with ice and fine strain into chilled glass.

1½	shot(s)	**La Fée Parisienne (68%) absinthe**
1	shot(s)	**Giffard Menthe Pastille liqueur**
1	shot(s)	**Chilled mineral water** (reduce if wet ice)

Origin: Adapted from Harry Craddock's 1930 'The Savoy Cocktail Book'.
Comment: This minty aniseed cocktail takes more than its colour from the green fairy.

●●●○○

GLASS TOWER

Glass: Collins
Method: SHAKE first 5 ingredients with ice and strain into ice-filled glass. TOP with lemonade and stir.

1	shot(s)	**Ketel One vodka**
1	shot(s)	**Bacardi Superior rum**
½	shot(s)	**Cointreau triple sec**
½	shot(s)	**Peach Tree peach schnapps**
¼	shot(s)	**Luxardo Sambuca dei Cesari**
Top up with		**Lemonade/Sprite/7-Up**

Comment: A heady, slightly sweet combination of spirits and liqueurs.

GLENN'S BRIDE

●●●●◐○

Glass: Martini
Garnish: Orange zest twist
Method: SHAKE all ingredients with ice and fine strain into chilled glass.

2	shot(s)	**Bulleit bourbon whiskey**
1	shot(s)	**St-Germain elderflower liqueur**
2	dashes	**Angostura aromatic bitters**
¼	shot(s)	**Rosewater**

Origin: Adapted from a drink created in 2005 by Julian Gibbs, England.
Comment: This serious, bourbon based cocktail ranks alongside the Sazerac in its aromatic complexity.

GLOOM CHASER COCKTAIL #1

●●●●◐○

Glass: Martini
Garnish: Orange zest twist
Method: SHAKE all ingredients with ice and fine strain into chilled glass.

¾	shot(s)	**Grand Marnier liqueur**
¾	shot(s)	**Cointreau triple sec**
1	shot(s)	**Freshly squeezed lemon juice**
¼	shot(s)	**Pomegranate (grenadine) syrup**
1	shot(s)	**Chilled mineral water** (reduce if wet ice)

Origin: Adapted from Harry Craddock's 1930 'The Savoy Cocktail Book'.
Comment: A sunny coloured drink for happy souls. And sweet orange and pomegranate soured with lemon would make anyone happy.

GLOOM CHASER COCKTAIL #2

●●●●◐○

Glass: Martini
Garnish: Berries on stick
Method: SHAKE all ingredients with ice and fine strain into chilled glass.

2	shot(s)	**Tanqueray London dry gin**
1	shot(s)	**Noilly Prat dry vermouth**
½	shot(s)	**La Fée Parisienne (68%) absinthe**
¼	shot(s)	**Pomegranate (grenadine) syrup**
½	shot(s)	**Chilled mineral water** (omit if wet ice)

Origin: Adapted from David A. Embury's 1948 'Fine Art of Mixing Drinks'.
Comment: A little absinthe goes a long way and may even chase your gloom away.

GLOOM LIFTER

●●●●●○

Glass: Martini
Garnish: Lime wedge
Method: SHAKE all ingredients with ice and fine strain into chilled glass.

1½	shot(s)	**Jameson Irish whiskey**
½	shot(s)	**Courvoisier V.S.O.P. cognac**
1	shot(s)	**Freshly squeezed lime juice**
¼	shot(s)	**Pomegranate (grenadine) syrup**
¼	shot(s)	**Sugar syrup** (2 sugar to 1 water)
½	fresh	**Egg white**

Comment: A whiskey and cognac sour with lime juice served straight-up.

GLORIA

●●●●◐○

Glass: Flute
Garnish: Lemon zest twist
Method: SHAKE first 3 ingredients with ice and fine strain into chilled glass. **TOP** with champagne.

1	shot(s)	**Don Julio reposado tequila**
½	shot(s)	**Freshly squeezed lemon juice**
½	shot(s)	**Sugar syrup** (2 sugar to 1 water)
Top up with		**Perrier Jouet brut champagne**

Comment: A tequila sour topped with champagne or a tequila French 75.

GODFATHER

●●●●◐○

Glass: Old-fashioned
Method: STIR all ingredients with ice and strain into ice-filled glass.

2	shot(s)	**Johnnie Walker Scotch whisky**
1	shot(s)	**Luxardo Amaretto di Saschira**

Variant: Based on vodka, this drink becomes a Godmother and when made with cognac it's known as a Godchild.
Comment: Scotch diluted and sweetened with almond – simple but good.

GODFREY

●●●●●○

Glass: Old-fashioned
Garnish: Three blackberries on drink
Method: MUDDLE blackberries in base of shaker. Add other ingredients, **SHAKE** with ice and fine strain into glass filled with crushed ice.

6	fresh	**Blackberries**
1½	shot(s)	**Courvoisier V.S.O.P. cognac**
½	shot(s)	**Grand Marnier liqueur**
¼	shot(s)	**Crème de mûre liqueur**
¼	shot(s)	**Freshly squeezed lemon juice**
¼	shot(s)	**Sugar syrup** (2 sugar to 1 water)

Origin: Created by Salvatore Calabrese at the Library Bar, Lanesborough Hotel, London, England.
Comment: Well balanced with a rich blackberry flavour.

GOLD

●●●●○○

Glass: Martini
Garnish: Orange zest twist
Method: SHAKE all ingredients with ice and fine strain into chilled glass.

1½	shot(s)	**Johnnie Walker Scotch whisky**
1	shot(s)	**Cointreau triple sec**
1	shot(s)	**Crème de banane liqueur**
¾	shot(s)	**Chilled mineral water** (omit if wet ice)

Comment: Sweet, ripe banana, Scotch and a hint of orange.

GOLD MEDALLION

Glass: Martini
Garnish: Flamed orange zest
Method: SHAKE all ingredients with ice and fine strain into chilled glass.

1½	shot(s)	**Courvoisier V.S.O.P. cognac**
1	shot(s)	**Galliano L'Autentico liqueur**
1½	shot(s)	**Freshly squeezed orange juice**
¼	shot(s)	**Freshly squeezed lime juice**
½	fresh	**Egg white** (optional)

Comment: Gold by name and golden in colour. Frothy, orange fresh and cognac based.

GOLD MEMBER

Glass: Martini
Garnish: Apple slice
Method: SHAKE all ingredients with ice and fine strain into chilled glass.

¾	shot(s)	**Goldschläger cinnamon schnapps**
¾	shot(s)	**Teichenné butterscotch schnapps**
¾	shot(s)	**Berentzen apple schnapps**
2¼	shot(s)	**Pressed apple juice**

Comment: Hints of cinnamon and apple – an interesting tipple, if a tad sweet.

GOLD RUSH SLAMMER

Glass: Shot
Method: SHAKE first 2 ingredients with ice and fine strain into chilled glass. **TOP** with champagne.

½	shot(s)	**Goldschläger cinnamon schnapps**
½	shot(s)	**Don Julio reposado tequila**
Top up with		**Perrier Jouet brut champagne**

Origin: Discovered in 2003 at Oxo Tower Bar, London, England.
Comment: Flakes of gold dance with the champagne's bubbles.

GOLDEN BIRD

Glass: Martini
Garnish: Orange 'beak' on rim
Method: SHAKE all ingredients with ice and fine strain into chilled glass.

1	shot(s)	**Bacardi Superior rum**
1	shot(s)	**Grand Marnier liqueur**
½	shot(s)	**Crème de banane liqueur**
1½	shot(s)	**Freshly squeezed orange juice**
1	shot(s)	**Pressed pineapple juice**

Comment: Fruity and sweet – an after dinner cocktail.

GOLDEN BRONX NEW #8

Glass: Martini
Garnish: Maraschino cherry
Method: SHAKE all ingredients with ice and fine strain into chilled glass.

2	shot(s)	**Tanqueray London dry gin**
¼	shot(s)	**Noilly Prat dry vermouth**
¼	shot(s)	**Martini Rosso sweet vermouth**
1	shot(s)	**Freshly squeezed orange juice**
⅛	shot(s)	**Sugar syrup** (2 sugar to 1 water)
1	fresh	**Egg yolk**

Origin: A vintage cocktail adapted from the classic Bronx Cocktail, created in 1906 by Johnny Solon, a bartender at New York's Waldorf-Astoria Hotel, and named after the newly opened Bronx Zoo.
Comment: A Bronx made 'golden' by the addition of egg yolk.

GOLDEN CADILLAC

Glass: Martini
Garnish: Dust with freshly ground nutmeg
Method: SHAKE all ingredients with ice and fine strain into chilled glass.

1	shot(s)	**White crème de cacao liqueur**
½	shot(s)	**Galliano L'Autentico liqueur**
1½	shot(s)	**Freshly squeezed orange juice**
½	shot(s)	**Double (heavy) cream**
½	shot(s)	**Milk**
2	dashes	**Angostura orange bitters**

Origin: Adapted from a drink reputedly created in the late sixties at Poor Red's, a barbecue joint favoured by 'sportbike pilots' in El Dorado, California.
Comment: A silky smooth but not very potent cocktail.

GOLDEN DAWN

Glass: Martini
Garnish: Orange zest twist
Method: SHAKE first 5 ingredients with ice and fine strain into chilled glass. Carefully **POUR** grenadine into centre of drink so that it sinks to create a sunrise effect.

¾	shot(s)	**Tanqueray London dry gin**
1	shot(s)	**Boulard Grand Solage calvados**
1	shot(s)	**Bols apricot brandy liqueur**
1	shot(s)	**Freshly squeezed orange juice**
2	dashes	**Angostura aromatic bitters**
⅛	shot(s)	**Pomegranate (grenadine) syrup**

Origin: Created in September 1930 by Tom Buttery at the Berkeley Hotel, London, England. There are now many versions of this classic drink (David Embury's 'The Fine Art of Mixing Drinks' lists three) but this is my favourite.
Comment: Although it spoils the sunrise effect, this drink is less tart if the syrup lying on the bottom is stirred into the drink (or, better, included when shaking).

GOLDEN DRAGON

Glass: Collins
Garnish: Green apple wedge
Method: SHAKE all ingredients with ice and strain into ice-filled glass.

2	shot(s)	**Don Julio reposado tequila**
¾	shot(s)	**Pisang Ambon liqueur**
2	shot(s)	**Pressed apple juice**
1	shot(s)	**Freshly squeezed lime juice**
½	shot(s)	**Passion fruit syrup**

Comment: Bright green, tangy and tropical.

GOLDEN DREAM

Glass: Martini
Garnish: Sponge biscuit on rim
Method: SHAKE all ingredients with ice and fine strain into chilled glass.

1	shot(s)	**Cointreau triple sec**
1	shot(s)	**Galliano L'Autentico liqueur**
2	shot(s)	**Freshly squeezed orange juice**
1	shot(s)	**Double (heavy) cream**

Comment: Tastes remarkably like syllabub.

GOLDEN FIZZ #1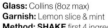

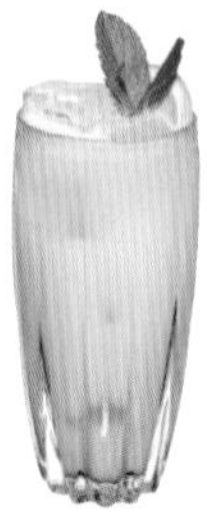

Glass: Collins (8oz max)
Garnish: Lemon slice & mint
Method: SHAKE first 4 ingredients with ice and fine strain into chilled glass. **TOP** with soda.

2	shot(s)	**Tanqueray London dry gin**
1	shot(s)	**Freshly squeezed lemon juice**
½	shot(s)	**Sugar syrup** (2 sugar to 1 water)
1	fresh	**Egg yolk**
Top up with		**Soda water** (from siphon)

Variant: Gin Fizz
Origin: Mid-19th century classic.
Comment: You may have some raw egg inhibitions to conquer before you can enjoy this drink.

GOLDEN FIZZ #2

Glass: Collins
Garnish: Orange slice or mint sprig
Method: STIR honey with gin in base of shaker until honey dissolves. Add next 3 ingredients, **SHAKE** with ice and strain into ice-filled glass. **TOP** with lemonade.

2	spoons	**Runny honey**
1½	shot(s)	**Tanqueray London dry gin**
1	shot(s)	**Cointreau triple sec**
1	shot(s)	**Freshly squeezed grapefruit juice**
¼	shot(s)	**Freshly squeezed lemon juice**
Top up with		**Lemonade/Sprite/7-Up**

Origin: Adapted from a drink created by Wayne Collins, UK.
Comment: More cloudy white than golden but a pleasant, refreshing long drink all the same.

GOLDEN GIRL

Glass: Martini
Garnish: Grated orange zest
Method: SHAKE all ingredients with ice and fine strain into chilled glass.

1¼	shot(s)	**Zacapa aged rum**
1	shot(s)	**Pressed pineapple juice**
1	shot(s)	**Warre's Otima tawny port**
¼	shot(s)	**Sugar syrup** (2 sugar to 1 water)
1	fresh	**Egg** (white & yolk)

Origin: Created by Dale DeGroff, New York City, USA. I've slightly increased the proportions of rum and port from Dale's original recipe.
Comment: This appropriately named velvety drink is a refined dessert in a glass.

GOLDEN MAC

Glass: Old-fashioned
Garnish: Orange zest twist
Method: MUDDLE ginger in base of shaker. Add honey and Scotch and **STIR** until honey dissolves. Add other ingredients, **SHAKE** with ice and fine strain into ice-filled glass.

2	slices	**Fresh root ginger** (thumbnail sized)
2	spoons	**Runny honey**
2	shot(s)	**Johnnie Walker Scotch whisky**
¼	shot(s)	**Teichenné butterscotch schnapps**
¼	shot(s)	**Frangelico hazelnut liqueur**

Origin: Adapted from a drink discovered in 2003 at Golden Mac, Glasgow, Scotland.
Comment: Looks, and even tastes golden.

GOLDEN NAIL

Glass: Old-fashioned
Garnish: Orange zest twist
Method: STIR all ingredients with ice and strain into ice-filled glass.

1½	shot(s)	**Bulleit bourbon whiskey**
¾	shot(s)	**Southern Comfort liqueur**
2	dashes	**Peychaud's aromatic bitters**

Comment: A warming taste of southern hospitality.

GOLDEN REIGN NEW #8

Glass: Martini
Garnish: Orange zest twist
Method: SHAKE all ingredients with ice and fine strain into chilled glass.

1½	shot(s)	**Bacardi Oro golden rum**
½	shot(s)	**Galliano L'Autentico liqueur**
½	shot(s)	**Grand Marnier liqueur**
1	shot(s)	**Double (heavy) cream**
⅛	shot(s)	**Sugar syrup** (2 sugar to 1 water)

Origin: Adapted from a drink created in 2002 by Peter Dorelli at The American Bar at The Savoy Hotel, London, England to celebrate the Queen's golden jubilee.
Comment: A lightly creamy, after dinner drink.

GOLDEN RETRIEVER UPDATED #8

Glass: Martini
Garnish: Orange zest twist
Method: STIR all ingredients with ice and strain into chilled glass.

1	shot(s)	**Bacardi Superior rum**
1	shot(s)	**Green Chartreuse liqueur**
1	shot(s)	**Cuarenta Y Tres (Licor 43) liqueur**

Origin: Created in 2002 by Dick Bradsell at Alfred's, London, England.
Comment: This powerful straw yellow cocktail offers a myriad of flavours. Benefits from the dilution of a long stir.

GOLDEN SCREW

Glass: Flute
Garnish: Physalis fruit
Method: POUR all ingredients into chilled glass and lightly stir.

½	shot(s)	**Courvoisier V.S.O.P. cognac**
½	shot(s)	**Bols apricot brandy liqueur**
1	shot(s)	**Freshly squeezed orange juice**
Top up with		**Perrier Jouet brut champagne**

Variant: With gin in place of brandy.
Comment: A favourite with Midas and others whose budgets extend beyond a Buck's Fizz or a Mimosa.

GOLDEN SHOT

Glass: Shot
Method: Refrigerate ingredients then LAYER in chilled glass by carefully pouring in the following order.

½	shot(s)	**Drambuie liqueur**
½	shot(s)	**Baileys Irish cream liqueur**
½	shot(s)	**Johnnie Walker Scotch whisky**

Comment: A whisky based layered shot with plenty of character.

GOLDEN SLIPPER

Glass: Martini
Garnish: Apricot slice on rim
Method: SHAKE all ingredients with ice and fine strain into chilled glass.

1½	shot(s)	**Yellow Chartreuse liqueur**
1½	shot(s)	**Bols apricot brandy liqueur**
1	fresh	**Egg yolk**

Comment: Rich in colour and equally rich in flavour. A dessert with a punch.

GOLDEN WAVE

Glass: Old-fashioned
Garnish: Pineapple wedge
Method: BLEND all ingredients with a 6oz scoop of crushed ice and serve with straws.

1	shot(s)	**Bacardi Superior rum**
½	shot(s)	**Cointreau triple sec**
½	shot(s)	**Velvet Falernum liqueur**
1	shot(s)	**Pressed pineapple juice**
¾	shot(s)	**Freshly squeezed lemon juice**

Origin: A Tiki drink created in 1969 by Jose 'Joe' Yatco at China Trader, California, USA.
Comment: Rum laced fruit served frozen.

GOLF COCKTAIL

Glass: Martini
Garnish: Orange zest twist
Method: STIR all ingredients with ice and strain into chilled glass.

2	shot(s)	**Tanqueray London dry gin**
1	shot(s)	**Noilly Prat dry vermouth**
1	dash	**Angostura aromatic bitters**

Comment: A 'wet' Martini with bitters.

GOOD HOPE PLANTATION RUM PUNCH NEW #8

Glass: Old-fashioned
Garnish: Cherry
Method: SHAKE first 4 ingredients with ice and strain into glass filled with crushed ice. TOP with soda.

1	shot(s)	**Myers's dark Jamaican rum**
1	shot(s)	**Cointreau triple sec**
1	shot(s)	**Grand Marnier liqueur**
1	shot(s)	**Freshly squeezed lime juice**
Top up with		**Soda water** (club soda)

Origin: Originally made at the Good Hope Hotel, Falmouth, Jamaica. The Good Hope is an 18th Century country house set in a 2,000-acre plantation high in the lush landscape of Cockpit Country near Montego Bay.
Comment: A classic citrus laced, big flavoured, punch.

GOODY-GOODY NEW #8

Glass: Martini
Garnish: Orange zest twist
Method: SHAKE all ingredients with ice and fine strain into chilled glass.

2	shot(s)	**Tanqueray London dry gin**
1	shot(s)	**Dubonnet Red** (French made)
¼	shot(s)	**Freshly squeezed lemon juice**
½	shot(s)	**Yellow Chartreuse liqueur**

Comment: Gin, lemon and Chartreuse. Not to everybody's taste.
Origin: In W.J. Tarling's 1937 Café Royal Cocktail Book Coronation Edition the invention of this cocktail is credited to G. Bongarzoni.

GOOMBAY SMASH

Glass: Collins
Garnish: Lime wedge
Method: SHAKE all ingredients with ice and strain into ice filled glass.

2	shot(s)	**Pusser's Navy rum**
¾	shot(s)	**Malibu coconut rum liqueur**
3	shot(s)	**Pressed pineapple juice**
¼	shot(s)	**Freshly squeezed lime juice**
½	shot(s)	**Cointreau triple sec**

Origin: The Goombay Smash is a speciality of Miss Emily's Blue Bee Bar in the Bahamas. Mrs Emily Cooper is now deceased but her daughter, Violet Smith, presides over her secret recipe.
Comment: Smashes are usually short drinks that include muddled mint, but this potent Tiki-style drink features rum, coconut and fruit.

> 'THE SECRET TO A LONG LIFE IS TO STAY BUSY, GET PLENTY OF EXERCISE AND DON'T DRINK TOO MUCH. THEN AGAIN, DON'T DRINK TOO LITTLE.'
> HERMANN SMITH JOHANNSON

GRAND COSMOPOLITAN

Glass: Martini
Garnish: Flamed orange zest twist
Method: SHAKE all ingredients with ice and fine strain into chilled glass.

1	shot(s)	**Ketel One Citroen vodka**
1	shot(s)	**Grand Marnier liqueur**
1½	shot(s)	**Ocean Spray cranberry juice**
¾	shot(s)	**Freshly squeezed lime juice**
2	dashes	**Angostura orange bitters** (optional)

Comment: A 'grand' Cosmo indeed.

GRAND DESIGNS NEW #8

Glass: Martini
Garnish: Rosemary sprig
Method: MUDDLE rosemary in base of shaker. Add other ingredients, **SHAKE** with ice and fine strain into chilled glass.

1	fresh	**Rosemary sprig**
1½	shot(s)	**Tanqueray London dry gin**
1	shot(s)	**St-Germain elderflower liqueur**
¼	shot(s)	**Noilly Prat dry vermouth**
¾	shot(s)	**Pressed pineapple juice**

Origin: Created in May 2008 for Grand Designs Live exhibition by Yours Truly (Simon Difford) at The Cabinet Room, London, England.
Comment: Easy drinking and slightly sweet, dried and made all to together grander by the rosemary.

LE GRAND FEU

Glass: Martini
Garnish: Mint sprig
Method: SHAKE all ingredients with ice and fine strain into chilled glass.

1½	shot(s)	**Courvoisier V.S.O.P. cognac**
1½	shot(s)	**Vanilla schnapps liqueur**
½	shot(s)	**Baileys Irish cream liqueur**
¾	shot(s)	**Cold chai tea**

Origin: Adapted from a recipe by Tony Venci, La Femme Bar, MGM Grand Hotel, Las Vegas, USA.
Comment: Cognac smoothed with vanilla and cream, spiced with chai tea.

GRAND MARGARITA UPDATED #8

Glass: Coupette
Garnish: Salt rim & lime wedge
Method: SHAKE all ingredients with ice and fine strain into chilled glass.

2	shot(s)	**Don Julio añejo tequila**
1	shot(s)	**Grand Marnier liqueur**
¾	shot(s)	**Freshly squeezed lime juice**

Comment: A balanced and flavoursome Margarita.

GRAND MIMOSA

Glass: Flute
Garnish: Strawberry on rim
Method: SHAKE first 2 ingredients with ice and strain into chilled glass. **TOP** with champagne.

1	shot(s)	**Grand Marnier liqueur**
2	shot(s)	**Freshly squeezed orange juice**
Top up with		**Perrier Jouet brut champagne**

Origin: The Mimosa was created in 1925 at the Ritz Hotel, Paris, and named after the Mimosa plant - probably because of its trembling leaves, rather like the gentle fizz of this mixture. The Grand Mimosa as shown here benefits from the addition of Grand Marnier liqueur.
Comment: As the name suggests, the orange of Grand Marnier heavily influences this drink. Basically a Buck's Fizz with more oomph.

GRAND PASSION

Glass: Martini
Garnish: Float half passion fruit
Method: Cut passion fruits in half and scoop flesh into shaker. Add other ingredients, **SHAKE** with ice and fine strain into chilled glass.

1	fresh	**Passion fruit**
2	shot(s)	**Bacardi Superior rum**
1	shot(s)	**Pressed apple juice**
½	shot(s)	**Sugar syrup** (2 sugar to 1 water)
3	dashes	**Angostura aromatic bitters**
½	fresh	**Egg white**

Comment: Are you lacking passion in your life? There's plenty in this fruity little number.

GRAND SAZERAC

Glass: Old-fashioned
Method: POUR absinthe into ice-filled glass and **TOP** with water. Leave the mixture to stand in the glass. Separately, **SHAKE** liqueur, bourbon and bitters with ice. Finally discard contents of absinthe-coated glass and fine strain contents of shaker into absinthe washed glass. (Note that there is no ice in the finished drink.)

½	shot(s)	La Fée Parisienne (68%) absinthe
Top up with		Chilled mineral water
1½	shot(s)	Grand Marnier liqueur
1½	shot(s)	Bulleit bourbon whiskey
2	dashes	Angostura aromatic bitters
3	dashes	Peychaud's aromatic bitters

Origin: Created in 2004 by Yours Truly (Simon Difford).
Comment: An orange twist on the classic Sazerac.

GRAND SIDECAR

Glass: Martini
Garnish: Orange zest twist
Method: SHAKE all ingredients with ice and fine strain into chilled glass.

2½	shot(s)	Grand Marnier liqueur
1	shot(s)	Freshly squeezed lemon juice
½	shot(s)	Chilled mineral water (omit if wet ice)

Origin: Created by Yours Truly (Simon Difford) in June 2005.
Comment: A twist on the classic, simple but very tasty. Also works well shaken and strained into an ice-filled old-fashioned glass.

GRAND SLAM NEW #8

Glass: Martini
Garnish: Strawberry (or other fruit garnish)
Method: STIR all ingredients with ice and strain into chilled glass.

2	shot(s)	Swedish Punch
1	shot(s)	Martini Rosso sweet vermouth
1	shot(s)	Noilly Prat dry vermouth

Origin: Vintage cocktail of unknown origin.
Comment: This after dinner libation is slightly sweet but incredibly aromatic.

GRANDE CHAMPAGNE COSMO

UPDATED #8

Glass: Martini
Garnish: Orange zest twist
Method: SHAKE all ingredients with ice and fine strain into chilled glass.

1½	shot(s)	Courvoisier V.S.O.P. cognac
¾	shot(s)	Grand Marnier liqueur
½	shot(s)	Freshly squeezed lemon juice
1	shot(s)	Ocean Spray cranberry juice
½	fresh	Egg white

Comment: 'Grande Champagne' refers to the top cru of the Cognac region: this drink is suitably elite.

GRANNY'S

Glass: Martini
Garnish: Apple wedge on rim
Method: SHAKE all ingredients with ice and fine strain into chilled glass.

1¾	shot(s)	Bacardi Superior rum
¼	shot(s)	Goldschläger cinnamon schnapps
½	shot(s)	Berentzen apple schnapps
1½	shot(s)	Pressed apple juice

Comment: Apple, rum and cinnamon were made for each other.

GRANNY'S MARTINI

Glass: Martini
Garnish: Dust with ground nutmeg
Method: SHAKE all ingredients with ice and fine strain into chilled glass.

1	shot(s)	Tanqueray London dry gin
½	shot(s)	Tio Pepe fino sherry
2	shot(s)	Bols advocaat liqueur

Origin: I have to own up to creating and naming this drink after three drink categories often identified with a stereotypical English granny. Sorry, mum.
Comment: Creamy, Christmassy drink just for nana.

GRAPE DELIGHT

Glass: Martini
Garnish: Grapes on stick
Method: MUDDLE grapes in base of shaker. Add rest of ingredients, **SHAKE** with ice and fine strain into chilled glass.

12	fresh	Seedless red grapes
2	shot(s)	Tanqueray London dry gin
½	shot(s)	Sloe gin liqueur
½	shot(s)	Pressed apple juice
¼	shot(s)	Sugar syrup (2 sugar to 1 water)
¼	shot(s)	Freshly squeezed lime juice
1	dash	Angostura aromatic bitters

Comment: This rust coloured drink is fruity and delicate.

GRAPE EFFECT

Glass: Martini
Garnish: Grapes on stick
Method: MUDDLE grapes in base of shaker. Add other ingredients, **SHAKE** with ice and fine strain into chilled glass.

12	fresh	Seedless white grapes
2	shot(s)	Bacardi Superior rum
1	shot(s)	St-Germain elderflower liqueur

Comment: Delicately flavoured but heavily laced with rum.

GRAPE ESCAPE

Glass: Collins
Garnish: Mint sprig
Method: MUDDLE grapes and mint in base of shaker. Add cognac and sugar, **SHAKE** with ice and strain into glass filled with crushed ice. **TOP** with champagne, stir and serve with straws.

8	fresh	**Seedless white grapes**
5	fresh	**Mint leaves**
2	shot(s)	**Courvoisier V.S.O.P. cognac**
½	shot(s)	**Sugar syrup** (2 sugar to 1 water)
Top up with		**Perrier Jouet brut champagne**

Origin: Created in 2000 by Brian Lucas and Max Warner at Long Bar @ Sanderson, London, England.
Comment: A cracking drink – subtle and refreshing.

GRAPE MARTINI #1 UPDATED #8

Glass: Martini
Garnish: Three white grapes on stick
Method: MUDDLE grapes in base of shaker. Add other ingredients, **SHAKE** with ice and fine strain into chilled glass.

12	fresh	**Seedless white grapes**
2	shot(s)	**Ketel One vodka**
¼	shot(s)	**Sugar syrup** (2 sugar to 1 water)

Origin: Formula by Yours Truly (Simon Difford) in 2004.
Comment: Simple but remarkably tasty.

GRAPE MARTINI #2 NEW #8

Glass: Martini
Garnish: Three red grapes on stick
Method: MUDDLE grapes in base of shaker. Add other ingredients, **SHAKE** with ice and fine strain into chilled glass.

10	fresh	**Seedless white grapes**
2	shot(s)	**Ketel One vodka**
¼	shot(s)	**Green Chartreuse liqueur**

Comment: Green Chartreuse adds extra complexity to what would otherwise be simply be vodka laced grape juice.

GRAPEFRUIT DAIQUIRI

Glass: Martini
Garnish: Maraschino cherry
Method: SHAKE all ingredients with ice and fine strain into chilled glass.

2	shot(s)	**Zacapa aged rum**
1½	shot(s)	**Freshly squeezed grapefruit juice**
¾	shot(s)	**Sugar syrup** (2 sugar to 1 water)

Comment: The flavours of rum and grapefruit combine perfectly – clean and fresh.

GRAPEFRUIT DAIQUIRI #2 (MOCKTAIL)

NEW #8

Glass: Old-fashioned
Garnish: Lime wedge on rim
Method: SHAKE all ingredients with ice and fine strain into chilled glass.

2	shot(s)	**Freshly squeezed grapefruit juice**
1	shot(s)	**Freshly squeezed lime juice**
½	shot(s)	**Sugar syrup** (2 sugar to 1 water)
2	dashes	**Angostura aromatic bitters***

*Note: Angostura aromatic bitters contain alcohol but in the finished drink the alcohol level is negligible.

Origin: Created in 2006 by Audrey Saunders, New York, USA.
Comment: Balanced and adult but cries out for rum. Take a cab instead.

GRAPEFRUIT JULEP

Glass: Collins
Garnish: Mint sprig
Method: STIR honey with vodka in base of shaker until honey dissolves. Add other ingredients, **SHAKE** with ice and strain into glass filled with crushed ice.

1	spoon	**Runny honey**
2	shot(s)	**Ketel One vodka**
4	fresh	**Mint leaves**
½	shot(s)	**Freshly squeezed lime juice**
½	shot(s)	**Pomegranate (grenadine) syrup**
¾	shot(s)	**Freshly squeezed grapefruit juice**

Origin: Created by Dale DeGroff, New York City, USA.
Comment: Wonderfully refreshing. Bring on the sun.

'IF YOU DRINK, DON'T DRIVE. DON'T EVEN PUTT.'
DEAN MARTIN

GRAPPA MANHATTAN

Glass: Martini
Garnish: Stemmed maraschino cherry
Method: STIR all ingredients with ice and strain into chilled glass.

2	shot(s)	**Francoli Moscato grappa**
1	shot(s)	**Martini Rosso sweet vermouth**
¼	shot(s)	**Maraschino syrup** (from cherry jar)
2	dashes	**Angostura aromatic bitters**

Comment: A great drink in which to appreciate modern style grappas, this remains very much a Manhattan.

AS LATE AS THE MID-17TH CENTURY, FRENCH WINE MAKERS DID NOT USE CORKS. INSTEAD, THEY USED OIL-SOAKED RAGS STUFFED INTO THE NECKS OF BOTTLES.

GRAPPACCINO

Glass: Martini
Garnish: Float 3 coffee beans
Method: SHAKE all ingredients with ice and fine strain into chilled glass.

2	shot(s)	**Francoli Moscato grappa**
½	shot(s)	**Luxardo Amaretto di Saschira**
½	shot(s)	**Sugar syrup** (2 sugar to 1 water)
1	shot(s)	**Espresso coffee**

Origin: Adapted from a drink created in 2006 by George Sinclair.
Comment: The character of the grappa shines through and is complimented by the amaretto and coffee.

GRAPPARITA

Glass: Coupette
Garnish: Lime wedge on rim
Method: SHAKE all ingredients with ice and fine strain into chilled glass.

2	shot(s)	**Francoli Moscato grappa**
1	shot(s)	**Luxardo limoncello liqueur**
1	shot(s)	**Freshly squeezed lemon juice**
½	fresh	**Egg white**

Origin: Adapted from a drink discovered in 2005 at Alfredo's of Rome, New York City, USA. The original called for sour mix.
Comment: Grappa replaces tequila and lemon liqueur triple sec in this Italian twist on the classic Margarita.

GRAPPLE MARTINI

Glass: Martini
Garnish: Grapes on stick
Method: MUDDLE grapes in base of shaker. Add other ingredients, **SHAKE** with ice and fine strain into chilled glass.

7	fresh	**Seedless white grapes**
2	shot(s)	**Ketel One vodka**
¾	shot(s)	**Sauvignon Blanc wine**
1	shot(s)	**Pressed apple juice**
¼	shot(s)	**Sugar syrup** (2 sugar to 1 water)

Origin: Adapted from a recipe created in 2003 by Chris Setchell at Las Iguanas, UK.
Comment: A rounded, fruity Martini-style drink.

GRASSHOPPER

Glass: Martini
Garnish: Mint leaf
Method: SHAKE all ingredients with ice and fine strain into chilled glass.

1	shot(s)	**Green crème de menthe liqueur**
1	shot(s)	**White crème de cacao liqueur**
1	shot(s)	**Double (heavy) cream**
1	shot(s)	**Milk**

Origin: Created at Tujague's, the second oldest restaurant in New Orleans, which was opened in 1856 by Guillaume Tujague. Some time before he died in 1912, Guillaume sold the restaurant to Philibert Guichet, who won second prize in a prestigious New York cocktail competition for this drink.
Comment: It's hard not to like this creamy, minty after dinner treat.

GRASSY FINNISH

Glass: Martini
Garnish: Lemongrass
Method: MUDDLE lemongrass in base of shaker. Add other ingredients, **SHAKE** with ice and fine strain into chilled glass.

1	stem	**Fresh lemongrass** (chopped)
2	shot(s)	**Lime flavoured vodka**
1	shot(s)	**Krupnik honey liqueur**
¼	shot(s)	**Sugar syrup** (2 sugar to 1 water)

Origin: Created in 2003 by Gerard McCurry at Revolution, UK.
Comment: Just like Finland, this drink is clean, green, wooded and safe, but deep down there's plenty of spice.

GRATEFUL DEAD

Glass: Sling
Garnish: Lime wedge
Method: SHAKE first seven ingredients with ice and strain into ice-filled glass. **TOP** with soda and serve with straws.

½	shot(s)	**Ketel One vodka**
½	shot(s)	**Tanqueray London dry gin**
½	shot(s)	**Bacardi Superior rum**
½	shot(s)	**Cointreau triple sec**
½	shot(s)	**Midori green melon liqueur**
1	shot(s)	**Freshly squeezed lime juice**
½	shot(s)	**Sugar syrup** (2 sugar to 1 water)
Top up with		**Soda water** (club soda)

Origin: LA Iced Tea with Midori in place of Chambord liqueur.
Comment: Don't be put off by the lime green colour. This fruity, sweet 'n' sour drink is actually quite pleasant.

DRINKS ARE GRADED AS FOLLOWS:

● DISGUSTING ●● PRETTY AWFUL ●● BEST AVOIDED
●●● DISAPPOINTING ●●● ACCEPTABLE ●●●● GOOD
●●●● RECOMMENDED ●●●●● HIGHLY RECOMMENDED
●●●●● OUTSTANDING / EXCEPTIONAL

GREAT MUGHAL MARTINI

Glass: Martini
Garnish: Lemon zest twist
Method: **MUDDLE** raisins in base of shaker. Add other ingredients, **SHAKE** with ice and fine strain into chilled glass.

20	dried	Raisins
1½	shot(s)	Bulleit bourbon whiskey
¼	shot(s)	Sugar syrup (2 sugar to 1 water)
¾	shot(s)	Passion fruit syrup
¼	shot(s)	Freshly squeezed lime juice
3	drops	Rosewater
1	shot(s)	Lime & lemongrass cordial

Origin: Created in 2001 by Douglas Ankrah for Red Fort, Soho, London, England.
Comment: Douglas' original recipe called for raisin infused bourbon and I'd recommend you make this drink that way if time permits.

GREEN APPLE & CUCUMBER MARTINI

Glass: Martini
Garnish: Float three cucumber slices
Method: **MUDDLE** cucumber in base of shaker. Add other ingredients, **SHAKE** with ice and fine strain into chilled glass.

1	inch	Cucumber (chopped & peeled)
2	shot(s)	Cucumber flavoured vodka
½	shot(s)	Sour apple liqueur
½	shot(s)	Pressed apple juice
⅛	shot(s)	Sugar syrup (2 sugar to 1 water)

Origin: Adapted from a recipe discovered in 2003 at Oxo Tower Bar, London, England.
Comment: Archetypal English flavours. Clean, green and refreshing.

GREEN BEETLE NEW #8

Glass: Martini
Garnish: Lemon zest twist
Method: **POUR** absinthe into ice-filled glass, **TOP** with water and leave to stand. Separately **SHAKE** other ingredients with ice. **DISCARD** contents of glass (absinthe, water and ice) and **STRAIN** contents of shaker into absinthe-coated glass.

---In glass---
½	shot(s)	La Fée Parisienne (68%) absinthe
Top up with		Chilled mineral water

---In shaker---
2	shot(s)	Don Julio reposado tequila
½	shot(s)	Agave syrup
½	shot(s)	Luxardo limoncello liqueur

Comment: Tequila and lemon aromatized by absinthe.
Origin: Created by Alex Richer at Bar Red, London, England.

GREEN DESTINY

Glass: Old-fashioned
Garnish: Kiwi slice
Method: **MUDDLE** cucumber and kiwi in base of shaker. Add other ingredients, **SHAKE** with ice and fine strain into glass filled with crushed ice.

1	inch	Chopped peeled cucumber
½	fresh	Kiwi fruit
2	shot(s)	Zubrówka bison vodka
1½	shot(s)	Pressed apple juice
¼	shot(s)	Sugar syrup (2 sugar to 1 water)

Origin: Created in 2001 by Andrew Tounos at Hakk, Warsaw, Poland.
Comment: Looks green and even tastes green, but pleasantly so.

GREEN DRAGON

Glass: Martini
Garnish: Mint sprig
Method: **SHAKE** all ingredients with ice and fine strain into chilled glass.

2	shot(s)	Tanqueray London dry gin
½	shot(s)	Green crème de menthe liqueur
¼	shot(s)	Kümmel liqueur
¼	shot(s)	Freshly squeezed lemon juice
3	dashes	Fee Brothers peach bitters
½	shot(s)	Chilled mineral water (omit if wet ice)

Origin: Adapted from Harry Craddock's 1930 'The Savoy Cocktail Book'.
Comment: Mint, juniper, caraway and fennel make for an unusual cocktail that's conducive to fresh breath.

GREEN EYES

Glass: Martini
Garnish: Lime wedge on rim
Method: **SHAKE** all ingredients with ice and fine strain into chilled glass.

2	shot(s)	Ketel One Citroen vodka
½	shot(s)	Bols blue curaçao liqueur
1	shot(s)	Freshly squeezed orange juice
½	shot(s)	Freshly squeezed lemon juice
¼	shot(s)	Almond (orgeat) syrup

Comment: A cross between a Blue Cosmo and a short Screwdriver.

GREEN FAIRY UPDATED #8

Glass: Martini
Garnish: Lemon zest twist
Method: **SHAKE** all ingredients with ice and fine strain into chilled glass.

1	shot(s)	La Fée Parisienne (68%) absinthe
1	shot(s)	Freshly squeezed lemon juice
1	shot(s)	Chilled mineral water
¾	shot(s)	Sugar syrup (2 sugar to 1 water)
1	dash	Angostura aromatic bitters
½	fresh	Egg white

Origin: Created in the 1990s by Dick Bradsell, London, England.
Comment: An Absinthe Sour style drink served straight-up.

GREEN FIZZ

Glass: Collins (8oz max)
Garnish: Slice of lemon & mint
Method: SHAKE first 4 ingredients with ice and strain into chilled glass. **TOP** with soda.

2	shot(s)	**Tanqueray London dry gin**
½	shot(s)	**Giffard Menthe Pastille liqueur**
1	shot(s)	**Freshly squeezed lemon juice**
¼	shot(s)	**Sugar syrup** (2 sugar to 1 water)
Top up with		**Soda water** (from siphon)

Variant: Gin Fizz
Origin: A mid-19th century classic.
Comment: Fresh, cleansing and refreshing - as only a minty Fizz can be.

GREEN FLY

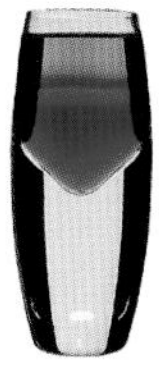

Glass: Shot
Method: Refrigerate ingredients then **LAYER** in chilled glass by carefully pouring in the following order.

½	shot(s)	**Midori green melon liqueur**
½	shot(s)	**Giffard Menthe Pastille liqueur**
½	shot(s)	**Green Chartreuse liqueur**

Origin: Created by Alex Turner at Circus, London, England.
Comment: A strong shot comprising three layers of different green liqueurs.

GREEN GLAZIER NEW #8

Glass: Martini
Garnish: Lime zest twist
Method: STIR all ingredients with ice and strain into chilled glass.

2	shot(s)	**Courvoisier V.S.O.P. cognac**
¾	shot(s)	**Green Chartreuse liqueur**
¼	shot(s)	**Brown crème de cacao liqueur**
2	dashes	**Angostura aromatic bitters**

Origin: Created in 2008 by Jamie Boudreau at Vessel, Seattle, USA.
Comment: This Martini-style drink doesn't take any prisoners. Go easy.

GREEN HORN

Glass: Martini
Garnish: Pineapple wedge & cherry
Method: SHAKE all ingredients with ice and fine strain into chilled glass.

1½	shot(s)	**Zacapa aged rum**
1	shot(s)	**Pressed pineapple juice**
1	shot(s)	**Midori green melon liqueur**
½	fresh	**Egg white**

Comment: Far more interesting and serious than the green hue from the melon liqueur would suggest.

GREEN HORNET

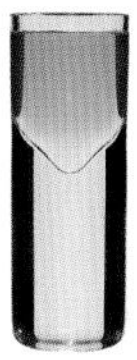

Glass: Shot
Method: SHAKE all ingredients with ice and fine strain into chilled glass.

¾	shot(s)	**Ketel One vodka**
⅛	shot(s)	**La Fée Parisienne (68%) absinthe**
¾	shot(s)	**Pisang Ambon liqueur**
½	shot(s)	**Rose's lime cordial**

Comment: A surprisingly palatable and balanced shot.

GREEN MELON SOUR NEW #8

Glass: Old-fashioned
Garnish: Lemon slice & cherry on stick (sail)
Method: SHAKE all ingredients with ice and strain into ice-filled glass.

2	shot(s)	**Midori green melon liqueur**
1	shot(s)	**Freshly squeezed lemon juice**
1	dash	**Angostura aromatic bitters**

Comment: Neon green in colour and a tad on the sweet side, but each to their own.

GREEN SWIZZLE

Glass: Old-fashioned
Method: POUR all ingredients into glass. Fill glass with crushed ice and **SWIZZLE** (stir) with bar spoon or swizzle stick to mix. Serve with straws.

2	shot(s)	**Bacardi Superior rum**
½	shot(s)	**Freshly squeezed lime juice**
¼	shot(s)	**Giffard Menthe Pastille liqueur**
¼	shot(s)	**Sugar syrup** (2 sugar to 1 water)
1	dash	**Angostura aromatic bitters**

Variant: With gin in place of rum
Origin: This 1940s classic features in 'The Rummy Affair Of Old Biffy' by P.G. Wodehouse. Bertie Wooster sings its praises after enjoying a few at the Panters' Bar of the West Indian stand at the 1924 Empire Exhibition.
Comment: A Daiquiri-like drink with a hint of peppermint.

GREEN TEA MARTINI #1

Glass: Martini
Garnish: Banana slice on rim
Method: SHAKE all ingredients with ice and fine strain into chilled glass.

2	shot(s)	**Zubrówka bison vodka**
¼	shot(s)	**Pisang Ambon liqueur**
⅛	shot(s)	**Giffard Menthe Pastille liqueur**
2	shot(s)	**Pressed apple juice**

Comment: It's green and, although it doesn't actually contain any tea, has something of the flavour of alcoholic peppermint tea.

GREEN TEA MARTINI #2

Glass: Martini
Garnish: Shiso (or mint) leaf
Method: SHAKE all ingredients with ice and strain into chilled glass.

2	shot(s)	**Tanqueray London dry gin**
1	shot(s)	**Zen green tea liqueur**
¼	shot(s)	**Noilly Prat dry vermouth**
¾	shot(s)	**Strong cold green tea**

Origin: Created in 2006 by Yours Truly (Simon Difford).
Comment: Exactly what it says on the tin: as subtle and delicate as green tea itself.

GREENBELT

Glass: Collins
Garnish: Grapes on stick
Method: MUDDLE grapes in base of shaker. Add other ingredients, **SHAKE** with ice and fine strain into ice-filled glass.

12	fresh	**Seedless white grapes**
2	shot(s)	**Macchu pisco**
1	shot(s)	**St-Germain elderflower liqueur**
Top up with		**Perrier Jouet brut champagne**

Origin: Created in 2007 by Yours Truly (Simon Difford).
Comment: This tastes as green as it looks - aromatic and refreshing.

GRETA GARBO

Glass: Martini
Garnish: Star anise
Method: SHAKE all ingredients with ice and fine strain into chilled glass.

2	shot(s)	**Bacardi Superior rum**
¼	shot(s)	**Luxardo maraschino liqueur**
½	shot(s)	**Sugar syrup** (2 sugar to 1 water)
1	shot(s)	**Freshly squeezed lime juice**
⅛	shot(s)	**Pernod anis**

Comment: A most unusual Daiquiri.

GREY MOUSE

Glass: Shot
Method: SHAKE all ingredients with ice and fine strain into chilled glass.

1	shot(s)	**Baileys Irish cream liqueur**
½	shot(s)	**Opal Nera black sambuca**

Comment: Aniseed and whiskey cream.

GREYHOUND

Glass: Collins
Garnish: Orange slice
Method: POUR ingredients into ice-filled glass and stir.

2	shot(s)	**Ketel One vodka**
Top up with		**Freshly squeezed grapefruit juice**

Comment: A sour Screwdriver.

GROG UPDATED #8

Glass: Old-fashioned
Garnish: Lime wedge
Method: STIR honey with rum in base of shaker until honey dissolves. Add other ingredients, **SHAKE** with ice and strain into ice-filled glass.

2	spoons	**Runny honey**
1½	shot(s)	**Pusser's Navy rum**
¼	shot(s)	**Freshly squeezed lime juice**
2½	shot(s)	**Chilled mineral water**
3	dashes	**Angostura aromatic bitters**

Variant: Hot Grog
Origin: For over 300 years the British Navy issued a daily 'tot' of rum, sometimes with double issues before battle. In 1740, as an attempt to combat drunkenness, Admiral Vernon gave orders that the standard daily issue of half a pint of neat, high-proof rum be replaced with two servings of a quarter of a pint, diluted 4:1 with water. The Admiral was nicknamed 'Old Grogram' due to the waterproof grogram cloak he wore, so the mixture he introduced became known as 'grog'. Lime juice was often added to the grog in an attempt to prevent scurvy, lending British sailors their 'limey' nickname.

The 'tot' tradition, which started in Jamaica in 1665, was finally broken on 31st July 1970, a day now known as 'Black Tot Day' – although by then the 'tot' had been reduced to a meagre two ounces.

Sounds plausible to me but drinks historians now say that grog is earlier than Old Grogram.
Comment: Strong, flavoursome Navy rum with a splash of scurvy-inhibiting lime. Too many and you'll be groggy in the morning.

THE GTO COCKTAIL

Glass: Collins
Garnish: Pineapple wedge on rim
Method: SHAKE all ingredients with ice and strain into ice-filled glass.

2	shot(s)	**Bulleit bourbon whiskey**
½	shot(s)	**Luxardo Amaretto di Saschira**
½	shot(s)	**Freshly squeezed lemon juice**
3	shot(s)	**Pressed pineapple juice**

Origin: Adapted from a recipe discovered in 2004 at Jones, Los Angeles, USA.
Comment: A fruity, punch-like drink.

GUARDABOSQUES NEW #8

● ● ● ● ○ ○

Glass: Old-fashioned
Garnish: Pineapple or lime wedge
Method: SHAKE ingredients with ice and strain into ice-filled glass.

| 1½ | shot(s) | Don Julio reposado tequila |
| 1 | shot(s) | Midori green melon liqueur |

Origin: Popular cocktail in Mexico.
Comment: Don't let the lime-green hue of this drink put you off. It tastes considerably more adult than it looks.

GUARD'S COCKTAIL NEW #8

● ● ● ● ○

Glass: Martini
Garnish: Orange zest twist
Method: SHAKE all ingredients with ice and fine strain into chilled glass.

1½	shot(s)	Tanqueray London dry gin
¾	shot(s)	Martini Rosso sweet vermouth
⅛	shot(s)	Grand Marnier liqueur
1	dash	Angostura orange bitters

Comment: Old Guard but this Sweet Martini made sweeter with a dash of orange liqueur well deserves a place on modern cocktail lists
Origin: Vintage cocktail of unknown origins.

GUILLOTINE

● ● ● ● ○ ○

Glass: Flute
Garnish: Berries on rim
Method: POUR first 2 ingredients into glass and TOP with champagne.

½	shot(s)	Crème de cassis liqueur
½	shot(s)	Poire William eau de vie
Top up with		Perrier Jouet brut champagne

Comment: Add some life to your bubbly.

GULF COAST SEX ON THE BEACH

● ● ● ● ○

Glass: Collins
Method: SHAKE all ingredients with ice and strain into ice-filled glass.

1½	shot(s)	Bacardi Superior rum
¾	shot(s)	Midori green melon liqueur
¾	shot(s)	Crème de banane liqueur
1½	shot(s)	Pressed pineapple juice
1½	shot(s)	Ocean Spray cranberry juice
¼	shot(s)	Freshly squeezed lime juice

Origin: Created in 1997 by Roberto Canino and Wayne Collins at Navajo Joe, London, England.
Comment: Golden tan in colour and tropical in flavour, complete with frothy top.

GUN CLUB PUNCH NO.1

● ● ● ● ● ◖

Glass: Cartridge mug or Collins
Garnish: Pineapple cube & cherry on stick plus mint sprig
Method: BLEND all ingredients with 12oz scoop crushed ice. Serve with straws.

1	shot(s)	Bacardi Superior rum
1	shot(s)	Pusser's Navy rum
1	shot(s)	Freshly squeezed lime juice
1½	shot(s)	Pressed pineapple juice
¼	shot(s)	Cointreau triple sec
¼	shot(s)	Pomegranate (grenadine) syrup

Origin: Victor Bergeron specified that this drink should be served in one of his bespoke green cartridge mugs (pictured here). This recipe comes from 'Trader Vic's Bartender's Guide' (1972 revised edition).
Comment: This Trader Vic classic is balanced rather than sweet. Fruit juice and ice tone down rum's powerful blast.

GUSTO

● ● ● ● ○

Glass: Collins
Garnish: Apple slice
Method: MUDDLE grapes in base of shaker. Add other ingredients, SHAKE with ice and fine strain into ice-filled glass.

7	fresh	Seedless white grapes
2	shot(s)	Don Julio reposado tequila
¾	shot(s)	Agavero tequila liqueur
2	shot(s)	Pressed apple juice

Origin: Created in 2003 by Thomas Gillgren at The Kingly Club, London, England.
Comment: A pleasing long drink flavoured with apple, grape and tequila.

GYPSY MARTINI

● ● ● ● ○

Glass: Martini
Garnish: Rosemary
Method: MUDDLE rosemary and raisins in base of shaker. Add other ingredients, SHAKE with ice and fine strain into chilled glass.

1	fresh	Rosemary sprig
10	dried	Raisins
2	shot(s)	Tanqueray London dry gin
½	shot(s)	Sugar syrup (2 sugar to 1 water)
1	shot(s)	Chilled mineral water (reduce if wet ice)

Origin: Adapted from a recipe created by Jason Fendick in 2002 for Steam, London, England.
Comment: Jason's original recipe called for raisin infused gin and I'd recommend you make this drink that way if time permits.

GYPSY

●●●●○

Glass: Martini
Garnish: Lime zest twist
Method: SHAKE all ingredients with ice and fine strain into chilled glass.

1½	shot(s)	**Tanqueray London dry gin**
¾	shot(s)	**St-Germain elderflower liqueur**
¼	shot(s)	**Green Chartreuse liqueur**
½	shot(s)	**Freshly squeezed lime juice**

Origin: Created in 2007 by Dominic Venegas at Bourbon & Branch, San Francisco, USA.
Comment: Dominic describes this drink as "a little homage to the 'Last Word' cocktail".

GYPSY QUEEN

●●●●○

Glass: Martini
Garnish: Orange zest twist
Method: STIR all ingredients with ice and strain into chilled glass.

1½	shot(s)	**Ketel One vodka**
¾	shot(s)	**Bénédictine D.O.M. liqueur**
¾	shot(s)	**Freshly squeezed orange juice**
¼	shot(s)	**Freshly squeezed lemon juice**

Origin: A long lost classic.
Comment: Tangy, herbal, predominantly orange and not overly sweet.

HABANERO NEW #8

●●●●○

Glass: Martini
Garnish: Orange zest twist
Method: MUDDLE ginger and chilli in base of shaker. Add other ingredients, **SHAKE** with ice and fine-strain into chilled glass.

1	slice	**Red chilli** (thin slice)
1	slice	**Fresh root ginger** (thumbnail sized)
2	shot(s)	**Bacardi Superior rum**
1	shot(s)	**Drambuie liqueur**
¾	shot(s)	**Freshly squeezed lime juice**
2	spoons	**Honey syrup** (4 honey to 1 water)
2	dashes	**Angostura orange bitters**
½	fresh	**Egg white**

Comment: A Daiquiri-style drink with honey, ginger and chilli.
Origin: Created in 2008 by Giuliano Morandin at The Bar at The Dorchester Hotel, Hotel, London, England.

HAIR OF THE DOG

●●●●○

Glass: Martini
Garnish: Grate fresh nutmeg
Method: STIR honey with Scotch until honey dissolves. Add other ingredients, **SHAKE** with ice and fine strain into chilled glass.

3	spoons	**Runny honey**
2	shot(s)	**Johnnie Walker Scotch whisky**
1	shot(s)	**Double (heavy) cream**
1	shot(s)	**Milk**

Origin: Traditionally drunk as a pick-me-up hangover cure.
Comment: This drink's name and reputation as a hangover cure may lead you to assume it tastes unpleasant. In fact, honey, whisky and cream combine wonderfully.

HAKKATINI

●●●●○

Glass: Martini
Garnish: Orange zest twist
Method: SHAKE all ingredients with ice and fine strain into chilled glass.

1	shot(s)	**Orange-infused Ketel One vodka**
1	shot(s)	**Grand Marnier liqueur**
¼	shot(s)	**Campari Bitter**
¾	shot(s)	**Pressed apple juice**

Origin: Adapted from a drink discovered in 2003 at Hakkasan, London, England.
Comment: Balanced bitter sweet orange and apple.

HAMMER OF THE GODS

●●●○○

Glass: Shot & pint glass
Method: LAYER ingredients by carefully pouring into shot glass in the following order. **IGNITE** and hold pint glass upside down a few inches above the flame. Allow the drink to burn for thirty seconds or so before killing the flame, being sure to keep the pint glass in place. Instruct your subject to suck the alcohol vapour from the inverted pint glass using a bendy straw. Finally, remove the pint glass and let your subject consume the drink through the straw.

1	shot(s)	**Tuaca Italian liqueur**
½	shot(s)	**La Fée Parisienne (68%) absinthe**

Origin: Created by Dick Bradsell at The Player, London, UK.
Comment: Killjoys would point out the dangers of fire and alcohol and observe that this is hardly 'responsible drinking'.

HOW TO MAKE SUGAR SYRUP

To make your own sugar syrup, gradually pour TWO cups of granulated sugar into a saucepan containing ONE cup of hot water. Stir as you pour and carry on stirring and simmering until the sugar is dissolved. Do not let the water even come close to boiling and only simmer for as long as it takes to dissolve the sugar. Allow syrup to cool and pour into an empty bottle. Ideally, you should finely strain your syrup into the bottle to remove any undissolved crystals which could otherwise encourage crystallisation. If kept in a refrigerator this mixture will last for a couple of months.

HAND GRENADE NEW #8

Glass: Collins (or Hand-Grenade)
Garnish: Whole lime with scored skin
Method: SHAKE all ingredients with ice and strain into glass filled with crushed ice.

1½	shot(s)	**Tanqueray London dry gin**
1½	shot(s)	**Bacardi Superior rum**
1½	shot(s)	**Ketel One vodka**
1½	shot(s)	**Midori green melon liqueur**

Comment: A blend of white spirits sweetened and melon flavoured by the addition of green-coloured liqueur. Classy!
Origin: The above recipe bares little similarity to the notorious Hand Grenade served by the three Tropical Isle Bars and the Funky Pirate bar in New Orleans, USA. Marketed as "New Orleans' most powerful drink" and served in long plastic half-yard hand-grenade shaped vessels this green melon flavoured proprietary drink is available as a pre-mix by mail order from www.tropicalisle.com. In the USA the operators of Tropical Isle have trademarked Hand Grenade so preventing other establishments not licensed by Tropical Isle from selling cocktails of this name.

HANKY-PANKY MARTINI UPDATED #8

Glass: Martini
Garnish: Orange zest twist
Method: STIR all ingredients with ice and strain into chilled glass.

1¾	shot(s)	**Tanqueray London dry gin**
1¾	shot(s)	**Martini Rosso sweet vermouth**
⅛	shot(s)	**Fernet Branca**

Origin: Created in the early 1900s by Ada 'Coley' Coleman at The Savoy's American Bar, London, for actor Sir Charles Hawtrey. He often said to Coley, "I am tired. Give me something with a bit of punch in it." This drink was her answer. After finishing his first one, Charles told Coley, "By Jove! That is the real hanky-panky!" And so it has since been named. Coley was the first Bar Manger of the famous American Bar. She perfected her craft at Claridge's and left to start at the Savoy in July 1903, where she stayed until her retirement in December 1924. The Hanky-Panky is her most famous creation.
Comment: A Sweet Martini made bitter and aromatic by Fernet Branca.

HAPPY NEW YEAR

Glass: Flute
Garnish: Orange slice on rim
Method: SHAKE first 3 ingredients with ice and fine strain into chilled glass. TOP with champagne.

¼	shot(s)	**Courvoisier V.S.O.P. cognac**
¾	shot(s)	**Warre's Otima tawny port**
¾	shot(s)	**Freshly squeezed orange juice**
Top up with		**Perrier Jouet brut champagne**

Origin: Created in 1981 by Charles Schumann, Munich, Germany.
Comment: Reminiscent of fizzy, fruity claret.

HARD LEMONADE

Glass: Collins
Garnish: Lemon slice
Method: SHAKE first 3 ingredients with ice and strain into ice-filled glass. TOP with soda and serve with straws.

2	shot(s)	**Ketel One vodka**
2	shot(s)	**Freshly squeezed lemon juice**
1	shot(s)	**Sugar syrup** (2 sugar to 1 water)
Top up with		**Soda water** (club soda)

Variants: Vodka Collins, Ray's Hard Lemonade
Origin: Discovered in 2004 at Spring Street Natural Restaurant, New York City, USA.
Comment: Refreshing lemonade with a kick. Great for a hot afternoon.

THE HARLEM

Glass: Martini
Garnish: Cherry in drink
Method: SHAKE all ingredients with ice and fine strain into chilled glass.

2	shot(s)	**Tanqueray London dry gin**
¼	shot(s)	**Luxardo maraschino liqueur**
2	shot(s)	**Pressed pineapple juice**

Origin: Thought to date back to the Prohibition era and the Cotton Club in Harlem.
Comment: Soft and fruity. Careful, it's harder than you think.

HARPOON NEW #8

Glass: Old-fashioned
Garnish: Lime wedge
Method: POUR ingredients into ice-filled glass and stir.

1	shot(s)	**Ketel One vodka**
2	shot(s)	**Ocean Spray cranberry juice**
¼	shot(s)	**Freshly squeezed lime juice**

Origin: Though to be the forerunner to the Cosmopolitan. A 1968 bottle label from Ocean Spray's archives lists the Harpoon as a "new cocktail". It was originally launched as being 2 ounces Ocean Spray cranberry and 1 ounce vodka or light rum served "over the rocks or tall with soda. Suggested garnish: a splash of lime or lemon optional." In 1970, it was updated to also list gin as a possible base spirit.
Comment: Innocuously light in both flavour and alcohol. Add a shot of triple sec and you are well on your way to making a Cosmopolitan.

DRINKS ARE GRADED AS FOLLOWS:

● DISGUSTING ●○ PRETTY AWFUL ●● BEST AVOIDED
●●○ DISAPPOINTING ●●● ACCEPTABLE ●●●○ GOOD
●●●● RECOMMENDED ●●●●○ HIGHLY RECOMMENDED
●●●●● OUTSTANDING / EXCEPTIONAL

SHOCHU WAS THE FAVOURITE BEVERAGE OF THE WORLD'S LONGEST-LIVING MAN, SHIGECHIYO IZUMI OF JAPAN, WHO LIVED FOR 120 YEARS AND 237 DAYS. HE WAS BORN ON JUNE 29, 1865 AND DIED ON FEBRUARY 21, 1986.

HARVEY WALLBANGER

Glass: Collins
Garnish: Orange slice
Method: SHAKE all ingredients with ice and strain into ice-filled glass.

2	shot(s)	**Ketel One vodka**
3½	shot(s)	**Freshly squeezed orange juice**
½	shot(s)	**Galliano L'Autentico liqueur**

Variant: Freddie Fudpucker
Origin: Legend has it that 'Harvey' was a surfer at Manhattan Beach, California. His favourite drink was a Screwdriver with added Galliano. One day in the late sixties, while celebrating winning a surfing competition, he staggered from bar to bar, banging his surfboard on the walls, and so a contemporary classic gained its name.

However, an article in Bartender Magazine credits the creation to Bill Doner, the host of a house party held in the mid-sixties in Newport Beach, California. One of the guests, Harvey, was found banging his head the next morning, complaining of the hangover this drink induced.
Comment: It's usual to build this drink and 'float' Galliano over the built drink. However, as the Galliano sinks anyway it is better shaken.

HARVARD UPDATED #8

Glass: Martini
Garnish: Lemon zest twist
Method: STIR all ingredients with ice and strain into chilled glass. **TOP** with a shot or so of chilled soda.

1½	shot(s)	**Courvoisier V.S.O.P. cognac**
2	shot(s)	**Martini Rosso sweet vermouth**
2	dashes	**Angostura orange bitters** (optional)
Top up with		**Soda water** (from siphon)

AKA: New Orleans Manhattan
Variant: Delmonico (with Angostura in place of orange bitters).
Origin: Recipe adapted from George J. Kappeler's 1895 'Modern American Drinks'. In his 1931 book 'Old Waldorf Bar Days', Albert Stevens Crockett, notes of this drink, "Named after a school for young men, whose site is contiguous to the Charles River, in a suburb of Boston. Alumni who drunk it sometimes lost the 'Harvard accent'.
Comment: Old-school, but approachably so. Dry and herbal. A great aperitif.

HAVANA COBBLER

Glass: Old-fashioned
Garnish: Lime zest twist
Method: SHAKE all ingredients with ice and strain into glass filled with crushed ice.

2	shot(s)	**Bacardi Superior rum**
1	shot(s)	**Warre's Otima tawny port**
½	shot(s)	**Stone's original green ginger wine**
¼	shot(s)	**Sugar syrup** (2 sugar to 1 water)

Comment: An unusual, spiced, Daiquiri-like drink.

HAVANA SPECIAL

Glass: Old-fashioned
Garnish: Lime zest twist
Method: SHAKE all ingredients with ice and strain into glass filled with crushed ice.

2	shot(s)	**Bacardi Superior rum**
1¾	shot(s)	**Pressed pineapple juice**
½	shot(s)	**Luxardo maraschino liqueur**

Comment: Daiquiri-like without the sourness. Fragrant and all too easy to drink.

HARVARD COOLER

Glass: Collins
Garnish: Lime wedge
Method: SHAKE first 3 ingredients with ice and strain into ice-filled glass. **TOP** with soda, stir and serve with straws.

2	shot(s)	**Boulard Grand Solage calvados**
1	shot(s)	**Freshly squeezed lime juice**
½	shot(s)	**Sugar syrup** (2 sugar to 1 water)
Top up with		**Soda water** (club soda)

Comment: Refreshing and not too sweet. Lime and sugar enhance the appley spirit.

DRINKS ARE GRADED AS FOLLOWS:

● DISGUSTING ●● PRETTY AWFUL ●● BEST AVOIDED
●●● DISAPPOINTING ●●● ACCEPTABLE ●●●● GOOD
●●●● RECOMMENDED ●●●●● HIGHLY RECOMMENDED
●●●●● OUTSTANDING / EXCEPTIONAL

HAVANATHEONE

Glass: Martini
Garnish: Mint leaf
Method: Lightly **MUDDLE** mint (just to bruise) in base of shaker. Add rum and honey and **STIR** until honey dissolves. Add other ingredients, **SHAKE** with ice and fine strain into chilled glass.

10	fresh	Mint leaves
2	spoons	Runny honey
2	shot(s)	Bacardi Superior rum
½	shot(s)	Freshly squeezed lime juice
1	shot(s)	Pressed apple juice

Origin: Discovered in 2003 at Hush, London, England.
Comment: A flavoursome Daiquiri featuring honey, apple and mint.

HAWAIIAN

Glass: Hurricane
Garnish: Pineapple wedge & cherry
Method: BLEND all ingredients with two 12oz scoops crushed ice and serve with straws.

2	shot(s)	Malibu coconut rum liqueur
½	shot(s)	Cointreau triple sec
½	shot(s)	Bacardi Superior rum
1½	shot(s)	Freshly squeezed orange juice
1½	shot(s)	Pressed pineapple juice
1	shot(s)	Freshly squeezed lime juice
½	shot(s)	Sugar syrup (2 sugar to 1 water)
1	shot(s)	Coco López cream of coconut

Comment: Coconut, rum and fruit juice. Aloha.

HAWAIIAN COCKTAIL

Glass: Martini
Garnish: Pineapple wedge & cherry on rim
Method: SHAKE all ingredients with ice and fine strain into chilled glass.

1½	shot(s)	Bacardi Superior rum
½	shot(s)	Southern Comfort liqueur
½	shot(s)	Luxardo Amaretto di Saschira
¾	shot(s)	Freshly squeezed orange juice
1½	shot(s)	Pressed pineapple juice

Origin: Discovered in Las Vegas in 2004.
Comment: Sweet, tangy and fruity.

HAWAIIAN COSMOPOLITAN

Glass: Martini
Garnish: Pineapple wedge on rim
Method: SHAKE all ingredients with ice and fine strain into chilled glass.

2	shot(s)	Ketel One Citroen vodka
1	shot(s)	Sour pineapple liqueur
1	shot(s)	Pressed apple juice
½	shot(s)	Freshly squeezed lime juice

Origin: Created in 2002 by Wayne Collins, UK.
Comment: Fresh, tangy and distinctly tropical.

HAWAIIAN EYE

Glass: Collins
Garnish: Pineapple wedge & cherry
Method: BLEND all ingredients with two 12oz scoops of crushed ice. Serve with straws.

1	shot(s)	Bacardi Superior rum
1	shot(s)	Bacardi Oro golden rum
½	shot(s)	Velvet Falernum liqueur
½	shot(s)	Freshly squeezed lime juice
½	shot(s)	Sugar syrup (2 sugar to 1 water)

Origin: A Tiki drink created in 1963 by Tony Ramos at China Trader, California, USA, for the cast of the TV series of the same name.
Comment: Tropical, rum laced cooler.

H

HAWAIIAN MARTINI

Glass: Martini
Garnish: Pineapple wedge & cherry
Method: SHAKE all ingredients with ice and fine strain into chilled glass.

1½	shot(s)	Tanqueray London dry gin
½	shot(s)	Noilly Prat dry vermouth
½	shot(s)	Martini Rosso sweet vermouth
1½	shot(s)	Pressed pineapple juice

Origin: Adapted from a drink discovered in 2005 at the Four Seasons, Milan, Italy.
Comment: An aptly named fruity twist on the classic Martini.

HAWAIIAN SEABREEZE

Glass: Collins
Garnish: Pineapple wedge on rim
Method: SHAKE all ingredients with ice and strain into ice-filled glass.

2	shot(s)	Mango flavoured vodka
2½	shot(s)	Ocean Spray cranberry juice
1½	shot(s)	Pressed pineapple juice

Variant: Bay Breeze
Comment: Easygoing, foam topped relative of the Seabreeze.

HAYDENISTIC

Glass: Martini
Garnish: Lime zest twist
Method: STIR all ingredients with ice and strain into chilled glass.

2	shot(s)	Ketel One vodka
⅛	shot(s)	St-Germain elderflower liqueur
⅛	shot(s)	Velvet Falernum liqueur

Origin: Created in 2007 by Hayden Lambert at The Merchant Hotel, Belfast, Northern Ireland.
Comment: Extremely subtle, like a very complex Wet Vodkatini.

HAZEL'ITO

Glass: Collins
Method: Lightly **MUDDLE** mint in base of glass (just to bruise). Add other ingredients, fill glass with crushed ice and **CHURN** (stir) with bar spoon to mix.

12	fresh	**Mint leaves**
2	shot(s)	**Bacardi Superior rum**
2	shot(s)	**Frangelico hazelnut liqueur**
1	shot(s)	**Freshly squeezed lime juice**
½	shot(s)	**Sugar syrup** (2 sugar to 1 water)

Origin: Created in January 2002 by Adam Wyartt, London, England.
Comment: Looks like a Mojito but has a nutty twang courtesy of the hazelnut liqueur.

HAZELNUT ALEXANDER

Glass: Martini
Garnish: Dust with cacao powder
Method: **SHAKE** all ingredients with ice and fine strain into chilled glass.

1¾	shot(s)	**Courvoisier V.S.O.P. cognac**
¾	shot(s)	**Frangelico hazelnut liqueur**
½	shot(s)	**Brown crème de cacao liqueur**
½	shot(s)	**Double (heavy) cream**
½	shot(s)	**Milk**
2	dashes	**Angostura aromatic bitters**

Origin: Created in 2005 by James Mellnor at Maze, London, England.
Comment: Great twist on a classic – the use of bitters is inspired.

HAZELNUT MARTINI

Glass: Martini
Garnish: Hazelnut in drink
Method: **STIR** all ingredients with ice and strain into chilled glass.

2	shot(s)	**Ketel One vodka**
½	shot(s)	**Frangelico hazelnut liqueur**
½	shot(s)	**White crème de cacao liqueur**
¾	shot(s)	**Chilled mineral water** (omit if wet ice)

Comment: A hazelnut Vodkatini with a hint of chocolate.

HEAD SHOT

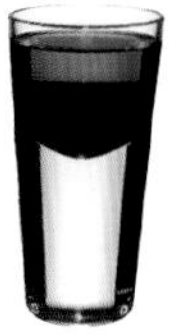

Glass: Shot
Method: Refrigerate ingredients then **LAYER** in chilled glass by carefully pouring in the following order.

| ¾ | shot(s) | **Opal Nera black sambuca** |
| ¾ | shot(s) | **Green Chartreuse liqueur** |

Comment: Please drink responsibly.

HEARST MARTINI

Glass: Martini
Garnish: Orange zest twist
Method: **STIR** all ingredients with ice and strain into chilled glass.

2	shot(s)	**Tanqueray London dry gin**
1	shot(s)	**Martini Rosso sweet vermouth**
1	dash	**Angostura orange bitters**
1	dash	**Angostura aromatic bitters**

Origin: This was supposedly a favourite of hacks who worked for the American newspaper magnate, William Randolph Hearst, and is believed to have been created at New York's Waldorf-Astoria. It is nicknamed 'The Disgruntled Journalist' and indeed, is not dissimilar to a Journalist with extra bitters.
Comment: A fantastically wet, sweet and aromatic Martini.

'YOU'RE NOT DRUNK IF YOU CAN LIE ON THE FLOOR WITHOUT HOLDING ON.'
DEAN MARTIN

HEATHER JULEP

Glass: Collins
Garnish: Mint sprig
Method: Lightly **MUDDLE** mint in base of shaker (just to bruise). Add other ingredients, **SHAKE** with ice and strain into glass filled with crushed ice. **CHURN** (stir) the drink using a bar spoon. Top the glass with more crushed ice so as to fill it and churn again. Serve with straws.

12	fresh	**Mint leaves**
2½	shot(s)	**Johnnie Walker Scotch whisky**
½	shot(s)	**Drambuie liqueur**
¾	shot(s)	**Sugar syrup** (2 sugar to 1 water)

Origin: Adapted from a drink discovered in 2001 at Teatro, London, England.
Comment: A Scottish twist on the classic bourbon based Mint Julep.

HEAVEN SCENT

Glass: Martini
Garnish: Orange zest twist
Method: **SHAKE** all ingredients with ice and fine strain into chilled glass.

1½	shot(s)	**Vanilla-infused Ketel One vodka**
1½	shot(s)	**Krupnik honey liqueur**
½	shot(s)	**Freshly squeezed lemon juice**
¾	shot(s)	**Chilled mineral water** (omit if wet ice)

Origin: Discovered in 2003 at Oxo Tower Bar, London, England.
Comment: Honey, vanilla and lemon – reminiscent of a chilled, straight-up toddy.

HEAVENS ABOVE

Glass: Collins
Garnish: Pineapple wedge on rim
Method: SHAKE all ingredients with ice and strain into glass filled with crushed ice.

2	shot(s)	**Bacardi Oro golden rum**
¼	shot(s)	**Kahlúa coffee liqueur**
¼	shot(s)	**Brown crème de cacao liqueur**
3	shot(s)	**Pressed pineapple juice**

Origin: A Tiki style drink adapted from a drink featured in Jeff Berry's 'Intoxica' and originally created circa 1970 at Top of Toronto, CN Tower, Toronto, Canada.
Comment: Slightly sweet, fruity rum – hard not to like

HEDGEROW SLING UPDATED #8

Glass: Sling
Garnish: Seasonal berries & lemon slice
Method: SHAKE first 4 ingredients with ice and strain into glass filled with crushed ice. **TOP** with soda and then **DRIZZLE** blackberry liqueur over drink. Serve with straws.

1	shot(s)	**Tanqueray London dry gin**
1	shot(s)	**Sloe gin liqueur**
1	shot(s)	**Freshly squeezed lemon juice**
½	shot(s)	**Sugar syrup** (2 sugar to 1 water)
Top up with		**Soda water** (club soda)
¼	shot(s)	**Crème de mûre liqueur**

Origin: Created by Brian Duell at Detroit, London, England.
Comment: Rich, long, berry drink.

HEMINGWAY

Glass: Flute
Garnish: Star anise on rim
Method: POUR anis into chilled glass. **TOP** with champagne.

1	shot(s)	**Pernod anis**
Top up with		**Perrier Jouet brut champagne**

AKA: Corpse Reviver #2
Origin: Created at Cantineros' Club, the famous Cuban bar school.
Comment: Why dilute your anis with water when you can use champagne?

HEMINGWAY MARTINI

Glass: Martini
Garnish: Maraschino cherry
Method: SHAKE all ingredients with ice and fine strain into chilled glass.

2	shot(s)	**Orange-infused Ketel One vodka**
½	shot(s)	**Vanilla schnapps liqueur**
1	shot(s)	**Freshly squeezed grapefruit juice**
⅛	shot(s)	**Noilly Prat dry vermouth**
⅛	shot(s)	**Maraschino syrup** (from cherry jar)

Origin: Created in 2005 by Claire Smith, London, England.
Comment: Fresh and refreshing in flavour, traditional yet modern in style.

HEMINGWAY SPECIAL DAIQUIRI

Glass: 10oz Martini (huge)
Garnish: Lime wedge on rim
Method: SHAKE all ingredients with ice and fine strain into chilled glass.

3½	shot(s)	**Bacardi Superior rum**
1	shot(s)	**Freshly squeezed grapefruit juice**
¾	shot(s)	**Luxardo maraschino liqueur**
1	shot(s)	**Freshly squeezed lime juice**
½	shot(s)	**Sugar syrup** (omit for original)

AKA: Papa Doble Daiquiri
Comment: A true Hemingway Special should be served without the addition of sugar. However, Hemingway had a hardened palate and more delicate drinkers may prefer the recipe above.
Origin: Created by Constantino (Constante) Ribalaigua Vert, the legendary head bartender of La Floridita, Havana, Cuba for Ernest Hemingway, after the great man wandered into the bar to use the toilet. When Hemingway tried the Floridita's standard frozen Daiquiri, he is quoted as saying, "That's good but I prefer it without sugar and with double rum," so the Hemingway Special was born.

Hemingway suffered from haemochromotosis, a rare and hereditary form of diabetes from which his father also suffered, hence his aversion to sugar. The original version was exactly as Hemingway requested a Daiquiri without sugar and heavy on the rum, basically rum shaken with a splash of lime juice. Years later after he took over the position of Head Bartender at La Floridita, Antonio Meilan added maraschino and grapefruit juice into the drink. Today sugar is commonly also added to balance this drink and make it more palatable to people with less sour palates than Hemingway.

Hemingway was affectionately known as 'Papa' in Cuba and this drink was originally named 'Daiquiri Like Papa' and then later 'Papa Doble'. After Meilan added maraschino and grapefruit the drink changed its name again to the Hemingway Special we recognise today.

HENRY VIII

Glass: Flute
Garnish: Orange zest twist
Method: Soak sugar cube with absinthe and drop into chilled glass. **POUR** other ingredients over sugar cube and serve.

1	cube	**Sugar**
⅛	shot(s)	**La Fée Parisienne (68%) absinthe**
½	shot(s)	**Ketel One Citroen vodka**
½	shot(s)	**Pepper flavoured vodka**
Top up with		**Perrier Jouet brut champagne**

Origin: Created in 2004 by Henry Besant, London, England.
Comment: A contemporary twist on the classic Champagne Cocktail.

DRINKS ARE GRADED AS FOLLOWS:

● DISGUSTING　●○ PRETTY AWFUL　●● BEST AVOIDED
●●○ DISAPPOINTING　●●● ACCEPTABLE　●●●○ GOOD
●●●● RECOMMENDED　●●●●○ HIGHLY RECOMMENDED
●●●●● OUTSTANDING / EXCEPTIONAL

●●●●○○

HE'S AT HOME NEW #8

Glass: Collins
Garnish: Lime zest twist
Method: SHAKE all ingredients with ice and fine strain into glass filled with crushed ice.

½	shot(s)	**Freshly squeezed lime juice**
2	shot(s)	**Green Chartreuse liqueur**
1	dash	**Fee Brothers mint bitters**

Origin: This recipe is adapted from one by Del Pedro, Alexander's, New York City. It came to me (in 1997) courtesy of the infamous LeNell Smothers. To quote from Del, "I used to call this a 'Gatsby cooler' at one time, because there seems something kinda evilly 'Hampton-ish' about this drink… but I also called it 'He's At Home' which was the name given to porcelain dildos that Nantucket ship's captain's wives kept stashed in the flue of their fireplaces for the lonely winter nights when the old dog was chasing whales."
Comment: LeNell's kind of drink and accompanying story. Other Chartreuse lover's should experiment.

●●●●○○

HESITATION NEW #8

Glass: Martini
Garnish: Lemon zest twist
Method: SHAKE all ingredients with ice and fine strain into chilled glass.

2	shot(s)	**Swedish Punch**
1	shot(s)	**Bulleit bourbon whiskey**
¼	shot(s)	**Freshly squeezed lemon juice**
½	shot(s)	**Chilled water** (omit if wet ice)

Comment: Lightly spiced and slightly sweet.
Origin: Vintage cocktail of unknown origin.

●●●●○○

HIBISCUS KISS NEW #8

Glass: Flute
Garnish: Lemon zest twist (discarded)
Method: Place hibiscus flower in base of chilled glass. Add rest of ingredients and gently stir.

1	candied	**Wild Hibiscus flower** (jarred)
¾	shot(s)	**Pear-flavoured vodka**
¾	shot(s)	**St-Germain elderflower liqueur**
Top up with		**Perrier Jouet brut champagne**

Comment: Pear and elderflower champagne over a candied hibiscus flower.
Origin: Created in 2008 by Francesco Lafranconi of Southern Wine & Spirits, USA.

●●●●●○

HIBISCUS MARGARITA NEW #8

Glass: Martini
Garnish: Wild Hibiscus flower from jar
Method: SHAKE all ingredients with ice and fine strain into chilled glass.

2	shot(s)	**Don Julio reposado tequila**
1	shot(s)	**Freshly squeezed lime juice**
1	shot(s)	**Homemade hibiscus tea syrup**

Comment: Hibiscus combines wonderfully with tequila in this flavoursome Margarita.

●●●●●◑

HIGHBALL (GENERIC NAME) UPDATED #8

Glass: Collins
Garnish: Slice of orange, lime or lemon as appropriate to the spirit and the carbonate
Method: POUR spirit into ice-filled glass and **TOP** with a carbonated soft drink (ginger ale, soda or tonic water). Stir gently so as not to kill the fizz.

| 2 | shot(s) | **Spirit** (whisk(e)y, brandy, vodka etc.) |
| Top up with | | **Ginger ale, soda, tonic water or other carbonated mixer** |

Comment: Simple, but simplicity can be beautiful.
Origin: Scotch & Soda, Gin & Tonic, Whiskey & Ginger, Vodka & Tonic and Rum & Coke are all examples of Highball cocktails. Highballs are a type of simple cocktail with only two ingredients, normally a spirit and a carbonate, served in a tall ice-filled glass (often referred to as a highball glass). Unlike Rickeys, Collinses and Fizzes, Highballs do not contain citrus fruit juice.

In his 1934 'The Official Mixer's Guide', Patrick Gavin Duffy writes, "It is one of my fondest hopes that the highball will again take its place as the leading American Drink. I admit to being prejudiced about this - it was I who first brought the highball to America, in 1895. Although the distinction is claimed by the Parker House in Boston, I was finally given due credit for this innovation in the New York Times of not many years ago."

That New York Times reference appears to be a letter written by Duffy on 22 October 1927 to the Editor in response to an editorial piece in the paper. He starts, "An editorial in The Times says that the Adams House, Boston, claims to have served the first Scotch highball in this country. This claim is unfounded." He goes on to tell of how in 1894 he opened a little cafe next the old Lyceum in New York City and that in the Spring of that year, an English actor and regular patron, E. J. Ratcliffe, one day asked for a Scotch and soda. At that time Duffy did not carry Scotch but this request and the growing number of English actors frequenting his bar led Duffy to order five cases of Usher's from Park & Tilford. Duffy claims that when the shipment arrived he "sold little but Scotch highballs", consisting of "Scotch, a lump of ice and a bottle of club soda". His letter finishes, "Shortly afterward every actor along Broadway, and consequently every New Yorker who frequented the popular bars, was drinking Scotch highballs. In a few years other Scotch distillers introduced their brands and many were enriched by the quantity consumed in this country. Actors on tour, and members of the Ancient and Honorable Artillery of Boston, who came here annually to attend the Old Guard Ball, brought the new drink to the Adams House."

Duffy's letter to The New York Times mentions Adam House in Boston while the reference in his subsequent book talks of "Parker House". Both are plausible Boston locations but does this confusion mean we should not take any of Duffy's claims for being the first to make Scotch Highballs in America seriously? The Times merely published Duffy's letter to the editor, the paper did not substantiate or even "give credit" to his claims.

In his 2003 'The Joy of Mixology', Gary Regan explains that "Highball is an old railroad term for the ball indicator connected to a float inside a steam train's water tank which told the conductor that there was enough water in the tank and so the train could proceed. Apparently when the train was set to depart, the conductor would give the highball – two short whistle blows and one long. Gary explains that this term was apt as the drinks consist of 2 shots of liquor and a long pour of mixer.

●●●●○○

HIGHLAND DRUM NEW #8

Glass: Coupette/Martini
Garnish: Orange zest twist
Method: SHAKE all ingredients with ice and fine strain into chilled glass.

2	shot(s)	**Singleton Speyside malt whisky**
1	shot(s)	**Noilly Prat dry vermouth**
¾	shot(s)	**Drambuie liqueur**
¼	shot(s)	**Freshly squeezed orange juice**
1	spoon	**Honey syrup** (4 honey to 1 water)
2	dash	**Angostura orange bitters**

Comment: The classic blend of Scotch and Drambuie with fresh orange and vermouth complexity.
Origin: Created by Salvatore Calabrese at Salvatore at Fifty, London, England.

HIGHLAND SLING

Glass: Sling
Garnish: Apple wedge
Method: SHAKE all ingredients with ice and strain into ice-filled glass.

1½	shot(s)	**Johnnie Walker Scotch whisky**
½	shot(s)	**Galliano L'Autentico liqueur**
1	shot(s)	**Ocean Spray cranberry juice**
½	shot(s)	**Bols apricot brandy liqueur**
2	shot(s)	**Pressed apple juice**

Comment: A surprisingly good combination of diverse flavours.

THE HIVE

Glass: Martini
Garnish: Orange zest twist
Method: STIR honey with vodka until honey dissolves. Add other ingredients, SHAKE with ice and fine strain into chilled glass.

2	spoons	**Runny honey**
1	shot(s)	**Ketel One vodka**
1	shot(s)	**Krupnik honey liqueur**
2	shot(s)	**Freshly squeezed grapefruit juice**

Origin: Discovered in 2004 at Circus, London, England.
Comment: Sour grapefruit balanced by sweet honey.

HOA SUA

Glass: Martini
Garnish: Pineapple wedge on rim
Method: SHAKE all ingredients with ice and fine strain into chilled glass.

1½	shot(s)	**POM Wonderful pomegranate juice**
1½	shot(s)	**Bacardi Superior rum**
¾	shot(s)	**Sake**
⅛	shot(s)	**Sugar syrup** (2 sugar to 1 water)
1	dash	**Angostura aromatic bitters**

Origin: Created in 2005 by Yours Truly (Simon Difford) for Hoa Sua catering school in Vietnam using locally available products.
Comment: Light and easy drinking – the rum flavour shines through.

HOBSON NEW #8

Glass: Old-fashioned
Garnish: Orange slice
Method: SHAKE all ingredients with ice and strain into glass filled with crushed ice.

2	shot(s)	**Sloe gin liqueur**
1	shot(s)	**Cointreau triple sec**
¼	shot(s)	**La Fée Parisienne (68%) absinthe**

Comment: Unbalanced towards sweetness. With drinks like this you can see why Hobson chose to be an abstainer. Originally served 'straight-up' but better over crushed ice.
Origin: Named after Richmond Pearson Hobson (1870-1937) the United States Navy Rear Admiral and not Thomas Hobson (1545–1631) from Cambridge, England who gave rise to the term 'Hobson's choice'. R.P. Hopson was a hero of the American-Spanish war of 1898 who went on to became a Congressman. An ardent abstainer, Hobson has been called 'The Father of American Prohibition' due of his advocacy for criminalizing alcohol and other drugs and was a prolific author on this subject.

HOBSON'S CHOICE (MOCKTAIL)

Glass: Collins
Garnish: Lime wedge on rim
Method: SHAKE all ingredients with ice and strain into ice-filled glass.

2½	shot(s)	**Freshly squeezed orange juice**
2½	shot(s)	**Pressed apple juice**
1	shot(s)	**Freshly squeezed lime juice**
¼	shot(s)	**Pomegranate (grenadine) syrup**

Comment: A fruity, non-alcoholic cocktail.

HOFFMAN HOUSE UPDATED #8

Glass: Martini
Garnish: Lemon zest twist
Method: SHAKE all ingredients with ice and fine strain into chilled glass.

2½	shot(s)	**Tanqueray London dry gin**
½	shot(s)	**Noilly Prat dry vermouth**
2	dashes	**Angostura orange bitters**

Comment: A shaken Wet (5:1) Martini with orange bitters.
Origin: Apparently the house cocktail at Manhattan's Hoffman House in the 1880s.

HOW TO MAKE SUGAR SYRUP

To make your own sugar syrup, gradually pour TWO cups of granulated sugar into a saucepan containing ONE cup of hot water. Stir as you pour and carry on stirring and simmering until the sugar is dissolved. Do not let the water even come close to boiling and only simmer for as long as it takes to dissolve the sugar. Allow syrup to cool and pour into an empty bottle. Ideally, you should finely strain your syrup into the bottle to remove any undissolved crystals which could otherwise encourage crystallisation. If kept in a refrigerator this mixture will last for a couple of months.

THE HOLLAND HOUSE COCKTAIL

●●●●○

Glass: Martini
Garnish: Lemon zest twist
Method: SHAKE all ingredients with ice and fine strain into chilled glass.

1¾	shot(s)	**Bokma oude genever**
¾	shot(s)	**Noilly Prat dry vermouth**
½	shot(s)	**Freshly squeezed lemon juice**
¼	shot(s)	**Luxardo maraschino liqueur**

Origin: A forgotten classic which is rightly being championed by the House of Bols, Amsterdam, The Netherlands.
Comment: Dry and reminiscent of an Aviation but with genever personality.

HONEY & MARMALADE DRAM

●●●●○

UPDATED #8

Glass: Martini
Garnish: Strips of orange peel
Method: STIR honey with Scotch in base of shaker until honey dissolves. Add other ingredients, **SHAKE** with ice and fine strain into chilled glass.

2	shot(s)	**Johnnie Walker Scotch whisky**
4	spoons	**Runny honey**
1	shot(s)	**Freshly squeezed lemon juice**
1	shot(s)	**Freshly squeezed orange juice**

Comment: This citrussy drink seems to enrich and enhance the flavour of Scotch.
Origin: I adapted this recipe from the Honeysuckle Daiquiri.

HONEY APPLE MARTINI

●●●●○

Glass: Martini
Garnish: Lemon zest twist
Method: SHAKE all ingredients with ice and fine strain into chilled glass.

1½	shot(s)	**Zubrówka bison vodka**
¾	shot(s)	**Krupnik honey liqueur**
1¼	shot(s)	**Pressed apple juice**
¼	shot(s)	**Freshly squeezed lemon juice**

Variant: Polish Martini
Comment: A classically Polish blend of flavours.

HONEY BEE UPDATED #8

●●●●○

Glass: Martini
Garnish: Lemon zest twist
Method: STIR honey with rum in base of shaker until honey dissolves. Add other ingredients, **SHAKE** with ice and fine strain into chilled glass.

2	shot(s)	**Bacardi Superior rum**
3	spoons	**Runny honey**
½	shot(s)	**Freshly squeezed lemon juice**
¾	shot(s)	**Chilled mineral water** (omit if wet ice)

Comment: Basically a honey Daiquiri – very nice.
Origin: Adapted from 1949 Esquire's 'Handbook For Hosts'.

HONEY BERRY SOUR #1 UPDATED #8

●●●●○

Glass: Old-fashioned
Garnish: Lemon wedge
Method: SHAKE all ingredients with ice and strain into ice-filled glass.

1½	shot(s)	**Krupnik honey liqueur**
¾	shot(s)	**Crème de cassis liqueur**
1	shot(s)	**Freshly squeezed lemon juice**
¼	shot(s)	**Sugar syrup** (2 sugar to 1 water)
½	fresh	**Egg white**

Comment: More sweet than sour but berry nice.
Origin: Created by Tim Hallilaj.

HONEY BLOSSOM

●●●○○

Glass: Old-fashioned
Garnish: Pineapple wedge on rim
Method: SHAKE all ingredients with ice and fine strain into ice-filled glass.

3	shot(s)	**Pressed pineapple juice**
1	shot(s)	**Freshly squeezed lemon juice**
¼	shot(s)	**Vanilla syrup**
½	fresh	**Egg white**
3	dashes	**Angostura aromatic bitters**

Origin: Created in 2003 by Tim Phillips at the GE Club, London, England.
Comment: Soft, fruity, yet adult. Note: contains trace amounts of alcohol.

HONEY DAIQUIRI

●●●●◖

Glass: Martini
Garnish: Lime wedge on rim
Method: STIR honey with rum in base of shaker until honey dissolves. Add other ingredients, **SHAKE** with ice and fine strain into chilled glass.

2	spoons	**Runny honey**
2	shot(s)	**Bacardi Superior rum**
½	shot(s)	**Freshly squeezed lime juice**
½	shot(s)	**Chilled mineral water** (omit if wet ice)

Comment: Sweet honey replaces sugar syrup in this natural Daiquiri. Try experimenting with different honeys. I favour orange blossom honey.

HONEY LIMEAID (MOCKTAIL)

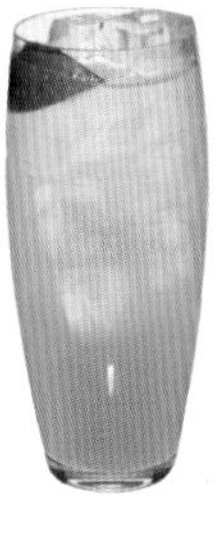

●●●●○

Glass: Collins
Garnish: Lime wedge
Method: STIR honey with lime juice in base of shaker until honey dissolves. **SHAKE** with ice and strain into ice-filled glass. **TOP** with soda.

1½	shot(s)	**Freshly squeezed lime juice**
7	spoons	**Runny honey**
Top up with		**Soda water** (club soda)

Origin: Discovered in 2005 at Hotel Quinta Real, Guadalajara, Mexico.
Comment: A refreshing Mexican variation on Real Lemonade.

HONEY VODKA SOUR

Glass: Old-fashioned
Garnish: Lemon wedge
Method: SHAKE all ingredients with ice and strain into ice-filled glass.

2	shot(s)	Krupnik honey liqueur
1½	shot(s)	Freshly squeezed lemon juice
½	shot(s)	Sugar syrup (2 sugar to 1 water)
½	fresh	Egg white
3	dashes	Angostura aromatic bitters

Comment: A vodka sour with true honey character.

HONEY WALL

Glass: Martini
Garnish: Flamed orange zest twist
Method: STIR all ingredients with ice and strain into chilled glass.

1¼	shot(s)	Zacapa aged rum
1¼	shot(s)	Tuaca Italian liqueur
1¼	shot(s)	Brown crème de cacao liqueur

Origin: Adapted from a drink created in 2002 by Dick Bradsell at Downstairs at Alfred's, London, England.
Comment: Strong, rich and chocolatey.

HONEYMOON

Glass: Martini
Garnish: Lemon zest twist
Method: SHAKE all ingredients with ice and fine strain into chilled glass.

1½	shot(s)	Boulard Grand Solage calvados
1	shot(s)	Bénédictine D.O.M. liqueur
¼	shot(s)	Cointreau triple sec
½	shot(s)	Freshly squeezed lemon juice
½	fresh	Egg white

AKA: Farmer's Daughter
Origin: A 1930s classic created in a long since departed New York bar called Brown Derby.
Comment: A romantic combination of apple, orange, lemon and herbs.

HONEYSUCKLE DAIQUIRI

Glass: Martini
Garnish: Mint leaf
Method: STIR honey with rum in base of shaker until honey dissolves. Add lemon and orange juice, SHAKE with ice and fine strain into chilled glass.

2	shot(s)	Bacardi Superior rum
4	spoons	Runny honey
1	shot(s)	Freshly squeezed lemon juice
1	shot(s)	Freshly squeezed orange juice

Variant: Made with gin in place of rum this drink becomes the 'Bee's Knees Martini'.
Origin: Adapted from a recipe in David Embury's 'The Fine Art Of Mixing Drinks'.
Comment: Honey – I love it!

THE HONEYSUCKLE ORCHARD

Glass: Martini
Garnish: Lemon wedge on rim
Method: STIR honey with vodka in base of shaker until honey dissolves. Add other ingredients, SHAKE with ice and fine strain into chilled glass.

1	spoon	Runny honey
2	shot(s)	Zubrówka bison vodka
1½	shot(s)	Pressed apple juice
¼	shot(s)	Freshly squeezed lemon juice

Origin: Discovered in 2005 at The Stanton Social, New York City, USA.
Comment: A back to nature Polish Martini - all the better for it.

HONG KONG FUEY UPDATED #8

Glass: Collins
Garnish: Lime wedge & cherry
Method: SHAKE first eight ingredients with ice and strain into ice-filled glass. TOP with lemonade, stir and serve with straws.

½	shot(s)	Ketel One vodka
½	shot(s)	Tanqueray London dry gin
½	shot(s)	Bacardi Superior rum
½	shot(s)	Don Julio reposado tequila
¾	shot(s)	Midori green melon liqueur
¼	shot(s)	Green Chartreuse liqueur
¼	shot(s)	Freshly squeezed lemon juice
¼	shot(s)	Rose's lime cordial
Top up with		Lemonade/Sprite/7-Up

Comment: You may recall Hong Kong Phooey, the 1970s Hanna-Barbera animated children's TV series featuring the mild-mannered janitor Penry and his superhero alter ego. This party drink is little better than Penry's kung fu but deadly all the same.
Variant: "Reloaded" with champagne in place of lemonade

HONI HONI NEW #8

Glass: Old-fashioned
Garnish: Pineapple cubes & cherry on stick, mint sprig
Method: SHAKE all ingredients with ice and fine strain into glass filled with crushed ice.

2	shot(s)	Bulleit bourbon whiskey
½	shot(s)	Cointreau triple sec
¾	shot(s)	Freshly squeezed lime juice
½	shot(s)	Almond (orgeat) syrup
¼	shot(s)	Sugar syrup (2 sugar to 1 water)

Comment: A Mai Tai based on whiskey rather than rum.
Origin: Adapted from Victor Bergeron's 'Trader Vic's Bartender's Guide' (1972 revised edition). The name of this vintage Tiki drink means 'Kiss Kiss'.

HONOLULU

Glass: Old-fashioned (or Tiki glass)
Garnish: Pineapple wedge and cherry
Method: BLEND all ingredients with 12oz scoop crushed ice and serve with straws.

1½	shot(s)	**Bacardi Superior rum**
1	shot(s)	**Pressed pineapple juice**
½	shot(s)	**Freshly squeezed lemon juice**
¼	shot(s)	**Pomegranate (grenadine) syrup**
¼	shot(s)	**Sugar syrup** (2 sugar to 1 water)

Origin: Adapted from Victor Bergeron's 'Trader Vic's Bartender's Guide' (1972 revised edition).
Comment: Cooling, fruity and pretty light on alcohol – perfect for a hot afternoon in Honolulu.

HONOLULU COCKTAIL NO.1

Glass: Martini
Garnish: Pineapple wedge & cherry on rim
Method: SHAKE all ingredients with ice and fine strain into chilled glass.

2	shot(s)	**Tanqueray London dry gin**
¼	shot(s)	**Freshly squeezed orange juice**
¼	shot(s)	**Pressed pineapple juice**
¼	shot(s)	**Freshly squeezed lemon juice**
¼	shot(s)	**Sugar syrup** (2 sugar to 1 water)

Origin: Adapted from Harry Craddock's 1930 'The Savoy Cocktail Book'.
Comment: Gin is hardly Hawaiian, but its bite works well in this tropically fruity cocktail.

HONOLULU COCKTAIL NO.2

Glass: Martini
Garnish: Maraschino cherry
Method: STIR all ingredients with ice and strain into chilled glass.

¾	shot(s)	**Tanqueray London dry gin**
¾	shot(s)	**Bénédictine D.O.M. liqueur**
¾	shot(s)	**Luxardo maraschino liqueur**
¾	shot(s)	**Chilled mineral water** (omit if wet ice)

Origin: Adapted from Harry Craddock's 1930 'The Savoy Cocktail Book'.
Comment: Spicy maraschino dominates this old-school after dinner cocktail.

HONOLULU JUICER

Glass: Collins
Garnish: Pineapple wedge & cherry
Method: SHAKE all ingredients with ice and strain into glass filled with crushed ice.

1	shot(s)	**Gosling's Black Seal rum**
1½	shot(s)	**Southern Comfort liqueur**
2	shot(s)	**Pressed pineapple juice**
¾	shot(s)	**Rose's lime cordial**
¾	shot(s)	**Freshly squeezed lemon juice**
¼	shot(s)	**Sugar syrup** (2 sugar to 1 water)

Origin: A classic Tiki drink.
Comment: A practically tropical, rum laced, fruity number.

HOOPLA

Glass: Martini
Garnish: Orange zest twist
Method: SHAKE all ingredients with ice and fine strain into chilled glass.

1	shot(s)	**Courvoisier V.S.O.P.cognac**
1	shot(s)	**Cointreau triple sec**
¾	shot(s)	**Noilly Prat dry vermouth**
¾	shot(s)	**Freshly squeezed lemon juice**
½	fresh	**Egg white**

Comment: Not far removed from a Sidecar.

HOP TOAD #1

Glass: Martini
Garnish: Apricot wedge on rim
Method: SHAKE all ingredients with ice and fine strain into chilled glass.

1¼	shot(s)	**Bacardi Superior rum**
1¼	shot(s)	**Bols apricot brandy liqueur**
1¼	shot(s)	**Freshly squeezed lime juice**
½	shot(s)	**Chilled mineral water** (omit if wet ice)

Variant: Made with brandy this is sometimes known as a Bullfrog.
Origin: First published in Tom Bullock's 'Ideal Bartender', circa 1917.
Comment: Resembles an apricot Daiquiri that's heavy on the lime yet balanced.

HOP TOAD #2

Glass: Martini
Garnish: Apricot wedge on rim
Method: SHAKE all ingredients with ice and fine strain into chilled glass.

1¾	shot(s)	**Zacapa aged rum**
1	shot(s)	**Bols apricot brandy liqueur**
¾	shot(s)	**Freshly squeezed lime juice**
½	shot(s)	**Chilled mineral water** (omit if wet ice)

Comment: Alcoholic apricot jam with a lovely twang of aged rum.

HOP TOAD #3

Glass: Martini
Garnish: Lemon zest twist
Method: SHAKE all ingredients with ice and fine strain into chilled glass.

1½	shot(s)	**Bols apricot brandy liqueur**
¾	shot(s)	**Freshly squeezed lemon juice**
¾	shot(s)	**Chilled mineral water** (omit if wet ice)

Origin: Adapted from Harry Craddock's 1930 'The Savoy Cocktail Book'.
Comment: Fresh apricot dessert – all it lacks is a dollop of whipped cream.

HORNITOS LAU

Glass: Collins
Garnish: Mint sprig
Method: Lightly **MUDDLE** mint (just to bruise) in base of shaker. Add other ingredients, **SHAKE** with ice and strain into glass filled with crushed ice. **CHURN** (stir) drink and add more crushed ice so drink meets rim of glass.

12	fresh	Mint leaves
2	shot(s)	Don Julio reposado tequila
1½	shot(s)	Cuarenta Y Tres (Licor 43) liqueur
½	shot(s)	Freshly squeezed lime juice

Origin: Created in 2005 by Jaspar Eyears at Bar Tiki, Mexico City, Mexico.
Comment: Jaspar recommends making a batch in their glasses and refreezing them with the straws already in the glass, like the old colonels and their julep freezers in Kentucky.

HORSE'S NECK WITH A KICK

Glass: Collins
Garnish: Peel rind of a large lemon in a spiral and place in glass with end hanging over rim.
Method: **POUR** ingredients into ice-filled glass and stir.

2	shot(s)	Bulleit bourbon whiskey
3	dashes	Angostura aromatic bitters
Top up with		Ginger ale

Variant: A Horse's Neck without a kick is simply ginger ale and bitters.
Comment: Whiskey and ginger with added shrubbery.

JOHN GORRIE PATENTED THE WORLD'S FIRST ICE-MAKING MACHINE IN 1851. HE DIED PENNILESS FOUR YEARS LATER.

THE HORSESHOE SLING

Glass: Collins
Garnish: Fresh seasonal fruit
Method: **SHAKE** first 5 ingredients with ice and strain into ice-filled glass. **TOP** with champagne.

2	shot(s)	Don Julio reposado tequila
¾	shot(s)	Freshly squeezed lime juice
½	shot(s)	Bénédictine D.O.M. liqueur
½	shot(s)	Heering cherry brandy liqueur
1½	shot(s)	Pressed pineapple juice
Top up with		Perrier Jouet brut champagne

Origin: Adapted from a drink created by Gary Regan, New York, USA.
Comment: Like its creator, this is upfront and refreshingly different.

HOT BUTTERED RUM

Glass: Toddy
Garnish: Cinnamon stick and slice of lemon studded with cloves
Method: Place bar spoon loaded with honey in warmed glass. Add other ingredients and **STIR** until honey and butter are dissolved.

2	spoons	Runny honey
1	knob	Unsalted butter
2	shot(s)	Bacardi Oro golden rum
¼	spoon	Freshly grated nutmeg
Top up with		Boiling water (or hot dry cider)

Comment: In 'The Fine Art of Mixing Drinks', David Embury says, "The Hot Spiced Rum is bad enough, but the lump of butter is the final insult. It blends with the hot rum just about as satisfactorily as warm olive oil blends with champagne!" It's rare for me to question Embury but I rather like this slightly oily, warming, spicy toddy.

HOT BUTTERED WHISKEY

UPDATED #8

Glass: Toddy
Garnish: Grate nutmeg over drink
Method: Place bar spoon in warmed glass. Add ingredients and **STIR** until butter dissolves.

1	knob	Unsalted butter
2	shot(s)	Bulleit bourbon whiskey
¾	shot(s)	Sugar syrup (2 sugar to 1 water)
Top up with		Boiling water

Comment: Warming and smooth – great on a cold day or whenever you fancy a warming treat.

HOT GROG

Glass: Toddy
Garnish: Lemon peel twist
Method: Place bar spoon loaded with honey in warmed glass. Add other ingredients and **STIR** until honey dissolves.

3	spoons	Runny honey
1	shot(s)	Pusser's Navy rum
¼	shot(s)	Freshly squeezed lime juice
2½	shot(s)	Boiling water

Variant: Black Stripe, with molasses replacing the honey.
Comment: Warming, honeyed, pungent rum with a hint of lime.

HOT PASSION

Glass: Collins
Garnish: Maraschino cherry
Method: **SHAKE** all ingredients with ice and strain into ice-filled glass.

1	shot(s)	Passoã passion fruit liqueur
1	shot(s)	Ketel One vodka
2	shot(s)	Ocean Spray cranberry juice
2	shot(s)	Freshly squeezed orange juice

Comment: A fruity, slightly sweet twist on a Madras.

HOT RED BLOODED FRENCHMAN

Glass: Toddy
Garnish: Orange zest twists
Method: Place bar spoon in warmed glass. Add other ingredients and **STIR.**

1	shot(s)	**Grand Marnier liqueur**
2	shot(s)	**Claret red wine**
½	shot(s)	**Freshly squeezed orange juice**
½	shot(s)	**Freshly squeezed lemon juice**
¼	shot(s)	**Sugar syrup** (2 sugar to 1 water)
Top up with		**Boiling water**

Comment: Warm, fruity red wine – great on a cold night.

HOT RUM PUNCH

Glass: Toddy
Garnish: Ground nutmeg
Method: Place bar spoon in warmed glass. Add ingredients and **STIR.**

1	shot(s)	**Bacardi Oro golden rum**
1	shot(s)	**Courvoisier V.S.O.P. cognac**
½	shot(s)	**Tio Pepe fino sherry**
¼	shot(s)	**Sugar syrup** (2 sugar to 1 water)
1	shot(s)	**Freshly squeezed lime juice**
Top up with		**Boiling water**

Origin: Punch originated in India, where it was most probably made with arrack. Rum punches were popular during the 1700s. This version is said to have been a favourite drink of Mozart the composer.
Comment: A great winter warmer.

HOT SHOT

Glass: Shot
Method: **LAYER** by carefully pouring ingredients in the following order.

¾	shot(s)	**Galliano L'Autentico liqueur**
¾	shot(s)	**Espresso coffee**
½	shot(s)	**Double (heavy) cream**

Origin: A huge drink in Scandinavia during the early 90s.
Comment: The Scandinavian answer to Irish coffee.

HOT TODDY #1

Glass: Toddy
Garnish: Cinnamon stick
Method: Place bar spoon loaded with honey in warmed glass. Add other ingredients and **STIR** until honey dissolves.

1	spoon	**Runny honey**
2	shot(s)	**Johnnie Walker Scotch whisky**
½	shot(s)	**Freshly squeezed lemon juice**
½	shot(s)	**Sugar syrup** (2 sugar to 1 water)
3	dried	**Cloves**
Top up with		**Boiling water**

Origin: Lost in time but Dickens refers to a "Whisky Toddy" in 'The Pickwick Papers'.
Comment: The smoky flavours in the Scotch add spice to this warming drink that's great when you're feeling down with a cold or the flu.

HOT TODDY #2

Glass: Toddy
Garnish: Lemon zest twist
Method: Place bar spoon loaded with honey in warmed glass. Add other ingredients and **STIR** until honey dissolves.

1	spoon	**Runny honey**
2	shot(s)	**Johnnie Walker Scotch whisky**
3	dried	**Cloves**
¼	spoon	**Freshly grated nutmeg**
Top up with		**Hot black English breakfast tea**

Comment: Tea and Scotch combine wonderfully in this hot and spicy winter warmer.

HOT TODDY #3

Glass: Toddy
Garnish: Lemon slice & cinnamon stick
Method: Place bar spoon in warmed glass. Add ingredients and **STIR.**

2	shot(s)	**Courvoisier VS.O.P. cognac**
½	shot(s)	**Freshly squeezed lemon juice**
¼	shot(s)	**Sugar syrup** (2 sugar to 1 water)
Top up with		**Boiling water**

Comment: Warms the cockles with cognac and a good dose of citrus.

HOT TUB

Glass: Martini
Garnish: Pineapple wedge on rim
Method: **SHAKE** first 3 ingredients with ice and fine strain into chilled glass. **TOP** with prosecco.

1½	shot(s)	**Ketel One vodka**
¼	shot(s)	**Chambord black raspberry liqueur**
1	shot(s)	**Pressed pineapple juice**
Top up with		**Prosecco sparkling wine**

Origin: Adapted from a drink discovered in 2004 at Teatro, Boston, USA.
Comment: Basically a French Martini with bubbles.

HOULA-HOULA COCKTAIL

Glass: Martini
Garnish: Orange zest twist
Method: **SHAKE** all ingredients with ice and fine strain into chilled glass.

2	shot(s)	**Tanqueray London dry gin**
1	shot(s)	**Freshly squeezed orange juice**
½	shot(s)	**Cointreau triple sec**
½	shot(s)	**Chilled mineral water** (omit if wet ice)

Origin: Adapted from Harry Craddock's 1930 'The Savoy Cocktail Book'.
Comment: Orange generously laced with gin.

HOYT'S DAIQUIRÍ NEW #8

Glass: Martini/Coupette
Garnish: Garnish with a seared lime slice
Method: Sear two halves of lime with a chef's blow torch and squeeze into a shaker. **SHAKE** all remaining ingredients with ice and fine strain into chilled glass.

2	shot(s)	Bacardi Superior rum
1	shot(s)	Burnt lime juice
¼	shot(s)	Jägermeister liqueur
½	shot(s)	Vanilla sugar syrup
½	fresh	Egg white

Comment: Most unusual and interesting. Recognisably a Daiquiri but with creamy mouth-feel and great depth of flavour.
Origin: Adapted from a recipe created in 2008 by Meimi Sanchez at Bramble, Edinburgh, Scotland.

HUAPALA UPDATED #8

Glass: Martini
Garnish: Lemon wedge on rim
Method: SHAKE all ingredients with ice and fine strain into chilled glass.

1	shot(s)	Bacardi Superior rum
1	shot(s)	Tanqueray London dry gin
½	shot(s)	Freshly squeezed lemon juice
¼	shot(s)	Pomegranate (grenadine) syrup
½	shot(s)	Chilled mineral water (omit if wet ice)

Origin: Adapted from Victor Bergeron's 'Trader Vic's Bartender's Guide' (1972 revised edition).
Comment: In his book Vic prefaces this cocktail with the comment, "Nice, easy drink". It's basically a lemon Daiquiri with gin and grenadine.

HULA HULA NEW #8

Glass: Martini/Coupette
Garnish: Pineapple wedge & cherry
Method: SHAKE all ingredients with ice and fine strain into chilled glass.

1½	shot(s)	Tanqueray London dry gin
1	shot(s)	Cointreau triple sec liqueur
1½	shot(s)	Freshly squeezed orange juice

Origin: Adapted from a drink created by Ray Buhen, one of Don The Beachcomber's original bartenders. In 1961 Ray opened his own Tiki-Ti Bar in Los Angeles, which today is run by his son and grandson.
Comment: Gin and juice – orange with a splash of orange liqueur.

HULK

Glass: Old-fashioned
Method: LAYER ingredients in ice-filled glass by carefully pouring in the following order.

2	shot(s)	Hpnotiq liqueur
1	shot(s)	Courvoisier V.S.O.P. cognac

Comment: Turns green when mixed. A crying waste of good cognac.

HUMMINGBIRD

Glass: Hurricane
Garnish: Banana slice
Method: BLEND all ingredients with 12oz scoop crushed ice and serve with straws.

1½	shot(s)	Bacardi Superior rum
½	shot(s)	Kahlúa coffee liqueur
1	shot(s)	Crème de banane liqueur
1	shot(s)	Coco López cream of coconut
1	fresh	Peeled banana

Origin: The house cocktail at the Hummingbird Beach Resort, Soufriere, St. Lucia.
Comment: With flavours of rum, coconut, banana and coffee, this tall, frozen drink tastes rather like dessert.

HUNK MARTINI

Glass: Martini
Garnish: Maraschino cherry
Method: SHAKE all ingredients with ice and fine strain into chilled glass.

2	shot(s)	Vanilla-infused Ketel One vodka
1¾	shot(s)	Pressed pineapple juice
½	shot(s)	Freshly squeezed lime juice
¼	shot(s)	Sugar syrup (2 sugar to 1 water)

Origin: The drink Carrie and co discovered in the summer of 2003. In this series the Sex And The City stars dropped Cosmopolitans in favour of Hunks – no change there then!
Comment: Pineapple and vanilla combine wonderfully. American readers may notice more than a passing resemblance to a Key Lime Pie served without the Graham Cracker rim.

HURRICANE #1

Glass: Hurricane
Garnish: Pineapple wedge & cherry on rim
Method: SHAKE all ingredients with ice and strain into ice-filled glass.

1½	shot(s)	Bacardi Superior rum
1	shot(s)	Pusser's Navy rum
1	shot(s)	Freshly squeezed orange juice
1	shot(s)	Pressed pineapple juice
¾	shot(s)	Rose's lime cordial
½	shot(s)	Freshly squeezed lime juice
¼	shot(s)	Passion fruit syrup

Origin: Named after the shape of a hurricane lamp and served in the tall, shapely glass of the same name. Thought to have originated in 1939 at The Hurricane Bar, New York City, but made famous at Pat O'Brien's in New Orleans. Some old cocktail books list a much earlier Hurricane made with cognac, absinthe and vodka.
Comment: A strong, tangy, refreshing drink packed with fruit and laced with rum.

HURRICANE #2

Glass: Hurricane
Garnish: Orange slice & cherry on stick (sail)
Method: Cut passion fruit in half and scoop flesh into shaker. Add other ingredients, **SHAKE** with ice and strain into ice-filled glass.

1	fresh	**Passion fruit**
1½	shot(s)	**Gosling's Black Seal rum**
1½	shot(s)	**Bacardi Superior rum**
1	shot(s)	**Freshly squeezed orange juice**
1	shot(s)	**Pressed pineapple juice**
½	shot(s)	**Freshly squeezed lime juice**
¼	shot(s)	**Passion fruit syrup**
¼	shot(s)	**Pomegranate (grenadine) syrup**

Comment: Sweet, tangy and potentially dangerous.

'I DON'T REGRET A DROP. NOT A DROP.'
PETER O'TOOLE

HURRICANE #3

Glass: Hurricane
Garnish: Pineapple wedge & cherry
Method: **SHAKE** all ingredients with ice and fine strain into ice-filled glass.

1	shot(s)	**Bacardi Superior rum**
1	shot(s)	**Gosling's Black Seal rum**
½	shot(s)	**Galliano L'Autentico liqueur**
2	shot(s)	**Pressed pineapple juice**
2	shot(s)	**Freshly squeezed orange juice**
¾	shot(s)	**Freshly squeezed lime juice**
¾	shot(s)	**Passion fruit syrup**
2	dashes	**Angostura aromatic bitters**

Origin: Adapted from a 2006 recipe by Chris McMillian, New Orleans, USA.
Comment: A veritable tropical fruit salad laced with rum.

HURRICANE NO.1 (ORIGINAL RECIPE) NEW #8

Glass: Hurricane
Garnish: Passion fruit half & lemon slice
Method: **SHAKE** all ingredients with ice and strain into glass filled with crushed ice.

4	shot(s)	**Myers's dark Jamaican rum**
2	shot(s)	**Passion fruit syrup**
2	shot(s)	**Freshly squeezed lemon juice**

Origin: Recipe adapted from Jeff Berry's 1998 'Beachbum Berry's Grog Log' and purported to be the 1960s recipe used at Pat O'Brien's in New Orleans. The recipe was adapted to a rum and juice combination where it was served in 1939 at the World's Fair in New York at the Hurricane bar.
Comment: The flavour of the passion fruit syrup predominates. Ok if you like that kind of thing.

THE HYPNOTIC MARGARITA

Glass: Coupette
Garnish: Lime wedge on rim
Method: **SHAKE** all ingredients with ice and fine strain into chilled glass.

1½	shot(s)	**Don Julio blanco tequila**
½	shot(s)	**Cointreau triple sec**
½	shot(s)	**Hpnotiq liqueur**
½	shot(s)	**Freshly squeezed lime juice**

Origin: Created in 2005 by Gary Regan at Painter's, Cornwall-on-Hudson, New York, USA.
Comment: Liqueurs combine harmoniously with lime and tequila in this tangy, fruity Margarita. However, I remain unconvinced by Hpnotiq.

I B DAMM'D

Glass: Martini
Garnish: Peach wedge
Method: **SHAKE** all ingredients with ice and fine strain into chilled glass.

2	shot(s)	**Bokma oude genever**
½	shot(s)	**St-Germain elderflower liqueur**
¼	shot(s)	**Peach Tree peach schnapps**
1	shot(s)	**Pressed apple juice**

Origin: Adapted from a drink discovered in 2003 at Oxo Tower Bar, London, England.
Comment: A subtle combination of fruit and floral flavours.

ICE MAIDEN MARTINI

Glass: Martini
Garnish: Orange zest twist
Method: **STIR** all ingredients with ice and strain into chilled glass.

1½	shot(s)	**Tanqueray London dry gin**
1	shot(s)	**Icewine**
¾	shot(s)	**Sauvignon Blanc wine**
¾	shot(s)	**Chilled mineral water** (reduce if wet ice)

Origin: Created in 2004 by Yours Truly (Simon Difford).
Comment: A subtle Martini with the honeyed flavours of icewine melding with botanicals in the gin and balanced by the acidity of the white wine.

ICE 'T' KNEE

Glass: Martini
Garnish: Lemon zest twist
Method: **STIR** all ingredients with ice and strain into chilled glass.

2	shot(s)	**Ketel One vodka**
1½	shot(s)	**Cold strong jasmine tea**
¾	shot(s)	**Icewine**

Origin: Created by Yours Truly (Simon Difford) in 2004.
Comment: Honeyed palate topped off with tannin and jasmine.

ICE WHITE COSMO

Glass: Martini
Garnish: Flamed orange zest twist
Method: SHAKE all ingredients with ice and fine strain into chilled glass.

2	shot(s)	Ketel One vodka
¾	shot(s)	Icewine
1¼	shot(s)	Ocean Spray white cranberry
¼	shot(s)	Freshly squeezed lime juice

Origin: Created by Yours Truly (Simon Difford) in 2004.
Comment: Recognisably from the Cosmo family but wonderfully different.

ICED SAKE MARTINI

Glass: Martini
Garnish: Float 3 slices cucumber
Method: STIR all ingredients with ice and strain into chilled glass.

2	shot(s)	Ketel One vodka
2	shot(s)	Sake
¼	shot(s)	Icewine

Origin: Created in 2004 by Yours Truly (Simon Difford).
Comment: The icewine adds interest and wonderfully honeyed notes to this Sake Martini.

ICED TEA

Glass: Collins
Garnish: Lime wedge
Method: SHAKE first 6 ingredients with ice and strain into glass filled with crushed ice. **TOP** with Coca-Cola.

½	shot(s)	Courvoisier V.S.O.P. cognac
½	shot(s)	Gosling's Black Seal rum
½	shot(s)	Cointreau triple sec
½	shot(s)	Freshly squeezed orange juice
½	shot(s)	Freshly squeezed lime juice
2	shot(s)	Cold English breakfast tea
Top up with		Coca-Cola

Origin: Created in 1990 by Charles Schumann, Munich, Germany.
Comment: Sweetened and fortified fruity cola.

ICED TEA MARTINI

Glass: Martini
Garnish: Lemon zest twist
Method: SHAKE all ingredients with ice and strain into chilled glass.

2	shot(s)	Tanqueray London dry gin
½	shot(s)	Noilly Prat dry vermouth
1	shot(s)	Cold earl grey tea
½	shot(s)	Sugar syrup (2 sugar to 1 water)

Origin: Created in 2006 by Yours Truly (Simon Difford).
Comment: Tannic and bittersweet - a very refreshing after dinner drink.

ICEWINE MARTINI

Glass: Martini
Garnish: Orange zest twist
Method: STIR all ingredients with ice and strain into chilled glass.

1½	shot(s)	Ketel One vodka
1½	shot(s)	Icewine
1½	shot(s)	Pressed apple juice

Origin: Created in 2004 by Yours Truly (Simon Difford)
Comment: Delicate with subtle flavours.

ICY PINK LEMONADE

Glass: Collins
Garnish: Lemon slice
Method: SHAKE first 4 ingredients with ice and strain into ice-filled glass. **TOP** with soda.

2	shot(s)	Ketel One vodka
½	shot(s)	Chambord black raspberry liqueur
2	shot(s)	Freshly squeezed lemon juice
½	shot(s)	Sugar syrup (2 sugar to 1 water)
Top up with		Soda water (club soda)

Comment: Tangy, citrussy, fruity and refreshing - just not that butch.

IDEAL NEW #8

Glass: Martini
Garnish: Almonds on side
Method: SHAKE all ingredients with ice and fine strain into chilled glass.

1	shot(s)	Tanqueray London dry gin
1	shot(s)	Noilly Prat dry vermouth
1	shot(s)	Martini Rosso sweet vermouth
¼	shot(s)	Freshly squeezed grapefruit juice
⅛	shot(s)	Luxardo maraschino liqueur

Origin: Recipe adapted from a 1937 Bar Florida menu (later renamed Floridita), Havana, Cuba.
Comment: Aromatic and herbal with grapefruit sourness balancing sweeter notes.

IGNORANCE IS BLISS UPDATED #8

Glass: Martini
Garnish: Lime wedge
Method: SHAKE all ingredients with ice and fine strain into chilled glass.

1	shot(s)	Campari Bitter
1	shot(s)	Ketel One Citron vodka
1	shot(s)	Pressed apple juice
½	shot(s)	Passion fruit syrup

Origin: Adapted from a drink created in the mid 1990s by Alex Kammerling, from whom I quote the following words of wisdom, "I once described Campari to a girl - It is like anal sex, it takes a few goes before you actually start liking it." Tsk.
Comment: Passion fruit syrup dominates.

IGUANA

Glass: Shot
Method: SHAKE all ingredients with ice and fine strain into chilled glass.

½   shot(s)   **Ketel One vodka**
½   shot(s)   **Don Julio reposado tequila**
½   shot(s)   **Kahlúa coffee liqueur**

Comment: Coffee and tequila's successful relationship is enhanced by the introduction of vodka.

IGUANA WANA

Glass: Old-fashioned
Garnish: Orange slice
Method: SHAKE all ingredients with ice and strain into ice-filled glass.

1   shot(s)   **Ketel One vodka**
¾   shot(s)   **Peach Tree peach schnapps**
2½   shot(s)   **Freshly squeezed orange juice**

Comment: Orange juice and peach schnapps, laced with vodka.

THE CONSUMPTION OF ALCOHOL WAS SO WIDESPREAD THROUGHOUT HISTORY THAT IT HAS BEEN CALLED 'A UNIVERSAL LANGUAGE.'

I'LL TAKE MANHATTAN

Glass: Martini
Garnish: Maraschino cherry
Method: STIR all ingredients with ice and strain into chilled glass.

2   shot(s)   **Bulleit bourbon whiskey**
1   shot(s)   **Martini Rosso sweet vermouth**
½   shot(s)   **Heering cherry brandy liqueur**
2   dashes   **Angostura aromatic bitters**

Origin: Adapted from a drink discovered in 2005 at The Stanton Social, New York City, USA.
Comment: Cherry is more than a garnish in this twist on the classic Manhattan.

ILLICIT AFFAIR

Glass: Old-fashioned
Garnish: Orange slice
Method: SHAKE all ingredients with ice and strain into ice-filled glass.

2   shot(s)   **Raspberry flavoured vodka**
1¾   shot(s)   **Freshly squeezed orange juice**
1¾   shot(s)   **Ocean Spray cranberry juice**

Comment: Fruity, easy drinking.

ILLUSION

Glass: Collins
Garnish: Watermelon wedge on rim
Method: SHAKE all ingredients with ice and strain into ice-filled glass.

2   shot(s)   **Ketel One vodka**
¾   shot(s)   **Cointreau triple sec**
¾   shot(s)   **Midori green melon liqueur**
2½   shot(s)   **Freshly pressed pineapple juice**

Comment: This medium-sweet, lime green drink is one for a summer's day by the pool.

IMPERIAL MARTINI

Glass: Martini
Garnish: Maraschino cherry
Method: STIR all ingredients with ice and strain into chilled glass.

1½   shot(s)   **Tanqueray London dry gin**
1½   shot(s)   **Noilly Prat dry vermouth**
3   dashes   **Angostura aromatic bitters**
⅛   shot(s)   **Luxardo maraschino liqueur**

Comment: This rust coloured Martini is very dry despite the inclusion of maraschino liqueur – not for everyone.

IN-AND-OUT MARTINI NEW #8

Glass: Martini
Garnish: Olive or lemon zest twist
Method: Gently **SHAKE** vermouth with ice. Strain and discard vermouth to leave the ice in the shaker coated with vermouth. Add gin, **SHAKE** again with coated ice and strain into chilled glass.

½   shot(s)   **Noilly Prat dry vermouth**
2½   shot(s)   **Tanqueray London dry gin**

Origin: Unknown but former U.S. President Richard Nixon is said to have preferred his Martini made this way.
Comment: A well diluted shaken Dry Martini.

IN-SEINE UPDATED #8

Glass: Martini
Garnish: 3 grapes on stick (or rubber ear if you have one to hand)
Method: SHAKE all ingredients with ice and fine strain into chilled glass.

1   shot(s)   **Courvoisier V.S.O.P. cognac**
1   shot(s)   **Bulleit bourbon whiskey**
1   shot(s)   **St-Germain elderflower liqueur**
⅛   shot(s)   **La Fée Parisienne (68%) absinthe**
½   fresh   **Egg white**

Origin: Created in 2006 by Simon Difford at The Cabinet Room, London, England. The name references the fact that St-Germain is a district of Paris on the left bank of the River Seine and absinthe was banned in Paris, partly because it was believed to induce insanity.
Comment: Elderflower liqueur mellows and boosts floral notes in the cognac with the merest dash of absinthe dries and adds a robust hint of aniseed.

●●●●◐○

INCOGNITO UPDATED #8

Glass: Martini
Garnish: Apricot slice or physalis fruit
Method: SHAKE all ingredients with ice and fine strain into chilled glass.

1½	shot(s)	Courvoisier V.S.O.P. cognac
1½	shot(s)	Noilly Prat dry vermouth
1	shot(s)	Bols apricot brandy liqueur
3	dashes	Angostura aromatic bitters

Comment: Dry with hints of sweet apricot – unusual.

●●●●◐○

INCOME TAX COCKTAIL UPDATED #8

Glass: Martini
Garnish: Orange zest twist
Method: SHAKE all ingredients with ice and fine strain into chilled glass.

2	shot(s)	Tanqueray London dry gin
¼	shot(s)	Noilly Prat dry vermouth
¼	shot(s)	Martini Rosso sweet vermouth
1	shot(s)	Freshly squeezed orange juice
2	dashes	Angostura aromatic bitters

Origin: A vintage cocktail adapted from the classic Bronx Cocktail, created in 1906 by Johnny Solon, a bartender at New York's Waldorf-Astoria Hotel.
Comment: A Bronx with the addition of two dashes of Angostura.

●●●●●○

INDIAN ROSE

Glass: Martini
Garnish: Edible rose petal
Method: SHAKE all ingredients with ice and fine strain into chilled glass.

2½	shot(s)	Tanqueray London dry gin
¼	shot(s)	Bols apricot brandy liqueur
¼	shot(s)	Rosewater
¼	shot(s)	Rose syrup
½	shot(s)	Chilled mineral water (omit if wet ice)

Origin: Adapted from a drink discovered in 2005 at Mie N Yu, Washington DC, USA.
Comment: Subtle rose hue and flavour.

●●●●◐○

INDIAN SUNSET NEW #8

Glass: Martini
Garnish: Mango slice
Method: MUDDLE cardamom in base of shaker. Add other ingredients, SHAKE with ice and fine strain into chilled glass.

2	pods	Cardamom seeds
2	shot(s)	Ketel One vodka
½	shot(s)	Domaine de Canton ginger liqueur
1	shot(s)	Boiron mango puree
½	shot(s)	Freshly squeezed lime juice
⅛	shot(s)	Sugar syrup (2 sugar to 1 water)

Comment: Mango, ginger and cardamom are all classic Indian flavours and here are rum laced with a splash of lime juice.
Origin: Created in 2008 by Yours Truly (Simon Difford) with David Furnish for Grey Goose's 'Character & Cocktails' 2008

●●●●●○

INDOCHINE NEW #8

Glass: Martini
Garnish: Slice fresh ginger
Method: SHAKE all ingredients with ice and fine strain into chilled glass.

2	shot(s)	Ketel One vodka
1	shot(s)	Domaine de Canton ginger liqueur
¾	shot(s)	Pressed pineapple juice

Origin: Adapted from a drink promoted at the end of 2007 by the makers of Canton ginger liqueur.
Comment: Slightly sweet and very frothy. Easy drinking with a ginger kick.

●●●●●○

INGA FROM SWEDEN

Glass: Collins
Garnish: Strawberry
Method: MUDDLE strawberries in base of shaker. Add other ingredients, SHAKE with ice and fine strain into ice-filled glass.

2	fresh	Strawberries (hulled)
1½	shot(s)	Belle de Brillet pear liqueur
½	shot(s)	Campari Bitter
2	shot(s)	Ocean Spray cranberry juice
¼	shot(s)	Sugar syrup (2 sugar to 1 water)
¼	shot(s)	Freshly squeezed lime juice

Comment: Inga must like a touch of bitter Italian with her fruit.

●●●●◐○

INK MARTINI #1

Glass: Martini
Garnish: Orange zest twist
Method: SHAKE all ingredients with ice and fine strain into chilled glass.

1¼	shot(s)	Tanqueray London dry gin
½	shot(s)	Bols blue curaçao liqueur
½	shot(s)	Peach Tree peach schnapps
2	shot(s)	Ocean Spray cranberry juice

Origin: Created in 2002 by Gentian Naci at Bar Epernay, Birmingham, England.
Comment: This simple, appropriately named drink is surprisingly quaffable.

●●●●●○

INK MARTINI #2

Glass: Martini
Garnish: Orange zest twist
Method: SHAKE all ingredients with ice and fine strain into chilled glass.

2	shot(s)	Ketel One vodka
½	shot(s)	Bols blue curaçao liqueur
1½	shot(s)	Ocean Spray cranberry juice

Origin: Discovered in 2005 at Halo, Atlanta, USA.
Comment: Surprisingly subtle and pleasant in flavour.

INSOMNIAC

Glass: Martini
Garnish: Float three coffee beans
Method: SHAKE all ingredients with ice and fine strain into chilled glass.

¾	shot(s)	**Ketel One vodka**
¾	shot(s)	**Frangelico hazelnut liqueur**
¾	shot(s)	**Kahlúa coffee liqueur**
1	shot(s)	**Espresso coffee**
½	shot(s)	**Double (heavy) cream**
½	shot(s)	**Milk**

Variant: Espresso Martini
Comment: Wonderfully balanced, creamy and caffeine laced.

INTERNATIONAL INCIDENT

Glass: Martini
Garnish: Dust with freshly grated nutmeg
Method: SHAKE all ingredients with ice and fine strain into chilled glass.

¾	shot(s)	**Ketel One vodka**
¾	shot(s)	**Kahlúa coffee liqueur**
¾	shot(s)	**Luxardo Amaretto di Saschira**
¾	shot(s)	**Frangelico hazelnut liqueur**
1½	shot(s)	**Baileys Irish cream liqueur**

Comment: Rich and creamy.

INTIMATE MARTINI

Glass: Martini
Garnish: Orange zest twist
Method: STIR all ingredients with ice and strain into chilled glass.

2	shot(s)	**Ketel One vodka**
½	shot(s)	**Noilly Prat dry vermouth**
1	shot(s)	**Bols apricot brandy liqueur**
3	dashes	**Angostura orange bitters**

Comment: Sweet apricot dried and balanced by vermouth and bitters. Surprisingly complex and pleasant.

IRISH ALEXANDER

Glass: Martini
Garnish: Crumbled Cadbury's Flake bar
Method: SHAKE all ingredients with ice and fine strain into chilled glass.

1½	shot(s)	**Baileys Irish cream liqueur**
1½	shot(s)	**Courvoisier V.S.O.P. cognac**
1	shot(s)	**Double (heavy) cream**

Comment: Rich, thick, creamy and yummy.

IRISH CHARLIE

Glass: Shot
Method: SHAKE all ingredients with ice and fine strain into chilled glass.

¾	shot(s)	**Baileys Irish cream liqueur**
¾	shot(s)	**Giffard Menthe Pastille liqueur**

Variant: Float Baileys on crème de menthe
Comment: The ingredients go surprisingly well together.

IRISH CHOCOLATE ORANJ'TINI

Glass: Martini
Garnish: Crumbled Cadbury's Flake bar
Method: SHAKE all ingredients with ice and fine strain into chilled glass.

1½	shot(s)	**Baileys Irish cream liqueur**
1½	shot(s)	**Kahlúa coffee liqueur**
1½	shot(s)	**Grand Marnier liqueur**

Comment: A B-52 served 'up'.

'I'M NOT SO THINK AS YOU DRUNK I AM.'
J. C. SQUIRE

IRISH COFFEE UPDATED #8

Glass: Toddy
Garnish: Three coffee beans
Method: Place bar spoon in glass. POUR whiskey into glass, TOP with coffee and stir. FLOAT a thin layer of cream.

1	shot(s)	**Jameson Irish whiskey**
Top up with		**Hot filter coffee**
Float		**Lightly whipped double cream**

Variant: Sweeten with sugar syrup or liqueur to taste before floating cream.
AKA: Gaelic Coffee
Tip: To ensure a good float, lightly whip or simply shake cream in container before pouring over the bowl of a spoon. It also helps if the cream is gently warmed.
Origin: This now ubiquitous cocktail was created in 1942 by Joe Sheridan, a bartender at Foynes airport (near the present-day Shannon airport). The majority of transatlantic flights used to stop to refuel in Ireland and in 1947 an American journalist, Stan Delaphane, found himself at Joe Sheridan's bar and tried his Irish Coffee. Delaphane was so impressed that on returning home he passed the recipe on to the bartender at his local bar, the Buena Vista Café in San Francisco. The recipe spread and the drink became a classic.
Comment: Like most great ideas, this one is very simple. Coffee with a whiskey kick.

IRISH COFFEE

IRISH COFFEE MARTINI

Glass: Martini
Garnish: Float three coffee beans
Method: SHAKE all ingredients with ice and fine strain into chilled glass.

1½	shot(s)	**Jameson Irish whiskey**
2	shot(s)	**Espresso coffee**
½	shot(s)	**Sugar syrup** (2 sugar to 1 water)
1	shot(s)	**Double (heavy) cream**

Origin: Created in 2003 by Yours Truly (Simon Difford).
Comment: Forget sipping warm java through a cold head of cream. This Martini version of the classic Irish Coffee offers all the flavour without the moustache.

IRISH ESPRESSO'TINI

Glass: Martini
Garnish: Float 3 coffee beans
Method: SHAKE all ingredients with ice and fine strain into chilled glass.

2	shot(s)	**Baileys Irish cream liqueur**
1¼	shot(s)	**Vanilla-infused Ketel One vodka**
1¼	shot(s)	**Espresso coffee**

Comment: Richly flavoured with a pleasingly bitter finish.

IRISH FLAG

Glass: Shot
Method: Refrigerate ingredients and **LAYER** in chilled glass by carefully pouring in the following order.

½	shot(s)	**Giffard Menthe Pastille liqueur**
½	shot(s)	**Baileys Irish Cream liqueur**
½	shot(s)	**Grand Marnier liqueur**

Origin: The Irish tricolour is the national flag of the Republic of Ireland. Its three equal stripes represent the political landscape. Orange stands for the Protestants because of William of Orange, the Protestant king of England who defeated the Roman Catholic James II in 1690. Green stands for the Catholic nationalists of the south and white for the hope for peace between Catholics and Protestants.
Comment: Tricoloured orange and mint smoothed with cream liqueur.

IRISH FRAPPÉ

Glass: Hurricane
Garnish: Float three coffee beans
Method: BLEND all ingredients with two 12oz scoops of crushed ice and serve with straws.

3	shot(s)	**Baileys Irish cream liqueur**
2	shot(s)	**Espresso coffee**
2	scoops	**Coffee ice cream**

Comment: A tasty frappé with coffee, cream and a hint of whiskey.

IRISH LATTE

Glass: Toddy
Method: POUR ingredients into warmed glass in the following order.

1	shot(s)	**Espresso coffee**
1½	shot(s)	**Baileys Irish cream liqueur**
Top up with		**Steamed foaming milk**

Comment: A latte with extra interest and flavour courtesy of Irish cream liqueur.

IRISH MANHATTAN

Glass: Martini
Garnish: Shamrock
Method: STIR all ingredients with ice and strain into chilled glass.

1½	shot(s)	**Bulleit bourbon whiskey**
1	shot(s)	**Tuaca Italian liqueur**
½	shot(s)	**Grand Marnier liqueur**
¼	shot(s)	**Vanilla sugar syrup**

Origin: Adapted from a drink discovered in 2001 at Detroit, London, England.
Comment: There's nothing Irish about this drink, but it's good all the same.

IRRESISTIBLE

Glass: Martini
Garnish: Lemon zest twist
Method: SHAKE all ingredients with ice and fine strain into chilled glass.

1½	shot(s)	**Bacardi Superior rum**
½	shot(s)	**Martini Rosso sweet vermouth**
¼	shot(s)	**Bénédictine D.O.M. liqueur**
¼	shot(s)	**Freshly squeezed lemon juice**
¾	shot(s)	**Chilled mineral water** (omit if wet ice)

Comment: Herbal yet delicate with hints of citrus.

ISLAND BREEZE

Glass: Collins
Garnish: Grapefruit wedge on rim
Method: SHAKE all ingredients with ice and strain into ice-filled glass.

2	shot(s)	**Malibu coconut rum liqueur**
2½	shot(s)	**Ocean Spray cranberry juice**
1½	shot(s)	**Freshly squeezed grapefruit juice**

Origin: Named after the Twelve Islands Shipping Company, the Caribbean producers of Malibu.
Comment: Great balance of sweet and sour flavours.

ITALIAN JOB # 1

Glass: Collins
Garnish: Orange slice
Method: SHAKE first 6 ingredients with ice and strain into ice-filled glass. **TOP** with tonic water, stir and serve with straws.

¾	shot(s)	Monasterium liqueur
¾	shot(s)	Campari Bitter
¾	shot(s)	Mandarine Napoléon liqueur
1½	shot(s)	Freshly squeezed grapefruit juice
½	shot(s)	Freshly squeezed lemon juice
¼	shot(s)	Sugar syrup (2 sugar to 1 water)
Top up with		Tonic water

Origin: Created by Tony Conigliaro in 2001 at Isola, Knightsbridge, London, England.
Comment: This orange coloured drink combines sweet and sour flavours in a most interesting and grown up way.

FAMOUS EX-BARTENDERS: SANDRA BULLOCK, BRUCE WILLIS, TOM ARNOLD, BILL COSBY, KRIS KRISTOFFERSON & CHEVY CHASE.

ITALIAN JOB #2

Glass: Sling
Garnish: Orange peel twist
Method: SHAKE first 3 ingredients with ice and strain into glass filled with crushed ice. **TOP** with wine and serve with straws.

1	shot(s)	Tuaca Italian liqueur
1	shot(s)	Luxardo Amaretto di Saschira
1	shot(s)	Ocean Spray cranberry juice
Top up with		Shiraz red wine

Origin: Discovered in 2002 at Rapscallion, London, England.
Comment: Mix layers with straw prior to drinking for vanillaed, almond, fruity wine.

ITALIAN MARGARITA

Glass: Martini
Garnish: Lime wedge on rim
Method: SHAKE all ingredients with ice and fine strain into chilled glass.

2	shot(s)	Don Julio reposado tequila
½	shot(s)	Cointreau triple sec
½	shot(s)	Luxardo Amaretto di Saschira
1	shot(s)	Freshly squeezed lime juice

Origin: Discovered in 2005 at the Club Bar, The Peninsula Beverly Hills, USA.
Comment: A liberal dash of amaretto adds very Italian subtexts of apricot and almond to your classic Margarita.

ITALIAN SOUR NEW #8

Glass: Old-Fashioned
Garnish: Lemon slice & cherry on stick (sail)
Method: SHAKE all ingredients and strain into ice-filled chilled glass.

½	shot(s)	Galliano L'Autentico liqueur
½	shot(s)	Strega liqueur
½	shot(s)	Campari Bitter
1	shot(s)	Freshly squeezed lemon juice
1	dash	Angostura aromatic bitters
½	fresh	Egg white

Comment: Perhaps a little too many powerful Italian flavours for one drink.

ITALIAN SUN

Glass: Martini
Garnish: Lemon zest twist
Method: SHAKE all ingredients with ice and fine strain into chilled glass.

2	shot(s)	Sauvignon Blanc wine
1½	shot(s)	Luxardo limoncello liqueur
¾	shot(s)	Frangelico hazelnut liqueur
½	shot(s)	Freshly squeezed lemon juice

Origin: Created in 2002 by Dan Spink at Browns, St Martin's Lane, London, England.
Comment: Tastes rather like a bon bon (a round, sugar coated, lemon flavoured sweet).

ITALIAN SURFER WITH A RUSSIAN ATTITUDE

Glass: Martini
Method: SHAKE all ingredients with ice and fine strain into chilled glass.

1½	shot(s)	Ketel One vodka
½	shot(s)	Luxardo Amaretto di Saschira
½	shot(s)	Malibu coconut rum liqueur
¾	shot(s)	Pressed pineapple juice
¾	shot(s)	Ocean Spray cranberry juice

Variant: Served as a long drink, over ice in a Collins glass.
Comment: Fruity and easy drinking but a tad sweet.

I.V.F. MARTINI

Glass: Martini
Garnish: Float three coffee beans
Method: SHAKE first 4 ingredients with ice and strain into glass. **FLOAT** cream on drink.

1	shot(s)	La Fée Parisienne (68%) absinthe
½	shot(s)	Kahlúa coffee liqueur
½	shot(s)	Tuaca Italian liqueur
2	shot(s)	Espresso coffee
1	shot(s)	Double (heavy) cream

Origin: Created by Giovanni Burdi, London, England. In this case I.V.F. stands for 'Italy v France' not 'in vitro fertilisation'.
Comment: Creamy, sweetened absinthe and coffee – hardcore but tasty.

JACK COLLINS

Glass: Collins
Garnish: Lemon slice
Method: SHAKE first 3 ingredients with ice and strain into ice-filled glass. **TOP** with soda, stir and serve with straws.

2	shot(s)	Boulard Grand Solage calvados
1	shot(s)	Freshly squeezed lemon juice
½	shot(s)	Sugar syrup (2 sugar to 1 water)
Top up with		Soda water (club soda)

Origin: A Collins named after its applejack (calvados) base.
Comment: Apple brandy makes a great base spirit in this refreshing classic.

JACK DEMPSEY

Glass: Martini
Garnish: Maraschino cherry
Method: SHAKE all ingredients with ice and fine strain into chilled glass.

1½	shot(s)	Bacardi Superior rum
1½	shot(s)	Tanqueray London dry gin
¼	shot(s)	Freshly squeezed lemon juice
¼	shot(s)	Sugar syrup (2 sugar to 1 water)
¾	shot(s)	Chilled mineral water (omit if wet ice)

Comment: Dilution makes or breaks this subtle, gin laced drink.

JACK FROST #1

Glass: Old-fashioned
Garnish: Orange zest twist
Method: SHAKE all ingredients with ice and strain into ice-filled glass.

2	shot(s)	Jack Daniel's Tennessee whiskey
½	shot(s)	Drambuie liqueur
¾	shot(s)	Freshly squeezed orange juice
½	shot(s)	Freshly squeezed lemon juice
¼	shot(s)	Pomegranate (grenadine) syrup

Comment: Tangy and fruity with the whiskey base dominating.

JACK FROST #2 NEW #8

Glass: Coupette/ Martini
Garnish: Sugar rim
Method: SHAKE all ingredients with ice and fine strain into chilled glass.

1½	shot(s)	Courvoisier V.S.O.P. cognac
1½	shot(s)	Chambord black raspberry liqueur
1½	shot(s)	Ocean Spay cranberry juice
½	shot(s)	Freshly squeezed lime juice

Comment: Fruits of the forest and cranberry burst forth from this cognac laced, slightly sweet drink.

JACK-IN-THE-BOX

Glass: Martini
Garnish: Pineapple wedge on rim
Method: SHAKE all ingredients with ice and fine strain into chilled glass.

2	shot(s)	Boulard Grand Solage calvados
2	shot(s)	Pressed pineapple juice
2	dashes	Angostura aromatic bitters

AKA: Jersey City
Variant: Pineapple Blossom
Origin: A classic cocktail of unknown origin.
Comment: Smooth 'n' easy apple and pineapple with spirity spice.

JACK MAPLES

Glass: Martini
Garnish: Dust with ground cinnamon
Method: SHAKE all ingredients with ice and fine strain into chilled glass.

2	shot(s)	Boulard Grand Solage calvados
¼	shot(s)	Maple syrup
1	dash	Angostura orange bitters

Comment: Maple syrup smoothes apple brandy, even as it enhances its character.

DURING WORLD WAR II, A GROUP OF ALPINE SOLDIERS WHO WERE STRANDED IN THE MOUNTAINS SURVIVED FOR AN ENTIRE MONTH ON NOTHING BUT A CASK OF SHERRY.

JACK PUNCH

Glass: Collins
Garnish: Pineapple wedge on rim
Method: Cut passion fruit in half and scoop flesh into shaker. Add other ingredients, **SHAKE** with ice and strain into ice-filled glass.

1	fresh	Passion fruit
2	shot(s)	Jack Daniel's Tennessee whiskey
½	shot(s)	Cuarenta Y Tres (Licor 43) liqueur
3	shot(s)	Pressed pineapple juice
⅛	shot(s)	Sugar syrup (2 sugar to 1 water)
3	dashes	Angostura aromatic bitters

Origin: Adapted from a recipe created in 2002 at Townhouse, London, England.
Comment: Vanilla hints in the whiskey and liqueur combine to dominate this fruity long drink.

JACK ROSE UPDATED #8

Glass: Martini
Garnish: Lemon wedge on rim
Method: SHAKE all ingredients with ice and fine strain into chilled glass.

2	shot(s)	Boulard Grand Solage calvados
¾	shot(s)	Freshly squeezed lemon juice
¼	shot(s)	Pomegranate (grenadine) syrup
¼	shot(s)	Sugar syrup (2 sugar to 1 water)
2	dashes	Peychaud's aromatic bitters (optional)
½	shot(s)	Chilled mineral water (omit if wet ice)

Variation: Made better by adding half fresh egg white (substitute for water).
Comment: An apple brandy sour sweetened with grenadine. Better when shaken with egg white.
Origin: Like many great classics this drink is served with numerous plausible origins:

1. The Jack Rose is named after the Jacqueminot rose, which in turn takes its name from the French general, Jean-François Jacqueminot. According to Albert S. Crockett's 1935 'The Old Waldorf-Astoria Bar Book', it is "So called because of its pink colour, the exact shade of a Jacqueminot rose, when properly concocted."

2. Some credit this drink's creation to the Colt's Neck inn in New Jersey, which was originally owned by a member of the Laird's family of applejack distillers. His name was Jack and 'Rose' is said to be a reference to the drink's reddish-pink hue. However, this theory has been discredited by Lisa Laird-Dunn, a ninth generation Laird family ancestor.

3. Other simply claim 'Jack' is short for 'applejack' and again hold that 'Rose' a reference to the drink's colour.

4. According to the Police Gazette of 1905, Frank J. May, better known as Jack Rose, a wrestling bartender who held bar at Gene Sullivan's Cafe, 187 Pavonia Avenue, Jersey City, New Jersey created this drink.

5. However, the most popular theory relates to a late 19th century New York small-time gangster called Jack Rose who was the informant in a notorious 1912 murder case. 'Bald' Jack Rose, whose favourite beverage is said to have been applejack brandy with lemon and grenadine, was heavily implicated in the 1912 the shooting of Herman Rosenthal, the owner of several New York gambling dens who was in throws of blowing the lid on police and municipal links to organised crime. Rosenthal had already squealed to the press and on the evening of July 15, after the lengthily delivery of his affidavit, left D.A. Charles Whitman's office at around midnight. Fatally he then headed to the Metropole Café at the Hotel Metropole on West 43rd Street, a favourite late night gambler's haunt, for a nightcap. As he exited the Metropole he was killed by four bullets, one to the chest and three to his head. The hit was pinned on a Lieutenant Charles Becker of the NYPD's antigambling squad and Rose was star witness in what was then the trial of the century. Becker went to the electric chair while Rose apparently went into the catering business, lending his name to his favourite drink.

6. Or, alternatively, it could be named after 'Jack Rose', an early 20th century brand of small cigars which sold for five cents a pack. Interestingly, these little cigars became known by the nickname 'squealers' after the Rosenthal case.

JACKIE O'S ROSE

Glass: Martini
Garnish: Lime wedge on rim
Method: SHAKE all ingredients with ice and fine strain into chilled glass.

2	shot(s)	Bacardi Superior rum
1	shot(s)	Freshly squeezed lime juice
½	shot(s)	Cointreau triple sec
½	shot(s)	Sugar syrup (2 sugar to 1 water)
½	spoon	Rosewater (optional)

Comment: In its simplest form this is a Daiquiri with added liqueur - or a Margarita with rum. Whatever, it's a good balance of sweet and sour.

JACKTINI

Glass: Martini
Method: SHAKE all ingredients with ice and fine strain into chilled glass.

1	shot(s)	Jack Daniel's Tennessee whiskey
1	shot(s)	Mandarine Napoléon liqueur
1¾	shot(s)	Freshly squeezed lemon juice
½	shot(s)	Sugar syrup (2 sugar to 1 water)

Comment: A citrus bite and a smooth Tennessee whiskey draw enhanced with rich mandarin liqueur.

JACUZZI

Glass: Flute
Garnish: Orange slice on rim
Method: SHAKE first 3 ingredients with ice and fine strain into chilled glass. TOP with champagne.

1	shot(s)	Peach Tree peach schnapps
½	shot(s)	Tanqueray London dry gin
1	shot(s)	Freshly squeezed orange juice
Top up with		Perrier Jouet brut champagne

Comment: A sweet, peachy champagne cocktail.

JADE DAIQUIRI

Glass: Martini
Garnish: Mint leaf
Method: SHAKE all ingredients with ice and fine strain into chilled glass.

2	shot(s)	Bacardi Superior rum
¼	shot(s)	Cointreau triple sec
¼	shot(s)	Giffard Menthe Pastille liqueur
½	shot(s)	Freshly squeezed lime juice
¼	shot(s)	Sugar syrup (2 sugar to 1 water)

Comment: A Daiquiri with a splash of orange and mint liqueurs. Fresh breath enhancing.

JADE GARDEN

Glass: Collins
Garnish: Lemon slice
Method: SHAKE all ingredients with ice and strain into ice-filled glass.

2	shot(s)	Ketel One vodka
1	shot(s)	St-Germain elderflower liqueur
1	shot(s)	Cold jasmine tea
1½	shot(s)	Pressed apple juice
½	shot(s)	Freshly squeezed lemon juice

Origin: Adapted from a drink created in 2004 by Michael Butt and Giles Looker of Soulshakers, England.
Comment: Not too dry (it has a hint of floral sweetness), nor too sweet (it offers notes of bitter tea and citrus) - just tasty, balanced and refreshing.

> ## 'COCKTAIL MUSIC IS ACCEPTED AS AUDIBLE WALLPAPER.'
> ### ALISTAIR COOKE

JADED LADY

Glass: Martini
Garnish: Grated nutmeg
Method: SHAKE first 4 ingredients with ice and fine strain into chilled glass. Carefully **POUR** blue curaçao through centre of drink (it should sink to the bottom).

1½	shot(s)	**Tanqueray London dry gin**
1½	shot(s)	**Bols advocaat liqueur**
½	shot(s)	**Freshly squeezed orange juice**
1	dash	**Angostura orange bitters**
⅛	shot(s)	**Bols blue curaçao liqueur**

Origin: First created by Yours Truly (Simon Difford) in 1996 but reinvented ten years on.
Comment: Distinctly Dutch in style, this thick, creamy drink delivers orange, vanilla and more than a hint of gin.

JAFFA MARTINI

Glass: Martini
Garnish: Float mini Jaffa Cake
Method: SHAKE all ingredients with ice and fine strain into chilled glass.

1	shot(s)	**Cointreau triple sec**
1	shot(s)	**Brown crème de cacao liqueur**
½	shot(s)	**Orange-infused Ketel One vodka**
½	shot(s)	**Freshly squeezed lemon juice**
1	shot(s)	**Freshly squeezed orange juice**
3	dashes	**Angostura orange bitters** (optional)
1	fresh	**Egg** (white & yolk)

Origin: Created by Yours Truly (Simon Difford) in 2004. McVitie's Jaffa Cakes have a tangy orange jelly centre on a hardish sponge base, covered in dark chocolate. Back in 1991 these tasty little snacks beat off UK Customs & Excise who sought to reclassify them as chocolate biscuits, which, unlike cakes, are categorised as luxuries and so subjected to Value Added Tax.
Comment: Sweet, dessert-style cocktail.

THE JÄGERITA NEW #8

Glass: Martini/Coupette
Garnish: Lime wedge
Method: SHAKE all ingredients with ice and fine strain into chilled glass.

2	shot(s)	**Jägermeister liqueur**
1	shot(s)	**Cointreau triple sec**
1	shot(s)	**Freshly squeezed lime juice**
¼	shot(s)	**Sugar syrup** (2 sugar to 1 water)

Origin: Created by David Cordoba and demonstrated at Difford's Cabinet Room in September 2008.
Comment: The bartender's favourite shot meets the bartender's favourite cocktail.

JALISCO

Glass: Martini
Garnish: Grapes on stick
Method: MUDDLE grapes in base of shaker. Add other ingredients, **SHAKE** with ice and fine strain into chilled glass.

12	fresh	**Seedless white grapes**
2½	shot(s)	**Don Julio reposado tequila**
½	shot(s)	**Sugar syrup** (2 sugar to 1 water)
3	dashes	**Angostura orange bitters**

Origin: Created in 2003 by Shelim Islam at GE Club, London, England. Pronounced 'Hal-is-co', this cocktail takes its name from the Mexican state that is home to the town of Tequila and the spirit of the same name.
Comment: It's amazing how well grapes combine with tequila.

JALISCO FLOWER NEW #8

Glass: Flute
Garnish: Grapefruit zest twist
Method: SHAKE first 3 ingredients with ice and fine strain into chilled glass. **TOP** with champagne. Lightly stir and serve.

½	shot(s)	**Don Julio reposado tequila**
¾	shot(s)	**St-Germain elderflower liqueur**
1	shot(s)	**Ruby grapefruit juice**
Top up with		**Perrier Jouet brut Champagne**

Origin: Created in 2008 by Vincenzo Marianella at Doheny, Los Angeles, USA.
Comment: Subtle, fruity and one of my favourite champagne cocktails.

JALISCO ESPRESSO

Glass: Martini
Garnish: Float 3 coffee beans
Method: SHAKE all ingredients with ice and fine strain into chilled glass.

2	shot(s)	**Don Julio reposado tequila**
1	shot(s)	**Espresso coffee**
1	shot(s)	**Kahlúa coffee liqueur**

Origin: Adapted from a drink created in 2005 by Henry Besant & Andres Masso, London, England, and named after the Mexican state where the tequila industry is centred.
Comment: A tequila laced wake up call.

JAM ROLL

Glass: Shot
Method: Refrigerate ingredients then **LAYER** in chilled glass by carefully pouring in the following order.

½	shot(s)	**Chambord black raspberry liqueur**
½	shot(s)	**Frangelico hazelnut liqueur**
½	shot(s)	**Baileys Irish cream liqueur**

Origin: Created in 2003 at Liquid Lounge, Marbella, Spain.
Comment: A very sweet jam roll laced with alcohol.

JAMAICAN ME CRAZY NEW #8

Glass: Hurricane
Garnish: Passion fruit boat, mint & fruit stick
Method: SHAKE all ingredients with ice and strain into glass filled with crushed ice.

1½	fresh	**Passion fruit juice**
2	shot(s)	**Bacardi Superior rum**
1	shot(s)	**Malibu coconut rum liqueur**
2	shot(s)	**Freshly squeezed orange juice**
2	shot(s)	**Ocean Spray cranberry juice**
1½	shot(s)	**Freshly squeezed lime juice**
¾	shot(s)	**Grenadine (pomegranate) juice**

Comment: A rum laced (originally Jamaican), fruity, Tiki-style cocktail.

JAMAICAN MULE

Glass: Collins
Garnish: Lime wedge
Method: POUR ingredients into ice-filled glass and lightly stir.

2	shot(s)	**Sailor Jerry spiced rum**
½	shot(s)	**Freshly squeezed lime juice**
½	shot(s)	**Sugar syrup** (2 sugar to 1 water)
Top up with		**Ginger beer**

Comment: A long, rum based drink with a spicy ginger taste.

JAMAICAN SUNSET

Glass: Collins
Garnish: Orange slice
Method: SHAKE all ingredients with ice and strain into ice-filled glass.

1½	shot(s)	**Wray & Nephew overproof rum**
1½	shot(s)	**Ocean Spray cranberry juice**
3	shot(s)	**Freshly squeezed orange juice**

Comment: Made with vodka as a base this drink would be called a Madras. Overproof rum adds both strength and flavour.

JAMBALAYA

Glass: Collins
Garnish: Orange slice & peach wedge
Method: SHAKE all ingredients with ice and strain into glass filled with crushed ice.

2	shot(s)	**Don Julio reposado tequila**
1	shot(s)	**Peach Tree peach schnapps**
2	shot(s)	**Freshly squeezed orange juice**
½	shot(s)	**Freshly squeezed lime juice**
¼	shot(s)	**Pomegranate (grenadine) syrup**

Comment: Peachy tropical fruit laced with tequila.

JAMBOUREE

Glass: Martini
Garnish: Orange zest twist
Method: STIR preserve with bourbon in base of shaker until mostly dissolved. Add other ingredients, SHAKE with ice and fine strain into chilled glass.

2	spoons	**Apricot preserve**
2	shot(s)	**Bulleit bourbon whiskey**
½	shot(s)	**Grand Marnier liqueur**
½	shot(s)	**Freshly squeezed lemon juice**
¾	shot(s)	**Chilled mineral water** (omit if wet ice)

Comment: Rich and jammy flavours balanced by bourbon and lemon juice.

JAMES JOYCE

Glass: Martini
Garnish: Maraschino cherry
Method: SHAKE all ingredients with ice and fine strain into chilled glass.

1½	shot(s)	**Jameson Irish whiskey**
¾	shot(s)	**Martini Rosso sweet vermouth**
¾	shot(s)	**Cointreau triple sec**
½	shot(s)	**Freshly squeezed lime juice**

Origin: Created in 2001 by the American drinks author Gary Regan. This recipe is taken from his book, 'The Joy of Mixology'.
Comment: A balanced adult sour blend.

JA-MORA

Glass: Flute
Garnish: Float single raspberry
Method: SHAKE first 4 ingredients with ice and fine strain into chilled glass. TOP with champagne.

1	shot(s)	**Ketel One vodka**
½	shot(s)	**Chambord black raspberry liqueur**
½	shot(s)	**Freshly squeezed orange juice**
½	shot(s)	**Pressed apple juice**
Top up with		**Perrier Jouet brut champagne**

Origin: Created by Jamie Terrell and Andres Masso in 1998. Named after 'mora', the Spanish for blackberry. The 'j' and 'a' stand for the names of its two creators.
Comment: Ja-more of this fruity champagne cocktail you drink, ja-more you'll like it.

JAPANESE COCKTAIL

Glass: Martini
Garnish: Lemon zest twist
Method: SHAKE all ingredients with ice and fine strain into chilled glass.

2	shot(s)	**Courvoisier V.S.O.P. cognac**
½	shot(s)	**Almond (orgeat) syrup**
2	dashes	**Angostura aromatic bitters**
¾	shot(s)	**Chilled mineral water** (reduce if wet ice)

Origin: Adapted from a recipe first published in Jerry Thomas' 1862 'Bartender's Guide or How To Mix Drinks'.
Comment: Lightly sweetened and diluted cognac flavoured with almond and a hint of spice.

JAPANESE PEAR

Glass: Martini
Garnish: Pear slice on rim
Method: SHAKE all ingredients with ice and fine strain into chilled glass.

1½	shot(s)	**Ketel One vodka**
1	shot(s)	**Sake**
½	shot(s)	**Poire William eau de vie**
¼	shot(s)	**Sugar syrup** (2 sugar to 1 water)

Origin: Adapted in 2002 from a recipe from Grand Pacific Blue Room, Sydney, Australia.
Comment: Originally made with Poire William liqueur, hence this version calls for a little sugar.

JAPANESE SLIPPER

Glass: Martini
Garnish: Salt rim
Method: SHAKE all ingredients with ice and fine strain into chilled glass.

2	shot(s)	**Don Julio reposado tequila**
1	shot(s)	**Midori green melon liqueur**
1	shot(s)	**Freshly squeezed lime juice**

Comment: A Melon Margarita.

JASMINE

Glass: Martini
Garnish: Lemon zest twist
Method: SHAKE all ingredients with ice and fine strain into chilled glass.

1½	shot(s)	**Tanqueray London dry gin**
¾	shot(s)	**Campari Bitter**
1	shot(s)	**Cointreau triple sec**
½	shot(s)	**Freshly squeezed lemon juice**

Origin: Created in 1999 by Paul Harrington, Berkeley, California, USA.
Comment: This bittersweet cocktail will only appeal to drinkers who have acquired the taste for Campari.

JASMINE & ELDERFLOWER MARTINI

Glass: Martini
Garnish: Mint leaf
Method: SHAKE all ingredients with ice and fine strain into chilled glass.

2	shot(s)	**Ketel One vodka**
1	shot(s)	**St-Germain elderflower liqueur**
¼	shot(s)	**Cold jasmine tea**
⅛	shot(s)	**Noilly Prat dry vermouth**

Origin: Created in 2006 by Yours Truly (Simon Difford).
Comment: Delicate and floral yet dry and serious. The tannins in the tea compliment and balance the drink.

JAYNE MANSFIELD

Glass: Flute
Garnish: Strawberry on rim
Method: MUDDLE strawberries in base of shaker. Add next 3 ingredients, **SHAKE** with ice and fine strain into glass. **TOP** with champagne.

4	fresh	**Strawberries** (hulled)
1	shot(s)	**Bacardi Superior rum**
1	shot(s)	**Crème de fraise de bois liqueur**
¼	shot(s)	**Sugar syrup** (2 sugar to 1 water)
Top up with		**Perrier Jouet brut champagne**

Origin: Named after the Hollywood actress.
Comment: Champagne is made to go with strawberries.

JEAN GABIN

Glass: Toddy
Garnish: Dust with freshly grated nutmeg
Method: POUR first 3 ingredients into glass. Add maple syrup and **STIR** until maple syrup dissolves.

1½	shot(s)	**Gosling's Black Seal rum**
¾	shot(s)	**Boulard Grand Solage calvados**
5	shot(s)	**Hot milk**
1	spoon	**Maple syrup**

Origin: Created in 1986 by Charles Schumann, Munich, Germany.
Comment: Beats hot chocolate as a nightcap.

VICTOR JULES BERGERON OPENED HINKY DINK'S RESTAURANT IN OAKLAND, SAN FRANSISCO, USA IN 1936 AND BECAME KNOWN AS THE TRADER.

JEAN LAFITTE COCKTAIL

Glass: Martini
Garnish: Orange zest twist
Method: SHAKE all ingredients with ice and fine strain into chilled glass.

2	shot(s)	**Zacapa aged rum**
¼	shot(s)	**La Fée Parisienne (68%) absinthe**
¼	shot(s)	**Cointreau triple sec**
⅛	shot(s)	**Sugar syrup** (2 sugar to 1 water)
1	fresh	**Egg yolk**
1	dash	**Peychaud's aromatic bitters**

Origin: My adaptation of the New Orleans classic named after the infamous privateer and hero of the Battle of New Orleans.
Comment: Not dissimilar to spicy, fortified advocaat.

JEAN MARC

Glass: Collins
Garnish: Mint sprig
Method: **MUDDLE** mint and ginger in base of shaker. Add next two ingredients, **SHAKE** with ice and fine strain into ice-filled glass. **TOP** with Appletiser, stir and serve with straws.

2	slices	**Fresh root ginger** (thumbnail sized)
4	fresh	**Mint leaves**
1½	shot(s)	**Green Chartreuse liqueur**
¼	shot(s)	**Berentzen apple schnapps**
Top up with		**Appletiser**

Origin: Created in 2003 by Yours Truly (Simon Difford) after judging a Chartreuse cocktail competition in London and realising which flavours best combine with Chartreuse. Named after my friend the President Directeur General of Chartreuse.
Comment: Chartreuse combines well with apple, ginger and mint in this summertime drink.

JELLY BELLY BEANY

Glass: Martini
Garnish: Jelly beans
Method: **SHAKE** all ingredients with ice and fine strain into chilled glass.

1½	shot(s)	**Bacardi Superior rum**
1	shot(s)	**Peach Tree peach schnapps**
1	shot(s)	**Malibu coconut rum liqueur**
2	dashes	**Angostura orange bitters**
½	shot(s)	**Chilled mineral water** (omit if wet ice)

Origin: Created in 2002 at Hush, London, England.
Comment: It's a sweetie but you're going to enjoy chewing on it.

JENEVER SOUR

Glass: Old-fashioned
Garnish: Maraschino cherry
Method: **SHAKE** all ingredients with ice and strain into ice-filled glass.

2	shot(s)	**Bokma oude genever**
1	shot(s)	**Freshly squeezed lemon juice**
½	shot(s)	**Sugar syrup** (2 sugar to 1 water)
½	fresh	**Egg white**

Comment: One of the more delicately flavoured sours.

JEREZ

Glass: Old-fashioned
Method: **STIR** all ingredients with ice and strain into ice-filled glass.

½	shot(s)	**Tio Pepe fino sherry**
½	shot(s)	**Noé Pedro Ximénez sherry**
1	shot(s)	**Peach Tree peach schnapps**
1	shot(s)	**Sauvignon Blanc wine**
1	shot(s)	**La Vieille Prune (prunelle)**
1	dash	**Angostura aromatic bitters**

Origin: This drink heralds from one of the noble houses of Spain – well that's what the sherry PR told me, anyway. I've changed the recipe slightly.
Comment: Sherry depth and stoned fruit flavours.

JERSEY SOUR

Glass: Old-fashioned
Garnish: Lemon zest twist
Method: **SHAKE** all ingredients with ice and fine strain into chilled glass.

2	shot(s)	**Boulard Grand Solage calvados**
1	shot(s)	**Freshly squeezed lemon juice**
½	shot(s)	**Sugar syrup** (2 sugar to 1 water)
½	fresh	**Egg white**

Origin: The classic name for an Applejack sour.
Comment: Apple brandy is possibly the best spirit on which to base a sour.

JEWEL COCKTAIL

Glass: Martini
Garnish: Maraschino cherry
Method: **STIR** all ingredients with ice and strain into chilled glass.

1	shot(s)	**Tanqueray London dry gin**
1	shot(s)	**Green Chartreuse liqueur**
1	shot(s)	**Martini Rosso sweet vermouth**
1	dash	**Angostura orange bitters**
½	shot(s)	**Chilled mineral water** (omit if wet ice)

Comment: Powerful in both alcohol and flavour. An old-school drink to challenge modern palates.

JOAN BENNETT

Glass: Collins
Garnish: Pineapple wedge on rim
Method: **SHAKE** all ingredients with ice and strain into glass filled with crushed ice.

2	shot(s)	**Bacardi Superior rum**
1	shot(s)	**Parfait Amour liqueur**
2½	shot(s)	**Pressed pineapple juice**

Origin: Adapted from a Tiki drink featured in Jeff Berry's 'Intoxica' and originally created in 1932 at Sloppy Joe's Bar, Havana, Cuba. Named after Hollywood ingénue, Joan Bennett, who in the same year starred in Fox's Careless Lady. Years later she hit the news when her husband, producer Walter Wanger, shot her agent in the crotch after catching them in bed together. Oo-err!
Comment: Fruity and floral, but an unfortunate colour.

JOCKEY CLUB

●●●●○

Glass: Martini
Garnish: Orange zest twist
Method: SHAKE all ingredients with ice and fine strain into chilled glass.

2	shot(s)	**Tanqueray London dry gin**
½	shot(s)	**Luxardo Amaretto di Saschira**
½	shot(s)	**Freshly squeezed lemon juice**
¾	shot(s)	**Chilled mineral water** (omit if wet ice)
1	dash	**Angostura orange bitters**
1	dash	**Angostura aromatic bitters**

Variant: Some old books, including 'The Fine Art of Mixing Drinks', describe the Jockey Club as a Manhattan with maraschino.
Origin: This classic drink from the 1930s originally called for crème de noyaux.
Comment: Peachy almond with gin.

JODI MAY

●●●●○○

Glass: Collins
Garnish: Orange slice
Method: SHAKE all ingredients with ice and fine strain into chilled glass.

1½	shot(s)	**Bulleit bourbon whiskey**
½	shot(s)	**Cointreau triple sec**
2½	shot(s)	**Freshly squeezed orange juice**
1½	shot(s)	**Ocean Spray cranberry juice**
¼	shot(s)	**Freshly squeezed lime juice**

Origin: Adapted from a drink discovered in 2003 at World Service, Nottingham, England.
Comment: Long, fruity and laced with whiskey.

JOHN COLLINS UPDATED #8

●●●●○

Glass: Collins
Garnish: Orange slice & cherry on stick (sail)
Method: SHAKE first 3 ingredients with ice and strain into ice-filled glass. **TOP** with soda, stir and serve with straws.

2	shot(s)	**Tanqueray London dry gin**
1	shot(s)	**Freshly squeezed lemon juice**
½	shot(s)	**Sugar syrup** (2 sugar to 1 water)
Top up with		**Soda water** (club soda)

Origin: In England, this drink is traditionally credited to John Collins, a bartender who worked at Limmer's Hotel, Conduit Street, London. The 'coffee house' of this hotel, a true dive bar, was popular with sporting types during the 19th century, and famous, according to the 1860s memoirs of a Captain Gronow, for its gin-punch as early as 1814.

John (or possibly Jim) Collins, head waiter of Limmer's, is immortalised in a limerick, which was apparently first printed in an 1892 book entitled 'Drinks of the World'. In 1891 a Sir Morell Mackenzie had identified John Collins as the creator of the Tom Collins, using this limerick, although both the words of the rhyme and the conclusions he drew from it were disputed. But, according to this version of the story, the special gin-punch for which John Collins of Limmer's was famous went on to become known as the Tom Collins when it was made using Old Tom gin.

The original Collins was probably based on genever gin, but there is also debate as to whether it was Old Tom or London Dry. To further complicate the issue a 'John Collins' appears to be exactly the same drink as a 'Tom Collins'. Thus I make a 'Collins' with genever gin, a 'Tom Collins' with old tom gin, and a 'John Collins' with London dry gin. Confused? Then you should also check out the 'Gin Punch' (which has the addition of bitters) and a 'Gin Fizz' which is topped with soda from a siphon.
Comment: A refreshing balance of sour lemon and sugar, laced with gin and lengthened with soda.

JOHN DALY

●●●●○

Glass: Collins
Garnish: Lemon slice
Method: SHAKE all ingredients with ice and strain into ice-filled glass.

1½	shot(s)	**Ketel One Citroen vodka**
¼	shot(s)	**Cointreau triple sec**
1½	shot(s)	**Freshly squeezed lemon juice**
¾	shot(s)	**Sugar syrup** (2 sugar to 1 water)
2	shot(s)	**Cold English breakfast tea**

Variants: Arnold Palmer, Tom Palmer.
Origin: Named after the American professional golfer noted for his victory in the 1991 PGA Championship and colourful personal life.
Comment: Essentially an alcoholic iced tea, this is bittersweet and refreshing - perfect for a hot afternoon.

JOLT'INI

●●●●○

Glass: Martini
Garnish: Float 3 coffee beans
Method: SHAKE all ingredients with ice and fine strain into chilled glass.

2	shot(s)	**Vanilla-infused Ketel One vodka**
½	shot(s)	**Kahlúa coffee liqueur**
1	shot(s)	**Espresso coffee**

Origin: Discovered in 2005 at Degrees, Washington DC, USA.
Comment: A flavoursome wake up call of espresso coffee laced with vanilla vodka.

> 'THE CONDITION OF ALIENATION, OF BEING ASLEEP, OF BEING UNCONSCIOUS, OF BEING OUT OF ONE'S MIND, IS THE CONDITION OF THE NORMAL MAN.'
> R. D. LAING

JOSE COLLINS

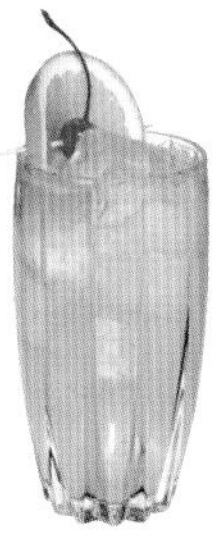

●●●●○

Glass: Collins
Garnish: Orange slice & cherry on stick (sail)
Method: SHAKE first 3 ingredients with ice and strain into ice-filled glass. **TOP** with soda, stir and serve with straws.

2	shot(s)	**Don Julio reposado tequila**
1	shot(s)	**Freshly squeezed lemon juice**
½	shot(s)	**Sugar syrup** (2 sugar to 1 water)
Top up with		**Soda water** (club soda)

AKA: Juan Collins
Comment: The classic long balance of sweet and sour with tequila adding Mexican spirit.

JOSEPHINE BAKER NEW #8

●●●●○○

Glass: Martini
Garnish: Dust with grated cinnamon
Method: SHAKE all ingredients with ice and fine strain into chilled glass.

1½	shot(s)	**Courvoisier V.S.O.P. cognac**
1½	shot(s)	**Warre's Otima tawny port**
1	shot(s)	**Bols apricot brandy liqueur**
¼	shot(s)	**Sugar syrup** (2 sugar to 1 water)
1	small	**Lemon zest twist**
1	fresh	**Egg yolk**

Origin: Recipe adapted from a 1937 Bar Florida menu, Havana, Cuba.
Comment: Smooth apricot and brandy with hints of wine and cold tea.

THE JOURNALIST

●●●●○

Glass: Martini
Garnish: Maraschino cherry
Method: SHAKE all ingredients with ice and fine strain into chilled glass.

2	shot(s)	**Tanqueray London dry gin**
½	shot(s)	**Noilly Prat dry vermouth**
½	shot(s)	**Martini Rosso sweet vermouth**
¼	shot(s)	**Cointreau triple sec**
¼	shot(s)	**Freshly squeezed lemon juice**
2	dashes	**Angostura aromatic bitters**

AKA: Periodista ('journalist' in Spanish).
Comment: Like some journalists I've met, this is bitter and sour.

JUBILANT

●●●●◐

Glass: Martini
Garnish: Orange slice on rim
Method: SHAKE all ingredients with ice and fine strain into chilled glass.

1½	shot(s)	**Tanqueray London dry gin**
¾	shot(s)	**Bénédictine D.O.M. liqueur**
½	shot(s)	**Freshly squeezed lemon juice**
½	shot(s)	**Freshly squeezed orange juice**
½	fresh	**Egg white**

Origin: A long lost classic.
Comment: Wonderfully balanced, aromatic, herbal and fruity.

'IT SHRINKS MY LIVER, DOESN'T IT? IT PICKLES MY KIDNEYS. YEAH. BUT WHAT DOES IT DO TO MY MIND? IT TOSSES THE SANDBAGS OVERBOARD SO THE BALLOON CAN SOAR. SUDDENLY, I'M ABOVE THE ORDINARY. I'M COMPETENT, SUPREMELY COMPETENT. I'M WALKING A TIGHTROPE OVER NIAGARA FALLS. I'M ONE OF THE GREAT ONES.'
BILLY WILDER

JUDGEMENT DAY NEW #8

●●●●○

Glass: Martini/Coupette
Garnish: Spray of Pimento Dram
Method: SHAKE with ice and fine strain into chilled glass.

1	shot(s)	**Macchu pisco**
⅛	shot(s)	**La Fée Parisienne (68%) absinthe**
½	shot(s)	**Freshly squeezed lime juice**
½	shot(s)	**Freshly squeezed lemon juice**
¼	shot(s)	**Sugar syrup** (2 sugar to 1 water)
½	fresh	**Egg white**

Origin: On 16th May 2008, superstar bartender Charles Vexenat was unjustly jailed in New Orleans during Tales of the Cocktail after Dre dropped a glass bottle in the Old Absinthe House. Fortunately for Charles he was saved a second day in the slammer by Melanie Asher, owner of Macchu Pisco who bailed him out. This cocktail, created at PDT, New York City, is Charles's tribute to Melanie.
Comment: Charles was pretty sour about his experience when he created this very aromatic sour.

JUDY (MOCKTAIL)

●●●●◐○

Glass: Collins
Garnish: Lime wedge
Method: SHAKE all ingredients with ice and strain into ice-filled glass.

2	shot(s)	**Freshly squeezed grapefruit juice**
3	shot(s)	**Pressed pineapple juice**
½	shot(s)	**Freshly squeezed lemon juice**
½	shot(s)	**Rose's lime cordial**

Comment: A refreshing, not sweet, driver's option. Consider adding a couple of dashes of Angostura aromatic bitters, although be aware that these contain some alcohol.

DRINKS ARE GRADED AS FOLLOWS:

● DISGUSTING ●◐ PRETTY AWFUL ●● BEST AVOIDED
●●◐ DISAPPOINTING ●●● ACCEPTABLE ●●●● GOOD
●●●● RECOMMENDED ●●●●◐ HIGHLY RECOMMENDED
●●●●● OUTSTANDING / EXCEPTIONAL

JULEP (GENERIC NAME) UPDATED #8

Glass: Collins
Garnish: Mint sprig
Method: Lightly **MUDDLE** mint leaves with spirit in base of shaker (just enough to bruise). (At this stage, if time allows, you should refrigerate the shaker, mint and spirit, and the glass in which the drink is to be served, for at least two hours.) Add other ingredients to shaker, **SHAKE** with ice and strain into glass filled with crushed ice. **CHURN** (stir) the drink with the crushed ice using a bar spoon. Top with more crushed ice to fill glass and churn again. Serve with straws.

12	fresh	**Mint leaves**
2½	shot(s)	**Spirit** (whisk(e)y, rum, gin, etc.)
¾	shot(s)	**Sugar syrup** (2 sugar to 1 water)
3	dashes	**Angostura aromatic bitters**

Origin: Juleps are tall drinks generally served in Collins glasses but originally served in julep cups and based on a spirit, liqueur or fortified wine. They are most often served with fresh mint over crushed ice.

The name ultimately derives from the Arabic word 'julab', meaning rosewater. Although this had been used to describe any sweetened drink, up to and including medicines. The Julep is thought to have originated in Persia, or there abouts, and it travelled to Europe (some say Southern France) where the rose petals were substituted for indigenous mint. The drink is then believed to have crossed the Atlantic where cognac was replaced with peach brandy and then whiskey – the Mint Julep we recognise today. The first known written reference to a cocktail-style Julep was by a Virginian gentleman in 1787.
Comment: The key to this drink is serving it ice cold and giving the flavours in the mint time to marry with the spirit. Hence, Juleps are ideally prepared hours in advance of serving. Adjust sugar to balance if using a fortified wine in place of a spirit.

JULEP MARTINI

Glass: Martini
Garnish: Mint leaf
Method: Lightly **MUDDLE** mint in base of shaker (just to bruise). Add other ingredients, **SHAKE** with ice and fine strain into chilled glass.

8	fresh	**Mint leaves**
2½	shot(s)	**Bulleit bourbon whiskey**
½	shot(s)	**Sugar syrup** (2 sugar to 1 water)
¾	shot(s)	**Chilled mineral water** (omit if wet ice)

Origin: Adapted from a recipe created in the mid 1990s by Dick Bradsell.
Comment: A short variation on the classic Julep: sweetened bourbon and mint.

JULES DELIGHT

Glass: Martini
Garnish: Strawberry
Method: **MUDDLE** strawberries in base of shaker. Add other ingredients, **SHAKE** with ice and fine strain into chilled glass.

3	fresh	**Strawberries** (hulled)
2	shot(s)	**Ketel One vodka**
¼	shot(s)	**White balsamic vinegar**
¾	shot(s)	**Pressed apple juice**
¼	shot(s)	**Freshly squeezed lemon juice**
½	shot(s)	**Sugar syrup** (2 sugar to 1 water)

Origin: Created in 2005 by Julien Gualdoni at Trailer Happiness, London, England.
Comment: Sweet fortified strawberries with a cleansing balsamic vinegar bite.

JULIETTE

Glass: Collins
Garnish: Pineapple wedge & cherry
Method: **SHAKE** all ingredients with ice and strain into ice-filled glass.

1	shot(s)	**Courvoisier V.S.O.P. cognac**
1	shot(s)	**Belle de Brillet pear liqueur**
¼	shot(s)	**Chambord black raspberry liqueur**
2½	shot(s)	**Ocean Spray cranberry juice**
1	shot(s)	**Pressed pineapple juice**

Comment: Fruity, medium sweet, cognac laced cooler.

JUMBLED FRUIT JULEP

Glass: Collins
Garnish: Strawberry & mint sprig
Method: **MUDDLE** strawberries and then mint in base of shaker (just to bruise mint). Add other ingredients, **SHAKE** with ice and strain into glass filled with crushed ice.

4	fresh	**Mint leaves**
3	fresh	**Strawberries** (hulled)
2	shot(s)	**Mango flavoured vodka**
1	shot(s)	**Pressed apple juice**
½	shot(s)	**Passion fruit sugar syrup**
½	shot(s)	**Freshly squeezed lime juice**

Origin: Created in 2005 by Michael Butt and Giles Looker of Soulshakers, England.
Comment: A fruity twist on the classic Julep.

JUMPING JACK FLASH

Glass: Martini
Glass: Pineapple wedge on rim
Method: **SHAKE** all ingredients with ice and fine strain into chilled glass.

1½	shot(s)	**Jack Daniel's Tennessee whiskey**
½	shot(s)	**Crème de banane liqueur**
½	shot(s)	**Galliano L'Autentico liqueur**
¾	shot(s)	**Freshly squeezed orange juice**
¾	shot(s)	**Pressed pineapple juice**

Comment: Whiskey further mellowed and sweetened by a tasty combo of liqueurs and juices.

JUNE BUG

Glass: Hurricane
Garnish: Pineapple wedge & cherry on rim
Method: **SHAKE** all ingredients with ice and strain into glass filled with crushed ice. Serve with straws.

1	shot(s)	**Midori green melon liqueur**
1	shot(s)	**Malibu coconut rum liqueur**
1	shot(s)	**Crème de banane liqueur**
4	shot(s)	**Pressed pineapple juice**
1	shot(s)	**Freshly squeezed lime juice**

Comment: Sweet & fruity.

JUNIPORT FIZZ NEW #8

Glass: Small Collins (max 8oz)
Garnish: Mint sprig
Method: SHAKE first 4 ingredients with ice and strain into empty chilled glass. **TOP** with soda from a siphon.

1½	shot(s)	Tanqueray London dry gin
½	shot(s)	Warre's Otima tawny port
¾	shot(s)	Freshly squeezed lemon juice
½	shot(s)	Sugar syrup (2 sugar to 1 water)
Top up with		Soda water (from siphon)

Comment: This straight forward fizz benefits from the unusual combination of gin and port.
Origin: Created in 2008 by Julian de Feral at Bureau, London, England.

JUNGLE BIRD

Glass: Old-fashioned (or Tiki mug)
Garnish: Orange slice & cherry on stick (sail)
Method: SHAKE all ingredients with ice and strain into glass filled with crushed ice.

1½	shot(s)	Gosling's Black Seal rum
½	shot(s)	Campari Bitter
½	shot(s)	Freshly squeezed lime juice
½	shot(s)	Sugar syrup (2 sugar to 1 water)
2	shot(s)	Pressed pineapple juice

Origin: Adapted from a drink featured in Jeff Berry's 'Intoxica' and originally created circa 1978 at the Aviary Bar, Kuala Lumpur, Malaysia.
Comment: Bittersweet and fruity with good rum notes.

> 'I RATHER LIKE MY REPUTATION, ACTUALLY, THAT OF A SPOILED GENIUS FROM THE WELSH GUTTER, A DRUNK, A WOMANIZER; IT'S RATHER AN ATTRACTIVE IMAGE.'
> RICHARD BURTON

JUNGLE FIRE SLING

Glass: Sling
Garnish: Orange slice & cherry on stick (sail)
Method: SHAKE first 4 ingredients with ice and strain into ice-filled glass. **TOP** with ginger ale, stir and serve with straws.

1	shot(s)	Courvoisier V.S.O.P. cognac
1	shot(s)	Heering cherry brandy liqueur
½	shot(s)	Parfait Amour liqueur
½	shot(s)	Bénédictine D.O.M. liqueur
Top up with		Ginger ale

Comment: Hardly the most refined of drinks, but it does have the refreshing zing of ginger with a soupcon of sticky fruit, herbs and cognac in the background.

JUNGLE JUICE

Glass: Collins
Garnish: Orange slice
Method: SHAKE all ingredients with ice and strain into ice-filled glass.

1	shot(s)	Ketel One vodka
1	shot(s)	Bacardi Superior rum
½	shot(s)	Cointreau triple sec
1	shot(s)	Ocean Spray cranberry juice
1	shot(s)	Freshly squeezed orange juice
1	shot(s)	Pressed pineapple juice
¾	shot(s)	Freshly squeezed lime juice
¼	shot(s)	Sugar syrup (2 sugar to 1 water)

Comment: If this is the juice of the jungle, I'm a monkey's uncle. That said, as fruity long drinks go this is not bad at all.

JUPITER MARTINI

Glass: Martini
Garnish: Orange zest twist
Method: SHAKE all ingredients with ice and fine strain into chilled glass.

2	shot(s)	Tanqueray London dry gin
¾	shot(s)	Noilly Prat dry vermouth
⅛	shot(s)	Parfait Amour liqueur
⅛	shot(s)	Freshly squeezed orange juice
½	shot(s)	Chilled mineral water (omit if wet ice)

Origin: A classic which is thought to have originated some time in the 1920s.
Comment: Bone dry and aromatic, this drink's colour is the grey hue of an overcast sky.

THE JUXTAPOSITION

Glass: Martini
Garnish: Two pineapple wedges on rim
Method: STIR honey with vodka in base of shaker until honey dissolves. Add other ingredients, **SHAKE** with ice and fine strain into chilled glass.

2	spoons	Runny honey
2	shot(s)	Cranberry flavoured vodka
1	shot(s)	Pressed pineapple juice
¾	shot(s)	Freshly squeezed lime juice
3	dashes	Angostura aromatic bitters

Origin: Adapted from a long drink created in 2003 by Michael Butt and Giles Looker of Soulshakers, England.
Comment: Tangy, complex with foaming pineapple.

KAMANIWANALAYA

Glass: Collins
Garnish: Pineapple wedge & cherry
Method: SHAKE all ingredients with ice and strain into ice-filled glass.

1½	shot(s)	Bacardi Superior rum
½	shot(s)	Pusser's Navy rum
1	shot(s)	Luxardo Amaretto di Saschira
3	shot(s)	Pressed pineapple juice

Comment: Try saying the name after a few of these rum laced, tropical pineapple concoctions.

KAMIKAZE

Glass: Shot
Method: SHAKE all ingredients with ice and fine strain into chilled glass.

1	shot(s)	Don Julio reposado tequila
½	shot(s)	Cointreau triple sec
½	shot(s)	Freshly squeezed lime juice

Variant: With vodka in place of tequila.
Comment: A bite-sized Margarita.

KANGAROO NEW #8

Glass: Martini/Coupette
Garnish: Lemon zest twist
Method: STIR all ingredients with ice and strain into chilled glass.

| 2 | shot(s) | Ketel One vodka |
| ½ | shot(s) | Noilly Prat dry vermouth |

AKA: Vodkatini
Origin: Bartending legend has it that 'Kangaroo' was the original name for a Vodkatini and the evidence usually put forward to collaborate this is the drinks listing in later editions of David A. Embury's 'Fine Art of Mixing Drinks'. However, the original 1948 edition omits this drink but does list a Vodka Martini served both 'dry' and 'perfect'.
Comment: Temperature is key to the enjoyment of this modern classic. Consume while icy cold.

KANU-NO NEW #8

Glass: Old-fashioned
Garnish: Orange zest twist
Method: STIR all ingredients with ice and strain into ice-filled glass.

2¼	shot(s)	Zacapa aged rum
¼	shot(s)	Matusalem Oloroso sherry
⅛	shot(s)	Harvey Bristol cream sherry
⅛	shot(s)	Taylor's Ruby Port

Comment: The rum's sherry notes are heightened by the addition of port and sherry.
Origin: Adapted from a drink created in 2007 by Mr Ueno at Star Bar, Ginza, Tokyo. Originally served straight-up.

KARAMEL SUTRA MARTINI

Glass: Martini
Garnish: Fudge on rim
Method: SHAKE all ingredients with ice and fine strain into chilled glass.

1½	shot(s)	Vanilla-infused Ketel One vodka
1½	shot(s)	Tuaca Italian liqueur
1	shot(s)	Toffee liqueur

Origin: Adapted from a drink discovered in 2003 at the Bellagio, Las Vegas, USA.
Comment: Liquid confectionery that bites back.

KATINKA UPDATED #8

Glass: Martini
Garnish: Lime wedge on rim
Method: SHAKE all ingredients with ice and fine strain into chilled glass.

1½	shot(s)	Ketel One vodka
½	shot(s)	Bols apricot brandy liqueur
1	shot(s)	Freshly squeezed lime juice
½	shot(s)	Sugar syrup (2 sugar to 1 water)

Comment: Medium sweet, yet also tart and tangy.

KATRINA COCKTAIL

Glass: Old-fashioned
Garnish: Dust with nutmeg
Method: SHAKE all ingredients with ice and fine strain into chilled glass. No ice!

2	shot(s)	Don Julio reposado tequila
¼	shot(s)	Kahlúa coffee liqueur
⅛	shot(s)	La Fée Parisienne (68%) absinthe
¼	shot(s)	Chambord black raspberry liqueur
1	shot(s)	Pressed apple juice

Origin: Adapted from a drink created in 2005 at Pirates Alley Café, New Orleans, and named after the hurricane which devastated the city in 2005. The name is an acronym of its original ingredients: Kahlúa, Absinthe, Tequila, Raspberry, Ice, Nutmeg and Apple juice.
Comment: Spicy, fruity tequila served in a style synonymous with the Crescent City – full on!

KAVA

Glass: Collins
Garnish: Pineapple wedge & cherry
Method: SHAKE all ingredients with ice and strain into glass filled with crushed ice.

1½	shot(s)	Bacardi Superior rum
½	shot(s)	Bacardi Oro golden rum
1	shot(s)	Pressed pineapple juice
1	shot(s)	Freshly squeezed lemon juice
¼	shot(s)	Pomegranate (grenadine) syrup
¼	shot(s)	Sugar syrup (2 sugar to 1 water)

Variant: Multiply ingredients by a factor of four to make a Kava Bowl and serve in an ice-filled Tiki bowl.
Origin: Adapted from a drink featured in Jeff Berry's 'Intoxica' and originally created circa 1942 by Trader Vic.
Comment: A wonderfully fruity, fluffy and kitsch Tiki drink.

KEE-WEE MARTINI

Glass: Martini
Garnish: Kiwi slice on rim
Method: Cut kiwi fruit in half, scoop out flesh into base of shaker and **MUDDLE**. Add other ingredients, **SHAKE** with ice and fine strain into chilled glass.

1	fresh	**Kiwi fruit**
2	shot(s)	**Tanqueray London dry gin**
¼	shot(s)	**Freshly squeezed lemon juice**
½	shot(s)	**Sugar syrup** (2 sugar to 1 water)

Origin: My version of this ubiquitous drink.
Comment: The citrus hints in the kiwi combine brilliantly with those in the gin and fresh lemon juice.

KENTUCKY JEWEL

Glass: Martini
Garnish: Berries on stick
Method: **SHAKE** all ingredients with ice and fine strain into chilled glass.

1½	shot(s)	**Bulleit bourbon whiskey**
¼	shot(s)	**Chambord black raspberry liqueur**
¼	shot(s)	**Cointreau triple sec**
2	shot(s)	**Ocean Spray cranberry juice**

Origin: Adapted from a drink created in 2004 by Jonathan Lamm, The Admirable Crichton, London, England.
Comment: Easy sipping, fruity bourbon.

KENTUCKY COLONEL

Glass: Old-fashioned
Garnish: Peach slice & mint sprig
Method: **SHAKE** all ingredients with ice and strain into glass filled with crushed ice.

1½	shot(s)	**Bulleit bourbon whiskey**
¼	shot(s)	**Southern Comfort liqueur**
¼	shot(s)	**Cointreau triple sec**
1	shot(s)	**Boiron peach puree**
½	shot(s)	**Freshly squeezed lemon juice**
¼	shot(s)	**Sugar syrup** (2 sugar to 1 water)

Origin: Created in 2001 by Morgan Watson of Apartment, Belfast, Northern Ireland.
Comment: Peach and bourbon with hints of orange and spice.

KENTUCKY MAC

Glass: Old-fashioned
Garnish: Mint sprig
Method: **MUDDLE** ginger and mint in base of shaker. Add other ingredients, **SHAKE** with ice and strain into glass filled with crushed ice.

2	slices	**Fresh root ginger** (thumbnail sized)
2	fresh	**Mint leaves**
1½	shot(s)	**Bulleit bourbon whiskey**
1	shot(s)	**Stone's original green ginger wine**
2	shot(s)	**Pressed apple juice**

Origin: Created in 1999 by Jamie Terrell, London, England.
Comment: Spicy, yet smooth and easy to sip.

KENTUCKY DREAM

Glass: Old-fashioned
Garnish: Lemon zest twist
Method: **STIR** vanilla liqueur and bitters with two ice cubes in a glass. Add half the bourbon and two more ice cubes. Stir some more and add another two ice cubes and the rest of the bourbon. Add the last two ingredients and more ice cubes, and stir lots more. The melting and stirring in of ice cubes is essential to the dilution and taste of the drink.

½	shot(s)	**Vanilla schnapps liqueur**
2	dashes	**Angostura aromatic bitters**
2	shot(s)	**Bulleit bourbon whiskey**
½	shot(s)	**Bols apricot brandy liqueur**
1	shot(s)	**Pressed apple juice**

Origin: Created in 2002 by Wayne Collins for Maxxium UK.
Comment: Tames bourbon and adds hints of apricot, vanilla and apple.

KENTUCKY MUFFIN UPDATED #8

Glass: Old-fashioned
Garnish: Blueberries
Method: **MUDDLE** blueberries in base of shaker. Add other ingredients, **SHAKE** with ice and strain into glass filled with crushed ice. Stir and serve with straws.

12	fresh	**Blueberries**
2	shot(s)	**Bulleit bourbon whiskey**
1	shot(s)	**Pressed apple juice**
½	shot(s)	**Freshly squeezed lime juice**
½	shot(s)	**Sugar syrup** (2 sugar to 1 water)

Origin: Created in 2000 at Mash, London, England.
Comment: Blueberries, lime and apple combine with and are fortified by bourbon.

HOW TO MAKE SUGAR SYRUP

To make your own sugar syrup, gradually pour TWO cups of granulated sugar into a saucepan containing ONE cup of hot water. Stir as you pour and carry on stirring and simmering until the sugar is dissolved. Do not let the water even come close to boiling and only simmer for as long as it takes to dissolve the sugar. Allow syrup to cool and pour into an empty bottle. Ideally, you should finely strain your syrup into the bottle to remove any undissolved crystals which could otherwise encourage crystallisation. If kept in a refrigerator this mixture will last for a couple of months.

KENTUCKY PEAR

Glass: Martini
Garnish: Pear slice on rim
Method: SHAKE all ingredients with ice and fine strain into chilled glass.

1	shot(s)	**Bulleit bourbon whiskey**
1	shot(s)	**Belle de Brillet pear liqueur**
1	shot(s)	**Freshly extracted pear juice**
1	shot(s)	**Pressed apple juice**

Origin: Created in 2003 by Jes at The Cinnamon Club, London, England.
Comment: Pear, apple, vanilla and whiskey are partners in this richly flavoured drink.

KENTUCKY TEA

Glass: Collins
Garnish: Lime wedge
Method: SHAKE first 4 ingredients with ice and strain into ice-filled glass. **TOP** with ginger ale.

2	shot(s)	**Bulleit bourbon whiskey**
1	shot(s)	**Cointreau triple sec**
1	shot(s)	**Freshly squeezed lime juice**
½	shot(s)	**Sugar syrup** (2 sugar to 1 water)
Top up with		**Ginger ale**

Comment: Spicy whiskey and ginger.

KEY LIME

Glass: Coupette
Garnish: Lime wedge on rim
Method: BLEND all ingredients without ice and serve.

1½	shot(s)	**Vanilla-infused Ketel One vodka**
1½	shot(s)	**Lime flavoured vodka**
½	shot(s)	**Sugar syrup** (2 sugar to 1 water)
½	shot(s)	**Rose's lime cordial**
3	scoops	**Häagen Dazs vanilla ice cream**

Comment: Tangy, smooth and rich! Alcoholic ice cream for the grown-up palate.

KEY LIME PIE #1

Glass: Martini
Garnish: Pie rim (wipe with cream mix and dip into crushed Graham Crackers or digestive biscuits)
Method: SHAKE first 3 ingredients with ice and fine strain into chilled, rimmed glass. **SHAKE** cream and Licor 43 without ice so as to mix and whip. **FLOAT** cream mix on surface of drink.

2	shot(s)	**Malibu coconut rum liqueur**
1	shot(s)	**Cointreau triple sec**
1	shot(s)	**Freshly squeezed lime juice**
2	shot(s)	**Double (heavy) cream**
½	shot(s)	**Cuarenta Y Tres (Licor 43) liqueur**

Origin: Created by Michael Waterhouse, owner of Dylan Prime, New York City, USA.
Comment: This extremely rich drink is great when served as a dessert alternative.

KEY LIME PIE #2

Glass: Martini
Garnish: Pie rim (wipe with cream mix and dip into crushed Graham Crackers or digestive biscuits)
Method: SHAKE all ingredients with ice and fine strain into chilled, rimmed glass.

2	shot(s)	**Vanilla-infused Ketel One vodka**
1¾	shot(s)	**Pressed pineapple juice**
½	shot(s)	**Freshly squeezed lime juice**
¼	shot(s)	**Rose's lime cordial**

Comment: Beautiful balance of pineapple, vanilla, sweet and sour.

KEY LIME PIE #3

Glass: Martini
Garnish: Pie rim (wipe with cream mix and dip into crushed Graham Crackers or digestive biscuits)
Method: SHAKE all ingredients with ice and fine strain into chilled, rimmed glass.

2	shot(s)	**Ketel One Citroen vodka**
½	shot(s)	**Vanilla schnapps liqueur**
1½	shot(s)	**Pressed pineapple juice**
½	shot(s)	**Freshly squeezed lime juice**
¼	shot(s)	**Rose's lime cordial**

Origin: Recipe adapted from one by Claire Smith in 2005, London, England.
Comment: My favourite rendition of this dessert-in-a-glass cocktail.

KEY WEST COOLER

Glass: Collins
Garnish: Lime wedge on rim
Method: SHAKE all ingredients with ice and strain into ice-filled glass.

2	shot(s)	**Ketel One vodka**
1	shot(s)	**Malibu coconut rum liqueur**
1½	shot(s)	**Ocean Spray cranberry juice**
1½	shot(s)	**Freshly squeezed orange juice**

Origin: Named after the island near the southern-most tip of the Florida Keys in Florida, USA.
Comment: A coconut laced Breeze that's suited to the poolside.

K.G.B.

Glass: Shot
Method: LAYER in glass by pouring carefully in the following order.

½	shot(s)	**Kahlúa coffee liqueur**
½	shot(s)	**Galliano L'Autentico liqueur**
½	shot(s)	**Courvoisier V.S.O.P. cognac**

Comment: The initials of this simple peppermint and coffee shooter stand for Kahlúa, Galliano and brandy.

KILLER PUNCH

Glass: Collins
Garnish: Lime wedge
Method: SHAKE all ingredients with ice and strain into ice-filled glass.

1	shot(s)	**Ketel One vodka**
½	shot(s)	**Midori green melon liqueur**
½	shot(s)	**Luxardo Amaretto di Saschira**
½	shot(s)	**Freshly squeezed lime juice**
3½	shot(s)	**Ocean Spray cranberry juice**

Comment: Pretty soft, sweet and fruity as killers go.

KING COLE COCKTAIL

Glass: Martini
Garnish: Orange & pineapple slices
Method: STIR all ingredients with ice and strain into chilled glass.

2	shot(s)	**Bulleit bourbon whiskey**
¼	shot(s)	**Fernet Branca**
½	shot(s)	**Sugar syrup** (2 sugar to 1 water)
½	shot(s)	**Chilled water** (omit if wet ice)

Origin: Adapted from Harry Craddock's 1930 'The Savoy Cocktail Book'.
Comment: My Fernet loving friends in San Francisco will appreciate this herbal number.

KIR

Glass: Goblet
Garnish: None
Method: POUR cassis into glass and TOP with chilled wine.

½	shot(s)	**Crème de cassis liqueur**
Top up with		**Sauvignon Blanc wine**

Variant: Kir Royale
Origin: This drink takes its name from a colourful politician and WWII resistance hero by the name of Canon Felix Kir, who served as the Mayor of Dijon, France, between 1945 and 1965. In order to promote local products, at receptions he served an aperitif made with crème de cassis and Bourgogne Aligoté white wine. The concoction quickly became known as Canon Kir's aperitif, then Father Kir's aperitif and finally as the 'Kir' aperitif.
Comment: Blackcurrant wine - clean, crisp and not too sweet.

KIR MARTINI

Glass: Martini
Garnish: Berries on stick
Method: STIR all ingredients with ice and strain into chilled glass.

2	shot(s)	**Ketel One vodka**
1	shot(s)	**Sauvignon Blanc wine**
1	shot(s)	**Crème de cassis liqueur**

Origin: Created by Yours Truly (Simon Difford) in 2004.
Comment: The Canon's traditional white wine and cassis aperitif with added oomph.

KIR ROYALE

Glass: Flute
Method: POUR cassis into glass and TOP with champagne.

½	shot(s)	**Crème de cassis liqueur**
Top up with		**Perrier Jouet brut champagne**

Variant: Kir
Comment: Easy to make, easy to drink.

KISS OF DEATH

Glass: Shot
Method: Take sambuca from freezer and Galliano from refrigerator then LAYER in chilled glass by carefully pouring in the following order.

¾	shot(s)	**Luxardo Sambuca dei Cesari**
¾	shot(s)	**Galliano L'Autentico liqueur**

Comment: Will give you fresh breath with which to apply that kiss.

KIWI BATIDA

Glass: Collins
Garnish: Kiwi slice
Method: Cut kiwi in half and scoop flesh into blender. Add other ingredients and BLEND with 18oz scoop crushed ice until smooth. Serve with straws.

1	fresh	**Kiwi**
2½	shot(s)	**Leblon cachaça**
1	shot(s)	**Sugar syrup** (2 sugar to 1 water)

Comment: The kiwi fruit flavour is a little lacking so this drink is improved by using kiwi-flavoured sugar syrup.

KIWI BELLINI

Glass: Flute
Garnish: Kiwi slice on rim
Method: Cut kiwi fruit in half, scoop out flesh into base of shaker and MUDDLE. Add next 3 ingredients, SHAKE with ice and fine strain into chilled glass. TOP with prosecco.

1	fresh	**Kiwi fruit**
1¼	shot(s)	**Ketel One vodka**
¼	shot(s)	**Freshly squeezed lemon juice**
¼	shot(s)	**Sugar syrup** (2 sugar to 1 water)
Top up with		**Prosecco sparkling wine**

Origin: Adapted from a drink discovered at Zuma, London, England, in 2004.
Comment: Lemon fresh kiwi, fortified with vodka and charged with prosecco.

KIWI COLLINS

Glass: Collins
Garnish: Kiwi slice
Method: Cut kiwi fruit in half, scoop out flesh into base of shaker and **MUDDLE**. Add next 3 ingredients, **SHAKE** with ice and fine strain into ice-filled glass. **TOP** with soda water.

1	fresh	**Kiwi fruit**
2	shot(s)	**Ketel One vodka**
1½	shot(s)	**Freshly squeezed lemon juice**
½	shot(s)	**Sugar syrup** (2 sugar to 1 water)
Top up with		**Soda water** (club soda)

Origin: Formula by Yours Truly (Simon Difford).
Comment: A fruity adaptation of a Vodka Collins.

KIWI CRUSH

Glass: Martini
Garnish: Kiwi slice
Method: Cut kiwi fruit in half, scoop out flesh into base of shaker and **MUDDLE**. Add other ingredients, **SHAKE** with ice and fine strain into chilled glass.

1	fresh	**Kiwi fruit**
2	shot(s)	**Ketel One Citroen vodka**
1	shot(s)	**Pressed apple juice**
½	shot(s)	**Freshly squeezed lemon juice**
¼	shot(s)	**Almond (orgeat) syrup**

Origin: Recipe adapted from one by Claire Smith in 2005, London, England.
Comment: Spirit laced kiwi, citrus and almond.

KIWI MARTINI (SIMPLE FORMULA)

Glass: Martini
Garnish: Kiwi slice on rim
Method: Cut kiwi fruit in half, scoop out flesh into base of shaker and **MUDDLE**. Add other ingredients, **SHAKE** with ice and fine strain into chilled glass.

1	fresh	**Kiwi fruit**
2	shot(s)	**Ketel One vodka**
½	shot(s)	**Sugar syrup** (2 sugar to 1 water)

Origin: Formula by yours Truly (Simon Difford) in 2004.
Comment: You may need to adjust the sugar depending on the ripeness of your fruit.

KLONDIKE UPDATED #8

Glass: Collins
Garnish: Orange slice
Method: **POUR** ingredients into ice-filled glass and gently stir.

2	shot(s)	**Bulleit bourbon whiskey**
2	shot(s)	**Freshly squeezed orange juice**
Top up with		**Ginger ale**

Origin: Recipe adapted from A. S. Crockett's 1935 'The Old Waldorf-Astoria Bar Book'.
Comment: A simple drink but the three ingredients combine well.

KNICKERBOCKER MARTINI

Glass: Martini
Garnish: Orange zest twist
Method: STIR all ingredients with ice and strain into chilled glass.

1¾	shot(s)	**Tanqueray London dry gin**
¾	shot(s)	**Noilly Prat dry vermouth**
½	shot(s)	**Martini Rosso sweet vermouth**

Origin: Thought to have been created at the Knickerbocker Hotel, New York City, USA.
Comment: Aromatic vermouth dominates this flavoursome Martini variant.

KNICKERBOCKER SPECIAL UPDATED #8

Glass: Martini
Garnish: Pineapple wedge & cherry on rim
Method: SHAKE all ingredients with ice and fine strain into chilled glass.

2	shot(s)	**Bacardi Superior rum**
½	shot(s)	**Grand Marnier liqueur**
½	shot(s)	**Pressed pineapple juice**
½	shot(s)	**Freshly squeezed orange juice**
½	shot(s)	**Freshly squeezed lemon juice**
¼	shot(s)	**Raspberry sugar syrup**

Origin: Thought to have been created sometime in the mid 19th century at the Knickerbocker Hotel, New York City, USA.
Comment: Easy drinking rum and orange curaçao, flavoured with pineapple and raspberry.

KNICKER DROPPER GLORY

Glass: Shot
Method: SHAKE all ingredients with ice and fine strain into chilled glass.

1	shot(s)	**Frangelico hazelnut liqueur**
½	shot(s)	**Freshly squeezed lemon juice**

Origin: Created circa 2000 by Jason Fendick, London, England.
Comment: Nutty sweetness sharpened with lemon.

KNOCKOUT MARTINI

Glass: Martini
Garnish: Star anise on rim
Method: STIR all ingredients with ice and strain into chilled glass.

1	shot(s)	**Tanqueray London dry gin**
1	shot(s)	**Noilly Prat dry vermouth**
¼	shot(s)	**La Fée Parisienne (68%) absinthe**
¼	shot(s)	**Giffard Menthe Pastille liqueur**

Comment: A Wet Martini with aniseed and mint. Stir well as it benefits from a little extra dilution.

KOI YELLOW

●●●●○

Glass: Martini
Garnish: Float rose petal
Method: SHAKE all ingredients with ice and fine strain into chilled glass.

2	shot(s)	**Raspberry flavoured vodka**
½	shot(s)	**Cointreau triple sec**
1	shot(s)	**Freshly squeezed lemon juice**
½	shot(s)	**Sugar syrup** (2 sugar to 1 water)

Origin: The signature drink at Koi Restaurant, Los Angeles, USA.
Comment: Sherbet and raspberry Martini with a sweet and citrus sour finish.

KOOL HAND LUKE

●●●●●

Glass: Rocks
Method: MUDDLE lime in base of glass to release its juices. Pour rum and sugar syrup into glass, add crushed ice and **CHURN**. Serve with straws.

1	fresh	**Lime cut into eighths**
2	shot(s)	**Myers's dark Jamaican rum**
1	shot(s)	**Sugar syrup** (2 sugar to 1 water)
2	dashes	**Angostura aromatic bitters**

Comment: This looks like a Caipirinha and has a similar balance of sweet, sour and spirit. The bitters bring out the spice in the rum, which is every bit as pungent as cachaça.

KOOLAID

●●●●●

Glass: Collins
Garnish: Lime wedge
Method: SHAKE all ingredients with ice and strain into ice-filled glass.

1½	shot(s)	**Ketel One vodka**
¾	shot(s)	**Midori green melon liqueur**
¾	shot(s)	**Luxardo Amaretto di Saschira**
½	shot(s)	**Freshly squeezed lime juice**
2	shot(s)	**Ocean Spray cranberry juice**
1	shot(s)	**Freshly squeezed orange juice**

Origin: A drink with unknown origins that emerged and morphed during the 1990s.
Comment: Tangy liquid marzipan with hints of melon, cranberry and orange juice.

KRAKOW TEA

●●●●○

Glass: Collins
Garnish: Mint sprig & lime wedge
Method: Lightly **MUDDLE** mint in base of shaker (just to bruise). **SHAKE** all ingredients with ice and fine strain into ice-filled glass.

12	fresh	**Mint leaves**
2	shot(s)	**Zubrówka bison vodka**
1	shot(s)	**Strong cold camomile tea**
3½	shot(s)	**Pressed apple juice**
¼	shot(s)	**Freshly squeezed lime juice**
¼	shot(s)	**Sugar syrup** (2 sugar to 1 water)

Origin: Created in 2002 by Domhnall Carlin at Apartment, Belfast, Northern Ireland.
Comment: Refreshing with a dry, citrus finish.

KRETCHMA

●●●●○○

Glass: Martini
Garnish: Dust with cocoa powder
Method: SHAKE all ingredients with ice and fine strain into chilled glass.

2	shot(s)	**Ketel One vodka**
¾	shot(s)	**White crème de cacao liqueur**
½	shot(s)	**Freshly squeezed lemon juice**
⅛	shot(s)	**Pomegranate (grenadine) syrup**

Variant: Without grenadine this is a 'Ninitchka'.
Origin: Adapted from a recipe in David Embury's 'The Fine Art Of Mixing Drinks'.
Comment: Fortified Turkish Delight.

KURRENT AFFAIR

●●●○○

Glass: Collins
Garnish: Lemon slice
Method: SHAKE all ingredients with ice and strain into ice-filled glass.

1½	shot(s)	**Ketel One Citroen vodka**
¾	shot(s)	**Berry flavoured vodka**
3	shot(s)	**Pressed apple juice**

Comment: Berry and citrus vodka combine with apple in this tall, refreshing summer drink.

HOW TO MAKE SUGAR SYRUP

To make your own sugar syrup, gradually pour TWO cups of granulated sugar into a saucepan containing ONE cup of hot water. Stir as you pour and carry on stirring and simmering until the sugar is dissolved. Do not let the water even come close to boiling and only simmer for as long as it takes to dissolve the sugar. Allow syrup to cool and pour into an empty bottle. Ideally, you should finely strain your syrup into the bottle to remove any undissolved crystals which could otherwise encourage crystallisation. If kept in a refrigerator this mixture will last for a couple of months.

●●●●○

THE LADY WEARS RED NEW #8

Glass: Martini
Garnish: Champagne foam (made by macerating orange zests in champagne overnight, adding gelatin and charging with N2O siphon).
Method: SHAKE all ingredients with ice and fine-strain chilled glass. Float on top a foam made from orange peel steeped in champagne.

1½	shot(s)	**Bacardi Superior rum**
½	shot(s)	**Aperol**
¼	shot(s)	**Grand Marnier liqueur**
¼	shot(s)	**Cointreau triple sec**
⅛	shot(s)	**Tio Pepe fino sherry**
⅛	shot(s)	**Noilly Prat dry vermouth**
⅛	shot(s)	**Velvet Falernum liqueur**
¾	shot(s)	**Freshly squeezed lime juice**
¼	shot(s)	**Sugar syrup** (2 sugar to 1 water)
1	dash	**Angostura orange bitters**
1	dash	**Fee Brothers grapefruit bitters**

Comment: This 'Lady' is high maintenance but she delivers a complex reward.
Origin: Adapted from a drink created in 2008 by Ben Carlotto at The Voodoo Rooms, Edinburgh, Scotland. The original recipe calls for homemade dry orange syrup made by macerating orange zests in a blend of different sugars with Lillet Blanc and fine sherry. It also calls for homemade citrus bitters, a complex mixture of kaffir lime leaves, various citrus elements, and spices like cardamom and cassia.

●●●●○

L'AMOUR EN FUITE

Glass: Old-fashioned
Garnish: Orange zest twist
Method: POUR absinthe into ice-filled glass, **TOP** with water and leave to stand. Separately **STIR** gin, vermouth and elderflower liqueur with ice. **DISCARD** contents of glass (absinthe, water and ice) and **STRAIN** contents of mixing glass into absinthe-coated glass. No ice!

½	shot(s)	**La Fée Parisienne (68%) absinthe**
1½	shot(s)	**Tanqueray London dry gin**
¾	shot(s)	**Noilly Prat dry vermouth**
¼	shot(s)	**St-Germain elderflower liqueur**

Origin: Created in 2007 by Jamie Boudreau, Seattle, USA, originally using Lillet. The name comes from a 1979 French film.
Comment: Serious yet approachably subtle with hints of vermouth and elderflower dominated by absinthe and gin.

> ## 'THE RELATIONSHIP BETWEEN A RUSSIAN AND A BOTTLE OF VODKA IS ALMOST MYSTICAL.'
> ### RICHARD OWEN

●●●○○

L.A. ICED TEA

Glass: Sling
Garnish: Split lime wedge
Method: SHAKE first 7 ingredients with ice and strain into ice-filled glass. **TOP** with soda.

½	shot(s)	**Ketel One vodka**
½	shot(s)	**Tanqueray London dry gin**
½	shot(s)	**Bacardi Superior rum**
½	shot(s)	**Cointreau triple sec**
½	shot(s)	**Midori green melon liqueur**
1	shot(s)	**Freshly squeezed lime juice**
½	shot(s)	**Sugar syrup** (2 sugar to 1 water)
Top up with		**Soda water** (club soda)

Comment: Long and lime green with subtle notes of melon and fresh lime.

●●●○○

LANDSLIDE

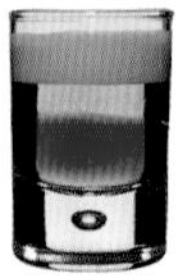

Glass: Shot
Method: Refrigerate ingredients then **LAYER** in chilled glass by carefully pouring in the following order.

½	shot(s)	**Luxardo Amaretto di Saschira**
½	shot(s)	**Crème de banane liqueur**
½	shot(s)	**Baileys Irish cream liqueur**

Comment: A sweet but pleasant combination of banana, almond and Irish cream liqueur.

●●●●○

LAGO COSMO

Glass: Martini
Garnish: Orange zest twist
Method: SHAKE all ingredients with ice and fine strain into chilled glass.

1½	shot(s)	**Cranberry flavoured vodka**
¾	shot(s)	**Cointreau triple sec**
1¾	shot(s)	**Freshly squeezed orange juice**
¼	shot(s)	**Freshly squeezed lime juice**
½	shot(s)	**Sugar syrup** (2 sugar to 1 water)

Origin: Discovered in 2003 at Nectar @ Bellagio, Las Vegas, USA.
Comment: A Cosmo with cranberry vodka in place of citrus vodka and orange juice in place of cranberry juice.

●●●●●

LARCHMONT

Glass: Martini
Garnish: Orange zest twist
Method: SHAKE all ingredients with ice and fine strain into chilled glass.

1½	shot(s)	**Bacardi Superior rum**
½	shot(s)	**Grand Marnier liqueur**
½	shot(s)	**Freshly squeezed lime juice**
¼	shot(s)	**Sugar syrup** (2 sugar to 1 water)
½	shot(s)	**Chilled mineral water** (omit if wet ice)

Origin: Created by David A. Embury, who in his 1948 'Fine Art of Mixing Drinks' writes of this drink: "As a grand finale to cocktails based on the Rum Sour, I give you one of my favorites which I have named after my favorite community."
Comment: I share Embury's appreciation of this fine drink, although I think of it more as a type of Orange Daiquiri.

THE LAST STRAW

Glass: Collins
Garnish: Apple wedge
Method: SHAKE all ingredients with ice and strain into ice-filled glass.

1½	shot(s)	**Boulard Grand Solage calvados**
1½	shot(s)	**St-Germain elderflower liqueur**
1½	shot(s)	**Dry cider**
1½	shot(s)	**Pressed apple juice**

Origin: Created in 2006 by Yours Truly (Simon Difford). We used the last straw we had left to sample the first one.
Comment: Three stages of the apple's alcoholic journey - juice, cider and brandy - are sweetened and aromatised by elderflower liqueur.

THE LAST WORD UPDATED #8

Glass: Martini
Garnish: Lime wedge on rim
Method: SHAKE all ingredients with ice and fine strain into chilled glass.

¾	shot(s)	**Tanqueray London dry gin**
¾	shot(s)	**Green Chartreuse liqueur**
¾	shot(s)	**Luxardo maraschino liqueur**
¾	shot(s)	**Freshly squeezed lime juice**
½	shot(s)	**Chilled mineral water** (omit if wet ice)

Origin: This vintage classic was first documented in Ted Saucier's 'Bottoms Up' in 1951 where its creation was attributed to the Detroit Athletic Club. It was practically forgotten until championed by the team at Pegu Club, New York City in 2005.
Comment: Chartreuse devotees will love this balanced, tangy drink. I'm one.

LAVENDER & BLACK PEPPER MARTINI

Glass: Martini
Method: Pour the syrup into an ice filled mixing glass. Add the vodka and black pepper. STIR and super-fine strain into chilled glass.

2½	shot(s)	**Ketel One vodka**
¼	shot(s)	**Lavender sugar syrup**
2	grinds	**Black pepper**

Origin: Adapted from a recipe created in 2006 by Richard Gillam at The Kenilworth Hotel, England.
Comment: Subtly sweetened and lavender flavoured vodka with a bump and grind of spicy pepper.

LAVENDER MARGARITA

Glass: Coupette
Garnish: Lime wedge
Method: SHAKE all ingredients with ice and fine strain into chilled glass.

2	shot(s)	**Don Julio reposado tequila**
1	shot(s)	**Freshly squeezed lime juice**
½	shot(s)	**Lavender sugar syrup**

Origin: Created in 2006 by Yours Truly (Simon Difford).
Comment: Lavender lime and tequila combine harmoniously.

LAVENDER MARTINI

Glass: Martini
Garnish: Lemon zest twist
Method: STIR all ingredients with ice and strain into chilled glass.

2½	shot(s)	**Lavender-infused Ketel One vodka**
¾	shot(s)	**Parfait Amour liqueur**
¼	shot(s)	**Noilly Prat dry vermouth**

Origin: Created in 2006 by Yours Truly (Simon Difford).
Comment: Infusing lavender in vodka tends to make it bitter but the parfait amour adds sweetness as well as flavour and colour.

LAZARUS

Glass: Martini
Garnish: Float three coffee beans
Method: SHAKE all ingredients with ice and fine strain into chilled glass.

1	shot(s)	**Ketel One vodka**
1	shot(s)	**Kahlúa coffee liqueur**
½	shot(s)	**Courvoisier V.S.O.P. cognac**
1	shot(s)	**Espresso coffee**

Origin: Created in 2000 by David Whitehead at Atrium, Leeds, England.
Comment: A flavoursome combination of spirit and coffee.

LCB MARTINI

Glass: Martini
Garnish: Lemon zest twist
Method: SHAKE all ingredients with ice and fine strain into chilled glass.

2	shot(s)	**Ketel One vodka**
¾	shot(s)	**Sauvignon Blanc wine**
2	shot(s)	**Freshly squeezed grapefruit juice**
¼	shot(s)	**Sugar syrup** (2 sugar to 1 water)

Origin: Created by Yours Truly (Simon Difford) in 2004 and named after Lisa Clare Ball, who loves both Sauvignon Blanc and pink grapefruit juice.
Comment: A sweet and sour, citrus fresh Martini.

LEAP YEAR MARTINI

Glass: Martini
Garnish: Lemon peel twist
Method: SHAKE all ingredients with ice and fine strain into chilled glass.

2	shot(s)	**Tanqueray London dry gin**
½	shot(s)	**Grand Marnier liqueur**
½	shot(s)	**Martini Rosso sweet vermouth**
¼	shot(s)	**Freshly squeezed lemon juice**

Origin: Harry Craddock created this drink for the Leap Year celebrations at the Savoy Hotel, London, on 29th February 1928 and recorded it in his 1930 Savoy Cocktail Book.
Comment: This drink, which is on the dry side, needs to be served ice-cold.

LEAVE IT TO ME MARTINI

Glass: Martini
Garnish: Lemon zest twist
Method: SHAKE all ingredients with ice and fine strain into chilled glass.

1½	shot(s)	Tanqueray London dry gin
½	shot(s)	Bols apricot brandy liqueur
¾	shot(s)	Martini Rosso sweet vermouth
½	shot(s)	Freshly squeezed lemon juice
¼	shot(s)	Pomegranate (grenadine) syrup

Origin: Adapted from a recipe in Harry Craddock's 1930 Savoy Cocktail Book.
Comment: Gin, apricot, vermouth and lemon create an old fashioned but well balanced drink.

THE LEAVENWORTH NEW #8

Glass: Martini/Coupette
Garnish: Orange zest twist
Method: STIR all ingredients with ice and strain into chilled glass.

2	shot(s)	Zacapa aged rum
1	shot(s)	Heering cherry brandy liqueur
10	drops	Tiki's Falernum Bitters (www.tradertiki.com)

Origin: Created in 2008 by Francesco Lafranconi of Southern Wine & Spirits, USA.
Comment: This great cocktail is dramatically influenced by the style of rum used. Francesco's original recipe calls for English Harbour rum.

LEFT BANK MARTINI UPDATED #8

Glass: Martini
Garnish: Lime zest twist
Method: SHAKE all ingredients with ice and fine strain into chilled glass.

2	shot(s)	Tanqueray London dry gin
¾	shot(s)	St-Germain elderflower liqueur
½	shot(s)	Noilly Prat dry vermouth
½	shot(s)	Chablis wine (or unoaked chardonnay)

Origin: Created in 2006 by Simon Difford at The Cabinet Room, London, England.
Comment: An aromatic, dry blend. For a sweet version, use equal parts of all three ingredients, for a dry one use two shots of gin.

LEKKER LEKKER NEW #8

Glass: Martini
Garnish: Apple slice
Method: SHAKE all ingredients with ice and fine strain into chilled glass.

1	shot(s)	Zubrówka bison vodka
¾	shot(s)	Frangelico hazelnut liqueur
½	shot(s)	Freshly squeezed lemon juice
½	shot(s)	Sugar syrup (2 sugar to 1 water)
2	shot(s)	Pressed apple juice

Comment: Most unusual with apple, hazelnut and lemon freshness.
Origin: Created by Tom Lawman at Snafu, Aberdeen. Lekker Lekker (pronounced 'Laker Laker') is Afrikaans for very nice, which is what Tom's South African friend exclaimed when he tasted this drink.

LEMON BEAT

Glass: Old-fashioned
Garnish: Lemon slice
Method: STIR honey with cachaça in the base of shaker to dissolve honey. Add other ingredients, SHAKE with ice and strain into ice-filled glass.

2	spoons	Clear runny honey
2	shot(s)	Leblon cachaça
1	shot(s)	Freshly squeezed lemon juice

Comment: Simple but effective. Use quality cachaça and honey and you'll have a great drink.

LEMON BUTTER COOKIE

Glass: Old-fashioned
Garnish: Lemon zest twist
Method: SHAKE all ingredients with ice and strain into glass filled with crushed ice.

¾	shot(s)	Zubrówka bison vodka
¾	shot(s)	Ketel One vodka
¾	shot(s)	Krupnik honey liqueur
2	shot(s)	Pressed apple juice
½	shot(s)	Almond (orgeat) syrup
⅛	shot(s)	Freshly squeezed lemon juice

Origin: Created in 2002 by Mark 'Q-Ball' Linnie and Martin Oliver at The Mixing Tin, Leeds, England.
Comment: An appropriate name for a most unusually flavoured drink modelled on the Polish Martini.

HOW TO MAKE SUGAR SYRUP

To make your own sugar syrup, gradually pour TWO cups of granulated sugar into a saucepan containing ONE cup of hot water. Stir as you pour and carry on stirring and simmering until the sugar is dissolved. Do not let the water even come close to boiling and only simmer for as long as it takes to dissolve the sugar. Allow syrup to cool and pour into an empty bottle. Ideally, you should finely strain your syrup into the bottle to remove any undissolved crystals which could otherwise encourage crystallisation. If kept in a refrigerator this mixture will last for a couple of months.

LEMON CAIPIROVSKA NEW #8

Glass: Old-fashioned
Garnish: None
Method: **MUDDLE** lemon in base of shaker, add other ingredients and **SHAKE** with 6oz scoop crushed ice. Pour into glass without straining and serve with straws.

¾	fresh	**Lemon cut into wedges**
2	shot(s)	**Ketel One Citroen vodka**
¾	shot(s)	**Sugar syrup** (2 sugar to 1 water)
1	dash	**Angostura orange bitters**

Origin: Created in 2002 by Tony Conigliaro at Isola, London, England.
Comment: A lemon-tastic Caipirovska.

LEMON CHIFFON PIE

Glass: Coupette
Garnish: Grated lemon zest
Method: **BLEND** all ingredients with crushed ice and serve with straws.

1	shot(s)	**Bacardi Superior rum**
1	shot(s)	**White crème de cacao liqueur**
1	shot(s)	**Freshly squeezed lemon juice**
2	scoops	**Häagen Dazs vanilla ice cream**

Comment: Creamy and tangy – like a lemon pie. Consume in place of dessert.

LEMON CURD MARTINI

Glass: Martini
Garnish: Lemon wedge on rim
Method: **SHAKE** all ingredients with ice and fine strain into chilled glass.

3	spoons	**Lemon curd**
2	shot(s)	**Ketel One Citroen vodka**
½	shot(s)	**Freshly squeezed lemon juice**

Origin: Created by Yours Truly (Simon Difford).
Comment: This almost creamy cocktail is named after and tastes like its primary ingredient. Martini purists may justifiably baulk at the absence of vermouth and the presence of fruit.

LEMON DROP

Glass: Shot
Garnish: Sugar coated slice of lemon
Method: **SHAKE** all ingredients with ice and fine strain into chilled glass.

½	shot(s)	**Ketel One vodka**
½	shot(s)	**Cointreau triple sec**
½	shot(s)	**Freshly squeezed lemon juice**

Comment: Lemon and orange combine to make a fresh tasting citrus shot.

LEMON DROP MARTINI

Glass: Martini
Garnish: Lemon zest twist
Method: **SHAKE** all ingredients with ice and fine strain into chilled glass.

2	shot(s)	**Ketel One Citroen vodka**
1	shot(s)	**Cointreau triple sec**
¾	shot(s)	**Freshly squeezed lemon juice**
½	shot(s)	**Sugar syrup** (2 sugar to 1 water)

Comment: Sherbety lemon.

LEMON LIME & BITTERS (MOCKTAIL)

UPDATED #8

Glass: Collins
Garnish: Lime wedge
Method: **POUR** lime and bitters into ice-filled glass. **TOP** with lemonade, lightly stir and serve with straws.

½	shot(s)	**Freshly squeezed lime juice**
4	dashes	**Angostura aromatic bitters***
Top up with		**Lemonade/Sprite/7-Up**

***Note:** Contains minute levels of alcohol due to use of Angostura bitters.

AKA: LLB
Origin: Very popular in its homeland, Australia.

LEMON MARTINI

Glass: Martini
Garnish: Lemon zest twist
Method: **MUDDLE** lemongrass in base of shaker. Add other ingredients, **SHAKE** with ice and fine strain into chilled glass.

1	inch	**Lemongrass** (chopped)
2	shot(s)	**Ketel One vodka**
¼	shot(s)	**Noilly Prat dry vermouth**
1	shot(s)	**Freshly squeezed lemon juice**
½	shot(s)	**Sugar syrup** (2 sugar to 1 water)

Origin: Created in 2006 by Yours Truly (Simon Difford).
Comment: A complex, delicately lemon Vodkatini.

LEMON MERINGUE MARTINI

Glass: Martini
Garnish: Lemon zest twist
Method: **SHAKE** all ingredients with ice and fine strain into chilled glass.

2	shot(s)	**Ketel One Citroen vodka**
1	shot(s)	**Baileys Irish cream liqueur**
1	shot(s)	**Freshly squeezed lemon juice**
¼	shot(s)	**Sugar syrup** (2 sugar to 1 water)

Origin: Adapted from a drink created in 2000 by Ben Reed, London, England.
Comment: Slightly creamy in consistency, this tangy lemon drink is indeed reminiscent of the eponymous dessert.

LEMON MERINGUE PIE'TINI

Glass: Martini
Garnish: Pie rim (wipe outside edge of rim with cream mix and dip into crunched up Graham Cracker or digestive biscuits)
Method: SHAKE first 3 ingredients with ice and fine strain into chilled and rimmed glass. **SHAKE** cream and Licor 43 without ice so as to mix and whip. **FLOAT** cream mix by pouring over back of a spoon.

1	shot(s)	Luxardo limoncello liqueur
1	shot(s)	Sugar syrup (2 sugar to 1 water)
1	shot(s)	Freshly squeezed lemon juice
2	shot(s)	Double (heavy) cream
½	shot(s)	Cuarenta Y Tres (Licor 43) liqueur

Origin: Created by Michael Waterhouse at Dylan Prime, New York City.
Comment: Rich and syrupy base sipped through a vanilla cream topping.

LEMON SORBET

Glass: Martini (saucer)
Garnish: Strips of lemon rind
Method: Heat water in pan and add sugar. Simmer and stir until sugar dissolves, add lemon juice and grated lemon rind and continue to simmer and stir for a few minutes. Take off the heat and allow to cool. Fine strain into a shallow container and stir in liqueur and orange bitters. Beat egg whites and fold into mix. Place in freezer and store for up to 3-4 days before use.

¾	cup(s)	Mineral water
1	cup(s)	Granulated white sugar
½	cup(s)	Freshly squeezed lemon juice
5	rinds	Fresh lemon (avoid the pith)
¼	cup	Luxardo limoncello liqueur
2	spoons	Angostura orange bitters
2	fresh	Egg whites

Variant: To make any other citrus flavour sorbet, simply substitute the juice and peel of another fruit such as grapefruit, lime or orange.
Comment: My favourite recipe for this dessert and occasional cocktail ingredient.

LEMONGRAD

Glass: Collins
Garnish: Lemon wedge squeezed over drink
Method: SHAKE first 4 ingredients with ice and strain into ice-filled glass. **TOP** with tonic and lightly stir.

1	shot(s)	Ketel One vodka
½	shot(s)	Ketel One Citroen vodka
½	shot(s)	St-Germain elderflower liqueur
½	shot(s)	Freshly squeezed lemon juice
Top up with		Tonic water

Origin: Adapted from a drink created in 2002 by Alex Kammerling, London, England.
Comment: A great summer afternoon drink. Fresh lemon with elderflower and quinine.

LEMONGRASS COSMO

Glass: Martini
Garnish: Lemon zest twist
Method: MUDDLE lemongrass in base of shaker. **ADD** other ingredients, **SHAKE** with ice and fine strain into chilled glass.

¼	stem	Fresh lemongrass (finely chopped)
1	shot(s)	Ketel One Citroen vodka
1	shot(s)	Cointreau triple sec
1½	shot(s)	Ocean Spray cranberry juice
½	shot(s)	Freshly squeezed lemon juice

Origin: Adapted from a drink discovered in 2005 at Opia, Hong Kong, China
Comment: Lemongrass adds complexity to this balanced Cosmo.

LEMONY

Glass: Martini
Garnish: Maraschino cherry
Method: SHAKE all ingredients with ice and fine strain into chilled glass.

2	shot(s)	Tanqueray London dry gin
½	shot(s)	Yellow Chartreuse liqueur
½	shot(s)	Luxardo limoncello liqueur
½	shot(s)	Freshly squeezed lemon juice
½	shot(s)	Chilled mineral water (omit if wet ice)

Comment: Lemon subtly dominates this complex, herbal drink.

LENINADE

Glass: Martini
Garnish: Orange zest twist
Method: SHAKE all ingredients with ice and fine strain into chilled glass.

1½	shot(s)	Ketel One Citroen vodka
1	shot(s)	Freshly squeezed lemon juice
¼	shot(s)	Sugar syrup (2 sugar to 1 water)
¼	shot(s)	Cointreau triple sec
3	dashes	Angostura orange bitters

Origin: Created by Dick Bradsell at Fred's, London, England, in the late 1980s.
Comment: Orange undertones add citrus depth to the lemon explosion.

THE LIBERTINE NEW #8

Glass: Old-fashioned
Garnish: Candied lime peel (see appendix)
Method: SHAKE first 4 ingredients with ice and fine strain into ice-filled glass. **TOP** with ginger beer and lightly stir.

1½	shot(s)	Kaffir lime flavoured vodka
¾	shot(s)	Green Chartreuse liqueur
¾	shot(s)	St-Germain elderflower liqueur
½	shot(s)	Freshly squeezed lime juice
1	shot(s)	Ginger beer

Origin: Created in 2008 by Joe Parrilli at Bacar, San Francisco, USA.
Comment: Huge flavours delicately combine in this surprisingly approachable drink.

LIFE (LOVE IN THE FUTURE ECSTASY)

Glass: Old-fashioned
Garnish: Mint leaf
Method: MUDDLE mint in base of shaker. Add next 3 ingredients, **SHAKE** with ice and fine strain into glass filled with crushed ice. **DRIZZLE** tea liqueur over drink.

7	fresh	**Mint leaves**
1½	shot(s)	**Ketel One vodka**
1	shot(s)	**Freshly squeezed lime juice**
½	shot(s)	**Sugar syrup** (2 sugar to 1 water)
1	shot(s)	**Tea liqueur**

Origin: Adapted from a drink created in 1999 by Nick Strangeway at Ché, London, England, for Martin Sexton (writer and artistic entrepreneur).
Comment: Refreshing tea and mint.

LIGHT BREEZE

Glass: Collins
Garnish: Lemon slice
Method: POUR all ingredients into ice-filled glass. Stir and serve with straws.

3	shot(s)	**Ocean Spray cranberry juice**
2	shot(s)	**Freshly squeezed grapefruit juice**
2	shot(s)	**Pernod anis**

Origin: Created in 2000 by Yours Truly (Simon Difford) at the Light Bar, London, England (hence the name).
Comment: A Seabreeze based on anis rather than vodka, with aniseed depth and sweetness.

LIGHTER BREEZE

Glass: Collins
Garnish: Apple wedge on rim
Method: POUR all ingredients into ice-filled glass. Stir and serve with straws.

2	shot(s)	**Pressed apple juice**
½	shot(s)	**Ocean Spray cranberry juice**
1	shot(s)	**St-Germain elderflower liqueur**
½	shot(s)	**Pernod anis**

Comment: Long, fragrant and refreshing.

LIMA SOUR

Glass: Old-fashioned
Garnish: Lemon zest string
Method: BLEND all ingredients with one 12oz scoop of crushed ice. Serve with straws.

2	shot(s)	**Macchu pisco**
½	shot(s)	**Luxardo maraschino liqueur**
¾	shot(s)	**Freshly squeezed grapefruit juice**
¾	shot(s)	**Freshly squeezed lime juice**
¾	shot(s)	**Sugar syrup** (2 sugar to 1 water)

Origin: Created before 1947 by Jerry Hooker.
Comment: A refreshing blend of pisco, maraschino and citrus.

LIME BLUSH (MOCKTAIL)

Glass: Old-fashioned
Garnish: Lime wedge
Method: SHAKE all ingredients with ice and strain into glass filled with crushed ice.

2	shot(s)	**Freshly squeezed lime juice**
½	shot(s)	**Rose's lime cordial**
½	shot(s)	**Pomegranate (grenadine) syrup**
½	shot(s)	**Sugar syrup** (2 sugar to 1 water)

Origin: Adapted from a drink discovered in 2005 at Blue Bar, Four Seasons Hotel, Hong Kong, China.
Comment: Refreshingly sweet and sour.

LIME BREEZE

Glass: Collins
Garnish: Lime wedge
Method: SHAKE all ingredients with ice and fine strain into ice-filled glass.

2	shot(s)	**Lime flavoured vodka**
3	shot(s)	**Ocean Spray cranberry juice**
1½	shot(s)	**Freshly squeezed grapefruit juice**

Comment: A lime driven Sea Breeze.

LIME SOUR

Glass: Old-fashioned
Garnish: Lime wedge on rim
Method: SHAKE all ingredients with ice and strain into ice-filled glass.

2	shot(s)	**Lime flavoured vodka**
1¼	shot(s)	**Freshly squeezed lime juice**
¼	shot(s)	**Sugar syrup** (2 sugar to 1 water)
½	fresh	**Egg white**

Comment: Fresh egg white gives this drink a wonderfully frothy top and smoothes the alcohol and lime juice.

LIMEADE (MOCKTAIL)

Glass: Collins
Garnish: Lime wedge
Method: SHAKE all ingredients with ice and fine strain into ice filled glass.

2	shot(s)	**Freshly squeezed lime juice**
1	shot(s)	**Sugar syrup** (2 sugar to 1 water)
3	shot(s)	**Chilled mineral water**

Variant: Shake first two ingredients & top with sparkling water.
Comment: A superbly refreshing alternative to lemonade.

LIMELITE

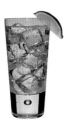

Glass: Collins
Garnish: Lime wedge
Method: SHAKE first 4 ingredients with ice and strain into ice-filled glass. **TOP** with lemonade.

2	shot(s)	**Lime flavoured vodka**
½	shot(s)	**Cointreau triple sec**
½	shot(s)	**Freshly squeezed lime juice**
¼	shot(s)	**Sugar syrup** (2 sugar to 1 water)
Top up with		**Lemonade/Sprite/7-Up**

Comment: Long and citrussy.

LIMEOSA

Glass: Flute
Method: SHAKE first two ingredients with ice and fine strain into chilled glass. **TOP** with champagne and gently stir.

1	shot(s)	**Lime flavoured vodka**
2	shot(s)	**Freshly squeezed orange juice**
Top up with		**Perrier Jouet brut champagne**

Comment: Why settle for a plain old Buck's Fizz when you could add a shot of lime-flavoured vodka?

LIMERICK

Glass: Collins
Garnish: Lime wedge squeezed over drink
Method: SHAKE first 3 ingredients with ice and strain into ice-filled glass. **TOP** with soda water and lightly stir.

2	shot(s)	**Lime flavoured vodka**
1	shot(s)	**Freshly squeezed lime juice**
½	shot(s)	**Sugar syrup** (2 sugar to 1 water)
Top up with		**Soda water** (club soda)

Origin: I created this twist on the classic Vodka Rickey in 2002.
Comment: A refreshing lime cooler.

LIMEY

Glass: Martini
Garnish: Lime zest twist
Method: SHAKE all ingredients with ice and fine strain into chilled glass.

2	shot(s)	**Lime flavoured vodka**
½	shot(s)	**Freshly squeezed lime juice**
½	shot(s)	**Sugar syrup** (2 sugar to 1 water)
⅛	shot(s)	**Rose's lime cordial**
3	dashes	**Angostura aromatic bitters**
½	shot(s)	**Chilled mineral water** (omit if wet ice)

Origin: I created and named this drink after the British naval tradition of mixing lime juice with spirits in an attempt to prevent scurvy. This practice gained British sailors the nickname 'limeys'.
Comment: A rust coloured drink with a delicately sour flavour.

LIMEY COSMO

Glass: Martini
Garnish: Lime wedge on rim
Method: SHAKE all ingredients with ice and fine strain into chilled glass.

1½	shot(s)	**Lime flavoured vodka**
1	shot(s)	**Cointreau triple sec**
1¼	shot(s)	**Ocean Spray cranberry juice**
¼	shot(s)	**Freshly squeezed lime juice**
½	shot(s)	**Rose's lime cordial**

Comment: If you like Cosmopolitans, you'll love this zesty alternative.

LIMEY MULE

Glass: Collins
Garnish: Lime wedge
Method: SHAKE first 3 ingredients with ice and strain into ice-filled glass. **TOP** with ginger ale, lightly stir and serve with straws.

2	shot(s)	**Lime flavoured vodka**
1	shot(s)	**Freshly squeezed lime juice**
½	shot(s)	**Sugar syrup** (2 sugar to 1 water)
Top up with		**Ginger ale**

Comment: Made with plain vodka this drink is a Moscow Mule. This variant uses lime flavoured vodka.

LIMINAL SHOT

Glass: Shot
Method: Refrigerate ingredients then **LAYER** in chilled glass by carefully pouring in the following order.

½	shot(s)	**Pomegranate (grenadine) syrup**
½	shot(s)	**Bols blue curaçao liqueur**
¾	shot(s)	**Lime flavoured vodka**

Comment: The name means transitional, marginal, a boundary or a threshold. Appropriate since the layers border each other.

LIMITED LIABILITY

Glass: Old-fashioned
Method: SHAKE all ingredients with ice and strain into ice-filled glass.

2	shot(s)	**Lime flavoured vodka**
¾	shot(s)	**Freshly squeezed lime juice**
1	shot(s)	**Bärenjäger honey liqueur**

Origin: Created in 2002 by Yours Truly (Simon Difford).
Comment: A sour and flavoursome short - honey and lime work well together.

LIMNOLOGY

Glass: Martini
Garnish: Lime zest twist
Method: STIR all ingredients with ice and fine strain into chilled glass.

2	shot(s)	**Lime flavoured vodka**
1	shot(s)	**Rose's lime cordial**
¾	shot(s)	**Chilled water** (reduce if wet ice)

Origin: The name means the study of the physical phenomena of lakes and other fresh waters – appropriate for this fresh green drink.
Comment: A vodka Gimlet made with lime flavoured vodka.

LIMONCELLO MARTINI

Glass: Martini
Garnish: Lemon zest twist
Method: SHAKE all ingredients with ice and fine strain into chilled glass.

1½	shot(s)	**Ketel One vodka**
1½	shot(s)	**Luxardo limoncello liqueur**
1	shot(s)	**Freshly squeezed lemon juice**

Origin: Adapted from a drink created in 2005 by Francesco at Mix, New York City, USA.
Comment: If you like the liqueur you'll love the cocktail.

LIMOUSINE

Glass: Old-fashioned
Method: Place bar spoon in glass. **POUR** ingredients into glass and stir.

2	shot(s)	**Lime flavoured vodka**
1	shot(s)	**Bärenjäger honey liqueur**
4	shot(s)	**Hot camomile tea**

Origin: Created in 2002 by Yours Truly (Simon Difford).
Comment: In winter this hot drink is a warming treat. In summer serve cold over ice, as pictured.

LINSTEAD

Glass: Martini
Garnish: Lemon zest twist
Method: SHAKE all ingredients with ice and fine strain into chilled glass.

2	shot(s)	**Johnnie Walker Scotch whisky**
2	shot(s)	**Pressed pineapple juice**
¼	shot(s)	**Sugar syrup** (2 sugar to 1 water)
⅛	shot(s)	**La Fée Parisienne (68%) absinthe**

Comment: Absinthe and pineapple come through first, with Scotch last. A great medley of flavours.

LIQUORICE ALL SORT

Glass: Collins
Garnish: Liquorice Allsort sweet
Method: SHAKE first 4 ingredients with ice and strain into ice-filled glass. **TOP** with lemonade.

1	shot(s)	**Opal Nera black sambuca**
1	shot(s)	**Crème de banane liqueur**
1	shot(s)	**Crème de fraise de bois liqueur**
1	shot(s)	**Bols blue curaçao liqueur**
Top up with		**Lemonade/Sprite/7-Up**

Origin: George Bassett (1818-1886), a manufacturer of liquorice sweets, did not invent the Liquorice Allsort that carries his name. That happened 15 years after George died when a salesman accidentally dropped a tray of sweets, they fell in a muddle and the famous sweet was born.
Comment: This aptly named, semi-sweet drink has a strong liquorice flavour with hints of fruit.

LIQUORICE MARTINI

Glass: Martini
Garnish: Piece of liquorice
Method: STIR all ingredients with ice and strain into chilled glass.

2	shot(s)	**Tanqueray London dry gin**
¼	shot(s)	**Opal Nera black sambuca**
⅛	shot(s)	**Sugar syrup** (2 sugar to 1 water)

Origin: Created in 2003 by Jason Fendick, London, England.
Comment: Gin tinted violet, flavoured with liquorice and slightly sweetened.

LIQUORICE SHOT

Glass: Shot
Method: SHAKE all ingredients with ice and fine strain into chilled glass.

½	shot(s)	**Ketel One vodka**
½	shot(s)	**Luxardo white sambuca**
½	shot(s)	**Crème de cassis liqueur**

Comment: For liquorice fans.

LIQUORICE WHISKY SOUR UPDATED #8

Glass: Old-fashioned
Garnish: Dust with grated liquorice
Method: SHAKE all ingredients with ice and strain into ice-filled glass.

2	shot(s)	**Johnnie Walker Scotch whisky**
1	shot(s)	**Freshly squeezed lemon juice**
½	shot(s)	**Homemade liquorice syrup**
1	dash	**Angostura aromatic bitters**
½	fresh	**Egg white**

Comment: Liquorice (or licorice for our American readers) dramatically changes the classic Sour, working harmoniously with the Scotch. I have also tried with bourbon and the result is not nearly so pleasing.
Origin: Created in 2006 by Tony Conigliaro at Shochu Lounge, London, England.

LISA B'S DAIQUIRI

Glass: Martini
Garnish: Grapefruit zest twist
Method: SHAKE all ingredients with ice and fine strain into chilled glass.

2½	shot(s)	**Vanilla-infused Bacardi rum**
½	shot(s)	**Freshly squeezed lime juice**
½	shot(s)	**Vanilla sugar syrup**
1	shot(s)	**Freshly squeezed grapefruit juice**

Origin: Created in 2003 by Yours Truly (Simon Difford) for a gorgeous fan of both Daiquiris and pink grapefruit juice.
Comment: Reminiscent of a Hemingway Special, this flavoursome, vanilla laced Daiquiri has a wonderfully tangy bitter-sweet finish.

LITTLE ITALY

Glass: Martini
Garnish: Orange zest twist
Method: STIR all ingredients with ice and fine strain into chilled glass.

2	shot(s)	**Bulleit bourbon whiskey**
1	shot(s)	**Martini Rosso sweet vermouth**
½	shot(s)	**Cynar artichoke liqueur**

Origin: Adapted from a drink discovered in 2006 at Pegu Club, New York City, USA.
Comment: A sweet, Manhattan-style drink, bittered with Cynar.

LITTLE VENICE NEW #8

Glass: Martini
Garnish: Orange zest twist (spray & discard) plus cherry
Method: STIR all ingredients with ice and strain into chilled glass.

2	shot(s)	**Sake**
1	shot(s)	**Bulleit bourbon whiskey**
1	shot(s)	**Martini Rosso sweet vermouth**

Origin: Discovered in 2007 at Yakitoria, London, England.
Comment: Simple and yet beautiful. Just the way a great drink should be.

LIVINGSTONE

Glass: Martini
Garnish: Lemon peel twist
Method: SHAKE all ingredients with ice and fine strain into chilled glass.

2	shot(s)	**Tanqueray London dry gin**
1	shot(s)	**Noilly Prat dry vermouth**
¼	shot(s)	**Sugar syrup** (2 sugar to 1 water)

Variant: Use pomegranate syrup in place of sugar and you have a Red Livingstone, named after London's 'lefty' ex-mayor, Ken.
Origin: This 1930s classic was named after Doctor Livingstone, the famous African missionary.
Comment: The classic gin and vermouth Martini made more approachable with a dash of sugar.

LOCH ALMOND

Glass: Collins
Garnish: Float amaretti biscuit
Method: POUR all ingredients into ice-filled glass, lightly stir and serve with straws.

1½	shot(s)	**Johnnie Walker Scotch whisky**
1½	shot(s)	**Luxardo Amaretto di Saschira**
Top up with		**Ginger ale**

Comment: If you haven't got to grips with Scotch but like amaretto, try this spicy almond combination.

LOLA

Glass: Martini
Garnish: Orange zest twist
Method: SHAKE all ingredients with ice and fine strain into chilled glass.

1½	shot(s)	**Bacardi Oro golden rum**
½	shot(s)	**Mandarine Napoléon liqueur**
½	shot(s)	**White crème de cacao liqueur**
1	shot(s)	**Freshly squeezed orange juice**
½	shot(s)	**Double (heavy) cream**

Origin: Created in 1999 by Jamie Terrell, London, England.
Comment: Strong, creamy orange.

LOLITA MARGARITA

Glass: Coupette
Garnish: Lime wedge on rim
Method: STIR honey with tequila in base of shaker to dissolve honey. Add other ingredients, **SHAKE** with ice and fine strain into chilled glass.

2	spoons	**Runny honey**
2	shot(s)	**Don Julio reposado tequila**
1	shot(s)	**Freshly squeezed lime juice**
2	dashes	**Angostura aromatic bitters**

Origin: Named after the novel by Vladimir Nabokov which chronicles a middle-aged man's infatuation with a 12 year old girl. Nabokov invented the word 'nymphet' to describe her seductive qualities.
Comment: A fittingly seductive Margarita.

LONDON CALLING

Glass: Martini
Garnish: Orange zest twist
Method: STIR all ingredients with ice and strain into chilled glass.

2	shot(s)	**Tanqueray London dry gin**
1¼	shot(s)	**Sloe gin liqueur**
½	shot(s)	**Martini Rosso sweet vermouth**
2	dashes	**Angostura orange bitters**

Origin: Discovered in 2003 at Oxo Tower Bar & Brasserie, London, England.
Comment: A traditionally styled sweet Martini with a dry, fruity finish.

LONDON COCKTAIL

Glass: Martini
Garnish: Orange zest twist
Method: SHAKE all ingredients with ice and fine strain into chilled glass.

2½	shot(s)	**Tanqueray London dry gin**
⅛	shot(s)	**La Fée Parisienne (68%) absinthe**
⅛	shot(s)	**Sugar syrup** (2 sugar to 1 water)
2	dashes	**Angostura orange bitters**
½	shot(s)	**Chilled mineral water** (omit if wet ice)

Origin: Adapted from a recipe in Harry Craddock's 1930 Savoy Cocktail Book.
Comment: Chilled, diluted and sweetened gin invigorated by a hint of absinthe.

LONDON COSMOPOLITAN NEW #8

Glass: Martini
Garnish: Orange zest twist (flamed)
Method: SHAKE all ingredients with ice and fine strain into chilled glass.

1	shot(s)	**Tanqueray London dry gin**
1	shot(s)	**Cointreau triple sec**
1½	shot(s)	**Ocean Spray cranberry juice**
½	shot(s)	**Freshly squeezed lime juice**

Origin: A subtle twist on the classic by Simon Difford in 2008 at The Cabinet Room, London, England.
Comment: Basically a Cosmopolitan but made with London dry gin instead of citrus vodka.

LONDON FOG UPDATED #8

Glass: Old-fashioned
Garnish: Orange zest twist
Method: Fill glass with ice. Add ingredients in the following order and **STIR**. Add more ice to fill.

1	shot(s)	**Tanqueray London dry gin**
2	shot(s)	**Chilled mineral water** (reduce if wet ice)
½	shot(s)	**Pernod anis**

Comment: Pernod clouds this drink and adds its distinctive aniseed flavour.

LONDON SCRAMBLE NEW #8

Glass: Old-fashioned
Garnish: Lemon zest twist spiral & 3 blackberries
Method: SHAKE first 4 ingredients with ice and fine strain into glass filled with crushed ice. **DRIZZLE** crème de mûre over drink (will slowly bleed through the cocktail).

2	shot(s)	**Don Julio blanco tequila**
½	shot(s)	**Freshly squeezed lemon juice**
½	shot(s)	**Freshly squeezed lime juice**
½	shot(s)	**Agave syrup**
¼	shot(s)	**Crème de mûre liqueur**

Comment: A tequila Bramble of which I'm sure Dick would be most approving.
Origin: Created in 2007 by Dre Masso & Henry Besant from the World Wide Cocktail Club, London.

LONELY BULL

Glass: Old-fashioned
Garnish: Dust with freshly grated nutmeg
Method: SHAKE all ingredients with ice and strain into ice-filled glass.

1½	shot(s)	**Don Julio reposado tequila**
1½	shot(s)	**Kahlúa coffee liqueur**
¾	shot(s)	**Double (heavy) cream**
¾	shot(s)	**Milk**

Comment: Like a creamy iced coffee – yum.

'I DO LIKE A DRY MARTINI TWO AT THE VERY MOST, AFTER THREE I'M UNDER THE TABLE, AFTER FOUR I'M UNDER THE HOST'
DOROTHY PARKER

LONG BEACH ICED TEA

Glass: Sling
Garnish: Lemon slice
Method: SHAKE all ingredients with ice and strain into ice-filled glass. Serve with straws.

½	shot(s)	**Kahlúa coffee liqueur**
½	shot(s)	**Don Julio reposado tequila**
½	shot(s)	**Bacardi Superior rum**
½	shot(s)	**Tanqueray London dry gin**
½	shot(s)	**Ketel One vodka**
1	shot(s)	**Freshly squeezed lime juice**
½	shot(s)	**Sugar syrup** (2 sugar to 1 water)
2	shot(s)	**Ocean Spray cranberry juice**

Comment: One of the more grown-up 'Iced Tea' cocktails.

LONG FLIGHT OF STAIRS

Glass: Collins
Garnish: Apple or pear slice
Method: SHAKE all ingredients with ice and strain into ice-filled glass. Serve with straws.

1	shot(s)	**Pear flavoured vodka**
1	shot(s)	**Boulard Grand Solage calvados**
1	shot(s)	**Belle de Brillet pear liqueur**
2½	shot(s)	**Pressed apple juice**

Origin: Created in 2005 by Yours Truly (Simon Difford) as a homage to the G.E. Club's 'Stairs Martini'.
Comment: A seriously tasty, strong, long drink. The name is a reversal of the London rhyming slang 'apples and pears' (stairs).

LONG ISLAND ICED TEA UPDATED #8

Glass: Sling
Garnish: Lemon slice
Method: SHAKE first 7 ingredients with ice and strain into ice-filled glass. TOP with Coca-Cola, stir and serve with straws.

½	shot(s)	**Bacardi Superior rum**
½	shot(s)	**Tanqueray London dry gin**
½	shot(s)	**Ketel One vodka**
½	shot(s)	**Don Julio blanco tequila**
½	shot(s)	**Cointreau triple sec**
1	shot(s)	**Freshly squeezed lime juice**
½	shot(s)	**Sugar syrup** (2 sugar to 1 water)
Top up with		**Coca-Cola**

Comment: A cooling, combination of five different spirits with a hint of lime and a splash of cola.
Origin: This infamous drink reached the height of its popularity in the early 1980s of the many stories surrounding its origin, perhaps the most credible attributes its creation to sometime in the late 1970s by Robert (Rosebud) Butt at Oak Beach Inn in Babylon, New York. This area of New York State is known as 'Long Island' and the drink looks like iced tea disguising its contents – a fact that has many claiming its true origins lie with Prohibition.

LONG ISLAND SPICED TEA

Glass: Collins
Garnish: Lime wedge on rim
Method: SHAKE first 7 ingredients with ice and strain into ice-filled glass. TOP with Coca-Cola, lightly stir and serve with straws.

½	shot(s)	**Sailor Jerry spiced rum**
½	shot(s)	**Ketel One vodka**
½	shot(s)	**Tanqueray London dry gin**
½	shot(s)	**Don Julio reposado tequila**
½	shot(s)	**Cointreau triple sec**
1	shot(s)	**Freshly squeezed lime juice**
½	shot(s)	**Sugar syrup** (2 sugar to 1 water)
Top up with		**Coca-Cola**

Comment: A contemporary spicy twist on an American classic.

THE LONG SHOT NEW #8

Glass: Collins
Garnish: Orange slice & lemon wedge
Method: SHAKE first 5 ingredients with ice and strain ice-filled glass. TOP with soda, lightly stir and serve with straws.

1½	shot(s)	**Don Julio reposado tequila**
½	shot(s)	**Orange curaçao** (or Grand Marnier)
¼	shot(s)	**Sugar syrup** (2 sugar to 1 water)
¾	shot(s)	**Freshly squeezed lemon juice**
1	dash	**Angostura aromatic bitters**
Top up with		**Soda water**

Comment: A simple variation on William Schmidt's Alabazam.
Origin: Created in 2008 by Julian de Feral at Bureau, London, England.

LONSDALE NEW #8

Glass: Collins
Garnish: Basil leaf & green apple slice
Method: STIR honey syrup with gin until honey dissolves. TEAR basil leaves and add to shaker with all other ingredients. SHAKE with ice and fine strain into chilled glass.

2	shot(s)	**Tanqueray London dry gin**
½	shot(s)	**Honey syrup** (4 honey to 1 water)
2-3	fresh	**Basil leaves**
¾	shot(s)	**Freshly squeezed lemon juice**
2½	shot(s)	**Pressed apple juice**

Origin: Created by Alexandra Fiot at Lonsdale Bar, London, England.
Comment: Not dry, not sweet, just balanced, long and refreshing.

LOOKS FAMILIAR NEW #8

Glass: Old-fashioned
Garnish: Orange zest twist
Method: STIR malt with ice and then strain and discard excess to leave the ice and mixing glass coated. Add other ingredients and STIR with the coated ice. Strain into ice-filled glass.

½	shot(s)	**Lagavulin 16yo malt whisky**
2	shot(s)	**Don Julio blanco tequila**
½	shot(s)	**Agave syrup**
2	dashes	**Angostura orange bitters**
¼	shot(s)	**Amer Picon liqueur**

Origin: Created by Jake Burger at Jake's Bar, Leeds, England.
Comment: I defy you not to love this herbal bitter-sweet tequila laced concoction.

'I DON'T HAVE A DRINKING PROBLEM EXCEPT WHEN I CAN'T GET A DRINK.'
TOM WAITS

LORRAINE #1 NEW #8

Glass: Old-fashioned
Garnish: Orange zest twist
Method: STIR all ingredients with ice and strain into ice-filled glass.

1½	shot(s)	**Tanqueray London dry gin**
1	shot(s)	**Noilly Prat dry vermouth**
½	shot(s)	**Grand Marnier liqueur**

Origin: Created by Joe Gilmore to mark Charles de Caulle's 1st state visit to Britain in the 1950s and named after the Cross of Lorraine, symbol of the Order of Liberation. The original recipe called for one whole shot of Grand Marnier.
Comment: A Wet Martini served on the rocks, sweetened and flavoured with a slug of orange liqueur.

LONG ISLAND ICED TEA

LORRAINE #2 NEW #8

Glass: Martini/Coupette
Garnish: Lime zest twist
Method: **SHAKE** all ingredients and fine strain into chilled glass.

¾	shot(s)	**Kirschwasser eau de vie**
¾	shot(s)	**Ketel One vodka**
¾	shot(s)	**Bénédictine D.O.M. liqueur**
½	shot(s)	**Freshly squeezed lime juice**
⅛	shot(s)	**Sugar syrup** (2 sugar to 1 water)

Origin: Adaptation by Yours Truly (Simon Difford). The original recipe called for 1¾ kirsch, ½ Bénédictine and ¾ lime juice.
Comment: Sweet and sour with fruity, herbal notes.

LOTUS ESPRESSO

Glass: Martini
Garnish: Float three coffee beans
Method: **SHAKE** all ingredients with ice and fine strain into chilled glass.

2	shot(s)	**Ketel One vodka**
½	shot(s)	**Kahlúa coffee liqueur**
½	shot(s)	**Maple syrup**
1	shot(s)	**Espresso coffee**

Origin: Adapted from a drink discovered in 2005 at Lotus Bar, Sydney, Australia.
Comment: Coffee to the fore but with complex, earthy bitter-sweet notes.

LOTUS MARTINI

Glass: Martini
Garnish: Mint leaf
Method: Lightly **MUDDLE** mint (just to bruise) in base of shaker. Add other ingredients, **SHAKE** with ice and fine strain into chilled glass.

7	fresh	**Mint leaves**
2	shot(s)	**Tanqueray London dry gin**
¼	shot(s)	**Bols blue curaçao liqueur**
1½	shot(s)	**Lychee syrup** (from tinned fruit)
¼	shot(s)	**Pomegranate (grenadine) syrup**

Origin: Created in 2001 by Martin Walander at Match Bar, London, England.
Comment: This violet coloured drink may have an unlikely list of ingredients, but definitely tastes great.

LOUD SPEAKER MARTINI

Glass: Martini
Garnish: Lemon peel twist
Method: **SHAKE** all ingredients with ice and fine strain into chilled glass.

1½	shot(s)	**Tanqueray London dry gin**
1½	shot(s)	**Courvoisier V.S.O.P. cognac**
½	shot(s)	**Martini Rosso sweet vermouth**
¼	shot(s)	**Freshly squeezed lemon juice**
¼	shot(s)	**Sugar syrup** (2 sugar to 1 water)

Origin: Adapted from a recipe in the 1930 Savoy Cocktail Book by Harry Craddock.
Comment: I've added a dash of sugar to the original recipe which I found too dry.

LOUISIANA TRADE

Glass: Old-fashioned
Garnish: Lime wedge
Method: **SHAKE** all ingredients with ice and strain into glass filled with crushed ice.

2	shot(s)	**Southern Comfort liqueur**
½	shot(s)	**Maple syrup**
1	shot(s)	**Freshly squeezed lime juice**
¼	shot(s)	**Sugar syrup** (2 sugar to 1 water)

Origin: Created in 2001 by Mehdi Otmann at Zeta, London, England.
Comment: Peach and apricot with the freshness of lime and the dense sweetness of maple syrup.

LOVE JUNK

Glass: Old-fashioned
Garnish: Apple wedge
Method: **SHAKE** all ingredients with ice and strain into ice-filled glass.

2	shot(s)	**Ketel One vodka**
½	shot(s)	**Midori green melon liqueur**
½	shot(s)	**Peach Tree peach schnapps**
1½	shot(s)	**Pressed apple juice**

Comment: A light, crisp, refreshing blend of peach, melon and apple juice, laced with vodka.

LOVE UNIT NEW #8

Glass: Martini
Garnish: Red bell pepper ring & basil sprig
Method: **MUDDLE** pepper in base of shaker. Add other ingredients, **SHAKE** with ice and fine strain into chilled glass.

2	rings	**Red bell pepper**
7	fresh	**Thai basil leaves**
1	shot(s)	**Bacardi Superior rum**
1	shot(s)	**Vanilla-infused Bacardi rum**
¾	shot(s)	**Freshly squeezed lime juice**
½	shot(s)	**Freshly squeezed grapefruit juice**
½	shot(s)	**Sugar syrup** (2 sugar to 1 water)

Origin: Created by Ryan Magarian, Seattle, USA.
Comment: Delicate, complex and balanced with enough fruit and veg to make your five-a-day.

LOVED UP

Glass: Martini
Garnish: Berries on stick
Method: **SHAKE** all ingredients with ice and fine strain into chilled glass.

1½	shot(s)	**Don Julio reposado tequila**
½	shot(s)	**Cointreau triple sec**
½	shot(s)	**Chambord black raspberry liqueur**
½	shot(s)	**Freshly squeezed lime juice**
1	shot(s)	**Freshly squeezed orange juice**
¼	shot(s)	**Sugar syrup** (2 sugar to 1 water)

Origin: Adapted from a cocktail discovered in 2002 at the Merc Bar, New York City, where the original name was listed as simply 'Love'.
Comment: Tequila predominates in this rusty coloured drink, which also features orange and berry fruit.

LUCIEN GAUDIN

Glass: Martini
Garnish: Orange zest twist
Method: **STIR** all ingredients with ice and strain into chilled glass.

1½	shot(s)	**Tanqueray London dry gin**
¾	shot(s)	**Cointreau triple sec**
¾	shot(s)	**Campari Bitter**
¾	shot(s)	**Noilly Prat dry vermouth**

Origin: Recipe from 'Vintage Spirits and Forgotten Cocktails' by Ted Haigh (Dr. Cocktail). Lucien Gaudin was a French fencer who achieved gold medals with two different weapons at the 1928 Olympics in Amsterdam.
Comment: A must try for anyone who loves Negronis.

LUCKY LILY MARGARITA

Glass: Coupette
Garnish: Pineapple wedge dusted with pepper on rim
Method: **STIR** honey with tequila in base of shaker to dissolve honey. **ADD** other ingredients, **SHAKE** with ice and fine strain into chilled glass.

2	spoons	**Runny honey**
2	shot(s)	**Don Julio reposado tequila**
1	shot(s)	**Pressed pineapple juice**
¾	shot(s)	**Freshly squeezed lime juice**
5	grinds	**Black pepper**

Origin: Adapted from a drink discovered in 2006 at All Star Lanes, London, England.
Comment: Spicy tequila and pineapple tingle with balance and flavour.

IN THE 1600'S THERMOMETERS WERE FILLED WITH BRANDY INSTEAD OF MERCURY.

LUCKY LINDY

Glass: Collins
Garnish: Lemon slice
Method: **STIR** honey with bourbon in base of shaker so as to dissolve honey. Add lemon juice, **SHAKE** with ice and strain into ice-filled glass. **TOP** with lemonade, lightly stir and serve with straws.

3	spoons	**Runny honey**
2	shot(s)	**Bulleit bourbon whiskey**
½	shot(s)	**Freshly squeezed lemon juice**
Top up with		**Lemonade/Sprite/7-Up**

Origin: Adapted from a drink discovered in 2003 at The Grange Hall, New York City, USA.
Comment: A long refreshing drink that combines whisky, citrus and honey – a long chilled toddy without the spice.

LUSH

Glass: Flute
Garnish: Raspberry in glass
Method: **POUR** vodka and liqueur into chilled glass, **TOP** with champagne and lightly stir.

1	shot(s)	**Ketel One vodka**
½	shot(s)	**Chambord black raspberry liqueur**
Top up with		**Perrier Jouet brut champagne**

Origin: Created in 1999 by Spike Marchant at Alphabet, London, England.
Comment: It is, are you?

LUTKINS SPECIAL MARTINI

Glass: Martini
Garnish: Orange zest twist
Method: **SHAKE** all ingredients with ice and fine strain into chilled glass.

1½	shot(s)	**Tanqueray London dry gin**
1	shot(s)	**Noilly Prat dry vermouth**
½	shot(s)	**Bols apricot brandy liqueur**
¾	shot(s)	**Freshly squeezed orange juice**

Origin: Adapted from a recipe in Harry Craddock's 1930 Savoy Cocktail Book.
Comment: I've tried many variations on the above formula and none are that special.

LUX DAIQUIRI

Glass: Martini (large)
Garnish: Maraschino cherry
Method: **BLEND** all ingredients with one 12oz scoop of crushed ice and serve in chilled glass.

3	shot(s)	**Bacardi Superior rum**
¾	shot(s)	**Freshly squeezed lime juice**
½	shot(s)	**Luxardo maraschino liqueur**
¼	shot(s)	**Sugar syrup** (2 sugar to 1 water)
¼	shot(s)	**Maraschino syrup** (from cherry jar)

Origin: This was one of two cocktails with which I won a Havana Club Daiquiri competition in 2002. I named it after Girolamo Luxardo, creator of the now famous liqueur, 'Luxardo Maraschino'. My educated sub also informs me Lux is Latin for light.
Comment: A classic frozen Daiquiri heavily laced with maraschino cherry.

LUXURY COCKTAIL

Glass: Martini
Method: **SHAKE** all ingredients with ice and fine strain into chilled glass.

2	shot(s)	**Tanqueray London dry gin**
¾	shot(s)	**Pimm's No.1 Cup**
½	shot(s)	**Crème de banane liqueur**
¾	shot(s)	**Martini Rosso sweet vermouth**
¼	shot(s)	**Rose's lime cordial**
3	dashes	**Angostura aromatic bitters**

Comment: Sticky banana followed by a bitter, refined aftertaste.

LUXURY MOJITO

Glass: Collins
Garnish: Mint sprig
Method: **MUDDLE** mint in glass with sugar and lime juice. Fill glass with crushed ice, add rum, Angostura and champagne, then gently stir.

12	fresh	**Mint leaves**
¼	shot(s)	**Sugar syrup** (2 sugar to 1 water)
1	shot(s)	**Freshly squeezed lime juice**
2	shot(s)	**Zacapa aged rum**
3	dashes	**Angostura aromatic bitters**
Top up with		**Perrier Jouet brut champagne**

Comment: A Mojito made with aged rum and topped with champagne instead of soda water: more complex than the original.

LYCHEE & BLACKCURRANT MARTINI

Glass: Martini
Garnish: Peeled lychee in glass
Method: **SHAKE** all ingredients with ice and fine strain into chilled glass.

2	shot(s)	**Tanqueray London dry gin**
½	shot(s)	**Soho lychee liqueur**
¼	shot(s)	**Crème de cassis liqueur**
¼	shot(s)	**Rose's lime cordial**
¾	shot(s)	**Chilled mineral water** (omit if wet ice)

Origin: Created by Yours Truly (Simon Difford) in 2004.
Comment: Light, fragrant and laced with gin.

LYCHEE & ROSE PETAL MARTINI

Glass: Martini
Garnish: Float rose petal
Method: **STIR** all ingredients with ice and strain into chilled glass.

2	shot(s)	**Tanqueray London dry gin**
1	shot(s)	**Lanique rose petal liqueur**
1	shot(s)	**Lychee syrup** (from tinned fruit)
2	dashes	**Peychaud's aromatic bitters**

Origin: Created in 2002 by Dick Bradsell for Opium, London, England.
Comment: Light pink in colour and subtle in flavour.

LYCHEE & SAKE MARTINI

Glass: Martini
Garnish: Peeled lychee in glass
Method: **STIR** all ingredients with ice and strain into chilled glass.

1½	shot(s)	**Tanqueray London dry gin**
2	shot(s)	**Sake**
¾	shot(s)	**Soho lychee liqueur**

Origin: Created in 2004 by Yours Truly (Simon Difford).
Comment: A soft, Martini styled drink with subtle hints of sake and lychee.

LYCHEE MAC

Glass: Old-fashioned
Garnish: Peeled lychee in drink
Method: **SHAKE** all ingredients with ice and strain into ice-filled glass.

2¼	shot(s)	**Johnnie Walker Scotch whisky**
1	shot(s)	**Soho lychee liqueur**
¾	shot(s)	**Stone's original green ginger wine**

Origin: Created by Yours Truly (Simon Difford) in 2004.
Comment: Peaty Scotch with sweet lychee and hot ginger.

LYCHEE MARTINI

Glass: Martini
Garnish: Whole lychee from tin
Method: **STIR** all ingredients with ice and fine strain into chilled glass.

2	shot(s)	**Ketel One vodka**
½	shot(s)	**Soho lychee liqueur**
½	shot(s)	**Noilly Prat dry vermouth**
1	shot(s)	**Lychee syrup** (from tinned fruit)

Origin: Thought to have been first made in 2001 at Clay, a Korean restaurant in New York City, USA.
Comment: If you like lychee you'll love this delicate Martini.

LYCHEE RICKEY

Glass: Collins (small 8oz)
Garnish: Immerse length of lime peel in drink.
Method: **SHAKE** first 3 ingredients with ice and strain into ice-filled glass. **TOP** with soda water.

2	shot(s)	**Tanqueray London dry gin**
1	shot(s)	**Soho lychee liqueur**
½	shot(s)	**Freshly squeezed lime juice**
Top up with		**Soda water** (club soda)

Origin: Adapted from a drink discovered in 2005 at Club 97, Hong Kong, China.
Comment: The lychee liqueur dominates this surprisingly dry Rickey.

LYNCHBURG LEMONADE

Glass: Collins
Garnish: Lemon slice
Method: **SHAKE** first 3 ingredients with ice and strain into ice-filled glass. **TOP** with lemonade.

1½	shot(s)	**Jack Daniel's Tennessee whiskey**
1	shot(s)	**Cointreau triple sec**
1	shot(s)	**Freshly squeezed lemon juice**
Top up with		**Lemonade/Sprite/7-Up**

Variant: With three dashes Angostura aromatic bitters.
Origin: Created for the Jack Daniel's distillery in - yep, you guessed it - Lynchburg, Tennessee.
Comment: Tangy, light and very easy to drink.

LYCHEE RICKEY

A
B
C
D
E
F
G
H
I
J
K
L
M
N
O
P
Q
R
S
T
U
V
W
X
Y
Z

M.G.F.

Glass: Martini
Garnish: Orange zest twist
Method: SHAKE all ingredients with ice and fine strain into chilled glass.

1	shot(s)	**Orange-infused Ketel One vodka**
1	shot(s)	**Ketel One Citroen vodka**
1	shot(s)	**Freshly squeezed grapefruit juice**
1	shot(s)	**Freshly squeezed lemon juice**
½	shot(s)	**Sugar syrup** (2 sugar to 1 water)

Origin: Discovered in 2003 at Claridge's Bar, London, England.
Comment: Short and sharp.

THE MACKINNON

Glass: Martini
Garnish: Lemon zest twist
Method: SHAKE all ingredients with ice and fine strain into chilled glass.

2	shot(s)	**Bacardi Oro golden rum**
1	shot(s)	**Drambuie liqueur**
½	shot(s)	**Freshly squeezed lemon juice**

Variant: Serve long over ice with soda.
Origin: Named after the MacKinnon family, the makers of Drambuie.
Comment: Honeyed rum with herbal and citrus nuances.

MAC ORANGE

Glass: Old-fashioned
Garnish: Orange zest twist
Method: SHAKE all ingredients with ice and fine strain into chilled glass.

2	shot(s)	**Johnnie Walker Scotch whisky**
1	shot(s)	**Stone's original green ginger wine**
1	shot(s)	**Freshly squeezed orange juice**
¼	shot(s)	**Sugar syrup** (2 sugar to 1 water)
3	dashes	**Angostura orange bitters**

Comment: A Whisky Mac with orange topping off the ginger.

MAD MONK MILKSHAKE

Glass: Collins
Garnish: Tie cord around glass
Method: SHAKE all ingredients with ice and strain into ice-filled glass.

2	shot(s)	**Frangelico hazelnut liqueur**
1	shot(s)	**Baileys Irish cream liqueur**
¼	shot(s)	**Kahlúa coffee liqueur**
1	shot(s)	**Double (heavy) cream**
2	shot(s)	**Milk**

Variant: Blend instead of shaking and serve frozen.
Comment: Long, creamy and slightly sweet with hazelnut and coffee.

M

MAÇÃ NEW #8

Glass: Martini/Coupette
Garnish: Apple slice & mint sprig
Method: SHAKE all ingredients with ice and fine strain into chilled glass.

2	shot(s)	**Leblon cachaça**
½	shot(s)	**St-Germain elderflower liqueur**
1½	shot(s)	**Pressed apple juice**
½	shot(s)	**Freshly squeezed lime juice**

Origin: Adapted from a recipe created in 2007 by Jamie Terrell, New York, USA and originally based of Sagatiba cachaça. Maçã means apple in Portuguese.
Comment: Subtle combination of cachaça, fresh lime, apple juice and elderflower.

MADRAS

Glass: Collins
Garnish: Orange slice
Method: SHAKE all ingredients with ice and strain into ice-filled glass.

2	shot(s)	**Ketel One vodka**
3	shot(s)	**Ocean Spray cranberry juice**
2	shot(s)	**Freshly squeezed orange juice**

Comment: A Seabreeze with orange juice in place of grapefruit juice, making it slightly sweeter.

MADROSKA

Glass: Collins
Garnish: Orange slice
Method: SHAKE all ingredients with ice and strain into ice-filled glass.

2	shot(s)	**Ketel One vodka**
2½	shot(s)	**Pressed apple juice**
1½	shot(s)	**Ocean Spray cranberry juice**
1	shot(s)	**Freshly squeezed orange juice**

Origin: Created in 1998 by Jamie Terrell, London, England.
Comment: A Madras with more than a hint of apple juice.

MACKA

Glass: Collins
Garnish: Lemon slice
Method: SHAKE first 4 ingredients with ice and strain into ice-filled glass. **TOP** with soda.

2	shot(s)	**Tanqueray London dry gin**
½	shot(s)	**Noilly Prat dry vermouth**
½	shot(s)	**Martini Rosso sweet vermouth**
½	shot(s)	**Crème de cassis liqueur**
Top up with		**Soda water** (club soda)

Comment: A long fruity drink for parched palates.

MAESTRO NEW #8

Glass: Martini/Coupette
Garnish: Half strawberry on rim & drop of balsamic vinegar.
Method: SHAKE all ingredients with ice and fine strain into chilled glass.

2	shot(s)	**Ketel One vodka**
1	shot(s)	**Crème de fraise liqueur**
1	shot(s)	**Freshly squeezed orange juice**
1/8	shot(s)	**Maple syrup**
1/16	shot(s)	**Balsamic vinegar** (8 year-old)

Origin: Created by Salvatore Calabrese at Salvatore At Fifty, London, England.
Comment: Strawberry and balsamic are a great combo – here served with orange juice, vodka and maple syrup.

MAE WEST MARTINI

Glass: Martini
Garnish: Melon wedge on rim
Method: SHAKE all ingredients with ice and fine strain into chilled glass.

2	shot(s)	**Ketel One vodka**
1/2	shot(s)	**Luxardo Amaretto di Saschira**
1/4	shot(s)	**Midori green melon liqueur**
1½	shot(s)	**Ocean Spray cranberry juice**

Comment: A rosé coloured, semi-sweet concoction with a cherry-chocolate flavour.

MAHUKONA NEW #8

Glass: Sling (10oz Pilsner glass)
Garnish: Pineapple cubes & cherry on stick, mint sprig
Method: BLEND all ingredients with 6oz scoop crushed ice and strain into glass half-filled with crushed ice. Serve with straws.

1	shot(s)	**Bacardi Superior rum**
1/2	shot(s)	**Cointreau triple sec**
1	shot(s)	**Pressed pineapple juice**
1/2	shot(s)	**Freshly squeezed lemon juice**
1/4	shot(s)	**Sugar syrup** (2 sugar to 1 water)
2	dashes	**Angostura aromatic bitters**

Origin: Adapted from Victor Bergeron's 'Trader Vic's Bartender's Guide' (1972 revised edition).
Comment: Citrus fresh and refreshing, not at all a sweetie.

MAISON CHARLES DAIQUIRI NEW #8

Glass: Martini/Coupette
Garnish: Rim with finely chopped mint leaves & powdered sugar.
Method: Lightly **MUDDLE** (just to bruise) mint in base of shaker. Add other ingredients, **SHAKE** with ice and fine strain into chilled glass.

8	fresh	**Mint leaves**
2	shot(s)	**Bacardi Superior rum**
1/2	shot(s)	**Freshly squeezed lime juice**
1/2	shot(s)	**Sugar syrup** (2 sugar to 1 water)
1/2	shot(s)	**Chilled water** (omit if wet ice)

Variant: Substitute triple sec for sugar to make a Madison Avenue.
Comment: Reminiscent of concentrated Mojito.
Origin: Pronounced 'May-Sawn Sharl', this recipe is adapted from David A. Embury's 1948 'Fine Art of Mixing Drinks'.

MAI TAI (VIC'S) UPDATED #8

Glass: Old-fashioned
Garnish: Half squeezed lime shell, mint sprig, pineapple cube & cherry on stick
Method: SHAKE all ingredients with ice and strain into glass filled with crushed ice.

2	shot(s)	**Zacapa aged rum**
1/2	shot(s)	**Orange curaçao liqueur**
3/4	shot(s)	**Freshly squeezed lime juice**
1/4	shot(s)	**Almond (orgeat) syrup**
1/4	shot(s)	**Sugar syrup** (2 sugar to 1 water)

Comment: I love Daiquiris and this is basically a classic Daiquiri with a few bells and whistles.
Origin: In 1934, Victor Jules Bergeron, or Trader Vic as he became known, opened his first restaurant in Oakland, San Francisco. He served Polynesian food with a mix of Chinese, French and American dishes cooked in wood-fired ovens. But he is best known for the rum based cocktails he created.

One evening in 1944 he tested a new drink on two friends from Tahiti, Ham and Carrie Guild. After the first sip, Carrie exclaimed, "Mai Tai-Roa Aé", which in Tahitian means 'Out of this world - the best!'.

So Bergeron named his drink the Mai Tai.

The original was based on 17 year old Jamaican J.Wray & Nephew rum which Vic in his own guide describes as being "surprisingly golden in colour, medium bodied, but with the rich pungent flavour particular to the Jamaican blends". Vic states he used "rock candy" syrup, an old term for the type of strong sugar syrup I prescribe in this guide. The term referred to the fact that you could dangle a piece of string in it to encourage crystallisation and make rock candy.

When supplies of the Jamaican 17-year-old rum dwindled, Vic started using a combination of dark Jamaican rum and Martinique rum to achieve the desired flavour. Sheer demand in his chain of restaurants later necessitated the introduction of a Mai Tai pre-mix (still available from www.tradervics.com).

Others, particularly Ernest Raymond Beaumont-Gantt, then owner of a Hollywood bar called Don the Beachcomber's, have also laid claim to the creation of this drink. But as Vic says in his own Bartender's Guide, "Anybody who says I didn't create this drink is a dirty stinker." This recipe is adapted from Victor Bergeron's 'Trader Vic's Bartender's Guide' (1972 revised edition).

HOW TO MAKE SUGAR SYRUP

To make your own sugar syrup, gradually pour TWO cups of granulated sugar into a saucepan containing ONE cup of hot water. Stir as you pour and carry on stirring and simmering until the sugar is dissolved. Do not let the water even come close to boiling and only simmer for as long as it takes to dissolve the sugar. Allow syrup to cool and pour into an empty bottle. Ideally, you should finely strain your syrup into the bottle to remove any undissolved crystals which could otherwise encourage crystallisation. If kept in a refrigerator this mixture will last for a couple of months.

MAI TAI #2 (BEAUMONT-GANTT'S FORMULA)

Glass: Old-fashioned
Garnish: Mint sprig
Method: Lightly muddle mint in base of shaker (just to bruise). Add other ingredients, **SHAKE** with ice and strain glass filled with crushed ice.

12	fresh	**Mint leaves**
1½	shot(s)	**Myers's dark Jamaican rum**
1	shot(s)	**Bacardi Superior rum**
¾	shot(s)	**Cointreau triple sec**
½	shot(s)	**Velvet Falernum liqueur**
1	shot(s)	**Freshly squeezed lime juice**
1	shot(s)	**Freshly squeezed grapefruit juice**
2	dashes	**Angostura aromatic bitters**

Origin: It is claimed that Ernest Raymond Beaumont-Gantt first served this drink in 1933 at his Don The Beachcomber's bar in Hollywood, California. This is some ten years earlier than Bergeron's Mai Tai-Roa Aé moment in cocktail history.
Comment: Whichever of the two created the drink; it is Trader Vic that made it famous and it is his recipe that endures.

METHYPHOBIA – THE IRRATIONAL FEAR OF ALCOHOL.

MAIDEN'S BLUSH

Glass: Martini
Garnish: Lemon zest twist
Method: SHAKE all ingredients with ice and fine strain into chilled glass.

2	shot(s)	**Tanqueray London dry gin**
½	shot(s)	**Cointreau triple sec**
½	shot(s)	**Pomegranate (grenadine) syrup**
¼	shot(s)	**Freshly squeezed lemon juice**
½	shot(s)	**Chilled mineral water** (omit if wet ice)

Origin: Adapted from a recipe in Harry Craddock's 1930 Savoy Cocktail Book.
Comment: Pale pink, subtle and light.

MAIDEN'S PRAYER

Glass: Martini
Garnish: Orange zest twist
Method: SHAKE all ingredients with ice and fine strain into chilled glass.

1½	shot(s)	**Tanqueray London dry gin**
1	shot(s)	**Cointreau triple sec**
1	shot(s)	**Freshly squeezed orange juice**
½	shot(s)	**Freshly squeezed lemon juice**

Origin: Adapted from a recipe in Harry Craddock's 1930 Savoy Cocktail Book.
Comment: Fresh, zesty orange with a pleasing twang of alcohol.

MAINBRACE UPDATED #8

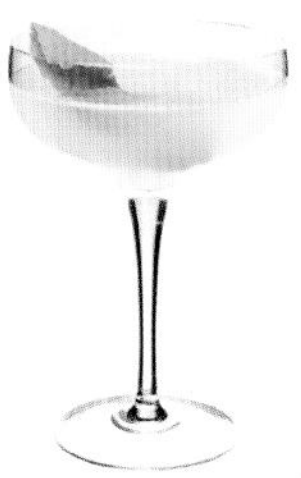

Glass: Martini
Garnish: Orange zest twist
Method: SHAKE all ingredients with ice and fine strain into chilled glass.

1¼	shot(s)	**Tanqueray London dry gin**
1¼	shot(s)	**Cointreau triple sec**
1¼	shot(s)	**Freshly squeezed grapefruit juice**

Comment: Tangy grapefruit laced with gin and a hint of orange. Tart finish.

MAJOR BAILEY #1

Glass: Sling
Garnish: Mint sprig
Method: Lightly **MUDDLE** (only bruise) mint with gin in base of shaker. Add other ingredients, **SHAKE** with ice and fine strain into glass half filled with crushed ice. **CHURN** (stir) drink with the ice using a barspoon. Top the glass to the brim with more crushed ice and churn again. Serve with straws.

12	fresh	**Mint leaves**
2	shot(s)	**Tanqueray London dry gin**
¼	shot(s)	**Freshly squeezed lime juice**
¼	shot(s)	**Freshly squeezed lemon juice**
½	shot(s)	**Sugar syrup** (2 sugar to 1 water)

Origin: Adapted from a recipe in the 1947 Trader Vic's Bartender's Guide by Victor Bergeron.
Comment: As Victor says of this gin based Julep, "This is a hell of a drink."

MAJOR BAILEY #2

Glass: Sling
Garnish: Mint sprig
Method: BLEND all ingredients with one 12oz scoop of crushed ice and serve with straws.

2	shot(s)	**Bacardi Superior rum**
1	shot(s)	**Cointreau triple sec**
1	shot(s)	**Pressed pineapple juice**
½	shot(s)	**Freshly squeezed lemon juice**
¼	shot(s)	**Sugar syrup** (2 sugar to 1 water)

Origin: Adapted from a drink created by Victor 'Trader Vic' Bergeron.
Comment: Made well, this is a long, fruity, brilliant frozen Daiquiri.

MAGIC BUS

Glass: Martini
Garnish: Lime wedge on rim
Method: SHAKE all ingredients with ice and fine strain into chilled glass.

1	shot(s)	**Don Julio reposado tequila**
1	shot(s)	**Cointreau triple sec**
1	shot(s)	**Ocean Spray cranberry juice**
1	shot(s)	**Freshly squeezed orange juice**

Comment: Orange and cranberry laced with tequila.

MALCOLM LOWRY

●●●●○

Glass: Old-fashioned
Garnish: Lime wedge
Method: SHAKE all ingredients with ice and strain into ice-filled glass.

1	shot(s)	Don Julio reposado tequila
½	shot(s)	Wray & Nephew overproof rum
¼	shot(s)	Cointreau triple sec
½	shot(s)	Freshly squeezed lime juice
¼	shot(s)	Sugar syrup (2 sugar to 1 water)

Origin: Created by drinks author David Broom. Named after Malcolm Lowry's 1947 novel 'Under the Volcano' which explores a man's battle with alcoholism in Mexico.
Comment: A suitably 'hard' and flavoursome Daiquiri-like drink.

MAMBO

●●●●○○

Glass: Collins
Garnish: Orange slice
Method: SHAKE all ingredients with ice and strain into ice-filled glass.

1	shot(s)	Ketel One vodka
1	shot(s)	Cointreau triple sec
1	shot(s)	Bols apricot brandy liqueur
¼	shot(s)	Campari Bitter
3	shot(s)	Freshly squeezed orange juice

Origin: Created by Nichole Colella.
Comment: A slightly bitter, tangy, orange, cooling drink.

> 'I SPENT A LOT OF MONEY ON BOOZE, BIRDS AND FAST CARS. THE REST I JUST SQUANDERED.'
> GEORGE BEST

MAÑANA DAIQUIRI NEW #8

●●●●○

Glass: Coupette/Martini
Garnish: Dried apricot
Method: SHAKE all ingredients with ice and fine strain into chilled glass.

2	shot(s)	Bacardi Superior rum
½	shot(s)	Bols apricot brandy liqueur
¼	shot(s)	Pomegranate (grenadine) syrup
¼	shot(s)	Freshly squeezed lemon juice
½	shot(s)	Chilled water (omit if wet ice)

Comment: Salmon pink in colour, the Manana has a subtle and delicate rum laced apricot flavour.
Origin: Mañana, literally meaning 'tomorrow' in Spanish but more usually used to mean some indefinite time in the future. This recipe is adapted from David A. Embury's 1948 'Fine Art of Mixing Drinks'.

MAN-BOUR-TINI

●●●●○

Glass: Martini
Garnish: Orange zest twist
Method: SHAKE all ingredients with ice and fine strain into chilled glass.

1	shot(s)	Mandarine Napoléon liqueur
¾	shot(s)	Bulleit bourbon whiskey
½	shot(s)	Freshly squeezed lime juice
2	shot(s)	Ocean Spray cranberry juice
¼	shot(s)	Sugar syrup (2 sugar to 1 water)

Origin: Created in 1999 by Yours Truly (Simon Difford).
Comment: A rounded, fruity, bourbon based drink with mandarin and lime sourness.

MANCHESTER SPECIAL RUM PUNCH NEW #8

●●●○○

Glass: Old-fashioned
Garnish: Grapefruit slice
Method: STIR honey with rum until honey dissolves. Add other ingredients, SHAKE with ice and strain into glass filled with crushed ice.

2	shot(s)	Myers's dark Jamaican rum
2	spoons	Runny honey
1	shot(s)	Freshly squeezed grapefruit juice
2	dashes	Angostura aromatic bitters

Origin: Originally made at the Manchester Hotel, Mandeville, Jamaica. The Manchester Hotel lies in a lush tropical setting in the centre of Jamaica high in the cool mountains of Manchester.
Comment: Fruity punch.

MANDARINE COLLINS

●●●○○

Glass: Collins
Garnish: Half orange slice
Method: SHAKE first 3 ingredients with ice and strain into ice-filled glass. TOP with soda.

1½	shot(s)	Tanqueray London dry gin
1	shot(s)	Mandarine Napoléon liqueur
1	shot(s)	Freshly squeezed lemon juice
Top up with		Soda water (club soda)

Comment: A tangy, long refreshing drink with an intense mandarin flavour.

MANDARINE SIDECAR

●●●●○

Glass: Martini
Garnish: Sugar rim (optional) & lemon zest twist
Method: SHAKE all ingredients with ice and fine strain into chilled glass.

1½	shot(s)	Courvoisier V.S.O.P. cognac
1	shot(s)	Mandarine Napoléon liqueur
1	shot(s)	Freshly squeezed lemon juice
¾	shot(s)	Chilled mineral water (omit if wet ice)
⅛	shot(s)	Sugar syrup (2 sugar to 1 water)

Comment: Wonderfully tart and strong in flavour.

MANDARINE SONGBIRD

Glass: Collins
Garnish: Orange slice
Method: SHAKE first 3 ingredients with ice and fine strain into ice-filled glass. **TOP** with ginger beer.

2	shot(s)	**Mandarine Napoléon liqueur**
½	shot(s)	**Freshly squeezed lemon juice**
¾	shot(s)	**Freshly squeezed orange juice**
Top up with		**Ginger beer**

Comment: Long, spicy orange.

MANDARINE SOUR

Glass: Old-fashioned
Garnish: Lemon slice
Method: SHAKE all ingredients with ice and strain into ice-filled glass.

2	shot(s)	**Mandarine Napoléon liqueur**
1	shot(s)	**Freshly squeezed lemon juice**
¼	shot(s)	**Sugar syrup** (2 sugar to 1 water)
½	fresh	**Egg white**

Comment: Sour, but with a strong mandarin sweetness.

MANDARINTINI

Glass: Martini
Garnish: Orange slice on rim
Method: SHAKE all ingredients with ice and fine strain into chilled glass.

1½	shot(s)	**Orange-infused Ketel One vodka**
½	shot(s)	**Campari Bitter**
½	shot(s)	**Grand Marnier liqueur**
1½	shot(s)	**Pressed apple juice**

Origin: Adapted from a drink discovered in 2005 at Aqua Spirit, Hong Kong, China.
Comment: This bittersweet palate cleanser looks like pink grapefruit juice.

MANDARITO

Glass: Collins
Garnish: Mint sprig
Method: Lightly **MUDDLE** mint (just to bruise) in base of glass. Add next 4 ingredients, half fill glass with crushed ice and **CHURN** (stir). Fill glass to brim with more crushed ice and churn some more. **TOP** with soda, stir and serve with straws.

12	fresh	**Mint leaves**
1½	shot(s)	**Mandarine Napoléon liqueur**
1	shot(s)	**Ketel One vodka**
1	shot(s)	**Freshly squeezed lime juice**
⅛	shot(s)	**Sugar syrup** (2 sugar to 1 water)
Top up with		**Soda water** (club soda)

Comment: A vodka Mojito with mandarin accents.

MANGO COLLINS

Glass: Collins
Garnish: Lemon slice
Method: SHAKE first 3 ingredients with ice and strain into ice-filled glass. **TOP** with soda, stir and serve with straws.

2	shot(s)	**Tanqueray London dry gin**
2	shot(s)	**Boiron mango purée**
1½	shot(s)	**Freshly squeezed lemon juice**
Top up with		**Soda water** (club soda)

Origin: Formula by Yours Truly (Simon Difford) in 2004.
Comment: Lemon juice and gin combine with mango in this refreshing tall drink.

MANGO DAIQUIRI

Glass: Martini
Garnish: Lime wedge on rim
Method: SHAKE all ingredients with ice and fine strain into chilled glass.

2	shot(s)	**Bacardi Superior rum**
2	shot(s)	**Boiron mango purée**
½	shot(s)	**Freshly squeezed lime juice**

Origin: Formula by Yours Truly (Simon Difford) in 2004.
Variant: Blended with 12oz scoop crushed ice and an additional half shot of sugar syrup.
Comment: Tropical yet potent and refreshing.

MANGO MARGARITA #1 (SERVED 'UP')

Glass: Coupette
Garnish: Lime wedge on rim
Method: SHAKE all ingredients with ice and fine strain into chilled glass.

2	shot(s)	**Don Julio reposado tequila**
1	shot(s)	**Boiron mango purée**
1	shot(s)	**Cointreau triple sec**
1	shot(s)	**Freshly squeezed lime juice**

Origin: Formula by Yours Truly (Simon Difford) in 2004.
Comment: The character of the tequila is not overwhelmed by the fruit.

MANGO MARGARITA #2 (FROZEN)

Glass: Coupette
Garnish: Mango slice on rim
Method: BLEND all ingredients with 6oz scoop crushed ice. Serve with straws.

2	shot(s)	**Don Julio reposado tequila**
¾	shot(s)	**Boiron mango purée**
1	shot(s)	**Cointreau triple sec**
½	shot(s)	**Freshly squeezed lime juice**
¼	shot(s)	**Sugar syrup** (2 sugar to 1 water)

Origin: Formula by Yours Truly (Simon Difford) in 2006.
Comment: Mango first and Margarita second.

MANGO MARTINI

Glass: Martini
Garnish: Mango slice on rim
Method: SHAKE all ingredients with ice and fine strain into chilled glass.

2½	shot(s)	**Ketel One Citroen vodka**
2	shot(s)	**Boiron mango purée**

Origin: Formula by Yours Truly (Simon Difford) in 2004.
Comment: This drink doesn't work nearly so well with plain vodka – if citrus vodka is not available, try using gin.

> 'THE SECRET TO A LONG LIFE IS TO STAY BUSY, GET PLENTY OF EXERCISE AND DON'T DRINK TOO MUCH. THEN AGAIN, DON'T DRINK TOO LITTLE.'
> HERMANN SMITH-JOHANNSON

MANGO PUNCH

Glass: Collins
Garnish: Mango slice (dried or fresh)
Method: SHAKE all ingredients with ice and fine strain into glass filled with crushed ice.

2	shot(s)	**Wray & Nephew overproof rum**
3	shot(s)	**Boiron mango purée**
¾	shot(s)	**Freshly squeezed lime juice**
¾	shot(s)	**Sugar syrup** (2 sugar to 1 water)

Origin: Formula by Yours Truly (Simon Difford) in 2004.
Comment: A distinctly tropical cocktail flavoured with mango.

MANGO RUM COOLER

Glass: Collins
Garnish: Mango slice (dried or fresh)
Method: SHAKE all ingredients with ice and strain into ice-filled glass.

2½	shot(s)	**Bacardi Superior rum**
1½	shot(s)	**Boiron mango purée**
1	shot(s)	**Pressed apple juice**
1½	shot(s)	**Freshly squeezed lemon juice**

Origin: Created in 2004 by Yours Truly (Simon Difford).
Comment: Long, fruity and cooling.

MANHATTAN DRY UPDATED #8

Glass: Martini
Garnish: Twist of orange (discarded) & two maraschino cherries
Method: STIR all ingredients with ice and strain into chilled glass.

2½	shot(s)	**Bulleit bourbon whiskey**
1	shot(s)	**Noilly Prat dry vermouth**
3	dashes	**Angostura aromatic bitters**

Variant: Manhattan Perfect and Manhattan Sweet. Also served over ice in an old-fashioned glass.
Origin: Like so many cocktails, the origins of the Manhattan are lost in time. And, as neither the name nor the ingredients are so unusual as to prevent inadvertent duplication, the mystery is likely to remain unsolved. The Democrat newspaper remarked in 1882 that, 'It is but a short time ago that a mixture of whiskey, vermouth and bitters came into vogue' and observed that it had been known as a Turf Club cocktail, a Jockey Club cocktail and a Manhattan cocktail.

Until fairly recently, the most popular story was that the drink was created in November 1874 at New York City's Manhattan Club for Lady Randolph Churchill (née Jenny Jerome), while she was celebrating the successful gubernatorial campaign of Samuel Jones Tilden. (The Manhattan Club was opposite the site which now houses the Empire State Building.) However, David Wondrich has pointed out that the banquet in question was held in November 1874, when Lady C was otherwise engaged, in England, giving birth to Winston.

A 1945 article claims that a drink under the name of the Manhattan appeared in an 1860 bar guide; it certainly appears in Harry Johnson's book of 1884.

A plausible story comes from a book published in 1923, 'Valentine's Manual of New York'. In this a William F. Mulhall who was a bartender at New York's Hoffman House in the 1880s recounts, "The Manhattan cocktail was invented by a man named Black who kept a place ten doors below Houston Street on Broadway in the [eighteen] sixties - probably the most famous drink in the world in its time."

Yet another story involves a Col. Joe Walker on a yachting trip in New York but as this specifically refers to sweet vermouth I have recounted it under 'Manhattan Sweet'.
Comment: A bone-dry Manhattan for those with dry palates.

MANHATTAN PERFECT UPDATED #8

Glass: Martini
Garnish: Twist of orange (discarded) & two maraschino cherries
Method: STIR all ingredients with ice and strain into chilled glass.

2½	shot(s)	**Bulleit bourbon whiskey**
½	shot(s)	**Martini Rosso sweet vermouth**
½	shot(s)	**Noilly Prat dry vermouth**
3	dashes	**Angostura aromatic bitters**

Variant: Manhattan Dry and Manhattan Sweet. Also served over ice in an old-fashioned glass.
Origin: Whatever the truth of its invention (see Manhattan Dry), the Manhattan was probably originally made with rye whiskey, rather than bourbon, as New York was a rye-drinking city, although early bar books just state 'whiskey'. Today it is common to use bourbon, although purists are beginning to revive rye.

When Scotch is substituted for bourbon the Manhattan becomes a Rob Roy, with brandy (cognac) it becomes a Harvard and with applejack it is a Star Cocktail when made with applejack.

Some time in 2005 it became conventional in some New York bars to garnish a Manhattan with two cherries as a 9/11 tribute.
Comment: The Manhattan version most popularly served – medium dry.

MANHATTAN SWEET UPDATED #8

Glass: Martini
Garnish: Twist of orange (discarded) & two maraschino cherries
Method: STIR all ingredients with ice and strain into chilled glass.

2½	shot(s)	**Bulleit bourbon whiskey**
1	shot(s)	**Martini Rosso sweet vermouth**
⅛	shot(s)	**Maraschino syrup** (from cherry jar)
3	dashes	**Angostura aromatic bitters**

Variant: Manhattan Dry and Manhattan Perfect. Also served over ice in an old-fashioned glass.
Origin: Various origins for this drink abound. They include: in November 1874 at New York City's Manhattan Club for Lady Randolph Churchill. Sometime in the 1880s "by a man named Black who kept a place ten doors below Houston Street on Broadway in the [eighteen] sixties", and by a Col. Joe Walker on a yachting trip in New York.

That last story is the most recent I have come across and comes courtesy of Barry Popik's website barrypopik.com where Barry notes an entry in the Daily Journal, Racine, Wisconsin, 8 March 1899. The article purports that Col. Joe Walker ran the then-famous Crescent Hall Saloon in New Orleans, at the corner of Canal and St. Charles Streets and that some years before he went on a little yachting trip with a party of friends while in New York. "By some oversight the liquid refreshments in the icebox were confined to Italian vermouth and plain whisky, and it occurred to the colonel that a palatable drink might be made by mixing the two. The results were so good that he experimented a little on his return to New Orleans, and soon perfected the Manhattan cocktail, as it is known today. It was christened in honor of his friends on Manhattan island, and the fame of the decoction soon spread all over the country. The true Manhattan cocktail is always made with Italian vermouth, but at half the places where they undertake to serve them, French [dry] vermouth is substituted, and the fine flavor is altogether destroyed. French vermouth is a sort of wine, while Italian vermouth is a cordial, pure and simple. They are as different as milk and molasses. A cocktail made from the French brand is no more a Manhattan cocktail than it is a Spanish omelette."
Comment: I must confess to preferring my Manhattans served sweet, or perfect at a push. The Manhattan is complex, challenging and moreish. Best of all, it's available in a style to suit every palate.

> **'I'VE ALWAYS BELIEVED THAT PARADISE WILL HAVE MY FAVORITE BEER ON TAP.'**
> RUDYARD WHEATLEY

MANHATTAN ISLAND

Glass: Martini
Garnish: Maraschino cherry
Method: STIR all ingredients with ice and fine strain into chilled glass.

2	shot(s)	**Courvoisier V.S.O.P. cognac**
1	shot(s)	**Martini Rosso sweet vermouth**
3	dashes	**Angostura aromatic bitters**
⅛	shot(s)	**Luxardo maraschino liqueur**

Comment: A twist on the classic Harvard, or brandy based Manhattan.

MAPLE OLD-FASHIONED

Glass: Martini
Garnish: Orange zest twist
Method: STIR one shot of the bourbon with two ice cubes in a glass. Add maple syrup and Angostura and two more ice cubes. Stir some more and add another two ice cubes and the rest of the bourbon. Stir lots more so as to melt the ice, then add fresh ice to complete the drink. The melting and stirring in of ice cubes is essential to the dilution and taste of this drink.

2	shot(s)	**Bulleit bourbon whiskey**
½	shot(s)	**Maple syrup**
2	dashes	**Angostura aromatic bitters**

Origin: Discovered in 2004 at Indigo Yard, Edinburgh, Scotland.
Comment: Maple syrup replaces sugar in this reworking of the classic Old-fashioned.

MAPLE LEAF

Glass: Old-fashioned
Garnish: Lemon zest twist
Method: SHAKE all ingredients with ice and strain into ice-filled glass.

2	shot(s)	**Bulleit bourbon whiskey**
½	shot(s)	**Freshly squeezed lemon juice**
¼	shot(s)	**Maple syrup**

Comment: This trio combine wonderfully.

MAPLE POMME

Glass: Collins
Garnish: Apple wedge
Method: SHAKE first 4 ingredients with ice and strain into ice-filled glass. **TOP** with ginger ale, lightly stir and serve with straws.

2	shot(s)	**Johnnie Walker Scotch whisky**
½	shot(s)	**Freshly squeezed lemon juice**
1	shot(s)	**Pressed apple juice**
½	shot(s)	**Maple syrup**
Top up with		**Ginger ale**

Origin: Adapted from a short drink created in 2005 by Tonin Kacaj at Maze, London, England.
Comment: Scotch based drink for warm weather.

MARAMA RUM PUNCH

Glass: Sling
Garnish: Mint sprig & lime wedge
Method: Lightly **MUDDLE** mint (just to bruise). Add next 5 ingredients, **SHAKE** with ice and strain into ice-filled glass. **TOP** with lemonade, lightly stir and serve with straws.

12	fresh	**Mint leaves**
1½	shot(s)	**Wray & Nephew overproof rum**
½	shot(s)	**Cointreau triple sec**
½	shot(s)	**Freshly squeezed lime juice**
½	shot(s)	**Almond (orgeat) syrup**
3	dashes	**Angostura aromatic bitters**
Top up with		**Lemonade/Sprite/7-Up**

Comment: A tangy, well-balanced punch.

MANHATTAN SWEET

MARGARET DUFFY NEW #8

Glass: Martini
Garnish: Lemon zest twist
Method: STIR all ingredients with ice and strain into chilled glass.

2	shot(s)	**Swedish Punch**
1	shot(s)	**Courvoisier V.S.O.P. cognac**
2	dashes	**Angostura aromatic bitters**
½	shot(s)	**Chilled water** (omit if wet ice)

Origin: Vintage cocktail of unknown origin.
Comment: Spiced and sweetened cognac.

MARGARITA #1 (STRAIGHT-UP) UPDATED #8

Glass: Coupette
Garnish: Salt rim & lime wedge
Method: SHAKE all ingredients with ice and fine strain into chilled glass.

2	shot(s)	**Don Julio blanco tequila**
1	shot(s)	**Cointreau triple sec**
1	shot(s)	**Freshly squeezed lime juice**

Variant: Margaritas made with premium tequilas are sometimes referred to as 'Deluxe' or 'Cadillac' Margaritas.
Origin: The Margarita can be considered a Tequila Sour, or a Tequila Sidecar, and two variations of this classic cocktail date back to the 1930s: the Tequila Daisy and the Picador. Both, however, lack the distinctive salt rim.

There are many people who claim to have invented the Margarita, which, as Spanish for 'daisy' and a popular woman's name, would have been a very common name for a drink. A brief summary of the top claimants:
Francisco 'Pancho' Morales, while working in a bar called Tommy's Place in Ciudad Juarez, Mexico, was asked to make a 'Magnolia' on the 4th July 1942, but couldn't remember it so created this drink. The customer's name may even have been Margarita.

Carlos 'Danny' Herrera created the cocktail either in 1947 or 1948 at his Rancho La Gloria bar in Rosarito, Mexico, for an actress called Marjorie King who drank no spirit but tequila. He added Cointreau and lime, and the unique salt rim that caught people's attention at the bar, then named his creation Margarita, the Spanish for Marjorie.

Daniel (Danny) Negrete created the drink in 1936 when he was the manager of Garci Crespo Hotel in Puebla, Mexico. His girlfriend, Margarita, apparently liked salt in her drinks and he is said to have created the drink for her as a present. In 1944 Danny moved to Tijuana, Mexico, and became a bartender at the Agua Caliente Racetrack, a place which has some claim to be the birthplace of the Margarita in the early 1930s.

Vernon Underwood was president of Young's Market Company, who in the 1930s had started distributing Cuervo tequila. He went to Johnny Durlesser, head bartender of the Tail O' The Cock in LA, and asked him to create something using his spirit, then named it after his wife Margaret (Margarita).

Sara Morales, an expert in Mexican folklore, claimed the Margarita was created in 1930 by Doña Bertha, owner of Bertha's Bar in Taxco, Mexico. The socialite Margaret Sames held a Christmas party in Acapulco, Mexico, in 1948, and created the first Margarita. She thought nothing of it until, when flying home to San Antonio from Acapulco airport, she saw a bar advertising 'Margarita's Drink', a cocktail with exactly the same ingredients as her own.

So… Plenty of Margarets and even Margaritas: there is also a popular holiday destination called Margarita Island, located in the Caribbean north of Venezuela, two-and-a-half hours from Miami.

It could simply be a twist on the 'Daisy', a classic cocktail dating back to Victorian times and made with citrus juice, sweetened with a syrup or liqueur, and fortified with a base spirit. Margarita is the Spanish word for daisy. A British antecedent of the Margarita called a 'Picador' has recently been unearthed.
Comment: For the perfect salt rim, liquidise sea salt to make it finer, then run a lime wedge around the outside edge of the glass before dipping the rim in salt. Rimming only half the glass with salt gives the drinker the option of enjoying the cocktail with or without salt.

MARGARITA #2 (ON THE ROCKS)

Glass: Old-fashioned
Garnish: Salt rim & lime wedge
Method: SHAKE all ingredients with ice and strain into ice-filled glass.

2	shot(s)	**Don Julio reposado tequila**
1	shot(s)	**Cointreau triple sec**
1	shot(s)	**Freshly squeezed lime juice**

Comment: Tangy citrus, tequila and salt.

MARGARITA #3 (FROZEN)

Glass: Martini
Garnish: Maraschino cherry
Method: BLEND all ingredients with 12oz scoop of crushed ice. Serve heaped in the glass and with straws.

1½	shot(s)	**Don Julio reposado tequila**
¾	shot(s)	**Cointreau triple sec**
¾	shot(s)	**Freshly squeezed lime juice**
½	shot(s)	**Sugar syrup** (2 sugar to 1 water)

Variant: With fruit and/or fruit liqueurs.
Comment: Citrus freshness with the subtle agave of tequila served frozen.

MARGARITA #4 (SALT FOAM FLOAT)

Glass: Coupette
Garnish: Lime wedge on rim
Method: Combine first 3 ingredients, POUR into cream whipping siphon and CHARGE with nitrous oxide. Shake and place siphon in a refrigerator for one hour prior to making drink. SHAKE next 3 ingredients with ice and fine strain into chilled glass. SQUIRT salt foam over surface of drink from siphon.

4	spoons	**Sea salt**
1	pint	**Chilled mineral water**
2	fresh	**Egg whites**
2	shot(s)	**Don Julio reposado tequila**
1	shot(s)	**Cointreau triple sec**
1	shot(s)	**Freshly squeezed lime juice**

Comment: Classic Margarita with a salty foam topping.

MARGUERITE MARTINI

Glass: Martini
Garnish: Orange zest twist
Method: SHAKE all ingredients with ice and fine strain into chilled glass.

2	shot(s)	**Tanqueray London dry gin**
½	shot(s)	**Noilly Prat dry vermouth**
1	dash	**Angostura orange bitters**

Origin: Adapted from a recipe in Harry Craddock's 1930 Savoy Cocktail Book.
Comment: A slightly wet yet bone dry classic Martini with a hint of orange.

MARGARITA

'THE PIANO HAS BEEN
DRINKING, NOT ME, NOT ME.'
TOM WAITS

MARIA THERESA MARGARITA

Glass: Martini
Garnish: Lime wedge on rim
Method: **STIR** honey with tequila in base of shaker
to dissolve honey. **ADD** other ingredients, **SHAKE**
with ice and fine strain into chilled glass.

2	spoons	**Runny honey**
2	shot(s)	**Don Julio reposado tequila**
1	shot(s)	**Ocean Spray cranberry juice**
½	shot(s)	**Freshly squeezed lime juice**

Origin: Adapted from a Tiki drink created by Victor
Bergeron (Trader Vic).
Comment: Originally sweetened with sugar syrup,
this is better smoothed with honey.

MARIE ROSE

Glass: Martini
Garnish: Rosemary sprig
Method: Strip leaves from rosemary and **MUDDLE**
with grapes in base of shaker. Add other
ingredients, **SHAKE** with ice and fine strain into
chilled glass.

½	sprig	**Fresh rosemary**
8	fresh	**Seedless white grapes**
2	shot(s)	**Tanqueray London dry gin**
¾	shot(s)	**St-Germain elderflower liqueur**
¼	shot(s)	**Freshly squeezed lime juice**

Origin: Created in 2007 by Renan Lejeune at Zeta
Bar, London, England.
Comment: Rosemary spiced gin with grape juice
and elderflower: very aromatic.

MARKET DAIQUIRÍ NEW #8

Glass: Coupette/Martini
Garnish: Pear slice
Method: SHAKE all ingredients with ice and fine
strain into chilled glass.

2	fresh	**Mint leaves**
2	shot(s)	**Bacardi Superior rum**
½	shot(s)	**Boiron pear purée**
¼	shot(s)	**Almond (orgeat) syrup**
½	shot(s)	**Freshly squeezed lime juice**

Comment: A classic Daiquiri influenced by the
addition of pear, mint and almond.
Origin: Created in 2008 by Dez O'Connell, London,
England.

MARMALADE COCKTAIL

Glass: Martini
Garnish: Orange zest twist
Method: **STIR** marmalade with gin until the
marmalade dissolves. **SHAKE** other ingredients
with ice and fine strain into chilled glass.

4	spoons	**Orange marmalade**
2	shot(s)	**Tanqueray London dry gin**
½	shot(s)	**Freshly squeezed lemon juice**

Origin: Adapted from a recipe in the 1930 'Savoy
Cocktail Book' by Harry Craddock (the original
recipe serves six people).
Comment: Harry wrote of his own drink, "By its
bitter-sweet taste this cocktail is especially suited to
be a luncheon aperitif."

MARMALADE SOUR NEW #8

Glass: Martini/Coupette
Garnish: Orange zest twist
Method: SHAKE all ingredients with ice and fine
strain into chilled glass.

1	spoon	**Orange or grapefruit marmalade**
2	shot(s)	**Leblon cachaça**
½	shot(s)	**Freshly squeezed lemon juice**
2	dashes	**Angostura orange bitters**
½	fresh	**Egg white**

Comment: Richly sour and citrussy.
Origin: Created by Jamie Boudreau.

MARMARITA UPDATED #8

Glass: Coupette
Garnish: Wipe Marmite (yeast extract) around rim
Method: SHAKE all ingredients with ice and fine
strain into chilled glass.

2	shot(s)	**Don Julio blanco tequila**
1	shot(s)	**Cointreau triple sec**
1	shot(s)	**Freshly squeezed lime juice**

Origin: Created in 2005 by Simon (Ginger)
Warneford at Blanch House, Brighton, England.
Comment: A Margarita with a Marmite rim. After all
yeast extract is slightly salty.

MARNY COCKTAIL

Glass: Martini
Garnish: Orange zest twist
Method: SHAKE all ingredients with ice and fine
strain into chilled glass.

2	shot(s)	**Tanqueray London dry gin**
1	shot(s)	**Grand Marnier liqueur**
2	dashes	**Angostura orange bitters** (optional)

Origin: Adapted from a recipe in Harry Craddock's
1930 Savoy Cocktail Book.
Comment: Spirit and liqueur in harmony.

MARQUEE

Glass: Martini
Garnish: Raspberries on stick
Method: SHAKE all ingredients with ice and fine strain into chilled glass.

1½	shot(s)	**Bulleit bourbon whiskey**
1½	shot(s)	**Ocean Spray cranberry juice**
½	shot(s)	**Chambord black raspberry liqueur**
½	shot(s)	**Freshly squeezed lemon juice**
¼	shot(s)	**Sugar syrup** (2 sugar to 1 water)

Origin: Created in 1998 by Giovanni Burdi at Match EC1, London, England.
Comment: Raspberry and bourbon combine perfectly in this short, slightly sweet, fruity drink.

MARTINEZ #1 (ORIGINAL GENEVER) NEW #8

Glass: Martini
Garnish: Orange zest twist
Method: STIR ingredients with ice and fine strain into chilled glass.

1½	shot(s)	**Bokma oude genever**
1½	shot(s)	**Martini Rosso sweet vermouth**
⅛	shot(s)	**Orange curaçao liqueur**
2	dashes	**Angostura aromatic bitters**

Comment: This medium dry Martini is somewhat more approachable than a Dry Martini.
Origin: Probably the forerunner of the Martini, the first known recipe for this drink appears in O.H. Byron's 1884 'The Modern Bartender' where it is listed as a variation to the Manhattan. Its first written standalone listing in a recipe book appears in Harry Johnson's 1888 Bartender's Manual.

Drinks historian David Wondrich and others believe it was first made using Dutch oude genever as this was the style of exported to America long before English Old Tom gin or London Dry gins. Although the drink appears in his 1887 Bartenders' Guide (as a variation), there is no evidence that Jerry Thomas invented the Martinez and significantly he omits the drink from the earlier 1862 edition of his Bartender's Guide.

Many claim that one Julio Richelieu created the drink in 1874 for a goldminer and that the drink is named after the Californian town of Martinez, where that unnamed goldminer enjoyed this libation.

MARTINEZ #2 (MODERN GENEVER) NEW #8

Glass: Martini
Garnish: Orange zest twist
Method: STIR ingredients with ice and fine strain into chilled glass.

2	shot(s)	**Bokma oude genever**
½	shot(s)	**Noilly Prat dry vermouth**
½	shot(s)	**Martini Rosso sweet vermouth**
⅛	shot(s)	**Luxardo maraschino liqueur**

Origin: This modern take on the vintage classic emerged in London during early 2008 with the introduction of Antica Formula.

MARTINEZ #3 (OLD TOM) NEW #8

Glass: Martini
Garnish: Orange zest twist
Method: STIR ingredients with ice and fine strain into chilled glass.

2	shot(s)	**Old Tom gin**
½	shot(s)	**Noilly Prat dry vermouth**
½	shot(s)	**Martini Rosso sweet vermouth**
⅛	shot(s)	**Luxardo maraschino liqueur**
2	dashes	**Angostura aromatic bitters**

Comment: Use an authentic tasting distilled with no added sugar Old Tom and this is a fabulous cocktail.

MARTINEZ #4 (LONDON DRY) NEW #8

Glass: Martini
Garnish: Orange zest twist
Method: STIR ingredients with ice and fine strain into chilled glass.

2	shot(s)	**Tanqueray London dry gin**
½	shot(s)	**Martini Rosso sweet vermouth**
¼	shot(s)	**Noilly Prat dry vermouth**
⅛	shot(s)	**Luxardo maraschino liqueur**
⅛	shot(s)	**Orange curaçao liqueur**
1	dashes	**Angostura aromatic bitters**

Comment: Aromatic, complex and very dry.

MARTINEZ #5 (ORANGE) UPDATED #8

Glass: Martini
Garnish: Orange zest twist
Method: STIR all ingredients with ice and strain into chilled glass.

2	shot(s)	**Tanqueray London dry gin**
1	shot(s)	**Martini Rosso sweet vermouth**
¼	shot(s)	**Orange curaçao liqueur**
2	dashes	**Angostura orange bitters** (optional)

Comment: Stir well as dilution helps to tame this old-school classic in which bitter orange predominates.

MARTINI ROYALE

Glass: Martini
Garnish: Lemon zest twist
Method: STIR vodka and crème de cassis with ice and strain into chilled glass. **TOP** with chilled champagne.

1½	shot(s)	**Ketel One vodka**
½	shot(s)	**Crème de cassis liqueur**
Top up with		**Perrier Jouet brut champagne**

Origin: Created in 2001 by Dick Bradsell at Monte's, London, England.
Comment: The Kir Royale meets the vodkatini in this pink but powerful drink.

> ## 'PROHIBITION IS BETTER THAN NO LIQUOR AT ALL.'
> ### WILL ROGERS

MARTINI SPECIAL

Glass: Martini
Garnish: Orange zest twist
Method: Fill glass with ice and **POUR** absinthe and Angostura over ice. **TOP** with chilled mineral water and leave to stand. **SHAKE** gin, vermouth and orange water with ice. **DISCARD** contents of standing glass and fine strain shaken drink into washed glass.

¼	shot(s)	La Fée Parisienne (68%) absinthe
4	dashes	Angostura aromatic bitters
Top up with		Chilled mineral water
2	shot(s)	Tanqueray London dry gin
¾	shot(s)	Martini Rosso sweet vermouth
⅛	shot(s)	Orange flower water

Origin: Adapted from a recipe in Harry Craddock's 1930 Savoy Cocktail Book.
Comment: Aromatic, very dry and very serious – yet it has a frothy head.

MARTINI THYME

Glass: Martini
Garnish: Thread three green olives onto thyme sprig
Method: **MUDDLE** thyme in base of shaker. **ADD** other ingredients, **SHAKE** with ice and fine strain into chilled glass.

2	sprigs	Lemon thyme (remove stalks)
1	shot(s)	Tanqueray London dry gin
¾	shot(s)	Green Chartreuse liqueur
¼	shot(s)	Sugar syrup (2 sugar to 1 water)

Origin: A combination of two very similar drinks, that both originally called for thyme infused gin. The first I discovered at The Lobby Bar (One Aldwych, London) and the other came from Tony Conigliaro at Isola, London, England.
Comment: A wonderfully fresh herbal Martini with the distinctive taste of Chartreuse. You'll either love it or hate it.

MARTINI WITH A SPOT NEW #8

Glass: Martini
Garnish: Lemon zest twist
Method: **STIR** gin and vermouth with ice and strain into chilled glass. Carefully **POUR** 'spot' of absinthe into centre of the drink.

2½	shot(s)	Tanqueray London dry gin
½	shot(s)	Noilly Prat dry vermouth
1	dash	La Fée Parisienne (68%) absinthe

Comment: Absinth adds bone-dry complexity to this otherwise Wet Martini.
Origin: Discovered in 2007 at Westbourne House, London, England.

MARTÍ'S MARTINI NEW #8

Glass: Martini/Coupette
Garnish: None
Method: **STIR** all ingredients with ice and strain into chilled glass.

1½	shot(s)	Bacardi Superior rum
¼	shot(s)	Galliano L'Autentico liqueur
¼	shot(s)	Genepi des Peres Chartreux
½	shot(s)	Noilly Prat dry vermouth
½	shot(s)	Chilled water (omit if wet ice)

Comment: Herbal, medium dry, rum-based, Martini-style drink.
Origin: Created in 2008 by Oli Gillespie at Bibendum Wine Ltd, London, England and named after José Martí (1853-1895) - a leader of the Cuban independence movement, writer and renowned poet.

MARY PICKFORD UPDATED #8

Glass: Martini **Garnish:** Maraschino cherry
Method: **SHAKE** all ingredients with ice and fine strain into chilled glass.

2	shot(s)	Bacardi Superior white rum
1½	shot(s)	Pressed pineapple juice
¼	shot(s)	Pomegranate (grenadine) syrup
⅛	shot(s)	Luxardo maraschino liqueur

Comment: When made correctly, this pale pink cocktail has a perfect balance between the fruit flavours and the spirit of the rum.
Origin: Created in the 1920s (during Prohibition) by Fred Kaufman at the Hotel Naćional de Cuba, Havana for the silent movie star and wife of Douglas Fairbanks. She was in Cuba filming a movie with her husband Douglas Fairbanks and Charlie Chaplin. This is recounted on page 40 of Basil Woon's 1928 book 'When It's Cocktail Time in Cuba'.

> ## 'WHEN LIFE HANDS YOU LEMONS, MAKE WHISKY SOURS.'
> ### W.C. FIELDS

MARY QUEEN OF SCOTS

Glass: Martini
Garnish: Sugar rim & maraschino cherry
Method: **SHAKE** all ingredients with ice and fine strain into chilled glass.

1½	shot(s)	Johnnie Walker Scotch whisky
¾	shot(s)	Drambuie liqueur
¾	shot(s)	Green Chartreuse liqueur

Origin: Discovered in 2006 on Kyle Branch's Cocktail Hotel blog cocktailhotel.blogspot.com). Mary Stuart, Mary Queen of Scots, was born on December 8th 1542 at Linlithgow Palace in West Lothian. On February 8th 1587, she was executed in the Great Hall of Fotheringhay.
Comment: Slightly sweet but herbal, serious and strong.

MARY ROSE

●●●●○

Glass: Martini
Garnish: Lime twist (discard) & rosemary sprig
Method: MUDDLE rosemary in base of shaker. Add other ingredients, **SHAKE** with ice and fine strain into chilled glass.

1	sprig	**Fresh rosemary**
2	shot(s)	**Tanqueray London dry gin**
1	shot(s)	**Green Chartreuse liqueur**
½	shot(s)	**Sugar syrup** (2 sugar to 1 water)
½	shot(s)	**Chilled mineral water** (omit if wet ice)

Origin: Created in 1999 by Philip Jeffrey at the Great Eastern Hotel, London, England. Named after King Henry VIII's warship, sunk during an engagement with the French fleet in 1545 and now on display in Portsmouth.
Comment: Herbal, herbal and herbal with a hint of spice.

MAT THE RAT

●●●●◐○

Glass: Collins
Garnish: Lime wedge
Method: SHAKE first 4 ingredients with ice and strain into ice-filled glass. **TOP** with lemonade, lightly stir and serve with straws.

2	shot(s)	**Sailor Jerry spiced rum**
½	shot(s)	**Cointreau triple sec**
1½	shot(s)	**Freshly squeezed orange juice**
½	shot(s)	**Freshly squeezed lime juice**
Top up with		**Lemonade/Sprite/7-Up**

Origin: A popular drink in UK branches of TGI Friday's, where it was created.
Comment: Whether or not Mat was a rat, we shall never know. However, the drink that's named after him is long and thirst-quenching.

MATADOR

●●●●○

Glass: Collins
Garnish: Pineapple wedge on rim
Method: SHAKE all ingredients with ice and strain into ice-filled glass.

2	shot(s)	**Don Julio reposado tequila**
1	shot(s)	**Cointreau triple sec**
1	shot(s)	**Freshly squeezed lime juice**
2	shot(s)	**Pressed pineapple juice**

Comment: A long Margarita-style drink. The lime and tequila work wonders with the pineapple.

MATADOR #2 (TOMMY'S STYLE) NEW #8

●●●●○

Glass: Martini
Garnish: Pineapple wedge on rim
Method: SHAKE all ingredients with ice and fine strain into chilled glass.

2	shot(s)	**Don Julio reposado tequila**
1	shot(s)	**Freshly squeezed lime juice**
½	shot(s)	**Agave syrup**
1½	shot(s)	**Pressed pineapple juice**

Comment: A pineapple Margarita with agave syrup in place of a sweet liqueur.

MAURESQUE

●●●○○

Glass: Collins (10oz max)
Method: POUR absinthe and almond syrup into glass. Serve iced water separately in a small jug (known in France as a 'broc') so the customer can dilute to their own taste (I recommend five shots). Lastly, add ice to fill glass.

1½	shot(s)	**La Fée Parisienne (68%) absinthe**
1	shot(s)	**Almond (orgeat) syrup**
Top up with		**Chilled mineral water**

AKA: Bureau Arabe
Origin: Pronounced 'Mor-Esk', this classic drink is very popular in the South of France, where it is now commonly made with pastis in place of absinthe. It was originally created by French soldiers serving in the Bataillon d'Afrique during the Algerian campaign of the 1830s and 40s, and was alternatively known as Bureau Arabe after the military department which dealt with local affairs and was said to act like "an iron fist in a velvet glove".
Comment: Long, refreshing aniseed, liquorice and almond.

MAURICE MARTINI

●●●●◐○

Glass: Martini
Garnish: Orange zest twist
Method: SHAKE all ingredients with ice and fine strain into chilled glass.

1½	shot(s)	**Tanqueray London dry gin**
¾	shot(s)	**Noilly Prat dry vermouth**
¾	shot(s)	**Martini Rosso sweet vermouth**
¼	shot(s)	**La Fée Parisienne (68%) absinthe**
¾	shot(s)	**Freshly squeezed orange juice**

Origin: Adapted from a recipe in Harry Craddock's 1930 Savoy Cocktail Book.
Comment: A perfect Martini with an aromatic burst of absinthe and a hint of orange.

MAYAN

●●●○○

Glass: Old-fashioned
Garnish: Float 3 coffee beans
Method: SHAKE all ingredients with ice and strain into ice-filled glass.

1½	shot(s)	**Don Julio reposado tequila**
½	shot(s)	**Kahlúa coffee liqueur**
2½	shot(s)	**Pressed pineapple juice**

Comment: Tequila, coffee and pineapple juice combine in this medium dry short drink.

MAYAN WHORE

●●●●○

Glass: Sling
Garnish: Split pineapple wedge
Method: SHAKE first 3 ingredients with ice and strain into ice-filled glass. **TOP** with soda, **DO NOT STIR** and serve with straws.

2	shot(s)	**Don Julio reposado tequila**
1½	shot(s)	**Pressed pineapple juice**
¾	shot(s)	**Kahlúa coffee liqueur**
Top up with		**Soda water** (club soda)

Comment: An implausible ménage à trois: coffee, tequila and pineapple, served long.

MAYFAIR COCKTAIL #1 UPDATED #8

Glass: Martini
Garnish: Orange zest twist
Method: MUDDLE cloves in base of shaker. Add other ingredients, **SHAKE** with ice and fine strain into chilled glass.

2	dried	Cloves
2	shot(s)	Tanqueray London dry gin
1	shot(s)	Bols apricot brandy liqueur
1	shot(s)	Freshly squeezed orange juice
⅛	shot(s)	Sugar syrup (2 sugar to 1 water)

Origin: Adapted from a recipe in Harry Craddock's 1930 Savoy Cocktail Book. Apparently this drink celebrates a fair that took place in the month of May during the rein of King Charles II.
Comment: Spiced apricot laced with gin. Slightly sweet.

MAYFAIR COCKTAIL #2 NEW #8

Glass: Martini
Garnish: Orange zest twist
Method: MUDDLE cloves in base of shaker. Add other ingredients, **SHAKE** with ice and fine strain into chilled glass.

2	dried	Cloves
2	shot(s)	Tanqueray London dry gin
1	shot(s)	Bols apricot brandy liqueur
¼	shot(s)	World's End Pimento Dram liqueur
1	shot(s)	Freshly squeezed orange juice

Comment: Gin with spicy cloves and hints of apricot and orange.

THE MAYFLOWER MARTINI UPDATED #8

Glass: Martini
Garnish: Lemon zest twist
Method: SHAKE all ingredients with ice and fine strain into chilled glass.

1½	shot(s)	Tanqueray London dry gin
½	shot(s)	St-Germain elderflower liqueur
½	shot(s)	Bols apricot brandy liqueur
½	shot(s)	Pressed apple juice
½	shot(s)	Freshly squeezed lemon juice

Comment: Fragrant balance of English fruits and flowers.
Origin: Adapted from a drink created in 2002 by Wayne Collins, London, England.

MAXIM'S COFFEE (HOT)

Glass: Toddy
Garnish: Float 3 coffee beans
Method: POUR all ingredients into warmed glass and **STIR**.

1	shot(s)	Courvoisier V.S.O.P. cognac
½	shot(s)	Bénédictine D.O.M. liqueur
¼	shot(s)	Galliano L'Autentico liqueur
Top up with		Hot filter coffee

Comment: An interesting herbal cognac laced coffee.

MEDICINAL SOLUTION

Glass: Collins
Garnish: Lime wedge
Method: SHAKE first 5 ingredients with ice and strain into ice-filled glass. **TOP** with tonic water, lightly stir and serve with straws.

1½	shot(s)	Bokma oude genever
½	shot(s)	Green Chartreuse liqueur
½	shot(s)	Freshly squeezed lime juice
¼	shot(s)	Sugar syrup (2 sugar to 1 water)
3	dashes	Angostura aromatic bitters
Top up with		Tonic water

Origin: Created in 2006 by Yours Truly (Simon Difford).
Comment: Every ingredient, apart from the sugar, has at some time been consumed for its medicinal qualities. Even the sugar is still used to make bitter tasting medicine more palatable. Some might say that's just what I've done here.

MEDIUM MARTINI

Glass: Martini
Garnish: Orange zest twist
Method: STIR all ingredients with ice and strain into chilled glass.

1½	shot(s)	Tanqueray London dry gin
¾	shot(s)	Noilly Prat dry vermouth
¾	shot(s)	Martini Rosso sweet vermouth

Origin: Adapted from a recipe in Harry Craddock's 1930 Savoy Cocktail Book.
Comment: A classic Martini served perfect and very wet. I prefer mine shaken which is the method Harry specifies in his guide.

MELLOW MARTINI

Glass: Martini
Garnish: Fresh lychee
Method: SHAKE all ingredients with ice and fine strain into chilled glass.

1½	shot(s)	Ketel One vodka
½	shot(s)	Soho lychee liqueur
½	shot(s)	Crème de banane liqueur
1½	shot(s)	Pressed pineapple juice

Comment: A fruity, tropical drink with a frothy head. Too fluffy to be a Martini.

MELON BALL

Glass: Shot
Method: SHAKE all ingredients with ice and fine strain into chilled glass.

½	shot(s)	Ketel One vodka
½	shot(s)	Midori green melon liqueur
¾	shot(s)	Freshly squeezed orange juice

Comment: A vivid green combination of vodka, melon and orange.

MELON COLLIE MARTINI

Glass: Martini
Garnish: Crumbled Cadbury's Flake bar
Method: SHAKE all ingredients with ice and fine strain into chilled glass.

1	shot(s)	Bacardi Superior rum
½	shot(s)	Malibu coconut rum liqueur
¾	shot(s)	Midori green melon liqueur
¼	shot(s)	White crème de cacao liqueur
¾	shot(s)	Double (heavy) cream
¾	shot(s)	Milk

Origin: Created in 2003 by Simon King at MJU, Millennium Hotel, London, England.
Comment: Something of a holiday disco drink but tasty all the same.

MELON DAIQUIRI #1 (SERVED 'UP')

Glass: Martini
Garnish: Melon slice or melon balls
Method: Cut melon into 8 segments and deseed. Cut cubes of flesh from skin of one segment and MUDDLE in base of shaker. Add other ingredients, SHAKE with ice and fine strain into chilled glass.

⅛	fresh	Cantaloupe melon
2	shot(s)	Bacardi Superior rum
½	shot(s)	Midori green melon liqueur
½	shot(s)	Freshly squeezed lime juice
⅛	shot(s)	Sugar syrup (2 sugar to 1 water)

Comment: A classic Daiquiri with the gentle touch of melon.

> 'I THINK A MAN OUGHT TO GET DRUNK AT LEAST TWICE A YEAR JUST ON PRINCIPLE, SO HE WON'T LET HIMSELF GET SNOTTY ABOUT IT.'
> RAYMOND CHANDLER

MELON DAIQUIRI #2 (SERVED FROZEN)

Glass: Martini (large 10oz)
Garnish: Melon slice or melon balls
Method: Cut melon into 8 segments and deseed. Cut cubes of flesh from skin of one segment and place in blender. Add other ingredients and BLEND with half scoop crushed ice. Serve with straws.

⅛	fresh	Cantaloupe melon
2	shot(s)	Bacardi Superior rum
½	shot(s)	Midori green melon liqueur
½	shot(s)	Freshly squeezed lime juice
¼	shot(s)	Sugar syrup (2 sugar to 1 water)

Comment: A cooling, fruity Daiquiri.

MELON MARGARITA #1 (SERVED 'UP')

Glass: Coupette
Garnish: Melon slice or melon balls
Method: Cut melon into 8 segments and deseed. Cut cubes of flesh from skin of one segment and MUDDLE in base of shaker. Add other ingredients, SHAKE with ice and fine strain into chilled glass.

⅛	fresh	Cantaloupe melon
2	shot(s)	Don Julio reposado tequila
1	shot(s)	Midori green melon liqueur
1	shot(s)	Freshly squeezed lime juice

Comment: Looks like stagnant pond water but tastes fantastic.

MELON MARGARITA #2 (SERVED FROZEN)

Glass: Coupette
Garnish: Melon slice or melon balls
Method: Cut melon into 8 segments and deseed. Cut cubes of flesh from skin of one segment and place in blender. Add other ingredients and BLEND with 6oz scoop crushed ice. Serve with straws.

⅛	fresh	Cantaloupe melon
2	shot(s)	Don Julio reposado tequila
1	shot(s)	Midori green melon liqueur
½	shot(s)	Freshly squeezed lime juice

Comment: Melon and tequila always combine well - here in a frozen Margarita.

MELON MARTINI #1

Glass: Martini
Garnish: Split lime wedge
Method: SHAKE all ingredients with ice and fine strain into chilled glass.

2¼	shot(s)	Ketel One vodka
1	shot(s)	Midori green melon liqueur
½	shot(s)	Freshly squeezed lime juice
¼	shot(s)	Sugar syrup (2 sugar to 1 water)

Comment: Bright green, lime and melon with more than a hint of vodka. Do it properly - have a fresh one.

MELON MARTINI #2 (FRESH FRUIT)

Glass: Martini
Garnish: Melon wedge on rim
Method: Cut melon into 8 segments and deseed. Cut cubes of flesh from skin of one segment and MUDDLE in base of shaker. Add other ingredients, SHAKE with ice and fine strain into chilled glass.

⅛	fresh	Cantaloupe melon
2	shot(s)	Ketel One vodka
¼	shot(s)	Sugar syrup (2 sugar to 1 water)

Variant: Substitute Midori melon liqueur for sugar syrup.
Comment: Probably the most popular of all the fresh fruit martinis.

MELONCHOLY MARTINI UPDATED #8

Glass: Martini
Garnish: Pineapple wedge on rim
Method: SHAKE all ingredients with ice and fine strain into chilled glass.

1	shot(s)	**Ketel One vodka**
1	shot(s)	**Midori green melon liqueur**
½	shot(s)	**Cointreau triple sec**
½	shot(s)	**Malibu coconut rum liqueur**
1	shot(s)	**Pressed pineapple juice**
¾	shot(s)	**Double (heavy) cream**
¼	shot(s)	**Freshly squeezed lime juice**

Origin: Created in 2002 by Daniel O'Brien at Ocean Bar, Edinburgh, Scotland.
Comment: A tad on the sweet side, but the flavours in this smooth, tangy, lime-green drink combine surprisingly well.

MENEHUNE JUICE

Glass: Old-fashioned
Garnish: Lime wedge, mint & Menehune
Method: SHAKE all ingredients with ice and strain into glass filled with crushed ice. Serve with straws.

2	shot(s)	**Bacardi Superior rum**
½	shot(s)	**Cointreau triple sec**
¾	shot(s)	**Freshly squeezed lime juice**
¼	shot(s)	**Almond (orgeat) syrup**
¼	shot(s)	**Sugar syrup** (2 sugar to 1 water)

Origin: Adapted from a recipe in the 1947-72 Trader Vic's Bartender's Guide by Victor Bergeron.
Comment: Slightly sweet and strong. According to Vic, "One sip and you may see a Menehune."

MERRY WIDOW #1

Glass: Martini
Garnish: Lemon zest twist
Method: STIR all ingredients with ice and strain into chilled glass.

1½	shot(s)	**Tanqueray London dry gin**
1½	shot(s)	**Noilly Prat dry vermouth**
¼	shot(s)	**La Fée Parisienne (68%) absinthe**
¼	shot(s)	**Bénédictine D.O.M. liqueur**
3	dashes	**Angostura aromatic bitters**
½	shot(s)	**Chilled mineral water** (omit if wet ice)

Origin: Adapted from a recipe in Harry Craddock's 1930 Savoy Cocktail Book.
Comment: Aromatic, complex, strong and bitter.

MERRY WIDOW #2

Glass: Martini
Garnish: Orange zest twist
Method: STIR all ingredients with ice and strain into chilled glass.

1¼	shot(s)	**Ketel One vodka**
1¼	shot(s)	**Dubonnet Red** (French made)
1¼	shot(s)	**Noilly Prat dry vermouth**
1	dash	**Angostura orange bitters**

Comment: Aromatic and complex - for toughened palates.

MESA FRESCA

Glass: Collins
Garnish: Lime slice
Method: SHAKE all ingredients with ice and strain into ice-filled glass.

2	shot(s)	**Don Julio reposado tequila**
3	shot(s)	**Freshly squeezed grapefruit juice**
1	shot(s)	**Freshly squeeezed lime juice**
½	shot(s)	**Sugar syrup** (2 sugar to 1 water)

Origin: Discovered in 2005 at Mesa Grill, New York City, USA.
Comment: Sweet and sour tequila and grapefruit.

MET MANHATTAN

Glass: Martini
Garnish: Orange zest twist
Method: SHAKE all ingredients with ice and fine strain into chilled glass.

2	shot(s)	**Bulleit bourbon whiskey**
1	shot(s)	**Grand Marnier liqueur**
½	shot(s)	**Teichenné butterscotch schnapps**
2	dashes	**Angostura orange bitters**

Origin: The Met Bar, Metropolitan Hotel, London, England.
Comment: Smooth and rounded bourbon with a hint of orange toffee.

METROPOLE UPDATED #8

Glass: Martini
Garnish: Maraschino cherry
Method: STIR all ingredients with ice and strain into chilled glass.

1½	shot(s)	**Courvoisier V.S.O.P. cognac**
1½	shot(s)	**Noilly Prat dry vermouth**
1	dash	**Peychaud aromatic bitters**
1	dash	**Angostura orange bitters**
¼	shot(s)	**Maraschino syrup** (from cherry jar)

Comment: I've added a dash of cherry syrup and changed the proportions of the original overly dry and hard classic recipe.
Origin: Named after The Hotel Metropole, located just off Times Square at 147 West 43rd Street. This was the first hotel in New York City to have running water in every room but had a less than salubrious reputation due to the clientele its all-night licensed street-level Café Metropole attracted. As Albert Stevens Crockett says in his 1935, 'The Old Waldorf Bar Days', "Attributed to a once well known and somewhat lively hotel, whose bar was a long centre of life after dark in the Times Square district."
In the early morning hours of 16th July 1912 Herman Rosenthal, the owner of several New York gambling dens, was murdered as he left Café Metropole (a crime recounted in the story of the Jack Rose). Just one week after the murder, The Hotel Metropole went bankrupt, later to become became the Hotel Rosoff.

METROPOLITAN UPDATED #8

●●●●○○

Glass: Martini
Garnish: Flamed orange twist
Method: SHAKE all ingredients with ice and fine strain into chilled glass.

1	shot(s)	**Raspberry flavoured vodka**
1	shot(s)	**Cointreau triple sec**
1½	shot(s)	**Ocean Spray cranberry juice**
½	shot(s)	**Freshly squeezed lime juice**
¼	shot(s)	**Rose's lime cordial**

Comment: A Cosmo with more than a hint of blackcurrant.
Origin: Created in 1993 by Chuck Coggins at Marion's Continental Restaurant & Lounge, New York City. Marion's was originally opened in 1950 by fashion model Marion Nagy, who came to the States after seeking asylum while swimming for Hungary in the Paris Peace Games after WWII.

> 'YOU CAN'T BE A REAL COUNTRY UNLESS YOU HAVE A BEER AND AN AIRLINE. IT HELPS IF YOU HAVE SOME KIND OF A FOOTBALL TEAM, OR SOME NUCLEAR WEAPONS, BUT AT THE VERY LEAST YOU NEED A BEER.'
> FRANK ZAPPA

MERRY-GO-ROUND MARTINI

●●●●○

Glass: Martini
Garnish: Olive & lemon zest twist
Method: STIR all ingredients with ice and fine strain into chilled glass.

2	shot(s)	**Tanqueray London dry gin**
½	shot(s)	**Noilly Prat dry vermouth**
½	shot(s)	**Martini Rosso sweet vermouth**

Origin: Long lost classic variation on the Dry Martini.
Comment: Stir this 'perfect' Martini around and then get merry.

MEXICAN

●●●●○

Glass: Martini
Garnish: Pineapple wedge on rim
Method: SHAKE all ingredients with ice and fine strain into chilled glass.

2	shot(s)	**Don Julio reposado tequila**
1½	shot(s)	**Pressed pineapple juice**
¼	shot(s)	**Pomegranate (grenadine) syrup**

Variant: Substitute sugar syrup for pomegranate syrup.
Comment: Fresh pineapple makes this drink.

MEXICAN 55 UPDATED #8

●●●●○

Glass: Collins
Garnish: Lime wedge
Method: SHAKE first 4 ingredients with ice and strain into ice-filled glass. **TOP** with champagne.

1½	shot(s)	**Don Julio reposado tequila**
1	shot(s)	**Freshly squeezed lemon juice**
½	shot(s)	**Sugar syrup** (2 sugar to 1 water)
2	dashes	**Angostura aromatic bitters**
Top up with		**Perrier Jouet brut champagne**

Variant: Orange bitters instead of Angostura, as discovered in 2008 at the Experimental Cocktail Club, Paris.
Origin: An adaptation of the classic French '75 created in 1988 at La Perla, Paris, France. The name comes from Fidel Castro's statement that bullets, like wine, came in vintages and Mexican '55 was a good year [for bullets].
Comment: Suitably hard, yet surprisingly refreshing and sophisticated.

MEXICAN COFFEE (HOT)

●●●●○○

Glass: Toddy
Garnish: Three coffee beans
Method: Place bar spoon in glass. **POUR** first 3 ingredients into glass and stir. **FLOAT** cream.

1	shot(s)	**Don Julio reposado tequila**
¼	shot(s)	**Sugar syrup** (2 sugar to 1 water)
Top up with		**Hot filter coffee**
Float		**Double (heavy) cream**

Tip: Lightly whip or simply shake cream in container before pouring over the bowl of a spoon. It also helps if the cream is gently warmed.
Comment: Tequila's answer to the Irish Coffee.

MEXICAN MANHATTAN

●●●●○

Glass: Martini
Garnish: Maraschino cherry
Method: STIR all ingredients with ice and strain into chilled glass.

2	shot(s)	**Don Julio reposado tequila**
1	shot(s)	**Martini Rosso sweet vermouth**
3	dashes	**Angostura aromatic bitters**

Comment: You've tried this with bourbon, now surprise yourself with an aged tequila.

MEXICAN MARTINI NEW #8

●●●●◐

Glass: Martini
Garnish: Jalapeno-stuffed olives
Method: SHAKE all ingredients with ice and fine strain into chilled glass.

2	shot(s)	**Don Julio añejo tequila**
1	shot(s)	**Freshly squeezed lime juice**
½	shot(s)	**Cointreau triple sec**
¼	shot(s)	**Agave syrup**

Comment: Basically a top-shelf Margarita garnished with Jalapeno-stuffed olives.

M

MEXICAN MELON BALL

Glass: Collins
Garnish: Melon balls on stick
Method: Cut melon into 8 segments and deseed. Cut cubes of flesh from skin of one segment and **MUDDLE** in base of shaker. Add other ingredients, **SHAKE** with ice and fine strain into ice-filled glass.

⅛	fresh	**Cantaloupe melon**
2	shot(s)	**Don Julio reposado tequila**
2	shot(s)	**Freshly squeezed orange juice**
¼	shot(s)	**Sugar syrup** (2 sugar to 1 water)

Origin: Adapted from a drink discovered at the Flying V Bar & Grill, Tucson, Arizona, USA.
Comment: Orange and melon laced with tequila.

MEXICANO (HOT)

Glass: Toddy
Garnish: Dust with nutmeg & cinnamon
Method: **POUR** tequila and liqueur into warmed glass and **TOP** with coffee. **FLOAT** cream over drink.

1	shot(s)	**Don Julio reposado tequila**
½	shot(s)	**Grand Marnier liqueur**
Top up with		**Hot filter coffee**
Float		**Double (heavy) cream**

Tip: Lightly whip or simply shake cream in container before pouring over the bowl of a spoon. It also helps if the cream is gently warmed.
Comment: A spicy, flavour-packed hot coffee.

MEXICAN MULE

Glass: Collins
Garnish: Lime wedge
Method: **SHAKE** first 3 ingredients with ice and strain into ice-filled glass. **TOP** with ginger beer, lightly stir and serve with straws.

1½	shot(s)	**Don Julio reposado tequila**
¾	shot(s)	**Freshly squeezed lime juice**
¼	shot(s)	**Sugar syrup** (2 sugar to 1 water)
Top up with		**Ginger beer**

AKA: El Burro
Comment: A tequila based version of the Moscow Mule.

MEXICO CITY

Glass: Coupette
Garnish: Lime wedge on rim
Method: **SHAKE** all ingredients with ice and fine strain into chilled glass.

1½	shot(s)	**Don Julio reposado tequila**
¾	shot(s)	**Grand Marnier liqueur**
½	shot(s)	**Freshly squeezed lime juice**
½	shot(s)	**Ocean Spray cranberry juice**
¼	shot(s)	**Sugar syrup** (2 sugar to 1 water)

Origin: Adapted from a cocktail discovered in 2002 at the Merc Bar, New York City.
Comment: This pinky-red Margarita benefits from a hint of cranberry.

MEXICAN SURFER

Glass: Martini
Garnish: Lime wedge on rim
Method: **SHAKE** all ingredients with ice and fine strain into chilled glass.

2	shot(s)	**Don Julio reposado tequila**
1½	shot(s)	**Pressed pineapple juice**
½	shot(s)	**Rose's lime cordial**

Comment: Frothy topped, easy to make, and all too easy to drink.

MEZCAL MARGARITA NEW #8

Glass: Old-fashioned
Garnish: Lime wedge
Method: **SHAKE** all ingredients with ice and fine strain into ice-filled glass.

2	shot(s)	**Mezcal**
1	shot(s)	**Cointreau triple sec**
1	shot(s)	**Freshly squeezed lime juice**

Comment: A smokin' Margarita.
Origin: Discovered in 2007 at Crazy Homies, London, England.

MEXICAN TEA (HOT)

Glass: Toddy
Garnish: Lime slice
Method: Place bar spoon in warmed glass. **POUR** all ingredients into glass and stir.

2	shot(s)	**Don Julio reposado tequila**
½	shot(s)	**Sugar syrup** (2 sugar to 1 water)
Top up with		**Hot black breakfast tea**

Comment: Tiffin will never be the same again.

MIAMI BEACH

Glass: Martini
Garnish: Pineapple wedge & cherry
Method: **SHAKE** all ingredients with ice and fine strain into chilled glass.

2	shot(s)	**Tanqueray London dry gin**
1½	shot(s)	**Pressed pineapple juice**
¼	shot(s)	**Sugar syrup** (2 sugar to 1 water)

Comment: Fruity and well proportioned – like the babes on Miami Beach. Sorry.

MIAMI DAIQUIRI

Glass: Martini
Garnish: Mint leaf
Method: SHAKE all ingredients with ice and fine strain into chilled glass.

2	shot(s)	**Bacardi Superior rum**
¼	shot(s)	**White crème de menthe liqueur**
½	shot(s)	**Freshly squeezed lime juice**
⅛	shot(s)	**Sugar syrup** (2 sugar to 1 water)
¾	shot(s)	**Chilled mineral water** (omit if wet ice)

Origin: My adaptation of a classic.
Comment: The merest hint of mint in a refreshing Daiquiri with a dry finish.

MICHELADA UPDATED #8

Glass: Beer Mug
Garnish: Lime wedge
Method: STIR first 6 ingredients in bottom of glass. Fill glass with ice and then TOP up with beer.

½	shot(s)	**Freshly squeezed lime juice**
1	dash	**Soy sauce**
2	drops	**Tabasco pepper sauce**
2	dashes	**Worcestershire sauce**
1	pinch	**Celery salt**
1	grind	**Black pepper**
Top up with		**Negra Modelo dark Mexican beer**

AKA: White Mary
Comment: This might be a huge and classic drink in Mexico but it still seems like either a waste of good beer or little improvement to bad beer. Only in this guide due to being something of a classic in its own parts.
Origin: Loosely translated as 'my cold beer', this drink, which is still popular in Mexico, is thought to have originated there sometime in the 1940s. There are many variations of this drink. It is sometimes served without ice and often with light Mexican lager. Even the spicy ingredients vary but the hot pepper sauce is a constant.

MIDNIGHT OVER TENNESSEE UPDATED #8

Glass: Martini
Garnish: Chocolate powder dust
Method: SHAKE first 3 ingredients with ice and fine strain into chilled glass. Separately SHAKE cream and crème de menthe and carefully strain over drink to layer.

2	shot(s)	**Jack Daniel's Tennessee whiskey**
½	shot(s)	**Kahlúa coffee liqueur**
½	shot(s)	**Brown crème de cacao liqueur**
½	shot(s)	**Green crème de menthe liqueur**
½	shot(s)	**Double (heavy) cream**

Origin: Created in 2006 by Leon Edwards at Restaurant Bar & Grill, Manchester, England.
Comment: One of the best dessert cocktails I've tried. Whiskey, coffee and chocolate sipped through a layer of minty cream.

MIKE ROMANOFF NEW #8

Glass: Martini
Garnish: Orange zest twist
Method: SHAKE all ingredients with ice and fine strain into chilled glass.

2	shot(s)	**Ketel One vodka**
⅛	shot(s)	**Cointreau triple sec**
⅛	shot(s)	**Bols apricot brandy liqueur**
¾	shot(s)	**Freshly squeezed lime juice**
¼	shot(s)	**Sugar syrup** (2 sugar to 1 water)

Comment: A Vodka Daisy sweetened with triple sec, apricot brandy and a touch of sugar.
Origin: Michael Romanoff (1890-1971) was a Hollywood impresario. Born Hershel Geguzin in Lithuania he immigrated to New York City aged ten and changed his name to Harry F. Ferguson. He moved to Hollywood where he took on the Michael Romanoff persona, claiming to be born Prince Michael Alexandrovitch Dimitri Obolensky Romanoff, nephew of Tsar Nicholas II. Scotland Yard described the former British and French convict as a "rouge of uncertain nationality." He was another actor in a town of actors and when a filmmaker needed a 'technical adviser' for a movie set in Europe, Romanoff was the obvious well paid expert. He was a popular Hollywood figure and he opened Romanoff's, a Beverly Hills restaurant popular with movie stars in the 1940s and 1950s. Humphrey Bogart was a good friend of Romanoff and a regular at the restaurant. Hollywood legend has it that one day in 1955 Bogie was lunching with Frank Sinatra, Judy Garland and Jimmy Van Heusen when Mrs Bogart, A.K.A. Lauren Bacall walked into the restaurant and on seeing the group exclaimed, "I see the rat pack is all here". Thus Romanoff's became the place where the Rat Pack term was first coined and also where this drink was created.
David Niven was also a close friend and in his book 'Bring on the Empty Horses' he devotes chapter eight, 'The Emperor', to the colourful Romanoff.

MILANO

Glass: Old-fashioned
Garnish: Orange slice
Method: STIR all ingredients with ice and strain into ice-filled glass.

1	shot(s)	**Ketel One vodka**
1	shot(s)	**Campari Bitter**
1	shot(s)	**Martini Rosso sweet vermouth**

AKA: Negrosky
Comment: A Negroni with vodka in place of gin.

MILANO SOUR

Glass: Old-fashioned
Garnish: Lemon slice & cherry on stick (sail)
Method: SHAKE all ingredients with ice and fine strain into ice-filled glass.

1½	shot(s)	**Tanqueray London dry gin**
1	shot(s)	**Galliano L'Autentico liqueur**
1	shot(s)	**Freshly squeezed lemon juice**
½	fresh	**Egg white**

Origin: Created in 2006 by Yours Truly (Simon Difford).
Comment: Delicate anise and peppermint with citrus freshness.

MILK & HONEY

Glass: Martini
Garnish: Grate fresh nutmeg over drink
Method: STIR Scotch with honey in base of shaker
to dissolve honey. Add other ingredients, **SHAKE**
with ice and fine strain into chilled glass.

2	shot(s)	Johnnie Walker Scotch whisky
3	spoons	Runny honey
½	shot(s)	Bärenjäger honey liqueur
¾	shot(s)	Double (heavy) cream
¾	shot(s)	Milk

Origin: Created in 2002 by Yours Truly (Simon Difford).
Comment: The rich flavour of Scotch is tamed by
honey and cream.

MILK PUNCH

Glass: Collins
Garnish: Dust with freshly grated nutmeg
Method: SHAKE all ingredients with ice and strain
into glass filled with crushed ice.

1	shot(s)	Courvoisier V.S.O.P. cognac
½	shot(s)	Goslings Black Seal rum
½	shot(s)	Vanilla sugar syrup
2	shot(s)	Milk
1	shot(s)	Double (heavy) cream

Comment: The cream, vanilla and sugar tame the
cognac and rum.

MILKY MOJITO

Glass: Collins
Garnish: Mint spring
Method: Lightly **MUDDLE** (just to bruise) mint in
glass. Fill glass with crushed ice, add other
ingredients. **TOP** with soda, stir and serve with straws.

12	fresh	Mint leaves
1	shot(s)	Freshly squeezed lime juice
¾	shot(s)	Sugar syrup (2 sugar to 1 water)
2	shot(s)	Pernod anis
Top up with		Soda water (club soda)

Comment: An anise laced alternative to a Mojito.
The name refers to the opaque white colour of the
drink after soda is added to the anis.

THE MILLION DOLLAR COCKTAIL

Glass: Martini
Garnish: Lemon zest twist (round like an egg yolk
in the foam)
Method: SHAKE all ingredients with ice and fine
strain into chilled glass.

2	shot(s)	Tanqueray London dry gin
1	shot(s)	Martini Rosso sweet vermouth
½	shot(s)	Pressed pineapple juice
¼	shot(s)	Pomegranate (grenadine) syrup
½	fresh	Egg white

Origin: This classic cocktail is thought to have been
created around 1910 by Ngiam Tong Boon at The
Long Bar, Raffles Hotel, Singapore. Boon is more
famous for the Singapore Sling.
Comment: Serious, yet superbly smooth and a bit fluffy.

MILLION DOLLAR MARGARITA

Glass: Old-fashioned
Garnish: Lime wedge
Method: SHAKE all ingredients with ice and strain
into ice-filled glass.

1½	shot(s)	Don Julio reposado tequila
1½	shot(s)	Grand Marnier (Cuvée du Centenaire)
½	shot(s)	Freshly squeezed lime juice

Origin: Discovered in 2006 at Maison 140 Hotel,
Los Angeles, USA where I paid a mere $41.14 plus
tip for the drink.
Comment: The proportions of this Margarita
accentuate the liqueur.

MILLIONAIRE UPDATED #8

Glass: Martini
Garnish: Quarter orange slice on rim
Method: SHAKE all ingredients with ice and fine
strain into chilled glass.

2	shot(s)	Rye whiskey (or bourbon)
½	shot(s)	Grand Marnier liqueur
¼	shot(s)	Pomegranate (grenadine) syrup
½	fresh	Egg white

Comment: Whiskey, orange liqueur and
pomegranate. This formula is recorded here due to
its classic status but its not a great drink.
Origin: There are numerous cocktails that go by the
name Millionaire and this particular recipe is
credited to London's Ritz Hotel, sometime pre
1925.

> **'WOE UNTO THEM THAT RISE UP EARLY IN THE MORNING, THAT THEY MAY FOLLOW STRONG DRINK.'**
> ISAIAH 5:11

MILLIONAIRE'S DAIQUIRI

Glass: Martini
Garnish: Star fruit
Method: SHAKE all ingredients with ice and fine
strain into chilled glass.

1¾	shot(s)	Bacardi Superior rum
¾	shot(s)	Sloe gin liqueur
¾	shot(s)	Bols apricot brandy liqueur
¾	shot(s)	Freshly squeezed lime juice
¼	shot(s)	Pomegranate (grenadine) syrup

Origin: This heralds from a classic cocktail known
simply as the Millionaire. Originally sloe gin was the
main base ingredient, but David Embury once
wrote, "Since the sloe gin, which is a liqueur, predominates in this drink, I do not regard it as a true
cocktail." Thus above is my modern adaptation.
Comment: The colour of this cocktail, due to sloe
liqueur and grenadine, belies a surprisingly dry finish.

MILLY MARTINI

Glass: Martini
Garnish: Pineapple wedge on rim
Method: Lightly **MUDDLE** basil (just to bruise) in base of shaker. Add other ingredients, **SHAKE** with ice and fine strain into chilled glass.

5	fresh	Basil leaves
2	shot(s)	Tanqueray London dry gin
2	shot(s)	Pressed pineapple juice
½	shot(s)	Sugar syrup (2 sugar to 1 water)
2	dashes	Angostura orange bitters

Origin: Created in 2003 by Shelim Islam at the GE Club, London, England.
Comment: Gin and pineapple with a pleasing hint of basil.

MILO NEW #8

Glass: Martini
Garnish: Raspberries on stick
Method: SHAKE all ingredients with ice and fine strain into chilled glass.

4	fresh	Raspberries
2	shot(s)	Tanqueray London dry gin
½	shot(s)	Cointreau triple sec
¼	shot(s)	Sugar syrup (2 sugar to 1 water)
1	dash	Peychard aromatic bitters

Origin: Created in 2002 by Tony Conigliaro at Isola, London, England.
Comment: Reminiscent of a Raspberry Cosmopolitan, only drier and stronger.

MIMOSA UPDATED #8

Glass: Flute
Garnish: Orange zest twist
Method: POUR ingredients into chilled glass and gently stir.

½	shot(s)	Grand Marnier liqueur
1¾	shot(s)	Freshly squeezed orange juice
Top up with		Perrier Jouet brut champagne

Variant: When made with mandarin juice this becomes a Puccini.
Origin: Created in 1925 at the Ritz Hotel in Paris and named after the tropical flowering shrub. In his 1948 'Fine Art of Mixing Drinks', David A. Embury writes of this drink, "Just another freak champagne mixture. It is not half bad and the ladies usually like it. Use a good quality domestic champagne, medium dry."
Comment: A liqueur-infused take on the Buck's Fizz.

MINCEMEAT PIE NEW #8

Glass: Martini/Coupette
Garnish: Dust with cinnamon
Method: SHAKE first 3 ingredients with ice and fine strain into chilled glass. FLOAT layer of cream on drink.

2	shot(s)	Zacapa aged rum
1	spoon	Mincemeat
1	shot(s)	Pressed apple juice
½	shot(s)	Double (heavy) cream

Comment: A festive tipple capturing the flavour of that Christmas staple, mince pies.
Origin: Created in 2008 by Bruce Borthwick, Scotland.

MINT & HONEY DAIQUIRI

Glass: Martini
Garnish: Mint sprig
Method: STIR honey and rum in base of shaker until honey dissolves. Add other ingredients, **SHAKE** with ice and fine strain into chilled glass.

2	spoons	Runny honey
2	shot(s)	Bacardi Superior rum
3	fresh	Mint leaves
½	shot(s)	Freshly squeezed lime juice
½	shot(s)	Chilled mineral water (omit if wet ice)

Origin: Created in 2006 by Yours Truly (Simon Difford).
Comment: A fresh-breath-tastic twist on the Daiquiri.

MINT COCKTAIL

Glass: Martini
Garnish: Mint leaf
Method: Lightly **MUDDLE** (just to bruise) mint in base of shaker. Add other ingredients, **SHAKE** with ice and fine strain into chilled glass.

12	fresh	Mint leaves
2	shot(s)	Tanqueray London dry gin
1	shot(s)	Sauvignon Blanc wine
¼	shot(s)	Giffard Menthe Pastille liqueur
¼	shot(s)	Sugar syrup (2 sugar to 1 water)

Origin: Adapted from a recipe in Harry Craddock's 1930 Savoy Cocktail Book.
Comment: A great grassy, minty digestif with a good balance between acidity and sweetness.

MINT COLLINS

Glass: Collins
Garnish: Mint sprig
Method: Lightly **MUDDLE** (just to bruise) mint in base of shaker. Add next 3 ingredients, **SHAKE** with ice and fine strain into chilled glass. **TOP** with soda, lightly stir and serve with straws.

12	fresh	Mint leaves
2	shot(s)	Tanqueray London dry gin
1	shot(s)	Freshly squeezed lemon juice
½	shot(s)	Sugar syrup (2 sugar to 1 water)
Top up with		Soda water (club soda)

Origin: Adapted from a recipe in the 1947-72 Trader Vic's Bartender's Guide by Victor Bergeron.
Comment: Exactly what the name promises.

DRINKS ARE GRADED AS FOLLOWS:

- ● DISGUSTING
- ●○ PRETTY AWFUL
- ●● BEST AVOIDED
- ●●○ DISAPPOINTING
- ●●● ACCEPTABLE
- ●●●○ GOOD
- ●●●● RECOMMENDED
- ●●●●○ HIGHLY RECOMMENDED
- ●●●●● OUTSTANDING / EXCEPTIONAL

MINT DAIQUIRI

Glass: Martini
Garnish: Mint leaf
Method: Lightly **MUDDLE** (just to bruise) mint in base of shaker. Add other ingredients, **SHAKE** with ice and fine strain into chilled glass.

12	fresh	**Mint leaves**
2	shot(s)	**Bacardi Superior rum**
½	shot(s)	**Freshly squeezed lime juice**
¼	shot(s)	**Sugar syrup** (2 sugar to 1 water)
½	shot(s)	**Chilled mineral water** (omit if wet ice)

Origin: Created in 2006 by Yours Truly (Simon Difford).
Comment: A short, concentrated Mojito.

MINT FIZZ

Glass: Collins
Garnish: Mint sprig
Method: Lightly **MUDDLE** mint (just to bruise) in base of shaker. Add other ingredients apart from soda, **SHAKE** with ice and fine strain into ice-filled glass. **TOP** with soda, lightly stir and serve with straws.

7	fresh	**Mint leaves**
2	shot(s)	**Tanqueray London dry gin**
1	shot(s)	**Freshly squeezed lime juice**
¼	shot(s)	**White crème de menthe liqueur**
½	shot(s)	**Sugar syrup** (2 sugar to 1 water)
Top up with		**Soda** (from siphon)

Comment: Long, refreshing citrus and mint fizz.

MINT JULEP

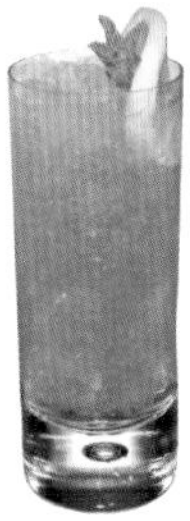

Glass: Collins
Garnish: Mint sprig and slice of lemon
Method: Lightly **MUDDLE** (only bruise) mint in base of shaker. Add other ingredients, **SHAKE** with ice and strain into glass half filled with crushed ice. **CHURN** (stir) the drink with the crushed ice using a bar spoon. Top up the glass with more crushed ice and **CHURN** again. Repeat this process until the drink fills the glass and serve.

12	fresh	**Mint leaves**
2½	shot(s)	**Bulleit bourbon whiskey**
¾	shot(s)	**Sugar syrup** (2 sugar to 1 water)
3	dashes	**Angostura aromatic bitters**

Comment: This superb drink is better if the shaker and its contents are placed in the refrigerator for several hours prior to mixing with ice. This allows the mint flavours to infuse in the bourbon.

MINT JULEP (MEXICAN STYLE) NEW #8

Glass: Old-fashioned
Garnish: Two cherries on stick
Method: **PLACE** lemon zest and mint in shaker. Add other ingredients, **SHAKE** with ice and fine strain into ice-filled glass.

1	twist	**Lemon zest**
8	leaves	**Fresh mint**
1	shot(s)	**Courvoisier V.S.O.P. cognac**
1	shot(s)	**Warre's Otima tawny port**
¼	shot(s)	**Luxardo maraschino liqueur**

Comment: Mint, cognac, port, lemon and maraschino – all subtly contribute to this Cuban take on Mexico.
Origin: Recipe adapted from a 1937 Bar Florida (later renamed Floridita) menu, Havana, Cuba.

MINT LIMEADE (MOCKTAIL)

Glass: Collins
Garnish: Mint sprig
Method: Lightly **MUDDLE** (just to bruise) mint in base of shaker. Add next 3 ingredients, **SHAKE** with ice and fine strain into ice-filled glass. **TOP** with lemonade, lightly stir and serve with straws.

12	fresh	**Mint leaves**
1½	shot(s)	**Freshly squeezed lime juice**
1	shot(s)	**Pressed apple juice**
¾	shot(s)	**Sugar syrup** (2 sugar to 1 water)
Top up with		**Lemonade/Sprite/7-Up**

Origin: Created in 2006 by Yours Truly (Simon Difford).
Comment: Superbly refreshing - mint and lime served long.

MINT MARTINI

Glass: Martini
Garnish: Mint leaf
Method: Lightly **MUDDLE** (just to bruise) mint in base of shaker. Add other ingredients, **SHAKE** with ice and fine strain into chilled glass.

12	fresh	**Mint leaves**
1½	shot(s)	**Ketel One vodka**
½	shot(s)	**Noilly Prat dry vermouth**
¼	shot(s)	**Green crème de menthe liqueur**
1½	shot(s)	**Sauvignon Blanc wine**
¼	shot(s)	**Sugar syrup** (2 sugar to 1 water)

Origin: Created in 2005 by Yours Truly (Simon Difford).
Comment: An after dinner palate cleanser.

HOW TO MAKE SUGAR SYRUP

To make your own sugar syrup, gradually pour TWO cups of granulated sugar into a saucepan containing ONE cup of hot water. Stir as you pour and carry on stirring and simmering until the sugar is dissolved. Do not let the water even come close to boiling and only simmer for as long as it takes to dissolve the sugar. Allow syrup to cool and pour into an empty bottle. Ideally, you should finely strain your syrup into the bottle to remove any undissolved crystals which could otherwise encourage crystallisation. If kept in a refrigerator this mixture will last for a couple of months.

MINT JULEP

A B C D E F G H I J K L **M** N O P Q R S T U V W X Y Z

LE MINUIT UPDATED #8

●●●●○

Glass: Martini
Garnish: Orange zest twist
Method: SHAKE all ingredients with ice and fine strain into chilled glass.

½	shot(s)	La Fée Parisienne (68%) absinthe
1	shot(s)	Sauvignon Blanc wine
1	shot(s)	Pressed apple juice
⅛	shot(s)	Sugar syrup (2 sugar to 1 water)
1	dash	Angostura orange bitters

Comment: Absinthe based but incredibly subtle. Absinthe combines wonderfully with wine and apple.
Origin: Adapted from a drink created in 2001 by Tony Conigliaro at Isola, Knightsbridge, London, England.

LO MISMO NEW #8

Glass: Old-fashioned
Garnish: Lime zest twist
Method: POUR ingredients into ice-filled glass.

| 2 | shot(s) | Bacardi Superior rum |
| Top up with | | Soda water (club soda) |

Comment: Light rum and soda makes for a fabulously subtle and refreshing drink. Don't serve too long or the dilution will kill it.
Origin: The Mismo was a craze said to be started by a group of Americans at the Cosmopolitan Club in Santiago in 1899. When ordering drinks, one of their Cuban colleagues asked for a Bacardi rum and seltzer (soda). His friend, also Cuban, called for 'Lo mismo' – Spanish for 'the same'. Not speaking Spanish, but eager to fit in, the Americans all also asked for 'lo mismos'. The next day, the Americans returned and ordered another round of 'Mismos' from the same barman. The name stuck.
'It spread with remarkable rapidity', reported the New York Tribune soon after. 'Now every barkeeper in Santiago knows what you are after if you ask for a "Mismo".

MISS MARTINI 🗝

●●●●◐○

Glass: Martini
Garnish: Raspberries on stick
Method: MUDDLE raspberries in base of shaker. Add other ingredients, SHAKE with ice and fine strain into chilled glass.

7	fresh	Raspberries
2	shot(s)	Ketel One vodka
½	shot(s)	Chambord black raspberry liqueur
¼	shot(s)	Double (heavy) cream
¼	shot(s)	Milk
⅛	shot(s)	Sugar syrup (2 sugar to 1 water)

Origin: Created in 1997 by Giovanni Burdi at Match EC1, London, England.
Comment: A pink, fruity and creamy concoction.

MISSIONARY'S DOWNFALL

●●●●●

Glass: Collins
Garnish: Mint sprig
Method: Lightly MUDDLE mint (just to bruise) in base of shaker. Add other ingredients, SHAKE with ice and strain into glass filled with crushed ice.

12	fresh	Mint leaves
2	shot(s)	Bacardi Superior rum
½	shot(s)	Peach Tree peach schnapps
1½	shot(s)	Freshly squeezed lime juice
½	shot(s)	Sugar syrup (2 sugar to 1 water)
2	shot(s)	Freshly squeezed pineapple juice

Origin: Created in the 1930s by Don The Beachcomber at his restaurant in Hollywood, California, USA.
Comment: Superbly balanced and refreshing rum, lime, mint and a hint of peach.

MISSISSIPPI PUNCH 🗝

●●●●○

Glass: Collins
Garnish: Lemon slice
Method: SHAKE all ingredients with ice and strain into glass filled with crushed ice.

1½	shot(s)	Bulleit bourbon whiskey
¾	shot(s)	Courvoisier V.S.O.P. cognac
¾	shot(s)	Freshly squeezed lemon juice
1	shot(s)	Sugar syrup (2 sugar to 1 water)
2	shot(s)	Chilled mineral water

Comment: Balanced and refreshing.

MISSISSIPPI SCHNAPPER

●●●●◐○

Glass: Martini
Garnish: Orange zest twist
Method: SHAKE all ingredients with ice and fine strain into chilled glass.

2	shot(s)	Bulleit bourbon whiskey
¾	shot(s)	Peach Tree peach schnapps
½	shot(s)	Cointreau triple sec
¼	shot(s)	Freshly squeezed lime juice
¼	shot(s)	Sugar syrup (2 sugar to 1 water)

Origin: Created in 1999 by Dan Cottle at Velvet, Manchester, England.
Comment: Orange predominates with peach sweetness balanced by whiskey and lime.

MISTER STU

●●●●◐○

Glass: Collins
Garnish: Pineapple wedge on rim
Method: SHAKE all ingredients with ice and strain into ice-filled glass. Serve with straws.

2	shot(s)	Don Julio reposado tequila
½	shot(s)	Luxardo Amaretto di Saschira
½	shot(s)	Malibu coconut rum liqueur
1½	shot(s)	Pressed pineapple juice
1½	shot(s)	Freshly squeezed orange juice

Comment: There's a touch of the disco about this foamy drink, but it is still complex and interesting.

LO MISMO

MITCH MARTINI ●●●●○

Glass: Martini
Garnish: Lemon zest twist
Method: SHAKE all ingredients with ice and fine strain into chilled glass.

2	shot(s)	**Zubrówka bison vodka**
¼	shot(s)	**Peach Tree peach schnapps**
1	shot(s)	**Pressed apple juice**
¼	shot(s)	**Boiron passion fruit syrup**

Origin: Created in 1997 by Giovanni Burdi at Match EC1, London, England.
Comment: One of London's contemporary classics. Far from a proper Martini, this is fruity and sweet, but not overly so.

MOCHA MARTINI ●●●●◐

Glass: Martini
Garnish: Dust with cocoa powder
Method: SHAKE first 4 ingredients with ice and fine strain into chilled glass. **FLOAT** cream in centre of drink.

1½	shot(s)	**Bulleit bourbon whiskey**
1	shot(s)	**Espresso coffee**
½	shot(s)	**Baileys Irish cream liqueur**
½	shot(s)	**Brown crème de cacao liqueur**
½	shot(s)	**Double (heavy) cream**

Comment: Made with great espresso, this drink is a superb, richly flavoured balance of sweet and bitter.

> ### 'LOVE MAKES THE WORLD GO ROUND? NOT AT ALL. WHISKY MAKES IT GO ROUND TWICE AS FAST.'
> #### COMPTON MACKENZIE

MODERNISTA ●●●●○○

Glass: Martini
Garnish: Lemon zest twist
Method: SHAKE all ingredients with ice and fine strain into chilled glass.

2	shot(s)	**Tanqueray London dry gin**
½	shot(s)	**Goslings Black Seal rum**
¼	shot(s)	**Pernod anis**
1	shot(s)	**Swedish Punch**
¼	shot(s)	**Freshly squeezed lemon juice**
1	dash	**Angostura orange bitters**

Origin: Adapted from a drink created by Ted Haigh (AKA Dr. Cocktail) and derived from the 'Modern Cocktail'. See Ted's book, 'Vintage Spirits & Forgotten Cocktails'.
Comment: A massive flavour hit to awaken your taste buds.

MOJITO #1 UPDATED #8 ●●●●●

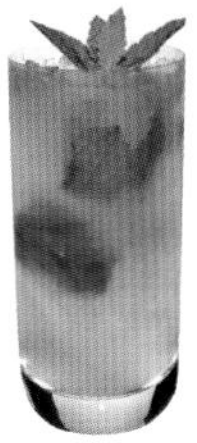

Glass: Collins
Garnish: Mint sprig
Method: Lightly **MUDDLE** mint (just to bruise) in base of glass. Add rum, lime juice and sugar. Half fill glass with crushed ice and **CHURN** (stir) with bar spoon. Fill glass with more crushed ice and **CHURN** some more. **TOP** with soda, stir and serve with straws.

12	fresh	**Mint leaves**
2	shot(s)	**Bacardi Superior rum**
¾	shot(s)	**Freshly squeezed lime juice**
½	shot(s)	**Sugar syrup** (2 sugar to 1 water)
Top up with		**Soda water** (club soda)

Variant: Add two dashes Angostura aromatic bitters
Comment: When well made, this Cuban cousin of the Mint Julep is one of the world's greatest and most refreshing cocktails.
Origin: The exact origins of the Mojito and its name are lost in the mists of time. Some trace it back to 1586 and a medicinal drink named after Sir Francis Drake. He was one of a band of privateers sponsored by England's Queen Elizabeth I to plunder Spanish cities in the New World and seize their riches.

Cuba was under Spanish rule and King Philip II of Spain had warned his governor in Cuba that he believed Drake intended to raid Havana in order to seize the Aztec gold stored in the city's royal treasury. Thus Havana was well defended but there was still surprised relief in the city when, after several days of waiting, Drake sailed away from the richest port in the West Indies after firing only a few shots.

Drake left Havana and its gold intact, but his visit was a major event – something perhaps worthy of naming a drink after. Others say the drink was not originally Cuban and it was actually invented upon board Drake's ship which carried mint to mix with cane spirit, sugar and lime to make a drink to relieve fever and colds.

What is for certain is that the Draque, Drak or Drac was certainly drunk for its perceived medicinal value. During one of the worst cholera epidemics ever to hit Havana, the author Ramon de Paula wrote, "Every day at eleven o' clock I consume a little Drake made from aguardiente (local cane spirit) and I am doing very well."

At some time in the late 1890s the local cane spirit in the Draque was replaced with Bacardi Carta Blanca rum and over the decades the drink started to be made long. This is supported by Frederick Villoch in 1940 "…when aguardiente was replaced with rum, the Drake was to be called a Mojito." However, some still maintain the Mojito was invented after Americans visiting Cuba's thriving bar culture between the wars, and especially during Prohibition, introduced the locals to the Mint Julep.

The origins of the name 'Mojito' are equally misty. Some say it comes from 'mojar', a Spanish verb suggesting wetness. Others claim it comes from the African word 'mojo', meaning spell.
Bodeguita del Medio bar in Havana is by urban myth credited with the first Mojito and this is apparently where Ernest Hemingway went for his. The great man wrote of Cuba's unofficial national drink, "it wasn't just a drink; it was a symbol of national pride."

MOJITO #2 (DIFFORD'S METHOD) UPDATED #8 ●●●●◐

Glass: Collins
Garnish: Mint sprig
Method: SHAKE all ingredients with ice and fine strain into ice-filled glass. **CHURN** (stir) with bar spoon. Fill glass with more crushed ice and **CHURN** some more. Keep adding ice and churning until drink fills glass. Serve with straws.

13	fresh	**Mint leaves**
2½	shot(s)	**Bacardi Superior rum**
¾	shot(s)	**Freshly squeezed lime juice**
½	shot(s)	**Sugar syrup** (2 sugar to 1 water)
⅛	shot(s)	**Giffard Menthe Pastille liqueur**
2	dashes	**Angostura aromatic bitters**

Comment: All the flavour of the Mojito but without unattractive mint leaves trapped in crushed ice. This only works when fresh, cold crushed ice is used. Otherwise the drink will be overly diluted.
Origin: Recipe by Yours Truly (Simon Difford), the man who likes his Mojito shaken and stirred.

MOJITO

MOJITO DE CASA

Glass: Collins
Garnish: Mint sprig
Method: Lightly **MUDDLE** mint (just to bruise) in base of glass. Add tequila, lime juice and sugar. Half fill glass with crushed ice and **CHURN** (stir) with bar spoon. Fill glass with more crushed ice and churn some more. **TOP** with soda, stir and serve.

12	fresh	**Mint leaves**
2	shot(s)	**Don Julio reposado tequila**
¾	shot(s)	**Freshly squeezed lime juice**
½	shot(s)	**Sugar syrup** (2 sugar to 1 water)
Top up with		**Soda water** (club soda)

Origin: Created at Mercadito, New York City, USA.
Comment: A tequila based Mojito.

MOJITO PARISIEN

Glass: Collins
Garnish: Mint sprig
Method: Lightly **MUDDLE** mint (just to bruise) in base of glass. Add other ingredients, half fill glass with crushed ice and **CHURN** (stir) with bar spoon. Fill glass to brim with more crushed ice and churn some more. Serve with straws.

12	fresh	**Mint leaves**
2	shot(s)	**Bacardi Superior rum**
1½	shot(s)	**St-Germain elderflower liqueur**
1	shot(s)	**Freshly squeezed lime juice**

Origin: Recipe in 2006 by Yours Truly (Simon Difford).
Comment: Those with a sweet tooth may want to add a dash of sugar syrup to taste.

MOLOTOV COCKTAIL

Glass: Martini
Garnish: Lemon zest
Method: **SHAKE** all ingredients with ice and fine strain into chilled glass.

1½	shot(s)	**Lime flavoured vodka**
1¼	shot(s)	**Parfait Amour liqueur**
½	shot(s)	**Freshly squeezed lemon juice**
½	shot(s)	**Opal Nera black sambuca**

Origin: Created after a visit to the Rajamäki distillery in Finland. At the start of the Second World War the plant was used to produce Molotov cocktails, inflammatory bombs with which the Finns put hundreds of Soviet tanks out of action.
Comment: The ingredients represent the four liquids used in the weapon. Vodka, stands for alcohol, parfait amour shares the purple hue of paraffin, lemon juice represents gasoline and black sambuca replaces tar.

LA MOMIE

Glass: Shot
Method: **POUR** pastis into chilled glass and **TOP** with chilled water.

| ½ | shot(s) | **Ricard pastis** |
| Top up with | | **Chilled water** |

Origin: Pronounced 'Mom-Ee', this shot is very popular in the South of France.

MOMISETTE

Glass: Collins (10oz max)
Method: **POUR** pastis and almond syrup into glass. Serve with bottle of sparkling water so the customer can dilute to their own taste. (I recommend five shots.) Lastly, add ice to fill glass.

1	shot(s)	**Ricard pastis**
¼	shot(s)	**Almond (orgeat) syrup**
Top up with		**Sparkling mineral water**

Origin: A traditional French drink, the name of which literally translates as 'tiny mummy'.
Comment: Complex balance of almond and liquorice.

MOMO SPECIAL

Glass: Collins
Garnish: Mint sprig
Method: Lightly **MUDDLE** mint (just to bruise) in base of shaker. Add next 3 ingredients, **SHAKE** with ice and strain into ice-filled glass. **TOP** with soda, lightly stir and serve with straws.

12	fresh	**Mint leaves**
2	shot(s)	**Ketel One vodka**
½	shot(s)	**Freshly squeezed lime juice**
½	shot(s)	**Sugar syrup** (2 sugar to 1 water)
Top up with		**Soda water** (club soda)

Origin: Created in 1998 by Simon Mainoo at Momo, London, England.
Comment: Enrich the minty flavour by macerating the mint in the vodka some hours before making.

MONA LISA

Glass: Collins
Garnish: Orange slice
Method: **SHAKE** first 3 ingredients with ice and strain into ice-filled glass. **TOP** with tonic water.

1	shot(s)	**Green Chartreuse liqueur**
3	shot(s)	**Freshly squeezed orange juice**
2	dashes	**Angostura aromatic bitters**
Top up with		**Tonic water**

Comment: Chartreuse fans will appreciate this drink, which is also an approachable way for novices to acquire a taste for the green stuff.

MONARCH MARTINI

Glass: Martini
Garnish: Lemon zest twist
Method: Lightly **MUDDLE** mint (just to bruise) in base of shaker. Add other ingredients, **SHAKE** with ice and fine strain into chilled glass.

7	fresh	**Mint leaves**
2	shot(s)	**Tanqueray London dry gin**
½	shot(s)	**St-Germain elderflower liqueur**
½	shot(s)	**Freshly squeezed lemon juice**
¼	shot(s)	**Sugar syrup** (2 sugar to 1 water)
2	dashes	**Fee Brothers peach bitters**

Origin: Adapted from a drink created in 2003 by Douglas Ankrah at Townhouse, London, England.
Comment: Wonderfully floral and minty – worthy of a right royal drinker.

MONKEY GLAND #1

Glass: Martini
Garnish: Orange zest twist
Method: SHAKE all ingredients with ice and fine strain into chilled glass.

2	shot(s)	**Tanqueray London dry gin**
¼	shot(s)	**La Fée Parisienne (68%) absinthe**
1½	shot(s)	**Freshly squeezed orange juice**
¼	shot(s)	**Pomegranate (grenadine) syrup**

Origin: Created in the 1920s by Harry MacElhone at his Harry's New York Bar in Paris. The Monkey Gland takes its name from the work of Dr Serge Voronoff, who attempted to delay the ageing process by transplanting monkey testicles.
Comment: Approach with caution. Due diligence reveals a dangerous base of gin and absinthe.

MONKEY GLAND #2

Glass: Old-fashioned
Garnish: Orange slice
Method: SHAKE all ingredients with ice and strain into ice-filled glass.

2	shot(s)	**Tanqueray London dry gin**
1¼	shot(s)	**Freshly squeezed orange juice**
½	shot(s)	**Bénédictine D.O.M. liqueur**
¼	shot(s)	**Pomegranate (grenadine) syrup**

Comment: A somewhat off-putting name for a very palatable cocktail.

MONKEY SHINE

Glass: Martini
Garnish: Cinnamon rim
Method: SHAKE all ingredients with ice and fine strain into chilled glass.

2	shot(s)	**Bacardi Oro golden rum**
1	shot(s)	**Malibu coconut rum liqueur**
1	shot(s)	**Pressed pineapple juice**

Origin: An adaptation of a drink discovered in 2003 at the Bellagio Resort & Casino, Las Vegas.
Comment: The sweet, tropical fruitiness of this drink is set off by the spicy rim.

MONKEY WRENCH

Glass: Collins
Method: POUR rum into ice-filled glass. Top with grapefruit juice, stir and serve with straws.

2	shot(s)	**Bacardi Oro golden rum**
Top up with		**Freshly squeezed grapefruit juice**

Comment: Simple but pleasant.

MONK'S CANDY BAR

Glass: Martini
Garnish: Sprinkle with nutmeg
Method: SHAKE all ingredients with ice and fine strain into chilled glass.

1	shot(s)	**Frangelico hazelnut liqueur**
½	shot(s)	**Teichenné butterscotch schnapps**
½	shot(s)	**Kahlúa coffee liqueur**
1	shot(s)	**Double (heavy) cream**
1	shot(s)	**Milk**

Comment: Creamy and sweet, with hazelnut, butterscotch and coffee.

MONK'S HABIT

Glass: Collins
Garnish: Orange slice
Method: SHAKE all ingredients with ice and strain into ice-filled glass.

1½	shot(s)	**Bacardi Superior rum**
½	shot(s)	**Cointreau triple sec**
1	shot(s)	**Frangelico hazelnut liqueur**
3	shot(s)	**Pressed pineapple juice**
¼	shot(s)	**Pomegranate (grenadine) syrup**

Comment: Fruit and nut laced with rum. Slightly sweet.

MONTE CARLO #1

Glass: Collins
Garnish: Maraschino cherry
Method: POUR first 3 ingredients into empty glass. **ADD** soda water to half fill glass. Fill glass with ice and then **TOP** with more soda. (This avoids 'shocking' the anis with the ice.) Serve with straws.

1	shot(s)	**Pernod anis**
½	shot(s)	**Luxardo maraschino liqueur**
¾	shot(s)	**Freshly squeezed lime juice**
Top up with		**Soda water** (club soda)

Origin: An adaptation of a Martini style drink created in 2002 by Alex Turner, London, England.
Comment: A long, fragrant, almost floral summer cooler with lots of aniseed.

MONTE CARLO #2 (AMERICAN VERSION) NEW #8

Glass: Coupette/Martini
Garnish: Lemon zest twist
Method: STIR all ingredients with ice and strain into chilled glass.

2¼	shot(s)	**Bulleit bourbon whiskey**
¾	shot(s)	**Bénédictine D.O.M. liqueur**
2	dashes	**Angostura aromatic bitters**

Comment: Spiced bourbon.

MONTE CARLO IMPERIAL

Glass: Martini
Garnish: Mint leaf
Method: SHAKE first 3 ingredients with ice and fine strain into chilled glass. **TOP** with champagne.

1½	shot(s)	Tanqueray London dry gin
½	shot(s)	Freshly squeezed lemon juice
½	shot(s)	Giffard Menthe Pastille liqueur
Top up with		Perrier Jouet brut champagne

Origin: Adapted from a recipe in Harry Craddock's 1930 Savoy Cocktail Book.
Comment: A classic, minty digestif.

MONTEGO BAY

Glass: Old-fashioned
Garnish: Lime wedge
Method: SHAKE all ingredients with ice and strain into ice-filled glass.

1½	shot(s)	Martinique agricole rum
½	shot(s)	Freshly squeezed lime juice
½	shot(s)	Cointreau triple sec
¼	shot(s)	Sugar syrup (2 sugar to 1 water)
2	dashes	Angostura aromatic bitters

Origin: Adapted from a recipe in the 1947-72 Trader Vic's Bartender's Guide by Victor Bergeron.
Comment: The name suggests Jamaica but the recipe requires agricole rum. This pungent style of rum is not Jamaican.

THE MONTFORD NEW #8

Glass: Coupette/Martini
Garnish: Lemon zest twist
Method: STIR all ingredients with ice and fine strain into chilled glass.

2	shot(s)	Tanqueray London dry gin
¾	shot(s)	Lillet Blanc
½	shot(s)	Noilly Ambre vermouth
2	dashes	Angostura orange bitters

Comment: A wonderfully wet Martini with the addition of Lillet and orange bitters.
Origin: Adapted from a drink created by Dan Warner at the Beefeater Distillery, London, England.

THE MONTGOMERY MARTINI NEW #8

Glass: Martini/Coupette
Garnish: Lemon zest twist
Method: STIR all ingredients with ice and fine strain into chilled glass.

2	shot(s)	Tanqueray London dry gin
⅛	shot(s)	Noilly Prat dry vermouth
1	dashes	Angostura orange bitters

Comment: Bone dry – a superbly cleansing Martini.
Origin: Unknown but this 15:1 gin to vermouth Martini was said to be Ernest Hemingway's favourite formula and is named after British Field Marshall Bernard Montgomery, who it is said, liked the gin in his Martini to outnumber the vermouth in roughly the same ratio as he liked to outnumber his opponents in battle.

MONZA

Glass: Collins
Garnish: Slice of apple
Method: Cut passion fruit in half and scoop flesh into shaker. Add other ingredients, **SHAKE** with ice and strain into ice-filled glass.

1	fresh	Passion fruit
2	shot(s)	Ketel One vodka
2	shot(s)	Campari Bitter
2	shot(s)	Pressed apple juice
¼	shot(s)	Sugar syrup (2 sugar to 1 water)

Origin: A classic cocktail promoted by Campari and named after the Italian Grand Prix circuit.
Comment: If you like Campari you'll love this.

MOOD INDIGO

Glass: Martini
Garnish: Violet blossom or mint sprig
Method: SHAKE all ingredients with ice and fine strain into chilled glass.

1½	shot(s)	Tanqueray London dry gin
½	shot(s)	Courvoisier V.S.O.P. cognac
½	shot(s)	Benoit Serres crème de violette
½	fresh	Egg white
⅛	shot(s)	Sugar syrup (2 sugar to 1 water)
½	shot(s)	Chilled mineral water (omit if wet ice)

Origin: Named after the jazz standard that was a hit for Nat King Cole.
Comment: Smooth, delicate and floral: the gin and brandy add just enough bite.

MOONDREAM NEW #8

Glass: Coupette/Martini
Garnish: Peach slice on rim
Method: STIR all ingredients with ice and strain into chilled glass.

3	shot(s)	Tanqueray London dry gin
1	shot(s)	Manzanilla sherry
¼	shot(s)	Crème pêche de vigne liqueur
¼	shot(s)	Noilly Prat dry vermouth

Origin: Created in 2007 by Thomas Waugh at Alembic, San Francisco, USA.
Comment: Also try with subtle styles of dry vermouth such as Dolin.

THE MOONLIGHT COCKTAIL NEW #8

Glass: Martini
Garnish: Orange zest twist
Method: SHAKE all ingredients with ice and fine strain into chilled glass.

1½	shot(s)	Tanqueray London dry gin
½	shot(s)	Cointreau triple sec
½	shot(s)	Benoit Serres crème de violette
½	shot(s)	Freshly squeezed lime juice
½	shot(s)	Chilled water (omit if wet ice)

Comment: A twist on the classic Aviation. This drink benefits from the optional addition of water.
Origin: Created in 2008 by Gary Regan, New York, USA. First published in his San Francisco Conical column.

MOONLIGHT MARTINI

Glass: Martini
Garnish: Lemon zest twist
Method: SHAKE all ingredients with ice and fine strain into chilled glass.

1½	shot(s)	Tanqueray London dry gin
¼	shot(s)	Kirschwasser eau de vie
1	shot(s)	Sauvignon Blanc wine
1¼	shot(s)	Freshly squeezed grapefruit juice

Origin: Adapted from a recipe in Harry Craddock's 1930 Savoy Cocktail Book.
Comment: Craddock describes this as "a very dry cocktail". It is, but pleasantly so.

MOONRAKER

Glass: Martini
Garnish: Maraschino cherry
Method: SHAKE all ingredients with ice and fine strain into chilled glass.

1½	shot(s)	Courvoisier V.S.O.P. cognac
1½	shot(s)	Dubonnet red (French made)
¾	shot(s)	Peach Tree peach schnapps
¼	shot(s)	Pernod anis

Origin: Adapted from a recipe in the 1947-72 Trader Vic's Bartender's Guide by Victor Bergeron.
Comment: A diverse range of flavours come together surprisingly well.

MOONSHINE MARTINI

Glass: Martini
Garnish: Maraschino cherry
Method: SHAKE all ingredients with ice and fine strain into chilled glass.

1½	shot(s)	Tanqueray London dry gin
1	shot(s)	Noilly Prat dry vermouth
½	shot(s)	Luxardo maraschino liqueur
⅛	shot(s)	La Fée Parisienne (68%) absinthe

Origin: Adapted from a recipe in the 1930 Savoy Cocktail Book by Harry Craddock.
Comment: A wet Martini with balanced hints of maraschino and absinthe.

MOON RIVER

Glass: Martini
Garnish: Mint leaf
Method: SHAKE all ingredients with ice and fine strain into chilled glass.

1½	shot(s)	Tanqueray London dry gin
½	shot(s)	Bols apricot brandy liqueur
½	shot(s)	Cointreau triple sec
¼	shot(s)	Galliano L'Autentico liqueur
½	shot(s)	Freshly squeezed lemon juice
½	shot(s)	Chilled mineral water (omit if wet ice)

Origin: Adapted from a drink discovered in 2005 at Bar Opiume, Singapore.
Comment: There's a hint of aniseed in this fruity, sweet and sour drink.

MORAVIAN COCKTAIL

Glass: Old-fashioned
Garnish: Orange slice & cherry on stick (sail)
Method: SHAKE all ingredients with ice and strain into ice-filled glass.

¾	shot(s)	Slivovitz plum brandy
¾	shot(s)	Becherovka liqueur
1½	shot(s)	Martini Rosso sweet vermouth

Origin: Discovered in 2005 at Be Bop Bar, Prague, Czech Republic.
Comment: The Czech answer to the Italian Negroni.

MORNING GLORY

Glass: Old-fashioned
Garnish: Lemon zest twist
Method: SHAKE all ingredients with ice and strain into ice-filled glass.

1	shot(s)	Courvoisier V.S.O.P. cognac
¾	shot(s)	Grand Marnier liqueur
⅛	shot(s)	La Fée Parisienne (68%) absinthe
½	shot(s)	Freshly squeezed lemon juice
¼	shot(s)	Sugar syrup (2 sugar to 1 water)
2	dashes	Angostura aromatic bitters
½	shot(s)	Chilled mineral water (omit if wet ice)

Origin: My interpretation of a classic.
Comment: Sophisticated and complex – one for sipping.

MORNING GLORY FIZZ UPDATED #8

Glass: Collins (small max 8oz)
Garnish: Lime slice
Method: Vigorously SHAKE first 6 ingredients with ice and strain into chilled glass (without ice). TOP with soda water from a siphon.

2	shot(s)	Johnnie Walker Scotch whisky
¾	shot(s)	Freshly squeezed lemon juice
½	shot(s)	Sugar syrup (2 sugar to 1 water)
½	fresh	Egg white
1/16	shot(s)	La Fée Parisienne 68% absinthe
Top up with		Soda water (from a siphon)

Comment: This classic, sour and aromatic cocktail is traditionally considered a morning after pick-me-up.
Origin: Recipe adapted from George Kappeler's 1895 'Modern American Drinks'.

MOSCOW LASSI

Glass: Collins
Garnish: Cucumber slices
Method: MUDDLE cucumber in base of shaker. Add other ingredients. SHAKE with ice and fine strain into ice-filled glass.

2	inches	Cucumber (peeled & chopped)
1	shot(s)	Boiron mango purée
1½	shot(s)	Ketel One vodka
2	shot(s)	Pressed apple juice
3	spoons	Natural yoghurt
¼	shot(s)	Sugar syrup (2 sugar to 1 water)

Origin: Created in 2001 by Jamie Stephenson at Gaucho Grill, Manchester, England.
Comment: One to serve with your Indian takeaway.

MOSCOW MULE UPDATED #8

Glass: Collins (or copper mug)
Garnish: Lime wedge & mint sprig
Method: SHAKE first 4 ingredients with ice and strain into ice-filled glass. **TOP** with ginger beer and stir.

2	shot(s)	**Ketel One vodka**
½	shot(s)	**Freshly squeezed lime juice**
3	dashes	**Angostura aromatic bitters**
Top up with		**Ginger beer**

Comment: A long, vodka based drink with spice provided by ginger beer and Angostura.
Origin: This classic combination was born in 1941. John G. Martin had acquired the rights to Smirnoff vodka for Heublein, a small Connecticut based liquor and food distributor. Jack Morgan, the owner of Hollywood's famous Cock'n'Bull Saloon, was trying to launch his own brand of ginger beer. The two men met at New York City's Chatham Bar and hit on the idea of mixing Martin's vodka with Morgan's ginger beer and adding a dash of lime to create a new cocktail, the Moscow Mule.
To help promote the drink, and hence their respective products, Morgan had the idea of marketing the Moscow Mule using specially engraved mugs. The five ounce mugs were embossed with a kicking mule and made at a copper factory a friend of his had recently inherited. The promotion helped turn Smirnoff into a major brand.

MOTOX

Glass: Martini
Garnish: Coriander leaf
Method: MUDDLE ginger and coriander in base of shaker. Add other ingredients, **SHAKE** with ice and fine strain into chilled glass.

1	slice	**Fresh root ginger** (thumbnail sized)
10	fresh	**Coriander leaves**
1½	shot(s)	**Ketel One Citroen vodka**
½	shot(s)	**Luxardo limoncello liqueur**
1	shot(s)	**Pressed pineapple juice**
1	shot(s)	**Pressed apple juice**

Origin: Adapted from a drink discovered in 2005 at Mo Bar, Landmark Mandarin Oriental Hotel, Hong Kong.
Comment: Each sip is fruity, lemon fresh and followed by a hot ginger hit.

MOUNTAIN

Glass: Martini
Garnish: Maraschino cherry
Method: SHAKE all ingredients with ice and fine strain into chilled glass.

2	shot(s)	**Bulleit bourbon whiskey**
¾	shot(s)	**Noilly Prat dry vermouth**
¾	shot(s)	**Martini Rosso sweet vermouth**
½	fresh	**Egg white**

Comment: A perfect Manhattan smoothed by egg white.

MOSQUITO NEW #8

Glass: Old-fashioned
Garnish: Mint sprig
Method: SHAKE all ingredients with ice and fine strain into ice-filled glass.

6	fresh	**Mint leaves**
2	shot(s)	**Quebranta pisco**
1	shot(s)	**Freshly squeezed lime juice**
¾	shot(s)	**Sugar syrup** (2 sugar to 1 water)

Comment: A short pisco based Mojito.
Origin: Adapted from a 2008 recipe created by Hans Hilburg at El Pisquerito, Cuzco, Peru.

MOUNTAIN COCKTAIL UPDATED #8

Glass: Martini
Garnish: Maraschino cherry
Method: SHAKE all ingredients with ice and fine strain into chilled glass.

1½	shot(s)	**Bulleit bourbon whiskey**
½	shot(s)	**Noilly Prat dry vermouth**
½	shot(s)	**Martini Rosso sweet vermouth**
½	shot(s)	**Freshly squeezed lemon juice**
½	fresh	**Egg white**

Comment: Bone dry – I prefer with the addition of half spoon sugar syrup.
Origin: This vintage cocktail is thought to have been originally made at New York's Hoffman House.

MOTHER RUM

Glass: Old-fashioned
Garnish: Cinnamon stick
Method: STIR all ingredients with ice and strain into ice-filled glass.

2	shot(s)	**Zacapa aged rum**
¼	shot(s)	**White crème de cacao liqueur**
¼	shot(s)	**Maple syrup**

Origin: Created in 2006 by Milo Rodriguez at Crazy Bear, London, England.
Comment: To quote Milo, this drink "is warm and comforting, just like the drinks my mother made."

MOUNTAIN SIPPER

Glass: Old-fashioned
Garnish: Orange zest twist
Method: SHAKE all ingredients with ice and strain into ice-filled glass.

2	shot(s)	**Bulleit bourbon whiskey**
1	shot(s)	**Cointreau triple sec**
1	shot(s)	**Ocean Spray cranberry juice**
1	shot(s)	**Freshly squeezed grapefruit juice**
⅛	shot(s)	**Sugar syrup** (2 sugar to 1 water)

Comment: Fruity citrus flavours balance the richness of the whiskey.

MOSCOW MULE

MRS ROBINSON #1

●●●●○

Glass: Old-fashioned
Garnish: Three raspberries
Method: **MUDDLE** raspberries in base of shaker. Add next 4 ingredients, **SHAKE** with ice and strain into ice-filled glass. **TOP** with soda, lightly stir and serve with straws.

8	fresh	**Raspberries**
2	shot(s)	**Bulleit bourbon whiskey**
1	shot(s)	**Crème de framboise liqueur**
¼	shot(s)	**Freshly squeezed lemon juice**
¼	shot(s)	**Sugar syrup** (2 sugar to 1 water)
Top up with		**Soda water** (club soda)

Origin: Created in 2000 by Max Warner at Long Bar, Sanderson, London, England.
Comment: Rich raspberry fruit laced with bourbon.

MRS. ROBINSON #2

●●●○○

Glass: Martini
Garnish: Quarter orange slice on rim
Method: **SHAKE** all ingredients with ice and fine strain into chilled glass.

2½	shot(s)	**Ketel One Vodka**
1	shot(s)	**Freshly squeezed orange juice**
½	shot(s)	**Galliano L'Autentico liqueur**

Origin: Discovered in 2006 on Kyle Branch's Cocktail Hotel blog. (www.cocktailhotel.blogspot.com).
Comment: A short Harvey Wallbanger.

MUCKY BOTTOM

●●●○○

Glass: Collins
Method: **SHAKE** first 3 ingredients with ice and strain into ice-filled glass. **POUR** coffee liqueur around top of drink - this will fall to the base of the glass and create the mucky bottom.

2	shot(s)	**Malibu coconut rum liqueur**
1	shot(s)	**Pernod anis**
3	shot(s)	**Freshly squeezed grapefruit juice**
¾	shot(s)	**Kahlúa coffee liqueur**

Origin: Created in 2003 by Yours Truly (Simon Difford). This was formerly and more tastefully named Red Haze.
Comment: Four very strong and distinctive flavours somehow tone each other down.

MUDDY WATER

●●●○○

Glass: Old-fashioned
Garnish: Float 3 coffee beans
Method: **SHAKE** all ingredients with ice and strain into ice-filled glass.

1	shot(s)	**Ketel One vodka**
1	shot(s)	**Kahlúa coffee liqueur**
1	shot(s)	**Baileys Irish cream liqueur**

Comment: Coffee and whiskey cream with added vodka.

MUDSLIDE

●●●●○

Glass: Hurricane
Garnish: Crumbled Cadbury's Flake bar
Method: **BLEND** all ingredients with two 12oz scoops of crushed ice and serve with straws.

1½	shot(s)	**Baileys Irish cream liqueur**
1½	shot(s)	**Kahlúa coffee liqueur**
1½	shot(s)	**Ketel One vodka**
3	scoops	**Häagen Dazs vanilla ice cream**

Comment: A simply scrumptious dessert drink with whiskey cream and coffee.

CAPTAIN RUSSELL ORDERS A BACARDI RUM AND COCA-COLA WITH A SQUEEZE OF LIME IN THE AMERICAN BAR, HAVANA, CUBA IN 1900. FREE CUBA!

MUJER VERDE

●●●●○

Glass: Martini
Garnish: Lime zest twist
Method: **SHAKE** all ingredients with ice and fine strain into chilled glass.

1	shot(s)	**Tanqueray London dry gin**
½	shot(s)	**Green Chartreuse liqueur**
½	shot(s)	**Yellow Chartreuse liqueur**
½	shot(s)	**Freshly squeezed lime juice**
¼	shot(s)	**Sugar syrup** (2 sugar to 1 water)
¾	shot(s)	**Chilled mineral water** (omit if wet ice)

Origin: Discovered in 2006 at Absinthe, San Francisco, where 'D Mexican' resurrected this drink from his hometown of Guadalajara.
Comment: The name means 'Green Lady'... and she packs a Chartreuse punch.

MULATA DAIQUIRI UPDATED #8

●●●●○

Glass: Martini
Garnish: Lime wedge on rim
Method: **SHAKE** all ingredients with ice and fine strain into chilled glass.

2	shot(s)	**Zacapa aged rum**
½	shot(s)	**Brown crème de cacao liqueur**
¼	shot(s)	**White crème de cacao liqueur**
½	shot(s)	**Freshly squeezed lime juice**

Variation: Blended with crushed ice.
Comment: A classic Daiquiri with aged rum and a hint of chocolate.
Origin: Thought to have been created by Constantino (Constante) Ribalaigua Vert at Havana's Floridita bar but in the Cuban book, 'Bartender's Sixth Sense' the cocktail is said to have been created in the 1940s by one Jose Maria Vazquez.

MULATA DAISY NEW #8

●●●●○

Glass: Coupette/Martini
Garnish: Dust with cocoa powder
Method: **MUDDLE** fennel seeds in base of shaker. Add other ingredients, **SHAKE** with ice and fine strain into chilled glass.

1½	spoon	Fennel seeds
1¾	shot(s)	Bacardi Superior rum
¾	shot(s)	Brown crème de cacao liqueur
½	shot(s)	Freshly squeezed lime juice
⅛	shot(s)	Galliano L'Autentico liqueur

Comment: Delicately spiced and subtly chocolaty.
Origin: Created in 2008 by Ago Perrone, The Connaught, London.

MULE'S HIND LEG

●●●●◐

Glass: Martini
Garnish: Apricot slice on rim
Method: **SHAKE** all ingredients with ice and fine strain into chilled glass.

1	shot(s)	Tanqueray London dry gin
1	shot(s)	Bénédictine D.O.M. liqueur
1	shot(s)	Boulard Grand Solage calvados
¼	shot(s)	Maple syrup
¾	shot(s)	Bols apricot brandy liqueur
½	shot(s)	Chilled mineral water (omit if wet ice)

Origin: My version of a classic 1920s recipe.
Comment: Apricot and maple syrup dominate this medium sweet drink.

MULLED WINE

●●●●○

Glass: Toddy
Garnish: Cinnamon stick
Method: **MUDDLE** cloves in base of mixing glass. Add rest of ingredients apart from boiling water, **STIR** and fine strain into warmed glass. **TOP** with boiling water and **STIR**.

5	dried	Cloves
1	pinch	Freshly grated nutmeg
1	pinch	Ground cinnamon
1½	shot(s)	Warre's Otima tawny port
1½	shot(s)	Shiraz red wine
¼	shot(s)	Grand Marnier liqueur
½	shot(s)	Freshly squeezed lemon juice
Top up with		Boiling water

Variant: Better if several servings are made and the ingredients warmed in a saucepan.
Comment: Warming, soothing and potent.

MYRTLE BANK SPECIAL RUM PUNCH NEW #8

●●●●◐

Glass: Old-fashioned
Garnish: Maraschino cherry
Method: **SHAKE** all ingredients with ice and strain into ice-filled glass.

2	shot(s)	Myer's dark Jamaican rum
1	shot(s)	Freshly squeezed lime juice
½	shot(s)	Sugar syrup (2 sugar to 1 water)
⅛	shot(s)	Heering cherry brandy liqueur
½	shot(s)	Chilled water (omit if wet ice)

Comment: A rich fruity Daiquiri with tangy molasses
Origin: Originally made at the Myrtle Bank Hotel, Kingston, Jamaica. Built in the mid-1800s, the Myrtle Bank, was converted from a shipyard but after the hotel was destroyed in the 1907 earthquake it was reconstructed in 1918 and was then the largest hotel in Jamaica with 205 rooms and a salt water pool.

MYRTLE MARTINI

●●●◐○

Glass: Martini
Garnish: Sugar rim
Method: **SHAKE** all ingredients with ice and fine strain into chilled glass.

2	shot(s)	Ketel One vodka
½	shot(s)	Crème de myrtille liqueur
2	shot(s)	Pressed apple juice
¼	shot(s)	Sugar syrup (2 sugar to 1 water)
¼	shot(s)	Freshly squeezed lime juice

Origin: Created in 2003 at Cheyne Walk Brasserie & Salon, London, England.
Comment: A fruity concoction to remember should you find yourself with a bottle of crème de myrtille.

MYSTIQUE UPDATED #8

●●●◐○

Glass: Martini
Garnish: Raspberries on stick
Method: **SHAKE** all ingredients with ice and fine strain into chilled glass.

2	shot(s)	Johnnie Walker Scotch whisky
1	shot(s)	Tuaca Italian liqueur
½	shot(s)	Chambord black raspberry liqueur

Comment: Rust coloured and fruit charged. Not the sweetie you might expect.
Origin: Created in 2002 by Tim Halilaj, Albania.

NACIONAL DAIQUIRI #1

●●●●◐

Glass: Martini
Garnish: Maraschino cherry
Method: **SHAKE** all ingredients with ice and fine strain into chilled glass.

2	shot(s)	Bacardi Superior rum
¾	shot(s)	Bols apricot brandy liqueur
½	shot(s)	Freshly squeezed lime juice
¾	shot(s)	Chilled mineral water (omit if wet ice)

Origin: An old classic named after the Hotel Nacional, Havana, Cuba, where it was created.
Comment: A sophisticated complex apricot Daiquiri.

NACIONAL DAIQUIRI #2 🗝

Glass: Martini
Garnish: Maraschino cherry
Method: SHAKE all ingredients with ice and fine strain into chilled glass.

2	shot(s)	**Bacardi Superior rum**
½	shot(s)	**Bols apricot brandy liqueur**
1½	shot(s)	**Pressed pineapple juice**
½	shot(s)	**Freshly squeezed lime juice**

Comment: An apricot Daiquiri with extra interest courtesy of pineapple.

NANTUCKET 🗝

Glass: Collins
Garnish: Lime wedge
Method: SHAKE all ingredients with ice and strain into ice-filled glass.

2	shot(s)	**Bacardi Superior rum**
3	shot(s)	**Ocean Spray cranberry juice**
2	shot(s)	**Freshly squeezed grapefruit juice**

Origin: Popularised by the Cheers bar chain, this is named after the beautiful island off Cape Cod.
Comment: Essentially a Seabreeze with rum in place of vodka.

NAPOLEON MARTINI

Glass: Martini
Garnish: Lemon peel twist
Method: SHAKE all ingredients with ice and fine strain into chilled glass.

2	shot(s)	**Tanqueray London dry gin**
¼	shot(s)	**Cointreau triple sec**
½	shot(s)	**Dubonnet Red** (French made)
¼	shot(s)	**Fernet Branca**
½	shot(s)	**Chilled mineral water** (omit if wet ice)

Origin: Adapted from a recipe in Harry Craddock's 1930 Savoy Cocktail Book.
Comment: A beautifully balanced, very approachable, rust coloured Martini.

NARANJA NEW #8

Glass: Old-fashioned
Garnish: Orange zest twist
Method: STIR one shot of rum with two ice cubes in a glass. Add sugar syrup, vermouth, bitters and two more ice cubes. STIR some more and add another two ice cubes and the rest of the rum. STIR lots more and add more ice.

2	shot(s)	**Bacardi Superior rum**
⅛	shot(s)	**Cinzano orange**
¼	shot(s)	**Sugar syrup** (2 sugar to 1 water)
2	dashes	**Angostura orange bitters**

Comment: Rum based twist on the classic Old Fashioned.
Origin: Created in 2008 by Chris Edwardes at Hanbury Club, Brighton, England.

NARANJA DAIQUIRI 🗝

Glass: Martini
Garnish: Orange slice on rim
Method: SHAKE all ingredients with ice and fine strain into chilled glass.

1¾	shot(s)	**Bacardi Superior rum**
¾	shot(s)	**Grand Marnier liqueur**
1	shot(s)	**Freshly squeezed orange juice**
½	shot(s)	**Freshly squeezed lime juice**
⅛	shot(s)	**Sugar syrup** (2 sugar to 1 water)

Comment: The Latino version of an orange Daiquiri.

NATHALIA

Glass: Old-fashioned
Garnish: Orange zest twist
Method: STIR all ingredients with ice and strain into ice-filled glass.

2	shot(s)	**Courvoisier V.S.O.P. cognac**
¾	shot(s)	**Yellow Chartreuse liqueur**
¾	shot(s)	**Crème de banane liqueur**
1	dash	**Angostura orange bitters**

Origin: Adapted from a drink discovered in 2006 at English Bar, Regina Hotel, Paris, France.
Comment: Herbal bananas and cognac. Be warned, the subtle sweetness conceals its strength.

NAUTILUS 🗝

Glass: Collins (or Nautilus seashell)
Garnish: Mint sprig
Method: SHAKE all ingredients with ice and strain into ice-filled glass. Serve with straws.

2	shot(s)	**Don Julio reposado tequila**
2	shot(s)	**Ocean Spray cranberry juice**
1	shot(s)	**Freshly squeezed lime juice**
½	shot(s)	**Sugar syrup** (2 sugar to 1 water)

Origin: Adapted from a drink created by Victor Bergeron (Trader Vic).
Comment: Basically a Margarita lengthened with cranberry juice.

NAVIGATOR UPDATED #8

Glass: Martini
Garnish: Lemon zest twist
Method: SHAKE all ingredients with ice and fine strain into chilled glass.

2	shot(s)	**Tanqueray London dry gin**
¾	shot(s)	**Luxardo limoncello liqueur**
1¼	shot(s)	**Freshly squeezed grapefruit juice**

Origin: Created in 2005 by Jamie Terrell, London, England.
Comment: This fruity, grapefruit-led drink is pleasantly bitter and sour.

NAVY GROG

Glass: Old-fashioned
Garnish: Lemon wedge
Method: STIR honey with rum in base of shaker to dissolve honey. Add next 3 ingredients, SHAKE with ice and strain into ice-filled glass.

3	spoons	**Runny honey**
1½	shot(s)	**Pusser's Navy rum**
¼	shot(s)	**Freshly squeezed lime juice**
2½	shot(s)	**Chilled mineral water**
2	dashes	**Angostura aromatic bitters**

Variant: Also great served hot. Top with boiling water and garnish with a cinnamon stick.
Comment: An extremely drinkable, honeyed cocktail.

> 'GIVING MONEY AND POWER TO GOVERNMENT IS LIKE GIVING WHISKEY AND CAR KEYS TO TEENAGE BOYS.'
> P.J. O'ROURKE

NEAL'S BARBADOS COSMOPOLITAN

Glass: Martini
Garnish: Orange zest twist
Method: SHAKE all ingredients with ice and fine strain into chilled glass.

1¼	shot(s)	**Bacardi Oro golden rum**
¾	shot(s)	**Cointreau triple sec**
½	shot(s)	**Freshly squeezed lime juice**
1½	shot(s)	**Ocean Spray cranberry juice**

Origin: Discovered in 2006 at Bix, San Francisco, USA.
Comment: Your standard Cosmo made more complex by a slug of warm Caribbean spirit.

NEGRONI UPDATED #8

Glass: Old-fashioned
Garnish: Orange zest twist
Method: POUR all ingredients into ice-filled glass and STIR.

1½	shot(s)	**Tanqueray London dry gin**
1½	shot(s)	**Campari Bitter**
1½	shot(s)	**Martini Rosso sweet vermouth**

Variant: Americano.
Comment: Bitter and dry, but very tasty. This no namby-pamby drink is traditionally assembled and mixed directly in the glass. There is something about this drink that does not suit fussing about with mixing glasses and strainers. To garnish with a lemon slice is a heinous crime.
Origin: This drink takes its name from Count Camillo Negroni. In the mid-1920s, while drinking at the Casoni Bar in Florence, Italy, he is said to have asked for an Americano 'with a bit more kick'.

NEGRONI SBAGLIATO NEW #8

Glass: Old-fashioned
Garnish: Orange slice
Method: POUR all ingredients into ice-filled glass and STIR.

1	shot(s)	**Martini Rosso sweet vermouth**
1	shot(s)	**Campari Bitter**
2	shot(s)	**Spumante (or brut champagne)**

Comment: This light style of Negroni has the bitterness but lacks the punch and character of the original.
Origin: Pronounced 'spal-yacht-oh' which in Italian means 'mistake', this drink was created in the late 1980s by Mirko Stocchetti at his Bar Basso in Milan when making a Negroni he mistakenly reached for a bottle of spumante instead of gin. They are still served at Basso today in enormous chalice-like glasses with a single, giant, rectangular ice cube.

NEGRONI SPUMANTE NEW #8

Glass: Old-fashioned
Garnish: Orange zest twist
Method: POUR first 3 ingredients into ice-filled glass. TOP with spumante and lightly STIR.

1	shot(s)	**Tanqueray London dry gin**
1	shot(s)	**Martini Rosso sweet vermouth**
1	shot(s)	**Campari Bitter**
Top up with		**Spumante (or champagne)**

Comment: A Negroni lengthened with sparkling wine. Every Negroni drinker should try this variation.

NEGROSKI NEW #8

Glass: Large wine
Garnish: Orange slice
Method: Pour ingredients into ice-filled glass and STIR.

1½	shot(s)	**Ketel One vodka**
1½	shot(s)	**Martini Rosso sweet vermouth**
1½	shot(s)	**Campari Bitter**

Comment: A Negroni where vodka is substituted for gin. I blame Italian fashionistas.

NEGUS (HOT)

Glass: Toddy
Garnish: Dust with freshly ground nutmeg
Method: Place bar spoon in warmed glass. POUR all ingredients into glass and STIR.

3	shot(s)	**Warre's Otima tawny port**
1	shot(s)	**Freshly squeezed lemon juice**
½	shot(s)	**Sugar syrup** (2 sugar to 1 water)
Top up with		**Boiling water**

Variant: Bishop
Origin: Colonel Francis Negus was the MP for Ipswich from 1717 to 1732. He created this diluted version of the original Bishop.
Comment: A tangy, citrussy hot drink.

THE NEUTRAL GROUND NEW #8

Glass: Coupette/Martini
Garnish: Orange zest twist
Method: STIR all ingredients with ice and fine strain into chilled glass.

2	shot(s)	**Rye whiskey (or bourbon)**
½	shot(s)	**Amontillado dry sherry**
½	shot(s)	**Bénédictine D.O.M. liqueur**
3	dashes	**Angostura orange bitters**

Comment: Sweet Manhattan-like with sherry and spiced notes.
Origin: Created in 2008 by Rhiannon Enlil at Bar Tonique, New Orleans, USA and named after the median area on Canal Street in New Orleans that formerly separated the American district from the Spanish/French district (now known as the French Quarter).

NEVADA DAIQUIRI

Glass: Martini
Garnish: Lime wedge on rim
Method: SHAKE all ingredients with ice and fine strain into chilled glass.

2	shot(s)	**Pusser's Navy rum**
1	shot(s)	**Freshly squeezed grapefruit juice**
½	shot(s)	**Freshly squeezed lime juice**
½	shot(s)	**Sugar syrup** (2 sugar to 1 water)

Comment: A pungent Daiquiri with the intense flavour of Navy rum.

NEVINS COCKTAIL NEW #8

Glass: Martini
Garnish: Lemon zest twist
Method: SHAKE all ingredients with ice and fine strain into chilled glass.

1½	shot(s)	**Bulleit bourbon whiskey**
½	shot(s)	**Bols apricot brandy liqueur**
½	shot(s)	**Freshly squeezed grapefruit juice**
¼	shot(s)	**Freshly squeezed lemon juice**
1	dash	**Angostura aromatic bitters**

Comment: Whiskey and apricot combine beautifully with a light burst of citrus in this easy sipper.

NEW ORLEANS BLACK NEW #8

Glass: Old-fashioned
Garnish: Lime wedge
Method: SHAKE first 4 ingredients with ice and strain into ice-filled glass. TOP with ginger beer.

1½	shot(s)	**Martinique agricole rum**
½	shot(s)	**Freshly squeezed lime juice**
⅛	shot(s)	**Sugar syrup** (2 sugar to 1 water)
2	dash	**Peychaud aromatic bitters**
Top up with		**Ginger beer**

Comment: Agricole character bursts out of this spiced Daiquiri.
Origin: Created in 2008 by Jonny Raglin at Absinthe, San Francisco, USA.

NEW ORLEANS MULE

Glass: Collins
Garnish: Lime wedge
Method: SHAKE first 4 ingredients with ice and fine strain into ice-filled glass. TOP with ginger beer.

2	shot(s)	**Bulleit bourbon whiskey**
1	shot(s)	**Kahlúa coffee liqueur**
1	shot(s)	**Pressed pineapple juice**
½	shot(s)	**Freshly squeezed lime juice**
Top up with		**Ginger beer**

Comment: A spicy, full-flavoured taste of the South.

NEW ORLEANS PUNCH

Glass: Collins
Garnish: Lemon slice
Method: SHAKE all ingredients with ice and strain into glass filled with crushed ice. Serve with straws.

1½	shot(s)	**Bulleit bourbon whiskey**
¾	shot(s)	**Zacapa aged rum**
1½	shot(s)	**Chambord black raspberry liqueur**
¾	shot(s)	**Freshly squeezed lemon juice**
3	shot(s)	**Cold black camomile tea**

Comment: Raspberry is the predominant flavour in this long drink.

NEW PORT CODEBREAKER

Glass: Collins
Method: SHAKE all ingredients with ice and strain into ice-filled glass.

1	shot(s)	**Don Julio reposado tequila**
1	shot(s)	**Pusser's Navy rum**
½	shot(s)	**Bols advocaat liqueur**
½	shot(s)	**Coco López cream of coconut**
4	shot(s)	**Freshly squeezed orange juice**

Origin: Adapted from a cocktail discovered in 1999 at Porter's Bar, Covent Garden, London.
Comment: This straw yellow drink is a most unusual mix of ingredients.

NEW YEAR'S ABSOLUTION

Glass: Old-fashioned
Garnish: Mint sprig
Method: STIR honey with absinthe in base of shaker until honey dissolves. Add apple juice, SHAKE with ice and strain into ice-filled glass. TOP with ginger ale and stir.

2	spoons	**Runny honey**
1	shot(s)	**La Fée Parisienne (68%) absinthe**
1	shot(s)	**Pressed apple juice**
Top up with		**Ginger ale**

Comment: The green fairy, tamed with honey and spiced with ginger.

NEW YORK FLIP NEW #8

Glass: Small wine glass
Garnish: Dust with freshly ground nutmeg
Method: Vigorously **SHAKE** all ingredients with ice and fine strain into chilled glass.

1½	shot(s)	**Bulleit bourbon whiskey**
½	shot(s)	**Warre's Otima tawny port**
1	fresh	**Egg** (white & yolk)
½	shot(s)	**Sugar syrup** (2 sugar to 1 water)

Comment: Flipping good. Easy and light.
Origin: One of the most famous flip-style drinks.

NEW YORKER

Glass: Martini
Garnish: Orange zest twist
Method: **SHAKE** all ingredients with ice and fine strain into chilled glass.

2	shot(s)	**Bulleit bourbon whiskey**
1	shot(s)	**Claret red wine**
½	shot(s)	**Freshly squeezed lemon juice**
½	shot(s)	**Sugar syrup** (2 sugar to 1 water)

Comment: Sweet 'n' sour whiskey and wine.

NIAGARA FALLS

Glass: Flute
Garnish: Physalis
Method: **SHAKE** first 4 ingredients with ice and strain into chilled glass. **TOP** with ginger ale and lightly stir.

1	shot(s)	**Ketel One vodka**
1	shot(s)	**Grand Marnier liqueur**
½	shot(s)	**Freshly squeezed lemon juice**
¼	shot(s)	**Sugar syrup** (2 sugar to 1 water)
Top up with		**Ginger ale**

Comment: Ginger ale and orange complement each other, fortified by vodka.

NICE PEAR-TINI

Glass: Martini
Garnish: Pear slice on rim
Method: **SHAKE** all ingredients with ice and fine strain into chilled glass.

1	shot(s)	**Courvoisier V.S.O.P. cognac**
½	shot(s)	**Belle de Brillet pear liqueur**
½	shot(s)	**Poire William eau de vie**
2	shot(s)	**Freshly extracted pear juice**
¼	shot(s)	**Sugar syrup** (2 sugar to 1 water)

Origin: Created in 2002 by Yours Truly (Simon Difford).
Comment: Spirited, rich and fruity.

NICKY FINN

Glass: Martini
Garnish: Lemon zest twist
Method: **SHAKE** all ingredients with ice and fine strain into chilled glass.

1	shot(s)	**Courvoisier V.S.O.P. cognac**
1	shot(s)	**Cointreau triple sec**
1	shot(s)	**Freshly squeezed lemon juice**
¼	shot(s)	**Pernod anis**

Origin: Adapted from a recipe in 'Cocktail: The Drinks Bible for the 21st Century' by Paul Harrington and Laura Moorhead.
Comment: Basically a Sidecar spiked with an aniseedy dash of Pernod.

NICKY'S FIZZ

Glass: Collins
Garnish: Orange slice
Method: **SHAKE** first 2 ingredients with ice and strain into ice-filled glass. **TOP** with soda, lightly stir and serve with straws.

2	shot(s)	**Tanqueray London dry gin**
2	shot(s)	**Freshly squeezed grapefruit juice**
Top up with		**Soda water** (from siphon)

Comment: A dry, refreshing, long drink.

NIGHT & DAY

Glass: Flute
Garnish: Orange zest twist
Method: **POUR** ingredients into chilled glass.

½	shot(s)	**Campari Bitter**
½	shot(s)	**Grand Marnier liqueur**
Top up with		**Perrier Jouet brut champagne**

Comment: Dry, aromatic, orange champagne.

NIGHTMARE MARTINI

Glass: Martini
Garnish: Maraschino cherry
Method: **SHAKE** all ingredients with ice and fine strain into chilled glass.

1	shot(s)	**Tanqueray London dry gin**
1	shot(s)	**Dubonnet Red** (French made)
½	shot(s)	**Heering cheery brandy liqueur**
2	shot(s)	**Freshly squeezed orange juice**

Comment: Pleasant enough, with hints of cherry. Hardly a nightmare.

NINE-20-SEVEN

Glass: Flute
Method: POUR ingredients into chilled glass and lightly stir.

¼	shot(s)	**Vanilla-infused Ketel One vodka**
¼	shot(s)	**Cuarenta Y Tres (Licor 43) liqueur**
Top up with		**Perrier Jouet brut champagne**

Origin: Created in 2002 by Damian Caldwell at Home Bar, London, England. Damian was lost for a name until a customer asked the time.
Comment: Champagne with a hint of vanilla.

THE NINTH WARD NEW #8

Glass: Martini/Coupette
Garnish: Lime zest twist
Method: SHAKE all ingredients with ice and fine strain into chilled glass.

1½	shot(s)	**Bulleit bourbon whiskey**
¼	shot(s)	**St-Germain elderflower liqueur**
½	shot(s)	**Velvet Falernum liqueur**
¾	shot(s)	**Freshly squeezed lime juice**
2	dashes	**Peychaud aromatic bitters**

Comment: Bourbon with a hint of elderflower, cloves and lime.
Origin: Adapted from a drink created by Brother Cleve, Boston, USA for Tales of the Cocktail 2008. The drink is a play on the classic Ward Eight and a homage to one of the New Orleans neighbourhoods hardest hit by Hurricane Katrina.

NO. 10 LEMONADE

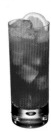

Glass: Collins
Garnish: Lemon slice
Method: MUDDLE blueberries in base of shaker. Add next 3 ingredients, **SHAKE** with ice and fine strain into ice filled glass. **TOP** with soda.

12	fresh	**Blueberries**
2	shot(s)	**Bacardi Superior rum**
1½	shot(s)	**Freshly squeezed lemon juice**
¾	shot(s)	**Sugar syrup** (2 sugar to 1 water)
Top up with		**Soda water** (club soda)

Origin: Adapted from a drink discovered in 2006 at Double Seven, New York City, USA.
Comment: Basically a long blueberry Daiquiri.

NOBLE EUROPE

Glass: Old-fashioned
Garnish: Orange slice
Method: SHAKE all ingredients with ice and strain into glass filled with crushed ice.

1½	shot(s)	**Tokaji Hungarian wine**
1	shot(s)	**Ketel One vodka**
1	shot(s)	**Freshly squeezed orange juice**
1	dash	**Vanilla essence**

Origin: Created in 2002 by Dan Spink at Browns, St Martin's Lane, London, England.
Variant: Also great served 'up' in a Martini glass.
Comment: A delicious cocktail that harnesses the rich, sweet flavours of Tokaji.

NOLA DAIQUIRI NEW #8

Glass: Old-fashioned
Garnish: Pineapple wedge
Method: SHAKE all ingredients with ice and fine strain into chilled glass.

1¾	shot(s)	**Bacardi Superior rum**
¾	shot(s)	**St-Germain elderflower liqueur**
⅛	shot(s)	**Freshly squeezed lemon juice**
⅛	shot(s)	**Freshly squeezed orange juice**
1	dash	**Peychaud aromatic bitters**

Comment: Light rum and elderflower with the merest hint of orange and lemon juice.
Origin: Created in 2007 by Lynnette Marrero at Freeman's, New York City, USA.

NOME

Glass: Martini
Garnish: Mint leaf
Method: STIR all ingredients with ice and strain into chilled glass.

1½	shot(s)	**Tanqueray London dry gin**
1	shot(s)	**Yellow Chartreuse liqueur**
1½	shot(s)	**Tio Pepe fino sherry**

AKA: Alaska Martini
Origin: A classic cocktail whose origin is unknown.
Comment: This dyslexic gnome is dry and interesting.

NOON

Glass: Martini
Garnish: Orange zest twist
Method: SHAKE all ingredients with ice and strain into chilled glass.

1½	shot(s)	**Tanqueray London dry gin**
¾	shot(s)	**Noilly Prat dry vermouth**
¾	shot(s)	**Martini Rosso sweet vermouth**
¾	shot(s)	**Freshly squeezed orange juice**
2	dashes	**Angostura aromatic bitters**
½	fresh	**Egg white**

Comment: This classic cocktail is smooth and aromatic.

NORTHERN LIGHTS

Glass: Martini
Garnish: Star anise
Method: SHAKE all ingredients with ice and fine strain into chilled glass.

1½	shot(s)	**Zubrówka bison vodka**
¾	shot(s)	**Berentzen apple schnapps**
1	shot(s)	**Pressed apple juice**
½	shot(s)	**Freshly squeezed lime juice**
½	shot(s)	**Pernod anis**
½	shot(s)	**Sugar syrup** (2 sugar to 1 water)

Origin: Created in 2003 by Stuart 'Holiday' Hudson at MJU Bar, Millennium Hotel, London, England.
Comment: Wonderfully refreshing: apple and anis served up on a grassy vodka base.

NORTHERN SUN NEW #8

Glass: Collins
Garnish: Pear slice
Method: MUDDLE ginger in base of shaker. Add other ingredients, **SHAKE** with ice and fine strain into ice-filled glass.

2	slices	Fresh root ginger (thumbnail sized)
2	shot(s)	Zacapa aged rum
3	shot(s)	Pressed pear juice
1	shot(s)	Ocean Spray cranberry juice
¼	shot(s)	Freshly squeezed lime juice
¼	shot(s)	Maple syrup

Comment: Subtle and easy. Hard to believe this drink contains two measures of rum.
Origin: Recipe adapted 2008 from LCBO Magazine and comes courtesy of Sean Murray, Aurora, Ontario, Canada.

NORTH POLE MARTINI

Glass: Martini
Method: SHAKE first 4 ingredients with ice and fine strain into chilled glass. **FLOAT** cream over drink.

2	shot(s)	Tanueray London dry gin
1	shot(s)	Luxardo maraschino liqueur
½	shot(s)	Freshly squeezed lemon juice
½	fresh	Egg white
Float		Double (heavy) cream

Origin: Adapted from a recipe in the 1947-72 Trader Vic's Bartender's Guide by Victor Bergeron.
Comment: An Aviation smoothed by egg white and cream.

NOSHINO MARTINI NEW #8

Glass: Martini
Garnish: Slice English cucumber
Method: STIR all ingredients with ice and strain into chilled glass.

| 2 | shot(s) | Sake |
| 2 | shot(s) | Shochu |

Origin: Adapted from a drink discovered in 2007 at Shochu Lounge, London, England.
Comment: If good quality sake and shochu are used then this can be a great drink. However, it lacks the alcoholic bite I associate with a true Martini, so I much prefer this drink when vodka is used in place of shochu.

NOT SO COSMO (MOCKTAIL)

Glass: Martini
Garnish: Orange zest twist
Method: SHAKE all ingredients with ice and fine strain into chilled glass.

1	shot(s)	Freshly squeezed orange juice
1	shot(s)	Ocean Spray cranberry juice
1	shot(s)	Freshly squeezed lime juice
1	shot(s)	Freshly squeezed lemon juice

Origin: Discovered in 2003 at Claridge's Bar, London, England.
Comment: This non-alcoholic cocktail may look like a Cosmo but it doesn't taste like one.

NOVEMBER SEABREEZE (MOCKTAIL)

Glass: Collins
Garnish: Lime wedge
Method: SHAKE first 3 ingredients with ice and strain into ice-filled glass. **TOP** with soda, gently stir and serve with straws.

2	shot(s)	Ocean Spray cranberry juice
2	shot(s)	Pressed apple juice
1	shot(s)	Freshly squeezed lime juice
Top up with		Soda water (club soda)

Comment: A superbly refreshing fruity drink, whatever the time of year.

NUCLEAR DAIQUIRI

Glass: Martini
Garnish: Lime wedge on rim
Method: SHAKE all ingredients with ice and fine strain into chilled glass.

1	shot(s)	Wray & Nephew overproof rum
¾	shot(s)	Green Chartreuse liqueur
1	shot(s)	Freshly squeezed lime juice
¼	shot(s)	Velvet Falernum liqueur
½	shot(s)	Chilled mineral water (omit if wet ice)

Origin: Created in 2005 by Gregor de Gruyther at LAB bar, London, England.
Comment: A great way to inflict mutually assured destruction, although there will be fallout the morning after.

N

NUEZ DAIQUIRI

Glass: Coupette/Martini
Garnish: Walnut
Method: SHAKE all ingredients with ice and fine strain into chilled glass.

2	shot(s)	Bacardi Superior rum
1	shot(s)	Nocello walnut liqueur
¾	shot(s)	Freshly squeezed lime juice
½	shot(s)	Pressed apple juice

Comment: A Daiquiri with nutty notes.
Origin: Named after the Spanish for Walnut.

NUTCRACKER SWEET

Glass: Martini
Garnish: Dust with cocoa powder
Method: SHAKE all ingredients with ice and fine strain into chilled glass.

2	shot(s)	Ketel One vodka
1	shot(s)	White crème de cacao liqueur
¾	shot(s)	Luxardo Amaretto di Saschira

Comment: After dinner, fortified almond and chocolate.

NUTS & BERRIES

Glass: Martini
Garnish: Float raspberry and almond flake
Method: STIR all ingredients with ice and strain into chilled glass.

1	shot(s)	Raspberry flavoured vodka
1	shot(s)	Almond flavoured vodka
¼	shot(s)	Frangelico hazelnut liqueur
¼	shot(s)	Chambord black raspberry liqueur
1	shot(s)	Lemonade/Sprite/7-Up

Origin: Created in 2004 by Yours Truly (Simon Difford).
Comment: The inclusion of a carbonate (lemonade) may annoy some classical bartenders but it adds flavour, sweetness and dilution.

NUTTY BERRY'TINI

Glass: Martini
Garnish: Float mint leaf
Method: SHAKE all ingredients with ice and fine strain into chilled glass.

2	shot(s)	Cranberry flavoured vodka
½	shot(s)	Heering cherry brandy liqueur
½	shot(s)	Frangelico hazelnut liqueur
¼	shot(s)	Luxardo maraschino liqueur
1	shot(s)	Ocean Spray cranberry juice
½	shot(s)	Freshly squeezed lime juice

Origin: Created by Yours Truly (Simon Difford) in 2003.
Comment: Cranberry vodka and juice, sweetened with cherry liqueur, dried with lime juice and flavoured with hazelnut.

NUTTY NASHVILLE

Glass: Martini
Garnish: Lemon zest twist
Method: STIR honey with bourbon in base of shaker to dissolve honey. Add other ingredients, SHAKE with ice and fine strain into chilled glass.

2	spoons	Runny honey
2	shot(s)	Bulleit bourbon whiskey
1	shot(s)	Frangelico hazelnut liqueur
1	shot(s)	Krupnik honey liqueur

Origin: Created in 2001 by Jason Fendick at Rockwell, Trafalgar Hotel, London, England.
Comment: Bourbon and hazelnut smoothed and rounded by honey.

NUTTY RUSSIAN

Glass: Old-fashioned
Method: SHAKE all ingredients with ice and strain into ice-filled glass.

1½	shot(s)	Ketel One vodka
¾	shot(s)	Frangelico hazelnut liqueur
¾	shot(s)	Kahlúa coffee liqueur

Comment: A Black Russian with hazelnut liqueur.

NUTTY SUMMER

Glass: Martini
Garnish: Drop three dashes of Angostura aromatic bitters onto surface of drink and stir around with a cocktail stick - essential to both the look and flavour.
Method: SHAKE all ingredients with ice and fine strain into chilled glass.

1½	shot(s)	Bols advocaat liqueur
¾	shot(s)	Luxardo Amaretto di Saschira
¾	shot(s)	Malibu coconut rum liqueur
¾	shot(s)	Pressed pineapple juice
½	shot(s)	Double (heavy) cream

Origin: Created in 2001 by Daniel Spink at Hush Up, London, England.
Comment: This subtle, dessert style cocktail is packed with flavour. A superb after dinner tipple for summer.

OATMEAL COOKIE

Glass: Shot
Method: SHAKE all ingredients with ice and fine strain into chilled glass.

½	shot(s)	Teichenné butterscotch schnapps
¼	shot(s)	Goldschläger cinnamon schnapps
¾	shot(s)	Baileys Irish cream liqueur

Comment: A well balanced, creamy shot with hints of butterscotch and cinnamon.

OÁZA

Glass: Old-fashioned
Garnish: Lime wedge
Method: SHAKE all ingredients with ice and strain into ice-filled glass.

2	shot(s)	Becherovka liqueur
¾	shot(s)	Freshly squeezed lime juice
¼	shot(s)	Sugar syrup (2 sugar to 1 water)

Origin: A popular drink in the Czech Republic where Becherovka, a herbal liquor, is the national drink.
Comment: Herbal and bittersweet. Not for everyone.

OBITUARY

Glass: Martini
Garnish: Olive on stick
Method: STIR all ingredients with ice and strain into chilled glass.

2	shot(s)	Tanqueray London dry gin
⅛	shot(s)	La Fée Parisienne (68%) absinthe
¼	shot(s)	Noilly Prat dry vermouth

Comment: What a way to go. A Dry Martini with a dash of the green fairy.

OCEANBREEZE NEW #8

● ● ● ◐ ○

Glass: Collins
Garnish: Lime wedge
Method: POUR cranberry juice into ice-filled glass.
SHAKE other ingredients with ice and carefully
strain into glass to LAYER over the cranberry juice.
Serve with straws so drinker can mix layers prior to
drinking.

2½	shot(s)	Ocean Spray cranberry juice
2	shot(s)	Ketel One vodka
1½	shot(s)	Freshly squeezed grapefruit juice
½	shot(s)	Pressed pineapple juice

Comment: Refreshingly juicy.
Origin: Created in 2007 by Yours Truly (Simon
Difford) for Ocean Spray.

OCEANS 21 NEW #8

● ● ● ● ○

Glass: Martini
Garnish: Flamed orange zest twist
Method: SHAKE all ingredients with ice and fine
strain into chilled glass.

1	shot(s)	Boulard Grand Solage calvados
½	shot(s)	Grand Marnier liqueur
1½	shot(s)	Ocean Spray cranberry juice

Comment: Apple, cranberry and orange.

ODDBALL MANHATTAN DRY

● ● ● ● ○

Glass: Martini
Garnish: Two maraschino cherries
Method: STIR all ingredients with ice and strain
into chilled glass.

2½	shot(s)	Bulleit bourbon whiskey
1	shot(s)	Noilly Prat dry vermouth
½	shot(s)	Yellow Chartreuse liqueur
3	dashes	Angostura aromatic bitters

Comment: Not as oddball as it sounds, the
Chartreuse combines harmoniously.

O'HENRY

● ● ● ◐ ○

Glass: Collins
Garnish: Lemon slice
Method: SHAKE first 2 ingredients with ice and
strain into ice-filled glass. TOP with ginger ale,
lightly stir and serve with straws.

2	shot(s)	Bulleit bourbon whiskey
1	shot(s)	Bénédictine D.O.M. liqueur
Top up with		Ginger ale

Origin: Discovered in 2006 at Brandy Library, New
York City, USA.
Comment: Herbal whiskey and ginger.

OH GOSH!

● ● ● ● ●

Glass: Martini
Garnish: Lemon zest twist
Method: SHAKE all ingredients with ice and fine
strain into chilled glass.

1½	shot(s)	Bacardi Superior rum
1	shot(s)	Cointreau triple sec
½	shot(s)	Freshly squeezed lime juice
¼	shot(s)	Sugar syrup (2 sugar to 1 water)
½	shot(s)	Chilled mineral water (omit if wet ice)

Origin: Created by Tony Conigliaro in 2001 at Isola,
London, England. A customer requested a Daiquiri
with a difference – when this was served he took
one sip and exclaimed "Oh gosh!".
Comment: A very subtle orange twist on the
classic Daiquiri.

OIL SLICK

● ● ● ◐ ○ ○

Glass: Shot
Method: Refrigerate ingredients then LAYER in
chilled glass by carefully pouring in the following
order.

¾	shot(s)	Opal Nera black sambuca
¾	shot(s)	Baileys Irish cream liqueur

Comment: Whiskey cream and liquorice.

OLD CRYSTAL SHRINE NEW #8

● ● ● ● ◐ ○

Glass: Old-fashioned
Garnish: Lemon & orange zests
Method: STIR all ingredients with ice and strain
over into glass over ice ball made from mineral
water.

1	spoon	White truffle honey
2	shot(s)	Yamazaki 12yo Japanese whisky
2	dashes	Regan's Orange Bitters No.6
1	dash	Peychaud aromatic bitters

Comment: Honeyed and spiced whiskey.
Origin: Created in 2008 by Stanislav Vadrna for the
Red Monkey Group, Slovakia.

OLD CUBAN NEW #8

● ● ● ● ◐

Glass: Martini/coupette
Garnish: Float mint leaf
Method: Lightly MUDDLE mint in base of shaker
(just to bruise). Add next 4 ingredients, SHAKE with
ice and fine strain into chilled glass. TOP with
champagne.

6	fresh	Mint leaves
2	shot(s)	Zacapa aged rum
¾	shot(s)	Freshly squeezed lime juice
½	shot(s)	Sugar syrup (2 sugar to 1 water)
2	shot(s)	Angostura aromatic bitters
¾	shot(s)	Perrier Jouet brut champagne

Comment: A luxurious, minty Daiquiri topped with
a splash of champagne.
Origin: Created in 2004 by Audrey Saunders, New
York, USA.

OLD FASHIONED #1 (CLASSIC VERSION)

UPDATED #8

●●●●●

Glass: Old-fashioned
Garnish: Orange (or lemon) twist
Method: STIR one shot of bourbon with two ice cubes in a glass. Add sugar syrup and Angostura and two more ice cubes. STIR some more and add another two ice cubes and the rest of the bourbon. STIR lots more and add more ice.

2½	shot(s)	**Bulleit bourbon whiskey**
½	shot(s)	**Sugar syrup** (2 sugar to 1 water)
3	dashes	**Angostura aromatic bitters**

Variation: Old Fashioned #2 (US Version)
Comment: The melting and stirring in of ice cubes is essential to the dilution and taste of this sublime classic.
Origin: As with the Martini, the glass this cocktail is served in has taken the name of the drink. Supposedly the cocktail was created at the Pendennis Club in Louisville, Kentucky, for a Kentucky Colonel (and bourbon distiller) named James E. Pepper. As the drink predates the club, this cannot be true, but Pepper seems to have promoted it heavily to help market his product and the story is given credence by appearing verbatim in A. S. Crockett's 1935 'The Old Waldorf-Astoria Bar Book'.

OLD FASHIONED #2 (US VERSION)

UPDATED #8

●●●●◐

Glass: Old-fashioned
Garnish: Orange zest twist & maraschino cherry
Method: MUDDLE orange and cherries in base of shaker. Add other ingredients, SHAKE with ice and fine strain into ice-filled glass.

2	whole	**Maraschino cherries**
1	fresh	**Orange slice** (cut into 8 segments)
2	shot(s)	**Bulleit bourbon whiskey**
⅛	shot(s)	**Maraschino syrup** (from cherry jar)
¼	shot(s)	**Sugar syrup** (2 sugar to 1 water)
2	dashes	**Angostura aromatic bitters**

Variation: Old Fashioned #1 (Classic Version)
Comment: This drink is often mixed in the glass in which it is to be served. Shaking better incorporates the flavours produced by muddling and fine straining removes the orange peel and cherry skin.
Origin: In the US orange segments and sometimes even a maraschino cherry are regularly muddled in this drink: the practice probably originated during Prohibition as a means of disguising rough spirits. This practice is almost unknown in England and as Crosby Gaige wrote in 1944, "Serious-minded persons omit fruit salad from Old Fashioneds."

DRINKS ARE GRADED AS FOLLOWS:

● DISGUSTING   ●◐ PRETTY AWFUL   ●● BEST AVOIDED
●●◐ DISAPPOINTING   ●●● ACCEPTABLE   ●●●◐ GOOD
●●●● RECOMMENDED   ●●●●◐ HIGHLY RECOMMENDED
●●●●● OUTSTANDING / EXCEPTIONAL

OLD FASHIONED CADDY

●●●●○

Glass: Old-fashioned
Garnish: Orange slice & cherry on stick (sail)
Method: SHAKE all ingredients with ice and strain into ice-filled glass.

2	shot(s)	**Johnnie Walker Scotch whisky**
½	shot(s)	**Heering cherry brandy liqueur**
½	shot(s)	**Martini Rosso sweet vermouth**
2	dashes	**Angostura aromatic bitters**

Origin: Created in 2005 by Wayne Collins, London, England.
Comment: Rich, red and packed with flavour.

OLD FLAME

●●●●○

Glass: Martini
Garnish: Flamed orange peel
Method: SHAKE all ingredients with ice and fine strain into chilled glass.

1	shot(s)	**Tanqueray London dry gin**
½	shot(s)	**Cointreau triple sec**
½	shot(s)	**Martini Rosso sweet vermouth**
¼	shot(s)	**Campari Bitter**
1½	shot(s)	**Freshly squeezed orange juice**

Origin: Created by Dale DeGroff, New York, USA.
Comment: Bittersweet, orchard fresh orange charged with gin.

OLD PAL

●●●●○○

Glass: Old-fashioned
Garnish: Orange slice
Method: STIR all ingredients with ice and strain into ice-filled glass.

1¼	shot(s)	**Canadian whiskey**
1¼	shot(s)	**Noilly Prat dry vermouth**
1¼	shot(s)	**Campari Bitter**

Origin: Adapted from Harry Craddock's 1930 'The Savoy Cocktail Book'.
Comment: A dry, bitter sipper for the more hardened palate.

OLE

●●●◐○

Glass: Martini
Garnish: Orange slice on rim
Method: SHAKE all ingredients with ice and fine strain into chilled glass.

2	shot(s)	**Courvoisier V.S.O.P. cognac**
¾	shot(s)	**Cuarenta Y Tres (Licor 43) liqueur**
1½	shot(s)	**Freshly squeezed orange juice**

Comment: Vanilla, orange and brandy combine well.

OLYMPIC

Glass: Martini
Garnish: Orange zest twist
Method: SHAKE all ingredients with ice and fine strain into chilled glass.

1¼	shot(s)	Courvoisier V.S.O.P. cognac
1¼	shot(s)	Grand Marnier liqueur
1¼	shot(s)	Freshly squeezed orange juice

Origin: Adapted from a recipe in Harry Craddock's 1930 Savoy Cocktail Book.
Comment: The perfect balance of cognac and orange juice. One to celebrate the 2012 Games perhaps.

ONION RING MARTINI

Glass: Martini
Garnish: Onion ring
Method: MUDDLE onion in base of shaker. Add other ingredients, SHAKE with ice and fine strain into chilled glass.

2	rings	Fresh red onion
1	shot(s)	Sake
2	shot(s)	Tanqueray London dry gin
3	dashes	Angostura orange bitters
⅛	shot(s)	Sugar syrup (2 sugar to 1 water)

Origin: Reputed to have been created at the Bamboo Bar, Bangkok, Thailand.
Comment: Certainly one of the most obscure Martini variations – drinkable, but does leave you with onion breath.

OOOH GINGER NEW #8

Glass: Martini
Garnish: Candied ginger slice
Method: STIR all ingredients with ice and fine strain into chilled glass.

2	shot(s)	Don Julio añejo tequila
½	shot(s)	Domaine de Canton ginger liqueur
½	shot(s)	Noilly Prat dry vermouth

Origin: Created in March 2008 by Dick Bradsell and Simon Difford at The Cabinet Room, London, England.
Comment: Subtle ginger spice flavours this dry tequila martini.

OPAL

Glass: Martini
Garnish: Orange zest twist
Method: SHAKE all ingredients with ice and fine strain into chilled glass.

2	shot(s)	Tanqueray London dry gin
½	shot(s)	Cointreau triple sec
1¼	shot(s)	Freshly squeezed orange juice
¼	shot(s)	Sugar syrup (2 sugar to 1 water)
⅛	shot(s)	Orange flower water (optional)

Origin: Adapted from the 1920s recipe.
Comment: Fresh, fragrant flavours of orange zest and gin.

OPAL CAFÉ

Glass: Shot
Method: SHAKE first 2 ingredients with ice and fine strain into chilled glass. FLOAT thin layer of cream over drink.

½	shot(s)	Opal Nera black sambuca
½	shot(s)	Espresso coffee
Float		Double (heavy) cream

Comment: A great liquorice and coffee drink to sip or shoot.

OPENING SHOT

Glass: Shot
Method: SHAKE all ingredients with ice and fine strain into chilled glass.

1	shot(s)	Bulleit bourbon whiskey
½	shot(s)	Martini Rosso sweet vermouth
⅛	shot(s)	Pomegranate (grenadine) syrup

Variant: Double the quantities and strain into a Martini glass and you have the 1920s classic I based this drink on.
Comment: Basically a miserly Sweet Manhattan.

OPERA

Glass: Martini
Garnish: Orange zest twist
Method: SHAKE all ingredients with ice and fine strain into chilled glass.

2	shot(s)	Tanqueray London dry gin
2	shot(s)	Dubonnet Red (French made)
¼	shot(s)	Luxardo maraschino liqueur
3	dashes	Angostura orange bitters

Origin: Adapted from the classic 1920s cocktail.
Comment: Dubonnet smoothes the gin while maraschino adds floral notes.

ORANG-A-TANG

Glass: Sling
Garnish: Orange slice on rim
Method: SHAKE first 5 ingredients with ice and strain into ice-filled glass. FLOAT layer of rum over drink.

1½	shot(s)	Ketel One vodka
¾	shot(s)	Cointreau triple sec
2	shot(s)	Freshly squeezed orange juice
½	shot(s)	Freshly squeezed lime juice
¼	shot(s)	Pomegranate (grenadine) syrup
½	shot(s)	Wood's 100 rum

Comment: Orange predominates in this long, tangy, tropical cooler.

ORANGE BLOOM MARTINI

Glass: Martini
Garnish: Maraschino cherry
Method: SHAKE all ingredients with ice and fine strain into chilled glass.

2	shot(s)	**Tanqueray London dry gin**
1	shot(s)	**Cointreau triple sec**
1	shot(s)	**Martini Rosso sweet vermouth**

Origin: Adapted from a recipe in the 1930s edition of the Savoy Cocktail Book by Harry Craddock.
Comment: Strong, fruity zesty orange laced with gin.

ORANGE BLOSSOM

Glass: Old-fashioned
Garnish: Orange zest twist
Method: SHAKE all ingredients with ice and strain into ice-filled glass.

1½	shot(s)	**Tanqueray London dry gin**
½	shot(s)	**Cointreau triple sec**
1½	shot(s)	**Freshly squeezed orange juice**
½	shot(s)	**Freshly squeezed lime juice**
⅛	shot(s)	**Pomegranate (grenadine) syrup**

Variant: Served long in a Collins glass this becomes a Harvester.
Comment: Gin sweetened with liqueur and grenadine, and soured with lime.

ORANGE BRÛLÉE

Glass: Martini
Garnish: Dust with cocoa powder
Method: SHAKE first 3 ingredients with ice and fine strain into chilled glass. **FLOAT** thin layer of cream over drink and turn glass to spread evenly.

1½	shot(s)	**Luxardo Amaretto di Saschira**
1½	shot(s)	**Grand Marnier liqueur**
¾	shot(s)	**Courvoisier V.S.O.P.cognac**
¼	shot(s)	**Double (heavy) cream**

Origin: Created in 2005 by Xavier Laigle at Bar Le Forum, Paris, France.
Comment: A great looking, beautifully balanced after-dinner drink.

ORANGE CUSTARD MARTINI

Glass: Martini
Garnish: Orange zest twist
Method: SHAKE all ingredients with ice and fine strain into chilled glass.

2	shot(s)	**Bols advocaat liqueur**
1	shot(s)	**Tuaca Italian liqueur**
½	shot(s)	**Grand Marnier liqueur**
¼	shot(s)	**Vanilla sugar syrup**

Origin: I created this drink in 2002 after rediscovering advocaat on a trip to Amsterdam.
Comment: A smooth, creamy orangey dessert cocktail

ORANGE DAIQUIRI #1

Glass: Old-fashioned
Garnish: Orange zest twist
Method: SHAKE all ingredients with ice and fine strain into ice-filled glass.

2	shot(s)	**Zacapa aged rum**
¾	shot(s)	**Freshly squeezed orange juice**
½	shot(s)	**Freshly squeezed lime juice**
¼	shot(s)	**Sugar syrup** (2 sugar to 1 water)

AKA: Bolo
Origin: My take on a popular drink.
Comment: Far more serious than it looks. Sweet and sour in harmony.

ORANGE DAIQUIRI #2

Glass: Martini
Garnish: Orange zest twist
Method: SHAKE all ingredients with ice and fine strain into chilled glass.

2	shot(s)	**Clément Créole Shrubb liqueur**
½	shot(s)	**Freshly squeezed lime juice**
¾	shot(s)	**Chilled mineral water** (omit if wet ice)

Variant: Derby Daiquiri
Origin: I conceived this drink in 1998, after visiting the company which was then importing Créole Shrubb. I took a bottle to London's Met Bar and Ben Reed made me my first Orange Daiquiri.
Comment: Créole Shrubb is an unusual liqueur made by infusing orange peel in casks of mature Martinique rum.

'I AM ONLY A BEER TEETOTALLER, NOT A CHAMPAGNE TEETOTALLER.'
GEORGE BERNARD SHAW

ORANGE MARTINI

Glass: Martini
Garnish: Orange zest twist
Method: SHAKE all ingredients with ice and fine strain into chilled glass.

2	shot(s)	**Tanqueray London dry gin**
1	shot(s)	**Freshly squeezed orange juice**
½	shot(s)	**Martini Rosso sweet vermouth**
¼	shot(s)	**Sugar syrup** (2 sugar to 1 water)
3	dashes	**Angostura orange bitters**

Origin: Adapted from the Orange Cocktail and Orange Martini Cocktail in the 1930s edition of the Savoy Cocktail Book by Harry Craddock.
Comment: A sophisticated, complex balance of orange and gin.

ORANGE MOJITO

Glass: Collins
Garnish: Mint sprig
Method: Lightly **MUDDLE** mint (just to bruise) in base of glass. Add other ingredients and half fill glass with crushed ice. **CHURN** (stir) with bar spoon. Fill with more crushed ice and churn some more. **TOP** with soda, stir and serve with straws.

8	fresh	**Mint leaves**
1½	shot(s)	**Orange-infused Ketel One vodka**
½	shot(s)	**Mandarine Napoléon liqueur**
½	shot(s)	**Bacardi Superior rum**
1	shot(s)	**Freshly squeezed lime juice**
½	shot(s)	**Sugar syrup** (2 sugar to 1 water)
Top up with		**Soda water** (club soda)

Origin: Created in 2001 by Jamie MacDonald while working in Sydney, Australia.
Comment: Mint and orange combine to make a wonderfully fresh drink.

ORANGE SPUR NEW #8

Glass: Coupette/Martini
Garnish: Star anise
Method: **STIR** all ingredients with ice and strain into chilled glass.

2	shot(s)	**Ketel One vodka**
½	shot(s)	**Marie Brizard anisette liqueur**
½	shot(s)	**Aperol**
2	dashes	**Angostura aromatic bitters**

Comment: Stir well – this bittersweet drink benefits from dilution.
Origin: Created in 2008 by Don Lee at PDT, New York City, USA.

ORANJINIHA

Glass: Collins
Garnish: Orange slice in glass
Method: **SHAKE** all ingredients with ice and strain into glass filled with crushed ice.

2	shot(s)	**Orange-infused Ketel One vodka**
3	shot(s)	**Freshly squeezed orange juice**
1	shot(s)	**Freshly squeezed lemon juice**
1	shot(s)	**Sugar syrup** (2 sugar to 1 water)

Origin: Created in 2002 by Alex Kammerling, London, England.
Comment: A tall, richly flavoured orange drink.

ORCHARD BREEZE

Glass: Collins
Garnish: Apple slice on rim
Method: **SHAKE** all ingredients with ice and strain into ice-filled glass.

2	shot(s)	**Ketel One vodka**
1	shot(s)	**St-Germain elderflower liqueur**
1	shot(s)	**Sauvignon Blanc wine**
2	shot(s)	**Pressed apple juice**
¼	shot(s)	**Freshly squeezed lime juice**

Origin: Adapted from a drink created in 2002 by Wayne Collins, London, England.
Comment: A refreshing, summery combination of white wine, apple, lime and elderflower laced with vodka.

ORCHARD CRUSH NEW #8

Glass: Old-fashioned
Garnish: freshberries
Method: **SHAKE** all ingredients with ice and strain into an ice-filled glass.

1	spoon	**Damson preserve**
2	shot(s)	**Boulard Grand Solage calvados**
1	shot(s)	**Freshly squeezed lemon juice**
¼	shot(s)	**Sugar syrup** (2 sugar to 1 water)

Origin: Created in 2008 by Jeffrey Morgenthaler at Bel Ami Lounge, Oregon, USA.
Comment: Apple brandy and damson jam combine brilliantly in this tangy but not at all sweet cocktail.

ORIENTAL NEW #8

Glass: Martini
Garnish: Orange zest twist
Method: **SHAKE** all ingredients with ice and fine strain into chilled glass.

2	shot(s)	**Rye whiskey (or bourbon)**
1	shot(s)	**Martini Rosso sweet vermouth**
1	shot(s)	**Grand Marnier liqueur**
½	shot(s)	**Freshly squeezed lime juice**

Comment: Be warned this dry, orangey bourbon based cocktail packs a punch.
Origin: Adapted from 1930 'The Savoy Cocktail Book' in which author Harry Craddock writes of this drink, In August, 1924, an American Engineer nearly died of fever in the Philippines, and only the extraordinary devotion of Dr. B- saved his life. As an act of gratitude the Engineer gave Dr. B- the recipe of this cocktail."

HOW TO MAKE SUGAR SYRUP

To make your own sugar syrup, gradually pour TWO cups of granulated sugar into a saucepan containing ONE cup of hot water. Stir as you pour and carry on stirring and simmering until the sugar is dissolved. Do not let the water even come close to boiling and only simmer for as long as it takes to dissolve the sugar. Allow syrup to cool and pour into an empty bottle. Ideally, you should finely strain your syrup into the bottle to remove any undissolved crystals which could otherwise encourage crystallisation. If kept in a refrigerator this mixture will last for a couple of months.

●●●●○

ORIENTAL GRAPE MARTINI UPDATED #8

Glass: Martini
Garnish: Grapes on stick
Method: MUDDLE grapes in base of shaker. Add other ingredients, **SHAKE** with ice and fine strain into chilled glass.

7	fresh	Seedless white grapes
2	shot(s)	Ketel One vodka
2	shot(s)	Sake
⅛	shot(s)	Sugar syrup (2 sugar to 1 water)

Variants: Double Grape Martini, Grape Martini, Grapple.
Origin: Created by Yours Truly (Simon Difford) in 2004.
Comment: Sake adds some oriental intrigue to what would otherwise be a plain old Grape Martini.

●●●●○

ORIENTAL TART

Glass: Martini
Garnish: Peeled lychee in drink
Method: SHAKE all ingredients with ice and fine strain into chilled glass.

1½	shot(s)	Tanqueray London dry gin
1	shot(s)	Soho lychee liqueur
2	shot(s)	Freshly squeezed grapefruit juice

Origin: Created in 2004 by Yours Truly (Simon Difford).
Comment: A sour, tart, fruity Martini with more than a hint of lychee.

●●●●◑

ORIGINAL SIN NEW #8

Glass: Martini
Garnish: Star anise
Method: POUR absinthe into ice-filled glass and top with water. Leave the mixture to stand in the glass. Separately, **STIR** all ingredients with ice. Finally discard contents of absinthe-coated glass and fine strain contents of shaker into absinthe washed glass.

½	shot(s)	La Fée Parisienne (68%) absinthe
2	shot(s)	Ketel One vodka
¾	shot(s)	Sake
⅛	shot(s)	Honey syrup (4 honey to 1 water)

Comment: Sake and vodka with a delicate hint of honey.
Origin: Created in 2009 by Spike Marchant and Simon Difford at the Cabinet Room, London, England.

●●●●◑

OSMO UPDATED #8

Glass: Martini
Garnish: Orange zest twist
Method: SHAKE all ingredients with ice and fine strain into chilled glass.

2	shot(s)	Sake
½	shot(s)	Cointreau triple sec
¼	shot(s)	Freshly squeezed lime juice
1½	shot(s)	Ocean Spray cranberry juice

Origin: Adapted from a drink discovered in 2005 at Mo Bar, Landmark Mandarin Oriental Hotel, Hong Kong, China.
Comment: A sake based Cosmopolitan.

●●●●○○

OUZI

Glass: Shot
Method: SHAKE all ingredients with ice and fine strain into chilled glass.

¾	shot(s)	Ketel One vodka
½	shot(s)	Ouzo 12 liqueur
¼	shot(s)	Sugar syrup (2 sugar to 1 water)
¼	shot(s)	Freshly squeezed lemon juice

Comment: A lemon and liquorice shooter.

●●●●○

PABLO ALVAREZ DE CAÑAS SPECIAL NEW #8

Glass: Coupette
Garnish: Pineapple cubes & cherry on stick, orange slice
Method: Place lemon zest in shaker, add other ingredients, **SHAKE** with ice and strain into chilled glass.

1	fresh	Lemon twist
1	shot(s)	Courvoisier V.S.O.P. cognac
1	shot(s)	Tio Pepe fino sherry
⅛	shot(s)	White crème de cacao liqueur
⅛	shot(s)	Heering cherry brandy liqueur
⅛	shot(s)	Sugar syrup (2 sugar to 1 water)

Origin: Recipe adapted from 1937 Bar Florida (later renamed Floridita) menu.
Comment: Sherry is most prevalent on the palate, but all the other ingredients, including the lemon zest, also contribute to this subtle, balanced and altogether a most unusual cocktail.

●●●●○

PADOVANI

Glass: Old-fashioned
Garnish: Lemon zest twist
Method: SHAKE all ingredients with ice and strain into ice-filled glass.

| 2 | shot(s) | Johnnie Walker Scotch whisky |
| 2 | shot(s) | St-Germain elderflower liqueur |

Origin: Created in 2006 and named after a fellow whisky fan, Xavier Padovani.
Comment: The peaty Scotch combines wonderfully with the floral, delicate elderflower liqueur.

●●●●◑○

PAGO PAGO

Glass: Martini
Garnish: Lime wedge on rim
Method: SHAKE all ingredients with ice and fine strain into chilled glass.

2	shot(s)	Bacardi Oro golden rum
¼	shot(s)	Green Chartreuse liqueur
½	shot(s)	White crème de cacao liqueur
½	shot(s)	Freshly squeezed lime juice
⅛	shot(s)	Sugar syrup (2 sugar to 1 water)
½	shot(s)	Chilled mineral water (omit if wet ice)

Comment: A Daiquiri with a liqueur twist.

PAINKILLER

Glass: Collins
Garnish: Pineapple wedge & cherry
Method: SHAKE all ingredients with ice and strain into ice-filled glass.

2	shot(s)	**Pusser's Navy rum**
2	shot(s)	**Pressed pineapple juice**
1	shot(s)	**Freshly squeezed orange juice**
1	shot(s)	**Coco López cream of coconut**

Origin: From the Soggy Dollar Bar on the island of Jost Van Dyke in the British Virgin Islands. The bar's name is logical, as most of the clientele are sailors and there is no dock. Hence they have to swim ashore, often paying for drinks with wet dollars.
Comment: Full-flavoured and fruity.

PAISLEY MARTINI

Glass: Martini
Garnish: Lemon zest twist
Method: STIR all ingredients with ice and strain into chilled glass.

2½	shot(s)	**Tanqueray London dry gin**
½	shot(s)	**Noilly Prat dry vermouth**
¼	shot(s)	**Johnnie Walker Scotch whisky**

Comment: A dry Martini for those with a penchant for Scotch.

PALE RIDER

Glass: Collins
Garnish: Lime wedge
Method: SHAKE all ingredients with ice and strain into ice-filled glass.

2	shot(s)	**Raspberry flavoured vodka**
½	shot(s)	**Peach Tree peach schnapps**
2	shot(s)	**Ocean Spray cranberry juice**
1	shot(s)	**Pressed pineapple juice**
1	shot(s)	**Freshly squeezed lime juice**
½	shot(s)	**Sugar syrup** (2 sugar to 1 water)

Origin: Created in 1997 by Wayne Collins at Navajo Joe, London, England.
Comment: Sweet and fruity.

PALERMO

Glass: Martini
Garnish: Vanilla pod
Method: SHAKE all ingredients with ice and fine strain into chilled glass.

1½	shot(s)	**Vanilla-infused Bacardi rum**
1	shot(s)	**Sauvignon Blanc wine**
1¼	shot(s)	**Pressed pineapple juice**
¼	shot(s)	**Sugar syrup** (2 sugar to 1 water)

Origin: Adapted from a cocktail discovered in 2001 at Hotel du Vin, Bristol, England.
Comment: This smooth cocktail beautifully combines vanilla rum with tart wine and the sweetness of the pineapple juice.

PALL MALL MARTINI

Glass: Martini
Garnish: Orange zest twist
Method: SHAKE all ingredients with ice and fine strain into chilled glass.

1	shot(s)	**Tanqueray London dry gin**
1	shot(s)	**Noilly Prat dry vermouth**
1	shot(s)	**Martini Rosso sweet vermouth**
¼	shot(s)	**White crème de cacao liqueur**
1	dashes	**Angostura orange bitters**

Comment: A classic Martini served 'perfect' with the tiniest hint of chocolate.

PALM BEACH

Glass: Martini
Garnish: Maraschino cherry
Method: SHAKE all ingredients with ice and fine strain into chilled glass.

2½	shot(s)	**Tanqueray London dry gin**
½	shot(s)	**Martini Rosso sweet vermouth**
1	shot(s)	**Freshly squeezed grapefruit juice**

Origin: A classic from the 1940s.
Comment: Dry, aromatic and packs one hell of a punch.

PALM SPRINGS

Glass: Collins
Garnish: Apple slice & mint sprig
Method: SHAKE all ingredients with ice and strain into glass filled with crushed ice.

4	fresh	**Mint leaves**
1	shot(s)	**Passoä passion fruit liqueur**
1	shot(s)	**Bacardi Oro golden rum**
¼	shot(s)	**Freshly squeezed lime juice**
1	shot(s)	**Pressed apple juice**
2	shot(s)	**Ocean Spray cranberry juice**

Comment: Sweet and aromatic.

PALMA VIOLET MARTINI

Glass: Martini
Garnish: Parma Violet sweets
Method: SHAKE all ingredients with ice and fine strain into chilled glass.

1½	shot(s)	**Ketel One vodka**
¼	shot(s)	**Peach Tree peach schnapps**
½	shot(s)	**Freshly squeezed lemon juice**
1	shot(s)	**Benoit Serres crème de violette**
¼	shot(s)	**Sugar syrup** (2 sugar to 1 water)
1	dash	**Angostura orange bitters**
½	shot(s)	**Chilled mineral water** (omit if wet ice)

Origin: Created in 2001 by Jamie Terrell at LAB, London, England.
Comment: A subtly floral drink with a delicate colour.

PALOMA UPDATED #8

●●●●◖

Glass: Collins
Garnish: Lime wedge & salt rim
Method: SHAKE first 4 ingredients with ice and strain into ice-filled glass. **TOP** with grapefruit soda, lightly stir and serve with straws.

2	shot(s)	**Don Julio reposado tequila**
2	shot(s)	**Freshly squeezed grapefruit juice**
½	shot(s)	**Freshly squeezed lime juice**
¼	shot(s)	**Agave syrup**
Top up with		**Grapefruit soda**

Origin: The name is Spanish for 'dove' and the cocktail is well-known in Mexico.
Comment: A long, fruity, Margarita-style drink.

PANACHÉE

●●●○○

Glass: Collins (10oz/290ml max)
Method: POUR first 2 ingredients into glass. Serve iced water separately in a small jug (known in France as a 'broc') so the customer can dilute to their own taste (I recommend four-and-a-half shots). Lastly, add ice to glass.

1	shot(s)	**La Fée Parisienne (68%) absinthe**
1	shot(s)	**Marie Brizard anisette liqueur**
Top up with		**Chilled mineral water**

Origin: This is one of the earliest known absinthe mixtures. Today if you order a 'panachée' at a French café, you will receive beer with lemonade (shandy).
Comment: Anisette sweetens the absinthe and adds a refreshing burst of herbal aniseed.

PANCHO VILLA

●●●●○

Glass: Martini (saucer)
Garnish: Pineapple wedge on rim
Method: SHAKE all ingredients with ice and fine strain into chilled glass.

1	shot(s)	**Bacardi Superior rum**
1	shot(s)	**Tanqueray London dry gin**
1	shot(s)	**Bols apricot brandy liqueur**
¼	shot(s)	**Heering cherry brandy liqueur**
¼	shot(s)	**Pressed pineapple juice**
½	shot(s)	**Chilled mineral water** (omit if wet ice)

Origin: Adapted from a recipe in the 1947-72 Trader Vic's Bartender's Guide by Victor Bergeron.
Comment: To quote Victor Bergeron, "This'll tuck you away neatly – and pick you up and throw you right on the floor".

PAPA BEAR NEW #8

●●●●◖

Glass: Coupette/Martini
Garnish: Honeycomb rim or lemon zest twist
Method: SHAKE all ingredients with ice and fine strain into chilled glass.

1	spoon	**Honey syrup** (4 honey to 1 water)
1½	shot(s)	**Courvoisier V.S.O.P. cognac**
1½	shot(s)	**Krupnik honey liqueur**
¾	shot(s)	**Freshly squeezed lemon juice**

Comment: Delicately spiced and honeyed cognac.
Origin: Created in 2008 by Tim Homewood, Dirty Martini Bar, London, England. Named after an old family friend who passed away. He was known to all of his children as 'daddy bear' so Papa Bear seemed appropriate.

PAPPY HONEYSUCKLE

●●●●◖

Glass: Martini
Garnish: Physalis fruit
Method: STIR honey with whiskey in base of shaker to dissolve honey. Add other ingredients, SHAKE with ice and fine strain into chilled glass.

1½	shot(s)	**Jameson Irish whiskey**
2	spoons	**Runny honey**
1¼	shot(s)	**Sauvignon Blanc wine**
1½	shot(s)	**Pressed apple juice**
¼	shot(s)	**Passion fruit syrup**
¼	shot(s)	**Freshly squeezed lemon juice**

Origin: Created in 2002 by Shelim Islam at the GE Club, London, England.
Comment: Fresh and fruity with honeyed sweetness.

PARADISE #1 ⚷

●●●●◖○

Glass: Martini
Garnish: Orange zest twist
Method: SHAKE all ingredients with ice and fine strain into chilled glass.

2	shot(s)	**Tanqueray London dry gin**
1	shot(s)	**Bols apricot brandy liqueur**
1	shot(s)	**Freshly squeezed orange juice**
¼	shot(s)	**Freshly squeezed lemon juice**

Origin: Proportioned according to a recipe in the 1930 edition of the Savoy Cocktail Book by Harry Craddock.
Comment: Orange predominates in this strong complex cocktail.

HOW TO MAKE SUGAR SYRUP

To make your own sugar syrup, gradually pour TWO cups of granulated sugar into a saucepan containing ONE cup of hot water. Stir as you pour and carry on stirring and simmering until the sugar is dissolved. Do not let the water even come close to boiling and only simmer for as long as it takes to dissolve the sugar. Allow syrup to cool and pour into an empty bottle. Ideally, you should finely strain your syrup into the bottle to remove any undissolved crystals which could otherwise encourage crystallisation. If kept in a refrigerator this mixture will last for a couple of months.

PARADISE #2

Glass: Martini
Garnish: Orange zest twist
Method: SHAKE all ingredients with ice and fine strain into chilled glass.

2	shot(s)	**Tanuqeray London dry gin**
¾	shot(s)	**Bols apricot brandy liqueur**
1¾	shot(s)	**Freshly squeezed orange juice**
3	dashes	**Angostura orange bitters** (optional)

Origin: This 1920s recipe has recently been revitalised by Dale DeGroff.
Comment: When well made, this wonderfully fruity cocktail beautifully harnesses and balances its ingredients.

PARADISE #3

Glass: Martini
Garnish: Orange zest twist
Method: Cut passion fruit in half and scoop flesh into shaker. Add other ingredients, **SHAKE** with ice and fine strain into chilled glass.

1	fresh	**Passion fruit**
2	shot(s)	**Tanqueray London dry gin**
¾	shot(s)	**Bols apricot brandy liqueur**
¾	shot(s)	**Freshly squeezed orange juice**

Comment: Thick, almost syrupy. Rich and fruity.

PARIS MANHATTAN UPDATED #8

Glass: Martini
Garnish: Maraschino cherry
Method: SHAKE all ingredients with ice and fine strain into chilled glass.

2	shot(s)	**Bulleit bourbon whiskey**
1	shot(s)	**St-Germain elderflower liqueur**
½	shot(s)	**Noilly Prat dry vermouth**
2	dashes	**Angostura aromatic bitters**

Origin: Created in 2006 by Yours Truly (Simon Difford), originally titled 'Elderflower Manhattan'.
Comment: Elderflower replaces sweet vermouth in this 'perfect' and aromatic Manhattan.

PARIS SOUR

Glass: Old-fashioned
Garnish: Lemon zest twist
Method: SHAKE all ingredients with ice and strain into ice-filled glass.

2	shot(s)	**Bulleit bourbon whiskey**
1¼	shot(s)	**Dubonnet Red** (French made)
¼	shot(s)	**Sugar syrup** (2 sugar to 1 water)
½	shot(s)	**Freshly squeezed lemon juice**
½	fresh	**Egg white**

Origin: Created in 2005 by Mark at Match Bar, London, England.
Comment: A wonderfully accommodating whiskey sour – it's easy to make and a pleasure to drink.

PARISIAN MARTINI #1

Glass: Martini
Garnish: Lemon peel twist
Method: SHAKE all ingredients with ice and fine strain into chilled glass.

1¼	shot(s)	**Tanqueray London dry gin**
1¼	shot(s)	**Crème de cassis liqueur**
1¼	shot(s)	**Noilly Prat dry vermouth**

Origin: A drink created in the 1920s to promote crème de cassis. This recipe is adapted from one in Harry Craddock's Savoy Cocktail Book.
Comment: Full-on rich cassis is barely tempered by gin and dry vermouth.

PARISIAN MARTINI #2

Glass: Martini
Garnish: Lime zest twist
Method: SHAKE all ingredients with ice and fine strain into chilled glass.

2	shot(s)	**Ketel One vodka**
1	shot(s)	**St-Germain elderflower liqueur**
¼	shot(s)	**Noilly Prat dry vermouth**

AKA: Can Can
Origin: Created in 2006 by Yours Truly (Simon Difford).
Comment: Floral, yet dry and aromatic. The character of the vodka shines through.

PARISIAN SIDECAR

Glass: Martini
Garnish: Lemon zest twist
Method: SHAKE all ingredients with ice and fine strain into chilled glass.

1½	shot(s)	**Courvoisier V.S.O.P. cognac**
1½	shot(s)	**St-Germain elderflower liqueur**
1	shot(s)	**Freshly squeezed lemon juice**

Origin: Created in 2006 by Yours Truly (Simon Difford).
Comment: An elderflower flavoured Sidecar named after the fashionable Left Bank area of Paris.

PARISIAN SPRING PUNCH

Glass: Collins
Garnish: Lemon zest knot
Method: SHAKE first 4 ingredients with ice and strain into ice-filled glass. **TOP** with champagne and serve with straws.

1	shot(s)	**Boulard Grand Solage calvados**
½	shot(s)	**Noilly Prat dry vermouth**
¼	shot(s)	**Freshly squeezed lemon juice**
¼	shot(s)	**Sugar syrup** (2 sugar to 1 water)
Top up with		**Perrier Jouet brut champagne**

Comment: Dry apple and champagne – like upmarket cider.

PARK AVENUE

Glass: Martini
Garnish: Maraschino cherry
Method: **SHAKE** all ingredients with ice and fine strain into chilled glass.

2	shot(s)	Tanqueray London dry gin
½	shot(s)	Grand Marnier liqueur
½	shot(s)	Martini Rosso sweet vermouth
1	shot(s)	Pressed pineapple juice

Origin: A classic from the 1940s.
Comment: Very fruity and well-balanced rather than dry or sweet.

PARK LANE

Glass: Martini
Garnish: Orange zest twist
Method: **SHAKE** all ingredients with ice and strain into chilled glass.

2	shot(s)	Tanqueray London dry gin
¾	shot(s)	Bols apricot brandy liqueur
¾	shot(s)	Freshly squeezed orange juice
⅛	shot(s)	Pomegranate (grenadine) syrup
½	fresh	Egg white

Comment: This smooth, frothy concoction hides a mean kick.

PARLAY PUNCH

Glass: Collins
Garnish: Lime wedge
Method: **SHAKE** all ingredients with ice and strain into ice-filled glass.

1½	shot(s)	Bulleit bourbon whiskey
1	shot(s)	Southern Comfort liqueur
1	shot(s)	Pressed pineapple juice
1	shot(s)	Ocean Spray cranberry juice
½	shot(s)	Freshly squeezed orange juice
½	shot(s)	Freshly squeezed lime juice

Origin: Adapted from a recipe discovered at Vortex Bar, Atlanta, USA.
Comment: Too many of these tangy punches and you'll be parlaying till dawn.

PARMA NEGRONI

Glass: Collins
Garnish: Orange slice
Method: **SHAKE** first 5 ingredients with ice and strain into ice-filled glass. **TOP** with tonic water, lightly stir and serve with straws.

1	shot(s)	Tanqueray London dry gin
1	shot(s)	Campari Bitter
1	shot(s)	Freshly squeezed grapefruit juice
2	dashes	Angostura aromatic bitters
½	shot(s)	Sugar syrup (2 sugar to 1 water)
Top up with		Tonic water

Origin: Discovered in 2005 at Club 97, Hong Kong, China.
Comment: Negroni drinkers will love this fruity adaptation.

PASS-ON-THAT

Glass: Collins
Garnish: Crown with passion fruit half
Method: Cut passion fruit in half and scoop flesh into shaker. Add other ingredients, **SHAKE** with ice and fine strain into ice-filled glass.

1	fresh	Passion fruit
1	shot(s)	Ketel One vodka
1	shot(s)	Passoã passion fruit liqueur
3	shot(s)	Ocean Spray cranberry juice

Comment: Full-on passion fruit and berries.

PASSBOUR COOLER

Glass: Collins
Garnish: Orange slice in glass
Method: **SHAKE** all ingredients with ice and strain into ice-filled glass.

1½	shot(s)	Bulleit bourbon whiskey
¾	shot(s)	Passoã passion fruit liqueur
¾	shot(s)	Heering cherry brandy liqueur
3	shot(s)	Ocean Spray cranberry juice

Comment: Cherry and bourbon with passion fruit.

PASSION FRUIT CAIPIRINHA

Glass: Old-fashioned
Method: **MUDDLE** lime wedges in the base of sturdy glass (being careful not to break the glass). Cut the passion fruit in half and scoop out the flesh into the glass. **POUR** cachaça and sugar syrup into glass, add crushed ice and **CHURN** (stir) with barspoon. Serve with straws.

1	fresh	Passion fruit
¾	fresh	Lime cut into wedges
2	shot(s)	Leblon cachaça
¾	shot(s)	Sugar syrup (2 sugar to 1 water)

Comment: A tasty fruit Caipirinha. You may end up sipping this from the glass as the passion fruit pips tend to clog straws.

PASSION FRUIT COLLINS

Glass: Collins
Garnish: Lemon slice
Method: Cut passion fruit in half and scoop out flesh into shaker. Add next 3 ingredients, **SHAKE** with ice and fine strain into ice-filled glass. **TOP** with soda, stir and serve with straws.

2	fresh	Passion fruit
2	shot(s)	Tanqueray London dry gin
1½	shot(s)	Freshly squeezed lemon juice
½	shot(s)	Passion fruit syrup
Top up with		Soda water (club soda)

Origin: Formula by Yours Truly (Simon Difford) in 2004.
Comment: This fruity adaptation of the classic Collins may be a tad sharp for some: if so, add a dash more sugar.

PASSION FRUIT DAIQUIRI

Glass: Martini
Garnish: Lime wedge on rim
Method: Cut passion fruit in half and scoop out flesh into shaker. Add other ingredients, **SHAKE** with ice and fine strain into chilled glass.

2	fresh	**Passion fruit**
2	shot(s)	**Bacardi Superior rum**
½	shot(s)	**Freshly squeezed lime juice**
½	shot(s)	**Sugar syrup** (2 sugar to 1 water)

Origin: Formula by Yours Truly (Simon Difford) in 2004.
Comment: The rum character comes through in this fruity cocktail.

PASSION FRUIT MARGARITA

Glass: Coupette
Garnish: Salt & lime wedge rim
Method: Cut passion fruit in half and scoop out flesh into shaker. Add other ingredients, **SHAKE** with ice and fine strain into chilled glass.

1	fresh	**Passion fruit**
2	shot(s)	**Don Julio reposado tequila**
1	shot(s)	**Cointreau triple sec**
1	shot(s)	**Freshly squeezed lime juice**
¼	shot(s)	**Passion fruit syrup**

Origin: Formula by Yours Truly (Simon Difford) in 2004.
Comment: The flavour of tequila is very evident in this fruity adaptation.

PASSION FRUIT MARTINI #1

Glass: Martini
Garnish: Physalis (cape gooseberry)
Method: Cut passion fruit in half and scoop out flesh into shaker. Add other ingredients, **SHAKE** with ice and fine strain into chilled glass.

1	fresh	**Passion fruit**
2	shot(s)	**Ketel One vodka**
½	shot(s)	**Sugar syrup** (2 sugar to 1 water)

Origin: Formula by Yours Truly (Simon Difford) in 2004.
Comment: A simple but tasty cocktail that wonderfully harnesses the flavour of passion fruit.

PASSION FRUIT MARTINI #2

Glass: Martini
Garnish: Star fruit on rim
Method: Cut passion fruit in half and scoop out flesh into shaker. Add other ingredients, **SHAKE** with ice and fine strain into chilled glass.

2	fresh	**Passion fruit**
2	shot(s)	**Ketel One vodka**
½	shot(s)	**Passion fruit syrup**

Origin: Formula by Yours Truly (Simon Difford) in 2004.
Comment: Not for Martini purists, but a fruity, easy drinking concoction for everyone else.

PASSION FRUIT MARTINI #3

Glass: Martini
Garnish: Float passion fruit half
Method: Cut passion fruit in half and scoop out flesh into shaker. Add other ingredients, **SHAKE** with ice and fine strain into chilled glass.

2	fresh	**Passion fruit**
2	shot(s)	**Tanqueray London dry gin**
½	shot(s)	**Cointreau triple sec**
¼	shot(s)	**Freshly squeezed lemon juice**
½	shot(s)	**Passion fruit syrup**
½	fresh	**Egg white**

Origin: Formula by Yours Truly (Simon Difford) in 2004.
Comment: Full-on passion fruit with gin and citrus hints.

PASSION KILLER

Glass: Shot
Method: Refrigerate ingredients then **LAYER** in chilled glass by carefully pouring in the following order.

½	shot(s)	**Midori green melon liqueur**
½	shot(s)	**Passoã passion fruit liqueur**
½	shot(s)	**Don Julio reposado tequila**

Comment: Tropical fruit and tequila.

PASSION PUNCH

Glass: Collins (or individual scorpion bowl)
Garnish: Half passion fruit
Method: Cut passion fruit in half and scoop flesh into blender. Add other ingredients and **BLEND** with 12oz scoop crushed ice. Serve with straws.

1	fresh	**Passion fruit**
2	shot(s)	**Tanqueray London dry gin**
¼	shot(s)	**Courvoisier V.S.O.P. cognac**
¾	shot(s)	**Freshly squeezed lime juice**
¾	shot(s)	**Sugar syrup** (2 sugar to 1 water)
2	dashes	**Angostura aromatic bitters**

Origin: Adapted from a recipe in the 1947-72 Trader Vic's Bartender's Guide by Victor Bergeron.
Comment: To quote the Trader, "A robust libation with the opulence of 'down under'."

PASSIONATE RUM PUNCH

Glass: Collins
Garnish: Passion fruit quarter
Method: Cut passion fruit in half and scoop out flesh into shaker. Add other ingredients, **SHAKE** with ice and fine strain into glass filled with crushed ice.

3	fresh	**Passion fruit**
2¼	shot(s)	**Wray & Nephew overproof rum**
¾	shot(s)	**Freshly squeezed lime juice**
1	shot(s)	**Sugar syrup** (2 sugar to 1 water)
½	shot(s)	**Passion fruit syrup**

Origin: Formula by Yours Truly (Simon Difford) in 2004.
Comment: Rum and fruit combine brilliantly in this tropical punch style drink.

PASSOVER

●●●○○

Glass: Collins
Garnish: Orange slice
Method: SHAKE all ingredients with ice and strain into ice-filled glass.

2	shot(s)	**Ketel One vodka**
1	shot(s)	**Passoã passion fruit liqueur**
3	shot(s)	**Freshly squeezed grapefruit juice**

Comment: Tropical and sweet.

PATRICK GAVIN DUFFY'S PUNCH NEW #8

●●●●○

Glass: Collins
Garnish: Mint sprig
Method: SHAKE all ingredients with ice and strain into ice-filled glass.

3	shot(s)	**Courvoisier V.S.O.P. cognac**
1½	shot(s)	**Bénédictine D.O.M. liqueur**
¼	shot(s)	**Sugar syrup** (2 sugar to 1 water)
2½	shot(s)	**Freshly squeezed orange juice**

Comment: Over four shots of alcohol per serve means this sure packs a tasty punch.

PAVLOVA SHOT

●●●●○

Glass: Shot
Method: Refrigerate ingredients then LAYER in chilled glass by carefully pouring in the following order.

¾	shot(s)	**Chambord black raspberry liqueur**
¾	shot(s)	**Ketel One vodka**

Comment: Pleasant, sweet shot.

PEACH DAIQUIRI

●●●●○

Glass: Martini
Garnish: Peach wedge on rim
Method: SHAKE all ingredients with ice and fine strain into chilled glass.

2	shot(s)	**Bacardi Superior rum**
1	shot(s)	**Peach Tree peach schnapps**
½	shot(s)	**Freshly squeezed lime juice**
½	shot(s)	**Chilled mineral water** (omit if wet ice)

Origin: My take on the Cuban Daiquiri de Melocoton.
Comment: A classic Daiquiri with a hint of peach liqueur.

PEACH MELBA MARTINI

●●●●◐○

Glass: Martini
Garnish: Float flaked almonds
Method: SHAKE all ingredients with ice and fine strain into chilled glass.

1½	shot(s)	**Vanilla-infused Ketel One vodka**
¾	shot(s)	**Peach Tree peach schnapps**
¾	shot(s)	**Chambord black raspberry liqueur**
1	shot(s)	**Double (heavy) cream**
1	shot(s)	**Milk**

Origin: Melba is a name given to various dishes dedicated to Dame Nellie Melba, the 19th century Australian opera singer. Peach Melba was created in 1892 by the world famous chef Georges-Auguste Escoffier, who was the business partner of César Ritz.
Comment: Not quite Peach Melba dessert, but rich and tasty all the same.

PEANUT BUTTER & JELLY SHOT

●●●●◐○

Glass: Shot
Method: SHAKE all ingredients with ice and fine strain into chilled glass.

½	shot(s)	**Chambord black raspberry liqueur**
½	shot(s)	**Frangelico hazelnut liqueur**
½	shot(s)	**Baileys Irish cream liqueur**

Comment: Does indeed taste a little like peanut butter and jelly (jam for the Brits).

PEAR & CARDAMOM SIDECAR

●●●●◐

Glass: Martini
Garnish: Pear slice on rim
Method: MUDDLE cardamom in base of shaker. Add other ingredients, SHAKE with ice and fine strain into chilled glass.

2	pods	**Green cardamom**
1	shot(s)	**Courvoisier V.S.O.P. cognac**
¾	shot(s)	**Cointreau triple sec**
¾	shot(s)	**Belle de Brillet pear liqueur**
¾	shot(s)	**Freshly squeezed lemon juice**
⅛	shot(s)	**Sugar syrup** (2 sugar to 1 water)
½	shot(s)	**Chilled mineral water** (omit if wet ice)

Origin: Adapted from a drink created in 2002 by Jason Scott at Oloroso, Edinburgh, Scotland.
Comment: A wonderful meld of aromatic ingredients.

HOW TO MAKE SUGAR SYRUP

To make your own sugar syrup, gradually pour **TWO cups of granulated sugar into a saucepan containing ONE cup of hot water.** Stir as you pour and carry on stirring and simmering until the sugar is dissolved. Do not let the water even come close to boiling and only simmer for as long as it takes to dissolve the sugar. Allow syrup to cool and pour into an empty bottle. Ideally, you should finely strain your syrup into the bottle to remove any undissolved crystals which could otherwise encourage crystallisation. If kept in a refrigerator this mixture will last for a couple of months.

PEAR & ELDERFLOWER COCKTAIL

Glass: Martini
Garnish: Pear slice on rim
Method: SHAKE all ingredients with ice and fine strain into chilled glass.

1½	shot(s)	**Ketel One vodka**
¾	shot(s)	**St-Germain elderflower liqueur**
1½	shot(s)	**Freshly extracted pear juice**

Origin: Adapted from a drink created in 2001 by Angelo Vieira at St. Martins, London, England.
Comment: Pear and elderflower are a match made in St Martin's Lane.

PEAR & VANILLA RICKEY

Glass: Collins
Garnish: Lime wedge
Method: SHAKE first 3 ingredients with ice and strain into ice-filled glass. **TOP** with lemonade, lightly stir and serve with straws.

1	shot(s)	**Vanilla-infused Ketel One vodka**
1	shot(s)	**Belle de Brillet pear liqueur**
1	shot(s)	**Freshly squeezed lime juice**
Top up with		**Lemonade/Sprite/7-Up**

Comment: Vanilla and pear create a creamy mouthful cut by lime juice.

PEAR DROP

Glass: Shot
Method: SHAKE all ingredients with ice and fine strain into chilled glass.

½	shot(s)	**Ketel One Citroen vodka**
½	shot(s)	**Soho lychee liqueur**
½	shot(s)	**Belle de Brillet pear liqueur**

Comment: Sweet, sticky and strong.

PEAR DROP MARTINI

Glass: Martini
Garnish: Pear drop sweet in drink
Method: SHAKE all ingredients with ice and fine strain into chilled glass.

1¼	shot(s)	**Belle de Brillet pear liqueur**
1	shot(s)	**Luxardo limoncello liqueur**
1	shot(s)	**Poire William eau de vie**
1	shot(s)	**Freshly extracted pear juice**

Origin: Created in 2002 by Yours Truly (Simon Difford).
Comment: Not as sticky as the sweet it takes its name from but full-on tangy pear.

THE FIRST 100% BLUE AGAVE TEQUILA WAS IMPORTED INTO AMERICA IN 1950 - BY BING CROSBY.

PEAR MARTINI

Glass: Martini
Garnish: Pear wedge on rim
Method: SHAKE all ingredients with ice and fine strain into chilled glass.

1½	shot(s)	**Pear flavoured vodka**
1½	shot(s)	**St-Germain elderflower liqueur**
⅛	shot	**Noilly Prat dry vermouth**

Comment: Aromatic pear vodka and floral elderflower liqueur are a match made in heaven. Vermouth adds complexity.

PEAR SHAPED #1 (DELUXE VERSION)

Glass: Martini
Garnish: Pear slice on rim
Method: Cut passion fruit in half and scoop out flesh into base of shaker. Add other ingredients, **SHAKE** with ice and fine strain into chilled glass.

1	fresh	**Passion fruit**
1½	shot(s)	**Johnnie Walker Scotch whisky**
1	shot(s)	**Belle de Brillet pear liqueur**
1	shot(s)	**Freshly extracted pear juice**
1	shot(s)	**Pressed apple juice**
¼	shot(s)	**Freshly squeezed lime juice**

Comment: Wonderful balance of flavours but pear predominates with a dry yet floral finish.

PEAR SHAPED #2 (POPULAR VERSION)

Glass: Collins
Glass: Pear wedge on rim
Method: SHAKE all ingredients with ice and strain into ice-filled glass.

2	shot(s)	**Johnnie Walker Scotch whisky**
1	shot(s)	**Belle de Brillet pear liqueur**
3	shot(s)	**Pressed apple juice**
½	shot(s)	**Freshly squeezed lime juice**
¼	shot(s)	**Vanilla sugar syrup**

Origin: Adapted from a drink created in 2003 by Jamie Terrell at Dick's Bar, Atlantic, London, England.
Comment: Scotch, pear and apple combine wonderfully in this medium-sweet long drink.

PEAR TREE COCKTAIL

●●●●◐

Glass: Martini
Garnish: Pear wedge on rim
Method: SHAKE first 2 ingredients with ice and fine strain into chilled glass. **TOP** with champagne.

1½	shot(s)	**Pear flavoured vodka**
1½	shot(s)	**St-Germain elderflower liqueur**
Top up with		**Perrier Jouet brut champagne**

Comment: Aromatic pear vodka and elderflower liqueur paired with biscuity champagne.

PEDRO COLLINS

●●●●○

Glass: Collins
Garnish: Lime wedge
Method: SHAKE first 3 ingredients with ice and strain into ice-filled glass. **TOP** with soda, lightly stir and serve with straws.

2	shot(s)	**Bacardi Superior rum**
1	shot(s)	**Freshly squeezed lime juice**
½	shot(s)	**Sugar syrup** (2 sugar to 1 water)
Top up with		**Soda water** (club soda)

Comment: This rum based Tom Collins is basically a long Daiquiri with soda.

EL PEDRONI NEW #8

●●●◐○

Glass: Old-fashioned
Garnish: Orange zest twist
Method: POUR ingredients into ice-filled glass and stir.

1½	shot(s)	**Don Julio reposado tequila**
1½	shot(s)	**Campari Bitter**
1½	shot(s)	**Punt e Mes**

Comment: Created by Teddy Joseph, UK.
Origin: Tequila replaces gin in this Negroni variation. Not an easy option.

PEGGY MARTINI

●●●○○

Glass: Martini
Garnish: Orange zest twist
Method: SHAKE all ingredients with ice and fine strain into chilled glass.

2	shot(s)	**Tanqueray London dry gin**
1	shot(s)	**Noilly Prat dry vermouth**
¼	shot(s)	**La Fée Parisienne (68%) absinthe**
¼	shot(s)	**Dubonnet Red** (French made)
½	shot(s)	**Chilled mineral water** (omit if wet ice)

Origin: Adapted from a recipe in the 1930s edition of the Savoy Cocktail Book by Harry Craddock.
Comment: Very dry and aromatic. Sadly this will appeal to few palates.

PEGU CLUB #1

●●●●○

Glass: Martini
Garnish: Lime wedge on rim
Method: SHAKE all ingredients with ice and fine strain into chilled glass.

2	shot(s)	**Tanqueray London dry gin**
1	shot(s)	**Cointreau triple sec**
½	shot(s)	**Freshly squeezed lime juice**
¼	shot(s)	**Sugar syrup** (2 sugar to 1 water)
1	dash	**Angostura aromatic bitters**
1	dash	**Angostura orange bitters**
½	shot(s)	**Chilled mineral water** (omit if wet ice)

Origin: Created in the 1920s at the Pegu Club, an expat gentlemen's club in British colonial Rangoon, Burma.

The recipe was first published in Harry MacElhone's 1927 'Barflies and Cocktails'. In his seminal 1930 Savoy Cocktail Book, Harry Craddock notes of this drink, "The favourite cocktail of the Pegu Club, Burma, and one that has travelled, and is asked for, round the world."
Comment: I've added a dash of sugar to the original recipe to reduce the tartness of this gin based Margarita-like concoction.

PEGU CLUB #2

●●●●◐

Glass: Martini
Garnish: Orange zest twist
Method: SHAKE all ingredients with ice and fine strain into chilled glass.

2	shot(s)	**Tanqueray London dry gin**
1	shot(s)	**Grand Marnier liqueur**
½	shot(s)	**Freshly squeezed lime juice**
1	dash	**Angostura aromatic bitters**
1	dash	**Angostura orange bitters**
½	shot(s)	**Chilled mineral water** (omit if wet ice)

Comment: This version of the Burmese classic is richer in orange.

PENDENNIS COCKTAIL

●●●●○

Glass: Martini
Garnish: Maraschino cherry
Method: SHAKE all ingredients with ice and fine strain into chilled glass.

2	shot(s)	**Tanqueray London dry gin**
1	shot(s)	**Bols apricot brandy liqueur**
½	shot(s)	**Freshly squeezed lime juice**
1	dash	**Peychaud's aromatic bitters**
¾	shot(s)	**Chilled mineral water** (omit if wet ice)

Origin: This classic is named after the Pendennis Club in Louisville, Kentucky, which is popularly supposed to be the birthplace of the Old-Fashioned.
Comment: Tangy, subtle, sweet and sour.

DRINKS ARE GRADED AS FOLLOWS:

● DISGUSTING ●● PRETTY AWFUL ●● BEST AVOIDED
●●◐ DISAPPOINTING ●●● ACCEPTABLE ●●●◐ GOOD
●●●● RECOMMENDED ●●●●◐ HIGHLY RECOMMENDED
●●●●● OUTSTANDING / EXCEPTIONAL

PENICILLIN NEW #8

●●●●●◐

Glass: Old-fashioned
Garnish: Candied ginger on rim
Method: SHAKE all ingredients with ice and strain into ice-filled glass.

1	shot(s)	**Johnny Walker Scotch whisky**
1	shot(s)	**Lagavulin 16yo malt whisky**
¼	shot(s)	**Domaine de Canton ginger liqueur**
¾	shot(s)	**Freshly squeezed lemon juice**
½	shot(s)	**Honey syrup** (4 honey to 1 water)

Origin: Adapted from a recipe by Sam Ross at Milk & Honey, New York City, USA.
Comment: Smoke and honey with subtle spice and plenty of Scottish attitude.

IN-FLIGHT COCKTAILS WERE SERVED FOR THE FIRST TIME TO PASSENGERS IN 1910 ON THE ZEPPELIN FLYING OVER GERMANY.

PEPIN RIVERO SPECIAL NEW #8

●●●●◐○

Glass: Coupette
Garnish: Cocoa dust
Method: SHAKE all ingredients with ice and fine strain into chilled glass.

1½	shot(s)	**Tanqueray London dry gin**
1	shot(s)	**White crème de cacao liqueur**
1	shot(s)	**Milk**

Origin: Created by Constantino (Constante) Ribalaigua Vert at the Floridita bar in Havana, Cuba. This recipe is adapted from a 1937 Bar Florida (later renamed Floridita) menu. The name refers to Pepin Rivero, who took over the Cuban El Diario de la Marina newspaper upon the death of his father Don Nicolas Rivero in 1944.
Comment: White chocolate come coconut ice-cream, only vaguely rescued from fluffiness by gin spirit.

PEPPER & VANILLA'TINI

●●●●●◐

Glass: Martini
Garnish: Strip yellow pepper
Method: SHAKE all ingredients with ice and fine strain into chilled glass.

1	shot(s)	**Vanilla-infused Ketel One vodka**
¾	shot(s)	**Pepper flavoured vodka**
1	shot(s)	**Cuarenta Y Tres (Licor 43) liqueur**
¾	shot(s)	**Tuaca Italian liqueur**
1	shot(s)	**Yellow bell pepper juice**

Origin: Formula by Yours Truly (Simon Difford) in 2002.
Comment: Vanilla and pepper seem to complement each other in a sweet and sour kind of way.

PEPPERED MARY

●●●●○

Glass: Collins
Garnish: Peppered rim & cherry tomato
Method: SHAKE all ingredients with ice and fine strain into chilled glass.

2	shot(s)	**Pepper flavoured vodka**
2	shot(s)	**Yellow bell pepper juice**
2	shot(s)	**Pressed tomato juice**
½	shot(s)	**Freshly squeezed lemon juice**
7	drops	**Tabasco pepper sauce**
1	spoon	**Lea & Perrins Worcestershire sauce**

Origin: Created in 2003 by Yours Truly (Simon Difford).
Comment: Hot and sweet pepper spice this Bloody Mary.

PEPPERMINT VANILLA DAIQUIRI

●●●○○

Glass: Old-fashioned
Garnish: Mint sprig
Method: SHAKE all ingredients with ice and strain into glass filled with crushed ice.

2	shot(s)	**Bacardi Superior rum**
¼	shot(s)	**Galliano L'Autentico liqueur**
¼	shot(s)	**Giffard Menthe Pastille liqueur**
½	shot(s)	**Freshly squeezed lime juice**
⅛	shot(s)	**Sugar syrup** (2 sugar to 1 water)

Origin: Discovered in 2005 at Bellini, Auckland, New Zealand.
Comment: An intriguing combination for folk who want their Daiquiris served 'fresh'.

PERFECT ALIBI

●●●●○

Glass: Collins
Garnish: Mint leaf & lime squeeze
Method: MUDDLE ginger in base of shaker. Add other ingredients, **SHAKE** with ice and fine strain into ice-filled glass.

2	slices	**Fresh root ginger** (thumbnail sized)
½	shot(s)	**Sugar syrup** (2 sugar to 1 water)
1½	shot(s)	**Krupnik honey liqueur**
½	shot(s)	**Bärenjäger honey liqueur**
3	shot(s)	**Cold black jasmine tea** (fairly weak)

Origin: Created in 2001 by Douglas Ankrah for Akbar, London, England.
Comment: A very unusual and pleasant mix of flavours.

PERFECT JOHN

●●●●○

Glass: Martini
Garnish: Orange zest twist
Method: SHAKE all ingredients with ice and fine strain into chilled glass.

1	shot(s)	**Ketel One vodka**
¾	shot(s)	**Cointreau triple sec**
1½	shot(s)	**Freshly squeezed orange juice**
¼	shot(s)	**Galliano L'Autentico liqueur**

Comment: A straight-up Harvey Wallbanger with Cointreau.

PERFECT LADY UPDATED #8

Glass: Martini
Garnish: Lemon zest twist (spray & discard) & peach slice
Method: SHAKE all ingredients with ice and fine strain into chilled glass.

2	shot(s)	Tanqueray London dry gin
¾	shot(s)	Crème pêche de vigne liqueur
¾	shot(s)	Freshly squeezed lemon juice
½	fresh	Egg white

Comment: This twist on a White Lady uses peach liqueur in place of triple sec to make a lighter, fruitier elaboration.
Origin: Created by S. Cox for a London cocktail competition in 1936 where it took the 1st Prize.

PERFECT MARTINI

Glass: Martini
Garnish: Orange zest twist
Method: SHAKE all ingredients with ice and fine strain into chilled glass.

1¼	shot(s)	Tanqueray London dry gin
1¼	shot(s)	Noilly Prat dry vermouth
1¼	shot(s)	Martini Rosso sweet vermouth
1	dash	Angostura orange bitters (optional)

Variant: Merry-Go-Round Martini
Origin: Adapted from a recipe in the 1930 edition of the Savoy Cocktail Book by Harry Craddock.
Comment: The high proportion of vermouth makes this Martini almost sherry-like.

PERFECT REGENT XV NEW #8

Glass: Coupette
Garnish: Berries on stick
Method: SHAKE all ingredients with ice and fine strain into chilled glass.

2	shot(s)	Courvoisier V.S.O.P. cognac
½	shot(s)	Crème de cassis liqueur
¼	shot(s)	Noilly Prat dry vermouth
¼	shot(s)	Martini Rosso sweet vermouth

Comment: Fruity and easy – perhaps not what you would expect.
Origin: Recipe adapted in 2008 by Yours Truly (Simon Difford) for Courvoisier.

PERIODISTA DAIQUIRI

Glass: Martini
Garnish: Lime wedge
Method: SHAKE all ingredients with ice and fine strain into chilled glass.

1½	shot(s)	Bacardi Superior rum
½	shot(s)	Freshly squeezed lime juice
½	shot(s)	Grand Marnier liqueur
½	shot(s)	Bols apricot brandy liqueur
½	shot(s)	Chilled mineral water (omit if wet ice)

Comment: Basically an orange and apricot Daiquiri.

PERISCOPE

Glass: Martini
Garnish: Grapefruit zest twist
Method: SHAKE all ingredients with ice and fine strain into chilled glass.

1½	shot(s)	Tanqueray London dry gin
1	shot(s)	St-Germain elderflower liqueur
⅛	shot(s)	Freshly squeezed lemon juice
⅛	shot(s)	Freshly squeezed lime juice
½	fresh	Egg white

Variant: Serve in an ice-filled Collins glass and top with soda.
Origin: Created by Matt Gee at Milk & Honey, New York City, USA.
Comment: Fabulously light, almost creamy, and very refreshing.

PERNELLE UPDATED #8

Glass: Collins
Garnish: Lemon zest twist & icing sugar dusted rosemary sprig
Method: SHAKE first 4 ingredients with ice and strain into glass filled with crushed ice. TOP with soda and serve with straws.

1	shot(s)	Ketel One vodka
1	shot(s)	St-Germain elderflower liqueur
1	shot(s)	Poire William eau de vie
1	shot(s)	Freshly squeezed lemon juice
Top up with		Soda water (club soda)

Comment: This long clear drink has a grassy, alpine aroma and a fresh pine finish.
Origin: Created in 2007 by Colin Asare-Appiah, London, England for U'Luvka vodka. This is named after the wife of the 14th century alchemist Nicolas Flamel, who supported him in his search for the Philosopher's Stone.

PERNOD & BLACK MARTINI

Glass: Martini
Garnish: Blackberries
Method: MUDDLE blackberries in base of shaker. Add other ingredients, SHAKE with ice and fine strain into chilled glass.

7	fresh	Blackberries
½	shot(s)	Pernod anis
1½	shot(s)	Ketel One vodka
½	shot(s)	Crème de mûre liqueur
1	shot(s)	Freshly squeezed lime juice
⅛	shot(s)	Vanilla sugar syrup
¾	shot(s)	Chilled mineral water (omit if wet ice)

Origin: Created in 2003 by Yours Truly (Simon Difford).
Comment: Pernod enhances the rich, tart flavours of blackberry.

PERROQUET

Glass: Collins (10oz / 290ml max)
Method: POUR pastis and mint syrup into glass. Serve iced water separately in a small jug (known in France as a 'broc') so the customer can dilute to their own taste (I recommend five shots). Add ice to fill glass.

1	shot(s)	**Ricard pastis**
¼	shot(s)	**Green mint (menthe) syrup**
Top up with		**Chilled mineral water**

Origin: Very popular throughout France, this drink is named after the parrot due to the bird's brightly coloured plumage.
Comment: The traditional French café drink with a hint of sweet mint.

PERRY-TINI

Glass: Martini
Garnish: Pear slice on rim
Method: SHAKE first 3 ingredients with ice and fine strain into chilled glass. **TOP** with champagne.

1	shot(s)	**Poire William eau de vie**
1	shot(s)	**Belle de Brillet pear liqueur**
2	shot(s)	**Freshly extracted pear juice**
Top up with		**Perrier Jouet brut champagne**

Origin: Created in 2002 by Yours Truly (Simon Difford).
Comment: Pear with a hint of sparkle.

PERUVIAN ELDER SOUR

Glass: Martini
Garnish: Lime wedge on rim
Method: SHAKE all ingredients with ice and fine strain into chilled glass.

2	shot(s)	**Barsol Quebranta pisco**
1	shot(s)	**St-Germain elderflower liqueur**
½	shot(s)	**Freshly squeezed lime juice**

Origin: Drinks writer Gary Regan created this in 2006 in New York, USA.
Comment: This tasty sour combines the aromatics of pisco and elderflower in an intriguing variation on the Margarita. Consider smoothing with fresh egg white.

PETER PAN COCKTAIL #1

Glass: Martini
Garnish: Orange zest twist
Method: SHAKE all ingredients with ice and fine strain into chilled glass.

1	shot(s)	**Tanqueray London dry gin**
1	shot(s)	**Noilly Prat dry vermouth**
1	shot(s)	**Freshly squeezed orange juice**
3	dashes	**Fee Brothers peach bitters**

Variant: Substitute Angostura aromatic bitters for peach bitters.
Origin: Adapted from a recipe in the 1930 edition of the Savoy Cocktail Book by Harry Craddock. The original recipe called for equal parts, including the bitters – surely a mistake.
Comment: Smoother, lighter and easier than most classic cocktails – perhaps a little too much so.

PETER PAN COCKTAIL #2

Glass: Martini
Garnish: Orange zest twist
Method: SHAKE all ingredients with ice and fine strain into chilled glass.

2	shot(s)	**Tanqueray London dry gin**
1	shot(s)	**Noilly Prat dry vermouth**
1	shot(s)	**Freshly squeezed orange juice**
3	dashes	**Fee Brothers peach bitters**

Origin: Adapted from a recipe in the 1930 edition of the Savoy Cocktail Book by Harry Craddock.
Comment: Orange predominates in this complex cocktail.

PETO MARTINI

Glass: Martini
Garnish: Orange zest twist
Method: SHAKE all ingredients with ice and fine strain into chilled glass.

2	shot(s)	**Tanqueray London dry gin**
1	shot(s)	**Noilly Prat dry vermouth**
1	shot(s)	**Martini Rosso sweet vermouth**
¼	shot(s)	**Freshly squeezed orange juice**
⅛	shot(s)	**Luxardo maraschino liqueur**

Origin: Adapted from a recipe in the 1930 edition of the Savoy Cocktail Book by Harry Craddock.
Comment: An aromatic classic Martini served 'perfect' with a hint of orange juice and maraschino.

PHARMACEUTICAL STIMULANT UPDATED #8

Glass: Medical cup or Old-fashioned
Garnish: Float three coffee beans
Method: SHAKE all ingredients with ice and strain into ice-filled glass.

2	shot(s)	**Ketel One vodka**
½	shot(s)	**Kahlúa coffee liqueur**
1½	shot(s)	**Espresso coffee**
¼	shot(s)	**Sugar syrup** (2 sugar to 1 water)

Comment: A real wake-up call and the drink that led to many an Espresso Martini.
Origin: Created in 1998 by Dick Bradsell at The Pharmacy, London, England.

PICADOR

Glass: Martini
Garnish: Lime zest twist
Method: SHAKE all ingredients with ice and fine strain into chilled glass.

2	shot(s)	**Don Julio reposado tequila**
1	shot(s)	**Freshly squeezed lime juice**
1	shot(s)	**Cointreau triple sec**

Origin: Yes, you're right! This drink is exactly the same as a classically proportioned Margarita. But... it was published in W. J. Tarling's 1937 'Café Royal Cocktail Book', 16 years before the first known written reference to a Margarita. Was the British recipe copied? Or did the Margarita independently evolve?
Comment: The name might be more masculine but it still tastes exactly like a classic Margarita.

PICCA

Glass: Martini
Garnish: Maraschino cherry
Method: SHAKE all ingredients with ice and fine strain into chilled glass.

1½	shot(s)	**Johnnie Walker Scotch whisky**
1	shot(s)	**Galliano L'Autentico liqueur**
1	shot(s)	**Martini Rosso sweet vermouth**
¾	shot(s)	**Chilled mineral water** (omit if wet ice)

Comment: Bittersweet whisky.

PICCADILLY MARTINI

Glass: Martini
Garnish: Lemon zest twist
Method: SHAKE all ingredients with ice and fine strain into chilled glass.

2	shot(s)	**Tanqueray London dry gin**
1	shot(s)	**Noilly Prat dry vermouth**
⅛	shot(s)	**La Fée Parisienne (68%) absinthe**
⅛	shot(s)	**Pomegranate (grenadine) syrup**

Origin: Adapted from a recipe in Harry Craddock's 1930 Savoy Cocktail Book.
Comment: A classic Martini tempered by a hint of pomegranate and absinthe.

PICHUNCHO MARTINI

Glass: Martini
Garnish: Orange zest twist
Method: SHAKE all ingredients with ice and fine strain into a chilled glass.

2¼	shot(s)	**Macchu pisco**
1½	shot(s)	**Martini Rosso sweet vermouth**
¼	shot(s)	**Sugar syrup** (2 sugar to 1 water)

Origin: Based on a traditional Chilean drink: pisco and vermouth served on the rocks.
Comment: This drink craves the best pisco and the best sweet vermouth. Find those and measure carefully and it's sublime.

THE [PICK OF] DESTINY NEW #8

Glass: Martini
Garnish: Orange zest twist
Method: SHAKE all ingredients with ice and fine strain into chilled glass.

2	shot(s)	**Rye whiskey (or bourbon)**
1	shot(s)	**St-Germain elderflower liqueur**
¾	shot(s)	**Freshly squeezed orange juice**
3	dashes	**Angostura orange bitters**

Comment: Fresh floral orange – just picked.
Origin: Adapted from a drink created in 2007 by Amanda Washington at Rye, San Francisco, USA.

PIERRE COLLINS

Glass: Collins
Garnish: Orange slice & cherry on stick (sail)
Method: SHAKE first 3 ingredients with ice and strain into ice-filled glass. **TOP** with soda, lightly stir and serve with straws.

2	shot(s)	**Courvoisier V.S.O.P. cognac**
1	shot(s)	**Freshly squeezed lemon juice**
½	shot(s)	**Sugar syrup** (2 sugar to 1 water)
Top up with		**Soda water** (club soda)

Comment: A Tom Collins made with cognac. The cognac's character shines through.

PILGRIM COCKTAIL

Glass: Martini
Garnish: Dust with grated nutmeg
Method: SHAKE all ingredients with ice and fine strain into chilled glass.

1½	shot(s)	**Bacardi Oro golden rum**
½	shot(s)	**Grand Marnier liqueur**
1	shot(s)	**Freshly squeezed orange juice**
¾	shot(s)	**Freshly squeezed lime juice**
¼	shot(s)	**World's End Pimento Dram liqueur**
3	dashes	**Angostura aromatic bitters**

Variant: Can also be served hot by simmering ingredients gently in a saucepan.
Comment: Whether you serve this hot or cold, it's a delicately spiced drink to warm the cockles.

> 'FRANKLY, I WAS HORRIFIED BY LIFE, AT WHAT A MAN HAD TO DO SIMPLY IN ORDER TO EAT, SLEEP AND KEEP HIMSELF CLOTHED. SO I STAYED IN BED AND DRANK.'
> CHARLES BUKOWSKI

PIMM'S COCKTAIL

Glass: Martini
Garnish: Lemon & orange zest twist
Method: SHAKE first 4 ingredients with ice and strain into chilled glass. **TOP** with champagne.

2	shot(s)	**Pimm's No.1 Cup**
½	shot(s)	**Tanqueray London dry gin**
¼	shot(s)	**Freshly squeezed lemon juice**
¼	shot(s)	**Sugar syrup** (2 sugar to 1 water)
Top up with		**Perrier Jouet brut champagne**

Comment: Luxuriate in this quintessentially English tipple.

PIMM'S CUP (OR CLASSIC PIMM'S) UPDATED #8

● ● ● ● ○ ○

Glass: Collins
Garnish: Mint sprig
Method: POUR Pimm's into glass half filled with ice. Add fruit and fill glass with more ice. **TOP** with lemonade (or ginger ale), lightly stir and serve with straws.

2	shot(s)	**Pimm's No. 1 Cup**
1	slice	**Fresh lemon**
1	slice	**Fresh orange**
2	slices	**Cucumber** (peeled & chopped)
1	fresh	**Strawberry** (hulled)
Top up with		**Lemonade/Sprite/7-Up** (or ginger ale)

Comment: You've not properly experienced an English summer until you've drunk one of these whilst sheltering from the rain.

Origin: This quintessential English summer tipple is usually accredited to James Pimm, who in 1823-4 began trading as a shellfish-monger in London's Lombard Street. He later moved to nearby number 3 Poultry, also in the City of London, where he established Pimm's Oyster Warehouse. It is here, in 1840, that he is said to have first served this drink.

Others dispute this, maintaining that James Pimm only unwittingly lent his name to the drink. They say the true credit lies with his successor, Samuel Morey, who is recorded as having taken out a retail liquor licence in 1860. This would appear to be when the oyster bar first offered its customers spirits. Many establishments of the day mixed house spirits to serve with liqueurs and juices as 'cups', in reference to the tankards in which they were sold. Naturally the 'cup' made at Pimm's Oyster Bar was named after the establishment which retained the goodwill of its founder.

Pimm's restaurant became very popular and changed hands a couple more times. Eventually Horatio David Davies, a wine merchant and owner of cafes in London bought the business. He became Sir Horatio, a Member of Parliament and between 1897-1898, Lord Mayor of London. He formed Pimm's into a private company in 1906, which, was controlled by family trusts for another 57 years after his death.

The precise date that the drink Pimm's was first sold outside restaurants and bars controlled by the Pimm's company is unknown. However, it is certain that the original product, No.1, was based on gin and flavoured with numerous botanicals including quinine. A second Pimm's product based on Scotch (Pimm's No.2 Cup) was launched and a third (Pimm's No.3 Cup) was based on brandy. Pimm's became popular in Britain in the 1920s and took off internationally after the Second World War. Other versions were then introduced: Pimm's No.4 based on rum, Pimm's No.6 on vodka and Pimm's No.7 on Rye whiskey.

PIMM'S ROYALE

● ● ● ○ ○ ○

Glass: Flute
Garnish: Berries on stick with cucumber peel
Method: POUR Pimm's into chilled glass and **TOP** with champagne.

1	shot(s)	**Pimm's No.1 Cup**
Top up with		**Perrier Jouet brut champagne**

Comment: Dry, subtle and refreshing.

DRINKS ARE GRADED AS FOLLOWS:

● DISGUSTING	● ● PRETTY AWFUL	● ● BEST AVOIDED
● ● ○ DISAPPOINTING	● ● ● ACCEPTABLE	● ● ● ● GOOD
● ● ● ● RECOMMENDED	● ● ● ● ○ HIGHLY RECOMMENDED	

● ● ● ● ● OUTSTANDING / EXCEPTIONAL

PIÑA COLADA #1 UPDATED #8

● ● ● ● ● ○

Glass: Hurricane (or hollowed out pineapple)
Garnish: Pineapple wedge & cherry
Method: BLEND all ingredients with one 12oz scoop crushed ice and serve with straws.

2	shot(s)	**Bacardi Oro golden rum**
4	shot(s)	**Pressed pineapple juice**
1	shot(s)	**Coco López cream of coconut**
1	shot(s)	**Double (heavy) cream**
1	pinch	**Salt**

Comment: A wonderful creamy, fruity concoction that's not half as sticky as the world would have you believe. Too much ice will detract from the creaminess and kill the drink.

Origin: Three Puerto Rican bartenders contest the ownership of this drink. Ramón Marrero Pérez claims to have first made it at the Caribe Hilton hotel's Beachcomber Bar in San Juan on 15th August 1954 using the then newly available Coco López cream of coconut. Ricardo Garcia, who also worked at the Caribe, says that it was he who invented the drink. But Ramón Portas Mingot says he created it in 1963 at the Barrachina Bar in Old San Juan.

It is, however, commonly accepted that the Piña Colada was adapted from an existing creation at the Caribe Hilton Hotel, which has since promoted itself as the home of the drink and today credits Ramón Marrero Pérez with its invention. Puerto Rico's famous Caribe Hilton Hotel sits on a 17-acre peninsula near Old San Juan. It was the first luxury hotel to open in the region and was a popular destination for the rich and famous who helped spread word of the drink.

The name 'Piña Colada' literally means 'strained pineapple', a reference to the freshly pressed and strained pineapple juice used in the drink's preparation. Another essential ingredient, 'cream of coconut', is a canned, non-alcoholic, thick, syrup-like blend of coconut juice, sugar, emulsifier, cellulose, thickeners, citric acid and salt.

PIÑA COLADA #2 (CUBAN STYLE)

● ● ● ● ○

Glass: Collins
Garnish: Lime wedge on rim
Method: SHAKE all ingredients with ice and strain into ice-filled glass.

1½	shot(s)	**Zacapa aged rum**
4	shot(s)	**Pressed pineapple juice**
¼	shot(s)	**Freshly squeezed lime juice**
¼	shot(s)	**Sugar syrup** (2 sugar to 1 water)

Origin: Touted by some as the original Piña Colada from Cuba.
Comment: This Colada has no coconut, but it is smooth, balanced and rather tasty.

PIÑA COLADA VIRGIN (MOCKTAIL)

● ● ● ● ○ ○

Glass: Hurricane
Garnish: Pineapple wedge & cherry on rim
Method: BLEND all ingredients with 18oz of crushed ice and serve with straws.

4	shot(s)	**Pressed pineapple juice**
1½	shot(s)	**Double (heavy) cream**
¾	shot(s)	**Milk**
2	shot(s)	**Coco López cream of coconut**

AKA: Snow White
Comment: A Piña Colada with its guts ripped out.

PIÑA MARTINI

Glass: Martini
Garnish: Pineapple wedge on rim
Method: SHAKE all ingredients with ice and fine strain into chilled glass.

2	shot(s)	**Ketel One vodka**
1¾	shot(s)	**Pressed pineapple juice**
¼	shot(s)	**Freshly squeezed lime juice**
⅛	shot(s)	**Sugar syrup** (2 sugar to 1 water)

Origin: Created in 2005 by Yours Truly (Simon Difford).
Comment: Rich pineapple but not too sweet.

PINEAPPLE & CARDAMOM DAIQUIRI

Glass: Martini
Garnish: Pineapple wedge on rim
Method: MUDDLE cardamom in base of shaker. Add other ingredients, **SHAKE** with ice and fine strain into chilled glass.

4	pods	**Green cardamom**
2	shot(s)	**Bacardi Superior rum**
1¾	shot(s)	**Pressed pineapple juice**
¼	shot(s)	**Freshly squeezed lime juice**
¼	shot(s)	**Sugar syrup** (2 sugar to 1 water)

Origin: Adapted from Henry Besant's Pineapple & Cardamom Martini.
Comment: One of the tastiest Daiquiris I've tried.

PINEAPPLE & CARDAMOM MARTINI

Glass: Martini
Garnish: Pineapple wedge on rim
Method: MUDDLE cardamom in base of shaker. Add other ingredients, **SHAKE** with ice and fine strain into chilled glass.

4	pods	**Green cardamom**
2	shot(s)	**Ketel One vodka**
2	shot(s)	**Pressed pineapple juice**
¼	shot(s)	**Sugar syrup** (2 sugar to 1 water)

Origin: Created in 2002 by Henry Besant at The Lonsdale, London, England.
Comment: This is about as good as it gets: a spectacular pairing of fruit and spice.

PINEAPPLE & GINGER MARTINI

Glass: Martini
Garnish: Pineapple wedge on rim
Method: MUDDLE ginger in base of shaker. Add other ingredients, **SHAKE** with ice and fine strain into chilled glass.

2	slices	**Fresh root ginger** (thumbnail sized)
2	shot(s)	**Ketel One vodka**
2	shot(s)	**Pressed pineapple juice**
⅛	shot(s)	**Sugar syrup** (2 sugar to 1 water)

Comment: Smooth, rich pineapple flavour with hints of vodka and ginger.

PINEAPPLE & SAGE MARGARITA

Glass: Coupette
Garnish: Pineapple wedge on rim
Method: Lightly **MUDDLE** sage in base of shaker. Add other ingredients, **SHAKE** with ice and fine strain into chilled glass.

5	fresh	**Sage leaves**
2	shot(s)	**Don Julio reposado tequila**
1	shot(s)	**Pressed pineapple juice**
½	shot(s)	**Freshly squeezed lime juice**
¼	shot(s)	**Agave syrup**

Origin: Adapted from a drink created in 2005 at Green & Red Bar, London, England.
Comment: Herbal tequila and sweet pineapple in harmony.

PINEAPPLE BLOSSOM

Glass: Martini
Garnish: Pineapple wedge on rim
Method: SHAKE all ingredients with ice and fine strain into chilled glass.

2	shot(s)	**Johnnie Walker Scotch whisky**
1	shot(s)	**Pressed pineapple juice**
½	shot(s)	**Freshly squeezed lemon juice**
½	shot(s)	**Sugar syrup** (2 sugar to 1 water)

Origin: My interpretation of a classic.
Comment: Richly flavoured but drier than you might expect.

PINEAPPLE DAIQUIRI #1
(ON-THE-ROCKS)

Glass: Old-fashioned
Garnish: Pineapple wedge & cherry
Method: SHAKE all ingredients with ice and fine strain into ice-filled glass.

2	shot(s)	**Bacardi Superior rum**
1	shot(s)	**Pressed pineapple juice**
½	shot(s)	**Freshly squeezed lime juice**
¼	shot(s)	**Sugar syrup** (2 sugar to 1 water)

Origin: Formula by Yours Truly (Simon Difford).
Comment: Rum and pineapple are just meant to go together.

PINEAPPLE DAIQUIRI #2 (FROZEN)

Glass: Martini (Large)
Garnish: Pineapple wedge & cherry
Method: BLEND all ingredients with 12oz scoop crushed ice and serve with straws.

2	shot(s)	**Bacardi Superior rum**
1½	shot(s)	**Pressed pineapple juice**
½	shot(s)	**Freshly squeezed lime juice**
¾	shot(s)	**Sugar syrup** (2 sugar to 1 water)

Origin: Formula by Yours Truly (Simon Difford).
Comment: Fluffy but very tasty.

●●●●○

PINEAPPLE FIX NEW #8

Glass: Old-fashioned
Garnish: Pineapple wedge
Method: SHAKE all ingredients with ice and strain into ice-filled glass.

2	shot(s)	**Zacapa aged rum**
1	shot(s)	**Pressed pineapple juice**
1	shot(s)	**Freshly squeezed lemon juice**
½	shot(s)	**Sugar syrup** (2 sugar to 1 water)

Comment: Rum and pineapple are a match made in heaven, here with lemon adding citrus freshness.

●●●●●

PINEAPPLE FIZZ

Glass: Collins
Garnish: Lime wedge & cherry
Method: SHAKE first 4 ingredients with ice and strain into ice-filled glass. **TOP** with soda, lightly stir and serve with straws.

2	shot(s)	**Bacardi Oro golden rum**
1½	shot(s)	**Pressed pineapple juice**
1	shot(s)	**Freshly squeezed lime juice**
½	shot(s)	**Sugar syrup** (2 sugar to 1 water)
Top up with		**Soda water** (club soda)

Comment: A Pineapple Daiquiri lengthened with soda. Surprisingly tasty and refreshing.

●●●●○

PINEAPPLE MARGARITA

Glass: Coupette
Garnish: Pineapple wedge on rim
Method: SHAKE all ingredients with ice and fine strain into chilled glass.

2	shot(s)	**Don Julio reposado tequila**
¾	shot(s)	**Cointreau triple sec**
1½	shot(s)	**Pressed pineapple juice**

Variant: Add half a shot of pineapple syrup, blend with 12oz scoop of crushed ice and serve frozen.
Comment: A Tequila Margarita with a pineapple fruit kick.

●●●●◐

PINEAPPLE MOJITO

Glass: Collins
Method: Lightly **MUDDLE** mint (just to bruise) in glass. **POUR** other ingredients into glass and half fill with crushed ice. **CHURN** (stir) with barspoon. Fill glass with more crushed ice, churn and serve with straws.

12	fresh	**Mint leaves**
2	shot(s)	**Bacardi Superior rum**
¾	shot(s)	**Cuarenta Y Tres (Licor 43) liqueur**
2	shot(s)	**Pressed pineapple juice**
1	shot(s)	**Freshly squeezed lime juice**

Origin: Discovered in 2003 at Apartment 195, London, England.
Comment: A fruity, vanilla-ed twist on the classic Mojito.

●●●●○○

PINEAPPLE SMOOTHIE (MOCKTAIL)

Glass: Collins
Garnish: Pineapple wedge
Method: BLEND all ingredients with 12oz scoop crushed ice. Serve with straws.

2	spoons	**Natural yoghurt**
2	spoons	**Runny honey**
4	shot(s)	**Pressed pineapple juice**

Comment: Fluffy in every sense of the word.

●●●●●◖

PINI

Glass: Martini
Garnish: Maraschino cherry
Method: SHAKE all ingredients with ice and fine strain into chilled glass.

2	shot(s)	**Macchu pisco**
½	shot(s)	**Courvoisier V.S.O.P. cognac**
¼	shot(s)	**White crème de cacao liqueur**
¼	shot(s)	**Sugar syrup** (2 sugar to 1 water)
½	shot(s)	**Chilled mineral water** (omit if wet ice)

Comment: Use a great pisco and you'll have a wonderfully complex drink.

●●●○○

PINK CLOUD

Glass: Martini
Method: SHAKE all ingredients with ice and fine strain into chilled glass.

1	shot(s)	**Luxardo Amaretto di Saschira**
1	shot(s)	**Pomegranate (grenadine) syrup**
1	shot(s)	**White crème de cacao liqueur**
¾	shot(s)	**Evaporated milk** (sweetened)

Origin: Adapted from a recipe in the 1947-72 Trader Vic's Bartender's Guide by Victor Bergeron.
Comment: To make this sweet after dinner drink I've used amaretto and pomegranate syrup in place of crème de noyaux. This almond flavoured liqueur made from apricot and peach stones is not currently available in the UK. US readers should use 2 shots of crème de noyaux in place of the first two ingredients.

●●●●○

PINK DAIQUIRI

Glass: Martini
Garnish: Lime wedge on rim
Method: SHAKE all ingredients with ice and fine strain into chilled glass.

2	shot(s)	**Bacardi Superior rum**
½	shot(s)	**Freshly squeezed lime juice**
½	shot(s)	**Pomegranate (grenadine) syrup**
¼	shot(s)	**Luxardo maraschino liqueur**
3	dashes	**Angostura aromatic bitters**
½	shot(s)	**Chilled mineral water** (omit if wet ice)

AKA: Daiquiri No.5
Origin: A classic from the 1930s.
Comment: The quality of pomegranate syrup will make or break this delicate Daiquiri.

PINK FLAMINGO

● ● ● ○ ○

Glass: Collins
Garnish: Apple slice
Method: SHAKE all ingredients with ice and fine strain into chilled glass.

2	shot(s)	**Orange-infused Ketel One vodka**
1	shot(s)	**Sour apple liqueur**
½	shot(s)	**Freshly squeezed lime juice**
1	shot(s)	**Ocean Spray cranberry juice**

Origin: Created in 2002 by Wayne Collins for Maxxium UK.
Comment: Soapy and citrus flavoured – but in a nice way.

PINK GIN (MODERN) UPDATED #8

● ● ● ● ○

Glass: Martini
Garnish: Lemon zest twist
Method: STIR all ingredients with ice and strain into chilled glass.

2	shot(s)	**Tanqueray London dry gin**
2	shot(s)	**Chilled mineral water** (reduce if wet ice)
1	dash	**Angostura aromatic bitters**

Comment: Normally I'd advocate liberal use of bitters but this refined and subtle drink benefits from frugality.
Origin: Gin was a favourite of the Royal Navy – along with rum, which was served as a daily ration right up until the 70s. It was often mixed with healthy ingredients to make them more palatable. Pink gin was originally used against stomach upsets, as Angostura aromatic bitters were considered medicinal. Traditionally this drink was made in a bitters swashed glass without the use of ice.

> **'BE WARY OF STRONG DRINK. IT CAN MAKE YOU SHOOT AT TAX COLLECTORS ... AND MISS.'**
> ROBERT A. HEINLEIN

PINK GIN & TONIC

● ● ● ● ○

Glass: Collins
Garnish: Lime slice
Method: POUR gin and Angostura bitters into ice-filled glass, **TOP** with tonic, lightly stir and serve with straws.

2	shot(s)	**Tanqueray London dry gin**
4	dashes	**Angostura aromatic bitters**
Top up with		**Tonic water**

Comment: Basically a G&T with an extra pep of flavour from Angostura, this has a wider appeal than the original Pink Gin.

PINK GRAPEFRUIT MARGARITA

● ● ● ● ○

Glass: Coupette
Garnish: Lime wedge on rim
Method: SHAKE all ingredients with ice and fine strain into chilled glass.

2	shot(s)	**Don Julio reposado tequila**
1	shot(s)	**Freshly squeezed grapefruit juice**
½	shot(s)	**Freshly squeezed lime juice**
¼	shot(s)	**Sugar syrup** (2 sugar to 1 water)

Comment: Delivers exactly what the name promises.

PINK HOUND

● ● ● ● ○

Glass: Martini
Garnish: Lemon zest twist
Method: SHAKE all ingredients with ice and fine strain into chilled glass.

2	shot(s)	**Tanqueray London dry gin**
1½	shot(s)	**Freshly squeezed grapefruit juice**
¼	shot(s)	**Pomegranate (grenadine) syrup**

Comment: A flavoursome balance of sweet and sour.

PINK LADY UPDATED #8

● ● ● ● ◐

Glass: Martini
Garnish: Maraschino cherry
Method: SHAKE all ingredients with ice and fine strain into chilled glass.

2	shot(s)	**Tanqueray London dry gin**
½	shot(s)	**Freshly squeezed lemon juice**
¼	shot(s)	**Pomegranate (grenadine) syrup**
½	fresh	**Egg white** (optional)

Variant: With the addition of half a shot apple brandy.
Origin: A classic cocktail named after a successful 1912 stage play.
Comment: Despite the colour, this is sharp and alcoholic.

PINK LEMONADE (MOCKTAIL)

● ● ● ○ ○

Glass: Collins
Garnish: Lemon slice
Method: SHAKE first 3 ingredients with ice and strain into ice-filled glass. **TOP** with soda and serve with straws.

2	shot(s)	**Freshly squeezed lemon juice**
½	shot(s)	**Pomegranate (grenadine) syrup**
¼	shot(s)	**Sugar syrup** (2 sugar to 1 water)
Top up with		**Soda water** (club soda)

Origin: Discovered in 2004 in New York City.
Comment: A tall, pink, tangy, alcohol free cocktail.

PINK PALACE

Glass: Martini
Garnish: Lemon twist
Method: SHAKE all ingredients with ice and fine strain into chilled glass.

2	shot(s)	**Tanqueray London dry gin**
½	shot(s)	**Grand Marnier liqueur**
½	shot(s)	**Freshly squeezed lemon juice**
¼	shot(s)	**Pomegranate (grenadine) syrup**

Origin: The signature drink at The Polo Lounge, Beverly Hills Hotel, Los Angeles, USA. The hotel, which is lovingly termed the 'Pink Palace', inspired The Eagles' Hotel California and graces the album cover.
Comment: A great drink but rarely done justice at the Polo Lounge.

PINK SIN MARTINI

Glass: Martini
Garnish: Dust with cinnamon powder
Method: SHAKE all ingredients with ice and fine strain into chilled glass.

1½	shot(s)	**Ketel One vodka**
1	shot(s)	**White crème de cacao liqueur**
¾	shot(s)	**Goldschläger cinnamon schnapps**
1	shot(s)	**Ocean Spray cranberry juice**

Comment: This looks a little like a Cosmo but delivers sweet cinnamon and chocolate.

PINK SQUIRREL

Glass: Martini
Garnish: Mint leaf
Method: SHAKE all ingredients with ice and fine strain into chilled glass.

1	shot(s)	**Crème de noyaux liqueur**
1	shot(s)	**White crème de cacao liqueur**
½	shot(s)	**Double (heavy) cream**
½	shot(s)	**Milk**

Origin: Adapted from Victor Bergeron's 'Trader Vic's Bartender's Guide' (1972 revised edition).
Comment: Crème de noyaux, a pink almond liqueur, is now very hard to obtain: if in doubt, substitute with ¾ amaretto ¼ grenadine.

PINK TUTU

Glass: Old-fashioned
Garnish: Orange slice
Method: SHAKE all ingredients with ice and strain into ice-filled glass.

1	shot(s)	**Peach Tree peach schnapps**
½	shot(s)	**Ketel One vodka**
½	shot(s)	**Campari Bitter**
1½	shot(s)	**Freshly squeezed grapefruit juice**
¼	shot(s)	**Sugar syrup** (2 sugar to 1 water)

Origin: Created in 1999 by Dominique of Café Rouge, Leeds, England.
Comment: A cocktail that's both bitter and sweet.

PINKY PINCHER

Glass: Old-fashioned
Garnish: Mint sprig, orange & lemon slice
Method: SHAKE all ingredients with ice and strain into ice-filled glass.

2	shot(s)	**Bulleit bourbon whiskey**
1	shot(s)	**Freshly squeezed orange juice**
1	shot(s)	**Freshly squeezed lemon juice**
¼	shot(s)	**Almond (orgeat) syrup**
¼	shot(s)	**Sugar syrup** (2 sugar to 1 water)

Origin: Adapted from a drink created by Victor Bergeron (Trader Vic).
Comment: Fruity, sweetened bourbon.

'I'M FOR ANYTHING THAT GETS YOU THROUGH THE NIGHT, BE IT PRAYER, TRANQUILIZERS, OR A BOTTLE OF JACK DANIEL'S.' FRANK SINATRA

PINO PEPE

Glass: Sling (or pineapple shell)
Garnish: Mint sprig
Method: BLEND all ingredients with 12oz scoop crushed ice. Pour into glass (or pineapple shell) and serve with straws. If using a pineapple shell, serve with ice cubes.

1	shot(s)	**Bacardi Superior rum**
1	shot(s)	**Ketel One vodka**
½	shot(s)	**Cointreau triple sec**
2	shot(s)	**Pressed pineapple juice**
½	shot(s)	**Freshly squeezed lime juice**
¼	shot(s)	**Freshly squeezed lemon juice**
½	shot(s)	**Sugar syrup** (2 sugar to 1 water)

Origin: Adapted from a recipe in the 1947-72 Trader Vic's Bartender's Guide by Victor Bergeron.
Comment: To quote Trader Vic, "Lethal but smooth – pineapple at its best".

PIRATE DAIQUIRI

Glass: Martini
Garnish: Lime wedge on rim
Method: SHAKE all ingredients with ice and fine strain into chilled glass.

¾	shot(s)	**Wray & Nephew overproof rum**
¾	shot(s)	**Pusser's Navy rum**
½	shot(s)	**Goldschläger cinnamon schnapps**
½	shot(s)	**Freshly squeezed lime juice**
¼	shot(s)	**Pomegranate (grenadine) syrup**
¾	shot(s)	**Chilled mineral water** (omit if wet ice)

Origin: Created in 2004 by Yours Truly (Simon Difford).
Comment: Why the name? Well, the rums are hard and nautical, the lime protects against scurvy, the liqueur contains gold and the syrup is red as blood.

PISCO COLLINS

Glass: Collins
Garnish: Orange slice & cherry on stick (sail)
Method: SHAKE first 3 ingredients with ice and strain into ice-filled glass. **TOP** with soda, lightly stir and serve with straws.

2	shot(s)	**Macchu pisco**
1	shot(s)	**Freshly squeezed lime juice**
½	shot(s)	**Sugar syrup** (2 sugar to 1 water)
Top up with		**Soda water** (club soda)

Comment: The most aromatic and flavoursome of the Collins family.

PISCO NARANJA

Glass: Collins
Garnish: Orange slice
Method: SHAKE all ingredients with ice and strain into ice-filled glass.

2	shot(s)	**Macchu pisco**
3	shot(s)	**Freshly squeezed orange juice**
1	shot(s)	**Grand Marnier liqueur**

Origin: I based this recipe on the traditional Chilean combination of pisco and orange juice.
Comment: Aromatic brandy and orange juice pepped up and sweetened with a slug of orange liqueur.

PISCO PUNCH #1 (DIFFORD'S FORMULA)

Glass: Collins
Garnish: Pineapple wedge on rim
Method: MUDDLE cloves in base of shaker. Add other ingredients except for champagne, **SHAKE** with ice and strain into ice-filled glass. **TOP** with champagne.

4	dried	**Cloves**
2¼	shot(s)	**Macchu pisco**
1¾	shot(s)	**Pressed pineapple juice**
¼	shot(s)	**Freshly squeezed orange juice**
½	shot(s)	**Freshly squeezed lemon juice**
½	shot(s)	**Sugar syrup** (2 sugar to 1 water)
Top up with		**Perrier Jouet brut champagne**

Origin: Created in 2003 by Yours Truly (Simon Difford).
Variant: This recipe is improved by using the marinade prescribed in Alfredo Micheli's Pisco Punch in place of sugar syrup. If using the marinade drop one of the marinated pineapple wedges and cloves into the drink as the garnish.
Comment: A tangy, balanced combination of rich flavours. The quality of pisco used is crucial to the success of a Pisco Punch.

PISCO PUNCH #2 (ALFREDO MICHELI'S FORMULA)

Glass: Goblet
Garnish: Pineapple wedge on rim
Method: MUDDLE orange and pineapple in base of shaker. Add pisco and pineapple marinade, **SHAKE** with ice and fine strain into ice-filled glass. **TOP** with no more than 2 shots of soda water.

2	fresh	**Orange slices**
3	fresh	**Marinated pineapple wedges**
2	shot(s)	**Macchu pisco**
¾	shot(s)	**Pineapple marinade**
Top up with		**Soda water** (club soda)

Recipe for marinade: Core and remove the rind from one ripe pineapple. Cut the pineapple into rings and then into wedges and place in a deep container. Add 30 cloves and one litre of sugar syrup and marinate for 24 hours.
Origin: Alfredo Micheli (who went by the nickname Mike) was employed at the Bank Exchange and spied on Duncan Nichol to learn how to make this legendary drink. After he believed he'd learnt the secret he left to start serving at a newly opened competitor to the Bank Exchange, Paoli's on Montgomery Street.
Comment: This subtly flavoured drink is justifiably legendary.

PISCO PUNCH #3 (LANES' FORMULA)

Glass: Collins
Garnish: Pineapple wedge on rim
Method: SHAKE first 4 ingredients with ice and strain into glass filled with crushed ice. **TOP** with soda, lightly stir and serve with straws.

2½	shot(s)	**Macchu pisco**
½	shot(s)	**Freshly squeezed lemon juice**
1	shot(s)	**Pressed pineapple juice**
½	shot(s)	**Sugar syrup** (2 sugar to 1 water)
Top up with		**Soda water** (club soda)

Origin: This recipe is said to herald from John Lanes, manager of the famous Bank Exchange when it closed in 1919.
Comment: Pisco's character comes through the fruit in this long, refreshing classic.

PISCO PUNCH #4 (PROSSER'S FORMULA)

Glass: Martini
Garnish: Grapes on rim
Method: MUDDLE grapes in base of shaker. Add other ingredients, **SHAKE** with ice and fine strain into chilled glass.

20	fresh	**Seedless white grapes**
2½	shot(s)	**Macchu pisco**
1	shot(s)	**Pressed pineapple juice**
⅛	shot(s)	**La Fée Parisienne (68%) absinthe**

Origin: Jack Koeppler, the bartender at the Buena Vista Café in San Francisco who's also famous for being the first bartender in America to serve Irish Coffee, was given this recipe by the son of its creator, a fellow San Franciscan by the name of Mr Prosser. I've adapted this recipe from his, which originally comprised: 2 shots white grape juice, 2 shots pisco, 1 spoon pineapple juice and 1 spoon absinthe.
Comment: An aromatic take on the Pisco Punch.

DRINKS ARE GRADED AS FOLLOWS:

● DISGUSTING ●◐ PRETTY AWFUL ●● BEST AVOIDED
●●◐ DISAPPOINTING ●●● ACCEPTABLE ●●●◐ GOOD
●●●● RECOMMENDED ●●●●◐ HIGHLY RECOMMENDED
●●●●● OUTSTANDING / EXCEPTIONAL

PISCO PUNCH

PISCO SOUR (TRADITIONAL RECIPE) UPDATED #8

Glass: Goblet
Garnish: Three drops of Angostura bitters
Method: BLEND all ingredients with 12oz scoop crushed ice and serve with straws.

2	shot(s)	**Macchu pisco**
1	shot(s)	**Freshly squeezed lime juice**
1	shot(s)	**Sugar syrup** (2 sugar to 1 water)
½	fresh	**Egg white**

Variation: Dust with cinnamon powder.
Origin: The national drink of both Peru and Chile and both countries lay claim to the origins of the drink and the spirit it is made from. The Pisco Sour is said to have been created in the early 1920s at Bar Morris located, 847 Calle Boza, Jiron de la Union, Lima, Peru. The drinks recent popularity outside of its native Peru and Chile is attributed to Joe Baum who promoted the drink in the 1960s at La Fonda Del Sol in New York.
Comment: One of the few really brilliant blended drinks.

PISCO SOUR (DIFFORD'S VERSION)

Glass: Old-fashioned
Garnish: Three drops of Angostura bitters
Method: SHAKE all ingredients with ice and fine strain into chilled glass.

2½	shot(s)	**Macchu pisco**
1	shot(s)	**Freshly squeezed lime juice**
½	shot(s)	**Sugar syrup** (2 sugar to 1 water)
½	fresh	**Egg white**
1	dash	**Orange flower water**

Origin: My adaptation of the Chilean and Peruvian classic.
Comment: Traditionally this drink is blended with crushed ice, but I prefer it served straight-up. Be sure to drink it quickly while it's cold.

THE IBA - THE INTERNATIONAL BARTENDERS ASSOCIATION - STARTED IN TORQUAY, UK IN 1951.

PISCOLA

Glass: Collins
Garnish: Lime wedge
Method: POUR pisco and bitters into ice-filled glass, top with Coca-Cola, stir and serve with straws.

2½	shot(s)	**Macchu pisco**
3	dashes	**Angostura aromatic bitters**
Top up with		**Coca-Cola**

Origin: A popular long drink in its native Chile.
Comment: A 'brandy' and cola with a hint of angostura. Try it and see why the Chileans enjoy it.

PLANTATION PUNCH

Glass: Collins
Garnish: Orange slice & mint sprig
Method: SHAKE first 5 ingredients with ice and strain into ice-filled glass. **TOP** with soda.

1½	shot(s)	**Southern Comfort liqueur**
1	shot(s)	**Bacardi Superior rum**
¾	shot(s)	**Freshly squeezed lemon juice**
¼	shot(s)	**Sugar syrup** (2 sugar to 1 water)
2	dashes	**Angostura aromatic bitters**
Top up with		**Soda water** (club soda)

Comment: Southern Comfort drives this tropical punch.

PLANTER'S PUNCH

Glass: Collins
Garnish: Orange slice & mint sprig
Method: SHAKE all ingredients with ice and strain into ice-filled glass.

1½	shot(s)	**Myers's dark Jamaican rum**
1	shot(s)	**Freshly squeezed lime juice**
½	shot(s)	**Sugar syrup** (2 sugar to 1 water)
2	shot(s)	**Chilled mineral water**
3	dashes	**Angostura aromatic bitters**

Origin: Invented in the late 19th century by the founder of Myers's rum, Fred L. Myers. The recipe on the back of each bottle is known as the 'Old Plantation formula' and uses the classic rum punch proportions of 1 sour (lime), 2 sweet (sugar), 3 strong (rum) and 4 weak (water). Rather than this or the American formula (1 sweet, 2 sour, 3 weak and 4 strong), I've followed David A. Embury's recommendation of 1 sweet, 2 sour, 3 strong and 4 weak.
Comment: A tangy punch which harnesses the rich flavours of Myers's rum.

PLANTER'S PUNCHLESS (MOCKTAIL)

Glass: Collins
Garnish: Lime wedge
Method: SHAKE first 3 ingredients with ice and strain into ice-filled glass. **TOP** with lemonade, lightly stir and serve with straws.

2	shot(s)	**Pressed apple juice**
¾	shot(s)	**Freshly squeezed lime juice**
¼	shot(s)	**Pomegranate (grenadine) syrup**
Top up with		**Lemonade/Sprite/7-Up**

Comment: A pleasant, if uninspiring, driver's option.

PLANTEUR

Glass: Collins
Garnish: Orange slice
Method: SHAKE all ingredients with ice and strain into ice-filled glass.

2	shot(s)	**Martinique agricole rum**
3½	shot(s)	**Freshly squeezed orange juice**
¼	shot(s)	**Pomegranate (grenadine) syrup**

Comment: Handle with extreme care.

PLATINUM BLONDE

Glass: Martini
Garnish: Freshly grated nutmeg
Method: **SHAKE** all ingredients with ice and fine strain into chilled glass.

1½	shot(s)	**Zacapa aged rum**
1½	shot(s)	**Grand Marnier liqueur**
½	shot(s)	**Double (heavy) cream**
½	shot(s)	**Milk**

Comment: An after dinner sipper.

PLAYA DEL MAR

Glass: Martini
Garnish: Pineapple wedge on rim
Method: **SHAKE** all ingredients with ice and fine strain into chilled glass.

1	shot(s)	**Don Julio reposado tequila**
½	shot(s)	**Cointreau triple sec**
1	shot(s)	**Ocean Spray cranberry juice**
¾	shot(s)	**Pressed pineapple juice**
½	shot(s)	**Freshly squeezed lime juice**
¼	shot(s)	**Sugar syrup** (2 sugar to 1 water)

Origin: This cocktail was created in 1997 by Wayne Collins at Navajo Joe, London, England. The name translates as 'Beach of the Sea'.
Comment: A fruity complex taste with a hint of tequila.

PLAYMATE MARTINI

Glass: Martini
Garnish: Orange zest twist
Method: **SHAKE** all ingredients with ice and fine strain into chilled glass.

1	shot(s)	**Courvoisier V.S.O.P. cognac**
1	shot(s)	**Grand Marnier liqueur**
1	shot(s)	**Bols apricot brandy liqueur**
1	shot(s)	**Freshly squeezed orange juice**
½	fresh	**Egg white**
3	dashes	**Angostura aromatic bitters**

Comment: Smooth and easy drinking.

PLUM COCKTAIL

Glass: Martini
Garnish: Plum quarter on rim
Method: Cut plum into quarters, remove stone and peel. **MUDDLE** plum in base of shaker. Add other ingredients, **SHAKE** with ice and fine strain into chilled glass.

1	fresh	**Plum** (stoned, peeled & chopped)
2	shot(s)	**Zuta Osa Slivovitz plum brandy**
¼	shot(s)	**Noilly Prat dry vermouth**
¼	shot(s)	**Sugar syrup** (2 sugar to 1 water)

Origin: Formula by Yours Truly (Simon Difford) in 2004.
Comment: The slivovitz adds woody, brandied notes to the plum.

PLUM DAIQUIRI

Glass: Martini
Garnish: Lime wedge on rim
Method: Cut plum into quarters, remove stone and peel. **MUDDLE** plum pieces in base of shaker. Add other ingredients, **SHAKE** with ice and fine strain into chilled glass.

1	fresh	**Plum** (stoned, peeled & chopped)
2	shot(s)	**Bacardi Superior rum**
½	shot(s)	**Freshly squeezed lime juice**
½	shot(s)	**Sugar syrup** (2 sugar to 1 water)

Origin: Formula by Yours Truly (Simon Difford) in 2004.
Comment: Depending on the ripeness of the plums, you may need to adjust the quantity of sugar.

PLUM MARTINI

Glass: Martini
Garnish: Plum quarter on rim (unpeeled)
Method: Cut plum into quarters, remove stone and peel. **MUDDLE** plum pieces in base of shaker. Add other ingredients, **SHAKE** with ice and fine strain into chilled glass.

1	fresh	**Plum** (stoned, peeled & chopped)
2	shot(s)	**Ketel One vodka**
¾	shot(s)	**Noilly Prat dry vermouth**
½	shot(s)	**Sugar syrup** (2 sugar to 1 water)

Origin: Formula by Yours Truly (Simon Difford) in 2004.
Variant: Substitute vanilla sugar syrup for plain sugar syrup.
Comment: Fortified plum juice in a Martini glass.

PLUM PUDDING MARTINI

Glass: Martini
Garnish: Grate fresh nutmeg over drink
Method: Cut plum into quarters, remove stone and peel. **MUDDLE** plum pieces in base of shaker. Add other ingredients, **SHAKE** with ice and fine strain into chilled glass.

1	fresh	**Plum** (stoned, peeled & chopped)
1	shot(s)	**Raspberry flavoured vodka**
1	shot(s)	**Vanilla-infused Ketel One vodka**
½	shot(s)	**Luxardo Amaretto di Saschira**
⅛	shot(s)	**Goldschläger cinnamon schnapps**

Origin: Created in 2004 by Yours Truly (Simon Difford).
Comment: Spicy and fruity.

PLUM SOUR

Glass: Old-fashioned
Garnish: Orange zest twist
Method: **MUDDLE** plum in base of shaker. Add other ingredients, **SHAKE** with ice and fine strain into ice-filled glass.

1	fresh	**Plum** (stoned, peeled & chopped)
2	shot(s)	**Ketel One vodka**
1	shot(s)	**Freshly squeezed lemon juice**
½	shot(s)	**Sugar syrup** (2 sugar to 1 water)
½	fresh	**Egg white**

Comment: Soft, ripe plums are key to this fruity sour.

POET'S DREAM

Glass: Martini
Garnish: Squeezed lemon zest twist
Method: STIR all ingredients with ice and strain into chilled glass.

1	shot(s)	**Tanqueray London dry gin**
1	shot(s)	**Bénédictine D.O.M. liqueur**
1	shot(s)	**Noilly Prat dry vermouth**
¾	shot(s)	**Chilled mineral water** (omit if wet ice)

Origin: Adapted from a recipe in the 1949 edition of Esquire's Handbook for Hosts.
Comment: Subtle, honeyed and herbal.

POGO STICK

Glass: Martini (large)
Garnish: Mint sprig
Method: BLEND all ingredients with 12oz scoop crushed ice. Serve with straws.

2	shot(s)	**Tanqueray London dry gin**
½	shot(s)	**Pressed pineapple juice**
½	shot(s)	**Freshly squeezed grapefruit juice**
½	shot(s)	**Freshly squeezed lime juice**
½	shot(s)	**Sugar syrup** (2 sugar to 1 water)

Origin: Adapted from a recipe in the 1947-72 Trader Vic's Bartender's Guide by Victor Bergeron.
Comment: To quote Trader Vic, "A refreshing blend of gin with pineapple and grapefruit juice… a real romper".

POINSETTIA

Glass: Flute
Garnish: Quarter slice of orange on rim
Method: POUR first 2 ingredients into chilled glass. TOP with champagne.

½	shot(s)	**Cointreau triple sec**
1	shot(s)	**Ocean Spray cranberry juice**
Top up with		**Perrier Jouet brut champagne**

Comment: Fruity champagne.

POLISH MARTINI UPDATED #8

Glass: Martini
Garnish: Apple slice
Method: SHAKE all ingredients with ice and fine strain into chilled glass.

¾	shot(s)	**Ketel One vodka**
¾	shot(s)	**Zubrówka bison vodka**
¾	shot(s)	**Krupnik honey liqueur**
¾	shot(s)	**Pressed apple juice**

Comment: Bison vodka and apple juice are a classic comb, here also an additional splash of Polish honey liqueur.
Origin: Created by Dick Bradsell, for his (Polish) father-in-law, Victor Sarge.

POLLY'S SPECIAL UPDATED #8

Glass: Martini **Garnish:** Grapefruit wedge on rim
Method: SHAKE all ingredients with ice and fine strain into chilled glass.

2	shot(s)	**Johnnie Walker Scotch whisky**
1	shot(s)	**Freshly squeezed grapefruit juice**
1	shot(s)	**Grand Marnier liqueur**
⅛	shot(s)	**Sugar syrup** (2 sugar to 1 water)

Comment: Sweet, sour, flavoursome and balanced.
Origin: Adapted from a recipe in the 1947 edition of Trader Vic's Bartender's Guide.

POMEGRANATE BELLINI

Glass: Flute
Method: SHAKE first 3 ingredients with ice and fine strain into chilled glass. TOP with sparkling wine.

1	shot(s)	**POM Wonderful pomegranate juice**
½	shot(s)	**Cuarenta Y Tres (Licor 43) liqueur**
⅛	shot(s)	**Freshly squeezed lemon juice**
Top up with		**Prosecco sparkling wine**

Origin: Created in 2005 by Yours Truly (Simon Difford).
Comment: This red drink is drier and more adult than it looks.

POMEGRANATE MARGARITA

Glass: Coupette
Garnish: Lime wedge on rim
Method: SHAKE all ingredients with ice and fine strain into chilled glass.

2	shot(s)	**Don Julio reposado tequila**
1	shot(s)	**POM Wonderful pomegranate juice**
½	shot(s)	**Freshly squeezed lime juice**
¼	shot(s)	**Pomegranate (grenadine) syrup**

Origin: Recipe by Yours Truly (Simon Difford) in 2006.
Comment: Pomegranate and tequila combine harmoniously in this Margarita.

POMEGRANATE MARTINI

Glass: Martini
Garnish: Orange zest twist
Method: SHAKE all ingredients with ice and fine strain into chilled glass.

2	shot(s)	**Ketel One vodka**
1½	shot(s)	**POM Wonderful pomegranate juice**
½	shot(s)	**Pomegranate (grenadine) syrup**

Origin: Adapted from a drink discovered in 2005 at Lotus Bar, Sydney, Australia.
Comment: This drink was originally based on gin but I find that juniper and pomegranate clash.

POMME ET SUREAU

Glass: Collins
Garnish: Apple wedge
Method: POUR first 2 ingredients into ice-filled glass. TOP with soda.

1	shot(s)	**Boulard Grand Solage calvados**
2	shot(s)	**St-Germain elderflower liqueur**
Top up with		**Soda water**

Origin: Created in 2006 by Yours Truly (Simon Difford). The name means 'Apple & Elderflower' in French.
Comment: Light, long and refreshing apple and elderflower.

POMPANSKI MARTINI

Glass: Martini
Garnish: Orange zest twist
Method: SHAKE all ingredients with ice and fine strain into chilled glass.

1¾	shot(s)	**Ketel One vodka**
½	shot(s)	**Cointreau triple sec**
1½	shot(s)	**Freshly squeezed grapefruit juice**
¼	shot(s)	**Sugar syrup** (2 sugar to 1 water)
1	spoon	**Noilly Prat dry vermouth**

Comment: Dry and zesty with the sharp freshness of grapefruit and a hint of orange.

PONCE DE LEON

Glass: Flute
Method: SHAKE first 4 ingredients with ice and fine strain into chilled glass. TOP with champagne.

½	shot(s)	**Bacardi Oro golden rum**
½	shot(s)	**Courvoisier V.S.O.P. cognac**
½	shot(s)	**Cointreau triple sec**
½	shot(s)	**Freshly squeezed grapefruit juice**
Top up with		**Perrier Jouet brut champagne**

Origin: A long lost classic.
Comment: A well-balanced champagne cocktail.

PONCHA

Glass: Collins
Garnish: Orange wedge
Method: STIR honey with aguardiente in base of shaker to dissolve honey. Add other ingredients, SHAKE with ice and strain into ice filled glass.

2	spoons	**Runny honey**
2½	shot(s)	**Torres Aqua d'Or aguardiente**
1	shot(s)	**Freshly squeezed lemon juice**
¼	shot(s)	**Sugar syrup** (2 sugar to 1 water)
1½	shot(s)	**Freshly squeezed orange juice**
1½	shot(s)	**Freshly squeezed grapefruit juice**

Origin: My adaptation of a tradtitional drink from the island of Madeira.
Comment: This citrus refresher is reputedly an excellent cold remedy.

PONCHE DE ALGARROBINA

Glass: Goblet
Garnish: Dust with cinnamon
Method: BLEND all ingredients with 12oz scoop crushed ice. Serve with straws.

2	shot(s)	**Macchu pisco**
1	fresh	**Egg yolk**
1	shot(s)	**Condensed milk**
1	spoon	**Algarrobo extract** (or malt extract from healthfood shops)

Tip: It pays to add the condensed milk and Algarrobo (or malt extract) after starting the blender.
Origin: A traditional Peruvian drink I discovered at Tito's Restaurant, London, England. Algarrobo is extracted from the fruits of the tree of the same name. It is a sticky honey-like liquid which I find tastes a little like malt extract.
Comment: A creamy frozen drink with real character.

PONTBERRY MARTINI

Glass: Martini
Garnish: Blackberries
Method: SHAKE all ingredients with ice and fine strain into chilled glass.

1½	shot(s)	**Ketel One vodka**
½	shot(s)	**Crème de mûre liqueur**
2	shot(s)	**Ocean Spray cranberry juice**

Origin: Created by Dick Bradsell in the late 90s for the opening of Agent Provocateur in Pont Street, London, England.
Comment: A light, fruity, easy drinking cocktail.

POOH'TINI

Glass: Martini
Garnish: Lemon zest twist
Method: STIR honey with vodka in base of shaker to dissolve honey. Add other ingredients, SHAKE with ice and fine strain into chilled glass.

2	spoons	**Runny honey**
2	shot(s)	**Zubrówka bison grass vodka**
½	shot(s)	**Krupnik honey liqueur**
1½	shot(s)	**Cold black camomile tea**

Origin: Adapted from a drink discovered in 1999 at Lot 61, New York City.
Comment: Grassy honey with a spicy, slightly tannic, camomile finish.

PORT FLIP NEW #8

Glass: Marini
Garnish: Dust with freshly ground nutmeg
Method: SHAKE all ingredients with ice and fine strain into chilled glass.

1	shot(s)	**Courvoisier V.S.O.P. cognac**
3	shot(s)	**Warre's Otima tawny port**
⅛	shot(s)	**Sugar syrup** (2 sugar to 1 water)
1	fresh	**Egg** (white & yolk)

Comment: Old-school and something of a meal in a glass.

PORT & MELON MARTINI

Glass: Martini
Garnish: Melon wedge on rim
Method: Cut melon into 8 segments and deseed. Cut cubes of flesh from skin of one segment and **MUDDLE** in base of shaker. Add other ingredients, **SHAKE** with ice and fine strain into chilled glass.

⅛	fresh	Cantaloupe melon
1½	shot(s)	Ketel One vodka
1½	shot(s)	Taylor's Chip dry white port
1	pinch	Ground ginger

Origin: Created in 2004 by Yours Truly (Simon Difford).
Comment: The classic seventies starter served as a Martini.

PORT & STARBOARD

Glass: Shot
Method: Refrigerate ingredients then **LAYER** in chilled glass by carefully pouring in the following order.

½	shot(s)	Pomegranate (grenadine) syrup
½	shot(s)	Giffard Menthe Pastille liqueur

Origin: Named after and inspired by the red and green running lights which respectively mark the 'Port' (left-hand) and 'Starboard' (right-hand) sides of a ship. The red light is called the Port side because port wine is red. The original name for the opposite side was Larboard, but over the years it was corrupted to Starboard.
Comment: Easy to layer but hard to drink. Very sweet.

> ## 'A MEDIUM VODKA DRY MARTINI — WITH A SLICE OF LEMON PEEL. SHAKEN AND NOT STIRRED.'
> ### IAN FLEMING

PORT LIGHT

Glass: Martini
Garnish: Passion fruit half
Method: **STIR** honey with bourbon in base of shaker to dissolve honey. Cut passion fruit in half and scoop flesh into shaker. Add other ingredients, **SHAKE** with ice and fine strain into chilled glass.

2	spoons	Runny honey
2	shot(s)	Bulleit bourbon whiskey
1	fresh	Passion fruit
1	shot(s)	Freshly squeezed lemon juice
½	shot(s)	Pomegranate (grenadine) syrup
½	fresh	Egg white

Origin: Adapted from a drink created by Victor Bergeron (Trader Vic).
Comment: Strong and very fruity. Too many will put your lights out.

PORT NO.2 NEW #8

Glass: Martini
Garnish: Orange zest twist
Method: **STIR** all ingredients with ice and strain into chilled glass.

2	shot(s)	Warre's Otima tawny port
½	shot(s)	Orange curaçao liqueur
2	dashes	Angostura orange bitters
1	dash	Angostura aromatic bitters

Origin: Vintage cocktail of unknown origin.
Comment: Sangria for grown-ups.

PORT SANGREE NEW #8

Glass: Martini
Garnish: Orange zest twist
Method: **STIR** all ingredients with ice and strain into chilled glass.

2	shot(s)	Warre's Otima tawny port
1	shot(s)	Chilled mineral water
¼	shot(s)	Sugar syrup (2 sugar to 1 water)

Comment: Wine-like, light and easy.
Origin: Vintage cocktail of unknown origin.

PORT WINE COCKTAIL

Glass: Martini
Garnish: Orange zest twist
Method: **STIR** all ingredients with ice and strain into chilled glass.

3	shot(s)	Warre's Otima tawny port
1	shot(s)	Courvoisier V.S.O.P. cognac

Origin: A classic from the early 1900s.
Comment: Port and brandy served straight-up and dressed up.

POTTED PARROT

Glass: Sling
Garnish: Parrot on stick & mint sprig
Method: **SHAKE** all ingredients with ice and strain into glass filled with crushed ice.

2	shot(s)	Bacardi Superior rum
½	shot(s)	Cointreau triple sec
2	shot(s)	Freshly squeezed orange juice
1	shot(s)	Freshly squeezed lemon juice
¼	shot(s)	Almond (orgeat) syrup
¼	shot(s)	Sugar syrup (2 sugar to 1 water)

Origin: Adapted from a recipe in the 1947-72 Trader Vic's Bartender's Guide by Victor Bergeron. Popular in Trader Vic's restaurants.
Comment: Tangy orange, not too sweet.

POUSSE-CAFÉ

Glass: Shot
Method: Refrigerate ingredients then **LAYER** in chilled glass by carefully pouring in the following order.

¼	shot(s)	**Pomegranate (grenadine) syrup**
¼	shot(s)	**Kahlúa coffee liqueur**
¼	shot(s)	**Green crème de menthe liqueur**
¼	shot(s)	**Cointreau triple sec**
¼	shot(s)	**Bulleit bourbon whiskey**
¼	shot(s)	**Wray & Nephew overproof rum**

Origin: A pousse-café is now a term for any multi-layered cocktail. (See 'Layer' in the 'Bartending Basics' chapter at the beginning of this guide.) The term originally seems to have been a general term for a mixture of liqueurs and/or spirits served after dinner, and most probably originated in France.
Comment: More a test of patience and a steady hand than a drink.

PRADO

Glass: Martini
Garnish: Lime wedge on rim
Method: **SHAKE** all ingredients with ice and fine strain into chilled glass.

2	shot(s)	**Don Julio reposado tequila**
1	shot(s)	**Freshly squeezed lime juice**
½	shot(s)	**Luxardo maraschino liqueur**
½	shot(s)	**Egg white**

Comment: Rather like a cross between an Aviation and a Margarita.

PRAIRIE OYSTER #1 (MOCKTAIL)

UPDATED #8

Glass: Coupette
Garnish: Dust with black pepper
Method: Taking care not to break the egg yolk, **PLACE** it in the centre if the glass. **SHAKE** the rest of the ingredients with ice and strain over egg. Instruct drinker to down in one.

1	fresh	**Egg yolk**
¼	shot(s)	**Malt vinegar**
1	spoon	**Worcestershire sauce**
1	spoon	**Tomato ketchup**
5	drops	**Tabasco pepper sauce**

Origin: Recipe adapted from Harry Craddock's 1930 'The Savoy Cocktail Book'. This drink is thought to have originally been created in Germany in the 1870s. Jeeves makes something similar for Bertie Wooster in a P.G. Wodehouse tale.
Comment: Like many supposed hangover cures, this works on the kill or cure basis. It tastes slightly better than it looks.

PRAIRIE OYSTER #2
(MODERN & ALCOHOLIC) NEW #8

Glass: Coupette
Method: Taking care not to break the egg yolk, **PLACE** it in the centre if the glass. **SHAKE** the rest of the ingredients with ice and strain over egg. Instruct drinker to down in one.

1	fresh	**Egg yolk**
1	shot(s)	**Courvoisier V.S.O.P. cognac**
¼	shot(s)	**Worcestershire sauce**
¼	shot(s)	**Tomato juice**
5	drops	**Tabasco pepper sauce**
2	grinds	**Pepper**
2	pinches	**Salt**
½	shot(s)	**Malt vinegar**

Variation: Use another spirit such as vodka in place of cognac.
Comment: This "pick-me-up" (A.K.A. hangover cure) may be a somewhat daunting prospect irrespective of the present state of your constitution.

SCHWEPPES FIRST LAUNCHED THEIR INDIAN TONIC WATER IN THE 1870s.

PRE SIESTA NEW #8

Glass: Martini
Garnish: Orange zest twist
Method: **SHAKE** all ingredients and fine strain into chilled glass.

2	shot(s)	**Don Julio reposado tequila**
½	shot(s)	**Aperol**
¾	shot(s)	**Cointreau triple sec**
3	dashes	**Angostura orange bitters**

Origin: Created in 2007 by Little Rich Hunt at Mahiki, London, England.
Comment: Orange liqueurs and bitters flavour this tequila-based, salmon-pink, dry and hard cocktail.

PRESIDENT

Glass: Martini
Garnish: Orange zest twist
Method: **SHAKE** all ingredients with ice and fine strain into chilled glass.

2	shot(s)	**Bacardi Superior rum**
1	shot(s)	**Freshly squeezed orange juice**
¼	shot(s)	**Freshly squeezed lemon juice**
¼	shot(s)	**Pomegranate (grenadine) syrup**
½	shot(s)	**Chilled mineral water** (omit if wet ice)

Origin: Adapted from a recipe in Harry Craddock's 1930 Savoy Cocktail Book.
Comment: A delicately fruity orange Daiquiri.

PRESIDENT VINCENT ●●●○○

Glass: Martini
Garnish: Lime zest twist
Method: SHAKE all ingredients with ice and fine strain into chilled glass.

2	shot(s)	**Bacardi Superior rum**
½	shot(s)	**Noilly Prat dry vermouth**
½	shot(s)	**Freshly squeezed lime juice**
¼	shot(s)	**Sugar syrup** (2 sugar to 1 water)

Origin: Probably 1930s.
Comment: A dry, spicy take on the Daiquiri.

PRESIDENTE UPDATED #8 ●●●●○

Glass: Coupette
Garnish: Orange zest twist (discarded) & maraschino cherry
Method: SHAKE all ingredients with crushed ice and strain into chilled glass.

1½	shot(s)	**Bacardi Superior rum**
1½	shot(s)	**Noilly Prat dry vermouth**
¼	shot(s)	**Grand Marnier liqueur**

Comment: Bone dry, light and delicate. The sweetness and colour of the maraschino cherry garnish makes this drink.
Origin: Thought to have created during the 1920s in Vista Alegre, Havana, Cuba. This recipe is adapted from a 1937 Bar Florida (later renamed Floridita) menu, Havana, Cuba. On page 40 of his 1928 book 'When it's cocktail time in Cuba', Basil Woon says of this drink, "It is the aristocrat of cocktails and is the one preferred by the better class of Cuban."

PRESIDENTE MENOCAL SPECIAL

NEW #8 ●●●●○

Glass: Coupette
Garnish: Mint sprig and two cherries
Method: SHAKE all ingredients with ice and fine strain into glass filled with crushed ice.

7	fresh	**Mint leaves**
2	shot(s)	**Bacardi Superior rum**
¼	shot(s)	**Sugar syrup** (2 sugar to 1 water)
⅛	shot(s)	**Freshly squeezed lime juice**

Comment: What hot Cuban summers are made for.
Origin: Created by Constantino (Constante) Ribalaigua Vert at the Floridita bar in Havana, Cuba. This recipe is adapted from a 1937 Bar Florida (later renamed Floridita) menu. The name refers to Mario García Menocal, who was president of Cuba from 1912 to 1920.

PRESTIGE COCKTAIL NEW #8 ●●●●◖

Glass: Martini
Garnish: Pineapple wedge & spiral lime peel
Method: SHAKE all ingredients with ice and strain into chilled glass.

1¾	shot(s)	**Zacapa aged rum**
1	shot(s)	**Pressed pineapple juice**
½	shot(s)	**Noilly Prat dry vermouth**
½	shot(s)	**Velvet Falernum liqueur**
½	shot(s)	**Freshly squeezed lime juice**

Origin: Created in 2002 by Dale Degroff, New York City, USA.
Comment: Slightly sweet but very more-ish. Aged rum, pineapple, clove and lime.

PRICKLY PEAR MULE ●●●●○

Glass: Collins
Garnish: Pear slice on rim
Method: SHAKE first 5 ingredients with ice and strain into ice-filled glass. TOP with ginger beer.

1¼	shot(s)	**Belle de Brillet pear liqueur**
1¼	shot(s)	**Poire William eau de vie**
3	shot(s)	**Freshly extracted pear juice**
¼	shot(s)	**Freshly squeezed lemon juice**
2	dashes	**Angostura aromatic bitters**
Top up with		**Jamaican ginger beer**

Origin: Created in 2002 by Yours Truly (Simon Difford).
Tip: Fill the glass with ice and go easy on the ginger beer which can predominate and overpower the pear.
Comment: Subtle pear with ginger spice.

PRINCE CHARLIE ●●●●○

Glass: Martini
Garnish: Lemon zest twist
Method: SHAKE all ingredients with ice and fine strain into chilled glass.

1	shot(s)	**Courvoisier V.S.O.P. cognac**
1	shot(s)	**Drambuie liqueur**
1	shot(s)	**Freshly squeezed lemon juice**
¾	shot(s)	**Chilled mineral water** (omit if wet ice)

Origin: A long lost classic.
Comment: Cognac and honey with sweet and sourness in harmony.

PRINCE OF WALES ●●●●○○

Glass: Flute
Garnish: Lemon peel twist
Method: Rub sugar cube with lemon peel, coat with bitters and drop into glass. POUR cognac and liqueur over soaked cube and TOP with champagne.

1	cube	**Brown sugar**
2	dashes	**Angostura aromatic bitters**
½	shot(s)	**Courvoisier V.S.O.P. cognac**
½	shot(s)	**Grand Marnier liqueur**
Top up with		**Perrier Jouet brut champagne**

Comment: More interesting than a classic Champagne Cocktail.

PRINCESS MARINA

Glass: Martini
Garnish: Orange zest twist
Method: SHAKE all ingredients with ice and fine strain into chilled glass.

1	shot(s)	**Tanqueray London dry gin**
½	shot(s)	**Boulard Grand Solage calvados**
½	shot(s)	**Dubonnet Red** (French made)
½	shot(s)	**Cointreau triple sec**
½	shot(s)	**Swedish Punch**
¾	shot(s)	**Chilled mineral water** (omit if wet ice)

Origin: Created in the late 1920s or early 1930s and named after Princess Marina, the late mother of The Duke of Kent, Prince Michael of Kent and Princess Alexandra.
Comment: Delicate yet loaded with alcohol and flavour.

PRINCESS MARY

Glass: Martini
Garnish: Dust with cocoa powder
Method: SHAKE all ingredients with ice and fine strain into chilled glass.

1½	shot(s)	**Tanqueray London dry gin**
1	shot(s)	**White crème de cacao liqueur**
¾	shot(s)	**Double (heavy) cream**
¾	shot(s)	**Milk**

Origin: Created in 1922 by Harry MacElhone to celebrate H.R.H. Princess Mary's marriage. The original recipe featured equal parts of all four ingredients.
Comment: Slightly sweet, very creamy - drink after dinner.

PRINCESS MARY'S PRIDE UPDATED #8

Glass: Martini
Garnish: Orange zest twist
Method: SHAKE all ingredients with ice and fine strain into chilled glass.

2	shot(s)	**Boulard Grand Solage calvados**
1	shot(s)	**Dubonnet Red** (French made)
1	shot(s)	**Noilly Prat dry vermouth**

Comment: Apple brandy to the fore, followed by aromatised wine.
Origin: Created by Harry Craddock on 28th February 1922 to mark the wedding of H.R.H. Princess Mary, daughter of King George V and Queen Mary to Henry, Viscount Lascelles. Recipe from 1930's Savoy Cocktail Book.

PRINCESS PRIDE

Glass: Martini
Garnish: Orange zest twist
Method: SHAKE all ingredients with ice and fine strain into chilled glass.

2	shot(s)	**Boulard Grand Solage calvados**
1	shot(s)	**Dubonnet Red** (French made)
1	shot(s)	**Martini Rosso sweet vermouth**

Origin: Adapted from a recipe in the 1947-72 Trader Vic's Bartender's Guide by Victor Bergeron.
Comment: Vic's improved version of the drink above.

PRINCETON

Glass: Martini
Garnish: Lemon zest twist
Method: STIR all ingredients with ice and strain into chilled glass.

2	shot(s)	**Tanqueray London dry gin**
1	shot(s)	**Warre's Otima tawny port**
¼	shot(s)	**Sugar syrup** (2 sugar to 1 water)
2	dashes	**Angostura orange bitters**

Origin: An old classic originally made with sweet 'Old Tom' gin and without the sugar syrup.
Comment: Overproof wine with a herbal orange garnish.

PRINCETON MARTINI

Glass: Martini
Garnish: Lime zest twist
Method: SHAKE all ingredients with ice and fine strain into chilled glass.

2	shot(s)	**Tanqueray London dry gin**
½	shot(s)	**Noilly Prat dry vermouth**
¼	shot(s)	**Rose's lime cordial**
½	shot(s)	**Chilled mineral water** (omit if wet ice)

Comment: The Dry Martini meets the Gimlet. They should meet more often.

PRUNE FACE

Glass: Old-fashioned
Garnish: Orange zest twist
Method: POUR bourbon into glass with 4 ice cubes and STIR until ice has at least half melted. Add other ingredients and additional ice and stir some more.

2	shot(s)	**Bulleit bourbon whiskey**
¾	shot(s)	**Vieille de prune eau de vie**
¼	shot(s)	**Mandarine Napoléon liqueur**
¼	shot(s)	**Sugar syrup** (2 sugar to 1 water)

Origin: Created in 2002 by Dan Warner at Zander, London, England and named after my friend's nickname for his stepmother.
Comment: Why muddle cherries into your Old Fashioned when you can add a hint of prune?

PRUNEAUX

Glass: Martini
Garnish: Prunes on stick
Method: SHAKE all ingredients with ice and fine strain into chilled glass.

1½	shot(s)	**Tanqueray Londo dry gin**
1	shot(s)	**Amontillado dry sherry**
½	shot(s)	**Noé Pedro Ximenez sherry**
¾	shot(s)	**Freshly squeezed orange juice**
¾	shot(s)	**Prune syrup** (from tinned fruit)

Origin: Adapted from a recipe in Harry Craddock's 1930 Savoy Cocktail Book.
Comment: Sherried prunes further fortified by gin.

P.S. I LOVE YOU

Glass: Martini
Garnish: Crumbled Cadbury's Flake bar
Method: SHAKE all ingredients with ice and fine strain into chilled glass.

1¼	shot(s)	**Baileys Irish cream liqueur**
1¼	shot(s)	**Luxardo Amaretto di Saschira**
¾	shot(s)	**Bacardi Oro golden rum**
¾	shot(s)	**Kahlúa coffee liqueur**
1	shot(s)	**Double (heavy) cream**

Comment: P.S. You'll love this creamy flavoursome drink.

PULP FICTION

Glass: Collins
Method: SHAKE all ingredients with ice and strain into ice filled glass. **TOP** with lemonade.

2	shot(s)	**Pressed apple juice**
2	shot(s)	**Courvoisier V.S.O.P. cognac**
1	shot(s)	**Berentzen apple schnapps**
Top up with		**Lemonade/Sprite/7-Up**

Origin: Discovered in 2001 at Teatro, London.
Comment: Originally made with apple pulp, this drink has a zingy apple taste.

> ## 'ZEN MARTINI: A MARTINI WITH NO VERMOUTH AT ALL. AND NO GIN, EITHER.'
> ### P.J. O'ROURKE

PUNCH NEW #8

Glass: Collins
Garnish: Lemon or lime slice
Method: SHAKE all ingredients with ice and fine strain into glass filled with crushed ice.

¾	shot(s)	**Freshly squeezed citrus** (1 x sour)
1½	shot(s)	**Sugar syrup** (2 x sweet)
2¼	shot(s)	**Spirit** (3 x strong)
3	shot(s)	**Water or fruit juice** (4 x weak)
3	dashes	**Angostura aromatic bitters** (spice)

Comment: Two traditional punches remain on today's cocktail lists, the 'Rum Punch' and the 'Hot Whisky Punch', now better known as the 'Hot Toddy'. Also bear in mind that the Gin Punch probably led to the creation of the Collins.
Origin: Long before the Martini, the V-shaped glass and the cocktail shaker, the drink of choice at society gatherings was punch and the punch bowl was the centre of activity at every party.

Punch had existed in India for centuries before colonialists brought it back to Europe some time in the latter half of the 1600s. The name derives from the Hindi word for five, 'panch', and refers to the five key ingredients: alcohol, citrus, sugar, water and spices.

In India, it was made with arrack (the Arabic word for liquor and a local spirit distilled from palm sap or sugar cane). Back in Britain it was common for punches to be spiced with nutmeg or tea.

The classic proportions of a punch follow a mnemonic, 'one of sour, two of sweet, three of strong and four of weak.' It refers to lime juice, sugar, rum and water - the fifth element, spice was added to taste.

The basic punch principle of balancing sweet and sour with spirit and dilution remains key to making a good cocktail to this day. Indeed, the essential punch ingredients - spirit, citrus, sugar and water - lie at the centre of most modern day cocktails including the Daiquiri, Sour, Margarita, Caipirinha and Sidecar. Today's bartenders are now also reintroducing the fifth punch ingredient by muddling or macerating herbs and spices in their cocktails.

PUCCINI

Glass: Flute
Garnish: Mandarin (tangerine) segment
Method: MUDDLE segments in base of shaker. Add liqueur, **SHAKE** with ice and fine strain into chilled glass. **TOP** with prosecco and lightly stir.

8	segments	**Fresh mandarin**
¾	shot(s)	**Mandarine Napoléon liqueur**
Top up with		**Prosecco sparkling wine**

Origin: Named after the composer of Madame Butterfly, this cocktail is popular in Venice and other areas of northern Italy. It is often made without mandarin liqueur.
Comment: The use of mandarin (tangerine) instead of orange makes the Puccini slightly sharper than the similar Mimosa.

HOW TO MAKE SUGAR SYRUP

To make your own sugar syrup, gradually pour TWO cups of granulated sugar into a saucepan containing ONE cup of hot water. Stir as you pour and carry on stirring and simmering until the sugar is dissolved. Do not let the water even come close to boiling and only simmer for as long as it takes to dissolve the sugar. Allow syrup to cool and pour into an empty bottle. Ideally, you should finely strain your syrup into the bottle to remove any undissolved crystals which could otherwise encourage crystallisation. If kept in a refrigerator this mixture will last for a couple of months.

PURGATORY NEW #8

Glass: Martini
Garnish: Lemon zest twist
Method: STIR all ingredients with ice and strain into chilled glass.

2½	shot(s)	Rye whiskey (or bourbon)
¾	shot(s)	Bénédictine D.O.M. liqueur
¾	shot(s)	Green Chartreuse liqueur

Comment: Too many and you're in it.
Origin: Created in 2007 by Ted Kilgore at Monarch Restaurant, Maplewood, USA. Adapted from an adapted recipe by Gary Regan and first [published in his column in The San Francisco Chronicle. Apparently, Kilgore created this drink as a pick-me-up.

THE PURITAN

Glass: Martini
Garnish: Orange zest twst
Method: STIR all ingredients with ice and strain into chilled glass.

1¾	shot(s)	Tanqueray London dry gin
½	shot(s)	Noilly Prat dry vermouth
¼	shot(s)	Yellow Chartreuse liqueur
1	dash	Angostura orange bitters
½	shot(s)	Chilled mineral water (omit if wet ice)

Origin: An often overlooked classic which is thought to have originated at the end of the nineteenth century.
Comment: Vermouth enhances the aromatics; Chartreuse and orange bitters add a hint of sweetness and complexity; gin underpins the whole.

THE PURL NEW #8

Glass: Pint
Method: POUR ingredients into chilled glass.

| 2 | shot(s) | Old Tom gin |
| Top up with | | British cask conditioned ale |

Comment: Somebody seems to have spiked my beer!
Origin: In 18th century London Gin tended to be mixed two to one with water and sold by the quarter pint. The Purl, simply gin and ale was another popular mix. Sometimes the beer was warmed first to make a 'hot purl', apparently popular with Thames boatman of the day.

PURPLE COSMO

Glass: Martini
Garnish: Orange zest twist
Method: STIR all ingredients with ice and strain into chilled glass.

2	shot(s)	Ketel One Citroen vodka
¾	shot(s)	Parfait Amour liqueur
1½	shot(s)	Ocean Spray white cranberry
¼	shot(s)	Freshly squeezed lime juice

Variant: Blue Cosmo
Comment: If shaken this becomes more of a grey Cosmo. The flavour and colour make for an interesting twist.

PURPLE FLIRT #1

Glass: Martini
Garnish: Orange zest twist
Method: SHAKE all ingredients with ice and fine strain into chilled glass.

1½	shot(s)	Ketel One vodka
¾	shot(s)	Opal Nera black sambuca
2	shot(s)	Ocean Spray cranberry juice

Comment: This purple drink is surprisingly balanced with subtle hints of liquorice.

'YOU CAN'T SERIOUSLY WANT TO BAN ALCOHOL. IT TASTES GREAT, MAKES WOMEN APPEAR MORE ATTRACTIVE, AND MAKES A PERSON VIRTUALLY INVULNERABLE TO CRITICISM.'
MAYOR QUIMBY, THE SIMPSONS

PURPLE FLIRT #2

Glass: Old-fashioned
Garnish: Orange slice & cherry on stick (sail)
Method: SHAKE all ingredients with ice and strain into ice-filled glass.

1	shot(s)	Goslings Black Seal rum
¼	shot(s)	Bols blue curaçao liqueur
1	shot(s)	Pressed pineapple juice
½	shot(s)	Freshly squeezed lemon juice
¼	shot(s)	Pomegranate (grenadine) syrup
½	fresh	Egg white

Comment: This popular drink is more brown than purple. It tastes OK, anyway.

PURPLE HAZE

Glass: Shot
Method: SHAKE first 3 ingredients with ice and strain into glass. **POUR** liqueur down the inside of the glass. This will fall to the bottom and form the purple haze.

1½	shot(s)	Ketel One vodka
½	shot(s)	Freshly squeezed lime juice
¼	shot(s)	Sugar syrup (2 sugar to 1 water)
⅛	shot(s)	Chambord black raspberry liqueur

Comment: A sweet and sour shot with a sweet, berry base.

PURPLE HOOTER

Glass: Collins
Garnish: Lime wedge
Method: SHAKE first 3 ingredients with ice and strain into ice-filled glass. **TOP** with soda.

2	shot(s)	Ketel One vodka
1	shot(s)	Chambord black raspberry liqueur
1	shot(s)	Freshly squeezed lime juice
Top up with		Soda water (club soda)

Comment: Tangy, fruity, long and refreshing.

PURPLE PEAR MARTINI UPDATED #8

Glass: Martini
Garnish: Pear slice on rim
Method: SHAKE all ingredients with ice and fine strain into chilled glass.

¾	shot(s)	Zubrówka bison vodka
¾	shot(s)	Poire William eau de vie
¾	shot(s)	Benoit Serres crème de violette
1	shot(s)	Lillet Blanc

Origin: Created in 2002 by Yours Truly (Simon Difford).
Comment: This floral drink suits its name.

PURPLE TURTLE

Glass: Shot
Method: SHAKE all ingredients with ice and fine strain into chilled glass.

½	shot(s)	Don Julio reposado tequila
½	shot(s)	Bols blue curaçao liqueur
½	shot(s)	Sloe gin liqueur

Comment: This aquamarine shooter goes down a treat.

PUSSYFOOT (MOCKTAIL)

Glass: Collins
Garnish: Orange slice
Method: MUDDLE mint in base of shaker. Add other ingredients, **SHAKE** with ice and fine strain into ice-filled glass.

7	fresh	Mint leaves
4	shot(s)	Freshly squeezed orange juice
½	shot(s)	Freshly squeezed lemon juice
½	shot(s)	Freshly squeezed lime juice
½	shot(s)	Pomegranate (grenadine) syrup
1	fresh	Egg yolk

Origin: Created in 1920 by Robert Vermeire at the Embassy Club, London, England. This non-alcoholic cocktail is named after 'Pussyfoot' (William E.) Johnson who was an ardent supporter of Prohibition.
Comment: Probably the best non-alcoholic cocktail ever.

PYRAMID PUNCH NEW #8

Glass: Collins
Garnish: Pineapple wedge on rim
Method: MUDDLE cloves in base of shaker. **ADD** other ingredients, **SHAKE** with ice and strain into ice-filled glass.

2	dried	Cloves
2	shot(s)	Macchu pisco
1	shot(s)	St-Germain elderflower liqueur
2	shot(s)	Pressed pineapple juice
½	shot(s)	Freshly squeezed grapefruit juice

Origin: Simon Difford's 2006 adaptation of the Pisco Punch made famous before Prohibition at San Francisco's legendary Bank Exchange's Bar. The Transamerica Pyramid skyscraper now stands on the site of The Bank Exchange, at the corner of Washington & Montgomery Streets, hence this drink's name and garnish.
Comment: Tangy, fruity and packed with flavour. Clove spice, fragrant floral pisco and elderflower with a hint of sweet pineapple and sour grapefruit.

QUARTER DECK

Glass: Martini
Garnish: Orange zest twist
Method: SHAKE all ingredients with ice and fine strain into chilled glass.

2	shot(s)	Bacardi Superior rum
1	shot(s)	Noé Pedro Ximenez sherry
¼	shot(s)	Freshly squeezed lemon juice
¾	shot(s)	Chilled mineral water (omit if wet ice)

Origin: Long lost classic.
Comment: Hints of prune, toffee and maple syrup. Very complex.

QUARTERBACK

Glass: Martini
Garnish: Orange zest twist
Method: SHAKE all ingredients with ice and fine strain into chilled glass.

1	shot(s)	Yellow Chartreuse liqueur
1	shot(s)	Cointreau triple sec
1	shot(s)	Double (heavy) cream
1	shot(s)	Milk

Comment: This white, creamy drink has a flavoursome bite.

QUEBEC UPDATED #8

Glass: Martini
Garnish: Orange zest twist
Method: STIR all ingredients with ice and strain into chilled glass.

2	shot(s)	Canadian whisky
2	shot(s)	Dubonnet Red (French made)
2	dashes	Angostura orange bitters

Origin: Created in 2004 by Goncalo de Sousa Monteiro at Victoria Bar, Berlin, Germany.
Comment: Canadian whiskey with French accents of aromatised wine – très Quebecois.

QUEEN MARTINI

Glass: Martini
Garnish: Maraschino cherry
Method: SHAKE all ingredients with ice and fine strain into chilled glass.

1½	shot(s)	**Tanqueray London dry gin**
½	shot(s)	**Noilly Prat dry vermouth**
½	shot(s)	**Martin Rosso sweet vermouth**
½	shot(s)	**Freshly squeezed orange juice**
½	shot(s)	**Pressed pineapple juice**

Comment: A 'perfectly' fruity Martini that's fit for a…

QUEEN'S PARK SWIZZLE

Glass: Collins
Garnish: Lime wedge & mint sprig
Method: Lightly **MUDDLE** mint (just to bruise) in base of glass, add other ingredients and half fill glass with crushed ice. **SWIZZLE** with a swizzle stick or **CHURN** (stir) with a bar spoon. Fill glass with more crushed ice and repeat. Serve with straws.

7	fresh	**Mint leaves**
2	shot(s)	**Zacapa aged rum**
¾	shot(s)	**Freshly squeezed lime juice**
½	shot(s)	**Sugar syrup** (2 sugar to 1 water)
3	dashes	**Angostura aromatic bitters**

Origin: Created at the Queen's Park Hotel, Port of Spain, Trinidad.
Comment: This close relation to the Mojito is drier, more complex and less minty than its sibling.

QUELLE VIE

Glass: Martini
Garnish: Orange zest twist
Method: STIR all ingredients with ice and fine strain into chilled glass.

2	shot(s)	**Courvoisier V.S.O.P. cognac**
½	shot(s)	**Kümmel liqueur**
¾	shot(s)	**Chilled mineral water** (omit if wet ice)

Origin: Adapted from a recipe in the 1930 Savoy Cocktail Book by Harry Craddock.
Comment: In Craddock's words, "Brandy gives you courage and Kümmel makes you cautious, thus giving you a perfect mixture of bravery and caution, with the bravery predominating."

QUINCE MUSTARD MARGARITA NEW #8

Glass: Old-fashioned
Garnish: Grind cracked black pepper & lime wedge
Method: SHAKE all ingredients with ice and fine strain into chilled glass.

1	spoon	**Quince mustard jam**
2	grinds	**Black pepper**
1½	shot(s)	**Don Julio reposado tequila**
½	shot(s)	**Cointreau triple sec**
1	shot(s)	**Freshly squeezed lime juice**
⅛	shot(s)	**Sugar syrup** (2 sugar to 1 water)

Origin: Created by Ryan Magarian, Seattle, USA.
Comment: A wonderfully quince influenced Margarita.

QUINCE SOUR

Glass: Old-fashioned
Garnish: Lemon slice & cherry on stick (sail)
Method: STIR quince jam with vodka in base of shaker to dissolve jam. Add other ingredients, **SHAKE** with ice and fine strain into ice-filled glass.

3	spoons	**Quince mustard jam**
2	shot(s)	**Ketel One vodka**
1	shot(s)	**Freshly squeezed lemon juice**
½	fresh	**Egg white**

Comment: The sweet quince both flavours and balances this sour.

THE QUINGENTI NEW #8

Glass: Martini/Coupette
Garnish: Lemon zest twist
Method: SHAKE all ingredients with ice and fine strain into chilled glass.

2	shot(s)	**Courvoisier V.S.O.P. cognac**
½	shot(s)	**Berentzen apple schnapps**
½	shot(s)	**Noilly Prat dry vermouth**
¼	shot(s)	**Sugar syrup** (2 sugar to 1 water)

Comment: Cognac with apple notes and a touch of herbal complexity by way of dry vermouth.
Origin: A created in 2008 by Yours Truly (Simon Difford) at the Cabinet Room, London, England to celebrate Courvoisier's Future 500 initiative. As every schoolboy knows, quingenti is Latin for five-hundred.

HOW TO MAKE SUGAR SYRUP

To make your own sugar syrup, gradually pour TWO cups of granulated sugar into a saucepan containing ONE cup of hot water. Stir as you pour and carry on stirring and simmering until the sugar is dissolved. Do not let the water even come close to boiling and only simmer for as long as it takes to dissolve the sugar. Allow syrup to cool and pour into an empty bottle. Ideally, you should finely strain your syrup into the bottle to remove any undissolved crystals which could otherwise encourage crystallisation. If kept in a refrigerator this mixture will last for a couple of months.

RAC COCKTAIL NEW #8

●●●●○

Glass: Martini/Couppette
Garnish: Orange zest twist (discarded) & cherry
Method: STIR all ingredients with ice and strain into chilled glass.

2	shot(s)	Tanqueray London dry gin
1	shot(s)	Noilly Prat dry vermouth
1	shot(s)	Martini Rosso sweet vermouth
⅛	shot(s)	Pomegranate (grenadine) syrup
1	dash	Angostura orange bitters

Comment: A one to one Perfect Martini with extra grenadine sweetness and orange bitters adding complexity.
Origin: The house cocktail at the Royal Automobile Club in London's Pall Mall. King Edward VII awarded this private members' club its royal title in 1907.

RAGING BULL

●●●●○○

Glass: Shot
Method: Refrigerate ingredients then **LAYER** in chilled glass by carefully pouring in the following order.

½	shot(s)	Kahlúa coffee liqueur
½	shot(s)	Luxardo Sambuca dei Cesari
½	shot(s)	Don Julio reposado tequila

Comment: Coffee and sambuca make a great combination, as do coffee and tequila.

RAMOS GIN FIZZ UPDATED #8

●●●●●

Glass: Small Collins (8oz)
Garnish: Half lemon slice & mint sprig
Method: 1/ Flash **BLEND** first 8 ingredients without ice (to emulsify mix). Then pour contents of blender into shaker and **SHAKE** with ice. Strain into chilled glass (no ice in glass) and **TOP** with soda from siphon. ALTERNATIVELY: 2/ Vigorously **DRY SHAKE** first 8 ingredients until bored/tired. Add ice to shaker, **SHAKE** again and strain into chilled glass (no ice). **TOP** with soda water from siphon.

2	shot(s)	Tanqueray London dry gin
½	shot(s)	Freshly squeezed lemon juice
½	shot(s)	Freshly squeezed lime juice
¾	shot(s)	Sugar syrup (2 sugar to 1 water)
⅛	shot(s)	Orange flower water
3	drops	Vanilla extract (optional)
1	fresh	Egg white
1	shot(s)	Double (heavy) cream
Top up with		Soda water (from siphon)

Comment: One of the great classic cocktails. The perfect balance of sweet and sour is enhanced by the incredibly smooth, almost fluffy mouth feel.
Origin: This was the secret recipe of Henry C. Ramos, who opened his Imperial Cabinet Bar in New Orleans in 1888. At the onset of Prohibition his brother, Charles Henry Ramos, published it in a full-page advertisement, and since 1935, the Roosevelt (now named the Fairmont) Hotel, New Orleans, has held the trademark on the name Ramos Gin Fizz.

To make a more traditional style of Ramos Gin Fizz try using full fat milk in place of cream and shake until bubbles disappear.

RANDY

●●●●○

Glass: Old-fashioned
Garnish: Orange zest twist
Method: STIR all ingredients with ice and strain into ice-filled glass.

1½	shot(s)	Courvoisier V.S.O.P. cognac
1½	shot(s)	Warre's Otima tawny port
½	shot(s)	Grand Marnier liqueur
¼	shot(s)	Vanilla sugar syrup

Origin: Created in 2003 by Yours Truly (Simon Difford).
Comment: Named after the rhyming slang for port and brandy, its base ingredients. Love interest comes courtesy of orange and vanilla.

> **'I DISTRUST CAMELS, AND ANYONE ELSE WHO CAN GO FOR A WEEK WITHOUT A DRINK.'**
> JOE E. LEWIS

RANGLIN NEW #8

●●●●○○

Glass: Old-fashioned
Garnish: Lime wedge.
Method: SHAKE all ingredients with ice and strain into ice-filled glass

2	shot(s)	Goslings Black Seal rum
½	shot(s)	Wray & Nephew overproof rum
¾	shot(s)	Velvet Falernum liqueur
1	shot(s)	Freshly squeezed lime juice
¼	shot(s)	Sugar syrup (2 sugar to 1 water)

Comment: This Tiki-style drink is rich and tangy with a hint of clove spice.
Origin: Created in 2008 by Gonçalo De Sousa Monteiro at Le Lion, Hamburg, Germany, apparently whilst listening to Ernest Ranglin, hence the name.

RASPBERRY CAIPIRINHA

●●●●○

Glass: Old-fashioned
Method: MUDDLE lime and raspberries in base of glass. Add other ingredients and fill glass with crushed ice. **CHURN** drink with barspoon and serve with short straws.

¾	fresh	Lime cut into wedges
8	fresh	Raspberries
2	shot(s)	Leblon cachaça
¾	shot(s)	Sugar syrup (2 sugar to 1 water)

Variants: Substitute other berries and fruits for raspberries. Add raspberry liqueur in place of sugar. Use rum in place of cachaça to make a Raspberry Caipirissima.
Comment: A fruity twist on the popular Caipirinha.

RASPBERRY COLLINS

Glass: Collins
Garnish: Three raspberries & lemon slice
Method: MUDDLE raspberries in base of shaker. Add next 5 ingredients, **SHAKE** with ice and strain into ice-filled glass. **TOP** with soda, lightly stir and serve with straws.

10	fresh	Raspberries
2	shot(s)	Tanqueray London dry gin
1½	shot(s)	Freshly squeezed lemon juice
½	shot(s)	Crème de framboise liqueur
½	shot(s)	Sugar syrup (2 sugar to 1 water)
3	dashes	Angostura orange bitters (optional)
Top up with		Soda water (club soda)

Variant: Raspberry Debonnaire
Origin: Created in 1999 by Cairbry Hill, London, England.
Comment: This fruity drink is the most popular modern adaptation of the classic Collins.

RASPBERRY COSMO

Glass: Martini
Garnish: Raspberries on stick
Method: SHAKE all ingredients with ice and fine strain into chilled glass.

1½	shot(s)	Ketel One Citroen vodka
¾	shot(s)	Crème de framboise liqueur
1	shot(s)	Ocean Spray cranberry juice
½	shot(s)	Freshly squeezed lime juice

Origin: Formula by Yours Truly (Simon Difford) in 2006.
Comment: Your classic Cosmo but with raspberry liqueur replacing orange liqueur.

RASPBERRY DEBONNAIRE

Glass: Collins
Garnish: Three raspberries & lemon slice
Method: MUDDLE raspberries in base of shaker. Add next 5 ingredients, **SHAKE** with ice and fine strain into ice-filled glass. **TOP** with soda, lightly stir and serve with straws.

10	fresh	Raspberries
2	shot(s)	Ketel One vodka
1½	shot(s)	Freshly squeezed lemon juice
½	shot(s)	Crème de framboise liqueur
½	shot(s)	Sugar syrup (2 sugar to 1 water)
3	dashes	Angostura orange bitters (optional)
Top up with		Soda water (club soda)

Variant: Raspberry Collins
Comment: If based on gin rather than vodka this would be a Raspberry Collins.

RASPBERRY LYNCHBURG

Glass: Collins
Garnish: Raspberries on drink
Method: SHAKE first 3 ingredients with ice and strain into ice-filled glass. **TOP** with lemonade and **DRIZZLE** liqueur around surface of drink. It will fall through the drink, leaving coloured threads.

2	shot(s)	Jack Daniel's Tennessee whiskey
¾	shot(s)	Freshly squeezed lime juice
¼	shot(s)	Sugar syrup (2 sugar to 1 water)
Top up with		Lemonade/Sprite/7-Up
½	shot(s)	Chambord black raspberry liqueur

Origin: Created in 1992 by Wayne Collins at Roadhouse, London, England.
Comment: This variation on a Lynchburg Lemonade has a sweet and sour flavour laced with whiskey.

RASPBERRY MARGARITA

Glass: Coupette
Garnish: Lime wedge on rim
Method: MUDDLE raspberries in base of shaker. Add other ingredients, **SHAKE** with ice and fine strain into chilled glass.

7	fresh	Raspberries
2	shot(s)	Don Julio reposado tequila
1	shot(s)	Cointreau triple sec
1	shot(s)	Freshly squeezed lime juice
⅛	shot(s)	Sugar syrup (2 sugar to 1 water)

Comment: Just as it says – a raspberry flavoured Margarita.

RASPBERRY MARTINI #1

Glass: Martini
Garnish: Three raspberries on stick
Method: MUDDLE raspberries in base of shaker. Add other ingredients, **SHAKE** with ice and fine strain into chilled glass.

10	fresh	Raspberries
2½	shot(s)	Ketel One vodka
½	shot(s)	Sugar syrup (2 sugar to 1 water)

Comment: The simplest of raspberry Martinis but still tastes good.

RASPBERRY MARTINI #2

Glass: Martini
Garnish: Three raspberries on stick
Method: MUDDLE raspberries in base of shaker. Add other ingredients, **SHAKE** with ice and fine strain into chilled glass.

7	fresh	Raspberries
2	shot(s)	Tanqueray London dry gin
1	shot(s)	Crème de framboise liqueur
2	dashes	Angostura orange bitters (optional)

Origin: Created in 1997 by Dick Bradsell, London, England.
Comment: Great raspberry flavour integrated with gin.

RASPBERRY MOCHA'TINI

Glass: Martini
Garnish: Three raspberries on stick
Method: SHAKE all ingredients with ice and fine strain into chilled glass.

1½	shot(s)	**Raspberry flavoured vodka**
¾	shot(s)	**Brown crème de cacao liqueur**
¾	shot(s)	**Crème de framboise liqueur**
1	shot(s)	**Espresso coffee**

Origin: Discovered in 2002 at Lot 61, New York City, USA.
Comment: Sweet chocolate and raspberry tempered by dry coffee and vodka.

RASPBERRY MULE

Glass: Collins
Garnish: Lime wedge
Method: MUDDLE raspberries in base of shaker. Add next 3 ingredients, SHAKE with ice and fine strain into ice-filled glass. TOP with ginger beer, lightly stir and serve with straws.

12	fresh	**Raspberries**
2	shot(s)	**Ketel One vodka**
1	shot(s)	**Freshly squeezed lime juice**
½	shot(s)	**Sugar syrup** (2 sugar to 1 water)
Top up with		**Ginger beer**

Comment: The fruity alternative to a Moscow Mule.

RASPBERRY SAKE'TINI

Glass: Martini
Garnish: Three raspberries.
Method: SHAKE all ingredients with ice and fine strain into chilled glass.

1½	shot(s)	**Raspberry flavoured vodka**
1½	shot(s)	**Sake**
½	shot(s)	**Chambord black raspberry liqueur**
½	shot(s)	**Pressed pineapple juice**

Comment: Fruity with wafts of sake – reminiscent of a French Martini.

RASPBERRY WATKINS

Glass: Sling
Garnish: Three raspberries
Method: SHAKE first 4 ingredients with ice and strain into ice-filled glass. TOP with soda, lightly stir and serve with straws.

2	shot(s)	**Ketel One vodka**
½	shot(s)	**Chambord black raspberry liqueur**
½	shot(s)	**Freshly squeezed lime juice**
¼	shot(s)	**Pomegranate (grenadine) syrup**
Top up with		**Soda water** (club soda)

Comment: A light, long, fizzy and refreshing drink.

RASPUTIN

Glass: Collins
Garnish: Lime wedge
Method: SHAKE all ingredients with ice and strain into ice-filled glass.

2	shot(s)	**Raspberry flavoured vodka**
2½	shot(s)	**Ocean Spray cranberry juice**
1½	shot(s)	**Freshly squeezed grapefruit juice**

Comment: This fruity adaptation of an Arizona Breeze is raspberry rich.

RAT PACK MANHATTAN

Glass: Martini
Garnish: Orange zest twist & maraschino cherry
Method: Chill glass, add Grand Marnier, swirl to coat and then DISCARD. STIR other ingredients with ice and strain into liqueur coated glass.

½	shot(s)	**Grand Marnier liqueur**
1½	shot(s)	**Bulleit bourbon whiskey**
¾	shot(s)	**Martini Rosso sweet vermouth**
¾	shot(s)	**Noilly Prat dry vermouth**
3	dashes	**Angostura aromatic bitters**

Origin: Created in 2000 by Wayne Collins at High Holborn, London, England. Originally Wayne used different whiskies to represent each of the Rat Pack crooners. The wash of Grand Marnier was for Sammy Davis, the wild card of the bunch.
Comment: A twist on the classic Manhattan.

RATTLESNAKE

Glass: Martini
Garnish: Lemon zest twist
Method: SHAKE all ingredients with ice and fine strain into chilled glass.

2	shot(s)	**Bulleit bourbon whiskey**
¼	shot(s)	**Freshly squeezed lemon juice**
¼	shot(s)	**Sugar syrup** (2 sugar to 1 water)
⅛	shot(s)	**La Fée Parisienne (68%) absinthe**
½	fresh	**Egg white**
½	shot(s)	**Chilled mineral water** (omit if wet ice)

Origin: Adapted from a recipe purloined from a 1930 edition of The Savoy Cocktail Book by Harry Craddock.
Comment: To quote Craddock, "So called because it will either cure rattlesnake bite, or kill rattlesnakes, or make you see them."

RATTLESNAKE SHOT

Glass: Shot
Method: Refrigerate ingredients then LAYER in chilled glass by carefully pouring in the following order.

½	shot(s)	**Kahlúa coffee liqueur**
½	shot(s)	**White crème de cacao liqueur**
½	shot(s)	**Baileys Irish cream liqueur**

Comment: Tastes rather like a strong cappuccino.

RAY GUN

Glass: Flute
Garnish: Orange zest twist
Method: POUR Chartreuse and blue curaçao into chilled glass. Top with champagne.

½	shot(s)	**Green Chartreuse liqueur**
¾	shot(s)	**Bols blue curaçao liqueur**
Top up with		**Perrier Jouet brut champagne**

Comment: Not for the faint-hearted.

RAY'S HARD LEMONADE

Glass: Collins
Garnish: Mint sprig
Method: Lightly **MUDDLE** (just to bruise) mint in base of shaker. Add next 4 ingredients, **SHAKE** with ice and fine strain into ice-filled glass. **TOP** with soda, lightly stir and serve with straws.

7	fresh	**Mint leaves**
2	shot(s)	**Ketel One vodka**
1	shot(s)	**Freshly squeezed lemon juice**
2	shot(s)	**Freshly squeezed lime juice**
1½	shot(s)	**Sugar syrup** (2 sugar to 1 water)
Top up with		**Soda water** (club soda)

Variant: Hard Lemonade
Origin: Discovered in 2004 at Spring Street Natural Restaurant, New York City, USA.
Comment: Alcoholic lemonade with mint? A vodka variation on the Mojito? However you describe it, it works.

RAZZITINI

Glass: Martini
Garnish: Lemon twist or raspberries on stick
Method: SHAKE first 2 ingredients with ice and fine strain into chilled glass. **TOP** with lemonade.

2½	shot(s)	**Ketel One Citroen vodka**
¾	shot(s)	**Chambord black raspberry liqueur**
Top up with		**Lemonade/Sprite/7-Up**

Origin: Discovered in 2003 at Paramount Hotel, New York City, USA.
Comment: This citrus and raspberry Martini is a tad on the sweet side.

RAZZMATAZZ

Glass: Martini
Garnish: Float mint sprig
Method: STIR honey with vodka until honey is dissolved. Add other ingredients, **SHAKE** with ice and fine strain into chilled glass.

3	spoons	**Runny honey**
1½	shot(s)	**Raspberry flavoured vodka**
½	shot(s)	**Cointreau triple sec**
1	shot(s)	**Pressed apple juice**
¼	shot(s)	**Freshly squeezed lime juice**
6	fresh	**Mint leaves**

Origin: Created by Wayne Collins, London, England.
Comment: Fruity with plenty of razzmatazz.

RAZZZZZBERRY MARTINI

Glass: Martini
Garnish: Three raspberries on stick
Method: SHAKE all ingredients with ice and fine strain into chilled glass.

2	shot(s)	**Vanilla-infused Ketel One vodka**
½	shot(s)	**Chambord black raspberry liqueur**
2	shot(s)	**Ocean Spray cranberry juice**

Comment: Raspberry and vanilla with characteristic dry cranberry fruit.

> ## 'THE REASON I DRINK IS BECAUSE WHEN I'M SOBER I THINK I'M EDDIE FISHER.'
> DEAN MARTIN

REAL LEMONADE (MOCKTAIL)

Glass: Collins
Garnish: Lemon slice
Method: POUR ingredients into ice-filled glass and lightly **STIR**. Serve with straws.

2	shot(s)	**Freshly squeezed lemon juice**
1	shot(s)	**Sugar syrup** (2 sugar to 1 water)
Top up with		**Soda water** (club soda)

Comment: The classic English summertime refresher.

REDBACK

Glass: Shot
Garnish: Maraschino cherry on rim
Method: POUR sambuca into glass, then pour advocaat down the side of the glass.

| 1 | shot(s) | **Opal Nera black sambuca** |
| ½ | shot(s) | **Bols advocaat liqueur** |

Comment: An impressive looking shot.

RED ANGEL

Glass: Martini
Garnish: Orange zest twist
Method: SHAKE all ingredients with ice and fine strain into chilled glass.

2	shot(s)	**Shiraz red wine**
1	shot(s)	**Grand Marnier liqueur**
¼	shot(s)	**Luxardo maraschino liqueur**
¾	shot(s)	**Chilled mineral water** (omit if wet ice)

Origin: Created in 2001 by Tony Conigliaro at Isola, Knightsbridge, London, England.
Comment: A subtly flavoured cocktail with a dry, almost tannic edge.

RED APPLE

Glass: Martini
Garnish: Maraschino cherry
Method: **SHAKE** all ingredients with ice and fine strain into chilled glass.

1½	shot(s)	**Bulleit bourbon whiskey**
½	shot(s)	**Sour apple liqueur**
2	shot(s)	**Ocean Spray cranberry juice**

Variant: Sour Apple Martini
Comment: As Apple Martinis go, this one is rather good.

THE RED ARMY

Glass: Old-fashioned
Garnish: Two raspberries
Method: **MUDDLE** raspberries in base of shaker. Add other ingredients, **SHAKE** with ice and fine strain into a glass filled with crushed ice.

12	fresh	**Raspberries**
2	shot(s)	**Raspberry flavoured vodka**
1	shot(s)	**Freshly squeezed lime juice**
½	shot(s)	**Sugar syrup** (2 sugar to 1 water)
½	shot(s)	**Cointreau triple sec**
½	shot(s)	**Crème de framboise liqueur**

Origin: Created in 2002 by Alex Kammerling, London, England.
Comment: Rather red and rather fruity.

RED BREAST

Glass: Collins
Garnish: Raspberry
Method: **POUR** first 3 ingredients into ice-filled glass and lightly stir. **DRIZZLE** raspberry liqueur over surface of drink.

2	shot(s)	**Johnnie Walker Scotch whisky**
½	shot(s)	**Freshly squeezed lime juice**
Top up with		**Ginger beer**
½	shot(s)	**Crème de framboise liqueur**

Origin: Created in 2004 by Wayne Collins, England.
Comment: Long and a tad pink but packs a tasty punch.

RED HOOKER

Glass: Martini
Garnish: Peach slice on rim
Method: **SHAKE** all ingredients with ice and fine strain into chilled glass.

1	shot(s)	**Boiron white peach puree**
2	shot(s)	**Don Julio reposado tequila**
¾	shot(s)	**Crème de framboise liqueur**
¾	shot(s)	**Freshly squeezed lemon juice**

Comment: An appropriately named red, fruity drink with more than a hint of tequila.

RED LION #1 (MODERN FORMULA)

Glass: Martini
Garnish: Orange slice on rim
Method: **SHAKE** all ingredients with ice and fine strain into chilled glass.

1¼	shot(s)	**Tanqueray London dry gin**
1¼	shot(s)	**Grand Marnier liqueur**
1	shot(s)	**Freshly squeezed orange juice**
1	shot(s)	**Freshly squeezed lemon juice**
⅛	shot(s)	**Pomegranate (grenadine) syrup**

Origin: This classic drink is said to have been created for the Chicago World Fair in 1933. However, it won the British Empire Cocktail Competition that year and was more likely created by W J Tarling for Booth's gin and named after the brand's Red Lion Distillery in London.
Comment: The colour of a summer's twilight with a rich tangy orange flavour.

> 'SHE SMOKES LIKE A CHIMNEY, DRINKS LIKE A FISH AND DRESSES LIKE HER MOTHER!'
> MARK DARCY,
> BRIDGET JONES' DIARY

RED LION #2 (EMBURY'S FORMULA)

Glass: Martini
Garnish: Orange slice on rim
Method: **SHAKE** all ingredients with ice and fine strain into chilled glass.

2	shot(s)	**Tanqueray London dry gin**
¼	shot(s)	**Grand Marnier liqueur**
½	shot(s)	**Freshly squeezed lime juice**
¼	shot(s)	**Pomegranate (grenadine) syrup**
¾	shot(s)	**Chilled mineral water** (reduce if wet ice)

Origin: Recipe adapted from one originally published in The Fine Art of Mixing Drinks by David Embury.
Comment: Embury is a Daiquiri fan and this is reminiscent of a Daiquiri in both style and proportions.

RED MARAUDER

Glass: Martini
Garnish: Raspberries on stick
Method: **SHAKE** all ingredients with ice and fine strain into chilled glass.

2	shot(s)	**Courvoisier V.S.O.P. cognac**
1½	shot(s)	**Ocean Spray cranberry juice**
½	shot(s)	**Chambord black raspberry liqueur**
¼	shot(s)	**Freshly squeezed lime juice**

Origin: Originally created for Martell, long term sponsors of the Grand National, this is named after the horse that won in 2001.
Comment: Slightly sweet and fruity with a hint of raspberry and cognac's distinctive flavour.

RED MELON'TINI

Glass: Martini
Garnish: Watermelon wedge on rim
Method: Cut watermelon into 16 segments, chop the flesh from one segment into cubes and **MUDDLE** in base of shaker. Add other ingredients, **SHAKE** with ice and fine strain into chilled glass.

1/16	fresh	**Watermelon** (diced)
2	shot(s)	**Pepper flavoured vodka**
1/4	shot(s)	**Sugar syrup** (2 sugar to 1 water)
4	grinds	**Black pepper**

Origin: Discovered in 2002 at the Fifth Floor Bar, London, England.
Comment: Watermelon pepped up with vodka and the subtlest peppery finish.

RED NECK MARTINI

Glass: Martini
Garnish: Orange zest twist
Method: SHAKE all ingredients with ice and fine strain into chilled glass.

2	shot(s)	**Johnnie Walker Scotch whisky**
1	shot(s)	**Dubonnet Red** (French made)
1	shot(s)	**Heering cherry brandy liqueur**

Origin: Created by Sylvain Solignac in 2002 at Circus Bar, London, England.
Comment: Nicely balanced, aromatic and not too sweet – the flavour of the Scotch shines through.

RED OR DEAD

Glass: Collins
Garnish: Lime wedge
Method: SHAKE all ingredients with ice and strain into ice-filled glass.

1½	shot(s)	**Southern Comfort liqueur**
3/4	shot(s)	**Campari Bitter**
3/4	shot(s)	**Freshly squeezed lime juice**
3	shot(s)	**Ocean Spray cranberry juice**

Comment: This long, ruby drink balances sweetness, sourness and bitterness.

RED ROVER

Glass: Old-fashioned
Garnish: Orange slice in glass
Method: SHAKE all ingredients with ice and strain into ice-filled glass.

3	shot(s)	**Shiraz red wine**
1	shot(s)	**Pusser's Navy rum**
1/2	shot(s)	**Chambord black raspberry liqueur**

Comment: Carpet-scaring red with the body of red wine but the palate of a cocktail.

RED RUM MARTINI

Glass: Martini
Garnish: Redcurrants draped over rim
Method: MUDDLE redcurrants in base of shaker. Add other ingredients, **SHAKE** with ice and fine strain into chilled glass.

24	fresh	**Redcurrants**
2	shot(s)	**Zacapa aged rum**
1/2	shot(s)	**Sloe gin liqueur**
1/2	shot(s)	**Freshly squeezed lemon juice**
1/2	shot(s)	**Vanilla sugar syrup**

Origin: Created by Jason Scott in 2002 at Oloroso, Edinburgh, Scotland. This cocktail, which is red and contains rum, is named after 'Red Rum', the only horse in history to win the Grand National three times (on his other two attempts he came second). He became a British hero, made an appearance on the BBC Sports Personality of the Year show and paraded right up until his death at the age of 30 in 1995.
Comment: A beautifully fruity, adult balance of bittersweet flavours.

RED SNAPPER UPDATED #8

Glass: Collins
Garnish: Rim the glass with black pepper and celery salt, add cherry tomato on a stick
Method: SHAKE all ingredients with ice and strain into ice-filled glass. Serve with straws.

2	shot(s)	**Tanqueray London dry gin**
4	shot(s)	**Pressed tomato juice**
1/2	shot(s)	**Freshly squeezed lemon juice**
7	drops	**Tabasco pepper sauce**
4	dashes	**Lea & Perrins Worcestershire sauce**
2	pinches	**Celery salt**
2	grinds	**Black pepper**

Variant: Bloody Mary
Origin: Today, the term Red Snapper means a Bloody Mary made with gin instead of vodka. But the first known recipes, from the 1940s, describe a 50-50 blend of vodka and tomato juice, with spices, just like an early Bloody Mary: one book even states that the Red Snapper is identical to the Bloody Mary.
Cocktail lore states that the Bloody Mary was officially renamed the Red Snapper at the St. Regis Hotel, at some point after the fabulously wealthy Vincent Astor bought it in 1935. Fernand Petiot, who most likely created the original drink (see 'Bloody Mary'), was working there, but Astor apparently found the title too crude for his clientele and insisted the drink be renamed. Customers, of course, continued to order Bloody Marys, but the Red Snapper found a drink of its own in due course.
Comment: Looks like a Bloody Mary but features gin's aromatic botanicals.

DRINKS ARE GRADED AS FOLLOWS:

- DISGUSTING
- PRETTY AWFUL
- BEST AVOIDED
- DISAPPOINTING
- ACCEPTABLE
- GOOD
- RECOMMENDED
- HIGHLY RECOMMENDED
- OUTSTANDING / EXCEPTIONAL

REEF JUICE

Glass: Collins
Garnish: Split pineapple wedge
Method: SHAKE all ingredients with ice and strain into ice-filled glass.

1½	shot(s)	**Pusser's Navy rum**
½	shot(s)	**Ketel One vodka**
1	shot(s)	**Crème de banane liqueur**
½	shot(s)	**Freshly squeezed lime juice**
2½	shot(s)	**Pressed pineapple juice**
½	shot(s)	**Pomegranate (grenadine) syrup**

Origin: Charles Tobias, proprietor of Pusser's, created this drink at the Beach Bar in Fort Lauderdale, Florida. It was a favourite of a friend who crashed his boat on the reef.
Comment: Tangy, fruity and dangerously moreish.

REGGAE RUM PUNCH

Glass: Collins
Garnish: Pineapple & cherry on rim
Method: SHAKE all ingredients with ice and strain into a glass filled with crushed ice.

1¾	shot(s)	**Wray & Nephew overproof rum**
½	shot(s)	**Crème de framboise liqueur**
¾	shot(s)	**Freshly squeezed lime juice**
¾	shot(s)	**Pomegranate (grenadine) syrup**
¾	shot(s)	**Pressed pineapple juice**
1½	shot(s)	**Freshly squeezed orange juice**

Origin: The most popular punch in Jamaica, where it is sold under different names with slightly varying ingredients. It always contains orange, pineapple and, most importantly, overproof rum.
Comment: Jamaicans have a sweet tooth and love their rum. This drink combines sweetness, strength and a generous amount of fruit.

'I'VE NEVER BEEN DRUNK, BUT OFTEN I'VE BEEN OVERSERVED.'
GEORGE GOBEL

RELÁJESE CON FACUNDO NEW #8

Glass: Martini
Garnish: Float extra-thin grapefruit slice
Method: SHAKE all ingredients with cubed ice and fine-strain into a chilled martini glass.

2	shot(s)	**Bacardi Superior rum**
1	shot(s)	**Freshly squeezed grapefruit juice**
½	shot(s)	**Lavender sugar syrup**
2	dashes	**Angostura orange bitters**

Comment: Floral but this rum-based drink is far from being a pansy.
Origin: Created in 2008 by Adam Elmegirab at Evo-lution Bar Consultancy, Aberdeen, Scotland. The name literally translates from Spanish as 'Relax with Facundo'.

REMEMBER THE MAINE UPDATED #8

Glass: Old-fashioned
Garnish: Lemon zest twist
Method: POUR absinthe into ice-filled glass, top up with water and set to one side. Separately, POUR other ingredients into an ice-filled mixing glass and STIR well. DISCARD absinthe, water and ice from serving glass. Finally strain contents of mixing glass into the absinthe rinsed glass.

1	shot(s)	**La Fée Parisienne (68%) absinthe**
Top up with		**Chilled mineral water**
2	shot(s)	**Bulleit bourbon whiskey**
¾	shot(s)	**Herring cherry brandy liqueur**
¾	shot(s)	**Martini Rosso sweet vermouth**

Origin: Adapted from a recipe by Charles H. Baker Junior. In his 1939 'The Gentleman's Companion' he writes of this drink, "a Hazy Memory of a Night in Havana during the Unpleasantnesses of 1933, when Each Swallow Was Punctuated with Bombs Going off on the Prado, or the Sound of 3" Shells Being Fired at the Hotel Nacional, then Haven for Certain Anti-Revolutionary Officers".
The drink is named after the press slogan, which allegedly provoked the 1898 Spanish-American War.
Comment: Charles H. Baker says of this twist on a Sazerac, "Treat this one with the respect it deserves, gentleman."

REMSEN COOLER

Glass: Collins
Garnish: Whole lemon peel
Method: POUR ingredients into ice-filled glass and serve with straws.

2½	shot(s)	**Johnnie Walker Scotch whisky**
Top up with		**Soda** (from siphon)

Origin: Adapted from a recipe purloined from David Embury's classic book, The Fine Art of Mixing Drinks, and so named because it was originally made with the now defunct Remsen Scotch whisky. Embury claims this is "the original cooler".
Comment: Scotch and soda for the sophisticate.

RESOLUTE

Glass: Martini
Garnish: Lemon zest twist
Method: SHAKE all ingredients with ice and fine strain into chilled glass.

2	shot(s)	**Tanqueray London dry gin**
1	shot(s)	**Bols apricot brandy liqueur**
½	shot(s)	**Freshly squeezed lemon juice**
¾	shot(s)	**Chilled mineral water** (omit if wet ice)

Origin: Adapted from a recipe purloined from a 1930 edition of The Savoy Cocktail Book by Harry Craddock.
Comment: Simple but tasty. All three flavours work in harmony.

REVERSE MARTINI NEW #8

Glass: Martini
Garnish: Lemon zest twist or olive
Method: STIR all ingredients with ice and strain into chilled glass.

2	shot(s)	**Noilly Prat dry vermouth**
1	shot(s)	**Tanqueray London dry gin**

Comment: Simply a Dry Martini with the proportions reversed to make a dripping Wet Martini.

REVERSED VESPER & TONIC NEW #8

Glass: Martini/Coupette
Garnish: Lemon zest twist
Method: SHAKE all ingredients with ice and fine strain into chilled glass.

1	shot(s)	**Tanqueray London Dry gin**
1	shot(s)	**Ketel One vodka**
1	shot(s)	**Lillet blonde aperitif**
⅛	shot(s)	**Becherovka liqueur**
⅛	shot(s)	**Pomegranate (grenadine) syrup**
½	shot(s)	**Tonic water**

Comment: Martini in style but with the hard edges shaken off and a hint of eastern spice added. Scarily, it took 14 attempts and 13 wasted drinks to arrive at the above formula.
Origin: Created in 2008 by Yours Truly (Simon Difford) at the Cabinet Room, London, England. James Bond named his favourite style of Martini after the beautiful Russian agent Vesper Lynd. This version is 'Reversed' due to the dramatically increased ratio of Lillet. It mixes east and west ingredients with the introduction of Becherovka, and where there is Becherovka there should be tonic water.

RHETT BUTLER

Glass: Old-fashioned
Garnish: Lime wedge
Method: SHAKE all ingredients with ice and fine strain into ice-filled glass.

1	shot(s)	**Grand Marnier liqueur**
1	shot(s)	**Southern Comfort liqueur**
2	shot(s)	**Ocean Spray cranberry juice**
1	shot(s)	**Freshly squeezed lime juice**

Comment: A simple and well-balanced classic drink.

RHINESTONE COWGIRL NEW #8

Glass: Collins
Garnish: Orange slice
Method: SHAKE all ingredients with ice and strain into chilled glass.

2	shot(s)	**Bulleit bourbon whiskey**
¾	shot(s)	**Crème de cassis liqueur**
2	shot(s)	**Ocean Spray cranberry juice**
1	shot(s)	**Freshly squeezed lemon juice**
½	shot(s)	**Sugar syrup** (2 sugar to 1 water)

Comment: Tangy, citrus, cranberry and berry fruit laced with sweetened bourbon.

RHUBARB & CUSTARD MARTINI

Glass: Martini
Garnish: Grate fresh nutmeg over drink
Method: SHAKE all ingredients with ice and fine strain into chilled glass.

1¼	shot(s)	**Tanqueray London dry gin**
1¼	shot(s)	**Bols advocaat liqueur**
1¼	shot(s)	**Rhubarb syrup** (from tinned fruit)

Origin: I created this drink in 2002. Rhubarb and Custard is a great British dessert and was a cult children's TV cartoon in the 1970s. It featured a naughty pink cat called Custard and a dog named Rhubarb who, like many British men, spent a lot of time in his garden shed.
Comment: As sharp, sweet, creamy and flavourful as the dessert it imitates.

RHUBARB & HONEY BELLINI

Glass: Flute
Garnish: Orange zest string
Method: SHAKE rhubarb syrup and honey liqueur with ice and fine strain into chilled glass. **TOP** with prosecco and gently stir.

1¼	shot(s)	**Rhubarb syrup** (from tinned fruit)
1¼	shot(s)	**Krupnik honey liqueur**
Top up with		**Prosecco sparkling wine**

Origin: A simplified adaptation of a drink created in 2003 by Tony Conigliaro at London's Shumi.
Comment: This implausible combination works surprisingly well.

> ## 'I ENVY PEOPLE WHO DRINK - AT LEAST THEY KNOW WHAT TO BLAME EVERYTHING ON.'
> OSCAR LEVAN

RHUBARB & LEMONGRASS MARTINI

Glass: Martini
Garnish: Stick of lemongrass in drink
Method: MUDDLE lemongrass in base of shaker. Add other ingredients, **SHAKE** with ice and fine strain into chilled glass.

4	inches	**Fresh lemongrass** (chopped)
2	shot(s)	**Tanqueray London dry gin**
2	shot(s)	**Rhubarb syrup** (from tinned fruit)
⅛	shot(s)	**Sugar syrup** (2 sugar to 1 water)

Origin: I based this drink on one I discovered in 2003 at Zuma, London, England.
Comment: Fragrant exotic lemon flavours combine with, well, rhubarb to make a surprisingly refreshing long drink.

ESQUIRE FIRST PUBLISHED
'HANDBOOK FOR HOSTS'
IN 1949.

RIBALAIGUA DAIQUIRI #3

Glass: Martini
Garnish: Mint leaf
Method: SHAKE all ingredients with ice and fine strain into chilled glass.

2	shot(s)	**Bacardi Superior rum**
½	shot(s)	**Luxardo maraschino liqueur**
1	shot(s)	**Freshly squeezed grapefruit juice**
½	shot(s)	**Chilled mineral water** (omit if wet ice)

Variant: With gin in place of rum this becomes Seventh Heaven No. 2.
Origin: Named for Constantino Ribalaigua, who introduced Hemingway to the Daiquiri at El Floridita, Havana, Cuba.
Comment: This unusual Daiquiri leads with sweet maraschino and finishes with sour grapefruit.

RICHMOND GIMLET NEW #8

Glass: Martini/Coupette
Garnish: Mint leaf
Method: SHAKE all ingredients with ice and fine strain into chilled glass.

8	fresh	**Mint leaves**
2	shot(s)	**Tanqueray London dry gin**
¾	shot(s)	**Freshly squeezed lime juice**
½	shot(s)	**Sugar syrup** (2 sugar to 1 water)
½	shot(s)	**Chilled mineral water** (omit if wet ice)

Comment: A properly grown-up Gimlet.
Origin: Adapted from a recipe created in 2008 by Jeffrey Morgenthaler at Bel Ami Lounge, Oregon, USA.

RICKEY (GENERIC NAME) UPDATED #8

Glass: Collins (small 8oz)
Garnish: Immerse length of lime peel in drink.
Method: SHAKE first 3 ingredients with ice and strain into ice-filled glass. **TOP** with soda.

2	shot(s)	**Spirit** (gin, vodka etc.)
½	shot(s)	**Freshly squeezed lime juice**
¼	shot(s)	**Sugar syrup** (2 sugar to 1 water)
Top up with		**Soda water**

Variant: Gin Rickey, Vodka Rickey, Apricot Rickey
Comment: Clean, sharp and refreshing.
Origin: Believed to have been created at the Shoemaker's restaurant in Washington, circa 1900, and named after Colonel Joe Rickey for whom it was invented. Coincidentally or not, Rickey went on to become a major importer of limes into the US.
  Many confuse the Rickey and the Collins. For the record a Rickey is made with lime juice and a Collins with lemon juice. A Rickey is also usually served in a shorter glass than a Collins but that difference is secondary.

THE RITZ COCKTAIL

Glass: Martini
Garnish: Orange zest twist
Method: STIR first 4 ingredients with ice and strain into chilled glass. **TOP** with a splash of champagne.

1	shot(s)	**Courvoisier V.S.O.P. cognac**
½	shot(s)	**Cointreau triple sec**
¼	shot(s)	**Luxardo maraschino liqueur**
¼	shot(s)	**Freshly squeezed lemon juice**
Top up with		**Perrier Jouet brut champagne**

Origin: Created in the mid-1980s by Dale DeGroff at Aurora, New York City, USA.
Comment: This combination of spirit, liqueurs, fruit and champagne tastes like alcoholic lemon tea.

RIVIERA BREEZE

Glass: Old-fashioned
Garnish: Orange slice in glass
Method: POUR pastis and orange juice into glass and then fill with ice. **TOP** with ginger ale and stir.

1½	shot(s)	**Ricard pastis**
2	shot(s)	**Freshly squeezed orange juice**
Top up with		**Ginger ale**

Origin: Created in 2003 by Roo Buckley at Café Lebowitz, New York City, USA.
Comment: An aniseed-rich summertime cooler.

RIZZO

Glass: Martini
Garnish: Float thin apple slice
Method: SHAKE all ingredients with ice and fine strain into chilled glass.

1	shot(s)	**Boulard Grand Solage calvados**
1	shot(s)	**Tanqueray London dry gin**
¾	shot(s)	**Freshly squeezed grapefruit juice**
½	shot(s)	**Freshly squeezed lime juice**
¼	shot(s)	**Passion fruit syrup**
¼	shot(s)	**Pomegranate (grenadine) syrup**

Origin: Created in 2006 by Gregor de Gruyther at Ronnie Scott's, London, England, and named for Betty Rizzo, the leader of the Pink Ladies in the film Grease.
Comment: The tangy, sharp grapefruit reveals hints of apple spirit smoothed by grenadine.

DRINKS ARE GRADED AS FOLLOWS:

● DISGUSTING   ●● PRETTY AWFUL   ●● BEST AVOIDED
●●● DISAPPOINTING   ●●● ACCEPTABLE   ●●●● GOOD
●●●● RECOMMENDED   ●●●●● HIGHLY RECOMMENDED
●●●●● OUTSTANDING / EXCEPTIONAL

ROA AÉ

Glass: Collins
Garnish: Pineapple wedge on rim
Method: SHAKE all ingredients with ice and strain into ice-filled glass.

1½	shot(s)	**Bacardi Superior rum**
½	shot(s)	**Bols apricot brandy liqueur**
½	shot(s)	**Grand Marnier liqueur**
½	shot(s)	**Belle de Brillet pear liqueur**
3	shot(s)	**Pressed pineapple juice**
¾	shot(s)	**Freshly squeezed lime juice**

Origin: Discovered in 2003 at Booly Mardy's, Glasgow, Scotland. Cocktail aficionados will be familiar with the Tahitian phrase 'Mai Tai – Roa Aé'. or 'out of this world – the best', which gave the Mai Tai its name. This cocktail means simply 'the best'.
Comment: Not quite the best, but this long, fruity thirst-quencher isn't half bad.

'PROFESSOR' JERRY THOMAS FIRST PUBLISHED 'HOW TO MIX DRINKS OR THE BON-VIVANT'S COMPANION' IN 1862.

THE ROADRUNNER

Glass: Martini
Garnish: Lemon zest twist
Method: SHAKE all ingredients with ice and fine strain into chilled glass.

2	shot(s)	**Vanilla-infused Don Julio tequila**
¾	shot(s)	**Freshly squeezed lemon juice**
½	shot(s)	**Maple syrup**
2	dashes	**Angostura aromatic bitters**
½	fresh	**Egg white**

Origin: Discovered in 2005 at The Cuckoo Club, London, England.
Comment: Citrus and tequila with a hint of maple and vanilla, smoothed with egg white.

ROB ROY #1

Glass: Martini
Garnish: Cherry & lemon zest twist (discard twist)
Method: STIR all ingredients with ice and strain into chilled glass.

2	shot(s)	**Johnnie Walker Scotch whisky**
1	shot(s)	**Martini Rosso sweet vermouth**
2	dashes	**Angostura aromatic bitters**
⅛	shot(s)	**Maraschino syrup** (optional)

Variant: 'Highland', made with orange bitters in place of Angostura.
Origin: Created in 1894 at New York's Waldorf-Astoria Hotel (the Empire State Building occupies the site today), and named after a Broadway show playing at the time.
Comment: A Sweet Manhattan made with Scotch in place of bourbon. The dry, peaty whisky and bitters ensure it's not too sweet.

ROB ROY #2

Glass: Martini
Garnish: Cherry & orange zest twist (discard twist)
Method: STIR all ingredients with ice and strain into chilled glass.

2	shot(s)	**Johnnie Walker Scotch whisky**
1	shot(s)	**Martini Rosso sweet vermouth**
2	dashes	**Peychaud's aromatic bitters**
½	shot(s)	**Chilled mineral water** (omit if wet ice)

Origin: This variation on the classic Rob Roy is recommended by author David Embury in his influential Fine Art of Mixing Drinks.
Comment: The Scotch answer to the Manhattan with added complexity courtesy of Peychaud's aromatic bitters.

ROBIN HOOD #1

Glass: Martini
Garnish: Apple wedge on rim
Method: SHAKE all ingredients with ice and fine strain into chilled glass.

1¾	shot(s)	**Bacardi Superior rum**
1¼	shot(s)	**Berentzen apple schnapps**
¾	shot(s)	**Rose's lime cordial**
½	shot(s)	**Freshly squeezed lime juice**

Origin: Adapted from a drink created in 2002 by Tony Conigliaro at The Lonsdale, London, England.
Comment: American readers might consider this an Apple Martini based on rum.

ROC-A-COE

Glass: Martini
Garnish: Maraschino cherry
Method: STIR all ingredients with ice and strain into chilled glass.

1½	shot(s)	**Tanqueray London dry gin**
2	shot(s)	**Amontillado dry sherry**
⅛	shot(s)	**Sugar syrup** (2 sugar to 1 water)
½	shot(s)	**Chilled mineral water** (omit if wet ice)

Origin: Adapted from a recipe purloined from a 1930 edition of The Savoy Cocktail Book by Harry Craddock.
Comment: Aromatic and balanced.

ROCKY MOUNTAIN ROOTBEER

Glass: Collins
Garnish: Lime wedge
Method: POUR vodka and liqueur into ice-filled glass, TOP with Coca-Cola and lightly stir.

2	shot(s)	**Ketel One vodka**
¾	shot(s)	**Galliano L'Autentico liqueur**
Top up with		**Coca-Cola**

Comment: Does indeed taste reminiscent of alcoholic root beer.

THE ROFFIGNAC

Glass: Collins
Garnish: Lime wedge
Method: SHAKE first 2 ingredients with ice and strain into ice-filled glass. **TOP** with soda, lightly stir and serve with straws.

2	shot(s)	**Courvoisier V.S.O.P. cognac**
1	shot(s)	**Crème de framboise liqueur**
Top up with		**Soda water** (club soda)

Origin: This classic cocktail is named after Count Louis Philippe Joseph de Roffignac, Mayor of New Orleans 1820-1828. Roffignac is noted for introducing street lights to the city and laying cobblestones on the roads in the French Quarter.
Comment: This bright red, fruity drink is simple but moreish.

ROGER

Glass: Martini
Garnish: Peach slice on rim
Method: SHAKE all ingredients with ice and fine strain into chilled glass.

2	shot(s)	**Ketel One vodka**
2	shot(s)	**Boiron white peach purée**
½	shot(s)	**Freshly squeezed lemon juice**
¼	shot(s)	**Sugar syrup** (2 sugar to 1 water)

Origin: A popular drink in Venice, where it is made using the peach purée mix prepared for Bellinis.
Comment: Thick and very fruity – one for a summer's afternoon.

ROMAN PUNCH

Glass: Collins
Garnish: Lemon slice
Method: SHAKE all ingredients with ice and strain into glass filled with crushed ice. Serve with straws.

1½	shot(s)	**Bénédictine D.O.M. liqueur**
¾	shot(s)	**Freshly squeezed lemon juice**
1½	shot(s)	**Courvoisier V.S.O.P. cognac**
¾	shot(s)	**Wray & Nephew overproof rum**
2	shot(s)	**Chilled mineral water**

Comment: Spirited and refreshing with herbal notes.

LA ROSA MARGARITA

Glass: Coupette
Garnish: Lime wedge on rim
Method: SHAKE all ingredients with ice and fine strain ino chilled glass.

2	shot(s)	**Don Julio reposado tequila**
¾	shot(s)	**Crème de mûre liqueur**
1	shot(s)	**Cold hibiscus tea** (strong brewed)
½	shot(s)	**Freshly squeezed lime juice**

Comment: A fruity yet dry crimson-coloured Margarita.

ROSARITA MARGARITA

Glass: Coupette
Garnish: Lime wedge & optional salted rim
Method: SHAKE all ingredients with ice and fine strain into chilled glass.

1½	shot(s)	**Don Julio reposado tequila**
¾	shot(s)	**Grand Marnier liqueur**
½	shot(s)	**Ocean Spray cranberry juice**
½	shot(s)	**Rose's lime cordial**
¾	shot(s)	**Freshly squeezed lime juice**
½	shot(s)	**Sugar syrup** (2 sugar to 1 water)

Origin: Created in 1999 by Robert Plotkin and Raymon Flores of BarMedia, USA.
Comment: This peachy coloured Margarita is well balanced and flavoursome.

THE ROSE #1 (ORIGINAL)

Glass: Martini
Garnish: Maraschino cherry
Method: STIR all ingredients with ice and fine strain into chilled glass.

2	shot(s)	**Noilly Prat dry vermouth**
1	shot(s)	**Kirsch eau de vie**
½	shot(s)	**Raspberry (or pomegranate) syrup**

Origin: Created in 1920 by Johnny Milta at the Chatham Hotel, Paris. This recipe is adapted from one in The Fine Art of Mixing Drinks by David Embury.
Comment: This salmon pink drink is wonderfully aromatic.

THE ROSE #2

Glass: Martini
Garnish: Maraschino cherry
Method: STIR all ingredients with ice and fine strain into chilled glass.

2	shot(s)	**Tanqueray London dry gin**
1	shot(s)	**Heering cherry brandy liqueur**
1	shot(s)	**Noilly Prat dry vermouth**

Origin: Adapted from a recipe in Harry Craddock's 1930 Savoy Cocktail Book.
Comment: Cherry and gin dried with vermouth.

THE ROSE #3

Glass: Martini
Garnish: Maraschino cherry
Method: SHAKE all ingredients with ice and fine strain into chilled glass.

1½	shot(s)	**Kirsch eau de vie**
1½	shot(s)	**Noilly Prat dry vermouth**
½	shot(s)	**Pomegranate (grenadine) syrup**

Origin: Adapted from a recipe in Harry Craddock's 1930 Savoy Cocktail Book.
Comment: Delicate, aromatic cherry – not too sweet.

ROSE-HYP MARTINI UPDATED #8

●●●●●

Glass: Martini
Garnish: Edible flower
Method: THROW all ingredients with ice and strain into chilled glass.

2	shot(s)	Tanqueray London dry gin
¾	shot(s)	St-Germain elderflower liqueur
½	shot(s)	Noilly Prat dry vermouth
¼	shot(s)	Lanique rose petal liqueur

Comment: Dry (but not bone dry), aromatic and floral.
Origin: Created in 2006 by Yours Truly (Simon Difford) in London, England.

ROSE PETALINI

●●●●○

Glass: Martini
Garnish: Float red rose petal
Method: STIR all ingredients with ice and strain into chilled glass.

1½	shot(s)	Rose vodka
1½	shot(s)	Tanqueray London dry gin
1	shot(s)	Lychee syrup (from tinned lychees)
3	dashes	Peychaud's aromatic bitters

Origin: Discovered in 2005 at Rain, Amsterdam, The Netherlands.
Comment: Peychaud's bitters give this fragrant cocktail a delicate pink hue.

ROSELYN MARTINI

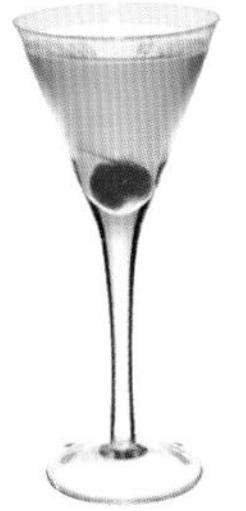

●●●●◐

Glass: Martini
Garnish: Maraschino cherry
Method: SHAKE all ingredients with ice and fine strain into chilled glass.

2	shot(s)	Tanqueray London dry gin
1	shot(s)	Noilly Prat dry vermouth
¼	shot(s)	Pomegranate (grenadine) syrup

Origin: Adapted from a recipe in Harry Craddock's 1930 Savoy Cocktail Book.
Comment: Subtle and beautifully balanced. A wet Martini made 'easy' by a dash of pomegranate syrup.

ROSITA

●●●●○

Glass: Old-fashioned
Garnish: Orange zest twist
Method: STIR all ingredients with ice and strain into ice-filled glass.

2	shot(s)	Don Julio reposado tequila
¾	shot(s)	Campari Bitter
¾	shot(s)	Noilly Prat dry vermouth
¾	shot(s)	Martini Rosso sweet vermouth
2	dashes	Angostura aromatic bitters

Comment: A bittersweet, tequila based, Negroni-like drink.

ROSSINI UPDATED #8

●●●●○

Glass: Flute
Garnish: Strawberry on rim
Method: MUDDLE strawberries in base of shaker. Add strawberry liqueur, SHAKE with ice and fine strain into chilled glass. TOP with prosecco and gently stir.

4	fresh	Strawberries (hulled)
¾	shot(s)	Crème de fraise liqueur
Top up with		Prosecco sparkling wine

Origin: Named for the 19th century Italian opera composer, Gioachino Antonio Rossini. This is one of the most popular Bellini variants in Venice.
Comment: Strawberries seem to complement Prosecco even better than white peaches.

ROSY MARTINI

●●●●○

Glass: Martini
Garnish: Orange zest twist
Method: STIR all ingredients with ice and strain into chilled glass.

2	shot(s)	Ketel One Citroen vodka
¾	shot(s)	Cointreau triple sec
¾	shot(s)	Dubonnet Red (French made)

Comment: An aptly named drink with hints of spice, citrus peel, honey and mulled wine.

ROULETTE

●●●●○

Glass: Martini
Garnish: Orange zest twist
Method: SHAKE all ingredients with ice and fine strain into chilled glass.

1½	shot(s)	Boulard Grand Solage calvados
¾	shot(s)	Bacardi Superior rum
¾	shot(s)	Swedish Punch
½	shot(s)	Chilled mineral water (omit if wet ice)

Origin: Adapted from a recipe in Harry Craddock's 1930 Savoy Cocktail Book.
Comment: Balanced apple and spice.

ROUSING CHARLIE

●●●●○○

Glass: Martini
Garnish: Lychee from tin in drink
Method: STIR all ingredients with ice and strain into chilled glass.

¾	shot(s)	Macchu pisco
¾	shot(s)	St-Germain elderflower liqueur
¾	shot(s)	Tio Pepe fino sherry
¾	shot(s)	Sake
½	shot(s)	Lychee syrup (from tinned fruit)

Origin: Adapted from a drink I created in 2002 and named after Charlie Rouse, a very lovely sherry lover.
Comment: Subtle with an interesting salty edge, this tastes almost like a wine.

ROY ROGERS (MOCKTAIL)

Glass: Collins
Garnish: Lime wedge
Method: POUR grenadine and Coca-Cola into ice-filled glass and stir. Serve with straws.

| ¼ | shot(s) | Pomegranate (grenadine) syrup |
| Top up with | | Coca-Cola |

Comment: I wouldn't bother.

ROYAL BERMUDA YACHT CLUB DAIQUIRI

Glass: Martini
Garnish: Lime wedge on rim
Method: SHAKE all ingredients with ice and fine strain into chilled glass.

2½	shot(s)	Bacardi Oro golden rum
¾	shot(s)	Freshly squeezed lime juice
½	shot(s)	Velvet Falernum liqueur
¼	shot(s)	Cointreau triple sec

Origin: Created at the eponymous club, established in Bermuda in 1844 and largely frequented by British Army officers.
This recipe is adapted from one in Trader Vic's Bartender's Guide.
Comment: A full-flavoured, tangy Daiquiri.

ROYAL COSMOPOLITAN

Glass: Martini
Garnish: Orange zest twist
Method: SHAKE first 4 ingredients with ice and fine strain into chilled glass. **TOP** with champagne.

1	shot(s)	Ketel One Citroen vodka
½	shot(s)	Cointreau triple sec
1	shot(s)	Ocean Spray cranberry juice
¼	shot(s)	Freshly squeezed lime juice
Top up with		Perrier Jouet brut champagne

Origin: Created in 2003 by Wayne Collins, London, UK.
Comment: The classic Cosmopolitan with a layer of fizz on top, adding a biscuity complexity. Sex And The City meets Ab Fab.

ROYAL GINGERSNAP NEW #8

Glass: Old-fashioned
Garnish: Cinnamon and sugar rim using orange juice plus famed orange zest twist
Method: MUDDLE the cherry in base of shaker. Add other ingredients, **SHAKE** with ice and fine strain into ice-filled glass.

1	whole	Maraschino cherry
2	shot(s)	Canadian whiskey
1	spoon	Orange marmalade
¼	shot(s)	Domaine de Canton ginger liqueur
½	shot(s)	Freshly squeezed orange juice
2	dashes	Angostura aromatic bitters

Comment: Variation on Old-Fashioned
Origin: Created by Dale DeGroff, this recipe is adapted from his 2008 book 'The Essential Cocktail'.

ROYAL MOJITO

Glass: Collins
Garnish: Mint sprig
Method: Lightly **MUDDLE** mint (just to bruise) in base of glass. Add rum, lime juice and sugar. Half fill glass with crushed ice and **CHURN** (stir) with bar spoon. Fill glass with more crushed ice and **CHURN** some more. **TOP** with champagne, lightly stir and serve with straws.

12	fresh	Mint leaves
2	shot(s)	Bacardi Superior rum
¾	shot(s)	Freshly squeezed lime juice
¼	shot(s)	Sugar syrup (2 sugar to 1 water)
Top up with		Perrier Jouet brut champagne

AKA: Luxury Mojito
Comment: A Mojito topped with champagne instead of soda water. There's posh!

ROYAL SMILE

Glass: Martini
Garnish: Lemon zest twist
Method: SHAKE all ingredients with ice and fine strain into chilled glass.

1	shot(s)	Tanqueray London dry gin
1	shot(s)	Boulard Grand Solage calvados
½	shot(s)	Freshly squeezed lemon juice
¼	shot(s)	Pomegranate (grenadine) syrup
½	shot(s)	Chilled mineral water (omit if wet ice)

Origin: Purloined from David Embury's classic book, The Fine Art of Mixing Drinks.
Comment: This balanced sweet and sour could put a smile on anyone's face. Unless one is not amused!

> **A TELEPHONE SURVEY SAYS THAT 51 PERCENT OF COLLEGE STUDENTS DRINK UNTIL THEY PASS OUT AT LEAST ONCE A MONTH. THE OTHER 49 PERCENT DIDN'T ANSWER THE PHONE.**

ROYAL VELVET MARGARITA

Glass: Coupette (or fresh pineapple shell)
Garnish: Lime wedge
Method: SHAKE all ingredients with ice and fine strain into chilled glass.

2	shot(s)	Don Julio reposado tequila
½	shot(s)	Chambord black raspberry liqueur
½	shot(s)	Luxardo Amaretto di Saschira
1	shot(s)	Freshly squeezed lime juice

Origin: Discovered in 2005 at Velvet Margarita Cantina, Los Angeles, USA.
Comment: An almond and berry flavoured Margarita.

GERRY'S SPECIALIST LIQUOR STORE OPENED IN SOHO, LONDON IN 1984.

R U BOBBY MOORE?

••••◐

Glass: Martini
Garnish: Apple wedge on rim
Method: STIR honey with Scotch and vodka in base of shaker until honey dissolves. Add other ingredients, **SHAKE** with ice and fine strain into chilled glass.

3	spoons	Runny honey
1	shot(s)	Johnnie Walker Scotch whisky
1	shot(s)	Zubrówka bison vodka
¾	shot(s)	Sauvignon Blanc wine
1	shot(s)	Pressed apple juice

Origin: Created in 2002 by Yours Truly (Simon Difford) and named after the rhyming slang for 'are you bloody sure?' Bobby Moore was the 60s England football captain and West Ham United defender who regrettably died young in 1993. My dictionary of rhyming slang claims 'Bobby Moore' means 'door' – well, not in East London it doesn't.
Comment: It's common to pair both Scotch and zubrówka with apple, but combining all three together with wine and honey really works.

RUBY MARTINI #1

•••••◐

Glass: Martini
Garnish: Lemon slice on rim
Method: SHAKE all ingredients with ice and fine strain into chilled glass.

1½	shot(s)	Ketel One Citroen vodka
1	shot(s)	Cointreau triple sec
1	shot(s)	Freshly squeezed grapefruit juice
¼	shot(s)	Sugar syrup (2 sugar to 1 water)

Origin: Several appearances in episodes of the hit US TV series, Sex And The City, helped this drink become fashionable in 2002, particularly in New York City. It is thought to have originated at the Wave restaurant in Chicago's W Hotel.
Comment: A sour, citrus-led variation on the Cosmopolitan.

RUBY MARTINI #2

•••••◐◐

Glass: Martini
Garnish: Raspberry & lemon twist
Method: SHAKE all ingredients with ice and fine strain into chilled glass.

1½	shot(s)	Courvoisier V.S.O.P. cognac
½	shot(s)	Cointreau triple sec
½	shot(s)	Crème de framboise liqueur
½	shot(s)	Martini Rosso sweet vermouth

Origin: Created by Wayne Collins, London, England.
Comment: Fruity and slightly sweet.

RUDE COSMOPOLITAN

•••••◐

Glass: Martini
Garnish: Orange zest twist
Method: SHAKE all ingredients with ice and fine strain into chilled glass.

1	shot(s)	Don Julio reposado tequila
1	shot(s)	Cointreau triple sec
1½	shot(s)	Ocean Spray cranberry juice
½	shot(s)	Freshly squeezed lime juice
2	dashes	Angostura orange bitters (optional)

AKA: Mexico City
Comment: Don't let the pink appearance of this Cosmopolitan (made with tequila in place of vodka) fool you into thinking it's a fluffy cocktail. It's both serious and superb.

RUDE GINGER COSMOPOLITAN

••••◐

Glass: Martini
Garnish: Orange zest twist
Method: MUDDLE ginger in base of shaker. Add other ingredients, **SHAKE** with ice and fine strain into chilled glass.

2	slices	Fresh root ginger (thumbnail sized)
1½	shot(s)	Don Julio reposado tequila
1	shot(s)	Cointreau triple sec
1	shot(s)	Ocean Spray cranberry juice
½	shot(s)	Freshly squeezed lime juice
¼	shot(s)	Rose's lime cordial

Origin: Created in 2003 by Jeremy Adderley at Halo, Edinburgh, Scotland.
Comment: To quote Halo's list, "Looks like a Cosmo, goes like a Mexican!"

RUM AMANDINE NEW #8

••••◐◐

Glass: Flute
Garnish: Maraschino cherry
Method: SHAKE all ingredients with ice and fine strain into chilled glass.

2	shot(s)	Bacardi Superior rum
⅛	shot(s)	Luxardo Maraschino liqueur
⅛	shot(s)	La Fée Parisienne (68%) absinthe
¾	shot(s)	Freshly squeezed lime juice
¼	shot(s)	Almond (orgeat) syrup
2	dashes	Orange flower water
½	shot(s)	Chilled water (omit if wet ice)

Comment: A classic Daquiri benefitting from the influence of almond and absinthe.
Origin: Marcis Dzelzainis, Quo Vadis, London, England.

DRINKS ARE GRADED AS FOLLOWS:

● DISGUSTING   ●◐ PRETTY AWFUL   ●● BEST AVOIDED
●●◐ DISAPPOINTING   ●●● ACCEPTABLE   ●●●◐ GOOD
●●●● RECOMMENDED   ●●●●◐ HIGHLY RECOMMENDED
●●●●● OUTSTANDING / EXCEPTIONAL

RUM & RAISIN ALEXANDRA

●●●●○

Glass: Martini
Garnish: Three red grapes on stick
Method: MUDDLE grapes in base of shaker. Add other ingredients, **SHAKE** with ice and fine strain into chilled glass.

7	fresh	Seedless white grapes
1½	shot(s)	Zacapa aged rum
½	shot(s)	Crème de cassis liqueur
½	shot(s)	Double (heavy) cream
½	shot(s)	Milk
¼	shot(s)	Sugar syrup (2 sugar to 1 water)

Origin: Created in 2003 by Ian Morgan, England.
Comment: Forgo the ice cream and try this creamy, quaffable, alcoholic dessert.

'I DON'T DRINK THESE DAYS. I AM ALLERGIC TO ALCOHOL AND NARCOTICS. I BREAK OUT IN HANDCUFFS.'
ROBERT DOWNEY JR

RUM PUNCH

●●●●●

Glass: Collins
Garnish: Orange slice & cherry on stick (sail)
Method: SHAKE all ingredients with ice and strain into glass filled with crushed ice.

¾	shot(s)	Freshly squeezed lime juice
1½	shot(s)	Sugar syrup (2 sugar to 1 water)
2¼	shot(s)	Wray & Nephew overproof rum
3	shot(s)	Chilled mineral water
3	dashes	Angostura aromatic bitters

Comment: The classic proportions of this drink (followed above) are 'one of sour, two of sweet, three of strong and four of weak' – referring to lime juice, sugar syrup, rum and water respectively. In Jamaica, the spiritual home of the Rum Punch, they like their rum overproof (more than 57% alc./vol.) and serving over crushed ice dilutes and tames this very strong drink.

RUM PUNCH-UP

●●●●●

Glass: Martini
Garnish: Lime wedge on rim
Method: SHAKE all ingredients with ice and fine strain into chilled glass.

1½	shot(s)	Wray & Nephew overproof rum
½	shot(s)	Freshly squeezed lime juice
½	shot(s)	Sugar syrup (2 sugar to 1 water)
1	shot(s)	Chilled mineral water (reduce if wet ice)
2	dashes	Angostura aromatic bitters

Origin: Adapted from a drink discovered in 2006 at Albannach, London, England.
Comment: Exactly what the name promises – a rum punch served straight-up, Daiquiri style.

RUMBA

●●●●○

Glass: Old-fashioned
Garnish: Lime wedge
Method: SHAKE all ingredients with ice and strain into glass filled with crushed ice. Serve with straws.

¾	shot(s)	Wray & Nephew overproof rum
1	shot(s)	Tanqueray London dry gin
1	shot(s)	Freshly squeezed lime juice
½	shot(s)	Pomegranate (grenadine) syrup
¼	shot(s)	Sugar syrup (2 sugar to 1 water)
½	shot(s)	Chilled mineral water (omit if wet ice)

Origin: Recipe adapted from David Embury's classic book, The Fine Art of Mixing Drinks.
Comment: To quote Embury, "Whoever thought up this snootful of liquid dynamite certainly liked his liquor hard!"

RUM RUNNER

●●●●○

Glass: Hurricane
Garnish: Pineapple wedge & cherry
Method: SHAKE all ingredients with ice and strain into glass filled with crushed ice.

1½	shot(s)	Pusser's Navy rum
½	shot(s)	Crème de mûre liqueur
1	shot(s)	Crème de banane liqueur
1	shot(s)	Freshly squeezed lime juice
2	shot(s)	Pressed pineapple juice
½	shot(s)	Pomegranate (grenadine) syrup

Comment: Fruity, sharp and rounded.

RUM SOUR

●●●●○

Glass: Old-fashioned
Garnish: Orange zest twist
Method: SHAKE all ingredients with ice and strain into ice-filled glass.

2	shot(s)	Zacapa aged rum
1	shot(s)	Freshly squeezed orange juice
1	shot(s)	Freshly squeezed lime juice
½	shot(s)	Sugar syrup (2 sugar to 1 water)
½	fresh	Egg white

Comment: Smooth and sour – well balanced.

RUM SWIZZLE NEW #8

●●●○○

Glass: Sling
Garnish: Mint sprig & orange slice
Method: POUR all ingredients into glass filled with crushed ice and **SWIZZLE** (stir).

2	shot(s)	Zacapa aged rum
½	shot(s)	Velvet Falernum liqueur
1	shot(s)	Freshly squeezed lime juice
½	shot(s)	Sugar syrup (2 sugar to 1 water)
1	dash	Angostura aromatic bitters

Comment: Sweet and sour with aged rum base. All too easy.
Origin: This drink emerged in the early 1800's in Guyana when British ex-pats mixed this drink on the terrace of the Georgetown club using a long five-pronged swizzle stick fashioned from a tree branch.

RUSSIAN

Glass: Martini
Garnish: Orange zest twist
Method: SHAKE all ingredients with ice and fine strain into chilled glass.

1½	shot(s)	Tanqueray London dry gin
1	shot(s)	Ketel One vodka
1	shot(s)	White crème de cacao liqueur

Origin: Adapted from a recipe in Harry Craddock's 1930 Savoy Cocktail Book.
Comment: Gin and vodka with a sweet hint of chocolate.

RUSSIAN BRIDE

Glass: Martini
Garnish: Dust with cocoa powder
Method: SHAKE all ingredients with ice and fine strain into chilled glass.

2	shot(s)	Vanilla-infused Ketel One vodka
¾	shot(s)	Kahlúa coffee liqueur
¼	shot(s)	White crème de cacao liqueur
½	shot(s)	Double (heavy) cream
½	shot(s)	Milk

Origin: Created in 2002 by Miranda Dickson, A.K.A. the Vodka Princess, for the UK's Revolution bar chain, where some 500,000 are sold each year.
Comment: A little on the sweet side for some but definitely a tasty combination.

RUSSIAN QUALUUDE SHOT

Glass: Shot
Method: Refrigerate ingredients then LAYER in chilled glass by carefully pouring in the following order.

½	shot(s)	Galliano L'Autentico liqueur
½	shot(s)	Green Chartreuse liqueur
½	shot(s)	Ketel One vodka

Comment: An explosive herb and peppermint shot.

RUSSIAN SPRING PUNCH

UPDATED #8

Glass: Sling
Garnish: Lemon slice & raspberry
Method: MUDDLE raspberries in base of shaker. Add next 5 ingredients, SHAKE with ice and strain into glass filled with crushed ice. TOP with champagne, lightly stir and serve with straws.

7	fresh	Raspberries
1	shot(s)	Ketel One vodka
¼	shot(s)	Crème de cassis liqueur
¼	shot(s)	Crème de framboise liqueur
1	shot(s)	Freshly squeezed lemon juice
¼	shot(s)	Sugar syrup (2 sugar to 1 water)
Top up with		Perrier Jouet brut champagne

Origin: Created in the 1990s by Dick Bradsell, London, England.
Comment: Well balanced, complex and refreshing.

RUSTY NEW #8

Glass: Old-fashioned
Garnish: Orange zest twist
Method: STIR all ingredients with ice and strain into ice-filled glass.

1½	shot(s)	Zacapa aged rum
1½	shot(s)	Amontillado dry sherry
¼	shot(s)	Lagavulin 16yo malt whisky
¼	shot(s)	Sugar syrup (2 sugar to 1 water)

Comment: The Sherry character of Zacapa is highlighted and its spicy notes built upon with smoky Islay malt.
Origin: Created in December 2008 by Yours Truly (Simon Difford) at The Cabinet Room, London, England.

RUSTY NAIL NEW #8

Glass: Old-fashioned
Garnish: Lemon zest twist
Method: STIR all ingredients with ice and strain into ice-filled glass.

2¼	shot(s)	Johnnie Walker Scotch whisky
¾	shot(s)	Drambuie liqueur

Comment: The liqueur smoothes and wonderfully combines with the Scotch.
Origin: Created in 1942 at a Hawaiian bar for the artist Theodore Anderson. The proportions of Scotch to Drambuie vary wildly and are a matter of taste. However, the 3:1 proportions used here appear most popular.

SAGE MARGARITA

Glass: Coupette
Garnish: Float sage leaf
Method: Lightly MUDDLE (just to bruise) sage in base of shaker. Add other ingredients, SHAKE with ice and fine strain into chilled glass.

3	fresh	Sage leaves
2	shot(s)	Don Julio reposado tequila
1	shot(s)	Cointreau triple sec
1	shot(s)	Freshly squeezed lime juice
⅛	shot(s)	Sugar syrup (2 sugar to 1 water)

Comment: Exactly as promised – a sage flavoured Margarita.

SAGE MARTINI

Glass: Martini
Garnish: Float sage leaf
Method: Lightly MUDDLE (just to bruise) sage in base of shaker. Add other ingredients, SHAKE with ice and fine strain into chilled glass.

3	fresh	Sage leaves
1½	shot(s)	Ketel One vodka
1½	shot(s)	Noilly Prat dry vermouth
¾	shot(s)	Pressed apple juice

Comment: Delicate sage and a hint of apple, dried with vermouth and fortified with vodka.

SAIGON COOLER

Glass: Collins
Garnish: Three raspberries
Method: MUDDLE raspberries in base of shaker. Add other ingredients, **SHAKE** with ice and fine strain into ice-filled glass.

7	fresh	**Raspberries**
2	shot(s)	**Tanqueray London dry gin**
½	shot(s)	**Chambord black raspberry liqueur**
3	shot(s)	**Ocean Spray cranberry juice**
¾	shot(s)	**Freshly squeezed lime juice**

Origin: Created at Bam-Bou, London, England.
Comment: Well balanced sweet 'n' sour with a rich fruity flavour.

SAIGON SLING

Glass: Sling
Garnish: Pineapple wedge & cherry on rim
Method: SHAKE first 7 ingredients with ice and strain into ice-filled glass. **TOP** with ginger ale.

1½	shot(s)	**Tanqueray London dry gin**
¾	shot(s)	**Ginger & lemongrass cordial**
½	shot(s)	**Krupnik honey liqueur**
¾	shot(s)	**Freshly squeezed lime juice**
1	shot(s)	**Pressed pineapple juice**
¼	shot(s)	**Passoã passion fruit liqueur**
2	dashes	**Peychaud's aromatic bitters**
Top up with		**Ginger ale**

Origin: Created in 2001 by Rodolphe Manor for a London bartending competition.
Comment: A fusion of unusual flavours.

SAILOR'S COMFORT

Glass: Old-fashioned
Garnish: Lime wedge
Method: SHAKE first 4 ingredients with ice and strain into ice-filled glass. **TOP** with soda, lightly stir and serve with straws.

1	shot(s)	**Sloe gin liqueur**
1	shot(s)	**Southern Comfort liqueur**
1	shot(s)	**Rose's lime cordial**
3	dashes	**Angostura aromatic bitters**
Top up with		**Soda water** (club soda)

Origin: Discovered in 2002 at Lightship Ten, London.
Comment: Lime, peach and hints of berry make a light, easy drink.

SAINT CLEMENTS (MOCKTAIL)

Glass: Collins
Garnish: Lime wedge
Method: POUR ingredients into ice-filled glass, lightly stir and serve with straws.

3	shot(s)	**Freshly squeezed orange juice**
Top up with		**Bitter lemon**

Comment: Only slightly more interesting than orange juice.

THE ST-GERMAIN

Glass: Collins (12oz)
Garnish: Lime slice
Method: POUR wine and then elderflower liqueur into ice-filled glass. **TOP** with soda (or champagne), lightly stir and serve with straws.

2	shot(s)	**Sauvignon Blanc wine**
1½	shot(s)	**St-Germain elderflower liqueur**
Top up with		**Soda water (or champagne)**

Variant: Also try 2 shots champagne, 1½ shots St-Germain topped with soda.
Origin: Created in 2006 by Yours Truly (Simon Difford), this is the signature drink of St-Germain elderflower liqueur.
Comment: A long, easy drinking summer cooler.

ST. KITTS (MOCKTAIL)

Glass: Collins
Garnish: Lime wedge
Method: SHAKE first 3 ingredients with ice and strain into ice-filled glass. **TOP** with ginger ale, lightly stir and serve with straws.

3	shot(s)	**Pineapple juice**
½	shot(s)	**Freshly squeezed lime juice**
¼	shot(s)	**Pomegranate (grenadine) syrup**
Top up with		**Ginger ale**

Variant: Add 3 dashes Angostura aromatic bitters. This adds a tiny amount of alcohol but greatly improves the drink.
Comment: Rust coloured and refreshing.

ST. PATRICK'S DAY

Glass: Old-fashioned
Garnish: Mint sprig/shamrock
Method: STIR all ingredients with ice and strain into ice-filled glass.

2	shot(s)	**Jameson Irish whiskey**
1	shot(s)	**Green Chartreuse liqueur**
1	shot(s)	**Green crème de menthe liqueur**
1	dash	**Angostura aromatic bitters.**

Origin: Created in 2006 by Yours Truly (Simon Difford).
Comment: Minty, herbal whiskey – a helluva craic.

SAKE MARTINI NEW #8

Glass: Coupette/Martini
Garnish: Float mandolin cut apple slice
Method: STIR all ingredients with ice and fine strain into chilled glass.

2	shot(s)	**Tanqueray London dry gin**
2	shot(s)	**Sake**
⅛	shot(s)	**Noilly Prat dry vermouth**

Comment: Dry, subtle, and depending on your choice of sake, possibly amazing.

SAKE'POLITAN

Glass: Martini
Garnish: Orange zest twist
Method: **SHAKE** all ingredients with ice and fine strain into chilled glass.

2¼	shot(s)	**Sake**
¾	shot(s)	**Cointreau triple sec**
¾	shot(s)	**Ocean Spray cranberry juice**
¼	shot(s)	**Freshly squeezed lime juice**
2	dashes	**Angostura orange bitters** (optional)

Comment: A Cosmo with more than a hint of sake.

SAKE-TINI #1

Glass: Martini
Garnish: Three thin slices of cucumber
Method: **STIR** all ingredients with ice and strain into chilled glass.

1	shot(s)	**Tanqueray London dry gin**
2½	shot(s)	**Sake**
½	shot(s)	**Grand Marnier liqueur**

Comment: Sake and a hint of orange liqueur add the perfect aromatic edge to this Martini-style drink.

SAKE-TINI #2

Glass: Martini
Garnish: Orange zest twist
Method: **SHAKE** all ingredients with ice and fine strain into chilled glass.

1½	shot(s)	**Ketel One vodka**
1	shot(s)	**Plum wine**
½	shot(s)	**Sake**
1	shot(s)	**Ocean Spray cranberry juice**

Origin: Discovered in 2005 at Nobu Berkeley, London, England.
Comment: Salmon-coloured, light and fragrant with plum wine and sake to the fore.

SAKINI

Glass: Martini
Garnish: Olives on stick
Method: **STIR** all ingredients with ice and strain into chilled glass.

| 1 | shot(s) | **Sake** |
| 2½ | shot(s) | **Ketel One vodka** |

Comment: Very dry. The sake creates an almost wine-like delicacy.

SALFLOWER SOUR

Glass: Martini
Garnish: Orange zest twist (discarded)
Method: **SHAKE** all ingredients with ice and fine strain into chilled glass.

2	shot(s)	**St-Germain elderflower liqueur**
¾	shot(s)	**Freshly squeezed orange juice**
¾	shot(s)	**Freshly squeezed lime juice**
1	dash	**Angostura orange bitters**
½	fresh	**Egg white**

Origin: Created on 12th April 2007 by Salvatore Calabrese at Fifty, London, England.
Comment: Classic sweet and sour enhanced by floral notes.

SALTECCA

Glass: Martini
Garnish: Lemon zest twist
Method: **STIR** all ingredients with ice and fine strain into chilled glass.

2	shot(s)	**Don Julio reposado tequila**
½	shot(s)	**Tio Pepe fino sherry**
⅛	shot(s)	**Caper brine** (from jar)
⅛	shot(s)	**Sugar syrup** (2 sugar to 1 water)
½	shot(s)	**Chilled mineral water** (omit if wet ice)

Comment: Reminiscent of salted water after boiling vegetables but you've got to try these things.

SALTY DOG

Glass: Martini
Garnish: Salt rim
Method: **SHAKE** all ingredients with ice and fine strain into chilled glass.

2	shot(s)	**Ketel One vodka**
2¼	shot(s)	**Freshly squeezed grapefruit juice**
⅛	shot(s)	**Luxardo maraschino liqueur** (optional)

Origin: Created in the 1960s.
Comment: For a more interesting drink, try basing this classic on gin rather than vodka.

SALTY LYCHEE MARTINI

Glass: Martini
Garnish: Lychee from tin
Method: **STIR** all ingredients with ice and strain into chilled glass.

2	shot(s)	**Tio Pepe fino sherry**
1	shot(s)	**Lanique rose petal liqueur**
1	shot(s)	**Lychee syrup** (from tinned fruit)

Origin: I created this drink in 2002 after trying Dick Bradsell's Lychee & Rose Petal Martini (also in this guide).
Comment: Light pink in colour and subtle in flavour with the salty tang of Fino sherry.

SAN FRANCISCO

●●●●◐○○

Glass: Collins
Garnish: Pineapple wedge on rim
Method: SHAKE all ingredients with ice and strain into ice-filled glass.

2	shot(s)	**Ketel One vodka**
½	shot(s)	**Cointreau triple sec**
½	shot(s)	**Crème de banane liqueur**
1½	shot(s)	**Freshly squeezed orange juice**
1½	shot(s)	**Pressed pineapple juice**
¼	shot(s)	**Pomegranate (grenadine) syrup**

Comment: Long, fruity, slightly sweet and laced with vodka.

SANDSTORM

●●●●●○

Glass: Collins
Garnish: Pineapple wedge on rim
Method: SHAKE all ingredients with ice and strain into ice-filled glass.

1½	shot(s)	**Tanqueray London dry gin**
1	shot(s)	**Grand Marnier liqueur**
½	shot(s)	**Vanilla schnapps liqueur**
1½	shot(s)	**Freshly squeezed grapefruit juice**
1½	shot(s)	**Pressed pineapple juice**
¼	shot(s)	**Sugar syrup** (2 sugar to 1 water)
¼	shot(s)	**Freshly squeezed lime juice**
¼	shot(s)	**Rose's lime cordial**

Origin: Created in 2003 by James Cunningham at Zinc, Glasgow, Scotland, and named for its cloudy yellow colour.
Comment: A long, fruity drink featuring well-balanced sweet and sourness.

LA SANG

●●●●●○

Glass: Collins
Garnish: Chopped fruit
Method: SHAKE all ingredients with ice and strain into ice-filled glass.

2	shot(s)	**Courvoisier V.S.O.P. cognac**
2	shot(s)	**Shiraz red wine**
2	shot(s)	**Freshly squeezed orange juice**
¼	shot(s)	**Sugar syrup** (2 sugar to 1 water)

Origin: French for 'blood', this cocktail is a twist on the classic Spanish Sangria, which also means 'blood'.
Comment: The tannin in the wine balances the fruit and sweetness nicely.

SANCTUARY NEW #8

●●●○○

Glass: Martini
Garnish: Orange zest twist
Method: STIR all ingredients with ice and strain into chilled glass.

2	shot(s)	**Dubonnet Red** (French made)
1	shot(s)	**Amer Picon liqueur**
½	shot(s)	**Cointreau triple sec**

Origin: Vintage cocktail of unknown origin.
Comment: Wine-like with strong hints of bittersweet orange.

SANGAREE

●●●●●○

Glass: Collins
Garnish: Dust grated nutmeg
Method: SHAKE all ingredients with ice and strain into ice-filled glass.

1	shot(s)	**Courvoisier V.S.O.P. cognac**
2	shot(s)	**Shiraz red wine**
½	shot(s)	**Grand Marnier liqueur**
1	shot(s)	**Freshly squeezed orange juice**
¼	shot(s)	**Freshly squeezed lemon juice**
¼	shot(s)	**Sugar syrup** (2 sugar to 1 water)
1	shot(s)	**Chilled mineral water** (reduce if wet ice)

Origin: This version of the Sangria was popular in 19th century America.
Comment: Basically red wine and orange liqueur, diluted with water, lemon juice and sugar.

SANGAREE (SANGRIA) UPDATED #8

●●●●○

Glass: Collins
Garnish: Apple & orange slice plus dust with freshly ground nutmeg
Method: SHAKE first 6 ingredients with ice and strain into ice-filled glass. Top with soda and lightly stir. Serve with straws.

½	shot(s)	**Courvoisier V.S.O.P. cognac**
½	shot(s)	**Grand Marnier liqueur**
3	shot(s)	**Shiraz red wine**
1	shot(s)	**Freshly squeezed orange juice**
¼	shot(s)	**Freshly squeezed lemon juice**
½	shot(s)	**Sugar syrup** (2 sugar to 1 water)
1	shot(s)	**Soda water**

Origin: This version of the Spanish Sangria was popular in 19th century America. The only real difference is that while a Sangria is usually made in batches, Sangaree are single serve.
Comment: Basically just red wine and orange liqueur, diluted with water, lemon juice and sugar. But tasty!

SANGRIA MARTINI

●●●●●○

Glass: Martini
Garnish: Quarter orange slice
Method: SHAKE all ingredients with ice and fine strain into chilled glass.

1	shot(s)	**Shiraz red wine**
¾	shot(s)	**Freshly squeezed orange juice**
1½	shot(s)	**Courvoisier V.S.O.P. cognac**
½	shot(s)	**Berentzen apple schnapps**
½	shot(s)	**Crème de framboise liqueur**

Origin: Created in 2003 by Angelo Vieira at Light Bar, St. Martins Hotel, London, England.
Comment: Brandy based and fruit laced – just like its namesake.

DRINKS ARE GRADED AS FOLLOWS:

● DISGUSTING   ●● PRETTY AWFUL   ●● BEST AVOIDED
●●◐ DISAPPOINTING   ●●● ACCEPTABLE   ●●●◐ GOOD
●●●● RECOMMENDED   ●●●●◐ HIGHLY RECOMMENDED
●●●●● OUTSTANDING / EXCEPTIONAL

SANGRITA

Glass: Shot
Method: SHAKE all ingredients with ice and fine strain into shot glass. Serve with a shot of tequila. The drinker can either down the tequila and chase it with sangrita or sip the two drinks alternately.

½	shot(s)	**Tomato juice**
½	shot(s)	**Pomegranate juice**
¼	shot(s)	**Freshly squeezed orange juice**
½	shot(s)	**Freshly squeezed lime juice**
⅛	shot(s)	**Pomegranate (grenadine) syrup**
2	drops	**Tabasco pepper sauce**
2	dashes	**Worcestershire sauce**
1	pinch	**Salt**
1	grind	**Black pepper**

Origin: The name means 'little blood' in Spanish and the drink is served with tequila in practically every bar in Mexico.
Comment: In Mexico the quality of the homemade Sangrita can make or break a bar. This recipe is spicy and slightly sweet and perfect for chasing tequila.

'ONE TEQUILA, TWO TEQUILA, THREE TEQUILA, FLOOR.'
GEORGE CARLIN

SANTIAGO #1

Glass: Collins
Garnish: Lime slices
Method: SHAKE first 5 ingredients with ice and strain into ice-filled glass. **TOP** with lemonade, lightly stir and serve with straws.

1	shot(s)	**Bacardi Superior rum**
1	shot(s)	**Sailor Jerry spiced rum**
½	shot(s)	**Freshly squeezed lime juice**
½	shot(s)	**Freshly squeezed orange juice**
3	dashes	**Angostura aromatic bitters**
Top up with		**Lemonade/Sprite/7-Up**

Comment: Light, refreshing and slightly spicy.

SANTIAGO #2 NEW #8

Glass: Martini/Coupette
Garnish: Float raspberry
Method: MUDDLE raspberries in base of shaker. Add other ingredients, **SHAKE** with ice and fine strain into chilled glass.

3	fresh	**Raspberries**
2	shot(s)	**Bacardi Superior rum**
1¼	shot(s)	**POM Wonderful pomegranate juice**
¾	shot(s)	**Luxardo limoncello liqueur**
½	shot(s)	**Freshly squeezed lemon juice**
¼	shot(s)	**Agave syrup**

Comment: Lemon-fresh pomegranate, sweetened with agave nectar and laced with white rum.
Origin: Created in 2008 by Simon Rowe at The Bar at The Dorchester Hotel, London, England.

SANTIAGO AL ANOCHECER NEW #8

Glass: Martini/Coupette
Garnish: Grapefruit zest twist
Method: SHAKE all ingredients with ice and fine strain into chilled glass.

2	shot(s)	**Bacardi Superior rum**
½	shot(s)	**Campari Bitter**
½	shot(s)	**Freshly squeezed grapefruit juice**
½	shot(s)	**Agave syrup**

Comment: The same colour as red sky at night. Bitter sweet, Negroni-like and a favourite with shepherd's.
Origin: Created in 2008 by Andrew Coyle at Montpeliers Group, Edinburgh, Scotland. The name literally translates from Spanish as 'Santiago at Dusk'.

SANTIAGO DAIQUIRI

Glass: Martini
Garnish: Maraschino cherry
Method: SHAKE all ingredients with ice and fine strain into chilled glass.

2	shot(s)	**Bacardi Superior rum**
1	shot(s)	**Freshly squeezed lemon juice**
½	shot(s)	**Pomegranate (grenadine) syrup**
½	shot(s)	**Chilled mineral water** (omit if wet ice)

Origin: Adapted from a recipe in Harry Craddock's 1930 Savoy Cocktail Book. Made with Bacardi rum this becomes the Bacardi Cocktail.
Comment: This Daiquiri is particularly delicate in its balance between sweet and sour.

SARATOGA COCKTAIL #1 NEW #8

Glass: Martini/Coupette
Garnish: Quarter slice of lemon
Method: Vigorously **SHAKE** all ingredients with just two cubes of ice and strain into glass.

1	shot(s)	**Courvoisier V.S.O.P. cognac**
1	shot(s)	**Rye whiskey (or bourbon)**
1	shot(s)	**Martini Rosso sweet vermouth**
2	dashes	**Angostura aromatic bitters**

Comment: Frothy topped yet hardcore.
Origin: Recipe adapted from Jerry Thomas' 1862 'The Bartenders Guide'.

SARATOGA COCKTAIL #2 NEW #8

Glass: Coupette/Martini
Garnish: Maraschino cherry
Method: SHAKE all ingredients with ice and fine strain into chilled glass.

2	shot(s)	**Courvoisier V.S.O.P. cognac**
¼	shot(s)	**Luxardo maraschino liqueur**
½	shot(s)	**Pressed pineapple juice**
½	shot(s)	**Freshly squeezed lemon juice**
1	dashes	**Angostura aromatic bitters**
½	shot(s)	**Chilled water** (omit if wet ice)

Comment: Dry and robust with cognac character combining well with maraschino and raspberry.

SATSUMA MARTINI

Glass: Martini
Garnish: Orange zest twist
Method: **SHAKE** all ingredients with ice and fine strain into chilled glass.

1½	shot(s)	Orange-infused Ketel One vodka
¾	shot(s)	Grand Marnier liqueur
2	shot(s)	Pressed apple juice
2	dashes	Angostura orange bitters

Origin: Discovered in 2002 at the Fifth Floor Bar, Harvey Nichol's, London, England.
Comment: Tastes like its namesake – hard to believe it's almost half apple.

SATAN'S WHISKERS (STRAIGHT)

Glass: Martini
Garnish: Orange zest twist
Method: **SHAKE** all ingredients with ice and fine strain into chilled glass.

1	shot(s)	Tanqueray London dry gin
1	shot(s)	Noilly Prat dry vermouth
1	shot(s)	Martini Rosso sweet vermouth
½	shot(s)	Grand Marnier liqueur
1	shot(s)	Freshly squeezed orange juice
1	dash	Angostura orange bitters (optional)

Variant: 'Curled' use triple sec in place of Grand Marnier.
Origin: Adapted from a recipe in Harry Craddock's 1930 Savoy Cocktail Book.
Comment: A variation on the Bronx. Perfectly balanced tangy orange.

SATIN SHEET NEW #8

Glass: Martini/Coupette
Garnish: Lime wedge on rim
Method: **SHAKE** all ingredients with ice and fine strain into chilled glass.

2	shot(s)	Don Julio reposado tequila
1	shot(s)	Freshly squeezed lime Juice
½	shot(s)	Velvet Falernum liqueur
¼	shot(s)	Sugar syrup (2 sugar to 1 water)

Comment: A spiced margarita-style drink.

SATURN MARTINI

Glass: Martini
Garnish: Grapes on stick
Method: **MUDDLE** grapes in base of shaker. **STIR** honey with vodka and grapes to dissolve honey. Add wine, **SHAKE** with ice and fine strain into chilled glass.

7	fresh	Seedless white grapes
1½	shot(s)	Ketel One Citroen vodka
2	shot(s)	Runny honey
1½	shot(s)	Sauvignon Blanc wine

Origin: Created in 2001 by Tony Conigliaro at Isola, Knightsbridge, London, England.
Comment: Delicate, beautifully balanced and subtly flavoured.

SAÚCO MARGARITA

Glass: Coupette
Garnish: Lime wedge & optional salt rim
Method: **SHAKE** all ingredients with ice and fine strain into chilled glass.

1½	shot(s)	Don Julio reposado tequila
1½	shot(s)	St-Germain elderflower liqueur
¾	shot(s)	Freshly squeezed lime juice

Origin: Created in 2006 by Yours Truly (Simon Difford) and named after 'flor saúco', which is Spanish for elderflower.
Comment: The floral notes of St-Germain combine wonderfully with the herbaceous tequila and citrusy lime.

SAVANNAH

Glass: Martini
Garnish: Orange zest twist
Method: **SHAKE** all ingredients with ice and fine strain into chilled glass.

2½	shot(s)	Tanqueray London dry gin
¾	shot(s)	Freshly squeezed orange juice
½	shot(s)	White crème de cacao liqueur
½	fresh	Egg white

Origin: Adapted from a recipe in the 1949 edition of Esquire's Handbook for Hosts.
Comment: Gin and orange with a hint of chocolate – smoothed by egg white.

SAVOY SPECIAL #1

Glass: Martini
Garnish: Orange zest twist
Method: **SHAKE** all ingredients with ice and fine strain into chilled glass.

2	shot(s)	Tanqueray London dry gin
1	shot(s)	Noilly Prat dry vermouth
¼	shot(s)	Pomegranate (grenadine) syrup
⅛	shot(s)	La Fée Parisienne (68%) absinthe
½	shot(s)	Chilled mineral water (omit if wet ice)

Origin: Adapted from a recipe in Harry Craddock's 1930 Savoy Cocktail Book.
Comment: Wonderfully dry and aromatic.

SAY SAY NEW #8

Glass: Coupette/Martini
Garnish: Lemon spiral on rim
Method: **MUDDLE** tomatoes in base of shaker. Add other ingredients, **SHAKE** with ice and fine strain into chilled glass.

3	fresh	Cherry tomatoes (chopped)
1½	shot(s)	Bacardi Superior rum
½	shot(s)	St-Germain elderflower liqueur
½	shot(s)	Pomegranate (grenadine) syrup
¾	shot(s)	Freshly squeezed lemon juice

Comment: This may have tomatoes in but it is no Bloody Mary. Possibly a tad on the sweet side, but complex none the less.
Origin: Adapted from a drink created in 2008 by J.P. Keating, Saba, Dublin, Republic of Ireland.

SAZERAC UPDATED #8

Glass: Old-fashioned
Garnish: Lemon zest twist (spray & discard)
Method: **POUR** absinthe into ice-filled glass, **TOP** with water and leave to stand. Separately **SHAKE** bourbon, cognac, sugar and bitters with ice. **DISCARD** contents of glass (absinthe, water and ice) and **STRAIN** contents of shaker into absinthe-coated glass.

---In glass---

¾	shot(s)	**La Fée Parisienne (68%) absinthe**
Top up with		**Chilled mineral water**

---In shaker---

1½	shot(s)	**Courvoisier V.S.O.P. cognac**
1	shot(s)	**Bulleit bourbon whiskey**
½	shot(s)	**Sugar syrup** (2 sugar to 1 water)
3	dashes	**Angostura aromatic bitters**
3	dashes	**Peychaud's bitters**

Comment: Don't be concerned about chucking expensive absinthe down the drain - its flavour will be very evident in the finished drink and worth the investment. Classically this drink is stirred but is better shaken.
Origin: The rounded, distinctive flavour of this classic New Orleans cocktail is reliant on one essential ingredient: Peychaud's aromatic bitters created by one Antoine Amedee Peychaud.

His story starts in 1795 when he arrives in New Orleans as a refugee in 1795 after his father was forced to flee the island of San Domingo, where his family owned a coffee plantation, after the slaves rebelled.

Antoine grew up to become a pharmacist and bought his own Drug and Apothecary Store at what was then No. 123 Royal Street in 1834. Here he created an 'American Aromatic Bitter Cordial' and marketed it as a medicinal tonic. Such potions were fashionable at the time and there were many similar products.

Antoine also served his bitters mixed with brandy and other liquors. (It has been falsely claimed that the word 'cocktail' originated with Antoine, from a measure known as a 'coquetier' he used to prepare drinks. But it is now undisputed that the term appeared in print in an upstate New York newspaper in 1806, when Antoine was still a child.)

Antoine Peychaud advertised his bitters in local newspapers and many New Orleans bars served drinks prepared with them. One such bar was the Sazerac Coffee House at 13 Exchange Alley, owned by John B. Schiller, also the local agent for a French cognac company 'Sazerac-du-Forge et Fils' of Limoges. It was here, in 1858, that a bartender called Leon Lamothe is thought to have created the Sazerac, probably using Peychaud's aromatic bitters, Sazerac cognac and sugar.

A decade or so later, one Thomas H Handy took over the coffee house and around the same time, Antoine Peychaud fell upon hard times and sold his pharmacy store, along with the formula and brand name of his bitters. A combination of the phylloxera aphid (which devastated French vineyards) and the American Civil War made cognac hard to obtain and Handy was forced to change the recipe of the bar's now established house cocktail. He still used the all-important Peychaud's bitters but substituted Maryland Club rye whiskey, retaining a dash of cognac and adding a splash of the newly fashionable absinthe.

The Sazerac was further adapted in 1912 when absinthe was banned in the US and Herbsaint from Louisiana was substituted. Today the name Sazerac is owned by the Sazerac Company, who licensed the name to the Sazerac Bar at New Orleans' Fairmont Hotel.

My formula for this classic uses cognac from the original recipe and also bourbon as is more communally used to make this drink today. Now that absinthe is widely available I would suggest its use as opposed to Herbaint.

DRINKS ARE GRADED AS FOLLOWS:

● DISGUSTING	●◐ PRETTY AWFUL	●● BEST AVOIDED
●●◐ DISAPPOINTING	●●● ACCEPTABLE	●●●◐ GOOD
●●●● RECOMMENDED	●●●●◐ HIGHLY RECOMMENDED	
●●●●● OUTSTANDING / EXCEPTIONAL		

'HELL IS FULL OF MUSICAL AMATEURS: MUSIC IS THE BRANDY OF THE DAMNED.'
GEORGE BERNARD SHAW

●●●◐○○

SCANDINAVIAN POP

Glass: Collins
Garnish: Lime wedge
Method: **SHAKE** first 3 ingredients with ice and strain into ice-filled glass. **TOP** up with ginger ale.

2	shot(s)	**Raspberry flavoured vodka**
2	shot(s)	**Ocean Spray cranberry juice**
½	shot(s)	**Freshly squeezed lime juice**
Top up with		**Ginger ale**

Origin: Created by Wayne Collins, London, England.
Comment: Berry fruit with a spicy splash of ginger.

●●●●○○

SCARLETT O'HARA UPDATED #8

Glass: Martini
Garnish: Cranberries or lime wedge
Method: **SHAKE** all ingredients with ice and fine strain into chilled glass.

1½	shot(s)	**Southern Comfort liqueur**
1½	shot(s)	**Ocean Spray cranberry juice**
¾	shot(s)	**Freshly squeezed lime juice**

Comment: The tang of lime and the dryness of cranberry balance the apricot sweetness of Southern Comfort.
Origin: This drink helped put Southern Comfort on the proverbial drink map and was created in 1939 and named after the heroine of the film Gone With The Wind, released that year.

●●●●●○

SCOFFLAW

S

Glass: Martini
Garnish: Lemon zest twist
Method: **SHAKE** all ingredients with ice and fine strain into chilled glass.

1½	shot(s)	**Bulleit bourbon whiskey**
1½	shot(s)	**Noilly Prat dry vermouth**
½	shot(s)	**Freshly squeezed lemon juice**
¼	shot(s)	**Pomegranate (grenadine) syrup**
1	dash	**Angostura orange bitters**

Origin: During the height of Prohibition The Boston Herald ran a competition asking readers to coin a new word for "a lawless drinker of illegally made or illegally obtained liquor". Out of 25,000 entries, 'Scofflaw' was chosen and on 15th January 1924 the $200 prize was shared between the two people who had submitted the word. This cocktail was created by Jock at Harry's American Bar, Paris, to celebrate the new term.
Comment: This rust-coloured drink is made or broken by the quality of pomegranate syrup used.

SCORCHED EARTH

Glass: Martini
Garnish: Lemon zest twist
Method: STIR all ingredients with ice and fine strain into chilled glass.

1½	shot(s)	**Courvoisier V.S.O.P. cognac**
½	shot(s)	**Martini Rosso sweet vermouth**
½	shot(s)	**Cynar artichoke liqueur**

Origin: Adapted from a recipe created in 2006 by Nicholas Hearin, at Restaurant Eugene in Atlanta, USA, and first published by Gary Regan.
Comment: Dry, very aromatic and bordering on bitter. Interesting but not to everybody's taste.

SCORPION

Glass: Collins
Garnish: Gardenia or orange slice & mint
Method: BLEND all ingredients with 12oz crushed ice and serve with straws.

1½	shot(s)	**Bacardi Superior rum**
¾	shot(s)	**Courvoisier V.S.O.P. cognac**
2	shot(s)	**Freshly squeezed orange juice**
1	shot(s)	**Freshly squeezed lemon juice**
½	shot(s)	**Almond (orgeat) syrup**

Variant: With pisco in place of cognac.
Origin: Created by Victor Bergeron and this recipe adapted from his 'Trader Vic's Bartender's Guide' (1972 revised edition).
Comment: Well balanced, refreshing spirit and orange. Not sweet.

SCOTCH BOUNTY MARTINI

Glass: Martini
Garnish: Orange zest twist
Method: SHAKE all ingredients with ice and fine strain into chilled glass.

1½	shot(s)	**Johnnie Walker Scotch whisky**
½	shot(s)	**White crème de cacao liqueur**
½	shot(s)	**Malibu coconut rum liqueur**
1½	shot(s)	**Freshly squeezed orange juice**
⅛	shot(s)	**Pomegranate (grenadine) syrup**

Comment: A medium-sweet combination of Scotch, coconut and orange.

SCOTCH MILK PUNCH

Glass: Martini
Garnish: Grate nutmeg over drink
Method: SHAKE all ingredients with ice and fine strain into chilled glass.

2	shot(s)	**Johnnie Walker Scotch whisky**
½	shot(s)	**Sugar syrup** (2 sugar to 1 water)
¾	shot(s)	**Double (heavy) cream**
¾	shot(s)	**Milk**

Comment: A creamy, malty affair.

SCOTCH NEGRONI

Glass: Old-fashioned
Garnish: Orange slice
Method: STIR all ingredients with ice and strain into ice-filled glass.

1	shot(s)	**Johnnie Walker Scotch whisky**
1	shot(s)	**Martini Rosso sweet vermouth**
1	shot(s)	**Campari Bitter**

Comment: Dry, slightly smoky – for palates that appreciate bitterness.

THE SCOTT

Glass: Martini
Garnish: Lemon zest twist
Method: STIR all ingredients with ice and strain into chilled glass.

2	shot(s)	**Johnnie Walker Scotch whisky**
1	shot(s)	**Noilly Prat dry vermouth**
½	shot(s)	**Drambuie liqueur**

Origin: Discovered in 2006 at The Clift Hotel, San Francisco, USA.
Comment: This golden drink is dry and sophisticated, yet honeyed and approachable.

SCREAMING BANANA BANSHEE

Glass: Hurricane
Garnish: Banana chunk on rim
Method: BLEND all ingredients with 12oz scoop of crushed ice and serve with straws.

2	shot(s)	**Ketel One vodka**
1	shot(s)	**Crème de banane liqueur**
1	shot(s)	**White crème de cacao liqueur**
1½	shot(s)	**Double (heavy) cream**
1½	shot(s)	**Milk**
½	fresh	**Peeled banana**

Origin: Without the vodka this is just a plain old Banana Banshee.
Comment: An alcoholic milkshake – not too sweet.

SCREAMING ORGASM

Glass: Hurricane
Garnish: Sprinkle with grated chocolate
Method: SHAKE all ingredients with ice and strain into glass filled with crushed ice.

1¼	shot(s)	**Ketel One vodka**
1¼	shot(s)	**Kahlúa coffee liqueur**
1¼	shot(s)	**Luxardo Amaretto di Saschira**
1¼	shot(s)	**Baileys Irish cream liqueur**
1¼	shot(s)	**Double (heavy) cream**
1¼	shot(s)	**Milk**

Origin: A dodgy drink from the 1980s.
Comment: Probably as fattening as it is alcoholic, this is a huge, creamy dessert in a glass.

● ● ● ● ○ ○

SCREWDRIVER

Glass: Collins
Garnish: Orange slice
Method: POUR vodka into ice-filled glass and **TOP** with orange juice. Lightly stir and serve with straws.

| 2 | shot(s) | **Ketel One vodka** |
| Top up with | | **Freshly squeezed orange juice** |

Origin: This cocktail first appeared in the 1950s in the Middle East. Parched US engineers working in the desert supposedly added orange juice to their vodka and stirred it with the nearest thing to hand, usually a screwdriver.
Comment: The temperature at which this drink is served and the freshness of the orange juice makes or breaks it.

● ● ● ● ○ ○

SEABREEZE #1 (SIMPLE)

Glass: Collins
Garnish: Lime slice
Method: SHAKE all ingredients with ice and strain into ice-filled glass.

2	shot(s)	**Ketel One vodka**
3	shot(s)	**Ocean Spray cranberry juice**
1½	shot(s)	**Freshly squeezed grapefruit juice**

Origin: Thought to have originated in the early 1990s in New York City.
Comment: Few bartenders bother to shake this simple drink, instead simply pouring and stirring in the glass.

● ● ● ● ○ ○

SEABREEZE #2 (LAYERED)

Glass: Collins
Garnish: Lime wedge
Method: POUR cranberry juice into ice-filled glass. **SHAKE** other ingredients with ice and carefully strain into glass to **LAYER** over the cranberry juice.

3	shot(s)	**Ocean Spray cranberry juice**
2	shot(s)	**Ketel One vodka**
1½	shot(s)	**Freshly squeezed grapefruit juice**
½	shot(s)	**Freshly squeezed lime juice**

Comment: This layered version requires mixing with straws prior to drinking.

● ● ● ● ○ ○

SEELBACH

Glass: Flute
Garnish: Orange zest twist
Method: POUR first 4 ingredients into chilled glass. **TOP** with champagne.

¾	shot(s)	**Bulleit bourbon whiskey**
½	shot(s)	**Cointreau triple sec**
1	dash	**Angostura aromatic bitters**
1	dash	**Peychaud's aromatic bitters**
Top up with		**Perrier Jouet brut champagne**

Origin: Created in 1917 and named after its place of origin, the Seelbach Hotel, Lousiville, Kentucky, USA.
Comment: This champagne cocktail is fortified with bourbon and orange liqueur.

● ● ● ● ○

SENSATION

Glass: Martini
Garnish: Maraschino cherry
Method: Lightly **MUDDLE** mint (just to bruise) in base of shaker. Add other ingredients, **SHAKE** with ice and fine strain into chilled glass.

12	fresh	**Mint leaves**
2	shot(s)	**Tanqueray London dry gin**
¾	shot(s)	**Freshly squeezed lemon juice**
¾	shot(s)	**Luxardo maraschino liqueur**
⅛	shot(s)	**Sugar syrup** (2 sugar to 1 water)
½	shot(s)	**Chilled mineral water** (omit if wet ice)

Origin: Adapted from a recipe in Harry Craddock's 1930 Savoy Cocktail Book.
Comment: Fresh, fragrant and balanced.

● ● ● ● ○

SENTIMENTAL MELODY NEW #8

Glass: Martini
Garnish: Flamed orange zest twist
Method: STIR preserve and rum in base of a shaker to dissolve the jam. Add other ingredients, **SHAKE** with ice and fine strain into chilled glass.

2	tspns	**Grapefruit preserve**
2	shot(s)	**Bacardi Superior rum**
¼	shot(s)	**Cointreau triple sec**
½	shot(s)	**St-Germain elderflower liqueur**
¾	shot(s)	**Ocean Spray cranberry juice**
¼	shot(s)	**POM Wonderful pomegranate juice**
½	shot(s)	**Freshly squeezed lime juice**

Comment: A twisted Daiquiri with rich berry fruit.
Origin: Adapted from a recipe created in 2008 by Peter Dorelli, London, England.

● ● ● ● ○

SERENDIPITY #1

Glass: Collins
Garnish: Slice of lemon
Method: MUDDLE blackberries in base of shaker. Add other ingredients, **SHAKE** with ice and strain into glass filled with crushed ice.

6	fresh	**Blackberries**
1	shot(s)	**Tanqueray London dry gin**
½	shot(s)	**Vanilla schnapps liqueur**
½	shot(s)	**Crème de cassis liqueur**
3	shot(s)	**Ocean Spray cranberry juice**
¼	shot(s)	**Freshly squeezed lemon juice**
¼	shot(s)	**Sugar syrup** (2 sugar to 1 water)

Origin: Created in 2002 by Jamie Stephenson, Manchester, England.
Comment: Long, red, fruity, vanilla.

DRINKS ARE GRADED AS FOLLOWS:

● DISGUSTING ● ○ PRETTY AWFUL ● ● BEST AVOIDED
● ● ○ DISAPPOINTING ● ● ● ACCEPTABLE ● ● ● ○ GOOD
● ● ● ● RECOMMENDED ● ● ● ● ○ HIGHLY RECOMMENDED
● ● ● ● ● OUTSTANDING / EXCEPTIONAL

SERENDIPITY #2

Glass: Old-fashioned
Garnish: Mint sprig
Method: Lightly **MUDDLE** mint (just to bruise) in base of shaker. Add calvados and apple juice, **SHAKE** with ice and strain into ice-filled glass. **TOP** with champagne.

7	fresh	Mint leaves
1½	shot(s)	Boulard Grand Solage calvados
3	shot(s)	Pressed apple juice
Top up with		Perrier Jouet brut champagne

Origin: My adaptation of one of Colin Field's drinks. He created it on 31 December 1994 in the Hemingway Bar of the Paris Ritz for Jean-Louis Constanza: upon tasting it, Jean-Louis exclaimed, "Serendipity".
Comment: Spirity, minty apple invigorated by a splash of champagne.

'PEOPLE WHO DRINK TO DROWN THEIR SORROW SHOULD BE TOLD THAT SORROW KNOWS HOW TO SWIM.'
ANN LANDERS

SETTLE PETAL

Glass: Martini
Garnish: Float rose petal
Method: STIR all ingredients with ice and strain into chilled glass.

2	shot(s)	Tanqueray London dry gin
1	shot(s)	Cucumber flavoured vodka
½	shot(s)	Rosewater
½	shot(s)	Vanilla sugar syrup

Origin: Created in 2003 by Andy Fitzmorris at Eclipse, Notting Hill, London, England.
Comment: An aptly named floral Martini.

SEVENTH HEAVEN #2

Glass: Martini
Garnish: Mint leaf
Method: SHAKE all ingredients with ice and fine strain into chilled glass.

2¼	shot(s)	Tanqueray London dry gin
¾	shot(s)	Luxardo maraschino liqueur
1½	shot(s)	Freshly squeezed grapefruit juice

Origin: Adapted from the Seventh Heaven No. 2 recipe in Harry Craddock's 1930 Savoy Cocktail Book.
Comment: Drink this and you'll be there.

THE 75

Glass: Martini
Garnish: Float star anise
Method: SHAKE all ingredients with ice and fine strain into chilled glass.

2	shot(s)	Boulard Grand Solage calvados
1	shot(s)	Tanqueray London dry gin
¼	shot(s)	La Fée Parisienne (68%) absinthe
¼	shot(s)	Pomegranate (grenadine) syrup
½	shot(s)	Chilled mineral water (omit if wet ice)

Origin: Like the French 75, this was named after the celebrated 75, a French 75mm field gun developed during the 1890s and used by the French army during the First World War and beyond. The gun was unusually lethal due to its fast rate of fire.
Comment: Hardened palates will appreciate this fantastically dry, aromatic and complex cocktail.

SEX ON THE BEACH #1

Glass: Collins
Garnish: Orange slice & cherry on stick (sail)
Method: SHAKE all ingredients with ice and strain into ice-filled glass.

2	shot(s)	Ketel One vodka
½	shot(s)	Chambord black raspberry liqueur
½	shot(s)	Peach Tree peach schnapps
1½	shot(s)	Freshly squeezed orange juice
1½	shot(s)	Ocean Spray cranberry juice

Variant: With melon liqueur in place of peach schnapps.
Origin: An infamous cocktail during the 1980s.
Comment: Sweet fruit laced with vodka.

SEX ON THE BEACH #2

Glass: Old-fashioned
Garnish: Orange slice & cherry on stick (sail)
Method: SHAKE all ingredients with ice and strain into ice-filled glass.

2	shot(s)	Ketel One vodka
½	shot(s)	Chambord black raspberry liqueur
½	shot(s)	Midori green melon liqueur
1½	shot(s)	Pressed pineapple juice

Comment: Sweeter than most.

SEX ON THE BEACH #3

Glass: Shot
Method: Refrigerate ingredients then **LAYER** in chilled glass by carefully pouring in the following order.

½	shot(s)	Chambord black raspberry liqueur
½	shot(s)	Midori green melon liqueur
½	shot(s)	Freshly squeezed lime juice
½	shot(s)	Pressed pineapple juice

Comment: A sweet and sour shot, combining raspberry, melon, lime and pineapple.

SGROPPINO

Glass: Flute
Garnish: Lemon zest twist
Method: BLEND all ingredients without additional ice and serve in chilled glass.

½	shot(s)	**Ketel One vodka**
¼	shot(s)	**Double (heavy) cream**
1½	shot(s)	**Prosecco sparkling wine**
2	scoops	**Lemon sorbet** (see recipe under L)

AKA: Sorbetto
Origin: Pronounced 'scroe-pee-noe', this hybrid of cocktail and dessert is often served after meals in Venice. The name comes from a vernacular word meaning 'untie', a reference to the belief that it relaxes your stomach after a hearty meal.
Comment: Smooth and all too easy to quaff. A great dessert.

SHADY GROVE COOLER

Glass: Collins
Garnish: Lime wedge on rim
Method: SHAKE first 3 ingredients with ice and strain into ice-filled glass. **TOP** with ginger ale, lightly stir and serve with straws.

2	shot(s)	**Tanqueray London dry gin**
1	shot(s)	**Freshly squeezed lime juice**
½	shot(s)	**Sugar syrup** (2 sugar to 1 water)
Top up with		**Ginger ale**

Comment: Long and refreshing with lime freshness and a hint of ginger.

SHAKERATO

Glass: Martini
Garnish: Lemon zest twist
Method: SHAKE all ingredients with ice and fine strain into chilled glass.

1½	shot(s)	**Campari Bitter**
¼	shot(s)	**Freshly squeezed lemon juice**
¼	shot(s)	**Sugar syrup** (2 sugar to 1 water)
1½	shot(s)	**Chilled mineral water**

Comment: Campari lovers only need apply.

SHAMROCK #1

Glass: Martini
Garnish: Twist of orange (discarded)
Method: STIR all ingredients with ice and strain into chilled glass.

2½	shot(s)	**Bulleit bourbon whiskey**
1	shot(s)	**Martini Rosso sweet vermouth**
¼	shot(s)	**Green crème de menthe liqueur**
2	dashes	**Angostura aromatic bitters**

Origin: Purloined from David Embury's classic book, The Fine Art of Mixing Drinks.
Comment: Basically a Sweet Manhattan with a dash of green crème de menthe.

SHAMROCK #2

Glass: Martini
Garnish: Mint leaf
Method: SHAKE all ingredients with ice and fine strain into chilled glass.

1½	shot(s)	**Jameson Irish whiskey**
1½	shot(s)	**Noilly Prat dry vermouth**
½	shot(s)	**Green Chartreuse liqueur**
½	shot(s)	**Green crème de menthe liqueur**
½	shot(s)	**Chilled mineral water** (omit if wet ice)

Origin: Adapted from a recipe in Harry Craddock's 1930 Savoy Cocktail Book.
Comment: A great drink for St. Patrick's Day.

SHAMROCK EXPRESS

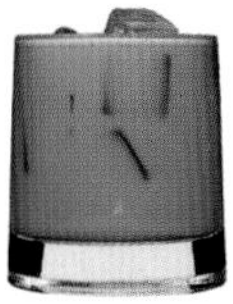

Glass: Old-fashioned
Method: SHAKE all ingredients with ice and strain into ice-filled glass.

1½	shot(s)	**Espresso coffee**
¾	shot(s)	**Teichenné butterscotch schnapps**
1	shot(s)	**Ketel One vodka**
1	shot(s)	**Baileys Irish cream liqueur**
¼	shot(s)	**Sugar syrup** (2 sugar to 1 water)

Origin: Created in 1999 by Greg Pearson at Mystique, Manchester, England.
Comment: Creamy coffee with the sweetness of butterscotch.

SHANDYGAFF UPDATED #8

Glass: Boston
Method: POUR ale into glass, **TOP** with ginger ale.

| 2/3rds fill | **Lager or dark ale** |
| Top up with | **Ginger ale** |

AKA: Sandygaff
Comment: Tastier than your average 'lager shandy'.
Origin: This drink and its name originated in England and dates back to at least the late 19th century. The name comes from the London slang for a pint of beer, 'shant of gatter' (shanty being a public house, gatter meaning water). The ginger ale serves as a flavoursome way to water down the strength of the beer, thus the literal translation, 'pub water'.

In the first chapter of The History of Mr. Polly, H. G. Wells describes a shandygaff as being, "two pints of beer and two bottles of ginger beer foaming in a huge round-bellied jug."

In London the beer is now usually diluted with lemonade and this drink is now simply known as a shandy. When ordering in a pub you are expected to call for 'lager shandy' or bitter shandy', the latter specifying the drink should be based on traditional real ale.

Today the term 'Shandygaff' is forgotten in London but popular in the Caribbean where this drink is made with beer and ginger ale or ginger beer.

SHARK BITE

Glass: Hurricane
Method: BLEND first 3 ingredients with 18oz scoop crushed ice and pour into glass. **POUR** grenadine around edge of the drink. Do not stir before serving.

2	shot(s)	**Pusser's Navy rum**
3	shot(s)	**Freshly squeezed orange juice**
½	shot(s)	**Freshly squeezed lime juice**
¾	shot(s)	**Pomegranate (grenadine) syrup**

Comment: Strong rum and orange juice. A tad sweet but easy to drink.

SHARK'S TOOTH NO.1 NEW #8

Glass: Sling (10oz Pilsner glass)
Garnish: Lime wedge
Method: SHAKE first 5 ingredients with ice and strain into ice-filled glass. **TOP** with soda and serve with straws.

1	shot(s)	**Wray & Nephew overproof rum**
½	shot(s)	**Freshly squeezed lime juice**
½	shot(s)	**Freshly squeezed lemon juice**
¼	shot(s)	**Sugar syrup** (2 sugar to 1 water)
¼	shot(s)	**Pomegranate (grenadine) syrup**
Top up with		**Soda water** (club soda)

Comment: Salmon-pink in colour and heavily influenced by the flavoursome overproof rum.
Origin: Adapted from Victor Bergeron's 'Trader Vic's Bartender's Guide' (1972 revised edition) where he writes, "One of the first drinks we ever made".

SHARK'S TOOTH NO.3 NEW #8

Glass: Sling (10oz Pilsner glass)
Garnish: Lime wedge
Method: SHAKE first 3 ingredients with ice and strain into ice-filled glass. **TOP** with soda and serve with straws.

2½	shot(s)	**Bacardi Superior rum**
1	shot(s)	**Freshly squeezed lemon juice**
½	shot(s)	**Pomegranate (grenadine) syrup**
Top up with		**Soda water** (club soda)

Origin: Adapted from Victor Bergeron's 'Trader Vic's Bartender's Guide' (1972 revised edition).
Comment: Sounds hard; looks pink. Tastes reminiscent of a dilute Bacardi Cocktail.

SHERRY SOUR NEW #8

Glass: Old-fashioned
Garnish: Maraschino cherry
Method: SHAKE all ingredients with ice and strain into ice-filled glass.

2	shot(s)	**Apostoles palo cortado sherry**
¾	shot(s)	**Freshly squeezed lemon juice**
½	shot(s)	**Sugar syrup** (2 sugar to 1 water)
½	fresh	**Egg white**

Comment: The huge flavour of sherry freshened by lemon juice and rounded by egg white.
Origin: Discovered in 2007 at Suba, New York City, USA.

SHIRLEY TEMPLE (MOCKTAIL)

Glass: Collins
Garnish: Maraschino cherry & lemon slice
Method: POUR ingredients into ice-filled glass, lightly stir and serve with straws.

¼	shot(s)	**Pomegranate (grenadine) syrup**
¼	shot(s)	**Freshly squeezed lemon juice**
Top up with		**Ginger ale**

Comment: I've added a splash of lemon juice to the usual recipe. It's still not that exciting.

> **'I HAVE DRUNK SINCE I WAS FIFTEEN AND FEW THINGS HAVE GIVEN ME MORE PLEASURE... THE ONLY TIME IT ISN'T GOOD FOR YOU IS WHEN YOU WRITE OR WHEN YOU FIGHT. YOU HAVE TO DO THAT COLD. BUT IT ALWAYS HELPS MY SHOOTING.'**
> ERNEST HEMINGWAY

SHOWBIZ

Glass: Martini
Garnish: Blackcurrants on stick
Method: SHAKE all ingredients with ice and fine strain into chilled glass.

1¾	shot(s)	**Ketel One vodka**
1	shot(s)	**Crème de cassis liqueur**
1¾	shot(s)	**Freshly squeezed grapefruit juice**

Comment: Sweet cassis soured with grapefruit and fortified with vodka.

SICILIAN NEGRONI

Glass: Old-fashioned
Garnish: Orange slice
Method: SHAKE all ingredients with ice and strain into ice-filled glass.

1½	shot(s)	**Tanqueray London dry gin**
1½	shot(s)	**Campari Bitter**
1½	shot(s)	**Fresh blood orange juice**

Origin: Discovered in 2006 at The Last Supper Club, San Francisco, USA.
Comment: Blood orange juice replaces sweet vermouth in this fruity Negroni.

SIDECAR (DIFFORD'S FORMULA) UPDATED #8

Glass: Martini
Garnish: Lemon zest twist
Method: SHAKE all ingredients with ice and fine strain into chilled glass.

1½	shot(s)	**Courvoisier V.S.O.P. cognac**
1	shot(s)	**Cointreau triple sec**
1	shot(s)	**Freshly squeezed lemon juice**
½	shot(s)	**Chilled mineral water** (omit if wet ice)

Variant: Apple Cart
Comment: Complex and very slightly on the sour side of balanced. There have been periods when it has been fashionable to coat the rim of the glass in which this drink is to be served with sugar. Thankfully sugar rims are now out of vogue and, as Embury writes in his book, "A twist of lemon may be used if desired and the peel dropped into the glass. Otherwise no decoration."

Origin: In his 1948 'Fine Art of Mixing Drinks', David A. Embury writes of the Sidecar: "It was invented by a friend of mine at a bar in Paris during World War I and was named after the motorcycle sidecar in which the good captain customarily was driven to and from the little bistro where the drink was born and christened."

Embury doesn't name the bar but it's commonly assumed that he meant Harry's New York Bar and that the cocktail was created by its owner, Harry MacElhone. However, in Harry's own book he credits the drink to Pat MacGarry of Buck's Club, London.

The proportions of this drink are debated as much as its origin. Perhaps due to ease rather than balance, the equal parts formula (1 x brandy, 1 x triple sec and 1 x lemon juice) was the earliest published recipe (Robert Vermeire's 1922 'Cocktails: How to Mix Them' and Harry McElhone's 1922 'ABC of mixing cocktails') and still seems popular to this day.

Embury writes of the 'equal parts' Sidecar, "This is the most perfect example of a magnificent drink gone wrong". He argues that "Essentially the Sidecar is nothing but a Daiquiri with brandy in the place of rum and Cointreau in the place of sugar syrup" and so the Daiquiri formula should be followed (2 x brandy, ½ x triple sec and ¼ x lemon juice). This may work for a Daiquiri but makes for an overly dry Sidecar.

I In his 1930 'The Savoy Cocktail Book', Harry Craddock calls for 2 x brandy; 1 x Cointreau and 1 x lemon juice. The formula I use here takes the middle ground between The Savoy and the 'equal parts' camp. I also find this drink benefits from a little extra dilution.

'I TRY NOT TO DRINK TOO MUCH BECAUSE WHEN I'M DRUNK, I BITE.'
BETTE MIDLER

SIDECAR NAMED DESIRE

Glass: Martini
Garnish: Lemon zest twist
Method: SHAKE all ingredients with ice and fine strain into chilled glass.

2	shot(s)	**Boulard Grand Solage calvados**
1	shot(s)	**Berentzen apple schnapps**
1	shot(s)	**Freshly squeezed lemon juice**

Comment: Take a classic Sidecar and add some love interest – apple!

SIDECARRIAGE

Glass: Martini
Garnish: Lemon zest twist
Method: SHAKE all ingredients with ice and fine strain into chilled glass.

1½	shot(s)	**Boulard Grand Solage calvados**
1½	shot(s)	**St-Germain elderflower liqueur**
1	shot(s)	**Freshly squeezed lemon juice**

Origin: Created in 2006 by Yours Truly (Simon Difford).
Comment: Hints of cider come through in this calvados based Sidecar with an elderflower twist.

SIDEKICK

Glass: Martini
Garnish: Quarter orange slice on rim
Method: SHAKE all ingredients with ice and fine strain into chilled glass.

2	shot(s)	**Belle de Brillet pear liqueur**
¾	shot(s)	**Cointreau triple sec**
1	shot(s)	**Freshly squeezed orange juice**
½	shot(s)	**Freshly squeezed lime juice**

Origin: Adapted from a drink discovered in 2003 at Temple Bar, New York City.
Comment: Rich pear and orange with a stabilising hint of sour lime.

SILENT THIRD UPDATED #8

Glass: Martini
Garnish: Lemon zest twist
Method: SHAKE all ingredients with ice and fine strain into chilled glass.

1½	shot(s)	**Johnnie Walker Scotch whisky**
1	shot(s)	**Cointreau triple sec**
¾	shot(s)	**Freshly squeezed lemon juice**
½	shot(s)	**Chilled mineral water** (omit if wet ice)

Comment: Basically a Sidecar made with Scotch in place of Cognac.

SILK PANTIES

Glass: Martini
Garnish: Peach wedge on rim
Method: SHAKE all ingredients with ice and fine strain into chilled glass.

2	shot(s)	**Ketel One vodka**
1	shot(s)	**Peach Tree peach schnapps**
2	dashes	**Fee Brothers peach bitters** (optional)

Origin: Created sometime in the 1980s.
Comment: This drink may be sweet but despite the silly name it is more serious than you might expect.

SILK STOCKINGS UPDATED #8

●●●●○○

Glass: Martini/Coupette
Garnish: Cinnamon or cocoa powder dust
Method: SHAKE all ingredients with ice and fine strain into chilled glass.

2	shot(s)	Don Julio blanco tequila
¾	shot(s)	White crème de cacao liqueur
¼	shot(s)	Pomegranate (grenadine) syrup
½	shot(s)	Double (heavy) cream
½	shot(s)	Milk

Comment: Smoothed and sweetened tequila with a hint of chocolate and fruit.

SILVER BRONX NEW #8

●●●●●

Glass: Martini
Garnish: Maraschino cherry
Method: SHAKE all ingredients with ice and fine strain into chilled glass.

2	shot(s)	Tanqueray London dry gin
¼	shot(s)	Noilly Prat dry vermouth
¼	shot(s)	Martini Rosso sweet vermouth
1	shot(s)	Freshly squeezed orange juice
½	fresh	Egg white

Comment: A Bronx made with egg white.
Origin: A vintage cocktail adapted from the classic Bronx Cocktail, created in 1906 by Johnny Solon, a bartender at New York's Waldorf-Astoria Hote.

SILVER BULLET MARTINI

●●●●○

Glass: Martini
Garnish: Lemon zest twist
Method: SHAKE all ingredients with ice and fine strain into chilled glass.

2	shot(s)	Tanqueray London dry gin
1	shot(s)	Kümmel liqueur
1	shot(s)	Freshly squeezed lemon juice
¼	shot(s)	Sugar syrup (2 sugar to 1 water)

AKA: Retreat from Moscow
Variant: A modern variation is to substitute sambuca for kümmel.
Origin: Thought to have been created in the 1920s.
Comment: Caraway and fennel flavour this unusual, sweet and sour drink.

SILVER FIZZ UPDATED #8

●●●●○

Glass: Collins (8oz max)
Garnish: Lemon slice
Method: DRY SHAKE first 4 ingredients with ice and strain into chilled glass (no ice). TOP with soda from siphon.

2	shot(s)	Spirit (gin, whisk(e)y, vodka, brandy)
1	shot(s)	Freshly squeezed lemon or lime juice
½	shot(s)	Sugar syrup (2 sugar to 1 water)
½	fresh	Egg white
Top up with		Soda water (from siphon)

Origin: A mid-19th century classic.
Variant: Omit the egg white and this is a mere Fizz.
Comment: I prefer my Fizzes with the addition of egg white. Why not also try a Derby Fizz.

SILVER MARTINI

●●●●○○

Glass: Martini
Garnish: Maraschino cherry
Method: SHAKE all ingredients with ice and fine strain into chilled glass.

1½	shot(s)	Tanqueray London dry gin
1½	shot(s)	Noilly Prat dry vermouth
¼	shot(s)	Luxardo maraschino liqueur
2	dashes	Angostura orange bitters

Origin: Adapted from a recipe in Harry Craddock's 1930 Savoy Cocktail Book.
Comment: Dry and aromatic – for serious imbibers only.

'CANDY IS DANDY, BUT LIQUOR IS QUICKER.'
OGDEN NASH

SINGAPORE SLING #1 (BAKER'S FORMULA) UPDATED #8

●●●●○○

Glass: Collins (10oz max)
Garnish: Lemon slice & cherry on stick (sail)
Method: SHAKE first 3 ingredients with ice and strain into ice-filled glass. TOP with soda, lightly stir and serve with straws.

2	shot(s)	Old Tom gin
¾	shot(s)	Bénédictine D.O.M. liqueur
¾	shot(s)	Heering cherry brandy liqueur
Top up with		Soda water (club soda)

Variant: Straits Sling
Comment: Lacks the citrus of other Singapore Slings but dilution cuts and so balances the sweetness of the liqueurs.

Origin: Adapted from a recipe by Charles H. Baker Jr. and published in his 1946 Gentleman's Companion. This drink was created some time between 1911 and 1915 by Chinese-born Ngiam Tong Boon at the Long Bar in Raffles Hotel, Singapore.

Raffles Hotel is named after the colonial founder of Singapore, Sir Stamford Raffles, and was the Near East's ex-pat central. As Charles H. Baker Jr. wrote in his 1946 Gentleman's Companion, "Just looking around the terrace porch we've seen Frank Buck, the Sultan of Johor, Aimee Semple McPherson, Somerset Maugham, Dick Halliburton, Doug Fairbanks, Bob Ripley, Ruth Elder and Walker Camp – not that this is any wonder". Raffles still sticks out of modern-day Singapore like a vast, colonial Christmas cake.

Although there is little controversy as to who created the Singapore Sling, where he created it and (roughly) when, there is huge debate over the original name and ingredients. Singapore and the locality was colonially known as the 'Straits Settlements' and it seems certain that Boon's drink was similarly named the 'Straits Sling'. The name appears to have changed sometime between 1922 and 1930.

Not even the Raffles Hotel itself appears sure of the original recipe and visiting the present day Long Bar in search of enlightenment is hopeless. Sadly, the Singapore Slings now served there are made from a powdered pre-mix, which is also available in the gift shop below.

While contemporary sources are clear that it was cherry brandy that distinguishes the Singapore Sling from another kind of sling, a great debate rages over the type of cherry brandy used. Was it a cherry 'brandy' liqueur or actually a cherry eau de vie? Did fruit juice feature in the original recipe at all? We shall probably never know, so I've listed several versions which are generally accepted to pass for a Singapore Sling today. Please also see the entry for 'Straits Sling'.

SINGAPORE SLING #2 UPDATED #8

●●●●○

Glass: Sling
Garnish: Lemon slice & cherry on stick (sail)
Method: **SHAKE** first 6 ingredients with ice and strain into ice-filled glass. **TOP** with soda, lightly stir and serve with straws.

2	shot(s)	Tanqueray London dry gin
½	shot(s)	Bénédictine D.O.M. liqueur
½	shot(s)	Heering cherry brandy liqueur
1	shot(s)	Freshly squeezed lemon juice
2	dashes	Angostura orange bitters
2	dashes	Angostura aromatic bitters
Top up with		Soda water (club soda)

Comment: On the sour side of dry, this is decidedly more complex than most Singapore Sling recipes.

SINGAPORE SLING #3 UPDATED #8

●●●●◐○

Glass: Sling
Garnish: Orange slice & cherry on stick (sail)
Method: **SHAKE** first 8 ingredients with ice and strain into ice-filled glass. **TOP** with soda, lightly stir and serve with straws.

2	shot(s)	Tanqueray London dry gin
½	shot(s)	Heering cherry brandy liqueur
¼	shot(s)	Bénédictine D.O.M. liqueur
¼	shot(s)	Cointreau triple sec
1½	shot(s)	Pressed pineapple juice
½	shot(s)	Freshly squeezed lime juice
¼	shot(s)	Pomegranate (grenadine) syrup
2	dashes	Angostura aromatic bitters
Top up with		Soda water (club soda)

Comment: Foaming, tangy and very fruity.

SIR CHARLES PUNCH

●●●●○

Glass: Old-fashioned
Garnish: Orange zest twist
Method: **STIR** all ingredients with ice and strain into ice-filled glass.

1	shot(s)	Warre's Otima tawny port
½	shot(s)	Courvoisier V.S.O.P. cognac
½	shot(s)	Grand Marnier liqueur
⅛	shot(s)	Sugar syrup (2 sugar to 1 water)

Origin: Adapted from a recipe in the 1949 edition of Esquire's Handbook for Hosts, which suggests serving it at Christmas.
Comment: Short but full of personality - like Kylie Minogue.

SIR THOMAS

●●●●○

Glass: Martini
Garnish: Maraschino cherry
Method: **STIR** all ingredients with ice and strain into chilled glass.

2	shot(s)	Bulleit bourbon whiskey
½	shot(s)	Cointreau triple sec
½	shot(s)	Heering cherry brandy liqueur
½	shot(s)	Martini Rosso sweet vermouth

Origin: Created in 2005 by Tom Ward, England.
Comment: Akin to a fruit laced Sweet Manhattan.

SIR WALTER COCKTAIL NEW #8

●●●○○

Glass: Martini
Garnish: Lemon zest twist
Method: **SHAKE** all ingredients with ice and fine strain into chilled glass.

¾	shot(s)	Bacardi Superior rum
¾	shot(s)	Courvoisier V.S.O.P. cognac
¼	shot(s)	Grand Marnier liqueur
¾	shot(s)	Freshly squeezed lemon juice
½	shot(s)	Pomegranate (grenadine) syrup
2	dashes	Angostura aromatic bitters

Origin: Adapted from Victor Bergeron's 'Trader Vic's Bartender's Guide' (1972 revised edition).
Comment: This blend of rum and cognac has more than a hint of Tiki fruitiness.

SKI BREEZE

●●●○○

Glass: Collins
Garnish: Apple slice
Method: **POUR** ingredients into ice-filled glass, lightly stir and serve with straws.

2	shot(s)	Raspberry flavoured vodka
3	shot(s)	Pressed apple juice
3	shot(s)	Ginger ale

Comment: A meld of apple and berries with hint of ginger.

SLEEPING BISON-TINI

●●●●○

Glass: Martini
Garnish: Pear slice on rim
Method: **SHAKE** all ingredients with ice and fine strain into chilled glass.

1½	shot(s)	Zubrówka bison vodka
¼	shot(s)	Bols apricot brandy liqueur
¼	shot(s)	Belle de Brillet pear liqueur
1	shot(s)	Freshly extracted pear juice
1	shot(s)	Pressed apple juice
1	shot(s)	Strong cold camomile tea

Comment: A light cocktail featuring a melange of subtle flavours.

SLEEPY HOLLOW

●●●●○

Glass: Old-fashioned
Garnish: Lemon slice
Method: Lightly **MUDDLE** mint in base of shaker (just to bruise). Add other ingredients, **SHAKE** with ice and fine strain into glass filled with crushed ice. Serve with straws.

10	fresh	Mint leaves
2	shot(s)	Tanqueray London dry gin
½	shot(s)	Bols apricot brandy liqueur
1	shot(s)	Freshly squeezed lemon juice
½	shot(s)	Sugar syrup (2 sugar to 1 water)

Origin: An adaption of a drink created in the early 1930s and named after Washington Irving's novel and its enchanted valley with ghosts, goblins and headless horseman.
Comment: Hints of lemon and mint with gin and apricot fruit. Very refreshing.

SLING (GENERIC NAME) UPDATED #8

Glass: Sling
Garnish: Lemon slice
Method: SHAKE first 3 ingredients with ice and strain into ice-filled glass. **TOP** with soda or ginger ale.

2	shot(s)	**Spirit** (gin, rum, scotch, whisk(e)y etc.)
½	shot(s)	**Freshly squeezed lemon juice**
¼	shot(s)	**Sugar syrup** (2 sugar to 1 water)
Top up with		**Soda water** (or ginger ale)

Origin: The word 'Sling' comes from the German 'schlingen', meaning 'to swallow', and Slings based on a spirit mixed with sugar and water were popularly drunk in the late 1800s.
Slings are similar to Toddies and like Toddies can be served hot. (Toddies, however, are never served cold.) The main difference between a Toddy and a Sling is that Slings are not flavoured by the addition of spices. Also, Toddies tend to be made with plain water, while Slings are charged with water, soda water or ginger ale.
The earliest known definition of 'cocktail' describes it as a bittered sling.
Comment: Sugar balances the citrus juice, the spirit fortifies and the carbonate lengthens.

SLIPPERY NIPPLE

Glass: Shot
Method: LAYER in glass by carefully pouring ingredients in the following order.

¼	shot(s)	**Pomegranate (grenadine) syrup**
¾	shot(s)	**Luxardo Sambuca dei Cesari**
¾	shot(s)	**Baileys Irish cream liqueur**

Comment: The infamous red, clear and brown shot. Very sweet.

SLOE GIN FIZZ

Glass: Sling
Garnish: Lemon slice or cucumber slice
Method: SHAKE first 5 ingredients with ice and strain into ice-filled glass. **TOP** with soda, stir and serve with straws.

1	shot(s)	**Tanqueray London dry gin**
1½	shot(s)	**Sloe gin liqueur**
1	shot(s)	**Freshly squeezed lime juice**
¼	shot(s)	**Sugar syrup** (2 sugar to 1 water)
½	fresh	**Egg white**
Top up with		**Soda water** (club soda)

Comment: A sour gin fizz with dark, rich sloe gin.

SLOE MOTION

Glass: Flute
Garnish: Lemon zest
Method: POUR liqueur into chilled glass and **TOP** with champagne.

| ¾ | shot(s) | **Sloe gin liqueur** |
| Top up with | | **Perrier Jouet brut champagne** |

Comment: Sloe gin proves to be an excellent complement to champagne.

SLOE TEQUILA

Glass: Old-fashioned
Garnish: Lime wedge
Method: SHAKE all ingredients with ice and strain into ice-filled glass.

1	shot(s)	**Sloe gin liqueur**
1	shot(s)	**Don Julio reposado tequila**
1	shot(s)	**Rose's lime cordial**

Comment: Berry fruit and tequila with a surprisingly tart, bitter finish.

SLOPPY JOE

Glass: Martini
Garnish: Lime wedge
Method: SHAKE all ingredients with ice and fine strain into chilled glass.

1	shot(s)	**Bacardi Superior rum**
1	shot(s)	**Noilly Prat dry vermouth**
¼	shot(s)	**Cointreau triple sec**
1	shot(s)	**Freshly squeezed lime juice**
½	shot(s)	**Sugar syrup** (2 sugar to 1 water)
¼	shot(s)	**Pomegranate (grenadine) syrup**

Comment: Nicely balanced sweet and sourness.

SLOW SCREW

Glass: Collins
Garnish: Orange slice
Method: SHAKE all ingredients with ice and strain into ice-filled glass.

1	shot(s)	**Sloe gin liqueur**
1	shot(s)	**Ketel One vodka**
4	shot(s)	**Freshly squeezed orange juice**

Comment: A Screwdriver with sloe gin.

SLOW COMFORTABLE SCREW

Glass: Collins
Garnish: Half orange slice
Method: SHAKE all ingredients with ice and strain into ice-filled glass.

1	shot(s)	**Ketel One vodka**
1	shot(s)	**Sloe gin liqueur**
1	shot(s)	**Southern Comfort liqueur**
3	shot(s)	**Freshly squeezed orange juice**

Comment: A Screwdriver with sloe gin and Southern Comfort. Fruity and fairly sweet.

SLOW COMFORTABLE SCREW AGAINST THE WALL

Glass: Collins
Method: **SHAKE** first 4 ingredients with ice and strain into ice-filled glass. Lastly **FLOAT** Galliano.

1	shot(s)	**Ketel One vodka**
1	shot(s)	**Sloe gin liqueur**
1	shot(s)	**Southern Comfort liqueur**
3	shot(s)	**Freshly squeezed orange juice**
½	shot(s)	**Galliano L'Autentico liqueur**

Comment: Galliano adds the wall (as in Harvey Wallbanger) and some herbal peppermint to this Slow Comfortable Screw.

SMARTINI

Glass: Martini
Garnish: Three Smarties in drink
Method: **SHAKE** all ingredients with ice and fine strain into chilled glass.

2	shot(s)	**Ketel One Citroen vodka**
1	shot(s)	**White crème de cacao liqueur**
¼	shot(s)	**Sugar syrup** (2 sugar to 1 water)
¾	shot(s)	**Chilled mineral water** (omit if wet ice)
3	dashes	**Angostura orange bitters**

Comment: Citrus with a crispy chocolate edge. A sweetie.

SMOKE OF SCOTLAND NEW #8

Glass: Martini
Garnish: Grapefruit zest twist (flamed)
Method: **STIR** all ingredients with ice and strain into chilled glass.

2	shot(s)	**Lagavulin 16yo malt whisky**
½	shot(s)	**Noilly Prat dry vermouth**
½	shot(s)	**St-Germain elderflower liqueur**
⅛	shot(s)	**Cynar artichoke liqueur**

Comment: Smoky, with floral and tropical fruit notes from the elderflower liqueur and added complexity from the vermouth and Cynar.
Origin: Created in 2007 by Vincenzo Marianella at Providence, Los Angeles, USA.

SMOKEY JOE NEW #8

Glass: Martini/Coupette
Garnish: Lemon zest spiral
Method: **STIR** all ingredients with ice and fine strain into chilled glass.

2	shot(s)	**Sake**
½	shot(s)	**Courvoisier V.S.O.P. cognac**
¼	shot(s)	**Lagavulin 16yo malt whisky**
1	shot(s)	**Sauternes wine**

Comment: Sake sweetened with sauternes and flavoured with cognac and Islay whisky.
Origin: Created in August 2008 by Simon Difford at The Cabinet Room, London, England.

SMOKIN ROSE NEW #8

Glass: Martini
Garnish: Maraschino cherry
Method: **SHAKE** all ingredients with ice and strain into chilled glass.

2	shot(s)	**Bacardi Superior rum**
¼	shot(s)	**Lanique rose petal liqueur**
⅛	shot(s)	**Lagavulin 16yo malt whisky**
⅛	shot(s)	**Sugar syrup** (2 sugar to 1 water)
¼	shot(s)	**Pressed apple juice**
½	shot(s)	**Freshly squeezed lime juice**
1	dashes	**Angostura aromatic bitters**

Comment: A bizarrely twisted Daiquiri with Islay malt, rose petal liqueur and vanilla.
Origin: Created in 2008 by Simon Difford, The Cabinet Room, London, England.

SMOKING STALLION NEW #8

Glass: Martini
Garnish: Dill sprig
Method: **STIR** all ingredients with ice and fine strain into chilled glass.

1	sprig	**Fresh dill**
2	shot(s)	**Ketel One vodka**
½	shot(s)	**Noilly Prat dry vermouth**
⅛	shot(s)	**Lagavulin 16yo malt whisky**
⅛	shot(s)	**Maple syrup**

Origin: Created in 2008 by Bart Van Ween at a Dutch World Class.
Comment: Subtly herbal and dry with a hint of whisky smokiness.

SMOKY APPLE MARTINI

Glass: Martini
Garnish: Maraschino cherry
Method: **SHAKE** all ingredients with ice and fine strain into chilled glass.

2½	shot(s)	**Johnnie Walker Scotch whisky**
1	shot(s)	**Sour apple liqueur**
½	shot(s)	**Rose's lime cordial**

Comment: Scotch adds some peaty character to this twist on the Sour Apple Martini.

S

SMOKY MARTINI #1

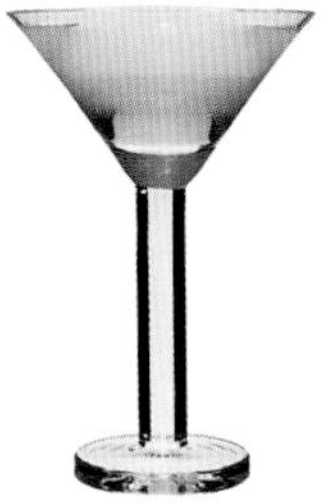

Glass: Martini
Garnish: Lemon zest twist
Method: **STIR** all ingredients with ice and strain into chilled glass.

2½	shot(s)	**Tanqueray London dry gin**
½	shot(s)	**Noilly Prat dry vermouth**
¼	shot(s)	**Johnnie Walker Scotch whisky**

Variant: Substitute vodka for gin.
Comment: A pleasant variation on the classic Dry Martini.

SMOKY MARTINI #2

Glass: Martini
Garnish: Orange zest twist
Method: STIR all ingredients with ice and strain into chilled glass.

2	shot(s)	Tanqueray London dry gin
1	shot(s)	Sloe gin liqueur
¼	shot(s)	Noilly Prat dry vermouth
2	dashes	Angostura orange bitters

Origin: Created in 1997 by Giovanni Burdi at Match EC1, London, England.
Comment: The basic Martini formula (gin plus vermouth) is enhanced with sloe gin and the traditional orange bitters variation, delivering a distinctive 'smoky' character.

SMOOTH & CREAMY'TINI

Glass: Martini
Garnish: Dust with grated nutmeg
Method: SHAKE all ingredients with ice and fine strain into chilled glass.

1½	shot(s)	Bacardi Oro golden rum
1	shot(s)	Malibu coconut rum liqueur
¼	shot(s)	Crème de banane liqueur
¾	shot(s)	Double (heavy) cream
¾	shot(s)	Milk

Comment: Creamy and moreish.

SNAKEBITE

Glass: Collins
Method: POUR lager into glass and **TOP** with cider.

| Half fill with | Lager |
| Top up with | Dry cider |

Variant: Add a dash of blackcurrant cordial to make a 'Snakebite & Black'.
Comment: The students' special.

SNOOD MURDEKIN

Glass: Shot
Method: SHAKE first 3 ingredients with ice and strain into chilled glass. **FLOAT** cream over drink.

½	shot(s)	Ketel One vodka
½	shot(s)	Chambord black raspberry liqueur
½	shot(s)	Kahlúa coffee liqueur
¼	shot(s)	Double (heavy) cream

Origin: Created in the late 90s by Dick Bradsell at Detroit, London, England, for Karin Wiklund, and named for the sad, flute-playing Moomin Troll.
Comment: Moreish combination of coffee and raspberries topped by cream.

SNOOPY

Glass: Old-fashioned
Garnish: Orange zest twist
Method: SHAKE all ingredients with ice and fine strain into ice-filled glass.

1	shot(s)	Galliano L'Autentico liqueur
1½	shot(s)	Bulleit bourbon whiskey
½	shot(s)	Campari Bitter
¾	shot(s)	Grand Marnier liqueur
¼	shot(s)	Freshly squeezed lemon juice

Comment: Tangy fruit with a balancing hint of citrus and bitterness.

SNOW FALL MARTINI

Glass: Martini
Garnish: Vanilla pod
Method: MUDDLE vanilla pod in base of shaker. Add other ingredients, **SHAKE** with ice and fine strain into chilled glass.

¼	pod	Vanilla
2	shot(s)	Vanilla-infused Ketel One vodka
1¼	shot(s)	Double (heavy) cream
1¼	shot(s)	Milk
¼	shot(s)	Sugar syrup (2 sugar to 1 water)

Origin: Discovered in 2002 at Lot 61, New York City.
Comment: An alcoholic version of a vanilla milkshake.

SNOW ON EARTH

Glass: Shot
Method: SHAKE first 3 ingredients with ice and strain into chilled glass. Carefully **FLOAT** cream on drink.

½	shot(s)	Kahlúa coffee liqueur
½	shot(s)	Chambord black raspberry liqueur
½	shot(s)	Krupnik honey liqueur
½	shot(s)	Double (heavy) cream

Comment: A sweet, flavoursome shot.

SNOW WHITE DAIQUIRI

Glass: Martini
Garnish: Pineapple wedge on rim
Method: SHAKE all ingredients with ice and fine strain into chilled glass.

2	shot(s)	Bacardi Superior rum
½	shot(s)	Pressed pineapple juice
½	shot(s)	Freshly squeezed lime juice
¼	shot(s)	Sugar syrup (2 sugar to 1 water)
½	fresh	Egg white

Origin: My adaptation of a classic cocktail.
Comment: The pineapple and egg white ensure that this delightful Daiquiri has an appropriately white frothy head.

SNOWBALL UPDATED #8

Glass: Collins
Garnish: Lime zest twist
Method: SHAKE first 3 ingredients with ice and strain into chilled glass. TOP with champagne.

2	shot(s)	**Bols advocaat liqueur**
1	shot(s)	**Tio Pepe fino sherry**
¾	shot(s)	**Rose's lime cordial**
¾	shot(s)	**Perrier Jouet brut champagne**

Comment: The classic light, fluffy concoction. Try it, you may like it.
Origin: This is thought to have originated in Britain in the late 1940s or early 1950s, reaching its peak of popularity in the 1970s.

SNYDER MARTINI

Glass: Martini
Garnish: Orange zest twist
Method: SHAKE all ingredients with ice and fine strain into chilled glass.

2	shot(s)	**Tanqueray London dry gin**
1	shot(s)	**Noilly Prat dry vermouth**
¼	shot(s)	**Grand Marnier liqueur**

Origin: Adapted from a recipe in Harry Craddock's 1930 Savoy Cocktail Book.
Comment: Dry, hardcore and yet mellow.

SOCIALITE

Glass: Old-fashioned
Method: SHAKE all ingredients with ice and strain into glass filled with crushed ice.

1	shot(s)	**Freshly squeezed lemon juice**
½	shot(s)	**Vanilla sugar syrup**
1	shot(s)	**Grand Marnier liqueur**
1	shot(s)	**Vanilla-infused Ketel One vodka**
1	shot(s)	**Luxardo limoncello liqueur**

Origin: Discovered in 2001 at Lab Bar, London, England.
Comment: Rich citrus with lashings of vanilla.

SODDEN GRAPE MARTINI

Glass: Martini
Garnish: Three grapes on stick
Method: MUDDLE grapes in base of shaker. Add other ingredients, SHAKE with ice and fine strain into chilled glass.

7	fresh	**Seedless white grapes**
2	shot(s)	**Zubrówka bison vodka**
¾	shot(s)	**Icewine**

Origin: Created by Yours Truly (Simon Difford) in 2004.
Comment: A 'sod' is a piece of turf. Here 'sodden' refers to the bison grass, the flavour of which combines well with the grapes and icewine.

SOL ARDIENTE NEW #8

Glass: Coupette/ Martini
Garnish: Crushed red peppercorns
Method: MUDDLE peppercorns in base of shaker. Add next 4 ingredients, SHAKE with ice and fine strain into chilled glass. TOP with splash soda.

1	spoon	**Red peppercorns**
2	shot(s)	**Bacardi Superior rum**
1	shot(s)	**Pressed pineapple juice**
1	shot(s)	**Freshly squeezed lime juice**
½	shot(s)	**Sugar syrup** (2 sugar to 1 water)
Top up with		**Soda water** (club soda)

Comment: Red pepper and pineapple influences this twisted Daiquiri.
Origin: Created in 2008 by Anthony Farrell, Sangreal Bartending Ltd, Belfast, Northern Ireland. The name translates from Spanish as 'Burning Sun'.

'EAT, DRINK, AND BE MERRY; FOR TOMORROW YOU MAY NOT BE ABLE TO AFFORD IT.'
UNKNOWN

SOLENT SUNSET

Glass: Collins
Garnish: Pineapple wedge & cherry on rim
Method: SHAKE all ingredients with ice and fine strain into ice-filled glass.

2	shot(s)	**Pusser's Navy rum**
¾	shot(s)	**Freshly squeezed lime juice**
3	shot(s)	**Pressed pineapple juice**
¼	shot(s)	**Pomegranate (grenadine) syrup**

Comment: A Naval style tropical rum punch for those occasional hot sunny days on the Solent (the stretch of sea which separates the Isle of Wight from mainland Britain).

SOPHISTICATED SAVAGE

Glass: Old-fashioned
Garnish: Lime wedge
Method: SHAKE all ingredients with ice and strain into ice-filled glass.

2	shot(s)	**Tuaca Italian liqueur**
1	shot(s)	**Leblon cachaça**
½	shot(s)	**Freshly squeezed lime juice**
½	fresh	**Egg white**

Origin: Created by: Poul Jensen, Brighton, England.
Comment: A sour drink with a horse's kick leading into a smooth subtle finish.

SORRELADE (MOCKTAIL)

Glass: Collins
Garnish: Lime wedge
Method: (Bulk recipe.) **SOAK** dried sorrel in water with ginger, ground cloves and honey for 12 hours. Bring this mixture to the **BOIL** then leave to cool and **SOAK** for a further 12 hours **STRAIN** and then keep refrigerated.

70	grams	**Sorrel** (hibiscus flowers)
1¼	litres	**Mineral water**
30	grams	**Root ginger** (sliced)
½	spoon	**Ground cloves**
3	spoons	**Runny honey**

Origin: Jamaican sorrel, also known by its scientific name 'Hibiscus Sabdariffa', is a plant propagated for its red petals. In Jamaica these are used to make this refreshing drink. (Jamaican sorrel is not related to the English garden herb of the same name.)
Comment: Sorrelade looks a little like cranberry juice and like cranberry juice has a bittersweet, slightly spicy taste.

SORREL RUM PUNCH

Glass: Collins
Garnish: Lime wedge
Method: **SHAKE** all ingredients with ice and strain into glass filled with crushed glass. Serve with straws.

2¼	shot(s)	**Wray & Nephew overproof rum**
3	shot(s)	**Sorrelade** (see recipe above)
¾	shot(s)	**Freshly squeezed lime juice**
1½	shot(s)	**Sugar syrup** (2 sugar to 1 water)

Origin: A classic Jamaican punch using the classic proportions of 'one of sour, two of sweet, three of strong and four of weak'.
Comment: This drink harnesses the flavour of sorrelade and combines it with the traditional strength and bittersweetness of rum punch. Jamaica in a glass.

SO-SO MARTINI UPDATED #8

Glass: Martini
Garnish: Float wafer thin apple slice
Method: **SHAKE** all ingredients with ice and fine strain into chilled glass.

1	shot(s)	**Tanqueray London dry gin**
1	shot(s)	**Noilly Prat dry vermouth**
½	shot(s)	**Boulard Grand Solage calvados**
½	shot(s)	**Pomegranate (grenadine) syrup**

Comment: This beautifully balanced, appley drink is so much more than so-so.
Origin: Adapted from a recipe in Harry Craddock's 1930 Savoy Cocktail Book. Harry McElhone's 1929 'ABC of Cocktails' credits this drink to "Mr P. Soso, the popular manager of Kit-Kat Club, London."

SOUR (GENERIC NAME) UPDATED #8

Glass: Old-fashioned
Garnish: Lemon slice & cherry on stick (sail)
Method: **SHAKE** all ingredients with ice and strain into ice-filled glass

2	shot(s)	**Spirit** (whisk(e)y, gin, rum or brandy etc.)
1	shot(s)	**Freshly squeezed lemon juice**
½	shot(s)	**Sugar syrup** (2 sugar to 1 water)
½	fresh	**Egg white**
3	dashes	**Angostura aromatic bitters**

Origin: Sours are aptly named drinks. Their flavour comes from either lemon or lime juice, which is balanced with sugar. Sours can be based on practically any spirit but the bourbon based Whiskey Sour is by far the most popular. Many (including myself) believe this drink is only properly made when smoothed with a little egg white. Sours are served either straight-up in a Sour glass (rather like a small flute) or on the rocks in an old-fashioned glass. They are traditionally garnished with a cherry and an orange slice, or sometimes a lemon slice.
Comment: This 4:2:8 formula is a tad sourer than the classic 3:4:8 which translates as: three quarter part of the sour ingredient (lemon juice), one part of the sweet ingredient (sugar syrup) and two parts of the strong ingredient (spirit). So if you find my formula to sour than best follow the classic proportions in future.

SOUR APPLE MARTINI #1
(POPULAR US VERSION)

Glass: Martini
Garnish: Cherry in glass
Method: **SHAKE** all ingredients with ice and fine strain into chilled glass.

2	shot(s)	**Ketel One vodka**
1½	shot(s)	**Sour apple liqueur**
¼	shot(s)	**Rose's lime cordial**

Variant: Some bars add sour mix in place of Rose's, others add a dash of fresh lime and sugar.
Comment: A hugely popular drink across North America.

SOUR APPLE MARTINI #2
(DELUXE US VERSION)

Glass: Martini
Garnish: Float wafer thin apple slice
Method: **SHAKE** all ingredients with ice and fine strain into chilled glass.

2	shot(s)	**Ketel One vodka**
1	shot(s)	**Sour apple liqueur**
½	shot(s)	**Freshly squeezed lime juice**
¼	shot(s)	**Sugar syrup** (2 sugar to 1 water)
½	fresh	**Egg white**

Comment: A sophisticated version of the contemporary classic.

SOURPUSS MARTINI

●●●●○

Glass: Martini
Garnish: Physalis (cape gooseberry) on rim
Method: SHAKE all ingredients with ice and fine strain into chilled glass.

1	shot(s)	**Ketel One Citroen vodka**
½	shot(s)	**Midori green melon liqueur**
½	shot(s)	**Sour apple liqueur**
2	shot(s)	**Pressed apple juice**

Origin: Created in 2001 by Colin 'Big Col' Crowden at Time, Leicester, England.
Comment: A lime-green, flavoursome cocktail that balances sweet and sour.

SOUTH BEACH

●●●●○

Glass: Martini
Garnish: Orange zest twist
Method: SHAKE all ingredients with ice and fine strain into chilled glass.

1	shot(s)	**Campari Bitter**
1	shot(s)	**Luxardo Amaretto di Saschira**
2½	shot(s)	**Freshly squeezed orange juice**
¼	shot(s)	**Sugar syrup** (2 sugar to 1 water)

Origin: Created in 1992 by Dale DeGroff, New York City, USA.
Comment: An unusual, bittersweet combination with a strong orange and almond flavour.

SOUTH CHINA BREEZE

●●●●○

Glass: Collins
Garnish: Orange slice
Method: SHAKE all ingredients with ice and strain into ice-filled glass.

2	shot(s)	**Orange-infused Ketel One vodka**
3	shot(s)	**Freshly squeezed grapefruit juice**
1½	shot(s)	**Lychee syrup** (from tinned fruit)
3	dashes	**Angostura aromatic bitters**

Comment: Orange and grapefruit with an oriental influence by way of lychee.

SOUTH OF THE BORDER

●●●●○○

Glass: Martini
Garnish: Three coffee beans
Method: SHAKE all ingredients with ice and fine strain into chilled glass.

2	shot(s)	**Don Julio reposado tequila**
1	shot(s)	**Kahlúa coffee liqueur**
¾	shot(s)	**Freshly squeezed lime juice**
½	fresh	**Egg white**

Comment: A strange mix of lime and coffee.

SOUTH PACIFIC

●●●●◑○

Glass: Martini
Garnish: Pineapple wedge on rim
Method: Cut passion fruit in half and scoop flesh into shaker. Add other ingredients, SHAKE with ice and fine strain into chilled glass.

1	fresh	**Passion fruit**
1	shot(s)	**Soho lychee liqueur**
1	shot(s)	**Ketel One Citroen vodka**
1	shot(s)	**Pressed pineapple juice**
½	shot(s)	**Freshly squeezed lime juice**

Origin: Adapted from a recipe created by Wayne Collins, London, England.

SOUTH PACIFIC BREEZE

●●●◑○

Glass: Collins
Garnish: Pineapple wedge on rim
Method: POUR gin and Galliano into ice-filled glass. TOP with lemonade to just below the rim. DRIZZLE blue curaçao around top of drink (it will sink leaving strings of blue). Serve with straws.

1½	shot(s)	**Tanqueray London dry gin**
¾	shot(s)	**Galliano L'Autentico liqueur**
Top up with		**Lemonade/Sprite/7-Up**
¾	shot(s)	**Bols blue curaçao liqueur**

Comment: Quite sweet but flavoursome – looks great.

SOUTHERN CIDER

●●●○○

Glass: Martini
Garnish: Lime wedge
Method: SHAKE all ingredients with ice and fine strain into chilled glass.

2	shot(s)	**Southern Comfort liqueur**
1	shot(s)	**Freshly squeezed lime juice**
1½	shot(s)	**Ocean Spray cranberry juice**

Origin: Discovered at Opryland Hotel, Nashville, USA.
Comment: Strangely, this cocktail does have a cidery taste.

SOUTHERN MANHATTAN

●●●●○

Glass: Martini
Garnish: Orange zest twist
Method: STIR all ingredients with ice and strain into chilled glass.

2	shot(s)	**Bulleit bourbon whiskey**
1	shot(s)	**Southern Comfort liqueur**
1	shot(s)	**Martini Rosso sweet vermouth**
3	dashes	**Peychaud's aromatic bitters**

Origin: Created in by Yours Truly (Simon Difford) in August 2005 for Tales of the Cocktail, New Orleans, USA.
Comment: A Manhattan with Southern Comfort and Peychaud's adding a hint of southern flavour.

SOUTHERN MINT COBBLER

Glass: Old-fashioned
Garnish: Mint sprig
Method: Lightly **MUDDLE** mint (just to bruise) in base of shaker. Add other ingredients, **SHAKE** with ice and fine strain into glass filled with crushed ice. Serve with straws.

7	fresh	**Mint leaves**
2	shot(s)	**Southern Comfort liqueur**
1	shot(s)	**Boiron white peach puree**
½	shot(s)	**Freshly squeezed lemon juice**

Comment: Very fruity and very easy to drink.

SOUTHERN MULE

Glass: Collins
Garnish: Lime wedge
Method: **SHAKE** first 3 ingredients with ice and strain into ice-filled glass. **TOP** with ginger beer, lightly stir and serve with straws.

2	shot(s)	**Southern Comfort liqueur**
½	shot(s)	**Freshly squeezed lime juice**
3	dashes	**Angostura aromatic bitters**
Top up with		**Ginger beer**

Comment: Tangy, fruity and spiced with ginger.

SOUTHERN PEACH

Glass: Collins
Garnish: Lime wedge
Method: **SHAKE** all ingredients with ice and strain into ice-filled glass. Serve with straws.

1	shot(s)	**Southern Comfort liqueur**
1	shot(s)	**Peach Tree peach schnapps**
3	shot(s)	**Ocean Spray cranberry juice**
1	shot(s)	**Freshly squeezed lime juice**

Comment: Fruity and slightly sweet but far from offensive.

SOUTHERN PUNCH

Glass: Collins
Garnish: Pineapple wedge on rim
Method: **SHAKE** all ingredients with ice and strain into ice-filled glass.

1½	shot(s)	**Southern Comfort liqueur**
½	shot(s)	**Bulleit bourbon whiskey**
2	shot(s)	**Pressed pineapple juice**
1	shot(s)	**Freshly squeezed lemon juice**
½	shot(s)	**Sugar syrup** (2 sugar to 1 water)
½	shot(s)	**Pomegranate (grenadine) syrup**

Comment: Tropical flavours with the warmth of the liquor trailed by a fresh lemon finish.

SOUTHERN TEA-KNEE

Glass: Martini
Garnish: Apricot slice on rim
Method: **SHAKE** all ingredients with ice and fine strain into chilled glass.

1	shot(s)	**Southern Comfort liqueur**
½	shot(s)	**Tanqueray London dry gin**
½	shot(s)	**Bols apricot brandy liqueur**
½	shot(s)	**Crème de banane liqueur**
2	shot(s)	**Strong cold earl grey tea**

Origin: Created by Yours Truly (Simon Difford) in 2002.
Comment: Sweet fruity flavours balanced by tannic bitterness in the tea.

SOUTHSIDE NEW #8

Glass: Martini
Garnish: Mint leaf
Method: **SHAKE** all ingredients (including mint) with ice and fine strain into chilled glass.

7	fresh	**Mint leaves**
2	shot(s)	**Tanqueray London dry gin**
1	shot(s)	**Freshly squeezed lime juice**
½	shot(s)	**Sugar syrup** (2 sugar to 1 water)

Origin: This vintage cocktail is purported to have originated at New York's Twenty-One Club. A long version served over crushed ice is said to have come from the southside of Chicago during Prohibition where it was drunk by the Southside mobsters, while on the other side of town hoodlums enjoyed the Northside (gin and ginger ale).
Comment: Gin and mint with a splash of lime. Refreshingly balanced.

DAVID A. EMBURY FIRST PUBLISHED 'FINE ART OF MIXING DRINKS' IN 1948.

SOUTHSIDE FIZZ NEW #8

Glass: Collins (small max 10oz)
Garnish: Mint sprig
Method: Lightly **MUDDLE** mint in base of shaker (just to bruise). Add next 3 ingredients, **SHAKE** with ice and fine strain into (empty) chilled glass. **TOP** with soda.

7	fresh	**Mint leaves**
2	shot(s)	**Tanqueray London dry gin**
1	shot(s)	**Freshly squeezed lemon juice**
½	shot(s)	**Sugar syrup** (2 sugar to 1 water)
Top up with		**Soda water** (from siphon)

Comment: A minty Collins.
Origin: Recipe adapted from Harry Craddock's 1930 'The Savoy Cocktail Book'.

HARRY CRADDOCK FIRST PUBLISHED 'THE SAVOY COCKTAIL BOOK' IN 1930.

SPENCER COCKTAIL

Glass: Martini
Garnish: Orange zest twist (discarded) & maraschino cherry
Method: SHAKE all ingredients with ice and fine strain into chilled glass.

2	shot(s)	Tanqueray London dry gin
1	shot(s)	Bols apricot brandy liqueur
¼	shot(s)	Freshly squeezed orange juice
1	dash	Angostura aromatic bitters

Origin: Adapted from a recipe in Harry Craddock's 1930 Savoy Cocktail Book.
Comment: To quote Craddock, "Very mellifluous: has a fine and rapid action: for morning work."

SOUTHSIDE ROYALE

Glass: Martini
Garnish: Mint leaf
Method: Lightly **MUDDLE** (just to bruise) mint in base of shaker. Add next 3 ingredients, **SHAKE** with ice and fine strain into chilled glass. **TOP** with a splash of champagne.

7	fresh	Mint leaves
2	shot(s)	Tanqueray London dry gin
1	shot(s)	Freshly squeezed lemon juice
½	shot(s)	Sugar syrup (2 sugar to 1 water)
Top up with		Perrier Jouet brut champagne

Variant: Topped with soda (from a siphon, please) in place of champagne this becomes a mere 'Southside'.
Origin: Created during Prohibition, either at a New York City speakeasy called Jack & Charlie's, or at Manhattan's Stork Club, or by Chicago's Southside gang to make their bootleg liquor more palatable.
Comment: A White Lady with fresh mint and champagne.

SPEYSIDE MARTINI

Glass: Martini
Garnish: Lemon zest twist
Method: MUDDLE grapes in base of shaker. Add other ingredients, **SHAKE** with ice and fine strain into chilled glass.

7	fresh	Seedless white grapes
2	shot(s)	Johnnie Walker Scotch whisky
¾	shot(s)	Bols apricot brandy liqueur
¾	shot(s)	Freshly squeezed grapefruit juice

Origin: Discovered in 2004 at Indigo Yard, Edinburgh, Scotland.
Comment: Scotch, grape juice, apricot liqueur and grapefruit may seem an unlikely combo but they get on well together.

SOYER AU CHAMPAGNE

Glass: Martini (Parfait glass)
Method: PLACE scoop of ice cream in base of glass. **SHAKE** next 3 ingredients with ice and strain over ice cream. **TOP** with champagne and serve while foaming with straws that the drinker should use to mix.

1	scoop	Häagen Dazs vanilla ice cream
½	shot(s)	Courvoisie V.S.O.P. cognac
½	shot(s)	Luxardo maraschino liqueur
½	shot(s)	Grand Marnier liqueur
Top up with		Perrier Jouet brut champagne

Origin: Adapted from a recipe in the 1949 edition of Esquire's Handbook For Hosts. Apparently this was "one of the most popular drinks at Christmas in the continental cafés".
Comment: A unique dessert of a drink.

SPICED APPLE DAIQUIRI

Glass: Martini
Garnish: Apple wedge on rim
Method: SHAKE all ingredients with ice and fine strain into chilled glass.

2	shot(s)	Bacardi Superior rum
½	shot(s)	Berentzen apple schnapps
¼	shot(s)	Goldschläger cinnamon schnapps
½	shot(s)	Freshly squeezed lime juice
¾	shot(s)	Pressed apple juice

Origin: Created in 1999 by Yours Truly (Simon Difford).
Comment: Sour apple and cinnamon laced with rum.

SPARKLING PERRY

Glass: Flute
Garnish: Pear slice on rim
Method: SHAKE first 3 ingredients with ice and fine strain into chilled glass. **TOP** with champagne and lightly stir.

¾	shot(s)	Poire William eau de vie
¾	shot(s)	Belle de Brillet pear liqueur
1	shot(s)	Freshly extracted pear juice
Top up with		Perrier Jouet brut champagne

Origin: Created in December 2002 by Yours Truly (Simon Difford).
Comment: Reminiscent of perry (pear cider).

SPICED CRANBERRY MARTINI

Glass: Martini
Garnish: Cranberry juice & cinnamon rim
Method: MUDDLE cloves in base of shaker. Add other ingredients, **SHAKE** with ice and fine strain into chilled glass.

7	dried	Cloves
1	shot(s)	Cranberry flavoured vodka
1	shot(s)	Pusser's Navy rum
2	shot(s)	Ocean Spray cranberry juice
½	shot(s)	Sugar syrup (2 sugar to 1 water)

Origin: Created in 2003 by Yours Truly (Simon Difford).
Comment: The cloves and the colour add a festive note to this notional Martini.

SPICED PEAR

Glass: Old-fashioned
Garnish: Pear slice
Method: SHAKE all ingredients with ice and strain into ice-filled glass.

1	shot(s)	**Belle de Brillet pear liqueur**
1	shot(s)	**Sailor Jerry spiced rum**
1	shot(s)	**Freshly extracted pear juice**
½	shot(s)	**Freshly squeezed lime juice**
½	shot(s)	**Sugar syrup** (2 sugar to 1 water)

Origin: Created in 2002 by James Stewart, Edinburgh, Scotland.
Comment: Just as it says on the tin – spiced pear.

SPICY FINN

Glass: Martini
Garnish: Blueberry or raspberry on rim
Method: MUDDLE ginger in base of shaker. Add other ingredients, SHAKE with ice and fine strain into chilled glass.

3	slices	**Fresh root ginger** (thumbnail sized)
2	shot(s)	**Cranberry flavoured vodka**
½	shot(s)	**Campari Bitter**
½	shot(s)	**Sugar syrup** (2 sugar to 1 water)
1	shot(s)	**Chilled mineral water** (reduce if wet ice)

Origin: Created by Michael Mahe at Hush, London.
Comment: The sugar syrup sweetens this up.

SPICY VEGGY

Glass: Martini
Garnish: Chunk of carrot on rim
Method: MUDDLE coriander seeds in base of shaker. Add other ingredients, SHAKE with ice and fine strain into chilled glass.

2	dozen	**Coriander seeds**
2	shot(s)	**Tanqueray London dry gin**
2	shot(s)	**Freshly extracted carrot juice**
¼	shot(s)	**Sugar syrup** (2 sugar to 1 water)
1	grind	**Black pepper**
1	pinch	**Salt**

Origin: Created in 2002 by Yours Truly (Simon Difford).
Comment: Reminiscent of alcoholic carrot and coriander soup.

SPIKED APPLE CIDER (HOT)

Glass: Toddy
Garnish: Cinnamon dust
Method: MUDDLE cloves in base of shaker. Add cognac and apple juice, DRY SHAKE and fine strain into glass. WARM in microwave then FLOAT double cream over drink.

2	dried	**Cloves**
2	shot(s)	**Courvoisier V.S.O.P. cognac**
3	shot(s)	**Pressed apple juice**
Float		**Double (heavy) cream**

Origin: Adapted from a drink discovered in 2006 at Double Seven, New York City, USA.
Comment: Warming and lightly spiced under a creamy head.

SPITFIRE NEW #8

Glass: Martini
Garnish: Lemon zest twist
Method: SHAKE all ingredients with ice and fine strain into chilled glass.

2	shot(s)	**Courvoisier V.S.O.P. cognac**
½	shot(s)	**Sauvignon Blanc wine**
1	shot(s)	**Freshly squeezed lemon juice**
½	shot(s)	**Sugar syrup** (2 sugar to 1 water)
½	fresh	**Egg white**

Comment: A brandy sour with a splash of dry white wine.
Origin: Created in 2006 by Tony Conigliaro at Shochu Lounge, London, England.

SPORRAN BREEZE

Glass: Collins
Garnish: Apple slice on rim
Method: SHAKE all ingredients with ice and strain into ice-filled glass. Serve with straws.

2	shot(s)	**Johnnie Walker Scotch whisky**
½	shot(s)	**Passion fruit syrup**
4	shot(s)	**Pressed apple juice**

Origin: Phillip Jeffrey created this drink for me in 2002 at the GE Club, London, England. I take credit (if any's due) for the name.
Comment: As with all simple drinks, the quality and flavour of the three ingredients used greatly affects the end product – choose wisely and you'll have a deliciously fresh blend of malty fruit.

SPRITZ AL BITTER

Glass: Old-fashioned
Garnish: Orange zest twist
Method: POUR ingredients into ice-filled glass and lightly stir.

1½	shot(s)	**Campari Bitter**
1½	shot(s)	**Sauvignon Blanc wine**
Top up with		**Soda water** (club soda)

Origin: The origins of this Venetian speciality date back to the end of the 19th century when the Austrians ruled the city.
Comment: Basically a Spritzer with a generous splash of Campari – dry and very refreshing.

SPRITZER

Glass: Goblet
Garnish: Lemon zest twist
Method: POUR ingredients into chilled glass and lightly stir. No ice!

3	shot(s)	**Sauvignon Blanc wine**
Top up with		**Soda water** (club soda)

Comment: The ultimate 'girlie' drink. To avoid ridicule when diluting a glass of white wine just try adding a couple of ice cubes instead.

●●●●○○

SPUTNIK #1

Glass: Martini
Garnish: Orange zest twist
Method: SHAKE all ingredients with ice and fine strain into chilled glass.

1	shot(s)	**Ketel One vodka**
1	shot(s)	**Peach Tree peach schnapps**
1½	shot(s)	**Freshly squeezed orange juice**
1	shot(s)	**Double (heavy) cream**

Comment: Blasts of fruit cut through this soft creamy drink.

●●●●●○

SPUTNIK #2

Glass: Old-fashioned
Garnish: Orange slice
Method: SHAKE all ingredients with ice and strain into ice-filled glass.

1	shot(s)	**Bacardi Superior rum**
1	shot(s)	**Courvoisier V.S.O.P. cognac**
2	shot(s)	**Freshly squeezed orange juice**
½	shot(s)	**Sugar syrup** (2 sugar to 1 water)

Origin: A cocktail served in underground clubs all over the former Eastern Bloc. It was originally made with Cuban rum, Georgian brandy and tinned orange juice.
Comment: Orange, cognac and rum meld well.

●●●●○○

SQUASHED FROG

Glass: Shot
Method: Refrigerate ingredients then **LAYER** in chilled glass by carefully pouring in the following order.

½	shot(s)	**Pomegranate (grenadine) syrup**
½	shot(s)	**Midori green melon liqueur**
½	shot(s)	**Bols advocaat liqueur**

Comment: Very sweet. However, the taste is not as offensive as the name might suggest.

●●●●●

STAIRS MARTINI

Glass: Martini
Garnish: Pear slice on rim
Method: SHAKE all ingredients with ice and fine strain into chilled glass.

2	shot(s)	**Ketel One vodka**
1	shot(s)	**Freshly extracted pear juice**
1	shot(s)	**Pressed apple juice**
¼	shot(s)	**Freshly squeezed lemon juice**
¼	shot(s)	**Sugar syrup** (2 sugar to 1 water)
2	dashes	**Angostura orange bitters**

Origin: Created in 2000 by Ian Baldwin at the GE Club, London, England.
Comment: In London's cockney rhyming slang 'apples and pears' means stairs. So this tasty cocktail is appropriately named.

●●●●●○

STANLEY COCKTAIL

Glass: Martini
Garnish: Lemon zest twist
Method: SHAKE all ingredients with ice and fine strain into chilled glass.

1½	shot(s)	**Tanqueray London dry gin**
1½	shot(s)	**Bacardi Superior rum**
½	shot(s)	**Freshly squeezed lemon juice**
½	shot(s)	**Pomegranate (grenadine) syrup**

Origin: Adapted from a recipe in Harry Craddock's 1930 Savoy Cocktail Book.
Comment: Salmon pink and reminiscent of a Daiquiri with a splash of gin.

●●●●●○

THE STAR #1

Glass: Martini
Garnish: Olive on stick
Method: STIR all ingredients with ice and fine strain into chilled glass.

1½	shot(s)	**Boulard Grand Solage calvados**
1½	shot(s)	**Martini Rosso sweet vermouth**
1	dash	**Angostura aromatic bitters**

Variant: T.N.T. Special - with the addition of a dash of sugar.
Origin: Recipe from Harry Craddock's 1930 Savoy Cocktail Book. Created in the 1870s by a bartender at the legendary Manhattan Club, which once stood at the north corner of 34th Street and 5th Avenue, New York City.
Comment: Like many old classics, this drink needs dilution so stir until you're bored and thirsty.

●●●○○○

STARS & STRIPES SHOT

Glass: Shot
Method: Refrigerate ingredients then **LAYER** in chilled glass by carefully pouring in the following order.

½	shot(s)	**Crème de cassis liqueur**
½	shot(s)	**Luxardo maraschino liqueur**
½	shot(s)	**Green Chartreuse liqueur**

Origin: Adapted from a recipe in Harry Craddock's 1930 Savoy Cocktail Book.
Comment: The taste is too sweet and the colours aren't quite right. A shame.

●●●●○○

S. TEA G.

Glass: Collins
Garnish: Lemon slice
Method: SHAKE first 3 ingredients with ice and strain into ice-filled glass. **TOP** with tonic water.

1½	shot(s)	**Tanqueray London dry gin**
1½	shot(s)	**St-Germain elderflower liqueur**
1	shot(s)	**Cold English breakfast tea**
Top up with		**Tonic water**

Origin: Created in 2006 by Yours Truly (Simon Difford).
Comment: Floral, long and refreshing.

STEALTH

Glass: Shot
Method: Refrigerate ingredients then **LAYER** in chilled glass by carefully pouring in the following order.

½	shot(s)	**Kahlúa coffee liqueur**
½	shot(s)	**Tuaca Italian liqueur**
½	shot(s)	**Baileys Irish cream liqueur**

Origin: Created by Poul Jensen, at St. James', Brighton, England. Another of the B-52 family of drinks, but named after Stealth bombers instead.
Comment: Reminiscent of a vanilla cappuccino.

STEEL BOTTOM

Glass: Collins
Method: POUR ingredients into glass and lightly stir.

1	shot(s)	**Wray & Nephew overproof rum**
Top up with		**Lager**

Origin: A very popular drink in Jamaica.
Comment: For those who like their beer turbo charged.

STEEP FLIGHT

Glass: Collins
Garnish: Apple or pear slice
Method: SHAKE all ingredients with ice and fine strain into ice-filled glass.

1	shot(s)	**Boulard Grand Solage calvados**
1	shot(s)	**Pear flavoured vodka**
1	shot(s)	**Belle de Brillet pear liqueur**
3	shot(s)	**Pressed apple juice**

Origin: Created in 2005 by Yours Truly (Simon Difford). Awarded a Gold in Long Drink category at the Drinks International Bartender's Challenge on 31st May 2006.
Comment: 'Apples and pears' is the cockney rhyming slang for stairs, hence the flavours in this particular flight.

THE STIG UPDATED #8

Glass: Old-fashioned
Garnish: Lime zest twist
Method: STIR all ingredients with ice and strain into ice-filled glass.

¾	shot(s)	**Boulard Grand Solage calvados**
¾	shot(s)	**Macchu pisco**
1	shot(s)	**St-Germain elderflower liqueur**
1	shot(s)	**Sauvignon Blanc wine**

Origin: Created in 2006 by Simon Difford, The Cabinet Room, London, England. Named partly for the 'St-G' on the screw cap of St-Germain and partly after 'The Stig', the mysterious racing driver on the 'Top Gear' TV series.
Comment: Whiter than white but yet mysterious.

STILETTO

Glass: Collins
Garnish: Lime wedge
Method: SHAKE all ingredients with ice and strain into ice-filled glass.

2	shot(s)	**Bulleit bourbon whiskey**
1	shot(s)	**Luxardo Amaretto di Saschira**
2½	shot(s)	**Ocean Spray cranberry juice**
½	shot(s)	**Freshly squeezed lime juice**
¼	shot(s)	**Sugar syrup** (2 sugar to 1 water)

Comment: Long and fruity with a hint of bourbon and almond.

STINGER

Glass: Old-fashioned
Garnish: Mint sprig
Method: SHAKE all ingredients with ice and strain into glass filled with crushed ice. Serve with straws.

2	shot(s)	**Courvoisier V.S.O.P. cognac**
¾	shot(s)	**White crème de menthe liqueur**

Origin: In the classic film 'High Society', Bing Crosby explains to Grace Kelly how the Stinger gained its name: "It's a Stinger. It removes the sting."
Comment: A refreshing, peppermint and cognac digestif.

STONE FENCE NEW #8

Glass: Boston
Garnish: Apple slice
Method: POUR ingredients into ice-filled glass and stir. Serve with straws.

2	shot(s)	**Courvoisier V.S.O.P. cognac**
Top up with		**Dry cider**

Variant: Substitute cognac with calvados, Scotch, bourbon or rum.
Origin: Although the origin of this simple mixed drink and its name are unknown history chronicles its being served at taverns since at least the early 1800s.
Comment: Dry cider fortified and made drier by cognac.

STONE & GRAVEL

Glass: Old-fashioned
Method: POUR ingredients into glass filled with crushed ice and stir.

1	shot(s)	**Wray & Nephew overproof rum**
3	shot(s)	**Stone's original green ginger wine**

Origin: A popular drink in Jamaica.
Comment: Simple, strong and surprisingly good.

STORK CLUB

Glass: Martini
Garnish: Orange zest twist
Method: SHAKE all ingredients with ice and fine strain into chilled glass.

1	shot(s)	**Tanqueray London dry gin**
1	shot(s)	**Cointreau triple sec**
1	shot(s)	**Freshly squeezed orange juice**
½	shot(s)	**Freshly squeezed lime juice**
2	dashes	**Angostura orange bitters** (optional)

Comment: Orange and gin with a souring splash of lime juice.

STRAITS SLING

Glass: Sling
Garnish: Orange slice & cherry on stick (sail)
Method: SHAKE first 6 ingredients with ice and strain into ice-filled glass. TOP with soda, lightly stir and serve with straws.

2	shot(s)	**Tanqueray London dry gin**
½	shot(s)	**Bénédictine D.O.M. liqueur**
½	shot(s)	**Kirsch eau de vie**
1	shot(s)	**Freshly squeezed lemon juice**
2	dashes	**Angostura orange bitters**
2	dashes	**Angostura aromatic bitters**
Top up with		**Soda water** (club soda)

Origin: Thought to be the original name of the Singapore Sling. Conjecture, partly based on a reference to 'Kirsch' in Embury's Fine Art of Mixing Drinks, has it that the drink was originally based on cherry eau de vie and not the cherry liqueur used in most Singapore Sling recipes today.
Comment: Dry cherry and gin come to the fore in this long, refreshing drink.

STRASBERI SLING

Glass: Sling
Garnish: Mint sprig
Method: SHAKE all ingredients with ice and strain into ice-filled glass.

1½	shot(s)	**Raspberry flavoured vodka**
1	shot(s)	**Pimm's No. 1 Cup**
½	shot(s)	**Sugar syrup** (2 sugar to 1 water)
1	shot(s)	**Freshly squeezed lime juice**
3	shot(s)	**Pressed apple juice**

Origin: Created in 2002 by Alex Kammerling, London, England.
Comment: Raspberry and apple combine beautifully in this refreshing drink with its clean citrus tang.

STRAWBERRY & BALSAMIC MOJITO

Glass: Collins
Garnish: Strawberry & lime wedge
Method: MUDDLE strawberries in base of shaker. Add next 5 ingredients, SHAKE with ice and fine strain into chilled glass. TOP with soda.

7	fresh	**Strawberries** (hulled)
2	shot(s)	**Bacardi Superior rum**
¾	shot(s)	**Freshly squeezed lime juice**
¼	shot(s)	**White balsamic vinegar**
½	shot(s)	**Sugar syrup** (2 sugar to 1 water)
12	fresh	**Mint leaves**
Top up with		**Soda water**

Origin: Adapted from a drink created in 2005 by Simon 'Ginger' Warneford at Blanch House, Brighton, England.
Comment: A fruity twist on the classic Mojito.

STRAWBERRY BLONDE NEW #8

Glass: Collins
Garnish: Strawberry on rim
Method: MUDDLE strawberries in base of shaker. Add next 3 ingredients, SHAKE with ice and fine strain into ice-filled glass. TOP with soda and serve with straws.

2	fresh	**Strawberries** (hulled)
2	shot(s)	**Ketel One vodka**
1½	shot(s)	**Freshly squeezed lemon juice**
¾	shot(s)	**Sugar syrup** (2 sugar to 1 water)
Top up with		**Soda water.**

Origin: Created in 2008 by Yours Truly (Simon Difford) at The Cabinet Room, London, England.
Comment: Lurid orange-red in colour and basically alcoholic strawberry flavoured real lemonade.

STRAWBERRY BLONDE MARTINI

Glass: Martini
Garnish: Float basil leaf
Method: MUDDLE basil in mixing glass. Add other ingredients, STIR with ice and fine strain into chilled glass.

4	fresh	**Basil leaves**
2½	shot(s)	**Raspberry flavoured vodka**
½	shot(s)	**Noilly Prat dry vermouth**
½	shot(s)	**Crème de fraise de bois liqueur**
⅛	shot(s)	**Sugar syrup** (2 sugar to 1 water)

Origin: Adapted from a recipe discovered in 2003 at Oxo Tower Bar, London, England.
Comment: Berry vodka dominates with hints of strawberry and basil.

HOW TO MAKE SUGAR SYRUP

To make your own sugar syrup, gradually pour TWO cups of granulated sugar into a saucepan containing ONE cup of hot water. Stir as you pour and carry on stirring and simmering until the sugar is dissolved. Do not let the water even come close to boiling and only simmer for as long as it takes to dissolve the sugar. Allow syrup to cool and pour into an empty bottle. Ideally, you should finely strain your syrup into the bottle to remove any undissolved crystals which could otherwise encourage crystallisation. If kept in a refrigerator this mixture will last for a couple of months.

STRAWBERRY COSMO

Glass: Martini
Garnish: Strawberry on rim
Method: SHAKE all ingredients with ice and fine strain into chilled glass.

2	shot(s)	**Ketel One Citroen vodka**
¾	shot(s)	**Crème de fraise de bois liqueur**
1¼	shot(s)	**Ocean Spray cranberry juice**
½	shot(s)	**Freshly squeezed lime juice**

Origin: Formula by Yours Truly (Simon Difford) in 2004.
Comment: Strawberry liqueur replaces the usual orange liqueur in this contemporary classic.

STRAWBERRY DAIQUIRI

Glass: Martini
Garnish: Strawberry on rim
Method: MUDDLE strawberries in base of shaker. Add other ingredients, **SHAKE** with ice and fine strain into chilled glass.

7	fresh	**Strawberries** (hulled)
2	shot(s)	**Bacardi Superior rum**
½	shot(s)	**Freshly squeezed lime juice**
¼	shot(s)	**Sugar syrup** (2 sugar to 1 water)

Origin: A popular drink in Cuba where it is known as a Daiquiri de Fresa.
Comment: Makes strawberries and cream appear very dull.

THE STRAWBERRY ÉCLAIR

Glass: Shot
Method: SHAKE all ingredients with ice and fine strain into chilled glass.

½	shot(s)	**Frangelico hazelnut liqueur**
½	shot(s)	**Crème de fraise de bois liqueur**
¼	shot(s)	**Freshly squeezed lime juice**

Origin: This drink heralds from Australia where it is a popular shot.
Comment: Far from sophisticated (some would say like Australia) but very appropriately named.

STRAWBERRY FROZEN DAIQUIRI

Glass: Martini
Garnish: Split strawberry
Method: BLEND all ingredients with 6oz scoop of crushed ice.

2	shot(s)	**Bacardi Superior rum**
¾	shot(s)	**Freshly squeezed lime juice**
½	shot(s)	**Sugar syrup** (2 sugar to 1 water)
5	fresh	**Strawberries** (hulled)

Comment: A delicious twist on a classic – Strawberry Mivvi for grown-ups.

STRAWBERRY MARGARITA

Glass: Martini
Garnish: Strawberry on rim
Method: MUDDLE strawberries in base of shaker. Add other ingredients, **SHAKE** with ice and fine strain into chilled glass.

5	fresh	**Strawberries** (hulled)
2	shot(s)	**Don Julio reposado tequila**
1	shot(s)	**Freshly squeezed lime juice**
¾	shot(s)	**Sugar syrup** (2 sugar to 1 water)

Origin: Formula by Yours Truly (Simon Difford) in 2004.
Comment: Fresh strawberries combine well with tequila in this fruity margarita.

STRAWBERRY MARTINI

Glass: Martini
Garnish: Strawberry on rim
Method: MUDDLE strawberries in base of shaker. Add other ingredients, **SHAKE** with ice and fine strain into chilled glass.

5	fresh	**Strawberries** (hulled)
2½	shot(s)	**Ketel One vodka**
½	shot(s)	**Sugar syrup** (2 sugar to 1 water)
2	grinds	**Black pepper**

Origin: Formula by Yours Truly (Simon Difford) in 2004.
Comment: Rich strawberries fortified with vodka and a hint of pepper spice.

STRAWBERRY 'N' BALSAMIC MARTINI

Glass: Martini
Garnish: Strawberry on rim
Method: MUDDLE strawberries in base of shaker. Add other ingredients, **SHAKE** with ice and fine strain into chilled glass.

5	fresh	**Strawberries** (hulled)
2½	shot(s)	**Ketel One vodka**
⅛	shot(s)	**Balsamic vinegar**
½	shot(s)	**Sugar syrup** (2 sugar to 1 water)

Origin: My version of a drink that became popular in London in 2002 and I believe originated in Che.
Comment: The balsamic adds a little extra interest to the fortified strawberries.

STRUDEL MARTINI

Glass: Martini
Garnish: Dust with cinnamon powder
Method: SHAKE all ingredients with ice and fine strain into chilled glass.

1½	shot(s)	**Ketel One vodka**
½	shot(s)	**Noé Pedro Ximénez sherry**
¾	shot(s)	**Pressed apple juice**
½	shot(s)	**Double (heavy) cream**
½	shot(s)	**Milk**

Origin: Created in 2002 by Jason Borthwick, Tiles, Edinburgh, Scotland.
Comment: Still think sherry is just for Granny?

STUPID CUPID

Glass: Martini
Garnish: Lemon zest twist
Method: SHAKE all ingredients with ice and fine strain into chilled glass.

2	shot(s)	**Ketel One Citroen vodka**
½	shot(s)	**Sloe gin liqueur**
1	shot(s)	**Freshly squeezed lime juice**
½	shot(s)	**Sugar syrup** (2 sugar to 1 water)

Comment: Citrussy with subtle sloe gin.

SUBURBAN

Glass: Old-fashioned
Garnish: Orange zest twist
Method: STIR all ingredients with ice and strain into ice-filled glass.

1½	shot(s)	**Bulleit bourbon whiskey**
¾	shot(s)	**Zacapa aged rum**
¾	shot(s)	**Warre's Otima tawny port**
1	dash	**Angostura orange bitters**
1	dash	**Angostura aromatic bitters**

Origin: Created at New York's old Waldorf-Astoria Hotel (the Empire State Building occupies the site today) for James R Keene, a racehorse owner whose steeds ran in the Suburban Handicap at Brooklyn's Sheepshead Bay track.
Comment: An interesting alternative to an Old-fashioned.

SUFFERING BASTARD NEW #8

Glass: Old-fashioned (large)
Garnish: Pineapple cubes and cherry on stick, lime wedge, lengthwise strip cucumber peel, mint sprig
Method: SHAKE all ingredients with ice and strain glass filled with crushed ice.

1	shot(s)	**Bacardi Superior rum**
2	shot(s)	**Martinique agricol rum**
1	shot(s)	**Freshly squeezed lime juice**
½	shot(s)	**Orange curaçao liqueur**
¼	shot(s)	**Almond (orgeat) syrup**
½	shot(s)	**Sugar syrup** (2 sugar to 1 water)

Comment: Pungent, heavily rum laced yet all too easy.
Origin: Adapted from Victor Bergeron's 'Trader Vic's Bartender's Guide' (1972 revised edition).

SUITABLY FRANK

Glass: Shot
Method: Refrigerate ingredients then LAYER in chilled glass by carefully pouring in the following order.

½	shot(s)	**Cuarenta Y Tres (Licor 43) liqueur**
½	shot(s)	**Heering cherry brandy liqueur**
½	shot(s)	**Ketel One vodka**

Comment: Frankly – it's a good shot.

SUMMER BREEZE

Glass: Collins
Garnish: Apple slice
Method: SHAKE all ingredients with ice and strain into ice-filled glass.

2	shot(s)	**Ketel One vodka**
1	shot(s)	**St-Germain elderflower liqueur**
2	shot(s)	**Pressed apple juice**
1	shot(s)	**Ocean Spray cranberry juice**

Origin: Adapted from a drink created in 1998 by Dick Bradsell, London, England.
Comment: Cranberry, apple and elderflower fortified with vodka.

SUMMER ROSE MARTINI

Glass: Martini
Garnish: Red rose petal (edible)
Method: STIR first 3 ingredients with ice and strain into chilled glass. POUR grenadine into the centre of the drink. This should sink and settle to form a red layer in the base of the glass.

1½	shot(s)	**Ketel One vodka**
¾	shot(s)	**White crème de cacao liqueur**
½	shot(s)	**Soho lychee liqueur**
½	shot(s)	**Pomegranate (grenadine) syrup**

Origin: Created in 2003 by Davide Lovison at Isola Bar, London, England.
Comment: This red and white layered drink could have been named War of the Roses. Unless you've a sweet tooth don't mix the factions – sip from the chocolate and lychee top and stop when you hit red.

SUMMER TIME MARTINI

Glass: Martini
Garnish: Kumquat
Method: SHAKE all ingredients with ice and fine strain into chilled glass.

1½	shot(s)	**Tanqueray London dry gin**
1	shot(s)	**Grand Marnier liqueur**
1½	shot(s)	**Freshly squeezed orange juice**
¼	shot(s)	**Pomegranate (grenadine) syrup**

Comment: Smooth, gin laced fruit for a summer's day.

SUMO IN A SIDECAR

Glass: Martini
Garnish: Orange zest twist
Method: SHAKE all ingredients with ice and fine strain into chilled glass.

2½	shot(s)	**Sake**
1	shot(s)	**Bols apricot brandy liqueur**
½	shot(s)	**Freshly squeezed lemon juice**

Comment: Hints of sake but retains the Sidecar style.

SUN KISSED VIRGIN (MOCKTAIL)

Glass: Sling
Garnish: Physalis (cape gooseberry) on rim
Method: SHAKE all ingredients with ice and strain into ice-filled glass.

2	shot(s)	Freshly squeezed orange juice
2	shot(s)	Pressed pineapple juice
1	shot(s)	Freshly squeezed lime juice
½	shot(s)	Almond (orgeat) syrup

Comment: Golden, slightly sweet and very fruity – just like a Sun Kissed Virgin should be. (Sorry.)

THE SUN SALUTATION

Glass: Collins
Garnish: Berries & mint sprig
Method: MUDDLE mint in base of shaker. Add next 3 ingredients, **SHAKE** with ice and fine strain into ice-filled glass. **TOP** with soda.

10	fresh	Mint leaves
1	shot(s)	Ketel One vodka
1½	shot(s)	Soho lychee liqueur
¾	shot(s)	Freshly squeezed lemon juice
Top up with		Soda (club soda)

Origin: Adapted from a recipe by David Nepove, Enrico's Bar & Restaurant, San Francisco.
Comment: Mint with a hint of lychee – long and refreshing.

SUNDOWNER #1

Glass: Martini
Garnish: Orange zest twist
Method: SHAKE all ingredients with ice and fine strain into chilled glass.

2	shot(s)	Courvoisier V.S.O.P. cognac
½	shot(s)	Grand Marnier liqueur
½	shot(s)	Freshly squeezed orange juice
¼	shot(s)	Freshly squeezed lemon juice
¾	shot(s)	Chilled mineral water (omit if wet ice)

Variant: Red Lion
Origin: This cocktail is popular in South Africa where it is made with locally produced brandy and a local orange liqueur called Van der Hum'.
Comment: Cognac and orange served 'up'.

SUNDOWNER #2

Glass: Old-fashioned
Garnish: Mint sprig
Method: SHAKE all ingredients with ice and strain into ice-filled glass.

1½	shot(s)	Southern Comfort liqueur
¾	shot(s)	Grand Marnier liqueur
2	shot(s)	Sauvignon Blanc wine

Origin: Adapted from a cocktail created in 2002 by Gary Regis at Bed Bar, London, England.
Comment: Subtle meld of summer and citrus flavours.

SUNNY BREEZE

Glass: Collins
Garnish: Half orange slice
Method: SHAKE all ingredients with ice and strain into glass filled with crushed ice.

1½	shot(s)	Pernod anis
½	shot(s)	Cointreau triple sec
½	shot(s)	Grand Marnier liqueur
3	shot(s)	Freshly squeezed grapefruit juice

Origin: Created in 2003 by Yours Truly (Simon Difford).
Comment: A suitably named refreshing long drink with an adult dry edge and kick.

SUNSHINE COCKTAIL #1

Glass: Martini
Garnish: Pineapple wedge on rim
Method: SHAKE all ingredients with ice and fine strain into chilled glass.

1½	shot(s)	Bacardi Superior rum
1½	shot(s)	Noilly Prat dry vermouth
1½	shot(s)	Pressed pineapple juice
⅛	shot(s)	Pomegranate (grenadine) syrup

Origin: Adapted from a recipe in my 1949 copy of Esquire's Handbook For Hosts.
Comment: Light, fruity and a tad on the sweet side, but could well brighten your day.

SUNSHINE COCKTAIL #2

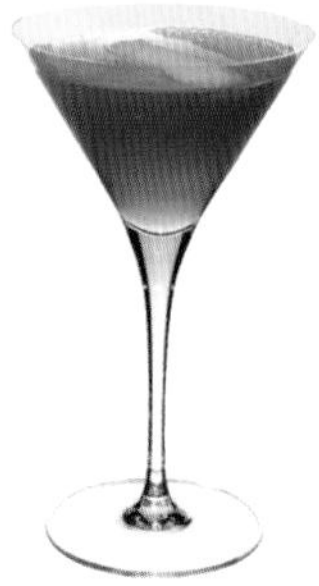

Glass: Martini
Garnish: Lemon zest twist
Method: SHAKE all ingredients with ice and fine strain into chilled glass.

1½	shot(s)	Bacardi Superior rum
1½	shot(s)	Noilly Prat dry vermouth
¼	shot(s)	Crème de cassis liqueur
¼	shot(s)	Freshly squeezed lemon juice

Origin: Adapted from a recipe in Harry Craddock's 1930 Savoy Cocktail Book.
Comment: More a sunset but fruity, flavoursome and well-balanced all the same.

SUNSTROKE

Glass: Martini
Garnish: Orange zest twist (round to make sun)
Method: SHAKE all ingredients with ice and fine strain into chilled glass.

1	shot(s)	Ketel One vodka
1	shot(s)	Cointreau triple sec
2	shot(s)	Freshly squeezed grapefruit juice

Comment: Fruity but balanced. One to sip in the shade.

SUPERMINTY-CHOCOLATINI

Glass: Martini
Garnish: Chocolate powder rim
Method: SHAKE all ingredients with ice and fine strain into chilled glass.

2	shot(s)	**Ketel One vodka**
1	shot(s)	**White crème de cacao liqueur**
1	shot(s)	**White crème de menthe liqueur**

Comment: Obvious but nicely flavoured.

SUPPERTIME DAIQUIRÍ NEW #8

Glass: Martini
Garnish: Lime wedge
Method: STIR preserve and rum in base of shaker to dissolve preserve. Add other ingredients, **SHAKE** with ice and fine strain into chilled glass.

3	spoons	**Rhubarb & orange preserve**
2	shot(s)	**Bacardi Superior rum**
¾	shot(s)	**Freshly squeezed lime juice**

Comment: Rhubarb and orange influence this Daiquiri twist.
Origin: Created in 2008 by Jamie MacDonald at Tigerlily, Edinburgh, England in honour of his good friend Sam Kershaw.

THE SURFER NEW #8

Glass: Collins
Garnish: Lemon slice
Method: POUR lemonade into ice-filled glass (approx two-thirds full). **FLOAT** cognac over lemonade. Serve with straws and instruct drinker to stir ingredients together before drinking.

4	shot(s)	**Fever Tree English lemonade**
2	shot(s)	**Courvoisier V.S.O.P cognac**

Origin: A 2008 adaptation of a Cognac Surfer by Yours Truly (Simon Difford). The original is made by floating cognac on mineral water.
Comment: Good quality lemonade adds lemon freshness and turns cognac into a refreshing afternoons drink.

SURFER ON A.C.D.

Glass: Shot
Method: SHAKE first 2 ingredients with ice and fine strain into chilled glass. **FLOAT** Jägermeister.

½	shot(s)	**Malibu coconut rum liqueur**
¾	shot(s)	**Pressed pineapple juice**
¼	shot(s)	**Jägermeister liqueur**

Comment: The spirity herbal topping counters the sweet coconut and pineapple base.

THE SUZY WONG MARTINI

Glass: Martini
Garnish: Orange zest twist
Method: MUDDLE basil in base of shaker. Add other ingredients, **SHAKE** with ice and fine strain into chilled glass.

7	fresh	**Basil leaves**
2	shot(s)	**Orange-infused Ketel One vodka**
½	shot(s)	**Grand Marnier liqueur**
1	shot(s)	**Freshly squeezed orange juice**
½	shot(s)	**Freshly squeezed lime juice**
¼	shot(s)	**Sugar syrup** (2 sugar to 1 water)

Origin: Discovered in 2005 at Suzy Wong, Amsterdam, The Netherlands.
Comment: Fresh tasting orange with a hint of basil.

SWAMP WATER

Glass: Collins
Garnish: Lime wedge & mint leaf
Method: SHAKE all ingredients with ice and strain into ice-filled glass.

1½	shot(s)	**Green Chartreuse liqueur**
4	shot(s)	**Pressed pineapple juice**
½	shot(s)	**Freshly squeezed lime juice**

Comment: Long and refreshing - the herbal taste of Chartreuse combined with the fruitiness of pineapple.

SWEDISH BLUE MARTINI

Glass: Martini
Garnish: Orange peel twist
Method: SHAKE all ingredients with ice and fine strain into chilled glass.

2	shot(s)	**Ketel One vodka**
½	shot(s)	**Bols blue curaçao liqueur**
½	shot(s)	**Peach Tree peach schnapps**
¼	shot(s)	**Freshly squeezed lime juice**
¼	shot(s)	**Sugar syrup** (2 sugar to 1 water)
2	dashes	**Angostura orange bitters**
½	shot(s)	**Chilled mineral water** (omit if wet ice)

Origin: Created in 1999 by Timothy Schofield at Teatro, London, England.
Comment: A fruity, blue concoction laced with vodka. Slightly sweet.

SWEDISH RUM PUNCH NEW #8

Glass: Old-fashioned
Garnish: Lime wedge
Method: SHAKE all ingredients with ice and strain into ice-filled glass.

1½	shot(s)	**Zacapa aged rum**
¾	shot(s)	**Swedish Punch**
½	shot(s)	**Freshly squeezed lime juice**

Origin: Created in 2008 by Yours Truly (Simon Difford).
Comment: A flavoursome Daiquiri-style with the subtle spice of Swedish punch.

S

SWEET LOUISE

Glass: Martini
Garnish: Blackberry
Method: Cut passion fruit in half and scoop out flesh into shaker. Add other ingredients, **SHAKE** with ice and fine strain into chilled glass.

1	fresh	**Passion fruit**
1	shot(s)	**Raspberry flavoured vodka**
½	shot(s)	**Chambord black raspberry liqueur**
½	shot(s)	**Luxardo Amaretto di Saschira**
¾	shot(s)	**Freshly squeezed lime juice.**
¼	shot(s)	**Pomegranate (grenadine) syrup**

Origin: Created in 2000 at Monte's Club, London, England
Comment: Lots of contrasting flavours but she's a sweet girl.

> 'IT WAS MY UNCLE GEORGE WHO DISCOVERED THAT ALCOHOL WAS A FOOD WELL IN ADVANCE OF MEDICAL THOUGHT.'
> P. G. WODEHOUSE

SWEET SCIENCE

Glass: Martini
Garnish: Orange zest twist
Method: **SHAKE** all ingredients with ice and fine strain into chilled glass.

2	shot(s)	**Johnnie Walker Scotch whisky**
¾	shot(s)	**Drambuie liqueur**
1½	shot(s)	**Freshly squeezed orange juice**

Origin: Created by Charles Schumann, Munich, Germany.
Comment: Herbal Scotch and orange.

SWEET TART

Glass: Sling
Garnish: Sugar rim & redcurrants
Method: **SHAKE** first 4 ingredients with ice and strain into ice-filled glass. **TOP** with lemonade.

2	shot(s)	**Ketel One vodka**
¾	shot(s)	**Chambord black raspberry liqueur**
¾	shot(s)	**Luxardo Amaretto di Saschira**
1	shot(s)	**Freshly squeezed lime juice**
Top up with		**Lemonade/Sprite/7-Up**

Comment: As the name suggests, a fruity combination of sweet and sour.

SWIZZLE (GENERIC NAME) UPDATED #8

Glass: Old-fashioned
Garnish: Fruit or mint sprigs
Method: **POUR** ingredients into glass filled with crushed ice. **SWIZZLE** with a swizzle stick and serve with straws.

2	shot(s)	**Spirit** (rum, brandy, gin, whisk(e)y etc.)
½	shot(s)	**Fresh lemon or lime juice**
¼	shot(s)	**Sugar syrup** (2 sugar to 1 water)

Variants: With rum try orgeat syrup or Velvet Falernum in place of the sugar syrup. With whiskey try Chartreuse.
Origin: Swizzles originated in the Caribbean. They are sour style drinks that, distinctively, must be churned with a swizzle stick.

Originally a twig from a species of tree called Quararibea turbinata which grow in the southern islands of the Caribbean. These trees have forked branches, which make perfect swizzle sticks. Today swizzle sticks are usually made of metal or plastic and have several blades or fingers attached to the base at right angles to the shaft. To use one, simply immerse the blades in the drink, hold the shaft between the palms of both hands and rotate the stick rapidly by sliding your hands back and forth against it. If you do not have a bona fide swizzle stick, use a barspoon in the same manner. Swizzles can be served as short drinks or lengthened with mineral water.
Comment: Match the appropriate citrus juice and sweetener to your spirit and you'll have a superb drink.

TABU NEW #8

Glass: Coconut shell or tiki mug
Garnish: Pineapple cubes & cherry on stick, mint sprig
Method: **BLEND** all ingredients with 12oz scoop crushed ice.

1	shot(s)	**Bacardi Superior rum**
1	shot(s)	**Ketel One vodka**
1½	shot(s)	**Pressed pineapple juice**
½	shot(s)	**Freshly squeezed lemon juice**
¼	shot(s)	**Sugar syrup** (2 sugar to 1 water)

Origin: Adapted from Victor Bergeron's 'Trader Vic's Bartender's Guide' (1972 revised edition) where Vic states the drink "originated in Seattle".
Comment: Ice-cold fresh pineapple laced with rum and vodka with a splash of citrus.

TAHITIAN HONEY BEE NEW #8

Glass: Martini
Garnish: Lemon zest twist
Method: **STIR** honey with rum in base of shaker s as to dissolve honey. Add lemon juice, **SHAKE** with ice and fine strain into chilled glass.

2	shot(s)	**Bacardi Superior rum**
2	spoons	**Runny honey**
½	shot(s)	**Freshly squeezed lemon juice**

Origin: Adapted from Victor Bergeron's 'Trader Vic's Bartender's Guide' (1972 revised edition).
Comment: Basically a honey Daiquiri – very tasty it is too.

TAILOR MADE

Glass: Martini
Garnish: Grapefruit zest twist
Method: **STIR** honey with bourbon in base of shaker to dissolve honey. Add other ingredients, **SHAKE** with ice and fine strain into chilled glass.

1	spoon	**Runny honey**
1½	shot(s)	**Bulleit bourbon whiskey**
¼	shot(s)	**Velvet Falernum liqueur**
1	shot(s)	**Freshly squeezed grapefruit juice**
1	shot(s)	**Ocean Spray cranberry juice**

Origin: Created by Dale DeGroff, New York City, USA.
Comment: Light, balanced fruit and bourbon.

TAINTED CHERRY

Glass: Martini
Garnish: Maraschino cherry
Method: **SHAKE** all ingredients with ice and fine strain into chilled glass.

1¾	shot(s)	**Ketel One vodka**
¾	shot(s)	**Heering cherry brandy liqueur**
1¾	shot(s)	**Freshly squeezed orange juice**

Comment: Orange and cherry combine to produce a flavour rather like amaretto.

TANGO MARTINI #1 UPDATED #8

Glass: Martini
Garnish: Orange zest twist
Method: **SHAKE** all ingredients with ice and fine strain into chilled glass.

1½	shot(s)	**Tanqueray London dry gin**
½	shot(s)	**Cointreau triple sec**
½	shot(s)	**Noilly Prat dry vermouth**
½	shot(s)	**Martini Rosso sweet vermouth**
1	shot(s)	**Freshly squeezed orange juice**

Comment: Balanced and complex with hints of gin and orange.
Origin: Adapted from a recipe in Harry Craddock's 1930 Savoy Cocktail Book. Harry McElhone's 1929 'ABC of Cocktails' credits this drinks creation to Harry, a bartender at Palermo, Rue Fontaine, Paris.

TANGO MARTINI #2

Glass: Martini
Garnish: Orange zest twist
Method: **SHAKE** all ingredients with ice and fine strain into chilled glass.

1¾	shot(s)	**Tanqueray London dry gin**
¾	shot(s)	**Passoã passion fruit liqueur**
2	shot(s)	**Freshly squeezed grapefruit juice**
¼	shot(s)	**Sugar syrup** (2 sugar to 1 water)

Origin: Adapted from a drink discovered in 2003 at the Bellagio, Las Vegas, USA.
Comment: Floral and balanced.

TANTRIS SIDECAR NO.1 UPDATED #8

Glass: Martini
Garnish: Lemon zest twist
Method: **SHAKE** all ingredients with ice and fine strain into chilled glass.

1	shot(s)	**Courvoisier V.S.O.P. cognac**
½	shot(s)	**Boulard Grand Solage calvados**
½	shot(s)	**Cointreau triple sec**
¼	shot(s)	**Green Chartreuse liqueur**
¼	shot(s)	**Pressed pineapple juice**
½	shot(s)	**Freshly squeezed lemon juice**
¼	shot(s)	**Sugar syrup** (2 sugar to 1 water)

Origin: Created in the late 1990s by Audrey Saunders at Bemelmans Bar at The Carlyle Hotel, New York City, USA.
Variant: Omit calvados and replace with an extra half shot cognac. An adaptation demonstrated by Audrey at a Cognac Summit on 22 January 2008.
Comment: A Sidecar with extra interest courtesy of Chartreuse, pineapple and Calvados.

TARRABERRY'TINI

Glass: Martini
Garnish: Tarragon sprig
Method: **MUDDLE** tarragon in base of shaker. Add other ingredients, **SHAKE** with ice and fine strain into chilled glass.

2	sprigs	**Fresh tarragon**
1½	shot(s)	**Cranberry flavoured vodka**
¼	shot(s)	**Pernod anis**
2	shot(s)	**Ocean Spray cranberry juice**
¼	shot(s)	**Freshly squeezed lemon juice**

Origin: Created in 2003 by Yours Truly (Simon Difford).
Comment: Cranberry with subtle hints of tarragon and lemon.

> ## 'WORK IS THE CURSE OF THE DRINKING CLASSES'.
> OSCAR WILDE

TARTE AUX POMMES

Glass: Collins
Garnish: Apple chevron
Method: **SHAKE** all ingredients with ice and strain into ice-filled glass.

1	shot(s)	**Boulard Grand Solage calvados**
½	shot(s)	**Crème de cassis liqueur**
¼	shot(s)	**Goldschläger cinnamon schnapps**
4	shot(s)	**Ocean Spray cranberry juice**
3	dashes	**Angostura aromatic bitters**

Origin: Created in 2001 by Jamie Stephenson at The Lock, Manchester, England.
Comment: Rich in flavour and well balanced.

TARTE TATIN MARTINI

Glass: Martini
Garnish: Cinnamon dust
Method: SHAKE first 3 ingredients with ice and strain into chilled glass. **SHAKE** cream with ice and carefully pour so as to **LAYER** over drink.

2	shot(s)	Vanilla-infused Ketel One vodka
¾	shot(s)	Berentzen apple schnapps
¾	shot(s)	Cartron caramel liqueur
2	shot(s)	Double (heavy) cream

Origin: Created in 2003 by Yours Truly (Simon Difford). The name means a tart of caramelised apples cooked under a pastry lid, a dish created by the Tatin sisters.
Comment: A creamy top hides a vanilla, apple and caramel combo.

TARTINI

Glass: Martini
Garnish: Raspberry
Method: MUDDLE raspberries in base of shaker. Add other ingredients, **SHAKE** with ice and fine strain into chilled glass.

12	fresh	Raspberries
2	shot(s)	Raspberry flavoured vodka
½	shot(s)	Chambord black raspberry liqueur
1½	shot(s)	Ocean Spray cranberry juice

Origin: Adapted from a cocktail I found at Soho Grand, New York City, USA.
Comment: Rich raspberry flavour, well balanced with bite.

TATANKA

Glass: Old-fashioned
Garnish: Apple slice
Method: SHAKE all ingredients with ice and strain into ice-filled glass.

| 2 | shot(s) | Zubrówka bison vodka |
| 2½ | shot(s) | Pressed apple juice |

Origin: This Polish drink takes its name from the film 'Dances with Wolves' (1990). Tatanka is a Native American word for buffalo and refers to the bison grass flavoured vodka the cocktail is based on.
Comment: The taste of this excellent drink (which is equally good served straight-up) is a little reminiscent of Earl Grey tea.

TATANKA ROYALE

Glass: Flute
Garnish: Apple slice
Method: SHAKE first 2 ingredients with ice and fine strain into chilled glass. **TOP** with champagne.

1	shot(s)	Zubrówka bison vodka
1	shot(s)	Pressed apple juice
Top up with		Perrier Jouet brut champagne

Origin: Discovered in 2004 at Indigo Yard, Edinburgh, Scotland.
Comment: Champagne with a subtle, grassy hint of apple.

TAWNY-TINI

Glass: Martini
Garnish: Orange zest twist
Method: SHAKE all ingredients with ice and fine strain into chilled glass.

2	shot(s)	Ketel One vodka
2	shot(s)	Warre's Otima tawny port
¼	shot(s)	Maple syrup

Comment: Dry yet rich. Port combines wonderfully with the maple syrup and is further fortified by the grainy vodka.

TEDDY BEAR'TINI

Glass: Martini
Garnish: Pear slice
Method: SHAKE all ingredients with ice and fine strain into chilled glass.

1½	shot(s)	Belle de Brillet pear liqueur
¾	shot(s)	Berentzen apple schnapps
1½	shot(s)	Pressed apple juice
1	pinch	Ground cinnamon

Origin: Created in 2002 at The Borough, Edinburgh, Scotland. Originally named after a well-known cockney duo but renamed after the rhyming slang for pear.
Comment: Beautifully balanced apple and pear with a hint of cinnamon spice.

TENNER MARTINI NEW #8

Glass: Martini/Coupette
Garnish: Grapefruit zest twist
Method: STIR all ingredients with ice and strain into chilled glass.

2	shot(s)	Tanqueray London dry gin
1	shot(s)	Noilly Prat dry vermouth
2	dashes	Fee Brothers grapefruit bitters

Comment: Very wet, aromatic Martini.

TENNESSEE BERRY MULE

Glass: Collins
Garnish: Three raspberries
Method: MUDDLE raspberries in base of shaker. Add next 4 ingredients, **SHAKE** with ice and strain into ice-filled glass. **TOP** with ginger beer, lightly stir and serve with straws.

8	fresh	Raspberries
1½	shot(s)	Jack Daniel's Tennessee whiskey
1	shot(s)	Luxardo Amaretto di Saschira
1½	shot(s)	Ocean Spray cranberry juice
½	shot(s)	Freshly squeezed lime juice
Top up with		Ginger beer

Origin: Adapted in 2003 from a recipe Alex Kammerling created for TGI Friday's UK. Named partly for the ingredients and partly as a reference to Jack Daniel's proprietor (and nephew), Lemuel Motlow, who took up mule trading during Prohibition.
Comment: A berry rich cocktail laced with whiskey, flavoured with amaretto and topped with ginger beer.

TENNESSEE ICED TEA

Glass: Sling
Garnish: Lemon wedge on rim
Method: SHAKE first 6 ingredients with ice and strain into ice-filled glass. **TOP** with Coca-Cola and serve with straws.

1	shot(s)	**Jack Daniel's Tennessee whiskey**
½	shot(s)	**Bacardi Superior rum**
½	shot(s)	**Ketel One vodka**
½	shot(s)	**Cointreau triple sec**
¾	shot(s)	**Freshly squeezed lemon juice**
¼	shot(s)	**Sugar syrup** (2 sugar to 1 water)
Top up with		**Coca-Cola**

Comment: JD and cola with extra interest courtesy of several other spirits and lemon juice.

TENNESSEE RUSH

Glass: Collins
Garnish: Lime wedge
Method: SHAKE all ingredients with ice and strain into ice-filled glass.

2	shot(s)	**Jack Daniel's Tennessee whiskey**
1	shot(s)	**Mandarine Napoléon liqueur**
2½	shot(s)	**Ocean Spray cranberry juice**
½	shot(s)	**Freshly squeezed lime juice**

Comment: This ruby red cocktail is long, fruity, refreshing and not too sweet.

TEQUILA FIZZ

Glass: Sling
Garnish: Orange zest twist
Method: SHAKE first 4 ingredients with ice and strain into ice-filled glass. **TOP** with lemonade.

2	shot(s)	**Don Julio reposado tequila**
1	shot(s)	**Freshly squeezed orange juice**
1	shot(s)	**Freshly squeezed lime juice**
½	shot(s)	**Sugar syrup** (2 sugar to 1 water)
Top up with		**Lemonade/Sprite/7-Up**

Comment: Refreshing with lingering lime.

TEQUILA GIMLET NEW #8

Glass: Martini
Garnish: Lime wedge on rim
Method: STIR all ingredients with ice and strain into chilled glass.

2½	shot(s)	**Don Julio reposado tequila**
¾	shot(s)	**Rose's lime cordial**

Comment: Tequila flavoured and slightly sweetened by lime cordial.

TEQUILA MOCKINGBIRD

Glass: Martini
Garnish: Mint leaf
Method: SHAKE all ingredients with ice and fine strain into chilled glass.

2	shot(s)	**Don Julio reposado tequila**
½	shot(s)	**Green crème de menthe liqueur**
½	shot(s)	**Freshly squeezed lime juice**
⅛	shot(s)	**Sugar syrup** (2 sugar to 1 water)

Variation: With white crème de menthe instead of green crème de menthe.
Origin: Named after Harper Lee's 1960 novel 'To Kill a Mockingbird', this is thought to have been created some time in the 1960s. Genius.
Comment: Minty tequila.

TEQUILA SLAMMER UPDATED #8

Glass: Shot
Method: POUR tequila into glass and then carefully **LAYER** with champagne. The drinker should hold and cover the top of the glass with the palm of their hand so as to grip it firmly and seal the contents inside. Then they should briskly pick the glass up and slam it down (not so hard as to break the glass), then quickly gulp the drink down in one while it is still fizzing.

1	shot(s)	**Don Julio reposado tequila**
1	shot(s)	**Perrier Jouet brut champagne**

Variants: With cream soda or ginger ale.
Origin: Originally topped with ginger ale and not champagne, this infamous libation is thought to have started out as a Hell's Angel drink – it needs no ice and can be carried in a bike bag.
The simplest slammer is a lick of salt, a shot of tequila and then a bite of lemon (or lime). A Bermuda Slammer involves straight tequila, salt, a slice of lemon and a partner: one has to lick the salt off the other one's neck and bite the lemon (held between their partner's teeth) before downing a shot of tequila.
To quote Victor Bergeron (Trader Vic), "You know, this rigmarole with a pinch of salt and lemon juice and tequila - in whatever order - was originally for a purpose: It's hot in Mexico. People dehydrate themselves. And they need more salt. Here, it's not so hot, and we don't need salt in the same way. So you can drink tequila straight right out of the bottle, if you want to."

TEQUILA SMASH

Glass: Old-fashioned
Garnish: Mint sprig
Method: SHAKE all ingredients with ice and fine strain into ice-filled glass.

7	fresh	**Mint leaves**
2	shot(s)	**Don Julio reposado tequila**
¼	shot(s)	**Agave syrup**

Origin: Adapted from the classic Brandy Smash.
Comment: Simple, not sweet: a great way to appreciate quality tequila.

TEQUILA SOUR

Glass: Old-fashioned
Garnish: Lime zest twist
Method: SHAKE all ingredients with ice and fine strain into ice-filled glass.

2	shot(s)	**Don Julio reposado tequila**
1	shot(s)	**Freshly squeezed lime juice**
½	shot(s)	**Sugar syrup** (2 sugar to 1 water)
½	fresh	**Egg white**

Comment: A standard sour but with tequila zing.

TEQUILA SUNRISE

Glass: Collins
Garnish: Orange slice & cherry
Method: SHAKE first 2 ingredients with ice and strain into ice-filled glass. **POUR** grenadine in a circle around the top of the drink. (It will sink to create a sunrise effect.)

2	shot(s)	**Don Julio reposado tequila**
3	shot(s)	**Freshly squeezed orange juice**
¾	shot(s)	**Pomegranate (grenadine) syrup**

Comment: Everyone has heard of this drink, but those who have tried it will wonder why it's so famous.

TEQUILA SUNSET

Glass: Sling
Garnish: Lemon slice
Method: STIR honey with tequila in base of shaker until honey dissolves. Add other ingredients, **SHAKE** with ice and strain into ice-filled glass.

7	spoons	**Runny honey**
2	shot(s)	**Don Julio reposado tequila**
2	shot(s)	**Freshly squeezed lemon juice**

Comment: A good sweet and sour balance with subtle honey hints.

TEQUILA'TINI

Glass: Martini
Garnish: Lime zest twist
Method: SHAKE all ingredients with ice and fine strain into chilled glass.

2	shot(s)	**Don Julio reposado tequila**
1	shot(s)	**Noilly Prat dry vermouth**
3	dashes	**Angostura aromatic bitters**
½	shot(s)	**Sugar syrup** (2 sugar to 1 water)

Comment: If you like tequila and strong drinks – this is for you.

TERESA

Glass: Martini
Garnish: Lime wedge on rim
Method: SHAKE all ingredients with ice and fine strain into chilled glass.

2	shot(s)	**Campari Bitter**
¾	shot(s)	**Crème de cassis liqueur**
1	shot(s)	**Freshly squeezed lime juice**

Origin: Created by Rafael Ballesteros of Spain, this recipe is taken from The Joy of Mixology by Gary Regan.
Comment: Bold, sweet and sour.

TESTAROSSA

Glass: Collins
Garnish: Orange slice
Method: POUR all ingredients into ice-filled glass, lightly stir and serve with straws.

1½	shot(s)	**Campari Bitter**
1½	shot(s)	**Ketel One vodka**
Top up with		**Soda water** (club soda)

Comment: Campari and soda with some oomph.

TEST PILOT

Glass: Old-fashioned
Garnish: Lime zest twist
Method: SHAKE all ingredients with ice and fine strain into ice-filled glass.

1½	shot(s)	**Zacapa aged rum**
¾	shot(s)	**Bacardi Superior rum**
¼	shot(s)	**Cointreau triple sec**
¼	shot(s)	**Velvet Falernum liqueur**
¼	shot(s)	**Freshly squeezed lemon juice**

Origin: Adapted from a recipe in the 1947-72 Trader Vic's Bartender's Guide by Victor Bergeron.
Comment: A fruity, sophisticated Daiquiri with hints of almond and spicy clove, served short over ice.

TEX COLLINS

Glass: Collins
Garnish: Lemon slice
Method: STIR honey with gin in base of shaker to dissolve honey. Add grapefruit juice, **SHAKE** with ice and strain into ice-filled glass. **TOP** with soda water.

2	shot(s)	**Tanqueray London dry gin**
2	spoons	**Runny honey**
2	shot(s)	**Freshly squeezed grapefruit juice**
Top up with		**Soda water** (club soda)

Origin: Adapted from a recipe in the 1949 edition of Esquire's Handbook For Hosts.
Comment: A dry, tart blend of grapefruit and gin.

TEXAS ICED TEA

Glass: Sling
Garnish: Lemon wedge on rim
Method: **SHAKE** first 6 ingredients with ice and strain into ice-filled glass. **TOP** with Coca-Cola.

1	shot(s)	**Don Julio reposado tequila**
½	shot(s)	**Bacardi Superior rum**
½	shot(s)	**Ketel One vodka**
½	shot(s)	**Cointreau triple sec**
¾	shot(s)	**Freshly squeezed lemon juice**
¼	shot(s)	**Sugar syrup** (2 sugar to 1 water)
Top up with		**Coca-Cola**

Comment: My favourite of the Iced Tea family of drinks. The tequila shines through.

TEXSUN

Glass: Martini
Garnish: Lemon zest twist
Method: **SHAKE** all ingredients with ice and fine strain into chilled glass.

1½	shot(s)	**Bulleit bourbon whiskey**
1½	shot(s)	**Noilly Prat dry vermouth**
1½	shot(s)	**Freshly squeezed grapefruit juice**

Origin: Adapted from a recipe in the 1949 edition of Esquire's Handbook for Hosts.
Comment: Bone dry with fruity herbal hints.

THAI LADY

Glass: Martini
Garnish: Lemon zest twist
Method: **MUDDLE** lemongrass in base of shaker. Add other ingredients, **SHAKE** with ice and fine strain into chilled glass.

2	inches	**Fresh lemongrass** (chopped)
2	shot(s)	**Tanqueray London dry gin**
½	shot(s)	**Cointreau triple sec**
1	shot(s)	**Freshly squeezed lemon juice**
¼	shot(s)	**Sugar syrup** (2 sugar to 1 water)

Origin: Adapted from a recipe created by Jamie Terrell, London, England.
Comment: A White Lady with the added flavour of lemongrass.

THAI LEMONADE (MOCKTAIL)

Glass: Collins
Garnish: Lime wedge
Method: **MUDDLE** coriander in base of shaker. Add next 2 ingredients, **SHAKE** with ice and fine strain into ice-filled glass. **TOP** with ginger beer.

5	sprigs	**Fresh coriander**
2	shot(s)	**Freshly squeezed lime juice**
½	shot(s)	**Almond (orgeat) syrup**
Top up with		**Ginger beer**

Origin: Adapted from a drink created in 2005 by Charlotte Voisey, London, England.
Comment: Lime lemonade with Thai influences courtesy of ginger, almond and coriander.

THAI RED DAIQUIRI NEW #8

Glass: Old-fashioned
Garnish: Slice of pepper in glass
Method: **MUDDLE** pepper in base of shaker. Add other ingredients, **SHAKE** with ice and fine strain into chilled glass.

¼	ring	**Red bell pepper**
3	fresh	**Thai basil leaves**
2	shot(s)	**Zacapa aged rum**
½	shot(s)	**Fresh coconut water**
½	shot(s)	**Freshly squeezed lime juice**
¼	shot(s)	**Sugar syrup** (2 sugar to 1 water)

Comment: Aged rum, delicately spiced by red pepper and basil.
Origin: Created in December 2008 by Yours Truly (Simon Difford) at the Cabinet Room, London, England.

THOMAS BLOOD MARTINI

Glass: Martini
Garnish: Apple wedge on rim
Method: **STIR** honey with vodka in base of shaker until honey dissolves. Add other ingredients, **SHAKE** with ice and fine strain into chilled glass.

2	spoons	**Runny honey**
1	shot(s)	**Ketel One vodka**
1	shot(s)	**Krupnik honey liqueur**
1	shot(s)	**Berentzen apple schnapps**
1	shot(s)	**Freshly squeezed lemon juice**

Comment: An appealing, honey led mélange of sweet and sour.

THREE MILER

Glass: Martini
Garnish: Lemon zest twist
Method: **SHAKE** all ingredients with ice and fine strain into chilled glass.

1½	shot(s)	**Courvoisier V.S.O.P. cognac**
1½	shot(s)	**Bacardi Superior rum**
½	shot(s)	**Freshly squeezed lemon juice**
½	shot(s)	**Pomegranate (grenadine) syrup**

Origin: Adapted from the Three Miller Cocktail in the 1930 Savoy Cocktail Book.
Comment: A seriously strong drink, in flavour and in alcohol.

THREESOME

Glass: Martini
Garnish: Pineapple wedge on rim
Method: **SHAKE** all ingredients with ice and fine strain into chilled glass.

1½	shot(s)	**Boulard Grand Solage calvados**
1	shot(s)	**Cointreau triple sec**
½	shot(s)	**Pernod anis**
1½	shot(s)	**Pressed pineapple juice**

Origin: Adapted from a drink discovered in 2002 at Circus Bar, London, England.
Comment: An interesting meld of apple, orange, anise and pineapple.

'ALWAYS DO SOBER WHAT YOU
SAID YOU'D DO WHEN YOU
WERE DRUNK. THAT WILL
TEACH YOU TO KEEP YOUR
MOUTH SHUT!'
CHARLES SCRIBNER, JR.

TI PUNCH UPDATED #8

Glass: Old-fashioned
Garnish: Lime disc (see note below)
Method: POUR the rum and sugar into glass. Then
SQUEEZE the lime disc between finger and thumb
before dropping into the drink. This expresses the
oil from the skin and little of the juice into the Ti
Punch. Lastly **STIR** and consider adding two or
three ice cubes.

1½	shot(s)	**Martinique agricole rum**
¼	shot(s)	**Martinique cane juice syrup**
1	fresh	**Lime disc** (see note below)

Note: Traditionally the limes used to make this drink
are not cut into slices or wedges. Instead a round
disc is cut from the side of the fruit. These are cut
large enough that some of the fruits pulp backs the
peel on the disc.
Origin: Named Ti from the French word 'Petit', this
is literally a small rum punch: unlike most rum
punches, it is not lengthened with water or juice. It
is popular in the French islands of Martinique,
Guadeloupe, Réunion and Maurice where it's often
drunk straight down without adding ice and chased
by a large glass of chilled water (called a 'crase' in
Martinique). These islands are also home to Rhum
Agricole (a style of rum distilled only from sugar
cane juice and usually bottled at 50% alc./vol.)
Comment: This drink only works with authentic
agricole rum and sugar cane juice. On its native
islands it is usual to use rhum blanc (unaged white
agricole rum) during the day and rhum vieux (aged
agricole rum) during the evening.

THRILLER FROM VANILLA

Glass: Martini
Garnish: Half vanilla pod
Method: SHAKE all ingredients with ice and fine
strain into chilled glass.

¾	shot(s)	**Vanilla-infused Ketel One vodka**
¾	shot(s)	**Tanqueray London dry gin**
½	shot(s)	**Cointreau triple sec**
2	shot(s)	**Freshly squeezed orange juice**

Origin: Adapted from a drink discovered in 2003 at
Oporto, Leeds, England. The 'Thriller in Manila' was
the name given to the 1975 heavyweight fight
between Muhammad Ali and Smokin' Joe Frazier.
Comment: Orange and creamy vanilla fortified with a
hint of gin.

THRILLER MARTINI

Glass: Martini
Garnish: Orange zest twist
Method: SHAKE all ingredients with ice and fine
strain into chilled glass.

2½	shot(s)	**Johnnie Walker Scotch whisky**
¾	shot(s)	**Stone's orginal green ginger wine**
¾	shot(s)	**Freshly squeezed orange juice**
⅛	shot(s)	**Sugar syrup** (2 sugar to 1 water)

Comment: Spiced Scotch with a hint of orange.

TICK-TACK MARTINI

Glass: Martini
Garnish: Three Tic-Tac mints
Method: STIR all ingredients with ice and strain
into chilled glass.

2	shot(s)	**Ketel One vodka**
½	shot(s)	**Luxardo Sambuca dei Cesari**
½	shot(s)	**White crème de menthe liqueur**

Origin: Created in 2001 by Rodolphe Sorel.
Comment: Strangely enough, tastes like a
Tic-Tac mint.

TIGER'S MILK

Glass: Old-fashioned
Garnish: Grate nutmeg over drink
Method: SHAKE all ingredients with ice and strain
into ice-filled glass.

2	shot(s)	**Courvoisier V.S.O.P. cognac**
2	drops	**Vanilla essence**
1	pinch	**Ground cinnamon**
¼	shot(s)	**Sugar syrup** (2 sugar to 1 water)
¾	shot(s)	**Double cream**
¾	shot(s)	**Milk**
½	fresh	**Egg white**

Origin: Adapted from a recipe purloined from
Charles H. Baker Jr's classic book, The
Gentleman's Companion. He first discovered this
drink in April 1931 at Gerber's Snug Bar,
Peking, China.
Comment: Creamy cognac and spice.

THUNDERBIRD

Glass: Martini
Garnish: Pineapple wedge on rim
Method: SHAKE all ingredients with ice and fine
strain into chilled glass.

1½	shot(s)	**Bulleit bourbon whiskey**
¾	shot(s)	**Luxardo Amaretto di Saschira**
1	shot(s)	**Pressed pineapple juice**
1	shot(s)	**Freshly squeezed orange juice**

Comment: Tangy bourbon with fruity almond.

TIKI BAR MARGARITA

Glass: Old-fashioned
Garnish: Mint leaf, pineapple wedge & lime wedge
Method: **SHAKE** all ingredients with ice and strain into glass filled with crushed ice.

2	shot(s)	**Don Julio reposado tequila**
1	shot(s)	**Freshly squeezed lime juice**
½	shot(s)	**Almond (orgeat) syrup**

Origin: Created in 2005 by Crispin Somerville and Jaspar Eyears at Bar Tiki, Mexico City.
Comment: A fantastic twist on the classic Margarita.

TIKI MAX

Glass: Old-fashioned
Garnish: Mint sprig & lime wedge
Method: **SHAKE** first nine ingredients with ice and strain into glass filled with crushed ice. **FLOAT** overproof rum on drink.

1	shot(s)	**Pusser's Navy rum**
½	shot(s)	**Myers's dark Jamaican rum**
½	shot(s)	**Grand Marnier liqueur**
½	shot(s)	**Bols apricot brandy liqueur**
¾	shot(s)	**Freshly squeezed lime juice**
1	shot(s)	**Almond (orgeat) syrup**
1½	shot(s)	**Pressed pineapple juice**
½	shot(s)	**Freshly squeezed orange juice**
6	dashes	**Angostura aromatic bitters**
½	shot(s)	**Wood's 100 rum**

Origin: Created by Yours Truly (Simon Difford).
Comment: This drink breaks the golden rule that simple is beautiful. However, it's tasty and very dangerous.

TILT

Glass: Sling
Garnish: Pineapple leaf garnish
Method: **SHAKE** first 5 ingredients with ice and strain into glass filled with crushed ice. **TOP** with bitter lemon.

1½	shot(s)	**Pineapple flavoured vodka**
½	shot(s)	**Malibu coconut rum liqueur**
1½	shot(s)	**Pressed pineapple juice**
1	shot(s)	**Freshly squeezed grapefruit juice**
¼	shot(s)	**Vanilla sugar syrup**
Top up with		**Bitter lemon**

Comment: Totally tropical taste.

TIPPERARY #1

Glass: Martini
Garnish: Cherries on stick
Method: **SHAKE** all ingredients with ice and fine strain into chilled glass.

2	shot(s)	**Jameson Irish whiskey**
½	shot(s)	**Green Chartreuse liqueur**
1	shot(s)	**Martini Rosso sweet vermouth**
½	shot(s)	**Chilled mineral water** (omit if wet ice)

Origin: Adapted from a recipe in Harry Craddock's 1930 Savoy Cocktail Book, which called for equal parts.
Comment: Chartreuse fans will love this serious drink.

TIPPERARY #2

Glass: Martini
Garnish: Mint leaf
Method: Lightly **MUDDLE** mint in base of shaker (just to bruise). Add other ingredients, **SHAKE** with ice and fine strain into chilled glass.

7	fresh	**Mint leaves**
2	shot(s)	**Tanqueray London dry gin**
1	shot(s)	**Noilly Prat dry vermouth**
¼	shot(s)	**Freshly squeezed orange juice**
¼	shot(s)	**Pomegranate (grenadine) syrup**

Origin: Adapted from a drink purloined from David Embury's classic book, The Fine Art of Mixing Drinks.
Comment: Delicate with subtle hints of mint, orange and gin.

TIRAMISU MARTINI

Glass: Martini
Garnish: Chocolate powder dust
Method: **SHAKE** all ingredients with ice and fine strain into chilled glass.

1	shot(s)	**Courvoisier V.S.O.P cognac**
½	shot(s)	**Kahlúa coffee liqueur**
½	shot(s)	**Brown crème de cacao liqueur**
½	shot(s)	**Double (heavy) cream**
½	shot(s)	**Milk**
1	fresh	**Egg yolk**
1	spoon	**Mascarpone cheese**

Origin: Created by Adam Ennis in 2001 at Isola, London, England.
Comment: The chef meets the bartender in this rich dessert cocktail.

TIZIANO

Glass: Flute
Garnish: Grapes on rim
Method: **MUDDLE** grapes in base of shaker. Add Dubonnet, **SHAKE** with ice and fine strain into chilled glass. Slowly **TOP** with prosecco and lightly stir.

10	fresh	**Seedless red grapes**
1	shot(s)	**Dubonnet Red** (French made)
Top up with		**Prosecco sparkling wine**

Origin: Named for the 15th century Venetian painter Titian, who was celebrated for his use of auburn red, this cocktail is commonplace in his home town, where it is made without Dubonnet.
Comment: Not dissimilar to a sparkling Shiraz wine.

TNT (TEQUILA 'N' TONIC) NEW #8

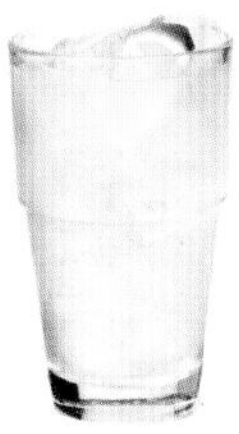

Glass: Collins
Garnish: Lime wedge
Method: **POUR** all ingredients into ice filled glass and **STIR**.

1½	shot(s)	**Don Julio blanco tequila**
½	shot(s)	**Freshly squeezed lime juice**
Top up with		**Tonic water**

Origin: Adapted from Victor Bergeron's 'Trader Vic's Bartender's Guide' (1972 revised edition).
Comment: A simple but tasty way to enjoy tequila.

TOAST & ORANGE MARTINI

Glass: Martini (5oz small)
Garnish: Orange zest twist
Method: SHAKE all ingredients with ice and fine strain into chilled glass.

2	shot(s)	**Bulleit bourbon whiskey**
1	spoon	**Orange marmalade**
3	dashes	**Peychaud's aromatic bitters**
⅛	shot(s)	**Sugar syrup** (2 sugar to 1 water)

Comment: Bourbon rounded and enhanced by bitter orange and Peychaud's bitters.

TOASTED ALMOND

Glass: Martini
Garnish: Dust with chocolate powder
Method: SHAKE all ingredients with ice and fine strain into chilled glass.

1	shot(s)	**Ketel One vodka**
1	shot(s)	**Luxardo Amaretto di Saschira**
¾	shot(s)	**Kahlúa coffee liqueur**
¾	shot(s)	**Double (heavy) cream**
¾	shot(s)	**Milk**

Comment: Slightly sweet but smooth, creamy and definitely toasted.

TODDY MARTINI

Glass: Martini
Garnish: Lemon zest twist
Method: SHAKE all ingredients with ice and fine strain into chilled glass.

1½	shot(s)	**Johnnie Walker Scotch whisky**
1	shot(s)	**Bärenjäger honey liqueur**
¾	shot(s)	**Freshly squeezed lemon juice**

Origin: Created in 2001 by Jamie Terrell at LAB, London, England.
Comment: An ice cold but warming combo of Scotch, honey and lemon.

TOFFEE APPLE

Glass: Sling
Garnish: Apple wedge on rim
Method: SHAKE all ingredients with ice and strain into ice-filled glass.

1	shot(s)	**Boulard Grand Solage calvados**
2	shot(s)	**Cartron caramel liqueur**
1	shot(s)	**Berentzen apple schnapps**
1	shot(s)	**Freshly pressed apple juice**
¼	shot(s)	**Freshly squeezed lime juice**

Origin: Created in 2002 by Nick Strangeway, London, England.
Comment: The taste is just as the name suggests.

TOFFEE APPLE MARTINI

Glass: Martini
Garnish: Apple and fudge on rim
Method: SHAKE all ingredients with ice and fine strain into chilled glass.

1	shot(s)	**Boulard Grand Solage calvados**
1	shot(s)	**Apple flavoured vodka**
1½	shot(s)	**Pressed apple juice**
1	shot(s)	**Toffee liqueur**

Origin: Created in 2003 by Yours Truly (Simon Difford).
Comment: This amber, liquid toffee apple is almost creamy on the palate.

TOKYO BLOODY MARY

Glass: Collins
Garnish: Stick of celery
Method: SHAKE all ingredients with ice and strain into ice-filled glass.

2	shot(s)	**Sake**
3½	shot(s)	**Tomato juice**
½	shot(s)	**Freshly squeezed lemon juice**
¼	shot(s)	**Warre's Otima tawny port**
7	drops	**Tabasco pepper sauce**
3	dashes	**Worcestershire sauce**
1	pinch	**Celery salt**
1	grind	**Black pepper**

Comment: Sake adds an interesting dimension to the traditionally vodka based Bloody Mary.

TOKYO ICED TEA

Glass: Sling
Garnish: Lemon slice
Method: SHAKE first 7 ingredients with ice and strain into ice-filled glass. **TOP** with lemonade, lightly stir and serve with straws.

½	shot(s)	**Bacardi Superior rum**
½	shot(s)	**Tanqueray London dry gin**
½	shot(s)	**Ketel One vodka**
½	shot(s)	**Don Julio reposado tequila**
½	shot(s)	**Cointreau triple sec**
1	shot(s)	**Freshly squeezed lime juice**
½	shot(s)	**Midori green melon liqueur**
Top up with		**Lemonade/Sprite/7-Up**

Comment: You will be surprised how the half shot of melon liqueur shows through the other ingredients.

TOKYO TEA

Glass: Collins
Garnish: Peeled lychee in drink
Method: SHAKE first 3 ingredients with ice and fine strain into ice-filled glass. **TOP** with Coca-Cola, lightly stir and serve with straws.

2	shot(s)	**Tanqueray London dry gin**
1½	shot(s)	**Soho lychee liqueur**
1	shot(s)	**Strong cold jasmine tea**
Top up with		**Coca-Cola**

Origin: Created by Yours Truly (Simon Difford) in 2004.
Comment: Light, floral and, due to the tannins in the jasmine tea, refreshingly dry.

TOLLEYTOWN PUNCH

Glass: Collins
Garnish: Cranberries, orange & lemon slices
Method: SHAKE first 4 ingredients with ice and strain into ice-filled glass. TOP with ginger ale.

2	shot(s)	**Jack Daniel's Tennessee whiskey**
2	shot(s)	**Ocean Spray cranberry juice**
½	shot(s)	**Pressed pineapple juice**
½	shot(s)	**Freshly squeezed orange juice**
Top up with		**Ginger ale**

Origin: A drink promoted by Jack Daniel's. Tolleytown lies just down the road from Lynchburg.
Comment: A fruity long drink with a dry edge that also works well made in bulk and served from a punch bowl.

TOM & JERRY

Glass: Toddy
Garnish: Grate nutmeg over drink
Method: Separately **BEAT** egg white until stiff and frothy and yolk until as liquid as water, then **MIX** together and pour into glass. Add rum, cognac, sugar and spices and **STIR** mixture together. **TOP** with boiling water, **STIR** and serve.

1	fresh	**Egg white**
1	fresh	**Egg yolk**
1½	shot(s)	**Bacardi Oro golden rum**
1½	shot(s)	**Courvoisier V.S.O.P. cognac**
¼	shot(s)	**Sugar syrup** (2 sugar to 1 water)
1	pinch	**Ground cloves**
1	pinch	**Ground cinnamon**
Top up with		**Boiling water**

Origin: Created in the early 19th century and attributed to Jerry Thomas. This recipe is adapted from (sometimes incorrectly attributed) Harry Craddock's 1930 Savoy Cocktail Book.
Comment: To quote Craddock, "The Tom and Jerry and the Blue Blazer – the latter a powerful concoction of burning whisky and boiling water – were the greatest cold weather beverages of that era."

TOM ARNOLD

Glass: Collins
Garnish: Lemon slice & cherry on stick (sail)
Method: SHAKE all ingredients with ice and strain into ice-filled glass.

1½	shot(s)	**Ketel One vodka**
1½	shot(s)	**Freshly squeezed lemon juice**
¾	shot(s)	**Sugar syrup** (2 sugar to 1 water)
2	shot(s)	**Cold breakfast tea**

Variants: Arnold Palmer, John Daly
Origin: This is one of a series of tea-based drinks that were originally named after golfers. It takes its name from the actor and comedian who starred in 'National Lampoon's Golf Punk'.
Comment: Traditional lemonade laced with vodka and lengthened with tea makes a light and refreshing drink.

TOM COLLINS UPDATED #8

Glass: Collins
Garnish: Lemon slice
Method: SHAKE first 3 ingredients with ice and strain into ice-filled glass. TOP with soda, lightly stir and serve with straws.

2	shot(s)	**Tanqueray London dry gin**
1	shot(s)	**Freshly squeezed lemon juice**
¾	shot(s)	**Sugar syrup** (2 sugar to 1 water)
Top up with		**Soda water** (club soda)

Comment: A medium-sweet gin Collins.
Origin: In England, this drink is traditionally credited to John Collins, a bartender who worked at Limmer's Hotel, Conduit Street, London. The 'coffee house' of this hotel, a true dive bar, was popular with sporting types during the 19th century, and famous, according to the 1860s memoirs of a Captain Gronow, for its gin-punch as early as 1814.

John (or possibly Jim) Collins, head waiter of Limmer's, is immortalised in a limerick, which was apparently first printed in an 1892 book entitled 'Drinks of the World'. In 1891 a Sir Morell Mackenzie had identified John Collins as the creator of the Tom Collins, using this limerick, although both the words of the rhyme and the conclusions he drew from it were disputed. But, according to this version of the story, the special gin-punch for which John Collins of Limmer's was famous went on to become known as the Tom Collins when it was made using Old Tom gin.

Others say that the Tom Collins originated in New York, and takes its name from the Great Tom Collins Hoax of 1874, a practical joke which involved telling a friend that a man named Tom Collins had been insulting them, and that he could be found in a bar some distance away, and took the city by storm. This is supported by the fact that the first known written occurrence of a Tom Collins cocktail recipe is found in the 1876 edition of Jerry Thomas' 'The Bartender's Guide'. Three drinks titled Tom Collins are listed: Tom Collins Whiskey, Tom Collins Brandy and Tom Collins Gin.

An alternative story attributes the drink to a Collins who started work at a New York tavern called the Whitehouse in 1873 and started pouring a thirst quencher made with gin. Another identifies a different Tom Collins, who worked as a bartender in New Jersey and New York area. There are apparently also versions of its creation in San Francisco and Australia, and it is not impossible that the drink evolved in two or more places independently.

TOMAHAWK

Glass: Collins
Garnish: Pineapple wedge
Method: SHAKE all ingredients with ice and strain into ice-filled glass.

1	shot(s)	**Don Julio reposado tequila**
1	shot(s)	**Cointreau triple sec**
2	shot(s)	**Ocean Spray cranberry juice**
2	shot(s)	**Pressed pineapple juice**

Comment: A simple recipe, and an effective drink.

TOMATE

Glass: Collins (10oz / 290ml max)
Method: POUR pastis and grenadine into glass. Serve iced water separately in a small jug (known in France as a 'broc') so the customer can dilute to their own taste (I recommend five shots). Lastly, add ice to fill glass.

1	shot(s)	**Ricard pastis**
¼	shot(s)	**Pomegranate (grenadine) syrup**
Top up with		**Chilled water**

Origin: Very popular throughout France. Pronounced 'Toh-Maht', the name literally means 'tomato' and refers to the drink's colour.
Comment: The traditional aniseed and liquorice French café drink with a sweet hint of fruit.

TOMMY'S MARGARITA UPDATED #8

Glass: Old-fashioned
Garnish: Lime wedge
Method: SHAKE all ingredients with ice and strain into ice-filled glass.

2	shot(s)	**Don Julio reposado tequila**
1	shot(s)	**Freshly squeezed lime juice**
½	shot(s)	**Agave syrup**

Origin: Created by Julio Bermejo and named after his family's Mexican restaurant and bar in San Francisco. Julio is legendary for his Margaritas and knowledge of tequila.
Comment: The flavour of agave is king in this simple Margarita, made without the traditional orange liqueur.

ERNEST BEAUMONT GANTT OPENED HIS DON THE BEACHCOMBER BAR IN 1934.

TONGA

Glass: Hurricane
Garnish: Orange, lime and lemon slices
Method: SHAKE all ingredients with ice and strain into ice-filled glass.

2	shot(s)	**Bacardi Superior rum**
½	shot(s)	**Courvoisier V.S.O.P. cognac**
¼	shot(s)	**Zacapa aged rum**
½	shot(s)	**Pomegranate (grenadine) syrup**
2	shot(s)	**Freshly squeezed orange juice**
¾	shot(s)	**Freshly squeezed lemon juice**
¾	shot(s)	**Freshly squeezed lime juice**
¼	shot(s)	**Sugar syrup** (2 sugar to 1 water)

Comment: The rum and cognac flavours are masked by zesty orange.

TONGUE TWISTER

Glass: Old-fashioned
Garnish: Maraschino cherry
Method: SHAKE all ingredients with ice and strain into glass filled with crushed ice.

¾	shot(s)	**Bacardi Superior rum**
¾	shot(s)	**Don Julio reposado tequila**
¾	shot(s)	**Ketel One vodka**
½	shot(s)	**Coco López cream of coconut**
3	shot(s)	**Pressed pineapple juice**
½	shot(s)	**Double (heavy) cream**
½	shot(s)	**Milk**
¼	shot(s)	**Pomegranate (grenadine) syrup**

Origin: Adapted from a drink featured in May 2006 on www.tikibartv.com.
Comment: This creamy, sweet Tiki number is laced with three different spirits.

TOO CLOSE FOR COMFORT

Glass: Martini
Garnish: Lemon zest twist
Method: SHAKE all ingredients with ice and fine strain into chilled glass.

1½	shot(s)	**Ketel One vodka**
1	shot(s)	**Southern Comfort liqueur**
1	shot(s)	**Freshly squeezed lemon juice**
½	shot(s)	**Sugar syrup** (2 sugar to 1 water)

Origin: Adapted from a drink discovered in 2005 at Mezza9, Singapore.
Comment: Sweet and sour with the distinctive flavour of Southern Comfort.

TOOTIE FRUITY LIFESAVER

Glass: Collins
Garnish: Pineapple wedge & cherry
Method: SHAKE all ingredients with ice and strain into ice-filled glass. Serve with straws.

1½	shot(s)	**Ketel One vodka**
¾	shot(s)	**Crème de banane liqueur**
¾	shot(s)	**Galliano L'Autentico liqueur**
1	shot(s)	**Ocean Spray cranberry juice**
1	shot(s)	**Pressed pineapple juice**
1	shot(s)	**Freshly squeezed orange juice**

Comment: Aptly named fruity drink.

TOP BANANA SHOT

Glass: Shot
Method: Refrigerate ingredients then LAYER in chilled glass by carefully pouring in the following order.

½	shot(s)	**Kahlúa coffee liqueur**
½	shot(s)	**White crème de cacao liqueur**
½	shot(s)	**Crème de banane liqueur**
½	shot(s)	**Ketel One vodka**

Comment: Banana, chocolate and coffee.

TOREADOR

Glass: Martini
Garnish: Lime zest twist
Method: SHAKE all ingredients with ice and fine strain into chilled glass.

2	shot(s)	**Don Julio reposado tequila**
1	shot(s)	**Bols apricot brandy liqueur**
1	shot(s)	**Freshly squeezed lime juice**

Origin: This drink was published in W. J. Tarling's 1937 'Café Royal Cocktail Book', 16 years before the first known written reference to a Margarita. He also lists a Picador, which is identical to the later Margarita.
Comment: Apricot brandy replaces triple sec, giving a fruity twist to the classic Margarita.

TOTAL RECALL

Glass: Collins
Garnish: Lime wedge
Method: SHAKE all ingredients with ice and strain into ice-filled glass.

¾	shot(s)	**Southern Comfort liqueur**
¾	shot(s)	**Don Julio reposado tequila**
¾	shot(s)	**Bacardi Oro golden rum**
1½	shot(s)	**Ocean Spray cranberry juice**
1½	shot(s)	**Freshly squeezed orange juice**
¾	shot(s)	**Freshly squeezed lime juice**

Comment: A long, burgundy coloured drink with a taste reminiscent of blood orange.

TRANSYLVANIAN MARTINI

Glass: Martini
Garnish: Pineapple wedge
Method: SHAKE ingredients with ice and fine strain into chilled glass.

2	shot(s)	**Ketel One vodka**
1	shot(s)	**Passoã passion fruit liqueur**
1	shot(s)	**Pressed pineapple juice**

Origin: Created for the 1994 International Bartenders cocktail competition.
Comment: A tad sweet and a tad dull.

TRE MARTINI

Glass: Martini
Garnish: Lemon zest twist
Method: SHAKE all ingredients with ice and fine strain into chilled glass.

2	shot(s)	**Bacardi Superior rum**
½	shot(s)	**Chambord black raspberry liqueur**
1½	shot(s)	**Freshly pressed apple juice**

Origin: Created in 2002 by Åsa Nevestveit at Sosho, London, England.
Comment: A simple, well balanced, fruity drink laced with rum.

TREACLE

Glass: Old-fashioned
Garnish: Lemon zest twist
Method: STIR sugar syrup and bitters with two ice cubes in glass. Add one shot of rum and two more ice cubes. **STIR** some more and add another two ice cubes and another shot of rum. **STIR** lots more and add more ice if required. Finally **FLOAT** apple juice.

¼	shot(s)	**Sugar syrup** (2 sugar to 1 water)
2	dashes	**Angostura aromatic bitters**
2	shot(s)	**Myers's dark Jamaican rum**
½	shot(s)	**Pressed apple juice**

Origin: This twist on the Old-Fashioned was created by Dick Bradsell. Like the original, it takes about five minutes to make and there are no shortcuts.
Comment: Almost like molasses – very dark flavour.

TRES COMPADRES MARGARITA

Glass: Coupette
Garnish: Lime wedge & salted rim (optional)
Method: SHAKE all ingredients with ice and fine strain into chilled glass.

1¼	shot(s)	**Don Julio reposado tequila**
½	shot(s)	**Cointreau triple sec**
½	shot(s)	**Chambord black raspberry liqueur**
½	shot(s)	**Rose's lime cordial**
¾	shot(s)	**Freshly squeezed lime juice**
¾	shot(s)	**Freshly squeezed orange juice**
¾	shot(s)	**Freshly squeezed grapefruit juice**

Origin: Created in 1999 by Robert Plotkin and Raymon Flores of BarMedia, USA.
Comment: A well balanced, tasty twist on the standard Margarita.

TRIANGULAR MARTINI

Glass: Martini
Garnish: Toblerone chocolate on rim
Method: STIR honey with vodka in base of shaker until honey dissolves. Add other ingredients, **SHAKE** with ice and fine strain into chilled glass.

2	spoons	**Runny honey**
1½	shot(s)	**Vanilla-infused Ketel One vodka**
½	shot(s)	**Luxardo Amaretto di Saschira**
1¼	shot(s)	**Brown crème de cacao liqueur**
¾	shot(s)	**Double (heavy) cream**
½	fresh	**Egg white**

Origin: Created by Yours Truly (Simon Difford) in 2003. The famous triangular Toblerone chocolate bar was invented in 1908 by the Swiss chocolate maker Theodor Tobler. The name is a blend of Tobler with Torrone, the Italian word for honey-almond nougat, one of its main ingredients.
Comment: Nibble at the garnish as you sip honeyed, chocolate and almond flavoured liquid candy.

TRIBBBLE

Glass: Shot
Method: Refrigerate ingredients then **LAYER** in chilled glass by carefully pouring in the following order.

½	shot(s)	**Teichenné butterscotch schnapps**
½	shot(s)	**Crème de banane liqueur**
½	shot(s)	**Baileys Irish cream liqueur**

Origin: A drink created by bartenders at TGI Friday's UK in 2002.
Comment: Named 'Tribbble' with three 'Bs' due to its three layers: butterscotch, banana and Baileys.

DRINKS ARE GRADED AS FOLLOWS:

● DISGUSTING ●◐ PRETTY AWFUL ●● BEST AVOIDED
●●◐ DISAPPOINTING ●●● ACCEPTABLE ●●●● GOOD
●●●● RECOMMENDED ●●●●◐ HIGHLY RECOMMENDED
●●●●● OUTSTANDING / EXCEPTIONAL

TRIFLE MARTINI

Glass: Martini
Garnish: Hundreds & thousands
Method: SHAKE all ingredients with ice and fine strain into chilled glass.

2	shot(s)	**Raspberry flavoured vodka**
½	shot(s)	**Chambord black raspberry liqueur**
2	shot(s)	**Drambuie cream liqueur**

Origin: Created by Ian Baldwin at GE Club, London, England.
Comment: A cocktail that tastes like its namesake.

TRIFLE'TINI

Glass: Martini
Garnish: Crumbled Cadbury's Flake bar
Method: MUDDLE raspberries and strawberries in base of shaker. Add next 4 ingredients, SHAKE with ice and fine strain into chilled glass. Lightly WHIP cream and FLOAT over drink.

10	fresh	**Raspberries**
2	fresh	**Strawberries** (hulled)
2	shot(s)	**Courvoisier V.S.O.P. cognac**
¾	shot(s)	**Luxardo Amaretto di Saschira**
½	shot(s)	**Crème de fraise de bois liqueur**
1	shot(s)	**Noé Pedro Ximénez sherry**
1½	shot(s)	**Double (heavy) cream**

Origin: Created in 2000 by Ian Baldwin at the GE Club, London, England.
Comment: Very rich – looks and tastes like a trifle.

TRILBY #1

Glass: Martini
Garnish: Orange zest twist
Method: STIR all ingredients with ice and strain into chilled glass.

1	shot(s)	**Johnnie Walker Scotch whisky**
1	shot(s)	**Parfait Amour liqueur**
1	shot(s)	**Martini Rosso sweet vermouth**
⅛	shot(s)	**La Fée Parisienne (68%) absinthe**
¾	shot(s)	**Chilled mineral water** (omit if wet ice)
2	dashes	**Angostura orange bitters**

Comment: An aromatic old classic of unknown origin.

TRILBY #2

Glass: Martini
Garnish: Lemon zest twist
Method: STIR first 3 ingredients with ice and strain into chilled glass. FLOAT Scotch over drink.

3	shot(s)	**Noilly Prat dry vermouth**
¼	shot(s)	**Cointreau triple sec**
1	dash	**Peychaud's aromatic bitters**
½	shot(s)	**Johnnie Walker Scotch whisky**

Comment: Salmon pink in colour and distinctly different in style. One of those drinks you just have to try.

TRINITY

Glass: Martini
Garnish: Orange twist (discarded) & two maraschino cherries
Method: STIR all ingredients with ice and strain into chilled glass.

2½	shot(s)	**Johnnie Walker Scotch whisky**
1	shot(s)	**Noilly Prat dry vermouth**
¼	shot(s)	**Bols apricot brandy liqueur**
¼	shot(s)	**Giffard Menthe Pastille liqueur**
1	dash	**Angostura orange bitters**

Origin: Recipe purloined from David Embury's classic book, The Fine Art of Mixing Drinks.
Comment: A Dry Manhattan based on Scotch with a dash of apricot liqueur and a touch of crème de menthe.

TRIPLE 'C' MARTINI

Glass: Martini
Garnish: Dark chocolate on rim
Method: SHAKE all ingredients with ice and fine strain into chilled glass.

2	shot(s)	**Vanilla-infused Ketel One vodka**
1	shot(s)	**Brown crème de cacao liqueur**
1¼	shot(s)	**Ocean Spray cranberry juice**

Origin: I created this drink in 2004 and originally called it the Chocolate Covered Cranberry Martini.
Comment: Rich vanilla, dark chocolate and cranberry juice.

TRIPLE ORANGE MARTINI

Glass: Martini
Garnish: Orange zest twist
Method: SHAKE all ingredients with ice and fine strain into chilled glass.

1	shot(s)	**Ketel One vodka**
1	shot(s)	**Grand Marnier liqueur**
¼	shot(s)	**Campari Bitter**
2	shot(s)	**Freshly squeezed orange juice**
½	fresh	**Egg white**

Origin: Created in 1998 by Yours Truly (Simon Difford).
Comment: A trio of orange flavours. The bitter orange of Campari adds character and balance.

TRIPLEBERRY

Glass: Martini
Garnish: Berries on stick
Method: MUDDLE raspberries in base of shaker. Add other ingredients, SHAKE with ice and fine strain into chilled glass.

7	fresh	**Raspberries**
2	shot(s)	**Ketel One vodka**
½	shot(s)	**Crème de cassis liqueur**
½	shot(s)	**Crème de fraise de bois liqueur**
¼	shot(s)	**Shiraz red wine**

Origin: Created in 2006 by Yours Truly (Simon Difford).
Comment: Rich berry fruit fortified with vodka and tamed by the tannins in a splash of red wine.

TROPIC

Glass: Collins
Garnish: Lemon slice
Method: SHAKE all ingredients with ice and strain into ice-filled glass.

1	shot(s)	**Bénédictine D.O.M. liqueur**
2	shot(s)	**Sauvignon Blanc wine**
2	shot(s)	**Freshly squeezed grapefruit juice**
½	shot(s)	**Freshly squeezed lemon juice**

Origin: Based on a recipe believed to date back to the 1950s.
Comment: A light, satisfying cooler.

TROPICAL BREEZE

Glass: Collins
Garnish: Lime wedge
Method: SHAKE all ingredients with ice and strain into ice-filled glass.

1	shot(s)	**Passoã passion fruit liqueur**
1½	shot(s)	**Ketel One vodka**
2½	shot(s)	**Ocean Spray cranberry juice**
1½	shot(s)	**Freshly squeezed grapefruit juice**

Comment: A sweet, fruity Seabreeze.

TROPICAL CAIPIRINHA

Glass: Old-fashioned
Garnish: Two squeezed lime wedges in drink
Method: SHAKE all ingredients with ice and strain into glass filled with crushed ice.

1	shot(s)	**Leblon cachaça**
1	shot(s)	**Malibu coconut rum liqueur**
1	shot(s)	**Pressed pineapple juice**
1	shot(s)	**Freshly squeezed lime juice**
¼	shot(s)	**Sugar syrup** (2 sugar to 1 water)

Origin: Created by Yours Truly (Simon Difford) in 2003.
Comment: In drink circles, tropical usually spells sweet. This drink has a tropical flavour but an adult sourness.

TROPICAL DAIQUIRI

Glass: Martini
Garnish: Pineapple wedge on rim
Method: SHAKE all ingredients with ice and fine strain into chilled glass.

2	shot(s)	**Goslings Black Seal rum**
1	shot(s)	**Pressed pineapple juice**
½	shot(s)	**Freshly squeezed lime juice**
¼	shot(s)	**Pomegranate (grenadine) syrup**

Origin: Adapted from a recipe in David Embury's classic book, The Fine Art of Mixing Drinks.
Comment: A seriously tangy Daiquiri.

TULIP COCKTAIL

Glass: Martini
Garnish: Lemon zest twist
Method: SHAKE all ingredients with ice and fine strain into chilled glass.

1	shot(s)	**Boulard Grand Solage calvados**
1	shot(s)	**Martini Rosso sweet vermouth**
½	shot(s)	**Freshly squeezed lemon juice**
½	shot(s)	**Bols apricot brandy liqueur**
½	shot(s)	**Chilled mineral water** (omit if wet ice)

Origin: Adapted from a recipe in Harry Craddock's 1930 Savoy Cocktail Book.
Comment: Rich but balanced with bags of fruit: apple, apricot and lemon.

'BEER THAT IS NOT DRUNK HAS MISSED ITS VOCATION'.
MEYER BRESLAU

TURF MARTINI

Glass: Martini
Garnish: Orange zest twist
Method: SHAKE all ingredients with ice and fine strain into chilled glass.

1½	shot(s)	**Tanqueray London dry gin**
1½	shot(s)	**Martini Rosso sweet vermouth**
⅛	shot(s)	**Luxardo maraschino liqueur**
⅛	shot(s)	**La Fée Parisienne (68%) absinthe**
2	dashes	**Angostura orange bitters**

Origin: Created before 1900 at the Ritz Hotel, Paris, France.
Comment: Old-school, full flavoured, aromatic and dry.

TURKISH COFFEE MARTINI

Glass: Martini
Garnish: Float three coffee beans
Method: MUDDLE cardamom pods in base of shaker. Add other ingredients, **SHAKE** with ice and fine strain into chilled glass.

9	pods	**Green cardamom**
2	shot(s)	**Ketel One vodka**
2	shot(s)	**Espresso coffee**
½	shot(s)	**Sugar syrup** (2 sugar to 1 water)

Origin: I created this in 2003.
Comment: Coffee is often made with cardamom in Arab countries. This drink harnesses the aromatic, eucalyptus, citrus flavour of cardamom coffee and adds a little vodka zing.

TURKISH DELIGHT

Glass: Martini
Garnish: Turkish Delight on rim
Method: STIR honey and vodka in base of shaker until honey dissolves. Add other ingredients, **SHAKE** with ice and fine strain into chilled glass.

2	spoons	Runny honey
1	shot(s)	Ketel One vodka
1	shot(s)	Vanilla-infused Ketel One vodka
½	shot(s)	White crème de cacao liqueur
⅛	shot(s)	Rosewater
¾	shot(s)	Chilled water (omit if wet ice)
½	fresh	Egg white

Origin: Created in 2003 by Yours Truly (Simon Difford).
Comment: Rosewater, honey, chocolate and vanilla provide a distinct flavour of Turkish Delight - fortified with vodka.

TURQUOISE DAIQUIRI

Glass: Martini
Garnish: Lime wedge on rim
Method: SHAKE all ingredients with ice and fine strain into chilled glass.

1½	shot(s)	Bacardi Superior rum
½	shot(s)	Cointreau triple sec
½	shot(s)	Bols blue curaçao liqueur
¾	shot(s)	Freshly squeezed lime juice
1	shot(s)	Pressed pineapple juice

Comment: A blue-rinsed Daiquiri with orange and pineapple – with tequila instead of rum it would be a twisted Margarita.

TUSCAN MULE

Glass: Collins
Garnish: Lime wedge
Method: SHAKE first 2 ingredients with ice and strain into ice-filled glass. **TOP** with ginger beer, lightly stir and serve with straws.

2	shot(s)	Tuaca Italian liqueur
¾	shot(s)	Freshly squeezed lime juice
Top up with		Jamaican ginger beer

Origin: Adapted from drink created in 2003 by Sammy Berry, Brighton, England.
Comment: A spicy long drink smoothed with vanilla.

TUTTI FRUTTI

Glass: Collins
Garnish: Split lime wedge
Method: SHAKE all ingredients with ice and strain into ice-filled glass.

1	shot(s)	Don Julio reposado tequila
1	shot(s)	Passoã passion fruit liqueur
1	shot(s)	Midori green melon liqueur
3	shot(s)	Ocean Spray cranberry juice

Comment: A berry drink with a tropical tinge.

TUXEDO MARTINI

Glass: Martini
Garnish: Orange zest twist
Method: STIR all ingredients with ice and fine strain into chilled glass.

1½	shot(s)	Tanqueray London dry gin
1½	shot(s)	Noilly Prat dry vermouth
½	shot(s)	Tio Pepe fino sherry
1	dash	Angostura orange bitters

Origin: Created at the Tuxedo Club, New York, circa 1885. A year later this was the birthplace of the tuxedo, when a tobacco magnate, Griswold Lorillard, wore the first ever tailless dinner jacket and named the style after the club.
Comment: Fino adds a nutty saltiness to this very wet, aromatic Martini.

TVR

Glass: Collins
Garnish: Lime wedge in drink
Method: POUR ingredients into ice-filled glass. Lightly stir and serve with straws.

1	shot(s)	Don Julio reposado tequila
1	shot(s)	Ketel One vodka
Top up with		Red Bull

Variant: Served as a shot.
Origin: A 90s drink named after its ingredients (tequila, vodka and Red Bull), which is also the name of a British sports car.
Comment: While I personally find the smell of Red Bull reminiscent of perfumed puke, this drink could be far worse.

TWENTIETH CENTURY MARTINI

Glass: Martini
Garnish: Lemon zest twist
Method: SHAKE all ingredients with ice and fine strain into chilled glass.

1½	shot(s)	Tanqueray London dry gin
¾	shot(s)	Noilly Prat dry vermouth
½	shot(s)	White crème de cacao liqueur
½	shot(s)	Freshly squeezed lemon juice

Origin: Thought to have been created in 1939 by one C. A. Tuck and named after the express train that travelled between New York City and Chicago.
Comment: Chocolate and lemon juice. 21st century tastes have moved on.

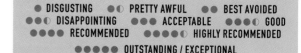

DRINKS ARE GRADED AS FOLLOWS:

● DISGUSTING   ●○ PRETTY AWFUL   ●● BEST AVOIDED
●●○ DISAPPOINTING   ●●● ACCEPTABLE   ●●●○ GOOD
●●●● RECOMMENDED   ●●●●○ HIGHLY RECOMMENDED
●●●●● OUTSTANDING / EXCEPTIONAL

TWINKLE

●●●●◐

Glass: Martini
Garnish: Lemon zest twist
Method: SHAKE first 2 ingredients with ice and fine strain into chilled glass. **TOP** with prosecco (or champagne).

3	shot(s)	Ketel One vodka
¾	shot(s)	St-Germain elderflower liqueur
Top up with		Prosecco sparkling wine

Origin: Adapted from a drink created in 2002 by Tony Conigliaro at Lonsdale House, London, England.
Comment: It's hard to believe this floral, dry, golden beauty contains three shots of vodka – until you've had a few.

TWISTED SOBRIETY

●●●●●

Glass: Flute
Method: SHAKE first 2 ingredients with ice and fine strain into chilled glass. **TOP** with champagne.

1	shot(s)	Courvoisier V.S.O.P. cognac
1	shot(s)	Poire William eau de vie
Top up with		Perrier Jouet brut champagne

Comment: Fortified champagne with a hint of pear.

TWO-ONE-TWO (212) NEW #8

●●●●○○

Glass: Collins
Garnish: Grapefruit zest twist
Method: SHAKE all ingredients with ice and strain into ice-filled glass.

2	shot(s)	Freshly squeezed grapefruit juice
1	shot(s)	Aperol
2	shot(s)	Don Julio reposado tequila

Origin: Created in 2008 by Willy Shine at Contemporary Cocktails Inc. in New York City. The name is a reference to NYC's 212 area code as well as the ounces in the recipe. Will is also the Partida Tequila Ambassador for NYC so I should point out that this is the brand originally called for in his recipe.
Comment: Earthy taste with freshness coming fro the grapefruit.

TWO 'T' FRUITY MARTINI

●●●●○

Glass: Martini
Garnish: Tooty Frooties
Method: SHAKE all ingredients with ice and fine strain into chilled glass.

2½	shot(s)	Ketel One vodka
¾	shot(s)	Passion fruit syrup
3	dashes	Angostura orange bitters

Origin: Created in 2002 at Hush, London, England.
Comment: Simple is beautiful – this drink is both. The rawness of vodka is balanced with sweet passion fruit and hints of orange bitterness.

TYPHOON

●●●○○

Glass: Old-fashioned
Method: STIR all ingredients with ice and strain into ice-filled glass.

1¾	shot(s)	Tanqueray London dry gin
½	shot(s)	Luxardo Sambuca dei Cesari
½	shot(s)	Rose's lime cordial

Comment: Great if you love sambuca.

UGURUNDU

●●●●◐○

Glass: Shot
Method: Lightly MUDDLE mint in base of shaker (just to bruise). Add other ingredients, SHAKE with ice and fine strain into chilled glass.

3	fresh	Mint leaves
½	shot(s)	Cranberry flavoured vodka
½	shot(s)	Rose's lime cordial

Origin: Created in 2004 by Peter Kubista at Bugsy's Bar, Prague, Czech Republic.
Comment: Fresh tasting and all too easy to knock back.

UMBONGO

●●●○○

Glass: Collins
Garnish: Orange slice in glass
Method: Cut passion fruit in half and scoop out flesh into shaker. Add next 3 ingredients, SHAKE with ice and fine strain into ice-filled glass. **TOP** with ginger ale.

1	fresh	Passion fruit
1	shot(s)	Passoã passion fruit liqueur
1	shot(s)	Ketel One vodka
1	shot(s)	Freshly squeezed orange juice
Top up with		Ginger ale

Comment: Pleasant, light and medium sweet tropical style drink.

UNCLE VANYA

●●●●○

Glass: Martini
Garnish: Lime wedge on rim
Method: SHAKE all ingredients with ice and fine strain into chilled glass.

1¾	shot(s)	Ketel One vodka
1	shot(s)	Crème de mûre liqueur
1	shot(s)	Freshly squeezed lime juice
½	shot(s)	Sugar syrup (2 sugar to 1 water)
½	fresh	Egg white

Origin: Named after Anton Chekhov's greatest play – a cheery tale of envy and despair. A popular drink in Britain's TGI Friday's bars, its origins are unknown.
Comment: Simple but great – smooth, sweet 'n' sour blackberry, although possibly a tad on the sweet side for some.

T.G.I. FRIDAYS HOSTED THE VERY FIRST KNOWN FLAIR BARTENDER CONTEST CALLED BAR OLYMPICS IN 1986. THE WINNER WAS JOHN JB BANDY WHO WENT ON TO TRAIN TOM CRUISE FOR HIS ROLE IN 'COCKTAIL'.

UNION CLUB

Glass: Martini
Garnish: Orange zest twist
Method: SHAKE all ingredients with ice and fine strain into chilled glass.

2	shot(s)	**Bulleit bourbon whiskey**
¼	shot(s)	**Cointreau triple sec**
½	shot(s)	**Freshly squeezed lime juice**
⅛	shot(s)	**Almond (orgeat) syrup**
⅛	shot(s)	**Pomegranate (grenadine) syrup**
½	fresh	**Egg white**

Origin: Adapted from a recipe purloined from David Embury's classic book, The Fine Art of Mixing Drinks.
Comment: Balanced sweet and sour with bourbon to the fore.

UNION CLUB COCKTAIL NEW #8

Glass: Coupette/Martini
Garnish: Orange zest twist
Method: SHAKE all ingredients with ice and fine strain into chilled glass.

2	shot(s)	**Bulleit bourbon whiskey**
½	shot(s)	**Luxardo Maraschino liqueur**
½	shot(s)	**Campari Bitter**
1½	shot(s)	**Freshly squeezed orange juice**

Comment: Maraschino and Campari balance perfectly. Fruity yet dry and complex.
Origin: Created in 2008 by Jamie Boudreau at Tini Bigs, Seattle, USA and named after a gambling joint Wyatt Earp opened in Seattle in 1899.

UNIVERSAL SHOT

Glass: Shot
Method: Refrigerate ingredients then LAYER in chilled glass by carefully pouring in the following order.

½	shot(s)	**Midori green melon liqueur**
½	shot(s)	**Freshly squeezed grapefruit juice**
½	shot(s)	**Ketel One vodka**

Comment: Sweet melon liqueur toned down by grapefruit and fortified by vodka.

UPSIDE-DOWN RASPBERRY CHEESECAKE

Glass: Martini
Garnish: Sprinkle crunched Graham Cracker or digestive biscuits
Method: First layer: MUDDLE raspberries in base of shaker. Add Chambord, SHAKE with ice and fine strain into centre of glass. Second layer: Grate lemon zest into shaker. Add rest of ingredients, SHAKE all ingredients with ice and strain into glass over spoon so as to LAYER over raspberry base.

---First Layer---

4	fresh	**Raspberries**
½	shot(s)	**Chambord black raspberry liqueur**

---Second Layer---

½	fresh	**Lemon zest** (grated)
2	shot(s)	**Vanilla-infused Ketel One vodka**
½	shot(s)	**Vanilla liqueur**
½	shot(s)	**Sugar syrup** (2 sugar to 1 water)
5	spoons	**Mascarpone cheese**
1	shot(s)	**Double (heavy) cream**

Origin: I created this in 2003 after adapting Wayne Collins' original cheesecake recipe.
Comment: Surprisingly, the biscuity top continues to float as you sip the vanilla cream layer right down to the point when you hit the raspberry topping – sorry, base.

URBAN HOLISTIC

Glass: Martini
Garnish: Lemon zest twist
Method: SHAKE first 2 ingredients with ice and fine strain into chilled glass. TOP with ginger ale.

2	shot(s)	**Sake**
1	shot(s)	**Noilly Prat dry vermouth**
Top up with		**Ginger ale**

Origin: Adapted from a drink discovered in 2005 at Mo Bar, Landmark Mandarin Oriental Hotel, Hong Kong, China.
Comment: East meets west in this dry refreshing cocktail.

URBAN OASIS

Glass: Martini
Garnish: Orange zest twist
Method: SHAKE all ingredients with ice and fine strain into chilled glass.

1½	shot(s)	**Orange-infused Ketel One vodka**
½	shot(s)	**Raspberry flavoured vodka**
¼	shot(s)	**Chambord black raspberry liqueur**
2	shot(s)	**Pressed pineapple juice**

Origin: Discovered in 2003 at Paramount Hotel, New York City, USA.
Comment: Alcoholic orange sherbet – how bad is that?

U.S. MARTINI

Glass: Martini
Garnish: Vanilla pod
Method: SHAKE all ingredients with ice and fine strain into chilled glass.

1½	shot(s)	**Vanilla-infused Courvoisier cognac**
1¼	shot(s)	**Sauvignon Blanc wine**
1½	shot(s)	**Pressed pineapple juice**
¼	shot(s)	**Sugar syrup** (2 sugar to 1 water)

Origin: Adapted from the Palermo cocktail discovered in 2001 at Hotel du Vin, Bristol, England. I created this drink in 2003 and named it after the grape varieties Ugni and Sauvignon. Ugni Blanc is the most common grape in Cognac, and Sauvignon Blanc is the grape used in the wine.
Comment: A relatively dry cocktail where the vanilla combines beautifully with the cognac and the acidity of the wine balances the sweetness of the pineapple juice.

UTTERLY BUTTERLY

Glass: Collins
Garnish: Apple wedge
Method: STIR peanut butter with vodka in base of shaker. Add other ingredients, **SHAKE** with ice and fine strain into ice-filled glass.

1	spoon	**Smooth peanut butter**
2	shot(s)	**Ketel One vodka**
¼	shot(s)	**Goldschläger cinnamon schnapps**
½	shot(s)	**Malibu coconut rum liqueur**
1½	shot(s)	**Pressed apple juice**
1½	shot(s)	**Pressed pineapple juice**
¾	shot(s)	**Freshly squeezed lime juice**

Comment: Yup, your eyes are not deceiving you and nor will your taste buds – it's made with peanut butter. Refreshingly different.

VACATION

Glass: Martini
Garnish: Pineapple wedge or orange slice on rim
Method: This drink can be finished with your choice of 3 different coloured and flavoured liqueurs. **SHAKE** first 5 ingredients with ice and fine strain into chilled glass. Then **POUR** your favoured final ingredient into the centre of the drink. It should sink.

2	shot(s)	**Vanilla-infused Ketel One vodka**
½	shot(s)	**Malibu coconut rum liqueur**
½	shot(s)	**Freshly squeezed lime juice**
1	shot(s)	**Pressed pineapple juice**
¼	fresh	**Egg white**
¼	shot(s)	**Chambord (red) or Midori (green)** **or Blue curaçao liqueur (blue)**

Origin: My adaptation (in 2003) of the signature drink at the Merc Bar, New York City, USA.
Comment: A great looking, fairly sweet cocktail with hints of vanilla, coconut and pineapple.

VALENCIA MARTINI NEW #8

Glass: Martini/coupette
Garnish: Flamed orange zest twist
Method: STIR all ingredients with ice and strain into chilled glass.

2½	shot(s)	**Tanqueray London dry gin**
½	shot(s)	**Tio Pepe fino sherry**

AKA: Spanish Martini
Variation: Flame of Love Martini
Comment: Fino sherry makes this Martini bone dry.

VALENCIA COCKTAIL #2

Glass: Flute
Garnish: Orange zest twist
Method: POUR first 3 ingredients into chilled glass. **TOP** with champagne.

½	shot(s)	**Bols apricot brandy liqueur**
¼	shot(s)	**Freshly squeezed orange juice**
4	dashes	**Angostura orange bitters** (optional)
Top up with		**Perrier Jouet brut champagne**

Variant: Also served as a Martini with gin in place of champagne.
Origin: Adapted from the Valencia Cocktail No. 2 in The Savoy Cocktail Book.
Comment: Floral and fruity – makes Bucks Fizz look a tad sad.

VALENTINO

Glass: Martini
Garnish: Lemon zest twist
Method: STIR all ingredients with ice and strain into a chilled glass.

2	shot(s)	**Tanqueray London dry gin**
½	shot(s)	**Campari Bitter**
1	shot(s)	**Martini Rosso sweet vermouth**

Comment: A variation on the Negroni. More gin and less Campari, make for an unusual bittersweet Martini.

VALKYRIE

Glass: Old-fashioned
Garnish: Lemon zest twist
Method: SHAKE all ingredients with ice and strain into glass filled with crushed ice. Serve with straws.

2	shot(s)	**Vanilla-infused Ketel One vodka**
½	shot(s)	**Freshly squeezed lemon juice**
½	shot(s)	**Vanilla sugar syrup**

Origin: Created in 2003 by Yours Truly (Simon Difford). The name comes from Norse mythology and literally translates as 'chooser of the slain'.
Comment: This sipping drink has a rich vanilla, sweet 'n' sour flavour.

VAMPIRO

Glass: Old-fashioned
Garnish: Lime wedge
Method: **SHAKE** all ingredients with ice and strain into ice-filled glass.

2	shot(s)	**Don Julio reposado tequila**
1	shot(s)	**Pressed tomato juice**
1	shot(s)	**Freshly squeezed orange juice**
½	shot(s)	**Freshly squeezed lime juice**
½	shot(s)	**Pomegranate (grenadine) syrup**
7	drops	**Tabasco pepper sauce**
1	pinch	**Celery salt**
1	grind	**Black pepper**

Origin: The national drink of Mexico where it's often made with pomegranate juice in place of tomato juice and without the grenadine.
Comment: Something of a supercharged Bloody Mary with tequila and a hint of sweet grenadine.

VANCOUVER

Glass: Martini
Garnish: Lemon zest twist
Method: **STIR** all ingredients with ice and fine strain into chilled glass.

1½	shot(s)	**Tanqueray London dry gin**
¾	shot(s)	**Martini Rosso sweet vermouth**
¼	shot(s)	**Bénédictine D.O.M. liqueur**
1	dash	**Angostura orange bitters**

Comment: A herbal medium dry Martini.

VANDERBILT

Glass: Martini
Garnish: Lemon zest twist
Method: **SHAKE** all ingredients with ice and fine strain into chilled glass.

2¼	shot(s)	**Courvoisier V.S.O.P. cognac**
¾	shot(s)	**Heering cherry brandy liqueur**
⅛	shot(s)	**Sugar syrup** (2 sugar to 1 water)
2	dashes	**Angostura aromatic bitters**

Origin: Adapted from a recipe in Harry Craddock's 1930 Savoy Cocktail Book.
Comment: Tangy, rich cherry and hints of vanilla fortified with brandy.

VANILLA & GRAPEFRUIT DAIQUIRI

Glass: Martini
Garnish: Grapefruit twist (discarded) & vanilla pod
Method: **SHAKE** all ingredients with ice and fine strain into chilled glass.

2½	shot(s)	**Vanilla-infused Bacardi rum**
½	shot(s)	**Freshly squeezed lime juice**
½	shot(s)	**Vanilla sugar syrup**
1	shot(s)	**Freshly squeezed grapefruit juice**

Origin: Created in 2003 by Yours Truly (Simon Difford).
Comment: Reminiscent of a Hemingway Special, this flavoursome, vanilla laced Daiquiri has a wonderfully tangy bittersweet finish.

VANILLA & RASPBERRY MARTINI

Glass: Martini
Garnish: Raspberries on stick
Method: **MUDDLE** raspberries in base of shaker. Add other ingredients, **SHAKE** with ice and fine strain into chilled glass.

12	fresh	**Raspberries**
2	shot(s)	**Vanilla-infused Ketel One vodka**
¼	shot(s)	**Shiraz red wine**
¼	shot(s)	**Sugar syrup** (2 sugar to 1 water)
½	shot(s)	**Chilled mineral water** (omit if wet ice)

Origin: Created in 2006 by Yours Truly (Simon Difford).
Comment: Exactly that – vanilla and raspberry.

VANILLA DAIQUIRI

Glass: Martini
Garnish: Lime wedge on rim
Method: **SHAKE** all ingredients with ice and fine strain into chilled glass.

2	shot(s)	**Vanilla-infused Bacardi rum**
½	shot(s)	**Freshly squeezed lime juice**
¼	shot(s)	**Sugar syrup** (2 sugar to 1 water)
¾	shot(s)	**Chilled mineral water** (omit if wet ice)

Comment: The classic 'Natural Daiquiri' with a hint of vanilla.

VANILLA LAIKA

Glass: Collins
Garnish: Berries
Method: **SHAKE** all ingredients with ice and strain into glass filled with crushed ice.

1½	shot(s)	**Vanilla-infused Ketel One Vodka**
¾	shot(s)	**Crème de mûre liqueur**
¼	shot(s)	**Freshly squeezed lemon juice**
¾	shot(s)	**Sugar syrup** (2 sugar to 1 water)
4	shot(s)	**Pressed apple juice**

Origin: Created by Jake Burger in 2002 at Townhouse, Leeds, England. Laika was a Russian dog and the first canine in space.
Comment: Vanilla berry fruit in a tall, refreshing drink.

VANILLA MARGARITA

Glass: Old-fashioned
Garnish: Lime wedge
Method: **SHAKE** all ingredients with ice and fine strain into ice filled chilled glass.

2	shot(s)	**Vanilla-infused Don Julio tequila**
1	shot(s)	**Freshly squeezed lemon juice**
1	shot(s)	**Cointreau triple sec**

Origin: I first discovered this drink in 1998 at Café Pacifico, London, England.
Comment: A classic Margarita with a hint of vanilla.

VANILLA SENSATION

Glass: Martini
Garnish: Float wafer thin apple slice
Method: SHAKE all ingredients with ice and fine strain into chilled glass.

2	shot(s)	**Vanilla-infused Ketel One vodka**
1	shot(s)	**Sour apple liqueur**
½	shot(s)	**Noilly Prat dry vermouth**

Origin: Created in 2003 but by whom is unknown.
Comment: A pleasing vanilla twist on an Apple Martini.

VANILLA VODKA SOUR

Glass: Flute
Garnish: Lemon & orange zest twists
Method: SHAKE all ingredients with ice and fine strain into chilled glass.

2	shot(s)	**Vanilla-infused Ketel One vodka**
¾	shot(s)	**Cuarenta Y Tres (Licor 43) liqueur**
¾	shot(s)	**Freshly squeezed lemon juice**
½	fresh	**Egg white**

Comment: A Vodka Sour with a blast of spicy vanilla.

VANILLA'TINI

Glass: Martini
Garnish: Half vanilla pod
Method: STIR all ingredients with ice and strain into chilled glass.

2½	shot(s)	**Vanilla-infused Ketel One vodka**
½	shot(s)	**Frangelico hazelnut liqueur**
1½	shot(s)	**Lemonade/Sprite/7-Up**

Origin: Discovered in 2003 at Paramount Hotel, New York City.
Comment: Vanilla, hazelnut and a hint of creamy citrus.

VANITINI

Glass: Martini
Garnish: Pineapple wedge on rim
Method: SHAKE all ingredients with ice and fine strain into chilled glass.

2	shot(s)	**Vanilla-infused Ketel One vodka**
2	shot(s)	**Sauvignon Blanc wine**
¾	shot(s)	**Sour pineapple liqueur**
¼	shot(s)	**Crème de mûre liqueur**

Comment: Vanilla and pineapple dried by the acidity of the wine, and sweetened and flavoured by blackberry liqueur.

VANTE MARTINI

Glass: Martini
Garnish: Orange zest twist
Method: MUDDLE cardamom in base of shaker. Add other ingredients, **SHAKE** with ice and fine strain into chilled glass.

4	pods	**Cardamom**
1½	shot(s)	**Vanilla-infused Ketel One vodka**
1½	shot(s)	**Sauvignon Blanc wine**
1	shot(s)	**Cuarenta Y Tres (Licor 43) liqueur**
¼	shot(s)	**Pressed pineapple juice**

Origin: Created in 2003 by Yours Truly (Simon Difford).
Comment: Bold, aromatic and complex flavours.

VAVAVOOM

Glass: Flute
Method: POUR ingredients into chilled glass and lightly stir.

½	shot(s)	**Freshly squeezed lemon juice**
½	shot(s)	**Cointreau triple sec**
¼	shot(s)	**Sugar syrup** (2 sugar to 1 water)
Top up with		**Perrier Jouet brut champagne**

Origin: Adapted from a drink created in 2002 by Yannick Miseriaux at The Fifth Floor Bar, London, England, and named after the Renault television advertisements.
Comment: The ingredients do indeed give champagne vavavoom.

VELVET FOG

Glass: Martini
Garnish: Orange peel twist (discarded) & freshly grated nutmeg
Method: SHAKE all ingredients with ice and fine strain into chilled glass.

1½	shot(s)	**Ketel One vodka**
1¼	shot(s)	**Freshly squeezed lime juice**
¾	shot(s)	**Velvet Falernum liqueur**
¾	shot(s)	**Freshly squeezed orange juice**
2	dashes	**Angostura aromatic bitters**

Origin: Created by Dale DeGroff, New York City, USA.
Comment: Tangy, fresh and bittersweet.

VELVET HAMMER

Glass: Martini
Garnish: Grate nutmeg over drink
Method: SHAKE all ingredients with ice and fine strain into chilled glass.

1	shot(s)	**Ketel One vodka**
¾	shot(s)	**Cointreau triple sec**
¾	shot(s)	**White crème de cacao liueur**
¾	shot(s)	**Double (heavy) cream**
¾	shot(s)	**Milk**
¼	shot(s)	**Pomegranate (grenadine) syrup**

Variant: With apricot brandy and coffee liqueur in place of cacao and grenadine.
Comment: Lots of velvet with a little bit of hammer courtesy of a shot of vodka.

VENETO

● ● ● ● ○ ○

Glass: Martini
Garnish: Lemon zest twist
Method: SHAKE all ingredients with ice and fine strain into chilled glass.

2	shot(s)	**Courvoisier V.S.O.P. cognac**
½	shot(s)	**Luxardo Sambuca dei Cesari**
½	shot(s)	**Freshly squeezed lemon juice**
⅛	shot(s)	**Sugar syrup** (2 sugar to 1 water)
½	shot(s)	**Egg white**

Comment: A serious, Stinger-like drink.

VENUS IN FURS

● ● ● ● ○ ○

Glass: Collins
Garnish: Berries & lemon slice in glass
Method: SHAKE all ingredients with ice and strain into ice-filled glass.

1	shot(s)	**Raspberry flavoured vodka**
1	shot(s)	**Ketel One Citroen vodka**
3½	shot(s)	**Pressed apple juice**
3	dashes	**Angostura aromatic bitters**

Origin: A cocktail which emerged in London's bars early in 2002.
Comment: Juicy flavours with a hint of spice make for a refreshing, quaffable drink.

VENUS MARTINI

● ● ● ● ●

Glass: Martini
Garnish: Raspberry in drink
Method: MUDDLE raspberries in base of shaker. Add other ingredients, **SHAKE** with ice and fine strain into chilled glass.

7	fresh	**Raspberries**
2	shot(s)	**Tanqueray London dry gin**
1	shot(s)	**Cointreau triple sec**
¼	shot(s)	**Sugar syrup** (2 sugar to 1 water)
3	dashes	**Peychaud's aromatic bitters** (optional)

Comment: Raspberry with hints of bitter orange and gin – surprisingly dry.

VERDANT

● ● ● ● ○

Glass: Martini
Garnish: Float mint leaf
Method: SHAKE all ingredients with ice and fine strain into chilled glass.

2	shot(s)	**Zubrówka bison vodka**
⅛	shot(s)	**Green Chartreuse liqueur**
2	shot(s)	**Pressed apple juice**
½	shot(s)	**Freshly squeezed lime juice**

Origin: I created this drink in 2003 and named it after the hue of its ingredients.
Comment: A herbal apple pie of a drink.

VERDI MARTINI

● ● ● ● ● ○

Glass: Martini
Garnish: Pineapple wedge on rim
Method: SHAKE all ingredients with ice and fine strain into chilled glass.

1¾	shot(s)	**Raspberry flavoured vodka**
½	shot(s)	**Midori green melon liqueur**
½	shot(s)	**Peach Tree peach schnapps**
1	shot(s)	**Pressed pineapple juice**
1	shot(s)	**Pressed apple juice**
¼	shot(s)	**Freshly squeezed lime juice**

Origin: Adapted from a drink discovered in 2002 at the Fifth Floor Bar, London, England.
Comment: A melange of fruits combine in a gluggable short drink.

VERT'ICAL BREEZE

● ● ● ● ○ ○

Glass: Collins
Garnish: Lemon wedge
Method: SHAKE all ingredients with ice and strain into ice-filled glass.

1	shot(s)	**La Fée Parisienne (68%) absinthe**
2½	shot(s)	**Ocean Spray cranberry juice**
2½	shot(s)	**Freshly squeezed grapefruit juice**

Comment: For those who don't speak French, 'vert' means green – the colour of absinthe. Vertical suggests takeoff – try it and see.

VESPER MARTINI UPDATED #8

● ● ● ● ●

Glass: Martini
Garnish: Lemon zest twist
Method: SHAKE all ingredients with ice and fine strain into chilled glass.

3	shot(s)	**Tanqueray London dry gin**
1	shot(s)	**Ketel One vodka**
½	shot(s)	**Noilly Prat dry vermouth**

Origin: This variation on the Dry Martini is said to have been created by Gilberto Preti at Duke's Hotel, London, for the author Ian Fleming. He liked it so much that he included it in his first James Bond novel, Casino Royale, published in 1951.

In chapter seven Bond explains to a Casino bartender exactly how to make and serve the drink: "In a deep champagne goblet. Three measures of Gordon's, one of vodka, half a measure of Kina Lillet [now called Lillet Blanc]. Shake it very well until it's ice-cold, then add a large slice of lemon peel."

When made, 007 compliments the bartender, but tells him it would be better made with a grain-based vodka. He also explains his Martini to Felix Leiter, the CIA man, saying, "This drink's my own invention. I'm going to patent it when I can think of a good name."

In chapter eight, Bond meets the beautiful agent Vesper Lynd. She explains why her parents named her Vesper and Bond asks if she'd mind if he called his favourite Martini after her. Like so many of Bond's love interests Vesper turns out to be a double agent and the book closes with his words, "The bitch is dead now."

Comment: Many bartenders advocate that a Martini should be stirred and not shaken, some citing the ridiculous argument that shaking will "bruise the gin". If you like your Martinis shaken (as I do) then avoid the possible look of distaste from your server and order a Vesper. This Martini is always shaken, an action that aerates the drink, and makes it colder and more dilute than simply stirring. It also gives the drink a slightly clouded appearance and can leave small shards of ice on the surface of the drink. This is easily prevented by the use of a fine strainer when pouring.

VIAGRA FALLS

●●●●○○

Glass: Martini
Garnish: Orange zest twist
Method: SHAKE all ingredients with ice and fine strain into chilled glass.

¾	shot(s)	**La Fée Parisienne (68%) absinthe**
1½	shot(s)	**Sour apple liqueur**
1¾	shot(s)	**Chilled mineral water**
2	dashes	**Angostura orange bitters**

Origin: Created by Jack Leuwens, London, England.
Comment: Aniseed and apple – sure to get your pecker up.

VICTORIAN LEMONADE

●●●●○○

Glass: Collins
Garnish: Lemon slice
Method: Lightly MUDDLE mint (just to bruise) in base of shaker. Add other ingredients, SHAKE with ice and fine strain into ice-filled glass.

12	fresh	**Mint leaves**
1½	shot(s)	**Tanqueray London dry gin**
1	shot(s)	**Freshly squeezed lemon juice**
¾	shot(s)	**Sugar syrup** (2 sugar to 1 water)
2½	shot(s)	**Chilled mineral water**

Comment: Gin laced, mint flavoured, traditional lemonade.

VICTORIA'S SECRET NEW #8

●●●○○

Glass: Collins
Garnish: Redcurrants
Method: SHAKE first layer ingredients with ice and strain into ice-filled glass. SHAKE second layer and FLOAT over first.

---First Layer---

1	shot(s)	**Sloe gin liqueur**
½	shot(s)	**Cox's Apple & Plum cordial**
½	shot(s)	**Freshly squeezed lemon juice**
1	shot(s)	**Pressed apple juice**

---Second Layer---

1½	shot(s)	**Bacardi Superior rum**
½	shot(s)	**Boiron mango purée**
½	shot(s)	**Passion fruit syrup**
¾	shot(s)	**Freshly squeezed orange juice**

Comment: Amber and red layer easily in this fruity drink.
Origin: Created in 2008 by Jamie Stephenson at The Bar Academy, Manchester, England.

VIEUX CARRÉ COCKTAIL

●●●●●○

Glass: Old-fashioned
Garnish: Lemon zest twist
Method: STIR all ingredients with ice and strain into ice-filled glass.

1	shot(s)	**Bulleit bourbon whiskey**
1	shot(s)	**Courvoisier V.S.O.P. cognac**
1	shot(s)	**Martini Rosso sweet vermouth**
¼	shot(s)	**Bénédictine D.O.M. liqueur**
1	dashes	**Peychaud's aromatic bitters**
1	dashes	**Angostura aromatic bitters**

Origin: Created in 1938 by Walter Bergeron, the head bartender at what is now the Carousel bar at the Monteleone Hotel, New Orleans, USA. Pronounced 'Voo-Ka-Ray', the name is French for the city's French Quarter and literally translates as 'old square'.
Comment: Rather like an ultra-smooth and complex Sweet Manhattan served on the rocks.

VIEUX MOT NEW #8

●●●○○

Glass: Coupette/Martini
Garnish: Maraschino cherry
Method: SHAKE all ingredients with ice and fine strain into chilled glass.

1½	shot(s)	**Tanqueray London dry gin**
¾	shot(s)	**St-Germain elderflower liqueur**
¾	shot(s)	**Freshly squeezed lemon juice**
¼	shot(s)	**Sugar syrup** (2 sugar to 1 water)

Comment: The ingredients combine to taste like lychee. Very fresh.
Origin: Created in 2007 by Don Lee at PDT, New York City, USA.

VIOLET AFFINITY

●●●●●○

Glass: Martini
Garnish: Lemon zest twist
Method: STIR all ingredients with ice and strain into chilled glass.

2	shot(s)	**Benoit Serres crème de violette**
1	shot(s)	**Martini Rosso sweet vermouth**
1	shot(s)	**Noilly Prat dry vermouth**

Origin: An adaptation of the classic Affinity.
Comment: Amazingly delicate and complex for such a simple drink.

VODKA COLLINS

●●●●○

Glass: Collins
Garnish: Orange slice & cherry on stick (sail)
Method: SHAKE first 3 ingredients with ice and strain into ice-filled glass. TOP with soda, lightly stir and serve with straws.

2	shot(s)	**Ketel One vodka**
1	shot(s)	**Freshly squeezed lemon juice**
½	shot(s)	**Sugar syrup** (2 sugar to 1 water)
Top up with		**Soda water** (club soda)

AKA: Joe Collins
Comment: A Tom Collins with vodka – a refreshing balance of sweet and sour.

VODKA ESPRESSO

Glass: Old-fashioned
Garnish: Three coffee beans
Method: SHAKE all ingredients with ice and strain into ice-filled glass.

2	shot(s)	**Ketel One vodka**
1½	shot(s)	**Espresso coffee**
½	shot(s)	**Kahlúa coffee liqueur**
¼	shot(s)	**Sugar syrup** (2 sugar to 1 water)

Origin: Created in 1983 by Dick Bradsell at the Soho Brasserie, London, England.
Comment: Vodka and coffee combine in this tasty wake up call.

VODKA GIMLET

Glass: Martini
Garnish: Lime wedge or cherry
Method: STIR all ingredients with ice and strain into chilled glass.

2½	shot(s)	**Ketel One vodka**
1¼	shot(s)	**Rose's lime cordial**

Variants: Shaken. The original Gimlet is based on gin.
Comment: Sweetened lime fortified with vodka.

VODKA SOUR

Glass: Old-fashioned
Garnish: Lemon slice & cherry on stick (sail)
Method: SHAKE all ingredients with ice and strain into ice-filled glass.

2	shot(s)	**Ketel One vodka**
1	shot(s)	**Freshly squeezed lemon juice**
½	shot(s)	**Sugar syrup** (2 sugar to 1 water)
3	dashes	**Angostura aromatic bitters**
½	fresh	**Egg white**

Comment: A great vodka based drink balancing sweet and sour.

VODKA RICKEY NEW #8

Glass: Collins (small 8oz)
Garnish: Immerse length of lime peel in drink.
Method: SHAKE first 3 ingredients with ice and strain into ice-filled glass. **TOP** with soda.

2	shot(s)	**Ketel One vodka**
½	shot(s)	**Freshly squeezed lime juice**
¼	shot(s)	**Sugar syrup** (2 sugar to 1 water)
Top up with		**Soda water**

Comment: Lacks interest but balanced and hard to fault as a simple refreshing drink.

VODKATINI UPDATED #8

Glass: Martini
Garnish: Lemon zest twist or olives
Method: SHAKE all ingredients with ice and fine strain into chilled glass.

2½	shot(s)	**Ketel One vodka**
¼	shot(s)	**Noilly Prat dry vermouth**

AKA: Kangaroo
Variant: Stir rather than shake.
Comment: Temperature is key to the enjoyment of this modern classic. Consume while icy cold.

VOLGA BOATMAN

Glass: Martini
Garnish: Orange zest twist
Method: SHAKE all ingredients with ice and fine strain into chilled glass.

1½	shot(s)	**Ketel One vodka**
¾	shot(s)	**Kirsch eau de vie**
1½	shot(s)	**Freshly squeezed orange juice**

Origin: Recipe adapted from David Embury's classic Fine Art of Mixing Drinks. Named after the epic (and somewhat camp) Cecil B. De Mille movie, which took its name from a Russian folksong hymning the Volga, Europe's longest river.
Comment: A Screwdriver served straight-up with a twist of cherry.

VOODOO

Glass: Collins
Garnish: Dust with cinnamon sprinkled through flame
Method: SHAKE all ingredients with ice and strain into ice-filled glass.

2	shot(s)	**Zacapa aged rum**
¾	shot(s)	**Martini Rosso sweet vermouth**
2½	shot(s)	**Pressed apple juice**
½	shot(s)	**Freshly squeezed lime juice**
¼	shot(s)	**Sugar syrup** (2 sugar to 1 water)

Origin: Created in 2002 by Alex Kammerling, London, England.
Comment: The rich flavour of the aged rum marries well with apple and lime juice.

VOWEL COCKTAIL

Glass: Martini
Garnish: Orange zest twist
Method: SHAKE all ingredients with ice and fine strain into chilled glass.

1¼	shot(s)	**Johnnie Walker Scotch whisky**
1	shot(s)	**Kümmel liqueur**
1	shot(s)	**Martini Rosso sweet vermouth**
¾	shot(s)	**Freshly squeezed orange juice**
2	dashes	**Angostura aromatic bitters**

Origin: Adapted from a recipe in Vintage Spirits & Forgotten Cocktails by Ted Haigh (AKA Dr. Cocktail).
Comment: Caraway from the Kümmel subtly dominates this aromatic drink.

WAGON WHEEL

Glass: Old-fashioned
Garnish: Lemon slice
Method: SHAKE all ingredients with ice and fine strain into glass filled with crushed ice.

1½	shot(s)	**Southern Comfort liqueur**
1½	shot(s)	**Courvoisier V.S.O.P. cognac**
¾	shot(s)	**Freshly squeezed lemon juice**
¼	shot(s)	**Pomegranate (grenadine) syrup**

Origin: Adapted from a recipe purloined from David Embury's Fine Art of Mixing Drinks.
Comment: This classic cocktail will be best appreciated by lovers of Southern Comfort.

WAH-WAH

Glass: Martini
Garnish: Orange zest twist
Method: SHAKE all ingredients with ice and fine strain into chilled glass.

1½	shot(s)	**Macchu pisco**
1	shot(s)	**St-Germain elderflower liqueur**
¾	shot(s)	**Aperol**
¾	shot(s)	**Freshly squeezed grapefruit juice**
1	dash	**Angostura aromatic bitters**

Origin: Created in 2007 at Range, San Francisco, USA.
Comment: Bittersweet and complex with hints of elderflower and grapefruit.

> ## 'I'VE HAD EIGHTEEN STRAIGHT WHISKIES. I THINK THAT'S THE RECORD.'
> ### DYLAN THOMAS

WALNUT ALEXANDER NEW #8

Glass: Martini
Garnish: Nutmeg dust
Method: SHAKE all ingredients with ice and fine strain into chilled glass.

2	shot(s)	**Courvoisier V.S.O.P. cognac**
¼	shot(s)	**Sugar syrup** (2 sugar to 1 water)
½	shot(s)	**Nocello walnut liqueur**
½	shot(s)	**Milk**
½	shot(s)	**Double (heavy) cream**

Origin: Created in 2008 by Simon Difford at The Cabinet Room, London, England.
Comment: One to accompany the nutty chocolates from the after-dinner selection box.

WALNUT MARTINI

Glass: Martini
Garnish: Float walnut half
Method: STIR all ingredients with ice and strain into chilled glass.

2	shot(s)	**Ketel One vodka**
¾	shot(s)	**Tuaca Italian liqueur**
¾	shot(s)	**Nocello walnut liqueur**
¾	shot(s)	**Noilly Prat dry vermouth**

Origin: Created in 2005 by Yours Truly (Simon Difford).
Comment: Nutty but nice.

WALDORF COCKTAIL NO.1 NEW #8

Glass: Martini/Coupette
Garnish: Lemon zest twist
Method: STIR all ingredients with ice and strain into chilled glass.

2	shot(s)	**Bulleit bourbon whiskey**
1	shot(s)	**Martini Rosso sweet vermouth**
⅛	shot(s)	**La Fée Parisienne (68%) absinthe**
2	dashes	**Angostura aromatic bitters**

Comment: A Sweet Manhattan dried by the merest hint of bitter absinthe.
Origin: The eponymous cocktail from the Waldorf Hotel occupied a site on New York's Fifth Avenue. The Empire State Building now stands occupies the hotel's original site and what has long been known as the Waldorf-Astoria Hotel now occupies a landmark Art-Deco building at 301 Park Avenue. Consisting of equal parts whiskey (probably originally rye), sweet vermouth and absinthe with a dash of bitters. This is the earlier of the two classic versions of this vintage cocktail which appeared in Jacques Straub's 1914 book 'Drinks' and later in A. S. Crockett's 1935 The Old Waldorf-Astoria Bar Book. The recipe above is adapted to better suit modern palates and ingredients.

WALDORF COCKTAIL NO.2 NEW #8

Glass: Martini
Garnish: Lemon zest twist
Method: SHAKE all ingredients with ice and fine strain into chilled glass.

2	shot(s)	**Swedish Punch**
1½	shot(s)	**Tanqueray London dry gin**
¾	shot(s)	**Freshly squeezed lime juice**

Variant: Astor
Comment: Lime works better than lemon but like the Astor, using a combination of lime and lemon makes for a better drink.
Origin: This is the later of the two versions of this vintage cocktail from New York's Waldorf-Astoria Hotel. It appears in the 1939 Café Royale book and in the 1955 United Kingdom Bartender's Book. Both books offer a choice between using lemon or lime juice. The original recipe calls for two parts Swedish punch to one part gin but with the punches I've tried this makes for an overly sweet drink.

W

WALTZING MATILDA

Glass: Collins
Garnish: Half orange slice
Method: Cut passion fruit in half and scoop out flesh into shaker. Add next 3 ingredients, **SHAKE** with ice and fine strain into ice-filled glass. **TOP** with ginger ale.

1	fresh	Passion fruit
1	shot(s)	Tanqueray London dry gin
2	shot(s)	Sauvignon Blanc wine
⅛	shot(s)	Grand Marnier liqueur
Top up with		Ginger ale

Origin: Adapted from a recipe from David Embury's classic book, The Fine Art of Mixing Drinks.
Comment: Passion fruit, gin, wine and ginger ale all combine well in this refreshing drink.

WANTON ABANDON

Glass: Martini
Garnish: Strawberry on rim
Method: **MUDDLE** strawberries in base of shaker. Add next 3 ingredients, **SHAKE** with ice and fine strain into chilled glass. **TOP** with champagne.

5	fresh	Strawberries (hulled)
2	shot(s)	Ketel One vodka
¾	shot(s)	Freshly squeezed lemon juice
½	shot(s)	Sugar syrup (2 sugar to 1 water)
Top up with		Perrier Jouet brut champagne

Comment: A crowd pleaser – looks great and its fruity, balanced flavour will offend few.

> ## 'I HAVE TAKEN MORE OUT OF ALCOHOL THAN ALCOHOL HAS TAKEN OUT OF ME.'
> ### WINSTON CHURCHILL

WARD EIGHT

Glass: Martini
Garnish: Orange slice & cherry
Method: **SHAKE** all ingredients with ice and fine strain into chilled glass.

2¼	shot(s)	Bulleit bourbon whiskey
¾	shot(s)	Freshly squeezed lemon juice
¾	shot(s)	Freshly squeezed orange juice
¼	shot(s)	Pomegranate (grenadine) syrup
½	shot(s)	Chilled mineral water (omit if wet ice)

Origin: Ward Eight was a voting district of Boston and famed for its political corruption. This drink was first served by Tom Hussion in November 1898 at Boston's Locke-Ober Café, in honour of Martin Lomasney, who owned the café and was running for election in Ward Eight.
Comment: This is a spirited, sweet and sour combination – like most politicians.

WARSAW

Glass: Martini
Garnish: Orange zest twist
Method: **STIR** all ingredients with ice and strain into chilled glass.

2	shot(s)	Ketel One vodka
½	shot(s)	Polska Wiśniówka cherry liqueur
¼	shot(s)	Cointreau triple sec
2	dashes	Angostura aromatic bitters
¾	shot(s)	Chilled mineral water (omit if wet ice)

Comment: Subtle cherry notes with orange.

WARSAW COOLER

Glass: Collins
Garnish: Mint sprig & orange zest
Method: **STIR** honey with vodka in base of shaker until honey dissolves. Add other ingredients, **SHAKE** with ice and strain into ice-filled glass.

2	spoons	Runny honey
1½	shot(s)	Żubrówka bison vodka
½	shot(s)	Sailor Jerry spiced rum
¼	shot(s)	Cointreau triple sec
½	shot(s)	Sugar syrup (2 sugar to 1 water)
¾	shot(s)	Freshly squeezed lemon juice
2	shot(s)	Pressed apple juice

Origin: Created in 2002 by Morgan Watson of Apartment, Belfast, Northern Ireland.
Comment: Orange, honey, apple and spice laced with Polish bison grass vodka.

WARSAW PACT NEW #8

Glass: Martini/Coupette
Garnish: Float mint leaf
Method: **SHAKE** all ingredients with ice and fine strain into chilled glass.

5	fresh	Mint leaves
2	shot(s)	Żubrówka bison vodka
½	shot(s)	Luxardo Amaretto di Saschira
1½	shot(s)	Pressed apple juice

Origin: Adapted from a drink discovered in 2007 at Paparazzi, Warsaw, Poland.
Comment: Complex fruit and mint flavours combine in this beautifully balanced easy cocktail.

WASABI MARTINI

Glass: Martini
Garnish: Float strips of yaki nori seaweed.
Method: Squeeze a pea-sized quantity of wasabi paste onto a barspoon and **STIR** with vodka until wasabi dissolves. Add other ingredients, **SHAKE** with ice and fine strain into chilled glass.

2	shot(s)	Ketel One vodka
1	pea	Wasabi paste
¾	shot(s)	Freshly squeezed lemon juice
½	shot(s)	Sugar syrup (2 sugar to 1 water)

Origin: Created in 2004 by Philippe Guidi at Morton's, London, England.
Comment: Wonderfully balanced with spicy heat and a zesty finish.

WASH HOUSE

Glass: Martini
Garnish: Fresh thyme sprig
Method: Lightly **MUDDLE** basil (just to bruise) in base of shaker. Add other ingredients, **SHAKE** with ice and fine strain into chilled glass.

4	fresh	**Basil leaves**
2	shot(s)	**Ketel One vodka**
½	shot(s)	**Freshly squeezed lime juice**
½	shot(s)	**Sugar syrup** (2 sugar to 1 water)
½	shot(s)	**Chilled mineral water** (omit if wet ice)

Origin: Adapted from a recipe by Neyah White at Nopa, San Francisco, USA. The building that now houses Nopa was once a laundry, hence the name.
Comment: Delicately herbal – simple but refreshing.

WASHINGTON APPLE

Glass: Collins
Garnish: Apple slice
Method: **SHAKE** first 4 ingredients with ice and fine strain into ice-filled glass. **DRIZZLE** grenadine over drink. Serve with straws.

2	shot(s)	**Ketel One vodka**
3	shot(s)	**Pressed apple juice**
¼	shot(s)	**Freshly squeezed lime juice**
½	shot(s)	**Sour apple liqueur**
¼	shot(s)	**Pomegranate (grenadine) syrup**

Origin: Created by Wayne Collins, London, England.
Comment: A long version of the once ubiquitous Sour Apple Martini.

WATERMELON & BASIL MARTINI

Glass: Martini
Garnish: Watermelon wedge on rim
Method: Cut watermelon into 16 segments, chop the flesh from one segment into cubes and **MUDDLE** in base of shaker. Add other ingredients, **SHAKE** with ice and fine strain into chilled glass.

¹/₁₆	fresh	**Watermelon** (diced)
7	fresh	**Basil leaves**
2	shot(s)	**Tanqueray London dry gin**
½	shot(s)	**Sugar syrup** (2 sugar to 1 water)

Comment: Refreshing watermelon with interesting herbal hints from the basil and gin.

WATERMELON & BASIL SMASH

Glass: Collins
Garnish: Watermelon wedge on rim
Method: Cut watermelon into 16 segments, chop the flesh from one segment into cubes and **MUDDLE** in base of shaker. Add next 3 ingredients, **SHAKE** with ice and fine strain into ice-filled glass. **TOP** with ginger ale.

¹/₁₆	fresh	**Watermelon** (diced)
8	fresh	**Basil leaves**
2	shot(s)	**Don Julio reposado tequila**
¾	shot(s)	**Luxardo limoncello liqueur**
Top up with		**Ginger ale**

Comment: Sweet and sour, long and refreshing with subtle hints of basil, ginger and tequila amongst the fruit.

WATERMELON COOLER NEW #8

Glass: Collins
Garnish: Watermelon wedge
Method: Shake all ingredients with ice and strain into ice-filled glass.

1½	shot(s)	**Bacardi Superior rum**
½	shot(s)	**Midori green melon liqueur**
3½	shot(s)	**Ocean Spray cranberry juice**
¼	shot(s)	**Freshly squeezed lime juice**

Comment: Summery, refreshing and light.

WATERMELON COSMO

Glass: Martini (large)
Garnish: Watermelon wedge on rim
Method: Cut watermelon into 16 segments, chop the flesh from one segment into cubes and **MUDDLE** in base of shaker. Add other ingredients, **SHAKE** with ice and fine strain into chilled glass.

¹/₁₆	fresh	**Watermelon** (diced)
2	shot(s)	**Ketel One Citroen vodka**
¾	shot(s)	**Freshly squeezed lime juice**
¾	shot(s)	**Ocean Spray cranberry juice**
½	shot(s)	**Midori green melon liqueur**
⅛	shot(s)	**Rose's lime cordial**
2	dashes	**Angostura orange bitters**

Origin: Created in 2003 by Eric Fossard at Cecconi's, London, England.
Comment: Looks like a standard Cosmo but tastes just as the name suggests.

HOW TO MAKE SUGAR SYRUP

To make your own sugar syrup, gradually pour TWO cups of granulated sugar into a saucepan containing ONE cup of hot water. Stir as you pour and carry on stirring and simmering until the sugar is dissolved. Do not let the water even come close to boiling and only simmer for as long as it takes to dissolve the sugar. Allow syrup to cool and pour into an empty bottle. Ideally, you should finely strain your syrup into the bottle to remove any undissolved crystals which could otherwise encourage crystallisation. If kept in a refrigerator this mixture will last for a couple of months.

WATERMELON MAN

Glass: Collins
Garnish: Lime wedge
Method: SHAKE first 5 ingredients with ice and strain into ice-filled glass. **TOP** with soda and serve with straws.

2	shot(s)	**Ketel One vodka**
1	shot(s)	**Watermelon liqueur**
1	shot(s)	**Freshly squeezed lime juice**
½	shot(s)	**Freshly squeezed orange juice**
1	shot(s)	**Pomegranate (grenadine) syrup**
Top up with		**Soda water** (club soda)

Origin: Named after the Herbie Hancock track and popularised by a club night promoter called Cookie in Berlin during the mid-1990s. He started serving this cocktail at his club nights and now practically every bar in Berlin offers it. Try the original at his Cookie Club.
Comment: Sweet and far from sophisticated, but better than the fodder peddled at most clubs.

WATERMELON MARTINI

Glass: Martini
Garnish: Watermelon wedge on rim
Method: Cut watermelon into 16 segments, chop the flesh from one segment into cubes and **MUDDLE** in base of shaker. Add other ingredients, **SHAKE** with ice and fine strain into chilled glass.

$1/16$	fresh	**Watermelon** (diced)
2	shot(s)	**Ketel One vodka**
½	shot(s)	**Sugar syrup** (2 sugar to 1 water)

Comment: So fruity, you can almost convince yourself this is a health drink!

WATERS OF CHAOS NEW #8

Glass: Old-fashioned
Garnish: Ti-Punch style lime zest disc
Method: SHAKE all ingredients with ice and strain into ice-filled glass.

1½	shot(s)	**Bokma oude genever**
¼	shot(s)	**Wray & Nephew overproof rum**
¼	shot(s)	**Green Chartreuse liqueur**
¾	shot(s)	**Freshly squeezed lime juice**
½	shot(s)	**Sugar syrup** (2 sugar to 1 water)
½	shot(s)	**Chilled mineral water** (omit if wet ice)

Comment: Overproof rum and Chartreuse do indeed have the potential to be waters of chaos.
Origin: Created by Yours Truly (Simon Difford) at the Cabinet Room, London, England and named after the words of the track Argha Noah by Nightmares on Wax.

DRINKS ARE GRADED AS FOLLOWS:

- DISGUSTING
- PRETTY AWFUL
- BEST AVOIDED
- DISAPPOINTING
- ACCEPTABLE
- GOOD
- RECOMMENDED
- HIGHLY RECOMMENDED
- OUTSTANDING / EXCEPTIONAL

WEBSTER MARTINI

Glass: Martini
Garnish: Lime zest twist
Method: SHAKE all ingredients with ice and fine strain into chilled glass.

2	shot(s)	**Tanqueray Londn dry gin**
1	shot(s)	**Noilly Prat dry vermouth**
½	shot(s)	**Bols apricot brandy liqueur**
½	shot(s)	**Freshly squeezed lime juice**

Origin: Adapted from a recipe in Harry Craddock's 1930 Savoy Cocktail Book. Craddock writes of this drink, "A favourite cocktail at the bar of the S.S. Mauretania."
Comment: Balanced rather than sweet. The old-school Dry Martini meets the contemporary fruit driven Martini.

WEEPING JESUS

Glass: Old-fashioned
Method: SHAKE first 3 ingredients with ice and strain into glass filled with crushed ice. **TOP** with lemonade.

1	shot(s)	**La Fée Parisienne (68%) absinthe**
1	shot(s)	**Peach Tree peach schnapps**
1	shot(s)	**Pomegranate (grenadine) syrup**
Top up with		**Lemonade/Sprite/7-Up**

Origin: Created in 2002 by Andy Jones at Yates's, London, England.
Comment: This bright red cocktail makes the strong aniseed flavours of absinthe approachable.

THE WENTWORTH

Glass: Martini
Garnish: Orange zest twist
Method: SHAKE all ingredients with ice and fine strain into chilled glass.

1¼	shot(s)	**Bulleit bourbon whiskey**
1¼	shot(s)	**Dubonnet Red** (French made)
1¼	shot(s)	**Ocean Spray cranberry juice**

Origin: Created in 2003 by Sharon Cooper at the Harvest Restaurant, Pomfret, Connecticut, USA.
Comment: Bourbon adds backbone to this fruity drink.

WET MARTINI

Glass: Martini
Garnish: Olive or twist?
Method: STIR all ingredients with ice and strain into chilled glass.

3	shot(s)	**Tanqueray London dry gin**
1½	shot(s)	**Noilly Prat dry vermouth**

Origin: A generous measure of vermouth to two of gin, hence the name 'Wet' Martini.
Comment: Reputed to be a favourite of HRH Prince Charles.

THE WET SPOT

Glass: Martini
Garnish: Lemon zest twist
Method: SHAKE all ingredients with ice and fine strain into chilled glass.

1½	shot(s)	**Tanqueray London dry gin**
½	shot(s)	**Bols apricot brandy liqueur**
1	shot(s)	**St-Germain elderflower liqueur**
1	shot(s)	**Pressed apple juice**
¾	shot(s)	**Freshly squeezed lemon juice**

Origin: Adapted from a drink created by Willy Shine and Aisha Sharpe at Bed Bar, New York City, USA.
Comment: Sharp but fresh tasting and moreish.

WHAT THE HELL

Glass: Martini
Garnish: Lime wedge on rim
Method: SHAKE all ingredients with ice and fine strain into chilled glass.

2	shot(s)	**Tanqueray London dry gin**
1	shot(s)	**Bols apricot brandy liqueur**
¾	shot(s)	**Noilly Pray dry vermouth**
¼	shot(s)	**Freshly squeezed lime juice**
⅛	shot(s)	**Sugar syrup** (2 sugar to 1 water)

Comment: Gin and dry apricots.

THE CRITERION WAS BRITAIN'S FIRST COCKTAIL BAR AND OPENED IN 1910 IN PICCADILLY CIRCUS, LONDON.

WHIP ME & BEAT ME

Glass: Shot
Method: SHAKE all ingredients with ice and fine strain into chilled glass.

½	shot(s)	**La Fée Parisienne (68%) absinthe**
½	shot(s)	**Malibu coconut rum liqueur**
½	shot(s)	**Double (heavy) cream**
½	shot(s)	**Milk**

Comment: A creamy, coconut, absinthe laden shot.

WHISKEY COBBLER

Glass: Goblet
Garnish: Lemon slice & mint sprig
Method: SHAKE all ingredients with ice and strain into glass filled with crushed ice.

2	shot(s)	**Johnnie Walker Scotch whisky**
½	shot(s)	**Courvoisier V.S.O.P. cognac**
½	shot(s)	**Grand Marnier liqueur**

Comment: A hardcore yet sophisticated drink.

WHISKEY COLLINS

Glass: Collins
Garnish: Orange slice & cherry on stick (sail)
Method: SHAKE first 4 ingredients with ice and strain into ice-filled glass. **TOP** with soda water, lightly stir and serve with straws.

2	shot(s)	**Bulleit bourbon whiskey**
¾	shot(s)	**Freshly squeezed lemon juice**
½	shot(s)	**Sugar syrup** (2 sugar to 1 water)
3	dashes	**Angostura aromatic bitters**
Top up with		**Soda water** (club soda)

Comment: A whiskey based twist on the classic Tom Collins.

WHISKEY DAISY #1

Glass: Martini
Garnish: Lemon zest twist
Method: SHAKE all ingredients with ice and fine strain into chilled glass.

1¾	shot(s)	**Bulleit bourbon whiskey**
¾	shot(s)	**Freshly squeezed lemon juice**
½	shot(s)	**Cointreau triple sec**
¼	shot(s)	**Pomegranate (grenadine) syrup**

Comment: This venerable, bourbon led classic has a strong citrus flavour.

WHISKEY DAISY #2 NEW #8

Glass: Goblet
Garnish: Lemon & orange zest twists
Method: SHAKE first 4 ingredients with ice and fine strain into glass filled with crushed ice. **TOP** with small dash soda.

1½	shot(s)	**Bulleit bourbon whisky**
1	spoon	**Honey syrup** (4 honey to 1 water)
½	shot(s)	**Grand Marnier liqueur**
¾	shot(s)	**Freshly squeezed lemon juice**
Top up with		**Soda water** (club soda)

Comment: Light, fresh and fruity. Perfect for a summer's afternoon.
Origin: Recipe adapted from Harry Johnson's 1888 'Bartender's Manual'.

WHISKEY SOUR #1 (CLASSIC FORMULA)

Glass: Old-fashioned
Garnish: Lemon slice & cherry on stick (sail)
Method: SHAKE all ingredients with ice and strain into ice-filled glass.

2	shot(s)	**Bulleit bourbon whiskey**
¾	shot(s)	**Freshly squeezed lemon juice**
1	shot(s)	**Sugar syrup** (2 sugar to 1 water)
3	dashes	**Angostura aromatic bitters**
½	fresh	**Egg white**

Origin: This recipe follows the classic sour proportions (3:4:8): three quarter part of the sour ingredient (lemon juice), one part of the sweet ingredient (sugar syrup) and two parts of the strong ingredient (whiskey).
Comment: I find the classic formulation more sweet than sour and prefer the 4:2:8 ratio below.

WHISKEY SOUR #2 (DIFFORD'S FORMULA)

Glass: Old-fashioned
Garnish: Lemon slice & cherry on stick (sail)
Method: SHAKE all ingredients with ice and strain into ice-filled glass.

2	shot(s)	Bulleit bourbon whiskey
1	shot(s)	Freshly squeezed lemon juice
½	shot(s)	Sugar syrup (2 sugar to 1 water)
3	dashes	Angostura aromatic bitters
½	fresh	Egg white

Origin: My 4:2:8 sour formula.
Comment: Smooth with a hint of citrus sourness and an invigorating blast of whiskey.

WHISKEY SQUIRT

Glass: Collins
Garnish: Peach slice
Method: SHAKE first 3 ingredients with ice and strain into ice-filled glass. **TOP** with soda from a siphon. Serve with straws.

2	shot(s)	Boiron peach puree
2	shot(s)	Bulleit bourbon whiskey
¼	shot(s)	Grand Marnier liqueur
Top up with		Soda (from siphon)

Origin: Adapted from a recipe purloined from David Embury's classic book, The Fine Art of Mixing Drinks.
Comment: Peach combines wonderfully with bourbon and this drink benefits from that marriage.

WHISKY FIZZ

Glass: Collins
Garnish: Lemon slice
Method: SHAKE first 3 ingredients with ice and strain into ice-filled glass. **TOP** with soda, lightly stir and serve with straws.

2	shot(s)	Johnnie Walker Scotch whisky
1	shot(s)	Freshly squeezed lemon juice
½	shot(s)	Sugar syrup (2 sugar to 1 water)
Top up with		Soda (from siphon)

Comment: The character of the whisky shines through this refreshing, balanced, sweet and sour drink.

WHISKY MAC

Glass: Old-fashioned
Method: POUR ingredients into ice-filled glass and lightly stir.

2	shot(s)	Johnnie Walker Scotch whisky
1	shot(s)	Stone's original green ginger wine

Comment: Ginger wine smoothes and spices Scotch.

WHITE CARGO NEW #8

Glass: Martini
Garnish: Freshly grated nutmeg dust
Method: SHAKE all ingredients with ice and fine strain into chilled glass.

2	shot(s)	Tanqueray London dry gin
1	scoop	Häagen Dazs vanilla ice cream
¼	shot(s)	Chardonnay white wine

Origin: Adapted from Harry Craddock's 1930 'The Savoy Cocktail Book'.
Comment: A delicious dessert-style drink.

WHITE COSMO

Glass: Martini
Garnish: Orange zest twist
Method: SHAKE all ingredients with ice and fine strain into chilled glass.

1	shot(s)	Ketel One Citroen vodka
1	shot(s)	Cointreau triple sec
1½	shot(s)	Ocean Spray white cranberry
½	shot(s)	Freshly squeezed lime juice

AKA: Cosmo Blanco
Origin: Emerged during 2002 in New York City.
Comment: Just what it says on the tin.

WHITE ELEPHANT

Glass: Martini
Garnish: Dust with cocoa powder
Method: SHAKE all ingredients with ice and fine strain into chilled glass.

1¾	shot(s)	Ketel One vodka
¾	shot(s)	White crème de cacao liqueur
¾	shot(s)	Double (heavy) cream
¾	shot(s)	Milk

AKA: White Beach
Comment: Smooth and creamy with a hint of chocolate.

WHITE GIN FIZZ

Glass: Collins
Garnish: Lemon wedge in drink
Method: SHAKE first 4 ingredients with ice and strain into ice-filled glass. **TOP** with soda from a siphon.

2	shot(s)	Tanqueray London dry gin
1	shot(s)	Freshly squeezed lemon juice
¼	shot(s)	Sugar syrup (2 sugar to 1 water)
2	scoops	Lemon sorbet (see recipe under 'L')
Top up with		Soda water (from siphon)

Origin: Created in 2003 by Tony Conigliaro at Shumi, London, England.
Comment: Almost creamy in consistency, this gin fizz reminds me of the Sgroppino found in Venice.

WHITE KNIGHT

Glass: Martini
Garnish: Grated nutmeg
Method: **SHAKE** all ingredients with ice and fine strain into chilled glass.

¾	shot(s)	Johnnie Walker Scotch whisky
¾	shot(s)	Kahlúa coffee liqueur
¾	shot(s)	Drambuie liqueur
¾	shot(s)	Double (heavy) cream
¾	shot(s)	Milk

Comment: This creamy after-dinner drink features Scotch and honey with a hint of coffee. Not too sweet.

WHITE LADY UPDATED #8

Glass: Martini
Garnish: Lemon zest twist
Method: **SHAKE** all ingredients with ice and fine strain into chilled glass.

1¾	shot(s)	Tanqueray London dry gin
1	shot(s)	Cointreau triple sec
1	shot(s)	Freshly squeezed lemon juice
1	fresh	Egg white

Variation: Chelsea Sidecar, Boxcar
Origin: In 1919 Harry MacElhone, while working at Ciro's Club, London, England, created his first White Lady with 2 shots triple sec, 1 shot white crème de menthe and 1 shot lemon juice. In 1923, he created the White Lady above at his own Harry's New York Bar in Paris, France.
Comment: A simple but lovely classic drink with a sour finish.

WHITE LION

Glass: Martini
Garnish: Lime wedge on rim
Method: **SHAKE** all ingredients with ice and fine strain into chilled glass.

2	shot(s)	Bacardi Superior rum
¼	shot(s)	Cointreau triple sec
½	shot(s)	Freshly squeezed lime juice
¼	shot(s)	Pomegranate (grenadine) syrup

Origin: Adapted from a recipe purloined from David Embury's classic book, The Fine Art of Mixing Drinks.
Comment: This fruity Daiquiri is superb when made with quality pomegranate syrup and rum.

WHITE RUSSIAN UPDATED #8

Glass: Old-fashioned
Garnish: Dust with grated nutmeg
Method: **SHAKE** all ingredients with ice and strain into ice-filled glass.

2	shot(s)	Ketel One vodka
1	shot(s)	Kahlúa coffee liqueur
½	shot(s)	Double (heavy) cream
½	shot(s)	Milk

Variant: Shake and strain vodka and coffee liqueur, then float cream.
Comment: A Black Russian smoothed with cream.

WHITE SANGRIA

Glass: Old-fashioned
Garnish: Fruit slices
Method: **SHAKE** first 3 ingredients with ice and strain into ice-filled glass. **TOP** with lemonade.

1	shot(s)	Grand Marnier liqueur
2	shot(s)	Sauvignon Blanc wine
1	shot(s)	Ocean Spray white cranberry
Top up with		Lemonade/Sprite/7-Up

Comment: A twist on the traditional Spanish and Portugese punch.

WHITE SATIN

Glass: Martini
Garnish: Cocoa dust
Method: **SHAKE** all ingredients with ice and fine strain into chilled glass.

1½	shot(s)	Galliano L'Autentico liqueur
1	shot(s)	Kahlúa coffee liqueur
¾	shot(s)	Double (heavy) cream
¾	shot(s)	Milk

Comment: Smoother than a cashmere codpiece!

WHITE STINGER

Glass: Old-fashioned
Method: **SHAKE** all ingredients with ice and strain into ice-filled glass.

2	shot(s)	Ketel One vodka
½	shot(s)	White crème de menthe liqueur
½	shot(s)	White crème de cacao liqueur

Comment: Liquid After Eights.

WIBBLE

Glass: Martini
Garnish: Lemon zest twist
Method: **SHAKE** all ingredients with ice and fine strain into chilled glass.

1	shot(s)	Tanqueray London dry gin
1	shot(s)	Sloe gin liqueur
1	shot(s)	Freshly squeezed grapefruit juice
¼	shot(s)	Freshly squeezed lemon juice
⅛	shot(s)	Sugar syrup (2 sugar to 1 water)
⅛	shot(s)	Crème de mûre liqueur

Origin: Created in 1999 by Dick Bradsell at The Player, London, England, for Nick Blacknell, a conspicuous lover of gin.
Comment: As Dick once said to me, "It may make you wobble, but it won't make you fall down." Complex and balanced.

NAKED MARTINIS BECAME INCREASINGLY POPULAR DURING THE SECOND WORLD WAR WHEN VERMOUTH WAS RATIONED IN BRITAIN.

WIDOW'S KISS UPDATED #8

Glass: Martini
Garnish: Mint leaf
Method: STIR all ingredients with ice and fine strain into chilled glass.

1½	shot(s)	**Boulard Grand Solage calvados**
¾	shot(s)	**Bénédictine D.O.M. liqueur**
¾	shot(s)	**Yellow Chartreuse liqueur**
2	dashes	**Angostura aromatic bitters**

Comment: Fantastically herbal with hints of apple, mint and eucalyptus. This classic is often made with green Chartreuse – I prefer mine with half yellow and half green and dare I say shaken.
Origin: Created before 1895 by George Kappeler at New York City's Holland House.

WILD BLOSSOM NEW #8

Glass: Martini
Garnish: Grapefruit twist
Method: SHAKE all ingredients with ice and fine strain into chilled glass.

2	shot(s)	**Tanqueray London dry gin**
¾	shot(s)	**St-Germain elderflower Liqueur**
¾	shot(s)	**Freshly squeezed grapefruit juice**
1	shot(s)	**Ocean Spray cranberry juice**

Origin: Adapted from a drink created in 2007 by James Scarito at BLT Market, New York City, USA.
Comment: Aptly named – It is indeed blossom-like, yet also dry and serious.

WILD HONEY

Glass: Martini
Garnish: Grate nutmeg over drink
Method: SHAKE all ingredients with ice and fine strain into chilled glass.

1	shot(s)	**Johnnie Walker Scotch whisky**
½	shot(s)	**Vanilla-infused Ketel One vodka**
¾	shot(s)	**Drambuie liqueur**
½	shot(s)	**Galliano L'Autentico liqueur**
½	shot(s)	**Double (heavy) cream**
½	shot(s)	**Milk**

Origin: Created in 2001 by James Price at Bar Red, London, England.
Comment: A serious yet creamy after dinner cocktail with whisky and honey.

WILD PROMENADE MARTINI

Glass: Martini
Garnish: Float 3 raspberries
Method: MUDDLE cucumber and raspberries in base of shaker. Add other ingredients, **SHAKE** with ice and fine strain into ice-filled glass.

2	inch	**Cucumber** (peeled & chopped)
5	fresh	**Raspberries**
1½	shot(s)	**Ketel One vodka**
½	shot(s)	**Raspberry flavoured vodka**
½	shot(s)	**Crème de framboise liqueur**
¼	shot(s)	**Sugar syrup** (2 sugar to 1 water)

Origin: Created in 2002 by Mehdi Otmann at The Player, London, England.
Comment: Rich raspberry with green hints of cucumber.

WILL OF ALAN NEW #8

Glass: Old-fashioned
Garnish: Lime wedge
Method: DRY SHAKE all ingredients without ice. Add ice, **SHAKE** again and strain into ice-filled glass.

2	shot(s)	**Zacapa aged rum**
½	shot(s)	**Velvet Falernam liqueur**
¾	shot(s)	**Pressed pineapple juice**
¾	shot(s)	**Freshly squeezed lime juice**
2	dashes	**Old-fashioned bitters**
¼	fresh	**Egg white**

Comment: Fantastic, spiced, tiki-style twisted Daiquiri.
Origin: Discovered in 2008 at Tonic, Edinburgh, Scotland.

'TEQUILA LOVES ME EVEN IF YOU DON'T.'
KENNY CHESNEY

WILTON MARTINI

Glass: Martini
Garnish: Float cinnamon dusted apple slice
Method: SHAKE all ingredients with ice and fine strain into chilled glass.

1	shot(s)	**Ketel One vodka**
1	shot(s)	**Boulard Grand Solage calvados**
½	shot(s)	**Berentzen apple schnapps**
⅛	shot(s)	**Goldschläger cinnamon schnapps**
1½	shot(s)	**Pressed apple juice**

Origin: An adaptation (2003) of the signature cocktail at The Blue Bar, London, England.
Comment: Refined cinnamon and apple.

WIMBLEDON MARTINI

Glass: Martini
Garnish: Strawberry on rim
Method: MUDDLE strawberries in base of shaker. Add other ingredients, **SHAKE** with ice and fine strain into chilled glass.

6	fresh	**Strawberries** (hulled)
1½	shot(s)	**Bacardi Superior rum**
1½	shot(s)	**Crème de fraise de bois liqueur**
¼	shot(s)	**Sugar syrup** (2 sugar to 1 water)
½	shot(s)	**Double (heavy) cream**
½	shot(s)	**Milk**

Comment: Takes some getting through the strainer, but when you do it's simply strawberries and cream.

THE WINDSOR ROSE

Glass: Martini
Garnish: Float rose petal
Method: SHAKE all ingredients with ice and fine strain into chilled glass.

1	shot(s)	**Orange-infused Ketel One vodka**
1	shot(s)	**Cointreau triple sec**
1½	shot(s)	**Ocean Spray cranberry juice**
½	shot(s)	**Freshly squeezed lime juice**
⅛	shot(s)	**Rosewater**

Origin: Discovered in 2005 at The Polo Club Lounge, New Orleans, USA.
Comment: An orange vodka and rosewater Cosmo.

WINDY MILLER

Glass: Collins
Garnish: Thin slices of lemon
Method: SHAKE first 3 ingredients with ice and strain into glass filled with crushed ice. **TOP** with lemonade.

1	shot(s)	**Ketel One Citroen vodka**
1	shot(s)	**Mandarine Napoléon liqueur**
½	shot(s)	**La Fée Parisienne (68%) absinthe**
Top up with		**Lemonade/Sprite/7-Up**

Origin: Discovered in 2000 at Teatro, London, England.
Comment: British readers over 40 may remember the children's TV series Trumpton, Chigley and Camberwick Green. If you do, then sing between sips, 'Pugh, Pugh, Barney McGrew, Cuthbert, Dibble and Grubb.'

WINE COOLER

Glass: Collins
Method: POUR first 4 ingredients into ice-filled glass. **TOP** with lemonade, lightly stir and serve with straws.

4	shot(s)	**Sauvignon Blanc wine**
½	shot(s)	**Ketel One Citroen vodka**
½	shot(s)	**Freshly squeezed lemon juice**
½	shot(s)	**Freshly squeezed orange juice**
Top up with		**Lemonade/Sprite/7-Up**

Comment: Like a citrussy white wine Spritzer.

WINK

Glass: Old-fashioned
Garnish: Wink as you serve
Method: POUR absinthe into ice-filled glass. **TOP** with chilled water and leave to stand. Separately **SHAKE** other ingredients with ice. **DISCARD** contents of glass and strain contents of shaker into empty (absinthe washed) glass.

½	shot(s)	**La Fée Parisienne (68%) absinthe**
2	shot(s)	**Tanqueray London dry gin**
½	shot(s)	**Sugar syrup** (2 sugar to 1 water)
¼	shot(s)	**Cointreau triple sec**
2	dashes	**Peychaud's aromatic bitters**
½	shot(s)	**Chilled mineral water** (omit if wet ice)

Origin: Created in 2002 by Tony Conigliaro at Lonsdale House, London, England.
Comment: A pink rinsed drink with a wonderfully aromatic flavour.

WINTER MARTINI UPDATED #8

Glass: Martini
Garnish: Lemon zest twist
Method: STIR all ingredients with ice and strain into chilled glass.

2	shot(s)	**Courvoisier V.S.O.P. cognac**
½	shot(s)	**Sour apple liqueur**
½	shot(s)	**Noilly Prat dry vermouth**
¼	shot(s)	**Sugar syrup** (2 sugar to 1 water)

Comment: Reminiscent of an Apple Cart (a Calvados Sidecar), this is simple, balanced and tastes great.

WISECRACK FIZZ

Glass: Collins
Garnish: Lemon zest twist
Method: SHAKE first 4 ingredients with ice and strain into an ice-filled glass. **TOP** with soda and serve with straws.

1½	shot(s)	**Macchu pisco**
1	shot(s)	**St-Germain elderflower liqueur**
1	shot(s)	**Freshly squeezed grapefruit juice**
½	shot(s)	**Freshly squeezed lemon juice**
Top up with		**Soda water** (club soda)

Origin: Created in 2007 by Matt Gee at Milk & Honey, New York City, USA.
Comment: Light, balanced and refreshing. The pisco character shines through.

DRINKS ARE GRADED AS FOLLOWS:

● DISGUSTING ●◐ PRETTY AWFUL ●● BEST AVOIDED
●●◐ DISAPPOINTING ●●● ACCEPTABLE ●●●◐ GOOD
●●●● RECOMMENDED ●●●●◐ HIGHLY RECOMMENDED
●●●●● OUTSTANDING / EXCEPTIONAL

WONKY MARTINI

Glass: Martini
Garnish: Orange zest twist
Method: STIR all ingredients with ice and strain into chilled glass.

1½	shot(s)	**Vanilla-infused Ketel One vodka**
1½	shot(s)	**Tuaca Italian liqueur**
1½	shot(s)	**Martini Rosso sweet vermouth**
2	dashes	**Angostura orange bitters**

Origin: Created in 2003 by Yours Truly (Simon Difford).
Comment: A sweet, wet Vodkatini invigorated with orange and vanilla.

WOODLAND PUNCH

Glass: Collins
Garnish: Lime wedge
Method: SHAKE first 4 ingredients with ice and strain into ice-filled glass. **TOP** with soda, lightly stir and serve with straws.

2	shot(s)	**Southern Comfort liqueur**
¼	shot(s)	**Heering cherry brandy liqueur**
½	shot(s)	**Freshly squeezed lime juice**
2	shot(s)	**Pressed pineapple juice**
Top up with		**Soda water**

Origin: Adapted from a drink created in 1997 by Foster Creppel. This is the signature drink at his Woodland Plantation, the great house on the west bank of the Mississippi that features on every bottle of Southern Comfort.
Comment: Tart, tangy and refreshing.

WOO WOO UPDATED #8

Glass: Old-fashioned
Garnish: Lime wedge
Method: SHAKE all ingredients with ice and strain into ice-filled glass.

2	shot(s)	**Ketel One vodka**
1	shot(s)	**Peach Tree peach schnapps**
2	shot(s)	**Ocean Spray cranberry juice**

Comment: Fruity, dry cranberry laced with vodka and peach. Not nearly as bad as its reputation, but still lost in the eighties.

YACHT CLUB

Glass: Martini
Garnish: Lemon zest twist
Method: STIR all ingredients with ice and strain into chilled glass.

2	shot(s)	**Bacardi Oro golden rum**
1	shot(s)	**Martini Rosso sweet vermouth**
¼	shot(s)	**Bols apricot brandy liqueur**

Origin: Adapted from a recipe purloined from David Embury's classic book, The Fine Art of Mixing Drinks.
Comment: Rich and slightly sweet with hints of apricot fruit.

YELLOW BELLY MARTINI

Glass: Martini
Garnish: Lemon zest twist
Method: SHAKE all ingredients with ice and fine strain into chilled glass.

1	shot(s)	**Ketel One Citroen vodka**
1	shot(s)	**Freshly squeezed lemon juice**
1	shot(s)	**Luxardo limoncello liqueur**
⅛	shot(s)	**Sugar syrup** (2 sugar to 1 water)
½	shot(s)	**Chilled mineral water** (omit if wet ice)

Comment: Lemon, lemon, lemon. Nice, though...

YELLOW BIRD

Glass: Martini
Garnish: Banana slice on rim
Method: SHAKE all ingredients with ice and fine strain into chilled glass.

1½	shot(s)	**Bacardi Oro golden rum**
½	shot(s)	**Crème de banane liqueur**
¼	shot(s)	**Bols apricot brandy liqueur**
1½	shot(s)	**Pressed pineapple juice**
¼	shot(s)	**Freshly squeezed lime juice**
¼	shot(s)	**Galliano L'Autentico liqueur**

Comment: A sweet and sour cocktail with four different fruits, rum and a splash of Galliano.

YELLOW FEVER MARTINI

Glass: Martini
Garnish: Pineapple wedge on rim
Method: SHAKE all ingredients with ice and fine strain into chilled glass.

2½	shot(s)	**Ketel One vodka**
½	shot(s)	**Galliano L'Autentico liqueur**
1½	shot(s)	**Pressed pineapple juice**
½	shot(s)	**Freshly squeezed lime juice**
⅛	shot(s)	**Sugar syrup** (2 sugar to 1 water)

Comment: Fortified pineapple with a subtle hint of cooling peppermint.

YELLOW PARROT

Glass: Martini
Garnish: Orange zest twist
Method: SHAKE all ingredients with ice and fine strain into chilled glass.

¼	shot(s)	**La Fée Parisienne (68%) absinthe**
1	shot(s)	**Yellow Chartreuse liqueur**
1	shot(s)	**Bols apricot brandy liqueur**
1	shot(s)	**Chilled mineral water** (reduce if wet ice)

Origin: Some say this was created in 1935 by Albert Coleman at The Stork Club, New York City, but the drink featured in Harry Craddock's Savoy Cocktail Book five years before that.
Comment: The aniseed of the absinthe combines well with the other ingredients. A bit of a sweety but a strong old bird.

YOKOHAMA NEW #8

Glass: Martini
Garnish: Orange zest twist
Method: **SHAKE** all ingredients and fine strain into chilled glass.

½	shot(s)	**Ketel One vodka**
1	shot(s)	**Freshly squeezed orange juice**
1	shot(s)	**Tanqueray London dry gin**
¼	shot(s)	**La Fée Parisienne (68%) absinthe**
½	shot(s)	**Pomegranate (grenadine) syrup**

Origin: One of the earliest published vodka recipes and credited to Harry McElhone who also created the Monkey Gland #1 to which this cocktail is practically identical, albeit a splash of vodka.
Comment: Gin and orange with a hint of absinthe.

YOU'VE GOT MAIL NEW #8

Glass: Collins
Garnish: Half orange slice
Method: **SHAKE** first 4 ingredients with ice and fine strain into ice-filled glass. **TOP** with champagne.

2	shot(s)	**Leblon cachaça**
¼	shot(s)	**Sugar syrup** (2 sugar to 1 water)
½	shot(s)	**Freshly squeezed lime juice**
½	shot(s)	**Freshly squeezed orange juice**
¼	shot(s)	**Honey syrup** (4 honey to 1 water)
Top up with		**Perrier Jouet brut champagne**

Comment: Cachaça and citrus balanced by honey and topped with champagne.
Origin: My adaptation of Dave Wondrich's adaptation of the classic Airmail.

YULE LUVIT

Glass: Shot
Garnish: Grate nutmeg over drink
Method: Refrigerate ingredients then **LAYER** in chilled glass by carefully pouring in the following order.

¾	shot(s)	**Frangelico hazelnut liqueur**
¾	shot(s)	**Bulleit bourbon whiskey**

Comment: Actually, 'yule' find it strongly nutty and sweet.

YUM

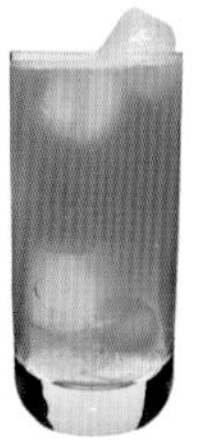

Glass: Collins
Garnish: Lemon wedge
Method: **SHAKE** all ingredients with ice and strain into ice-filled glass.

1½	shot(s)	**Mandarine Napoléon liqueur**
½	shot(s)	**Peach Tree peach schnapps**
¼	shot(s)	**Chambord black raspberry liqueur**
1	shot(s)	**Freshly squeezed lemon juice**
3	shot(s)	**Pressed apple juice**

Comment: If you like sweet, fruity 'disco drinks' then this is indeed yummy.

Z MARTINI

Glass: Martini
Garnish: Hand stuffed blue cheese olives
Method: **STIR** all ingredients with ice and strain into chilled glass.

2½	shot(s)	**Ketel One vodka**
1¼	shot(s)	**Taylor's Chip dry white port**

Origin: Discovered in 2004 at Les Zygomates, Boston, USA.
Comment: Grainy vodka with dry, wine-like notes. Top marks for the garnish alone.

ZABAGLIONE MARTINI

Glass: Martini
Method: Separately **BEAT** egg white until stiff and frothy and yolk until this is as liquid as water, then pour into shaker. Add other ingredients, **SHAKE** with ice and fine strain into chilled glass.

1	fresh	**Egg yolk**
1	fresh	**Egg white**
1½	shot(s)	**Bols advocaat liqueur**
½	shot(s)	**Courvoisier V.S.O.P. cognac**
1	shot(s)	**Marsala wine**
¾	shot(s)	**Freshly squeezed lemon juice**

Origin: I created this drink in 2003 after the classic Italian dessert, which incidentally derives its name from the Neapolitan dialect word 'zapillare', meaning 'to foam'.
Comment: Like the dessert, this is sweet and rich with flavours of egg and fortified wine.

ZAC'S DAIQUIRI NEW #8

Glass: Martini/Coupette
Garnish: Lemon zest twist
Method: **SHAKE** all ingredients with ice and strain into chilled glass.

2	shot(s)	**Zacapa aged rum**
½	shot(s)	**Freshly squeezed lemon juice**
½	shot(s)	**Pressed apple juice**
¼	shot(s)	**Sugar syrup** (2 sugar to 1 water)

Origin: Created in January 2009 by Yours Truly (Simon Difford) at the Cabinet Room, London, England.
Comment: Zacapa has whiskey hints, which suit lemon rather than lime in a Daiquiri. Daiquiris benefit from dilution and here a dash of apple juice adds a barely perceptible amount of fruit as well.

ZAKUSKI MARTINI

Glass: Martini
Garnish: Lemon zest & cucumber peel
Method: **MUDDLE** cucumber in base of shaker. Add other ingredients, **SHAKE** with ice and fine strain into chilled glass.

1	inch	**Cucumber** (peeled & chopped)
2	shot(s)	**Ketel One Citroen vodka**
½	shot(s)	**Cointreau triple sec**
½	shot(s)	**Freshly squeezed lemon juice**
¼	shot(s)	**Sugar syrup** (2 sugar to 1 water)

Origin: Created in 2002 by Alex Kammerling, London, England.
Comment: Appropriately named after the Russian snack.

Z

THE ZAMBOANGA 'ZEINIE' COCKTAIL

●●●●○

Glass: Martini
Garnish: Lime zest twist (discarded) & cherry
Method: SHAKE all ingredients with ice and fine strain into chilled glass.

2	shot(s)	**Courvoisier V.S.O.P. cognac**
1	shot(s)	**Pressed pineapple juice**
½	shot(s)	**Freshly squeezed lime juice**
¼	shot(s)	**Maraschino syrup** (from cherry jar)
2	dashes	**Angostura aromatic bitters**

Origin: Adapted from a recipe in Charles H. Baker Jr's classic book, The Gentleman's Companion. He describes this as "another palate twister from the land where the Monkeys Have No Tails. This drink found its way down through the islands to Mindanao from Manila…".
Comment: Reminiscent of a tropical Sidecar.

ZANZIBAR

●●●●○○

Glass: Old-fashioned
Garnish: Lime zest twist
Method: SHAKE all ingredients with ice and strain into glass filled with crushed ice.

2	shot(s)	**Goslings Black Seal rum**
¼	shot(s)	**Bols apricot brandy liqueur**
¼	shot(s)	**Grand Marnier liqueur**
½	shot(s)	**Freshly squeezed orange juice**
½	shot(s)	**Freshly squeezed lime juice**
⅛	shot(s)	**Almond (orgeat) syrup**

Origin: Discovered in 2005 at Zanzi Bar, Prague, Czech Republic.
Comment: Tangy rum and citrus with fruit and hints of almond.

ZAZA

●●●●○

Glass: Martini
Garnish: Orange zest twist
Method: SHAKE all ingredients with ice and fine strain into chilled glass.

| 2 | shot(s) | **Tanqueray London dry gin** |
| 2 | shot(s) | **Dubonnet Red** (French made) |

AKA: Dubonnet Cocktail
Variant: Substitute sloe gin or fino sherry for gin.
Origin: I've adapted this from a recipe in Harry Craddock's 1930 'Savoy Cocktail Book'. It is named after a French play which was a hit around the verge of the 20th century and was followed by opera and film versions.
Comment: Zaza is a diminutive of Isabelle. But there's nothing diminutive about this simple, yet fantastic drink.

ZEE DEE NEW #8

●●●●○

Glass: Martini/Coupette
Garnish: Lemon zest twist
Method: STIR all ingredients with ice and strain into chilled glass.

1½	shot(s)	**Zacapa aged rum**
1½	shot(s)	**Pressed apple juice**
1½	shot(s)	**Amontillado dry sherry**

Origin: Created in January 2009 by Yours Truly (Simon Difford) at the Cabinet Room, London, England.
Comment: Aged rum and sherry with a delicate hint of apple fruit.

ZELDA MARTINI

●●●●○

Glass: Martini
Garnish: Mint sprig
Method: Lightly **MUDDLE** mint (just to bruise) in base of shaker. Add other ingredients, **SHAKE** with ice and fine strain into chilled glass.

5	fresh	**Mint leaves**
2	shot(s)	**Zubrówka bison vodka**
1	shot(s)	**Freshly squeezed lime juice**
¾	shot(s)	**Almond (orgeat) syrup**
½	shot(s)	**Chilled mineral water** (omit if wet ice)

Origin: Created in May 2002 by Phillip Jeffrey at the GE Club, London, England. He made it for a friend called Zelda – and the name really wouldn't have worked if she'd been called Tracy.
Comment: Bison grass vodka combines brilliantly with mint and almond.

ZESTY

●●●●○

Glass: Old-fashioned
Garnish: Lime zest twist
Method: SHAKE all ingredients with ice and strain into glass filled with crushed ice.

| 2 | shot(s) | **Frangelico hazelnut liqueur** |
| ½ | shot(s) | **Freshly squeezed lime juice** |

Comment: Citrus fresh with a nutty touch.

ZEUS MARTINI

●●●●●

Glass: Martini
Garnish: Float three coffee beans
Method: POUR Fernet Branca into frozen glass, swirl round and **DISCARD. MUDDLE** raisins with cognac in base of shaker. Add other ingredients, **SHAKE** with ice and fine strain into chilled glass.

1	shot(s)	**Fernet Branca**
25	dried	**Raisins**
2	shot(s)	**Courvoisier V.S.O.P. cognac**
¼	shot(s)	**Maple syrup**
⅛	shot(s)	**Kahlúa coffee liqueur**
1	shot(s)	**Chilled mineral water** (reduce if wet ice)

Origin: Adapted from Dr Zeus, a cocktail created by Adam Ennis in 2001 at Isola, London, England.
Comment: Rich, pungent and not sweet.

DRINKS ARE GRADED AS FOLLOWS:

- ● DISGUSTING
- ●○ PRETTY AWFUL
- ●● BEST AVOIDED
- ●●○ DISAPPOINTING
- ●●● ACCEPTABLE
- ●●●○ GOOD
- ●●●● RECOMMENDED
- ●●●●○ HIGHLY RECOMMENDED
- ●●●●● OUTSTANDING / EXCEPTIONAL

ICE WAS FIRST SOLD IN THE UNITED STATES IN 1800 – IN THE FORM OF SLABS HACKED FROM FROZEN LAKES.

ZHIVAGO MARTINI

Glass: Martini
Garnish: Float wafer thin apple slice
Method: **SHAKE** all ingredients with ice and fine strain into chilled glass.

1½	shot(s)	**Vanilla-infused Ketel One vodka**
½	shot(s)	**Bulleit bourbon whiskey**
½	shot(s)	**Sour apple liqueur**
1	shot(s)	**Freshly squeezed lime juice**
¾	shot(s)	**Sugar syrup** (2 sugar to 1 water)

Origin: Created in by Alex Kammerling, London.
Comment: Perfectly balanced sweet and sour – sweet apple, vanilla and bourbon balanced by lime juice..

ZINGY GINGER MARTINI

Glass: Martini
Garnish: Lemon zest twist
Method: **SHAKE** all ingredients with ice and fine strain into chilled glass.

2½	shot(s)	**Ketel One Citroen vodka**
½	shot(s)	**Freshly squeezed lemon juice**
½	shot(s)	**Ginger cordial**
½	shot(s)	**Chilled mineral water** (omit if wet ice)

Origin: Created in 2001 by Reece Clark at Hush Up, London, England.
Comment: It sure is both zingy and gingery..

ZOMBIE #1 (INTOXICA! RECIPE)

Glass: Hurricane
Garnish: Mint sprig
Method: **STIR** brown sugar with lemon juice in base of shaker until it dissolves. Add other ingredients, **SHAKE** with ice and strain into ice-filled glass.

1	spoon	**Brown sugar**
1	shot(s)	**Freshly squeezed lemon juice**
1	shot(s)	**Bacardi Superior rum**
1	shot(s)	**Bacardi Oro golden rum**
1	shot(s)	**Demerara 151° overproof rum**
1	shot(s)	**Pressed pineapple juice**
1	shot(s)	**Freshly squeezed lime juice**
1	shot(s)	**Passion fruit syrup**
1	dash	**Angostura aromatic bitters**

Origin: The above recipe for Don the Beachcomber's classic cocktail is based on one published in Intoxica! by Jeff Berry.
Comment: Plenty of flavour and alcohol with tangy rum and fruit.

ZOMBIE #2 (VIC'S FORMULA)

Glass: Collins (14oz)
Garnish: Mint sprig
Method: **BLEND** all ingredients with one 12oz scoop crushed ice. Serve with straws.

¾	shot(s)	**Bacardi Superior rum**
¾	shot(s)	**Zacapa aged rum**
½	shot(s)	**Grand Marnier liqueur**
1½	shot(s)	**Freshly squeezed orange juice**
2½	shot(s)	**Pressed pineapple juice**
1	shot(s)	**Freshly squeezed lemon juice**
½	shot(s)	**Freshly squeezed lime juice**
¼	shot(s)	**Pomegranate (grenadine) syrup**

Origin: Adapted from a recipe in the 1947-72 Trader Vic's Bartender's Guide by Victor Bergeron.
Comment: More fruit than alcohol but tangy not sweet.

ZOMBIE #3 (MODERN FORMULA)

Glass: Hurricane
Garnish: Pineapple wedge
Method: **SHAKE** first 9 ingredients with ice and strain into glass filled with crushed ice. **FLOAT** rum.

¾	shot(s)	**Bacardi Superior rum**
¾	shot(s)	**Pusser's Navy rum**
¾	shot(s)	**Bacardi Oro golden rum**
½	shot(s)	**Bols apricot brandy liqueur**
½	shot(s)	**Grand Marnier liqueur**
2½	shot(s)	**Freshly squeezed orange juice**
2½	shot(s)	**Pressed pineapple juice**
1	shot(s)	**Freshly squeezed lime juice**
½	shot(s)	**Pomegranate (grenadine) syrup**
½	shot(s)	**Wray & Nephew overproof rum**

Comment: A heady mix of four different rums with pineapple, orange, lime and grenadine.

ZOOM

Glass: Martini
Garnish: Dust with cocoa powder
Method: **SHAKE** all ingredients with ice and fine strain into chilled glass.

2½	shot(s)	**Courvoisier V.S.O.P. cognac**
3	spoons	**Runny honey**
½	shot(s)	**Double (heavy) cream**
½	shot(s)	**Milk**

Variant: Base on other spirits or add a dash of cacao.
Comment: Cognac is smoothed with honey and softened with milk and cream in this classic cocktail.

ZUB-WAY

Glass: Collins
Garnish: Three raspberries
Method: Chop watermelon and **MUDDLE** in base of shaker with raspberries. Add other ingredients, **SHAKE** with ice and fine strain into ice-filled glass.

1/16	fresh	**Watermelon** (diced)
2½	shot(s)	**Zubrówka bison vodka**
½	shot(s)	**Sugar syrup** (2 sugar to 1 water)

Origin: Created in 1999 by Jamie Terrell, London.
Comment: Few ingredients, but loads of flavour.

z

INGREDIENTS INDEX

THE FOLLOWING PAGES INDEX OUR FAVOURITE COCKTAILS MADE WITH MOST OF THE BOTTLES COMMONLY FOUND ON BAR SHELVES.

FOR YOUR CONVENIENCE OUR WEBSITE 'DIFFORDSGUIDE.COM' ENABLES A COMPLETE SEARCH OF ALL THE COCKTAILS ON OUR DATABASE ACCORDING TO NAME OR MULTIPLE INGREDIENTS.
THUS - IDENTIFY THE COCKTAILS YOU WANT TO MAKE USING INGREDIENTS YOU ACTUALLY HAVE - ONLINE AND THEN FOLLOW THE RECIPE FROM THE PAGES OF THIS BOOK.
A HARMONIOUS MARRIAGE OF OLD AND NEW MEDIA HOPEFULLY RESULTING IN AN EQUALLY HAPPY UNION IN YOUR GLASS.

ALMOND (ORGEAT) SYRUP

Almond Martini #1
Army & Navy
Cameron's Kick
Cool Orchard
Cosmopolitan Delight
Daiquiri De Luxe
Gin Daisy #2
Japanese Cocktail
Kiwi Crush
Lemon Butter Cookie
Marama Rum Punch
Menehune Juice
Momisette
Pinky Pincher
Rum Amandine
Scorpion
Tiki Bar Margarita
Union Club
Zanzibar
Zelda Martini

ANGOSTURA ORANGE BITTERS

Adonis
Bamboo
Bicardar
Bluegrass
Boulevard
Casino #2
Coronation Cocktail No.1
Dubliner
Elder Fashioned
Grand Cosmopolitan
Guard's Cocktail
Habanero
Hearst Martini
Hoffman House
Hoffman House
Metropole
Naranja
Salflower Sour
Stairs Martini
The Montgomery Martini

BACARDI ORO GOLDEN RUM

Abacaxi Ricaco
Airmail
Bajan Mojito
Bermuda Rum Swizzle
Bossa Nova #1
Butterscotch Martini
Chocolate Puff
Club Cocktail #3
Commodore #1
Fat Sailor
Fish House Punch #1
Four W Daiquiri
Funky Monkey
Ginger Punch
Golden Reign
Heaven's Above
Pina Colada
The MacKinnon
Total Recall
Zombie #1

BAILEYS IRISH CREAM LIQUEUR

Bananas & Cream
Barnamint
Bumblebee
Carrot Cake
Cream Cake
Creamy Bee
FBI
International Incident
Irish Espresso'Tini
Lemon Meringue Martini
Mocha Martini
Mudslide
PS I Love You
Shamrock Express

BENEDICTINE D.O.M.

Argentina Cocktail
Aztec
B&T
Brighton Punch
De La Louisiane #1
Frisco Sour
Gypsy Queen
Honeymoon
Jubilant
Lorraine #2
Mule's Hind Leg
O'Henry
Poet's Dream
Purgatory
Roman Punch
Singapore Sling #2
Straits Sling
The Horseshoe Sling
The Neutral Ground
Tropic

ANGOSTURA AROMATIC BITTERS

Alfonso
Brubaker Old-Fashioned
Call Me Old-fashioned
Champs-Elysées
Club Cocktail #3
Dandy Cocktail
Fancy Free
Flying Scotsman
Four W Daiquiri
French Whisky Sour
Liquorice Whisky Sour
Lolita Margarita
Manhattan Perfect
Old Fashioned #2
Rat Pack Manhattan
Rob Roy #1
Royal Gingersnap
The Long Shot
The Roadrunner
The Zamboanga 'Zeinie' Cocktail

APEROL

Amarita
Bitter Grapefruit
Bluegrass
Facundo's Flare
Orange Spur
Pre Siesta
The Lady Wears Red
Two-One-Two
Wah-Wah

BACARDI SUPERIOR RUM

Bacardi Cocktail
Breakfast Club
Clara Astie Cocktail
Daiquiri No.1 Natural
Don Daisy
El Coco
El Presidente No.1 #1
Fireman's Sour
Florida Daiquiri
Hemingway Special Daiquiri
Honeysuckle Daiquiri
Love Unit
Mary Pickford
Mint & Honey Daiquiri
Mojito #1
Oh Gosh!
Presidente Menocal Special
Sol Ardiente
Tahitian Honey Bee
The 1862

BENOIT SERRES CRÈME DE VIOLETTE

Aviation No.1
Blue Moon
Bramblette
Fizz a la Violette
Flower Power Martini
Mood Indigo
Purple Pear Martini
The Atty Cocktail
The Moonlight Cocktail
Violet Affinity

BERENTZEN APPLE SCHNAPPS LIQUOUR

Amber
Apple Strudel #2
Appleissimo
Applesinth
Cider Apple Cooler
Cider Apple Martini
Frisky Bison
Fuego Manzana No.2
Granny's
Northern Lights
Robin Hood #1
Sangria Martini
Sidecar Named Desire
Spiced Apple Daiquiri
Tarte Tatin Martini
Teddy Bear'Tini
The Quingenti
Thomas Blood Martini
Toffee Apple
Wilton Martini

BOKMA OUDE GENEVER

Amsterdam Cocktail
Death in The Gulf Stream
Dutch Martini
Flying Dutchman Martini
Gin Daisy #2
Gin Punch
I B Damm'd
Jenever Sour
Martinez #2
Medicinal Solution
Medicinal Solution
The Alamagoozlum Cocktail
The Holland House Cocktail
Waters of Chaos

BOLS ADVOCAAT LIQUEUR

Beach Blonde
Bessie & Jessie
Brandy Flip
Canary Flip
Crème Anglaise Martini
Dutch Breakfast Martini
Dutch Courage
Egg Custard Martini
Fluffy Duck
Granny's Martini
Jaded Lady
New Port Codebreaker
Nutty Summer
Orange Custard Martini
Rhubarb & Custard Martini
Snowball
Zabaglione Martini

BOLS APRICOT BRANDY LIQUEUR

Angel Face
Apricot Rickey
Brooklyn #2
Claridge Cocktail
Fruit Tree Daiquiri
Manana Daiquiri
Mayfair Cocktail
Moon River
Nacional Daiquiri #1
Pancho Villa
Paradise #2
Periodista Daquiri
Resolute
Sleepy Hollow
Spencer Cocktail
Sumo in a Sidecar
The Mayflower Martini
The Wet Spot
Toreador
What the Hell

BOLS BLUE CURACAO

Bikini Martini
Black Mussel
Blue Hawaii
Blue Margarita
Blue Monday
Blue Passion
Blue Velvet Margarita

Cactus Jack
Darlington
Green Eyes
Ink Martini #1
Ink Martini #2
Lotus Martini
Swedish Blue Martini
Turquoise Daiquiri

BOULARD GRAND SOLAGE CALVADOS

A.J.
Autumn Leaves
Calvados Cocktail
Cyder Press
Dempsey
Elysian
Fallen Leaves
First of July
Jack Rose
Ocean's 21
Orchard Crush
Pomme Et Sureau
Princess Marina
Rizzo
Roulette
Sidecarriage
So-So Martini
Steep Flight
The 75
The Star #1

BULLEIT BOURBON WHISKEY

Avenue
Black Rose
Blinker
Bourbon Crusta
Caramel Manhattan
Devil's Share
Don's Delight
East Meets West Julep
Frisco Sour
Glenn's Bride
Kentucky Dream
Little Venice
Manhattan
Millionaire
Mint Julep
Old Fashioned #1
Rat Pack Manhattan
The Apple One
The Currier
Toast & Orange Martini

CAMPARI

Blood Orange
Campirinha
Cardinale
Champino
Copper Illusion
Cornwall Negroni
Hakkatini
Jungle Bird
Lucien Gaudin
Negroni
Negroni Sbagliato
Old Flame
Rosita
Sicilian Negroni
South Beach
Spicy Finn
Spritz al Bitter
The Beauty Beneath
Triple Orange Martini
Valentino

CHAMBORD

Basil Grande
Black Cherry Martini
Black Forest Gateau Martini
Cham Cham
Crimson Blush
Dirty Sanchez
Eclipse
Encantado
Estes
Finitaly
First of July
French Bison-Tini
French Martini
Hot Tub
Ja-Mora
Kentucky Jewel
Marquee
Tre Martini
Tres Compadres Margarita
Urban Oasis

COINTREAU TRIPLE SEC

Margarita #2
White Lady
Chelsea Sidecar
Casablanca #1
Dry Orange Martini

The Journalist
Pear & Cardomom Sidecar
Fine & Dandy
Pompanski Martini
Rude Cosmopolitan
Sage Margarita
Sidecar #1
Sidekick
Stork Club
Sunstroke
Thriller From Vanilla
Union Club

COURVOISIER V.S.O.P. COGNAC

Between The Sheets #1
Brandy Fix
Call Me Old Fashioned
Classic Cocktail
Cobblers
Dr Zeus
Eastern Raspberry Sidecar
Grape Escape
La Sang
Nicky Finn
Ponce de Leon
Randy
Sazerac
Sidecar
Sidecar #2
Spitfire
Stinger
The Roffignac
The Surfer
Winter Martini

CRÈME DE CASSIS

Arnaud Martini
Aviator #1
Black Jack Cocktail
Bolshoi Punch
Cassini
Epestone Daiquiri
French Daisy
Gina
Kir Martini
Lychee & Blackcurrant Martini
Martini Royale
Mexican Martini
Parisian Martini #1
Perfect Regent XV
Rum & Raisin Alexander
Russian Spring Punch
Serendipity #1
Showbiz
Sunshine Cocktail #2
Tarte aux Pommes

DON JULIO 100% AGAVE TEQUILA

Almond Old Fashioned
Buena Vida
Cider House Rules
East Village Athletic Club
El Torado
Elegante Margarita
Estilo Viejo
Jalisco
Lavender Margarita
Lolita Margarita
London Scramble
Lucky Lilly Margarita
Margarita #1
Marmarita
Matador #2
Million Dollar Margarita
Paloma
Pineapple & Sage Margarita
Quince Mustard Margarita
Tommy's Margarita

DUBONNET RED

Aviator
Barney Barnato Cocktail
Bartender's Martini
Blackthorn Cocktail
Dandy Cocktail
De La Louisiane #3
Dolores #1
Fly Like A Butterfly
Goody-Goody
Moonraker
Napoleon Martini
Opera
Paris Sour
Quebec
Red Neck Martini
Rosy Martini
The Dubonnet Cocktail
The Wentworth
Tiziano
Zaza

DRAMBUIE

Argha Noah
Bonnie Prince Charles
Daiquiri Noir

Embassy Royal
Habanero
Heather Julep
Highland Drum
Mary Queen of Scots
Prince Charlie
Rusty Nail
The MacKinnon
The Scott

FRANGELICO

Casse Noisette
Cherry & Hazelnut Daiquiri
Clairvoyant
Cuppa Joe
DC Martini
Fosbury Flip
Hazel'ito
Hazelnut Alexander
Insomniac
Nuts & Berries
Nutty Nashville
The Bistro Sidecar
The Strawberry Éclair
Vanilla'Tini
Yule Luvit
Zesty

BOIRON FRUIT PUREE

Batida de Carnaval
Bellini
Bellini'Tini
Bourbon Cookie
Indian Sunset
Kentucky Colonel
Mango Collins
Mango Daiquiri
Mango Margarita #1
Market Daiquiri
Mitch Martini
Roger
Southern Mint Cooler
Victoria's Secret
Whiskey Squirt

GALLIANO L'AUTENTICO

Adam & Eve
Bossa Nova #1
California Root Beer
Caribbean Punch

Daiquiri Authentico
Don's Passion
Giuseppe's Habit
Golden Dream
Highland Sling
Hurricane #3
Italian Sour
Jumping Jack Flash
Marti's Martini
Maxim's Coffee
Milano Sour
Mulata Daisy
Picca
Snoopy
Wild Honey
Yellow Fever Martini

GIFFARD MENTHE PASTILLE

Afterburner
American Beauty #1
Chiclet Daiquiri
Chocolate Mint Martini
Delmarva Cocktail No.1
Dixie Dew
Fu Manchu Daiquiri
Green Fizz
Green Swizzle
Jade Daiquiri
Knock Out Martini
Mint Cocktail
Monte Carlo Imperial
Peppermint Vanilla Daiquiri
Trinity

GOSLING'S BLACK SEAL RUM

Baltimore Egg Nog
Bella Donna Daiquiri
Bermuda Rum Swizzle
Black Strap
Dark 'n' Stormy
Dino Sour
Georgetown Punch
Honolulu Juicer
Hurricane #2
Iced Tea
Jean Gabin
Jungle Bird
Milk Punch
Modernista
Ranglin
Tropical Daiquiri
Zanzibar

LA FEE (68%) PARISIENNE ABSINTHE

Absinthe Cocktail #1
Absinthe Frappé
Applesinth
Bobby Burns #2
Bombay No.2
Chrysanthemum
Corpse Reviver No.2 #1
Dempsey
Green Fairy
In-Seine
Knockout Martini
Le Minuit
Moonshine Martini
New Year's Absolution
Original Sin
Piccadilly Martini
Remember The Maine
Savoy Special #1
The Atty Cocktail
Wink

LAGAVULIN 16YO MALT WHISKY

Fumigator Flip
Looks Familiar
Penicillin
Rusty
Smoke of Scotland
Smokey Joe
Smokin' Rose
Smoking Stallion

LUXARDO AMARETTO DI SASCHIRA

Bananas & Cream
Bella Donna Daiquiri
Blueberry Tea
Brooklyn
Chas
French Connection
Grappaccino
Hawaiian Cocktail
International Incident
Italian Job #2
Jockey Club
Loch Almond
Mae West Martini
Nutcracker Sweet

Nutty Summer
Orange Brûlée
South Beach
Tennessee Berry Mule
Thunderbird
Toasted Almond

LUXARDO LIMONCELLO

Basilico
Clementine
Cuban Heal
Grapparita
Italian Sun
Lemon Meringue Pie'Tini
Lemony
Limoncello Martini
Motox
Navigator
Pear Drop Martini
Santiago #2
Socialite
Watermelon & Basil Smash
Yellow Belly Martini

LUXARDO MARASCHINO

Bensonhurst
Bicardar
Boomerang
Bourbon Crusta
Casino #1
East India #1
Feather Dusta Crusta
Fifth Degree
Full Monte
Great Garbo
Havana Special
Hemingway Special Daiquiri
Mae West Martini
Opera
Ribalaigua Daiquiri #3
Saratoga Cocktail #2
Sensation
Seventh Heaven #2
The Harlem
The Ritz Cocktail

LUXARDO SAMBUCA DEI CESARI

All White Frappe
Anis'Tini

Bumble Bee
Crème de Café
Glass Tower
Raging Bull
Tick-Tack Martini
Typhoon
Veneto

MACCHU PISCO

Algeria
Cola De Mono
Doheny Pisco Punch
Dulchin
Elderflower Pisco Punch
Extradition
Greenbelt
Judgement Day
Lima Sour
Pichuncho Martini
Pini
Pisco Collins
Pisco Naranja
Pisco Punch
Pisco Sour
Poncho De Algarrobina
Pyramid Punch
Rousing Charlie
The Stig
Wisecrack Fizz

MALIBU COCONUT RUM LIQUEUR

Bahama Mama
Bahamas Daiquiri
Black & White Daiquiri
Caribbean Punch
Coco Cabana
Coconut Daiquiri
Coconut Water
Goombay Smash
Jamaican Me Crazy
Key Lime Pie #1
Melon Collie Martini
Melon Daiquiri #1
Melon Margarita #1
Meloncholy Martini
Monkey Shine
Scotch Bounty Martini
Smooth and Creamy'Tini
Tilt
Vacation
Whip Me & Beat Me

MARTINI ROSSO SWEET VERMOUTH

Addington
Adonis
Club Cocktail #2
Cornwall Negroni
Froupe Cocktail
Grand Slam
Guard's Cocktail
Harvard
Income Tax Cocktail
Manhattan Sweet
Martinez #1
Martini Special
Merry-Go-Round Martini
Milano
Queen Martini
Tulip Cocktail
Turf Martini
Vieux Carré Cocktail
Waldorf Cocktail No.1
Wonky Martini

MIDORI GREEN MELON LIQUEUR

Apple & Melon Maritni
Apple Blossom Cocktail
Congo Blue
Evita
Grateful Dead
Green Fly
Green Horn
Guardabosques
Hand Grenade
Hong Kong Fuey
Illusion
Japanese Slipper
Killer Punch
Koolaid
Lovejunk
Mae West Martini
Melon Daiquiri
Meloncholy Martini
Sourpuss Martini
Verdi Martini

MANDARIN NAPOLEAN LIQUEUR

Breakfast at Terrell's
Clementine
Donegal

Italian Job #1
Jacktini
Lola
Man-Bour-Tini
Mandarine Collins
Mandarine Sidecar
Mandarine Songbird
Mandarine Sour
Mandarito
Orange Mojito
Prune Face
Puccini
Tennessee Rush
Windy Miller
Yum

NOILLY PRAT DRY VERMOUTH

Bearskin Martini
Brooklyn #1
Caprice
Coronation Cocktail No.1
Dicken's Martini
Diplomat
Falconi
Fifty-Fifty Martini
Ideal
In-And-Out Martini
Parisian Martini #2
RAC Martini
Reverse Martini
Satan's Whiskers
Scofflaw
Snyder Martini
Sunshine Coxktail #1
The Rose #1
Tipperary #2
Trilby #2

OCEAN SPRAY CRANBERRY JUICE

Bald Eagle
C C Kazi
Cassini
Cosmogroni
Creole Cocktail
Eclipse
Estes
London Cosmopolitan
Nautilus
Northern Sun
Ocean Breeze
Osmo
Red Maurader
Rosarita Margarita
Rude Ginger Cosmopolitan
Sake'Politan

Tartini
The Windsor Rose
Watermelon Cosmo
Wild Blossom

OPAL NERA BLACK SAMBUCA

Allesandro
Black Dream
Black Widow
Liquorice All Sort
Liquorice Martini
Molotov Cocktail
Opal Café
Purple Flirt #1

PEACH TREE PEACH SCHNAPPS

Aku Aku
Apple Spritz
Bellini-Tini
Bermuda Cocktail
Bohemian Iced Tea
Encantado
Georgia Julep
I B Damm'd
Jelly Belly Martini
Missionary's Downfall
Mississippi Schnapper
Mitch Martini
Moonraker
Mystique
Palma Violet Martini
Peach Daquiri
Peach Tree Daiquiri
Perfect Lady
Verdi Martini
Woo Woo

PERNOD ANIS

Anis'Tini
Appleissimo
Asylum Cocktail
Blackthorn Irish
Doctor Funk
Drowned Out
French Kiss #1
French Leave
Greta Garbo
Hemingway

London Fog
Modernista
Monte Carlo
Moonraker
Nicky Finn
Northern Lights
Pernod & Black Martini
Sunny Breeze
Tarraberry'Tini
Threesome

PERRIER JOUET BRUT CHAMPAGNE

Apple Spritz
Autumn Punch
Black Magic
Bling! Bling!
Champagne Cup
Champagne Pick-Me-Up
Champino
Chin Chin
Elle For Leather
French 75
Jalisco Flower
Parisian Spring Punch
Royal Mojito
Serendipity #2
Southside Royale
Soyer au Champagne
Tatanka Royale
Twinkle
Valencia
VaVaVoom

PUSSER'S NAVY RUM

Alexandra
Aunt Agatha
Bahama Mama
Bee's Knees #1
Caribbean Breeze
Charles Daquiri
Dark Daiquiri
Fat Sailor
Grog
Gun Club Punch
Hurricane #1
Navy Grog
Nevada Daquiri
Painkiller
Red Rover
Reef Juice
Rum Runner
Solent Sunset
Spiced Cranberry Martini
Zombie #3

ST-GERMAIN ELDERFLOWER LIQUEUR

Amber Room #2
Apple & Elderflower Collins
Apple, Cucumber & Elderflower Cup
Bermondsey Breeze
Beverly Hills Hotel Martini
Cyder Press
Eden
Elder & Wiser
Floral Martini
Flower Power Martini
Left Bank Martini
Padovani
Paris Martini
Periscope
Rosehip Martini
St-Germain Sidecar
The [Pick Of] Destiny
The Stig
Wild Blossom
Wisecrack Fizz

TANQUERAY LONDON DRY GIN

Bebbo
Bee's Knees #2
Blood Sage
Breakfast Martini
Clover Club No.3 #1
English Breakfast Martini
Franklin Martini
Gibson
Gin & Sin
Lonsdale
Martinez #5
Negroni Spumante
Pegu Club
Pink Gin
Pink Lady
Ramos Gin Fizz
Silver Bronx
Tenner Martini
The Last Word
White Cargo

TIO PEPE FINO SHERRY

Adonis
Alaska Martini
Alberto Martini
Bamboo #1
Bronze Adonis
Club Cocktail #1

Coronation Cocktail No.1
Damn It Jimmy
Damn It Jimmy
Dolores #1
Dutch Master
East Indian
Jerez
Nome
Pablo Alvarez de Cañas Special
Rousing Charlie
Saltecca
Snowball
The Lady Wears Red
Tuxedo Martini

VELVET FALERNUM LIQUEUR

Bajan Daiquiri
Bermuda Rum Swizzle
Caribe Daiquiri
Chartreuse Swizzle
Coquetail au Vanilla
Especie
Golden Wave
Hawaiian Eye
Haydenistic
Nuclear Daiquiri
Prestige Cocktail
Royal Bermuda Yacht Club Daiquiri
Rum Swizzle
Satin Sheet
Tailor Made
Test Pilot
The Lady Wears Red
The Ninth Ward
Velvet Fog
Will of Alan

WARRE'S OTIMA PORT

A.B.C. Cocktail
Bishop
Bloody Maria
Byculla
Chancellor
Chatham Hotel Special
Coffee Cocktail
Devil's
Falconi
Free Town
Golden Girl
Havana Cobbler
Josephine Baker
Juniport Fizz
Negus
New York Flip
Princeton
Sir Charles Punch
Suburban
Tawny-tini

WHITE CRÈME DE CACAO

Ace of Clubs Daiquiri
Barbary Coast
Behemoth
Bird of Paradise
Cherry Alexander
Chocolate Sazerac
Commodore #1
Delmarva Cocktail No.2
Easter Martini
Fruit & Nut Chocolate Martini
Mother Rum
Mulata Daiquiri
Pago Pago
Pall Mall Martini
Pink Cloud
Smartini
Summer Rose Martini
Turkish Delight
Velvet Hammer
White Elephant

WRAY & NEPHEW OVERPROOF RUM

Afterburner
AWOL
Beach Blonde
Bolshoi Punch
Caribbean Punch
Coco Naut
Cold Comfort
Jamaican Sunset
Malcolm Lowry
Mango Punch
Marama Rum Punch
Nuclear Daqiuiri
Pirate Daiquiri
Ranglin
Reggae Rum Punch
Rum Punch
Rum Punch-Up
Rumba
Sorrel Rum Punch
Stone & Gravel

YELLOW CHARTREUSE

Alaskan Martini
Ambrosia Cocktail
Brandy Fix
Cheeky Monkey
Cloyster
Corpse Reviver No.2 #2

Daisy Cutter Martini
East Village Athletic Club
Episcopal
Gin Daisy
Golden Slipper
Lemony
Mujer Verde
Nathalia
Oddball Manhattan Dry
Quarterback
The Alamagoozlum Cocktail
The Puritan
Widow's Kiss
Yellow Parrot

ZACAPA AGED RUM

Aged Honey Daiquiri
Bolero Sour
Brass Rail
Dolores #1
East India House
Flip That's Good
Golden Girl
Honey Wall
Kanu-No
Mai Tai (Vic's Formula)
Old Cuban
Orange Daquiri #1
Pineapple Fix
Prestige Cocktail
Queen's Park Swizzle
Rum Sour
Thai Red Daiquiri
The Leavenworth
Zac's Daiquiri
Zee Dee

ZUBROWKA BISON VODKA

Apple, Cucumber & Elderflower Cup
Coolman Martini
Cucumber Martini
Earl Grey Fizz
Green Tea Martini #1
Krakow Tea
Lekker Lekker
Lemon Butter Cookie
Mitch Martini
Polish Martini
Pooh'Tini
R U Bobby Moore?
Sleeping Bison-Tini
Sodden Grape Martini
Tatanka
Verdant
Warsaw Cooler
Warsaw Pact
Zelda Martini
Zub-Way

INGREDIENTS
APPENDIX

Absinthe

Our recommendation: La Fée Parisienne

Absinthe, like gin, is basically flavoured vodka. In the same way as gin distillers use different botanical recipes, different absinthe manufacturers use slightly different ingredients and production methods.

Essentially, oil of wormwood is macerated with herbs and spices including hyssop, mint, fennel, cinnamon and lemon balm, along with lesser amounts of angelica, star anise, dittany, juniper, nutmeg and veronica, in neutral ethanol alcohol. Antimony chloride was also used to help the drink turn cloudy when added to water. Today some manufacturers add other ingredients to produce the emerald green colour that was originally due to the presence of chlorophyll from the plants.

There are two basic styles of absinthe commonly available – French and Czech. French styles, which are mostly still banned in their country of origin, have a full-bodied aniseed flavour and a deep green colour. When served with water the colour should change and eventually go cloudy. This process of precipitation is known as the louche.

Czech absinth (spelt without the 'e') usually has a bluer tinge to its green colour. The aniseed flavour is more subtle than in its French counterpart and it is not usual for it to turn cloudy with the addition of water.

Advocaat

Our recommendation: Bols advocaat

This Dutch liqueur is made of brandy, egg yolks and sugar. Although the origins of advocaat are unclear, some say it is derived from an alcoholic drink that Dutch colonists made from the abacate, a variety of avocado. Dutch texts from the 17th century describe a yellow-coloured drink popular with sailors of the period and made on the Dutch Antilles from an avocado mousse mixed with alcohol. In the absence of avocado at home, they used egg yolk to imitate the colour (an obvious substitution, the yellow flesh of fruit for egg yolk?). The name, which had already evolved into 'advocate' by Portuguese colonists in Brazil, became advocaat in Dutch.In the Netherlands there are many different brands of Advocaat, some flavoured with fruit or vanilla.

Others, including my Oxford English Dictionary, place Advocaat's origins more recently in the 1930s with the name from the Dutch for 'advocate', "being originally considered a lawyer's drink".

Whatever the origin, due to stereotyping with the Snowball, the cocktail enjoyed by British grannies in the 1970s, sadly, advocaat now struggles in the UK drink style stakes. However, those that knock this thick bright yellow liqueur usually haven't tried it for years. I must profess to being an advocaat fan, particularly of the super-thick style sold in the Netherlands. This comes in a wide-necked bottle to facilitate its slow glug by glug pour and is traditionally served in small dishes and eaten with a spoon.

Whilst on the subject of drinks made from avocados, in Africa, the plant leaves are fermented to make a sparkling and mildly alcoholic drink known as 'babine'.

Agave Syrup (Agave Nectar)

Agave syrup (also called agave nectar) is a sweetener which can be used in place of sugar or honey, and pairs particularly well with tequila, the spirit from its parent plant. It is as much as two-thirds sweeter than sugar but is less viscous than honey.

Agave syrup is commercially produced in Jalisco, Mexico, from several species of agave, in a roughly similar way to maple syrup. Juices are tapped from the core of the agave, the piña, and filtered, then heated, to turn carbohy-drates into sugars. Agave syrup has a much lower glycemic index than sugar.

Agavero®

www.agavero.com

A liqueur based on 100% agave añejo and reposado tequilas with an average age of 18 months. Agavero is a blend of Gran Centenario Tequila flavoured with Damiana essence - taken from a flower indigenous to the Jalisco region in Mexico, and allegedly an aphrodisiac.

Aguardiente

This Spanish pomace brandy is similar to Italian Grappa and French Marc and is generally known as aguardiente (confusingly, this term is used of all kinds of distillates all over the Spanish-speaking world). It is little exported.

Akvavit (Aquavit)

The word akvavit, like the word whisky, originates from the alchemical term 'water of life' - in Latin, aqua vitae. It is also known as aquavit. This flavoured white spirit is popular in Scandinavian countries, especially Denmark, where production centres on the town of Aalborg, its place of origin some 400 years ago.

Akvavit is distilled from potatoes or grain, and the resulting spirit is then redistilled with flavourings, which must include caraway. The EU definition states that akvavit must be 38% abv or more and must be flavoured with caraway, though additional flavourings such as honey, whisky and sherry are also permitted and used.

Like Eastern European vodkas, akvavits are typically drunk from a frosted shot glass as a chaser. Alternatively, try adding akvavit to black coffee.

Alcohol by Volume (alc. /vol. & abv)

Abbreviated as 'alc. /vol.' and also commonly abbreviated as 'abv', this term is a measure of a spirit's strength, recorded as a percentage of alcohol by volume at a given temperature (15°C). This measure, now the most commonly used method of recording alcoholic strength in Europe is more properly known is the 'Gay-Lussac Scale', named after its originator, a French physicist. At one end of this scale, zero alcohol (water) is equal to 0% alc. /vol., while at the opposite end, pure alcohol (proof) is measured at 100% alc. /vol.

Algarrobo Extract (Algarrobina)

The algarrobina is a product derivative from the algarrobo tree (also known as the carob tree in some countries) and is often used Peruvian cuisine. The tree's fruit, algarrobo pods, are rich in vitimans and sugars. These are cooked and the extract processed to produce a sweet syrup.

In Peru, algarrobina is commonly mixed with pisco to form the base of the Algarrobina Cocktail.

Almond (Orgeat) Sugar Syrup

This is a sweet syrup traditionally made from almonds, sugar and rose water or orange flower water. It is known in French as 'orgeat sirop' (pronounced 'Ohr-Zhat'), and many older recipes will call for simply 'Orgeat'.

Almond Flavoured Vodka

Commercial almond flavoured vodka is now widely available. These are usually flavoured using natural essences. Alternatively flavour your own vodka by infusing ground almonds in vodka and then filtering.

Amaretto Liqueur

Our recommendation: Luxardo Amaretto di Saschira

An Italian liqueur with an almond-apricot flavour. The flavours of the bitter almond and the apricot marry together well as they are both from the same fruit genus, Prunus. Bitter almonds are the kernels of the Prunus amygdalus amara from which amaretto's slight bitterness comes. There are hundreds of brands of amaretto made in Italy, but DiSaronno Originale Amaretto claims to be the original.

Amaro

The Italian word for bitter - this name is given to Italian liqueur bitters, which are usually dark brown in colour and produced from herbs, plants, tree bark and other botanicals. As well as the many commercially produced brands available it is common for Italian restaurants to make their own amaro to family recipes.

Amer Picon®

'Amer' is French for bitter and this bittersweet, orange and gentian aperitif was created in 1837, in Philippeville, Algeria by Gaetan Picon, a French cavalry sergeant serving in Algeria. Like a number of other French aperitifs created at the time (including Dubonnet Red and St Raphaël), Amer Picon includes quinine and owed part of its popularity to its perceived health benefits, particularly amongst the military keen to ward off malaria whilst on campaigns in North Africa, hence its nickname 'African Amer'.

Fresh and dried orange peel are macerated in neutral alcohol and then distilled. Dried gentian roots and quinquina are macerated separately. These two base flavoured spirits are then blended together along with sugar and caramel.

Two different styles of Amer Picon are produced to suit different mixers. Amer Picon Bière is usually mixed with beer (one part Picon to five parts beer) while Amer Picon Club is best mixed with white wine, champagne, tonic or mineral water.

Traditionally served over ice with a dash of grenadine, soda and a slice of orange or with lemon syrup and topped with soda water. Now more commonly drunk mixed with wine or beer.

Angostura Aromatic Bitters®

www.angostura.com

Johann Gottlieb Benjamin Siegert (1796-1870) was a German doctor who sought adventure and, it would seem, liked a battle. He tended troops in the Napoleonic Wars, including the Battle of Waterloo, and during the independence wars in Venezuela. It was here he chose to settle after being appointed Surgeon-General of a military hospital in the town of Angostura. Siegert's fellow settlers suffered chronic stomach complaints, partly due to the forced change in diet. So in 1820 the good doctor began experimenting with gentian root and other aromatic herbs. In 1824 he created the now famous bitters, which he originally called Amargo Aromatico and used them to treat stomach disorders and indigestion.

Siegert soon changed the name of his creation to Angostura, after the town where he was working (not, as is often presumed, after Angostura bark, which is not an ingredient). The town (now called Ciudad Bolivar) was in turn named after the native word for narrow, a reference to the nearby Orinoco River, which was reduced to a trickle in summer months. When the doctor died in 1870, production of the bitters was taken over by his sons who, in 1875, due to unrest in Venezuela, moved to Trinidad.

The truth behind Angostura's quirky packaging stems from the Caribbean's laid-back attitude. One day a new batch of labels was ordered and a simple mistake led to them being too big for the bottles. The error was spotted in time but everyone thought somebody else would deal with the problem. No one did, so when the crunch came they simply stuck the labels on the bottles intending to fix the next batch. No one quite got round to it and the oversized label became a trademark of the brand.

Angostura Aromatic Bitters are used in a great number of cocktails and cooking and are even great over vanilla ice cream.

Anis

Our recommendations: Pernod

The origins of anis pastis lie around the 19th century French fashion for absinthe. This potent greenish-yellow spirit, infused with herbs and spices (chiefly star anise and wormwood) was invented by a Frenchman - Dr Ordinaire, in Couvet, Switzerland. Most Western countries banned absinthe early in the twentieth century due to the supposed toxic nature of the wormwood root from which it was made and a series of media horror stories. Anis was manufactured as a replacement to absinthe, and Pernod Fils and Hemard Distilleries created the first brand – Pernod in 1920. Pastis followed later in 1932 with the creation of Ricard.

Both anis and pastis are produced by flavouring ethyl alcohol (neutral spirit) with natural extracts of star anise (Lllicium Verum) and/or anise (Pimpinella Anisum) and/or fennel (Foeniclum Vulgare). As well as anise (which tastes somewhat like wormwood) both anis and pastis also contain angelica and cloves. Brands may use as many as 40 other different herbs and spices, including cardamom, black and white pepper, artemisia, centaury, nutmeg and cinnamon.

Anis is the French word for anise. As well as the popular French drink described above, Anis is also a Spanish aniseed flavoured liqueur available in Secco (dry) and, since 1920, Dulce (sweet) versions. The anise plant widely used in Spain to flavour this drink is matalauva.

Anisette Liqueur

Our recommendation: Marie Brizard

This sweet, aniseed-flavoured liqueur often includes coriander and various other herbs. It is popular throughout the Mediterranean - in France, Spain and North Africa.

Aperitif

An aperitif is any drink taken before a meal to sharpen the appetite and some brands are still produced and marketed with this use in mind. The word 'aperitif' is derived from the Latin word 'aperire', meaning to open, a reference to warming up the digestive tract before eating. This is a hard category into which to pigeonhole brands as most vermouths, aromatized wines and many liqueurs are aperitifs. Brands based on spirits tend to be described as liqueur aperitifs and those based on wine as aromatized wines or vermouths. Some styles of Sherry are also great aperitifs.

Old-style cocktail books often categorise aperitif cocktails under the heading of 'pre-dinner drinks'. These tend to be short, bitter rather than sweet cocktails.

Vermouths and aromatic wines are often termed aperitifs. Brands include: Aperol, Campari, Commandaria St. John, Punt E Mes.

Aperol®

www.aperol.com

The Barbieri company was established in 1891 by Giuseppe Barbieri in Padua, Italy to produce and market a wide range of liqueurs. The company's most famous and enduring product, Aperol, was especially created in 1919 by his two sons, Luigi and Silvio for a large exhibition attracting international visitors which was held in the their home. The concept of making an aperitif with an alcohol content of only 11% was revolutionary, and perhaps a little before its time, as it did not take off and only became a major success after the Second World War.

In 1991 the Barbieri Company was acquired by Ireland's C&C International and as a result, later that same year, merged with Barbero (now part of Campari) who continued to build Aperol and today it is enjoyed by over 3.4 million Italians and is commonly available across Europe and North America.

This spirit based aperitif's unique flavour and orange/red colour comes from a secret infusion of 16 ingredients, including bitter orange essence, gentian, cinchona bark (quinine) and Chinese rhubarb. The majority of herbs and roots used come from the Piedmont region of Northern Italy and the recipe remains unchanged since it was first created in 1919. Aperol does not undergo any aging process and is ready to be bottled immediately after blending.

Apostoles Palo Cortado

Prounounced 'Ap-Ost-O-Less' this Palo Cortado is part of the González Byass 'Very Rare Solera' range. Made from Palomino Fino grapes aged in a Solera created in honour of her Majesty Queen Isabel II of Spain, when she visited the company's bodegas in 1862.

Apple Flavoured Vodka

Proprietary apple flavoured vodka is now widely available. These are usually flavoured using natural essences.

Apple Juice

The best way to use apples in cocktails is as a juice. You can make your own in a standard electric juice extractor. There's no need to peel or core apples, as the skin and core contain over half the fruit's nutrients. Simply remove the stalks and chop the fruit into small enough chunks to fit through the feeder. Choose a flavoursome variety like Bramley over more bland types like Washington Red or Golden Delicious.

Unchecked, the juice will quickly oxidise and discolour but a splash of lime juice helps prevent this without too much effect on the flavour. You'll find that crisper apples yield clearer juice.

Most supermarkets carry at least one quality pressed apple juice and the best of these cloudy juices makes DIY juicing unnecessary. Unless clarity of appearance is essential, avoid the packaged 'pure', clear apple juices as these tend to be overly sweet and artificial tasting.

Apple Schnapps Liqueur

Our recommendation: Berentzen apfelkorn

The term schnapps traditionally suggests a clear strong spirit. However, over the last decade or so the term has come to refer to sweet liqueurs of only 20-24% abv, which bear no resemblance to the strong, dry, almost vodka-style schnapps from which they take their name. I tend to refer to such products 'schnapps liqueurs' to avoid confusion.

Applejack

Applejack is the term generally applied to North American apple brandy distilled from cider, mainly in New England and Eastern Canada. Applejack is similar to English cider brandy and French Calvados.

When settlers arrived in New England in the 17th century, they tried to grow hops to make beer. The hops did not do well but apple trees thrived so they started making applejack instead. There are more than 800 varieties of apple and of these, 120-odd are suitable for making cider, which can then be distilled to make a brandy. Different kinds of apple add different elements to the finished brandy: sweet apples yield a high proportion of the sugars from which alcohol is made, bitter apples add tannins for taste and aroma, while tart apples add freshness.

The best applejacks are distilled in pot stills and matured in oak for at least two years. While similar to Calvados, applejack usually has a lighter flavour and aroma than its French counterpart, partly because the apples used are generally less bitter.

Apricot Brandy Liqueur

Our recommendation: Bols apricot brandy

Also known as 'apry' in French, these liqueurs are produced either by infusing apricots in brandy and sweetening, or by infusing apricots in neutral spirit. The best examples are distilled from apricots. In the United States the term 'apricot brandy' refers to a flavoured brandy that is based on grape brandy.

Armagnac

Armagnac is a fine French brandy from the Gascony region, an inland area between Bordeaux and Toulouse, stretching to the Pyrenees. This area was once home to many swashbuckling characters: the most famous being Charles de Batz Castelmore, Seigneur d'Artagnan, who led the King's Musketeers under Louis XIV and has been immortalised as one of the Three Musketeers.

The winemakers of Gascony were among the first in France to learn methods of distillation. This is probably because of its close proximity to the Spanish border – it seems highly likely that the vintners learnt distillation from the Moors who ruled Spain during the Middle Ages. The first documentary evidence of Armagnac distillation dates back to 1411, so Armagnac predates the other great brandy of France, Cognac, by some two centuries. Unlike Cognac, the Armagnac region lacks easy access to a large river or the sea so Armagnac remained a local drink and has never enjoyed the wide popularity that Cognac has over the centuries.

Like Cognac, Armagnac is still made by hundreds of small farmers who sell their brandy to larger companies, who age and blend the Armagnac. However, it has a very different style to Cognac – tending to have a more robust flavour.

Armagnacs tend to be sold in two types of traditional bottle. One is oval shaped and flat sided with a long neck; the other, known as a 'basquaise' or 'pot gascon' is round and squat. Some producers have now moved to different 'more modern' bottles.

Aromatized Wines

Any product based on wines fortified with spirit and flavoured with herbs and spices is a 'aromatized wine'. There is a very fine and somewhat misty line between vermouths and aromatized wines. In this guide I've taken my lead from how the producers categorize their own products. The production methods of both are similar if not identical. For further information see 'vermouth'.

Averna Amaro Siciliano®

www.avernausa.com

Amaro liqueur was created in 1868 for Salvatore Averna by the herbalist monks of the Holy Spirit Abbey. Averna was the first licensed spirit in Sicily and over generations the brand and distillery have grown to become Italy's best-selling brand of Amaro. It is now owned by Crupo Campari.

Amero is made from an infusion of aromatic herbs, dried flowers, spices and liquorice but the exact recipe is a closely guarded secret.

Bacardi Superior Rum®

www.bacardi.com

The story of Bacardi starts with Don Facundo Bacardi Massó, a carpenter's son who at the age of 15 left his Spanish hometown of Sites near Barcelona. He travelled to Cuba, then Spain's prized colonial possession, in search of his fortune and in 1830 arrived at the port of Santiago de Cuba on the eastern side of the island where he established a grocer's store.

Over the years he gradually built the business, also importing wines and spirits from Spain. All was well until 1852 when two successive earthquakes just nine days apart decimated the eastern side of the island and resulted in an outbreak of cholera that claimed the lives of two of his children. He left for Spain with his wife, Doña Amalia, and his remaining children until the epidemic was over. On his return he found that his store had been looted and that the business was bankrupt.

Together with an inheritance from his grandfather and a loan from his wife's godmother, Don Facundo was able to restart the business and resolved to create his own product rather than simply trade in those made by others. Although modern distillation processes were employed throughout the Caribbean at the time, the rum they produced was harsh and inconsistent, so he set out to develop a consistently high quality rum product to rival the spirits that he imported from Europe.

Don Facundo experimented to create a more controlled distillation process and after ten years research into techniques of fermentation, distillation and maturation on the 4th February 1862 he purchased a simple tin-roofed distillery on Matadero Street with a single copper and cast iron pot still and established Bacardi y Compania.

Before Don Facundo created what we now know today as Bacardi 'Superior' (the original 'Carta Blanca' name remains on the modern label) white rum did exist but it was harsh and unrefined being bottled straight from the still. The rum Don Facundo created was the world's first premium aged white rum and became a pioneer of white rum production, setting the standards others followed for rum production.

Don Facundo spent many years experimenting with various yeast samples to find the one that allowed for a fast fermentation so producing a mash with fewer impurities, less contamination and a higher alcohol content. When distilled this produced a lighter rum with a consistent flavour profile. He discovered the perfect yeast growing naturally in the sugarcane plantations near Santiago de Cuba. Now known as La Levadura Bacardi, Don Facundo was the first rum producer to isolate and later culture a proprietary strain of yeast. Bacardi Superior is still made with the same strain of yeast that Don Facundo used to this day.

Don Facundo chose molasses over the more common and cheaper 'guarapo', or sugarcane juice due to the low water content of molasses reducing the risk of contamination and concentrating the mineral content. Molasses are also pasteurised, preventing bacteria, mould and natural yeasts from causing spontaneous fermentation. This allows the flavour development in the mash to be controlled, and produces a lighter, cleaner spirit.

In his quest to produce a more refined and lighter rum Don Facundo created two different mashes. One with a flavour profile containing a high level of congeners to make a spirit with a more pronounced flavour for the distillation of Aguardiente, and one with a lighter profile to create a more delicate and refined spirit for the distillation of Redestilado.

Today, Bacardi still distil two different rum bases from two different mashes: 'Aguardiente', a fruity, heavy-bodied rum with a high level of congeners and strong flavours made from in a single continuous distillation in a copper and cast iron column still to 70-80% abv and 'Redestilado', a drier light-bodied rum with few congeners and a subtler flavour. This is distilled through five separate continuous stainless steel columns to 92.5%-94.5% abv. These

contrasting light and heavy rums are aged and blended to make Bacardi Superior rum.

Don Facundo was the first person to distil both Aguardiente and Redestilado to be aged and then blended together to produce a balanced rum. In doing so, he created what has become known in rum-making as the 'Parallel Process'.

As an importer of spirits Don Facundo was aware that barrel maturation caused the spirit to become mellow and complex. Before Don Facundo started aging rums in 1862, rum was generally only stored in wooden casks for transportation, so the action of maturation was coincidental rather than deliberate. Don Facundo was the first person to mature his rum in oak barrels until a specific flavour profile had been reached.

Bacardi Superior rum is blended only from rums aged for at least 12 months, and as long as 2 years, depending on the characteristics of the individual barrel. The Aguardiente and Redestilado are aged separately in lightly charred American white-oak barrels formerly used to mature American whiskey. The inside of each barrel is shaved and recharged with a light toast to open the pores of the oak and activate the wood sugars.

Don Facundo's quest to produce a smoother, more elegant rum led him to experiment with filtration techniques. He found that natural charcoal was perfect for filtering harsh and undesirable components and impurities from his rum, making it smoother and more harmonious. Different charcoals made from different woods remove different componants. The recipe for the charcoal filter that Don Facundo created, like the recipe for the rum itself, remains a carefully guarded secret but is known to be a mix of tropical woods and coconut shells.

One of the specific charcoals, chosen for the flavour compounds that it removes from the rum, also has the side effect of removing the rum's colour. Bacardi Superior rum is the original aged and charcoal-filtered clear rum. Charcoal filtration is used at three key points of Bacardi Superior's production process - before and after ageing the Aguardiente, and after ageing the Redestilado (but not before).

Soon after buying the distillery in 1862, Don Facundo's wife, discovered a colony of fruit bats roosting high in the rafters, and knowing that bats were considered lucky in both local and Spanish folklore, she suggested using a bat as a symbol for the new Bacardi Superior rum. In 1860s Cuba, many people were illiterate and so the bat symbol made Bacardi rum easily recognisable.

When Don Facundo launched what became known as 'El Ron del Murcielago' (The Rum of the Bat), it quickly established a reputation for being incredibly smooth and drinkable. Although the design has evolved over the years, the iconic bat symbol has appeared on every product carrying the Bacardi family name since.

In 1862 Don Facundo's son and namesake planted a coconut palm in front of the new distillery. When the distillery was expanded work had to go around what became affectionately known as El Coco. The palm survived fires, earthquakes and hurricanes and came to symbolise the company's strength and vitality. Local prophecy spoke of the Bacardi Company surviving in Cuba as long as the coconut palm lived.

The business prospered and was eventually taken over by Don Facundo's three sons. One of them, Emilio, was a major influencer in Cuban independence and was arrested and deported twice by the Spanish for anti-colonial activities. He became the first freely elected Mayor of Santiago de Cuba and eventually Senator of Cuba's Eastern province. However, he became disenchanted by the American government's interference in Cuba's politics and so resigned his post to focus on managing his family business. Emilio expanded his father's company to Spain and the United States. When he died, shortly after the completion of a new distillery in 1922, Santiago's shops closed for two days in mourning.

Enrique Schueg, Don Facundo's son-in-law, was also politically active and in 1894 was arrested by the Spanish Governors. Thanks to the intervention of France's Minister of External Affairs he escaped execution but was deported to Haiti until the end of the Civil War. He would later become the Bacardi Company's third president.

Pepín Bosch, Don Facundo's grandson-in-law, was another family member to hold high office when in 1949 Cuban President Carlos Prio Socarras persuaded him to become Cuba's Ministro de Hacienda (Home Secretary). During his term of office, Bosch turned Cuba's $18 million deficit into a $15 million surplus. Time Magazine wrote: 'The secret to Pepín Bosch's success was uncommon ministerial honesty and an un-answering drive to collect taxes uncollected by lax predecessors. Worldwide demand for Bacardi grew rapidly and the company's distilleries were working at full capacity. In 1931 they opened a distillery in Mexico and another in Puerto Rico in 1936.

Back in Cuba, the 1950s saw a turbulent political situation erupt with a

series of coups d'etat. It was a time of widespread corruption and Government interference in business. Bacardi's CEO, Pepin Bosch, feared Bacardi would fall prey to such interference by the corrupt right wing dictatorship of Fulgencio Batista and so wisely transferred the assets of Compania Ron Bacardi S.A. to Nassau in the Bahamas. In doing so, he moved the ownership of trademarks and the Bacardi Company's proprietary formulas outside Cuba.

Meanwhile Fidel Castro's revolutionary movement promised democratic elections and an end to government corruption. He was supported financially and politically by people throughout the country, including members of the Bacardi family. On 31st December 1959, Castro succeeded in his revolt to overthrow the Batista Government. Castro was welcomed as a liberating hero and the Bacardi family believed Cuba was finally a free and just place.

However, in October 1960 Castro's administration instigated a program of forceful expropriation and confiscated all privately-owned companies and assets on the island without compensation. Il Coco, the emblematic palm tree at the original distillery, inexplicably started to wither and finally died. The prophecy proved to be correct: and all of the Bacardi Company's assets were confiscated and the company was nationalised by the Cuban Administration. The Bacardi family were exiled from their homeland.

Fortunately, due to Pepin Bosch's foresight, the company's intellectual property was safely off the island. It was not just the trademarks that eluded Castro's Government. An oversight led to the company's headquarters being raided a full day after the sales office in Havana, so giving Bacardi's distillers (the Maestros de Ron Bacardi) time to destroy the all important yeast cultures (La Levadura Bacardi) and their secret charcoal recipe. Without these the Cuban Government could not produce rum that tasted like Bacardi Superior. This could have been the end of Bacardi rum if it were not for the other cultures of La Levadura Bacardi, charcoal recipes and other proprietary processes still safely held in the company's other distilleries in Mexico and Puerto Rico.

Bacardi was awarded its first medal in 1876 in Philadelphia and in its first seventy years amassed a further 29 awards, ten of which appear on the label. Bacardi is now the most popular rum brand in the world, and the most popular brand-called spirit, sold in more than 170 countries and the company, which is still controlled by the Bacardi family, is the fifth largest liquor company in the world. The Bacardi family remain in exile from Cuba to this day.

Bacardi Oro Golden Rum®

www.bacardi.com

This golden rum (Oro is Spanish for gold) was first produced in 1862 and is made to original specifications by Don Facundo Bacardi. Bacardi Oro is blended from rums aged for a longer period than Bacardi Superior, generally between 2-3 years, for a richer, mellower flavour profile, and is filtered through a different recipe of charcoals to give a light background of oak and caramel.

Baileys Original Irish Cream®

www.baileys.com

The story of Baileys (the registered trademark omits the apostrophe) began in 1971 when the idea of blending Irish whiskey and Irish cream originated due to what was then Grand Metropolitan (now part of Diageo plc) owning both the spirits firm W&A Gilbey & Co and Express Dairies.

The bottle has always proclaimed its producer as being the fictional R&A Bailey. In reality, it is owned and made by the British based spirits conglomerate Diageo. The rather quaint sounding R&A Bailey was the brainwave of one of the golf obsessed original brand development managers after reading an article about the Royal and Ancient Golf Club. The brand's surname comes from The Bailey Pub in Duke Street, Dublin where the brand team often met. First launched in November 1974 Baileys is the world's original cream liqueur and it creation was only possible thanks to two men, Matt Gluckman and Matt McPherson, perfecting the technique of combining spirits and fresh cream without souring the cream. They borrowed a process from the ice-cream industry, which removes and replaces the protein in the cream thus giving it a positive charge. When this is blended with the negatively charged alcohol the two combine harmoniously.

Baileys is now the world's bestselling liqueur, selling over seven million nine-litre cases a year in some 130 countries. Wherever in the world Baileys is sold, it is produced in Ireland, at two plants in Dublin and Belfast, which receive daily deliveries of fresh cream. Some 40,000 cows on 1,500 dairy farms jointly supply the more than 275 million litres of milk required each year, principally processed by Glanbia PLC's Virginia facility in County Cavan, which has supplied cream to Baileys for over thirty years.

The makers of Baileys are very specific about the cream used in Baileys and insist it comes from happy Holstein-Friesian cows. Happy? They are kept happy due to being fed on four specific varieties of grass, after all, and to quote Baileys, "they don't call Ireland the Emerald Isle for nothing."

Cream makes up half of every bottle. Other ingredients include triple distilled pot-still Irish whiskey, neutral spirit, vanilla, cocoa and sugar. Baileys does not contain any artificial preservatives but due to the spirit acting as a natural preservative has a shelf life of two years once opened. That said I'd recommend stashing yours in a refrigerator, as it is best served cold over ice.

Bailey's continues to grow from strength to strength and in 2005 'Baileys with a hint of Mint Chocolate' and 'Baileys with a hint Crème Caramel' line extensions were launched in UK airports.

When making cocktails, mixing Baileys with citrus and acidic ingredients (tonic, wine etc.) should be avoided as these will cause the cream to coagulate. There is of course no truth in the urban legend that combining Baileys and tonic is lethal. Baileys is best served neat over ice and is popular in layered shots such as a B52 and as a float in place of cream. It also mixes well with coffee and I particularly recommend serving in a Mocha Martini, the creamy version of an Espresso Martini.

Banana

The fruit of a perennial herb that looks like a tree, bananas come in a range of hues from purple to yellow, although we are most familiar with the yellow kind. These are transported green and ripened prior to sale in dedicated ripening warehouses, and should not be stored in refrigerators as exposure to low temperatures turns the fruit black. They bring a distinctively sweet, smooth tropical flavour to drinks but suffer from association with disco drinks.

Bärenjäger®

www.barenjagerhoney.com

This honey-flavoured liqueur is said to have been developed in Eastern Prussia during the late 15th century. The name means 'bear hunter' or bear trap and Bärenjäger is sold in a distinctive bottle with a plastic beehive-shaped cap.

Basil

This aromatic herb has strong flavours of lemon and jasmine. Unless stipulated, recipes in this guide calling for basil leaves refer to the common sweet variety and not the more pungent Thai varieties (see also Thai Basil). Basil leaves don't generally require muddling when used in a shaken cocktail as the action of shaking is usually sufficient to release the flavour of the leaves into the drink.

Becherovka (Carlsbad Becher)®

www.janbecher.cz

An English physician, Dr Frobridge, who was visiting the small Czech spa town of Karlovy Vary as the personal physician to Count Zu Pletenberg-Mietingen, originally produced Becherovka as a stomach 'medicine' in 1805. Demand led to factory production, which started in 1807 at Karlovy-Vary, west of Prague (which, under the Austrians, was Karlsbad - hence the drink's alternative name, Carlsbad Becher).

Now the Czech national liqueur, Becherovka is matured in oak and contains cinnamon, cloves, nutmeg and other herbs. It can be drunk neat over ice but is more commonly drunk with tonic water and lime, a mix known as a Beton.

Belle de Brillet®

www.brillet.fr

Around twenty pounds of ripe Williams pears are required to make each bottle of Belle de Brillet pear liqueur. The pears are macerated in neutral alcohol and the essence blended with Brillet Cognac and sugar.

Bénédictine D.O.M.®

www.benedictine.fr

Bénédictine is believed to have been first formulated in 1510 by Dom Bernardo Vincelli, a keen botanist and Bénédictine monk at the Abbey of Fécamp on the Normandy Coast, France. His elixir attracted considerable attention and in 1524, François I of France travelled to Fécamp to sample it. The abbey was destroyed during the French Revolution, but a local merchant, Alexandre Le Grand, who is said to have been a descendant of the trustee of the abbey, found a recipe to the lost drink in one of the many abbey books in his possession and in 1863 succeeded in making an elixir that satisfied the palates of those who could still remember the original.

Le Grand was a brilliant marketer and named his elixir Bénédictine and incorporated the initials D.O.M. on the label to reinforce its monastic origins. These initials stand for Deo Optimo Maximo, meaning 'To God, most good, most great'. So successful was he, that towards the end of the 19th century he built a fantastically opulent distillery and offices on the site of the former Abbey. His extravagant edifice is still the home of the liqueur and dominates the small town.

Bénédictine is based on brandy and neutral spirit and flavoured with 56 different herbs and spices including: hyssop, balm, angelica, aloe, apricot, cinnamon, genepi, cloves, nutmeg, myrrh, pine, tea, cardamom, mace, thyme, vanilla and honey, along with saffron to give the amber hue. These herbs are used in four different preparations, three using distillation and one using maceration, all aged independently before being blended and left to marry and further age. The whole process takes some two years.

When the men of the 11th battalion of the East Lancashire regiment were fighting in the Normandy trenches, they discovered the local liqueur, Bénédictine, which they drunk as a grog with hot water. This firm favourite of the regiment became known as a 'Benny and Hot' and is still popular in Lancashire towns such as Accrington and Burnley.

Benoit Serres Crème de Violette®

www.benoit-serres.com

This vivid purple liqueur looks like methylated spirits and is flavoured by the infusion of violets and vanilla.

Benoit Serres is a family concern in Villefrance-de-Lauragais, southeast of Toulouse in the south of France and is widely regarded to be the best producer of crème de violette liqueur.

Berentzen Apfelkorn®

www.berentzen.de

Established in 1758, Berentzen are famous for this world-leading apple schnapps. In 1976 the brothers Berentzen dramatically changed their company's fortunes by creating a new product, which almost instantly became an international success.

German students traditionally mixed Berentzen Korn Schnapps (a dry, clear spirit) with apple juice. Recognising this, the brothers worked on an apple flavoured schnapps, blending apple juice with wheat spirit, which proved an instant success.

Bitter Lemon

Bitter lemon is a carbonated soft drink flavoured with quinine, lemon and sugar. It is the quinine that gives this drink its bitter taste and is basically tonic water with additional lemon flavour.

Bitter Lemon is thought to have first been produced by Schweppes in 1950's.

Bitters

A term for bitter liqueurs and aperitifs made from roots, flowers, fruits and peels, macerated in neutral spirits. Popular ingredients include gentian, quinine and orange. Many originated from medieval therapeutic drinks. Although bitters are essential ingredients in a good proportion of the world's classic cocktails, they are usually the smallest bottles on a bar and the ones that the smallest quantities are poured from. Though brands such as

Angostura, Peychaud's and Fee Brothers now predominate, historically bars would produce their own bitters.

Blackcurrants

The fruit of a native northern European shrub that is now widely cultivated in France, Germany, the Netherlands and Belgium. In the French Côte d'Or blackcurrants are heavily used in the production of cassis liqueur.

Blueberries

Blueberry pie is as much an American icon as the Stars and Stripes. This bushy shrub, which is virtually identical to the bilberry, is native to the States and many different types grow there – not all of them blue.

The lowbush blueberry, which is called the 'bleuet' in Quebec, tends to be smaller and sweeter than other varieties and is often marketed as 'wild blueberry'. The larger, highbush blueberry is the variety most cultivated in the US.

These soft berries are best muddled in the base of your shaker or glass. Recipes in this guide specify the number required for each drink. Alternatively, you can make a purée. Just stick them in the blender and add a touch of sugar syrup. Fresh blueberries should not be stored in the refrigerator.

Boiron Fruit Purées®

www.boironfreres.com

Les vergers Boiron was established in 1970 and has since become one of the most respected and best known producers of frozen fruit purées. Fruits are picked from around the world at their optimum ripeness to ensure the most intense flavour. These fruits are frozen as soon as they are picked which allows them to release all their original qualities when later used. The fruit is transported back to the factory in Valence, in the Drôme area, at the heart of one of France's biggest orchards where a special method of flash pasteurization is used to maintain the natural flavours, colours and textures of the fruit within the purée.

Les vergers Boiron purées should be stored at -18°C and should be defrosted for 24 – 48 hours at a temperature between +2°C and +4°C to use at their best.

Bokma Oude Genever®

www.bokma.com

This famous Dutch genever was first created by the Bokma family in 1826 in the Frisian capital of Leeuwarden. 'Bok' means a male goat, hence the goat emblem on the crest. Bokma's unique square bottle was designed in 1894 and I believe predates other famous quadrilaterals such as Cointreau.

Bokma make excellent jonge but I particularly like their oude and according to authorities such as David Wondrich in his excellent 'Imbibe', it was this oude style of genever that pioneering American bartenders such as Jerry Thomas used back in the 1800s.

Bols Advocaat®

www.bols.com

This Dutch liqueur is made from brandy, egg yolks and sugar. It is derived from an alcoholic drink that Dutch colonists in South Africa made from the yellowish pulp of the abacate fruit. In Holland, egg yolks took the place of the fruit and the name, which had already evolved into avocado by Portuguese colonists in Brazil, became Advocaat in Dutch.

Bols Advocaat is an entirely natural product, made only using brandy, egg yolks, sugar and vanilla without any preservatives or artificial thickeners.

Bols Apricot Brandy®

www.bols.com

In 1575, the Bols family arrived in Amsterdam to open 'het Lootsje' (which translates as 'The Little Shed') to distill liqueurs. Despite 'het Lootsje' being a wooden shed, fire risks dictated that the distillery had to be built outside

Amsterdam's city walls. As the distillery grew, new stone buildings replaced the original wooden structure, but the name 'Lootsje' stuck.

Lucas Bols was born in 1652 and is the man credited with first taking Bols into the international market. He was also a major shareholder of The Dutch East India Company who, during the prolific time of the Dutch Golden Age, brought exotic herbs, spices and fruits back to Amsterdam. These unusual new flavours were used to create new liqueurs – the hand written recipes of many of which still remain today.

After years of prosperity the last male member of the Bols family died in 1813 and the company was offered for conditional sale - requesting that the name Lucas Bols should always be retained.

Bols Apricot brandy liqueur is produced by infusing apricots in selected cognacs and flavouring the infusion with various herbs to bring out the best flavour and aroma of the apricots. Enriched with a hint of almond, this amber coloured liqueur is one of Bols most popular. With an aroma of juicy apricots, this distinctively flavoured liqueur is suited to use in a variety of different cocktails. The light clean taste features apricot with a hint of brandy and almond.

Bols Blue®

www.bols.com

The Latin words "Semper Idem" inscribed in the coat of arms of the Bols family mean "always the same", which to the distiller means "Always the same end product of the same high quality". Distillation of quality products requires a lot of experience and knowledge.

Distilled from the peel of the bitter Curaçao oranges, this vivid blue curaçao liqueur is probably the best known of the Bols range. Lucas Bols B.V., the modern Dutch beverage company, originated from a firm started in 1575 by a Dutchman called Lucas Bols. Prevented from distilling within the city walls due to the fire risk, Lucas distilled from a wooden shed outside Amsterdam. Today the Bols is one of the largest liqueur producers in the world.

Bols Blue is distilled from a blend of predominantly natural products from around the world – herbs, sweet red oranges, the characteristically flavourful bitter Curaçao oranges and the rare Kinnow oranges. This gives Bols Blue a fresh, yet complex orange scent and taste.

Bols Blue is frequently used by bartenders due to its distinctive colour and refreshing taste, which features orange zest with a hint of spice.

Boulard Grand Solage®

www.calvados-boulard

Boulard Grand Solage is a Pays d'Auge Calvados produced by traditional methods and aged from three to five years. The house of Boulard was founded in 1825 by Pierre-August Boulard, and is still owned by his fifth generation descendant Vincent.

120 different varieties of apple are used in Boulard's production: their own orchards contribute 20% of the total, while a network of 500 local growers supply the remainder.

Boulard applies strict quality controls in the production of cider for distillation and double distil it in their eight copper pot stills before ageing in seasoned oak casks.

Bourbon Whiskey

Our recommendation: Bulleit bourbon

For a whiskey to be Bourbon, it must be produced according to specific rules easily remembered by the seven A to G letters which stand for these specifications. Bourbon must be:

(A=American) Made anywhere in the USA but only Kentucky Bourbon can advertise the state where it is made.

(B = Barrels) Aged at least 2 years in charred new white oak barrels. Any whiskey which has been aged for less than four years must state its age on the label. Generally 2 to 4 year old whiskies are best avoided.

(C = Corn) Contain at least 51% corn but not more than 80%.

(D = Distillation) Distilled to a strength of not more than 80% abv.

(E = Entry Proof) Placed in cask to age at 62.5%abv or less.
(F = Fill Proof) Reduced at the time of bottling to no lower than 40% abv.
(G = Genuine) Only water may be added. No colouring or flavouring may be added to straight whiskey.

A bourbon distiller must first determine the 'mashbill', essentially a recipe of different grains from which the whiskey is to be made. In the case of Bourbon this will consist of a minimum of 51% corn (but usually 70%) with the balance made up by 'small grains', usually malted barley and then either rye or wheat. Rye produces a heavier whiskey, while wheat results in a lighter one. Limestone water is then added to the grain and the mix is cooked in a pressure cooker to produce a 'mash'. The cooking reduces the starch present into fermentable sugars.

Then yeast is added, along with modern American whiskey's essential ingredient – 'sour mash'. Sour mash is the mash from the last batch of whiskey made. Generally about 25% is held back and added to the latest batch. This will contain some of the yeast needed for fermentation, and helps to keep out wild yeasts and ensure a consistency between different batches. The beer-like fermented liquid is then distilled. In some distilleries, this is a huge industrial process employing Coffey stills, in other, smaller businesses, a cross between a pot and Coffey still is used. The beer is distilled twice, usually once in a column still which takes the strength up to approximately 50% abv and then again in a 'doubler', which continues to remove fusel-oils and impurities and also further increases the strength. (Few Bourbons are triple distilled). The whiskey is then casked, unless the spirit is to be a Tennessee Whiskey (see Tennessee Whiskey).

The most important part of the creation of any Bourbon is the method of ageing. Bourbon must be aged for at least two years in a charred oak barrel, which may not then be re-used for the same purpose. (There are degrees of charring, light to heavy.) While the spirit matures in the fluctuating temperatures of the warehouse, the charred oak adds vanilla and caramel flavours to the whiskey.

Whiskies termed 'small batch' are bottled from casks stored in one section of the warehouse, or even from an individual barrel. This category is still to be recognised in law and is a concept rather than a specific term where legislation can be enforced. This is not helped by the many different producers, who have not agreed, and probably never will agree, on a specific number of litres and casks to determine what constitutes 'small batch'.

Brown Crème de Cacao

Crème de cacao is a dark chocolate-flavoured liqueur based on neutral spirit. Its flavour chiefly derives from roasted cacao beans but each producer of the various different brands available adds their own proprietary blend of additional herbs and spices, usually including vanilla.

Brown crème de cacao liqueurs are sometimes alternatively named 'dark crème de cacao' in reference to the liqueurs dark colour. Most brands of crème de cacao liqueur also bottle a clear or 'white' version. The brown and white versions of crème de cacao are differentiated by more than colour. Typically the brown versions derive their flavour from percolation while the cacao beans flavouring the clear version will be distilled. Brown crème de cacao liqueurs tend to have a more robust flavour than their more delicately flavoured white counterparts.

Bulleit Bourbon

www.bulleitbourbon.com
Augustus Bulleit first created Bulleit Bourbon in Louisville, Kentucky around 1830. He came from a family of brandy makers who had emigrated from France to New Orleans in the 1700s and when Augustus moved from New Orleans to Louisville to open a tavern, he used his knowledge of French brandy making to experiment with his own small batch distilling of Kentucky bourbon.

Bulleit's popularity grew and the bourbon was sold throughout Kentucky and Indiana but in 1860 Augustus disappeared whilst transporting liquor to New Orleans. Some say he was murdered by his business partner, while others believe he was seduced by the sumptuous life in the city's French Quarter. The recipe for Bulleit Bourbon seemed to disappear with him and it was not until 1987 when Augustus' great-great grandson Tom Bulleit finally recreated Bulleit Bourbon.

For bourbon to be classified as such, it needs to meet certain criteria, introduced by the American Government in May 1964. It must be a mix of corn, rye, wheat and barley but the major component (at least 51%) must be corn. It must be distilled to no more than 80% abv. It must be 100% natural – with only water added, and it must be aged in new, charred oak barrels. If all criteria are met, it is then recognised as "a distinctive product of the United States"

Today Bulleit Bourbon is distilled and aged in small batches and stored in a single-story warehouse to reduce inconsistencies in the maturation process. It is aged in American White Oak barrels that are flame charred for at least six years, which creates maturity and smoothness. In true bourbon fashion, only limestone-filtered water is used plus unlike most other producers, Bulleit Bourbon has its own Grain Division, which acquires distiller's grade grains, grown to their own specification.

It is made up of 30% Rye – the highest rye content of any other bourbon – and initially has a sweet and buttery taste, which becomes spicier with buttery corn notes and hints of dark chocolate and coffee.

Butterscotch Schnapps Liqueur

Our recommendation: Teichenne butterscotch schnapps
Butterscotch is one of those indulgent flavours that take us back to our youth, being commonly used in cookies, ice-cream toppings and candies. The flavour is sweet, creamy but also has a wonderfully tangy bite.

The word 'butterscotch' has nothing to do with Scotch whisky or even Scotland. In this context 'scotch' means to cut or score a surface, a reference to when butterscotch candy is poured out to cool, it's 'scotched' to make it easier to break into pieces later.

Simple butterscotch is made with dark brown sugar, butter and lemon juice. Butterscotch's distinctive flavour comes from what chemists call the Maillard reaction, in which sugars and proteins react under heat to create roasted and browned flavours.

Butterscotch candy is made in a similar manner to that of caramel, fudge and toffee. The difference being the boiling temperature and the ways in which they are cooled.

Cachaça

Our recommendation: Leblon cachaça
Outside of Brazil, Cachaça is most often encountered as part of a Caipirinha, the cocktail served in a tumbler with crushed ice, crushed lime wedges and sugar. Pronounced 'Ka-Shah-Sa', cachaça is the spirit of Brazil and the Caipirinha its national drink. (The name actually means 'a little countryside drink'.)

In Brazil, Cachaça is also marketed under the name Caninha ('little cane') or as 'Aguardente de Cana', which means 'distillate of cane' but could be uncharitably translated as 'cane firewater'.

Cachaça is made from sugar cane and so is a kind of rum (although as traditionally maze meal is used to start the fermentation, many brands of cachaça are not strictly rums according to EU regulations). Sugar cane has been cultivated in Brazil since 1532 when the country came under Portuguese rule and the crop has played a major role in the socio-economic history of the country. Large estates growing only sugar cane were the basis of Brazil's economy until well into the 20th century. Cachaça production in Brazil quickly followed.

Unlike most rums, which are produced from molasses, a by-product of sugar refining, the best cachaça is distilled from fermented sugar cane juice. However, this is not always the case and many brands are made from sugar syrup or molasses. The big brands tend to burn the sugar to accelerate the breakdown of sugars, while the smaller distillers tend to use cane syrup.

Cachaça is only distilled to a maximum of 75% alcoholic strength, unlike most light rums, which are usually distilled to 96% strength. This lower distillation strength means cachaça is less refined with more impurities and consequently retains more of the aroma and flavour of the sugar cane.

Calisay®

This traditional, quinine-based Catalan herb liqueur has a history that goes back to the Middle Ages and the monks of the Bohemia monastery.

The calisaya is a type of cinchona tree, which is native to the South

American Andes. Its yellow bark is a source of quinine (70-80% of alkaloids in cultivated tree bark are quinine). Cinchonas are grown in plantations, mainly in Java, and mature for ten years before being stripped of the yellow bark, roots and branches.

Calisaya is a traditional Spanish bitters made with calisaya bark in a brandy base, sweetened with sugar syrup and matured in oak. It is usually served neat as a digestive but alternatively serve in a Glamis cocktail.

Calvados

Our recommendation: Boulard Grand Solage

Calvados is a French brandy made from apples (though it can also contain pears). The name is an appellation controlee, meaning that Calvados can only be produced in defined areas of North-Western France.

Like Cognac and Armagnac, the Calvados-making district is divided into smaller areas. Two of these sub-regions have their own appellations controlees: Pays d'Auge and Domfront. Pays d'Auge, the area around the villages of Orne and Eure, is generally considered to produce the best Calvados and by law all AOC Pays d'Auge Calvados must be double-distilled in pot stills. Domfront Calvados, which acquired its AOC at the end of 1997, must contain at least 30% perry pears.

Calvados production starts with selecting the fruit, which is washed, crushed and pressed. It is then fermented, using natural yeasts from the skin of the fruit, a process that lasts from one to three months. The result is a cider with an alcoholic strength of at least 4.5%.

This cider is then either single-distilled in a column still or double-distilled in a pot still, the distillate emerging at around 68-72% abv. Most of the better quality Calvados and all Pays d'Auge Calvados are made in a pot still.

Calvados must be aged in oak casks for a minimum of one year although most good Calvados will be aged for several years and some for 20 years or more. Generally, different batches are blended to produce a consistent product, although some distillers offer vintage bottlings from a single barrel. After blending, the Calvados is bottled at between 40-45% abv. Most producers will blend the spirit with water to reach this strength, but a few will allow the alcohol to evaporate naturally as the Calvados ages.

The age stated on a bottle is that of the youngest brandy in the blend and a Calvados is deemed to have been born on the 30th September following its distillation (in winter or early spring). The youngest Calvados, called 'Vieux' (old) have usually been aged for three years. VO Calvados are usually at least four years old, while VSOP and Extra are aged for five to ten years.

Camomile Tea

Camomile (or Chamomile) is the common name for several plants but camomile tea is commonly made from Matricaria recutita (German or blue chamomile). The name camomile is derived from ancient Greek and translates as 'ground apple' in reference to the fruity aroma.

The best quality camomile comes from the Nile Delta in Egypt and brews a pleasant aromatic tea with a fruity flavour enhanced by the addition of honey.

Campari Bitter®

www.campari.com

Gaspare Campari created this bright red aperitif, flavoured with 68 different herbs and spices, between 1860 and 1867 in the cellars of his Caffè Campari coffee shop in Milan. The new drink became locally famous when he moved his business to the newly built Galleria Vittorio Emanuele in September 1867. Campari Bitters proved instantly popular with the upmarket clientele the new, elegant, upmarket arcade attracted. If you visit Milan and the Galleria, you can see the premises that were originally Gaspare's bar – now Bar Zucca it's on the left-hand side of the Galleria entrance facing the Duomo.

The Campari brand we know today was propelled to become an internation-ally recognised brand by Davide Campari, a son from Gaspare's second marriage who took over the running of the family business in 1882. Davide Campari was in love with beautiful opera singer and as he pursued her across Europe and to New York so he established export markets for Campari as he went.

Campari should be served chilled and the bottle must be kept from direct sunlight and heat, ideally in a refrigerator.

When adding a garnish to a drink containing Campari, always use a slice of orange, as lemon impairs the true flavour. When serving Campari with a mixer such as tonic, soda or grapefruit juice, mix 50/50.

Candied Peel

To make candied peel boil citrus peels in a pot of cold water, strain and repeat three times. On the third time add sugar to the boiling water until it reaches the consistency of a rich simple syrup, continue to boil lime peels until they turn translucent, remove from heat, and allow to cool.

Caper Brine

Capers are the bud of a spiny bush, which thrives in Mediterranean climates. Caper brine is simply the vinegar and salt solution from jarred pickled caper berries.

Caramel Liqueur

Derived from the Latin 'canna mella' for sugar cane, caramel means melted sugar that has been browned by heating. Tiny amounts of caramel have long been used to colour spirits and liqueurs but caramel flavoured liqueurs are a relatively recent phenomenon.

Carlshamns Flaggpunsch Torr®

In its native Sweden, punch is inextricably connected to Karlshamn, a small port in southern Sweden the name of which literally translates as 'Karl's Harbour'. The manufacture of punch was one of the town's key industries and was owned by the town's politicians and aristocrats.

Lars Olsson Smith of Absolut Vodka fame bought the C.G. Berg factory in 1876 and launched the 'Carlshamns Flaggpunsch' brand in 1885. Like Absolut, Carlshamns Flaggpunsch is now made by V&S Vin & Sprit.

While Carlshamns Flaggpunsch is no longer made in the town, Karlshamn does boast its own Swedish Punsch museum with exhibits from one of the two large factories, which manufactured punsch there in the 1800s. Carlshamns Flaggpunsch is now also available in a new dry (Torr) formulation, which is not as sweet as the 'Original'.

Carpano Antica Formula®

Legend has it that sometime in the late 18th century, Antonio Benedetto Carpano set up his wine bar in the Piazza Castello, in the centre of Turin. Soon after opening he created a new drink and in 1786 launched Carpano, the world's first commercial vermouth. Made from dry white wine, fortified with alcohol, sweetened and flavoured with an infusion of aromatic herbs, Antica Formula is reportedly based on Antonio's original 1786 recipe.

Caster Sugar

Caster (or Castor) sugar is a refined sugar with a particle size approximately half the size of granulated sugar.

Celery Salt

Celery salt is a flavoured salt made from either ground lovage or celery seeds mixed with either table or sea salt and is most commonly used in the Bloody Mary family of cocktails.

Chambord Liqueur Royale de France®

www.chambordonline.com

Chambord was created in 1981 by N. J. 'Sky' Cooper using a bottle design borrowed from a now defunct brand called Forbidden Fruit which was packaged in a orb-shaped bottle. After building the brand over some 20 years, in 2007, Sky and his two sons, John and Rob, sold Chambord to Brown-Forman.

Chambord is a rich framboise-style liqueur based on neutral spirit with blackberries and raspberries flavoured with herbs and honey. It is named after Chambord, the largest chateau in France's Loire Valley.

This liqueur is very popular in the United States where it is often mixed as a Kir-like drink with Champagne.

Champagne

Our recommendation: Perrier Jouet

The vineyards of the Champagne region are the most northerly in France, lying north-east of Paris, on either side of the River Marne. Most of the Champagne houses are based in one of the two towns synonymous with Champagne: Epernay and Reims.

Champagne, surprisingly, is made predominantly from black grapes. The three grape varieties used are Pinot Noir (the red grape of Burgundy), Pinot Maunier (a fruitier relative of Pinot Noir) and lastly Chardonnay. Pinot Maunier is the most commonly used of these three varieties with Chardonnay, the only white grape, accounting for less than 30% of vines in the Champagne region. There are three other grape varieties permitted in the region: Petit Meslier, Arbanne and Pinot Blanc Vrai. In practice however, these lesser-known varieties are rarely grown.

Due to champagne being predominantly being made from red grapes to produce a white wine the grapes must be handled very carefully to avoid the black skins from tinting the wine. Thus picking is by hand and pressing takes place soon after picking.

Fermentation usually takes place in the producer's cellars, either in wood, or, increasingly often, in stainless steel. The next stage is known as 'assemblage'. This is the blending of different wines from different vintages, pressings, grapes and villages to achieve a consistent house style (except vintage bottlings which must be made from wines of the same vintage).

After blending and prior to, or during, bottling a small amount of 'liqueur de tirage' is added. This is a mixture of wine, sugar and yeast. The bottle is sealed with a temporary crown cork and laid to rest in horizontal position in one of Champagne's miles of chalky tunnels. When the yeast starts acting on the sugar, a second fermentation starts, which increases the alcohol content of the wine and produces carbon dioxide. This gas is unable to escape and so dissolves into the wine, creating Champagne's fizz.

The second fermentation in the bottle also produces dead yeast cells, which eventually break down and interact with the wine, adding a distinctive flavour. These dead yeast cells are known as 'lees' and the length of time a Champagne has spent on its lees greatly affects the quality of the final product. (The time counted from the time of bottling.)

The next stage is known as 'remuage': here the sediment is worked from the side of the bottle down to its neck. This is achieved by gradually altering the position of the bottle from horizontal to vertical with its neck facing downward. As the angle of the bottle is changed it is turned, forcing the yeast particles down the bottle towards the neck.

The dead yeast cells must now be removed from the neck of the bottle and the cork replaced without losing too much of the wine or its dissolved gas. This is known as 'dégorgement' and is achieved by dipping into a frozen brine solution. This freezes the yeast particles together and forms an ice plug. The temporary bottle cap is removed, allowing the pressure within the bottle to force out the plug, so removing the dead yeast cells.

Inevitably a little wine is lost from each bottle during this process. The level in the bottle is topped up with a mixture of wine and sugar, known as the 'liqueur d'expedition'. The amount of sugar used is dependent on the required sweetness of the finished champagne. This part of the champagne process is known as 'dosage'.

The processes described in the last two paragraphs, along with the final cork being driven into the bottle, are carried out at some speed. Before being driven into the bottle, champagne corks are cylindrical, and several times the diameter of the bottle neck they are to seal. The characteristic mushroom shape of champagne is only acquired after corking.

Chartreuse Elixir Végétal®

www.chartreuse.fr

The secret recipe for Chartreuse originated as an elixir of life (or at least youth). In the 16th century many alchemists were engaged in the search for an elixir – and in 1605 Marshall d'Estrees, a friend of King Henry IV of France, gave a recipe to the monks of the Carthusian order. The manuscript was hand-written and signed by Estrees, so it is assumed he was the original creator of the Elixir, a fact apparently supported by his living to the age of 97. But the fifty page recipe lay untouched in a monastery at Vauverre near Paris for 132 years

before it was eventually taken to the Monastery of Grand Chartreuse where Brother Jérôme Maubec, a master apothecary, worked to decipher the recipe and perfect the elixir.

Brother Jérôme passed on the secrets to Brother Antoine while on his deathbed. Two years after his death, in 1764, Brother Antoine completed the task of combining 130 different herbs from around the world with health giving and aromatic properties to create the 'Herbal Elixir Of The Grande Chartreuse' (which is still made to the original recipe today). The monks lived on the proceeds of making and selling the elixir which quickly gained a reputation for its flavour and curing properties, as did 'Green Chartreuse' a 'health liqueur' also developed by Brother Antoine from the same recipe.

The French Revolution dispersed the monks and for several decades interrupted production of Chartreuse. However, the manuscript and monks returned to the monastery and sometime around 1840 the formula was further adapted by Brother Bruno Jacquet to produce another liqueur, yellow in colour and with a sweeter, lighter taste. In 1869 the trademark was officially registered and the signature of L. Garnier, the monk responsible, still appears on all Chartreuse labels.

Further troubles for the monks lay ahead. The worldwide reputation of Chartreuse liqueurs and the profits raised by the monks attracted the attention of the French government, to the degree that in 1904 both the monastery and the distillery were nationalised. The monks refused to give up their distilling secrets and fled to Tarragona in Spain where they built a new distillery to continue the production of Chartreuse.

While the monks were exiled from France, other distillers worked at the monastery with government support to produce a copy of the famous liqueur. Unable to discover the recipe or the production secrets, the copy never came close to genuine Chartreuse. Due to lack of sales the company (La Compagnie Fermière) producing the counterfeit liqueur went bankrupt in 1929. When the monks returned to France and the Grande Chartreuse they resumed production at a distillery in the nearby town of Voiron where Chartreuse is still made today.

The three brothers entrusted with the preparation of Chartreuse by their order carefully mix the herbs at Grand Chartreuse to the original formula. They monitor every stage of production from their retreat in the mountains over 15 miles away via a computer link and visit the distillery to supervise blending and bottling.

All the liqueurs manufactured by the Carthusian fathers are made from entirely natural products with their vivid colours coming only from the plants they contain. The Chartreuse production process includes four distillations and three macerations. The result of the different processes are blended together and left to mature and marry in oak casks, many of which are more than 100 years old.

Elixir Végétal de la Grande Chartreuse is classified in France as a pharmaceutical product, this is the original tonic (elixir of life) first created by Brother Antoine in 1764.

Chartreuse Jaune®

www.chartreuse.fr

Around 1840 the formula was adapted by Brother Bruno Jacquet to produce this lighter, sweeter and more approachable version of the classic elixir.

Chartreuse Verte®

www.chartreuse.fr

The original liqueur formulated by Brother Antoine from the 'elixir' (See Chartreuse Elixir Végétal). The strong and distinctive flavour, coupled with its 55% abv strength make this a challenging but rewarding drink for the uninitiated.

Cherry Brandy

Our recommendation: Heering cherry brandy

Cherry Brandy is a liqueur made by macerating cherries in neutral spirit and then flavouring with spices such as cinnamon and cloves. As the name suggests the blend may also contain brandy but in most markets this is not a legal requirement.

Some brands also include crushed cherry kernels to add a distinctive almond note to the finished liqueur.

Chilled Water
Controlled dilution is essential to a well made and balanced cocktail and some drinks benefit from more dilution than others. Hence some recipes call for a little water to be added to provide more dilution than would normally be archived by just shaking or stirring with ice.

Obviously if you are using wet ice rather than ice freshly removed from the freezer then you are already in danger of having an overly diluted drink and the addition of water should be omitted.

Chillies
Fresh chillies are used to add their distinctive heat to some cocktails but care should be taken when handling them and consider wearing kitchen gloves to handle them but be sure not to touch your eyes while, or after, handling chillies. Be sure to wash your hands thoroughly.

Surprisingly it is not the seeds or the flesh, which holds chillies heat but the fine white membrane, which surrounds the seeds. Thus when you deseed a chilli you should also scrape out this membrane as well.

Choya Umeshu-Dento liqueur®

Pronounced 'wu-meh-shoo', this is a traditional Japanese liqueur from Choya (largest producers of Umeshu) is flavoured with a type of Japanese plum, the ume which are actually a type of apricot. The ume is only grown in Japan, China, Korea and Taiwan and the best fruits are grown in the Minabe district of Wakayama prefecture near Osaka.

Choya Umeshu is aged for 12 years and the bottle contains whole plums. The miniature version (5cl bottle) also contains a whole plum and has a natty rip top lid. Choya Umeshu-Dento is sweetened with honey and contains no added sugar.

Cider Brandy
The first written record of cider brandy production in England goes back to 1678 but by the late eighteenth century heavy taxation had left it virtually extinct. Then in 1984 the Cider Museum in Hereford was granted the first licence to distil cider brandy in England for over two centuries. There are now several producers making English cider brandy.

There are more than 800 varieties of apple. Of these, 120-odd are suitable for making cider, which can then be distilled to make a brandy. Different kinds of apple add different elements to the finished brandy: sweet apples yield a high proportion of the sugars from which alcohol is made, bitter apples add tannins for taste and aroma, while tart apples add freshness. It takes 7-13 kilograms (15-28lb) of apples to make one bottle of cider brandy.

English cider apples with names like Dabinett, Harry Masters, Kingston Black, Stoke Red and Yarlington Mill are picked in the autumn; pressed and blended. The juice is then fermented in vats for three months to produce cider. This is distilled and aged in oak barrels until it reaches the desired maturity for bottling.

Somerset is the home of English cider brandy. The soil, climate and apple varieties are very different from those used in France's better-known Calvados, and this spirit has a very different character.

Cinnamon Schnapps Liqueur

Our recommendation: Goldschläger cinnamon schnapps
Cinnamon is obtained from the bark of several tropical trees. Sri Lanka and China are the largest producers. Cinnamon liqueurs have a warm, sweet, spicy flavour.

Cinnamon Syrup
Buy proprietary brand or make your own by boiling 1/2 cup water with 1 cup caster sugar and 2 cinnamon sticks which have been ground to a powder using a pestle and mortar. Use a low heat and do not let the mix even come close to boiling. Stir until all the sugar dissolves. Remove from heat, allow to cool and strain into an empty bottle. Store in the refrigerator and use within three months.

Clément Creole Shrubb®

www.rhumclement.net
Clement Shrubb is a blend of unaged and six-year-old Clément Martinique Rum rum, which are mixed and then aged with orange peels in 250 litre oak casks for a year. The resulting blend is sweetened with cane syrup prior to bottling.

Coca-Cola®

www.coca-cola.com
Coca-Cola is perhaps the best-known carbonated soft drink in the world and is often simply referred to as Coke. Originally formulated as a medicine it was invented in the late 19th century by John Pemberton but was developed into a successful brand by businessman Asa Griggs Candler.

The Coca-Cola Company in Atlanta, Georgia make the concentrated base syrup which is then shipped to contracted bottling companies around the world who fill the familiar cans and bottles.

Coco López®

www.cocolopez.com
An essential ingredient to a Piña Colada, this is a canned, non-alcoholic, thick, syrup-like blend of coconut juice, sugar, emulsifier, cellulose, thickeners, citric acid and salt.

The original brand, Coco López, was created in the early 1950s by Don Ramón López-Irizarry after receiving a development grant from the Puerto Rican government. Cream of coconut had previously been made but López-Irizarry mechanised the labour intensive process. The brand was launched in 1954 and is an essential part of many a Piña Colada.

Coconut Rum Liqueur

Our recommendation: Malibu coconut rum liqueur
Coconut rums are mostly made in the Caribbean but are also found in France and Spain. They are made by blending rectified white rum with coconut extracts and tend to be presented in opaque white bottles.

Coconut Syrup
This is simply a cloudy coconut-flavoured sugar syrup and numerous commercial brands are available.

Coffee

Our recommendation: Illy
Coffee beans are the dried and roasted seed of a cherry, which grows on a bush in the tropics. When the coffee fruit is ripe, it is a small, scarlet berry. After harvesting, the producer processes the cherry so that the scarlet flesh is sloughed away from the two green seeds inside. These seeds are then dried and roasted, turning them into the hard, dark brown bean we recognise as coffee.

There are two main species of coffee plant: Coffea Arabica and Coffea Canephora. These are commonly known as Arabica and Robusta and produce beans of very different quality. Arabica is relatively low in caffeine, more delicate and requires more intensive cultivation. Robusta is higher in caffeine, more tolerant of climate and parasites and can be grown fairly cheaply. Robusta beans tend to be woody and bitter while Arabica has well-rounded, subtle flavours. Unsurprisingly, Arabica is more expensive than Robusta.

Most of the recipes in this guide that use coffee call for espresso and, as with other ingredients, the quality of this will greatly affect the finished drink. I strongly recommend using an Arabica coffee such as Illy brewed in an espresso machine or a moka pot.

Coffee Liqueur

Our recommendation: Kahlua coffee liqueur

Coffee flavoured liqueurs are made by infusing coffee beans in alcohol or by infusing beans in hot water and then blending with alcohol. Look for brands made using Arabica coffee beans.

Cognac

Our recommendation: Courvoisier V.S.O.P. cognac
www.bnic.fr

Cognac is a fine French brandy (eau-de-vie) from the region around the little town of Cognac in southwest France. It is recognised with its own appellation controlee and the production area this covers is divided into six sub-regions, reflecting variations in climate and soil – as a general rule, the finest have more chalk in their soil and are at the centre of the region with the most regarded region, Grande Champagne, having only a very thin layer of top soil over solid chalk.

Grande Champagne – The top (premier) cru centres on the town of Segonzac and spreads out north and east.

Petite Champagne – To the south of Grande Champagne, and extending west of Segonzac, this is the second finest cru.

Borderies – literally meaning 'edges' is the smallest, and due to its geography, the coolest of the cognac regions. Borderies cognac tends to be nutty as opposed to the Christmas cake-like flavours associated with the Fine Champagnes. Floral flavours, particularly violet are also associated with Borderies.

Fins Bois – The largest of the cognac regions surrounds the first three crus. The name means 'fine woods' since when the vines were planted much of this area was wooded.

Bons Bois – Meaning 'good woods' although again little of this area remains wooded, this surrounds the Fin Bois region.

Bois Ordinaires – This cru includes two areas, one to the northwest, including the islands of Oléron and Ré, the other to the northeast of Segonzac. The name means 'ordinary woods' (although the woods have long been cleared) and the vineyards' sandy soil and closeness to the sea impact unfavourably on their wines.

Fine Grande Champagne is a term that can only be applied to cognacs made from grapes grown in Cognac's Grande Champagne region. Fine Champagne Cognacs must be made only from Grande Champagne and Petite Champagne, with at least 50% of the blend coming from Grande Champagne.

Three kinds of grape are grown in cognac: Ugni Blanc, Folle Blanche and Colombard. Due to its resistance to frost, pests and rot, 90% of grapes grown in the region are Ugni Blanc.

Cognac distillation is tightly controlled by the terms of the appellation and must be double distilled using copper pot stills. Distillation, which usually starts at the beginning of November must be completed before 31 March. The 'eau-de-vie' produced by distillation must spend a minimum of three years ageing in oak casks before it can be termed Cognac. The wood from which these casks are made generally comes from the French forests of Limoges.

Confusingly, a cognac's age is counted from its second birthday, which is deemed to be on 1 April. Thus a cognac which is officially four years old was actually distilled from grapes picked more than 5 years ago. Cognac is the result of blending at least two different aged eaux-de-vie together. There are many different ways of blending cognacs, and the process often happens gradually over a period of years, as spirits are moved from barrel to barrel and combined.

Cognac rules on age statement and quality are confused by the fact that different producers will use the same term for different ages.

VS or Three Star – The initials stand for 'Very Special'. This is the youngest and cheapest blend; the youngest eau-de-vie in the blend must be at least 2½ years old.

VSOP – An abbreviation of 'very superior old pale', the youngest element in a VSOP or Reserve Cognac must be aged for at least 4½ years.

Napoléon/X.O./Hors d'Age/Extra etc. – Legally, these must be aged for a minimum of 6½ years, but they are often very much older. Generally, X.O. Cognacs are at least 15-20 years old.

Cointreau®

www.cointreau.com

The distilling firm of Cointreau was founded in 1849 by two brothers - Adolphe and Edouard-Jean Cointreau, who were confectioners in Angers. The liqueur we know today was created by Edouard Cointreau, the son of Edouard-Jean, and first marketed in 1871. Cointreau is made with the peel of bitter oranges from the Caribbean, sweet orange peel from Spain, neutral alcohol, sugar and water.

The popularity of Cointreau was originally driven in Britain by an English wine shipper, George Glendenning, who discovered the liqueur when visiting Bordeaux in 1902. He was so impressed that he travelled to Angers to meet Edouard and subsequently started importing Cointreau. However, in 1923 Glendenning informed the Cointreau family that their product was too sweet for the British palate and an extra dry version for the British market was created. It is this 'triple sec' (triple dry) version that has since been marketed around the world.

In the period between the two World Wars, Cointreau removed the term 'triple sec' from the label to differentiate it from any similar liqueur produced by other liqueur houses. However, if you are following a cocktail recipe that calls for 'triple sec' then Cointreau is almost certainly the liqueur the author intended to be used.

Cordials

In Europe, particularly the UK, people tend to think that a cordial is a non-alcoholic mixer (like Rose's lime cordial). But the words 'liqueur' and 'cordial' actually mean the same thing (see 'liqueur'). Cordial comes from the Latin 'cor' for heart, reflecting the medieval custom of serving liqueurs as medicines to stimulate the heart.

In Britain non-alcoholic (or low alcohol) mixer style cordials have developed since the 1980s with many new brands and flavours being developed.

Courvoisier V.S.O.P. Exclusif®

www.courvoisier.com

The story of the Cognac house of Courvoisier starts early in the 19th century when Emmanuel Courvoisier established his Cognac business in Jarnac and Louis Gallois separately established his wine and spirit wholesale business.

The Gallois family sold the Cognacs produced by the Courvoisier family until in 1835 the sons of the original founders merged the two businesses. The visit of Napoléon I to the Gallois warehouse in 1811 heralded the beginning of a close relationship between the imperial courts of Napoléon I, II and III and Courvoisier, a relationship which led to Courvoisier establishing the Napoléon standard.

In 1909 two English brothers, the Simmons, bought the House of Courvoisier, adopted the slogan 'The Brandy of Napoleon' and introduced the silhouette of the emperor on the Josephine bottle. In 1964 heirs of the Simmons family sold the business to Hiram Walker, the US distributor of Courvoisier. Several mergers and acquisitions later in 1993 this company became known as Allied Domecq, itself broken as part of an acquisition, which resulted in Courvoisier now being owned and distributed by Fortune Brands. Launched 1996 in Asia and then worldwide travel retail (duty free) in 2000, Exclusif is a blend of Grande Champagne, Petite Champagne (6 to 10 years old), Fine Bois (min 5 years old) and around 20% Borderies (10 to 15 years old), has an average age of 5 to 12 years.

Exclusif was originally developed for the Japanese market where Cognac is drunk mixed with water, and so is richer, spicier and more concentrated than Courvoisier's other VSOP. Unusually this blend containing Cognacs from four of Cognac's regions is sold at a premium to Courvoisier's Fine Champagne VSOP, containing only Grande and Petite Champagne.

Cream (Double/Heavy)

I've specified 'double' or 'heavy' cream in preference to lighter creams. In many recipes this is diluted with an equal measure of milk – a combination known as 'half & half'. You'll find these ingredients are always specified separately in this guide.

Cream of Coconut

This is a non-alcoholic, sticky blend of coconut juice, sugar, emulsifier, cellulose, thickeners, citric acid and salt. Fortunately it tastes better than it sounds and is an essential ingredient of a good Piña Colada.

One 15oz/425ml can will make approximately 25 drinks. Once opened the contents should be transferred to a suitable container and stored in a refrigerator. This may thicken the product, so gentle warming may be required prior to use. Coconut milk is very different and cannot be used as a substitute.

Crème de...

This French term indicates that one particular flavour predominates in the liqueur; it does not imply that the liqueur contains cream. Many fruit liqueurs are described as 'crème de' followed by the name of a fruit. This refers to the liqueur's quality, as in the French phrase 'crème de la crème'.

French liqueurs prefixed with 'crème de' must contain at least 250 grams of sugar per litre. The exception is crème de cassis, which must contain a minimum of 400 grams of sugar per litre.

Crème de Banane Liqueur

Banana flavoured liqueurs made by infusion or maceration of the fruit in neutral spirit. Some brands also include pineapple juice, and herbs and spices such as cocoa, vanilla and even tea.

Crème de Cacao

A chocolate flavoured liqueur based on cacao beans. Available in clear (white) or brown (dark) versions, brown crème de cacao is often flavoured with vanilla. The word Chouao on the label indicates the cacao beans came from Chouao, a suburb of Caracas, Venezuela, which is reputed to grow the best cocoa beans in the world. (See 'Brown Crème de Cacao' and 'White Crème de Cacao'.)

Crème de Cassis

Like other 'crème de' liqueurs, this term comes from de French phrase "crème de la crème" meaning 'best of the best' and does not mean the liqueur contains any cream. Crème de cassis is a blackcurrant liqueur, which originated in France and is made by both infusion and maceration. The original recipe for a crème de cassis is thought to have been formulated by Denis Lagoute in 1841 in the French Dijon region. Many of the best examples are still produced in this region.

EEC law states that crème de cassis must have a minimum of 400g of sugar per litre and a minimum alcoholic strength of 15%. Unfortunately no minimum is set for the fruit content although the best brands will contain as much as 600g of blackcurrants per litre. Brands with a high fruit content will have a more fruity taste and a deeper colour than low-fruit brands. Some French brands are labelled 'double crème de cassis'. Although this term is not officially recognised it implies a sugar and fruit content higher than standard crème de cassis so less of this concentrated liqueur is required in mixed drinks.

While taste is obviously the best test of the quality of crème de cassis, the following tests are also a good indication:
Turn the bottle of upside-down and then back again. Note how the liqueur clings to the glass. An inferior crème de cassis will leave little or no colour on the glass, while a quality brand will cling to the glass for some time.

Add water to the cassis and see how dilution affects the colour of the liqueur. Lesser brands will turn pink in colour, while quality brands will retain their rich red colour. Smell watered down samples of cassis - poor products will lose their aroma while better brands will retain it.
Surprisingly the biggest market for crème de cassis is Japan and indeed most of the Pacific Rim, where one of the most popular mixed drink is crème de cassis-and-soda.

Crème de Fraise

'Fraise' is French for strawberry and Crème de Fraise is a strawberry liqueur made by infusion and maceration. Some are labeled 'Crème de Fraise des bois' referring to the tiny wild strawberries from which these liqueurs are produced.

Crème de Fraise should have a rich ripe strawberry flavour with light hints of citrus fruit. There are great served chilled, in a cocktail, over strawberries or in a fruit salad.

Crème de Framboise

The French word for raspberry is 'framboise' and crème de framboise liqueurs are made both by infusion and maceration.

Crème de Menthe

French peppermint flavoured liqueur, most commonly sold with added green colouring. 'Menthe' is French for mint.

Crème de Mûre

The French refer to blackberry liqueurs as 'crème de mûre'. This comes from the French word for blackberry 'mûre' and 'crème', meaning 'cream' or 'essence'.

Crème de Myrtille

A French liqueur produced from wild bilberries. Related to the blueberry, this is a low, heathland shrub native to northern regions of Europe, America and Asia. Bilberries are small purplish-blue berries with a slightly acidic flavour.

Crème de Noisette

A generic term for French hazelnut-flavoured liqueurs.

Crème de Noyeaux

Also known as Crème de Noyaux, this is a pink coloured liqueur flavoured apricot and peach stones with an almond flavour. Substitute with amaretto liqueur and a dash of pomegranate (grenadine) syrup.

Crème de Peche de Vigne

Our recommendation: Giffard Crème de Peche de Vigne
Crème de Peche is the French term for peach liqueurs but you should particularly look out for those labelled 'de Vigne' – literally meaning 'of bush'. These are made from small, red, incredibly concentrated peaches and tend to be of a higher quality and so more flavoursome.

Cremova

Cremova is a sticky yellow drink made by adding egg yolks to Marsala: it is used for making the Italian dessert Zabaglione. Until 1984, it was often called 'Marsala Cremova', but due to changes in the DOC regulations it is no longer allowed to carry the name Marsala.

Crown Royal®

www.crownroyal.com
This "fine de luxe" Canadian whisky blend was created in 1939 for a state tour by King George VI, and ceremoniously presented to him when he travelled across Canada in a special train. The bottle shape is designed to resemble a crown and the label illustrates a crown sat on a blue cushion. The bottle is packed in a plush purple velvet bag.

Crown Royal was introduced into the USA in 1965 where it has subsequently become the best selling Canadian whisky. In fact Crown Royal is the eighth largest spirits brand in the US and the number one Canadian whisky in the world.

Cuarenta Y Tres®

www.licor43.com
The name of this yellow Spanish liqueur means forty three, and happily for us Anglo-Saxons, also goes by the more pronounceable, 'Licor 43'. Not entirely coincidentally, this vanilla-flavoured liqueur is made from 43 different herbs and spices. Serve chilled over ice, mixed with orange juice or as a cocktail ingredient.

Cucumber

The fruit of a climbing plant originating from the foothills of the Himalayas, cucumbers should be used as fresh as possible, so look for firm, unwrinkled fruit. The skin can be quite bitter so cucumber is best peeled before use in cocktails. Either muddle in the base of your shaker or juice using an extractor.

Cynar®

www.campari.com

A bittersweet Italian aperitif created in 1949. Toffee-brown in colour and spirit based, it is flavoured with a blend of artichoke leaves and herbs. Cynar has long been marketed with the 'medicinal' slogan 'Cynar, against the stress of modern life'.

Serve on-the-rocks with a slice of orange and soda or tonic. Alternatively serve mixed with aguardente to make the famous Tail of Rooster.

Domaine de Canton®

www.domainedecanton.com

Canton Delicate Ginger liqueur was originally launched back in 1980s by N. J. 'Sky' Cooper. The new, reinvigorated Canton ginger liqueur is the brainchild of Sky's son, John Cooper, who has named his company after his grandfather, 'Maurice Cooper', also a liqueur maker.

The original 1980s Canton liqueur was said to have been created centuries ago for the emperors of old Canton who "treasured the value of ginger" and was produced from six different varieties of fresh ginger with gentle herbs and ginseng, blended with brandy and a touch of honey. It was said to originate from Jing An Town, Doumen, Guangdong Province, China.

This latest Canton liqueur from Cooper junior is an infusion of baby ginger with cognac, ginseng, vanilla and honey. The ginger is picked, washed and cubed – all by hand, before being cooked with a "secret blend of herbs and spices". The ginger is then shipped to Jarnac in France's Cognac region where it is infused with cognac.

Tales of old emperors and China have been dropped and the company now says the ginger used to flavour this liqueur comes from colonial Indochina (now Vietnam), and a ginger estate called Domaine de Canton. The bottle is designed to look like a bamboo shoot but is also somewhat reminiscent of a Chinese lantern.

Don Julio Tequila®

www.donjulio.com

Pronounced 'Don-Hoo-Li-O', this tequila is named after Don Julio González (born 1925), who started working in his uncle's tequila distillery in 1932 as a child aged just seven and established his own distillery, Tres Magueyes, in 1942, when he was only 17.

Don Julio tequila comes from the Highlands – Los Altos region, famous for its iron and copper rich red soil. Many tequila aficionados attribute the apparent sweetness of Highland tequilas to the high altitude of some 2,000 feet above sea level and the thinness of the air stressing the agave so making the plant produce more fermentable sugars as it strives to build reserves of energy.

When cultivating new plants by removing the offshoots, 'hijuelos', which grow in the soil around established plants from its rhizomes (ground roots), Don Julio are careful to ensure as much of the root system of the baby plant as possible is retained so when planted it can immediately start drawing nutriments from the soil.

Unlike most other producers, Don Julio believes that fields should be planted allowing each plant room to develop at 1.5 meters apart. This not only prevents root systems from crossing each other until the plants are mature, but also allows maximum levels of sunlight and so photosynthesis.

It is common practice amongst some producers to cut the agave leaves at 3, 4 and 5 years to stress the plant so forcing early maturation. The root systems have to work harder and the piña draws in water looking for nutriments and swells. This practice allows the plants to be harvested some two years earlier than if left to mature naturally, as is the practice at Don Julio where there is absolutely no pruning of the agave.

Whilst some producers harvest an entire field when it reaches a specific age, Don Julio only harvest individual plants as they are judged to have reached perfect maturity, regardless of how young or old they are. The company leases some 90% of its land with 30 year term leases thus allowing two complete growing cycles of 8-15 years per field.

When harvesting the agave the jimadors shave off the leaves close to the

piña as Don Julio believe the green stems add a bitter flavour. Once harvested the piñas are cut in half or thirds and roasted for 24 hours in traditional brick ovens and then left in the ovens to cool for a further 48 hours to allow greater complexity of flavour to develop. This long 72 hour cooking period compares to the mere 6-8 hours employed by some other producers who use pressurised auto claves. At Don Julio the ovens have top vents allowing the steam, which is introduced at the base, to escape so that pressure does not build within the oven. Don Julio operates 18 such brick ovens with a capacity of 20 tonnes.

As the piñas roast in the ovens their juices fall to the floor to be collected in a runoff trough. These juices are initially bitter and it is common practice for producers to discard the first 3 hours of this runoff. In contrast, Don Julio set aside the first 8 hours of this by-product before starting to collect the sweet 'aguamiel', literally 'honey water'.

The cooked piñas then pass through a set of five shredding machines to release their sweet juices. Water is sprayed over the piñas as they are shredded to wash the aguamiel (honey water) from the spent husks, which are collected for recycling.

The aguamiel collected from the roasting run-off and the juice produced by shredding the piña are blended together to make a musto, which has a relatively low brix (sugar content) of 4% for fermentation.

The yeast used during the fermentation process is an isolated wild yeast strain specifically cultured for Don Julio and kept in a laboratory in Mexico City. Each year a sample is sent to the distillery where it is cultivated on-site for fresh use each week. Fermentation takes place in small closed stainless steel tanks where inoculation is employed to eliminate the presence of any wild yeasts and ensure constancy between batches.

The fermented liquid is distilled twice, with only the heart of each distillation taken (about 65-70% of the total run). The final spirit comes off the stills at a relatively low strength of around 58% abv to maximise its flavour. The stills used at Don Julio are steam coil heated stainless steel pot stills and of these 15 stills, numbers 1-3 are only used for the first distillation and one smaller still, number 6, is reserved specifically for the second distillation of '1942' and 'Real'.

The Don Julio variants that are aged (all but blanco) are matured in American white oak casks previously used to age whiskey. The exception to this is Don Julio Real which also includes tequila aged in casks previously used to age Canadian Crown Royal whisky in its blend.

Don Julio Blanco®

www.donjulio.com

Launched 1996, this blanco tequila is un-aged - merely rested for a short period in inert containers before bottling. It is presented in a round, squat, clear bottle with a creamy-white wooden screw cap.

Don Julio Reposado®

www.donjulio.com

Launched 1989, this reposado is aged for 8 months in recharged American white oak casks previously used to age Tennessee whiskey.

Don Julio Reposado originated in 1987 when Don Julio threw a party to commemorate his 45th anniversary in the tequila industry. To celebrate the occasion he created a special 100% agave tequila as a gift for his family and friends. That original family reserve was what we now term 'reposado' and it is considered by many to be the original of the category. It was also presented in the distinctive square hand-blown bottle with a stopper made from native Mexican Chechen wood, as still used for Don Julio Reposado today, and that too was the first of its style.

Don Julio Añejo®

www.donjulio.com

Launched in 1996, Don Julio Añejo is aged from 18 months to 2 years in

recharged American white oak casks previously used to age Tennessee whiskey. It is presented in a round, squat, clear bottle with a white wooden screw cap.

Don Julio 1942 Añejo®

www.donjulio.com

Launched in 2002 and positioned as a super premium, this añejo tequila is aged for 30 months in recharged American white oak casks previously used to age Tennessee whiskey. This two-and-a-half year ageing period is just six months short of qualifying to be termed an Extra Añejo but is judged by Don Julio to be perfect at this age.

Don Julio 1942 is presented in a tall, greeny-brown bottle, the shape of which mimics that of an agave leaf.

Don Julio Real Extra Añejo®

www.donjulio.com

Released in 1996, this extra añejo was released 10 years before the category was created and so seemingly takes pride in not actually proclaiming to be an extra añejo on the bottle. Real is blended from tequila aged between 3 and 5 years. And unlike all other aged tequilas in the Don Julio range, Real is blended from tequila aged in both American ex-whiskey casks and unusually also casks previously used to age Crown Royal Canadian whisky. It is presented in a decanter-style bottle with three silvered agave plants clutching its sides. This rather flashy bottle is topped with a piña-shaped silvered cork stopper.

Drambuie®

www.drambuie.com

Scotland's most famous liqueur is based on Scotch whiskies, many of which are 15-17 year old malts, blended with homemade heather honey syrup and a secret herbal essence.

Bonnie Prince Charlie is said to have given the recipe to Captain John MacKinnon of Strathaird in 1746 in gratitude for his steadfast loyalty during the Jacobite uprising. A descendant, Malcolm MacKinnon, started commercial production in 1906.

The name is taken from the Gaelic phrase 'an dram buidheach' meaning 'the drink that satisfies'.

Dry Cider

Cider is an alcoholic beverage usually made from the fermented juice of apples, although for some inexplicable reason non-alcoholic apple juice is often called cider in North America and the real alcoholic stuff is termed 'hard cider'. Cider can be made from any variety of apples, although certain bitter varieties known as cider apples are preferred. Cider is very popular in the United Kingdom, especially in South West England and the UK has the highest per capita consumption of cider in the world.

Dubonnet Red®

In the 1840s, thousands of French colonists were dying of malaria in North Africa. Quinine, from the South American cinchona tree, was known to ward off malaria – but tasted vile. The French government was keen to encourage people to consume more quinine, and pronounced a reward for anyone that produced a palatable drink including the bitter drug. In 1846 Joseph Dubonnet successfully created his wine based aperitif, by blending Roussillon wines made from five different grape varietals with an infusion of herbs and spices including bitter bark and quinine, then ageing the blend for three years to four years in oak vats.

In 1896 Mrs Dubonnet's cat appeared on the label, and in 1932 the famous French artist Cassandre created the character of the 'Dubonnet Man' with the legendary slogan 'Dubo, Dubon, Dubonnet'.

Grapes from the sunny Languedoc-Roussillon region including muscat, grenache, carignan and macabeo are pressed and the juice mixed with a neutral base alcohol at 15% abv to prevent fermentation. This ensures the grape juice retains its flavours, aromas and sugars. (In contrast to fortified wines where the grape juice is allowed to start fermenting before being stopped by the addition of alcohol to kill the yeast.) Capturing the natural sugars in the grape allows Dubonnet to be produced without the need to add sugar.

The fortified grape juice, which is called 'mistelle' is then aged for three to four years in oak. Other flavours are then added to this mistelle by pumping it under pressure through percolators containing cocoa beans, quinine, colombo (mild variation on curry powder), orange peel, Columbian green coffee, cinnamon, camomile and elderflower. Lasting eight hours the process is repeated to fully extract the flavours. The blender then has the task of blending the different flavoured mistelles together to produce Dubonnet which is stabilised by holding close to freezing point at -9°C and then chill filtered prior to bottling.

In the 10-15 years before the Millennium, Dubonnet Red underwent some dramatic changes being first reduced in strength from 18% to 16% abv and then finally to today's 14.8% abv. Each time the alcohol content has been lowered the recipe has also been adapted to maintain the product's balance. If you want to enjoy a product more akin to the original try Dubonnet 21°. Taking its name from its 21% alc./volume strength this has a higher quinine content and is altogether spicier and less floral than the standard product.

Dubonnet also produces a green labelled 'Dubonnet Blanc' and a gold labelled 'Dubonnet Doré'. This last line extension is often termed 'amber' due to its colour and has an aroma akin to lime cordial and a flavour that resembles oak aged lime cordial.

Many years ago the American rights to the Dubonnet Red brand were sold. The Dubonnet available in the US is now American-produced and is made from California wine that has been fortified with grape brandy. It is quite different from the French made product and is available in red and white styles.

Eaux-de-vie

Eau-de-vie means 'water of life' and this is the French term for brandies made from a fruit other than grapes. (Confusingly, this is also used in France for brandies that will become Cognac and Armagnac when they are older, but have not yet reached the statutory age.) Produced in France, Germany, Yugoslavia and Scandinavia, these 'fruit brandies' are clear and colourless and generally sold at 40 - 45% abv.

Two quite different production methods are used to make fruit eaux-de-vie. Stoned fruits, such as cherries and peaches, are crushed with their kernels, which add a pleasantly bitter component to the brandy. The mash is encouraged to ferment with the addition of yeast, a process that can take weeks or months. The resulting wine is then distilled in a pot still.

Stoneless fruits are lower in sugar, and so could not ferment to a sufficient alcoholic strength to be distilled. So a different process is employed for stoneless fruits. Instead of being crushed and fermented they are finely chopped and macerated in neutral alcohol. This mixture is then distilled in a pot still.

Eaux-de-vie are bottled as soon as possible after distillation to preserve their elegance and fruit fragrances. They are rarely cask matured because the woody flavours would detract from the delicate aromas and fruit flavours. Generally, the only eaux-de-vie to be aged are those made from fruits with stones. To contribute a little more flavour in lieu of ageing, there is a growing tendency to infuse fruit in the distillate prior to bottling. In Germany the two products are differentiated by calling pure distillates 'wasser' (water) and infused distillates 'geist' (spirit).

Eggs

Raw eggs can be hazardous to health so you may decide it is safer to use commercially produced pasteurised egg white, particularly if you are infirm or pregnant (but then you probably shouldn't be drinking cocktails anyway). Many cocktails only taste their best when made with fresh eggs but you should take steps to reduce the risk of Salmonella poisoning. Therefore I recommend you store small, free range eggs in a refrigerator and use them well before the sell-by-date. Always wash before use and don't consume raw eggs if:

1. You are uncertain about their freshness.
2. There is a crack or flaw in the shell.
3. They don't wobble when rolled across a flat surface.
4. The egg white is watery instead of gel-like.
5. The egg yolk is not convex and firm.
6. The egg yolk bursts easily.
7. They smell foul.

Fernet Branca®

www.brancaproducts.com

A famous Italian bitters founded in Milan by the noble Branca di Romanico family in 1845. Fernet Branca is made from 30 different roots and herbs, including gentian, camomile, saffron and rhubarb, and aged in Slovenian oak vats for one year. Best served with a slice of lemon or orange over plenty of ice. In 1965 a mintier 'summertime version', appropriately named 'Branca Menta' was launched, which is more approachable.

Frangelico®

www.frangelico.com

This Italian liqueur is produced from berries, herbs and hazelnuts. It is named after a monk named Father Angelico who lived as a hermit in the Piedmont area in the 17th Century. When originally launched in the USA in 1987, this liqueur used an abbreviation of his name 'Fra. Angelico'.

It's not known whether Father Angelico actually made liqueurs, but early Christian monks living in the Piedmont hills in the 17th century did understand the art of distillation and used local hazelnuts and herbs. Frangelico liqueur uses hazelnuts from the Piedmont region, which are toasted and distilled with alcohol before infusing the result with cocoa, coffee, vanilla, berries, rhubarb root, sweet orange flowers and other natural flavours. This is aged in oak casks for months prior to bottling.

Frangelico is instantly recognisable by its eye-catching monk-shaped bottle and rope tie (which incidentally was tied by hand until 2003).

French Vermouth

Our recommendation: Noilly Prat

Popular belief has it that Italian vermouth was originally sweet and produced from red wine, while French vermouth was typically dry and white. Hence, many old cocktail books refer to 'French' for dry vermouth and 'Italian' where sweet vermouth is called for.

The truth is that the division between the styles of the two countries was never that defined and producers in both countries now make both sweet (rosso) and dry styles.

Although red vermouth was initially based on red wine, now virtually all is made from white wine with caramel blended in to give an amber colour.

Fruit Cups

Fruit cups were invented by the Victorians and were originally a mixture of fruit, liqueurs and spices with a base spirit of gin and usually made in the kitchen for home consumption. The best known modern day commercial brand of fruit cup is Pimm's.

Fruit Juice

The vast majority of cocktails are made with some kind of fruit juice. Often, in fact, fruit juice is the main ingredient. So naturally enough the quality of that juice affects the finished drink as much, if not more, than the quality of its alcoholic ingredients.

The most flavoursome and nutritious juices are those which you extract yourself immediately before use. However, that's not always practical so when considering pre-packaged juice please opt for 'freshly squeezed' juice from the chill cabinet rather than cartons from the ambient shelf.

Before you buy juice, please bear the following in mind.
Juices labelled 'pure' are usually made from concentrate. To make this, fresh juice is reduced by boiling. Up to two years later it is reconstituted by adding water. The concentrate can also contain undesirable additives like citric acid, sugar and antioxidants.

Many packaged juices are pasteurised to make them last longer. The heat involved adversely affects their vitamin C content and their flavour. Juices marketed as "a rich source of vitamin C" may actually be pasteurised juices with added ascorbic acid.

Another potentially misleading term is "free from artificial sugars". This could suggest that fructose, a natural fruit sugar, has been added to sweeten the juice. Natural or not, fructose is an additive and contains just as many calories as artificial sugars.

Both 'pure' and pasteurised juices are often placed in supermarket chill cabinets and can be easily confused with better quality 'freshly squeezed' juices. Even the term 'freshly squeezed' hardly guarantees freshness – especially if it has a two week use-by date. Bits of pulp in the juice are definitely not a guarantee of freshness: these are often dried and then reconstituted.

All that said, some fruits are best purchased in juice form, while others should be muddled or pureed. Please see notes on individual fruits for guidance.

Fruit Purée

Our recommendation: Boiron

Fruit purees are made from fresh fruit, which have been chopped up and liquidised. Buy a proprietary brand or make your own puree by adding roughly five to ten percent sugar syrup depending on the fruit's ripeness.

Galliano Authentico®

www.galliano.com

Galliano is a vibrant, golden, vanilla flavoured liqueur from Italy, easily recognised by its tall, fluted bottle, inspired by Roman columns.

Galliano was invented in 1896 by Arturo Vaccari, a distiller from Livorno in Tuscany, and is made from over 30 ingredients including star anise, lavender, ginger, juniper, musk yarrow, peppermint, cinnamon and vanilla. The complex production process includes seven infusions and six distillations.

The name honours a war hero whose exploits were being celebrated by Italians at the time Vaccari created his liqueur. Maggiore Galliano was a major in the Italian 1887-1896 campaign in Abyssinia (today known as Ethiopa). In December 1895 he held the Fort of Enda Jesus near the ancient city of Makallè against bewildering odds (outnumbered some 36 to one against 80,000 adversaries) for 44 days until receiving orders on 20 January 1896 to abandon the fort. Galliano's label used to depict Fort Enda, unfortunately the origin of the name is no longer commemorated on the bottle.

The versatility of Galliano ensures that it can be enjoyed in cocktails and as a long drink. It also works particularly well as a hot shot with coffee and cream. The lovely smell of Galliano is reminiscent of a pack of Tic-Tac sweets, while its smooth vanilla taste is complimented by peppermint and spiced with cinnamon, ginger, nutmeg and citrus.

Génépi des Pères Chartreux®

www.chartreuse.fr

Génépi is the name used for several different aromatic Alpine plants (also known as Mugwort). This Génépi liqueur is made to a secret recipe under the supervision of the Carthusian monks of Chartreuse.

Genever

Our recommendation: Bokma oude genever

Also known as hollands, genever (or jenever) this is a juniper-flavoured spirit originally from Holland and also made in Belgium. The juniper flavouring means that genever is technically a gin, and it was the forerunner of the London gin styles, which dominate today's market.

But genever is a very distinctive style of juniper spirit. Unlike most gins, it is a blend of two very different spirits – botanical-infused neutral spirit and malt-wine, a kind of unaged whiskey. Due to this, it retains more of the flavour of some of its base ingredients - rye, malted barley and maize - than most common gin styles, which are based on neutral spirit alone.

There are three basic styles of genever - 'oude' (literally, 'old'), 'jonge' ('young') and 'korenwijn' ('corn wine'). They differ in their use of botanicals and the percentage of malt-wine contained.

Jonge genever is so named because it is a modern, young style. It was first developed in the 1950s in response to consumer demand for a lighter flavoured, more mixable genever. Jonge genevers contain a lower percentage of malt-wine than either oude or korenwijn styles.

Oude genevers, despite the name, are not aged. They are so called because they are traditional, old-style genevers, as opposed to the more modern jonge genevers. They must contain at least 15% malt-wine and often feature more botanicals than jonge styles.

The third category of genever is 'korenwijn' (corn wine), which Bols spell

'corenwyn'. Confusingly, unlike oude genevers, korenwijn styles are cask aged. By law they must contain at least 51% malt-wine.

The traditional Dutch way to drink genever is known as Kopstoot (pronounced 'Cop-Stout') and literally translates as 'a blow for your head': simply sip a shot of ice-cold genever from a small, tulip-shaped glass, then follow with a sip of beer. In the worthy pursuit of responsible drinking I must stress you repeatedly take a sip of each - savour the combination rather than shoot.

Gin

Our recommendation: Tanqueray London dry

To produce a decent (i.e. distilled) gin is a two stage process – first a base spirit is made, now referred to as a 'neutral spirit' and then that is flavoured through re-distillation with seeds, berries, roots, fruits and herbs and spices – collectively known as 'botanicals'.

Early British distillers would distil the fermented wash (type of beer) in a traditional pot-still. The first distillation of such a still produces a weak, rough spirit known as 'low wines'. Repeated distillation of these low wines (rectification) strengthens and purifies the spirit and this process can be repeated several times. Different distillers use completely different recipes of botanicals (see below), but the main three extraction processes used run roughly as follows, although there are many technical variations between distilleries.

One-shot Method: Under the one-shot method, a mix of juniper and other botanicals is macerated in neutral spirit and water. Some producers leave the botanicals to steep for as long as 48 hours before distillation; others believe that maceration 'stews' the flavours and so distil the mixture immediately. Whichever, as soon as maceration is deemed to be completed, the resulting mixture is distilled in a pot still, producing a spirit full of the aromas and tastes of the botanicals. Water is added to reduce it to bottling strength.

Two-shot Method: The two-shot method is quicker and saves on still usage, increasing production capacity. A mix of juniper and botanicals several times stronger than usual is macerated then distilled, producing a spirit with a super-concentrated flavour. This is mixed with neutral spirit; then water is added to reduce to bottling strength.

Vapour Infusion Method: With the vapour infusion method, the mix of juniper and botanicals do not come into contact with liquid spirit at all. Instead, they are placed in baskets inside elaborate modified stills and only encounter the spirit as steam. The botanical-infused vapour then condenses into a botanical-infused spirit, and water is added to reduce to bottling strength.

Hardly any of today's gins are aged, although there are signs of a revival of this historic practice.

Every gin has a different recipe, but all gins are flavoured with botanicals – seeds, berries, roots, fruits, peel, spices or herbs – and all must contain juniper. After juniper, coriander and angelica are the most popular botanicals and these three are the main flavours in a London Dry gin.

Ginger (Fresh Root)

Ginger is an edible rhizome that is commonly used as a spice in cooking. Although often referred to as a root, it is in fact the horizontal, subterranean stem of the plant which is used.

Recipes in this guide call for fresh root ginger. Clean the stem by cutting away the outer skin and slice into thin, thumbnail-sized pieces. Muddle a number of these in the base of your shaker as specified in the recipe.

Ginger Ale

Make this non-alcoholic drink by adding ginger essence, colouring and sweeteners to carbonated water. It is not as powerful in flavour as ginger beer.

Ginger Beer

This fizzy drink is flavoured with ginger and sometimes contains small quantities of alcohol. Buy a quality brand or brew your own as follows:
Combine 2oz/56 grams of peeled and crushed root ginger, 2 lemons sliced into thick rings, 1 teaspoon of cream of tartar, 1lb/450 grams sugar and 1 gallon/4 litres water in a large stainless steel saucepan and bring to the boil. Stir and leave to cool to blood temperature. Stir in 1oz/ 28 grams of yeast and leave to ferment for 24 hours. Skim off the yeast from the surface and fine strain the liquid into four sterilised 1 litre plastic bottles with screw caps. (Leave at least 2 inches/5cm of air at the top of each bottle and ensure all utensils are scrupulously clean.). Place bottles upright and release excess pressure after 12 hours. Check again after another 12 hours. Once the bottles feel firm and under pressure, place them in the refrigerator and consume their contents within three days.

Ginger Syrup

Buy a proprietary brand of ginger syrup or make your own by gradually pouring and stirring two cups of granulated sugar into a saucepan containing one cup of hot water and simmer until the sugar is dissolved. Add half a cup of thinly sliced fresh ginger and simmer for ten minutes stirring occasionally and being careful not to let the mixture even come close to boiling. Remove from heat and allow to cool before adding two tablespoons of freshly squeezed lemon juice. Fine strain the mixture as you decant into an empty bottle. If kept in a refrigerator this mixture will last for a couple of months.

Ginger Wine

Our recommendation: Stone's Ginger Wine

Ginger Wine is a fortified wine made from a fermented blend of ground ginger and raisins. The first documented ginger wine was made in 1740 by The Finsbury Distilling Company in the City of London, England. Their main customer for this new product was Joseph Stone, a grocer in London's High Holborn and so his name was added to the ginger wine.

Although ginger wine can be drunk on its own or over ice it is most commonly used as an ingredient in mixed drinks, most notably with whisky to make a 'Whisky Mac'.

Golden Rum

Our recommendation: Bacardi Oro

As the name would suggest 'golden rums' are amber coloured due to a period of maturation in wood and often the addition of caramel. They tend to be light or medium bodied in character and are produced in most rum making regions by a number of producers.

Goldschläger®

www.schlager.com

Goldschläger is an Italian cinnamon schnapps with tiny flakes of 24-carat gold leaf flakes suspended in the clear liqueur. Goldschläger takes its name from German word meaning 'gold beater' referring to gold leaf makers who hammered and worked bars of gold into wafer-thin sheets.

Gomme Sirop

The term 'gomme sirop' or 'gum syrup' refers to commercially made sugar syrups with the addition of gum arabic, the crystallised sap of the acacia tree, which prevents the sugar from crystallizing and adds mouth-feel and smoothness. Gomme syrups also have hints of rose water flavouring added.

Goslings Black Seal®

www.blackseal.com

In the spring of 1806 James Gosling, a London wine and spirits merchant, chartered the ship Mercury, loaded it with £10,000 worth of merchandise, and sent his eldest son James to set sail for America. After ninety-one desperate days on rough seas the charter ran out and they pulled into the nearest port, St. George's, Bermuda.

Determined to make the best of the situation he found himself in, James opened a shop on the King's Parade, St. George's, in December 1806 to sell the goods he'd shipped from England. James returned to England in 1824 but his brother Ambrose took a shop on Front Street in the new capital of Hamilton. In 1857 the firm, know as Ambrose Gosling and Son, was renamed Gosling Brothers.

Sometime around 1860 the company imported the first casks of rum to Bermuda and created this distinctive dark blend, originally sold to locals at cask strength straight from the barrel it was simply called 'Old Rum'. This continued until the First World War, when the company began filling champagne bottles reclaimed from the British Officer's mess. The corks were secured in place with the use of black sealing wax, prompting people to refer to the brand as 'Black Seal'.

People began asking for the rum with the 'black seal and eventually a play on words gave birth to the barrel juggling 'Black Seal' which still graces the label today.

Gosling's Black Seal is a full-flavoured dark, barrel-aged rum, which is blended in Bermuda from three distinctly different, triple pot distilled rums. The rum is then aged for 3 years in re-charred American oak barrels previously used to age bourbon.

Gosling's Black Seal is Bermuda's largest export and is most popularly served in bars around the world, mixed with ginger beer, in the popular 'Dark 'n' Stormy' cocktail.

Grand Marnier Cordon Rouge®

www.grand-marnier.com

In 1827 Jean-Baptiste Lapostolle founded a modest distillery in Neauphle-le-Château, a small village near Paris. His company, which would become Marnier-Lapostolle, soon acquired a reputation for fine fruit liqueurs but Jean-Baptiste could never have dreamt that his fledgling distillery's drinks would be known around the globe.

It was Eugéne, Jean-Baptiste's son, who transformed the company's fortunes. In 1870, fleeing the Franco-Prussian war, he travelled to Cognac. There he met with distillers, visited cellars and returned home laden with fine Cognac and impressed by the distillers' expertise.

At home, Eugéne invited friends and family to appraise his samples, among them his son-in-law, Louis-Alexandre Marnier-Lapostolle. Louis-Alexandre was so inspired by his father-in-law's enthusiasm and the quality of the Cognacs that he immediately set about experimenting in the distillery's laboratory. His great idea was to blend Cognac with orange, which was then an exotic fruit and hard to obtain. In 1880, after ten years of blending, experimenting and ageing, and sampling different test batches, he finally created a liqueur with perfectly balanced flavours.

César Ritz was one of many influential people impressed by the new liqueur and he immediately introduced it to the Savoy Hotel in London. He also advised Louis-Alexandre to go against the prevailing trend of dubbing every product 'petit'. The distiller duly called his creation 'Grand' Marnier. Today the Grand Marnier bottle, designed by Louis-Alexandre in homage to the Cognac pot still, is a familiar sight in bars around the world. Marnier-Lapostolle is still owned by Louis-Alexandre's descendants and the red ribbon on every bottle is still tied by hand.

The 16th century Chateau de Bourg lies in a small village just outside the town of Jarnac, in the Cognac region of South-West France. The picturesque house is owned by Marnier-Lapostolle and the Cognacs which make up the Grand Marnier blend are aged in its cellars before being moved to the company's distillery, in Neauphle-le-Château near Versailles. Grand Marnier Cordon Rouge is made with a blend of over 200 different cognacs all aged for at least 3 years and some very much longer.

Grand Marnier is flavoured at the distillery using Citrus Bigaradia essence, a delicately perfumed variety of bitter orange from the Caribbean, selected due to its high concentration of natural oils and hence flavour. The orange peels are macerated in neutral alcohol at Neauphle-le-Château before being distilled to extract the essence of their rich flavour.

Finally, the Cognac is blended with the orange essence and sugar syrup. The resulting liqueur is casked in oak, where it marries and ages. This final maturation helps give Grand Marnier its characteristic roundness and complexity.

For the finishing touches, the liqueur goes to the company's bottling plant where the liqueur is finished with its distinctive bottle, complete with moiré ribbon and wax seal.

Grapefruit Juice

This citrus fruit may take its name from the way the unripe fruit hangs in green clusters from the tree like bunches of grapes. Or maybe some early botanist just got confused.

As a rule of thumb, the darker the flesh, the sweeter the juice and the more antioxidants and vitamins. But even the sweetest of grapefruits are wonderfully sharp and tart.

Grapefruit is an easy fruit to juice yourself using a citrus press or an electric spinning juicer so there is no excuse for using inferior packaged juices. Simply cut the fruit in half and juice away, taking care to avoid the pith, which can make the juice bitter. As with other citrus fruits, avoid storing in the refrigerator immediately prior to use as cold fruit yield less juice.

Grapes

Oddly, many of the grapes which are classically used for winemaking are not particularly good to eat. Only a few, like Gamay, Tokay, Zinfandel and Muscat, are used for both purposes.

The main commercially available table grapes are Concord, which gives a purple juice which is used for concentrates and jellies, Emperor, which is red and thick-skinned, and Thompson Seedless, which is green and sweet. Seedless grapes are easiest to use in cocktails and produce a fresh juice with a delicate, subtle flavour, which is very different from the syrupy stuff in cartons.

The best way to extract juice is to muddle the required number of grapes in the base of your shaker. Recipes in this guide call for 'seedless red grapes' or 'seedless white grapes'. Obviously, if you've opted for a grape that has seeds you'll need to remove them yourself before you muddle the grapes. Crushing the seeds releases bitter flavours, which can spoil a drink.

Grappa

Unsurprisingly, given that it is made from the waste products of another drink, grappa used to have a reputation for being closer to rocket fuel than a subtle taste experience. While there are still many unremarkable grappas produced on an industrial scale, there are some superb modern grappas. The best of these are produced in relatively small quantities and are delicate with an oily, mouth-filling palate.

Most of the best grappas are made from a particular grape variety, the aromas and character of which can be found in the finished spirit, and from grapes which have only been gently pressed, rather than completely stripped of all their juice.

According to the European Union, grappa must be distilled in Italy from Italian pomace and have an alcoholic strength of not less than 37.5%. Once the juice has been extracted for wine making, pomace from white grape varieties is taken to the distillery and left to ferment. Red grape pomace has usually begun fermenting with the wine and so does not require further fermentation, while pomace used for making rose wines is semi-fermented. At this stage red pomace is around 4% abv, white around 2.5% abv and pomace used for rose is somewhere in-between.

The pomace (in Italian, 'vinaccia') is then processed to remove larger stalks and wood. Premium grappa producers are extremely careful to remove the stalks and stems, as they are a source of methanol (wood alcohol). The soggy mass is then distilled using one of several different processes. The 'discontinuous' method is the most classic. Fermented pomace is distilled in batches only large enough to fill the retort of the still. After each batch, the head and tails of the distillate are separated off, leaving only the heart. The still is then emptied, cleaned and refilled with fresh pomace, and the process begins again.

In the 'continuous' method the disalcolatore (which literally translates as 'alcohol-stripper') is fed continuously with fresh marc. The apparatus uses steam to strip the pomace of its alcohol. (Steam is used as the pomace is so solid that it would burn if heated directly). The disalcolatore produces 'flemma', an unappealing slurry of water and alcohol (at 15-20% abv). The flemma is then distilled and cut to produce grappa (at 80-86% abv).

The spirit is then stocked in vats to marry for at least six months. Unaged grappa is hydrated prior to bottling to reduce the strength to 40-50% abv. Aged Grappa is kept in oak for 1 to 5 years before bottling. The ageing process mellows the grappa and gives it a dry, woody character. Some grappa is aged in glass to produce a crystal clear but oily spirit.

A grappa can take the name of a DOCG or DOC (appellation controlee) wine such as Chianti or Amarone if the pomace that it was made from derived from the production of that wine. The term 'Monovarietal' is used to describe grappa made from the vinaccia of a single grape variety.

Green Crème de Menthe

Green Crème de Menthe is a classic, green coloured liqueur flavoured with peppermint - extracted, of course, from fresh mint leaves. The mint oils are distilled; to deliver a high quality and very refreshing mint flavour, which has stood the test of time as a digestive liqueur.

Guinness®

www.guinness.com

A dry stout beer based upon London's 18th century original porter style and brewed at Arthur Guinness' St. James's Gate Brewery in Dublin, Ireland.

Arthur Guinness started brewing ales initially in Leixlip, then from 1759 at the St. James's Gate Brewery where he took a 9,000 year lease at £45 per annum for the then unused brewery. The Guinness brewery in Park Royal, London closed in 2005 and production of all Guinness moved to the Dublin brewery.

Guinness stout is made from water, malt, barley, hops and brewer's yeast. A portion of the barley is flaked and roasted to give Guinness its dark colour and characteristic taste.

Draught and canned Guinness attains its creamy head and smooth character by use of nitrogen (N2) as well as carbon dioxide while the Original Extra Stout contains only carbon dioxide so has a more acidic taste.

Half & Half

This blend of 50% milk and 50% cream is relatively unknown in the UK. I've listed milk and cream as separate ingredients in both the American and the British versions of this guide.

Heering Cherry Liqueur®

www.heering.com

On 1st December 1818, Peter Heering opened his grocer's shop in Copenhagen. As well as selling groceries, Peter produced and sold his homemade cherry liqueur to a recipe originally given to him by Mrs Carstensen, the wife of the grocer in whose shop Peter served his apprenticeship.

Cherry Heering is still made to the same recipe from Danish Steven's cherries, harvested in August. The fruit is crushed together with the stones, which give Heering its characteristic hint of almond. A secret combination of herbs and spices is added to the product, which then undergoes maturation in oak barrels for at least three years. These barrels are only partially emptied before being topped up so each bottle contains traces of the original liqueur produced in 1818.

Honey

Many bartenders dilute honey with hot water to make it easier to mix. Some mix to equal parts but I find that a 4 parts runny honey to 1 part water mix is enough to liquefy the honey sufficiently to use. To do this simply empty a fifth of the honey from our jar or bottle (spread on your toast) and replace with moderately hot water. Reseal and shake. This extra dilution should enable your honey to be stored in the refrigerator.

If you don't want to dilute precious honey stocks then dissolve it by stirring it into the cocktail's base spirit prior to adding the other ingredients.

I favour a good quality runny orange blossom honey for general bar use and find those packaged in squeezy plastic bottles with a fine nozzle easiest to dispense.

Hpnotiq Tropical®

www.hpnotiq.com

Prounounced 'Hip-Not-Ick' this aqua-blue coloured liqueur was launched in 2002. It is made in France from a blend of triple pot still distilled, charcoal filtered vodka, cognac and fruit juices (pineapple, grape, passion fruit and orange).

Presented in a tall shapely frosted flint bottle, the packaging is certainly distinctive. Despite the obvious use of colourings, Hpnotiq does not contain any flavourings, sweeteners or preservatives.

Ice

Apart from rare exceptions such as hot drinks, ice is simply the most important cocktail ingredient so ensure a plentiful supply. Avoid the hollow, tubular or wafers of ice. Instead look for large, solid cubes of ice. I recommend a Kold Draft (kold-draft.com) or Hoshizaki (hoshizaki.com) ice machines producing large (inch/25mm square) solid cubes.

When filling ice cube trays, use bottled or filtered water to avoid the taste of chlorine often apparent in municipal water supplies. Your ice should be dry, almost sticky to the touch. Avoid 'wet' ice that has started to thaw.

Unless otherwise stated, all references to ice mean cubed ice. If crushed ice is required for a particular recipe, the recipe will state 'crushed ice'. This is available commercially. Alternatively you can crush cubed ice in an ice-crusher or simply bash a bag or tea towel of cubed ice with a rolling pin.

Icewine

Is a type of sweet dessert wine produced from grapes, which have not been harvested until frosts have caused them to freeze while still on the vine. This causes water within the grapes to freeze while sugars and other dissolved solids do not. Thus the wine made from these grapes has a very concentrated, usually very sweet flavour.

Infusions

Some recipes call for an infused spirit, such as 'vanilla-infused rum'. You make this by putting three split vanilla pods in a bottle of rum and leaving it to stand for a fortnight. Warming and turning the bottle frequently can speed the infusion.

Other herbs, spices and even fruits can be infused in a similar manner in vodka, gin, rum, whiskey and tequila. Whatever spirit you decide to use, pick a brand that is at least 40% alcohol by volume.

Be aware that when the level of spirit in a bottle drops below the flavouring, the alcohol loses its preservative effect and the flavouring can start to rot. Also be careful not to load the spirit with too much flavour or leave it to infuse for too long. Sample the infusion every couple of days to ensure the taste is not becoming overpowering.

Irish Cream Liqueur

Our recommendation: Baileys Irish Cream Liqueur

In November 1974 R&A Bailey perfected the technique of combining Irish whiskey, cocoa and fresh cream without souring the cream. Sales grew quickly and it is now the world's best selling liqueur.

Irish Whiskey

Our recommendation: Jameson Irish Whiskey

Irish whiskey has an undeserved reputation as a harsh, rough spirit only suited to pepping up coffee. It may be great in an Irish Coffee, but rough and harsh it is not. In fact, the very opposite is true. Due to years of domination by Irish Distillers, the producers' group is now owned by Pernod-Ricard. As a rule Irish whiskey is triple-distilled and not peated and hence light and smooth (although the independent Cooley Distillery produces some notable exceptions to these rules).

Both grain and malt whiskies are produced in Ireland, although grain whiskies are only used in blends. Whiskies may be made from malted barley, unmalted barley and other cereals.

For malt whiskies, as in Scotland, the barley is malted – i.e., it is encouraged to start to germinate and then dried. Unlike its Scottish counterpart, generally no smoke is allowed to come into contact with the grain and so no smoky taste is imparted. (Recently, however, Cooley Distillery has launched peated brands including Connemara and Inishowen.)

Distillation methods vary according to the distillery and the whiskey which is being produced. Grain whiskies are continuously distilled. Malt whiskies are generally distilled three times in a pot still (Connemara is only distilled twice), meaning that the spirit leaves the still at a much higher alcoholic strength than Scotch – often as high as 85% abv.

By law, the grain spirit which leaves the still cannot be called Irish whiskey until it has been aged for at least three years in oak casks in Ireland. Casks which have previous contained sherry, rum, brandy and Bourbon are used for ageing the whiskey.

Blending or 'vatting' is the final part of the process. Here single malt and grain whiskies are mixed and allowed to marry for anything from two days to a month. They are then reduced to bottling strength with the addition of water.

Italian Vermouth

Our recommendation: Martini Rosso

Popular belief has it that Italian vermouth was originally sweet and produced from red wine, while French vermouth was typically dry and white. Hence, many old cocktail books refer to 'French' for dry vermouth and 'Italian' where sweet vermouth is called for.

The truth is that the division between the styles of the two countries was never that defined and producers in both countries now make both sweet (rosso) and dry styles.

Although red vermouth was initially based on red wine, now virtually all is made from white wine with caramel blended in to give an amber colour.

Jack Daniel's Old No.7 Brand®

www.jackdaniels.com

Jack Daniel's is a Tennessee whiskey (not a Bourbon) and was named No.7 by Jack himself in 1887 – no one knows why.

Jasper Newton (Jack) Daniel was introduced to distilling at the tender age of seven, when he went to live with a lay preacher called Daniel Houston Call who operated a whiskey still, store and farm. Originally, he was taken on as something of an errand boy but he was soon learning the art of making whiskey from Dan Call's distiller, Nearest Green. In 1863 a temperance preaching woman known as Lady Love convinced Call to choose between his ministry and his whiskey, so Dan sold his still to Jack, then aged thirteen. Jack's actual birth date is not known but it is commonly accepted that he was born in September 1850, one of thirteen children. The distillery makes the most of this uncertainty, celebrating his birthday for the whole month of September. A life size bronze statue of Jack in front of Cave Spring which was unveiled on his 150th birthday (or thereabouts) illustrates just how short in stature he was. Standing only 5' 2" tall and mounted on a chunk of local limestone, the statue is nicknamed, 'Jack On The Rocks'.

In 1866 and already an established distiller, Jack moved to a new site, setting up a distillery about five miles down the road alongside the excellent Cave Spring water source. This is America's oldest registered distillery. Jack died on 8th October 1911, aged 61, from a gangrenous infection. In 1905 he had broken a toe kicking his safe in a fit of temper when he could not open it. The infection led to the amputation of his leg and ultimately his death. Jack never married (although he is reputed to have been something of a ladies' man) and so left the distillery to his nephew, Lemuel Motlow and a cousin, Richard Daniel. Lem bought Richard's share and took over the running of the distillery. He still features as 'proprietor' on the bottom of the whiskey's label.

The township of Lynchburg, where Jack Daniel's is based, is in Moore County, deep in the religious South. In 1910 the area voted to go 'dry', forcing Lem to mothball his distillery and set up operations in St. Louis and Birmingham. These too were forced to close on the advent of national Prohibition in 1919 and Lem turned to mule trading instead. His mule barn can still be seen just outside Lynchburg on the road to Tullahoma and it is still possible to shop at the hardware store he built on Lynchburg's town square in 1912. It is famous for the motto: 'all goods worth price charged'.

Even when Prohibition was repealed in 1933, Moore County remained dry, as it does to this day. Lem was elected to the legislature and in 1938 a special state law was passed allowing whiskey to be made, though not sold, in Moore County. At the age of 69, 29 years after he had been forced to stop, he resumed production. While he waited for his whiskey to reach sufficient age to sell, he made peach and apple brandy.

Lem had four sons who jointly took over the distillery after his death in 1947. The sons, who had no male children, sold their business to Brown Forman, the huge distilling conglomerate, in 1956, after receiving assurances that the whiskey would not be changed. Today Jack Daniel's is still made from a mash bill consisting 80% corn, 8% rye and 12% malted barley, all sourced from America's Midwest. This is milled and mixed with water from Cave Spring Hollow, a limestone cave spring whose iron-free water runs at a constant temperature of 13°C (56°F). Fermentation takes place in huge vats using the sour mash method.

The wash is distilled in 30 metre continuous stills to 70% abv and the clear distillate is dripped through one of 60 large vats filled with 10 feet of densely packed hard sugar maple charcoal. This takes between 10 and 12 days and is known as the Lincoln County Process – so named because 'charcoal mellowing' was developed in the county, whose borders used to include Lynchburg. The charcoal is made from hard sugar maples (Acer saccharum) and tall trees growing on high ground are favoured. These are split into strips about 4 foot (1.2m) long and approximately 2 inches (5cm) square, then stacked in ricks and burned to produce charcoal.

The charcoal mellowed spirit is then aged in new white oak barrels, which have been charred in a two-stage process, for over four years (around 52 months). The casks are stored in ageing warehouses, on top of the hills overlooking Lynchburg. Greater changes in temperature occur higher up so

maturation proceeds slightly faster. When the whiskey reaches maturity, the contents of a number of casks are blended together and reduced to bottling strength using cave spring water.

Jägermeister®

www.jager.com

This German bitter-sweet liqueur is made from 56 varieties of herbs, fruits and spices, macerated in spirit for up to six weeks and then matured in oak before blending. Although established in 1878, Jägermeister did not produce this drink until 1935.

Pronounced 'Yey-Ger-My-Stir', the name means 'master of the hunt'. The logo has a deer with a cross between its antlers, recalling a vision in the life of St Hubert, the patron saint of hunters.

Serve mixed with tonic, lemonade or cola, or alternatively drink frozen straight as a shooter or chaser.

Jameson®

www.jamesonwhiskey.com

John Jameson was a Scot who married into the Haig family of Scotch whisky distillers before taking over his distillery in Bow Street, Dublin, around 1780. At this time it was Irish whiskey, which dominated the whiskey industry rather than Scotch so while the move was bold, it was also a shrewd one for an ambitious young whiskey distiller.

The Jameson crest on every bottle features the family motto, 'Sine Metu' meaning 'without fear' in reference to their bravery in battling pirates on the high seas in the 1950s, a family trait that John would appear to have inherited. The world's best selling Irish whiskey, Jameson is triple distilled from an even mixture of Irish malted and unmalted barley and other cereals, aged for an average of seven years in oak casks previously used for Sherry and Bourbon. Owing to the demands of expansion, production was moved to Power's Distillery in 1971 and then in 1975 to Middleton in Ireland's County Cork, where it is distilled today.

Jameson Signature Reserve®

www.jamesonwhiskey.com

Signature Reserve takes its name from a time before distilleries began bottling their own whiskey and this bottling celebrates Jameson's practice of sending their own labels, each bearing the John Jameson & Son signature, with every delivery of casks to the whiskey bonders. Thus the Jameson signature became synonymous with the whiskey, something still recognised to this day.

Signature Reserve has a high pot still content and is aged in selected American bourbon barrels and Spanish oloroso sherry casks, the latter significantly contributing to the style of this whiskey.

Jameson 12 Year Old Special Reserve®

www.jamesonwhiskey.com

First produced in the mid-eighties under the name Jameson 1780 in reference to the year the original Jameson distillery in Bow Street, Dublin, was founded. Old Special Reserve contains around 75% pot still whiskey and a third of the whiskies used in the blend are aged in sherry casks, and of course all the whiskies are aged for at least 12 years.

Jameson Gold Reserve®

www.jamesonwhiskey.com

Launched in 1996, until recently this rich pot still character whiskey bottling was only to be found in airports. Jameson Gold Reserve is a blend of three well-aged whiskies, one uniquely matured in virgin oak barrels, one in bourbon barrels and the other in sherry casks.

Jameson 18 Year Old Limited Reserve®

www.jamesonwhiskey.com

This exceptional Jameson bottling is matured for no less than 18 years in a combination of bourbon and oloroso sherry casks, it's given a final finish in fresh fill American bourbon barrels. Since its launch in 2002, stocks of Jameson 18 Year Old have been appropriately limited, something evidenced by its being packaged in individually numbered bottles.

Johnnie Walker Red®

www.johnniewalker.com

In 1820, John Walker, the son of an Ayrshire farmer, established the family grocer's business at the age of fifteen in Kilmarnock and began selling Scotch whisky. His son, Alexander, joined the business a year before his father died in 1857, and by the time his sons joined the business, it was no longer a grocers, but a firm of whisky merchants.

John Walker's grandsons patented the name Johnnie Walker in 1908 and launched a White Label, Special Red Label and Extra Special Black label whisky. The white was dropped, but the red and black in their easily recognisable square bottles with the 'striding dandy' became internationally successful blends - the red became the world's best-selling Scotch.

Johnnie Walker Black®

www.johnniewalker.com

Johnnie Walker Black Label contains around forty single malt whiskies including Talisker, Cardhu, and Lagavulin. It has a high proportion of Islay malts and is matured for twelve years in oak casks. The brand was originally called 'Extra Special Old Highland Whisky' – the name was changed to 'Black Label' because customers always ordered by the colour of the label.

Johnnie Walker was Sir Winston Churchill's favourite Scotch and his 1932 oil painting 'Bottlescape' features a bottle of Johnnie Walker Black Label.

Johnnie Walker Gold®

www.johnniewalker.com

This 'Centenary Blend' was created by Sir Alexander Walker in 1920 to celebrate the founding of the company by John Walker 100 years before. The blend consists of whiskies from both the Highlands and Islay, each matured in oak for at least 18 years.

Johnnie Walker Blue®

www.johnniewalker.com

An even more premium version of the already deluxe Johnnie Walker Black Label, with a proportion of malts as old as 60 years in the blend. The blue-green flint glass, square sided bottle which tapers to the base is a replica of the original Johnnie Walker bottle. The cork stopper has cord seal with a dangling medallion commemorating the brands establishment in 1820.

Kahlúa®

www.kahlua.com

First created in Mexico in 1936, Kahlùa is the original coffee liqueur and is made by blending roasted and ground Arabica coffee beans with water, sugar cane spirit, vanilla and sugar.

Kahlùa was almost unknown until the early sixties when an American entrepreneur, Jules Berman bought the brand and started to promote it in the United States.

Berman, who became known as 'Mr Kahlùa', began his phenomenally successful business career by opening the first liquor store in Beverly Hills shortly after the repeal of Prohibition. Berman went on to open five more Llord's stores before selling out and taking a job at the import division of Schenley Industries. After serving in the Navy during World War II, Berman started his own wine and liquor import company 'Berman Enterprises' which popularized brands as Cinzano, J&B Rare, Heineken and of course Kahlùa, which incidentally he acquired from Schenley Industries.

Berman was a keen pre-Columbian art collector and used West Mexican ceramics in advertisements for Kahlùa, employing fellow collector and horror actor Vincent Price to lend artefacts and his own deep voice to one of the brand's early promotions.

After successfully establishing the brand Berman sold Kahlùa to Hiram Walker and Sons in 1964 but remained as a corporate officer in charge of brand development until 1970.

Ketel One®

www. KetelOne.com

Ketel One is the creation of one of Holland's oldest distilling dynasties, the Nolet family of Schiedam, who have been making spirits since Johannes Nolet started his business in 1691.

Johannes Nolet opened his distillery near the mouth of the great river Mass on the North Sea, attracted to the area due to its accessibility to shipping and its close proximity to one of Holland's largest grain auctions. By 1882 the Nolet Distillery was one of 394 distilleries operating in Schiedam. Today there are only four. Ten generations after Johannes, Carolus Nolet now runs the company with the help of his two sons, Carl and Bob.

Like the families of great wineries, the Nolets have dedicated themselves to the traditional craft of distilling premium spirits. Also like many of the great names in wine, Ketel One is a descriptive name with its own heritage, not merely a contrived marketing device. The name heralds from the original 'Distilleerketel #1', the centuries-old alembic copper pot still that is still used to produce Ketel One Vodka at the Nolet Distillery today.

It is from this traditional copper pot still method of distillation that the living legacy of the Nolet family originates. Recipes found in Johannes Nolet's journals dating back to when he first established the business in 1691 are all based around small-batch pot still distillation. These journals have been passed down the generations through to the company's current chairman, who with the help of these secret family formulas continues to build upon the family's commitment to maintaining and strengthening the distillery's reputation for excellence.

The family's pride in their distilling traditions and reputation is obvious when they talk about their heritage and use of traditional methods today. They insist upon the best raw materials, always ensuring that the focus is on quality rather than quantity. These are used in small batch distillations requiring the painstaking attention of a master distiller to hand-stoke the fire, oversee the distillation process and regulate the temperature. The first 100 gallons (known as the head) of every distillation is discarded due to being too harsh. The last 100 gallons (the tail) are also discarded because they are too weak. Only the heart of the distillate has the purity, clarity and smoothness required to make Ketel One Vodka. Multiple distillations and charcoal filtration are used to produce a superbly smooth, ultra premium wheat grain vodka. As a final check, each batch of Ketel One must be tasted by a member of the Nolet family before it is approved for release and deemed worthy of the family name.

Ketel One Citroen®

www.ketelone.com

Having already created what they and many top bartenders consider the perfect vodka for Martinis, the Nolet family wanted to create a flavoured vodka of equal excellence for making the ultimate Cosmopolitan. The family spent more than two years researching and evaluating different blending and infusion methods, before arriving at the costly but effective process of hand-crafting in small batches as is the case with their original, unflavoured vodka, and infusing with natural citrus oils comprising 95% lemon and 5% lime. Ketel One Citroen combines the smooth qualities of the original Ketel One Vodka with the refreshing natural essence of citrus fruit. To ensure continuity in the quality of Ketel One Citroen, a member of the Nolet family personally samples each batch produced prior to release.

Kina Lillet®

The former name for what is now known as Lillet blonde.

Kirschwasser Eau de Vie

'Kirsch' is German for cherry, and kirsch eau de vie is a clear, cherry-flavoured spirit made from cherry kernels, traditionally produced in the area where France, Germany and Switzerland meet.

Alsace is the most noted area for kirsch production in France and French kirsch is graded by law by the following categories: 'pur' - pure cherry distillate, 'commerce' - cherry distillate with added alcohol, 'fantaisie' alcohol flavoured with kirsch and other elements, 'artificiel' - neutral grain alcohol flavoured with artificial essences. The latter two are only suitable for cooking use.

The picturesque Black Forest is the area most associated with kirsch production in Germany. Kirschgeist is a German kirsch where the fruit has been macerated in alcohol then redistilled ('geist' is German for 'spirit'). Kirschwasser indicates a spirit distilled from fermented fruit ('wasser' means 'water' in German).

This German product tends to be drier and stronger than French kirsch, which is distilled at a lower point to retain more of the fruit flavour.

Kirsch Liqueur

'Kirsch' is German for cherry, and kirsch is a clear, cherry-flavoured liqueur made from cherry kernels, traditionally produced in the area where France, Germany and Switzerland meet. 'Cuisine' or 'culinary' in the name suggests a lower alcohol product intended for use in the kitchen.

Kiwi Fruit

The kiwi is also known as the Chinese gooseberry. Seeds from China's Yangtze valley reached New Zealand in the early 20th century and were cultivated commercially 40 years later. It was rebranded as a kiwi fruit, partly for reasons of Cold War politics and partly because it's brown, furry exterior resembles New Zealand's national bird. Despite the fruit's name, New Zealand no longer enjoys an export monopoly, but remains the largest producer.

Preparation: The kiwi fruit is best muddled. Simply slice the fruit in half, scoop out the juicy flesh and muddle. Alternatively use a commercially available kiwi fruit puree, our recommendation being Boiron, a frozen puree without added sugar.

Krupnik®

There are many varieties of honey liqueur but the Polish brands claim the oldest heritage. Traditional Polish vodka-based honey liqueurs are thought to have originated in the 16th century. Besides use in cocktails, these liqueurs are worth enjoying neat and slightly warmed in a balloon glass – I have seen bars warm the bottle in a baby's bottle warmer so always ready for chilled winter drinkers.

Kümmel

This clear liqueur is distilled from grain or potatoes and flavoured with caraway seeds, fennel, orris and other herbs. Kümmel is said to have been developed by the Dutch distiller Lucas Bols in the late sixteenth century, with the first written recipe dating back to 1575.

Kwai Feh®

www.dekuyper.nl

This lychee-flavoured liqueur is named after the beautiful consort of the Tang Dynasty Emperor Ming who is said to have craved lychees.

La Fée Parisienne®

www.lafeeabsinthe.com

La Fée is made in Paris to a 19th century recipe containing wormwood (Artemisia absinthium) and flavoured with anise, hyssop and other aromatic herbs. It was launched in 2000 by George Rowley, the man responsible for

importing the first absinthe into the UK since before the Second World War, and the originator of absinthe's renaissance.

This was the first traditional absinthe to be commercially produced in France since it was banned in 1914-15. A mark of La Fée's authenticity is its endorsement by Marie-Claude Delahaye, founder and curator of the Absinthe Museum in Auvers-sur-Oise, France.

As should be the case in a traditional French absinthe, La Fée turns cloudy with the addition of water. The bottle is as distinctive as its contents, with its label dominated by an illustration of an eye.

La Fée has the flavour profile of a traditional French absinthe. It has clean, fresh and rounded aniseed flavours and well-balanced liquorice, mint, lemon, angelica, and rootier notes.

La Fée Bohemian®

www.lafeeabsinthe.com

La Fée Bohemian absinth is distilled south of Prague, in the heart of Bohemia. (Note the missing 'e' in the Czech spelling of absinth.) Bohemian absinth has a bluer tinge to its green colour and a more subtle aniseed flavour than its French counterpart and has subtle undertones of fennel and mint.

It is not usual for Czech absinth to turn cloudy when water is added as you would expect from La Fée, this is completely authentic.

Lagavulin 16 Year Old®

www.malts.com

Lagavulin is a single malt Scotch whisky from the island of Islay. It is pronounced 'Lagga-Voolin', after the Gaelic Laggan Mhouillin, meaning 'the mill in the valley'. The distillery sits on the water's edge in a small sheltered bay on Islay's south-eastern coast close to the ruins of Dunyveg Castle. This is where Robert Bruce took refuge after his defeat by the Earl of Pembroke, and was also the bastion of the Lords of the Isles. Lagavulin is instantly recognisable due to its long, low white warehouses and tall red brick chimney.

One of the oldest distilleries on Islay with illicit distilling recorded on the site as early as 1742. The Lagavulin distillery dates from 1816, when John Johnston constructed Kildalton Distillery at Lagavulin. The following year Archibald Campbell built a second distillery named Lagavulin alongside Kildalton which Johnston also acquired in 1825. The two distilleries merged to become Lagavulin in 1837 under the ownership of the Graham brothers and James Logan Mackie.

Peter Mackie worked for his uncle, James Logan, at the distillery before establishing his own company, Mackie & Co. Distillers Limited, in 1883 before inheriting Lagavulin in 1890. Mackie went on to establish the White Horse blend of which Lagavulin remains an important part. After his death in 1924 the company adopted the name 'White Horse Distillers Limited'. Three years later it became part of the Distillers Company Limited (DCL), now part of Diageo who market Lagavulin as part of their Classic Malts range. The label still carries the Mackie name and rearing horse crest.

Lagavulin is noted for its pronounced peaty character. Islay boasts miles of peat bog and the water used to charge Lagavulin's stills runs brown down the burn from the Solan Lochs in the hills above the distillery. Thanks to a legal battle fought by Peter Mackie - Lagavulin has exclusive rights over this water course.

The barley used to distil Lagavulin is malted at nearby Port Ellen and where it is exposed to some 20 times as much peat smoke as is in Speyside. Of the four stills at Lagavulin two have an unusual pear shape. These along with one of the slowest distillations of any Islay malt (around five hours for the first distillation and more than nine hours for the second) is said to give Lagavulin its roundness.

A long 16 year maturation period finishes this very characterful and highly regarded malt.

Lanique Rose Petal®

www.laniquevodka.com

Lanique is the brand name under which Lancut (pronounced 'Wan-tsut') Distillery in southeast Poland exports to the UK. The distillery was founded in 1784 by Princess Lubomirska and it is said that this is where Pierre Smirnoff learnt his trade.

Lanique Rose Petal liqueur is flavoured with attar of roses from the East giving it a flavour reminiscent of Turkish delight.

Lapponia Lakka Cloudberry®

This Finnish liqueur is flavoured with cloudberries (hjortron), a rare wild berry that grows in bogs and wetlands and in some Arctic areas. Lapponia is very popular in its home country and Sweden.

Lapponia Polar Karpalo Cranberry®

This Finnish liqueur is flavoured with cranberries harvested in the spring from Finland's arctic marshlands, which are apparently a delicacy for passing cranes flying north.

Leblon®

www.leblonspirit.com

Leblon is an ultra-premium white cachaça inspired by its namesake and place of origin, Leblon Beach in Rio de Janeiro, Brazil. While relaxing at a beach bar in Leblon, Roberto Nogueira dreamt of producing a world class Brazilian cachaça. Insisting on the very best, Roberto called upon a team of international specialists to lend their expertise to producing this unique cachaça.

Leblon is made from fresh cane juice obtained within three hours of harvesting by pressing only the middle and best part of the sugar cane. This fresh sweet juice is fermented through a strictly controlled process and then carefully distilled through an alambic distillation process to fully harness the flavour. The cachaça is then lightly aged in French vintage cognac barrels for one month to form a perfectly blended, fresh and smooth super premium white spirit.

Leblon is a modern light, clean spirit but yet retains the distinctive flavour profile of traditional cachaças. Thus Leblon is perfect for Caipirinhas, Batidas and other traditional Brazilian drinks but with the versatility to also use in contemporary cocktails.

Lemon Juice

Originally from India or Malaysia, lemons are available throughout the year and in many different varieties, distinguishable by their shape, size and thickness of skin.

Lemon juice is a key cocktail ingredient and ideally should be freshly squeezed for each drink as its flavour quickly deteriorates when exposed to oxygen in the atmosphere. For further information see 'Limes' below.

Lemonade

An 'ade' is a non-alcoholic beverage made from diluted fruit juice and sugar and may be carbonated. Thus when used as a suffix, as in lemonade it simply means a sweetened lemon flavoured drink. Achieving a harmonious balance between the sweetener and the sour citrus fruit.

There are numerous types of lemonade and in this guide recipes call for the clear fizzy lemonade commonly found in the UK, US, Australia, New Zealand and France. We recommend 'Fever Tree' lemonade.

Lemoncello

Our recommendation: Luxardo Limoncello

Pronounced '(lee-mohn-CHEH-loh), this is a generic term for Italian citrus (usually lemon but sometimes also with lime) based liqueurs. Not dissimilar to alcoholic lemonade, this is a very traditional style of liqueur in Italy with most families claiming a recipe made for generations, particularly in the lemon-producing region along the Italian Amalfi Coast in Capri and Sorrento. Typically, these recipes involve the maceration of lemon rind in neutral alcohol and sweetening with the addition of sugar syrup. This simple mix of spirit, citrus and sugar is one of the most basic drinks mixes, a formula that's found in classics such as the Daiquiri, Caipirinha and rum punch.

In Italy Lemoncello moved from being largely home produced to become a fashionable commercial product during the nineties and is now one of the most popular styles of liqueur. This sudden surge in popularity gave rise to a plethora of brands, most claiming old family recipes as their origin. These brands often us alternative spelling of the name such as 'Limoncello' and 'Lemonello'.

Limes

Although smaller and more fragrant than lemons, limes are closely related to the lemon. Limes are cultivated in tropical countries and are widely used in Caribbean and Brazilian cuisine.

Both these citrus fruits are bartender staples and their juice is used to balance sweetness and add depth to a bewildering range of cocktails. Lemon and lime juice will curdle cream and cream liqueurs but will happily mix with most other spirits and liqueurs. Limes generally pair well with rum while lemons are preferable in drinks based on whiskey or brandy.

Limes and lemons last longer if stored in the refrigerator, although you'll get more juice out of them if you let them warm up to room temperature then roll the fruit on a surface under the palm of your hand before you cut them. Save hard fruits for garnishing: soft fruits have more juice and flavour.

To juice, simply cut in half widthways and juice using a press, squeezer or spinning juicer, taking care not to grind the pith. Ideally you should juice your lemons and limes immediately prior to use as the juice will oxidise after a couple of hours.

Light Rum

Our recommendation: Bacardi Superior

Rum is termed 'light' or 'heavy', depending on the purity to which it was distilled. Essentially, the flavour of any spirit comes from 'congeners' – products of fermentation which are not ethyl alcohol. When alcohol is concentrated during distillation, the levels of congeners are reduced. The fewer congeners, the lighter the rum. The more congeners, the heavier.

The fermentation process also affects whether a rum is light or heavy. A longer, slower fermentation will result in a heavier rum.

The odour, texture and taste of light rums are more subtle and refined than those of heavy rums, which have a heavy, syrupy flavour to match their dark colour.

Light rums tend to originate from countries originally colonised by the Spanish, such as Cuba, the Dominican Republic, Puerto Rico and Venezuela.

Lillet Blanc®

www.lillet.com

The Lillet Frères company was formed in 1865 by two brothers, Paul and Raymond Lillé who were merchants of fine wine and spirits in Bordeaux. The brothers first produced their Kina Lillet in 1887 after an idea by father Kermann, a monk and doctor who had returned to Bordeaux after a stay in Brazil.

Lillet Blanc is a blend of 85 percent Sémillon and Sauvignon Blanc wine with 15 percent fruit liqueurs, which are made by macerating sweet oranges from Spain, bitter oranges from Haiti, green oranges from Morocco and quinine from Peru, in brandy for several months. The resulting blend is aged in Yugoslav oak casks in Lillet's Podensac cellars for a year before bottling. Lillet Frères was purchased in 1985 by Bruno Borie of the famed Borie family (the owners of several Bordeaux châteaux) who invested in the company's production facilities and in 1986 re-launched the brand with the name and recipe changed. The original name 'Kina Lillet', derived from the Peruvian Indian name for the cinchona tree, kin-kina. 'Kina' was dropped from the name and the amount of quinine reduced to create a lighter, fruitier, less syrupy drink to appeal to modern tastes.

Lillet is the only aperitif from Bordeaux and is not flavoured with herbs, nor is it oxidized like vermouth meaning it is classified an aperitif and not a vermouth.

Lillet has greatly benefited from Ian Fleming's Casino Royale, in which James Bond specifies that his Martini should be made with a half measure of Kina Lillet. Later in the book he names his bespoke Martini 'Vesper' after the beautiful double agent Vesper Lynd.

Lillet Rouge®

www.lillet.com

Originally created in 1965, Lillet Rouge is made in a similar way to Lillet Blanc but is based on Cabernet Sauvignon and Merlot grapes. Like the Blanc, this is aged in Yugoslav oak casks for a year before bottling. Between 1990 and 1993, Lillet Rouge was reformulated with higher-quality base wines to produce a more complex flavour.

Lime Cordial
Our recommendation: Rose's Lime Cordial
Lauchlan Rose started importing lime juice from the West Indies to England in the 1860s, when ships were compelled to carry lime or lemon juice to prevent scurvy. In 1867 he devised a method for preserving juice without alcohol and so created lime cordial, the world's first concentrated fruit drink.

Liqueurs
Liqueurs can be flavoured with practically everything including herbs, flowers, roots, spices, fruit and fruit stones. Unfortunately, for many the word 'liqueur' connotes a sweet and sticky (or creamy), low-alcohol, unchallenging drink. True, many liqueurs fit this description – and many of these are very pleasant – but there are also many more serious liqueurs out there for the discerning drinker.

All liqueurs have one thing in common - they all have spirits as a base. They are sweetened alcoholic drinks made by mixing or redistilling spirits with flavourings and colourings.

The French word liqueur also has Latin roots; it is derived from the word 'liquefacere' meaning to melt or dissolve. The Italian word for liqueur is 'liquori', which also encompasses dry spirits and fortified wines. Within the EEC a liqueur must have an alcohol content of at least 15%abv and a minimum sugar content of 100g per litre - this law harks back to the days when sugar was an expensive luxury.

In Victorian England liqueurs came into vogue – they were drunk from small glasses by ladies at the end of the meal. One of the popular liqueurs of the period was Ratafia; the name probably derives from the Creole word for molasses spirit, Tafia. Many liqueurs went under this title, most coloured and flavoured with red fruits. Liqueurs dropped in popularity at the turn of the 20th century, but the boom in cocktail bartending has begun to bring liqueurs back in from the cold.

Liqueurs are generally made by adding flavourings to a base spirit or spirits and then sweetening with sugar syrup – although most producers keep their secret recipes heavily guarded. The following methods can be used to extract flavours from fruit and other botanicals.

Maceration - Fruit and botanicals are steeped in cold alcohol – for days, weeks, months, or sometimes as long as a year. Liqueur flavourings made by maceration or infusion are known as 'tinctures'.
Infusion - Fruit and botanicals are steeped in warm alcohol (usually 40°-50°C, but occasionally up to 60°C). This process is sometimes known as 'digestion'.
Percolation - This is an intensive, more efficient method of maceration. Pure alcohol is forced through the botanicals to extract the flavour as quickly as possible. The alcohol may be cold, hot or even a vapour, and the process may be continuously repeated in a closed cycle.
Distillation - Botanicals are distilled with neutral alcohol, producing a clear distillate with some of the flavour of the botanicals. The richly perfumed distillate produced is a mixture of alcohol and essential oils and is known as an 'esprit'.
Maturation - Some liqueurs are then aged in oak or just left to marry before being reduced to the required bottling strength and bottled.

Liquorice (UK) or Licorice (U.S.) Syrup
This is made by dissolving half a stick of Italian unsweetened pure liquorice stick in three-quarters of a mug of water by heating and stirring in a saucepan. When liquorice has dissolved, let the water cool a little and start adding 1 cup of sugar, keep stirring over low heat until all the sugar has fully dissolved. Allow to cool, bottle and store in refrigerator.

Luxardo Amaretto di Saschira®

www.luxardo.it
This delicate liqueur is an Italian classic, packed with the unique flavour of sweet almond. The Luxardo family have been distilling fine liqueurs in the Veneto region of Italy for six generations. They make their amaretto with the pure paste of the finest almonds, from Avola in southern Sicily, and age it for eight months in larch vats to impart its distinctive, well-rounded taste. Their very contemporary amaretto has a palate of almond and marzipan, making it a vital tool in any mixologist's flavour armoury.

Luxardo Limoncello®

www.luxardo.it
Limoncello has been made by Luxardo since 1906 and it delivers a rich sweet lemon flavour in a blast of sour citrus, lemon zest and candied citrus, which somehow remains pure and balanced. It is increasingly popular among bartenders seeking new ways of delivering that vital citrus tang.

Luxardo Maraschino Originale®

www.luxardo.it
Originally from Genova, Girolamo Luxardo moved with his family to the town of Zara in 1817 as consular representative of the Kingdom of Sardinia. Zara, a port city on the Dalmatian coast is now Croatia but then was under Austrian sovereignty after the fall of Venetian republic in 1797.

Dalmatia was the only habitat of the Marasca cherry until well into the 20th century. This bitter tasting cherry is ideal for liqueur production and for centuries the farmers around Zara produced a macerated 'rose water' (rosolio maraschino) from the cherry for which the town was famous. Luxardo's wife, Maria Canevari, was interested in this liqueur, and began making it at home. So regarded was her product that in 1821 her husband, Girolamo, founded a distillery in Zara to mass-produce it.

Girolamo became the largest liqueur producer in the region and he exported his brand of Maraschino to markets worldwide. The carrier doves, which he used for sending messages, became a mark of the company and still feature on bottles today. When Girolamo died (aged 81) in 1865, his son, Nicolo, took over the business.

In 1913 the 3rd generation Michelangelo Luxardo built a new distillery, one of the largest in the entire Austro-Hungarian Empire. At the end of the First World War, Zara was incorporated into the Kingdom of Italy as 85% of its population were Italians.

The company prospered until the Second World War when after repeated Anglo-American bombing raids during 1943-44 the city and the distillery was almost completely destroyed. The German troops withdrew and followed the occupation by Tito's communist partisans. The majority of the surviving Italian population fled into exile but many were killed by the partisans. Sadly the unlucky ones included Pietro Luxardo as well as Nicolo II and his wife who were drowned in the Adriatic by Tito's forces.

Giorgio, the only surviving fourth generation brother, with the help of Nicolo III (the young fifth generation) temporarily refounded the business at Venice before Giorgio found the perfect location in Torreglia, Padova. Here on the Euganean Hills the climate is ideal to grow Marasca cherries and so it is here that in 1947 they planted the first orchard. Today that orchard boasts 20,000 cherry trees and is where the family-owned business still continues to operate.

Luxardo Maraschino is aged for two years in white Finnish ashwood vats before being put in bottles encased in hand-plaited straw - originally to make transportation safe and now a trade mark exported to over 60 countries.
Taste: An almost smoky, nutty nose leads to a silky palate with hints of dark chocolate and vanilla; trace of orange marmalade and subtle cherry notes. White chocolate cherry finish.

Luxardo Sambuca dei Cesari®

www.luxardo.it
Traditionally all the countries of the Mediterranean basin boast an anise based national liqueur and Italy is no exception.

Luxardo Sambuca is a sweet and strong liqueur made from green Sicilian aniseed.

The essential oils of the star anise are extracted by steam distilling and are soluble in pure alcohol. Uniquely, Luxardo's Sambuca is macerated in pure spirit and matured in Finnish ash wood vats.
Taste: Clean rich aniseed palate that's lighter and less syrupy than some other sambuca brands. Subtle hints of lemon zest.

Lychee Liqueur
Native to South China, the lychee's distinctive floral, fragrant flavour has a luscious delicacy, which is distinctly Asian. Revered for over two thousand years as a symbol of love and romance, in part for its flavour and in part for its similarity to the heart, lychee is making waves around the world.

Macchu La Diablada Pisco®

www.macchupisco.com

Peruvian Melanie de Trindade-Asher was studying at Harvard Business School when she decided to apply her education toward establishing her own brand of premium Pisco - the result being Macchu Pisco. Her first bottling of just 500 bottles, 'Poción 9', was a blend of carefully selected Peruvian Pisco. Distillation to Melanie's own specification did not commence until 2004 when 6,000 bottles where produced.

The Macchu 'La Diablada' blend is named after an Andean dance that re-enacts a legendary fight between angels and demons. The distillate of three different varieties of Muscat grapes is used in the blend - Italia, Moscatel and Quebranta. Each is single pot distilled from the first pressing with the run from each batch distillation averaging 42%abv. The resulting spirits are rested in oak casks for four months before blending and bottling. During this aging process, the spirit loses 2%abv so no dilution is necessary, or allowed according to Peruvian law, to reach bottling strength. It should be noted that no sugar is added either.

Madeira

Madeira is a fortified wine from the semi-tropical island of the same name in the Atlantic, 600km off the coast of Morocco. The island is only 57km east to west and 23km north to south and is divided into two halves by a mountain range that forms its backbone.

Until the opening of the Suez Canal, Madeira enjoyed a strategic position on the Atlantic shipping lanes and during the 17th and 18th Centuries ships sailing from Britain carried the local wine as ballast. The wine was slowly warmed during the voyage through the tropics concentrating the flavour and developing a mellow, "baked" flavour. This unusual, richly flavoured wine became popular so the ships' effects were replicated on the island using a heating process called 'estufagem'.

The principle grape varieties used to make Madeira are Malmsey (traditionally known as Malvasia), Bual, Verdelho, Sercial (all white grapes) and Tinta Negra Mole (the only red variety). Ninety percent of all Madeira is now made from Tinta Negra Mole, which have a thin skin and so are soft to touch, hence the term 'mole', which means 'soft'.

Better quality Madeira is usually made from a single grape variety (one of the four 'noble' grapes, rather than Tinta Negra). The grape from which it originated is shown on the label, which also serves to indicate the style. Other less common grape varieties include Terrantez and Bastardo - both now rare and hard to find wines.

Traditionally, estufagem took place in large lofts called 'canteiros', which were designed to soak up the island's strong sunlight. It now more usually takes place in special lodges called 'estufas', which use the circulation of hot water to heat the wines. Madeira termed 'canteiro' are aged only in the cask and do not undergo artificial heating. After estufagem the wine continues to mature in conventional, relatively cool warehousing.

Madeira's age is counted from when the estufagem is completed. The fortified wine starts its ageing process at around 17%abv, but as it ages it loses water due to evaporation, meaning that the relative alcohol content is increased as is the concentration of flavours in the wine. Some well-aged vintage Madeira can be over 20%abv with very concentrated flavours.

All Madeiras are aged in wood and are normally bottled ready for sale when 3, 5, 10 or 15 years old, depending on their inherent quality and ageing potential. The finest Madeiras will become vintages and are made from the best wines of an excellent year.

'Colheitas' are wines from a single good year and can be made from a single grape variety or a blend of several. Wines labelled as colheita (meaning harvest) must have spent a minimum of five years ageing in oak casks.
Vintage Madeiras are only made from a single grape variety and must remain in the cask for a minimum of 20 years, after which they spend two further years in the bottle prior to sale.

Madeiras aged for five years or more are known as Reserves; ten-year-old Madeiras are termed Special Reserve; while Exceptional Reserves are aged for a minimum of fifteen years.

Apart from those selected for 'vintage' or 'colheita' bottling, almost all Madeiras are blends and the winemaker must use his experience to achieve a blend to match the house style.

There are four predominant styles of Madeira available. While all styles of Madeira go well with dried fruit, certain styles are better accompaniments to particular foods than others.

Sercial (Dry) – An invigorating pale dry wine with appealing citrus flavours.
Verdelho (Medium Dry) - Soft and sweet, honeyed, often with smoky hints. In the US, medium dry Madeira is traditionally referred to as 'Rainwater' while Verdelho's market share in Britain is only 1%.
Bual (Medium Sweet) - Rich wine with raisiny fruit, a full flavour and a smoky complexity.
Malmsey (Sweet) – This sweet (or as the Madeira shippers would prefer, 'rich') dessert wine is a soft, honeyed, fragrant after dinner drink. The term 'Malmsey' is an Anglicisation of the Portuguese 'Malvasia'. This style has been popular in Britain for several centuries and more than three-quarters of the Madeira sold in the UK today is Malmsey.

All Madeira will keep for up to ten years after opening without the need for vacuum sealing. The estufagem process and the wine's high acidity means Madeira does not deteriorate due to contact with oxygen, so it's possible to enjoy a bottle over a ten year period by simply replacing the cork each time and standing the bottle back on the shelf.

Malibu Coconut®

www.malibu-rum.com

A rum based coconut flavoured liqueur. Malibu is based on rectified white Barbados rum blended with natural coconut extracts and presented in a iconic opaque white bottle with the palm tree logo, sadly much copied by other 'me-too' coconut flavoured rum liqueurs.

Malibu was created in the 1980s and is produced in Barbados at the West Indies Rum Distillery which was established in 1893. The Twelve Island Shipping Company named on the bottle was responsible for the early distribution of Malibu in the dozen islands of the lower Antilles and later the rest of the world.

Malibu is based on a triple distilled light-bodied rum produced from molasses using specially designed column stills at the West Indies Rum Distillery in Barbados. This white rum is then blended with natural coconut extract and sugar to produce the world's best-known coconut-flavoured rum.

Mandarine Napoléon Grande Liqueur Impériale®

www.mandarinenapoleon.com

Mandarine Napoléon is claimed to have been created in 1892 by Antoine-François de Fourcroy, a chemist and son of a pharmacist who served as member of Emperor Napoléon's State Council. Antoine had frequent meetings with Emperor Napoléon and used to make notes about these meetings in his private diary. One such entry pertains to the recipe of Mandarine Napoléon liqueur, which it is believed Antoine created especially for the Emperor based on aged cognacs and exotic mandarin oranges. Mandarins, often known as tangerines, had been introduced into Europe from China in the 18th century and grew particularly well in Corsica, Bonaparte's birthplace.

During the late 19th century, a Belgian chemist interested in the work of Fourcroy discovered the ingredients to Napoléon's liqueur in Fourcroy's diary. This chemist, Louis Schmidt had a small distillery in Brussels and in 1892 decided to create a liqueur based on the recipe. Production was continued by members of Mr Schmidt's family until shortly after the Second World War, when they closed their distillery in Brussels. Members of the Fourcroy Company, which had coincidentally been in the wine and spirit trade since 1862 took over production of the liqueur. Thus, Mandarine Napoléon was once again connected with the Fourcroy family.

This liqueur's flavour comes from Mediterranean mandarin peel, which is macerated in alcohol with a secret combination of twenty other botanicals (including green tea, clover, coriander and cumin) before being triple-distilled. The distillate is then aged for a period of at least three years before being blended with cognac.

Mango

Our recommendation: Boiron Mango puree
The mango is part of the cashew family and nicknamed "apple of the tropics". It has been cultivated in India for at least four thousand years and Indian varieties remain the best - especially the widely available, kidney-shaped Alphonso, which has highly perfumed orange to yellow flesh and a smooth,

almost custard-like consistency. The best variety from South America is 'Mango de Azúcar' (sugar mango).

There are over a thousand varieties of this fruit, which can vary from 2 to 10 inches in length and from 4oz to 4lbs in weight. To check whether a mango is ripe, squeeze the fruit (it should give slightly), look for black freckles on the skin and check for a rich, honeyed scent. The shade of the skin is irrelevant as mangos come in many different colours.

Mangos are packed with vitamins A, B, C and E and are one of the higher energy fruits. They mix well with apple, lemon and lime, as well as dairy products.

The best way to use mango in cocktails is as a puree. Buy a commercially made mango puree (we recommend 'Boiron' frozen purees) or slice the fruit lengthways on each side of the central flat stone. Scoop the flesh from the fruit slices into a blender or food processor and blend. Add approximately 5% sugar syrup and blend some more. Decant into a squeezy plastic bottle and store in the refrigerator until required.

Maple Syrup
The boiled-down sap of the North American sugar maple, authentic maple syrup has a complex sweetness appreciated all over the world. A maple tree needs to be about 40 years old and have a diameter of around 10 inches before it can be tapped. Each tree produces several gallons of sap each year, but it takes 40 gallons of sap to produce one gallon of syrup and consequently the price is high.

Please be wary of synthetic imitations, which are nowhere near as good as the real thing. Maple syrups are graded A or B – grade B, which is dark and very strongly flavoured, is sometimes known as 'cooking syrup'.

The A grade syrups are divided into categories, according to their hue and level of flavour: 'light amber', 'medium amber' and 'dark amber'. Confusingly, Canadian and different US states apply slightly different names to their different grades. There is no difference in quality between these grades but there is a definite difference in flavour.

Maple syrup should be stored in the refrigerator and consumed within a month of opening. To use in a cocktail, simply pour into a thimble measure and follow the recipe.

Maraschino Cherries
Strictly speaking the term 'maraschino cherries' should only be applied to marasca cherries preserved in maraschino. A liqueur produced by distilling the fermented juice of the same species of cherries, a small variety of the European wild cherry indigenous to the Dalmatian Mountains.

However, in many countries including the UK, maraschino cherries are often prepared from the Royal Anne variety of cherry and artificially coloured and flavoured and packaged in flavoured sugar syrup rather than maraschino liqueur. Properly these should be labelled 'imitation maraschino cherries' or simply 'artificially coloured and flavoured preserved cherries'.

Maraschino Syrup
The sweet syrup from a jar of maraschino cherries.

Maraschino Liqueur

Our recommendation: Luxardo Maraschino
Pronounced 'Mara-Sk-Eno', this is a clear Italian liqueur distilled from the Marasca sour cherry and aged in ashwood. The bottle is traditionally encased in straw.

What we now recognise as Maraschino liqueur has been produced since medieval times originated in North and Middle Dalmatia, particularly around the town of Zadar in what is now Croatia. The liqueur is made from a particular variety of cherry, the Prunus Cerasus Marasca. This is not indigenous to Europe and exactly how it came to Croatia from Central Asia is unknown. Marasca cherries are much more bitter and less juicy than their Western European and North American counterparts.

Early 16th Century Monks of the Dominican Monastery are credited with creating the liqueur and giving it the name 'Rosolj' from the Latin 'Ros Solis' - The Sun Rose. It was not until a century later that the Zadar Italians gave this liqueur the name we are familiar with today, 'Maraschino'.

Marie Brizard Anisette®

www.mariebrizard.com

Fable has it that on 11 January 1750, at 8.30 in the morning, at the port of Bordeaux, Marie Brizard, then aged 36 discovered Thomas, a West Indian sailor from the ship Intrépide who was lying on the ground stricken with a severe fever. She took him in and nursed him. In gratitude he gave her the recipe to this aniseed liqueur.

Five years later in partnership with her nephew Jean-Baptiste Roger, the Marie Brizard Company was established to produce the liqueur, which was named Marie Brizard Anisette. Another nephew, Captain Paul Brizard, supplied the eleven plants, spices and fruits from around the world that flavour the liqueur. These include green aniseed, cinnamon, oranges, lemons, angelica, iris, coriander and cloves.

Marie Brizard Anisette is still made to the original recipe in Bordeaux. A silver labelled dry version launched in 2001 has less sugar but consequently also lacks the flavour delivery of the original.

Marsala
Marsala is a sweet, amber coloured fortified wine which takes its name from its home, the port of Marsala in Sicily.

Marsala was first made in 1773 by a Liverpool merchant, John Woodhouse, who settled in the port of Marsala and began fortifying the local wine in an attempt to emulate Sherry. But it was Admiral Horatio Nelson who popularised it. His victuallers bought Marsala as an alternative to rum for the Navy's Mediterranean fleet before the battle of the Nile in 1798.

Nelson was given a vineyard in Marsala by the King of the Two Sicilies in thanks for his protection from Napoleon, and persuaded the British Admiralty that his Marsala should be used to toast victories. Ironically, it was this Marsala that British sailors were drinking to the victory at Trafalgar in 1805 as Nelson lay dying on H.M.S Victory.

Marsala is made from a blend of wines – usually from three local grape varieties (Grillo, Cataratto and Inzolia). The blend is fortified with neutral grape brandy then sweetened, either with boiled down must (mosto cotto) or with grape juice whose fermentation has been stopped with spirit (mistela). Older Marsala is aged using the Solera system. Marsala production is strictly controlled by the Italian government controlled DOC (Denominazione di Origine Controllata), which determines the areas in which it can be made.

Martini Rosso®

www.martini.com

In 1847 several Italian businessmen started a company called 'Michel Agnel Re and Banding' based in Pessione, near Turin, producing spirits, vermouth and bitters. Those interested in dynasties may be interested to learn that the Agnel in this company was the grandfather of Giovanni Agnelli, the founder of Fiat.

In the 1850s Alessandro Martini became a commercial director in the company, joining the board in 1863 along with Luigi Rossi and Teofilo Sola. The company name was changed to 'Martini, Sola & Cia. The importance of the 1863 date is commemorated on the modern day bottle as this is the year Rossi, a wine expert, created the vermouth which we know today as Martini Rosso. They started exporting vermouth around the world with New York receiving its first shipment in 1867.

The company prospered and when Sola died in 1879 his sons sold their shares and consequently the company was renamed Martini & Rossi after the two remaining directors. Martini Extra Dry was launched in 1900 and Martini Bianco a few years later.

When Alessandro Martini died in 1905, Luigi Rossi's three sons inherited the company. In 1922 both the company and brand name was simplified to 'Martini'. The exception being the United States where due to Martini already being identified with the cocktail the brand remains Martini & Rossi to this day.

The same image now embossed on the bottle is used throughout the range of vermouths sold under the Martini brand name. This depicts Vittoria, the mythological Roman goddess of victory, blowing her trumpet over the flags of conquered nations, and signifies the many countries where Martini is sold. Also shown is the bull of Turin, the city's coat of arms and the Italian royal coat of arms.

Martinique Agricole Rum
Correctly termed 'rhum agricole' this is made from fresh pressed sugar cane juice rather than the more usual molasses, a by-product of refining sugar. The Caribbean island of Martinique has seven distilleries producing rhum agricole and the island is by far the best known region for production of this style of rum.

Martinique rhum (French spelling) received its Appellation d'Origine Contrôlée (A.O.C.) designation in 1996 so production is strictly regulated by the French government. The rules allow the use of 12 different types of sugar cane but blue cane has the highest sugar content so considered premium.

Rhum agricole cannot be distilled to a higher strength than 75% abv so maintains much of the sugar cane character. If the distillate is to be bottled as 'blanc rhum' (white rum) it must be rested for at least 3 months before bottling, usually in stainless steel vats but often in old oak barrels, which due to their age contribute little flavour or colour to the rum.

Distillate destined to become 'ambre rhum' (amber rum) must be aged in oak barrels (usually previously used for American whiskey) for at least 18 months. 'Vieux Rhum' (old rum) must be aged a minimum of 3 years but confusingly the initials 'VS' also denote a 3 year old rum. 'VSOP' denotes 4 years and 'XO' 6 years. Rhums labelled 'hors d'age' must be aged for at least 7 years. The A.O.C. also permits Rhums from exceptional years to be labelled with their vintage date.

Martinique Sugar Cane Syrup

This is quite simply genuine sugar cane syrup. Sugar cane is squeezed to extract is rich juice which is then filtered and bottled.

Matúsalem Oloroso Dulce®

www.gonzalezbyass.es

Pronounced 'Ollow-Ross-O' 'Dul-Che' and part of the González Byass 'Very Rare Solera' range, this Rich Oloroso is made from Palomino Fino blended over many years with wines from Pedro Ximénez grapes.

The biblical character of Methuselah (Matúsalem in Spanish) lived to the ripe old age of 969 years and like its namesake, this Sherry is the oldest in the González Byass 'Rare Old Soleras' range, although by law it's only allowed to state 30 years on the label. Serve after a meal or as an accompaniment to mince pies, Christmas pudding or Stilton cheese.

Menthe Pastille®

www.giffard.com

More than a century ago, Emile Giffard was a dispensing chemist in Angers. Whilst working late one night a patron from the hotel next door arrived on his doorstep complaining of indigestion. She asked if Emile could concoct a drink from mint tablets. He ground the tablets into a fine powder, to which he added some spirit. The mixture cured her indigestion and left Emile with a great idea. He set about formulating a liqueur and imported peppermint leaves from England, which he used to distil a clear liqueur he called 'Menthe Pastille'. He began to market the liqueur, which proved an instant success, leading him to establish his own distillery.

Menthe Pastille is still made to the original recipe at a distillery run by Emile's great grandson, Bruno Giffard, who also produces a range of over 30 different liqueurs including blue curaçao, apricot brandy and crème de banane.

Mezcal

The word mezcal originates from the Aztec language and refers to a potent Mexican spirit made from the maguey plant. The main difference between products labelled tequila and those labelled mezcal is that tequila is distilled in and around the northern state of Jalisco, while mezcal is distilled in the south near the gulf of Mexico, in and around the state of Oaxaca (pronounced 'Wo-Ha-Ka').

Mezcal is distilled from the fermented juice of the maguey (or meztl) plant, a member of the agave family of succulents which have been cultivated in Mexico for millennia. Since Mezcal was granted its Denominación de Origin status in 2005, 18 types of agave collectively known as 'maguey' may be used for making mezcal. These are cultivated and harvested in a similar manner to the Blue Webber Agave used in tequila production. (See 'tequila'.)

However, most mezcals, unlike most tequilas, are made from piñas which have been roasted, not baked. It is this heating process which gives mezcal its distinctive smoky flavour.

The piñas, which tend to be smaller than that of the blue agave (weighing 65-100lb), are cut into halves and thrown into an oven, which is basically a large hole in the ground, lined with fireproof bricks and preheated with wood.

The hole is covered with maguey leaves, stones and clay and is left to slowly cook the piña for two to three days.

After cooking, the piña is crushed in order to separate the pulp from the fibre. The product is then steeped in pure water. Airborne yeasts start fermentation, which lasts several days and produces a 'mosto', vaguely similar to the pulque mentioned above. The fermented liquid is then distilled to around 43%-46% abv. Most mezcal destined for the domestic market is single distilled, while that made for the export market is usually distilled twice. Unlike tequila, products labelled mezcal can only be exported in bottles and not in bulk.

Some bottles of mezcal contain a 'gusano', which means worm. These creatures are actually moth larvae of the Night Butterfly. The white larva emerges from a small egg left by its parent moth on the leaves of the maguey and burrows into its heart where it is protected from predators while it grows. Once mature, it transforms into a chrysalis and then a moth - unless it is captured and pickled in mezcal. The red larva lives in the roots of the maguey. Mezcal 'worms' are falsely reputed to have hallucinogenic properties, so its addition to mezcal to add extra flavour and 'something special' is hardly surprising. (As mezcal can also be spelt mescal, many have also wrongly assumed it contains the hallucinogenic drug mescaline.

You will sometimes find mezcal with a small cotton bag tied to the neck of the bottle. Inside the bag is Gusano salt made up from crushed dried worms, salt and chilli powder. A pinch of this powder should be sprinkled onto the surface of the mezcal before it is drunk.

Be warned: As a rule of thumb I would avoid any mescal so embellished as the better quality mescals are usually sold without a worm inside.

Midori®

www.midori-world.com

Midori is flavoured with extracts of honeydew melons and can rightly claim to be the original melon liqueur. When Midori was launched in 1978, John Travolta attended the launch party held at New York's famed Studio 54 nightclub.

'Midori' is Japanese for green and this liqueur is fittingly vibrant green in colour. It is owned by Suntory, Japan's leading producer and distributor of alcoholic beverages.

Milk

We recommend homogenised and pasteurised semi-skimmed milk (1.5 – 1.8% fat). As with all fresh products, please store in a refrigerator and pay particular attention to sell by dates.

Mint

This perennial herb grows in most temperate parts of the world. The varieties which non-botanists call 'mint' belong to the genus mentha. Mentha species include apple mint, curly mint, pennyroyal, peppermint, pineapple mint, spearmint and water or bog mint.

Spearmint or garden mint is the most common kind and you may well find it growing in your garden. It has a fruity aroma and flavour and, like peppermint, has bright green leaves and purple flowers. Spearmint is generally used for cooking savouries, such as mint sauce.

Peppermint is the second most common kind. The leaves produce a pungent oil which is used to flavour confectionery, desserts and liqueurs such as crème de menthe.

The main visible difference between peppermint and spearmint is in the leaves. Spearmint leaves have a crinkly surface and seem to grow straight out of the stem, while peppermint leaves have smoother surfaces and individual stems. Peppermint can also tend towards purple.

Which type of mint you choose to use in drinks is largely a matter of personal taste: some recommend mentha nemorosa for Mojitos.

Growing your own mint, be it spearmint, peppermint or otherwise is easy – but be sure to keep it in a container or it will overrun your garden. Either buy a plant or place a sprig in a glass of water. When it roots, pot it in a large, shallow tub with drainage holes. Place bricks under the tub to prevent the roots from growing through the holes.

To keep harvested mint at optimum freshness, first soak in cold water to clean and restore. Then store in an airtight container and with damp paper towels at base and top and one interleaved in middle of box to help maintain moisture. Fresh mint prepared and stored in this way in a refrigerator will last up to a week.

Mint leaves have long been used in cocktails. The Mojito and Mint Julep are two of the best known. Generally, you should muddle the mint lightly in the glass or shaker base, aiming to bruise it. If you pulverise the mint, both stems and leaves will release bitter juices and spoil your drink. Many argue that simply shaking with ice is enough to tease the flavour out of mint and that muddling is unnecessary.

Montilla

A fortified wine from the Southern Spanish province of Cordoba, particularly the town from which it takes its name. Originally part of the Sherry region, the soils are similar, but being further inland, the climate has more extremes than that of Sherry. Officially known as Montilla-Moriles, the main difference between Montilla wines and those of Sherry, is that they have naturally high alcohol levels without fortification - in fact the addition of grape brandy is rare for Montilla wines. Montilla is still the main production area for Pedro Ximénez grapes used to sweeten sherry and originally leant its name to the Sherry term Amontillado.

In the UK these wines tend to be sold from supermarket shelves as cheap alternatives to sherry. This is because the duty on alcoholic products increases considerably above 15% abv and Montillas can be produced between 14-16% abv. Not surprisingly almost all Montilla sold in the UK is below 15%. This tax break also affects the labelling of Montilla in the UK – while the same styles are found as those in sherry, to be labelled Fino, the Montilla must be over 15% and to be Amontillado or Oloroso over 16%. Thus in the UK they tend to be termed simply dry, medium and cream.

Myer's Planter's Punch®

Produced since 1879, this is a blend of Jamaican rums distilled using traditional pot stills. All the rums in the blend are aged in American white oak casks for a minimum of five years to produce this rich, nutty brown rum. Myer's is still presented in its original oval shaped bottle and classic livery.

Nocello Liqueur de Noix®

www.toschi.it

Nocello is a walnut and hazelnut-flavoured liqueur from Italy produced by the Toschi Vignola s.r.l. company of Savignano sul Panaro, Province of Modena, Emilia-Romagna, Italy. Its packaging is made all the more distinctive by the walnut glued to the top of each cork stopper.

It is perhaps not surprising that the best-known walnut liqueur should come from Italy - after all the ancient Romans highly regarded the walnut, considering it a portrait of the human brain. The outer husk was the scalp, the shell the protective skull, and the convoluted nut itself represented the two hemispheres of the brain.

Nocello was first produced by Monasteries in the Middle Ages as a medicinal elixir. According to superstition, the green walnuts must be picked on Midsummer's Day. The harvested walnuts are shelled and then soaked in oak casks of neutral alcohol on their shells for two years. The infused alcohol is then redistilled and herbs and spices added

Noé Pedro Ximénez®

www.gonzalezbyass.es

Pronounced 'No-E' 'Him-En-Eth, this Sherry is part of the González Byass 'Very Rare Solera' range, made purely from Pedro Ximénez grapes picked and spread out on grass mats to dry in the sun in the traditional 'soleo' manner. Noé is aged in oak casks for over 30 years.

According to the bible, Noah, Noé in Spanish, lived to be 950 which made him just slightly junior to Methuselah. (Hope they had a good pension plan.) This Sherry is named after the biblical hero and is the sweetest in the González Byass range.

Noilly Prat Blanc®

www.noillyprat.com

At the turn of the 18th century, Joseph Noilly was a herbalist making both perfumes and liqueurs and also a wine merchant in Lyons. After some experimentation in 1813 he came up with the recipe for a new, wine based apéritif,

the first dry vermouth to compete with the sweet vermouth styles being produced in Turin. Vermouths were fashionable at the time due to their perceived health benefits and Joseph sought to capitalise on this.

Joseph sourced most of the ingredients he used to produce his new white-wine aperitif then simply called Noilly from Marseilles, where in 1837 an eccentric English traveller called Claudius Prat (1814-1859) started to work for him. Prat would go on to be a major influence on the company.

Meanwhile, in 1843 Louis Noilly (1801-1865) took over the running of his father's thriving business and relocated the company to Marseilles on the Côte d'Azur, renaming the company Louis Noilly & Cie. Afraid of losing the secret to producing his aperitif, Louis sought to separate the various processes, so in 1850 he moved the maturation of the base wines to Marseillan, a small fishing village on the Etang de Thau, an inland lake on the French Mediterranean coast southwest of Montpellier. Marseillan was a natural location due to its proximity to the famous wine producing villages of Pinet and Pomérols, in the white wine producing area of the Languedoc, a region otherwise associated with red wines.

Louis had a beautiful young daughter, Joséphine Noilly, who fell in love with Claudius Prat. Louis made his new son-in-law a partner in 1855 and the business became known as Noilly Prat & Cie. Knowing the story behind the brand name it becomes obvious that Noilly Prat is correctly pronounced as an English 'Prat' with a 't', not the 'Praah' used by some uniformed Francophiles. Joséphine remained a director of the firm after the death of both her husband and father, when the company was run by her two children. Vicomtesse Vigier, Joséphine's granddaughter joined the firm in 1939 and continued to run the business until she died in 1970 when she was well over 100 years old – hence the stories of the revivifying and restorative qualities of Noilly Prat abound. In 1973 the business was sold due to there being no heirs and the whole production process, with only the exception of bottling, moved to Marseillan. Noilly Prat is now part of the Bacardi-Martini Corporation.

Noilly Prat is based on light, fruity Languedoc wine made from three grape varieties; Picoul and Bourett - which are dry and high in acidity along with the fuller flavoured Clairett grape. These wines are fortified to 16% abv and aged in 10,600 gallon/40,000 litre Canadian oak vats for eight months before being transferred into smaller 160 gallon/600 litre casks.

These casks are then placed in L'enclos (the enclosure) a large yard where thousands of casks are left in the open air for a further year where the effect of oak casks, cold winters and hot Mediterranean summers combined with the sea air to give the wine an amber hue and distinctive slightly salty taste. This process was introduced to replicate the temperature changes and atmosphere once experienced by wines as they were transported on slow sailing ships. The importance of this incidental aging was only recognised when faster steam ships were introduced in the 19th century and the fine French wines lost their rich flavour.

Locally, this aged wine is known as 'vin cuit' (cooked wine) and the controlled oxidisation of wine is a process some call 'maderization'. Visit Google and take a look at satellite images of Marseillan and you will see the rows of barrels in the L'enclos which boundaries Quai de Toulon and Rue du Canal.

The wine is then transferred to large 530 gallon/2,000 litre vats where it is blended with a sweet muscat mistelle (grape juice where fermentation has been stopped by the addition of alcohol) and an in-house distilled essence of lemon and raspberry. To each cask a secret 44lb/20kg blend of dried botanicals is added. This is known to include: French camomile flowers, coriander, teasel, Egyptian cornflower, bitter orange peel, quinine, orris root, and nutmeg.

The blend is stirred daily by hand for three weeks before being filtered and left to rest for a further six weeks before final chill-filtration and bottling. The whole process takes two years.

Ocean Spray Classic®

www.oceanspray.com

Cranberries are native to North America and are grown in rich acid peat bogs. The fields are flooded during harvesting when large machines, fondly known as egg beaters, release the berries from the vines. Air pockets in the fruit allow them to bob to the surface to create a stunning crimson carpet. You can tell when a cranberry is good enough to eat because it bounces – all part of the quality test.

Cranberries are rich in unique antioxidants which help protect you inside

and are best known as a natural remedy for a number of infections. Some brands of cranberry only contain a tiny proportion of cranberry concentrate and consequently taste weak and sometimes far too sweet. Ocean Spray Cranberry Classic and Cranberry Select contain a high proportion of natural cranberry juice, providing the authentic taste of the fruit. Ocean Spray is an agricultural co-operative, formed in 1930 by just three cranberry growers and now has more than 650 growers

Ocean Spray White Cranberry®

www.oceanspray.com
Ocean Spray White cranberry juice drinks are made with natural white cranberries which are harvested in late summer before they fully develop: the red are harvested in the autumn. This early harvesting not only affects the colour, but means the berries' flavour is milder and less tart than the more familiar red cranberry juice.

Opal Nera®

www.opalnera.com
In 1989 Alessandro Francoli was on his honeymoon in America, where he took time to present his company's traditional Italian grappa and sambucas to a potential buyer. He noticed the interest the buyer showed in a coffee sambuca. This dark sambuca set Alessandro, a trained chemist, thinking. On his return home he experimented with different flavours combined with traditional sambuca and created this black coloured version with a hint of lemon. The inspiration for the colour came from the rich purple-black colour of the elderberries, the key ingredient of all Sambucas, and the colour inspired the suitably dark name.

Opal Nera's seductive and unmistakable colour comes from macerating the purple-black skins of the elderberries.

Orange Bitters

Our recommendation: Angostura orange bitters
A term for orange-flavoured bitter liqueurs and aperitifs made bitter by gentian, quinine and other herbal roots. Orange bitters date back to the early 1900s reaching the height of their popularity in the early 20th century so consequently are commonly found in cocktail recipes from that period.

Sadly, this key cocktail ingredient is hard to find in modern liquor stores. There are a number of brands that profess to be 'orange bitters' but many hardly taste of orange and are more like sweet liqueurs than bitters.

Orange Curaçao Liqueur
Curaçao liqueurs are traditionally made from the dried peel of the small bitter Curaçao orange, named for the island of Curaçao. As Curaçao was a Dutch colony, it supplied oranges to the liqueur makers of Holland, but Curaçao is now also produced from bitter oranges of other origins.

Curaçao can be clear, blue, red and orange. The colours are purely decorative and were developed for the cocktail barman, though the flavour of each colour may differ slightly according to different producers.

Curacao is a generic name for an orange-flavoured liqueur produced by many different companies. Only one brand is actually distilled on the Caribbean island of Curacao. This bottling is called Senior's Curacao of Curacao and is available in a few different colours, though the sweet orange flavour remains constant throughout the range.

Orange Flower Water
Orange flower water, or orange blossom water, is made by macerating bitter orange blossoms in water and then distilling the broth. It is most often used in Middle Eastern cooking, though has established itself as a cocktail ingredient through its inclusion in the Ramos Gin Fizz.

Orange Infused Vodka
Buy a proprietary brand or orange-flavoured vodka or make your own orange infused vodka:

1. Scrub two large oranges to clean and remove any wax coating.
2. Peel the zest from oranges using a knife or potato peeler. Be careful not to cut into white pith: alternatively trim off white pith from peel.
3. Feed orange zest into an empty and clean Ketel One Vodka bottle.
4. Fill bottle containing orange zest with Ketel One Vodka using a funnel to help pour from new bottle.
5. Replace cap securely and shake.
6. Leave to infuse for at least a week, turning daily.

Oranges & Orange Juice
The orange is now so commonly available in our shops and markets that it's hard to believe it was once an exotic and expensive luxury. Although native to China, its name originates from 'naranga' in the old Indian language of Sanskrit. Oranges now come mainly from Algeria, Australia, Cyprus, Israel, Italy, Morocco, Sicily, South Africa, Spain, Tunisia, Turkey and the United States.

There are many different types of orange but the best ones for bartending purposes are Washington Navels, which are in season from the end of October. These have a firm, rough skin perfect for cutting twists from and are juicy and slightly sour.

Orange juice is high in antioxidants and vitamin C. A small glass of freshly squeezed orange juice contains all the vitamin C an adult needs in a day. To juice simply cut in half and juice with a hand press. If using an electric spinning citrus juicer take care not to grind the pith. Be sure to strain the juice prior to measuring into your cocktails.

Oranges are so widely available and easy to juice that there is little reason to buy packaged juice from the supermarket. If you really must, always buy freshly squeezed, refrigerated juice.

Orange marmalade (medium cut)
English marmalade is a sweet citrus fruit preserve with a tangy, bitter aftertaste. American marmalade is often missing this tang. Made from fruit, sugar, water and zest the cut refers to the amount of fruit peel within the preserve.

Ouzo 12®

www.ouzo12.com
The first bottled Ouzo and still the world's best selling brand - Ouzo 12 was first produced by the Kaloyannis brothers in 1880 and its name comes from one of the first batches produced. It was the blend in cask number twelve that the brothers agreed would be their house style.

Ouzo 12 is made by double distilling grape alcohol with anise, cardamom, cinnamon, coriander and nutmeg.

Pacharán Liqueur

Our recommendation: Zoco
A digestif from the northern province of Navarra in Spain. Pacharán is made by macerating sloe berries or 'pacharanes' in alcohol to which aniseed essence is added. Some brands also add other flavourings such as cinnamon and coffee.

Parfait Amour Liqueur
A French, lilac coloured curaçao liqueur flavoured with rose petals, vanilla pods and almonds. The name means 'perfect love'.

Passion Fruit

Our recommendation: Boiron passion fruit puree
The fruit of the passion flower (Passiflora), a climbing plant which is native to South America but grown around the world, is an ugly, spherical outgrowth about the size of a hen's egg.

Known in Spanish as 'granadilla' ('little pomegranate'), the passion fruit has a thick, leathery, yellowish-green or brownish-red skin, which is smooth and shiny when unripe and pockmarked, almost wrinkly when ripe. The inside yields intensely flavoured, slightly acidic, yellow flesh with small, edible, crunchy black seeds. Select heavy fruits as the light ones tend to be dried out and lacking in juice.

Preparation: Cut the fruit in half with a sharp knife and scoop the flesh out of the shell into your shaker (or simply push flesh out by squeezing the fruit half between your fingers). If you are making a blended drink it is advisable to pass the flesh through a sieve to strain out the seeds before combining it with other ingredients. However, this isn't necessary with shaken drinks, as the seeds should be removed when the drink is fine strained into the glass.

Alternatively use a commercially available puree such as Boiron Fruit Purees.

Passion Fruit Sugar Syrup
Passion fruit syrup is sugar syrup flavoured with passion fruit juice. Make your own or buy commercially available products such as Monin or Giffard brands.

Passoã®

www.passoa.com

The passion fruit was first discovered in South America, during the colonisation by Spanish missionaries in the 1500s. They first noticed the amazing flowers of the fruit in the jungle. Nobody knows exactly why it became known as the passion fruit. Was it because the crown-like flower reminded people of the thornbush of Christ's Passion? Or because of its supposed qualities as an aphrodisiac?

Passoã is a passion fruit flavoured liqueur launched in the Netherlands in 1986. The matt black Passoã bottle features a brightly coloured tropical motif of palm trees suggesting its tropical fruit taste.

Pastis

Our recommendation: Ricard

Both anis and pastis are produced by flavouring ethyl alcohol of agricultural origin with natural extracts of star anise (Lllicium verum) from Southern China and North Vietnam. There are numerous varieties of anise, notably green anise (pimpiniclum anisum) and fennel (Foeniclum vulgare) from the south of France, but star anise is considered the best for flavouring.

As well as anise (which tastes somewhat like wormwood) both anis and pastis also contain angelica and cloves. Brands may use as many as 40 other different herbs and spices, including cardamom, black and white pepper, artemisia, centaury, nutmeg and cinnamon.

According to EU law, Pastis must also contain natural extracts of liquorice root (Glycyrrhiza glabra), which implies the presence of colorants known as 'chalcones' as well as glycrrhizic acid (the active ingredient of liquorice), the minimum and maximum levels of which must be 0.05 and 0.05 grams per litre respectively.

Pastis must contain less than 100 grams of sugar per litre meaning that it is classified as a spirit and not a liqueur. Conversely, anis brands tend to have over 100 grams of sugar per litre and so are classified liqueurs.

Pastis is best served with chilled water as an aperitif. Most brands recommend one part of pastis to five parts water. The pastis should be poured into the glass, and then water that is chilled to 4°C added. The small jug of water that should be served with a glass of pastis is called a 'broc'. If ice is to be used to cool the drink then this should be added last. Ice should never be added directly to Pastis as the extreme cold will upset the delicate suspension of anise in the spirit.

Peach eau de vie (de pêche)
Ripe peaches are harvested, crushed and fermented and then distilled. Because eau de vie are not usually aged there is no colour to this spirit. Bottling happens very quickly in order to preserve the fruits original flavour.

Peach Schnapps

Our recommedation: Peach Tree peach schnapps
A clear liqueur based on neutral alcohol and flavoured with natural peach essence.

Peach Tree Peach Schnapps®

www.dekuyper.com

Peachtree schnapps is produced by DeKuyper Royal Distillers in Schiedam, Holland – a company which can trace its roots back to 1695 when Petrus de Kuyper started as a manufacturer of barrels and casks to transport beer and spirits.

In 1752 his son Jan de Kuyper took over a small distillery in Schiedam and originally made and exported Dutch genever to Europe, the UK and Canada. In 1911, they built a new distillery and began making liqueurs – which became their main line of business as genevers became less fashionable. In 1986 the right to manufacture and market DeKuyper's brands in the USA was sold to Jim Beam Brands and in 1995, after 300 years of trading, DeKuyper was given the 'Royal' title by Queen Beatrix of the Netherlands.

DeKuyper's Peachtree was originally created for the American market and is the world's best selling peach schnapps.

Peaches

Our recommendation: Boiron white peach puree

The fruit of the peach tree peach which originated in China where it has grown since the 5th century BC. The English name came from the French 'pêche' and the fruit's Latin name Prunus persica, literally Persian Plum.

Cultivated peaches are classified according to whether the flesh sticks to the stone or not and the two types can have either white or yellow flesh. Both colours often have some red on their skin. As a general rule, peaches with white flesh tend to be sweeter and less acidic than those with yellow flesh hence white peaches are preferable for cocktail use.

The lack of consistent availability of ripe white peaches means it is common practice to use a commercially made white peach puree such Boiron frozen puree.

Peanut Butter
Peanut butter was patented in Canada in 1884 by Marcellus Gilmore Edson and is described as having "a consistency like that of butter, lard or ointment". Peanuts are roasted and ground and then oil is added to create the paste. Use peanut butter as a cocktail ingredient at your own peril.

Pears

Our recommendation: Boiron pear puree

The earliest known mention of pear is in Sumeria, around 2750BC, where one was used to make a poultice, but it was almost three thousand years later that the Romans introduced the fruit to Britain.

Western varieties of pear soften when ripe and tend to have quite a grainy texture; Asian types, such as the nashi pear, are crisp when ripe. Unless otherwise stated, pear in this guide means the Western varieties. Conference is widely available and works well in cocktails.

Pears will ripen after they are picked, but spoil quickly, so care is needed in storage. The easiest way to use pear in your cocktails is as a puree (we recommend Boiron frozen purees). Alternatively extract the flavour of a pear using an electric juice extractor, blender or food processor. Surprisingly, you'll find that beautifully ripe fruits yield little and much of that is in the form of slush. Instead, look for pears which are on their way to ripeness but still have a good crunch. Remove the stalk but don't worry about peeling or removing the core. Cut the fruit into chunks small enough to push into the juicer.

Pernod Anis®

www.pernod.net

The story of Pernod starts in 1789 when Dr Pierre Ordinaire, a retired French physician living in Switzerland blended alcohol with 15 herbs including wormwood oil to create an elixir, which he called absinthe. He prescribed his pain relieving & special reviving 'absinthe elixir' in Switzerland. Ten years later, Major Dubied bought the formula and set up a absinthe factory in Couvet,

Switzerland with son-in-law, Henri-Louis Pernod. In 1805, Henri-Louis Pernod established the Pernod Fils company in Pontarlier, France to produce his absinthe named after himself.

The original absinthe, the original Pernod was created from a recipe of green anise, fennel, hyssop and the 'artemisa absinthium': the plant of absinthe. Pernod quickly gained fame as the absinthe of Parisian café society. But a prohibitionist propaganda movement which included wine makers keen to regain lost custom started a press campaign blaming absinthe abuse for causing insanity, tuberculosis and even murder. Pressure grew and on 7th January 1915 a decision to ban absinthe was passed by ministerial decree. Pernod Fils was forced to close.

Pernod Fils and Hemard Distilleries created Pernod in 1920 without using the now-notorious wormwood and so while tasting of anise it did not fall foul of the law banning absinthe. In its new guise Pernod regained its popularity. In 1926, the production centres of 'Maisons Hémard, Pernod Père et Fils et Pernod Fils Réunis' joined to be renamed later 'Etablissements Pernod'. Pernod is made from distillates of star anise and fennel, married with distillates of 14 herbs including camomile, coriander and veronica. Pernod has a low liquorice content, which sets it apart from pastises like Ricard and Pastis 51 which have a pronounced liquorice flavour.

When liquid is added to Pernod it turns milky as the essential oils and resins for an emulsion: the ethanol is not soluble, the molecules become opaque and stay in suspension in the mixer. Pernod is best served long one part Pernod to five parts mixer, typically cranberry juice, apple juice or bitter lemon.

Perrier Jouet

www.perrier-jouet.com

The Perrier family owned vines and presses within the Grands Cru regions since 1811 when the company was established taking its name from founder Pierre-Nicolas-Marie Perrier, who then added the maiden name of his wife, Ad le Jouët. The business was family owned until 1959, when it was bought out by Seagrams, then Allied Domecq and finally Pernod Ricard in 2005. There are now sixty-five hectares of vines almost entirely in Grands Crus vineyards. Perrier Jouet is made up of predominantly Chardonnay grapes, which gives freshness – though the house favours older vines which bring additional depth and structure. The red grapes used to blend are Pinot Noir and Pinot Meunier, which are also long grown on the northern Montagne de Reims. Their ripe delicacy contrasts with the fuller flavours from the white grapes grown further south.

The first vintage of Belle Epoque, a Brut style, was the 1964, released in 1969. However, the recognisable anemone-adorned Belle Epoque Perrier Jouet bottle was actually designed in 1902 by the Art Noveau artist Emile Gallé.

Peychaud's Aromatic Bitters®

www.sazerac.com

Peychaud's aromatic bitters were created by one Antoine Amedee Peychaud. His story starts in 1795 when he arrives in New Orleans as a refugee in 1795 after his father was forced to flee the island of San Domingo, where his family owned a coffee plantation, after the slaves rebelled.

Antoine grew up to become a pharmacist and bought his own Drug and Apothecary Store at what was then No. 123 Royal Street in 1834. Here he created an 'American Aromatic Bitter Cordial' and marketed it as a medicinal tonic. Such potions were fashionable at the time and there were many similar products.

Antoine also served his bitters mixed with brandy and other liquors. (It has been falsely claimed that the word 'cocktail' originated with Antoine, from a measure known as a 'coquetier' he used to prepare drinks. But it is now undisputed that the term appeared in print in an upstate New York newspaper in 1806, when Antoine was still a child.)

Antoine Peychaud advertised his bitters in local newspapers and many New Orleans bars served drinks prepared with them. One such bar was the Sazerac Coffee House at 13 Exchange Alley, owned by John B. Schiller, also the local agent for a French cognac company 'Sazerac-du-Forge et Fils' of Limoges. It was here, in 1858, that a bartender called Leon Lamothe is thought to have created the Sazerac, probably using Peychaud's aromatic

bitters, Sazerac cognac and sugar.

A decade or so later Peychaud fell upon hard times and sold his pharmacy store, along with the formula and brand name of his bitters.

Pimento Dram (Allspice)

A spicy liqueur made by steeping pimento berries in rum. Pimento Dram is a dried, unripe berry from a West Indian tree called Pimenta dioica, which is related to the eucalyptus.

Pimm's No. 1 Cup®

www.anyoneforpimms.com

James Pimm is usually credited with creating this quintessentially English tipple. He began trading as a shellfish-monger in 1823-4 on London's Lombard Street, before moving to nearby number 3 Poultry, also in the heart of the City. There he established Pimm's Oyster Warehouse. According to legend, it was here that he first served his creation, in 1840.

As so often, however, the story appears more complex. Some maintain that the true credit lies with Pimm's successor – Samuel Morey. Morey is recorded as taking out a retail liquor license in 1860, which suggests that Pimm's oyster bar was not serving spirits prior to this time.

Many establishments of the day mixed house spirits to serve with liqueurs and juices and called them "cups" after the tankards in which the cocktails were sold. Naturally the "cup" made at Pimm's was named after the restaurant, which retained the goodwill of its founder.

The original Pimm's Cup, No.1, was based on gin and flavoured with numerous botanicals including quinine. Subsequently six further versions were introduced, based on Scotch, brandy, rum, rye, vodka and Bourbon (inter alia).

In 1969 the brand was taken over by the company now known as Diageo and the original, gin-based, Pimm's was catapulted into the international league. The company focused on marketing No. 1, and the remaining versions were soon dropped – although No. 6, which is based on vodka, was later reprieved. In 2004 Pimm's Winter Cup was launched. Like the original no. 3, it is based on brandy with such suitably wintry additions as orange zest, cinnamon and caramel. Its flavour is altogether more robust and spicy than Pimm's No.1.

Pineapple Juice

The pineapple is native to South America and was brought to Europe by the Spanish under its indigenous name of anana. The English soon noticed its resemblance to a pine cone, then known as a 'pineapple' and renamed it to match.

Pineapples are widely grown in the West Indies, Africa and Asia and are particularly abundant in European markets in the winter months. There are many varieties which vary significantly in both size and flavour. When pineapples are ripe the skin changes colour from yellow-green to brown, then moves to yellow-brown once over-ripe.

Pineapples are tropical and tend to deteriorate at temperatures below 7°C (45°F) so are best left out of the refrigerator.

Pineapple is one of the most satisfying fruits to chop up and pass through an electric juice extractor due to the quantity of juice it yields. Chop the crown and bottom off, then slice the skin off, without worrying too much about the little brown dimples that remain. Finally slice the fruit along its length around the hard central core, and chop into pieces small enough to fit into your juice extractor.

It's best to use a large serrated knife to slice pineapple and I find a bread knife particularly suited to the task. The base is the sweetest part of a pineapple, so if you are only juicing half be sure to divide the fruit lengthways. For convenience I sometimes end up buying cartons of 'pressed pineapple juice' from the supermarket chill cabinet. As with all such juices, look for those labelled "not from concentrate".

Pineau des Charentes

This is a fortified wine from the Charentes (Cognac) region of France, with its own appellation contrôlée. It is produced by blending partially fermented grape juice with a one-year-old cognac from the same producer and then maturing the blend in oak casks for at least three years.

There are hundreds of small producers of Pineau, each with their own brand name. Many of the big Cognac houses also make it. Pineau des Charentes is available in both red and white styles.

Pisang Ambon®

www.bols.com
A Dutch liqueur made with banana, other fruits and herbs, supposedly to an old Indonesian recipe. 'Pisang' means banana and 'Ambon' means island, hence literally banana island.

Pisco

Our recommendation: Macchu Pisco
Pisco is a type of brandy and is the national drink of Chile and Peru, which some time ago were both under the rule of the Viceroyalty of Peru. Its name probably comes from the port of Pisco in Peru, a hotbed of smuggling. Other theories relate it to 'pisquo', the old Peruvian word for a 'flying bird', on the basis that Pisco gives you wings, or to 'pisquillo', the term for a container used to carry spirits.

Pisco's origins date back to the conquistadors, who planted vineyards in the early 1600s so that they could have wine for Communion (and drinking), then began to distil the wine. The resulting spirit became known as Pisco in the second half of the 19th century, and in 1931 was given an appellation. The best Pisco is made from the fermented juice of the Muscat grape, which grow in the Ica region of southwestern Peru and in Chile's Elqui Valley. There are many varieties of Muscat. The Quebranta grape is favoured in Peru where it is usually blended with one or two of the other six varietals permitted: Moscatel, Albilla, Negra, Mollar and Torontel. In Chile Common Black, Mollar, Pink Muscat, Torontel, Pedro Jimenez and Muscat of Alexandria are all used. After distillation, some grades of Chilean Pisco are aged in wooden vats made of American oak and Rauli, the native Chilean beechwood.

Pisco production in Peru is highly regulated and only certain methods of production are allowed. Grades of Pisco include 'acholado' (half breed), which can be made from any variety of grapes, 'aromático' (aromatic), which must be made only from Muscat, and 'puro', which must be made primarily from Quebranta grapes.

Chilean law states that Pisco must be produced in the area between Copiapo and Illapel. This area is full of fertile valleys enclosed by sunny hills of which the most famous is the Elqui Valley, which is now part of Chile but was once in Peru. In the native language its name means 'the given in heritage by God' and this is generally considered the best area in Chile for Pisco production. It is noted for its lack of clouds and clean air, so much so that an astronomical observatory is sited there.

Pisco is used to make Chile and Peru's national drink, the Pisco Sour, which is based on lime and sugar. Another popular Pisco cocktail is the Pisco Punch, which originated in San Francisco over a hundred years ago and is basically a Pisco Sour with the addition of pineapple juice and soda water or Champagne. Pisco is also popularly served with cola as a 'Piscola'.

Plums

Plums originated in Asia but were introduced to Western Europe by the Crusaders. They can be yellow, green, red or purple. Dried plums, or prunes, were used in a great deal of English cuisine before the raisin began to replace them in the seventeenth century. British plums are in season from late July to September but imported varieties are available all year round.
Ideally plums should be left until ripe, but not overripe, when they turn soft and wrinkled. The matt, whitish 'bloom' on the fruit's surface is easily rubbed off: the lack of this can be a sign of over-handling.
Preparation: When plums are ripe they are best muddled. Cut the fruit into quarters, remove the stone and peel each segment. Muddle the skinned flesh in the base of your shaker.

Unripe plums are best quartered, stoned and put through an electric juice extractor. The skin adds colour.

Plymouth Sloe Gin®

www.plymouthgin.com
The making of fruit liqueurs is a long tradition in the British countryside and Plymouth stays true to a unique 1883 recipe. The sloe berries are slowly and gently steeped in high strength gin, soft Dartmoor water and a further secret ingredient. The drink is bottled only when the Head Distiller decides the perfect flavour has been reached. The result is an entirely natural product with no added flavouring or colouring.

This richly flavoured liqueur is initially dry but opens with smooth, sweet, lightly jammy, juicy cherry and raspberry notes alongside a complimentary mixture of figs, cloves, set honey and stewed fruits. The finish has strong almond notes.

Poire William Eau de Vie

Eau-de-vie means 'water of life' and is the French term for brandies made from a fruit other than grapes. Produced in France, Germany, Yugoslavia and Scandinavia, these 'fruit brandies' are clear and colourless and generally sold at 40 - 45% alc. /vol.

Poire William is a particular variety of pear favoured by distillers for making eau-de-vie.

POM Wonderful Pomegranate Juice®

www.pomwonderful.com
POM Wonderful is made from 100% pomegranate juice – a juice that is extremely high in antioxidants. The pomegranates used to make POM are all grown in California and are picked by hand to avoid damaging the fruit. Each bottle contains the juice of five-and-a-half fruits.

Pomegranate (Grenadine) Syrup

Originally grenadine was syrup flavoured with pomegranate. Sadly, most of today's commercially available grenadine syrups are flavoured with red berries and cherry juice. They may be blood red but they don't taste of pomegranate. Hunt out one of the few genuine commercially made pomegranate syrups or make your own.
1. Simple method: Gradually pour and stir two cups of granulated sugar into a saucepan containing one cup of pomegranate juice (POM Wonderful works well) and gently warm until the sugar is dissolved (do not let the juice even simmer!). Consider adding half a split vanilla pod for extra flavour. Allow syrup to cool and fine strain into an empty bottle. If kept in a refrigerator this mixture will last for a week or so (please be aware of the use-by date of your pomegranate juice).
2. Messy method: Separate the seed cells from the outer membranes and skin of eight pomegranates. Simmer these in a saucepan with 25ml/1oz of sugar syrup and ¼ of a vanilla pod for each pomegranate for at least an hour. Allow to cool, strain through a cheesecloth-layered sieve and store in a refrigerator.

Ponche Liqueur

A Spanish liqueur invented by Jose de Soto Ruiz. The word 'ponche' means punch, and is derived from the Moorish word for five. The key ingredients are brandy and matured Sherry, sweetened and flavoured with orange peel, plums, raisins and vanilla marinated in syrup. Ponche originates from Jerez, the Sherry growing area of Spain, and is traditionally sold in a distinctive silver bottle.

Port/Porto

Port, or to give it its full name 'vinho do porto', is a Portuguese wine from the area known as the Upper Douro which starts 45 miles from the coast at the town of Oporto and stretches east to the Spanish border. Wine is fortified with grape brandy, which stops fermentation before it is complete by raising the alcoholic strength beyond that at which the yeasts can survive. This produces wines with residual sugars, giving Port its inherently sweet style.

Wood matured Ports are aged in oak casks, called 'pipes', or large oak vats. Port which has been stored in vats is subject to less contact with the wood, so these are used to age lighter, fruitier Ports.

Wood aged Ports should be stored at a reasonably cool and constant temperature. They are not improved by further ageing in the bottle, so drink and enjoy.

Wood matured Ports do not require decanting as they are filtered before bottling and hence have no sediment. However, decanting will allow them to breathe and can often improve their flavour. Once open they will keep for a week to ten days providing the cork is replaced, or better, a Vacuvin is used. However, after a fortnight oxidation will wreck the Port.

Bottle matured ports are initially aged in pipes and vats in the same way as wood matured Ports, they are not fined and filtered prior to bottling. This preserves more of the fruit flavours and allows them to continue to develop in the bottle.

Bottle matured Port should be stored lying on the same side as it was in the Port producer's warehouse. A white splash of paint on a bottle indicates the top and an indentation in the base of the bottle indicates the bottom, though bottles may be marked with only one of these signs.

Bottle matured Ports throw a sediment or 'crust' during maturation, which must be separated from the Port by decanting prior to serving. As a rule, any Port with a cork that requires a corkscrew is bottle matured and will require decanting. Before opening, stand the bottle upright for 24 hours. Draw the cork and pour steadily and carefully so that the sediment remains undisturbed at the bottom of the bottle. A simple way of making sure that no sediment finds its way into your decanter is to cover the top of a funnel with clean stockings and pour your Port though this and into the decanter. All bottle matured Ports are best drunk within a day or two of decanting to best appreciate their superb nose and flavour.

There are seven different styles of wood matured Port and four different bottle matured styles. These offer different flavour profiles and affordability, and require different handling and serving methods as explained below.

White Port (wood matured) - Made using only white grapes to achieve a light golden colour, white Ports are usually aged for three years in large oak vats prior to bottling. They can be either very dry or sweet – the label should state which. Sweet white Ports are often served with melon. Dry whites make great aperitifs.

Ruby Port (wood matured) - A rich, fruity and sweet Port created from a blend of both young and old wines. Usually aged three years in large oak vats prior to bottling, Rubys are everyday drinking Ports.

Tawny Port (wood matured) - Blended Ports from different harvests aged for a longer period in wood, which changes the colour and gives the wine a smooth consistency. They are aged in 'pipes' for about three years to produce a very soft and smooth style of Port. Good tawny Ports can be recognised by their red-brown as opposed to pink rim and should be served slightly chilled to enjoy their full potential.

Vintage Character (wood matured) - Made from a blend of the highest quality ruby Ports with extra age, these are sometimes referred to as VC, premium ruby or reserve Ports. After maturation for 3-5 years in oak vats, they are blended to give full bodied, round and fruity Ports with vintage characteristics. Serve slightly chilled.

Colheita (wood matured) - A tawny Port from a single year, rather than a blend of a number of years. Colheitas are aged in 'pipes' for 8-40 years and are generally excellent wines displaying the character of a particular year, but with a consistent soft, smooth style. Serve slightly chilled.

Old Tawnies (wood matured) - These wines are aged in 'pipes' for 10-40 years and can only be labelled 10, 20, 30 and over 40 years old. The stated age is an average age of the wines in the blend. The best are among the best wines from this region. Soft and smooth in style, they should be served slightly chilled.

Late Bottled Vintage (wood matured) - LBV Ports are from a good single harvest and are aged 4-6 years in wood, then filtered prior to bottling, meaning that they will not develop in the bottle. The term is also applied to some bottle matured Ports (see below). Wood matured LBVs have more depth and complexity than Vintage Character Ports and tend to be more full-bodied than bottle matured LBV Ports. Serve slightly chilled.

Late Bottled Vintage (bottle matured) - Bottle matured LBV Ports are made from better quality grapes than are used in wood matured LBV Ports, and come from a good single harvest. They are matured in wood for 4-6 years before bottling, where further maturation will develop. They are not as full-bodied as wood matured LBV Ports, but generally more complex, and should benefit from being left for 5 years before opening.

Crusted (bottle matured) - Ports from different, but excellent years are blended together and bottled to create this British style of Port, which is not generally available in Portugal. They are matured 3½-4 years in wood prior to bottling then left to develop in the bottle for a further four years or more. Crusted Ports are usually sold ready to drink, but may benefit from an additional few years.

Single Quinta (bottle matured) - Pronounced 'Kin-Ta', these are the product of a single estate (quinta) and are only made from 'A grade' grapes matured for 2–2½ years in large oak vats prior to bottling. Further maturation takes place in the bottle. Single Quintas are produced in the good quality years not declared vintage by the general Port Producing House and are the closest style to vintage Port, but not sold at vintage price. Mature for at least a further 10-15 years to allow the Port to develop in the bottle.

Vintage (bottle matured) - On average a vintage is declared only three times a decade, 18 months after the wine goes into wood, and with the

agreement of the general Port Producing House. Vintage Port is made from outstanding wine from an outstanding year and by only a handful of vineyards in the Alto Douro. Mature for a minimum of 10-15 years to allow the Port to develop in the bottle.

Powdered Sugar
Sometimes referred to as 'bar sugar' this is simply caster (or castor) sugar that has been ground to reduce its particle size to a fine dust. Make your own powdered by crushing caster sugar in a pestle and mortar.

Proof
A term used to indicate alcoholic strength. Originally gunpowder was used to determine the strength of a spirit. The tester would mix the spirit with gunpowder and attempt to light it. If the spirit did not ignite, it was under-proof; if it burned steadily, it was proof; if it exploded, it was over-proof. Proof is measured differently in the USA to the UK, 100% proof in the states is equivalent to 87.7% British proof (Sikes Scale). US proof is double alcohol by volume (Gay-Lussac). British proof was the result of a complex calculation based on the relative volumes of alcohol and water at a temperature of 51° Fahrenheit and fortunately has now been abandoned in favour of the Gay-Lussac alcohol-by-volume (abv) scale. To convert British Proof to a percentage of alcohol by volume divided by 0.571.

Scale	Water	Proof	Pure Alcohol
Gay-Lussac (abv) Europe	0°	57°	100°
Sikes scale % of proof (old UK scale)	0°	100°	175°
Proof USA	0°	114°	200°

Prosecco Sparkling Wine
Prosecco is a wine produced around the towns of Conegliano and Valdobbiadene in the Italian province of Treviso. It can be still, semi-sparkling or sparkling, dry, off-dry or sweet. The style called for in this guide, and the preferred style for export, is dry and sparkling. 'Frizzante' means 'semi-sparkling' and 'spumante' means 'sparkling'.

The better wines from hillside vineyards are labelled 'Prosecco di Conegliano-Valdobbiadene'. The best are 'Prosecco Superiore di Cartizze' from the great hill of Cartizze in the Valdobbiadene sub-region.

Punt E Mes®

www.puntemes.com

In the late 18th century, Antonio Benedetto Carpano set up his wine bar in the Piazza Castello, in the centre of Turin. Soon after opening he set about creating a new drink to better suit delicate palates still favouring the robust table wines of the region. In 1786 he launched Carpano. This was the first commercial vermouth and was basically a dry white wine, lightly fortified with alcohol, sweetened and flavoured with an infusion of aromatic herbs. His business was a great success and he was succeeded by his nephew, Guiseppe Bernardino whose initials still front the company name - G B Carpano.

Punt E Mes was created in 1870 and its popularity soon ousted the bars other vermouths. In those days individual customers would specify the style of vermouth they wanted, choosing between bitter and sweet and requesting particular herbs and spices which would be drawn from bottles behind the bar. As in today's coffee shops, a language grew around the terms for each style of drink being ordered. The Carpano bar was frequented by many customers from the nearby Turin Stock Exchange. At the end of a particular days trading, when some key stocks had just fallen by one and a half points and the bar was full of traders, a businessman ordered a particular style of bitter-sweet vermouth in Piadmontese dialect, "Ca'm dag'n punt e mes' (Give me a point and a half). He was simply requesting one and a half points of bitterness to be added, but those around him laughed at the coincidence to their discussions on that days trading fall. So the drink was created and named.

Stockbrokers at the Carpano bar used to show off by ordering the drink using a stock broking hand signal. They would hold up one thumb (a point) and then draw their hand horizontally through the air, indicating a half.

The company remained family owned until being taken over by Sylvio Turati, a Turin industrialist and then by Fratelli Branca, makers of Fernet Branca. Sadly an air raid in 1943 destroyed the original Carpano bar.

Punt E Mes is made by adding over fifty herbs and spices to white wine, these include: orange peel and quinine. It is traditionally served in a tumbler over ice with the merest splash of soda and a slice of orange. It should be accompanied by a piece of dark cocoa rich chocolate – try it!

Pusser's British Navy Admiralty Strength®

www.pussers.com

The name 'Pusser' is slang in the Royal Navy for purser, the officer with responsibility for the issue of rum on board ship. For more than 300 years the British Navy issued a daily 'tot' of Pusser's rum, with a double issue before battle. This tradition, which started in Jamaica in 1665, was finally broken on 31st July 1970, a day now known as 'Black Tot Day'.

In 1979 the Admiralty approved the re-blending of Pusser's rum to the original specifications by Charles Tobias in the British Virgin Islands. A significant donation from the sale of each bottle accrues to the benefit of The Royal Navy Sailor's Fund, a naval charity established to compensate sailors for their lost tot.

Pusser's is a blend of six pot still rums from different Caribbean distilleries in Guyana, Trinidad, and The British Virgin Islands.

Quince Jam (Membrillo)

Quince fruit can often be sour and hard though with long cooking times, either stewing or roasting, they can be made into a jam or marmalade. The fruit colour darkens as it is cooked resulting in the deep orange colour of Quince jam.

Quinquina

The generic term for sweetened fortified aperitif wines containing quinine and spices. Brands within this category include: Byrrh, Dubonnet and St. Raphael.

Raspberries & Blackberries

Both raspberries and blackberries are high in vitamins C and E, grow on brambly bushes and are related to the rose. Both can be cultivated in a wide range of colours, from white or yellow to orange, pink or purple, as well as the more common red and black.

The loganberry is a cross between a blackberry and a raspberry and is named after its Californian creator, James H Logan. Other later hybrids of the two fruits include the tayberry (named after the Scottish river) and the boysenberry (named after its creator).

The juice of both raspberries and blackberries is intense and a little goes a long way. This is just as well because there's precious little juice in each berry and you'll find putting them through an electric juicer a complete waste of time. Instead, either blend them into a puree or (as I do) muddle the fruits in the base of your shaker or in the glass.

Red Bull®

www.redbull.com

Red Bull was launched in Thailand in 1987 and was inspired by existing brand 'Kraitang Daeng' (translates as Red Bull). An energy drink that promises to improve performance and aid concentration, it contains a lot of caffeine and sugar. The product dominates the global market for energy drinks selling more than 3 billion cans in 2006.

Red Wine

The acidity in table wine can balance a cocktail in a similar way to citrus juice. Avoid heavily oaked wines.

Ricard® Pastis

www.ricard.fr

This French liquorice based spirit is Europe's best-selling spirit brand and the world's third biggest selling spirit brand. It dates back to 1932 when the 22 year-old Paul Ricard created his aniseed-flavoured drink and established a firm in Marseille to produce and market what he called pastis. Although the firm of Ricard is still based in Marseille, production now takes place in Bessan, a small village in Southern France (blending and bottling also takes place in Bordeaux and Lille).

Ricard is flavoured with liquorice root, the bark of which is shaved off by hand to leave the core which is then shredded and placed in a percolator through which alcohol and purified water at 42% abv is forced under pressure. This is repeated three times so that the alcohol takes on the flavour and aroma of the liquorice. This same process is also used to extract flavours of seven different aromatic herbs from Provence. The other key ingredient to Ricard is green anise and fennel, the essence of which is rectified to produce anethole essence.

These three separate ingredients are blended together with neutral alcohol, and sugar (less than 100 grams sugar per litre). Caramel is also added, which adds to the distinctive yellow colour the liquorice content gives Ricard. The anethole is extremely rich in flavour and only 1.5 to 2 grams are required to flavour a litre of Ricard. The finished product is then triple filtered through mineral and cellulose filters before bottling.

It is the delicate dilution of anethole in Ricard which makes the spirit turn milky when water is added. Ricard should be stored at above 12°C and away from direct light. If exposed to colder temperatures the anethole will start to crystallise and impair the look and flavour of the product. To return the product to its normal state, place the bottle in hot water and shake it from time to time until the crystals disappear. To enjoy Ricard at its best, it should be consumed within three years of purchase.

Ricard's label has always featured an acanthus leaf, an ornamental plant from the south of France. This leaf is now recognised as a distinctive mark of the brand and of pastis in general. In more recent years a bright yellow sun logo has also been introduced to the bottles neck.

Ricard is traditionally served one part to five parts chilled water with ice. Due to the anethole within pastis being so sensitive to the cold, the water should be added first and then, a few moments later – the ice cubes. The dilution on one to five and the use of chilled water is critical to enjoying the finished drink. In France, Ricard tends to be served in 20ml measures diluted with 100ml of chilled water.

Rose Water

Rose water is a by-product when making rose oil for perfumes. Damask roses are most often used which are grown in Iran, Bulgaria and more recently Spain, Italy and France. Rosewater has a delicate flavour and is also used in cosmetics, as it has a calming affect for the skin.

Rosemary

Rosemary is an evergreen, perennial herb with woody, needle-like leaves. The name rosemary has nothing to do with roses and translates from the latin 'ros' - dew and marinus – 'sea' as apparently it grows easily by the sea. The herb has a fresh, green, piney flavour.

Rum

Our recommendation: Bacardi rum

The spectrum of rums available ranges from light, vodka-like white rums through to cognac-like aged rums.

Rum can be made from fermented fresh sugar cane juice, cane syrup or molasses. Cane juice is simply the juice which results from crushing the harvested sugar cane. Cane syrup is cane juice which has been boiled to remove some of the water content. Molasses is a black, liquid by-product of commercial sugar extraction from the juice. In most cases rum is produced from molasses. Rum distilled from fresh cane juice tends to come from the French islands where it is called 'rhum agricole'. Rum distilled from molasses is referred to as 'rhum traditional'.

Whatever base ingredient is chosen, this is fermented with water and cultured (almost always) or naturally occurring yeast, until it reaches a strength of 5-9% abv. The resulting 'wash' can then be distilled.

Rum is termed 'light' or 'heavy', depending on the purity to which it was distilled. Essentially, the flavour of any spirit comes from 'congeners' – products of fermentation which are not ethyl alcohol. When alcohol is concentrated during distillation, the levels of congeners are reduced. The fewer congeners, the lighter the rum, the more congeners, the heavier.

Rum produced from a pot still or single distillation column is usually described as heavy. Multiple-column stills can produce both heavy and light rums depending on where the spirit is removed from the still. Premium rums tend to be pot distilled.

The fermentation process can also affect whether a rum is light or heavy. A longer, slower fermentation will result in a heavier rum due to other contaminating bacteria reproducing during the process. Different yeasts also affect the final wash and the distilled rum.

The odour, texture and taste of light rums are more subtle and refined than those of heavy rums, which have a heavy, syrupy flavour to match their dark colour. The level of impurities in light rum is less than a third of those found in heavy rums. Distilleries producing light and heavy rums often blend the two to produce a rum having characteristics of both.

Light rums tend to originate from countries originally colonised by the Spanish, such as Cuba, the Dominican Republic, Puerto Rico and Venezuela. The heavy rums come from countries from the former French and English colonies, including Haiti, Jamaica, Martinique, Aruba, Guyana and the Virgin Islands.

Like other distillates, rum is clear when it condenses after distillation. White rum can simply be a sugar cane distillate watered down and bottled. The fact that ageing in oak barrels improved the raw rum was discovered when ships carried rum on the long passage to Europe: it arrived darker in colour and with an enhanced flavour.

Today, rum is aged in barrels from France or the United States, which have previously been used to age Cognac, Bourbon or whiskey. They may be charred or scraped clean to remove any previous charring before receiving the rum: the treatment of the barrels is reflected in the character they impart to the finished rum.

Blending is the final process which the distiller can use to alter the character of a rum. Many rums are blends of different aged rums, light rums and dark rums. Some even have added spices or flavourings.

It is common for caramel to be added to aged rums to 'correct' the colour, and let's be honest, often to darken the colour so potentially giving the rum an older appearance. Conversely, some aged rums are charcoal filtered to remove any colour and are bottled completely clear. So with rum what you see is not necessarily what you get.

Sailor Jerry Spiced Rum®

www.sailorjerry.com
A continuously distilled light Caribbean rum flavoured with five spices including ginger, cinnamon, clove, vanilla and an infusion of natural lime. The recipe is claimed to be based on an original by the famous tattoo artist, 'Sailor Jerry Collins', who died in 1973 and the bottle is decorated with Collins tattoos, including Hula girls printed on the inside back label which are hidden until the bottle has been emptied.

St-Germain®

www.stgermain.fr
St-Germain is the world's first elderflower liqueur and unlike other elderflower products, which tend to be made from freeze dried and frozen blossoms, St-Germain is produced only using freshly picked flowers.

The fresh elderflowers used to make St-Germain are harvested from the foothills of the French Alps, in Haute Savoie, where elder trees grow abundantly. The elder shrubs (sambucus nigra) flower for a few weeks in late spring but are only at their ripest for about a week. A group of local French farmers harvest the flowers by hand, as has long been the tradition in this region of France. Incredibly, several of the farmers ride blossom-laden bicycles between the elder trees, which grow along side rural country roads. Once picked, speed is of the essence in order to capture the blossoms' fragrance and flavour as the flowers dull and fade.

The elderflowers are macerated in eau-de-vie made from a blend of Chardonnay and Gamay grapes. The elderflower infused spirit is then blended with just enough Caribbean cane sugar to enhance the natural flavours. With just 180 grams of sugar per litre, St-Germain has a lot less sugar than many other liqueurs. It mixes well with all white fruits, particularly apple, pear and white grapes. The acidity of white wine also superbly balances St-Germain.

Sake

Sometimes described as a rice wine, sometimes as a rice beer, sake shares qualities of both. It is fermented from specially developed rice and water by brewmasters ('toji'). But, although sake is brewed like a beer, it is served like a wine and, like a wine, can either be dry or sweet, heavy or light. But it is slightly more alcoholic than wine, and much more boozy than beer, at 14-18% abv. Sake (pronounced Sar-Keh – heavy on the K!) is native to Japan (and parts of

China). The basic outline of production has changed little since the 11th century, but complex and fragrant sake has only been generally available since the 1970s.

Sambuca

Our recommendation: Luxardo Sambuca dei Cesari & Opal Nera
Sambuca is considered by many as the national liqueur of Italy. It takes its name from the Latin name for elder, a shrub which, along with anise, is an essential ingredient in all Sambucas. The medicinal properties of these two main ingredients helped its popularity as a therapeutic drink.

The anise plant was appreciated in ancient times for its therapeutic properties. Originating from China, it became widespread through the centuries along the Mediterranean coast. Its name derives from the Arab word Zammut (anise). The word zammù still exists in the Sicilian dialect, meaning an anise drink diluted with water

First produced in the 20th century, sambuca must contain between 1 gram & 2 grams per litre of natural anethol – an essential oil extracted from the distillation of either star anise, Mediterranean anise or bitter fennel. Sambuca must have 350 grams per litre of sugar and a minimum 38% of alcohol.

Sambuca is traditionally served 'Con Mosca' meaning 'with flies' - flamed in a shot glass with three floating coffee beans. The number signifies health, wealth and happiness and is said to bestow good luck on the drinker.

Schnapps

In most countries the term schnapps traditionally suggests a clear strong spirit or clear liqueur that may be flavoured and served in a shot glass. (Although today schnapps often refers to sweet liqueurs of only 20-24% abv, these have no resemblance to the strong dry schnapps from which they take their name. In Austria, schnapps are clear eaux-de-vie, produced from anything from pears to rowanberries to juniper.

In Germany, schnaps (with one 'p') is a term for almost any hard liquor. Kornbranntwein is a German term for a clear, light, quality schnapps produced from only corn and distilled in a pot still. The name literally means 'corn brandy' and is often shortened to korn. Korns may resemble rye whisky or be flavoured with herbs and spices. In northern Germany these spirits are a popular chaser to beer.

And they can all be referred to as schnapps (or schnaps, or snaps) – a term which comes from the Old Norse 'snappen', meaning to gulp, snatch or (in this case) down in one.

Scotch Whisky

Our recommendation: Johnnie Walker Scotch
For whisky to be called 'Scotch whisky' it must be a) made in Scotland and b) be aged in oak casks in Scotland for a minimum of three years.

Until the 1830s almost all Scottish whisky was made exclusively from malted barley and produced in pot stills – i.e., it was what we would today call 'malt whisky'. However, two developments brought about 'Scottish grain whisky' and 'Scotch blended whisky'. The first was the development of a new type of still, known variously as the column still, patent still, continuous still or Coffey still; the second was the repeal of the British Corn Laws.

Thanks to cheap grain and the new continuous column stills, distilleries could produce a light 'grain' whisky very cheaply. Small independent Scottish distillers sought to prevent the new grain distillers calling their produce 'whisky' but in 1909 a Royal Commission was appointed and ruled against the malt distillers. The grain distillers were free to call their grain whisky 'Scotch whisky' - but 'malt whisky' must be made from barley using a pot still.

Continuous stills are far more efficient compared to traditional pot stills. The spirit from a malt whisky pot still (termed 'New Make Spirit'), leaves the still at around 70% abv while the spirit made in continuous stills can be up to 95% abv.

Like all distillates, grain spirit is clear when it leaves the still - it smells rather like rum and raisin ice cream. Before the clear spirit can be termed Scotch whisky it must (like malt whisky) be aged in oak casks for a minimum of three years.

Very little single grain whisky is bottled and sold as such. Grain whisky is mainly used for blending with malt whisky to produce Scotch blended whisky. Blended Scotch whisky, or 'Scotch' for short is by far the world's most popular

whisky and accounts for well over 85% of all Scottish whisky. Although malt was the original Scottish whisky, and although it has recently become extremely popular, the majority of pot still malt whisky is still sold in blends, not as 'single malt whisky'.

Like cognac, the quality of Scotch is reliant on the blender's ability and experience to select from the ever-changing casks available and skilfully blend them to match the style of the brand time after time, providing the drinker with a consistent product. Although the style of a brand may vary over the years, this is generally due to a conscious decision to improve it.
A standard blended Scotch whisky will probably contain 15-40% malt and have no age statement (though every whisky in it will have been aged at least three years). Some blends describe themselves as 'deluxe' - this is a reference to the percentage of malt whisky in the blend and the average age of the whisky. A deluxe brand will usually contain more than 45% pot still malt and will show an age statement of 12 years or more.

Sherry – Amontillado
An Amontillado sherry begins as a Fino, a pale, dry sherry produced under a layer of a kind of yeast known as 'flor'. Once the flor dies, increasing the oxidisation and changing the flavour of the wine, the sherry becomes an Amontillado. There are two distinct Amontillado styles. One is naturally dry, while the other is sweetened. Recipes in this guide which call for Amontillado sherry require the better quality, dry style.

Sherry – Fino
Pronounced 'Fee-No' this pale, dry style of sherry is best drunk young. It is produced under a layer of a kind of yeast known as 'flor' which protects the wine from oxidation.

Sherry - Pedro Ximénez
This superbly rich dessert sherry is made from sun-dried Pedro Ximénez grapes.

Single Malt Scotch Whisky
The term 'Single Malt Scotch' refers to a whisky that fulfils all three elements of the term: 'Single' - the whisky must be from only one distillery. 'Malt' - the raw material used must be barley malt. No other grain or fermentable material can be used. The barley malt is infused with water, fermented with yeast and distilled in a pot still. 'Scotch' – the whisky must be distilled and matured in Scotland.

Slivovitz
This plum flavoured brandy is produced in the Balkan countries. The best examples come from the former Yugoslavia and are made from Pozega plums taken from trees that are at least 20 years old. The plums are fermented for several months before being double distilled. Part of the kernel is used which imparts the characteristically dry, almond bitterness. Unusually for a fruit brandy, Slivovitz is aged in wood for 3-5 years, giving it a brown-yellow colour. Slivovitz has a rich, spicy plum taste, and is generally 40-50% abv.

Sour Apple Liqueur
There are several brands of this style of liqueur available and they tend to be bright green in colour with sweet & sour character and a strong apple flavour. Noted brands include Puckers Sour Apple and Sourz Sour Apple (launched 1999).

Southern Comfort®

www.southerncomfort.com
Whisky was a popular drink in 1860s New Orleans. Paddle-wheel steamers brought barrels of it down the Ohio and Mississippi rivers from Tennessee and Kentucky. In the saloons it was served straight from the barrel - and the quality of the product varied greatly from cask to cask.

Martin Wilkes 'M.W' Heron, a local barman at McCauley's Tavern in New Orleans wanted to find a way to make particularly harsh casks of whiskey more palatable.

In 1874, Heron began experimenting, using local fruits such as lemons, limes, oranges and cherries. His family had a restaurant business, so he also had some knowledge of spices – and as New Orleans was a booming port he had access to exotic ingredients such as Moroccan cinnamon and Mexican vanilla. Heron experimented with different blends selling his concoctions straight from the whiskey barrel.

In 1889, Heron move up the Mississippi River to Memphis, where he opened his own bar near Beale Street, an area famous for Blues music. Around this time a competitor's brandy based liqueur called 'Hats & Tails' was becoming popular so Heron started bottling his whiskey liqueur under the cheeky name 'Cuffs & Buttons'. Each label had his signature and the phrase 'None Genuine but Mine'.

Sometime in the late 1990s he opened a blues club further north in St. Louis and a factory to produce his liqueur which he renamed 'Southern Comfort', for an important exhibition in New York. The newly titled liqueur prospered until the onset of Prohibition.

In 1933, after Prohibition was repealed, the Fowler family acquired the secret recipe for Southern Comfort and began producing it again. While flicking through a book of sketches, they found the perfect image for their new label: a sketch entitled 'Home on the Mississippi', produced in 1894 by Nathaniel Currier and James Ives, two of the century's most popular lithographers.

The mansion featured in the print is known as the Woodland Plantation, and was originally built in 1834 as the grand house of sugar cane planters. Situated on Highway 23, today it is operated as a guesthouse and fishing lodge.

Sales of Southern Comfort took off in 1939, helped by being the key ingredient in the Scarlett O'Hara cocktail, which was named after the heroine of the Gone With the Wind movie released that year. M.W. Heron's concoction has since become an international mega-brand, now owned and distributed by Brown Forman.

Southern Comfort has much evolved over the years. First in name, then image with the introduction of the Woodland's Plantation illustration, and in more recent decades, in base alcohol, taste and alcoholic strength. Brown Forman has long since stopped using whisky as the base spirit in Southern Comfort, instead basing the liqueur on neural alcohol. Other changes to Heron's original recipe have seen a reduction in the apricot and peach flavours, as well as less sugar to balance a reduction in alcoholic strength.

Spiced Rum

Our recommendation: Sailor Jerry
Spiced rums are continuously distilled light rums flavoured with spices including ginger, cinnamon, clove and vanilla.

Stone's Original® Ginger Wine

www.stonesgingerwine.com
The green ginger wine recipe used to make Stones is said to date from 1740 while brand name dates from the mid-nineteenth century, when the wine was sold by Joseph Stone, a London grocer.

Strawberries
Like the raspberry and the blackberry, the strawberry is a member of the rose family, indigenous to both Old and New Worlds. Wild strawberries are small and fine-flavoured, with an intensely musky scent: sadly they are also expensive. Most strawberries for the last few centuries have been a hybrid of old world and new.

Strawberries are delicate and do not keep much longer than 48 hours in the refrigerator. Opt for smaller, darker berries, and wash them briefly in warm water.

Preparation: You can do pretty much what you like with strawberries: stick them through the electric juicer, puree them or muddle them. I muddle mine, probably because I hate cleaning the blender, let alone the juicer.

Strega Liqueur®

www.strega.it
'Strega' is Italian for 'witch', so named because witches are reputed to have held a coven every Saturday night on the banks of the River Sabato in Benevento, just north of Naples where they danced around a gigantic walnut tree. They are also said to have made a love potion, which would ensure that any couple drinking it would remain in love.

This famous Italian liqueur was first invented by a wine merchant, Guiseppe Alberti of Benevento (the town of witches fame above) in 1860. However, it was his sons who first marketed the liqueur which is flavoured with over 70 different herbs and spices. The distillates are produced in pot stills and the liqueur is aged in wood after blending.

Sugar Syrup

Many cocktails benefit from sweetening but granulated sugar does not dissolve easily in cold drinks. Hence pre-dissolved sugar syrup (also known as 'simple syrup') is used. Commercially made 'gomme sirop' (gum syrup) is sugar syrup with the addition of gum arabic, the crystallised sap of the acacia tree, which adds mouth-feel and smoothness to some drinks, but not all.

Make your own sugar syrup by gradually pouring and stirring two cups of granulated sugar into a saucepan containing one cup of hot water and simmer until the sugar is dissolved. Heating helps the sugar to dissolve in the water but also changes the sugars physical properties. The more the sugar is heated, the more the sucrose will break down to the less viscous but sweeter glucose and fructose. So do not let the water even come close to boiling and only simmer for as long as it takes to dissolve the sugar. Allow syrup to cool and pour into an empty bottle. Ideally, you should finely strain your syrup into the bottle to remove any undissolved crystals which could otherwise encourage crystallisation. If kept in a refrigerator this mixture will last for a couple of months.

A wide range of flavoured sugar syrups are commercially available. Orgeat (almond), passion fruit and vanilla are among the most popular. See also 'Pomegranate (Grenadine) Syrup'.

Suze®

www.suze.com

This slightly bitter aperitif was created in 1885 and launched in 1889 by its creator Fernand Moureaux to immediate success. Suze is made from gentian roots macerated in alcohol for several years. This alcohol is then double distilled and blended with herbs and other botanicals that have also been macerated. The distinctive amber coloured bottle was introduced in 1896, when Henri Porte joined forces with Moureaux.

Swedish Punch

Our recommendation: Carlshamns Flaggpunsch

Swedish Punch (also known as Arrack Punch, Caloric Punch, Punch or Punsch) is a style of liqueur popular in Sweden and other Nordic countries. Punsch was introduced to Sweden by the East Indian Company in 1773, when Batavia arrack was imported for the first time from the island of Java (now part of Indonesia). Batavia arrack is made from fermented rice and distilled in a pot still, then aged in local hardwood.

To make Swedish Punch, the arrack is blended with grain neutral spirit, sweetened and flavoured with cardamom, nutmeg and cinnamon. This distinctive liqueur which is best served mixed with rum.

Talisker®

www.diageo.com

This 10yo Scotch Single Malt Whisky takes its name from its place of origin. Dwarfed by the 23 jagged peaks of the jagged Cuillin Hills, Talisker nestles on the shores of Loch Harport on the west coast of Skye – the name means 'sloping rock' and comes from the Norse name for the mountain above it, 'Thalas Gair'. Dunvegan Castle, the seat of the Clan Macleod, is nearby. The distillery was originally built in 1830 by two brothers, Hugh and Kenneth MacAskill and is the last surviving distillery on the Isle of Skye. Much of the present day distillery dates from the 1960s following a rebuild necessitated by a still house fire.

Talisker was originally triple distilled, with double distillation starting in 1928. Supplies are still sent to the distillery by sea and the influence of the Atlantic is very evident in this Island malt. Talisker is one of Diageo's six 'Classic Malts' and the company also releases old and rare bottlings as part of its 'Rare Malts' and 'Special Releases' range.

Tanqueray Special Dry®

www.tanqueray.com

The Tanqueray family were originally silversmiths and left France for England early in the 18th century, where three successive Tanquerays became rectors in Bedfordshire. In 1830 Charles Tanqueray, then aged just twenty, broke with family tradition and rather than become a clergyman, established a distillery in London's Finsbury, then noted for its spa water.

Until 1947, Tanqueray was sold in many different shaped bottles. The design we recognise today was inspired by a 1920s range of Tanqueray pre-mixed cocktails that were sold in bottles designed to resemble a cocktail shaker - not a fire hydrant as some mistakenly believe. The name 'Special Dry' was introduced in 1950 and today is still applied to Tanqueray 47.3% abv.

Tanqueray Export Strength®

www.tanqueray.com

The Tanqueray Special Dry iconic bottle is used for this Tanqueray Export Strength introduced in 1999. It is made to the same recipe but with a lower 43.1% abv strength that is perfect for cocktail use.

Both Special Dry and Export strength Tanqueray gins are distilled by the traditional one-shot process in a 200 year old copper pot still nicknamed 'Old Tom'. The recipe which has remained unchanged since 1830 has three dominant botanicals: Tuscan juniper, angelica and coriander, giving both these gins the same crisp, dry style with a rich juniper flavour.

Tanqueray No. Ten Gin®

www.tanqueray.com

Launched in 2000, Tanqueray No. Ten is an ultra premium gin based on the traditional Tanqueray botanical recipe but with unusual extras such as camomile and fresh grapefruit. It takes its name from the distillery's number 10 still, known as Tiny Ten. Dating back to the 30s, this small pot still was originally used as an experimental, or trial-run, still and is a scale replica of the Old Tom still.

Tiny Ten is used for the first distillation, which produces the citrus spirit known as the 'citrus heart' of No. Ten. Wheat grain neutral spirit is distilled with chopped Florida oranges, Mexican limes and grapefruits to produce this essence.

The second and final distillation takes place in the larger Old Tom still. This is charged with the citrus heart previously distilled in Tiny Ten and wheat grain neutral spirit. Traditional botanicals such as juniper, coriander, angelica and liquorice are added, along with camomile flowers and slices of fresh limes. While the juniper, coriander, angelica and liquorice come from the same sources as those used in standard Tanqueray production, their proportions differ: in particular, substantially less juniper is used, so as not to dominate No. Ten's fresh citrus character.

Taylor's Chip Dry®

www.taylor.pt

Taylor's were the pioneers of white port, having introduced it in 1934. It is made in exactly the same way as conventional port, but using white grapes rather than red. Chip Dry is made from selected dry white ports from Douro Superior grapes, mainly Malvasia Fina. The dry style is due to later fortification than for most ports - leaving a lower level of residual sugar in the finished wine. Indeed, Taylors Chip Dry has enough acidity to be mistaken for a sweetish white table wine rather than a port.

Teichenné® Butterscotch Schnapps

www.teichenne.com

A family owned distiller and liqueur producer, the Teichenné firm was founded in 1956 when Juan Teichenné Senaux launched his distillery in the small town of L'Arboç (40 miles south of Barcelona). Born in France, Teichenné moved to Spain as part of the French wine industry's search for new production sources. In those early days, production was very small, concentrating on 'handmade' brandies and liqueurs for sale locally in the Penedès Region. Expansion did not start until the 70s, when Joan Teichenné Canals took over the business after his father's death. In the 1980s Teichenné led the Spanish boom in liqueur schnapps.

Teichenné butterscotch schnapps has a rich butterscotch and fudge flavour with a hint of cinnamon, baked apple and nutmeg.

Tennessee Whiskey

The main difference between bourbon and Tennessee whiskey lies in the Lincoln County Process, a form of charcoal filtration. In the 1820s someone (possibly Alfred Eaton) started filtering whiskey through maple charcoal. Tennessee whiskeys are now filtered through 10-12 feet of maple charcoal before they are bottled, removing impurities and giving a 'sooty' sweetness to the finished spirit.

A Tennessee whiskey must be made from at least 51% of one particular grain. This could be rye or wheat, but most often, as with bourbon, corn is the favoured base.

Tequila

Our recommendation: Don Julio 100% agave
Tequila is the native drink of Mexico and is named after the town of the same name located about forty miles west of Guadalajara in the state of Jalisco. In the local Nahuatl language the word tequila means 'volcanic rock' or 'rock that cuts', a reference to the dormant volcano that shadows the town.

Tequila is a recognised Appellation of Origin (AOC) and can only originate from five designated regions of Mexico, being the entire state of Jalisco and specific areas in the four states of Guanajuanto, Michoacan, Nayarit and Tamaulipas.

Tequila is made from the agave (pronounced 'Uh-Gah-Vee'), a native plant to Mexico, which despite its spiky appearance, is not a cactus and instead is commonly defined as being a member of the lily family.

There are more than 200 different (some say 400) varieties of agave but legally only one can be used to make tequila, Agave Tequilana A. Weber Blue azul, better known as blue agave. Other Mexican spirits such as mezcal and sotol are produced from other varieties of agave.

The agave usually reaches maturity after 5 to 8 years when its piña (core) swells and ripens ready for harvesting.

There is no minimum statutory age before agave can be harvested and plants are selected for harvesting according to their maturity. The harvesters, called 'jimadors', use a long handled knife (coa) to remove the long, spiky blue/green leaves to expose the piña, which looks rather like a huge pineapple.

The harvested piñas are traditionally sliced into either two or four pieces depending on size before being steam-baked in an oven to convert the starchy sap contained within the piña into sugar.

The cooked piñas are then shredded to release their sugary sap. If the tequila being made is to be mixto, cane or corn sugar may be added at this point, but the best quality tequilas are made from agave plants which are ripe enough not to require the addition of sugar. In 100% agave tequila, only agave juice is fermented.

Traditionally, natural yeast is formed in the vats where fermentation takes place. (Some distilleries now introduce cultivated yeasts.) Fermentation takes between thirty-six hours and three days. At this stage in the process the mixture, which contains agave fibres, is known as 'mosto'.

The mosto is distilled twice in copper pot stills. The product of this first dis-tillation is known as 'ordinario'. Only after a second distillation can the product be described as Tequila. Some distillers will distil the product a third time.

Blanco (or silver) Tequilas can be reduced with water and bottled straight from the still without any barrel ageing. Reposado and añejo tequilas are aged in oak, so that, over time, the wood can impart tannins that soften and mellow the spirit and add character. Most are blended with water before bottling but a few producers allow the alcoholic strength of their aged tequilas to reduce naturally through evaporation.

As touched on earlier, tequila is categorised according to the percentage of agave spirit it contains: mixto and 100% agave.

Mixto – Is a tequila distilled from a must fermented from a minimum of 51% agave sugars and additional other sugars (usually sugar cane).
100% agave – Is pure agave tequila, where no sugar has been added during production. These are generally considered to be the best tequilas.

These two types of tequila (Mixto and 100% agave) are further categorised according to whether or not it undergoes and ageing period, and if so how long. They are Blanco (unaged), Reposado (aged minimum of 60 days and a maximum of 11 months and 30 days), Añejo (aged in white oak casks with a capacity no larger than 600 litres for at least a year and less than 2 years and 11 months and 30 days) and Extra Añejo (aged in government sealed white oak casks with a capacity no larger than 600 litres for a minimum of three years). Any of these categories can also be Curados (flavoured with natural ingredients such as lemon, orange, tangerine, strawberry, pineapple and pear). Additives such as glycerine, caramel, sugar and oak extract are permitted to all categories but must be less than one percent.

Thai basil leaves

Thai basil has a more assertive flavour than the more usual sweet basil varieties. The leaves are smaller and the stems purple. The flavour has hints of liquorice (licorice) and mint.

Basil leaves don't generally require muddling when used in a shaken cocktail, as the action of shaking is usually sufficient to release the flavour of the leaves into the drink.

Tío Pepe®

www.gonzalezbyass.es
In 1835, the 23 year-old Manuel María González Angel founded his Sherry business when he rented a small warehouse in the centre of old Jerez and begun ageing his first casks. During a business visit to England he met Mr Robert Blake Byass, a wine importer who became the British agent and later in 1855, a partner in the company. Hence the firm's name of González Byass.

Another figure that played an important role in the success of González Byass was Manuel's uncle - José Angel, then an acknowledged expert in Sherry. He was known locally as 'Tío Pepe', meaning 'Uncle Joe' in Spanish and so the name of world's best selling Fino sherry produced and exported since 1844, is a fitting recognition of his advice.

Tío Pepe is made from Palomino Fino grapes with an estimated ageing period of five years. The Tío Pepe guitar-player logo was first created at the end of the 1920s to symbolise the Andalucian origins of the brand. Now the largest Sherry producer, González Byass is still a family owned business.

Tobacco syrup

To make tobacco syrup, peel apart a large cigar and add to the pan when making standard two parts sugar to one part water sugar syrup. Don't leave on heat for any longer than is necessary to dissolve sugar and then strain to remove tobacco leaves before leaving to cool and bottle.

Tomato Juice

Originally from Peru, the tomato was imported into Spain in the 16th century. Although technically a fruit, its sharp, fresh, slightly salty qualities have associated it with a range of savoury cocktails for over 80 years. Buy a quality, chilled, freshly pressed juice or make your own. Avoid sweet, packaged juices made from concentrate.

Triple Sec

Our recommendation: Cointreau
Although the name means Triple Dry, these orange liqueurs are very sweet. Made like Curacao, from orange peel, but triple-distilled, they are a key ingredient in many cocktails.

The first triple sec was created in 1834 by Combier at Saumur in France's Loire Valley.

Tuaca®

www.tuaca.com

Pronounced 'Two-Wa-Ka' this golden amber, brandy based spirit liqueur is flavoured with citrus fruits, vanilla, caramel and orange essence. Tuaca comes from Italy's Tuscany region and is said to have been created at the height of the 16th century Renaissance for Lorenzo di Medici, a ruler of Florence and patron to Michelangelo and Botticelli. Tuaca's original 1930s label played tribute to the Medicis with a gilded scene based on a bible panel created by Lorenzo Ghiberti, within the baptistery door of Florence's Duomo Cathedral, which Michelangelo called 'The Gates of Paradise'. A new, less religious label was introduced in 2004.

During World War II, American servicemen stationed in Livorno, Italy (a seaside resort on Tuscany's Mediterranean Coast) discovered Tuaca's smooth flavour. On their return home they searched for the brand but were unable to find it – that was until the late 1950s when an astute importer brought Tuaca across the ocean. Tuaca is now well established in the States and was introduced to the UK in the mid 1990s.

Vanilla
The cured pods of a tropical plant which belongs to the orchid family, vanilla has long been a prized flavouring. It is native to Mexico and Central America, where the Aztecs originally used it to flavour chocolate, but its name derives from the Spanish 'vainilla', meaning 'little sheath', a reference to the long thin shape of the pod.

The vanilla orchid is now cultivated in many different tropical regions. Bourbon vanilla is generally considered the finest kind, and Mexico and the Indian Ocean islands are popularly the best producers.

Once the pods are harvested from the parent vine, they undergo months of curing to develop and refine their distinctive flavour.

Vanilla Infused Spirits (Rum, Vodka & Tequila)
The pods of a tropical plant which belongs to the orchid family, vanilla has long been a prized flavouring. In this guide, recipes utilise its magic by infusing it in a spirit, most often light rum or vodka. Simply take two quality vanilla pods (roughly 6in/15cm long) and split them lengthwise with a sharp knife. Place them in the bottle of spirit you want to flavour and leave it to infuse for a fortnight, turning occasionally

Velvet Falernum®

www.velvetfalernum.com
A flavoursome non-alcoholic syrup and liqueur developed by John D. Taylor of Bridgetown, Barbados in 1890. Based on sugar cane its flavour comes from an infusion of lime and 'botanicals' including almonds and cloves.

Vermouth

Our recommendation: Noilly Prat (dry) & Martini Rosso (sweet)
The word 'vermouth' comes from the German word 'vermud', meaning 'wormwood', the name of a family of legendarily bitter plants of the genus Artemisia. Wormwoods were used for everything from insect repellents to antiseptics; to improve digestion, enhance the appetite and even to clear worms from patients – hence the name. The bitter herbs were added to wine to make the medicine more palatable – other herbs and spices were added with alcohol and so vermouth was born. Bizarrely, although the name derives from 'wormwood', many modern vermouth producers no longer use wormwood as flavouring.

Vermouths are sometimes also categorised as aromatized wines. Any product based on wines fortified with spirit and flavoured with herbs and spices is a 'aromatized wine'.

Vermouth as we know it today was invented during the 18th century in the ancient Kingdom of Savoy, which is now divided between northwest Italy and parts of southern and eastern France. At that time the region had an abundance of grapes and had only produced very ordinary wines, hence it became common to pep up the wine and pursue new markets by fortification and the addition of herbs and spices. The French and Italian side of the Alps, where vermouth production was centred, has a wealth of the herbs needed for flavouring.

Although the production methods of different vermouths vary greatly, all are based on fermented grape juice (wine). Some are sweetened with added sugar while others use the natural sweetness of the grapes by checking fer-

mentation with the addition of alcohol so killing the yeast before it is able to convert all the natural sugars to alcohol. This low alcohol and high sugar wine is known as mistelle.

The base wine may be aged before being flavoured with herbs, spices, roots and barks using various methods. In addition to wormwood, popular flavourings include: coriander, lime, camomile, hyssop, elderflower, cinnamon, quinine, mint, orange peel, angelica, cardamom, nutmeg and orris. Further aging in casks or vats may also take place prior to bottling.

Popular believe has it that Italian vermouth was originally sweet and produced from red wine, while French vermouth which was typically dry white, followed later. Hence, many old cocktail books refer to 'French' for dry vermouth and 'Italian' where sweet vermouth is called for. The truth is that the division between the styles of the two countries was never that defined and producers in both countries now produce both sweet (rosso) and dry styles with some also producing the medium sweet Bianco, a much later style which did not become popular until the 1960s. Although red vermouth was initially based on red wine, now virtually all is made from white wine with caramel blended in to give an amber colour.

French vermouth producers discovered that ageing the wine in oak after fortification improved the vermouth considerably. They also found that if the oak barrels were left out in the open, exposed to the weather and atmospheric changes, then the ageing process would be accelerated. Some people, particularly those in southern France, refer to this style as 'vin cuit' or cooked wine.

It is fair to generalise that French vermouth tends to be aged in oak casks and usually has a spicy aroma. (Well known names include Noilly Prat and Chambéry.) While Italian vermouth has a broader range of styles (Cinzano and Martini are by far the best known) with production centred around Turin. It is common to flavour vermouth with fruits, particularly orange, lemon and strawberry. A well-known example is the traditional French strawberry flavoured Chambéryzette, while Cinzano and Martini now also offer flavoured versions.

Vermouth should be stored refrigerated and drunk within two to four weeks of opening as it is based on wine and so is liable to oxidise (go off). The dryer the vermouth, the sooner it will deteriorate once opened and so exposed to the air.

Vodka

Our recommendation: Ketel One
Vodka is a clear spirit (Blavod and flavoured vodkas aside) which can be produced from anything containing starch or sugar - including potatoes, molasses and, most commonly, grain.

According to a recent agreement by the European Commission, vodka made from cereals and potatoes will be labelled 'vodka', while vodka made from other materials (e.g. grapes) will carry the indication 'produced from'. Vodka is most commonly made from molasses and grain, though grain is generally favoured for the production of premium or super-premium brands. The types of grain used will affect the taste of the finished vodka. Types of grain and the flavour associated include barley (lightly nutty, spicy sweetness), maize/corn (buttery), rye (nutty rye bread sweetness) and wheat (aniseedy). Vodka can be made from anything that contains starch, as starch can be converted into sugar and alcohol is fermented from sugar. As well as using potatoes, made famous by Poland, vodka can be made from apples, bread, beetroots, carrots or even onions, and there are at least a couple of grape vodkas on the market.

The other important raw ingredient common to all vodka is water. The quality of the water used vastly affects the finished product and many brands pin their marketing story on the water they use. Most producers, however, are more vocal about the source of the water they use to distil their product than the purified tap water with which many still dilute it to bottling strength. Like all spirits, vodka can only be distilled from a liquid that is already alcoholic. So before distillation the base ingredient must be mixed with water and yeast and then fermented. This produces a type of beer known as a 'wash' – generally around 8% alc./vol.

Distillation of the wash normally takes place in continuous (column) stills, ensuring that the final distillate is extremely pure and neutral tasting (it usually leaves its final distillation at 96% abv). However, an increasing number of top-end producers now choose to use pot stills, which leave more of the character and flavour of the raw material in the distillate.

Many producers filter the distillate through active charcoal or other

substances. This process was originally designed to remove the bad fusel oils (toxic alcohols) from the distillate, which inefficient older stills could not remove.

There is a trend among marketers to state on the label and in the literature that a vodka is 'triple distilled' or even 'quadruple distilled'. When, as often is, this refers to distillation in a column still (or stills), such terms are meaningless. The purity of a column still distillate derives from the number of distilling plates the still houses – a 50-plate still will produce a much purer spirit than a 3-plate still.(Pot still distillates, to which such terms originally referred, become purer and purer the more times they are distilled.)

Claims such as 'triple filtered' are almost equally laughable. The quality of a filtration depends on how long the spirit has been filtered, through what material and through what size filter. How many times it passes through the filter is irrelevant without this information.

In general, you should look for vodkas whose labels contain concrete information about the type of still used, the base ingredient – the kind of grain and where it comes from, for example - and the filtration method.

Watermelon
Botanically unrelated to other melons, the watermelon is native to Africa. It was eaten in Egypt well before 2000 BC and was taken to the US by slave traders in the early 17th century.

The juice is more refreshing than flavoursome, with a faint sweetness; the seeds, usually discarded, are nonetheless edible.

Preparation: Watermelons are best muddled in cocktails. Cut chunks of flesh from a segment, taking care to avoid the rind, and muddle in a shaker. Be sure to strain the drink to exclude the seeds.

White Crème de Cacao
A number of cocktails benefit from the chocolate flavour of crème de cacao yet not the dark brown colour. In order to preserve the taste but eliminate the colour, the flavour of the finest roasted cacao beans is extracted by means of distillation instead of percolation. This process also gives white crème de cacao a lighter flavour than brown crème de cacao.

White crème de cacao adds a rich chocolate flavour to any cocktail.

White Crème de Menthe

Our recommendation: Giffard Menthe Pastille
A French peppermint flavoured liqueur, most commonly sold with added green colouring. 'Menthe' is French for mint thus 'white' version omits the green colouring and is clear.

White Port (Porto)

Our recommendation: Taylor's Chip Dry
Made using only white grapes to achieve a light golden colour, white Ports are usually aged for three years in large oak vats prior to bottling. They can be either very dry or sweet – the label should state which. Sweet white Ports are often served with melon. Dry whites make great aperitifs.

Wray & Nephew®

www.rum.co.uk
Wray & Nephew is the world's top selling high strength rum. Any spirit equal to or over 57% abv is termed 'overproof' and this unaged white rum is one such example. Wray & Nephew is an intrinsic part of Jamaica's culture, heritage and tradition, and a staple in every Jamaican household. Fondly known as 'Whites' it is used as part of medicine, ritual and everyday living, and accounts for over 90% of all rum consumed.

It is made by Wray & Nephew, the oldest distiller in Jamaica which was founded by a Scotchman, Charles John Wray. He settled in Jamaica in the early 1800s and first blended rums at his tavern in Kingston, the capital of Jamaica, in 1825. He soon started bottling his blends to sell to other tavern keepers on the Island and in 1862 won three gold medals at the London International Exhibition. During this year he also formed a partnership with his nephew, Charles James Ward, and the business became John Wray & Nephew.

Ron Zacapa 23 solera®

The Ron Zacapa distillery sits one and a half miles above sea level in the shadows of soaring Guatemalan mountains and active volcanoes. Unusually, instead of being made from molasses (as is the case with most rums) Ron Zacapa is produced from the first pressing of sugar cane juice, referred to as 'virgin honey'. It is also set apart from other rums by a complex Solera maturation system.

Barrels previously used to age bourbon and sherry are used in a five stage ageing process during which there is repeated reblending with very old aged rums introduced at each stage of the blending process. Scrapping and recharging of casks also plays an important part in this maturation process which concludes in a final marrying vat. This process takes place in warehouses perched at 7,650 feet (2,332 meters) so unusual atmospheric conditions are also at play.

Ron Zacapa is presented in a bottle made distinctive by a band of 'Royal Palm'. This is made from hand-woven palm leaves prepared by local people. However, it is the flavour of Ron Zacapa that really sets it apart with its hugely complex palate appearing slightly sweet while giving rich notes of coffee, roast chestnut, smoky wood and tobacco. Incredibly for such a well age rum Zacapa is also wonderfully fruity with cherry and sweet molasses.

Zen® Green Tea Liqueur

www.zen-greentea.com
Zen is made in Japan by Suntory using high grade Kyoto green tea leaves grown by one of the most famous producers of fine teas in Japan, Marukyu-Koyama-En, who have been cultivating tea for more than 300 years. Suntory infuses neutral spirits with whole and ground green tea leaves, then blends this with lemongrass and other herbs and natural flavourings to produce this distinctively green coloured liqueur.

Zoco®

www.zoco.info
Pronounced 'Thock-O' and first sold in 1956, Zoco is the oldest and leading brand of Pacharán, a Spanish liqueur made by macerating sloe berries collected from the blackthorn, in an anise-flavoured spirit (anisette).

Zoco was founded by the family of Ambrosio Velasco who had been producing patxaran in the Viana area since 1816. Marketed in a distinctive square bottle it is now owned by Pernod Ricard.

Zubrówka®

www.zubrowka.net
Pronounced 'Zhu-bruff-ka', this Polish vodka is flavoured with Hierochloe Odorata grass, a blade of which is immersed in each bottle, giving the vodka a translucent greenish colour and a subtle flavour. The area where this grass grows in the Bialowieza Forest is the habitat of wild Polish bison – so, although the bison don't eat this variety of grass, the vodka has the nickname 'Bison vodka'. The Hierochloe Odorata grass is harvested by hand in early summer when its flavour is best, then dried, cut to size and bound in bunches for delivery to the Bialystok distillery. The vodka is forced through the grass to absorb its aromatic flavour rather as espresso coffee machines force water through coffee.

The palate is herby and grassy with flavours of citrus, vanilla, lavender, tobacco, cold jasmine tea and caffè latte, plus hints of dry chocolate/vanilla. This subtle and delicately flavoured vodka is extremely mixable.

Zucca Rabarbaro®
www.illva.com
Zucca is Italian for 'pumpkin' and Rabarbaro (pronounced 'ra-barb-bar-row') translates as 'rhubarb'. The name refers to the fact that this Italian bittersweet liqueur is based on rhubarb and flavoured with citrus zest, cardamom and other herbs.

COCKTAIL TIMELINE

1732 – The Fish House Punch was created at the State Fishing and Social Club in Schuylkill, Philadelphia. It would have originally been made using peach brandy, though peach schnapps are often substituted now.

1740 – Admiral Edward Vernon (nicknamed 'Old Grogram' due to his waterproof grogram cloak) reduced rum rations in the British Navy to combat drunkenness. The quarter of a pint of rum, diluted 4:1 with water became known as grog.

1747 – Scottish surgeon James Lind proved citrus fruit prevented scurvy whilst serving in the British Navy. Lemons and limes were added to grog to maintain levels of Vitamin C and British sailors subsequently became known as 'limeys'.

1767 – Dr Joseph Priestley, an English clergyman and chemist created the first artificially carbonated water (soda water).

1787 – The first written reference to a Julep appeared in Virginia - "The Virginian rises in the morning, about six o'clock. He then drinks a julap, made of rum, water and sugar, but very strong." The author is unknown.

1792 – Dr Pierre Ordinaire perfected his recipe for absinthe. He wanted to find a way to make the healing herb wormwood more palatable as although it is one of the bitterest substances known - aty the time it was one of the best available remedies for stomach upsets, parasitic infestations, and fever.

1800 – Ice was first sold commercially in the United States in the form of slabs hacked from frozen lakes.

1803 – American Thomas Moore patented the term 'refrigerator'. Two years later, Oliver Evans designed the first closed circuit refrigerating machine, which was then patented another four years later by his colleague Jacob Perkins.

1806 – The word 'cocktail' appeared in print in a New York newspaper. After a reader wrote in and asked for an explanation of the term, the following was published "Cock tail, then is a stimulating liquor, composed of spirits of any kind, sugar, water and bitters it is vulgarly called a bittered sling, and is supposed to be an excellent electioneering potion inasmuch as it renders the heart stout and bold, at the same time that it fuddles the head. It is said also, to be of great use to a democratic candidate: because, a person having swallowed a glass of it, is ready to swallow any thing else."

1814 – Bartender John Collins created the Gin Punch (the forerunner to Gin Collins) at Limmer's Hotel, Conduit Street, London. It is unclear if it would have originally been made with genever, Old Tom or London dry gin.

1824 – Angostura Aromatic Bitters were invented, originally designed to help improve digestion and appetite.

1825 – The Oxford English Dictionary cited the first instance of Eggnog in the written English language.

1826 – Robert Stein patented continuous distillation and installed his invention in his distillery at Kilbagie in Central Scotland. Only four Stein Stills were ever made and used, as they were extremely complicated.

1830 – The Coffey Still was created and patented by Aeneas Coffey, an Irishman with no technical engineering skills. Coffey managed to create a machine capable of processing almost 14,000 litres of wash per hour. By 1860 there were twenty-eight of his stills in use in Britain.

1840(s) – Joseph Santina created the Brandy Crusta at Jewel of the South, Gravier Street, New Orleans. Crustas always contain a spirit, lemon juice and sugar – sometimes in the form of a liqueur. They are so named because of their sugar rim or crust, which should be applied hours before the drink is served. Some historians believe that the Crusta is the forerunner of the Sidecar and in turn the Margarita. Logical.

1858 – Leon Lamothe claimed he created the Sazerac in the Sazerac Coffee House, New Orleans. The original recipe was probably made with Peychaud's aromatic bitters, Sazerac cognac and sugar. Today the name Sazerac is owned by the Sazerac Company, who license the name to the Sazerac Bar at the Fairmont Hotel.

1860(s) – 'Professor' Jerry Thomas created the Blue Blazer at the Occidental Hotel, San Francisco. Born in 1830, Thomas toured the world as a travelling bartender and showman often juggling bottles or in this case pouring flaming alcohol from cup to cup.

1862 – 'Professor' Jerry Thomas published 'How To Mix Drinks or The Bon-Vivant's Companion' – the first drink book to be published in the United States.

1867 – Lauchlin Rose patented a process to preserve fruit juice without alcohol – Rose's lime cordial. In the same year, the Merchant Shipping Act required all ships in the Royal Navy and Merchant Navy to provide a daily lime ration (often in the form of Rose's Lime Cordial) to prevent scurvy.

1870(s) – Schweppes launched Indian Tonic Water. It was originally popular with the British in India, as it contained quinine, which was used as a preventative measure against malaria. The amount of quinine in today's Schweppes Tonic is too small to have any medicinal effect.

1870 – 'Professor' Jerry Thomas created the Martinez using Old Tom gin. This was possibly the forerunner to the Dry Martini.

1876 – 'Professor' Jerry Thomas published 'The Bartender's Guide'.

1880(s) – The first Martini recipe was recorded. Initially, Martinis would have been quite sweet – developing from the Martinez made with Old Tom gin and sweet vermouth. The first Dry Martini probably came in with the emergence of London dry gin some years later.

1882 – Harry Johnson published 'New and Improved Bartender's Manual'.

1886 – Coca-Cola was invented by Dr John Pemberton - a pharmacist from Atlanta, Georgia. Pemberton apparently concocted the Coca-Cola formula in his backyard and the name was a suggestion by his book-keeper.

1887 – 'Professor' Jerry Thomas published 'The Bartenders Guide or How To Mix All Kinds of Plain and Fancy Drinks'.

1892 – William Schmidt published 'The Flowing Bowl'.

1894 – The Rob Roy is created at the Waldorf-Astoria Hotel, New York and named after a Broadway show playing at the time.

1895 – George J. Kappeler published 'Modern American Drinks'.

1895 – Patrick Gavin Duffy was credited for the popularity of the Scotch Highball in New York. He wrote in his 1934 publication " It is one of my fondest hopes that the highball will again take its place as the leading American Drink. I admit to being prejudiced about this – it was I who first brought the highball to America, in 1895."

1898 – American-Spanish War.

1898 – Jennings Stockton Cox, an American engineer created the Daiquiri, and named it after the town of Daiquiri, Cuba. Drinks legend has it that another engineer called Pagliuchi was viewing mines in the region and met with Cox. During their meeting they set about making a drink from the ingredients Cox had to hand: Bacardi rum, limes and sugar. Cox's granddaughter recounts a slightly different tale; namely that Cox ran out of gin when entertaining American guests. Wary of serving them straight rum, he added lime and sugar.

1900(s) – Ada 'Coley' Coleman created the Hanky Panky Martini at The American Bar, Savoy Hotel, London where she worked from 1903 until retirement in 1924.

1900 – The Rickey was created at Shoemaker's Restaurant, Washington and name after Colonel Joe Rickey, a Confederate soldier and lobbyist, for whom it was invented.

1900 – A Captain during the American-Spanish war ordered a Bacardi Rum and Coca-Cola with a squeeze of lime in the American Bar, Havana, Cuba . The drink was renamed the Cuba Libre after a toast to 'Free Cuba'.

1906 – Johnny Solon created the Bronx Cocktail at the Waldorf-Astoria Hotel, New York. He named the drink after the newly opened Bronx Zoo and it was supposedly the first cocktail to use fruit juice.

1909 – Paul E. Lowe published 'Drink – How to Mix and Serve'.

1910 – The first in-flight cocktails were served to passengers on the Zeppelin flying over Germany.

1910 – Britain's first cocktail bar, The Criterion opened in Piccadilly Circus. In the same year – the first electric advertisements also appeared.

1912 – Absinthe was banned in the United States. It was believed the spirit caused addiction and hallucinations.

1914 – World War One began.

1916 – Hugo R. Ensslin published 'Recipes for Mixed Drinks'. The key cocktail to come from this book was the Aviation.

1917 – Tom Bullock published 'The Ideal Bartender'.

Sazerac - 1858

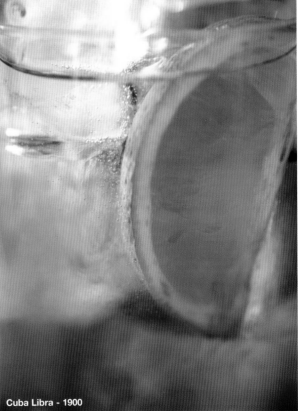

Cuba Libra - 1900

1917 – The Bacardi Cocktail is created in Cuba. In 1936 Bacardi issued a lawsuit against The Barbizon Plaza Hotel and The Wivel Restaurant both in NYC for not using Bacardi rum within the Bacardi Cocktail. The case was built on the premise that the rum was unique and uncopyable. The judge ruled in Bacardi's favour and the law still stands that a Bacardi Cocktail must contain its namesakes rum.

1918 – World War One ends.

1919 – Harry MacElhone created the first version of the White Lady at Ciro's Club, London. This was made using white crème de menthe instead of gin. MacElhone also published 'The ABC of Mixing Drinks' in this year.

1920(s) – Count Camillo Negroni asked for an Americano with 'more kick' and so created the Negroni at the Casoni Bar, Florence.

1920(s) – The Pisco Sour was created and became the national drink of both Chile and Peru where Pisco is produced. Peru has a National Pisco Sour Day, which is celebrated on the first Saturday of February. Chile's National Pisco Day is celebrated later on May 15.

1920 – Prohibition began in America.

1920 (or 1921) – Fernand Petiot created the Bloody Mary at Harry's New York Bar, Paris. The name most likely comes from one of Petiot's customers – the entertainer Roy Barton. He had worked at a nightclub called the Bucket of Blood where there was a waitress who was known as Bloody Mary. Apparently the drink reminded him of her. The celery garnish dates back to the 1960s when a bartender at the Ambassador Hotel in Chicago noticed a lady stirring her drink with a celery stick.

1921 – Pat MacGarry created the Buck's Fizz at Buck's Club, London. Famous members included Winston Churchill and P.G. Wodehouse. MacGarry is also credited with creating the Sidecar whilst at Buck's.

1922 – Stephen J. Poplawski, owner of the Stevens Electric Company, invented and patented the electric blender. It was designed to make Horlick's milkshakes.

1923 – Harry MacElhone created the more famous version of the White Lady at Harry's New York Bar, Paris using gin as the base spirit.

1924 – The Club de Cantineros (Professional Barmen's Association) was created in Cuba.

1927 – Harry MacElhone published 'Barflies and Cocktails'.

1928 – Ernest Hemingway arrived in Havana, Cuba. He spent his time drinking Daiquiris at El Floridita and eventually christened his own Hemingway Daiquiri - made with additional grapefruit juice.

1928 – British playwright Basil Woon published 'When its Cocktail Time in Cuba'.

1928 – Herbert Asbury republished Jerry Thomas' 1862 'How To Mix Drinks or the Bon-Vivant's Companion'. He went onto write 'Gangs of New York' amongst other things.

1929 – Wall Street Crash.

1930 – Harry Craddock published 'The Savoy Cocktail Book'.

1931 – Albert S. Crockett published 'Old Waldorf Bar Days' – the full title reads 'Old Waldorf Bar Days. With the Cognomina and Composition of Four Hundred and Ninety-one Appealing Appetizers and Salutary Potations Long Known ... Also a Glossary for the Use of Antiquarians and Students of American Mores' Catchy.

1933 – Prohibition ended.

1934 – Ernest Beaumont Gantt opened his Don the Beachcomber bar in Hollywood, California and changed his name by deed poll to Donn Beach. The menu included a drink called the Original Beachcomber Rum Concoction. He claimed it was this drink that later became known as the Mai Tai, meaning he would have predated Trader Vic's recipe by ten years.

1934 – Patrick Gavin Duffy published 'The Official Mixers Guide'.

1935 – The Roosevelt (now Fairmont) Hotel won the trademark for the Ramos Gin Fizz although the drink was actually created in the 1880's by Henry C. Ramos at Meyer's Restaurant, New Orleans. The favourite drink of Senator Huey Long – he once flew the bartender from New Orleans to New York just to make the cocktail. He called it 'his gift to New York'.

1936 – Victor Jules Bergeron opened the first Trader Vic's restaurant in Oakland, San Francisco and assumed the name The Trader. He had previously opened a restaurant called Hinky Dinks in 1934.

1937 – Head bartender of the Café Royal, W.J. Tarling published 'Café Royal Cocktail Book' (Coronation Edition). Funds raised from the sales of the book went towards the United Kingdom Bartenders Guild Sickness Fund and the Cafe Royal Sports Club Fund.

1938 – Stanley Clisby published 'Famous New Orleans Drinks and How To Mix 'Em'.

1939 – World War Two began.

1939 – Charles H. Baker, a food and drink journalist for Esquire and Gourmet magazines published the two-volume set - 'The Gentleman's Companion: Being an Exotic Cookery and Drinking Book'

1939 – The Hurricane was first served at the World's Fair, New York at the Hurricane Bar. The drink was named after the lamp-shaped 'hurricane' glass the first drinks were served in.

1940 – Rationing began in the UK, which was later credited for the creation of the Naked Martini due to dwindling Vermouth supplies.

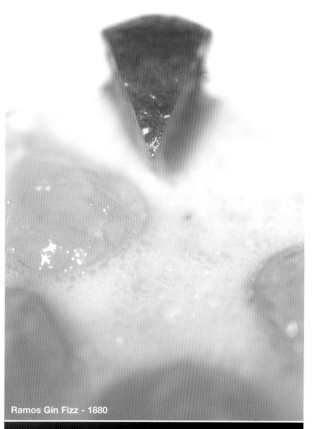
Ramos Gin Fizz - 1880

1941 – John G. Martin and Jack Morgan created the Moscow Mule in the Chatham Bar, New York. Martin had just acquired the rights to Smirnoff vodka and Morgan who owned the Cock 'n' Bull saloon was trying to launch his own ginger beer. Mixed together in a specially engraved copper mug with a squeeze of lime turned both Smirnoff and the Moscow Mule recipe into iconic brands.

1942 – Joe Sheridan created the Irish Coffee at Foynes airport, Ireland. The majority of transatlantic flights used to stop to refuel in Ireland and journalist Stan Delaphane was so impressed with Sheridan's recipe he passed it on to his local bartender at the Buena Vista Café in San Francisco.

1944 – Trader Vic claims he created the Mai Tai at his restaurant in Oakland, San Francisco. As he served this drink, one of his Tahitian customers said "Mai Tai - Roa Aé" which means 'Out of this world – The Best!' The original recipe was based on 17 yo Jamaican J Wray & Nephew rum. In his 1947 bartenders' guide he wrote, "Anybody who says I didn't create this drink is a dirty stinker."

1945 – Giuseppe Cipriani created the Bellini at Harry's Bar, Venice. Cipriani named the drink after the 15th century painter Giovanni Bellini due to the drink's pink hue and the painter's penchant for using rich pinks on his canvasses.

1945 – World War Two ends.

Irish Coffee - 1942

1946 – Charles H. Baker published both 'The Gentleman's Companion: Being an Exotic Drinking Book or Around the World with Jigger, Beaker and Flask' and 'The Gentleman's Companion: Being an Exotic Cookery Book or Around the World with Knife, Fork, and Spoon'.

1948 – David A. Embury published 'Fine Art of Mixing Drinks'. He is quoted as saying, "I have always possessed an insatiable curiosity about the whys and wherefores of many things and particularly of food and drinks."

1949 – Esquire published 'Handbook for Hosts - A Practical Guide to Party Planning and Gracious Entertaining'.

1950 – Bing Crosby imported the first 100% blue agave tequila to America. The brand was Herradura.

1951 – The International Bartenders Association (IBA) was started in Torquay, UK. The Association, which is still going strong today, is now based in Italy.

1953 – Coronation of Queen Elizabeth II.

1954 – Rationing finally ends in United Kingdom.

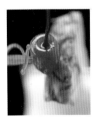

1954 – Ramón Marrero Pérez claimed he created the Piña Colada at the Caribe Hilton's Beachcomber Bar, San Juan. The Caribe was the first luxury hotel in San Juan and became a popular destination for the rich and famous who helped the drink gain notoriety. The name literally translates as 'strained pineapple'.

1956 – James A. Beard, the eccentric American chef and writer republished Patrick Gavin Duffy's 'The Official Mixers Manual'. He also wrote twenty of his own books plus started the James Beard Foundation Awards, which are held annually on the first Monday in May. The awards celebrate the finest chefs, restaurants and food journalists in the USA.

1965 – First TGI Friday venue opened in New York at the corner of First Avenue and 63rd Street.

1965 – American troops are first sent to Vietnam.

1972 – Victor Bergeron republished 'Trader Vic's Bartender's Guide' (revised edition).

1975 – American troops leave Vietnam.

1980(s) – Dick Bradsell created the Bramble at Fred's Club, London.

1980(s) – Cheryl Cook created the Cosmopolitan at The Strand on Washington Avenue, South Beach, Miami.

1984 – Gerry's liquor store opened in Soho, London.

1986 – T.G.I. Fridays hosted the very first known flair bartender contest called Bar Olympics for T.G.I. Friday bartenders. John JB Bandy won and went on to train Tom Cruise for his role in 'Cocktail' which was released in 1988.

1989 – Margaret Thatcher's government introduced a legislation known as the 'Beer Orders', which changed the breweries ownership over the Great British pub. This encouraged entrepreneurs to move in and with them came gastro pubs and crucially something occupying the ground between a pub and club, which became known as 'style bars'.

1990(s) – Salvatore Calabrese, National President of the UKBG, created the Breakfast Martini at the Library Bar, Lanesborough Hotel London.

1994 – Atlantic Bar & Grill opened in Soho, London with Oliver Peyton at the helm.

1997 – Simon Difford launched CLASS Magazine in the UK. The name was an acronym for Cocktails, Liqueur And Speciality Spirit.

1997 – Jonathan Downey opened the first Match Bar & Grill in Clerkenwell.

1998 – Robert Hess created drinkboy.com – an online forum for bartenders. It had to close in 2008 but has been reincarnated at chanticleersociety.org

2000 – Sasha Petraske opened private members club Milk & Honey in New York and starts a trend for prohibition style bars in both NYC and London.

2002 – Dale 'King Cocktail' DeGroff published 'Craft of the Cocktail'.

2003 – LeNell's Liquor Store opened in Red Hook, Brooklyn. It had to close in 2009 due to issues with the lease.

2003 – Gary Regan published 'Joy of Mixology'.

2004 – Museum of the American Cocktail opened in New Orleans. Founders include Robert Hess, Ted Haigh, Anistatia Miller, Chris McMillian, Laura McMillian, Jill DeGroff, Dale DeGroff, Jared Brown, and Phil Greene.

2004 – Ted Haigh published 'Vintage Spirits and Forgotten Cocktails'.

2004 – Henry Besant and Dre Masso formed the Worldwide Cocktail Club.

2005 – Anistatia Miller and Jared Brown published 'Mixologist: The Journal of the American Cocktail Volume I'. Volume II followed in 2006 and Volume III in 2009.

2007 – Absinthe was finally legalized in the USA. It was previously presumed that absinthe contained a toxic chemical, known as thujone, that has mind-altering properties. However, scientists have now found that there is only a very small amount of this chemical within absinthe and so don't have a leg to stand on anymore.

2007 – Flair bartenders - The Bar Wizards reached the final of ITV's 'Britains Got Talent'. They lost to a seven year old girl and an opera singing Welshman. Shame.

2007 – Cocktail historian David Wondrich published 'Imbibe! - From Absinthe Cocktail to Whiskey Smash, a Salute in Stories and Drinks to Professor Jerry Thomas, Pioneer of the American Bar'.

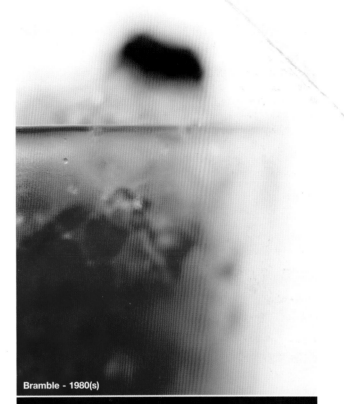

Bramble - 1980(s)

Cosmopolitan - 1980(s)